AMERICAN GOVERNMENT

Institutions and Policies

SIXTH EDITION

James Q. Wilson
University of California, Los Angeles

John J. DiIulio, Jr.
Princeton University

D. C. HEATH AND COMPANY
Lexington, Massachusetts   Toronto

Address editorial correspondence to

D. C. Heath and Company
125 Spring Street
Lexington, MA 02173

Acquisitions Editor: Paul Smith
Production Editor: Karen Wise
Designer: Cornelia Boynton
Photo Researcher: Mark Corsey
Art Editor: Penny Peters
Production Coordinator: Richard Tonachel
Permissions Editor: Margaret Roll
Cover: (photo) Maxwell MacKenzie / Uniphoto,
    (design) Linda Manly Wade

International Standard Book Number: 0–669–34088–X

Library of Congress Catalog Number: 94–75275

10 9 8 7 6 5 4   VHP   00 99 98 97

For Roberta, Matthew, Rebecca, Annie, and Bob.
And Winston, Clementine, and Sarah.
J.Q.W.

Dedicated to the memory of Aaron H. Crasner.
J.J.D.

James Q. Wilson

is the Collins Professor of Management and Political Science at the University of California, Los Angeles. He was previously the Shattuck Professor of Government at Harvard University. Raised in California, Wilson received a B.A. degree from the University of Redlands and a Ph.D. degree from the University of Chicago. He is the author or coauthor of thirteen books, including *Negro Politics, The Amateur Democrat, City Politics* (with Edward C. Banfield), *Varieties of Police Behavior, Political Organizations, Thinking about Crime, The Investigators, Bureaucracy, The Moral Sense, Watching Fishes: Life and Behavior on Coral Reefs* (with Roberta Wilson), and *Crime and Human Nature* (with Richard J. Herrnstein).

Wilson has served in a number of advisory posts in the federal government. He was chairman of the White House Task Force on Crime in 1967, chairman of the National Advisory Council on Drug Abuse Prevention in 1972–1973, a member of the Attorney General's Task Force on Violent Crime in 1981, and a member of the President's Foreign Intelligence Advisory Board in 1986–1990.

In 1977 the American Political Science Association conferred on him the Charles E. Merriam Award for advancing the art of government through the application of social science knowledge and in 1990 the James Madison Award for distinguished scholarship. In 1991–1992 he was President of the Association.

He is a Fellow of the American Academy of Arts and Sciences and a member of the American Philosophical Society. When not writing, teaching, or advising, he goes scuba diving. He says that it clears the brain.

John J. DiIulio, Jr.

is Professor of Politics and Public Affairs at Princeton University, teaching in both the Princeton Politics Department and the Woodrow Wilson School of Public and International Affairs. Raised in Philadelphia, DiIulio received a B.A. from the University of Pennsylvania and a Ph.D. from Harvard University. He is the author, coauthor, or editor of seven books, including *Making Health Reform Work* (with Richard P. Nathan), *Improving Government Performance* (with Donald F. Kettl and Gerald J. Garvey), *Deregulating the Public Service, Governing Prisons,* and *Courts, Corrections, and the Constitution.*

DiIulio is Director of the Brookings Institution's Center for Public Management, and in that capacity has worked with officials of the National Performance Review, the Office of Management and Budget, the General Accounting Office, and other federal agencies. In 1990 he chaired the New Jersey Governor's Task Force on Corrections and has been a member of the National Commission on the State and Local Public Service since 1991. He has served as an advisor to the Office of National Drug Control Policy (1989–1992), directed leadership training programs for the U.S. Justice Department (1991–1992), and chaired the Department's performance measurement project (1991–1994).

In 1987 he received the American Political Science Association's Leonard D. White Award in public administration. In 1991–1994 he chaired the Association's standing committee on professional ethics. He also serves on the editorial boards of several public management and criminal justice journals.

He spends all his free time with family and friends who live in or around Philadelphia, and gets to the New Jersey shore whenever possible.

Preface

For the Sixth Edition of *American Government*, James Q. Wilson has been joined by a coauthor, Professor John J. DiIulio, Jr., of Princeton University. DiIulio studied with Wilson at Harvard, and the two have maintained a close intellectual relationship ever since. Their collaboration has resulted in a thorough revision and the addition of many new features, all presented in a freshly designed and reset volume.

These changes have not altered the essential structure or themes of the text. It remains an effort to show not only who governs but what difference—in policies adopted or rejected—it makes who governs. The process by which policy decisions are made (or not made) is presented with the aid of a simple but useful conceptual scheme that helps students understand why some political coalitions form and others do not and why some groups gain advantages and others suffer burdens.

Moreover, the text continues to stress the importance of the Constitution and American political culture in shaping governmental activities and to present the historical evolution of our practices and institutions. To make clear how distinctive our political habits are, frequent reference is made to the way in which other democratic nations manage similar issues.

The first five editions of this text have benefited from many criticisms and suggestions offered by its users, but the bulk of these comments have supported the general approach that gives the book its distinctive perspective.

The Sixth Edition

More new material has been added to this edition than to any preceding revision. Beyond updating everything through the 1994 elections and incorporating many of the recent findings of political scien-

tists, we have added to the text these major new themes and issues:

- *Representative versus direct democracy* Throughout the book, but especially in the chapters on Congress and public opinion, we have highlighted the tension between two conceptions of popular rule. We draw out, with concrete examples, the implications of having the government mirror public opinion or interpret it and of having the Congress "do what the people want" versus "do what is best for the people." This theme is especially important in evaluating proposals for reforming Congress.

- *Critical thinking* A number of boxes have been added that help the student think critically about political matters. For instance, there are boxes on "How to Read the *Federalist* Papers 10 and 51" and "How to Read a Newspaper."

- *The culture war* Today citizens seem more divided over such issues as crime, abortion, contraception, gay rights, and school prayer than they are over economic or military policy. At the root of these cultural conflicts are religious and philosophical beliefs about human nature, personal freedom, and social order. A discussion of the nature, origins, and consequences of what is often called "the culture war" has been added to Chapter 4.

- *Crime and criminal justice* In 1994, crime topped the list of popular concerns, yet the national government has relatively little impact on crime rates or even on criminal-justice policies. To show why this is so, we added to the chapter on state and local government a detailed discussion of federal efforts to shape crime policy.

- *Aliens and immigration* Many people have only the vaguest idea about the rights of aliens, documented and undocumented, or of the process by which one becomes a citizen. We have added boxes on these subjects together with a discussion of the changing pattern of immigration into this country.

- *Health care* As we go to press, health-care reform is an unresolved issue of the greatest potential importance. We discuss in Chapter 17 the politics of the problem, emphasizing the difficulty of making radical changes in a system with which most people are reasonably content and around which countless interest groups have organized. If and when the issue is resolved, we will update this section in subsequent printings.

Some of the unique features of the Fifth Edition have been retained here, including two in particular. The series of boxes headed "Politically Speaking" that give the origin of certain common political terms (such as *litmus test, lame duck, logrolling, boycott,* and *muckraker*) have proved to be useful ways of making unfamiliar words accessible and interesting. Another series of boxes headed "What Would You Do?" present to the student something very much like a presidential decision memorandum (albeit ones for a variety of political actors). Should we send troops? Rule a state statute unconstitutional? Take money from a political action committee? These boxes can be the basis of classroom debates or term papers.

The lists of "Political Trivia" and "Laws of Politics" remain; students (like the authors of this text) seem to have an unflagging appetite for such minutiae and folk wisdom.

Finally, a much-expanded Glossary in the Appendix and lists of Key Terms at the end of each chapter have been added to serve as easy references and to help students review for examinations.

A New Kind of Text: CD-ROM

The Interactive Edition of *American Government,* Sixth Edition, represents a revolution in education, providing students with an integrated learning environment for American government. Including the complete text of the book, this CD-ROM version also contains an impressive array of special features and tools, so that students can access materials as diverse as the text of the *Federalist* papers or video footage of speeches and campaign commercials or pointed lectures by Professors Wilson and DiIulio on complex or high-interest subjects. Many trusted pedagogical devices find new life in this interactive environment, including chapter overviews, glossaries of key terms, self-tests, and a customizable notebook. It is available in both Macintosh and Windows versions.

Supplements

The outstanding ancillary program that has always supported *American Government* has been improved and enlarged:

Student Handbook Now including sample practice midterm and final exams, this handbook is an indispensable tool for students using *American Government,* Sixth Edition. For each textbook chapter, the handbook includes focus points, a study outline, key terms, notes about possible misconceptions, a data check, examination practice, special application projects, and a selection of primary-source readings excerpted from significant documents in American government. It is ideal for class preparation, reviewing class reading, and especially preparing for examinations.

Instructor's Guide This guide helps instructors using the Sixth Edition to plan their course, lectures, and discussion sections. Elements new to the Sixth Edition are summarized, and the Videotape Guide is completely updated.

Test Item File Now conveniently grouping question variations together, the *Test Item File* includes more than 4000 questions—conceptual, analytical, and factual. It is available in print or on disk for MS-DOS, Macintosh, and Apple computers.

Transparencies Approximately 50 full-color transparencies will be drawn from the exciting new illustration program of *American Government,* Sixth Edition.

Video Study Guide Unique to the textbook market, this 120-minute videotape consists of twenty 6-minute segments on the text's key chapters. Each segment offers students a focused overview of the chapter's content, key points, and themes, augmented with graphics, photos, and video footage chosen to bring the concepts to life.

Guest Lectures To supplement classroom lectures, college adopters will regularly receive papers on timely subjects by experts in the field. These informative lectures will reflect contemporary topics of interest to both instructors and students. Past papers have included William Lasser's "The Supreme Court: Where Has It Been and Where Is It Going?" and Peter Skerry's "The Politics of Hispanic Americans."

California Government Organized to parallel *American Government*, Sixth Edition, this 80-page text, written by Professor John L. Korey of California State Polytechnic University, introduces students to the specific issues of California politics and policy, covering everything from the California state constitution to the local media to the state institutions, offices, and parties. California instructors will find this a useful and inexpensive solution to the state's curricular requirements.

The Help of Others

In preparing to produce the Sixth Edition, we benefited greatly from the work of others. Heather Elms, Mary Flood, and Robert Wargo served as Wilson's research assistants, and Dana Ansel and Meena Bose as DiIulio's. Several individuals called to our attention some factual errors; we are grateful to C. R. Alexander, Randall Bland, Charles W. Gossett, W. Lee Johnston, and Lee A. Sanders, Jr. In addition, David Leege provided us with some detailed suggestions on the relationship between religion and politics.

A number of scholars also participated in a survey of textbook users and made many helpful suggestions. They include Nikki Bennett, Valencia Community College; Steven Bennett, University of Cincinnati; Don Broyles, California State University at Fresno; Don Carson, Memphis State University; Jack Citrin, University of California at Berkeley; Robert Delorme, California State University at Long Beach; Robert DiClerico, West Virginia University; Jeff Hughston, Pasadena State College; Arthur Levy, University of South Florida; Joel Lieske, Cleveland State University; Gerald Long, Rogers State College; John McAdams, Marquette University; Clifton McCleskey, University of Virginia; Daniel Reagan, Ball State University; Helen Ridley, Kenessaw College; and Howard Scarough, State University of New York at Stony Brook.

Our editors at D. C. Heath—Paul Smith and Karen Wise—have been with us for many years and, as always, were splendid guides and colleagues.

J.Q.W. and J.J.D.

Contents

PART THREE

Institutions of Government
281

PART FOUR

The Politics of Public Policy *449*

American Government

PART ONE

The American System

"*In framing a government which is to be administered by men over men, the great difficulty lies in this: You must first enable the government to control the governed; and in the next place oblige it to control itself.*"

— FEDERALIST NO. 51

1

The Study of American Government

There are two questions about politics: Who governs? To what end?

We want to know the answer to the first question because we believe that those who rule—their personalities and beliefs, their virtues and vices—will affect what they do to and for us. Many people think they already know the answer to the question, and they are prepared to talk and vote on that basis. That is their right and the opinions they express may be correct. But they may also be wrong. Indeed many of these opinions *must* be wrong because they are in conflict. When asked, "Who governs?" some people will say "the unions" and some will say "big business"; others will say "the politicians" or "the people" or "the special interests." Still others will say "Wall Street," "the military," "crackpot liberals," "the media," "the bureaucrats," or "white males." Not all these answers can be correct—at least not all of the time.

The answer to the second question is important because it tells us how government affects our lives. We want to know not only who governs, but what difference it makes who governs. In our day-to-day lives, we may not think government makes much difference at all. In one sense that is right because our most pressing personal concerns—work, play, love, family, health—are essentially private matters on which government touches but slightly. But in a larger and longer perspective, government makes a substantial difference. Consider: in 1935, 96 percent of all American families paid no federal income tax, and for the 4 percent or so who did pay, the average rate was only about 4 percent of their incomes. Today almost all families pay federal income taxes, and the average rate is 20 percent of their incomes. Through laws that have been enacted since the 1930s, the federal government has taken charge of an enormous amount of the nation's income, with results that are still being debated. Or consider: in 1960, in many parts of the country, blacks could ride only in the backs of buses, had to use washrooms and drinking fountains that were labeled "colored," and could not be served in most public restaurants. Such restrictions have been almost eliminated, in large part because of decisions by the federal government.

It is important to bear in mind that we wish to answer two different questions, and not two versions of the same question. You cannot always predict what goals government will establish knowing only who governs, nor can you always tell who governs by knowing what activities government undertakes. Most people holding national political office are middle-class, middle-aged, white Protestant males, but we cannot then conclude that the government will only adopt policies that are to the narrow advantage of the middle class, or the middle-aged, or whites, or Protestants, or men. If we thought that, we would be at a loss to explain why the rich are taxed more heavily than the poor, why a War on Poverty was declared, why constitutional amendments giving rights to blacks and women passed Congress by large majorities, or why Catholics and Jews have been appointed to so many important governmental posts.

This book is chiefly devoted to answering the question, Who governs? It is written in the belief that this question cannot be answered without looking at how government makes—or fails to make—decisions about a large variety of concrete issues. Thus, especially in Part 4, we shall inspect government policies to see what individuals, groups, and institutions seem to exert the greatest power in the continuous struggle to define the purposes of government. We shall see that power and purpose are inextricably intertwined.

What Is Political Power?

By **power** we mean the ability of one person to get another person to act in accordance with the first person's intentions. Sometimes an exercise of power is obvious, as when the president tells the air force that it can or cannot build the B-1 bomber. More often, power is exercised in subtle ways that may not be evident even to the participants, as when the president's economic advisers persuade him to impose or lift wage and price controls. The advisers may not think they are using power—after all, they are the president's subordinates—but if the president acts in accord with their intentions as a result of their arguments, they have used power.

Power is found in all human relationships, but we shall be concerned here only with power as it is used to affect who will hold government office and how government will behave. This fails to take into account many important things. If a corporation closes a factory in a small town where it was the major employer, it is using power in ways that affect deeply the lives of people. When a university refuses to admit a student or a medical society refuses to license a would-be physician, it is also using power. But to explain how all these things happen would be tantamount to explaining how society as a whole, and in all its particulars, operates. We limit our view to government, and chiefly to the American federal government. However, we shall repeatedly pay special attention to how things once thought to be "private" matters become "public"—that is, how they manage to become objects of governmental action. In Chapter 15, where we begin the discussion of policy-making, we will look closely at how issues get onto the governmental agenda. Indeed one of the most striking transformations of American politics has been the extent to which, in recent decades, almost every aspect of human life has found its way onto the governmental agenda. In the 1950s the federal government would have displayed no interest in a factory closing its doors, a university refusing an applicant, or a profession not accrediting a member. Now government actions can and do affect all these things.

People who exercise political power may or may not have the authority to do so. By **authority** we mean the right to use power. The exercise of rightful power—that is, of authority—is ordinarily easier than the exercise of power that is not supported by any persuasive claim of right. We accept decisions, often without question, if they are made by people who we believe have the right to make them; we may bow to naked power because we cannot resist it, but by our recalcitrance or our resentment we put the users of naked power to greater trouble than the wielders of authority. We will on occasion speak of "formal authority." By this we mean that the right to exercise power is vested in a governmental office. A president, a senator, and a federal judge have formal authority to take certain actions.

What makes power rightful varies from time to time and from country to country. In the United States we usually say that a person has political authority if his or her right to act in a certain way is

Dramatic changes have occurred in what people believe it is legitimate for the government to do. We now submit to searches before boarding an aircraft, unthinkable before hijackings made such government regulations seem necessary.

conferred by a law or by a state or national constitution. But what makes a law or constitution a source of right? That is the question of **legitimacy**. In the United States the Constitution today is widely, if not unanimously, accepted as a source of legitimate authority, but that was not always the case.

Much of American political history has been a struggle over what constitutes legitimate authority. The Constitutional Convention in 1787 was an effort to see whether a new, more powerful federal government could be made legitimate; the succeeding administrations of George Washington, John Adams, and Thomas Jefferson were in large measure preoccupied with disputes over the kinds of decisions that were legitimate for the federal government to make. The Civil War was a bloody struggle over the legitimacy of the federal union; the New Deal of Franklin Roosevelt was hotly debated by those who disagreed over whether it was legitimate for the federal government to intervene deeply in the economy.

In the United States today no government at any level would be considered legitimate if it were not in some sense democratic. That was not always the prevailing view, however; at one time people disagreed over whether democracy itself was a good idea. In 1787 Alexander Hamilton worried that the new government he helped create might be too democratic, while George Mason, who refused to sign the Constitution, worried that it was not democratic enough. Today virtually everyone believes that "democratic government" is the only proper kind. Most people probably believe that our existing government is democratic; and a few believe that other institutions of public life—schools, universities, corporations, trade unions, churches—should be run on democratic principles if they are to be legitimate. We shall not discuss the question of whether democracy is the best way of governing all institutions. Rather we shall consider the different meanings that have been attached to the word *democratic* and which, if any, best describes the government of the United States.

What Is Democracy?

Democracy is a word used to describe at least three different political systems. In one system the government is said to be democratic if its decisions will serve the "true interests" of the people whether or not those people directly affect the making of those decisions. It is by using this definition of democracy that various authoritarian regimes—China, Cuba, and

Before Boris Yeltsin came to power in Russia, the old Soviet Union was run on the principle of what the communists called "democratic centralism."

certain European, Asian, and Latin American dictatorships—have been able to claim that they were "democratic." Presidents of the now-defunct Soviet Union, for example, used to claim that they operated on the principle of **democratic centralism** whereby the true interests of the masses were discovered through discussion within the Communist party and then decisions were made under central leadership to serve those interests. The collapse of the Soviet Union occurred in part because many average Russians doubted that the Communist party knew or would act in support of the people's true interests.

Second, the term *democracy* is used to describe those regimes that come as close as possible to Aristotle's definition—the "rule of the many."[1] A government is democratic if all, or most, of its citizens participate directly in either holding office or making policy. This is often called **direct** or **participatory**

democracy. In Aristotle's time—Greece in the fourth century B.C.—such a government was possible. The Greek city-state, or *polis*, was quite small, and within it citizenship was extended to all free adult male property holders. (Slaves, women, minors, and those without property were excluded from participation in government.) In more recent times the New England town meeting approximates the Aristotelian ideal. In such a meeting the adult citizens of a community gather once or twice a year to vote directly on all major issues and expenditures of the town. As towns have become larger and issues more complicated, many town governments have abandoned the pure town meeting in favor of either the representative town meeting (in which a large number of elected representatives, perhaps two or three hundred, meet to vote on town affairs) or representative government (in which a small number of elected city councillors make decisions).

The third definition of democracy is the principle of governance of most nations that are called democratic. It was most concisely stated by the economist Joseph Schumpeter: "The democratic method is that institutional arrangement for arriving at political decisions in which individuals [that is, leaders] acquire the power to decide by means of a competitive struggle for the people's vote."[2] Sometimes this method is called approvingly **representative democracy**; at other times it is referred to, disapprovingly, as the elitist theory of democracy. It is justified by one or both of two arguments: First, it is impractical, owing to limits of time, information, energy, interest, and expertise, for the people to decide on public policy, but it is not impractical to expect them to make reasonable choices among competing leadership groups. Second, some people (including, as we shall see in the next chapter, many of the Framers of the Constitution) believe that direct democracy is likely to lead to bad decisions because people often decide large issues on the basis of fleeting passions and in response to popular demagogues. This fear of direct democracy persists today, as can be seen from the statements of those who do not like what the voters have decided. For example, politicians who favored Proposition 13, the referendum measure that in 1978 sharply cut property taxes in California, spoke approvingly of the "will of the people." Politicians who disliked Proposition 13 spoke disdainfully of "mass hysteria."

Direct Versus Representative Democracy: Which Is Best?

Whenever the word *democracy* is used alone in this book, it will have the meaning Schumpeter gave it. As we shall see in the next chapter, the men who wrote the Constitution did not use the word *democracy* in that document. They wrote instead of a "republican form of government," but by that they meant what we call "representative democracy." Whenever we refer to that form of democracy involving the direct participation of all or most citizens, we shall use the term *direct* or *participatory* democracy.

For representative government to work, there must, of course, be an opportunity for genuine leadership competition. This requires in turn that individuals and parties be able to run for office, that communication (through speeches, the press, and in meetings) be free, and that the voters perceive that a meaningful choice exists. Many questions still remain to be answered. For instance: How many offices should be elective and how many appointive? How many candidates or parties can exist before the choices become hopelessly confused? Where will the money come from to finance electoral campaigns? There is more than one answer to such questions. In some European democracies, for example, very few offices—often just those in the national or local legislature—are elective, and much of the money for campaigning for these offices comes from the government. In the United States many offices—executive and judicial as well as legislative—are elective, and most of the money the candidates use for campaigning comes from industry, labor unions, and private individuals.

Some people have argued that the virtues of direct or participatory democracy can and should be reclaimed even in a modern, complex society. This can be done either by allowing individual neighborhoods in big cities to govern themselves (community control) or by requiring those affected by some government program to participate in its formulation (citizen participation). In many states a measure of direct democracy exists when voters can decide on referendum issues—that is, policy choices that appear on the ballot. The proponents of direct democracy defend it as the only way to ensure that the "will of the people" prevails.

In ancient Athens citizens participated directly in politics by meeting in the Agora.

How Is Power Distributed in a Democracy?

Representative democracy is any system of government in which leaders are authorized to make decisions by winning a competitive struggle for the popular vote. It is obvious then that very different sets of hands can control political power depending on what kinds of people can become leaders, how the struggle for votes is carried on, how much freedom to act is given to those who win the struggle, and what other sorts of influence (besides the desire for popular approval) affect the leaders' actions.

In some cases the leaders will be so sharply constrained by what most people want that the actions of officeholders will follow the preferences of citizens very closely. We shall call such cases examples of majoritarian politics. In this case elected officials are the delegates of the people, acting as the people (or a majority of them) would act were the matter put to a popular vote. The issues handled in a majoritarian fashion can only be those that are sufficiently important to command the attention of most citizens, sufficiently clear to elicit an informed opinion from citizens, and sufficiently feasible so that what citizens want done can in fact be done. In Chapter 15 we shall discuss what features of an issue create the circumstances that facilitate majoritarian decision making, and in other chapters in Part 4 we give examples of them.

When circumstances do not permit majoritarian decision making, then some group of officials will have to act without knowing (and perhaps without caring) exactly what people want. Indeed, even on issues that do evoke a clear opinion from a majority of citizens, the shaping of the details of a policy will reflect the views of those people who are sufficiently motivated to go to the trouble of becoming active

Direct or participatory democracy can still be found in the New England town meeting.

participants in policy-making. These active participants usually will be a small, and probably an unrepresentative, minority. Thus the actual distribution of political power even in a democracy will depend importantly on the composition of the political elites who are actually involved in the struggles over policy. By **elite**, we mean an identifiable group of persons who possess a disproportionate share of some valued resource—in this case, political power.

Four Theories of Who Governs

At least four theories purport to describe and explain the actions of political elites. One theory is associated with the writings of Karl Marx. To Marxists—or at least to some of them, since not all Marxists agree—government, whatever its outward form, is merely a reflection of underlying economic forces, primarily the pattern of ownership of the means of production. All societies, they claim, are divided into classes on the basis of the relations of people to the economy—capitalists (the bourgeoisie), workers, farmers, intellectuals. In modern society two major classes contend for power—capitalists and workers. Whichever class dominates the economy also controls the government, which is nothing more than a piece of machinery designed to express and give legal effect to underlying class interests. In the United States the government "is but a committee for managing the common affairs of the whole bourgeoisie."[3] To a traditional Marxist it would be pointless to study the government since, as it is controlled by the dominant social class, it would have no independent power. There are many variations, some quite subtle, on this fundamental argument, and some newer Marxists find it more interesting to study how the government actually operates than did Marx himself, for whom government was a mere "epiphenomenon." But even neo-Marxists believe that the answer to the questions of who really governs, and to what ends, is to be found in the pattern of economic interests, especially those represented by the large corporation.

A second theory, closely related to the first, argues that a nongovernmental elite makes most of the major decisions but that this elite is not composed exclusively, or even primarily, of corporate leaders. C. Wright Mills, an American sociologist, expresses this view in his book *The Power Elite*.[4] To him, the most

CRITICAL ★ THINKING

Do We Want Push-Button Democracy?

The choice between representative and direct democracy is a profound one. Today many Americans are dissatisfied with representative government, which, they argue, acts too slowly, serves only special interests, and is unresponsive to majority opinion. During the 1992 presidential campaign, independent candidate Ross Perot promised to bring televised town hall–style meetings to the nation. Viewers would listen to experts debate an issue and then "vote" via toll-free telephone services capable of processing tens of thousands of calls per minute. Although he came in third in the 1992 election behind Bill Clinton and George Bush, Perot received 19.2 million votes, or 19 percent of all votes cast. (See Chapter 8 for details on the 1992 election.)

This type of "push-button" democracy is rapidly becoming technologically feasible, but is it desirable? Is government by electronic plebiscite preferable to government by deliberative institutions? Do you believe that most citizens have the time, information, interest, and expertise to make reasonable choices among competing policy positions? Or do you suspect that even highly educated people can be manipulated by demagogic leaders who play on their fears and prejudices?

How you respond to such questions ought not to depend on how you feel about any particular public figure, whether you like watching television, or how much you enjoy playing with computers. Rather, your answer ought to depend primarily on what you believe about the arguments for and against representative government versus direct democracy. For example, it is true that representative democracy often proceeds slowly and prevents sweeping changes in government policy. But it is also true that a government that is capable of doing great good quickly is just as capable of doing great harm quickly.

Representative democracy is often plagued by special interests, but it is by no means clear that direct democracy would solve rather than exacerbate this problem. For example, in California in 1990 about $125 million was spent to influence voters on initiatives (laws and amendments proposed by citizens with a required number of signatures on a petition and then decided by popular vote). That is more than was spent in 1990 by all special interests to lobby California legislators on all legislation (over one thousand bills).

Majority opinion figures in the enactment of many government policies, but few Americans would want the protection of their civil rights or civil liberties to hinge on a majority vote—the right to a

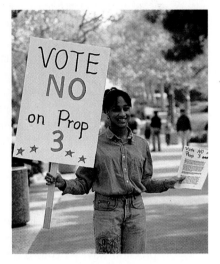

When people vote on referenda, the "special interests" are *us.*

fair trial, the freedoms of speech, press, and religion, or the right to vote itself.

As we will discuss in Chapter 2, the Framers of the United States Constitution believed strongly that government should mediate, not mirror, popular views, and that elected officials should represent, not register, majority sentiments. They favored representative democracy as a way of minimizing the chances that power would be abused either by a tyrannical popular majority or by self-serving office holders.

---

important policies are set by a loose coalition of three groups—corporate leaders, top military officers, and a handful of key political leaders. Different people have different versions of the "power elite" theory. Some would add to the triumvirate listed by Mills the leaders of the major communications media; others would add major labor leaders or the heads of various special-interest groups. The essential argument is the same, however: government is dominated by a few top leaders, most of whom are outside the government and enjoy great advantages in wealth, status, or organizational position. They act in concert, and

Karl Marx (left) (1818–1883), a German philosopher and radical political leader, was the founder of modern socialist thought. A brilliant, complex, and vituperative writer, Marx was best known for his *Communist Manifesto*. His major work was *Das Kapital*, a four-volume analysis of nineteenth-century capitalism.

Max Weber (right) (1864–1920), a German scholar, was a founder of sociology. Trained in law and history, he produced a major analysis of the evolution of modern society, which stressed the role of bureaucracy.

the policies they make serve the interests of the elite. Some people have such leaders in mind when they use the term *the Establishment*, though when that expression was first coined it referred to the influence exercised by Wall Street lawyers who alternated between governmental and private employment.[5]

A third theory directs attention to the appointed officials—the **bureaucrats**—who operate government agencies from day to day. Max Weber, a German historian and sociologist who wrote in the early years of this century, criticized the Marxist position because it assigned exclusive significance to economic power. Weber thought Marx had neglected the dominant social and political fact of modern times—that all institutions, governmental and nongovernmental, have fallen under the control of large bureaucracies whose expertise and specialized competence are essential to the management of contemporary affairs. Capitalists or workers may come to power, but the government agencies they create will be dominated by those who operate them on a daily basis. This dominance would have advantages, Weber thought, because decisions would be made more rationally; but it would also have disadvantages because the political power of the bureaucrats would become "overtowering."[6]

A fourth answer has no single intellectual parent but can be described loosely as the **pluralist** view. Political resources, such as money, prestige, expertise, organizational position, and access to the mass media, are so widely scattered in our society and in the hands of such a variety of persons that no single elite has anything like a monopoly on them. Furthermore there are so many governmental institutions in which power may be exercised—city, state, and federal governments and, within these, the offices of mayors, managers, legislators, governors, presidents, judges, bureaucrats—that no single group, even if it had many political resources, could dominate most, or even much, of the political process. Policies are the outcome of a complex pattern of political haggling, innumerable compromises, and shifting alliances.[7] Pluralists do not argue that political resources are distributed equally—that would be tantamount to saying that all decisions are made on a majoritarian basis. They believe that political resources are sufficiently divided among such different kinds of elites (businesspeople, politicians, union leaders, journalists, bureaucrats, professors, environmentalists, lawyers, and whomever) that all, or almost all, relevant interests have a chance to affect the outcome of decisions. Not only are the elites divided, they are responsive to their followers' interests, and thus they provide representation to almost all citizens affected by a policy.

Contemplating these contending theories may lead some people to the cynical conclusion that, whichever theory is correct, politics is a self-seeking enterprise in which everybody is out for personal gain. Though there is surely plenty of self-interest among political elites (at least as much as there is among college students!), it does not necessarily follow that the resulting policies will be wholly self-serving. For one thing, a policy may be good or bad independently of the motives of the person who decided it, just as a product sold on the market may be useful or useless regardless of the profit-seeking or wage-seeking motives of those who produced it. For another thing, the self-interest of individuals is often an incomplete guide to their actions. People must frequently choose between two courses of action, neither of which has an obvious "payoff" to them. We caution against the cynical explanation of politics that Americans seem especially prone to adopt. Alexis de Tocqueville, the French author of a perceptive account of American life and politics in the early nineteenth century, noticed this trait among us.

> *Americans . . . are fond of explaining almost all the actions of their lives by the principle of self-interest rightly understood. . . . In this respect I think they frequently fail to do themselves justice; for in the United States as well as elsewhere people are sometimes seen to give way to those disinterested and spontaneous impulses that are natural to man; but the Americans seldom admit that they yield to emotions of this kind; they are more anxious to do honor to their philosophy than to themselves.[8]*

The belief that people will usually act on the basis of their self-interest, narrowly defined, is a theory to be tested, not an assumption to be made. Two examples of how such an assumption can prove misleading will suffice for now. In the 1960s leaders of the AFL-CIO in Washington were among the most influential forces lobbying Congress for the passage of certain civil rights bills. Yet at the time they did this, the leaders did not stand to benefit either personally (they were almost all white) or organizationally (rank-and-file labor union members were not enthusiastic about such measures).[9] Another example: In the late 1970s, many employees of the Civil Aeronautics Board worked hard to have their agency abolished, even though this meant that they would lose their jobs. To understand why they took these positions, it is not enough to know their incomes or their jobs; one must also know something about their attitudes, their allies, and the temper of the times. In short, political preferences cannot invariably be predicted simply by knowing economic or organizational position.

Political Change

The question of who governs will be answered differently at different times. Circumstances change, as does our knowledge about politics. As we shall see in Part 3, the presidency and Congress in the second half of the nineteenth century were organized rather differently from how they are today. Throughout this book we shall make frequent reference to the historical evolution of institutions and policies. We shall do this partly because what government does today is powerfully influenced by what it did yesterday, and partly because the evolution of our institutions and policies has not stopped but is continuing. If we get some sense of how the past has shaped the government, we may better understand what we see today and are likely to see tomorrow.

When we view American government from the perspective of the past, we will find it hard to accept as generally true any simple, mechanistic, theory of politics. Economic interests, powerful elites, entrenched bureaucrats, and competing pressure groups have all played a part in shaping our policies, but the great shifts in the direction of that policy respond to changing *beliefs* about what government is supposed to do.

In the 1920s it was widely assumed that the federal government would play a small role in our lives.

Direct Democracy and the Computerized Presidency

Shortly after being elected to office, President Clinton starred in a television program that was billed as a "nationwide electronic town meeting" on jobs and the economy. The White House communications staff also employed a former disc jockey to develop "BC TV" (Bill Clinton TV), an interactive cable television station that would provide twenty-four-hour coverage of the presidency. Subscribers to major on-line computer services such as CompuServe can now punch in the command "GO WHITEHOUSE" to hook into the "White House forum," send or receive messages and information on dozens of subjects, or gain instant access to presidential speeches and photographs. During the Reagan years (1980–1988), the White House operators received five thousand calls on a busy day. But in the first months of the Clinton presidency, about forty thousand calls a day lit up the White House switchboard.

What the Majority Wants: Of Government and Baseball

The choice between representative and direct democracy is central to governance. According to public opinion surveys, a majority of Americans would:

- sentence all rapists to death

- oppose extending civil rights laws to homosexuals

- not allow anyone accused of a violent crime to get out on bail while awaiting trial

- spend less on foreign aid

- oppose military intervention if Arab forces invaded Israel

- spend more government money on medical care, protecting the environment, big cities, and transportation

- spend either the same amount or less government money on welfare, unemployment insurance, and programs that benefit minority citizens

- oppose the construction of nuclear power plants

- oppose giving financial aid to Russia

- have rejected the Marshall Plan (the financial support America gave to rebuild Europe after World War II)

- favor term limits for members of Congress

- favor amending the Constitutions to require a balanced budget

Most Americans are in the majority on some issues but not on others. (Are you in the majority on some, all, or none of the issues listed above?) Thus, for most Americans simply knowing what the majority wants is not a way to resolve the tension between direct and representative democracy.

As it is in government, so it is in major-league baseball. Most baseball fans like getting a chance to vote on which players merit selection to the All-Star teams. In 1992 at the All-Star break, Edgar Martinez of the Seattle Mariners was

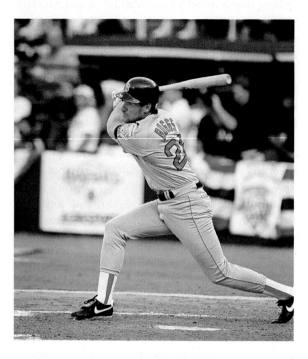

hitting .319 (third in the American League), with forty-six runs-batted-in, and fourteen home runs; he was a standout fielder. Wade Boggs of the Boston Red Sox was hitting .268 (sixty-fourth in the American League), with just twenty-five runs-batted-in, and only six home runs; he was having an average year fielding. But Boggs received 1.2 million votes versus Martinez's 500,000. Boggs played third base on the All-Star team; Martinez watched the game on TV. Direct democracy in baseball appeals to the fans, but does it produce the best All-Star teams?

SOURCE: Adapted from Christopher J. Georges, "Perot or Con," *The Washington Monthly* (June 1993): 38–43, and *The Gallup Monthly Poll* (April 1993): 31–34.

From the 1930s through the 1970s it was generally believed that the federal government would try to solve whatever social or economic problem existed. From 1981 through 1988 the administration of Ronald Reagan sought to reverse that assumption and to cut back on the taxes Washington levied, the money it spent, and the regulations it imposed. It is clear that no simple theory of politics is likely to explain both the growth of federal power after 1932 and the effort to cut back on that power starting in 1981. Every student of politics sooner or later learns that the hardest things to explain are usually the most important ones.

Take the case of foreign affairs. During certain periods in our history we have taken an active interest in the outside world—at the time the nation was founded when France and England seemed to have it in their power to determine whether or not America would survive as a nation; in the 1840s when we sought to expand the nation into areas where Mexico and Canada had claims; in the late 1890s when many leaders believed we had an obligation to acquire an overseas empire in the Caribbean and the Pacific; and in the period from the 1940s to the 1960s when we openly accepted the role of the world's police officer. At other times America has looked inward, spurning opportunities for expansion and virtually ignoring events that in other periods would have been a cause for war, or at least mobilization.

Deep-seated beliefs, major economic developments, and widely shared (or competing) opinions about what constitutes the dominant political problem of the time shape the nature of day-to-day political conflict. What this means is that, in any broad historical or comparative perspective, politics is *not just* about "who gets what," though that is part of the story. It is about how people, or elites claiming to speak for people, define the public interest. Lest one think that such definitions are mere window dressing, signifying nothing of importance, bear in mind that on occasion men and women have been prepared to fight and die for one definition or another. Suppose you, the reader, had been alive in 1861. Do you think you would have viewed slavery as a matter of gains and losses, costs and benefits, winners and losers? Some people did. Or do you think you would have been willing to fight to abolish or preserve it? Many others did just that. The differences in these ways of thinking about such an issue are at least as important as how institutions are organized or elections conducted.

Finding Out Who Governs

Ideally political scientists ought to be able to give clear answers, amply supported by evidence, to the questions, How is political power distributed? and To what purposes will it be used under various circumstances? In reality they can (at best) give partial, contingent, and controversial answers. The reason is to be found in the nature of our subject. Unlike economists, who assume that people have more or less stable preferences and can compare ways of satisfying those preferences by looking at the relative prices of various goods and services, political scientists are interested in how preferences are formed, especially for those kinds of services, such as national defense or pollution control, that cannot be evaluated chiefly in terms of monetary costs.

Understanding preferences is vital to understanding power. Who did what in government is not hard to find out, but who wielded power—that is, who made a difference in the outcome and for what reason—is much harder to discover. *Power* is a word that conjures up images of deals, bribes, power plays, and arm-twisting. In fact most power exists because of shared understanding, common friendships, communal or organizational loyalties, and different degrees of prestige. These are hard to identify and almost impossible to quantify.

Nor can the distribution of political power be inferred simply by knowing what laws are on the books or what administrative actions have been taken. The enactment of a consumer-protection law does not mean that consumers are powerful any more than the absence of such a law means that corporations are powerful. The passage of such a law could reflect an aroused public opinion, the lobbying of a small group claiming to speak for consumers, the ambitions of a senator, or the intrigues of one business firm seeking to gain a competitive advantage over another. A close analysis of what the law entails and how it was passed and administered is necessary before much of anything can be said.

This book will avoid sweeping claims that we have an "imperial" presidency (or an impotent one), an "obstructionist" Congress (or an innovative one), or "captured" regulatory agencies. Such labels do an injustice to the different roles that presidents, members of Congress, and administrators play in different kinds of issues and in different historical periods.

The view taken in this book is that judgments about institutions and interests can be made only after one has seen how they behave on a variety of important issues or potential issues. Thus Part 4 of this book on policy-making is an essential component of the analysis, not an appendage. The issues discussed there—economic policy, the regulation of business, social welfare, civil rights and liberties, foreign and military affairs—are the daily business of government. The policies adopted or blocked, the groups

Direct political action can be peaceful or violent, as when abortion-rights advocates march (top) or opponents bomb an abortion clinic (bottom).

way other democratic nations handle it, and differs as well from the way our own institutions once treated it. The description of our institutions in Part 3 will therefore include not only an account of how they work today but also a brief historical background on their workings and a comparison with similar institutions in other countries. There is a tendency to assume that how we do things today is the only way they could possibly be done. In fact there are other ways to operate a government based on some measure of popular rule. History, tradition, and belief weigh heavily on all that we do.

In any event the place to begin a search for how power is distributed in national politics and what purposes that power serves is with the founding of the federal government in 1787: the Constitutional Convention and the events leading up to it. Though the decisions of that time were not made by philosophers or professors, the practical men who made them had a philosophic and professorial cast of mind, and thus they left behind a fairly explicit account of what values they sought to protect and what arrangements they thought ought to be made for the allocation of political power.

SUMMARY

There are two major questions about politics: Who governs? To what ends? This book will focus mainly on answering the first.

Four answers have traditionally been given to the question of who governs.

- The *Marxist*—those who control the economic system will control the political one.

- The *elitist*—a few top leaders, not all of them drawn from business, make the key decisions without reference to popular desires.

- The *bureaucratic*—appointed civil servants run things.

- The *pluralist*—competition among affected interests shapes public policy.

To choose among these theories or to devise new ones requires more than describing governmental institutions and processes. In addition one must examine the kinds of issues that do (or do not) get taken

heeded or ignored, the values embraced or rejected—these constitute the raw material out of which one can fashion an answer to the central questions we have asked: Who rules? and To what ends?

The way in which our institutions of government handle social welfare, for example, differs from the up by the political system and how that system resolves them.

The distinction between different types of democracies is important. The Framers of the Constitution intended that America be a representative democracy in which the power to make decisions is determined by means of a free and competitive struggle for the citizens' votes.

KEY TERMS

power   *p. 4*

authority   *p. 4*

legitimacy   *p. 5*

democracy   *p. 5*

democratic centralism   *p. 6*

direct *or* participatory democracy   *p. 6*

representative democracy   *p. 6*

elite   *p. 8*

Marxist   *p. 8*

bureaucrats   *p. 10*

pluralist   *p. 10*

SUGGESTED READINGS

Banfield, Edward C. *Political Influence*. New York: Free Press, 1961. A method of analyzing politics—in this case, in the city of Chicago—comparable to the approach adopted in this book.

Crick, Bernard. *The American Science of Politics*. London: Routledge & Kegan Paul, 1959. A critical review of the methods of studying government and politics.

Marx, Karl, and Friedrich Engels. "The Manifesto of the Communist Party." In *The Marx-Engels Reader*, edited by Robert C. Tucker. 2d ed. New York: Norton, 1978, 469–500. The classic statement of the Marxist view of history and politics. Should be read in conjunction with Engels, "Socialism: Utopian and Scientific," in the same collection, 683–717.

Mills, C. Wright. *The Power Elite*. New York: Oxford University Press, 1956. An argument that self-serving elites dominate American politics.

Schumpeter, Joseph A. *Capitalism, Socialism, and Democracy*. 3d ed. New York: Harper, 1950, Chs. 20–23. A lucid statement of the theory of representative democracy and how it differs from participatory democracy.

Truman, David B. *The Government Process*. 2d ed. New York: Knopf, 1971. A pluralist interpretation of American politics.

Weber, Max. *From Max Weber: Essays in Sociology*. Translated and edited by H. H. Gerth and C. Wright Mills. London: Routledge & Kegan Paul, 1948, Ch. 8. A theory of bureaucracy and its power.

Congress of the United States,
begun and held at the City of New-York, on
Wednesday the fourth of March one thousand seven hundred and eighty nine.

2

The Constitution

The goal of the American Revolution was liberty. It was not the first revolution with that object; it may not have been the last; but it was perhaps the clearest case of a people altering the political order violently, simply in order to protect their liberties. Subsequent revolutions had more complicated, or utterly different, objectives. The French Revolution in 1789 sought not only liberty, but "equality and fraternity." The Russian Revolution (1917) and the Chinese Revolution (culminating in 1949) chiefly sought equality and were little concerned with liberty as we understand it.

The Problem of Liberty

What the American colonists sought to protect when they signed the Declaration of Independence in 1776 were the traditional liberties to which they thought they were entitled as British subjects. These liberties included the right to bring their legal cases before truly independent judges rather than ones subordinate to the king; to be free of the burden of having British troops quartered in their homes; to engage in trade without burdensome restrictions; and, of course, to pay no taxes voted by a British Parliament in which they had no direct representation. During the ten years or more of agitation and argument leading up to the War of Independence, most colonists believed that their liberties could be protected while they remained a part of the British Empire.

Slowly but surely opinion shifted. By the time war broke out in 1775, a large number of colonists (though perhaps not a majority) had reached the conclusion that the colonies would have to become independent of Great Britain if their liberties were to be assured. The colonists had many reasons for regarding independence as the only solution, but one is especially important: they no longer had confidence in the English constitution. This constitution was not a single written document but rather a collection of laws, charters, and traditional understandings that

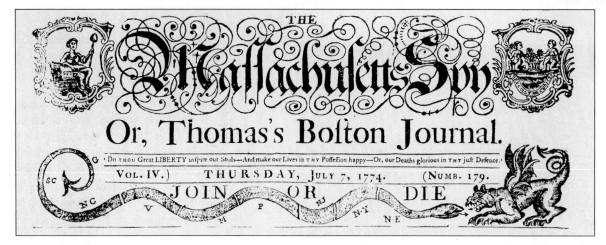

Even before the Revolutionary War, many felt that some form of union would be necessary if the rebellious colonies were to survive. In 1774 the *Massachusetts Spy* portrayed the colonies as segments of a snake that must "Join or Die."

proclaimed the liberties of British subjects. Yet these liberties, in the eyes of the colonists, were regularly violated despite their constitutional protection. Clearly, then, the English constitution was an inadequate check on the abuses of political power. The revolutionary leaders sought an explanation of the insufficiency of the constitution and found it in human nature.

The Colonial Mind

"A lust for domination is more or less natural to all parties," one colonist wrote.[1] Men will seek power, many colonists believed, because they are ambitious, greedy, and easily corrupted. John Adams denounced the "luxury, effeminacy, and venality" of English politics; Patrick Henry spoke scathingly of the "corrupt House of Commons"; and Alexander Hamilton described England as "an old, wrinkled, withered, worn-out hag."[2] This was in part flamboyant rhetoric designed to whip up enthusiasm for the conflict, but it was also deeply revealing of the colonial mind. Their belief that English politicians—and by implication, most politicians—tended to be corrupt was the colonists' explanation of why the English constitution was not an adequate guarantee of the liberty of the citizens. This opinion was to persist and, as we shall see, profoundly affect the way the Americans went about designing their own governments.

The liberties the colonists fought to protect were, they thought, widely understood. They were based not on the generosity of the king or the language of statutes but on a "higher law" embodying "natural rights" that were ordained by God, discoverable in nature and history, and essential to human progress. These rights, John Dickinson wrote, "are born with us; exist with us; and cannot be taken away from us by any human power."[3] There was general agreement that the essential rights included life, liberty, and property long before Thomas Jefferson wrote them into the Declaration of Independence. (Jefferson changed "property" to "the pursuit of happiness," but almost everybody else went on talking about property.)

This emphasis on property did not mean that the American Revolution was thought up by the rich and wellborn to protect their interests or that there was a struggle between property owners and the property-less. In late eighteenth-century America most people (except the black slaves) had property of some kind. The overwhelming majority of citizens was self-employed—as farmers or artisans—and rather few people benefited financially by gaining independence from England. Taxes were higher during and after the war than before, trade was disrupted by the conflict, and debts mounted perilously as various expedients were invented to pay for the struggle. There were, of course, war profiteers and those who tried to manip-

The American colonists' desire to assert their liberties led in time to a deep hostility to British government, as when these New Yorkers toppled a statue of King George III, melted it down, and used the metal to make bullets.

ulate the currency to their own advantage, but most Americans at the time of the war saw the conflict clearly in terms of political rather than economic issues. It was a war of ideology.

Everyone recognizes the glowing language with which Jefferson set out the case for independence in the second paragraph of the Declaration:

We hold these truths to be self-evident, that all men are created equal, that they are endowed by their Creator with certain unalienable Rights, that among these are Life, Liberty, and the pursuit of Happiness.—That to secure these rights, Governments are instituted among Men, deriving their just powers from the consent of the governed—that whenever any Form of Government becomes destructive of these ends, it is the Right of the People to alter or to abolish it, and to institute new Government, laying its foundation on such principles, and organizing its powers in such form, as to them shall seem most likely to effect their Safety and Happiness.

What almost no one recalls, but what is an essential part of the Declaration, are the next twenty-seven paragraphs in which, item by item, Jefferson listed the specific complaints the colonists had against George III and his ministers. None of these items spoke of social or economic conditions in the colonies; all spoke instead of specific violations of political liberties. The Declaration was in essence a lawyer's brief prefaced by a stirring philosophical claim that the rights being violated were **unalienable**—that is, based on nature and Providence, and not on the whims or preferences of people. Jefferson, in his original draft, added a twenty-eighth complaint—that the king had allowed the slave trade to continue *and* was inciting slaves to revolt against their masters. Congress, faced with so contradictory a charge, decided to include a muted reference to slave insurrections and omit all reference to slave trade.

The Real Revolution

The Revolution was more than the War of Independence. It began before the war, continued after it, and involved more than driving out the British army by force of arms. The *real* Revolution, as John Adams afterward explained in a letter to a friend, was the *"radical change in the principles, opinions, and sentiments, and affections of the people."*[4] This radical change had to do with a new vision of what could make political

NORTH AMERICA IN 1787

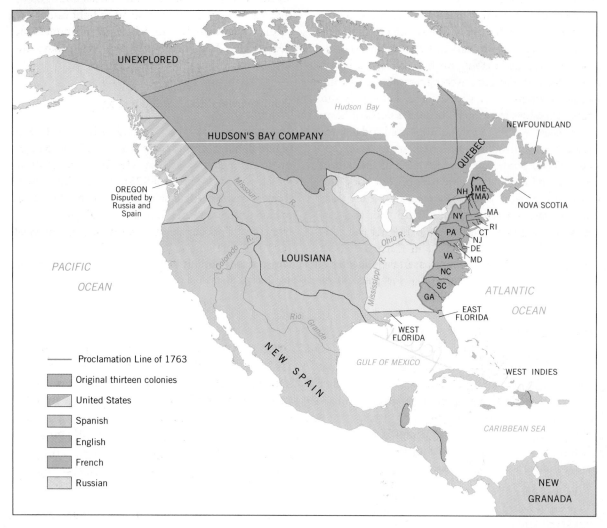

authority legitimate and personal liberties secure. Government by royal prerogative was rejected; instead legitimate government would require the consent of the governed. Political power could not be exercised on the basis of tradition but only as a result of a direct grant of power contained in a written constitution. Human liberty existed before government was organized, and government must respect that liberty. The legislative branch of government, in which the people were directly represented, should be superior to the executive branch.

These were indeed revolutionary ideas. No government at the time had been organized on the basis of these principles. And to the colonists such notions

were not empty words but rules to be put into immediate practice. In 1776 eight states adopted written constitutions. Within a few years every former colony had adopted one except Connecticut and Rhode Island, two states that continued to rely on their colonial charters. Most state constitutions had detailed bills of rights defining personal liberties, and most placed the highest political power in the hands of elected representatives.

Written constitutions, representatives, and bills of rights are so familiar to us now that we forget how bold and unprecedented those innovations were in 1776. Indeed many Americans did not think they would succeed: such arrangements would be either so strong that they would threaten liberty or so weak that they would permit chaos.

The eleven years that elapsed between the Declaration of Independence and the signing of the Constitution in 1787 were years of turmoil, uncertainty, and fear. George Washington had to wage a bitter, protracted war without anything resembling a strong national government to support him. The supply and financing of his army were based on a series of hasty improvisations, most badly administered and few adequately supported by the fiercely independent states. When peace came, many parts of the nation were a shambles. At least a quarter of New York City was in ruins, and many other communities were nearly devastated. Though the British lost the war, they still were powerful on the North American continent, with an army available in Canada (where many Americans loyal to Britain had fled)and a large navy at sea. Spain claimed the Mississippi River Valley and occupied what are now Florida and California. Men who had left their farms to fight came back to discover themselves in debt with no money and heavy taxes. The paper money printed to finance the war was now virtually worthless.

Weaknesses of the Confederation

The thirteen states had formed only a faint semblance of a national government with which to bring order to the nation. The **Articles of Confederation**, which went into effect in 1781, created little more than a "league of friendship" that could not levy taxes or regulate commerce. Each state retained its sovereignty and independence, each state (regardless of size) had one vote in Congress, nine (of thirteen) votes were required to pass any measure, and the

John Hancock was proud to have signed the Declaration of Independence, but thought so little of the presidency under the Articles of Confederation that he never bothered to accept the job.

The Articles of Confederation had made it plain that the United States was not to have a true national government but was to be governed by a compact among sovereign and independent states.

ARTICLES

Of Confederation and perpetual Union between the States of *New-Hampshire, Massachusetts-Bay, Rhode-Island* and *Providence Plantations, Connecticut, New-York, New-Jersey, Pennsylvania, Delaware, Maryland, Virginia, North-Carolina, South-Carolina* and *Georgia.*

ARTICLE I.   THE ſtile of this confederacy ſhail be " The United " States of America."   Stile of the Confederacy

ART. II.   EACH ſtate retains its ſovereignty, freedom and independence, and every power, juriſdiction and right, which is not by this confederation expreſly delegated to the United States, in Congreſs aſſembled.   Sovereignty and Independence of the reſpective States.

ART. III.   THE ſaid ſtates hereby ſeverally enter into a firm league of friendſhip with each other, for their common defence, the ſecurity of their liberties, and their mutual and general welfare, binding themſelves to aſſiſt each other, againſt all force offered to, or attacks made upon them, or any of them, on account of religion, ſovereignty, trade, or any other pretence whatever.   Deſign of the Confederation, as it regards common ſecurity.

ART. IV.   THE better to ſecure and perpetuate mutual friendſhip and intercourſe among the people of the different ſtates in this union, the free inhabitants of each of theſe ſtates, paupers, vagabonds, and fugitives from juſtice excepted, ſhall be entitled to all privileges and immunities of free citizens in the ſeveral ſtates ; and the people of each ſtate ſhall have free ingreſs and regreſs to and from any other ſtate, and ſhall enjoy therein all the privileges of trade and commerce, ſubject to the ſame duties, impoſitions and reſtrictions as the inhabitants thereof reſpectively, provided that ſuch reſtriction ſhall not extend ſo far as to prevent the removal of property imported into any ſtate, to any other ſtate of which the owner is an inhabitant ; provided alſo that no impoſition, duties or reſtriction ſhall be laid by any ſtate, on the property of the united ſtates, or either of them.   Social and mutual intercourſe among the States.

Independence Hall in Philadelphia, where the Declaration of Independence and the Constitution were signed.

delegates who cast these votes were picked and paid for by the state legislatures. Congress did have the power to make peace, and thus it was able to ratify the treaty with England in 1783. It could coin money, but there was precious little to coin; it could appoint the key army officers, but the army was small and dependent for support on independent state militias; it was allowed to run the post office, then, as now, a thankless task that nobody else wanted. John Hancock, who in 1785 was elected to the meaningless office of "president" under the Articles, never showed up to take the job. Several states claimed the unsettled lands in the West, and occasionally pressed those claims with guns. Pennsylvania and Virginia went to war near Pittsburgh, and Vermont threatened to become part of Canada. There was no national judicial system to settle these or other claims among the states. To amend the Articles of Confederation, all thirteen states had to agree.

Many of the leaders of the Revolution, such as George Washington and Alexander Hamilton, believed that a stronger national government was essential. They lamented the disruption of commerce and travel caused by the quarrelsome states and deeply feared the possibility of foreign military intervention, with England or France playing one state off against another. A small group of men, conferring at Washington's home at Mount Vernon in 1785, decided to call a meeting to discuss trade regulation. That meeting, held at Annapolis, Maryland, in September 1786, was not well attended (no delegates arrived from New England), and so another meeting, this one in Philadelphia, was called for the following spring—in May 1787—to consider ways of remedying the defects of the Confederation.

The Constitutional Convention

The delegates assembled at Philadelphia for what was advertised (and authorized by Congress) as a meeting to revise the Articles; they adjourned four months later having written a wholly new constitution. When they met, they were keenly aware of the problems of the confederacy but far from agreeing as to what should be done about those problems. The protection of life, liberty, and property was their objective in 1787 as it had been in 1776, but they had no accepted political theory that would tell them what kind of national government, if any, would serve that goal.

The Lessons of Experience

They had read ancient and modern political history, only to learn that nothing seemed to work. James Madison spent a good part of 1786 studying books sent to him by Thomas Jefferson, then in Paris, in hopes of finding some model for a workable American republic. He took careful notes on various confederacies in ancient Greece and on the more modern confederacy of the United Netherlands. He reviewed the history of Switzerland and Poland and the ups and downs of the Roman republic. He concluded that there was no model; as he later put it in one of the *Federalist* papers, history consists only of beacon lights "which give warning of the course to be shunned, without pointing out that which ought to be pursued."[5] The problem seemed to be that confederacies were too weak to govern and tended to collapse from internal dissension, while all stronger forms of government were so powerful as to trample the liberties of the citizens.

State Constitutions   Madison and the others did not need to consult history, or even the plight of the Articles of Confederation, for illustrations of the problem. These could be found in the government of the American states at the time. Pennsylvania and Massachusetts exemplified two aspects of the problem. The Pennsylvania constitution, adopted in 1776, created the most radically democratic of the new state regimes. All power was given to a one-house (unicameral) legislature, the Assembly, the members of which were elected annually for one-year terms. No legislator could serve more than four years. There was no governor or president, only an Executive Council that had few powers. Thomas Paine, whose pamphlets had helped precipitate the break with England, thought the Pennsylvania constitution was the best in America, and in France philosophers hailed it as the very embodiment of the principle of rule by the people. Though popular in France, it was a good deal less popular in Philadelphia. The Assembly disfranchised the Quakers, persecuted conscientious objectors to the war, ignored the requirement of trial by juries, and manipulated the judiciary.[6] To Madison and his friends the Pennsylvania constitution demonstrated how a government, though democratic, could be tyrannical as a result of concentrating all powers into one set of hands.

The Massachusetts constitution, adopted in 1780, was a good deal less democratic. There was a clear separation of powers among the various branches of government, the directly elected governor could veto acts of the legislature, and judges served for life. Both voters and elected officials had to be property owners; the governor, in fact, had to own at least £1,000 worth of property. The principal officeholders had to swear they were Christians.

Shays's Rebellion   But if the government of Pennsylvania was thought to be too strong, that of Massachusetts seemed too weak, despite its "conservative" features. In January 1787 a group of ex–Revolutionary War soldiers and officers, plagued by debts and high taxes and fearful of losing their property to

The presiding officer at the Constitutional Convention was George Washington (1732–1799). He participated just once in the debates, but the effect of his presence was great. He was a national military hero, and it was generally expected that he would be the nation's first president.

creditors and tax collectors, forcibly prevented the courts in western Massachusetts from sitting. This became known as **Shays's Rebellion**, after one of the officers, Daniel Shays. The governor of Massachusetts asked the Continental Congress to send troops to suppress the rebellion, but it could not raise the money or the manpower. Then he turned to his own state militia, but discovered he did not have one. In desperation private funds were collected to hire a volunteer army that marched on Springfield and, with the firing of a few shots, dispersed the rebels, who fled into neighboring states.

Shays's Rebellion, occurring between the aborted Annapolis and the coming Philadelphia conventions had a powerful effect on opinion. Delegates who might have been reluctant to attend the Philadelphia meeting, especially those from New England, were galvanized by the fear that state governments were about to collapse from internal dissension. George Washington wrote a friend despairingly: "For God's sake . . . , if they [the rebels] have *real* grievances, redress them; if they have not, employ the force of government against them at once."[7] Thomas Jefferson, living in Paris, took a more detached view: "A little rebellion now and then is a good thing," he wrote.

Commonwealth of MASSACHUSETTS,

By BENJAMIN LINCOLN, ESQUIRE,
Commanding General of the Troops now in the Field, by Order of
GOVERNMENT.

WHEREAS there are some of the Citizens of this Commonwealth, who have acted in Arms as Non-Commissioned Officers and
Privates against the Government of this State, who have caused it
to be represented, that they would willingly return to their Allegiance and Duty, could they hope for a Pardon.

To all such I declare, That if they will come in, surrender their
Arms, and take and subscribe the Oath of Allegiance to this Commonwealth, that they will be recommended to a Pardon.

B. LINCOLN.

Dated at Head-Quarters, Pittsfield, *February* 19, 1787.

Shays's Rebellion in western Massachusetts in 1786–1787 stirred deep fears of anarchy in America. The ruckus was put down by a hastily assembled militia, and the rebels were eventually pardoned.

"The tree of liberty must be refreshed from time to time with the blood of patriots and tyrants."[8] Though Jefferson's detachment might be explained by the fact that he was in Paris and not in Springfield, there were others, like Governor George Clinton of New York, who shared the view that no strong central government was required. (Whether Clinton would have agreed about the virtues of spilled blood, especially his, is another matter.)

The Framers

The Philadelphia convention attracted fifty-five delegates, only about thirty of whom participated regularly in the proceedings. One state, Rhode Island, refused to send anyone. The convention met during a miserably hot Philadelphia summer, with the delegates pledged to keep their deliberations secret. The talkative and party-loving Benjamin Franklin was often accompanied by other delegates to make sure that neither wine nor his delight in telling stories would lead him to divulge delicate secrets.

Those who attended were for the most part young (Hamilton was thirty; Madison, thirty-six) but experienced. Eight delegates had signed the Dec-

laration of Independence, seven had been governors, thirty-four were lawyers and reasonably well-to-do, a few were wealthy. They were not "intellectuals," but men of practical affairs. Thirty-nine had served in the ineffectual Congress of the Confederation; a third were veterans of the Continental army.

Some names made famous by the Revolution were conspicuously absent. Thomas Jefferson and John Adams were serving as ministers abroad; Samuel Adams was ill; Patrick Henry was chosen to attend but refused, commenting that he "smelled a rat in Philadelphia, tending toward monarchy."

The convention produced not a revision of the Articles of Confederation, as it had been authorized to do, but instead a wholly new written constitution creating a true national government unlike any that had existed before. That document is today the world's oldest written national constitution. Those who wrote it were neither saints nor schemers, and the deliberations were not always lofty or philosophical—much hard bargaining, not a little confusion, and the accidents of personality and time helped shape the final product. The delegates were split on many issues—what powers should be given to a central government, how the states should be represented, what was to be done about slavery, the role of the people—each of which was resolved by a compromise. The speeches of the delegates (known to us from the detailed notes kept by Madison) did not explicitly draw on political philosophy or quote from the writings of philosophers. Everybody present was quite familiar with the traditional arguments and, on the whole, well read in history. But though the leading political philosophers were only rarely mentioned, the debate was profoundly influenced by philosophical beliefs, some formed by the revolutionary experience and others by the eleven-year attempt at self-government.

From the debates leading up to the Revolution, the delegates had drawn a commitment to liberty, which, despite the abuses sometimes committed in its name, they continued to share. Their defense of liberty as a natural right was derived from the writings of the English philosopher John Locke and based on his view that such rights are discoverable by reason. In a "state of nature," Locke argued, all men cherish and seek to protect their life, liberty, and property. But in a state of nature—that is, a society without a government—the strong can use their liberty to deprive the weak of theirs. The instinct for self-preservation leads people to want a government that will prevent this exploitation. But if the government is not itself to deprive its subjects of their liberty, it must be limited. The chief limitation on it, he said, should derive from the fact that it is created, and

Patrick Henry

James Madison

Thomas Jefferson

Edmund Randolph

John Locke

William Paterson

The Federalist *Papers*

*I*n 1787, to help win ratification of the new Constitution in the New York state convention, Alexander Hamilton decided to publish a series of articles defending and explaining the document in the New York City newspapers. He recruited John Jay and James Madison to help him, and the three of them, under the pen name "Publius," wrote eighty-five articles that appeared from late 1787 through 1788. The identity of the authors was kept secret at the time, but we now know that Hamilton wrote fifty-one of them, Madison twenty-six, Jay five, and Hamilton and Madison jointly authored three. The two most famous articles—Numbers 10 and 51—were by Madison alone (and are reprinted here in the Appendix).

The *Federalist* papers probably played only a small role in securing ratification. Like most legislative battles, this one was not decisively influenced by philosophical writings. But these essays have had a lasting value as an authoritative and profound explanation of the Constitution. Though written for political purposes, the *Federalist* has become the single most important piece of American political philosophy ever produced. Ironically Hamilton and Madison were later to become political enemies; even at the Philadelphia convention they had different views of the kind of government that should be created. But in 1787–1788 they were united in the belief that the new Constitution was the best that could have been obtained under the circumstances.

James Madison

Alexander Hamilton

For the Independent Journal.

The FŒDERALIST. No. X.

To the People of the State of New-York.

AMONG the numerous advantages promised by a well constructed Union, none deserves to be more accurately developed than its tendency to break and control the violence of faction. The friend of popular governments, never finds himself so much alarmed for their character and fate, as when he contemplates their propensity to this dangerous vice. He will not fail therefore to set a due value on any plan which, without violating the principles to which he is attached, provides a proper cure for it. The instability, injustice and confusion introduced into the public councils, have in truth been the mortal diseases under which popular governments have every where perished; as they continue to be the favorite and fruitful topics from which the adversaries to liberty derive their most specious declamations. The valuable improvements made by the American Constitutions on the popular models, both ancient and modern, cannot certainly be too much admired; but it would be an unwarrantable partiality, to contend that they have as effectually obviated the danger on this side as was wished and expected. Complaints are every where heard from our most considerate and virtuous citizens, equally the friends of public and private faith, and of public and personal liberty; that our governments are too unstable; that the public

John Jay

governs, by the consent of the governed. People will not agree to be ruled by a government that threatens their liberty; therefore the government to which they freely choose to submit themselves will be a limited government designed to protect liberty.

The Pennsylvania experience as well as the history of British government led the Framers to doubt whether popular consent alone would be a sufficient guarantor of liberty. A popular government may prove too weak (as in Massachusetts) to prevent one faction from abusing another, or a popular majority can be tyrannical (as in Pennsylvania). In fact the tyranny of the majority can be an even graver threat than rule by the few. In the former case there may be no defenses for the individual—one lone person cannot count on the succor of public opinion or the possibility of popular revolt.

The problem, then, was a delicate one: how to devise a government strong enough to preserve order but not so strong that it would threaten liberty. The answer, the delegates believed, was not "democracy" as it was then understood. To many conservatives in the late eighteenth century, democracy meant mob rule—it meant, in short, Shays's Rebellion (or if they had been candid about it, the Boston Tea Party). On the other hand, *aristocracy*—the rule of the few—was no solution, since the few were likely to be self-seeking. Madison, writing later in the *Federalist* papers, put the problem this way:

> If men were angels, no government would be necessary. If angels were to govern men, neither external nor internal controls on government would be necessary. In framing a government which is to be administered by men over men, the great difficulty lies in this: you must first enable the government to control the governed; and in the next place oblige it to control itself.[9]

Striking this balance could not be done, Madison believed, simply by writing a constitution that set limits on what government could do. The example of British rule over the colonies proved that laws and customs were inadequate checks on political power. As he expressed it, "A mere demarcation on parchment of the constitutional limits [of government] is not a sufficient guard against those encroachments which lead to a tyrannical concentration of all the powers of government in the same hands."[10]

The Challenge

The resolution of political issues, great and small, often depends crucially on how the central question is phrased. The delegates came to Philadelphia in general agreement that there were defects in the Articles of Confederation that ought to be remedied. Had they, after convening, decided to make their business that of listing these defects and debating alternative remedies for them, the document that emerged would in all likelihood have been very different from what in fact was adopted. But immediately after the convention had organized itself and chosen Washington to be its presiding officer, the Virginia delegation, led by Governor Edmund Randolph but relying heavily on the draftsmanship of James Madison, presented to the convention a comprehensive plan for a wholly new national government. The plan quickly became the major item of business of the meeting; it, and little else, was debated for the next two weeks.

The Virginia Plan

When the convention decided to make the Virginia Plan its agenda, it had fundamentally altered the nature of its task. The business at hand was not to be the Articles and their defects, but rather how one should go about designing a true national government. The Virginia Plan called for a strong national union organized into three governmental branches—the legislative, executive, and judicial. The legislature was to be composed of two houses, the first elected directly by the people and the second chosen by the first house from among the people nominated by state legislatures. The executive was to be chosen by the national legislature, as were members of a national judiciary. The executive and some members of the judiciary were to constitute a "council of revision" that could veto acts of the legislature; that veto, in turn, could be overridden by the legislature. There were other interesting details, but the key features of the Virginia Plan were two: (1) a national legislature would have supreme powers on all matters on which the separate states were not competent to act, as well as the power to veto any and all state laws, and (2) at least one house of the legislature would be elected directly by the people.

The New Jersey Plan

As the debate went on, the representatives of New Jersey and other small states became increasingly worried that the convention was going to write a constitution in which the states would be represented in both houses of Congress on the basis of population. If this happened, the smaller states feared they would always be outvoted by the larger ones and so, with William Paterson of New Jersey as their spokesman, they introduced a new plan. The New Jersey Plan proposed to amend, not replace, the old Articles of Confederation. It enhanced the power of the national government (though not as much as the Virginia Plan), but it did so in a way that left the states' representation in Congress unchanged from the Articles—each state would have one vote. Thus not only would the interests of the small states be protected, but Congress itself would remain to a substantial degree the creature of state governments.

If the New Jersey resolutions had been presented first and taken up as the major item of business, it is quite possible that they would have become the framework for the document that finally emerged. But they were not. Offered after the convention had been discussing the Virginia Plan for two weeks, the resolutions encountered a reception very different from what they would have received if introduced earlier. The debate had the delegates already thinking in terms of a national government that was more independent of the states, and thus it had accustomed them to proposals that, under other circumstances, might have seemed quite radical. On June 19 the first decisive vote of the convention was taken: seven states preferred the Virginia Plan, three states the New Jersey Plan, and one state was split.

With the tide running in favor of a strong national government, the supporters of the small states had to shift their strategy. They now began to focus their efforts on ensuring that the small states could not be outvoted by the larger ones in Congress. One way was to have the members of the lower house elected by the state legislatures rather than the people, with each state getting the same number of seats rather than seats proportional to its population.

The debate was long and feelings ran high, so much so that Benjamin Franklin, at eighty-one the oldest delegate present, suggested that each day's meeting begin with a prayer. It turned out that the convention could not even agree on this: Hamilton is supposed to have objected that the convention did not need "foreign aid," and others pointed out that the group had no funds with which to hire a minister. And so the argument continued.

The Compromise

Finally a committee was appointed to meet during the Fourth of July holidays to work out a compromise, and the convention adjourned to await its report. Little is known of what went on in that committee's session, though some were later to say that Franklin played a key role in hammering out the plan that finally emerged. That compromise, the most important reached at the convention, and later called the **Great Compromise** (or sometimes the Connecticut Compromise), was submitted to the full convention on July 5 and debated for another week and a half. The debate might have gone on even longer, but suddenly the hot weather moderated, and Monday, July 16, dawned cool and fresh after a month of misery. On that day the plan was adopted: five states were in favor, four opposed, and two not voting.* Thus, by the narrowest of margins, the structure of the national legislature was set, as follows:

- A House of Representatives consisting initially of sixty-five members apportioned among the states roughly on the basis of population and elected by the people.

- A Senate consisting of two senators from each state to be chosen by the state legislatures.

The Great Compromise reconciled the interests of small and large states by allowing the former to predominate in the Senate and the latter in the House. This reconciliation was necessary to ensure that there would be support for a strong national

---

*The states in favor were Connecticut, Delaware, Maryland, New Jersey, and North Carolina. Those opposed were Georgia, Pennsylvania, South Carolina, and Virginia. Massachusetts was split down the middle; the New York delegates had left the convention. New Hampshire and Rhode Island were absent.

government from small as well as large states. It represented major concessions on the part of several groups. Madison, for one, was deeply opposed to the idea of having the states equally represented in the Senate. He saw in that a way for the states to hamstring the national government and much preferred some measure of proportional representation in both houses. Delegates from other states worried that representation on the basis of population in the House of Representatives would enable the large states to dominate legislative affairs. Although the margin by which the compromise was accepted was razor-thin (five states in favor, four opposed), it held firm. In time most of the delegates from the dissenting states accepted it.

After the Great Compromise many more issues had to be resolved, but by now a spirit of accommodation had developed. When one delegate proposed having the Congress choose the president, another, James Wilson, proposed that he be elected directly by the people. When neither side of that argument prevailed, a committee invented a plan for an "Electoral College" that would choose a president. When some delegates wanted a president chosen for a life term, others proposed a seven-year term, and still others wanted the term limited to three years without eligibility for reelection. The convention settled on a four-year term with no bar to reelection. Some states wanted the Supreme Court picked by the Senate; others wanted it chosen by the president. They finally agreed to let the justices be nominated by the president and then confirmed by the Senate.

Finally, on July 26, the proposals that were already accepted, together with a bundle of unresolved issues, were handed over to a "Committee of Detail" of five delegates. This committee included Madison and Gouverneur Morris, who was to be the chief draftsman of the document that finally emerged. The committee hardly contented itself with mere "details," however. It inserted some new proposals and made changes in old ones, drawing for inspiration on existing state constitutions and the members' beliefs as to what the other delegates might accept. On August 6 the report—the first complete draft of the Constitution—was submitted to the convention. There it was debated, item by item, revised, amended, and finally, on September 17, approved by all twelve states in attendance. (Not all *delegates* approved, however; three, including Edmund Randolph, who first submitted the Virginia Plan, refused to sign.)

The Constitution and Democracy

A debate continues to rage over whether the Constitution created, or was even intended to create, a democratic government. The answer is complex. The Framers did not intend to create a "pure democracy"—one in which the people rule directly. For one thing the size of the country and the distances between settlements would have made that physically impossible. But more important, the Framers worried that a government in which all citizens directly participate, as in the New England town meeting, would be a government excessively subject to temporary popular passions and one in which minority rights would be insecure. They intended instead to create a **republic**, by which they meant a government in which a system of representation operates. In designing that system the Framers chose, not without argument, to have the members of the House of Representatives elected directly by the people. Some delegates did not want to go even that far. Elbridge Gerry of Massachusetts, who refused to sign the Constitution, argued that though "the people do not want [that is, lack] virtue," they are often the "dupes of pretended patriots." Roger Sherman of Connecticut agreed. But George Mason of Virginia and James Wilson of Pennsylvania carried the day when they argued that "no government could long subsist without the confidence of the people," and this required "drawing the most numerous branch of the legislature directly from the people." Popular elections for the House were approved: six states were in favor, two opposed.

But though popular rule was to be one element of the new government, it was not to be the only one. State legislatures, not the people, would choose the senators; electors, not the people directly, would choose the president. As we have seen, without these arrangements, there would have been no Constitution at all, for the small states adamantly opposed any proposal that would have given undue power to the large ones. And direct popular election of the president would clearly have made the populous states the dominant ones. In short the Framers wished to observe the principle of majority rule, but they felt that, on the most important questions, two kinds of majorities were essential—a majority of the voters and a majority of the states.

The power of the Supreme Court to declare an act of Congress unconstitutional—**judicial review**—is also a way of limiting the power of popular majorities. It is not clear whether the Framers intended that there be judicial review, but there is little doubt that in the Framers' minds the fundamental law, the Constitution, had to be safeguarded against popular passions. They made the process for amending the Constitution easier than it had been under the Articles but still relatively difficult.

An amendment can be proposed either by a two-thirds vote of both houses of Congress *or* by a national convention called by Congress at the request of two-thirds of the states.* Once proposed, an amendment must be ratified by three-fourths of the states, either through their legislatures or through special ratifying conventions in each state. Twenty-seven amendments have survived this process, all of them proposed by Congress and all but one (the Twenty-first) ratified by state legislatures rather than state conventions.

In short the answer to the question of whether the Constitution brought into being a democratic government is yes, if by democracy is meant a system of representative government based on popular consent. The degree of that consent has changed since 1787, and the institutions embodying that consent can take different forms. One form, rejected in 1787, gives all political authority to one set of representatives, directly elected by the people (That is the case, for example, in most parliamentary regimes, such as Great Britain, and in some city governments in the United States.) The other form of democracy is one in which different sets of officials, chosen directly or indirectly by different groups of people, share political power. (That is the case with the United States and a few other nations where the separation of powers is intended to operate.)

Key Principles

The American version of representative democracy was based on two major principles, the separation of powers and federalism. In America political power was to be shared by three separate branches of government; in parliamentary democracies that power was concentrated in a single, supreme legislature. In America political authority was divided between a national government and several state governments—**federalism**—whereas in most European systems authority was centralized in the national government. Neither of these principles was especially controversial at Philadelphia. The delegates began their work in broad agreement that separated powers and some measure of federalism were necessary, and both the Virginia and New Jersey plans contained a version of each. How much federalism should be written into the Constitution was quite controversial, however.*

Government and Human Nature

The desirability of separating powers and leaving the states equipped with a broad array of rights and responsibilities was not controversial at the Philadelphia convention because the Framers' experiences with British rule and state government under the Articles had shaped their view of human nature.

These experiences had taught most of the Framers that people would seek their own advantage in and out of politics; this pursuit of self-interest, unchecked, would lead some people to exploit others. Human nature was good enough to make it pos-

---

*There have been many attempts to get a new constitutional convention. In the 1960s thirty-three states, one short of the required number, requested a convention to consider the reapportionment of state legislatures. In the 1980s efforts were made to call a convention to consider amendments to ban abortions and to require a balanced federal budget.

*To the delegates a truly "federal" system was one, like the New Jersey Plan, that allowed for very strong states and a weak national government. When the New Jersey Plan lost, the delegates who defeated it began using the word *federal* to describe their plan even though it called for a stronger national government. Thus men who began as "Federalists" at the convention ultimately became known as "Antifederalists" during the struggle over ratification.

sible to have a decent government that was based on popular consent, but it was not good enough to make it inevitable. One solution to this problem would be to improve human nature. Ancient political philosophers such as Aristotle believed that the first task of any government was to cultivate virtue among the governed.

Many Americans were of the same mind. To them, Americans would first have to become good people before they could have a good government. Samuel Adams, a leader of the Boston Tea Party, said that the new nation must become a "Christian Sparta." Others spoke of the need to cultivate frugality, industry, temperance, and simplicity.

But to James Madison and the other architects of the Constitution, the deliberate cultivation of virtue would require a government too strong and thus too dangerous to liberty, at least at the national level. Self-interest, freely pursued within reasonable limits, was a more practical and durable solution to the problem of government than any effort to improve the virtue of the citizenry. He wanted, he said, to make republican government possible "even in the absence of political virtue."

Madison argued that the very self-interest that leads people toward factionalism and tyranny might, if properly harnessed by appropriate constitutional arrangements, provide a source of unity and a guarantee of liberty. This harnessing was to be accomplished by dividing the offices of the new government among many people and giving to the holder of each office the "necessary means and personal motives to resist encroachments of the others." In this way "ambition must be made to counteract ambition" so that "the private interest of every individual may be a sentinel over the public rights."[11] If men were angels, all this would be unnecessary. But Madison and the other delegates pragmatically insisted on taking human nature pretty much as it was, and therefore they adopted "this policy of supplying, by opposite and rival interests, the defect of better motives."[12] The **separation of powers** (see box) would work, not in spite of the imperfections of human nature, but because of them.

So also with federalism. By dividing power between the states and the national government, one level of government can serve as a check on the other. This should provide a "double security" to the rights

Checks and Balances

*T*he Constitution creates a system of *separate* institutions that *share* powers. Because the three branches of government share powers, each can (partially) check the powers of the others. This is the system of **checks and balances**. The major checks possessed by each branch are listed below.

CONGRESS

1. Can check the president in these ways.
   a. By refusing to pass a bill the president wants
   b. By passing a law over the president's veto
   c. By using the impeachment powers to remove the president from office
   d. By refusing to approve a presidential appointment (Senate only)
   e. By refusing to ratify a treaty the president has signed (Senate only)
2. Can check the federal courts in these ways:
   a. By changing the number and jurisdiction of the lower courts
   b. By using the impeachment powers to remove a judge from office
   c. By refusing to approve a person nominated to be a judge (Senate only)

PRESIDENT

1. Can check Congress by vetoing a bill it has passed
2. Can check the federal courts by nominating judges

COURTS

1. Can check Congress by declaring a law unconstitutional
2. Can check the president by declaring actions by him or his subordinates to be unconstitutional or not authorized by law

In addition to these checks specifically provided for in the Constitution, each branch has informal ways of checking the others. For example, the president can try to withhold information from Congress (on the grounds of "executive privilege"), and Congress can try to get information by mounting an investigation.

The exact meaning of the various checks is explained in Chapter 11 on Congress, Chapter 12 on the presidency, and Chapter 14 on the courts.

RATIFICATION OF THE FEDERAL CONSTITUTION BY STATE CONVENTIONS, 1787–1790

Strongly in favor, ratified early

Initially opposed, later ratified

Ratified initially after close struggle

ers among several governments would give to virtually every faction an opportunity to gain some—but not full—power.

The Constitution and Liberty

A more difficult question is whether the Constitution created a system of government that would respect personal liberties. And that in fact is the question that was debated in the states when the document was presented for ratification. The proponents of the Constitution called themselves the **Federalists** (though they might more accurately be called "nationalists"). The opponents came to be known as the **Antifederalists** (though they might more accurately be called "states' righters"). To be put into effect, the Constitution had to be approved at ratifying conventions in at least nine states. This was perhaps the most democratic feature of the Constitution: it had to be accepted, not by the existing Congress (still limping along under the Articles of Confederation), nor by the state legislatures, but by special conventions elected by the people

Though democratic, the process established by the Framers for ratifying the Constitution was technically illegal. The Articles of Confederation, which still governed, could be amended only with the approval of all thirteen state legislatures. The Framers wanted to bypass these legislatures because they feared that, for reasons of ideology or out of a desire to retain their powers, the legislators would oppose the Constitution. The Framers wanted ratification with less than the consent of all thirteen states because they knew that such unanimity could not be attained. And indeed the conventions in North Carolina and Rhode Island did initially reject the Constitution.

The Antifederalist View

The great issue before the state conventions was liberty, not democracy. The opponents of the new Constitution, the Antifederalists, had a variety of objections but were in general united by the belief that liberty could be secure only in a small republic in which the rulers were physically close to—and closely checked by—the ruled. Their central objec-

of the people: "The different governments will control each other, at the same time that each will be controlled by itself."[13] This was especially likely to happen in America, Madison thought, because it was a large country filled with diverse interests—rich and poor, Protestant and Catholic, northerner and southerner, farmer and merchant, creditor and debtor. Each of these interests would constitute a **faction** that would seek its own advantage. One faction might come to dominate government, or a part of government, in one place, and a different and rival faction might dominate it in another. The pulling and hauling among these factions would prevent any single government—say, that of New York—from dominating all of government. The division of pow-

By steadily moving westward, Americans both searched for economic opportunity and sought to protect their freedom from government. Here George Caleb Bingham depicts Daniel Boone escorting settlers through the Cumberland Gap.

tion was stated by a group of Antifederalists at the ratifying convention in an essay published just after they had lost: "a very extensive territory cannot be governed on the principles of freedom, otherwise than by a confederation of republics."[14]

These dissenters argued that a strong national government would be distant from the people and would use its powers to annihilate or absorb the functions that properly belonged to the states. Congress would tax heavily, the Supreme Court would overrule state courts, and the president would come to head a large standing army. (Since all these things have occurred, we cannot dismiss the Antifederalists as cranky obstructionists who opposed without justification the plans of the Framers.) These critics argued that the nation needed, at best, a loose confederation of states, with most of the powers of government kept firmly in the hands of state legislatures and state courts.

But if a stronger national government was to be created, the Antifederalists argued, it should be hedged about with many more restrictions than those in the Constitution then under consideration.

They proposed several such limitations, including narrowing the jurisdiction of the Supreme Court, checking the president's power by creating a council that would review his actions, leaving military affairs in the hands of the state militias, increasing the size of the House of Representatives so that it would reflect a greater variety of popular interests, and reducing or eliminating the power of Congress to levy taxes. Most important, they insisted that a bill of rights be added to the Constitution.

James Madison gave his answer to these criticisms in *Federalist* papers 10 and 51 (reprinted in the Appendix). It was a bold answer, for it flew squarely in the face of widespread popular sentiment and much philosophical writing. Following the great French political philosopher Montesquieu, many Americans believed that liberty was safe only in small societies governed either by direct democracy or by large legislatures with small districts and frequent turnover among members.

Madison argued quite the opposite—that liberty is safest in *large* (or as he put it, "extended") republics. In a small community, he said, there will be

C R I T I C A L ★ T H I N K I N G

How to Read the Federalist *Papers 10 and 51*

James Madison is rightly regarded as the single most important mind behind the Constitution and his ideas are worth knowing first-hand. The Appendix to this book contains reprints of Madison's *Federalist* papers 10 and 51. After you have finished this chapter, turn to the Appendix and try to read them. On your first reading of the papers you may find Madison's language difficult to understand and his ideas overly complex. The following pointers will help you decipher his meaning.

In *Federalist* No. 10, Madison begins by stating that "a well constructed Union" can "break and control the violence of faction." He goes on to define a "faction" as any group of citizens who attempt to advance their ideas or economic interests at the expense of other citizens, or in ways that conflict with "the permanent and aggregate interests of the community" or "public good." Thus, what Madison terms "factions" are what we today call "special interests."

One way to defeat factions, according to Madison, is to remove whatever causes them to arise in the first place. This can be attempted in two ways. First, government can deprive people of the liberty they need to organize: "Liberty is to faction what air is to fire." But that is surely a cure "worse than the disease." Second, measures can be taken to make all citizens share the same ideas, feelings, and economic interests. However as Madison observes, some people are smarter or more hard working than others and this "diversity in the faculties" of citizens is bound to result in different economic interests as some people acquire more property than others. Consequently, protecting property rights, not equalizing property ownership, "is the first object of government." Even if everyone shared the same basic economic interests they would still find reasons "to vex and oppress each other" rather than cooperate "for their common good." Religious differences, loyalties to different leaders, even "frivolous and fanciful distinctions" (not liking how other people dress or their taste in music) can be fertile soil for factions. In Madison's view people are factious by nature; the "causes of faction" are "sown" into their very being.

Madison thus proposes a second and, he thinks, more practical and desirable way of defeating faction. The way to cure "the mischiefs of faction" is not by removing its causes but by "controlling its effects." Factions will always exist, so the trick is to establish a form of government that is likely to serve the public good through the even-handed "regulation of these various and interfering interests." Wise and public-spirited leaders can "adjust these clashing interests and render them all subservient to the public good," but, he cautions, "Enlightened statesmen will not always be at the helm." (Madison implies that "enlightened statesmen"—such as himself, Washington, and Jefferson—*were* at the "helm" of government in 1787.)

Madison's proposed cure for the evils of factions is in fact nothing other than a republican form of government. Use the following questions to guide your own analysis of Madison's ideas. Why does Madison think the problem of a "minority" faction is easy to handle? Conversely, why is he so troubled by the potential of a majority faction? How does he distinguish direct democracy from republican government? What is he getting at when he terms elected representatives "proper guardians of the public weal," and why does he think that "extensive republics" are more likely to produce such representatives than small ones?

When you are finished with *Federalist* No. 10, try your hand at *Federalist* No. 51. You will find that the ideas in the former paper anticipate many of those in the latter. And you will find many points on which you may or may not agree with Madison. For example, do you agree with his assumption that people—even your best friends or college roommates—are factious by nature? Likewise, do you agree with his view that government is "the greatest of all reflections on human nature"?

By attempting to meet the mind of James Madison, you can sharpen your own mind and deepen your understanding of American government.

relatively few differences in opinion or interest; people will tend to see the world in much the same way. If anyone dissents or pursues an individual interest, he or she will be confronted by a massive majority and will have few, if any, allies. But in a large republic there will be many opinions and interests; as a result it will be hard for a tyrannical majority to form or organize, and anyone with an unpopular view will find it easier to acquire allies. If Madison's argument seems strange or abstract, ask yourself the following question: If I have an unpopular opinion, an exotic lifestyle, or an unconventional interest, will I find greater security living in a small town or a big city?

By favoring a large republic, Madison was not trying to stifle democracy. Rather he was attempting to show how democratic government really works, and what can make it work better. To rule, different interests must come together and form a **coalition**—that is, an alliance. In *Federalist* No. 51, he was arguing that the coalitions that formed in a large republic would be more moderate than those that formed in a small one because the bigger the republic, the greater the variety of interests, and thus the more a coalition of the majority would have to accommodate a diversity of interests and opinions if it hoped to succeed. He concluded that in a nation the size of the United States, with its enormous variety of interests, "a coalition of a majority of the whole society could seldom take place on any other principles than those of justice and the general good." Whether he was right in that prediction is a matter to which we shall return repeatedly.

The implication of Madison's arguments was daring, for he was suggesting that the national government should be at some distance from the people and insulated from their momentary passions because the people did not always want to do the right thing. Liberty was threatened as much (or even more) by public passions and popularly based factions as by strong governments. Now the Antifederalists themselves had no very lofty view of human nature, as is evidenced by the deep suspicion with which they viewed "power-seeking" officeholders. What Madison did was take this view to its logical conclusion, arguing that if people could be corrupted by office, they could also be corrupted by factional self-interest. Thus the government had to be designed to prevent both the politicians and the people from using it for ill-considered or unjust purposes.

To argue in 1787 against the virtues of small democracies was like arguing against motherhood, but the argument prevailed, probably because many citizens were convinced that a reasonably strong national government was essential if the nation were to stand united against foreign enemies, facilitate commerce among the states, guard against domestic insurrections, and keep one faction from oppressing another. The political realities of the moment and the recent bitter experiences with the Articles probably counted for more in ratifying the Constitution than did Madison's arguments. His cause was helped by the fact that, for all their legitimate concerns and their uncanny instinct for what the future might bring, the Antifederalists could offer no agreed-upon alternative to the new Constitution. In politics, then as now, you cannot beat something with nothing.

But this does not explain why the Framers failed to add a bill of rights to the Constitution. If they were so preoccupied with liberty, why didn't they take this most obvious step toward protecting liberty, especially since the Antifederalists were demanding it? Some historians have suggested that this omission was evidence that liberty was not as important to the Framers as they claimed. In fact, when one delegate suggested that a bill of rights be drawn up, the state delegations at the convention unanimously voted the idea down. There were several reasons for this.

First, the Constitution, as written, *did* contain a number of specific guarantees of individual liberty, including the right of trial by jury in criminal cases and the privilege of the writ of habeas corpus. The liberties guaranteed in the Constitution (before the Bill of Rights was added) are listed below.

- **Writ of habeas corpus*** may not be suspended (except during invasion or rebellion).

- No **bill of attainder** may be passed by Congress or the states.

- No **ex post facto law** may be passed by Congress or the states.

- Right of trial by jury in criminal cases is guaranteed.

- The citizens of each state are entitled to the privileges and immunities of the citizens of every other state.

- No religious test or qualification for holding federal office is imposed.

- No law impairing the obligation of contracts may be passed by the states.

Second, most states in 1787 had bills of rights. When Elbridge Gerry proposed to the convention that a federal bill of rights be drafted, Roger Sherman

*For a definition of this and the following terms used in connection with certain rights, see the Glossary.

The Bill of Rights

The First Ten Amendments to the Constitution Grouped by Topic and Purpose

PROTECTIONS AFFORDED CITIZENS TO PARTICIPATE IN THE POLITICAL PROCESS

Amendment 1: Freedom of religion, speech, press, and assembly; the right to petition the government.

PROTECTIONS AGAINST ARBITRARY POLICE AND COURT ACTION

Amendment 4: No unreasonable searches or seizures.

Amendment 5: Grand jury indictment required to prosecute a person for a serious crime.

No "double jeopardy"—being tried twice for the same offense.

Forcing a person to testify against himself or herself prohibited.

No loss of life, liberty, or property without due process.

Amendment 6: Right to speedy, public, impartial trial with defense counsel and right to cross-examine witnesses.

Amendment 7: Jury trials in civil suits where value exceeds $20.

Amendment 8: No excessive bail or fines, no cruel and unusual punishments.

PROTECTIONS OF STATES' RIGHTS AND UNNAMED RIGHTS OF PEOPLE

Amendment 9: Unlisted rights are not necessarily denied.

Amendment 10: Powers not delegated to the United States or denied to states are reserved to the states.

OTHER AMENDMENTS

Amendment 2: Right to bear arms.

Amendment 3: Troops may not be quartered in homes in peacetime.

rose to observe that it was unnecessary because the state bills of rights were sufficient.[15]

But third, and perhaps most important, the Framers thought they were creating a government with specific, limited powers. It could do, they thought, only what the Constitution gave it the power to do, and nowhere in that document was there permission to infringe on freedom of speech or of the press or to impose cruel and unusual punishments. Some delegates probably feared that if any serious effort were made to list the rights that were guaranteed, later officials might assume that they had the power to do anything not explicitly forbidden.

Need for a Bill of Rights

Whatever their reasons, the Framers made at least a tactical and perhaps a fundamental mistake. It quickly became clear that without at least the promise of a bill of rights, the Constitution would not be ratified. Though the small states, pleased by their equal representation in the Senate, quickly ratified (in Delaware, New Jersey, and Georgia, the vote in the conventions was unanimous), the battle in the large states was intense and the outcome uncertain. In Pennsylvania Federalist supporters dragged boycotting Antifederalists to the legislature in order to ensure that a quorum was present so that a convention could be called. There were rumors of other rough tactics.

In Massachusetts the Constitution was approved by a narrow majority, but only after key leaders promised to obtain a bill of rights. In Virginia James Madison fought against the fiery Patrick Henry, whose climactic speech against ratification was dramatically punctuated by a noisy thunderstorm outside. The Federalists won by ten votes. In New York Alexander Hamilton argued the case for six long weeks against the determined opposition of most of the state's key political leaders; he carried the day, but only by three votes, and then only after New York City threatened to secede from the state if it did not ratify. By June 21, 1788, the ninth state—New Hampshire—had ratified and the Constitution was law.

Despite the bitterness of the ratification struggle, the new government that took office in 1789–1790, headed by President Washington, was greeted enthusiastically. By the spring of 1790 all thirteen states had ratified. There remained, however, the task of fulfilling the promise of a bill of rights. To that end James Madison introduced into the first session of the First Congress a set of proposals, many based on the existing Virginia bill of rights. Twelve were approved by Congress; ten of these were ratified by the states and went into effect in 1791. These amendments did not limit the power of state governments over citizens, only the power of the federal government. Later the Fourteenth Amendment, as interpreted by the Supreme Court, extended many of the guarantees of the Bill of Rights to cover state governmental action.

The Constitution and Slavery

Nowhere in the Constitution can one find the word *slave* or *slavery*. Yet at the time the document was written, one-third of the population of five southern states was made up of black slaves. Everyone at the Philadelphia convention was fully aware of this fact, but there was little debate on the morality of slaveholding. The only major argument was over the im-

plications of slavery for the apportioning of seats in the House of Representatives, the power of the government to restrict the slave trade, and certain related issues.

To some the failure of the Constitution to address the question of slavery was a great betrayal of the promise of the Declaration of Independence that "all men are created equal."[16] For the Constitution to be silent on the subject of slavery, and thereby to allow that odious practice to continue, was to convert, by implication, the wording of the Declaration to, "all *white* men are created equal."

It is easy to accuse the signers of the Declaration and the Constitution of hypocrisy. They knew of slavery, many of them owned slaves, and yet they were silent. Indeed British opponents of the independence movement took special delight in taunting the colonists about their complaints of being "enslaved" to the British Empire while ignoring the slavery in their very midst. Increasingly, revolutionary leaders during this period spoke to this issue. Thomas Jefferson had tried to get a clause opposing the slave trade put into the Declaration of Independence. James Otis

The Constitution was silent on slavery, and so buying and selling black slaves continued for many years.

of Boston had attacked slavery and argued that black as well as white men should be free. As revolutionary fervor mounted, so did northern criticisms of slavery. The Massachusetts legislature and then the Continental Congress voted to end the slave trade; Delaware prohibited the importation of slaves; Pennsylvania voted to tax it out of existence; and Connecticut and Rhode Island decided that all slaves brought into those states would automatically become free.

Slavery continued unabated in the South, defended by some whites because they thought it right, by others because they found it useful. But even in the South there were opponents, though rarely conspicuous ones. George Mason, a large Virginia slaveholder and a delegate to the convention, warned prophetically that "by an inevitable chain of causes and effects, providence punishes national sins [slavery] by national calamities."[17]

The blunt fact, however, was that any effort to use the Constitution to end slavery would have meant the end of the Constitution. The southern states would never have signed a document that seriously interfered with slavery. Without the southern states there would have been a continuation of the Articles of Confederation, which would have left each state entirely sovereign and thus entirely free of any prospective challenge to slavery.

Thus the Framers compromised with slavery; political scientist Theodore Lowi calls this their Greatest Compromise.[18] Slavery is dealt with in three places in the Constitution, though never by name. In determining the representation each state was to have in the House, "three-fifths of all other persons" (that is, of slaves) are to be added to "the whole number of free persons."[19] The South originally wanted slaves to count fully even though, of course, none would be elected to the House; they settled for counting 60 percent of them. The convention also agreed not to allow the new government by law or even constitutional amendment to prohibit the importation of slaves until the year 1808.[20] The South thus had twenty years in which it could acquire more slaves from abroad; after that, Congress was free (but not required) to end the importation. Finally, the Constitution guaranteed that if a slave were to escape his or her master and flee to a nonslave state, the slave would be returned by that state to "the party to whom . . . service or labour may be due."[21]

The unresolved issue of slavery was to prove the most explosive question of all and, in the end, led to the Civil War. Nor did the problem go away with the war's end, for the legacy of slavery continues to the present. The enslavement of the blacks in the United States has proved to be a social and political catastrophe of the first magnitude. The Framers managed to postpone that catastrophe in order to create a union that, they hoped, would eventually be strong enough to deal with the problem when it could no longer be postponed.

The Motives of the Framers

The Framers were not saints or demigods. They were men with political opinions who also had economic interests and human failings. It would be a mistake to conclude that everything they did in 1787 was motivated by a disinterested commitment to the public good. But it would be an equally great mistake to think that what they did was nothing but an effort to line their pockets by producing a government that would serve their own narrow interests. As in almost all human endeavors, the Framers acted out of a mixture of motives. What is truly astonishing is that economic interests played only a modest role in their deliberations.

Economic Interests at the Convention

Some of the Framers were wealthy; some were not. Some owned slaves; some had none. Some were creditors (having loaned money to the Continental Congress or to private parties); some were deeply in debt. For nearly a century scholars have argued over just how important these personal interests were in explaining the provisions of the Constitution.

Charles Beard, a historian, published in 1913 a book—*An Economic Interpretation of the Constitution*—arguing that the better-off urban and commercial classes, especially those members who held the IOUs issued by the government to pay for the Revolutionary War, favored the new Constitution because they stood to benefit from it.[22] But in the 1950s that view was challenged by historians who, after looking carefully at what the Framers owned or owed, concluded that one could not explain the Constitution exclusively or even largely in terms of the economic interests of those who wrote it.[23] Some of the richest delegates, such as Elbridge Gerry of Massachusetts and George Mason of Virginia, refused to sign the document, while many of its key backers—James Madison and James Wilson, for example—were men of modest means or heavy debts.

In the 1980s a new group of scholars, primarily economists applying more advanced statistical techniques, found evidence that some economic considerations influenced how the Framers voted on some issues during the Philadelphia convention. Interestingly, however, the economic position of the *states* from which they came had a greater effect on their votes than did their *own* monetary condition.[24]

We have already seen how delegates from small states fought to reduce the power of large states and

Elbridge Gerry (1744–1814) was a wealthy Massachusetts merchant and politician who participated in the convention but refused to sign the new Constitution.

James Wilson (1742–1798) of Pennsylvania, a brilliant lawyer and terrible businessman, was the principal champion of the popular election of the House. Near the end of his life he was jailed repeatedly for debts incurred by his business speculations.

how those from slaveowning states made certain that the Constitution would contain no provision that would threaten slavery.

But contrary to what Beard asserted, the individual interests of the Framers themselves did not dominate the convention except in a few cases where a constitutional provision would have affected them directly. As you might expect, all slaveowning delegates, even those who did not live in states where slavery was commonplace (and several northern delegates owned slaves), tended to vote for provisions that would have kept the national government's power over slavery as weak as possible. However, the effects of other personal business interests were surprisingly weak. Some delegates owned a lot of public debt that they had purchased for low prices. A strong national government of the sort envisaged by the Constitution was more likely than the weak Continental Congress to pay off this debt at face value, thus making the delegates who owned it much richer. Despite this, the ownership of public debt had no significant effect on how the Framers voted in Philadelphia. For example, five men who among them owned one-third of all the public securities held by all the delegates voted against the Constitution. Nor did the big land speculators vote their interests. Some, such as George Washington and Robert Morris, favored the Constitution, while others, such as George Mason and William Blount, opposed it.[25]

In sum, the Framers tended to represent their states' interests on important matters. Since they were picked by the states to do so, this is exactly what one would expect. If they had not met in secret, perhaps they would have voted even more often as their constituents wanted. But except with respect to slavery, they usually did not vote their own economic interests. They were, in short, reasonably but not wholly disinterested delegates who were probably influenced as much by personal beliefs as by economic factors.

Economic Interests and Ratification

At the popularly elected state ratifying conventions, economic factors played a larger role. Delegates who were merchants, who lived in cities, who owned large amounts of western land, who held government IOUs, and who did not own slaves were more likely to vote to ratify the new Constitution than were delegates who were farmers, who did not own public debt, and who did own slaves.[26] There were plenty of exceptions, however. Small farmers dominated the conventions in some states where the vote to ratify was unanimous.

Though interests made a difference, they were not simply elite interests. In most states the great majority of adult white males could vote for delegates to the ratifying conventions. This means that women and blacks were excluded from the debates, but by the standards of the time—standards that did not change for over a century—the ratification process was remarkably democratic.

The Constitution and Equality

Ideas counted for as much as interests. At stake were two views of the public good. One, espoused by the Federalists, was that a reasonable balance of liberty, order, and progress required a strong national government. The other, defended by the Antifederalists, was that liberty would not be secure in the hands of a powerful, distant government; freedom required decentralization.

Today that debate has a new focus. The defect of the Constitution, to some contemporary critics, is not that the government it created is too strong but that it is too weak. In particular the national government is too weak to resist the pressures of special interests that reflect and perpetuate social inequality.

This criticism reveals how our understanding of the relationship between liberty and equality has changed since the Founding. To Jefferson and Madison citizens naturally differed in their talents and qualities. What had to be guarded against was the use of governmental power to create *un*natural and undesirable inequalities. This might happen, for example, if political power was concentrated in the hands of a few people (who could use that power to give themselves special privileges) or if it was used in ways that allowed some private parties to acquire exclusive charters and monopolies. To prevent the inequality that might result from having too strong a government, its powers must be kept strictly limited.

Today some people think of inequality quite differently. To them it is the natural social order—the marketplace and the acquisitive talents of people operating in that marketplace—that leads to undesirable inequalities, especially in economic power. The government should be powerful enough to restrain these natural tendencies and produce, by law, a

CRITICAL ★ THINKING

Were Women Left Out of the Constitution?

In one sense, yes: Women were nowhere mentioned in the Constitution when it was written in 1787. Moreover Article 1, which set forth the provisions for electing members of the House of Representatives, granted the vote to those people who were allowed to vote for members of the lower house of the legislature in the states in which they resided. In no state at the time could women participate in those elections. In no state could they vote in any elections or hold any offices. Furthermore, wherever the Constitution uses a pronoun, it uses the masculine form—*he* or *him.*

In another sense, no: Wherever the Constitution or the Bill of Rights defines a right that people are to have, it either grants that right to "persons" or "citizens," not to "men," or it makes no mention at all of people or gender. For example:

• "The *citizens* of each State shall be entitled to all privileges and immunities of citizens of the several States."

[Art. I, sec. 9]

• "No *person* shall be convicted of treason unless on the testimony of two witnesses to the same overt act, or on confession in open court."

[Art. III, sec. 3]

• "No bill of attainder or ex post facto law shall be passed." [Art. I sec. 9]

• "The right of the *people* to be secure in their persons, houses, papers, and ef-

fects, against unreasonable searches and seizures, shall not be violated. . . ."

[Amend. IV]

• "No *person* shall be held to answer for a capital, or otherwise infamous crime, unless on presentment or indictment of a grand jury. . . . nor shall any *person* be subject for the same offense to be twice put in jeopardy of life or limb; . . . nor be deprived of life, liberty, or property, without due process of law. . . ." [Amend. V]

• "In all criminal prosecutions the *accused* shall enjoy the right to a speedy and public trial, by an impartial jury. . . ." [Amend. VI]

Moreover, when the qualifications for elective office are stated, the word *person*, not *man*, is used.

• "No *person* shall be a Representative who shall not have attained to the age of twenty-five years. . . ." [Art. 1, sec. 2]

• "No *person* shall be a Senator who shall not have attained to the age of thirty years. . . ." [Art. 1, sec. 3]

• "No *person* except a natural born citizen, . . . shall be eligible to the office of President; neither shall any *person* be eligible to that office who shall not have attained to the age of thirty-five years. . . ." [Art. 2, sec. 1]

In places the Constitution and the Bill of Rights used the pronoun *he*, but always in the context of referring back to a *person* or *citizen.* At the time, and until quite

recently, the male pronoun was often used in legal documents to refer generically to both men and women.

Thus, though the Constitution did not give women the right to vote until the Nineteenth Amendment was ratified in 1920, it did use language that extended fundamental rights, and access to office, to women and men equally.

Of course what the Constitution permitted did not necessarily occur. State and local laws denied to women rights that in principle they ought to have enjoyed. Except for a brief period in New Jersey, no women voted in statewide elections until, in 1869, they were given the right to cast ballots in territorial elections in Wyoming.

When women were first elected to Congress, there was no need to change the Constitution; nothing in it restricted office-holding to men.

When women were given the right to vote by constitutional amendment, it was not necessary to amend any existing language in the Constitution because nothing in the Constitution itself denied women the right to vote; the amendment simply added a new right:

• "The right of citizens of the United States to vote shall not be denied or abridged by the United States or any state on account of sex." [Amend. XIX]

SOURCE: Adapted from Robert Goldwin, "Why Blacks, Women and Jews Are Not Mentioned in the Constitution," *Commentary* (May 1987): 28–33.

greater degree of equality than society allows when left alone.

To the Framers liberty and (political) equality were not in conflict; to some people today these two principles are deeply in conflict. To the Framers the

task was to keep government so limited as to prevent it from creating the worst inequality—political privilege. To some modern observers the task is to make government strong enough to reduce what they believe is the worst inequality—differences in wealth.

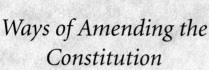

Ways of Amending the Constitution

Under Article V there are two ways to *propose* amendments to the Constitution and two ways to *ratify* them.

TO PROPOSE AN AMENDMENT

1. Two-thirds of both houses of Congress vote to propose an amendment, *or*
2. Two-thirds of the state legislatures ask Congress to call a national convention to propose amendments

TO RATIFY AN AMENDMENT

1. Three-fourths of the state legislatures approve it, *or*
2. Ratifying conventions in three-fourths of the states approve it.

SOME KEY FACTS

- Only the first method of proposing an amendment has been used.
- The second method of ratification has been used only once, to ratify the Twenty-first Amendment (repealing Prohibition).
- Congress may limit the time within which a proposed amendment must be ratified. The usual limitation has been seven years.
- Thousands of proposals have been made, but only thirty-three have obtained the necessary two-thirds vote in Congress.
- Twenty-seven amendments have been ratified.
- The first ten amendments, ratified on December 15, 1791, are known as the Bill of Rights.

Constitutional Reform—Modern Views

Almost from the day it was ratified, the Constitution has been the object of debate over ways in which it might be improved. These debates have rarely involved the average citizen, who tends to revere the document even if he or she cannot recall all its details. Because of this deep and broad popular support, scholars and politicians have been wary of attacking the Constitution or suggesting many wholesale changes. But such attacks have occurred. During the 1980s—the decade in which we celebrated the bicentennial of its adoption—we heard a variety of suggestions for improving the Constitution, ranging from particular amendments to wholesale revisions. In general there are today, as in the eighteenth century, two kinds of critics: those who think the federal government is too weak and those who think it is too strong.

Reducing the Separation of Powers

To the first kind of critic the chief difficulty with the Constitution is the separation of powers. By making every decision the uncertain outcome of the pulling and hauling between the president and Congress, the Constitution precludes the emergence—except perhaps in times of crisis—of the kind of effective national leadership the country needs. In this view our nation today faces a number of challenges that require prompt, decisive, and comprehensive action. Our problem is gridlock. Our position of international leadership, the dangerous and unprecedented proliferation of nuclear weapons among the nations of the globe, and the need to find ways of stimulating economic growth while reducing our deficit and conserving our environment—all these situations require that the president be able to formulate and carry out policies free of some of the pressures and delays from interest groups and members of Congress tied to local interests.

Not only would this increase in presidential authority make for better policies, these critics argue, it would also help the voters hold the president and his party accountable for their actions. As matters now stand, nobody in government can be held responsible for policies: everybody takes the credit for successes and nobody takes the blame for failures. Typically the president, who tends to be the major source of new programs, cannot get his policies adopted by Congress without long delays and much bargaining, the result of which often is some watered-down compromise that neither the president nor Congress really likes but that each must settle for if anything is to be done at all.

The Twenty-seventh Amendment: A Rip Van Winkle Ratification

*T*he Twenty-sixth Amendment to the Constitution gave citizens of the United States who are eighteen years of age or older the right to vote. It cleared Congress on March 23, 1971, and was ratified by the states on June 30, 1971. Since 1971 five other proposed constitutional amendments have come to a vote in one or both chambers of Congress:

- *Equal Rights Amendment* Cleared Congress in 1972; ratification deadline extended by Congress in 1978; deadline expired in 1982 after 35 states (of 38 needed) had approved it.

- *Voting representation in Congress for the District of Columbia* Cleared Congress in 1978; ratification deadline expired in 1985 after 16 states (of 38 needed) had approved it.

- *Prohibition of busing for school desegregation* House rejected in 1979.

- *Balanced Budget Amendment* Passed Senate in 1982, but rejected in House.

- *Denial of a constitutional right to abortion* Senate rejected in 1983.

Most amendments proposed in recent times have been sent to the states with a seven-year deadline for ratification; however there is no constitutional requirement that Congress impose such deadlines. A dozen amendments sent to the states in 1789 had no deadline; ten of them became the Bill of Rights (see box on page 36). The other two were a proposal to change the apportionment of the House and a proposal to keep congressional pay increases from taking effect until after an election has intervened. The former proposal was never ratified. The latter, after a 203-year ratification process, became the Twenty-seventh Amendment in 1992.

The Twenty-seventh Amendment states: "No law varying the compensation for the services of Senators and Representatives, shall take effect, until an election of Representatives shall have intervened." Between 1789 and 1992 forty states (of thirty-eight needed) ratified the amendment. The amendment was certified by the United States Archivist on May 18, 1992, and printed in the *Federal Register* the day after. On May 18, 1992, the Senate passed two resolutions recognizing the amendment by a vote of 99–0. On May 19, 1992, the House passed a resolution recognizing it by a vote of 414–3. And on May 20, 1992, both chambers of Congress passed resolutions endorsing the amendment.

But Congress did not need to pass any resolutions in order to make the amendment official. Because there is no limit on the amount of time it can take to ratify an amendment (unless Congress specifically imposes a deadline), the Twenty-seventh Amendment automatically became law once the requisite thirty-eight states had ratified it. Still, some members of Congress recommended holding hearings on the 203-year-old amendment's constitutionality, but because of the political furor over congressional pay increases, they did not do so. Despite its Rip Van Winkle–like ratification, the Twenty-seventh Amendment is now as much a part of the Constitution as the Bill of Rights.

Finally, critics of the separation of powers complain that the government agencies responsible for implementing a program are exposed to undue interference from legislators and special interests. In this view the president is supposed to be in charge of the bureaucracy but in fact must share this authority with countless members of Congress and congressional committees.

Not all critics of the separation of powers agree with all these points, nor do they all agree on what should be done about the problems. But they all have in common a fear that the separation of powers makes the president too weak and insufficiently accountable.

Their proposals for reducing the separation of powers include the following:

- Allow the president to appoint members of Congress to serve in the cabinet (the Constitution forbids members of Congress from holding any federal appointive office while in Congress).

- Allow the president to dissolve Congress and call for a special election (elections now can be held only on the schedule determined by the calendar).

- Allow the Congress to require a president who has lost its confidence to face the country in a special election before his term would normally end.

- Require the presidential and congressional candidates to run as a team in each congressional district so that each voter would have to vote for the team as a whole; thus a presidential candidate who carries a given district could be sure that the congressional candidate of his party would also win in that district.

- Have the president serve a single six-year term instead of being eligible for up to two four-year terms; this would presumably free the president to lead without having to worry about reelection.

- Lengthen the terms of members of the House of Representatives from two to four years so that the entire House would stand for reelection at the same time as the president.[27]

Some of these proposals are offered by critics out of a desire to make the American system of government work more like the British parliamentary system, in which, as we shall see in Chapters 11 and 12,

the prime minister is the undisputed leader of the majority in the British parliament. The parliamentary system is the major alternative in the world today to the American separation-of-powers system.

Both the diagnosis and the remedies proposed by these critics of the separation of powers have been challenged. Many defenders of our present constitutional system believe that nations, such as Great Britain, with a different, more unified political system have done no better than the United States in dealing with the problems of economic growth, national security, and environmental protection. Moreover, they argue, close congressional scrutiny of presidential proposals has improved these policies more often than it has weakened them. Finally, congressional "interference" in the work of government agencies is a good way of ensuring that the average citizen can fight back against the bureaucracy; without that so-called interference, citizens and interest groups might be helpless before big and powerful agencies.

Each of the specific proposals, defenders of the present constitutional system argue, would either make matters worse or have, at best, uncertain effects. Adding a few members of Congress to the president's cabinet would not provide much help in getting his program through Congress; there are 535 senators and representatives, and probably only about half a dozen would be in the cabinet. Giving either the president or Congress power to call a special election in between the regular elections (every two or four years) would cause needless confusion and great expense; the country would live under the threat of being in a perpetual political campaign with even weaker political parties. Linking the fate of the president and congressional candidates, by having them run as a team in each district, would reduce the stabilizing and moderating effect of having them separately elected. A Republican presidential candidate who wins in the new system would have a Republican majority in the House; a Democratic candidate winner would have a Democratic majority. We might as a result expect dramatic changes in policy as the political pendulum swings back and forth. Giving presidents a single six-year term would indeed free them from the need to worry about reelection, but it is precisely that worry that keeps presidents reasonably concerned about what the American people want.

Making the System Less Democratic

The second kind of critic of the Constitution thinks the government does too much, not too little. Though the separation of powers at one time may have slowed the growth of government and moderated the policies it adopted, in the last few decades government has grown helter-skelter. The problem, these critics argue, is not that democracy is a bad idea but that democracy can produce bad, or at least unintended, results if the government caters to the special-interest claims of the citizens rather than to their long-term values.

To see how these unintended results might occur, imagine a situation in which every citizen thinks the government grows too big, taxes too heavily, and spends too much. Each citizen wants the government made smaller by reducing the benefits other people get—but not by reducing the benefits he or she gets. In fact such citizens may even be willing to see their own benefits cut, provided everybody else's are cut as well, and by a like amount.

But the political system attends to individual wants, not general preferences. It gives aid to farmers, contracts to industry, grants to professors, pensions to the elderly, and loans to students. As someone once said, the government is like an adding machine: during elections candidates campaign by promising to do more for whatever group is dissatisfied with what the incumbents are doing for it. As a result most elections bring to office men and women who are committed to doing more for somebody. The grand total of all these additions is more for everybody. Few politicians have an incentive to do less for anybody.

To remedy this state of affairs, these critics suggest various mechanisms, but principally a constitutional amendment that would either set a limit on the amount of money the government could collect in taxes each year, or require that each year the government have a balanced budget (that is, not spend more than it takes in in taxes), or both. In some versions of these plans an extraordinary majority (say, 60 percent) of Congress could override these limits, and the limits would not apply in wartime.

The effect of such amendments, the proponents claim, would be to force Congress and the president to look at the big picture—the grand total of what they are spending—rather than just to operate the adding machine by pushing the "add" button over and over again. If they could only spend so much during a given year, they would have to allocate what they spend among all rival claimants. For example, if more money were to be spent on the poor, less could then be spent on the military, or vice versa.

Some critics of an overly powerful federal government think these amendments will not be passed or may prove unworkable; instead they favor enhancing the president's power to block spending by giving him a **line-item veto**. As we shall see in Chapter 12, the president must now sign or veto a bill as a whole, take it or leave it. Most state governors, however, can veto a particular part of a bill and approve the rest, using a line-item veto. The theory is that such a veto would better equip the president to stop unwarranted spending without vetoing the other provisions of a bill.

Finally, some of these critics of a powerful government feel that the real problem arises not from an excess of "adding-machine" democracy but from the growth in the power of the federal courts, as described in Chapter 14. What these critics would like

As governor of Massachusetts, William Weld can veto specific items in a spending bill passed by the legislature. The president of the United States is not allowed a line-item veto.

to do is devise a set of laws or constitutional amendments that would narrow the authority of federal courts.

The opponents of these suggestions argue that constitutional amendments to restrict the level of taxes or to require a balanced budget are unworkable, even assuming—which they do not—that a smaller government is desirable. There is no precise, agreed-upon way to measure how much the government spends or to predict in advance how much it will receive in taxes during the year (see Chapter 16); thus defining and enforcing a "balanced budget" is no easy matter. Since the government can always borrow money, it might easily evade any spending limits. It has also shown great ingenuity in spending money in ways that never appear as part of the regular budget.

The line-item veto may or may not be a good idea, these people argue, but we can never know without trying it, since the states, where some governors now have such a veto, are quite different from the federal government in power and responsibilities. And if we tried it, we might well discover that the president would use it not to spend less but to spend more—by threatening, for example, to veto something of modest cost that Congress wants in order to get Congress to vote for a far more costly item that the president wants.

Finally, proposals to curtail judicial power are thinly veiled attacks, the opponents argue, on the ability of the courts to protect essential citizen rights. If Congress and the people do not like the way the Supreme Court has interpreted the Constitution, they can always amend the Constitution to change a specific ruling; there is no need to adopt some general, across-the-board limitation on court powers.

Who Is Right?

Some of the arguments of these two sets of critics of the Constitution may strike you as plausible or even entirely convincing. Whatever you may ultimately decide, decide nothing for now. One cannot make or remake a Constitution based entirely on abstract reasoning or unproven factual arguments. Even when the Constitution was first written in 1787, it was not an exercise in abstract philosophy but rather an effort to solve pressing, practical problems in the light of a theory of human nature, the lessons of past experi-

ence, and a close consideration of how governments in other countries and at other times had worked.

Just because the Constitution is over two hundred years old does not mean that it is out of date. The crucial questions are these: How well has it worked over the long sweep of American history? How well has it worked compared to the constitutions of other democratic nations?

The only way to answer those questions is to study American government closely—with special attention to its historical evolution and to the practices of other nations. That is what this book is about. Of course, even after close study, people will still disagree about whether our system should be changed. People want different things and evaluate human experience according to different beliefs. But if we first understand how, in fact, the government works and why it has produced the policies it has, we can then argue more intelligently about how best to achieve our wants and give expression to our beliefs.

SUMMARY

The Framers of the Constitution sought to create a government capable of protecting both liberty and order. The solution they chose—one without precedent at that time—was a government that was based on a written constitution that combined the principles of popular consent, the separation of powers, and federalism.

Popular consent was embodied in the procedure for choosing the House of Representatives but limited by the indirect election of senators and the Electoral College system for selecting a president. Political authority was to be shared by three branches of government in a manner deliberately intended to produce conflict among these branches. This conflict, motivated by the self-interest of the people occupying each branch, would, it was hoped, prevent tyranny, even by a popular majority.

Federalism came to mean a system in which both the national and state governments had independent authority. Allocating powers between the two levels of government and devising means to ensure that neither large nor small states would dominate the national government required the most delicate compromises at the Philadelphia convention. The decision to do nothing about slavery was another such compromise.

In the drafting of the Constitution and the struggle over its ratification in the states, the positions people took were not chiefly determined by their economic interests but by a variety of factors. Among these were profound differences of opinion over whether state governments or national government would be the best protector of personal liberty.

KEY TERMS

unalienable rights   *p. 19*

Articles of Confederation   *p. 21*

Constitutional Convention   *p. 22*

Shays's Rebellion   *p. 23*

The *Federalist* Papers   *p. 26*

Great Compromise   *p. 28*

republic   *p. 29*

judicial review   *p. 30*

federalism   *p. 30*

separation of powers   *p. 31*

checks and balances   *p. 31*

faction   *p. 32*

Federalists   *p. 32*

Antifederalists   *p. 32*

coalition   *p. 35*

writ of habeas corpus   *p. 35*

bill of attainder   *p. 35*

ex post facto law   *p. 35*

Bill of Rights   *p. 36*

amendment   *p. 42*

line-item veto   *p. 45*

SUGGESTED READINGS

Bailyn, Bernard. *The Ideological Origins of the American Revolution.* Cambridge, Mass.: Harvard University Press, 1967. A brilliant account of how the American colonists formed and justified the idea of independence.

Becker, Carl L. *The Declaration of Independence.* New York: Vintage, 1942. The classic account of the meaning of the Declaration.

Farrand, Max. *The Framing of the Constitution of the United States.* New Haven, Conn.: Yale University Press, 1913. A good, brief account of the Philadelphia convention, by the editor of Madison's notes on the convention.

Federalist papers. By Alexander Hamilton, James Madison, and John Jay. The definitive edition, edited by Jacob E. Cooke, was published in Middletown, Conn., in 1961, by the Wesleyan University Press.

Goldwin, Robert A., and William A. Schambra, eds. *How Capitalistic Is the Constitution?* Washington, D.C.: American Enterprise Institute, 1982. Essays from different viewpoints discussing the relationship between the Constitution and the economic order.

————. *How Democratic Is the Constitution?* Washington, D.C.: American Enterprise Institute, 1980. Collection of essays offering different interpretations of the political meaning of the Constitution.

McDonald, Forrest. *Novus Ordo Seclorum.* Lawrence: University of Kansas Press, 1985. A careful study of the intellectual origins of the Constitution. The Latin title means "New World Order," which is what the Framers hoped they were creating.

Robinson, Donald L., ed. *Reforming American Government.* Boulder, Colo.: Westview Press, 1985. Collection of essays advocating constitutional reform.

Storing, Herbert J. *What the Anti-Federalists Were For.* Chicago: University of Chicago Press, 1981. Close analysis of the political views of those opposed to the ratification of the Constitution.

Wood, Gordon S. *The Creation of the American Republic.* Chapel Hill, N.C.: University of North Carolina Press, 1969. A detailed study of American political thought before the Philadelphia convention.

————. *The Radicalism of the American Revolution.* New York: Alfred P. Knopf, 1992. Magisterial study of the nature and effects of the American Revolution and the relationship between the socially radical revolution and the Constitution.

3

Federalism

Since the adoption of the Constitution in 1787, the single most persistent source of political conflict has been the relations between the national and state governments. The political conflict over slavery, for example, was intensified because some state governments condoned or supported slavery, while others took action to discourage it. The proponents and opponents of slavery were thus given territorial power centers from which to carry on the dispute. Other issues, such as the regulation of business and the provision of social welfare programs, were in large part fought out, for well over a century, in terms of "national interests" versus "states' rights." While other nations, such as Great Britain, were debating the question of whether the national government *ought* to provide old-age pensions or regulate the railroads, the United States debated a different question—whether the national government *had the right* to do these things. Even after these debates had ended—almost invariably with a decision favorable to the national government—the administration and financing of the programs that resulted have usually involved a large role for the states. In short, federalism has long been a central issue in American politics. It continues to be even today, when most Americans think of the government in Washington as vastly powerful and state governments as weak or unimportant.

Governmental Structure

Federalism refers to a political system in which there are local (territorial, regional, provincial, state, or municipal) units of government, as well as a national government, that can make final decisions with respect to at least some governmental activities and whose existence is specially protected.[1] Almost every nation in the world has local units of government of some kind, if for no other reason than to decentralize the administrative burdens of governing. But these governments are not federal unless the local units

On the Evolving Meaning of Federalism

I t is customary in textbooks to distinguish among three forms of government—the unitary, the federal, and the confederal—and to claim that the United States is an instance of the federal form.

These three terms describe different places in which political sovereignty can be located. **Sovereignty** means supreme or ultimate political authority: a sovereign government is one that is legally and politically independent of any other government. A unitary system is one in which sovereignty is wholly in the hands of the national government, so that the states and localities are dependent on its will. A **confederation** or **confederal system** is one in which the states are sovereign and the national government is allowed to do only that which the states permit. A **federal system** is one in which sovereignty is shared, so that on some matters the national government is supreme and on others the states are supreme.

These definitions, though neat and systematic, do not correspond either to the intentions of the Founders or to the realities of American politics. The Founders at the Philadelphia convention, and later in the *Federalist* papers, did not make precise distinctions among these three kinds of governments. Indeed there is some evidence that they took *confederal* and *federal* to mean much the same thing. Nor did they establish a government in which there was a clear and systematic division of sovereign authority between the national and state governments. They created something quite new—a government that combined some characteristics of a unitary regime with some of a confederal one.

In this text little is made of the conventional definitions and distinctions. Instead a federal regime is defined in the simplest possible terms—as one in which local units of government have a specially protected existence and can make some final decisions over some governmental activities. Where "sovereignty" is located is a matter that the Founders did not clearly answer, and no one else has been able to answer since.

exist independently of the preferences of the national government and can make decisions on at least some matters without regard to those preferences.

The United States, Canada, Australia, India, Germany, and Switzerland are federal systems, as are a few other nations. France, Great Britain, Italy, and Sweden are not: they are **unitary systems,** because such local governments as they possess can be altered or even abolished by the national government and cannot plausibly claim to have final authority over any significant governmental activities.

The special protection that subnational governments enjoy in a federal system derives in part from the constitution of the country but also from the habits, preferences, and dispositions of the citizens and the actual distribution of political power in society. The constitution of the former Soviet Union in theory created a federal system, as claimed by that country's full name—the Union of Soviet Socialist Republics—but for most of their history, none of these "socialist republics" were in the slightest degree independent of the central government. Were the American Constitution the only guarantee of the independence of the American states, they would long since have become mere administrative subunits of the government in Washington. Their independence results in large measure from the commitment of Americans to the idea of local self-government and from the fact that Congress consists of people who are selected by and responsive to local constituencies.

"The basic political fact of federalism," writes David B. Truman, "is that it creates separate, self-sustaining centers of power, prestige, and profit."[2] Political power is locally acquired by people whose careers depend for the most part on satisfying local interests. As a result, though the national government has come to have vast powers, it exercises many of those powers through state governments. What many of us forget when we think about "the government in Washington" is that it spends much of its money and enforces most of its rules not on citizens directly but on other, local units of government. A large part of the welfare system, all of the interstate highway system, virtually every aspect of programs to improve cities, the largest part of the effort to supply jobs to the unemployed, the entire program to clean up our water, and even much of our military manpower (in the form of the National Guard) are enterprises in which the national government does not govern so much as it seeks, by regulation, grant, plan, argument, and cajolery, to get the states to govern in accordance with nationally defined (though often vaguely defined) goals.

In France welfare, highways, education, the police, and the use of land are all matters that are directed nationally. In the United States highways and some welfare programs are largely state functions (though they make use of federal money), while education, policing, and land-use controls are primarily local (city, county, or special-district) functions.

Federalism: Good or Bad?

A measure of the importance of federalism is the controversy that surrounds it. To some, federalism means allowing states to block action, prevent progress, upset national plans, protect powerful local interests, and cater to the self-interest of hack politicians. Harold Laski, a British observer, described American states as "parasitic and poisonous,"[3] and William H. Riker, an American political scientist, argued that "the main effect of federalism since the Civil War has been to perpetuate racism."[4] By contrast another political scientist, Daniel J. Elazar, believes that the "virtue of the federal system lies in its ability to develop and maintain mechanisms vital to the perpetuation of the unique combination of governmental strength, political flexibility, and individual liberty, which has been the central concern of American politics."[5]

So diametrically opposed are the Riker and the Elazar views that one wonders whether they are talking about the same subject. They are, of course, but they are stressing different aspects of the same phenomenon. Whenever the opportunity to exercise political power is widely available (as among the fifty states, three thousand counties, and many thousands of municipalities), it is obvious that in different places different people will make use of that power for different purposes. There is no question that allowing states and cities to make autonomous, binding political decisions will allow some people in some places to make those decisions in ways that maintain racial segregation, protect vested interests, and facilitate corruption. It is equally true, however, that this arrangement also enables other people in other

In this country, unlike most others, police work is almost entirely under local control.

places to pass laws that attack segregation, regulate harmful economic practices, and purify politics, often long before these ideas gain national support or become national policy.

For example, in a unitary political system, such as that of France, a small but intensely motivated group could not have blocked civil rights legislation for as long as some southern senators blocked it in this country. But by the same token it would have been equally difficult for another small but intensely motivated group to block plans to operate a nuclear power plant in their neighborhood, as citizens have done in this country but not in France. An even more dramatic illustration involved the efforts of citizens in England, France, and the United States to prevent the Concorde supersonic transport from landing at airports near certain populated areas. Such groups had no success in England or France, where the

Federalism has permitted experimentation. Women were able to vote in the Wyoming territory in 1888, long before they could do so in most states.

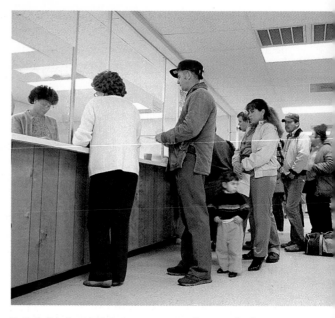

Both federal and state governments share authority over the provision of welfare benefits.

national government alone makes these decisions. But they enjoyed considerable (albeit temporary) success in the United States, where they were able to persuade the Port of New York Authority to deny landing rights to the Concorde. British and French officials were incredulous that such matters could be decided by local authorities. (Eventually the courts ruled that these restrictions had to be lifted.)

The existence of independent state and local governments means that different political groups pursuing different political purposes will come to power in different places. (While groups opposed to the

Concorde had the most influence in New York, those welcoming it were most influential in Dallas.) The smaller the political unit, the more likely it is to be dominated by a single political faction. James Madison understood this fact perfectly and used it to argue (in *Federalist* No. 10) that it would be in a large (or "extended") republic, such as the United States as a whole, that one would find the greatest opportunity for all relevant interests to be heard. When William Riker condemns federalism, he is thinking of the fact that in some places the ruling factions in cities and states have opposed granting equal rights to blacks. When Daniel Elazar praises federalism, he is recalling that, in other states and cities, the ruling factions have taken the lead (long in advance of the federal government) in developing measures to protect the environment, extend civil rights, and improve social conditions. If you live in California, whether you like federalism depends in part on whether you like the fact that California has, independent of the federal government, cut property taxes, strictly controlled coastal land use, heavily regulated electric utilities, and increased (at one time) and decreased (at another time) its welfare rolls.

CRITICAL ★ THINKING

Federalism American-Style:
Should Who Gets What Depend on Where?

Ronald A. Harmelin learned about federalism the hard way. On June 27, 1991, the U.S. Supreme Court ruled 5 to 4 that the life-without-parole prison sentence imposed on him by the state of Michigan did not violate the Constitution. In 1978 Michigan adopted a law requiring a mandatory life sentence for persons convicted of possessing more than 650 grams (about one and one-half pounds) of cocaine. Mr. Harmelin had 672.5 grams of cocaine in the trunk of his car when the police stopped him for running a red light. When he was convicted in 1986, Michigan was the only state to impose a mandatory life sentence for the possession of this amount of cocaine. For the same crime under the federal sentencing guidelines he would have received about ten years. In Alabama and some other states he would have received only about five years.

Politics, argued the political scientist Harold Lasswell, is about deciding "who gets what." In a federal system, many decisions about who gets what depend on who lives where. Criminal justice furnishes some of the most dramatic examples: a conviction for first-degree murder in some states means the death penalty, but a conviction for the same crime in other states normally means only ten years (or fewer) behind bars. Criminal justice is not the only area in which who gets what depends on where. As the following table illustrates, states differ widely in the benefits they pay to persons on public assistance.

Likewise, states differ widely in the degree to which they restrict minors' access

Selected Monthly State Benefits[a]

Top Five	
Alaska	$1,184
Connecticut	$862
Vermont	$857
California	$850
New York	$806
Bottom Five	
Mississippi	$412
Alabama	$441
Texas	$476
Tennessee	$477
Arkansas	$496

[a] Maximum monthly benefits from Aid to Families with Dependent Children (AFDC) and food stamps for a family of three as of January 1992.

SOURCE: Adapted from *The New York Times* (July 5, 1992): 16.

to abortion. For instance, there are no such restrictions in Florida or New York, whereas a minor in Pennsylvania must obtain consent of one parent or find a judge who will waive that requirement.

Federalism permits intrastate as well as interstate differences. A study by the Congressional Research Service based on 1986–1987 data from the U.S. Census Bureau documented big intrastate gaps in public school expenditures. In at least ten states the average annual expenditures per pupil in the ten wealthiest school districts were twice or more the expenditures of the ten poorest school districts. For example, in New York the ten wealthiest school districts spent an annual average of about ten thousand dollars per student while the ten poorest spent barely four thousand dollars per student. Similarly, average annual spending per pupil in Texas ranges from about twenty-seven hundred dollars in some school districts to nearly ten thousand dollars in others.

Much else depends on the state and local government under which you happen to live or under whose jurisdiction you happen to be passing: whether you can legally drive faster than fifty-five miles per hour on designated highways without risking a speeding ticket, whether you can purchase a bottle of beer at a neighborhood restaurant or have to go dry, whether you can get divorced quickly or have to show grounds, and whether your property taxes are light or heavy.

Other countries that have federal systems limit the extent of such differences more than we do in the United States. What criteria should be used in deciding which matters of public law and policy are allowed to vary, and to what degree, among and between states and localities? Who should decide? Congress? Federal and state judges? Governors? State legislatures? City officials? Trying to answer such questions is one way to begin to come to grips with the pros and cons of federalism American-style.

SOURCES: *Governing* (April 1993): 23; Jill Zuckerman, "The Next Education Crisis," *Congressional Quarterly Weekly* (March 27, 1993): 749–754; Linda Greenhouse, "Mandatory Life Term Is Upheld in Drug Cases," *New York Times* (June 28, 1991).

Increased Political Activity

Federalism has many effects, but its most obvious effect has been to facilitate the mobilization of political activity. Unlike Don Quixote, the average citizen does not tilt at windmills. He or she is more likely to

FIGURE 3.1 Lines of Power in Three Systems of Government

UNITARY SYSTEM

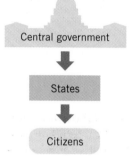

Power centralized.
State or regional governments derive authority from central government.
Examples: United Kingdom, France.

FEDERAL SYSTEM

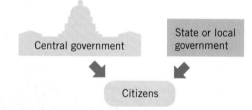

Power divided between central and state or local governments.
Both the government and constituent governments act directly
   upon the citizens.
Both must agree to constitutional change.
Examples: Canada, United States since adoption of Constitution.

**CONFEDERAL SYSTEM
(or CONFEDERATION)**

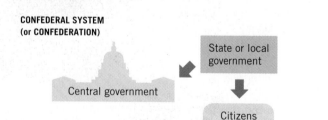

Power held by independent states.
Central government is a creature of the constituent governments.
Example: United States under the Articles of Confederation.

become involved in organized political activity if he or she feels there is a reasonable chance of having a practical effect. The chances of having such an effect are greater where there are many elected officials and independent governmental bodies, each with a relatively small constituency, than where there are few elected officials, most of whom have the nation as a whole for a constituency. In short a federal system, by virtue of the decentralization of authority, lowers the cost of organized political activity; a unitary system, because of the centralization of authority, raises the cost. We may disagree about the purposes of organized political activity, but the fact of widespread organized activity can scarcely be doubted—or if it can be doubted, it is only because you have not yet read Chapters 6 and 9.

It is impossible to say whether the Founders, when they wrote the Constitution, planned to produce such widespread opportunities for political participation. Unfortunately they were not very clear (at least in writing) about how the federal system was supposed to work, and thus most of the interesting questions about the jurisdiction and powers of our national and state governments had to be settled by a century and a half of protracted, often bitter, conflict.

The Founding

The goal of the Founders seems clear: federalism was one device whereby personal liberty was to be protected. (The separation of powers was another.) They feared that placing final political authority in any one set of hands, even in the hands of persons popularly elected, would so concentrate power as to risk tyranny. But they had seen what happened when independent states tried to form a compact, as under the Articles of Confederation; what the states put together, they could also take apart. The alliance among the states that existed from 1776 to 1787 was a confederation: that is, a system of government in which the people create state governments, which, in turn, create and operate a national government (see Figure 3.1). Since the national government in a confederation derives its powers from the states, it is dependent on their continued cooperation for its survival. By 1786 that cooperation was barely forthcoming.

A Bold, New Plan

A federation—or a "federal republic," as the Founders called it—derives its powers directly from the people, as do the state governments. As the Founders envisioned it, both levels of government, the national and the state, would have certain powers but neither would have supreme authority over the other. Madison, writing in *Federalist* No. 46, said that both the state and federal governments "are in fact but different agents and trustees of the people, constituted with different powers." In *Federalist* No. 28 Hamilton explained how he thought the system would work: the people could shift their support between state and federal levels of government as needed to keep the two in balance. "If their rights are invaded by either, they can make use of the other as the instrument of redress."

It was an entirely new plan, for which no historical precedent existed. Nobody came to the Philadelphia convention with a clear idea of what a federal (as opposed to a unitary or a confederal) system would look like, and there was not much discussion at Philadelphia of how the system would work in practice. Few delegates then used the word *federalism* in the sense in which we now employ it (it was originally used as a synonym for *confederation* and only later came to stand for something different).[6] The Constitution does not spell out the powers that the states are to have, and until the Tenth Amendment was added at the insistence of various states, there was not even a clause in it saying (as did the amendment) that "the powers not delegated to the United States by the Constitution, nor prohibited by it to the states, are reserved to the states respectively, or to the people." The Founders assumed from the outset that the federal government would have only those powers given to it by the Constitution; the Tenth Amendment was an afterthought, added to make that assumption explicit and allay fears that something else was intended.[7]

The Tenth Amendment has rarely had much practical significance, however. From time to time the Supreme Court has tried to interpret that amendment as putting certain state activities beyond the reach of the federal government, but invariably the Court has later changed its mind and allowed Washington to regulate such matters as the hours that employees of a city-owned mass-transit system may work. The Court did not find that running such a transportation system was one of the powers "reserved to the states."[8]

Elastic Language

The need to reconcile the competing interests of large and small states and of northern and southern states, especially as they affected the organization of Congress, was sufficiently difficult without trying to spell out exactly what relationship ought to exist between the national and state systems. For example, Congress was given the power to regulate commerce

Thomas Jefferson (1743–1826) was not at the Constitutional Convention. His doubts about the new national government led him to oppose the Federalist administration of John Adams and to become an ardent champion of states' rights.

"among the several states." The Philadelphia convention would have gone on for four years rather than four months if the Founders had decided that it was necessary to describe, in clear language, how one was to tell where commerce *among* the states ended and commerce wholly *within* a single state began. The Supreme Court, as we shall see, devoted over a century to that task before giving up.

Though some clauses bearing on federal-state relations were reasonably clear (see the accompanying box), other clauses were quite vague. The Founders knew, correctly, that they could not make an exact and exhaustive list of everything the federal government was empowered to do—circumstances would change, new exigencies would arise. Thus they added the following elastic language to Article I: Congress

The States and the Constitution

*T*he Framers made some attempt to define the relations between the states and the federal government and how states were to relate to one another. The following points were made in the original Constitution—before the Bill of Rights was added.

RESTRICTIONS ON POWERS OF THE STATES

States may not make treaties with foreign nations, coin money, issue paper currency, grant titles of nobility, pass a bill of attainder or an ex post facto law,* or, without the consent of Congress, levy any taxes on imports or exports, keep troops and ships in time of peace, or enter into an agreement with another state or with a foreign power.   [Art. I, sec. 10]

GUARANTEES BY THE FEDERAL GOVERNMENT TO THE STATES

The national government guarantees to every state a "republican form of government" and protection against foreign invasion and (provided the states request it) protection against domestic insurrection.   [Art. IV, sec. 4]

An existing state will not be broken up into two or more states or merged with all or part of another state without that state's consent.   [Art. IV, sec. 3]

Congress may admit new states into the Union.
[Art. IV, sec. 3]

Taxes levied by Congress must be uniform throughout the United States: they may not be levied on some states but not others.   [Art, I, sec. 8]

The Constitution may not be amended to give states unequal representation in the Senate.   [Art. V]

RULES GOVERNING HOW STATES DEAL WITH EACH OTHER

"Full faith and credit" shall be given by each state to the laws, records, and court decisions of other states. (For example, a civil case settled in the courts of one state cannot be retried in the courts of another.)
[Art. IV, sec. 1]

The citizens of each state shall have the "privileges and immunities" of the citizens of every other state. (No one is quite sure what this is supposed to mean.)
[Art. IV, sec. 2]

If a person charged with a crime by one state flees to another, he or she is subjected to extradition—that is, the governor of the state that finds the fugitive is supposed to return the person to the governor of the state that wants him or her.   [Art. IV, sec. 2]

*For definitions of *bill of attainder* and *ex post facto law*, see the Glossary.

shall have the power to "make all laws which shall be necessary and proper for carrying into execution the foregoing powers."

The Founders themselves carried away from Philadelphia different views of what federalism meant. One view was championed by Hamilton. Since the people had created the national government, since the laws and treaties made pursuant to the Constitution were "the supreme law of the land" (Article VI), and since the most pressing needs were the development of a national economy and the conduct of foreign affairs, Hamilton thought that the national government was the superior and leading force in political affairs and that its powers ought to be broadly defined and liberally construed.

The other view, championed by Jefferson, was that the federal government, though important, was the product of an agreement among the states; and though "the people" were the ultimate sovereigns, the principal threat to their liberties was likely to come from the national government. (Madison, a strong supporter of national supremacy at the convention, later became a champion of states' rights.) Thus the powers of the federal government should be narrowly construed and strictly limited. As Madison put it in *Federalist* No. 45, in language that probably made Hamilton wince, "The powers delegated by the proposed Constitution to the federal government are few and defined. Those which are to remain in the State governments are numerous and indefinite."

Hamilton argued for national supremacy, Jefferson for states' rights. Though their differences were greater in theory than in practice (as we shall see in Chapter 12, Jefferson while president sometimes acted in a positively Hamiltonian manner), the differing interpretations they offered of the Constitution were to shape political debate in this country until well into the 1960s.

The Debate on the Meaning of Federalism

The Civil War was fought, in part, over the issue of national supremacy versus states' rights, but it settled only one part of that argument—namely, that the national government was supreme, its sovereignty derived directly from the people, and thus the states could not lawfully secede from the Union. Virtually every other aspect of the national-supremacy issue continued to animate political and legal debate for another century.

The Supreme Court Speaks

As arbiter of what the Constitution means, the Supreme Court became the focal point of that debate. In Chapter 14 we shall see in some detail how the Court made its decisions. For now it is enough to know that during the formative years of the new Republic, the Supreme Court was led by a staunch and brilliant advocate of the Hamilton position, Chief Justice John Marshall. In a series of decisions he and the Court powerfully defended the national-supremacy view of the newly formed federal government.

The most important decision was in a case, seemingly trivial in its origins, that arose when James McCulloch, the cashier of the Baltimore branch of the Bank of the United States, which had been created by Congress, refused to pay a tax levied on that bank by the state of Maryland. He was hauled into state court and convicted of failing to pay a tax. In 1819 McCulloch appealed all the way to the Supreme Court in a case known as *McCulloch* v. *Maryland*. The Court, in a unanimous opinion, answered two questions in ways that expanded the powers of Congress and confirmed the supremacy of the federal government in the exercise of those powers.

The first question was whether Congress had the right to set up a bank, or any other corporation, since such a right is nowhere explicitly mentioned in the Constitution. Marshall said that, though the federal government possessed only those powers enumerated in the Constitution, the "extent"—that is, the meaning—of those powers required interpretation. Though the word *bank* is not in that document, one finds there the power to manage money: to lay and collect taxes, issue a currency, and borrow funds. To carry out these powers Congress may reasonably decide that chartering a national bank is "necessary and proper." Marshall's words were carefully chosen to endow the **"necessary and proper" clause** with the widest possible sweep:

Let the end be legitimate, let it be within the scope of the Constitution, and all means which are appropriate, which are plainly adapted to that end, which are not prohibited, but consistent with the letter and spirit of the Constitution, are constitutional.[9]

The second question was whether a federal bank could lawfully be taxed by a state. To answer it, Marshall went back to first principles. The government of the United States was not established by the states, but by the people, and thus the federal government was supreme in the exercise of those powers conferred upon it. Having already concluded that chartering a bank was within the powers of Congress, Marshall then argued that the only way for such powers to be supreme was for their use to be immune from state challenge and for the products of their use to be protected against state destruction. Since "the power to tax involves the power to destroy," and since the power to destroy a federal agency would confer upon the states using it supremacy over the federal government, the states may not tax any federal instrument. Hence the Maryland law was unconstitutional.

McCulloch won, and so did the federal government. Half a century later, the Court decided that what was sauce for the goose was sauce for the gander. It held that, just as state governments could not tax federal bonds, the federal government could not tax the interest people earn on state and municipal bonds. In 1988 the Supreme Court changed its mind and decided that Congress was now free, if it wished, to tax the interest on such state and local bonds. Municipal bonds, which for nearly a century were a tax-exempt investment protected, so their holders thought, by the Constitution, were now protected only by politics. So far Congress hasn't wanted to tax them.[10]

Nullification

The Supreme Court can decide a case without settling the issue. The struggle over states' rights versus national supremacy continued to rage in Congress, during presidential elections, and ultimately on the battlefield. The issue came to center on the doctrine of **nullification.** When Congress passed laws (in 1798) to punish newspaper editors who published stories critical of the federal government, James Madison and Thomas Jefferson opposed the laws, suggesting (in statements known as the Virginia and Kentucky Resolutions) that the states had the right to "nullify" (that is, declare null and void) a federal law that, in the states' opinion, violated the Constitution. The laws expired before the claim of nullification could be settled in the courts.

Later the doctrine of nullification was revived by John C. Calhoun of South Carolina, first in opposition to a tariff enacted by the federal government and later in opposition to federal efforts to restrict slavery. Calhoun argued that if Washington attempted to ban slavery, the states had the right to declare such

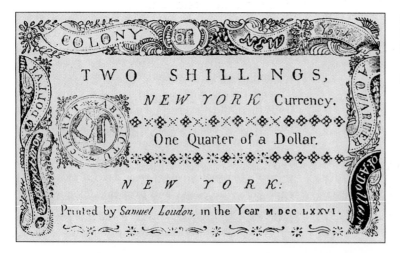

At one time the states could issue their own paper money, such as this New York currency worth 25 cents in 1776. Under the Constitution this power was reserved to Congress.

acts unconstitutional and thus null and void. This time, the issue was settled—by war. The northern victory in the Civil War determined once and for all that the federal union is indissoluble and that states cannot declare acts of Congress unconstitutional, a view later confirmed by the Supreme Court.[11]

Dual Federalism

After the Civil War the debate about the meaning of federalism focused on the interpretation of the commerce clause of the Constitution. Out of this debate there emerged the doctrine of **dual federalism,** which held that though the national government was supreme in its sphere, the states were equally supreme in theirs, and that these two spheres of action should and could be kept separate. Applied to commerce, the concept of dual federalism implied that there was such a thing as *inter*state commerce, which Congress could regulate, and *intra*state commerce, which only the states could regulate, and that the Court could tell which was which.

For a long period the Court tried to decide what was interstate commerce based on the kind of business that was being conducted. Transporting things between states was obviously interstate commerce, and so subject to federal regulation. Thus federal laws affecting the interstate shipment of lottery tickets,[12] prostitutes,[13] liquor,[14] and harmful foods and drugs[15] were upheld. On the other hand manufacturing,[16] insurance,[17] and farming[18] were in the past considered *intra*state commerce, and so only the state governments were allowed to regulate them.

Such product-based distinctions turned out to be hard to sustain. For example, if you ship a case of whiskey from Kentucky to Kansas, how long is it in interstate commerce (and thus subject to federal law), and when does it enter intrastate commerce and become subject only to state law? For a while the Court's answer was that the whiskey was in interstate commerce so long as it was in its "original package,"[19] but that only precipitated long quarrels as to what was the original package, and how one is to treat things, like gas and grain, that may not be shipped in packages at all. And how could one distinguish between manufacturing and transportation when one company did both or when a single manufacturing corporation owned factories in different states? And if an insurance company sold policies to customers both inside and outside a given state, were there to be different laws regulating identical policies that happened to be purchased from the same company by persons in different states?

In time the effort to find some clear principles that distinguished interstate from intrastate commerce was pretty much abandoned. Commerce was like a stream flowing through the country, drawing to itself contributions from thousands of scattered enterprises and depositing its products in millions of individual homes. The Court began to permit the federal government to regulate almost anything that affected this stream, so that by the 1940s not only had farming and manufacturing been redefined as part of interstate commerce,[20] but even the janitors and window washers in buildings that housed companies engaged in interstate commerce were now said to be part of that stream.[21]

The current Court interpretation of various laws pertaining to commerce is immensely complex, difficult to summarize, and impossible to explain. (For example, lawyers are said to engage in interstate commerce but professional baseball players are not, so that federal antitrust laws affect the former but not the latter.)[22] It would be only a mild overstatement, however, to say that the doctrine of dual federalism is virtually extinct and that, provided it has a good reason for wanting to do so, Congress can pass a law that will regulate constitutionally almost any kind of economic activity located anywhere in the country. In short the principle of national supremacy has triumphed over that of states' rights.

Federal-State Relations

Though constitutionally the federal government may be supreme, politically it must take into account the fact that the laws it passes have to be approved by members of Congress selected from, and responsive to, state and local constituencies. Thus what Washington lawfully may do is not the same thing as what it politically may wish to do. For example, in 1947 the Supreme Court decided that the federal government and not the states had supreme authority over oil beneath the ocean off the nation's coasts.[23] Six years later, after an intense debate, Congress passed and the president signed a law transferring title to these tidelands oil reserves back to the states.

Some of the nation's greatest universities, such as the University of California at Berkeley, began as land-grant colleges.

Grants-in-Aid

The best illustration of how political realities modify legal authority can be found in federal **grants-in-aid.** The first of these programs began even before the Constitution was adopted, in the form of land grants made by the national government to the states in order to finance education. (State universities all over the country were built with the proceeds from the sale of these land grants; hence the name *land-grant colleges.*) Land grants were also made to support the building of wagon roads, canals, railroads, and flood-control projects. These measures were hotly debated in Congress (President Madison thought some were unconstitutional) even though the use to which the grants were put was left almost entirely to the states.

Cash grants-in-aid began almost as early. In 1808 Congress gave $200,000 to the states to pay for their militia, with the states in charge of the size, deployment, and command of these troops. However, grant-in-aid programs remained few in number and small in price until the twentieth century, when scores of new ones came into being. In 1915 less than $6 million was spent per year in grants-in-aid; by

1925 over $114 million was spent; by 1937 nearly $300 million.[24] The great growth began in the 1960s: between 1960 and 1966 federal grants to the states doubled; from 1966 to 1970 they doubled again; between 1970 and 1975 they doubled yet again. By 1985 they amounted to over $100 billion a year and were spent through more than four hundred separate programs. The five largest programs accounted for over half the money spent and reflected the new priorities that federal policy had come to serve: housing assistance for low-income families, Medicaid, highway construction, services to the unemployed, and welfare programs for mothers with dependent children and for the disabled.

The grant-in-aid system, once under way, grew rapidly because it helped state and local officials resolve a dilemma. On the one hand they wanted access to the superior taxing power of the federal government. On the other hand prevailing constitutional interpretation, at least until the late 1930s, held that the federal government could not spend money for purposes not authorized by the Constitution. The solution was obviously to have federal money put into state hands: Washington would pay the bills, the states would run the programs.

There were four reasons why federal money seemed, to state officials, so attractive. First, the money was there. During most of the nineteenth century and the early decades of the twentieth, the federal government was taking in more money than it was spending. The high-tariff policies of the Republicans produced a large budget surplus; in the 1880s Washington literally had more money than it knew what to do with. Some went to pay off a big part of the national debt, some was given to Civil War veterans as a pension, and some went to the states or was otherwise used for internal improvements.[25]

By the mid–twentieth century, when budget surpluses had pretty much become a thing of the past, a second reason for turning to Washington became evident: the federal income tax. Inaugurated in the 1920s, it proved to be a marvelously flexible tool of public finance, for it automatically brought in more money as economic activity (and thus personal income) grew.

Third, the federal government, unlike the states, managed the currency and thus could print more money whenever it needed it. (Technically it borrowed this money, and of course it paid interest on what it had borrowed, but it was under no obligation to pay it all back because, as a practical matter, it had borrowed from itself.) The size of the federal public debt stayed more or less constant, or even declined, in the second half of the nineteenth century. By the mid–twentieth century, for reasons to be explained in Chapter 16, people no longer worried about the national debt so much, or at least worried about it for reasons other than the fear of being in debt. Thus the federal government came to accept, as a matter of policy, the proposition that when it needed money, it would print it. States could not do this: if they borrowed (and many could not), they had to pay it all back, in full.

These three economic reasons for the attractiveness of federal grants were probably not as important as a fourth reason: politics. Federal money seemed to a state official to be "free" money. If Alabama could get Washington to put up the money for improving navigation on the Tombigbee River, the citizens of the entire nation, not just those of Alabama, would pay for it. Of course, if Alabama gets money for that purpose, every state will want it (and will get it). Even so, it was still an attractive political proposition: the governor of Alabama did not have to propose, collect, or take responsibility for federal taxes. Indeed the governor could denounce the federal government for being profligate in its use of the people's money. Meanwhile he or she would cut the ribbon opening the new dam on the Tombigbee.

That every state had an incentive to ask for federal money to pay for local programs meant, of course, that it would be very difficult for one state to get money for a given program without every state's getting it. The senator from Alabama who votes for the project to improve navigation on the Tombigbee will have to vote in favor of projects improving navigation on every other river in the country if the senator expects his or her Senate colleagues to support such a request. Federalism as practiced in the United States means that when Washington wants to send money to one state or congressional district, it must send money to many states and districts.

In 1966, for example, President Lyndon Johnson proposed a "Model Cities" plan under which federal funds would be spent on experimental programs in a small number of large cities that had especially acute problems. When the bill went to Congress, it quickly became clear that no such plan could be passed un-less the number of cities to benefit was increased. Senator Edmund Muskie of Maine, whose support was crucial, would not vote for a bill that did not make Augusta, Bangor, and Portland eligible for aid originally intended to help New York, Chicago, and Philadelphia.[26]

Meeting National Needs

Until the 1960s most federal grants-in-aid were conceived by or in cooperation with the states and were designed to serve essentially state purposes. Large blocs of voters and a variety of organized interests would press for grants to help farmers, build highways, or support vocational education. During the 1960s, however, an important change occurred: the federal government began devising grant programs based less on what states were demanding and more on what federal officials perceived to be important *national* needs (see Figure 3.2). Federal officials, not state and local ones, were the principal proponents of

FIGURE 3.2 The Changing Purposes of Federal Grants to State and Local Governments

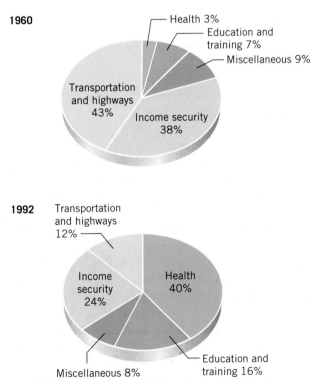

1960

Health 3%
Education and training 7%
Miscellaneous 9%
Transportation and highways 43%
Income security 38%

1992

Transportation and highways 12%
Income security 24%
Health 40%
Miscellaneous 8%
Education and training 16%

SOURCE: *Budget of the U.S. Government, Fiscal Year 1994,* 51–85

TABLE 3.1   Federal Aid to State and Local Governments, 1955–1995

| Year | Total Federal Aid (in billions)[a] | Federal Aid as a Percentage of | |
		Federal Outlays	State and Local Outlays
1955	$15.1	4.7%	10.1%
1960	29.1	7.6	14.7
1965	41.8	9.2	15.3
1970	73.6	12.3	19.2
1975	105.4	15.0	23.0
1980	127.6	15.5	26.3
1985	113.0	11.2	21.0
1990	119.7	10.8	20.0
1995	175.3 (est.)	15.3 (est.)	NA

[a] In constant 1987 dollars.

SOURCE: Total aid figures, percentages of federal outlays, and 1995 estimates from *Budget of the Government of the U.S. Government, Fiscal Year 1993*, Table 12.1, part 5, 164–165. Percentages of state and local outlays 1955–1985 from *Budget of the U.S. Government, Fiscal Year 1991*, Table 12.1, A-321. Percentage of state and local outlays in 1990 from *Budget of the U.S. Government, Fiscal Year 1994*, 79.

grant programs to aid the urban poor, combat crime, reduce pollution, and deal with drug abuse. Some of these programs even attempted to bypass the states, providing money directly to cities or even to local citizen groups. These were worrisome developments for governors who were accustomed to being the conduit for money on its way from Washington to local communities.

The rise in federal activism in setting goals and the efforts, on occasion, to bypass state officials occurred at a time when the total amount of federal aid to states and localities had become so vast that many jurisdictions were completely dependent on it for the support of vital services. Whereas federal aid amounted to less than 2 percent of state and local spending in 1927, by 1970 it amounted to 19 percent and by 1980 to 26 percent (see Table 3.1 and Figure 3.3). Some of the older, larger cities had become what one writer called "federal-aid junkies," so dependent were they on these grants. In 1978 in Detroit 77 percent of the revenue the city raised came from Washington.[27]

FIGURE 3.3   Federal Aid to State and Local Governments, 1980–1994

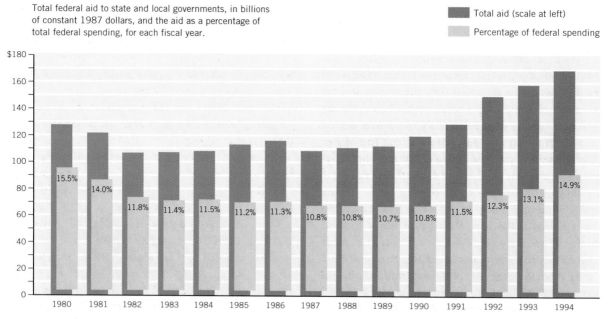

Total federal aid to state and local governments, in billions of constant 1987 dollars, and the aid as a percentage of total federal spending, for each fiscal year.

■ Total aid (scale at left)
■ Percentage of federal spending

NOTE: Data for 1992, 1993, and 1994 are estimated.

SOURCE: *Budget of the U.S. Government, Fiscal Year 1991 Supplement*, Table 12.1, 164–165.

TABLE 3.2 State and Local Governments Lobby in Washington

Organization	Number of Employees 1990	Approximate Budget 1990	Percentage of Budget from Federal Governments	
			1980	1990
National Governors' Association (55 state and territorial governors)	100	$10 million	42%	33%
National Conference of State Legislatures (50 state legislatures)	140	$10 million	36	15
National League of Cities (14,700 cities)	65	$8 million	43	2
U.S. Conference of Mayors (1,000 large cities)	50	$7 million	60	35
National Association of Counties (2,000 counties)	70	$10 million	30	9

SOURCES: Updated by Xandra Kayden from *National Journal* (August 1, 1981). Copyright © 1981 by National Journal, Inc. All rights reserved. Reprinted by permission.

The Intergovernmental Lobby

State and local officials, both elected and appointed, began to form an important new lobby—the "intergovernmental lobby," made up of mayors, governors, superintendents of schools, state directors of public health, county highway commissioners, local police chiefs, and others who had come to count on federal funds.[28] The five largest of these lobbies employed, in 1990, over four hundred people and spent about $45 million (see Table 3.2), nearly half of which came from the federal government. Even this has proved insufficient. After all, national organizations of governors or mayors can press for more federal money but not for increased funding for any particular state or city. Thus over thirty-one individual states, more than two dozen counties, and over one hundred cities have opened their own offices in Washington. Some are small, some share staff with other communities, but a few are quite large. Texas alone employs two dozen people in Washington to look after its interests.

The purpose of this intergovernmental lobby was the same as that of any private lobby—to obtain more federal money with fewer strings attached. For a while the cities and states did in fact get more money, but by 1980 federal grants had stopped growing.

Categorical Grants versus Revenue Sharing

The effort to loosen the strings took the form of shifting, as much as possible, the federal aid from **categorical grants** to **block grants** or to **revenue sharing.** A categorical grant is one for a specifc purpose defined by federal law: to build an airport or a college dormitory, for example, or to make welfare payments to low-income mothers. Such grants usually require that the state or locality put up money to "match" some part of the federal grant, though the amount of matching funds can be quite small. (In the federal highway program Washington pays about 90 percent of the construction costs and the states only about 10 percent.) Governors and mayors complained about these categorical grants because their purposes were often so narrow that it was impossible for a state to adapt federal grants to local needs. A mayor seeking federal money to build parks might have discovered that the city could get money only if it launched an urban renewal program that entailed bulldozing several blocks of housing or small businesses.

One response to this problem was to consolidate several categorical or project grant programs into a single block grant devoted to some general purpose and with fewer restrictions on its use. Block grants (sometimes called "special revenue sharing" or "broad-based aid") began in the mid-1960s, when such a grant was created in the health field. Though many block grants were proposed between 1966 and 1980, only five were enacted. Of the three largest, one consolidated various categorical grant programs aimed at cities (Community Development Block Grants); another created a program to aid local law enforcement (Law Enforcement Assistance Act); and a third authorized new kinds of locally managed programs for the unemployed (CETA, or the Comprehensive Employment and Training Act). In 1981 President Reagan persuaded Congress to raise the number of block grants to nine. In 1987 block grants accounted for about 12 percent of all federal aid programs.

Revenue sharing (sometimes called *general revenue sharing*, or GRS) was even more permissive. Adopted in 1972 with the passage of the State and Local Fiscal Assistance Act, GRS provided for the distribution of about $6 billion a year in federal funds to the states and localities, with no requirement as to matching funds and freedom to spend the money on almost any governmental purpose. Distribution of the money was determined by a statistical formula that took into account population, local tax effort, and the wealth of the state in a way intended to send more money to poorer, heavily taxed states and less to richer, lightly taxed ones. In 1986 the program was ended after having distributed about $85 billion over a fourteen-year period.

In theory block grants and revenue sharing were supposed to give the states and cities considerable freedom in deciding how to spend the money while helping to relieve their tax burdens. To some extent they did. However neither the goal of "no strings" nor the one of fiscal relief was really attained. First, the amount of money available from block grants and revenue sharing did not grow as fast as the states had hoped nor as quickly as did the money available through categorical grants. Second, the federal government steadily increased the number of strings attached to the spending of this supposedly "unrestricted" money.

The Slowdown in "Free" Money

Block grants grew more slowly than categorical grants because of the different kinds of political coalitions supporting each. Congress and the federal bureaucracy liked categorical grants for the same reason the states disliked them—the specificity of these programs enhanced federal control over how the money was to be used. Federal officials, joined by liberal interest groups and organized labor, tended to

Federal aid now supports almost every local government program, including school lunches.

distrust state governments. Whenever Congress wanted to address some national problem, its natural inclination was to create a categorical grant program so that it, and not the states, would decide how the money would be spent.

Moreover, even though governors and mayors like block grants and revenue sharing, these programs cover such a broad range of activities that no single interest group has a vital stake in pressing for their enlargement. Revenue sharing, for example, provided a little money to many city agencies but rarely provided all or even most of the money for any single agency. Thus no single agency acted as if the expansion of revenue sharing were a life-and-death matter. Categorical grants, on the other hand, are often a matter of life and death for many agencies—state departments of welfare, of highways, and of health, for example, are utterly dependent on federal aid. Accordingly the administrators in charge of these programs will press strenuously for their expansion. Moreover categorical programs are supervised by special committees of Congress, and as we shall see in Chapter 11, many of these committees have an interest in seeing their programs grow.

As a result of the political differences between categorical grants and block grants or revenue sharing, the amount spent on the former tends to increase faster than the amount spent on the latter. Between 1975 and 1978 the amount spent on revenue sharing increased by 11 percent, but that spent on categorical grants increased by 56 percent.[29] One observer explained: "You dilute the constituency when you make aid more general. Say you had a program to control a disease. You'd get everyone in the country interested in that disease to focus on that one subject, and a congressman to become the champion of it. . . . There just is not that much sympathy to increase revenue sharing."[30] So little support did general revenue sharing have that, in their debate over the 1986 budget, almost the only thing Democrats and Republicans could agree on was abolishing revenue sharing, which they did.

Not only did general revenue sharing lack a constituency, but it was a wasteful way of trying to help poor communities. The waste resulted from the fact that *every* community—some thirty-nine thousand in all—got revenue-sharing money whether it was rich or poor. Paw Paw, West Virginia, a town devastated by a loss of jobs, received only $11,874 from revenue sharing, but that amounted to more than one-third of all the tax money it collected, and was enough to pay the salary of its lone police officer. Beverly Hills, California, a city so affluent and exclusive that, as the joke goes, the police department has an unlisted phone number, also got revenue-sharing money.

Rivalry Among the States

The more important that federal money becomes to the states, the more likely they are to compete among themselves for the largest share of it. For a century or better, the growth of the United States—in population, business, and income—was concentrated in the industrial Northeast. In recent decades, however, that growth—at least in population and employment, if not in income—has shifted to the South, Southwest, and Far West. This change has precipitated an intense debate over whether the federal government, by the way it distributes its funds and awards its contracts, is unfairly helping some regions and states at the expense of others. Journalists and politicians have dubbed the struggle as one between "Snowbelt" (or "Frostbelt") and "Sunbelt" states.

Whether in fact there is anything worth arguing about is far from clear: the federal government has had great difficulty in figuring out where it ultimately spends what funds for what purposes. For example, a $1 billion defense contract may go to a company with headquarters in California, but much of the money may actually be spent in Connecticut or New York, as the prime contractor in California buys from subcontractors in the other states. It is even less clear whether federal funds actually affect the growth rate of the regions. The uncertainty about the facts has not prevented a debate about the issue, however. That debate focuses on the formulas written into federal laws by which block grants are allocated. These formulas take into account such factors as a county's or city's population, personal income in the area, and housing quality. A slight change in a formula can shift millions of dollars in grants in ways that favor either the older, declining cities of the Northeast or the newer, still-growing cities of the Southwest.

With the advent of grants based on distributional formulas (as opposed to grants for a particular project), the results of the census, taken every ten years, assume monumental importance. A city or state shown to be losing population may, as a result, forfeit millions of dollars in federal aid. There are over one hundred programs (out of some five hundred federal grant programs in all) that distribute money on the basis of population. When the director of the census in 1960 announced figures showing that many big cities had lost population, he was generally ignored. When he made the same announcement in 1980, after the explosion in federal grants, he was roundly denounced by the mayors of those cities.

Senators and representatives now have access to computers that can tell them instantly the effect on their states and districts of even minor changes in a formula by which federal aid is distributed. These formulas rely on objective measures, but the exact measure is selected with an eye to its political consequences. There is nothing wrong with this in principle, since any political system must provide some benefits for everybody if it is to stay together. Given the competition among states in a federal system, however, the struggle over allocation formulas becomes especially acute. The results are sometimes plausible, as when Congress decides to distribute money intended to help disadvantaged local school systems in large part on the basis of the proportion of poor children in each school district. But sometimes the results are a bit strange, as when the formula by which federal aid for mass transit is determined gives New York, a city utterly dependent on mass transit, a federal subsidy of two cents per transit passenger but gives Grand Rapids, a city that relies chiefly on the automobile, a subsidy of forty-five cents per passenger.[31]

Federal Aid and Federal Control

So important has federal aid become for state and local governments that mayors and governors, along with others, began to fear that Washington was well on its way to controlling other levels of government. "He who pays the piper calls the tune," they muttered. In this view the constitutional protection of state government to be found in the Tenth Amendment was in jeopardy as a result of the strings being attached to the grants-in-aid on which the states were increasingly dependent.

Block grants and revenue sharing were efforts to reverse this trend by allowing the states and localities

freedom (considerable in the case of block grants; almost unlimited in the case of revenue sharing) to spend money as they wished. But as we have seen, these new devices did not in fact reverse the trend. Until 1978 block grants and revenue sharing increased until they amounted to 27 percent of all federal grants to states and localities but then began to decline, so that by 1986 they accounted for only 18 percent of such aid. Categorical grants—those with strings attached—continued to grow even faster.

There are two kinds of federal controls on state governmental activities. The traditional control tells the state government what it must do if it wants to get some grant money. These strings are often called **conditions of aid**. The newer form of control tells the state government what it must do, period. These rules are called **mandates.** Sometimes the mandates must be observed only if the state takes any federal grants, but sometimes the mandates have nothing to do with federal aid—they apply to all state governments whether or not they accept grants.

Mandates

Most mandates concern civil rights and environmental protection. States may not discriminate in the operation of their programs, no matter who pays for them. Initially the antidiscrimination rules applied chiefly to distinctions based on race, sex, age, and ethnicity, but of late they have been broadened to include physical and mental disabilities as well. Various pollution-control laws require the states to comply with federal standards regarding clean air, pure drinking water, and sewage treatment.[32]

Stated in general terms, these mandates seem reasonable enough. It is hard to imagine anyone arguing that state governments should be free to discriminate against people because of their race or national origin. In practice, however, some mandates create administrative and financial problems, especially when the mandates are written in vague language, thereby giving federal administrative agencies the power to decide for themselves what state and local governments are supposed to do.

In 1980 there were thirty-six mandates affecting state and local governments, twenty-two of them enacted in the 1970s. Both the Reagan administration and the Bush administration opposed the growth of mandates. Nevertheless, between 1982 and 1991 Congress passed twenty-seven additional mandates (see Table 3.3).

All mandates are not created equal. Some mandates take the form of regulatory statutes and amendments that expand on previous legislation; the 1982 Voting Rights Act Amendment was based on federal civil rights laws dating back to the 1960s. Other mandates represent new areas of federal involvement. For example, the 1986 Handicapped Children's Protection Act introduced federal regulations intended to improve the life prospects of disabled youngsters. Some mandates are easy to understand, simple to administer, and relatively inexpensive; for example, the 1988 Ocean Dumping Ban Act, which prohibits any additional dumping of municipal sewage sludge in ocean waters. However many mandates are hard to interpret, difficult to administer, and have high or uncertain costs. The 1990 Americans with Disabilities Act (ADA), which required businesses and state and local governments to provide the disabled with equal access to services, employment, buildings, and transportation systems, was one of twenty mandates signed into law by President Bush in 1990. Unfortunately the ADA was enacted with no clear-cut definition of "equal access," no unambiguous blueprint of how it was to be administered, and no reliable estimates of how much it would cost to implement.

The Clinton administration has expressed sympathy for the complaints that state and local officials have made about the administrative and fiscal burdens of mandates. President Clinton, who served as governor of Arkansas, was a leader of the National Governors' Association, which has taken a strong position against the unfettered growth of mandates. When the Republicans took control of Congress in 1995, they immediately set to work drafting a bill that would reduce "unfunded mandates." But doing that is not easy. For example, what are "mandates?" The minimum wage law? The clean air act? The endangered species act? Another question: what do they really cost? No one can say for certain. Now some states are taking matters into their own hands. Governor Pete Wilson of California refused to comply with the "motor voter" law (see page 132) because Washington would not pay what it would cost the state to implement it. Other governors have followed suit. Congress struggled to find a solution.

TABLE 3.3 Major Mandate Enactments Regulating State and Local Governments, 1982–1991

1982	Surface Transportation Assistance Act
	Voting Rights Act Amendments
1983	Social Security Amendments
1984	Child Abuse Amendments
	Hazardous and Solid Waste Amendments
	Highway Safety Amendments
	Voting Accessibility for the Elderly and Handicapped Act
1985	Consolidated Omnibus Budget Reconciliation Act
1986	Age Discrimination in Employment Act Amendments
	Asbestos Hazard Emergency Response Act
	Commercial Motor Vehicle Safety Act
	Education of the Handicapped Act Amendments
	Emergency Planning and Community Right-to-Know Act
	Handicapped Children's Protection Act
	Safe Drinking Water Act Amendments
1987	Civil Rights Restoration Act
	Water Quality Act
1988	Drug-Free Workplace Act
	Fair Housing Act Amendments
	Lead Contamination Control Act
	Ocean Dumping Ban Act
1990	Americans with Disabilities Act
	Cash Management Improvement Act
	Clean Air Act Amendments
	Education of the Handicapped Act Amendments
	Older Workers Benefit Protection Act
1991	Social Security Fiscal Budget Reconciliation Act

SOURCE: Adapted from Timothy J. Conlan and David R. Beam, "Federal Mandates: The Record of Reform and Future Prospects," *Intergovernmental Perspective* (Fall 1992): 8.

The courts have helped fuel the growth of mandates. As interpreted in this century by the United States Supreme Court, the Tenth Amendment provides state and local officials no protection against the march of mandates. Indeed, many of the more controversial mandates result not from congressional action but from court decisions. For example, many state prison systems have been, at one time or another, under the control of federal judges who required major changes in prison construction and management in order to meet standards the judges derived from their reading of the Constitution. School-desegregation plans are of course the best-known example of federal mandates. Those involving busing—an unpopular policy—have typi-

Federal Golfing Mandates

During the debate on the Americans with Disabilities Act (ADA), no one mentioned golf courses. Nevertheless, the ADA has changed the way that public golf courses are administered. There is an Association of Disabled American Golfers and a National Blind Golfers Association. The March 1993 issue of *Golf Course News* offered the following guidelines to public golf course operators, who must comply with the ADA:

- Reserve one or two handicapped parking spaces near the bag drop rather than next to the clubhouse.

- Cut out spots on raised curbs so carts can pass through.

- Build ramps to tees where possible.

- Provide a spot for disabled golfers to get in and out of the bunker.

- Keep bunker grades no more than one foot of elevation for every five feet of length.

- Install a Telecommunication Device for the Deaf (TDD) in the reservation office so the hearing impaired can make tee-time reservations by phone.

SOURCE: Joanne Desky, "Park Facilities Meet ADA Challenges: Even Public Golf Course Managers Must Comply," *PA Times*, 16, no. 5 (May 1, 1993): 1, 16.

cally been the result of court orders rather than of federal law or regulation (see Chapter 19).

Judges—usually, but not always, in federal courts—have ordered Massachusetts to change the way it hires fire fighters, required Philadelphia to institute new procedures to handle complaints of police brutality, and altered the location in which Chicago was planning to build housing projects. Note that in most of these cases nobody in Washington was placing a mandate on a local government; rather a local citizen was using the federal courts to change a local practice.

The Supreme Court has made it much easier of late for citizens to control the behavior of local officials. A federal law, passed in the 1870s to protect newly freed slaves, makes it possible for a citizen to sue any state or local official who deprives that citizen of any "rights, privileges, or immunities secured by the Constitution and laws" of the United States.[33] In 1980 the Court decided that this law permitted a cit-

izen to sue a local official if the official deprived the citizen of *anything* to which the citizen was entitled under federal law (and not just those federal laws protecting civil rights).[34] For example, a citizen can now use the federal courts to obtain from a state welfare office a payment to which he or she may be entitled under federal law. No one yet knows how this development will affect the way local government operates.

Conditions of Aid

By far the most important federal restrictions on state action are the conditions attached to the grants the states receive. In theory accepting these conditions is voluntary—if you don't want the strings, don't take the money. But when the typical state depends for a quarter or more of its budget on federal grants, many of which it has received for years and on which many of its citizens depend for their livelihoods, it is not clear exactly how "voluntary" such acceptance is. During the 1960s some strings were added, the most important of which had to do with civil rights. But beginning in the 1970s the number of conditions proliferated. One study of federal grant programs in five large states found that between 1951 and 1978 over a thousand conditions had been added to these programs; nearly 90 percent had been added after 1971.[35]

Some conditions are specific to particular programs. For example, if a state does not establish a highway-beautification program, it will lose 10 percent of its federal highway aid money.[36] Others are general, covering most or all grants. For instance, if a state builds something with federal money, it must first conduct an environmental-impact study, it must pay construction workers the "prevailing wage" in the area, it often must provide an opportunity for citizen participation in some aspects of the design or location of the project, and it must ensure that the contractors who build the project have nondiscriminatory hiring policies.

The states and the federal government, not surprisingly, disagree about the costs and benefits of such rules. Members of Congress and federal officials feel they have an obligation to develop uniform national policies with respect to important matters and to prevent states and cities from misspending federal tax dollars. State officials, on the other hand, feel these national rules fail to take into account diverse local conditions, require the states to do things that the states must then pay for, and create serious inefficiencies.

The dispute over the best way to make city transit facilities accessible to disabled persons illustrates the difficulty of reconciling national objectives and a decentralized system of government. In 1973 Congress passed the Rehabilitation Act, which forbids discrimination against disabled people in any program receiving federal aid. Since there was virtually no discussion of this provision as the bill moved through Congress, no one was quite certain what it would mean when applied to a city transit system receiving federal money. Narrowly read, the law might mean only that the city could not refuse to hire an otherwise qualified disabled person to work in the transit system. Broadly read, it might mean that the buses and subway cars in the city had to be made physically accessible to disabled persons.

Under pressure from organizations representing the disabled, various federal agencies decided that the law should be given the broader interpretation. Accordingly they issued regulations requiring that city transit systems receiving federal aid equip their buses and subway cars with devices to lift wheelchairs on board.

Disabled people were pleased with these rules, believing that the benefits to them were well worth the cost. State and local officials took a different view. The then mayor of New York City, Edward Koch, argued that rebuilding existing buses and subways and buying new ones would make each trip by a wheelchair user cost thirty-eight dollars. It would be cheaper, he said, for the city to give free taxicab rides to every disabled person, but the federal regulations would not permit that. Billions would be spent by cities for a program to benefit 2 percent of the transit users, deserving though they may be.[37] (In 1981 the Reagan administration relaxed the requirement that buses be able to lift wheelchairs aboard.)

What local officials discovered, in short, was that "free" federal money was not quite free after all. In the 1960s federal aid seemed to be entirely beneficial; what mayor or governor would not want such money? But just as local officials found it attractive to do things that another level of government then paid

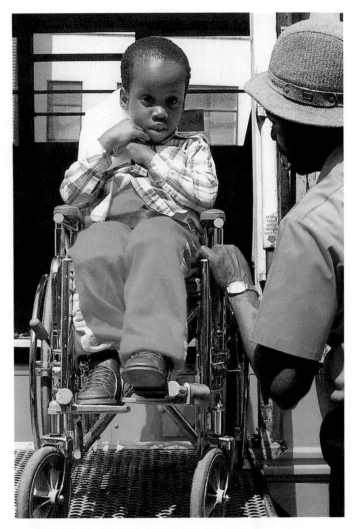

With more federal aid has come more federal control. City transportation systems getting federal money must be accessible to disabled persons.

for, in time federal officials learned the same thing. Passing laws to meet the concerns of national constituencies—leaving the cities and states to pay the bills and manage the problems—began to seem attractive to Congress.

One's perspective depends on what office one holds, as is revealed by this statement of Mayor Koch, who once had been a congressman from New York:

As a member of Congress I voted for many of the laws imposing grant conditions, and did so with every confidence that we were enacting sensible

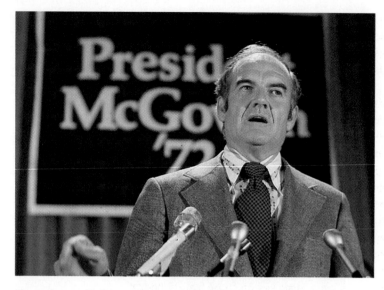

When George McGovern was a senator (left), he voted for many federal regulations that he later found burdensome when he became an innkeeper in Connecticut (right).

permanent solutions to critical problems. It took a plunge into the mayor's job to drive home how misguided my congressional outlook had been. The bills I voted for came to the floor in a form that compelled approval. After all, who can vote against clean air and water or better access and education for the handicapped? But as I look back it is hard to believe I could have been taken in by the simplicity of what the Congress was doing and by the flimsy empirical support . . . offered to persuade the members that the proposed solution would work throughout the country.[38]

As is evident from the mayor's remarks, the tensions in the federal system do not arise from one level of government or another being callous or incompetent, but from the kinds of political demands with which each must cope. Because of these competing demands, federal and local officials find themselves in a bargaining situation in which each side is trying to get some benefit (solving a problem, satisfying a pressure group) while passing on to the other side most of the costs (taxes, administrative problems).

The bargains struck in this process used to favor the local officials because members of Congress were essentially servants of local interests: they were elected by local political parties, they were part of local political organizations, and they supported local autonomy. Beginning in the 1960s, however, changes in American politics that will be described in later chapters—especially the weakening of political parties, the growth of public-interest lobbies in Washington, and the increased activism of the courts—shifted the orientation of many in Congress toward favoring Washington's needs over local needs.

Various presidents have tried to reverse this trend, but with little success. President Nixon proclaimed the "new federalism" and helped create revenue sharing and block grants, but as we have seen, federal mandates and conditions of aid *grew* rather than declined during his administration.

In 1981 President Reagan asked Congress to consolidate eighty-three categorical grants into six large block grants, none of which would seriously restrict how the states could spend the money. Congress went along in name only—it consolidated fifty-seven programs into nine small block grants, each of which had many restrictions attached. The debate over this plan showed that what is at stake is not simply differing views on how best to "streamline" or make "more efficient" the way in which federal money supports local programs, but rather competing philosophies of governance.

The Reagan administration believed that giving money without strings to the states was good because state governments are generally more conservative than the federal government. The reasons are that state governments must have balanced budgets (and thus cannot spend on social programs by running up deficits) and that liberal interest groups are less influential at the state level than at the national level. The critics of the Reagan view distrusted state governments for the very reason he admired them—they are less responsive to liberal causes. And members of Congress, whether they are liberal or conservative, are exposed to the demands of state officials who wish to have particular federal programs that benefit them protected by "categorization."

The States Respond

No state likes losing federal money, and most continue to ask for more. At the same time, however, the cutback in the amount of such aid, coupled with changes in state government, as described in Chapter 25, has led many states to experiment with new ways of delivering services. They have once again become "laboratories," trying out new ideas.

Some of this has been encouraged by federal laws, such as the Family Support Act of 1988, which allows states to test new ways of paying welfare benefits. However, some has occurred despite burdensome federal rules designed to standardize service delivery. Here are some examples:

Child Care   Some states subsidize day care for the children of working parents, by giving tax deductions either to the parents who pay for this care or to the employers who supply it. Over half the states pay for preschool education.

Welfare   Many states are trying to find ways to get people off welfare and into jobs. In Wisconsin a family with teenage children loses part of its welfare check if the child drops out of school before finishing. In New York and elsewhere state governments are trying to get absent parents—usually, the fa-

ther—to pay more in child support. Ohio offers a bonus to young welfare mothers if they stay in school (or, if they have dropped out, to go back to school).

Education   Many state governors have aggressively sought new ways of organizing the schools. In 1989 the governors held an "educational summit meeting" with President Bush to discuss these plans. Among the ideas that are being tried: a Minnesota plan that allows parents to send their children to any public school in the state, not just to the one in the neighborhood; a Rhode Island plan to pay part of the college tuition of high school students who promise to stay in school, to obey the law, to keep off drugs, and to avoid becoming teenage parents; a Maryland plan to give bonuses to schools that do a good job and to impose penalties on those that do poorly

No one is sure which of these ideas, or others like them, will work out and which will be failures. Moreover, people who don't like a state experiment will often try to get the federal government to withdraw its support or to adopt rules ending the project. The politics of federalism is a pendulum that over the last half century has swung between giving the states a lot of leeway and giving them very little.

Sorting Things Out

Some observers think that our federal system would work better if the endless conflict between Washington and the states over the hundreds of programs for which they are jointly responsible were reduced by sorting out in a more rational manner the functions performed by national and state governments. In this view the federal government should pay all the cost of those programs that are truly national in scope, such as environmental protection and welfare and medical programs for the disadvantaged, while the states should pay the full cost of programs that are primarily local in nature, such as education and community development.

Every so often, a president tries to accomplish this sorting out. None has succeeded. In 1957 President Eisenhower formed a committee to decide which federal programs should be returned to full state control. After two years of deliberation, it found just two such programs (vocational education and

What Should the Federal Government Do?

Interstate Issues Problems cannot be solved without federal action, because state and local governments lack leverage, incentives, etc.

Uniform Standards Solutions require uniform national standards (e.g., social security, environmental regulation, civil rights).

Destructive Competition Policies are so sensitive to competition between states or localities that such competition creates negative consequences that outweigh the benefits of decentralization.

Fiscal Redistribution Solutions require redistribution of national resources, because poor regions cannot generate the necessary resources.

The Clinton Administration's Blueprint

Program Types	Reason
Federal action is strongly justified	
Housing	Fiscal redistribution
Food and Nutrition	Fiscal redistribution
Employment and Training	Uniform standards, fiscal redistribution
Community Development	Fiscal redistribution
Public Assistance	Uniform standards, fiscal redistribution
Environmental, Water Pollution Control	Interstate issues, destructive competition
Medical Assistance	Destructive competition, fiscal redistribution
Economic Opportunity	Fiscal redistribution
Education (higher)	Interstate issues
Occupational Safety and Health	Uniform standards, destructive competition
Medical Research	Interstate issues
Vocational Rehabilitation	Uniform standards
Some federal role is justified, but most responsibility should be state/local	
Airports	Uniform standards (safety regulation only)
Highways	Interstate issues (interstate highways)
Public Transit	Fiscal redistribution
Education (K-12)	Fiscal redistribution
Resource Conservation, Development	Interstate issues, destructive competition
Civil Preparedness (disaster relief only)	Uniform standards, fiscal redistribution
Energy	Interstate issues
No federal role is justified	
Highway (non-interstate)	
Criminal Justice (state and local)	
Volunteer Services	
Libraries	
Economic Development (state and local)	
Other Transportation (state and local)	
Arts and Humanities	
Rural Development	
Fire Protection	

SOURCE: David Osborne, "A New Federal Compact: Sorting Out Washington's Proper Role." In *Mandate for Change,* edited by Will Marshall and Martin Schram (New York: Berkeley Books, 1993), 250–251.

When President Clinton met with Los Angeles County supervisor Gloria Molina and Catholic archbishop Roger Mahoney, he was acknowledging the federal government's need to respond to local demands.

sewage-treatment plants), and even these recommendations were defeated in Congress. In 1981 President Reagan proposed a new sorting out involving a swap—the states would take over certain federal programs, and Washington would take over some state programs. This, too, failed.

The reason is the Constitution. The Founders did not produce a document that drew clear lines between national and state responsibilities. They left them vague, subject to political determination. Two hundred years of political history have not clarified them very much or made it possible to devise some "rational" scheme for deciding which government will do what. The Clinton administration's blueprint for sorting out federal and state responsibilities (see box on page 72) is unlikely to change the complicated character of American federalism any more than did the efforts of the Eisenhower administration in the late 1950s or the Reagan administration in the early 1980s. In the words of one student of the subject, American federalism will continue to look more like a marble cake than a layer cake.

Changes have occurred, but not as a result of any master plan. When federal aid to the states began de-clining in the late 1970s and early 1980s, state governments had to face up to a loss of "free" money. Many of them did so by creating innovative new ways of running existing programs (such as welfare) or by increasing state influence over programs once run by counties and cities. One unanticipated result of the slowdown in federal grants to the states was an increase in the power and imagination of state governments.

Federalism and Public Policy

The growing importance of federal laws, regulations, and court orders in shaping the conduct of state and local affairs does not mean that we have become a wholly centralized nation. Far from it. There remains more political and policy diversity in the United States than one is likely to find in any other large industrialized nation.

The reason is not only that state and local governments have retained certain constitutional protections but that the members of Congress continue to think of themselves chiefly as the representatives of

The Complex Web of Federal, State, and Local Agencies

The Case of Oakland, California   To get an aircraft hangar and a ship terminal built in a way that would help reduce minority unemployment in Oakland, California, the following groups and agencies had to cooperate.

Federal

- Economic Development Administration (EDA), U.S. Department of Commerce
- Seattle Regional Office of the EDA
- Oakland Office of the EDA
- U.S. General Accounting Office
- U.S. Department of Health, Education and Welfare
- U.S. Department of Labor
- U.S. Navy

Local

- Mayor of Oakland
- Oakland City Council
- Port of Oakland

Private

- World Airways Company
- Oakland business leaders
- Oakland black leaders
- Conservation and environmental groups in Oakland

There were at least seventy important decisions to which some or all of these groups had to agree.

SOURCE: Jeffrey L. Pressman and Aaron B. Wildavsky, *Implementation* (Berkeley, University of California Press, 1973), 95–96, 102–107.

localities *to* Washington and not as the representatives *of* Washington to the localities. As we shall see in Chapter 11, American politics, even at the national level, remains local in orientation.

But if this is true, why do these same members of Congress pass laws that create so many problems for, and stimulate so many complaints from, mayors and governors? One reason is that members of Congress represent different constituencies from the same localities. Two members of Congress from Los Angeles may feel that they are in Washington to look out for Los Angeles, but one may think of Los Angeles as a collection of businesspeople, homeowners, and taxpayers while the other may think of Los Angeles as a group of blacks, Hispanics, and nature lovers. When Washington simply sent money to Los Angeles, these two representatives usually voted together. When Washington began sending mandates and restrictions to Los Angeles, these two would often vote on opposite sides, but each voted as his or her Los Angeles constituents probably preferred.

Another reason is that the organizational forms that once linked members of Congress to local political groups have eroded. As we shall see in Chapter 7, the political parties that once allowed many localities to speak with a single voice in Washington have decayed to the point where most members of Congress now operate as individuals, free to judge local needs and national moods as they see fit. In the 1960s these needs and moods seemed to require creating new grant programs; in the 1970s they seemed to require voting for new mandates; in the 1980s they seemed to require letting the cities and states alone to experiment with new ways of meeting their needs.

There are exceptions. In some states parties continue to be strong, to dominate decision making in the state legislatures, and to significantly affect the way in which a state's congressional delegation will behave. Democratic members of Congress from Cook County (Chicago), Illinois, typically have a common background in party politics and share at least some allegiance to important party leaders.

But these exceptions are becoming fewer and fewer. As a result, when somebody tries to speak "for" a city or state in Washington, that person has little claim to any real authority. The mayor of Philadelphia may favor one program, the governor of

Pennsylvania may favor another, and individual local and state officials in that state—school superintendents, the insurance commissioner, public-health administrators—may favor still others. In bidding for federal aid, those parts of the state or city that are best organized often do the best; but increasingly the best-organized groups are not the political parties but rather the specialized occupational groups, such as doctors or schoolteachers. If one is to ask, therefore, why a member of Congress does not listen to his or her state anymore, the answer is, "What do you mean by 'the state'?" Which official, which occupational group, which party leader, speaks "for" the state?

Given the great complexity and individualism of American federal politics, the national government has not been able to achieve anything like a single national policy in most policy areas, even when Washington is paying most of the bills. For example, the federal government puts up most of the money for what is commonly called "welfare" (more precisely, aid to families with dependent children, or AFDC). Washington sets a lot of conditions, but it lets the states decide how much money each family gets. As a result there is a wide variation in cash payments. In 1990, the average monthly payment nationally was $169 but in California it was $640.[39] This difference may strike you as unjustifiable, but remember two things—it costs less to live in, say, Louisiana than in California and in both states AFDC families get a package of other benefits as well, such as Medicaid and food stamps. One government study found that, after adding up all the benefits, an AFDC family in San Francisco received about 66 percent of the median household income in that city, while an AFDC family in New Orleans received about 65 percent of the local income.[40] Federalism produces differences in policies, but some of the variation may reflect real differences in local conditions.

This variation seems to be characteristic of all federal systems. The United States, like Canada, Switzerland, and Germany, allows the amount of money spent on education to vary much more among regions than do such unitary political systems as England and Sweden.[41]

Not only does federalism lead to variation in public policy, but it also increases the difficulty of managing complex programs. It is never easy to build

an airport or a ship terminal, but when one wants to build these within a federal system, it becomes even harder. One has to obtain the participation of many more groups, public and private. For example, the Economic Development Administration, a part of the U.S. Department of Commerce, sought to reduce unemployment and ease racial tensions in Oakland, California, by giving agencies in that city over $2 million to build an aircraft maintenance hangar and a ship terminal. Many jobs on these projects were earmarked for the unemployed, especially blacks and other minorities. Four years later, the terminal was only partially built, the plans for the hangar were not yet complete, and only a small number of jobs for minorities had been created. The poor showing was not the result of incompetence or indifference but rather of complexity. Several different goals had to be achieved by many different agencies at every level of government, as well as by private groups. Some groups emphasized employing minorities, others wanted speedy construction whether or not minorities were employed, and still others worried that any construction would harm the environment. It is rarely possible to get independent organizations to agree by "issuing orders"; it is never possible to do so when they belong to legally distinct levels of government.[42]

Any judgment about the worth of a federal system is fundamentally a judgment about important competing values. And very few of us have a consistent set of values. To the extent that we favor equal treatment of individuals by government, we will prefer uniform national policies instead of diverse state policies. But since we also favor personal liberty and the opportunity for local diversity, we also will support decentralization and be suspicious of Washington.

And we differ in the extent to which we like federal as opposed to local decisions. As Figure 3.4 shows, when people are asked which level of government gives them the most for their money, relatively poor people are likely to mention the federal government first, whereas relatively well-to-do people are more likely to mention local government.

If we added to income other measures of our social diversity—race, religion, and region—we would probably see even sharper differences of opinion

FIGURE 3.4   From Which Level of Government Do You Feel You Get the Most for Your Money?

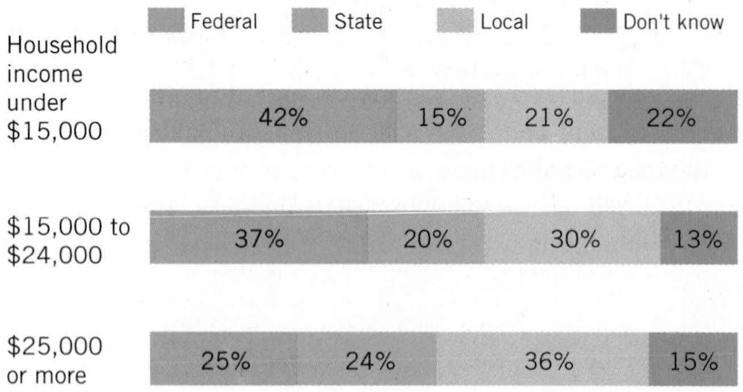

Legend: Federal | State | Local | Don't know

Household income	Federal	State	Local	Don't know
under $15,000	42%	15%	21%	22%
$15,000 to $24,000	37%	20%	30%	13%
$25,000 or more	25%	24%	36%	15%

SOURCE: Advisory Commission on Intergovernmental Relations (1982): *Changing Public Attitudes on Governments and Taxes,* as cited in David C. Nice, *Federalism: The Politics of Intergovernmental Relations* (New York: St. Martin's Press, 1987), 210.

about which level of government works best. It is this social diversity that helps explain why federalism is so important. We simply do not agree on enough things, or even on which level of government ought to decide on those things, to make possible a unitary system.

SUMMARY

States participate actively both in determining national policy and in administering national programs. Moreover they reserve to themselves or the localities within them important powers over public services, such as schooling and law enforcement, and important public decisions, such as land-use control, that in unitary systems are dominated by the national government.

How one evaluates federalism depends in large part on the value one attaches to the competing criteria of equality and participation. Federalism means that citizens living in different parts of the country will be treated differently, not only in spending programs, such as welfare, but in legal systems that assign in different places different penalties to similar offenses or that differentially enforce civil rights laws. But federalism also means that there are more oppor-

tunities for participation in making decisions: in influencing what is taught in the schools and in deciding where highways and government projects are to be built. Indeed differences in public policy—that is, unequal treatment—are in large part the result of participation in decision making. It is difficult, perhaps impossible, to have more of one of these values without having less of the other.

Politics and public policy have become decidedly more nationalized of late, with the federal government, and especially the federal courts, imposing increasingly uniform standards on the states in the form of both mandates and conditions of aid. Efforts to reverse this trend by shifting to revenue sharing and block grants have been only partially successful.

KEY TERMS

federalism   *p. 49*

sovereignty   *p. 50*

confederation *or* confederal system   *p. 50*

federal system   *p. 50*

unitary systems   *p. 50*

"necessary-and-proper" clause   *p. 57*

nullification   *p. 58*

dual federalism   *p. 59*

grants-in-aid   *p. 60*

categorical grants   *p. 63*

block grants   *p. 63*

revenue sharing   *p. 63*

conditions of aid   *p. 66*

mandates   *p. 66*

SUGGESTED READINGS

Beer, Samuel H. *To Make a Nation: The Rediscovery of American Federalism.* Cambridge, Mass.: Harvard University Press, 1993. The definitive study of the philosophical bases of American federalism.

Derthick, Martha. *The Influence of Federal Grants.* Cambridge, Mass.: Harvard University Press, 1970. Considers the extent to which federal aid leads to federal control in the area of welfare.

Diamond, Martin. "The Federalist's View of Federalism." In *Essays in Federalism,* edited by George C. S. Benson. Claremont, Calif.: Institute for Studies in Federalism of Claremont Men's College, 1961, 21–64. A profound analysis of what the Founders meant by federalism.

Elazar, Daniel J. *American Federalism: A View from the States.* 2d ed. New York: Crowell, 1972. A sympathetic analysis of historical development and present nature of American federalism.

Grodzins, Morton. *The American System.* Chicago: Rand McNally, 1966. Argues that American federalism has always involved extensive sharing of functions between national and state governments.

Peterson, Paul E., Barry G. Rabe, and Kenneth K. Wong. *When Federalism Works.* Washington, D.C.: Brookings Institution, 1986. A careful analysis of how various federal grant-in-aid programs actually work.

Pressman, Jeffrey L., and Aaron B. Wildavsky. *Implementation.* Berkeley: University of California Press, 1973. An excellent case study of how federalism affected the implementation of a single economic development project in Oakland, California.

Riker, William H. *Federalism: Origin, Operation, Significance.* Boston: Little, Brown, 1964. An explanation and critical analysis of federalism here and abroad.

Wright, Deil S. *Understanding Intergovernmental Relations.* 2d ed. Monterey, Calif.: Brooks/Cole, 1982. Useful survey of how state and local officials try to influence federal policies.

4

American Political Culture

If the Republic, created in 1787, had depended for its survival entirely on the constitutional machinery designed by the Founders, it probably would not have endured. That machinery was copied by many other nations, notably those of Latin America, but in virtually no other country did such devices as federalism, the elected president, the bicameral legislature, and the separation of powers produce a political system capable of both effective government and the protection of liberty. In many nations (such as Argentina, Brazil, and the Philippines) that adopted the American model, there have been, at best, brief periods of democratic rule interrupted by military takeovers, the rise to power of demagogues, or the spread of wholesale corruption. The Constitution of the United States, like an old wine, has rarely survived an ocean crossing.

Alexis de Tocqueville, the perceptive French observer of American politics, noticed this as early as the 1830s. One reason a democratic republic took root in the United States but not in other countries that had copied its constitution was that this country offered more abundant and fertile soil in which the roots could grow.[1] The vast territory of the United States created innumerable opportunities for people to acquire land and make a living. No feudal aristocracy monopolized the land, the government imposed only minimal taxes, few legal restraints existed. As one place after another filled up, people kept pushing west to find new opportunities. A nation of small, independent farmers, unlike the traditional European one of landless peasants or indentured servants, could make democracy work.

But other nations that were similarly favored did not achieve the same result. As Tocqueville noted, much of South America contains fertile lands and rich resources, but democracy has not flourished there.[2] Had he returned to the United States fifty years later, when the frontier was no longer expanding and Americans were crowding into big cities, he would have found that democratic government was still more or less intact.

Alexis de Tocqueville (1805–1859) was a young French aristocrat who came to the United States to study the American prison system. He wrote the brilliant *Democracy in America* (2 vols., 1835–1840), a profound analysis of our political culture.

Neither the Constitution nor the physical advantages of the country can alone explain the persistence of democratic institutions. In addition we must consider the customs of the people—what Tocqueville called their "moral and intellectual characteristics,"[3] and what modern social scientists call their political culture.

Political Culture

If you travel abroad, you will quickly become aware that other people often behave differently from Americans. Spaniards may eat dinner at 10:00 P.M., whereas Americans eat at 6:00 or 7:00 P.M. Italians may close their shops for three hours in the middle of the day, while American shops are open continuously from 9:00 to 5:00. The Germans address people more formally than Americans, using last names when we would use first names. Japanese business executives attach a lot of importance to working together as a group, while their American counterparts often are more individualistic. In these and countless other ways, we observe cultural differences among people.

Such differences are not limited to eating, shop-keeping, or manners. They include differences in political culture as well. A **political culture** is a distinctive and patterned way of thinking about how political and economic life ought to be carried out (see the accompanying box). Beliefs about economic life are part of the political culture because politics affects economics.

Americans do not judge their political and economic systems in the same way. As we shall see, this difference makes them somewhat unique, for in many other nations people apply the same standards to both systems. For example, Americans think it very important that everybody should be equal politically, but they do not think it important that everybody should be equal economically. By contrast people in some other nations believe that the principle of equality should be applied to both economic and political life.

The Political System

There are at least five important elements in the American view of the political system:

- **Liberty:** Americans are preoccupied with their rights. With some exceptions they believe they should be free to do pretty much as they please so long as they don't hurt other people.

- **Equality:** Everybody should have an equal vote and an equal chance.

- **Democracy:** Government officials should be accountable to the people.

- **Civic duty:** Americans ought to take community affairs seriously and help out when they can.[4]

- **Individual responsibility:** Barring some disability, individuals are responsible for their actions and well-being.

By vast majorities Americans believe that every citizen should have an equal chance to influence government policy and to hold public office, and they

The Meaning of Political Culture

A political culture is a patterned set of ways of thinking about how politics and governing ought to be carried out. A nation, if it is made up of people who are quite similar to one another, may have a single political culture, part of what is sometimes referred to as a "national character." Most nations are not homogeneous, however, being made up instead of distinctive regions, religions, and ethnic groups. Each of these parts may have a distinctive political subculture. The American South, for example, has a political culture that differs in important ways from that of the Northeast.

Because a political culture consists of our fundamental assumptions about how the political process should operate, we often take it for granted or are completely unaware of how important these assumptions are. For instance, we assume that a person who loses an election should not try to prevent the winner from taking office, that it is wrong to use public office to enrich oneself or one's family, and that nobody should have a greater claim to political authority simply because he or she comes from a rich or wellborn family. In many other societies these are not widely shared assumptions, and in some societies the opposite is often believed.

A political culture is not the same as a **political ideology.** The concept of ideology will be explained in Chapter 5. As used there, it will refer to more or less consistent sets of views as to the policies government ought to pursue. A doctrinaire conservative, liberal, or radical has an ideology. Up to a point people can disagree on ideology (what government should do) but still share a common political culture (how government ought to be operated). Some ideologies, however, are so critical of the existing state of affairs that they require a fundamental change in the way politics is carried on, and thus they embody a different political culture as well.

America has both a shared political culture and some distinctive subcultures associated with various ethnic and religious groups.

At the height of immigration to this country there was a striking emphasis on creating a shared political culture. Schoolchildren, whatever their national origin, were taught to salute this country's flag.

oppose the idea of letting people have titles, such as "Lord" or "Duke," as in England. By somewhat smaller majorities they believe that people should be allowed to vote even if they can't read or write or vote intelligently.[5] Though Americans recognize that people differ in their abilities, they overwhelmingly agree with the statement that "teaching children that all people are really equal recognizes that all people are equally worthy and deserve equal treatment."[6]

At least three questions can be raised about this political culture. First, how do we know that people share these beliefs? For most of our history there have been no public-opinion polls, and even after they became commonplace, they were rather crude tools for measuring the existence and meaning of complex, abstract ideas. There is in fact no way to prove that such values as those listed above are important to Americans. But neither is there good reason for dismissing the list out of hand. One can infer, as have many scholars, the existence of certain values by a close study of the kinds of books Americans read, the speeches they hear, the slogans to which they respond, and the political choices they make, as well as by noting the observations of insightful foreign visitors. Personality tests as well as opinion polls, particularly those asking similar questions in different

countries, also supply useful evidence, some of which will be reviewed in the following paragraphs.

Second, if these values are important to Americans, how can we explain behavior that is so obviously inconsistent with them? For example, if white Americans say that they believe in equality of opportunity, why did so many of them for so long deny that equality to black Americans? That people act contrary to their professed beliefs is an everyday fact of life: people believe in honesty, yet they steal from their employers and sometimes underreport their taxable income. Self-interest and social circumstances, as well as values, shape behavior. Gunnar Myrdal, a Swedish observer of American society, described race relations in this country as "an American dilemma" resulting from the conflict between the "American creed" (a belief in equality of opportunity) and American behavior (denying blacks full citizenship).[7] But the creed remains important because it is a source of change: as more and more persons become aware of the inconsistency between their values and their behavior, that behavior slowly changes.[8] Race relations in this country would take a very different course if, instead of the abstract but widespread belief in equality, there were an equally widespread belief that one race is inherently inferior to another. (No doubt some Americans believe that, but most do not.)

Third, if there is agreement on certain political values, why has there been so much political conflict in our history? How can Americans who agree on fundamentals fight a bloody civil war, engage in violent labor-management disputes, take to the streets in riots and demonstrations, and sue each other in countless court battles? Conflict, even violent struggle, can occur over specific policies even among those who share, at some level of abstraction, common beliefs. Many political values may be irrelevant to specific controversies: there is no abstract value, for example, that would settle the question of whether steelworkers ought to organize unions. More important, much of our conflict has occurred precisely because we have strong beliefs that happen, as each of us interprets them, to be in conflict. Equality of opportunity seems an attractive idea, but sometimes it can be pursued only by curtailing personal liberty, another attractive idea. The states went to war in 1861 over one aspect of that conflict—the rights of slaves versus the rights of slaveowners.

Indeed the Civil War is a remarkable illustration of the extent to which certain fundamental beliefs about how a democratic regime ought to be organized have persisted despite bitter conflict over the policies adopted by particular governments. When the southern states seceded from the Union, they formed not a wholly different government but one modeled, despite some important differences, on the United States Constitution. Even some of the language of the Constitution was duplicated, suggesting that the southern states believed not that a new form of government or a different political culture ought to be created but that the South was the true repository of the existing constitutional and cultural order.[9]

Perhaps the most frequently encountered evidence that Americans believe themselves bound by common values and common hopes has been the persistence of the word *Americanism* in our political vocabulary. Throughout the nineteenth and most of the twentieth centuries, *Americanism* and *American way of life* were familiar terms not only in Fourth of July speeches but in everyday discourse. For many years a committee of the House of Representatives existed, called the House UnAmerican Activities

When in the 1950s a committee of the House of Representatives investigated alleged subversion, it was called the committee on *"UnAmerican"* activities—a term that seemed strange to nations that did not understand the great appeal of the concept of "Americanism."

Committee. There is hardly any example to be found abroad of such a way of thinking: there is no "Britishism" or "Frenchism," and when Britons and French people become worried about subversion, they call it a problem of internal security, not a manifestation of "un-British" or "un-French" activities.

The Economic System

Americans judge the economic system using many of the same standards by which they judge the political one, albeit with some very important differences. As with politics, so with economics, liberty is important. Thus Americans support the idea of a free-enterprise economic system, calling it "generally fair and efficient" and denying that it "survives by keeping the poor down."[10] However there are limits to how much freedom they think should exist in the marketplace. People support government regulation of business in order to keep some firms from becoming too powerful and to correct specific abuses.[11]

Americans are more willing to tolerate economic inequality than political inequality. They believe in equality, but when applied to the economy they mean "equality of opportunity," not "equality of results." If everyone has an equal opportunity to get ahead, then it is all right for people with more ability to earn higher salaries and for wages to be set based on how hard people work rather than on their economic needs.[12] Although Americans are quite willing to support education and training programs to help disadvantaged people get ahead, they are strongly opposed to anything that looks like preferential treatment (for example, hiring quotas) in the workplace.[13]

The leaders of very liberal political groups, such as civil-rights and feminist organizations, are more willing than the average American to support preferential treatment in hiring and promoting minorities and women. They do so because, unlike most citizens, they believe that whatever disadvantages blacks and women face are the result of failures of the economic system rather than the fault of individuals.[14] Even so, these leaders strongly support the idea that earnings should be based on ability and oppose the idea of having any top limit on what people can earn.[15]

This popular commitment to economic individualism and personal responsibility may help explain how Americans think about particular public policies, such as welfare and civil rights. As we shall see in Chapter 17, Americans are willing to help people "truly in need" (this includes the elderly and the disabled) but not those deemed "able to take care of themselves" (this includes, in the public's mind, people "on welfare"). As we shall see in Chapter 19, Americans dislike preferential hiring programs and quotas to deal with racial inequality.

At the core of these policy attitudes is a widely (but not universally) shared commitment to economic individualism and personal responsibility. Some scholars, among them Donald Kinder and David Sears, interpret these individualistic values as "symbolic racism"—a kind of plausible camouflage for antiblack attitudes.[16] But other scholars, such as Paul M. Sniderman and Michael Gray Hagen, argue that these views are not a smoke screen for bigotry or insensitivity, but a genuine commitment to the ethic of self-reliance.[17] Since there are many Americans on both sides of this issue, debates about welfare and civil rights tend to be especially intense. What is striking about the American political culture is that in this country the individualist view of social policy is by far the most popular.[18]

Views about specific economic policies change. Americans now are much more inclined than they once were to believe that the government should help the needy and regulate business. But the commitment to certain underlying principles has been remarkably enduring. In 1924 most of the high school students in Muncie, Indiana, said that "it is entirely the fault of the man himself if he cannot succeed" and disagreed with the view that differences in wealth showed that the system was unjust. In 1977, over half a century later, the students in this same high school were asked the same questions again, and with the same results (see Table 4.1)[19]

TABLE 4.1   Responsibility for Success or Failure

Statement	Percentage of High School Students Agreeing	
	1924	1977
It is entirely the fault of the man himself if he cannot succeed.	47%	47%
The fact that some men [in 1977: people] have so much more money than others shows there is an unjust condition in this country that ought to be changed.	30	34

SOURCE: Theodore Caplow and Howard M. Bahr, "Half a Century of Change in Adolescent Attitudes: Replication of a Middletown Survey by the Lynds," *Public Opinion Quarterly* 43 (Spring 1979): 1–17, Table 1. Reprinted by permission of University of Chicago Press.

Comparing America with Other Nations

The best way to learn what is distinctive about the American political culture is to compare it with that of other nations. When we make this comparison, we find that Americans have somewhat different beliefs about the political system, the economic system, and religion.

Political System

Sweden has a well-developed democratic government, with a constitution, free speech, an elected legislature, competing political parties, and a reasonably honest and nonpartisan bureaucracy. But the Swedish political culture is significantly different from ours; it is more deferential than participatory. Though almost all adult Swedes vote in national elections, few participate in politics in any other way. They defer to the decisions of experts and specialists who work for the government, rarely challenge governmental decisions in court, believe leaders and legislators ought to decide issues on the basis of "what is best" more than on "what the people want," and value equality as much as (or more than) liberty.[20] Where Americans are contentious, Swedes value harmony; where Americans tend to assert their rights, Swedes tend to observe their obligations.

The contrast in political cultures is even greater when one looks at a nation, such as Japan, with a wholly different history and set of traditions. One study compared the values expressed by a small number of upper-status Japanese with those of some similarly situated Americans. Where the Americans emphasized the virtues of individualism, competition, and equality in their political, economic, and social relations, the Japanese attached greater value to maintaining good relations with colleagues, having decisions made by groups, preserving social harmony, and displaying respect for hierarchy. Americans were more concerned than the Japanese with rules and with treating others fairly but impersonally, with due regard for their rights. The Japanese, on the other hand, stressed the importance of being sensitive to the personal needs of others, avoiding conflict, and reaching decisions through discussion rather than the application of rules.[21] These cultural differences affect in profound but hard-to-measure ways the workings of the political and economic systems of the two countries, making them function quite differently despite the fact that both are industrialized, capitalist nations.

It is easy to become carried away by the more obvious differences among national cultures and to overgeneralize from them. Thinking in stereotypes about the typical American, the typical Swede, or the typical Japanese is as risky as thinking of the typical white or the typical black American. This can be especially misleading in nations, such as the United States and Canada, that have been settled by a variety of ethnic and religious groups (English-speaking versus French-speaking Canadians, for example, or Jewish, Protestant, and Catholic Americans). But it is equally misleading to suppose that the operation of a political system can be understood entirely as the result of the nation's objective features—its laws, economy, or physical circumstances.

In 1959–1960 Gabriel Almond and Sidney Verba published a study of political culture in five nations. In general they found that Americans, and to a lesser degree citizens of Great Britain, had a stronger sense of civic duty (a belief that one has an obligation to participate in civic and political affairs) and a stronger sense of **civic competence** (a belief that one can affect government policies) than did the citizens of Germany, Italy, or Mexico. Over half of all Americans and a third of all Britons believed that the average citizen ought to "be active in one's community," compared to only a tenth in Italy and a fifth in Germany. Moreover many more Americans and Britons than Germans, Italians, or Mexicans believed that they could "do something" about an unjust national law or local regulation.[22]

Since 1960 nobody has asked people in these five countries the same questions, and hence we do not know whether these views have changed in recent years. In the United States, at least, people have less trust in government today than they once did. But even so, popular confidence in political institutions remains higher here than in many places abroad. In 1987 a survey in the United States and four European nations showed that Americans and Britons were much more likely than people in West Germany, France, or Spain to say that they had a "great deal of" or "some" confidence in the armed forces, the police, and Congress (or in Europe, parliament). With respect to the judicial system and labor unions, Americans displayed less confidence but still more than did Europeans (see Table 4.2).[23]

TABLE 4.2 Popular Confidence in Institutions in Europe and America, 1987

Institution	*Percentage Saying They Have a "Great Deal of" or "Some" Confidence*				
	U.S.	Great Britain	West Germany	France	Spain
Armed forces	86%	79%	69%	59%	36%
Police	88	80	80	72	44
Congress (Parliament)	83	52	64	55	30
Schools	82	53	82	82	59
Church	85	56	66	53	38
Business	84	55	44	30	26
Press / media / TV	69	38	41	48	46
Labor unions	52	29	43	36	26
Judicial system	77	56	72	62	35

SOURCE: Laurence Parisot, "Attitudes About the Media: A Five-Country Comparison," *Public Opinion* (January–February 1988): 18. Reprinted with the permission of the American Enterprise Institute for Public Policy Research, Washington, D.C.

By the same token, Americans were more likely to say that they were "very proud" of their national identity and that, if a war came, they would be "willing to fight" for their country (see Table 4.3).[24] Of course Americans know that their country has a lot of faults. But even the most disaffected voters believe the United States needs to change only certain policies, not the system of government.[25]

A television picture of a U.S. serviceman captured by the enemy (here, Michael Durant, a prisoner of war in Somalia) powerfully unites the nation.

Economic System

The political culture of Sweden is not only more deferential than ours, but also more inclined to favor equality of results over equality of opportunity. Sidney Verba and Gary Orren have compared the views of Swedish and American trade-union and political-party leaders on a variety of economic issues. In both countries the leaders were chosen from either blue-collar unions or the major liberal political party (the Democrats in the United States, the Social Democrats in Sweden).

The results (see Table 4.4) are quite striking. By margins of four or five to one, the Swedish leaders were more likely to believe in giving workers equal pay than were their American counterparts. Moreover, by margins of at least three to one, the Swedes were more likely than the Americans to favor putting a top limit on incomes.[26]

Just what these differences in beliefs mean in dollars-and-cents terms was revealed by the answers to another question. Each group was asked what should be the ratio between the income of an executive and that of a menial worker (a dishwasher in Sweden, an elevator operator in the United States). The Swedish leaders said the ratio should be a little over two to one. That is, if the dishwasher earned $200 a week, the executive should earn no more than $440 to $480 a week. But the American leaders were ready to let

TABLE 4.3 Patriotism in America and Europe, 1991

Statement	*Percentage Agreeing*				
	U.S.	Germany	Great Britain	Italy	France
I am very patriotic.	88%	77%	72%	69%	64%
We should all be willing to fight for our country whether it is right or wrong.	55	28	56	39	37

SOURCE: Adapted from *The Public Perspective* (November/December 1991): 6. Reprinted by permission of *The Public Perspective,* a publication of the Roper Center for Public Opinion Research, University of Connecticut.

the executive earn between $2,260 and $3,040 per week when the elevator operator was earning $200.

Americans, compared to people in many other countries, are more likely to think that freedom is more important than equality and less likely to think that hard work goes unrewarded or that government should guarantee citizens a basic standard of living (see Table 4.5). These cultural differences make a difference in politics. In fact there is less income inequality in Sweden than in the United States—the government sees to that.

The Role of Religion

In the 1830s Tocqueville was amazed by how religious Americans were in comparison to his fellow Europeans. As political sociologist Seymour Martin Lipset has observed, "from the early nineteenth century down to the present, the United States has been among the most religious countries in the world."[27]

The average American is more likely than the average European to believe in God, to pray on a daily basis, and to acknowledge clear standards of right and wrong (see Table 4.6).

Religious beliefs have always played a significant role in American politics. The religious revivalist movement of the late 1730s and early 1740s (known as the First Great Awakening) transformed the political life of the American colonies. Religious ideas fueled the break with England for violating, in the words of the Declaration of Independence, "the laws of nature and nature's God." Religious leaders were central to the struggle over slavery in the nineteenth century and the temperance movement of the early twentieth century.

Both liberals and conservatives have used the pulpit to promote political change. The civil rights movement of the 1950s and 1960s was led mainly by black religious leaders, most prominently Martin Luther King, Jr. In the 1980s a conservative religious

TABLE 4.4 Commitment to Income Equity in Sweden and the United States

	Political-Party Leaders		*Blue-Collar Union Leaders*	
	Sweden (Social Democrats)	U.S. (Democrats)	Sweden	U.S.
Favor equality of results (%)	21%	9%	14%	4%
Favor equal pay (%)	58	12	68	11
Favor top limit on income (%)	44	17	51	13
Fair income ratio of executive to menial worker[a]	2 : 1	15 : 1	2 : 1	11 : 1

[a] In Sweden, menial worker was a dishwasher; in U.S., menial worker was an elevator operator.
SOURCE: Sidney Verba and Gary R. Orren, *Equality in America: The View from the Top* (Cambridge, Mass.: Harvard University Press, 1985), 255.

TABLE 4.5　Attitudes Toward Economic Equality in America and Europe, 1991

Statement	Percentage Agreeing				
	U.S.	Great Britain	Germany	Italy	France
It is government's responsibility to take care of the very poor who can't take care of themselves.	23%	62%	50%	66%	62%
Hard work guarantees success.	63	46	38	51	46
Government should *not* guarantee every citizen food and basic shelter.	34	9	13	14	10

SOURCE: Adapted from *The Public Perspective* (November/December 1991): 5, 7. Reprinted by permission of *The Public Perspective*, a publication of the Roper Center for Public Opinion Research, University of Connecticut.

group known as the Moral Majority advocated constitutional amendments that would require prayer in public schools and ban abortion. If history is any guide, religious beliefs will continue to shape American political culture well into the next century.

The Sources of Political Culture

That Americans bring a distinctive way of thinking to their political life is easier to demonstrate than to explain. But even a brief, and necessarily superficial, effort to understand the sources of our political culture can help make its significance clearer.

The American Revolution, as we discussed in Chapter 2, was essentially over liberty: an assertion by colonists of what they took to be their rights. Though the Constitution, produced eleven years after the Revolution, had to deal with other issues as well, its animating spirit reflected the effort to reconcile personal liberty with the needs of social control. These founding experiences, and the political disputes that followed, have given to American political thought and culture a preoccupation with the assertion and maintenance of rights. This tradition has imbued the daily conduct of politics with a kind of adversary spirit quite foreign to the political life of countries that did not undergo a libertarian revolution or that were formed out of an interest in other goals, such as social equality, national independence, or ethnic supremacy.

The adversary spirit of the American political culture reflects not only our preoccupation with rights but also our long-standing distrust of authority and of people wielding power. Our experiences with British rule over the American colonies was one source of that distrust. But another, older source was the religious belief of many Americans that human

TABLE 4.6　Religious Belief in America and Europe, 1991

Statement	Percentage Agreeing				
	U.S.	Great Britain	Germany	Italy	France
I never doubt the existence of God.	60%	31%	20%	56%	29%
Prayer is an important part of my daily life.	77	37	44	69	32
There are clear guidelines about what is good and evil.	79	65	54	56	64

SOURCE: Adapted from *The Public Perspective* (November/December 1991): 5, 8. Reprinted by permission of *The Public Perspective*, a publication of the Roper Center for Public Opinion Research, University of Connecticut.

nature was fundamentally depraved. To them, all of mankind suffered from original sin, symbolized by Adam and Eve eating the forbidden fruit in the Garden of Eden. Since no one was born innocent, no one could be trusted with power. Thus, the Constitution had to be designed in such a way as to curb the darker side of human nature. Otherwise, everyone's rights would be in jeopardy.

The contentiousness of a people animated by a suspicion of government and devotion to individualism could easily have made democratic politics so tumultuous as to be impossible. After all, one must be willing to trust others with power if there is to be any kind of democratic government. And sometimes those others will be people not of one's own choosing. The first great test case took place around 1800 in a battle between the Federalists, led by John Adams and Alexander Hamilton, and the Democratic-Republicans, led by Thomas Jefferson and James Madison. The two factions deeply distrusted each other: the Federalists had passed laws (see Chapter 18) designed to suppress Jeffersonian journalists; Jefferson suspected the Federalists were out to subvert the Constitution; the Federalists believed he intended to sell out the country to France. But as we shall see in Chapter 7, the threat of civil war never materialized, and the Jeffersonians came to power peacefully. Within a few years the role of an opposition party had become legitimate, and serious efforts to suppress one's opponents had been abandoned. By happy circumstance people were reconciled to the view that liberty and orderly political change could coexist.

The Constitution, by creating a federal system and dividing political authority among competing institutions, provided ample opportunity for widespread—though hardly universal—participation in politics. The election of Jefferson in 1800 produced no political catastrophe, and those who had predicted one were, to a degree, discredited. But other, more fundamental features of American life contributed to the same end. One of the most important of these was religious diversity.

The absence of an established or official religion for the nation as a whole, reinforced by a constitutional prohibition of such an establishment and the migration to this country of people with different religious backgrounds, meant that religious diversity

Religion plays a larger role in the lives of Americans than it does in the lives of the citizens of most other western countries.

was inevitable. Since there could be no orthodox or official religion, it became difficult for a corresponding political orthodoxy to emerge. Moreover the conflict between the Puritan tradition, with its emphasis on faith and good works, and the Catholic church, with its devotion to the sacraments and priestly authority, provided a recurrent source of cleavage in American public life. The differences in values between these two groups showed up not only in their religious practices but in areas involving the regulation of manners and morals, and even in the choice of a political party. For more than a century candidates for state and even national office were deeply divided over whether the sale of liquor should be prohibited, a question that arose ultimately out of competing religious doctrines.

Even though there was no established church, there was certainly a dominant religious tradition, and that was Protestantism and especially Puritanism. The Protestant churches provided both a set of beliefs and an organizational experience that had profound effects on American political culture. Those beliefs were consistent with, and even required, a life of personal achievement as well as religious conviction: a believer had an obligation to work, save money, obey the secular law, and do good works. Max Weber explained the rise of capitalism in part by what he called the Protestant ethic and what we now sometimes call the **work ethic**.[28] Such values had political consequences as well; people holding them were motivated to engage in civic and communal action.

Churches offered a ready opportunity for developing and practicing civic and political skills. Since most Protestant churches were organized along congregational lines—that is, the church was controlled by its members, who put up the building, hired the preacher, and supervised the finances—they were, in effect, miniature political systems, with leaders and committees, conflict and consensus. Developing a participant political culture was undoubtedly made easier by the existence of a particular religious culture. Even some Catholic churches in early America were under a degree of lay control. Parishioners owned the church property, negotiated with priests, and conducted church business.

All aspects of culture, including the political, are preserved and transmitted to new generations primarily by the family. Though some believe that the weakening of the family unit has eroded the extent to which it transmits anything, particularly culture, and has enlarged the power of other sources of values—the mass media and the world of friends and fashion, leisure and entertainment—there is still little doubt that the ways in which we think about the world are largely acquired within the family. In Chapter 5 we shall see that the family is the primary source of one kind of political attitude—identification with one or another political party. Even more important, the family shapes in subtle ways how we think and act on political matters. Erik Erikson, the psychologist, noted certain traits that are more characteristic of American than of European families—the greater freedom enjoyed by children, for example, and the larger measure of equality among family members. These familial characteristics promote a belief, carried through life, that every person has rights deserving protection, and that a variety of interests have a legitimate claim to consideration when decisions are made.[29]

The combined effect of religious and ethnic diversity, an individualistic philosophy, fragmented political authority, and the relatively egalitarian American family can be seen in the absence of a high degree of **class consciousness** among Americans. Class consciousness means thinking of oneself as a worker whose interests are in opposition to those of management, or vice versa. In this country most people, whatever their jobs, think of themselves as "middle class."

If any group of Americans were likely to think and act in terms of their economic class, one would suppose it would be the unemployed. Nonetheless a careful study of their political views in 1976 showed that, though unemployed people feel deprived, the great majority do not identify with other unemployed persons or think that their interests as a class are in opposition to those of management. The political views of the unemployed do not seem to differ much from those of the employed, and even when the former think in class terms, their political views do not seem to be affected. Moreover we know that even in the late 1930s, when the country was in the grip of a massive depression, only a small minority of the unemployed expressed a strong sense of class consciousness.[30]

Though the writings of Horatio Alger are no longer popular, Americans still seem to believe in the message of those stories—the opportunity for success available to people who work hard. This may help explain why the United States is the only large industrial democracy without a significant socialist party and why, as we shall see in Chapter 17, the nation has been slow to adopt certain welfare programs.

The Culture War

Almost all Americans share some elements of a common political culture. Why, then, is there so much cultural conflict in American politics? For many years, the most explosive political issues have included abortion, gay rights, drug use, school prayer, and pornography. Viewed from a Marxist perspective, politics in the United States is utterly baffling: instead of two economic classes engaged in a bitter struggle over wealth, we have two cultural classes locked in a war over values.

To say that there are two cultural classes is, of course, an oversimplification, but to say that there is a culture war is not an exaggeration.[31] Groups supporting and opposing a right to abortion have had many angry confrontations in recent years. The latter have been arrested while attempting to block access

The changing American family. At the top is an extended family in Black River Falls, Wisconsin, around 1900; on the lower left a nuclear family in contemporary America; on the lower right a single-parent family.

to abortion clinics, some clinics have been fire-bombed, and at least one physician has been killed. A controversy over what school children should be taught about homosexuals was responsible, in part, for the firing of the head of the New York City school system; in other states, there have been fierce arguments in state legislatures and before the courts over whether gay and lesbian couples should be allowed to adopt children. Although most Americans want to keep heroin, cocaine, and other drugs illegal, a significant number of people want to legalize (or at least decriminalize) their use. The Supreme Court has ruled that children cannot pray in public schools, but this has not stopped many parents and school authorities from trying to reinstate school prayer, or at least prayer-like moments of silence. The discovery that a federal agency, the National Endowment for the Arts, had given money to support exhibitions and performances that contained what many people thought were obscene materials led to a furious congressional struggle over the future of the agency. The

1992 presidential election centered, in part, on a passionate argument over which candidate best exemplified "family values."

The culture war differs from other political disputes (over such matters as taxes, business regulation, and foreign policy) in several ways: money is not at stake, compromises are almost impossible to arrange, and the conflict is more profound. The cultural conflict is animated by deep differences in people's beliefs about private and public morality—about, that is, the standards that ought to govern individual behavior and social arrangements. The culture war is about what kind of country we ought to live in, not just about what kinds of policies our government ought to adopt.

To simplify, there are two opposed camps, the **orthodox** and the **progressive**. On the orthodox side are people who believe that morality is as important as, or more important than, self-expression and that moral rules derive from the commands of God or the laws of nature—commands and laws that are relatively clear, unchanging, and independent of individual preferences. On the progressive side are people who think that personal freedom is as important as, or more important than, certain traditional rules and that these rules depend on the circumstances of modern life—circumstances that are quite complex, changeable, and dependent on individual preferences.

Most conspicuous among the orthodox are fundamentalist Protestants and born-again Christians, and so critics who dislike orthodox views often dismiss them as the fanatical expressions of "the Religious Right." But many people who hold orthodox views are not fanatical or deeply religious or right-wing on most issues; they simply have strong views about drugs, pornography, and sexual morality. Similarly, the progressive side often includes the leaders of mainline Protestant denominations (for example, Episcopalians and Unitarians) and people with no strong religious beliefs, and so their critics often denounce them as immoral, anti-Christian radicals who have embraced the ideology of secular humanism, the belief that moral standards do not require religious justification. But in all likelihood few progressives are immoral or anti-Christian and most do not regard secular humanism as an insidious ideology.

As chancellor of the New York City public school system, Joseph Fernandez supported condom distribution and a curriculum that included nontraditional families. His contract was not renewed.

Moreover, the culture war is occurring not just between different religious denominations but also within them. Catholic, Protestant, and Jewish leaders with an orthodox perspective tend to assign great importance to two-parent families, condemn pornography, denounce homosexuality, oppose ratification of the Equal Rights Amendment to the Constitution, and think the United States is in general a force for good in the world. Leaders of the same faiths who have a progressive outlook are instead more likely to say that many legitimate alternatives to the traditional two-parent family exist, that pornography and homosexuality are private matters protected by individual rights, and that the United States has been at best a neutral and at worst a bad force in world affairs.[32] This conflict between the orthodox and progressive view of American culture is similar to, and has many of the same causes, as the cleavage (described in Chapter 5) between the traditional middle class and the new middle class.

American history has always had conflicts of this sort, but they have acquired special importance today as a result of two major changes in American society. The first is the great increase in the proportion of people who consider themselves progressive. Once, almost everyone was religiously orthodox even if politically liberal; today, fewer are. The second factor is the rise of technologies (such as television, talk shows, and direct-mail advertising) that make it easy to wage a cultural war on a large scale. In the past, preachers, writers, and lecturers could reach at most a few hundred people at a time; today, television evangelists, radio talk-shows hosts, and the authors of mail messages can wage a furious war of words reaching tens of millions of people and recruiting hundreds of thousands of followers. A cultural war that once enlisted only a few activists can now mobilize mass armies.

The tensions generated by the culture war affect our views as to how well our government works, how much influence ordinary people can have over it, and how large a measure of freedom we ought to grant to our opponents. Trust in government, a sense of political efficacy, and tolerance for views we dislike are always fragile under the best of circumstances. Have the cultural tensions of recent decades made matters worse? In the rest of this chapter we shall try to answer these questions.

Mistrust of Government

In 1979 President Jimmy Carter, taking note of numerous public-opinion polls that showed a dramatic decline in the proportion of Americans who said they had a great deal of confidence in our system, made a nationwide television address on the subject of the American malaise, which he defined as a crisis of confidence evident in the "growing disrespect" for government, schools, churches, and other institutions.

Though it probably wasn't a politically astute speech—Americans don't like to be told they suffer from a malaise, and the following year they voted against Carter and for a man, Ronald Reagan, who offered a much more upbeat assessment of the American condition—it was based on some solid, factual evidence. As can be seen in Figure 4.1, various measures of mistrust in government rose steadily for about fifteen years beginning in the mid–1960s. By 1976 nearly twice as many Americans as in 1958 thought that there were "quite a few" crooks in government, that government was run for the benefit of a "few big interests," that a "lot" of tax money was wasted and that we can expect government to do the right thing only "some of the time."[33]

In part this decline in trust was the result of some dramatic events. The largest single increase in mistrust occurred between 1972 and 1974—the time of the Watergate scandal when close aides to President Nixon authorized a burglary of the Democratic party headquarters and the president himself participated in the cover-up of the bungled break-in. But the decline began long before Watergate (or the war in Vietnam) and continued after both events were history.

This rising mistrust is worrisome, but should be seen in context. There is evidence that the mistrust is chiefly aimed not at the *system* of government but at specific leaders and policies.[34] We have already seen that Americans have more confidence in governmental institutions than do citizens of many other countries. Even in 1972–1974, when distrust of government was especially high, 86 percent of those interviewed in a national survey agreed with the following statement: "I am proud of many things about our form of government."[35]

FIGURE 4.1   The Growth of Mistrust of Government

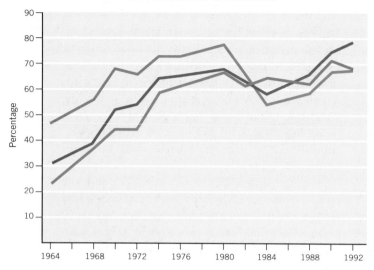

QUESTIONS

Do you think that people in the government waste a lot of the money we pay in taxes, waste some of it, or don't waste very much of it?

⎯⎯⎯ Percentage who responded:
       Waste a lot

Would you say that the government is pretty much run by a few big interests looking out for themselves or that it is run for the benefit of all the people?

⎯⎯⎯ Percentage who responded:
       A few big interests

How much of the time do you think you can trust the government in Washington to do what is right — just about always, most of the time, or only some of the time?

⎯⎯⎯ Percentage who responded:
       Only some of the time

SOURCES: Survey Research Center, University of Michigan. Supplied by the SRC/CPS American National Election Studies, University of Michigan. 1990 and 1992 figures supplied by *ICPSR American National Election Studies*, University of Michigan.

Intense press coverage of scandals has deepened popular distrust of government. Here, former special counsel Lawrence Walsh talks about his investigation of the Iran-Contra affair.

Moreover there are reasons for thinking that the current level of trust in government is close to the historical norm and that the much higher levels of trust of the late 1950s and early 1960s were unusual. Though polling was then in its infancy, there is evidence that Americans in the 1930s were not much more trustful of their government than they are now.[36] Between the 1930s and the 1960s this nation overcame an economic depression and won World War II, events that gave to citizens an unusually high degree of confidence in the capacity of their government. The 1960s and 1970s, when that confidence weakened, were years of great turmoil—the civil-rights movement, the war in Vietnam, the sharp rise in crime rates, the assassination of various leaders, urban riots and campus demonstrations, and economic inflation. Small wonder that people thought that things were getting out of hand and that political leaders ought to take some of the blame.

The decline in popular confidence in government was part and parcel of a general loss of confidence in almost all institutions. As we can see in Table 4.7, the percentage of Americans saying they had "a great deal of confidence in" the people running major companies and the press also declined sharply between 1966 and the early 1990s.

The impassioned conflict over American involvement in Vietnam brought out protesters on both sides, each side seeking to associate important symbols ("peace" and "patriotism") with its cause.

There was a brief and small improvement in trust during the early Reagan years,[37] but that gain was washed out, and then some, by a big drop in the early 1990s. Owing to the combined effects of an economic recession, political scandals (such as the revelation that members of the House of Representatives were writing checks without money in the House bank to cover them), and the continued growth in such problems as crime, drug abuse, and the federal debt, Americans in record numbers expressed disgust at politics and politicians. Ross Perot, the Texas businessman who ran for president in 1992 as an independent, tried to capitalize on that anger. But there was no sign of a popular revolt against the Constitutional system.

In sum, Americans have not lost confidence in themselves or in their governmental system, but they no longer so readily give to political leaders and their policies the kind of support they gave in the less troubled years of the 1950s.

TABLE 4.7   Confidence in People Running American Institutions, 1966–1992

Percentage saying they have "a great deal of confidence" in "people in charge of running" various institutions

Institution	1966	1971–1979	1980–1989	1990–1992	Change 1966 to 1990s
Congress	42%	16%	19%	10%	−32%
U.S. Supreme Court	50	29	29	28	−22
Federal bureaucracy	41	19	20	14	−27
The press	29	23	18	15	−14
Major companies	55	22	18	14	−41

SOURCE: Humphrey Taylor, "The American Angst of 1992," *The Public Perspective* (July/August 1992): 3, reporting survey data from Louis Harris and Associates. Reprinted by permission of *The Public Perspective,* a publication of the Roper Center for Public Opinion Research, University of Connecticut.

Americans' trust in government was especially high in the 1950s when Eisenhower was president.

Political Efficacy

Perhaps the most worrisome aspect of recent changes in American political culture is the decline in the extent to which citizens feel that the political system will respond to their needs and beliefs. These changes are in what scholars call a citizen's sense of **political efficacy**, by which they mean a citizen's capacity to understand and influence political events.

This sense of efficacy has two parts—**internal efficacy** (confidence in one's own abilities to understand and take part in political affairs) and **external efficacy** (a belief that the system will respond to what citizens do). Since the mid-1960s there has been a fairly sharp drop in the sense of external efficacy (or system responsiveness) but not much change in the sense of internal efficacy (personal competence).

As we can see in Figure 4.2, people today are not much different from people in 1952 with respect to whether they can understand what is going on in government (most find it too complicated to fathom) or whether they have much say in what the

FIGURE 4.2   Changes in the Sense of Political Efficacy

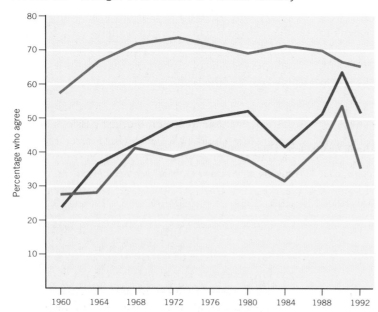

Internal Efficacy

STATEMENTS

Sometimes politics and government seem so complicated that a person like me can't really understand what's going on.

People like me don't have any say about what the government does.

External Efficacy

STATEMENT

I don't think public officials care much what people like me think.

SOURCES: Center for Political Studies, University of Michigan, as reported in Seymour Martin Lipset and William Schneider, *The Confidence Gap: Business, Labor, and Government in the Public Mind* (New York: Free Press, 1983). 1990 and 1992 figures supplied by *ICPSR American National Election Studies*, University of Michigan.

government does. But there has been a big change in how responsive people think the government is to their interests. In 1980 people were twice as likely as those in the late 1950s to say that public officials don't "care much what people like me think." And in 1980 they were much more likely than they had been (even as recently as 1968) to say "those we elect to Congress in Washington lose touch with the people pretty quickly" and "parties are only interested in people's votes, not their opinions."[38]

Unlike the increase in the mistrust of government, the increase in the feeling that government was unresponsive was not shaped by any particular events; the sense of external efficacy dropped more or less steadily throughout the 1960s and 1970s. What seems to have happened is that Americans gradually have come to the view that government has become too big and pervasive for it to be sensitive to citizen preferences. In 1976 half of all Americans thought the federal government was too powerful; in 1964 less than a third did.[39]

Though Americans may feel less effective as citizens than they once did, their sense of efficacy remains much higher than it is among Europeans. In 1974 a poll taken in five nations found that the average American scored significantly higher on the efficacy scale than the average person in Austria, Germany, Great Britain, or the Netherlands. Moreover Americans were much more likely than the Europeans to say they regularly discussed politics, signed petitions, and worked to solve community problems.[40] Though Americans, are less likely to vote than Europeans, they are more likely to do the harder chores that make up democratic politics.

Because Americans are less likely than they once were to hold their leaders in high esteem, to have confidence in governmental policies, and to believe the system will be responsive to popular wishes, some observers like to say that Americans today are more "alienated" from politics. It probably would be better to say that they are simply more realistic.

Political Tolerance

Democratic politics depends crucially on citizens' being reasonably tolerant of the opinions and actions of others. If unpopular speakers were always shouted down, if government efforts to censor newspapers

Americans may not vote at as high a rate as citizens in European countries, but they probably sign more petitions than any other people anywhere.

were usually met with popular support or even public indifference, if peaceful demonstrations were regularly broken up by hostile mobs, if the losing candidates in an election refused to allow their victorious opponents to take office, then the essential elements of a democratic political culture would be missing, and democracy would fail. Democracy does not require perfect tolerance; if it did, the passions of human nature would make democracy forever impossible. But at a minimum citizens must have a political culture that allows the discussion of ideas and the selection of rulers in an atmosphere reasonably free of oppression.

Public-opinion surveys show that the overwhelming majority of Americans agree with such concepts as freedom of speech, majority rule, and the right to circulate petitions—at least in the abstract.[41]

But when we get down to concrete cases, a good many Americans are not very tolerant of groups they dislike. Suppose you must decide which groups will be permitted to espouse their causes at meetings held

TABLE 4.8 **Percentage of Americans Willing to Permit Demonstrations and Petitions, by Various Causes**

Cause	Percentage Tolerant of	
	Demonstrations	Petitions
About crime in community	81%	95%
About pollution from a factory	80	93
By black militants	61	69
By radical students	60	72
To legalize marijuana	41	52
To protect blacks buying or renting homes in white neighborhoods (asked of whites only)	55	70

SOURCE: David G. Lawrence, "Procedural Norms and Tolerance: A Reassessment," *American Political Science Review* 70 (March 1976): 88. Reprinted by permission.

in your community's civic auditorium. Which of these groups would *you* allow to run such a meeting?

1. Protestants holding a revival meeting.

2. Right-to-life groups opposing abortion.

3. People protesting a nuclear power plant.

4. Feminists organizing a march for the Equal Rights Amendment.

5. The gay liberation movement organizing for homosexual rights.

6. Atheists preaching against God.

7. Students organizing a sit-in to shut down the city hall.

In a national opinion poll conducted by Herbert McClosky and Alida Brill in 1978–1979, a majority of Americans would have allowed the first four groups to hold their meetings but would have refused to allow the last three. (Similar findings from another opinion survey are shown in Table 4.8.) Leaders in the communities where this survey was done would have allowed the first five groups to meet. Lawyers and judges in these communities would have allowed all seven to meet.[42]

Clearly community leaders, and especially lawyers and judges, are more tolerant of specific political

activities than are most citizens. But two things need to be said on behalf of the average citizen.

First, Americans are willing to allow many people with whom they disagree to do a great deal politically. In the McClosky-Brill study, for example, the general public supported the right of the movie industry to make movies on any subject it chose, upheld the right of reporters to keep confidential their sources of information, defended the right of newspapers and television stations to hire "radical reporters," believed that college officials should allow nonviolent protest demonstrations by students, and supported freedom of worship for even extremist religious groups.[43]

Second, Americans have become more tolerant over the last few decades. For instance, in the 1970s people were much more willing to allow communists, socialists, and atheists to meet and disseminate their views than they were in the early 1950s, even though Americans in the 1970s were probably no more sympathetic to these causes than they were in the 1950s.[44] Similarly there has been a general increase in the willingness of citizens to say that they would vote for a Catholic, Jew, black, or woman for president (see Figure 4.3).

Nonetheless this majority tolerance for many causes should not blind us to the fact that for most of us there is some group or cause from which we are willing to withhold political liberties—even though we endorse those liberties in the abstract.

If most people dislike one or another group strongly enough to deny it certain political rights that we usually take for granted, how is it that such groups (and such rights) survive? The answer, in part, is that most of us don't act on our beliefs. We rarely take the trouble—or have the chance—to block another person from making a speech or teaching school. And among people who are in a position to deny other people rights—officeholders and political activists, for example—the level of political tolerance is somewhat greater than among the public at large.[45]

But another reason may be just as important. Most of us are ready to deny *some* group its rights, but we usually can't agree on which group that should be. Sometimes we can agree, and then the disliked group may be in for real trouble. As we shall see in Chapter 18, there have been times (1919–1920, and again in the early 1950s) when socialists or com-

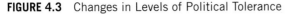

FIGURE 4.3 Changes in Levels of Political Tolerance

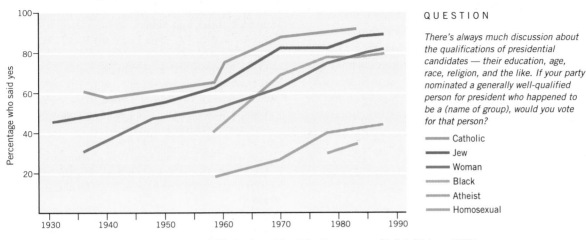

QUESTION

There's always much discussion about the qualifications of presidential candidates — their education, age, race, religion, and the like. If your party nominated a generally well-qualified person for president who happened to be a (name of group), would you vote for that person?

— Catholic
— Jew
— Woman
— Black
— Atheist
— Homosexual

SOURCE: Gallup poll data, various years, as compiled by Professor John Zaller, Department of Political Science, UCLA.

munists were disliked by most people. The government on each occasion took strong actions against them. Today fewer people agree that these left-wing groups are a major domestic threat, and so their rights are now more secure.

Finally, the courts are sufficiently insulated from public opinion that they can act against majority sentiments and enforce constitutional protections (see Chapter 14). Most of us are not willing to give all rights to all groups, but most of us are not judges.

These facts should be a sober reminder that political liberty cannot be taken for granted. Men and women are not, it would seem, born with an inclination to live and let live, at least politically, and many—possibly most—of them never acquire that inclination. Liberty must be learned and protected. Happily the United States during much of its recent history has not been consumed by a revulsion against one group that is strong enough to place its rights in jeopardy.

Nor should any part of society pretend that it is always more tolerant than another. In the 1950s, for example, ultraconservatives outside the universities were attacking the rights of professors to say and teach certain things. In the 1960s and 1970s ultraliberal students and professors inside the universities were attacking the rights of other students and professors to say certain things.

SUMMARY

The American constitutional system is supported by a political culture that fosters a sense of civic duty, that takes pride in the nation's constitutional arrangements, and that provides support (sometimes out of indifference or diversity more than principle) for the exercise of essential civil liberties. In recent decades mistrust of government officials (though not of the system itself) has increased, and confidence in their responsiveness to popular feelings has declined.

Although Americans value liberty in both the political and economic systems, they believe that equality is important only in the political realm. In economic affairs they wish to see equality of opportunity but accept inequality of results.

Not only is our culture generally supportive of democratic rule, it also has certain distinctive features that make our way of governing different from what one finds in other democracies. Americans are preoccupied with their rights, and this fact, combined with a political system that (as we shall see) encourages the vigorous exercise of rights and claims, gives to our political life an *adversarial* style. Unlike Swedes or Japanese, we do not generally reach political decisions by consensus, and we often do not defer to the authority of administrative agencies. American politics, more than that of many other nations, is shot through at every stage with protracted conflict.

But as we shall learn in the next chapter, that conflict is not easily described as always pitting liberals against conservatives. Not only do we have a lot of conflict, it is often messy conflict, a kind of political Tower of Babel. Foreign observers sometimes ask how we stand the confusion. The answer of course is that we have been doing it for over two hundred years. Maybe our Constitution is two centuries old not in spite of this "confusion" but because of it. We shall see.

KEY TERMS

political culture   *p. 80*

civic duty   *p. 80*

political ideology   *p. 81*

civic competence   *p. 85*

work ethic   *p. 90*

class consciousness   *p. 90*

orthodox   *p. 92*

progressive   *p. 92*

political efficacy   *p. 96*

internal efficacy   *p. 96*

external efficacy   *p. 96*

SUGGESTED READINGS

Almond, Gabriel, and Sidney Verba. *The Civic Culture.* Princeton, N.J.: Princeton University Press, 1963. A survey of the political cultures of five nations—the United States, Germany, Great Britain, Italy, and Mexico—as they were in 1959.

Devine, Donald J. *The Political Culture of the United States.* Boston: Little, Brown, 1972. Useful summary of several studies of American political values.

Hartz, Louis. *The Liberal Tradition in America.* New York: Harcourt Brace Jovanovich, 1955. A stimulating interpretation of American political thought since the Founding, emphasizing the notion of a liberal consensus.

Hochschild, Jennifer L. *What's Fair? American Beliefs About Distributive Justice.* Cambridge, Mass.: Harvard University Press, 1981. Revealing, in-depth interviews that compare the attitudes of rich and poor people toward inequality.

Lipset, Seymour Martin. *The First New Nation.* Rev. ed. New York: Norton, 1979. How the origins of American society gave rise to the partially competing values of equality and achievement and the ways in which these values shape political institutions.

McClosky, Herbert, and Alida Brill. *Dimensions of Tolerance: What Americans Believe About Civil Liberties.* New York: Russell Sage Foundation, 1983. How—and whether—different kinds of Americans learn political tolerance.

McClosky, Herbert, and John Zaller. *The American Ethos: Public Attitudes Toward Capitalism and Democracy.* Cambridge, Mass.: Harvard University Press, 1984. Study of the ways in which Americans evaluate political and economic arrangements.

Tocqueville, Alexis de. *Democracy in America.* Edited by Phillips Bradley. 2 vols. New York: Knopf, 1951. First published in 1835–1840, this was and remains the greatest single interpretation of American political culture.

Verba, Sidney, and Gary R. Orren. *Equality in America: The View from the Top.* Cambridge, Mass.: Harvard University Press, 1985. Elite views on political and economic equality.

Wald, Kenneth. *Religion and Politics in the United States,* 2nd ed. Washington, D.C.: Congressional Quarterly Press, 1992. A thoughtful look at how religious beliefs and organizations shape American politics.

PART TWO

Opinions, Interests, and Organizations

"The latent causes of faction are thus sown in the nature of man; and we see them everywhere brought into different degrees of activity, according to the different circumstances of civil society."

— FEDERALIST NO. 10

5

Public Opinion

In the Gettysburg Address Abraham Lincoln said that the United States has a government "of the people, by the people, and for the people." That suggests that the government should do what the people want. If that is the case, it is puzzling that:

• The federal government has a large budget deficit, but the people want a balanced budget.

• Courts order children bused in order to balance the schools racially, but the people oppose busing.

• The Equal Rights Amendment to the Constitution was not ratified, but polls showed that most people supported it.

• President Reagan sent aid to Nicaraguans fighting against the Marxist government there, but the people said they did not think our government should do this.

• Most people believe that there should be a limit on the number of terms to which U.S. senators and members of the U.S. House of Representatives can be elected, but Congress has taken no action on term limits.

Some people, reflecting on the many gaps between what the government does and what the people want, may become cynical and think our system is democratic in name only. That would be a mistake. There are several very good reasons why government policy will often appear to be at odds with public opinion.

First, the Framers of the Constitution did not try to create a government that would do from day to day "what the people want." They created a government for the purpose of achieving certain substantive goals. The preamble to the Constitution lists six of these: "to form a more perfect union, establish justice, ensure domestic tranquility, provide for the common defense, promote the general welfare, and secure the blessings of liberty. . . . "

One means to achieve these goals was popular rule, as provided for by the right of the people to vote

Korean Americans in Los Angeles express their opinion about the riots that burned so many of their stores.

imagine that they tell us what the public believes. That may be true on a few rather simple, clear-cut, and widely discussed issues, but it is not true with respect to most matters on which government must act. The best pollsters know the limits of their methods, and the citizen should know them as well.

Third, the more people are active in and knowledgeable about politics, the more weight their opinions carry in governmental affairs. For most of us, politics ranks way down on the list of things to think about, well below families, jobs, health, sweethearts, entertainment, and sports. Some people, however, are political activists, and so come to know as much about politics as the rest of us know about batting averages, soap operas, and car repair. Not only do these activists, or political elites, *know more* about politics than the rest of us, they *think differently* about it—they have different views and beliefs. The government attends more to the elite views than to popular views, at least on many matters.

In this chapter we shall take a close look at what "public opinion" is, how it is formed, the major cleavages in those opinions, and especially how political elites differ from ordinary citizens. In later chapters we shall examine the workings of political parties, interest groups, and government institutions and consider what impact those workings have on which opinions affect what kinds of policies.

for members of the House of Representatives (and later for senators and presidential electors). But other means were provided as well: representative government, federalism, the separation of powers, a Bill of Rights, and an independent judiciary. These were all intended to be checks on public opinion. In addition the Framers knew that in a nation as large and diverse as the United States, there would rarely be any such thing as "public opinion"; rather there would be many "publics" (that is, factions) holding many opinions. The Framers hoped that the struggle among these many publics would protect liberty (no one "public" would dominate) while at the same time permitting the adoption of reasonable policies that commanded the support of many factions.

Second, it is not as easy as one may suppose to know what the public thinks. We are so inundated these days with public-opinion polls that we may

What Is Public Opinion?

A few years ago some researchers at the University of Cincinnati asked twelve hundred local residents whether they favored passage of the Monetary Control Bill of 1983. About 21 percent said that they favored the bill, 25 percent said that they opposed it, and the rest said that they hadn't thought much about the matter or didn't know.

The members of Congress from Cincinnati would have been surprised to learn of this expression of "public opinion" from their constituents, for there was no such thing as the Monetary Control Bill. The researchers had made it up. Nor is there anything unusual about people in Cincinnati. A few years earlier, about 26 percent of the people questioned in a national survey also expressed opinions on the same piece of "legislation."[1]

Ignorance (or an inclination to pretend that one is informed) is not limited to arcane bits of legislation. In 1986 a national survey found that only a third of the people polled could identify Caspar Weinberger (he was then the secretary of defense) and only 14 percent knew who William Rehnquist was (the chief justice of the United States). Robert Dole was running for president (and according to some polls, doing reasonably well), but only 12 percent of the people could identify him accurately.[2] Given this low level of name recognition, how much confidence should we place in polls that presumably tell us what "the American people" think about our defense policy, the posture of the Supreme Court, and presidential candidates?

Even if people have heard of the matter, how we word the question can dramatically affect the answer we get. Suppose we want to know whether the public believes that the federal government should provide housing for people. In Table 5.1 we see the results obtained from asking that question in three different ways. In the first example people are asked whether they agree or disagree with a one-sided statement ("The federal government should see to it that all people have adequate housing"). A majority agree. In the second example we give people a choice between two statements, one favoring a federal housing policy (mentioned first) and the other favoring individual

TABLE 5.1   The Effects of Question Wording: The Issue of Public Housing

One-sided question		
Do you agree or disagree with the following statement: The federal government should see to it that all people have adequate housing.	Agree: government responsible Disagree: government not responsible	55.0% 45.0%
Two-sided question, government option first		
Some people feel that the federal government should see to it that all people have adequate housing, while others feel each person should provide for his own housing. Which comes *closest* to how you feel about this?	Government responsible Government not responsible	44.6% 55.4%
Two-sided question, government option second		
Some people feel that each person should provide for his own housing, while others feel the federal government should see to it that all people have adequate housing. Which comes *closest* to how you feel about this?	Government responsible Government not responsible	29.5% 70.5%

SOURCE: Howard Schuman and Stanley Presser, *Questions and Answers in Attitude Surveys* (New York: Academic Press, 1981), 70–71.

responsibility ("each person should provide for his own housing"). Given this choice, a small majority now opposes federal housing programs. In the third example the question is repeated, but this time with the individual responsibility option mentioned first. Now over 70 percent of the respondents oppose federal housing programs. Obviously just altering the *order* in which people are presented with options

affects which option they choose and thus what is "public opinion" on housing programs.

Moreover, opinions on public issues may not be stable—that is, firmly held. In January 1980 and again in June of the same year, the same people were asked the same questions. The first had to do with how tough we should be in dealing with Russia, the second with whether spending should be cut on things like health and education programs. As Table 5.2 shows, many people gave one opinion in January and then a different one in June. Of those who said in January that we should cooperate more with Russia, one-quarter said in June that we should get together with Russia. Of those who said in January that the government should cut the services it provides, more than one-quarter said in June that they wanted to keep those services at the same level or expressed a middle-of-the-road position.

In sum, public opinion on many matters suffers from ignorance, instability, and sensitivity to the way the question is worded. This does not mean that the American people are ignorant, unstable, or gullible, only that most Americans do not find it worth their while to spend the amount of time thinking about politics they they spend on their jobs, families, and friends. Moreover just because people do not think much about politics does not mean that democracy is impossible, only that it can work best when people are given relatively simple, clear-cut choices—like those between Democrats and Republicans, or between one presidential candidate and another.

Furthermore our specific attitudes about particular matters may be much less important for the health of the society than our underlying political culture—our commitment, discussed in Chapter 4, to liberty, equality, individualism, and civic duty. As we shall see, different people give different weight to parts of this culture in ways that can be described as producing a political ideology.

TABLE 5.2   Response Stability over Repeated Interviews: Two Examples

AMERICAN RELATIONS WITH RUSSIA[a]

Some people feel it is important for us to try very hard to get along with Russia. Others feel it is a big mistake to try too hard to get along with Russia. Where would you place yourself on this scale, or haven't you thought about this?

Attitudes in **June** 1980	Attitudes in **January** 1980			
	Cooperate	Middle	Tougher	Unsure
Cooperate	**52%**	25%	13%	19%
Middle	14	**24**	17	16
Tougher	23	41	**60**	18
Unsure	10	11	11	**47**
Number	338	153	266	74

LEVEL OF GOVERNMENT SERVICES[b]

Some people think the government should provide fewer services, even in areas such as health and education, in order to reduce spending. Other people feel it is important for the government to continue the services it now provides even if it means no reduction in spending. Where would you place yourself on this scale, or haven't you thought about this?

Attitudes in **June** 1980	Attitudes in **January** 1980			
	Cut	Middle	Keep Same	Unsure
Cut	**54%**	38%	18%	34%
Middle	18	**24**	10	10
Keep same	11	25	**59**	15
Unsure	17	14	13	**41**
Number	362	122	208	138

[a] Respondents were asked to place themselves on a seven-point scale. In this table, points 1, 2, and 3 have been counted as "cooperate"; 4 is counted as "middle"; 5, 6, and 7 have been counted as "tougher."
[b] Points 1, 2, and 3 have been counted as "cut"; 4 is counted as "middle"; 5, 6, and 7 have been counted as "keep same."
SOURCE: National Election Studies, 1980 panel study.

The Origins of Political Attitudes

Because our attitudes are often unstable or uninformed, some critics of American society have argued that we are brainwashed—duped by television or demagogic leaders into thinking one way or another. Often we are told that presidential candidates are "sold" as if they were boxes of soap flakes. Naturally these critics never say that *they* are brainwashed; only the rest of us.

However shallow their analysis, the argument is a serious one. If the government (or the media) can by plan manipulate our political attitudes, then democracy would be a joke. It is akin to what would happen in the marketplace if automobile dealers could "brainwash" us into buying Chevrolets, Fords, Chryslers, or Toyotas. The car manufacturers would no longer have to strive to achieve greater efficiency and produce better products; they would only have to "persuade" us what to like. We would be happy not because we owned a good car but because Madison Avenue told us we owned a good car.

Of course advertising does affect our choice of candidates and policies just as it affects our choice of automobiles. Otherwise why would companies and politicians spend so much money on advertising? But there are real and important limits to the impact of that advertising. Those limits exist because we have learned, independently of government and the market, some things that help us make our own choices.

The Role of the Family

The best-studied (though not necessarily the most important) case of opinion formation is that of party identification. The majority of young people identify with their parents' political party. A study of high school seniors showed that, of these young men and women, almost all (91 percent) knew accurately the presidential preference of their parents, the great majority (71 percent) knew accurately their parents' party identification, and most shared that identification (only 9 percent identified with the party opposite to that of their parents).[3] (See Table 5.3.) This process begins fairly early in life: by the time they are in the fifth grade (age eleven), over half of all schoolchildren identify with one party or the other and another fifth claim to be independents.[4]

Naturally, as people grow older, they become more independent of their parents in many ways, including politically, but there nonetheless remains a great deal of continuity between youthful partisanship, learned from one's parents, and adult partisanship. One study of adults found that around 60 percent still had the party identification—Democrat,

"Yes, son, we're Republicans."

Drawing by Richter; © 1991 The New Yorker Magazine, Inc.

Republican, or independent—of their parents. Of those who differ with at least one parent, the overwhelming majority do so not by identifying with the opposite party but by describing themselves as "independents."[5]

The ability of the family to inculcate a strong sense of party identification has declined in recent years. The proportion of citizens who say they consider themselves to be Democrats or Republicans has become steadily smaller since the early 1950s. This drop has been greatest among those who *strongly* identify with one party or another. In 1952, 22 percent of the voters said they were strong Democrats

TABLE 5.3 Parent and Child Agreement in Party Identification

| | Parents | | |
Child	Democrat	Independent	Republican
Democrat	**66%**	29 %	13 %
Independent	27	**53**	36
Republican	7	17	**51**
Number	914	442	495

SOURCE: M. Kent Jennings and Richard G. Niemi, *The Political Character of Adolescence: The Influence of Families and Schools* (Princeton, N.J.: Princeton University Press, 1974), 41. Copyright © 1974 by Princeton University Press. Reprinted by permission.

and 13 percent said they were strong Republicans; by 1976 only 15 percent claimed to be strong Democrats and 9 percent to be strong Republicans. Accompanying this decline in partisanship has been a sharp rise in the proportion of citizens describing themselves as independents.

Part of this change results from the fact that young voters have always had a weaker sense of partisanship than older ones, and today there are proportionally a larger number of young voters than there were thirty years ago. But the youthfulness of the population cannot explain all the changes, for the decline in partisanship has occurred at all age levels. Moreover those who reached voting age in the 1960s were less apt than those who matured in the 1950s to keep the party identification of their parents.[6]

Though we still tend to acquire some measure of partisanship from our parents, the meaning of that

Religion shapes more aspects of political life in the United States than in almost any other industrialized nation.

identification is far from clear. There are, after all, liberal and conservative Democrats, as well as liberal and conservative Republicans. So far the evidence suggests that children are more independent of their parents in policy preferences than in party identification. The correlation of children's attitudes with parental attitudes on issues involving civil liberties and racial questions is much lower than the correlation of party identification. This may be because issues change from one generation to the next, because children are more idealistic than their parents, or because most parents do not communicate to their children clear, consistent positions on a range of political issues. The family dinner table is not a seminar in political philosophy, but a place where people discuss jobs, school, dates, and chores.

In some families, however, the dinner table *is* a political classroom. Fairly clear political ideologies (a term we shall define in a later section) seem to be communicated to that small proportion of children raised in families where politics is a dominant topic of conversation and political views are strongly held. Studies of the participants in various student radical movements in the 1960s suggested that college radicals were often the sons and daughters of people who had themselves been young radicals; some commentators dubbed them the "red-diaper babies." Presumably, deeply conservative people come disproportionately from families that were also deeply conservative. This transfer of political beliefs from one generation to the next does not appear in large national studies because such a small a proportion is at either the far left or the far right of the political spectrum.

Religion

One way in which the family forms and transmits political beliefs is by its religious tradition. In general, Catholic families are somewhat more liberal on economic issues than white Protestant ones, while Jewish families are much more liberal on both economic and social issues than families of either Catholics or Protestants.[7]

There are two theories as to why this should be so. The first has to do with the **social status** of religious groups in America. When they immigrated to this country, Catholics and Jews were often poor and the object of discrimination. As a result they often affiliated themselves with whichever party and social doctrine seemed most sympathetic to their plight. In many places the Democratic party and a liberal social doctrine seemed to offer the most support. Today Catholics and Jews enjoy greater economic prosperity and face much less discrimination, and so their support for Democrats and liberal candidates has weakened.

The status explanation cannot be the whole story, for if it were simply a matter of low status and discrimination, born-again Christians, many of whom are poor and all of whom are treated with contempt by the national media, would be liberal Democrats.

The second theory emphasizes the content of the **religious tradition** more than the social status of its adherents. In this view the Jewish faith has always emphasized social justice as much as personal rectitude. By contrast evangelical Protestant denominations emphasize personal salvation (becoming "born again") more than questions of social policy. This difference in teachings has led Jews to be disproportionately liberal and fundamentalist Protestants to be disproportionately conservative on many social issues.

Whatever the source, religious differences make for political differences. In Table 5.4 we can see how the religious beliefs of white voters affected their policy preferences in 1986. People who believe that the Bible is God's word and literally true are more likely than those who think the Bible is not inspired by God to favor more defense spending, to want the government to be tougher in its dealings with Russia, to oppose abortions, and to favor prayer in the public schools. (These differences remain essentially the

TABLE 5.4   The Relationship Between Politics and Religion (Among White Voters Only)

Which of these statements comes closest to describing your feelings about the Bible?
The Bible is the actual word of God and is to be taken literally, word for word.
The Bible is the word of God but not everything in it should be taken literally word for word.
The Bible is a book written by men and is not the word of God.

	Believes Bible should be taken literally (36%)	Believes Bible should not be taken literally (50%)	Believes Bible is written by men (14%)
Believes U.S. did the right thing in sending military forces to the Persian Gulf	82%	83%	70%
Favors more defense funding	28	17	9
Believes that abortion should be legal	38	70	90
Opposes government job guarantees	52	51	51
Believes racial and ethnic groups should maintain their distinct cultures	38	31	32
Favors cuts in level of government services and reduced government spending	37	32	33
Believes U.S. would be better off if we stayed home and did not concern ourselves with problems in other parts of the world	30	22	20
Believes government should make special effort to improve social and economic position of blacks	15	18	32
Thinks of himself/herself as a Democrat	29	36	40
Favors a law that would limit members of Congress to twelve years of service	84	83	77
Believes women and men should have equal roles	60	80	90
Considers himself/herself a liberal	13	26	52

SOURCE: American National Election Study, 1992: Pre- and Post-Election Surveys.

TABLE 5.5   The Gender Gap: Differences in Political Views of Men and Women

Issue	Men	Women
Federal spending for welfare programs should be increased.	13%	20%
Abortion should be permitted by law.	65	60
Sexual harassment is a very serious problem in the workplace.	24	38
This country would be better off if we just stayed home and did not concern ourselves with problems in other parts of the world.	21	33
The United States did the right thing in sending military forces to the Persian Gulf.	83	71
All things considered, the Persian Gulf War was worth it.	66	47
I voted for Clinton in 1992.	41	53
Generally speaking, I think of myself as a Democrat.	30	39
The United States should increase defense spending.	22	18
The United States should increase spending on solving the problems of the homeless.	66	78
Over the past year, America's ability to compete in the world economy has gotten better.	18	11

SOURCE: ICPSR American National Election Survey, 1992: Pre- and Post-Election Surveys.

same even after you divide the respondents between those who have a lot of political information and those who have rather little.)

Interestingly there are no significant differences in how people holding differing views of the Bible feel about economic, as opposed to social or foreign-policy, issues. Fundamentalists and nonfundamentalists have about the same opinion on government job guarantees and spending on government services. This suggests that both social status and religious tradition help explain the effect of religion on politics: the poor status of many fundamentalists inclines them to back liberal government economic policies, but the religious tradition of this group leads them to take a conservative position on social and foreign-policy matters.

The Gender Gap

In recent elections much has been made of the **gender gap**—that is, the differences in political views between women and men. In fact such differences have existed for as long as we have records. What has changed about the gender gap is which party benefits from it.

During the 1950s women were more likely to be Republicans than men; since the late 1960s they have been more likely to be Democrats. The reason for the shift is that the political parties have changed their positions on the kinds of issues to which women respond differently than men—certain social questions (such as prohibition and gun control) and foreign policy (especially the threat of war). For example, in the 1930s and 1940s more women than men wanted to ban the sale of liquor and keep the country out of war; this helped the Republicans, who were then more sympathetic to such policies than the Democrats. In 1980 the aversion that women felt to any policy that might increase the risk of war hurt the Republicans, whom they saw being led by a president (Reagan) who was ready to send troops into combat (even so, in 1984 a clear majority of women voted for Reagan).[8]

The gender gap tends to disappear during years in which sex-sensitive policies—war, gun control, or pornography—are not in the limelight and to reemerge during those years in which these topics become hotly partisan. As we see in Table 5.5, the biggest male-female differences are over the use of force and confidence in the future. The gender gap is not unique to the United States; it can be found throughout the world.

Analysts disagree about the electoral significance of the gender gap. One unresolved question is whether, other things being equal, female voters are more likely than male voters to support female candidates. For example, in 1992 there were ten U.S. Senate races with female candidates. As we see in Table 5.6, women gave a higher fraction of their votes to female candidates than did men in all of these races. But the size of the gender gap varied from race to race, and the gender gap was also a party gap. A hard-to-specify fraction of the gender gap in voting reflects the tendency of women to identify more strongly than men with the Democratic party.[9]

Schooling and Information

Studies going back over half a century seem to show that attending college has a big impact on political attitudes, usually making them more liberal. College students are more liberal than the population generally, and students at the most prestigious or selective colleges are the most liberal of all.[10] For example, the undergraduates at Harvard College in 1984 preferred Mondale to Reagan, 61 percent to 28 percent, while the country at large favored Reagan over Mondale, 59 percent to 41 percent.[11] Moreover the longer students stay in college, the more liberal they are, with seniors more liberal than freshmen and graduate students more liberal than undergraduates.[12] Harvard seniors were more supportive of Mondale than Harvard freshmen were. Students studying the social sciences tend to be more liberal than those studying engineering or the physical sciences.[13] As we shall see in the next chapter, having gone to college increases the rate at which people participate in politics.

Why schooling should have this effect on attitudes is not clear. One possibility is that it has nothing to do with schooling, but rather with the individual traits typically possessed by people who go to college and beyond. Some combination of temperament, intelligence, and family background may lead to greater liberalism, with the contents of a college education playing no role at all.

A second possibility is that college and postgraduate schooling expose people to more information about politics from all sources. College graduates, compared to high school graduates, read more newspapers and periodicals, join more organizations and social movements, and participate in more election campaigns and lobbying efforts. Their political beliefs may be shaped by these experiences as much as, or more than, by what they learn in the college classroom. In addition evidence collected by John Zaller shows that the level of political information one has is the best single predictor of being liberal on some kinds of issues, such as civil liberties and civil rights.[14] Information on these matters, he suggests, is today produced by a predominantly liberal cultural elite (see Chapter 10). The longer you stay in school, the more you are exposed to the views of that elite.

The third possibility is that college somehow teaches liberalism. We know that professors are more

TABLE 5.6 The Gender Gap in Selected U.S. Senate Races, 1992

		Men	Women	Gender Gap[a]
Selected Senate races involving women				
California	Barbara Boxer (D)	43%	57%	28%
	Bruce Herschensohn (R)	51	37	
	Dianne Feinstein (D)	50	64	27
	John Seymour (R)	46	33	
Illinois	Carol Moseley Braun (D)	50	57	14
	Richard Williamson (R)	47	40	
Missouri	Geri Rothman-Serot (D)	39	48	17
	Christopher Bond (R)	58	50	
Pennsylvania	Lynn Yeakel (D)	42	52	19
	Arlen Specter (R)	54	45	
Selected Senate races not involving women				
Georgia	Wyche Fowler (D)	47	54	14
	Paul Coverdell (R)	53	46	
New York	Robert Abrams (D)	43	52	18
	Alfonse D'Amato (R)	54	45	
Oregon	Les AuCoin (D)	39	55	31
	Robert Packwood (R)	58	43	

[a] The gender gap is the difference between the margin of support women gave women (or Democratic) candidates and their opponents and the margin of support men gave women (or Democratic) candidates and their opponents.
SOURCE: *The American Enterprise* (January/February 1993): 100.

liberal than members of other occupations, professors at the most prestigious schools are more liberal than those at the less-celebrated ones, professors in the social sciences are more liberal than those in engineering or business, and younger faculty members are more liberal than older ones.[15] (College faculty members often develop a lifestyle that reveals their political convictions. As shown in Table 5.7, a professor who drives a Volvo or Mercedes tends to be politically more liberal than one who drives a Chevrolet or Ford.)

The political disposition of professors is in part the result of the kinds of people who become college teachers, but it is also the result of the nature of intellectual work. Intellectuals require freedom to explore new or unpopular ideas and thus tend to be strong

TABLE 5.7   Automobiles and Ideology: Kinds of Automobiles Owned by College Faculty Members Who Have Differing Political Ideologies (in percentages)

	Political Ideology				
	liberal ←			→	conservative
Automobile	1	2	3	4	5
GM	12%	18%	18%	23%	29%
Ford	15	19	20	22	24
Chrysler	19	22	18	21	20
AMC	21	17	12	23	26
Japanese	22	22	17	20	18
Volkswagen	26	26	16	17	15
Fiat	27	18	30	11	13
Mercedes-Benz	32	19	21	17	11
Volvo	32	19	18	18	14
No car	31	28	23	11	7

NOTE: The more liberal the faculty member, the more likely he or she is to own no car or an imported car, especially a Volvo or a Mercedes-Benz. The more conservative the faculty member, the more likely he or she is to own an American car, especially a General Motors product.

SOURCE: Data from survey of faculty opinion by Everett Carll Ladd, Jr., and Seymour Martin Lipset, 1975. B. Bruce-Briggs, *The War against the Automobile* (New York: Dutton, 1977), 184.

supporters of civil liberties. Intellectuals work with words and numbers to develop general or abstract ideas; frequently they do not take personal responsibility for practical matters. Thus they are often critical of people who do take such responsibility and who, in the management of complex human affairs, inevitably make compromises. Intellectuals are by training and profession skeptical of common opinions, and thus they are often critical of accepted values and existing institutions. They are interested in ideas and the ideal and thus are sometimes disdainful of the interests and institutions of society.

At one time the liberalizing effect of college had only a small impact on national politics because so few persons were college graduates. In 1900 only 6 percent of Americans seventeen years of age had even graduated from high school, and less than 1 percent of twenty-three-year-olds were college graduates. By 1982, 71 percent of all Americans ages twenty-five and over were high school graduates, and 18 percent of those ages twenty-five and over were college graduates.[16] College, or the exposure to ideas and move-

ments that one encounters there, has become, along with the family, an important source of political opinion for the American electorate.

Some people believe that college students today are more conservative than ten or twenty years ago. That is partly true and partly false. As indicated in Table 5.8, contemporary college freshmen are less likely to favor legalizing marijuana or abortion but more willing to support busing to integrate schools. Their opinions about government-sponsored environmental protection are unchanged.

How long the liberalizing effect of college persists depends on a number of factors. One study found that former college students still described themselves as more liberal than their parents seven years after graduation.[17] Another study found that students who changed in college from being conservative to being liberal tended to maintain that liberalism for at least twenty years if they acquired, after graduation, liberal friends and spouses.[18] College graduates who go on to get a postgraduate degree — say, a law degree or a Ph.D. — tend to become decidedly more liberal than those who stop with just a B.A. degree.[19] A scholar who tracked students graduating from college in 1969 found that those who had taken part in protests remained very liberal well into the 1980s, while nonprotesters became somewhat more conservative over the years.[20]

Cleavages in Public Opinion

The way in which political opinions are formed helps explain the cleavages that exist among these opinions and why these cleavages do not follow any single political principle, but instead overlap and crosscut in bewildering complexity. If, for example, the United States were composed almost entirely of white Protestants, the great majority of whom did not attend college, and all of whom lived in the North, there would still be plenty of political conflict — the rich would have different views from the poor; the workers, different views from the farmers — but that conflict would be much simpler to describe and explain. It might even lead to political parties that were more clearly aligned with competing political philosophies than those we now have. In fact, of course, some democratic nations in the world today do have a population very much like the one we have asked you to imagine, and the United States itself, during the first half of the nineteenth century, was overwhelmingly white, Protestant, and without much formal schooling.

Today, however, there are crosscutting cleavages based on race, ethnicity, religion, region, and education, in addition to those created by income and occupation. To the extent that politics is sensitive to public opinion, it is sensitive to a variety of different and even competing publics. Not all these publics have influence proportionate to their numbers or even to their numbers adjusted for the intensity of their feelings. As will be described later, a filtering process occurs that makes the opinions of some publics more influential than those of others.

Whatever this state of affairs may mean for democracy, it creates a messy situation for political scientists. It would be so much easier if everyone's opinion on political affairs reflected some single feature of one's life—one's income, occupation, age, race, or sex. Of course some writers have argued that political opinion *is* a reflection of one such feature, social class, usually defined in terms of income or occupation, but that view, though containing some truth, is beset with inconsistencies: poor blacks and poor whites disagree sharply on many issues involving race; well-to-do Jews and well-to-do Protestants often have opposing opinions on social welfare policy; and low-income elderly people are much more worried about crime than are low-income graduate students. Plumbers and professors may have similar incomes, but they rarely have similar views, and businesspeople in New York City often take a very different view of government from businesspeople in Houston or Birmingham.

In some other democracies a single factor such as class may explain more of the differences in political attitudes than it does in the more socially heterogeneous United States. Most blue-collar workers in America think of themselves as being "middle-class," whereas most such workers in Britain and France describe themselves as "working-class." In England the working class prefers the Labour party by a margin of three to one, while in the United States workers prefer the Democratic party by less than two to one, and in 1980 and 1984 they gave most of their votes to Ronald Reagan.[21]

TABLE 5.8   The Changing College Student

Since the 1970s college freshmen have become more conservative on some issues and more liberal on others.

Issue	Percentage Agreeing	
	1970s[a]	1993
Abolish death penalty	33%	22%
Legalize abortion	83	62
Legalize marijuana	47	28
Increase military spending	39	23
Criminals have too many rights	52	68
Government not doing enough to:		
Control pollution	91	84
Protect consumers	77	72

NOTE: We have no comparable figures for college seniors. Freshmen may change their opinions on these matters while in school.

[a] Exact year the question was asked in 1970s varies between 1970 and 1976, depending on the question.

SOURCE: Richard C. Braungart and Margaret M. Braungart, "Black Colleges: Freshmen Attitudes," *Public Opinion* (May–June 1989): 14. Reprinted with the permission of the American Enterprise Institute for Public Policy Research, Washington, D.C. Updated to 1993 from Alexander W. Astin, William S. Korn, and Ellyne R. Riggs, *The American Freshman* (Los Angeles, CA: UCLA Graduate School of Education, 1993), p. 25.

Social Class

Americans speak of "social class" with embarrassment. The norm of equality tugs at our conscience, urging us to judge people as individuals, not as parts of some social group ("the lower class"). Social scientists speak of "class" with confusion. They know it exists but quarrel constantly about how to define it: By income? Occupation? Wealth? Schooling? Prestige? Personality?

Let's face up to the embarrassment and skip over the confusion. Truck drivers and investment bankers look different, talk differently, and vote differently. There is nothing wrong with saying that the first group consists of "working-class" (or "blue-collar") people and the latter of "upper-class" (or "management") people. Moreover, though different definitions of class produce slightly different groupings of people, most definitions overlap to such an extent that it does not matter too much which we use.

However defined, public opinion and voting have been less determined by class in the United States

The Art of Public-Opinion Polling

A survey of public opinion—popularly called a **poll**—can provide us with a reasonably accurate measure of how people think, provided certain conditions are met. There are five key criteria that must be met in designing and interpreting surveys.

1. **The persons interviewed must be a *random sample* of the entire population.** In a random sample any given person, or any given voter or adult, has an equal chance of being interviewed. Most national surveys draw a sample of between a thousand and fifteen hundred persons by a process called stratified or multi-stage area sampling. The pollster makes a list of all geographical units in the country (say, all counties) and groups (or "stratifies") them by sizes of their populations. The pollster then selects at random units from each group or stratum in proportion to their total population. For example, if one stratum contains counties whose total population is 10 percent of the national population, then in the sample 10 percent of the counties will be drawn from this stratum. Within each selected county, smaller and smaller geographical units (cities, towns, census tracts, blocks) are chosen and then, within the smallest unit, individuals are selected at random (by, for example, choosing the occupant of every fifth house). The key is to stick to the sample and not let people volunteer to be interviewed—volunteers often have views different from those who do not volunteer.

2. **The questions must be comprehensible.** The questions must ask people about things of which they have some knowledge and some basis for forming an opinion. Most people know, at least at election time, whom they would prefer as president; most people also have views about what they think the most important national problems are. But relatively few voters will have any opinion about our policy toward El Salvador (if indeed they have even heard of it) or about the investment tax credit. If everybody refused to answer questions about which they are poorly informed, no problem would arise, but unfortunately many of us like to pretend that we know things that in fact we don't, or to be helpful to interviews by inventing opinions on the spur of the moment.

3. **The questions must be asked fairly.** They should be worded in clear language, without the use of "loaded" or "emotional" words. They must give no indication of what the "right" answer is, but offer a reasonable explanation, where necessary, of the consequences of each possible answer. For example, in 1971 the Gallup poll asked people whether they favored a proposal "to bring home all U.S. troops [from Vietnam] before the end of the year." Two-thirds of the public agreed with that. Then the question was asked in a different way: Do you agree or disagree with a proposal to withdraw all U.S. troops by the end of the year "regardless of what happens there [in Vietnam] after U.S. troops leave"? In this form substantially less than half the public agreed.

4. **The answer categories offered to a person must be carefully considered.** This is no problem when there are only two candidates for office—say, Michael Dukakis and George Bush—and you want only to know which one the voters prefer. But it can be a big problem when you want more complex information. For example, if you ask people (as does George Gallup) whether they "approve" or "disapprove" of how the president is handling his job, you will get one kind of answer—let us say that 55 percent approve and 45 percent disapprove. On the other hand if you ask them (as does Louis Harris)

---

than in Europe, and the extent of class cleavage has declined in the last few decades in both the United States and Europe. In the 1950s V. O. Key, Jr., found that differences in political opinion were closely associated with occupation. He noted that people holding managerial or professional jobs had distinctly more conservative views on social welfare policy and more internationalist views on foreign policy than did manual workers.[22]

During the next decade this pattern changed greatly. Opinion surveys done in the late 1960s showed that business and professional people had views quite similar to those of manual workers on such matters as the poverty program, health insur-

how they rate the job the president is doing, "excellent, pretty good, only fair, or poor," you will get very different results. It is quite possible that only 46 percent will pick such positive answers as "excellent" or "pretty good," and the rest will pick the negative answers, "only fair" and "poor." If you are president, you can choose to believe Mr. Gallup (and feel pleased) or Mr. Harris (and be worried). The differences in the two polls do not arise from the competence of the two pollsters, but entirely from the choice of answers that they include with their questions.

5. **Not every difference in answers is a significant difference.** A survey is based on a sample of people. Select another sample, by equally randomized methods, and you might get slightly different results. This difference is called a **sampling error,** and

its likely size can be computed mathematically. In general the bigger the sample and the bigger the differences between the percentage of people giving one answer and the percentage giving another, the smaller the sampling error. If a poll of fifteen hundred voters reveals that 47 percent favor Bill Clinton, we can be 95 percent certain that the *actual* proportion of *all* voters favoring Clinton is within three percentage points of this figure—that is, it lies somewhere between 44 and 50 percent. In a close race an error of this size could be quite important. It could be reduced by using a bigger sample, but the cost of interviewing a sample big enough to make the error much smaller is huge.

As a result of sampling error and for other reasons, it is very hard for pollsters to predict the winner in a close

election. Since 1952 every major national poll has in fact picked the winner of the presidential election, but there may have been some luck involved in such close races as the 1960 Kennedy-Nixon and the 1976 Carter-Ford contests. In 1980 the polls greatly underestimated the Reagan vote, partly because many voters made up their minds at the last minute and partly because a bigger percentage of Carter supporters decided not to vote at all. In contrast, pollsters did remarkably well in forecasting the results of the 1992 presidential election, a volatile three-way race between Bill Clinton, George Bush, and Ross Perot. Although they tended to overestimate Clinton's margin and to underestimate Perot's, twenty of the most frequently cited national polls came close to predicting the actual results. Polling is not an exact science, but done right, it is a highly skilled art.

ance, American policy in Vietnam, and government efforts to create jobs.[23]

The voting patterns of different social classes have also become somewhat more similar. Class voting has declined sharply since the late 1940s in the United States, France, Great Britain, and West Germany and declined moderately in Sweden.

Class differences remain, of course. Unskilled workers are more likely than affluent white-collar workers to be Democrats and to have liberal views on economic policy. And when economic issues pinch—for example, when farmers are hurting or steelworkers are being laid off—the importance of economic interests in differentiating the opinions of various groups rises sharply. Moreover there is some evidence that during the Reagan administration, income once again began to make a large difference in the party affiliation of voters.

Why should social class, defined along income lines, have become less important over the long term? One reason has to do largely with schooling. At one time the income of people did not depend so heavily as it now does on having educational credentials. Most people had only a high school education, whatever their job might be, and only a small minority had a college or postgraduate degree. Today access to higher-paying jobs (outside of sports and entertainment) is increasingly restricted to people with extensive schooling. Since, as we have seen, college and (especially) postgraduate education tends to make people more liberal than they would otherwise be, the arrival of millions of college graduates, lawyers, and Ph.D.'s into the ranks of the financially affluent has brought into the upper classes a more liberal political outlook than once was the case.

Another reason is that the issues that now lead us to choose which party to support and determine

Hispanic voters are divided between relatively liberal Mexicans and Puerto Ricans and relatively conservative Cubans.

whether we think of ourselves as liberals or conservatives have increasingly become noneconomic issues. In recent years our political posture has been shaped by the positions we take on race relations, abortion, school prayer, arms control, and environmentalism, issues that do not clearly affect the rich differently from the poor (or at least do not affect them as differently as do the union movement, the minimum wage, and unemployment). Moral, symbolic, and foreign-policy matters do not divide rich and poor in the same way as economic ones. Thus we have many well-off people who think of themselves as liberals because they take liberal positions on these noneconomic matters, and many not-so-well-off people who think of themselves as conservatives because that is the position they take on these issues.

Race and Ethnicity

If class has become a less clear-cut political cleavage, race has become more so. Whites and blacks differ profoundly over whether children should be bused to achieve racially balanced schools and whether a person should be able to sell his or her home to anyone, even if it means refusing to sell it to a black. The differences extend to nonracial matters as well. Whites are more likely than blacks to support the death penalty for murder and to favor increased spending on national defense; they are less likely to endorse national health insurance. In the 1960s blacks were more opposed than whites to the war in Vietnam. An issue that divides blacks and whites in the 1990s is how to remedy the effects of past racial discrimination. As Seymour Martin Lipset has observed, "every national survey still shows that a sizable majority of whites is opposed to remedying the effects of past discrimination by giving special consideration to the less formally qualified with respect to hiring or school admissions."[24] For example, a 1991 Gallup poll asked, "Do you believe that because of past discrimination against black people, qualified blacks should receive preference over equally qualified whites in such matters as getting into college or getting jobs?" Only 19 percent of whites compared to 48 percent of blacks responded positively.[25]

There are, however, many issues on which the two races feel pretty much the same, such as allowing the police to search the homes of known drug dealers without a warrant, opposing a woman's right to abortion on demand, and opposing the legalization of marijuana (see Table 5.9). And despite broad differences over how to remedy the effects of past discrimination, majorities of both blacks and whites oppose policies requiring specific quotas and numerical goals for integration.[26]

Blacks have become the most consistently liberal group within the Democratic party.[27] Nevertheless a majority of blacks believe they are as a group better off today than they were ten years ago and that their children's opportunities will be better yet.[28]

There appears to be less class cleavage among blacks than among whites—that is, the differences in opinion between poor and better-off blacks is less than it is between poor and better-off whites.[29] This means that at every income level blacks are more liberal than whites.* However, there is a significant gap between the leaders of black organizations and black people generally. A 1985 survey of over one hundred black leaders and six hundred black citizens found that the leaders were much more likely than the rank and file to favor abortions, school busing, affirmative action, and forcing U.S. corporations to pull out of South Africa. Most black leaders deny that blacks are making progress, while most black citizens think they are.[30] This cleavage between the black political elite and black voters should not surprise us; as we shall see, there are similar cleavages between white political elites and white voters.

Though there are an estimated 20 million Hispanics and 7 million Asian-Americans in this country, they tend to be concentrated in a few locations, and so not enough appear in the usual national opinion polls to permit us to say much about their views.

However, a survey of ethnic groups in California, a state where fully one-third of all recent immigrants to this country live, gives us some knowledge of how

TABLE 5.9   White versus Black Opinions

Issue	Whites	Blacks
Favor busing children to achieve better racial balance in schools[a]	18%	67%
Favor homeowner's right to refuse to sell to black[a]	55	26
Favor spending more on national defense[b]	52	29
Favor national health insurance by government[c]	47	75
Favor mandatory death penalty for drug traffickers[d]	74	64
Favor allowing police to search houses of known drug dealers without a court order[d]	57	56
Favor woman's right to obtain a legal abortion if she wants it for any reason[d]	36	39
Do *not* oppose the death penalty[c]	74	43
Favor registration of young men for draft[b]	85	68
Favor harsher treatment of criminals by the courts[a]	86	76
Favor legalization of marijuana use[a]	25	29

SOURCES: [a] *Public Opinion* (April–May 1981): 32–40, citing polls by Gallup, NORC, and ABC News–*Washington Post*. [b] Philip E. Converse et al., *American Social Attitudes, 1947–1978* (Cambridge, Mass.: Harvard University Press, 1980), 109. [c] Robert S. Erikson, Norman R. Luttbeg, and Kent L. Tedin, *American Public Opinion,* 2d ed. (New York: Wiley, 1980), 169, citing polls by University of Michigan and Gallup. [d] Adapted from *The American Enterprise* (September/October 1991): 84, citing polls by NORC and Princeton Survey Associates, Inc.

Latinos and Asian-Americans feel about political parties and issues. As you can see in Table 5.10, Latinos identify themselves as Democrats, but much less so than do blacks, and Asian-Americans are even more identified with the Republican party than Anglo-whites. On such issues as spending on the military and welfare programs, prayer in the public schools, and the imposition of the death penalty for murder, Asian-American views are much more like those of Anglo-whites than either blacks or Hispanics. Latinos are somewhat more liberal than Anglos or Asian-Americans, but much less liberal than blacks, except with respect to bilingual education programs.[31]

These figures conceal important differences within these ethnic groups. For example, Japanese-Americans are among the more conservative of

---

*One problem in interpreting opinion polls on race issues is that responses will differ depending on whether the interviewee is being questioned by a person of the same or a different race. In 1986 a *New York Times*–CBS poll found that 56 percent of all blacks said that they approved of how Reagan was handling the presidency, but a *Washington Post*–ABC poll, asking the same question at about the same time, found that only 23 percent of all blacks said that they approved of Reagan as president. One major difference: the *Washington Post*–ABC poll used only black interviewers to question blacks, and they prefaced their questions by saying that they were doing a survey of blacks only, perhaps inducing respondents to "think black." There is no way to know which responses were the "right" ones.

TABLE 5.10 Party Identification and Political Attitudes of Ethnic Groups in California (1984)

	Anglo-White	Black	Latino	Asian-American
Party identification				
Democrat	37%	78%	54%	35%
Republican	35	3	20	38
In between, other	28	18	26	27
Political attitude				
Favor increased military spending	32	18	28	38
Favor increased welfare spending	59	84	73	66
Favor prayer in public schools	50	62	53	46
Favor death penalty for murder	75	47	57	73
Favor abortion on demand	60	47	40	53
Favor bilingual education programs	41	63	69	51
Number	409	335	593	305

SOURCE: Bruce Cain and Roderick Kiewit, "California's Coming Minority Majority," *Public Opinion* (February–March 1986): 50–52. Reprinted with permission of American Enterprise Institute for Public Policy Research.

Asian-Americans, whereas Korean-Americans (perhaps because they are among the most recent immigrants) are more liberal. Similarly, Latinos, the fastest-growing ethnic group in the United States, are a diverse mix of Cuban-Americans, Mexican-Americans, and Puerto Ricans with distinct political views. A study of Latino voting in the 1988 presidential election found that Mexican-Americans were the most Democratic, Cuban-Americans the most Republican, and Puerto Ricans were in between the other two groups.[32]

Region

It is widely believed that geographic region affects political attitudes and in particular that southerners and northerners disagree importantly on many policy questions. As we will see, southern members of Congress tend to vote differently—and more conservatively—than northern ones, and it should stand to reason that this is because their constituents, southern voters, expect them to vote differently. At one time white southerners were conspicuously less liberal than easterners, midwesterners, or westerners on such questions as aid to minorities, legalizing marijuana, school busing, and enlarging the rights of

those accused of crimes. Although more conservative on these issues, they held views on economic issues similar to those of whites in other regions of the country. This helps to explain why the South was for so long a part of the Democratic party coalition: on national economic and social welfare policies, southerners expressed views not very different from northerners. That coalition was always threatened, however, by the divisiveness produced by issues of race and liberty.

Today the political views of white southerners are less distinct from those of whites living in other parts of the country. As Table 5.11 illustrates, the proportion of white Protestants in the South who gave liberal answers to questions regarding both civil liberties/civil rights issues and economic/welfare issues in 1992 was only somewhat different from that of white Protestants in other regions. (The table is limited to white Protestants to eliminate the effect of the very different proportions of Catholics, Jews, blacks, and other ethnic groups living in various regions.)

The southern lifestyle is in fact different from that of other regions of the country. The South has, on the whole, been more accommodating to business enterprise and less so to organized labor than, for example, the Northeast; it gave greater support to the

TABLE 5.11   Does the South Differ?

Percentage giving "liberal" response among white Protestants living in different regions, 1992.

Issue	Northeast[a]	North Central[b]	South[c]	West[d]
Economic and welfare issues				
More government services	26.4	27.4	28.8	26.5
More government job guarantees	23.0	19.2	20.7	21.2
Increase social security	55.1	39.7	43.8	42.0
Cut defense spending	47.3	36.4	37.0	44.4
Civil rights and civil liberties issues				
Government aid to black citizens	10.4	13.8	12.0	21.7
Laws to protect homosexuals against job discrimination	61.1	45.8	50.3	56.8
Women's equality	72.5	66.8	72.1	75.8
Right to abortion	50.0	40.6	34.7	53.8
Average percentage liberal, all issues	43.2	36.2	37.4	42.8

[a] Northeast: Connecticut, Massachusetts, New Hampshire, New Jersey, New York, Pennsylvania
[b] North Central: Illinois, Indiana, Iowa, Kansas, Michigan, Minnesota, Missouri, Nebraska, Ohio, Wisconsin
[c] South: Alabama, Arkansas, Delaware, District of Columbia, Florida, Georgia, Louisiana, Maryland, North Carolina, Tennessee, Texas, Virginia, West Virginia
[d] West: Arizona, California, Colorado, Oregon, Washington, Wyoming
SOURCE: Compiled by Meenekshi Bose, using data from the ICPSR *1992 American National Election Survey*, University of Michigan.

third-party candidacy of George Wallace in 1968, which was a protest against big government and the growth of national political power as well as against civil rights; and it was in the South that the greatest opposition arose to income-redistribution plans, such as the Family Assistance Plan of 1969 (to be discussed in Chapter 17). Moreover there is some evidence that white southerners became by the 1970s more conservative than they had been in the 1950s, at least when compared to white northerners.[33] Finally, white southerners have become less attached to the Democratic party: whereas over three-fourths described themselves as Democrats in 1952, only a third did by 1990 (see Figure 5.1).

These changes in the South can have great significance, as we shall see in the next three chapters when we consider how elections are fought out. It is enough for now to remember that, without the votes of the southern states, no Democrat except Lyndon Johnson in 1964 would have been elected president from 1940 through 1976. (Without the South, Roosevelt would have lost in 1944, Truman in 1948, Kennedy in 1960, and Carter in 1976. And even

Governor Bill Clinton of Arkansas made his successful bid for the Democratic presidential nomination by finding positions that both northern and southern Democrats could support.

though Carter carried the South, he did not win a majority of white southern votes.) Clinton won in 1992 without carrying the South, but that was a three-man race.

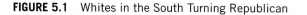

FIGURE 5.1 Whites in the South Turning Republican

Percentage of southern white registered voters who identified with each party

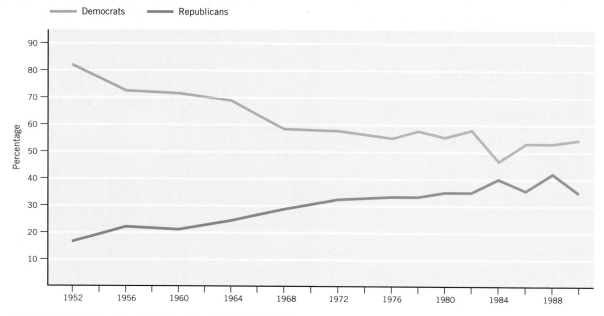

SOURCE: ICPSR National Election Studies, Cumulative Data File, 1952–1990.

Political Ideology

Up to now the words **liberal** and **conservative** have been used here as if everyone agreed on what they meant and as if they accurately described general sets of political beliefs held by large segments of the population. Neither of these assumptions is correct. Like many useful words—*love, justice, happiness*—they are as vague as they are indispensable.

When we refer to people as liberals, conservatives, socialists, or radicals, we are implying that they have a patterned set of beliefs about how government and other important institutions in fact operate and how they ought to operate, and in particular about what kinds of policies government ought to pursue. They are said to display to some degree a **political ideology**—that is, a coherent and consistent set of beliefs about who ought to rule, what principles rulers ought to obey, and what policies rulers ought to pursue. Political scientists measure the extent to which people have a political ideology in two ways:

first, by seeing how frequently people use broad political categories (such as "liberal," "conservative," "radical") to describe their own views or to justify their preferences for various candidates and policies and, second, by seeing to what extent the policy preferences of a citizen are consistent over time or based at any one time on certain consistent principles. This second method involves a simple mathematical procedure: measuring how accurately one can predict a person's view on a subject at one time from having known his or her view on that subject at an earlier time or measuring how accurately one can predict a person's view on one issue from knowing his or her view on a different issue. The higher the accuracy of such predictions (or correlations), the more we say a person's political opinions display "constraint" or ideology. Despite annual fluctuations, ideological self-identification surveys typically find that moderates are the largest group among American voters, conservatives the second largest, and liberals the smallest (see Figure 5.2).

Except when asked by pollsters most Americans do not actually employ the words *liberal* or *conservative* in explaining or justifying their preferences for candidates or policies; not many more than half can give plausible meanings for these terms; and there are relatively low correlations among the answers to similar questions given by people at different times and to comparable questions asked at one time. From this, many scholars have concluded that the great majority of Americans do not think about politics in an ideological or even in a very coherent manner and make little use of such concepts, so dear to political commentators and professors alike, as "liberal" or "conservative."[34]

Consistent Attitudes

This does not settle the question entirely, however. Critics of the view that Americans are nonideological have argued that people can have general, and strongly felt, political predispositions even though they are not able to use such terms as *liberal* correctly. Moreover public opinion polls must of necessity ask rather simple questions, and the apparent "inconsistency" in the answers people give in different time periods may mean only that the nature of the problem and the wording of the question have changed in ways not obvious to people analyzing the surveys.[35]

People can have an ideology without using the words *liberal* or *conservative* and without having beliefs that line up neatly along the conventional liberal-versus-conservative dimension. We saw in Chapter 4 that most Americans had a distinctive political culture—a belief in freedom, equality (of political condition and economic opportunity), and civic duty. They also attach a great deal of importance to "Americanism." Though these words may be vague, they are not trivial—at some level they are an ideology.

Scholars regularly discover that people have what some would consider "inconsistent" opinions. For example, a voter may want the government to spend more on education and the environment *and* he or she may favor a bigger military budget and a tough posture toward unfriendly nations. These views are "inconsistent" only in the sense that they violate a political rule of thumb, common in the media and in national policy debates, that expects people who fa-

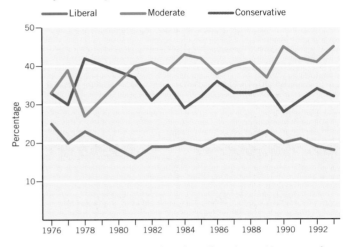

FIGURE 5.2 Ideological Self-Identification, 1976–1993

QUESTION

How would you describe your views on most political matters? Generally, do you think of yourself as a liberal, moderate, or conservative?

SOURCE: *The American Enterprise* (March/April 1993): 84, citing surveys by CBS/*New York Times*.

vor a bigger welfare state to favor a smaller military establishment as well. That is the conventional "liberal" view. Similarly the rule of thumb in the media is that people who support a strong military posture are also going to favor prayer in the schools and oppose abortion on demand. That is the conventional "conservative" position. But of course many citizens violate these rules of thumb, picking and choosing their positions without regard to the conventional definitions of liberalism and conservatism.

What Do *Liberalism* and *Conservatism* Mean?

Just because most people are not consistent liberals or consistent conservatives does not prove that these terms are meaningless. As we shall see, they are very meaningful for political elites. And they even have meaning for ordinary citizens, but this meaning is a complicated one that requires careful analysis.

The definition of these words has changed since they first came into use in the early nineteenth century. At that time a liberal was a person who favored personal and economic liberty—that is, freedom from the controls and powers of the state. An economic liberal, for example, supported the free market and opposed government regulation of trade. A conservative was originally a person who opposed the excesses of the French Revolution and its emphasis on personal freedom, and favored instead a restoration of the power of the state, the church, and the aristocracy.

Beginning around the time of Franklin Roosevelt and the New Deal, the meaning of these terms began to change. Roosevelt used the term *liberal* to refer to his political program—one that called for an active

national government that would intervene in the economy, create social welfare programs, and assist certain groups (such as organized labor) to acquire greater bargaining power. In time the opponents of an activist national government began using the term *conservative* to describe themselves. (Barry Goldwater, in 1964, was the first major U.S. politician to proclaim himself a conservative.) In general a conservative favored a free market rather than a regulated one, states' rights over national supremacy, and greater reliance on individual choice in economic affairs.

Though the meaning of these terms changed, it did not in the process become more precise. Two persons may describe themselves as liberals even though the first favors both the welfare state and a strong national defense and the second favors the welfare state but wants a sharp reduction in military spending. Similarly one conservative may favor enforcement of laws against drug abuse and another may believe that the government should let people decide for themselves what drugs to take. Once liberals favored laws guaranteeing equality of opportunity among the races; now some liberals favor "affirmative-action" plans involving racial quotas or goals. Once conservatives opposed American intervention abroad; today many conservatives believe the United States should play an active role in foreign affairs.

In view of this confusion one is tempted to throw up one's hands in disgust and consign words like *liberal* and *conservative* to the garbage can. While understandable, such a reaction would be a mistake because, in spite of their ambiguities, these words remain in general use, convey some significant meaning, and point to real differences between, for example, the liberal and conservative wings of the Democratic and Republican parties. Our task is to clarify these differences by showing the particular meanings these words have.

Various Categories

We can imagine certain broad categories of opinion to which different people subscribe. These categories are found by analyzing the answers people give to dozens of questions about political issues. Different analysts come up with slightly different categories, but on the whole there is a substantial amount of agreement. Three categories in particular have proved useful.

POLITICALLY **P.S.** SPEAKING

Ideology: You Versus Your Enemies

A political ideology is a coherent set of political rules for explaining how the world works and prescribing how it ought to work.

Liberals describe

- *themselves* as "caring," "committed," "an activist," or "progressive";
- *their enemies* as "reactionary," "right-wing," and "extremist."

Conservatives describe

- *themselves* as "moderate," "responsible," "prudent," or "mainstream";
- *their enemies* as "crackpot," "knee-jerk," "left-wing," or "bleeding-heart."

An easy way to tell whether a politician, newspaper, or magazine is liberal or conservative is to see whether, in describing liberals or conservatives, it uses terms from the "nice" (themselves) list or the "hostile" (their enemies) list.

The first category involves questions about government policy with regard to the *economy*. We will describe as liberal those persons who favor government efforts to ensure that everyone has a job, to spend more money on medical and educational programs, and to increase rates of taxation for well-to-do persons.

The second involves questions about *civil rights* and race relations. We will describe as liberal those who favor strong federal action to desegregate schools, to increase hiring opportunities for minorities, to provide compensatory programs for minorities, and to enforce civil-rights laws strictly.

The third involves questions about public and political *conduct*. We will describe as liberal those who are tolerant of protest demonstrations, who favor legalizing marijuana and in other ways wish to "decriminalize" so-called victimless crimes, who emphasize protecting the rights of the accused over punishing criminals, and who see the solution to crime in eliminating its causes rather than in getting tough with offenders.

Analyzing Consistency

Now it is obvious that people can take a liberal position on one of these issues and a conservative position on another without feeling in the slightest degree "inconsistent." Several studies, such as those by Herbert McClosky and John Zaller and by Seymour Martin Lipset and Earl Raab, show that this is exactly what most people do.[36]

This fact does not mean that people are unideological but that we need more than two labels to describe their ideology. If we considered all possible combinations of the three sets of views described above, we would have nine categories of opinion; if people always stuck with whichever category they were in, we would need nine different ideological labels to describe those people.

To invent those labels and describe the people who have those views would take countless pages and bore the reader to tears. To avoid all that pain and suffering, let's use just two sets of views—those on economic policy and those on personal conduct—and describe the kinds of people that have each of the four combinations (liberal or conservative on each set). The data are from a study by William S. Maddox and Stuart A. Lilie.

1. *Pure liberals:* These people are liberal on both economic policy and personal conduct. They want the government to reduce economic inequality, regulate business, tax the rich heavily, cure the (presumably) economic causes of crime, allow abortions, protect the rights of the accused, and guarantee the broadest possible freedoms of speech and press.

   Number: In 1980 about one-fourth of the population were pure liberals.

   Traits: Pure liberals are more likely than the average citizen to be young, college-educated, and either Jewish or nonreligious. They voted heavily against Ronald Reagan.

2. *Pure conservatives:* These people are conservative on both economic and conduct issues. They want the government to cut back on the welfare state, allow the market to allocate goods and services, keep taxes low, lock up criminals, and curb forms of conduct they regard as antisocial.

   Number: In 1980 about one-sixth of the population were pure conservatives.

   Traits: Pure conservatives are more likely than the average citizen to be older, to have higher incomes, to be white, and to live in the Midwest. They voted overwhelmingly for Ronald Reagan.

3. *Libertarians:* These people are conservative on economic matters and liberal on social ones. The common theme is that they want a small, weak government—one that has little control over either the economy or the personal lives of citizens.

   Number: In 1980 about one-sixth of the population were libertarians.

   Traits: Libertarians are more likely than the average citizen to be young, college-educated, and white, to have more high incomes and no religion, and to live in the West. They voted for Ronald Reagan, but many also supported the third-party ticket of John Anderson.

4. *Populists:* These people are liberal on economic matters and conservative on social ones. They want a government that will reduce economic inequality and control business, but they also want it to regulate personal conduct, lock up criminals, and permit school prayer.

CRITICAL ✪ THINKING

Public Opinion on Homosexuality: Liberal, Conservative, or Neither?

When President Clinton announced his plan to end the U.S. military's ban on homosexuals, leaders on both sides of the issue claimed that the people were on their side. But numerous surveys indicate that public opinion is much more complicated than such assertions imply.

In thirteen national surveys conducted between 1973 and 1991, an average of about 71 percent of all Americans agreed with the statement that "homo-

sexual relations between adults are always wrong." But during these same years, Americans became more likely to agree that "homosexuality should be considered an acceptable lifestyle." Whether people agree that homosexuality is acceptable depends somewhat on their sex, age, party affiliation, and schooling. Men, older persons, Republicans, and those without a high school education are least tolerant; women, younger persons, Democrats, and people with a postgraduate

education are most tolerant. But even with all of these differences, most people in every group think homosexuality is wrong.

Opinion on the issue of allowing homosexuals in the military is much more closely divided than is opinion on the morality of homosexuality. In 1992, 50 percent supported the ban, while 43 percent were in favor of lifting it. The strongest opposition came from within the military: 74 percent of enlisted personnel supported the ban; only 18 percent wanted it ended.

However, attitudes toward gays and lesbians in the military are not the same as feelings about them in other occupations. In 1992 large majorities felt that it was all right to hire homosexuals as salespersons, doctors, high school teachers, and members of the president's cabinet. In 1993 the public was evenly split as to whether "civil rights laws" should be extended to "include homosexuals."

Clearly, public opinion on this matter is complicated and changing. Labels such as *liberal* and *conservative* are not very precise.

SOURCES: *The American Enterprise* (March/April 1993): 82, 83; the National Opinion Research Center; the Gallup Organization; *The Gallup Poll Monthly* (April 1993): 33.

Number: In 1980 about one-fourth of the population were populists.

Traits: Populists are more likely than the average citizen to be older, poorly educated, low-income, religious, and female, and to live in the South or Midwest. In 1980 they voted for Jimmy Carter, but in 1984 they voted for Reagan.[37]

Obviously this classification is an oversimplification. There are many exceptions, and the number of people in each category changes from time to time. Moreover this categorization leaves out about one-seventh of the population—their views do not fit any of these categories. Nonetheless it is a useful way to explain how complex are the political ideologies in this country and why such terms as *liberal* and *conservative*, in their "pure" form, only describe the views of relatively few people.

Political Elites

There is one group that can be classified as liberals or conservatives in a pure sense, and it is made up of people who are in the **political elite**. By "elite" we do not mean people who are "better" than others. *Elite* is a technical term used by social scientists to refer to people who have a disproportionate amount of some valued resource—money, schooling, prestige, athletic ability, political power, or whatever. Every society, capitalist or communist, has an elite because in every society government officials will have more power than ordinary folk, some persons will make more money than others, and some people will be more popular than others. (In the former Soviet Union they even had an official name for the political elite—the *nomenklatura*.)

In this country we often refer to the political elite as "activists"—people who hold office, run for office, work in campaigns or on newspapers, lead interest groups and social movements, and speak out on public issues. Being an activist is not an all-or-nothing proposition; people will display differing degrees of activism, from full-time politicians to persons who occasionally get involved in a campaign (see Chapter 6). But the more a person is an activist, the more likely he or she will display ideological consistency on the conventional liberal-conservative spectrum.

The reasons for this greater consistency seem to be information and peers. First, information: In general the better informed people are about politics and the more interest they take in politics, the more likely they are to have consistently liberal or conservative views.[38] This higher level of information and interest may lead them to find relationships among issues that others don't see and to learn from the media and elsewhere what are the "right" things to believe. This does not mean that there are no differences within liberal elites (or within conservative ones), only that the differences occur within a liberal (or conservative) consensus that is more well defined, more consistent, and more important to those who share it than would be the case among ordinary citizens.

Second, peers: Politics does not make strange bedfellows. On the contrary, politics is a process of likes attracting likes. The more active you are in

Activists tend to take political ideology more seriously than do most voters.

Public Opinion on Abortion: Liberal, Conservative, or Neither?

*T*he media often depict abortion as a hotly divisive issue that pits pro-choice liberals against pro-life conservatives. But numerous surveys indicate that public opinion on abortion transcends conventional ideological definitions. The politics of abortion are complex because most people's ideas and feelings about abortion are complex. For example:

- Between 1975 and 1992 the majority of Americans believed that abortion should be legal "only under certain circumstances." There were no national majorities either for the position that abortion should be "legal under any circumstances" or for the position that it should be "illegal in all circumstances."[a]

- Between 1973 and 1989 most Americans *favored* a woman's right to obtain a legal abortion if her health was seriously endangered by the pregnancy, if she became pregnant as the result of rape, or if there was a strong chance of a serious defect in the baby.[b]

- Over the same years most Americans *opposed* a woman's right to obtain a legal abortion for any of the following reasons: she had a low income (or was unable to afford more children), she was unmarried and did not want to marry the child's father, or she was married but did not want to have any more children.[b]

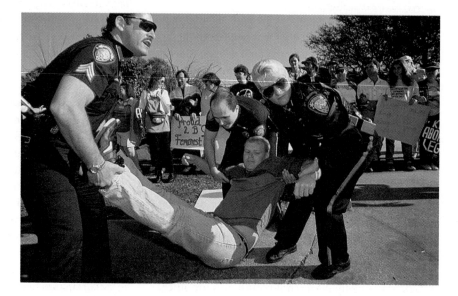

- Democratic leaders and activists tend to be strongly pro-choice; their Republican counterparts tend to be strongly pro-life. But rank-and-file members of the two parties hold strikingly similar views on the issue. In surveys taken from 1984 through 1988, 34 percent of those who identified themselves as strongly committed Democrats said they favored abortion for any reason and 66 percent opposed abortion on demand. Among strong Republicans the distribution was identical—34 percent in favor, 66 percent opposed.[c]

- Jewish voters, women with post-graduate degrees, and persons with no religion are the most consistently pro-choice; born-again Christian voters, Asian-Americans, and persons who did not graduate from high school are the most strongly pro-life.[d] However, even among these groups there are many individual differences of opinion.

SOURCES: (a) *The American Enterprise,* May/June 1992, p. 99, citing surveys by the Gallup Organization. (b) *Public Opinion,* May/June 1989, p. 37, citing surveys by NORC (1975–1988) and the *Los Angeles Times* (1989). (c) Everett Carll Ladd, "The Partisan Consequences," *Public Opinion* (May/June 1989): 6, analyzing and citing data from NORC surveys (1984–1988). (d) *The American Enterprise* (January/February 1993): 103, citing 1992 surveys by the Voter Research & Surveys Consortium.

politics, the more you will associate with people who agree with you on some issues; the more time you spend with those people, the more your other views will shift to match theirs.

The greater ideological consistency of political elites can be seen in the case of Congress. As we shall

note in Chapter 11, Democratic members of Congress tend to be consistently liberal and Republican members of Congress tend to be consistently conservative—*far more* consistently than Democratic voters and Republican voters. By the same token, we shall see in Chapter 7 that the delegates to presidential nominating conventions are far more ideological (liberal in the Democratic convention, conservative in the Republican one) than is true of voters who identify with the Democratic or Republican parties.

Is There a "New Class"?

Some writers have speculated that political elites now represent a "new class" in American politics. The old classes were those who owned the means of production (the capitalists) and those who were employed by those owners (the workers). The "new class" consists of people who are advantaged, not by the power, resources, and growth of business, but by the power, resources, and growth of government.[39]

Politicians, bureaucrats, members of the media, interest-group leaders—these people and others like them have, it is claimed, a stake in the growth of government. Because of that, they often have liberal (that is, progovernment) views even though they also have high incomes. The emergence of the new class helps explain, in this theory, why affluent people are not as consistently conservative as they were in the 1940s and 1950s.

It is true, as we have already seen, that many well-off people are liberals. That these people benefit from big government may be one explanation for this fact. But there is another explanation: the spread of higher education.

High levels of schooling, especially at the post-graduate level, tend to make people more liberal. This was not always the case. For example, in the 1940s and 1950s a clear majority of Harvard students, and probably of most college students, preferred Republican candidates for president.[40] For whatever reason things are different now. Some people with law degrees and Ph.D.'s may favor government because they get grants and jobs from it, but most people probably favor it because they have acquired an ideology that is consistent with a more activist government.

In any event it is striking how strongly postgraduate education affects political preferences. John McAdams has analyzed the voting results for several presidential, gubernatorial, and senatorial elections and for various state referenda elections on issues such as the death penalty, school busing, nuclear energy, gun control, environmental protection, and the Equal Rights Amendment. In each and every case he discovered that those with a postgraduate education were much more likely to take a liberal position even after holding constant age, race, and income.[41]

On the basis of his findings, McAdams suggests that the middle class in the United States has been split in two—one part he calls the "traditional middle class," the other he calls the "new class" (though it might more appropriately be called the "liberal middle class").[42] The traditional middle class consists of people who often have gone to college but not beyond and who live in the suburbs, go to church, are well disposed toward business, have conservative views on social issues, and usually vote Republican. The liberal middle class is more likely to consist of people who have a postgraduate education, live in or near big cities, are critical of business, have liberal views on social issues, and usually vote Democratic. The cleavage between the traditional and the liberal middle class has many of the same causes as the growing rift between orthodox and progressive ideologies discussed in Chapter 4.

As we shall see in Chapter 7, the strain within the middle class has been particularly felt by the Democratic party. That strain has made it harder to hold together the coalition (often called the New Deal coalition) that once made that party so strong, a coalition among blue-collar workers, southerners, blacks, and intellectuals. Increasingly the workers and white southerners have displayed their conservatism on social issues, while members of the liberal middle class have displayed their liberalism on these issues. Each side has a label for the other: the workers in the Democratic party call the members of the liberal middle class the "cheese and white wine set," while the people in the liberal middle class call the workers "Joe Six-Pack."

Political Elites, Public Opinion, and Public Policy

Though the elites and the public see politics in very different ways and though there are often intense antagonisms between the two groups, the elites influence public opinion in at least two important ways.

First, elites, especially those in or having access to the media (see Chapter 10), raise and frame political issues. At one time environmentalism was not on the political agenda; at a later time not only was it on the

Hollywood has worked hard to generate public support for AIDS victims, encouraging stars such as Elizabeth Taylor to wear a red ribbon.

agenda, but it was up near the top of government concerns. At some times the country has had little interest in what we should do in South Africa or Central America; at other times the government is preoccupied with these matters. Though world events help shape the political agenda, so also do political elites. A pathbreaking study by John Zaller shows in fact that elite views shape mass views by influencing both what issues capture public attention and how those issues are debated and decided.[43]

Second, elites state the norms by which issues should be settled. (A **norm** is a standard of right or proper conduct.) By doing this, they help determine the range of acceptable and unacceptable policy options. For example, elites have for a long time emphasized that racism is wrong. Of late they have emphasized that sexism is wrong. Over a long period the steady repetition of views condemning racism and sexism will at least intimidate, and perhaps convince, those of us who are racist and sexist.

A recent example of this process has been the public discussion of AIDS and its relationship to

homosexuality. The initial public reaction to AIDS was one of fear and loathing. But efforts to quarantine people infected with AIDS were met with firm resistance from the medical community and from other policy elites. The elites even managed to persuade some legislatures to bar insurance companies from testing insurance applicants for the disease.

There are limits to how much influence elites can have on the public. As we shall see in Chapter 16, elites do not define economic problems—people can see for themselves that there is or is not unemployment, that there is or is not raging inflation, that there are or are not high interest rates. Elite opinion may shape the policies, but it does not define the problem. Similarly, elite opinion has little influence on whether we think there is a crime or drug problem; it is, after all, *our* purses being snatched, cars being stolen, and children being drugged. On the other hand elite opinion will define the problem as well as the policy options with respect to most aspects of foreign affairs (see Chapter 20). The public has little firsthand experience with which to judge what is going on in Panama or Iraq.

Because elites affect how we see some issues and determine how other issues get resolved, it is important to study the differences between elite and public opinion. But it is wrong to suppose that there is one elite, unified in its interests and opinions. Just as there are many publics, and hence many public opinions, there are many elites, hence many different elite opinions. Whether there is enough variety of opinion and influence among elites to justify calling our politics "pluralist" is one of the central issues confronting any student of government. It is a matter to which we shall return in Part 4 of this book.

SUMMARY

"Public opinion" is a slippery notion, partly because there are many publics with many different opinions and partly because opinion on all but relatively simple matters tends to be uninformed, unstable, and sensitive to different ways of asking poll questions.

The chief sources of political opinion are the family, religion, information, and schooling. Once occupation (or income) was a central determinant of opinion, but with the spread of higher education the connection between occupational status (or income) and opinion is no longer quite as close.

The chief cleavages in opinion are race and ethnicity, class (in which schooling is an important component), and region.

Americans are divided by their political ideologies, but not along a single liberal-conservative dimension. There are several kinds of issues on which people may take "liberal" or "conservative" positions, and they often do not take the same position on all issues. Just using two kinds of issues—economic and social—it is possible to define four kinds of ideologies: pure liberal, pure conservative, libertarian, and populist.

Political elites are much more likely to display a consistently liberal or consistently conservative ideology. Elites are important because they have a disproportionate influence on public policy and even an influence on mass opinion (through the dissemination of information and the evocation of political norms).

KEY TERMS

middle America   *p. 105*

silent majority   *p. 105*

social status   *p. 108*

religious tradition   *p. 109*

gender gap   *p. 110*

poll   *p. 114*

random sample   *p. 114*

sampling error   *p. 115*

liberal   *p. 120*

conservative   *p. 120*

political ideology   *p. 120*

libertarians   *p. 123*

populists   *p. 123*

political elite   *p. 125*

norm   *p. 128*

SUGGESTED READINGS

Dionne, E. J. *Why Americans Hate Politics.* New York: Simon and Schuster, 1991. Misnamed, this book actually describes the emergence of various elite ideologies since the 1960s and why, in the author's view, none is relevant to actually solving problems.

Erikson, Robert S., Norman Luttbeg, and Kent L. Tedin. *American Public Opinion: Its Origins, Content and Impact.* 2d ed. New York: Wiley, 1980. A good summary of studies of public opinion and its relation to politics.

Jennings, M. Kent, and Richard G. Niemi. *The Political Character of Adolescence: The Influence of Families and Schools.* Princeton, N.J.: Princeton University Press, 1974. A study of political attitudes among high school students.

——. *Generations and Politics.* Princeton, N.J.: Princeton University Press, 1981. A study of persistence and change in the political views of young adults and their parents.

Key, V. O., Jr. *The Responsible Electorate.* Cambridge, Mass.: Harvard University Press, 1966. An argument, with evidence, that American voters are not fools.

Ladd, Everett Carll, Jr. *Where Have All the Voters Gone?* New York: Norton, 1978. A stimulating essay on recent changes in public opinion and its connection with political parties.

Lane, Robert E. *Political Ideology.* New York: Free Press, 1962. A sensitive account of the average American voter based on in-depth interviews that explore the beliefs of a small number of citizens.

Lipset, Seymour Martin. *Political Man: The Social Bases of Politics.* Garden City, N.Y.: Doubleday, 1959. An exploration of the relationship between society, opinion, and democracy in America and abroad.

Nie, Norman H., Sidney Verba, and John R. Petrocik. *The Changing American Voter.* Cambridge, Mass.: Harvard University Press, 1976. Traces shifts in American voter attitudes since 1960.

Zaller, John. *The Nature and Origins of Mass Opinion.* Cambridge, England: Cambridge University Press, 1992. A pathbreaking study of how the public forms an opinion, illustrating the ways in which elite views help shape mass views.

6

Political Participation

- ➤ The problem of nonvoting
- ➤ The rise of the American electorate
- ➤ Voter turnout
- ➤ Who participates?
- ➤ Different forms of participation
- ➤ Causes of participation

Americans are often embarrassed by their low rates of participation in national elections. Data such as those shown in Figure 6.1 are frequently used to make the point: whereas well over 80 percent of the people vote in many European elections, fewer than 60 percent of the people vote in American presidential elections (and a much smaller percentage vote in congressional contests). Many observers blame this low turnout on the fact that Americans are apathetic, and urge the government and private groups to mount campaigns to get out the vote.

There are only three things wrong with this view. First, it is a misleading description of the problem; second, it is an incorrect explanation of the problem; third, it proposes a remedy that won't work.

A Closer Look at Nonvoting

First, the problem: The conventional data on voter turnout here and abroad are misleading because they compute participation rates by two different measures. Figure 6.1 shows what proportion of the **registered voters** in various European nations went to the polls, but it shows what percentage of the **voting-age population** in the United States went to the polls. In this country only two-thirds of the voting-age population is registered to vote. To understand what this means, look at Table 6.1. In column A are several countries ranked in terms of the percentage of the voting-age population that voted in the 1984 national election. As you can see, the United States, where 52.6 percent voted, ranked near the bottom; only Switzerland was lower. Now look at column B, where the same countries are ranked in terms of the percentage of the registered voters who participated in the last national election. The United States, where almost 87 percent of the registered voters turned out at the polls, is now up in the middle of the pack.[1]

Second, explaining the problem: "Apathy" on election day is clearly not the source of the problem.

131

Of those who are registered, the overwhelming majority vote. The real source of the participation problem in the United States is that a relatively low percentage of the adult population is registered to vote.

Third, curing the problem: Mounting a get-out-the-vote drive won't make much difference. What would make a difference is a plan that would get more people to register to vote. But doing that does not necessarily involve overcoming the "apathy" of unregistered voters. Some people may not register because they don't care about politics or their duty as citizens. But there are other explanations for being unregistered. In this country the entire burden of registering to vote falls on the individual voters. They must learn how and when and where to register; they must take the time and trouble to go someplace and fill out a registration form; and they must reregister in a new county or state if they happen to move. In most European nations registration is done for you, automatically, by the government. Since it is costly to register in this country and costless to register in other countries, it should not be surprising that fewer people are registered here than abroad.

In 1993 Congress passed a law designed to make it easier to register to vote. Known as the **motor-voter bill**, the law requires states to allow people to register to vote when applying for driver's licenses and to provide registration through the mail and at some state offices that serve the disabled or provide public assistance (such as welfare checks). As we can see in Figure 6.2, some 49 million voting-age people who are not registered to vote have driver's licenses or state-issued identification cards. The motor-voter bill takes effect in 1995; thus it will be some years before we know how many people it will add to the registration rolls and lead into the voting booths.

FIGURE 6.1 Average Voter Turnout from the 1950s to 1980s

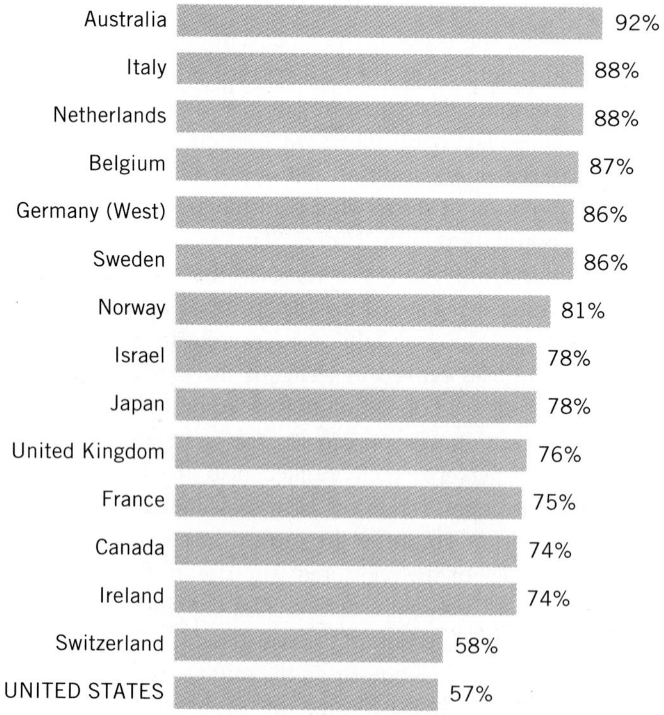

Country	Turnout
Australia	92%
Italy	88%
Netherlands	88%
Belgium	87%
Germany (West)	86%
Sweden	86%
Norway	81%
Israel	78%
Japan	78%
United Kingdom	76%
France	75%
Canada	74%
Ireland	74%
Switzerland	58%
UNITED STATES	57%

SOURCE: Russell J. Dalton and Martin P. Weinberg, "The Not So Simple Act of Voting," in *Political Science: The State of the Discipline,* ed. Ada Finifter, 2nd ed. (Washington, D.C.: APSA,1993), 210. Reprinted by permission.

TABLE 6.1 Two Ways of Calculating Voting Turnout

A Turnout as Percentage of Voting-Age Population		B Turnout as Percentage of Registered Voters	
Austria	89.3%	Belgium	94.6%
Belgium	88.7	Australia	94.5
Sweden	86.8	Austria	91.6
Netherlands	84.7	Sweden	90.7
Australia	83.1	New Zealand	89.0
Denmark	82.1	West Germany	88.6
Norway	81.8	Netherlands	87.0
West Germany	81.1	UNITED STATES	86.8
New Zealand	78.5	France	85.9
France	78.0	Denmark	83.2
United Kingdom	76.0	Norway	82.0
Japan	74.4	United Kingdom	76.3
Canada	67.4	Japan	74.5
Finland	63.0	Canada	69.3
UNITED STATES	52.6	Finland	64.3
Switzerland	39.4	Switzerland	48.3

SOURCE: Adapted from tables in David Glass, Peverill Squire, and Raymond Wolfinger, "Voter Turnout: An International Comparison," *Public Opinion* (December–January 1984): 50, 52. Reprinted with permission of American Enterprise Institute for Public Policy Research.

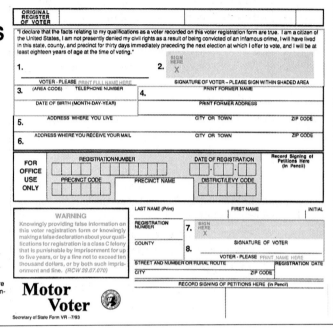

MOTOR VOTER
REGISTRATION INSTRUCTIONS

You must complete steps 1-3. Failure to provide
this information may jeopardize your registration.

BOX 1   <u>Print</u> your name on the line in box # 1.

BOX 2   Please read the oath and then sign your name in the grey shaded area next to the RED
X. This signature attests that you meet the qualifications of the oath.

BOX 3   Enter your daytime phone number, and date of birth.

BOX 4   If you are changing your address, or name, or have been registered to vote before,
please write the name and address at which you were previously registered in box 4.

BOX 5   Do you want to be registered at the address on your current license or I.D. card?
- If Yes, skip box #5.
- If No, please write the address where you live in box #5. (You may not use a
work address as your residence address.)

BOX 6   If your mailing address is different from the address where you live please write your
mailing address in box #6. (You may not use a work address for mailing purposes.)

BOX 7   Please sign your name next to the RED X on the lower half of the form.

BOX 8   Please print your name.

OATH

"I declare that the facts relating to my qualifications as a voter recorded on this voter registration form are
true. I am a citizen of the United States, I am not presently denied my civil rights as a result of being convicted of an infamous crime, I will have lived in this state, county, and precinct for thirty days immediately
preceding the next election at which I offer to vote, and I will be at least eighteen years of age at the time
of voting."

When you apply for a driver's license in the state of Washington, you are given this form so that you can register to vote at the same time. This "motor-voter" idea became the basis of a federal law passed in 1993.

A final point: Voting is only one way of partici-pating in politics. It is important (we could hardly be considered a democracy if nobody voted), but it is not all-important. Joining civic associations, sup-porting social movements, writing to legislators, fighting city hall—all these and other activities are ways of participating in politics. It is possible that, by these measures, Americans participate in politics *more* than most Europeans—or anybody else, for that matter. Moreover it is possible that low rates of registration indicate that people are reasonably well satisfied with how the country is governed. If 100 percent of all adult Americans registered and voted (especially under a system that makes registering rel-atively difficult), it could mean that people are deeply upset about how things are run. In short it is not at all clear whether low rates of voting are symptoms of political disease or political good health.

The important question about participation is not how much there is but how different kinds of participation affect the kind of government we get. This question cannot be answered just by looking at

FIGURE 6.2   The Motor-Voter Bill, 1992

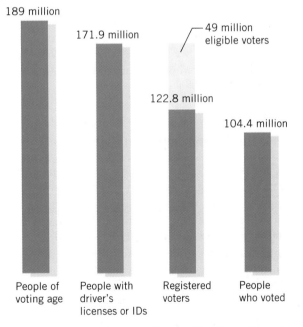

189 million

171.9 million

49 million
eligible voters

122.8 million

104.4 million

People of voting age | People with driver's licenses or IDs | Registered voters | People who voted

NOTE: The voting-age figure includes 11 million illegal aliens and 600,000 convicted felons who are not eligible to vote. It does not in-clude about 600,000 Americans overseas who are eligible to vote.

SOURCE: Richard Sammon, "Senate Filibuster Kills Threat, Clears 'Motor-Vote' Bill," *Congressional Quarterly* (May 15, 1993): 1221.

In the first years of the republic, voting was frequently restricted to male property owners.

voting turnout, the subject of this chapter; it also requires us to look at the composition and activities of political parties, interest groups, and the media (the subjects of later chapters).

Nonetheless, voting is important. To understand why participation in American elections takes the form that it does, we must first understand how laws have determined who shall vote and under what circumstances.

The Rise of the American Electorate

It is ironic that relatively few citizens vote in American elections, since it was in this country that the mass of people first became eligible to vote. At the time the Constitution was ratified, the vote was limited to property owners or taxpayers, but by the administration of Andrew Jackson it had been broadened to include virtually all white male adults. Only in a few states did property restrictions persist: they were not abolished in New Jersey until 1844 or in North Carolina until 1856. And of course in many parts of the North as well as in the South, black males could not vote in many states, even if they were not slaves. Women could not vote in most states until the twentieth century; Chinese-Americans were widely

denied the vote; and being in prison is grounds for losing the franchise even today. Aliens, on the other hand, were often allowed to vote if they had at least begun the process of becoming a citizen. By 1880 only an estimated 14 percent of all adult males in the United States could not vote; in England in the same period about 40 percent of adult males were disfranchised.[2]

From State to Federal Control

Initially it was left entirely to the states to decide who could vote and for what offices. The Constitution gave to Congress only the right to pick the day on which presidential electors would gather and to alter state regulations regarding congressional elections. The only provision of the Constitution requiring a popular election was the clause in Article I stating that members of the House of Representatives be chosen by the "people of the several states."

Because of this permissiveness, early federal elections varied greatly. Several states picked their members of the House at large (that is, statewide) rather than by district; others used districts but elected more than one representative from each. Still others had their elections in odd-numbered years, and some even required that a congressional candidate win a

After the Civil War, while Union forces were still in control, blacks began to vote in the South, as here in Richmond, Virginia, in 1871.

When Reconstruction ended in 1876, black voting shrank under the attack of white supremacists.

majority, rather than simply a plurality, of votes to be elected (when that requirement was in effect, runoff elections — in one case as many as twelve — were necessary). Furthermore presidential electors were at first picked by state legislatures rather than by the voters directly.

Congress, by law and constitutional amendment, has steadily reduced state prerogatives in these matters. In 1842 a federal law required that all members of the House be elected by districts; other laws over the years required that all federal elections be held in even-numbered years on the Tuesday following the first Monday in November.

The most important changes in elections have been those that extended the suffrage to women, blacks, and eighteen-year-olds and made mandatory the direct popular election of United States senators. The Fifteenth Amendment, adopted in 1870, said that the "right of citizens of the United States to vote shall not be denied or abridged by the United States or by any state on account of race, color, or previous condition of servitude." Reading those words today, one would assume that they gave blacks the right to vote. That is not what the Supreme Court during the 1870s thought that they meant. By a series of decisions, it held that the Fifteenth Amendment did not necessarily confer the right to vote on anybody; it

merely asserted that if someone was denied that right, the denial could not be explicitly on the grounds of race. And the burden of proving that it was race that led to the denial fell on the black who was turned away at the polls.[3]

This interpretation opened the door to all manner of state stratagems to keep blacks from voting. One was a **literacy test** (a large proportion of former slaves were illiterate), another was a requirement that a **poll tax** be paid (most former slaves were poor), a third was the practice of keeping blacks from voting in primary elections (in the one-party South the only meaningful election was the Democratic primary). To allow whites to vote who were illiterate or poor, a **grandfather clause** was added to the law saying that you could vote, even though you did not meet the legal requirements, if you or your ancestors voted before 1867 (blacks, of course, could not vote before

TABLE 6.2 Voter Registration in the South

		Ala.	Ark.	Fla.	Ga.	La.	Miss.	N.C.	S.C.	Tenn.	Tex.	Va.	Total
					Percentage of Voting-Age Population That Is Registered								
1960	White	63.6	60.9	69.3	56.8	76.9	63.9	92.1	57.1	73.0	42.5	46.1	61.1
	Black*	13.7	38.0	39.4	29.3	31.1	5.2	39.1	13.7	59.1	35.5	23.1	29.1
1970	White	85.0	74.1	65.5	71.7	77.0	82.1	68.1	62.3	78.5	62.0	64.5	62.9
	Black	66.0	82.3	55.3	57.2	57.4	71.0	51.3	56.1	71.6	72.6	57.0	62.0
1986	White	77.5	67.2	66.9	62.3	67.8	91.6	67.4	53.4	70.0	79.0	60.3	69.9
	Black	68.9	57.9	58.2	52.8	60.6	70.8	58.4	52.5	65.3	68.0	56.2	60.8

*Includes other minority races.
SOURCE: Voter Education Project, Inc., of Atlanta, Georgia, as reported in *Statistical Abstract of the United States, 1990*, 264.

1867). When all else failed, blacks were intimidated, threatened, or harassed if they showed up at the polls.

There began a long, slow legal process of challenging in court each of these restrictions in turn. One by one the Supreme Court set most of them aside. The grandfather clause was declared unconstitutional in 1915[4] and the **white primary** finally fell in 1944.[5] Some of the more blatantly discriminatory literacy tests were also overturned.[6] The practical result of these rulings was slight: only a small proportion of voting-age blacks were able to register and vote in the South, and they were found mostly in the larger cities. A dramatic change did not begin until 1965, with the passage of the Voting Rights Act. This act suspended the use of literacy tests and authorized the appointment of federal examiners who could order the registration of blacks in states and counties (mostly in the South) where fewer than 50 percent of the voting-age population were registered or had voted in the last presidential election. It also provided criminal penalties for interfering with the right to vote.

Though implementation in some places was slow, the number of blacks voting rose sharply throughout the South. For example, in Mississippi the proportion of voting-age blacks who registered rose from 5 percent to over 70 percent in just ten years (see Table 6.2). These changes had a profound effect on the behavior of many white southern politicians: Governor George Wallace stopped making prosegregation speeches and began courting the black vote.

Women were kept from the polls by law more than by intimidation, and when the laws changed, women almost immediately began to vote in large numbers. By 1915 several states, mostly in the West, had begun to permit women to vote. But it was not until the Nineteenth Amendment to the Constitution was ratified in 1920, after a struggle lasting many decades, that women generally were allowed to vote. At one stroke the size of the eligible voting population almost doubled. Contrary to the hopes of some and the fears of others, no dramatic changes occurred in the conduct of elections, the identity of the winners, or the substance of public policy. Initially, at least, women voted more or less in the same manner as men, though not quite as frequently.

The political impact of the youth vote was also less than expected. The Voting Rights Act of 1970 gave the right to vote in federal elections to eighteen-year-olds, beginning January 1, 1971. It also contained a provision lowering the voting age to eighteen in state elections, but the Supreme Court declared this unconstitutional. As a result a constitutional amendment, the Twenty-sixth, was proposed by Congress and ratified by the states in 1971. The 1972 elections became the first in which all people between the ages of eighteen and twenty-one could cast ballots (before then, four states had allowed those under twenty-one to vote). About 25 million people suddenly became eligible to participate in elections, but their turnout was lower than for the population as a whole, and they did not flock to any particular party or candidate. George McGovern, the Democratic candidate for president in 1972, counted heavily on attracting the youth vote, but did not. Most young voters supported Nixon (though college students favored McGovern).[7]

National standards now govern almost every aspect of voter eligibility. All persons eighteen years of age and older may vote; there may be no literacy test or poll tax; states may not require residency of more than thirty days in that state before a person may vote; areas with significant numbers of citizens not speaking English must give those people ballots written in their own language; and federal voter registrars and poll watchers may be sent into areas where less than 50 percent of the voting-age population participates in a presidential election. Before 1961 residents of the District of Columbia could not vote in presidential elections; the Twenty-third Amendment to the Constitution gave them this right.

The campaign to win the vote for women nationwide succeeded with the adoption of the Nineteenth Amendment in 1920.

Voting Turnout

Given all these legal safeguards, one might expect that participation in elections would have risen sharply. In fact the proportion of the voting-age population that has gone to the polls in presidential elections has remained about the same — between 50 percent and 60 percent of those eligible — at least since 1932 and appears today to be much smaller than it was in the latter part of the nineteenth century (see Figure 6.3). In every presidential election between 1860 and 1900, at least 70 percent of the eligible population apparently went to the polls, and in some years (1860 and 1876) over 80 percent seem to have voted. Since 1900 not a single presidential election turnout has reached 70 percent, and on two

FIGURE 6.3 Voter Participation in Presidential Elections, 1860–1992

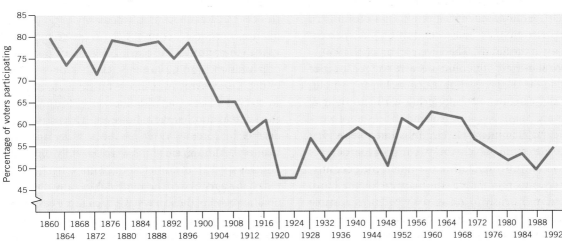

NOTE: Several southern states did not participate in the 1864 and 1868 elections.

SOURCES: For 1860–1928: Bureau of the Census, *Historical Statistics of the United States, Colonial Times to 1970*, Pt. 2, 1071; 1932–1992: *Statistical Abstract of the United States, 1992*, 517.

CRITICAL ⭐ THINKING

Voter Turnout: Some Myths and Realities

MYTH	REALITY
Turnout is declining because the poor are dropping out of politics.	Turnout is declining because *all* groups — the poor, the middle class, and the rich — have become less likely to vote.
Today's voters see no differences between Democrats and Republicans.	More voters see more important differences between the parties today than they did in the 1960s.
Nonvoters don't vote because the policies they prefer haven't been debated or adopted.	Voters and nonvoters differ very little in their policy preferences.
Many elections are decided by levels of voter turnout.	Levels of turnout do not, as a rule, make much of a difference to election outcomes.
Registration reform (for example, the "motor-voter" bill, Figure 6.2) would definitely help the Democrats (the majority party nationally) and hurt the Republicans.	Nobody really knows, but surveys suggest that the political leanings of voters and nonvoters do not differ enough for the addition of even millions of nonvoters to make much of a partisan impact.

SOURCE: Adapted from Ruy A. Teixeira, "Voter Turnout in America," *The Brookings Review* (Fall 1992): 28–31.
Reprinted with permission of the Brookings Institution.

occasions (1920 and 1924) it did not even reach 50 percent.[8] Even outside the South (where efforts to disfranchise blacks make data on voting turnout especially hard to interpret) turnout seems to have declined: over 84 percent of the voting-age population participated in presidential elections in nonsouthern states between 1884 and 1900, but only 68 percent between 1936 and 1960 and even fewer since 1960.[9]

Scholars have vigorously debated the meaning of these figures. One view is that this decline in turnout, even allowing for the shaky data on which the estimates are based, has been real and the result of a decline of popular interest in elections and a weakening of the extent to which the two major parties are closely competitive. During the nineteenth century, according to this theory, the parties fought hard, worked strenuously to get as many voters as possible to the polls, afforded the mass of voters a chance to participate in party politics through caucuses and conventions, kept the legal barriers to participation (such as complex registration procedures) low, and

looked forward to close, exciting elections. After 1896, by which time the South had become a one-party Democratic region and the North heavily Republican, both parties became more conservative, national elections usually resulted in lopsided victories for the Republicans, and citizens began to lose interest in politics because it no longer seemed relevant to their needs. The parties ceased functioning as organizations to mobilize the mass of voters and fell under the control of leaders, mostly conservative, who resisted mass participation.[10]

There is another view, however. It argues that the decline in voter turnout has been more apparent than real. Though elections were certainly more of a popular sport in the nineteenth century than they are today, the parties were no more democratic then than now, and voters then may have been more easily manipulated. Until around the beginning of the twentieth century, vote frauds were commonplace because they were easy to pull off. The political parties, not the government, printed the ballots; they were often cast in public, not private, voting booths; there were few serious efforts to decide who was eligible to vote, and the rules that did operate were easily evaded.

Under these circumstances it was easy for a person to vote more than once, and the party machines made heavy use of these "floaters" or repeaters. "Vote early and often" was not a joke but a fact. "Big Tim" Sullivan, a boss in New York's old Tammany Hall, once had his party's ballots soaked in perfume so that he could use scent as well as sight to ensure that his voters put the right ballot in the right box.[11] The parties often controlled the counting of votes, padding the totals whenever they feared losing. As a result of these machinations, the number of votes counted was often larger than the number cast, and the number cast was in turn often larger than the number of individuals eligible to vote. For example, in 1888 West Virginia officially claimed that there were 147,408 persons in the state eligible to vote, but mysteriously 159,440 votes were cast in the presidential election, for a "voter turnout" of 108 percent![12]

Around 1890 the states began adopting the **Australian ballot.** This was a government-printed ballot of uniform size and shape that was cast in secret to replace the old party-printed ballot cast in public. By 1910 only three states were without the Australian ballot. Its use cut back on (but certainly did not eliminate) vote buying and fraudulent vote counts.

In short, if votes had been legally cast and honestly counted in the nineteenth century, the statistics on election turnout might well be much lower than the inflated figures we now have.[13] To the extent that this is true, we may not have had a decline in voter participation as great as some have suggested. Nevertheless most scholars believe that, even accurately measured, turnout probably did decline somewhat after the 1890s. One reason was that voter-registration regulations became more burdensome: there were longer residency requirements; aliens who had announced their intention of becoming citizens could no longer vote in most states; it became harder for blacks to vote; educational qualifications for voting were adopted by several states; and voters had to register long in advance of the elections. These changes, designed to purify the electoral process, were aspects of the Progressive reform impulse described in Chapter 7 and served to cut back on the number of persons who could participate in elections.

MTV's efforts to encourage young people to vote in the 1992 election included a televised question-and-answer session with Al Gore.

Strict voter-registration procedures tended, like most reforms in American politics, to have unintended as well as intended consequences. These changes not only reduced fraudulent voting but also reduced voting generally because they made it more difficult for certain groups of perfectly honest voters — those with little education, for example, or those who had recently moved — to register and vote. This was not the first time, and it will not be the last, that a reform designed to cure one problem created another.

Even after all the legal changes are taken into account, there has still been a decline in citizen participation in elections. Between 1960 and 1980 the proportion of voting-age people casting a ballot in presidential elections fell by about 10 percentage points, a drop that cannot be explained by how ballots were printed or registration rules were rewritten. By the same token, these factors cannot explain the 5 percentage point increase in turnout from the 1988 (50 percent turnout) to the 1992 presidential election (55 percent turnout).

Who Participates in Politics?

To understand better why voting turnout declined and what, if anything, that decline may mean, we must first look at who participates in politics.

Forms of Participation

Table 6.3 shows the results of asking Americans about their involvement in various kinds of political activities. As can be seen, voting is by far the most common form of political participation, while giving money to a candidate and being a member of a political organization are the least common. And even these figures overstate matters, since most persons

TABLE 6.3   Political Involvement

Type of Political Participation	Percentage
Report regularly voting in presidential elections[a]	72%
Report always voting in local elections	47
Active in at least one organization involved in community problems	32
Have worked with others in trying to solve some community problems	30
Have attempted to persuade others to vote as they were	28
Have ever actively worked for a party or candidates during an election	26
Have ever contacted a local government official about some issue or problem	20
Have attended at least one political meeting or rally in last three years	19
Have ever contacted a state or national government official about some issue or problem	18
Have ever formed a group or organization to attempt to solve some local community problem	14
Have ever given money to a party or candidate during an election campaign	13
Presently a member of a political club or organization	8

[a] Composite variable created from reports of voting in 1960 and 1964 presidential elections. Percentage is equal to those who report they have voted in both elections.
SOURCE: Sidney Verba and Norman H. Nie, *Participation in America* (New York: Harper & Row, 1972), 21, Table 2.1, "Percentage Engaging in Twelve Different Acts of Political Participation." Copyright © 1972 by Sidney Verba and Norman H. Nie. Reprinted by permission of Harper & Row, Publishers, Inc.

tend to exaggerate how frequently they vote or how active they are in politics. Consider: in Table 6.3, 72 percent of those interviewed said that they vote "regularly" in presidential elections. Yet we know that since 1960 on average only 58 percent of the voting-age population has actually cast presidential ballots. Careful studies of this discrepancy suggest that 8 percent to 10 percent of Americans interviewed misreport their voting habits: they claim to have voted when in fact they have not. Young, low-income, less-educated, and nonwhite people are most likely to misreport than others.[14] If people misreport their voting behavior, it is likely that they also misreport—that is, exaggerate—the extent to which they participate in other ways.

Sidney Verba and Norman H. Nie did an elaborate statistical analysis of the ways in which people participate in politics and came up with six forms of participation that are characteristic of six different kinds of U.S. citizens. About one-fifth (22 percent) of the population is completely inactive: they rarely vote, they do not get involved in organizations, and they probably do not even talk about politics very much. These inactives typically have little education and low incomes, are relatively young, and many of them are black. At the opposite extreme are the complete **activists,** constituting about one-ninth of the population (11 percent), who are highly educated, have high incomes, and tend to be middle-aged rather than young or old. They tend to participate in all forms of politics.

Between these extremes are four categories of limited forms of participation. The voting specialists are people who vote but do little else; they tend not to have much schooling or income, and to be substantially older than the average person. Campaigners not only vote but like to get involved in campaign activities as well. They are better educated than the average voter, but what seems to distinguish them most is their interest in the conflicts, passions, and struggle of politics, their clear identification with a political party, and their willingness to take strong positions. Communalists are much like campaigners in social background but have a very different temperament: they do not like the conflict and tension of partisan campaigns. They tend to reserve their energies for community activities of a more nonpartisan nature—forming and joining organizations to deal with local problems and contacting local officials about these problems. Finally, there are some parochial participants who do not vote and stay out of election campaigns and civic associations, but who are willing to contact local officials about specific, often personal, problems.[15]

The Causes of Participation

Whether participation takes the form of voting or being a complete activist, it is higher among persons who have gone to college than among persons who have not and higher among persons who are over thirty-five years of age than among persons who are under thirty-five. (The differences in voting rates for these groups are shown in Figure 6.4.) Even after controlling for differences in income and occupation, the more schooling one has, the more likely one is to vote. Of course it may not be schooling itself that causes participation but something that is strongly correlated with schooling, such as high levels of political information.[16]

In fact the differences in participation that are associated with schooling (or its correlates) are probably even greater than reported in this figure, since we have already seen that less-educated persons exagger-

ate how frequently they vote. An excellent study of turnout concludes that people are more likely to vote when they have those personal qualities that "make learning about politics easier and more gratifying."[17]

Religious involvement also increases political participation. If you are a regular church-goer who takes your faith seriously, the chances are that you will be more likely to vote and otherwise take part in politics than if you are a person of the same age, sex, income, and educational level who does not go to church. Church involvement leads to social connectedness, teaches organizational skills, increases one's awareness of larger issues, and puts one in contact with like-minded people.[18]

Men and women vote at about the same rates, but blacks and whites do not. Although at one time that difference was largely the result of discrimination, today it can be explained mostly by differences in social class—blacks are poorer and have less schooling, on the average, than whites. However, among people of the same socioeconomic status—that is, having roughly the same level of income and schooling—blacks tend to participate *more* than whites.[19]

Because the population became younger (during the baby boom of the 1960s and 1970s) and because blacks have increased in numbers faster than whites,

FIGURE 6.4 Voter Turnout in Presidential Elections, by Age, Schooling, and Race, 1964–1992

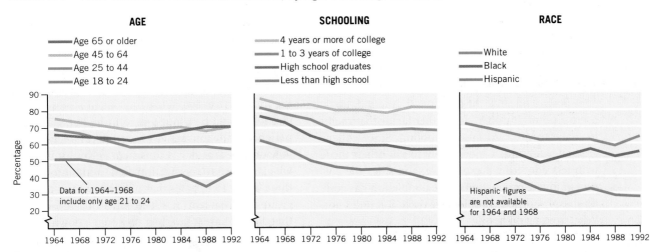

SOURCE: Gary R. Orren, "The Linkage of Policy to Participation," in *Presidential Selection*, ed. Alexander Heard and Michael Nelson (Durham, N.C.: Duke University Press, 1987) and tabulated by Daron Shaw; data for 1992 are from *Statistical Abstract of the United States, 1993,* 283.

In the 1840 presidential campaign, political parties strove to increase political participation by slogans ("Tippecanoe and Tyler Too!") and by less subtle appeals (free hard cider).

one might suppose that these demographic changes explain why the turnout in presidential elections has gone down a bit since the early 1960s. And they do—up to a point. But there is another factor that ought to make turnout go *up*—schooling. Since college graduates are much more likely to vote than those with less educational experience, and since the college-graduate proportion of the population has gone up sharply, turnout should have risen. But it did not. What is going on here?

Perhaps turnout has declined despite the higher levels of schooling due to the rising level of distrust of government. We saw in Chapter 4 that, well into the 1990s, more and more people were telling pollsters that they lacked confidence in political leaders. Ris-

ing distrust seems a plausible explanation for declining turnout until one looks at the facts. The data show that there is *no correlation* between expressing distrust of political leaders and not voting.[20] People who are cynical about our leaders are just as likely to vote as people who are not.

Because turnout is powerfully affected by the number of people who register to vote, perhaps in recent years it has become harder to register. But in fact exactly the opposite is true. Since 1970 federal law has prohibited residency requirements longer than thirty days for presidential elections, and a Supreme Court decision in 1972 held that requirements much in excess of this were invalid for state and local elections.[21] By 1982 twenty-one states and the District of Columbia, containing about half the nation's population, had adopted laws permitting voters to register by mail. In four states—Maine, Minnesota, Oregon, and Wisconsin—voters can register and vote on the same day, all at once.

What is left? Several small things. First, the greater youthfulness of the population, together with the presence of growing numbers of blacks and other minorities, has pushed down the percentage of voters who are registered and vote.

Second, political parties today are no longer as effective as they once were in mobilizing voters, ensuring that they are registered, and getting them to the polls. As we shall see in Chapter 7, the parties once were grassroots organizations with which many people strongly identified. Today parties are somewhat distant, national bureaucracies with which most of us do not identify very strongly.

Third, the remaining impediments to registration exert some influence. One study estimated that if every state had registration requirements as easy as the most permissive states, turnout in a presidential election would be about 9 percent higher.[22] The experience of the four states where you can register and vote on the same day is consistent with this: in 1976, when same-day registration first went into effect, three of the four states that had it saw their turnout go up by 3 percent or 4 percent, while those states that did not have it saw their turnout go down.[23] If an even bolder plan were adopted, such as the Canadian system of universal enrollment whereby the government automatically puts on the voter list every eligible citizen, there would probably be some additional gain in turnout.[24]

Fourth, if *not* voting is costless, then there will be more nonvoting. Several nations with higher turnouts than ours make voting compulsory. For example, in Italy a person who does not vote has his or her government identification papers stamped "*DID NOT VOTE.*"[25] In Australia and other countries fines can be levied on nonvoters. As a practical matter such fines are rarely imposed, but just the threat of them probably induces more people to register and vote.

Finally, voting (and before that, registering) will go down if people do not feel that elections matter much. There has been a decline in the proportion of

Registering to vote will become easier now that the "motor-voter" law has been passed.

Democracy

League of Women Voters

Contact your local League of Women Voters for information about registration and voting.

This poster has been made possible by a contribution from the LTV Corporation.

Keep it strong
Pass it along

Register and Vote

Latino Americans tend to participate less frequently in elections than other groups. This billboard tries to change that: "Don't leave yourself out. Arm yourself. Register to vote."

people who feel that elections matter a lot, corresponding to the decrease in those who do participate in elections.

In short there are a number of reasons why we register and vote less frequently here than do citizens abroad. Two careful studies of all these factors found that almost all of the differences in turnout among twenty-four democratic nations, including the United States, could be explained by party strength, automatic registration, and compulsory voting laws.[26]

The presence of these reasons does not necessarily mean that somebody ought to do something about them. We could make registration automatic—but that might open the way to voter fraud, since here people move around so much and change names often enough to enable some of them, if they wanted to, to vote more than once. We could make voting compulsory, but Americans have an aversion to government compulsion in any form and probably would object strenuously to any plan for making citizens carry identification papers that the government would stamp.

Democrats and Republicans fight over various measures designed to increase registration and voting because one party (usually the Democrats) thinks that higher turnout will help them and the other (usually the Republicans) fears that higher turnout will hurt them. In fact no one really knows whether either party would be helped or hurt by higher voter turnout.

Nonvoters are more likely than voters to be poor, black or Hispanic, or uneducated. However, the proportion of nonvoters with some college education rose from 7 percent in 1960 to 18 percent in 1980. In addition, the percentage of nonvoters who held white-collar jobs rose from 33 percent to 50 percent in the same period. Many of these better-off nonvoters might well have voted Republican if they had gone to the polls. And even if the turnout rates only of blacks and of Hispanics had increased, there would not have been enough votes added to the Democratic column to affect the outcome of the 1984 or 1988 presidential elections.[27]

Both political parties try to get a larger turnout among voters likely to be sympathetic to them, but it is hard to be sure that these efforts will produce real gains. If one party works hard to get its nonvoters to the polls, the other party will work just as hard to get its people there. For example, when Jesse Jackson ran for the presidency in 1984, registration of southern blacks increased, but registration of southern whites increased even more.

The Meaning of Participation Rates

Americans may be voting less, but there is evidence that they are participating more. One survey found that the proportion of people who had ever written a letter to a public official increased from about 17 percent in 1964 to over 27 percent in 1976. People participate when they give money to a political campaign or cause, and such giving, too, has increased in recent years.

Public demonstrations such as sit-ins and protest marches have become much more common in recent decades than they once were. By one count there were only 6 demonstrations per year between 1950 and 1959 but over 140 per year between 1960 and 1967. Though these demonstrations began with civil-rights and antiwar activists, these means were later employed by farmers demanding government aid, truckers denouncing the national speed limit, the disabled seeking to dramatize their needs, parents

Participation can mean much more than voting, as when these disabled persons protested what they felt were inadequate wheelchair facilities for hockey games at Boston Garden.

objecting to busing to achieve racial balance in the schools, conservationists hoping to block nuclear power plants, and construction workers urging that nuclear power *not* be blocked.[28]

These other forms of participation are more common in the United States than in many places abroad. Table 6.4 compares the percentage of people in seven countries who said they regularly voted, joined in a political campaign, engaged in communal activity, or contacted public officials. As expected, the proportion of the population who voted was lower in the United States than in most of the other nations, but the percentage working for a party, being active in a community organization, working with a local group on a local problem, or contacting a local official was in this country as high as or higher than in most other places.

Even though we vote at lower rates here than people do abroad, the meaning of our voting is also different. For one thing we elect far more public officials than do the citizens of any other nation. One scholar has estimated that there are 521,000 elective offices in the United States, and that almost every week of the year there is an election going on somewhere in this country.[29]

A citizen of Massachusetts, for example, votes not only for president, but for senator, governor, member of the House of Representatives, state representative, state senator, attorney general, state auditor, state treasurer, secretary of state, county commissioner, sheriff, and clerks of various courts, as well as (in the cities) for mayor, city councillor, and school committee members, and (in towns) for selectmen, town-meeting members, moderator, library trustees, health-board members, assessors, water commissioners, town clerk, housing-authority members, tree warden, and commissioner of the public burial ground. (There are probably others that I have forgotten.)

In many European nations, by contrast, the voters get to make one choice once every four or five years: they can vote for or against a member of parliament. When there is only one election for one office every several years, that election is bound to assume more importance to the voter than many elections for scores of offices. But one election for one office probably has less effect on how the nation is governed than many elections for thousands of offices. Americans may not vote at high rates, but voting affects a far greater part of the political system here than abroad.

The kinds of people who vote here are also different from those who vote abroad. Since almost everybody votes in many other democracies, the votes cast there mirror almost exactly the social composition of those nations. Since only slightly over half of the vot-

ing-age population turns out even for presidential elections here, the votes cast in the United States may not reflect the country accurately.

That is in fact the case. Figure 6.5 shows the proportion of each major occupational group that usually votes in Japan, Sweden, and the United States. As is obvious, each occupational group — or if you prefer, social class — votes at about the same rate in Japan and Sweden. But in the United States the turnout is heavily skewed toward higher-status per-

TABLE 6.4   How Citizens Participate in Seven Countries

	Austria	India	Japan	Netherlands	Nigeria	United States	Yugoslavia
Voting							
Regular voters[a]	85%	48%	93%	77%	56%	63%	82%
Campaign activity							
Members of a party or political organization	28	5	4	13	[b]	8	15
Worked for a party	10	6	25	10	[b]	25	45
Attended a political rally	27	14	50	9	[b]	19	45
Communal activity							
Active members in a community action organization	9	7	11	15	34	32	39
Worked with a local group on a community problem	3	18	15	16	35	30	22
Helped form a local group on a community problem	6	5	5	[b]	26	14	[b]
Contacted an official in the community on some social problem	5	4	11	6	2	13	11
Contacted an official outside the community on a social problem	3	2	5	7	3	11	[b]
Particularized contacting							
Contacted a local official on a personal problem	15	12	7	38	2	6	20
Contacted an official outside the community on a personal problem	10	6	3	10	1	6	[b]
Number	1,769	2,637	2,657	1,746	1,799	2,544	2,995

[a] Vote regularly in both local and national elections.   [b] Not asked.
SOURCE: Norman H. Nie and Sidney Verba, "Political Participation," in *Handbook of Political Science,* ed. Fred I. Greenstein and Nelson W. Polsby (Reading, Mass.: Addison-Wesley, 1975), Vol. 4 24–25. Reprinted with permission.

sons: those in professional, managerial, and other white-collar occupations are overrepresented among the voters.

Although nonwhites and Latinos are the fastest growing segment of the population, they tend to be the most underrepresented of American voters. Little is known about the relationship between political participation and such political resources as command of the language and involvement in nonpolitical institutions that provide information or impart skills relevant to politics (such as workplaces and voluntary associations). However, such factors could be quite important in explaining differences in political participation rates among poor and minority citizens. As we can see in Figure 6.6, although less involved than whites, blacks participate in voting and political activities at higher rates than do Latino citizens. One excellent study suggests that these differences are due in part to the fact that blacks are more likely than Latinos to be members of churches that stimulate political interest, activity, and mobilization.[30] Language barriers also make it harder for many Latinos to get in touch with a public official, serve on local governing boards, and engage in other forms of political participation in which command of English is an asset. The lower participation rates of minority citizens are likely compounded by their being disproportionately of low socioeconomic status compared to white Americans.

Exactly what these differences in participation mean in terms of how the government is run is not entirely clear. But since we know from evidence

FIGURE 6.5   Voter Turnout in National Elections in Three Countries, by Occupation

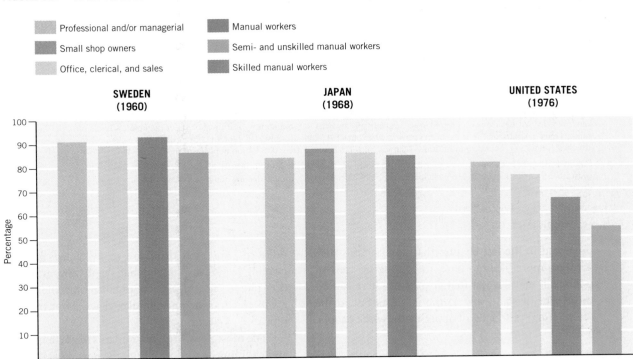

SOURCES: For Japan: The Society for Promotion of Clean Elections, Survey of 34th General Election, 1976. Reprinted from an unpublished paper by Gary Orren, "Political Participation and Public Policy: The Case for Institutional Reform" (Cambridge, Mass., November 1985), 16A. For Sweden and the United States: Samuel P. Huntington and Joan M. Nelson, *No Easy Choice* (Cambridge, Mass.: Harvard University Press, 1976), 88.

FIGURE 6.6 Electoral and Nonelectoral Political Participation Among Anglo-Whites, African-Americans, and Latinos

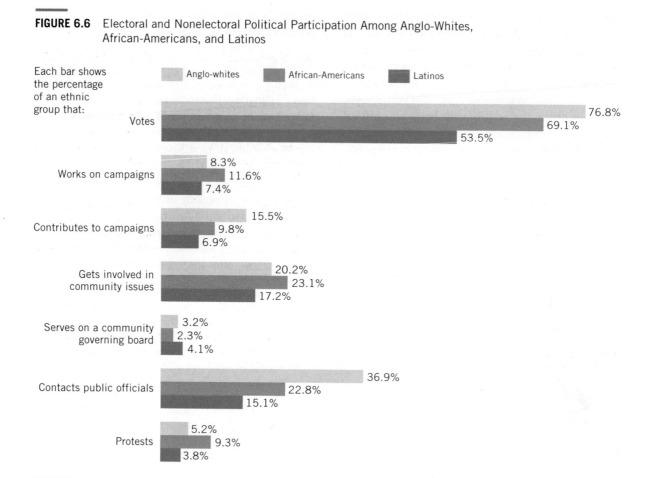

NOTE: "Community activists" were defined as persons who got "involved informally on local community issues"; "board members" were defined as persons who served in an "unpaid capacity on a local community governing board, for example, a school or zoning board"; "contactors" were defined as persons who contacted public officials; and "protesters" were defined as persons who attended "protests or other demonstrations." "Latinos" includes Latino citizens plus Latino noncitizens living in the U.S.

SOURCE: Adapted from Sidney Verba, Kay Lehman Scholzman, Henry Brady, and Norman H. Nie, "Race, Ethnicity, and the Resources for Participation: the Role of Religion," paper delivered at the 1992 Annual Meeting of the American Political Science Association, September 3–6, 1992. Reprinted by permission.

presented in the last chapter that upper-status persons are more likely to have an ideological view of politics, it may suggest that governance here is a bit more sensitive not only to the interests but to the (conflicting) ideologies of upper-status white people.

SUMMARY

The popular view that Americans "don't vote" as a result of "apathy" is not quite right. The correct view is that we don't register to vote (but once registered, we

do vote), and that there are many factors having nothing to do with apathy that shape our participation rates—age, race, party organization, the barriers to registration, and popular views about the significance of elections.

The most powerful determinants of participation are schooling and information; the next most powerful is age. Race makes a difference, but black participation rates approximate white rates once you control for socioeconomic status.

Compared to other nations, Americans vote at lower rates but more frequently and for many more offices, so that elections make a bigger difference in the conduct of public affairs here than abroad. We also engage somewhat more frequently than do people abroad in various nonelectoral forms of participation.

KEY TERMS

registered voters   *p. 131*

voting-age population   *p. 131*

motor-voter bill   *p. 132*

literacy test   *p. 135*

poll tax   *p. 135*

grandfather clause   *p. 135*

white primary   *p. 136*

Australian ballot   *p. 139*

activists   *p. 140*

SUGGESTED READINGS

Burnham, Walter Dean. *Critical Elections and the Mainsprings of American Politics.* New York: Norton, 1970. An argument about the decline of voter participation, linking it to changes in the economic system.

Conway, M. Margaret. *Political Participation in the United States.* 2d ed. Washington, D.C.: Congressional Quarterly Press, 1991. Good brief summary of what we need to know about who participates in politics and why.

Orren, Gary R. "The Linkage of Policy to Participation." In *Presidential Selection*, edited by Alexander Heard and Michael Nelson. Durham, N.C.: Duke University Press, 1987. Carefully evaluates various proposals for increasing electoral turnout in the United States.

Teixeira, Ruy. *Why Americans Don't Vote.* Westport, Conn.: Greenwood Press, 1987. Good summary of what we know about nonvoting.

Verba, Sidney, and Norman H. Nie. *Participation in America.* New York: Harper & Row, 1972. The effect of social class on various forms of political participation.

Verba, Sidney, Norman H. Nie, and Jae-on Kim. *Participation and Political Equality.* Cambridge, England: Cambridge University Press, 1978. A comparative study of political participation in seven nations.

Wolfinger, Raymond E., and Steven R. Rosenstone. *Who Votes?* New Haven, Conn.: Yale University Press, 1980. Excellent analysis of what factors determine turnout.

7

Political Parties

One of the reasons why voter turnout is higher abroad than in this country is that political parties in other democratic nations are more effective at mobilizing voters than here. The sense of being a party member and the inclination to vote the party ticket are greater in France, Italy, or Sweden than in the United States. From this fact you might suppose that political parties here are recent inventions with little experience at organizing and no history of attracting voter identification.

Quite the contrary. American political parties are the oldest in the world, and at one time being a Democrat or a Republican was a serious commitment that people did not make lightly or abandon easily. In those days it would have been hard to find anything in Europe that could match the vote-getting power of such party organizations as those in Chicago, New York, and Philadelphia.

Parties in the United States are relatively weak today, not because they are old but because the laws and rules under which they operate have taken away much of their power at the same time that many voters have lost their sense of commitment to party identification. This weakening has proceeded unevenly, however, because our constitutional system has produced a decentralized party system just as it has produced a decentralized governmental system, with the result that parties in some places are strong and in other places almost nonexistent.

Parties—Here and Abroad

A **political party** is a group that seeks to elect candidates to public office by supplying them with a label—a "party identification"—by which they are known to the electorate.[1] This definition is purposefully broad so that it will include both familiar parties (Democratic, Republican) and unfamiliar ones (Whig, Libertarian, Socialist Worker) and will cover periods in which a party is very strong (having an elaborate and well-disciplined organization that

151

provides money and workers to its candidates) as well as periods in which it is quite weak (supplying nothing but the label to candidates). The label by which a candidate is known may or may not actually be printed on the ballot opposite the candidate's name: in the United States it does appear on the ballot in all national elections but in only a minority of municipal ones; in Australia and Israel (and in Great Britain before 1969) it never appears on the ballot at all.

This definition suggests the three political arenas within which parties may be found. A party exists as a *label* in the minds of the voters, as an *organization* that recruits and campaigns for candidates, and as a *set of leaders* who try to organize and control the legislative and executive branches of government. A powerful party is one whose label has a strong appeal for the voters, whose organization can decide who will be candidates and how their campaigns will be managed, and whose leaders can dominate one or all branches of government.

American parties have become weaker in all three arenas. As a *label* with which voters identify, the parties are probably much weaker than they were in the nineteenth century but only somewhat weaker than they were thirty years ago (see Figure 7.1). In 1952, 22 percent of the voters described themselves as "strong" Democrats; by 1992 only 18 percent did. In 1952, 13 percent said that they were "strong" Republicans; in 1992, 11 percent did. There has been an increase in the proportion of people saying that they either were "independent" or had no preference between the two major parties. (Many of the "independents," of course, lean more to one party than the other, and many of the "no preference" voters simply don't care about politics, period.) After 1980 the number of Republicans increased owing, apparently, to the popularity of President Reagan; however scholars are not sure that this increase will last. But the best evidence of weakening party identification is what voters *do*. As we shall see in the next chapter, they increasingly have been voting split tickets—that is, supporting a president from one party and member of Congress from the other.

As a *set of leaders* who organize government, especially Congress, political parties have become weaker in ways that will be described in Chapter 11. As *organizations* that nominate and elect candidates, parties have become dramatically weaker just since the 1960s. In most states parties have very little con-

FIGURE 7.1 Party Identification, 1952–1992

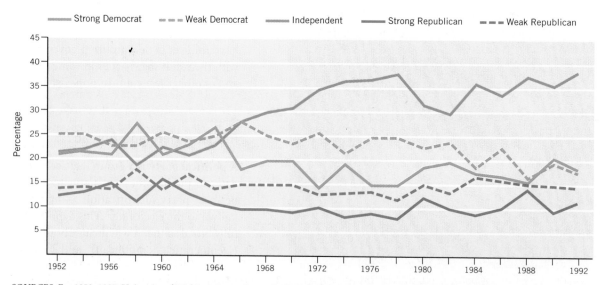

SOURCES: For 1952–1987: University of Michigan Survey Research Center (1952–1982) and University of Chicago National Opinion Research Center (1984–1987) as reported in *National Journal* (November 14, 1987), 2866, updated by Daron Shaw; for 1990–1992: ICPSR American National Election Studies, University of Michigan.

trol over who gets nominated to office. The causes and consequences of that change are the subject of this chapter.

In Europe things are very different. Almost the only way a person can become a candidate for elective office is to be nominated by party leaders. Campaigns are run by the party, using party funds and workers, not by the candidate. Once in office, the elected officials are expected to vote and act together with other members of their party. The principal criterion by which voters choose among candidates is their party identification or label. (This has been changing somewhat of late: European parties, like American ones, have not been able to count as heavily as in the past on party loyalty among the voters.)

Several factors explain the striking differences between American and European political parties. First, the federal system of government in the United States decentralizes political authority and thus decentralizes political-party organizations. For nearly two centuries most of the important governmental decisions were made at the state and local levels— decisions regarding education, land use, business regulation, and public welfare—and thus it was at the state and local levels that the important struggles over power and policy occurred. Moreover most people with political jobs—either elective or appointive—worked for state and local government, and thus a party's interest in obtaining these jobs for its followers meant that it had to focus attention on who controlled city hall, the county courthouse, and the state capitol. Federalism, in short, meant that political parties would acquire jobs and money from local sources and fight local contests. This, in turn, meant that the national political parties would be coalitions of local parties, and though these coalitions would have a keen interest in capturing the presidency (with it, after all, went control of large numbers of federal jobs), the national party leaders rarely had as much power as the local ones. The Republican leader of Cuyahoga County, Ohio, for example, could often ignore the decisions of the Republican national chairman and even of the Ohio state chairman.

Political authority in the United States has of late come to be far more centralized: the federal government now makes decisions affecting almost all aspects of our lives, including those—such as school-

The weakening of parties can be seen in these campaign buttons—they mention the candidates but not the parties.

ing and welfare—once left entirely in local hands. Yet the political parties have not become more centralized as a result. If anything, they have become even weaker and more decentralized. One reason for this apparent paradox is that in the United States, unlike in most other democratic nations, political parties are closely regulated by state and federal laws, and these regulations have had the effect of weakening the power of parties substantially. Perhaps the most important of these regulations are those that prescribe how a party's candidates are to be selected.

In the great majority of American states, the party leaders do not select people to run for office; by law those people are chosen by the voters in primary elections. Though sometimes the party can influence

Party means more in Italy than in the United States, as is evident from this party rally.

who will win a primary contest, in general people running for state or national office in this country owe little to party leaders. In Europe, by contrast, there is no such thing as a primary election—the only way to become a candidate for office is to persuade party leaders to put your name on the ballot. In a later section of this chapter, the impact of the direct primary will be discussed in more detail; for now, it is enough to note that its use removes from the hands of the party leadership its most important source of power over officeholders.

Furthermore, if an American political party wins control of Congress, it does not—as in most European nations with a parliamentary system of government—also win the right to select the chief executive of the government. The American president, as we have seen, is independently elected, and this means that he will choose his principal subordinates not from among members of Congress but from among persons out of Congress. Should he pick a representative or senator for his cabinet, the Constitution requires that person to resign from Congress in order to accept the job. Thus an opportunity to be a cabinet secretary is not an important reward for members of

Congress, and so the president cannot use the prospect of that reward as a way of controlling congressional action. All this weakens the significance and power of party as a means of organizing the government and conducting its business.

Political Culture

The attitudes and traditions of American voters reinforce the institutional and legal factors that make American parties relatively weak. Political parties in this country have rarely played an important part in the life of the average citizen; indeed one does not usually "join" a party here except by voting for its candidates. In many European nations, on the other hand, large numbers of citizens will join a party, pay dues, and attend regular meetings. Furthermore, in countries such as France, Austria, and Italy, the political parties sponsor a wide range of activities and dominate a variety of associations to which a person may belong—labor unions, youth groups, educational programs, even chess clubs.

In the United States we tend to keep parties separate from other aspects of our lives. As Democrats or

Republicans, we may become excited by a presidential campaign and a few of us may even participate in helping elect a member of Congress or state senator. Our social, business, working, and cultural lives, however, are almost entirely nonpartisan. Indeed most Americans, unlike many Europeans, would resent partisanship's becoming a conspicuous feature of other organizations to which they belong. All this is a way of saying that American parties play a segmental, rather than comprehensive, role in our lives and that even this role is diminishing as more and more of us proclaim ourselves to be "independents."

The Rise and Decline of the Political Party

Our nation began without parties; today parties, though far from extinct, are about as weak as at any time in our history. In between the Founding and the present, however, parties arose and became powerful. We can see this process in four broad periods of party history: when political parties were created (roughly from the Founding to the 1820s); when the more or less stable two-party system emerged (roughly from the time of President Jackson to the Civil War); when parties developed a comprehensive organizational form and appeal (roughly from the Civil War to the 1930s); and finally when party "reform" began to alter the party system (beginning in the early 1900s but taking effect chiefly since the New Deal).

The Founding

The Founders disliked parties, thinking of them as "factions" motivated by ambition and self-interest. George Washington, dismayed by the quarreling between Hamilton and Jefferson in his cabinet, devoted much of his Farewell Address to condemning parties. This hostility to party was understandable: the legitimacy and success of the newly created federal government were still very much in doubt. When Jefferson organized his followers to oppose Hamilton's policies, it seemed to Hamilton and *his* followers that Jefferson was opposing not just a policy or a leader but the very concept of a national government. Jefferson for his part thought that Hamilton was not simply pursuing bad policies but was subverting the Constitution itself. Before political parties could be-

 **Two Views of Parties**

President George Washington, in his 1796 Farewell Address: "Let me warn you in the most solemn manner against the baneful effects of the spirit of party generally. This spirit . . . exists under different shapes in all government, more or less stifled, controlled, or repressed; but in those of the popular form it is seen in its greatest rankness and is truly their worst enemy."

Political scientist E. E. Schattschneider, in a 1942 book: "Political parties created democracy and . . . modern democracy is unthinkable save in terms of the parties."

come legitimate, it was necessary for people to be able to separate in their minds quarrels over policies and elections from disputes over the legitimacy of the new government itself. The ability to make that distinction was slow in coming, and thus parties were objects of profound suspicion, defended, at first, only as temporary expedients.

The first organized political party in American history was made up of the followers of Jefferson, who, beginning in the 1790s, called themselves *Republicans* (hoping to suggest thereby that their opponents were secret monarchists).* The followers of Hamilton kept the label *Federalist* that once had been used to refer to all supporters of the new Constitution (hoping to imply that *their* opponents were "Antifederalists," or enemies of the Constitution).

These parties were loose caucuses of political notables in various localities, with New England being strongly Federalist and much of the South passionately Republican. Jefferson and his ally James Madison thought that their Republican party was a temporary arrangement designed to defeat John Adams, a Federalist, in his bid to succeed Washington in 1796. (Adams narrowly defeated Jefferson, who, under the system then in effect, became vice president because he had the second most electoral votes.) In 1800 Adams' bid to succeed himself intensified party activity even more, but this time Jefferson won and the Republicans assumed office. The Federalists

*The Jeffersonian Republicans were not the party that today we call Republican. In fact, present-day Democrats consider Jefferson to be their founder.

feared that Jefferson would dismantle the Constitution, but Jefferson adopted a conciliatory posture, saying in his inaugural address that "we are all Republicans, we are all Federalists."[2] It was not true, of course: the Federalists detested Jefferson and some were planning to have New England secede from the Union. But it was good politics, expressive of the need that every president has to persuade the public that, despite partisan politics, the presidency exists to serve all the people.

So successful were the Republicans that the Federalists virtually ceased to exist as a party. Jefferson was reelected in 1804 with almost no opposition; Madison easily won two terms; James Monroe carried sixteen out of nineteen states in 1816 and was reelected without opposition in 1820. Political parties had seemingly disappeared, just as Jefferson had hoped. The weakness of this so-called first party system can be explained by the fact that it *was* the first: nobody had been born a Federalist or a Republican; there was no ancestral party loyalty to defend; the earliest political leaders did not think of themselves as professional politicians; and the Federalist party had such a limited sectional and class base that it could not compete effectively in national elections. The parties that existed in these early years were essentially small groups of local notables. Political participation was limited, and nominations for most local offices were arranged rather casually.

Even in this early period, the parties, though they had very different views on economic policy and somewhat different class bases, did not represent clear, homogeneous economic interests. Farmers in Virginia were Republicans, but farmers in Delaware were Federalists; the commercial interests of Boston were firmly Federalist, but commercial leaders in urban Connecticut were likely to be Republican. From the beginning to the present, elections have created heterogeneous coalitions as Madison had anticipated.

The Jacksonians

What is often called the second party system emerged around 1824 with Andrew Jackson's first run for the presidency and lasted until the Civil War became inevitable. Its distinctive feature was that political participation became a mass phenomenon. For one thing the number of voters to be reached had become

When Andrew Jackson ran for president in 1828, over a million votes were cast for the first time in American history. This poster, from the 1832 election, was part of the emergence of truly mass political participation.

quite large. Only about 365,000 popular votes were cast in 1824. But as a result of laws that enlarged the number of people eligible to vote and of an increase in the population, by 1828 well over a million votes were tallied and by 1840 well over 2 million. (In England at this time there were only 650,000 eligible voters.) In addition by 1832 presidential electors were selected by popular vote in virtually every state. (As late as 1816 electors were chosen by the state legislatures, rather than by the people, in about half the states.) Presidential politics had become a truly national, genuinely popular activity; indeed in many communities election campaigns had become the principal public spectacle.

The party system of the Jacksonian era was built from the bottom up rather than—as during the period of the Founding—from the top down. No change better illustrates this transformation than the abandonment of the system of having caucuses composed of members of Congress nominate presidential candidates. The caucus system was an effort to unite the legislative and executive branches by giving the former some degree of control over who would have a chance to capture the latter. The caucus system became unpopular when the caucus candidate for president in 1824 ran third in a field of four in the general election and was completely discredited that same year when Congress denied the presidency to Jackson, the candidate with the most popular votes.

To replace the caucus, the party convention was invented. The first convention in American history was that of the Anti-Masonic party in 1831; the first convention of a major political party was that of the anti-Jackson Republicans later that year (it nominated Henry Clay for president). The Democrats held a convention in 1832 that ratified Jackson's nomination for reelection and picked Martin Van Buren as his running mate. The first convention to select a man who would be elected president and who was not already the incumbent president was held by the Democrats in 1836; it chose Van Buren.

Considering the many efforts made in recent years to curtail or even abolish the national nominating convention, it is worth remembering that the convention system was first developed in part as a reform—a way of allowing for some measure of local control over the nominating process. Virtually no other nation adopted this method, just as no other nation was later to adopt the direct primary after the convention system became the object of criticism. It is interesting, but perhaps futile, to speculate on how American government would have evolved if the legislative caucus had remained as the method for nominating presidents.

The Civil War and Sectionalism

Though the party system created in the Jacksonian period was the first truly national system, with Democrats (followers of Jackson) and Whigs (opponents of Jackson) fairly evenly balanced in most regions, it could not withstand the deep split in opinion created by the agitation over slavery. Both parties tried, naturally, to straddle the issue since neither wanted to divide its followers and thus lose the election to its rival. But slavery and sectionalism were issues that could not be straddled. The old parties divided and new ones emerged. The modern Republican party (not the old Democratic-Republican

party of Thomas Jefferson) began as a third party. As a result of the Civil War, it came to be a major party (the only third party ever to gain major-party status) and to dominate national politics with only occasional interruptions for three-quarters of a century.

Republican control of the White House, and to a lesser extent of Congress, was in large measure the result of two events that gave to Republicans a marked advantage in the competition for the loyalties of

The Donkey and the Elephant

Since 1874, when Thomas Nast published political cartoons using these figures, the elephant has been the symbol of the Republican party and the donkey (originally the jackass) the symbol of the Democratic party.

The association of the Democrats with donkeys may have begun with a remark by Ignatius Donnelly, a Republican in the Minnesota legislature, who said that the "Democratic party is like a mule—without pride of ancestry or hope of posterity." An equally uncharitable explanation for the link between Republicans and elephants was offered by Democratic presidential candidate Adlai Stevenson, who in the 1950s observed that "the elephant has a thick skin, a head full of ivory, and as everyone who has seen a circus parade knows, proceeds best by grasping the tail of its predecessor."

SOURCE: Adapted from William Safire, *Safire's Political Dictionary* (New York: Ballantine Books, 1978). Used by permission.

★ Old-Style Party Loyalties

*T*oday we take party loyalties rather lightly. In the latter part of the nineteenth century and well into the twentieth, however, such loyalties were deep and powerful. Brand Whitlock recalls what it meant to be a Republican in Ohio during his youth:

> In the Ohio of those days it was natural to be a Republican; it was more than that, it was inevitable that one should be a Republican; it was not a matter of intellectual choice, it was a process of biological selection. The Republican party was not a faction, not a group, not a wing, it was an institution, . . . rooted like oak-trees. . . . It was elemental, like gravity, the sun, the stars, the ocean. . . . One became, in Urbana and Ohio for many years, a Republican just as the Eskimo dons fur clothes. It was inconceivable that any self-respecting person should be a Democrat.*

By changing the place to Georgia, the same could have been written about what it meant to be a Democrat.

*From Brand Whitlock, *Forty Years of It* (New York: Appleton, 1914), 27. Quoted in James L. Sundquist, *Dynamics of the Party System* (Washington, D.C.: Brookings Institution, 1973), 91.

In 1968, older party leaders were still to be seen at national conventions, but they were already being replaced by younger activists.

voters. The first of these was the Civil War. This bitter, searing crisis deeply polarized popular attitudes. Those who supported the Union side became, for generations, Republicans; those who supported the Confederacy, or who had opposed the war, became Democrats.

As it turned out, this partisan division was, for a while, nearly even: though the Republicans usually won the presidency and the Senate, they often lost control of the House. There were many northern Democrats. In 1896, however, another event—the presidential candidacy of William Jennings Bryan—further strengthened the Republican party. Bryan, a Democrat, alienated many voters in the populous northeastern states while attracting voters in the South and Midwest. The result was to confirm and deepen the split in the country, especially North versus South, begun by the Civil War. From 1896 to the 1930s, with only rare exceptions, the northern states were solidly Republican, the southern ones solidly Democratic.

This split had a profound effect on the organization of political parties, for it meant that most states were now one-party states. As a result, competition for office at the state level had to go on *within* a single dominant party (the Republican party in Massachusetts, New York, Pennsylvania, Wisconsin, and elsewhere; the Democratic party in Georgia, Mississippi, South Carolina, and elsewhere). Consequently there emerged two major factions within each party, but especially within the Republican. One was composed of the party regulars, the professional politicians, the "stalwarts," or the Old Guard. They were preoccupied with building up the party machinery, developing party loyalty, and acquiring and dispensing patronage—jobs and other favors—for themselves and their faithful followers. Their great skills were those of organization, negotiation, bargaining, compromise; their great interest was in winning.

The other faction, variously called **mugwumps** or **progressives** (or "reformers"), was opposed to the heavy emphasis on patronage, disliked the party machinery because it only permitted bland candidates to rise to the top, was fearful of the heavy influx of immigrants into American cities and of the ability of the party regulars to organize them into "machines," and wanted to see the party take unpopular positions on certain issues (such as free trade). Their great skills were those of advocacy and articulation; their great interest was in principle.

At first the mugwumps tried to play a balance-of-power role, sometimes siding with the Republican party of which they were members, at other times defecting to the Democrats (as when they bolted the Republican party to support Grover Cleveland, the Democratic nominee, in 1884). But later, as the Republican strength in the nation grew, progressives within that party became less and less able to play a balance-of-power role, especially at the state level. Wisconsin, Michigan, Ohio, and Iowa were solidly Republican; Georgia, the Carolinas, and the rest of the Old South by 1880 had become so heavily Democratic that the Republican party in many areas had virtually ceased to exist. If the progressives were to have any power, it would require, they came to believe, an attack on the very concept of partisanship itself.

The Era of Reform

Progressives began to espouse measures to curtail or even abolish political parties. They favored primary elections to replace nominating conventions because the latter were viewed as manipulated by party bosses; they favored nonpartisan elections at the city level and in some cases at the state level as well; they argued against corrupt alliances between parties and businesses. They wanted strict voter-registration requirements that would reduce vote frauds but that would also, as it turned out, keep ordinary citizens who found the requirements cumbersome from voting; they pressed for civil-service reform to eliminate patronage; and they made heavy use of the mass media as a way of attacking the abuses of partisanship and of promoting their own ideas and candidacies.

The progressives were more successful in some places than in others. In California, for example, progressives led by Governor Hiram Johnson in 1910–1911 were able to institute the direct primary and to adopt procedures—called the *initiative* and the *referendum*—so that citizens could vote directly

This was Tammany Hall in its heyday as Democratic party head-quarters in Manhattan.

on proposed legislation, thereby bypassing the state legislature. Governor Robert La Follette brought about similar changes in Wisconsin.

The effect of these changes was to reduce substantially the worst forms of political corruption and ultimately to make boss rule in politics difficult if not impossible. But they also had the effect of making political parties, whether led by bosses or by statesmen, weaker, less able to hold officeholders accountable, and less able to assemble the power necessary for governing the fragmented political institutions created by the Constitution. In Congress party lines began to grow fainter, as did the power of congressional leadership. Above all, the progressives did not

FIGURE 7.2   Cleavages and Continuity in the Two-Party System

1787	Federalists	Antifederalists
1789	(no organized parties)	(no organized parties)
1792		
1796		
1800	Federalists	Democratic-Republicans
1804		
1808		
1812		
1816		
1820		
1824		
1828	National Republicans	Democrats
1832		
1836		
1840	Whigs	
1844		
1848	Republicans Whigs	
1852		
1856	Republicans Democrats Southern Constitutional
1860		Democrats Unionists
1864		
1868	Democrats	
1872		
1876		
1880		
1884		
1888		
1892	National Bryan
1896	Democrats Democrats
1900		
1904	Democrats	
1908	Republicans Bull Moose
1912	Progressive	
1916		
1920	Republicans	
1924		
1928		
1932		
1936		
1940		
1944	Henry Wallace States' Rights
1948	Progressives Democrats
1952		
1956	Democrats	
1960	George Wallace
1964	Democrats[a] Democrats
1968		
1972	Democrats	
1976		
1980		
1984	John Anderson
1988	Independents	
1992		
		Ross Perot
		Independents[b]

[a]American Independent party.

[b]United We Stand America party.

Ross Perot ran for president in 1992 not only as an independent candidate but as a symbol of popular opposition to political parties.

have an answer to the problem first faced by Jefferson: if there is not a strong political party, by what other means will candidates for office be found, recruited, and supported? Political candidacies, like people, are not the products of a virgin birth. Some group or organization must arrange a candidacy, and if that group is not a party, then it can only be another kind of interest group, the mass media, or the personal supporters and family of the candidate. These alternatives are best seen by looking at the forms of party structure now operating.

The National Party Structure Today

Since political parties exist at the national, state, and local levels, you might suppose that they are arranged like a big corporation, with a national board of directors giving orders to state managers, who in turn direct the activities of rank-and-file workers at the county and city level.

Nothing could be further from the truth. At each level a separate and almost entirely independent organization exists that does pretty much what it wants, and in many counties and cities there is virtually no organization at all.

On paper the national Democratic and Republican parties look quite similar. In both parties ultimate authority is in the hands of the **national convention** that meets every four years to nominate a presidential candidate. Between these conventions party affairs are managed by a **national committee,** made up of delegates from each state and territory. In the Congress each party has a **congressional campaign committee** that helps members who are running for reelection or would-be members running for an open seat or challenging a candidate from the opposition party. The day-to-day work of the party is managed by a full-time, paid **national chairman** who is elected by the committee.

For a long time the two national parties were alike in behavior as well as description. The national chairman, if his party held the White House, would help decide who among the party faithful would get federal jobs. Otherwise the parties did very little.

But beginning in the late 1960s and early 1970s, the Republicans began to convert their national party into a well-financed, highly staffed organization devoted to finding and electing Republican candidates, especially to Congress. At about the same time, the Democrats began changing the rules governing how presidential candidates are nominated in ways that profoundly altered the distribution of power within the party. As a consequence the Republicans became a bureaucratized party and the Democrats became a factionalized one. After the Republicans won four out of five presidential elections from 1968 to 1984 and briefly took control of the Senate, the Democrats began to suspect that maybe an efficient bureaucracy was better than a collection of warring factions, and so they made an effort to emulate the Republicans.

What the Republicans had done was to take advantage of a new bit of technology—computerized mailings. They built up a huge file of names of people who had given or might give money to the party, usually in small amounts, and used that list to raise a big budget for the national party. In 1983 the Republican National Committee (RNC) raised $35 million from over 1.7 million individual donors; by the time of the

TRIVIA

Political Parties

First national political convention	*Anti-Masonic party, 1831, in Baltimore*
First time incumbent governors were nominated for president	*Rutherford B. Hayes of Ohio (by Republicans in 1876) Samuel J. Tilden of New York (by Democrats in 1876)*
First black to receive a vote at a national party convention	*Frederick Douglass (at Republican convention in 1888)*
First year in which women attended conventions as delegates	*1900 (one woman at both Democratic and Republican conventions)*
Most ballots needed to choose a presidential nominee	*103, by Democrats in 1924 to select John W. Davis*
Closest vote in convention history	*543 ³/₂₀ to 542 ⁷/₂₀, defeating a motion to condemn the Ku Klux Klan at 1924 Democratic convention*
First Catholic nominated for president by major party	*Al Smith, by Democrats in 1928*
Only person nominated for president four times by major political party	*Franklin D. Roosevelt (by Democrats in 1932, 1936, 1940, and 1944)*
First presidential nominee to make an acceptance speech at the party convention	*Franklin D. Roosevelt*

Franklin D. Roosevelt

Frederick Douglass

No longer deliberative bodies, party conventions have become arenas for made-for-television hoopla.

1986 election, the RNC was able to raise $75 million from 1.8 million donors. In presidential election years it raised even more.

The RNC used this money to run, in effect, a national political consulting firm. Money went to recruit and train Republican candidates, give them legal and financial advice, study issues and analyze voting trends, and conduct national advertising campaigns on behalf of the party as a whole. No one can be sure how much political success this money bought (after all, the Republicans lost control of the Senate in 1986), but many observers believed that Republican losses in Congress in 1982 and 1986 would have been even greater if the RNC had not worked so vigorously on behalf of its candidates.

When the Democratic National Committee (DNC) decided to play catch-up, it followed the RNC strategy. Using the same computerized, direct-mail techniques, the DNC managed to raise $15 million in the 1985–1986 election period, only one-fifth of what the Republicans raised, but still a lot better than what it had done in the 1970s. (Though the DNC raised less money than the RNC, Democratic candidates still outspent their Republican opponents. The Democrats more than made up the difference with money raised by individual candidates.)

A lot of RNC money goes to commission public-opinion polls, not only to find out which candidate is likely to win an election, but more important, to find out what issues are troubling the voters, how different segments of the population respond to different kinds of issues and news stories, and how people react to the campaign efforts of specific candidates. During the Reagan administration the RNC's principal pollster, Richard Wirthlin, was doing polls at least monthly, and sometimes daily.[3] For reasons explained in Chapter 5, these polls can take you just so far; they are helpful, but they are not a surefire guide to public opinion or how to change it.

The Democrats still have a long way to go to catch up with the Republicans organizationally. Though the RNC began the new era in national politics by backing individual candidates, it now tries to help state and local party organizations as well. In 1986 it spent about $2.5 million on state Republican parties (the DNC, by contrast, spent $160,000). Polling is done less frequently. But the differences are not just monetary ones. Whereas the RNC has been able to develop a smooth-running organization that often has good relations with state and local parties, the DNC is still to some degree a collection of feuding factions. To see why this should be, we must look closely at how the parties nominate their presidential candidates.

National Conventions

The national committee selects the time and place of the next national convention and issues a "call" for the convention that sets forth the number of delegates each state and territory is to have and also the rules under which delegates must be chosen. The number of delegates, and their manner of selection, can significantly influence the chances of various presidential candidates, and considerable attention is thus devoted to these matters. In the Democratic party, for example, a long struggle took place between those who wished to see southern states receive a large share of delegates to the convention in recognition of their firm support of Democratic candidates in presidential elections and those who preferred to see a larger share of delegates allotted to northern and western states that, though less solidly Democratic, were larger or more liberal.

The national nominating convention was created to broaden political participation, but by 1880, when the Republicans met in Chicago, the convention was often under the control of party bosses. Today the bosses are gone but the spectacle endures.

A similar conflict within the Republican party has pitted conservative Republican leaders in the Midwest against liberal ones in the East. Though a compromise formula is usually chosen, the drift of these formulas over the years has gradually shifted voting strength in the Democratic convention away from the South and toward the North and West and in the Republican convention away from the East and toward the South and Southwest. These delegate-allocation formulas are but one sign (others will be mentioned later in this chapter) of the tendency of the two parties' conventions to move in opposite ideological directions—Democrats more to the left, Republicans more to the right.

The exact formula for apportioning delegates is extremely complex. For the Democrats it takes into account the vote each state cast for Democratic candidates in past elections and the number of electoral votes of each state; for the Republicans it takes into account the number of representatives in Congress and whether the state in past elections cast its electoral votes for the Republican presidential candidate and elected Republicans to the Senate, the House, and the governorship. Thus the Democrats give extra delegates to large states while the Republicans give extra ones to loyal states.

The way in which delegates are chosen can be even more important than their allocation. The Democrats, beginning in 1972, have developed an elaborate set of rules designed to weaken the control over delegates by local party leaders and to increase the proportion of women, young people, blacks, and Native Americans attending the convention. These rules were first drafted by a party commission chaired by Senator George McGovern (who was later to make skillful use of these new procedures in his successful bid for the Democratic presidential nomination). They were revised in 1974 by another commission chaired by Barbara Mikulski, whose decisions were ratified by the 1974 midterm convention. After the 1976 election yet a third commission, chaired by Morley Winograd, produced still another revision of the rules, which took effect in 1980. Then a fourth commission, chaired by North Carolina

Governor James B. Hunt, recommended in 1981 yet another set of rules, which became effective with the 1984 convention.

The general thrust of the work of the first three rules commissions was to broaden the antiparty changes started by the progressives at the beginning of this century. Whereas the earlier reformers tried to minimize the role of parties in the election process, those of the 1970s sought to weaken the influence of leaders within the party. In short the newer reforms were aimed at creating *intra*party democracy as well as *inter*party democracy. This was done by rules that, for the 1980 convention, required:

- Equal division of delegates between men and women.

- Establishment of "goals" for the representation of blacks, Hispanics, and other groups in proportion to their presence in a state's Democratic electorate.

- Open delegate-selection procedures, with advance publicity and written rules.

- Selection of 75 percent of the delegates at the level of the congressional district or lower.

- No "unit rule" that would require all delegates to vote with the majority of their state delegation.

- Restrictions on the number of party leaders and elected officials who could vote at the convention.

- Requirement that all delegates pledged to a candidate vote for that candidate.

In 1981 the Hunt Commission changed some of these rules—in particular the last two—in order to increase the influence of elected officials and to make the convention a somewhat more deliberative body. The commission reserved about 14 percent of the delegate seats for party leaders and elected officials, who would not have to commit themselves in advance to a presidential candidate, and it repealed the rule requiring that delegates pledged to a candidate vote for that candidate.

Rules have consequences. Whereas in 1980 only one-seventh of the Democratic senators and representatives got to be delegates to the national convention, in 1984 more than half were delegates. In the 1984 presidential primaries, Walter Mondale was the chief beneficiary of the delegate-selection rules. He won the support of the overwhelming majority of elected officials—the so-called **superdelegates**—and he did especially well in those states that held winner-take-all primaries. Had different rules been in effect (if, for example, the delegates had been allocated strictly in proportion to the primary votes that the candidates won), Mondale probably would not have entered the Democratic convention with an assured majority.

But the "reform" of the parties, especially the Democratic party, has had far more profound consequences than merely helping one candidate or another. Before 1968 the Republican party represented, essentially, white-collar voters and the Democratic party represented blue-collar ones. After a decade of "reform" the Republican and the Democratic parties each represented two ideologically different sets of upper-middle-class voters (see Table 7.1). In the terminology of Chapter 5, the Republicans came to represent the more conservative wing of the traditional middle class and the Democrats the more leftist wing of the liberal middle class (or the "new class").

This was more troubling to the Democrats than to the Republicans because the traditional middle class (and thus the Republican national convention) is somewhat closer to the opinions of most citizens than is the liberal middle class (and thus the delegates to the Democratic national convention). And for whatever reason the Republicans won five out of six presidential races between 1968 and 1988.

Before the 1988 convention the Democrats took a long, hard look at their party procedures. Under the leadership of DNC chairman Paul Kirk, they decided against making any major changes, especially ones that would increase the power of grassroots activists at the expense of elected officials and party leaders. The number of such officials (or superdelegates) to be given delegate seats was increased. For example, 80 percent of the Democratic members of Congress and all Democratic governors were automatically made convention delegates in 1988. The official status of some special-interest caucuses (such as those organized to represent blacks, homosexuals, and various ethnic groups) was reduced in order to lessen the perception that the Democrats were simply a party of factions.

The surface harmony was a bit misleading, however, as some activists, notably supporters of Jesse

Jackson, protested that the rules made it harder for Jackson to win delegates in proportion to his share of the primary vote. (In 1984 he got 18 percent of the primary votes but only 12 percent of the delegates.) The DNC responded by changing the rules for the 1992 campaign. Former DNC chairman Ronald H. Brown (later President Clinton's secretary of commerce) won approval for three important requirements:

- The winner-reward systems of delegate distribution, which gave the winner of a primary or caucus extra delegates, were banned. (In 1988 fifteen states used winner-reward systems, including such vote-rich states as Florida, Illinois, New Jersey, and Pennsylvania.)

- The proportional representation system was put into use. This system divides a state's publicly elected delegates among candidates who receive at least 15 percent of the vote.

- States that violate the rules are now penalized with the loss of 25 percent of their national convention delegates.

Even though the Democrats have retreated a bit from the reforms of the 1960s and 1970s, the conventions of both parties have changed fundamentally, and probably permanently. Delegates once selected by party leaders are now chosen by primary elections and grassroots caucuses. As a result the convention is no longer a place where party leaders meet to bargain over the identity of their presidential candidate; it is instead a place where delegates come together to ratify choices already made by party activists and primary voters.

Most Americans dislike bosses, deals, and manipulation and prefer democracy, reform, and openness. These are commendable instincts. But such instincts, unless carefully tested against practice, may mislead us into supposing that anything carried out in the name of reform is a good idea. Rules must be judged by their practical results as well as by their conformity to some principle of fairness. Rules affect the distribution of power: they help some people win and others lose. Later in this chapter we shall try to assess delegate-selection rules by looking more closely at how they affect who attends conventions and which presidential candidates are selected there.

TABLE 7.1   Who Are the Party Delegates?

Characteristics of delegates to Democratic and Republican national conventions in 1988

	Democrats	Republicans
Women	52%	37%
Blacks	21	3
Under age 30	4	4
Religion		
Catholic	30	24
Jewish	6	2
Protestant	51	70
Education		
College degree or beyond	73	68
Postgraduate degree	52	42
Occupation		
Lawyer	16	17
Teacher	14	5
Union member	25	3
Hold elective office	26	28

SOURCE: *New York Times* (August 14, 1988): 14. Copyright © 1988 by the New York Times Company. Reprinted by permission.

State and Local Parties

While the national party structures have changed, the grassroots organizations have withered. In between, state party systems have struggled to redefine their roles.

In every state there is a Democratic and Republican state party organized under state law. Typically each will consist of a state central committee below which will be found county committees and sometimes city, town, or even precinct committees. The members of these committees are chosen in a variety of ways—sometimes in primary elections, sometimes by conventions, sometimes by a building-block process whereby people elected to serve on precinct or town committees choose the members of county committees, who in turn choose state committee members.

Knowing these formal arrangements is much less helpful than knowing the actual distribution of power in each state party. In a few places strong party bosses handpick the members of these committees;

in other places powerful elected officials—key state legislators, county sheriffs, or judges—control the committees. And in many places no one is in charge, so that either the party structure is largely meaningless or it is made up of the representatives of various local factions.

To understand how power is distributed in a party, we must first know what *incentives* motivate people in a particular state or locality to become active in a party organization. Different incentives lead to different ways of organizing parties.

The Machine

A **political machine** is a party organization that recruits its members by the use of tangible incentives—money, political jobs, an opportunity to get favors from government—and that is characterized by a high degree of leadership control over member activity. At one time many local party organizations were machines, and the struggle over political jobs—patronage—was the chief concern of their members. Though Tammany Hall in New York City began as a caucus of well-to-do notables in the local Democratic party, by the late nineteenth century it had be-

come a machine organized on the basis of political clubs in each assembly district. These clubs were composed of party workers whose job it was to get out the straight party vote in their election districts and who hoped for a tangible reward if they were successful.

And there were abundant rewards to hope for. During the 1870s it was estimated that one out of every eight voters in New York City had a federal, state, or city job.[4] The federal bureaucracy was one important source of those jobs. The New York Custom House alone employed thousands of people, virtually all of whom were replaced if their party lost the presidential election. The postal system was another source, and it was frankly recognized as such. When James N. Tyner became postmaster general in 1876, he was "appointed not to see that the mails were carried, but to see that Indiana was carried."[5] Elections and conventions were so frequent and the intensity of party competition so great that being a party worker was for many a full-time paid occupation.

Well before the arrival of vast numbers of poor immigrants from Ireland, Italy, and elsewhere, old-stock Americans had perfected the machine, run up the cost of government, and systematized vote frauds. Kickbacks on contracts, payments extracted from officeholders, and funds raised from business-people made some politicians rich but also paid the huge bills of the elaborate party organization. When the immigrants began flooding the eastern cities, the party machines were there to provide them with all manner of services in exchange for their support at the polls: the machines were a vast welfare organization operating before the creation of the welfare state.

The abuses of the machine were well known and gradually curtailed. Stricter voter-registration laws reduced fraud, civil-service reforms cut down the number of patronage jobs, and competitive-bidding laws made it harder to award overpriced contracts to favored businesses. The Hatch Act (passed by Congress in 1939) made it illegal for federal civil-service employees to take an active part in political management or political campaigns by serving as a party officer, soliciting campaign funds, running for partisan office, working in a partisan campaign, endorsing partisan candidates, taking voters to the polls, counting ballots, circulating nominating petitions, or being a delegate to a party convention. (They may still vote and make campaign contributions.)

Ex-Senator George Washington Plunkitt of Tammany Hall explains machine politics from atop the bootblack stand in front of the New York County Court House, around 1905.

These restrictions gradually took federal employees out of machine politics, but they did not end the machines. In many cities—Chicago, Philadelphia, and Albany—ways were found to maintain the machine even though city employees were technically under civil service. Far more important than the various progressive reforms that weakened machines were changes among voters. As voters grew in education, income, and sophistication, they depended less and less on the advice and leadership of local party officials. And as the federal government created a bureaucratic welfare system, the party's welfare system declined in value.

It is easy either to scorn the machine as a venal and self-serving organization or to romanticize it as an informal welfare system. In truth it was a little of both. Above all it was a frank recognition of the fact that politics requires organization; the machine was the supreme expression of the value of organization. Even allowing for vote frauds, in elections where machines were active, voter turnout was huge: more people participated in politics when mobilized by a machine than when appealed to by television or good-government associations.[6] Moreover, because machines were interested in winning, they would subordinate any other consideration to that end. This has meant that machines were usually willing to support the presidential candidate with the best chance of winning, regardless of his policy views (provided, of course, that he was not determined to wreck the machine once in office). Republican machines helped elect Abraham Lincoln as well as Warren G. Harding; Democratic machines were of crucial importance in electing Franklin D. Roosevelt and John F. Kennedy.

The old-style machine is almost extinct, though important examples still can be found in the Democratic organization in Cook County (Chicago) and the Republican organization in Nassau County (New York). But a new-style machine has emerged in a few places. It is a machine in the sense that it uses money to knit together many politicians, but it is new-style in that the money comes not from patronage and contracts, but from campaign contributions supplied by wealthy individuals and the proceeds of direct-mail campaigns.

The political organization headed by Democratic congressmen Henry A. Waxman and Howard L. Berman on the west side of Los Angeles is one such new-style machine. By the astute use of campaign funds, the "Waxman-Berman organization" builds loyalties to it among a variety of elected officials at all levels of government. Moreover this new-style machine, unlike the old ones, has a strong interest in issues, especially at the national level. In this sense it is not a machine at all, but a cross between a machine and an ideological party.

Ideological Parties

At the opposite extreme from the machine is the **ideological party.** Where the machine values winning above all else, the ideological party values principle above all else. Where the former depends on money incentives, the latter spurns them. Where the former is hierarchical and disciplined, the latter is usually contentious and factionalized.

The most firmly ideological parties have been independent "third parties," such as the Socialist, Socialist Workers, Libertarian, and Right-to-Life parties. But there have been ideological factions within the Democratic and Republican parties; in some places these ideological groups have taken over the regular parties.

In the 1950s and 1960s these ideological groups were "reform clubs" within local Democratic and Republican parties. In Los Angeles, New York, and many parts of Wisconsin and Minnesota, issue-oriented activists fought to take over the party from election-oriented regulars. Democratic reform clubs managed to defeat the head of Tammany Hall in Manhattan; similar activist groups became the dominant force in California state politics.[7] The Democratic club leaders were more liberal than rank-and-file Democrats; Republican club leaders were often more conservative than rank-and-file Republicans.

The 1960s and 1970s saw these "reform" movements replaced by more focused social movements. The "reform" movement was based on a generalized sense of liberalism (among Democrats) or conservatism (among Republicans). With the advent of social movements concerned with civil rights, peace, feminism, environmentalism, libertarianism, abortion, and right to life, the generalized ideology of the clubs was replaced by the specific ideological demands of single-issue activists.

Today, for example, the Christian Coalition is an active group within the Republican party. Strongly

Television evangelist Pat Robertson (left) became a leader of the Christian Coalition.

pro-life and conservative on social issues, in the early 1990s these religiously oriented Republican party activists were influential in everything from local school board races to congressional races.

The result is that in many places the party has become a collection of people drawn from various social movements. For a candidate to win the party's support, he or she often has to satisfy the "litmus-test" demands of the ideological activists in the party. Democratic Senator Barbara Mikulski put it this way: "The social movements are now our farm clubs."

With social movements as their farm clubs, the big-league teams—the Democrats and Republicans at the state level—behave very differently than they did when political machines were the farm clubs. Internal factionalism is more intense, and the freedom of action of the party leader (say, the chairperson of the state committee) has been greatly reduced. A leader who demands too little or gives up too much,

or who says the wrong thing on a key issue, is quickly accused of having "sold out." Under these circumstances many "leaders" are that in name only.

Solidary Groups

Many people who participate in state and local politics do so not in order to earn money or vindicate some cause, but simply because they find it fun. They enjoy the game, they meet interesting people, and they like the sense of being "in the know" and rubbing shoulders with the powerful. When people get together out of gregarious or game-loving instincts, we say that they are responding to **solidary incentives;** if they form an organization, it is a solidary association.

Some of these associations were once machines. When a machine loses its patronage, some of its members—especially the older ones—may continue to serve in the organization out of a desire for camaraderie. In other cases precinct, ward, and district committees are built up on the basis of friendship networks. One study of political activists in Detroit found that most of them mentioned friendships and a liking for politics, rather than an interest in issues, as their reasons for joining the party organization.[8] Members of ward and town organizations in St. Louis County gave the same answers when asked why they joined.[9] Since patronage has declined in value and since the appeals of ideology are limited to a minority of citizens, the motivations for participating in politics have become very much like those for joining a bowling league or a bridge club.

The advantage of such groups is that they are neither corrupt nor inflexible; the disadvantage is that they often do not work very hard. Knocking on doors on a rainy November evening to try to talk people into voting for your candidate is a chore under the best of circumstances; it is especially unappealing if you joined the party primarily because you like to attend meetings or drink coffee with your friends.[10]

Sponsored Parties

Sometimes a relatively strong party organization can be created among volunteers without heavy reliance on money or ideology and without depending entirely on people's finding the work fun. This type of **sponsored party** occurs when another organization

Political parties have come increasingly to consist of social movements. People opposing abortion are well represented in the Republican party; those supporting it are well represented in the Democratic party.

exists in the community that can create, or at least sponsor, a local party structure. The clearest example of this is the Democratic party in and around Detroit, which has been developed, led, and to a degree financed by the political-action arm of the United Auto Workers union. The UAW has had a long tradition of rank-and-file activism, stemming from its formative struggles in the 1930s, and since the city is virtually a one-industry town, it was not hard to transfer some of this activism from union organizing to voter organizing.

By the mid-1950s union members and leaders made up over three-fourths of all the Democratic party district leaders within the city.[11] On election day union funds were available for paying workers to canvass voters; between elections political work on an unpaid basis was expected of union leaders. Though the UAW–Democratic party alliance in Detroit has not always been successful in city elections (the city is nonpartisan), it has been quite successful in carrying the city for the Democratic party in state and national elections.

Not many areas have organizations as effective or as dominant as the UAW that can bolster, sponsor, or even take over the weak formal party structure. Thus sponsored local parties are not common in the United States.

Personal Following

Because most candidates can no longer count on the backing of a machine, because sponsored parties are limited to a few unionized areas, and because solidary groups are not always productive, a person wanting to get elected will often try to form a **personal following** that will work for him or her during a campaign and then disband until the next election rolls around. Sometimes a candidate tries to meld a personal following with an ideological group, especially during the primary-election campaign, when one needs the kind of financial backing and hard work that only highly motivated activists are likely to supply.

To form a personal following, the candidate must have an appealing personality, a lot of friends, or a big bank account. The Kennedy family has had all three, and the electoral success of the personal followings of John F. Kennedy, Edward M. Kennedy, Robert Kennedy, and Joseph Kennedy, Jr., became legendary.

Southern politicians who have had to operate in one-party states with few, if any, machines have been the grand masters at building personal followings, such as those of the Talmadge family in Georgia, the Long family in Louisiana, and the Byrd family in

Virginia. But the strategy is increasingly followed wherever party organization is weak. The key asset is to have a known political name. That has helped the electoral victories of the son of Hubert Humphrey in Minnesota, the son and daughter of Pat Brown in California, the son of Birch Bayh in Indiana, the son of George Wallace in Alabama, and the son and grandson of Robert La Follette in Wisconsin.

The traditional party organization—one that is hierarchical, lasting, based on material incentives, and capable of influencing who gets nominated for office—exists today, according to political scientist David Mayhew, in only about eight states, mostly the older states in the Northeast. Another five states, he feels, have faction-ridden versions of the traditional party organization.[12] The states in the rest of the country display the weak party system of solidary clubs, personal followings, ideological groups, and sponsored parties. What that means can be seen in the composition of recent Democratic national conventions. More than half of the delegates are drawn from the ranks of the AFL-CIO, the National Education Association, and the National Organization for Women.[13]

The Two-Party System

With so many different varieties of local party organizations (or nonorganizations) and with such a great range of opinion found within each party, it is remarkable that we have had only two major political parties for most of our history. In the world at large a two-party system is a rarity; by one estimate only 15 nations have it.[14] Most European democracies are multiparty systems. We have only two parties with any chance of winning nationally, and these parties have been, over time, rather evenly balanced—between 1888 and 1992, the Republicans won fifteen presidential elections and the Democrats twelve. Furthermore, whenever one party has achieved a temporary ascendancy and its rival has been pronounced dead (as were the Democrats in the first third of this century and as were the Republicans during the 1930s and the 1960s), the "dead" party has displayed remarkable powers of recuperation, coming back to win important victories.

At the state and congressional-district levels, however, the parties are not evenly balanced. For a

The Kennedy family succeeded in developing strong political followings for three of its members—John F. Kennedy (center, standing), Robert F. Kennedy (to the right of John), and Edward M. Kennedy (seated, right).

long time the South was so heavily Democratic at all levels of government as to be a one-party area while upper New England and the Dakotas were strongly Republican. All regions are more competitive today than once was the case, but even now one party tends to enjoy a substantial advantage in at least half the states and in perhaps two-thirds of the congressional districts. Nevertheless, though the parties are not as competitive in state elections as they are in presidential ones, states have rarely had, at least for any extended period, political parties other than the Democratic and Republican (see Table 7.2).

Scholars do not entirely agree on why the two-party system should be so permanent a feature of American political life, but two kinds of explanations are of major importance. The first has to do with the system of elections, the second with the distribution of public opinion.

Elections at every level of government are based on the plurality, winner-take-all method. The **plurality system** means that in all elections for representative, senator, governor, and president, and in almost all elections for state legislator, mayor, and city councillor, the winner is that person who gets the most votes, even if they do not constitute a majority of the votes. We are so familiar with this system that we sometimes forget that there are other ways of running an election. For example, one could require that the winner get a majority of the votes, thus producing runoff elections if nobody got a majority on the

TABLE 7.2   The Rise of Republican Politics in the South, 1956–1994

Year	Number of Representatives		Number of Senators		Number of Governors		Number of States Voting for Presidential Nominee	
	Dem.	Rep.	Dem.	Rep.	Dem.	Rep.	Dem.	Rep.
1956	99	7	22	0	11	0	6	5
1958	99	7	22	0	11	0		
1960	99	7	22	0	11	0	8[a]	2
1962	95	11	21	1	11	0		
1964	89	17	21	1	11	0	6	5
1966	83	23	19	3	9	2		
1968	80	26	18	4	9	2	1	5[b]
1970	79	27	16 (1)[c]	5	9	2		
1972	74	34	14 (1)[c]	7	8	3	0	11
1974	81	27	15 (1)[c]	6	8	3		
1976	82	26	16 (1)[c]	5	9	2	10	1
1978	77	31	15 (1)[c]	6	8	3		
1980	55	53	11 (1)[c]	10	6	5	1	10
1982	80	33	11	11	11	0		
1984	72	41	11	11	10	1	0	11
1986	77	39	16	6	6	5		
1988	80	36	15	7	6	5	0	11
1990	77	39	15	7	8	3		
1992	82	43	14	8	8	3	4	7
1994	61	64	9	13	5	6		

[a] Eight Mississippi electors voted for Harry Byrd.
[b] George Wallace won five states on the American Independent ticket.
[c] Harry Byrd, Jr., was elected in Virginia in 1970 and 1976 as an independent.

In France, as in many European countries, parties are both more numerous and more influential than in the United States. In this French election the voter can choose one of six lists of candidates offered by six different parties.

first try. France does this in choosing its national legislature. In the first election candidates for parliament who win an absolute majority of the votes cast are declared elected. A week later the remaining candidates who received at least one-eighth but less than one-half the vote go into a runoff election; those who then win an absolute majority are also declared elected.

The French method encourages many political parties to form, each hoping to win at least one-eighth of the vote in the first election and then to enter into an alliance with its ideologically nearest rival in order to win the runoff. In the United States the plurality system means that a party must make all of the alliances it can before the first election—there is no second chance. Hence every party must be as broadly based as possible; a narrow, minor party has no hope of winning.

The winner-take-all feature of American elections has the same effect. Only one member of Congress is elected from each district. In many European countries the elections are based on proportional representation. Each party submits a list of candidates for parliament, ranked in order of preference by the party leaders. The nation votes. A party winning

37 percent of the vote gets 37 percent of the seats in parliament; a party winning 2 percent of the vote gets 2 percent of the seats. Since even the smallest parties have a chance of winning something, minor parties have an incentive to organize.

The most dramatic example of the winner-take-all principle is the electoral college (see pages 348–351). In every state but Maine and Nebraska, the candidate who wins the most popular votes in a state wins *all* of that state's electoral votes. In 1992, for example, Bill Clinton won only 45 percent of the popular vote in Missouri, but he got all of Missouri's eleven electoral votes because his two rivals (George Bush and Ross Perot) each got fewer popular votes. Minor parties cannot compete under this system. Voters are often reluctant to "waste" their vote on a minor-party candidate who cannot win.

The United States has experimented with other electoral systems. Proportional representation was used for municipal elections in New York City at one time and is still in use for that purpose in Cambridge, Massachusetts. Many states have elected more than one state legislator from each district. In Illinois, for example, three legislators have been elected from each district, with each voter allowed to cast two votes, thus virtually guaranteeing that the minority party will be able to win one of the three seats. But none of these experiments has altered the national two-party system, probably because of the existence of a directly elected president chosen by a winner-take-all electoral college.

The presidency is the great prize of American politics; to win it, you must form a party with as broad appeal as possible. As a practical matter, that means there will be, in most cases, only two serious parties—one made up of those who support the party already in power and the other made up of everybody else. Only one third party ever won the presidency—the Republicans in 1860—and it had by then pretty much supplanted the Whig party.

The second kind of explanation for the persistence of two parties is to be found in the opinions of the voters. Though there have been periods of bitter dissent, most of the time most citizens have agreed enough to permit them to come together into two broad coalitions. There has not been a massive and persistent body of opinion that has rejected the prevailing economic system (and thus we have not had a Marxist party with mass appeal); there has not been in our history an aristocracy or monarchy (and thus there has been no party that has sought to restore aristocrats or monarchs to power). Churches and religion have almost always been regarded as matters of private choice that lie outside politics (and thus there has not been a party seeking to create or abolish special government privileges for one church or another). In some European nations the organization of the economy, the prerogatives of the monarchy, and the role of the church have been major issues with long and bloody histories. So divisive have these issues been that they have helped prevent the formation of broad coalition parties.

But Americans have had other deep divisions—between white and black, for example, or between North and South—and yet the two-party system has endured. This suggests that electoral procedures are of great importance—the winner-take-all, plurality

United We Stand America: Third Party in the Making?

*I*n the 1992 presidential election Ross Perot captured 19 percent of the popular vote, an impressive showing for a third-party candidate (see Chapter 8 for more details). But Perot won no states in the electoral college and arguably did not affect the outcome of the election.

Most third-party candidates soon fade from the scene. After the defeat of his Bull Moose party candidacy in 1912, Theodore Roosevelt left America to study the flora and fauna of Brazil. John Anderson foreswore electoral politics and became a television commentator in Chicago following his unsuccessful independent bid in 1980.

But after the 1992 election, Ross Perot took to the airwaves with campaign-style programs on the nation's deficit and trade problems, and testified frequently in Congress, continuing to make headlines. In January of 1993 Perot announced the formation of United We Stand America (UWSA), an advocacy group for governmental and political reform. In the first few months of UWSA's existence, Perot visited thirty-seven cities in fourteen states. UWSA now boasts more than 1 million members, with each member paying at least fifteen dollars in annual dues.

Organizationally, UWSA resembles a political party. For example, UWSA is organized by state chapters, each with a director paid by the national headquarters in Dallas. The directors oversee elections for state chairmen and other officers.

Will UWSA develop into a viable third party? Stay tuned.

SOURCE: James A. Barnes, "Still on the Trail," *National Journal* (April 10, 1993): 863–864.

" SORRY, FOLKS... BUT YOUR SET'S NOT BROKEN...HE _REALLY_ IS ON EVERY CHANNEL... "

Types of Minor Parties

Ideological parties: Parties professing a comprehensive view of American society and government radically different from that of the established parties. Most have been Marxist in outlook, but some are quite the opposite, such as the Libertarian party.

Examples:
Socialist party (1901 to 1960s)
Socialist Labor party (1888 to present)
Socialist Workers party (1938 to present)
Communist party (1920s to present)
Libertarian party (1972 to present)

One-issue parties: Parties seeking a single policy, usually revealed by their names, and avoiding other issues.

Examples:
Free Soil party—to prevent spread of slavery (1848–1852)
American or "Know-Nothing" party—to oppose immigration and Catholics (1856)
Prohibition party—to ban the sale of liquor (1869 to present)
Woman's party—to obtain the right to vote for women (1913–1920)

Economic-protest parties: Parties, usually based in a particular region, especially involving farmers, that protest against depressed economic conditions. These tend to disappear as conditions improve.

Examples:
Greenback party (1876–1884)
Populist party (1892–1908)

Factional parties: Parties that are created by a split in a major party, usually over the identity and philosophy of the major party's presidential candidate.

Examples:
Split off from the Republican party:
  "Bull Moose" Progressive party (1912)
  La Follette Progressive party (1924)
Split off from the Democratic party:
  States' Rights ("Dixiecrat") party (1948)
  Henry Wallace Progressive party (1948)
  American Independent (George Wallace) party (1968)

election rules have made it useless for anyone to attempt to create an all-white or an all-black national party except as an act of momentary defiance or in the hope of taking enough votes away from the two major parties to force the presidential election into the House of Representatives. (That may have been George Wallace's strategy in 1968.)

For many years there was an additional reason for the two-party system: the laws of many states made it difficult, if not impossible, for third parties to get on the ballot. In 1968, for example, the American Independent party of George Wallace found that it would have to collect 433,000 signatures (15 percent of the votes cast in the last statewide election) in order to get on the presidential ballot in Ohio. Wallace took the issue to the Supreme Court, which ruled, six to three, that such a restriction was an unconstitutional violation of the equal-protection clause of the Fourteenth Amendment.[15] Wallace got on the ballot. In 1980 John Anderson, running as an independent, was able to get on the ballot in all fifty states; in 1992 Ross Perot did the same. For the reasons already indicated, the two-party system will probably persist even without the aid of these legal restrictions.

Minor Parties

The electoral system may prevent minor parties from winning, but it does not prevent them from forming. Minor parties—usually called, erroneously, "third parties"—have been a permanent feature of American political life. Four major kinds of minor parties, with examples of each, are described in the box at left.

The minor parties that have endured have been the ideological ones. Their members feel themselves to be outside the mainstream of American political life and sometimes, as in the case of various Marxist parties, look forward to a time when a revolution or some other dramatic change in the political system will vindicate them. They are usually not interested in immediate electoral success and thus persist despite their poor showing at the polls. One such party, however, the Socialist party of Eugene Debs, won nearly 6 percent of the popular vote in the 1912 presidential election and during its heyday elected some twelve hundred candidates to local offices, including seventy-nine mayors. Part of the Socialist appeal arose from its opposition to municipal corruption, part from its opposition to American entry into World War I, and part from its critique of American society. No ideological party has ever carried a state in a presidential election.

Apart from the Republicans, who quickly became a major party, the only minor parties to carry states and thus win electoral votes were one party of economic protest (the Populists, who carried five states in 1892) and several factional parties (most recently, the States' Rights Democrats in 1948 and the American Independent party of George Wallace in 1968). Though factional parties may hope to cause the defeat of the party from which they split, they have not always been able to achieve this. Harry Truman was elected in 1948 despite the defections of both the leftist progressives, led by Henry Wallace, and the right-wing Dixiecrats, led by J. Strom Thurmond. In 1968 it seems likely that Hubert Humphrey would have lost even if George Wallace had not been in the race (Wallace voters would probably have switched to Nixon rather than to Humphrey, though of course one cannot be certain). It is quite possible, on the other hand, that a Republican might have beaten Woodrow Wilson in 1912 if the Republican party had not split in two (the regulars supporting William Howard Taft, the progressives supporting Theodore Roosevelt).

What is striking is not that we have had so many minor parties but that we have not had more. There have been several major political movements that did not produce a significant third party: the civil-rights movement of the 1960s, the antiwar movement of the same decade, and most important the labor movement in this century. Blacks were part of the Republican party after the Civil War and part of the Democratic party after the New Deal (even though the southern wing of that party for a long time kept them from voting). The antiwar movement found candidates with whom it could identify within the Democratic party (Eugene McCarthy, Robert F. Kennedy, George McGovern) even though it was a Democratic president, Lyndon B. Johnson, who was chiefly responsible for our commitment in Vietnam. After Johnson only narrowly won the 1968 New Hampshire primary, he withdrew from the race. Unions in this century have not tried to create a labor party—

indeed they were for a long time opposed to almost any kind of national political activity. Since labor became a major political force in the 1930s, the largest industrial unions have been content to operate as a part (and a very large part) of the Democratic party.

One reason why some potential sources of minor parties never formed such parties, in addition to the dim chance of success, is that the direct primary and the national convention have made it possible for dissident elements of a major party, unless they become completely disaffected, to remain in the party and influence the choice of candidates and policies. The antiwar movement had a profound effect on the Democratic conventions of 1968 and 1972; blacks have played a growing role in the Democratic party, especially with the candidacy of Jesse Jackson in 1984 and 1988; only in 1972 did the unions feel that the Democrats nominated a presidential candidate (McGovern) unacceptable to them.

The impact of minor parties on American politics is hard to judge. One bit of conventional wisdom holds that minor parties develop ideas that the major parties later come to adopt. The Socialist party, for example, is supposed to have called for major social and economic policies that the Democrats under Roosevelt later embraced and termed the New Deal. It is possible that the Democrats did steal the thunder of the Socialists, but it hardly seems likely that they did it because the Socialists had proposed these things or proved them popular. (In 1932 the Socialists got only 2 percent of the vote and in 1936 less than one-half of 1 percent.) Roosevelt probably adopted the policies he did in part because he thought them correct and in part because dissident elements within his *own* party—leaders such as Huey Long of Louisiana—were threatening to bolt the Democratic party if it did not move to the left. Even Prohibition was adopted more as a result of the efforts of interest groups such as the Anti-Saloon League than as the consequence of its endorsement by the Prohibition party.

The minor parties that have probably had the greatest influence on public policy have been the factional parties. Mugwumps and liberal Republicans, by bolting the regular party, may have made that party more sensitive to the issue of civil-service reform; the Bull Moose and La Follette progressive parties probably helped encourage the major parties to

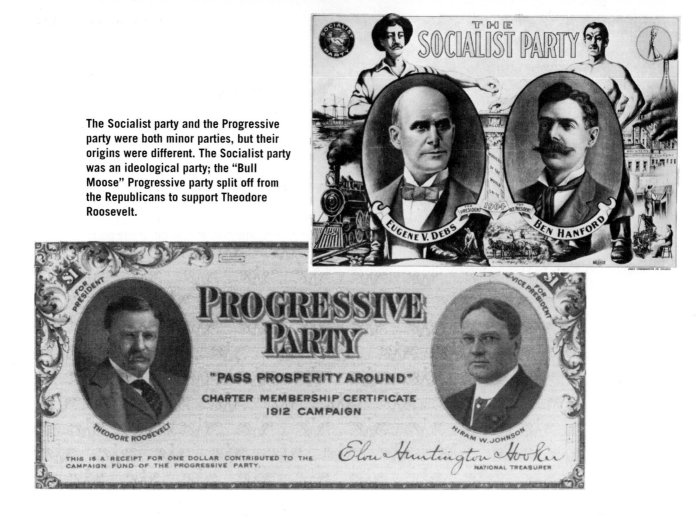

The Socialist party and the Progressive party were both minor parties, but their origins were different. The Socialist party was an ideological party; the "Bull Moose" Progressive party split off from the Republicans to support Theodore Roosevelt.

pay more attention to issues of business regulation and party reform; the Dixiecrat and Wallace movements probably strengthened the hands of those who wished to go slow on desegregation. The threat of a factional split is a risk that both major parties must face, and it is in the efforts that each makes to avoid such splits that one finds the greatest impact, at least in this century, of minor parties.

Nominating a President

The major parties face, as we have seen, two contrary forces: one, generated by the desire to win the presidency, pushes them in the direction of nominating a candidate who can appeal to the majority of voters and who will thus have essentially middle-of-the-road views. The other, produced by the need to keep dissident elements in the party from bolting and forming a third party, leads them to compromise

with dissidents or extremists in ways that may damage the party's standing with the voters.

The Democrats and Republicans have always faced these conflicting pressures, but of late they have become especially acute. When the presidential nomination was made by a party convention that was heavily influenced, if not controlled, by party leaders and elected officials, it was relatively easy to ignore dissident factions and pick candidates on the basis of who could win. The *electoral* objectives of the party were predominant. The result was that often a faction left the party and ran a separate ticket—as in 1912, 1924, 1948, 1968, and 1980. Today the power of party leaders and elected officials within the parties is greatly diminished, with most delegates now selected by primary elections. A larger proportion of the delegates is likely to be more interested in issues and to be less amenable to compromise over those issues than formerly. In these circumstances the *policy* interests of the party activists are likely to be important.

Are the Delegates Representative of the Voters?

There would be no conflict between the electoral and policy interests of a political party if the delegates to its nominating convention had the same policy views as most voters, or at least as most party supporters. In fact this is not the case: in parties, as in many organizations, the activists and leaders tend to have views different from those of the rank and file.[16] In American political parties in recent years, this difference has become very great.

In 1964 the Republican party nominated the highly conservative Barry Goldwater for president. We have no opinion data for delegates to that convention as detailed and comprehensive as those available for subsequent conventions, but it seems clear that the Republican delegates selected as their nominee a person who was not the most popular candidate among voters at large and thus not the candidate most likely to win.

At every Democratic national convention since 1972, the delegates have had views on a variety of important issues that were vastly different from those of rank-and-file Democrats. On welfare, military policy, school desegregation, crime, and abortion, Democratic delegates expressed opinions almost diametrically opposed to those of most Democrats. The delegates to the 1980, 1984, and (to a lesser extent) 1988 and 1992 conventions were ideologically very different from the voters at large. The Democratic delegates were more liberal than the Democratic voters, the Republican delegates were more conservative than the Republican voters (see Table 7.3).[17]

What accounts for the sharp disparity between delegate opinion (and often delegate candidate preference) and voter attitudes? Some blame the discrepancy on the rules, described earlier in this chapter, under which Democratic delegates are chosen, especially those that require increased representation for women, minorities, and the young. Close examination suggests that this is not a complete explanation. For one thing it will not explain why the Republicans nominated Goldwater in 1964 (and almost nominated Ronald Reagan instead of Gerald Ford in 1976). For another, women, minorities, and youth have among them all shades of opinions: there are many middle-of-the-road women and young people as well as very liberal or very conservative ones.

TABLE 7.3 How Party Delegates and Party Voters Differ in Liberal Ideology

Liberal Ideology	1984	1988	1992
Democrats			
Delegates	66%	39%	47%
Voters	31	25	28
Republicans			
Delegates	2	1	1
Voters	15	12	12

SOURCES: For 1984: *Los Angeles Times* (August 19,1984); for 1988: *New York Times*–CBS News poll, in *New York Times* (August 14, 1988); for 1992: *New York Times* (July 13, 1992), *New York Times* (August 17, 1992), and unpublished CBS News poll, "The 1992 Republican Convention Delegates."

(There are not many very conservative blacks, at least on race issues, but there are certainly plenty who are moderate on race and conservative on other issues.) The question is why only *certain* elements of these groups are heavily represented at the conventions.

Who Votes in Primaries?

Maybe delegates are unrepresentative because they are chosen in caucuses and primary elections whose participants are themselves unrepresentative of the party rank and file. Before 1972 most delegates were picked by party leaders; primaries were relatively unimportant, and voter caucuses were almost unheard of. Adlai Stevenson in 1952 and Hubert Humphrey in 1968 won the Democratic presidential nominations without even entering a primary. Harry Truman once described primaries as "eyewash."[18]

After 1972 they were no longer eyewash. The vast majority of delegates were selected in primaries and caucuses. In 1992 forty states and territories held primaries, and twenty held caucuses (some places had both primaries and caucuses).

Only about half as many people vote in primaries as in general elections. If these primary voters have more extreme political views than do the rank-and-file party followers, then they might support presidential delegates who also have extreme views. However, there is not much evidence that such is the case. Studies comparing the ideological orientations of primary voters with those of rank-and-file party voters do not reveal many strong differences.[19]

Popular Preferences and Convention Nominations

*U*sually the presidential candidate nominated by a party's convention is the person who has the most support in opinion polls of the party rank and file. There are exceptions, however. In 1952 and 1972 the Democrats nominated someone other than the most popular Democrat, and in 1964 the Republicans nominated a man who was tied with his rival in voter popularity.

Election Year		Candidate Preferred by Party Voters	Candidate Nominated by Party Convention
1948	Democrats	Truman	Truman
	Republicans	Dewey	Dewey
1952	**Democrats**	**Kefauver**	**Stevenson**
	Republicans	Eisenhower	Eisenhower
1956	Democrats	Stevenson	Stevenson
	Republicans	Eisenhower	Eisenhower
1960	Democrats	Kennedy	Kennedy
	Republicans	Nixon	Nixon
1964	Democrats	Johnson	Johnson
	Republicans	**Goldwater or Nixon** (tie)	**Goldwater**
1968	Democrats	Humphrey	Humphrey
	Republicans	Nixon	Nixon
1972	**Democrats**	**Humphrey or Wallace** (tie)	**McGovern**
	Republicans	Nixon	Nixon
1976	Democrats	Carter	Carter
	Republicans	Ford	Ford
1980	Democrats	Carter	Carter
	Republicans	Reagan	Reagan
1984	Democrats	Mondale	Mondale
	Republicans	Reagan	Reagan
1988	Democrats	Dukakis	Dukakis
	Republicans	Bush	Bush
1992	Democrats	Clinton	Clinton
	Republicans	Bush	Bush

NOTE: Poll data are from last poll taken before convention.
SOURCE: Reprinted by permission of Elsevier North Holland, Inc. from James R. Beniger, "Winning the Presidential Nomination: National Polls and State Primary Elections, 1936–1972," *Public Opinion Quarterly* 40:27. Copyright © 1976 by The Trustees of Columbia University. 1976, 1980, 1984, 1988, and 1992 entries based on Gallup poll data.

Caucuses are a different matter. A **caucus** is a meeting of party followers, often lasting for hours and held in the dead of winter in a schoolhouse miles from home, in which party delegates are picked. Only the most dedicated partisans attend. For the Demo-

crats, these have been liberals; for the Republicans, conservatives. In 1988 the most liberal Democratic candidate, Jesse Jackson, got more delegates in the Alaska, Delaware, Michigan, and Vermont caucuses than did Michael Dukakis, the eventual nominee. On the Republican side, evangelist Pat Robertson did not win a single primary, but he won the caucuses in Alaska, Hawaii, and Washington.

Who Are the New Delegates?

However delegates are chosen, they are a different breed today than they once were. Whether picked by caucuses or primaries, and of whatever sex or race, a far larger proportion of convention delegates, both Republican and Democratic, are issue-oriented activists—people with an "amateur" or "purist" view of politics. Far fewer delegates are in it for the money (there is no longer much patronage to pass around) or to help their own reelection prospects. For example, in 1980 only 14 percent of the Democratic senators and 15 percent of the Democratic members of the House were delegates to the national convention. In 1956, by contrast, 90 percent of the senators and 33 percent of the representatives were delegates.[20]

Party activists, especially those who work without pay and who are in politics out of an interest in issues, are not likely to resemble the average citizen, for whom politics is merely an object of observation, discussion, and occasional voting. In 1972 such activists at the Democratic convention were most likely to support one of the two candidates with the strongest ideological appeal—McGovern or Wallace—and least likely to support those candidates that represented party regularity (Edmund Muskie or Hubert Humphrey).[21] It seems likely that the same thing was true at the Republican conventions of 1964, 1976, and 1980; the activists favored the more ideological candidates.

In sum, the changing incentives for participation in party work, in addition to the effects of the primary system, have contributed to the development of a national presidential nominating system different from that which once existed. The advantage of the new system is that it increases the opportunity for those with strong policy preferences to play a role in the party and thus reduces the chance that they will bolt the party and form a factional minor party. The disadvantage of the system is that it increases the

TABLE 7.4 Political Opinions of Delegates and Voters, 1988

	Democrats		Republicans	
	Delegates	Voters	Voters	Delegates
Political philosophy				
Conservative	5%	22%	43%	60%
Liberal	39	25	12	1
Taxes and spending				
Favor balanced budget amendment to Constitution	38	77	80	77
Favor increasing top tax rate	67	63	61	19
Favor smaller government providing fewer services	16	33	59	87
Social issues				
Favor school prayer	22	67	72	51
Keep abortion legal	72	43	39	29
Favor federal funding of abortions	57	32	28	16
Favor gay rights law	65	43	28	26
Favor death penalty	49	64	79	88
Favor Equal Rights Amendment to Constitution	86	80	68	34
Military policy				
Don't cut military spending	32	59	73	84
Use military to stop drugs	54	61	63	67

SOURCE: *New York Times*–CBS News polls as reported in *New York Times* (August 14, 1988): 14, and in Martin Plissner and Warren J. Mitofsky, "The Making of the Delegates, 1968–1988," *Public Opinion* (September–October 1988): 46. Copyright © 1988 by the New York Times Company. Reprinted by permission.

chances that one or both parties may nominate presidential candidates who are not appealing to the average voter or even to a party's rank and file.

Parties versus Voters

Since 1968 the Democratic party has had no trouble winning congressional elections but great difficulty winning presidential contests. Except for 1980–1986 and 1994, the Democrats have controlled both houses of Congress; except for 1976 and 1992, they have lost every presidential election. The Republican party has had the opposite problem: though it won five out of seven presidential elections between 1968 and 1992, it did not control Congress for the forty years preceding its big win in 1994.

There are many reasons for this odd state of affairs, most of which will be discussed later. But one requires attention here. The difficulty the Democrats have had in competing for the presidency is in part because their candidates for the presidency have had on certain issues—chiefly social and taxation issues—views very different from those of the average voter. That disparity to a large degree mirrors (and may be caused by) the gulf that separates the opinions of delegates to Democratic nominating conventions from the opinions of most citizens.

The Republicans have not been immune to this problem. In 1964 they nominated a candidate, Barry Goldwater, whose beliefs placed him well to the right of most voters. Not surprisingly, he lost. And the delegates to recent Republican conventions have held opinions on some matters that continue to be very different from those of most people. Nevertheless the problem has been more acute for the Democrats.

The problem can be seen in Table 7.4. A lot of information is shown there; to understand it, study the table step by step. First, look at the two middle columns. Here are the views of Democratic and Republican voters as of 1988. (Because there are about the same number of Democratic and Republican voters, the opinion of the average voter is about halfway between those of the followers of the two parties.)

The first thing you learn is that George Wallace was wrong when he said that "there is not a dime's worth of difference between Democrats and Republicans." Democratic voters are more likely than Republican voters to say that they are liberal, to favor the Equal Rights Amendment, to support a gay-rights law, and to oppose making the government smaller. However, on most issues, the differences are not very large, and on some issues—such as favoring amending the Constitution to require a balanced budget, supporting higher taxes on the rich, and keeping abortions legal—Democrats and Republicans are quite similar.

Now look at the columns on the far left and the far right. These show the views of delegates to the 1988 Democratic and Republican conventions. On almost every issue, the delegates are in sharp disagreement. There were hardly any conservatives at the Democratic convention or liberals at the Republican convention. On every social issue and on every tax or spending issue, the delegates were at opposite ends of the political spectrum. About the only thing they agreed on was using the military to stop drug trafficking.

Finally, compare the views of Democratic delegates with those of Democratic voters (the first two columns) and the beliefs of Republican delegates with those of Republican voters (the last two columns). The Democratic delegates disagreed with Democratic voters on the balanced budget amendment, school prayer, legalized abortion, federal funding for abortions, gay rights, the death penalty, and cutting military spending. The Republican delegates disagreed with Republican voters on higher taxes for the rich and on the Equal Rights Amendment. (The percentages of Republican delegates favoring many other measures were different from those of the voters, but on most measures both groups were on the same side.)

This means that the Democratic national convention was filled with people who wanted to support a candidate who disagreed on many key issues with the people who said they were leaning toward the Democratic party (and of course who disagreed even more with those who said they thought of themselves as Republicans). If the 1988 presidential candidate had the views of the delegates and if the election were fought out on the issues, he would lose. He did, it was, and he lost.

The Democratic party has had this problem since 1972; indeed the cleavage between Democratic delegates and the average voter was even wider in 1972 than it was in 1988.[22]

This does not mean that the Democrats cannot win the presidency. They can win *if* the delegates nominate a candidate whose views put him or her closer to the average citizen than to the average delegate *or* if the campaign is fought out over issues on which the delegates and the voters agree. For example, if the election turned on what to do about an economic recession, the delegates, the voters, and the candidate would probably all agree: do whatever is necessary to end the recession. Exactly that happened in 1992, and the Democrats won.

Of course even without a scandal, recession, or some other unifying issue, the need to win an election will lead all candidates to move toward the middle of the road. That is where the votes are. But this creates a dilemma for a candidate of either party. The stance one takes to win support from party activists in the caucuses and primaries will often be quite different from the stance one should take to win votes from the general public. In the next chapter we shall look more closely at how politicians try to cope with that dilemma.

SUMMARY

A political party exists in three arenas: among the voters who psychologically identify with it, as a grassroots organization staffed and led by activists, and as a group of elected officials who follow its lead in lawmaking. In this chapter we have looked at the party primarily as an organization and seen the various forms it takes at the local level—the machine, the ideological party, the solidary group, the sponsored party, and the personal following.

Nationally the parties are weak, decentralized coalitions of these local forms. As organizations that influence the political systems, parties are getting weaker. Voters no longer strongly identify with one of the major parties as they once did. The spread of the direct primary has made it harder for parties to control who is nominated for elective office, thus making it harder for the parties to influence the behavior of these people once elected. Delegate-selection rules, especially in the Democratic party, have helped shift the center of power in the national nominating convention. Because of the changes in rules, power has moved away from officeholders and party regulars and toward the more ideological wings of the parties.

Minor parties have arisen from time to time, but the only ones that have affected the outcome of presidential elections have been those that represented a splinter group within one of the major parties (such as the Bull Moose Progressives). The two-party system is maintained, and minor parties are discouraged, by an election system (winner-take-all, plurality elections) that makes voters reluctant to waste a vote on a minor party and by the ability of potential minor parties to wield influence within a major party by means of the primary system.

In the next chapter we shall look at the role of parties in shaping voter attitudes, and in Chapter 11 at the role of parties in Congress. In each of these areas we will find more evidence of party decay.

KEY TERMS

political party   *p. 151*

mugwumps *or* progressives   *p. 158*

national convention   *p. 161*

national committee   *p. 161*

congressional campaign committee   *p. 161*

national chairman   *p. 161*

superdelegates   *p. 164*

political machine   *p. 166*

ideological party   *p. 167*

solidary incentives   *p. 168*

sponsored party   *p. 168*

personal following   *p. 169*

two-party system   *p. 170*

plurality system   *p. 171*

caucus   *p.178*

SUGGESTED READINGS

Chambers, William Nisbet, and Walter Dean Burnham, eds. *The American Party Systems: Stages of Political Development.* 2d ed. New York: Oxford University Press, 1975. Essays tracing the rise of the party system since the Founding.

Goldwin, Robert A., ed. *Political Parties in the Eighties.* Washington, D.C.: American Enterprise Institute, 1980. Essays evaluating parties and efforts to reform them.

Kayden, Xandra, and Eddie Mahe, Jr. *The Party Goes On.* New York: Basic Books, 1985. How the Democratic and Republican national parties have adjusted to new political conditions.

Key, V. O., Jr. *Southern Politics.* New York: Knopf, 1949. A classic account of how politics operated in the one-party South.

Mayhew, David R. *Placing Parties in American Politics.* Princeton, N.J.: Princeton University Press, 1986. A state-by-state description of state party organizations.

Polsby, Nelson W. *Consequences of Party Reform.* New York: Oxford University Press, 1983. Fine analysis of how changed party rules have affected the parties and the government.

Ranney, Austin. *Curing the Mischiefs of Faction: Party Reform in America.* Berkeley: University of California Press, 1975. History and analysis of party "reforms," with special attention to the 1972 changes in the Democratic party rules.

Riordan, William L. *Plunkitt of Tammany Hall.* New York: Knopf, 1948 (first published in 1905). Amusing and insightful account of how an old-style party boss operated in New York City.

Schattschneider, E. E. *Party Government.* New York: Holt, Rinehart and Winston, 1942. An argument for a more disciplined and centralized two-party system.

Shafer, Byron E. *Quiet Revolution: The Struggle for the Democratic Party and the Shaping of Post-Reform Politics.* New York: Russell Sage Foundation, 1983. Detailed, insightful history of how the Democratic party came to be reformed.

Sundquist, James L. *Dynamics of the Party System.* Rev. ed. Washington, D.C.: Brookings Institution, 1983. History of the party system, emphasizing the impact of issues on voting.

Wilson, James Q. *The Amateur Democrat.* Chicago: University of Chicago Press, 1962. Analysis of the issue-oriented political clubs that rose in the Democratic party in the 1950s and 1960s.

8

Elections and Campaigns

I f you want to be elected to Congress or to the presidency, you must develop a game plan that is in tune with the unique legal, political, and financial realities of American politics. A plan that will work here would be useless in almost any other democratic nation; one that would work abroad would be useless here.

Elections have two crucial phases—getting nominated and getting elected. Getting nominated means getting your name on the ballot. In the great majority of states winning the nomination for either the presidency or Congress requires an *individual* effort— you decide to run, you raise money, you and your friends collect signatures to get your name on the ballot, and you appeal to voters in primary elections on the basis of your personality and your definition of the issues. In most European nations winning the nomination for parliament involves an *organizational* decision—the party looks you over, the party decides whether to allow you to run, and the party puts your name on its list of candidates.

Political parties do play a role in determining the outcome of American elections, but even that role involves parties more as labels in the voters' minds than as organizations that get out the vote. By contrast many other democratic nations conduct campaigns that are almost entirely a contest between parties as organizations. In Israel and the Netherlands the names of the candidates for the legislature do not even appear on the ballot; only the party names are listed there. And even where candidate names are listed, as in Great Britain, the voters tend to vote "Conservative" or "Labour" more than they vote for Smith or Jones. European nations (except France) do not have a directly elected president; instead the head of the government—the prime minister—is selected by the party that has won the most seats in parliament.

At one time parties played a much larger role in elections in the United States than they do now. Until well into this century they determined, or powerfully influenced, who got nominated. In the early nineteenth century the members of Congress from a given party would meet in a caucus to pick their presidential candidate. After these caucuses were replaced by national nominating conventions, the real power over presidential nominations was wielded by local party leaders, who came together, sometimes in the legendary "smoke-filled rooms," to choose the candidate whom the rest of the delegates would then endorse.

Congressional candidates were often handpicked by powerful local party bosses. In the election campaign people then were much more likely than people today to vote the straight-party ticket.

The last chapter described the factors that weakened parties as organizations able to control nominations. There is little chance that they will ever regain that control. Thus you, the candidate, are pretty much on your own. What do you do?

Presidential versus Congressional Campaigns

Presidential and congressional races differ in important ways. The most obvious, of course, is size: more voters participate in the former than the latter contest, and so as a presidential candidate you must work harder and spend more. But there are some less obvious differences that are equally important.

First, presidential races are more competitive than those for the House of Representatives. In the thirty-one elections between 1932 and 1994, the Republicans won control of the House only three times (10 percent of the time); in the sixteen presidential elections during the same period, the Republicans won the White House on seven occasions (44 percent of the time). In the typical presidential race the winner gets less than 55 percent of the two-party vote; in the typical House race, the incumbent wins and receives over 60 percent of the vote. A president cannot serve more than two terms, so at least once every eight years you have a chance of running against a nonincumbent; members of Congress can serve for an unlimited number of terms, and so the chances are you will run against an incumbent. If you do, the odds are very much against you. Most years over 90 percent of all House incumbents who stand for reelection are reelected; in 1986 and 1988 over *98 percent* retained their seats.

Second, a much smaller proportion of people vote in congressional races during off years (that is, when there is no presidential contest) than vote for president. This lower turnout (around 36 percent of the voting-age population) means that in a congressional race you will be appealing to the more motivated and partisan voter.

Third, members of Congress can do things for their constituents that a president cannot do. They take credit—sometimes deserved, sometimes not—for every grant, contract, bridge, canal, and highway that the federal government supplies to the district or state. They send letters (at the government's expense) to a large fraction of their constituents and visit their district every weekend. Presidents get little credit for district improvements and must rely on the mass media to communicate with voters.

Fourth, a candidate for Congress can deny that he or she is responsible for "the mess in Washington," even when the candidate is an incumbent. As we shall see in Chapter 11, incumbents tend to run as individuals, even to the point of denouncing the very Congress of which they are a part. An incumbent president can't get away with this; rightly or wrongly he is often held responsible for whatever has gone wrong, not only in the government but in the nation as a whole.

These last three factors—low turnout, service to constituents, the ability to duck responsibility—probably help explain why so high a percentage of congressional incumbents get reelected.

But they do not enjoy a completely free ride. Members of Congress who belong to the same party as the president often feel voters' anger about national affairs, particularly economic conditions. When the economy turns sour and a Republican is in the White House, Republican congressional candidates lose votes; if a Democrat is in the White House, Democratic congressional candidates lose votes.

At one time the coattails of a popular presidential candidate could help congressional candidates in his own party. But there has been a sharp decline in the value of presidential coattails; indeed some scholars doubt whether they still exist.

The net effect of all these factors is that, to a substantial degree, congressional elections have become independent of presidential ones. Though economic factors may still link the fate of a president and some members of his party, by and large the incumbent members of Congress enjoy enough of a cushion to protect them against whatever political storms engulf an unpopular president. This fact further reduces the meaning of party—members of Congress can get reelected even though their party's "leader" in the White House has lost popular support, and nonincumbent candidates for Congress may lose despite the fact that a very popular president from their party is in the White House.

Running for President

The first task facing anyone who wishes to be president is to get "mentioned" as someone who is of "presidential caliber." No one is quite sure why some people are mentioned and others are not. The journalist David Broder has suggested that somewhere there is "The Great Mentioner," who announces from time to time who is of presidential caliber (and only The Great Mentioner knows how big that caliber is).

But if The Great Mentioner turns out to be as unreal as the Easter bunny, you have to figure out for yourself how to get mentioned. One way is to let it be known to reporters ("off the record") that you are thinking about running for president. Another is to travel around the country making speeches (Ronald Reagan, while working for General Electric, made a dozen or more speeches *a day* to audiences all over the country). Another way is to already have a famous name (John Glenn, the former astronaut, was in the public eye long before he declared for the presidency in 1984). Another way to get mentioned is to be identified with a major piece of legislation. Senator Bill Bradley of New Jersey was known as an architect of the Tax Reform Act of 1986; Representative Richard Gephardt of Missouri was known as an author of a bill designed to reduce foreign imports. Still another way is to be the governor of a big state. New York governors, such as Mario Cuomo, are often viewed as presidential prospects, partly because New York City is the headquarters of the television and publishing industries.

Once mentioned, it is wise to set aside a lot of time to run, especially if you are only "mentioned" as opposed to being really well known. Ronald Reagan devoted the better part of six years to running; Walter Mondale spent four years campaigning; Howard

POLITICALLY **P.S.** SPEAKING

Coattails

Today the word is used in the sense of riding into office on the coattails of a better-known or more popular candidate for office. The political carrying power of coattails depends on the voters' casting a straight-ticket ballot so that their support for a popular presidential candidate is translated into support for lesser candidates on the same party ticket. Scholars are skeptical that such a coattail effect exists today.

The word first came into popular usage in 1848 when Abraham Lincoln defended the Whig party's effort to take shelter under the military coattail of that party's presidential candidate, General Zachary Taylor. Lincoln argued that in the past the Democrats had run under the coattail of General Andrew Jackson.

Later the military connotation of *coattail* fell by the wayside and the term came to mean any effort to obtain straight-ticket voting.

SOURCE: Adapted from William Safire, *Safire's Political Dictionary* (New York: Ballantine Books, 1978). Used by permission.

Baker resigned from the Senate in 1984 to prepare to run in 1988 (he finally dropped out of the race). However, most 1988 and 1992 candidates—George Bush, Senators Bob Dole, Al Gore, Tom Harkin, Bob Kerrey, and Paul Simon, Governors Michael Dukakis and Bill Clinton, and House members Richard Gephardt and Jack Kemp—made the run while holding elective office.

✪ Mobilization Politics in the Nineteenth Century

*P*olitics was a national sport during much of the nineteenth century. Torchlight parades, massive rallies, colorful banners, and public orations were commonplace then; today they have been replaced with television interviews and sedate meetings in auditoriums.

Morton Keller notes that in 1888 twenty-five possible presidential candidates were pictured on cards placed in packages of Honest Long Cut Tobacco. The cards were collected and traded as if they were pictures of baseball players.*

The very language of politics emphasized the warlike nature of the effort to mobilize voters, as suggested by this pastiche of typical phrases:

*From the **opening gun** of the **campaign** the **standard bearer**, along with other **war-horses** fielded by the party, **rallied** the **rank and file** around the party **standard**, the **bloody shirt**, and other **slogans**. Precinct **captains** aligned their **phalanxes** shoulder-to-shoulder to **mobilize** votes for the **Old Guard**. . . . Finally the **well-drilled fuglemen** in the **last ditch** closed **ranks**, overwhelmed the enemy **camp**, and divided the **spoils** of victory.†*

*Morton Keller, *Affairs of State* (Cambridge, Mass.: Harvard University Press, 1977), 535.
†Richard Jensen, *The Winning of the Midwest* (Chicago: University of Chicago Press, 1971), 11.

PRESIDENTIAL POSSIBILITIES
JOHN M. PALMER,
OF ILLINOIS

Money One reason why running takes so much time is that it takes so long to raise the necessary money and build up an organization of personal followers. As we shall see later in the chapter, federal law restricts the amount that any single individual can give you to $1,000 in each election (a **political-action committee,** or PAC, which is a committee set up by and representing a corporation, labor union, or other special-interest group, can give up to $5,000). Moreover, to be eligible for federal matching grants to pay for your primary campaign, you must first raise at least $5,000, in individual contributions of $250 or less, in each of twenty states.

Organization Raising and accounting for this money requires a staff of fund-raisers, lawyers, and accountants. You also need a press secretary, a travel scheduler, an advertising specialist, a direct-mail company, and a pollster, all of whom must be paid, plus a large number of volunteers in at least those states that hold early primary elections or party caucuses. These volunteers will brief you on the facts of each state, try to line up endorsements from local politicians and celebrities, and put together a group of people who will knock on doors, make telephone calls, organize receptions and meetings, and try to keep you from mispronouncing the name of the town in which you are speaking. Finally you have to assemble advisers on the issues. These advisers will write "position papers" for you on all sorts of things that you are supposed to know about (but probably don't). Because a campaign is usually waged around a few broad themes, these position papers rarely get used or even read. The papers exist so that you can show important interest groups that you have taken "sound" positions, so that you can be prepared to answer tough questions, and so that journalists can look up your views on matters that may become topical.

Strategy and Themes Every candidate picks a strategy for the campaign. In choosing one, much depends on whether you are the incumbent. Incumbents must defend their record, like it or not. (An incumbent ran for president in 1964, 1972, 1976, 1980, 1984, and 1992.) The challenger attacks the incumbent. Where there is no incumbent (as in 1960, 1968, and 1988), both candidates can announce their own programs; however, the candidate from the party that holds the White House must take, whether he thinks he deserves it or not, some of the blame for whatever has gone wrong in the preceding four years. Within these limits a strategy consists of the answer to questions about tone, theme, timing, and targets:

- What *tone* should the campaign have? Should it be a positive (build-me-up) or negative (attack-the-opponent) campaign? In 1988 George Bush began with a negative campaign; Michael Dukakis followed suit.

- What *theme* can I develop? A theme is a simple, appealing idea that can be repeated over and over again. For Jimmy Carter in 1976 it was "trust"; for Ronald Reagan in 1980 it was "competence," and in 1984 it was "it's morning again in America"; for Bush in 1988 it was "stay the course"; for Clinton in 1992 it was "we need to change."

- What should be the *timing* of the campaign? If you are relatively unknown, you will have to put everything into the early primaries and caucuses, try to emerge a front-runner, and then hope for the best. If you are already the front-runner, you may either go for broke early (and try to drive out all opponents) or hold back some reserves for a long fight.

- Whom should you *target*? Only a small percentage of voters change their vote from one election to the next. Who is likely to change this time—unemployed steelworkers? Unhappy farmers? People upset by inflation?

Primary versus General Campaigns

These four strategic decisions are not easily made, however, because you are (you hope) entering *two* elections, not just one. The first consists of primary elections and caucuses, designed to win the nomination; the second is the general election, designed to win office. Each election attracts a different mix of voters, workers, and media attention. What works in

The Road to the Nomination

A campaign for the presidential nomination must begin early. Among the key steps are these:

Create an organization: A campaign manager, fund-raiser, pollster, and several lawyers and accountants must be hired early—two or even three years before the election. Money cannot legally be raised until an organization exists to receive and account for it.

Start raising money: To be eligible for federal matching dollars for your primary-election campaign, you must raise $250 from each of at least twenty donors in each of twenty states. You cannot receive more than $1,000 from any individual or $5,000 from any PAC. There are national and state-by-state limits on what you can spend.

Prepare for the early primaries and caucuses: To show that you are a serious contender and have "momentum," you should enter the early primaries and caucuses. In 1992 some key early ones were

- February 10: Iowa caucus
- February 18: New Hampshire primary
- March 10: "Super Tuesday" (primaries in eight states, mostly in the South)

To win a primary you must campaign hard and often; to win a caucus you must have an organization that can get your supporters to attend and vote at the local caucuses.

Pick a strategy: If you are relatively unknown, you must campaign heavily in the early primaries (this is called a "front-loaded" campaign). But then you risk running out of money before the later primaries in the big states. If you are the front-runner, you are in better shape, but then you must worry about losing even one primary (as did Mondale to Hart in New Hampshire in 1984), thereby tarnishing your "unbeatable" image.

Control the convention: If you win the most delegates in the primaries and caucuses, you will be nominated. (From 1956 through 1992 the winning candidate was nominated on the first ballot at the Democratic and Republican conventions.) Then your problem is to control everything else that goes on at the convention—the platform, the speeches, the vice presidential nomination—so nothing happens that will embarrass you.

The campaign before the Iowa caucuses in 1988 was retail politics—countless meetings with small groups of likely participants.

the primary election may not work in the general one, and vice versa.

To win the nomination you must mobilize political activists who will give money, do volunteer work, and attend local caucuses. As we saw in Chapters 5 and 6, the activists are more ideologically polarized than the voters at large. To motivate these activists you must be more liberal (if you are a Democrat) in your tone and theme than are the rank-and-file Democrats, or more conservative (if you are a Republican) than are the rank-and-file Republicans.

Consider the caucuses held in Iowa in early February of a presidential-election year. This is the first real test of the candidates vying for the nomination. Anyone who does poorly here is at a disadvantage, in media attention and contributor interest, for the rest of the campaign.

The several thousand Iowans who participate in their party caucuses are not representative of the followers of their party in the state, much less nationally. In 1988 Senator Robert Dole came in first and evangelist Pat Robertson came in second in the Iowa Republican caucus, with Vice President George Bush finishing third. As it turned out, there was little support for Dole or Robertson in the rest of the country.

Democrats who participate in the Iowa caucuses tend to be more liberal than Democrats generally.[1] Moreover, the way the caucuses are run is a far cry from how most elections are held. To vote in the Republican caucus, you need not prove you are a Republican or even a voter. The Democratic caucus is not an election at all; instead, a person supporting a certain candidate stands in one corner of the room with people who also support him, while those supporting other candidates stand in other corners with other groups. There is a lot of calling back and forth designed to persuade people to leave one group and join another. No group with fewer than 15 percent of the people in attendance gets to choose any delegates, so people in these small groups then go to other, larger ones. It is a cross between musical chairs and fraternity pledge week.

Suppose you, as a Democrat, do well in the Iowa caucuses. Suppose you go on to win your party's nomination. Now you have to go back to Iowa to campaign for general-election votes. Since 1940 Iowa has voted Republican in every presidential election but three (1948, 1964, and 1988). Your Republican opponent is not going to let you forget all of the liberal slogans you uttered nine months before. The

Republican candidate faces the mirror image of this problem—sounding very conservative to get support from Republican activists in states such as Massachusetts and New York and then having to defend those speeches when running against his Democratic opponent in those states.

The problem is not limited to Iowa but exists in every state where the activists are more ideologically polarized than the average voters. To get activist support candidates move to the ideological extremes; to win elections they try to move back to the ideological center. The typical voter looks at the results and often decides that neither candidate appeals to him or her very much, and so casts a "clothespin vote" (see the box on page 191).

Occasionally even the voters in the primary elections will be more extreme ideologically than are the general-election voters. This certainly happened in 1972. George McGovern won the Democratic nomination with the support of voters who were well to the left of the public at large (and even of rank-and-file Democratic voters) on such issues as U.S. policy in Vietnam, amnesty for draft resisters, decriminalizing marijuana, and helping minorities.[2] His general-election opponent, Richard Nixon, was able to take advantage of this by portraying McGovern as a leftist. But even when primary voters are not too different from general-election voters, the activists who contribute the time, money, and effort to mount a campaign are very different from the voters—in both parties.

Television, Debates, and Direct Mail

Once campaigns mostly involved parades, big rallies, "whistle-stop" train tours, and shaking hands outside factory gates and near shopping centers. All of this still goes on, but increasingly presidential and senatorial candidates (and those House candidates with radio and television stations in their districts) use broadcasting.

There are two ways to use television—by running paid advertisements and by getting on the nightly news broadcasts. In the language of campaigners short television ads are called *spots,* and a campaign activity that appears on a news broadcast is called a *visual.* Much has been written about the preparation of spots, usually under titles such as "the

TRIVIA

Elections

Only two men to have been elected president by the House of Representatives after failing to win a majority in the Electoral College.	*Thomas Jefferson (1800) and John Quincy Adams (1824)*
Only Democratic senator to be the running mate of a Republican presidential candidate	*Andrew Johnson (1864)*
The candidate for president who received more popular votes than his opponent but was not elected	*Grover Cleveland got more popular votes but fewer electoral votes than Benjamin Harrison in 1888*
President who won the largest percentage of the popular vote	*Lyndon B. Johnson, 61.7 percent (1964)*
Only person to serve as vice president and president without having been elected to either post	*Gerald Ford (1973–1976)*
President who won the most electoral votes	*Ronald Reagan (525 in 1984)*
First woman to run for national office on a major-party ticket	*Geraldine Ferraro (Democratic candidate for vice president, 1984)*

Geraldine Ferraro

Kinds of Elections

There are two kinds of elections in the United States: general and primary. A **general election** is used to fill an elective office. A **primary election** is used to select a party's candidates for an elective office, though in fact those who vote in a primary election may not consider themselves party members. Some primaries are closed. In a **closed primary** you must declare in advance (sometimes several weeks in advance) that you are a registered member of the political party in whose primary you wish to vote. About forty states have closed primaries.

Other primaries are open. In an **open primary** you can decide when you enter the voting booth in which party's primary you wish to participate. You are given every party's ballot; you may vote on one. Idaho, Michigan, Minnesota, Montana, North Dakota, Utah, Vermont, and Wisconsin have open primaries. A variant on the open primary is the **blanket** (or "free love") **primary**—in the voting booth you mark a ballot that lists the candidates of all the parties, and thus you can help select the Democratic can-didate for one office and the Republican candidate for another. Alaska and Washington have blanket primaries.

The differences among these kinds of primaries should not be exaggerated, for even the closed primary does not create any great barrier for a voter who wishes to vote in the Democratic primary in one election and the Republican in another. Some states also have a **runoff primary:** if no candidate gets a majority of the votes, there is a runoff between the two with the most votes. Runoff primaries are common in the South.

A special kind of primary, a **presidential primary,** is that used to pick delegates to the presidential nominating conventions of the major parties. Presidential primaries come in a bewildering variety. A simplified list looks like this:

- **Delegate selection only** Only the names of prospective delegates to the convention appear on the ballot. They may or may not indicate their presidential preference.

- **Delegate selection with advisory presidential preference** Voters pick delegates and indicate their preferences among presidential candidates. The delegates are not legally bound to observe these preferences.

- **Binding presidential preference** Voters indicate their preferred presidential candidate. Delegates must observe these preferences, at least for a certain number of convention ballots. The delegates may be chosen in the primary or by a party convention.

In 1981 the Supreme Court ruled that political parties, not state legislatures, have the right to decide how delegates to national conventions are selected. Thus Wisconsin could not retain an "open" primary if the national Democratic party objected (*Democratic Party* v. *La Follette,* 101 Sup. Ct. 1010, 1981). Now the parties can insist that only voters who declare themselves Democrats or Republicans can vote in presidential primaries. The Supreme Court's ruling may have relatively little practical effect, however, since the "declaration" might occur only an hour or a day before the election.

The ballots from a state with an "open" primary election.

OFFICIAL BALLOT
FOR PRESIDENTIAL PREFERENCE VOTE
DEMOCRA[...]

NOTICE TO ELECTORS: THIS BALLOT MAY [...]
ELECTION INSPECTORS. IF CAST AS AN A[...]
BEAR THE INITIALS OF THE MUNICIPAL C[...]

MARK THIS BALLOT IN ONE SPACE ONLY. [...]

Express your preference for one of t[...]
printed on this ballot (in that case, [...]
square at the RIGHT of that person['...]

Vote for an uninstructed delegation [...]
convention of the Democratic party [...]
square at the RIGHT of "Uninstruc[...]

Write in the name of another pers[...]
candidate of the Democratic party [...]
name into the space following "Wr[...]

LARRY AGRAN . . . .

PAUL E. TSONGAS . . . .

BILL CLINTON . . . .

EUGENE McCARTHY . . . . .

LYNDON H. LaROUCHE, JR.

BOB KERREY

OFFICIAL BALLOT
FOR PRESIDENTIAL PREFERENCE VOTE
REPUBLICAN PARTY

NOTICE TO ELECTORS: THIS BALLOT MAY BE INVALID UNLESS INITIALED BY 2 ELECTION INSPECTORS. IF CAST AS AN ABSENTEE BALLOT, THE BALLOT MUST BEAR THE INITIALS OF THE MUNICIPAL CLERK OR DEPUTY CLERK.

MARK THIS BALLOT IN ONE SPACE ONLY. YOU HAVE ONE OF 3 CHOICES:

Express your preference for one of the persons whose names are printed on this ballot (in that case, make a cross (X) in the square at the RIGHT of that person's name); or

Vote for an uninstructed delegation from Wisconsin to the national convention of the Democratic party (in that case, make a cross (X) in the square at the RIGHT of "Uninstructed delegation"); or

Write in the name of another person to become the presidential candidate of the Democratic party (in that case, write that person's name into the space following "Write-in candidate").

GEORGE BUSH . . . . ☐

HAROLD E. STASSEN . . . . ☐

DAVID [...]

selling of the president" or "packaging the candidate"—mostly by advertising executives, who are not especially known for underestimating their own abilities. No doubt spots can have an important effect in some cases. A little-known candidate can increase his or her visibility by frequent use of spots (this is what Jimmy Carter did in the 1976 presidential primaries). Sometimes a complete unknown can win a primary by clever use of television, as allegedly happened when Mike Gravel became the Democratic nominee for senator from Alaska in 1968 and Milton Shapp became the Democratic nominee for governor of Pennsylvania in 1966. Nelson Rockefeller was helped in his difficult campaign for reelection as governor of New York in 1966 by television spots that did *not* show Rockefeller—his advertising agency decided that he did not come across well on TV—but showed instead clever commercials describing his policies and programs.

The effect of television advertising on general elections is probably a good deal less than on primaries; indeed, as we shall see in Chapter 10, most scientific studies of television influence on voting decisions show that either it has no effect or the effect is subtle and hard to detect. Nor is it surprising that this should be the case. In a general election, especially one for high-visibility offices (such as president or governor), the average voter has many sources of information—his or her own party or ideological pref-

POLITICALLY P.S. SPEAKING

Clothespin Vote

The vote cast by a person who does not like either candidate and so votes for the less objectionable of the two, putting a clothespin over his or her nose to keep out the unpleasant stench.

erence, various kinds of advertising, the opinions of friends and family, and newspaper and magazine stories. Furthermore both sides will use TV spots; if well done, they are likely to cancel each other out. In short it is not yet clear that a gullible public is being sold a bill of goods by slick Madison Avenue advertisers, whether the goods are automobiles or politicians.

Visuals are a vital part of any major campaign effort because, unlike spots, they cost the campaign little and, as "news," they may have greater credibility with the viewer. A visual is a brief filmed episode showing the candidate doing something that a reporter thinks is newsworthy. Simply making a speech, unless the speech contains important new facts or charges, is often thought by TV editors to be uninteresting: television viewers are not attracted by pictures of "talking heads," and in the highly competitive world of TV, audience reactions are all-important determinants of what gets on the air. Knowing

In the 1888 presidential campaign, supporters of Benjamin Harrison rolled a huge ball covered with campaign slogans across the country. The gimmick, first used in 1840, gave rise to the phrase, "keep the ball rolling."

Candidates first made phonographic recordings of their speeches in 1908. Warren G. Harding is shown here recording a speech during the 1920 campaign.

Urbanization and the movement of people to big cities made railroad tours of small towns an increasingly inefficient way to meet voters. Thus the motorcade through city streets began to take its place, such as this one in 1968 where the public greeted Robert F. Kennedy.

"Whistle-stop" tours were popular in the railroad era; in 1992, Bill Clinton and Al Gore substituted a bus tour.

this, campaign managers will strive to have their candidates do something visually interesting every day, no later than 3:00 P.M. (if the visual is to be on the 6:00 P.M. news)—talk to elderly folks in a nursing home, shake hands with people waiting in an unemployment line, commiserate about inflation with shoppers in a supermarket, or sniff the waters of a polluted lake. Obviously all these efforts are for nought if a TV camera crew is not around; great pains are therefore taken to schedule these visuals at times and in places that make it easy for the photographers to be present.

Ironically the visuals—and television newscasts generally—may give the viewer less information than commercial spots. This, of course, is the exact opposite of what many people believe. It is commonplace to deplore political advertising, especially the short spot, on the grounds that it is either devoid of information or manipulative, and to praise television news programs, especially longer debates and interviews, because they are informative and balanced. In fact the best research we have so far suggests that the reverse is true: news programs covering elections tend to convey very little information (they often show scenes of crowds cheering or candidates shouting slogans) and to make little or no impression on viewers, if indeed they are watched at all. Paid commercials, on the other hand, especially the shorter spots, often contain a good deal of information that is seen, remembered, and evaluated by a public that is quite capable of distinguishing between fact and humbug.[3]

A special kind of television campaigning is the campaign debate. Incumbents or well-known candidates have little incentive to debate their opponents; by so doing, they only give more publicity to lesser-known rivals. Despite the general rule among politicians never to help an opponent, Vice President Nixon debated the less-well-known John Kennedy in 1960, and President Gerald Ford debated the less-well-known Jimmy Carter in 1976. Nixon and Ford lost. Lyndon Johnson would not debate Barry Goldwater in 1964, nor would Nixon debate Humphrey in 1968 or McGovern in 1972. Johnson and Nixon won. Carter debated the equally well known Reagan in 1980 (but refused to join in a three-way debate with Reagan and John Anderson). Carter lost. It is hard to know what effect TV debates have on election out-comes, but poll data suggest that in 1980 voters who watched the debates were reassured by Reagan's performances; after the second debate with Carter, he took a lead in the polls that he never relinquished.[4] In 1984 most people thought that Mondale did better than Reagan in the first debate, but there is little evidence that the debate affected the outcome of the election.

In 1988, the televised debate became a major activity during—and even before—the primary elections. The half dozen or so contenders for both the Democratic and the Republican presidential nominations participated in so many debates that one journalist was led to compare the campaign to a political version of the television program "The Dating Game," with the candidates, like bachelors trying to impress a woman, describing, over and over again, all their good qualities. Other than providing free television exposure (and probably boring the candidates to tears), it is hard to see what this accomplished.

Though TV visuals and debates are free, they are also risky. The risk is the slip of the tongue. You may have spent thirty years of your life in unblemished public service, you may have thought through your position on the issues with great care, you may have

The first televised presidential campaign debate occurred in 1960 between John F. Kennedy and Richard M. Nixon.

In 1992 Ross Perot bought "infomercials"—half-hour television broadcasts devoted to his discussion of national issues.

rehearsed your speeches until your dog starts to howl, but just make one verbal blunder and suddenly the whole campaign focuses on your misstep. In 1976 President Ford erroneously implied that Poland was not part of the Soviet bloc. For days the press dwelt on this slip. His opponent, Jimmy Carter, admitted in a *Playboy* interview that he sometimes had lust in his heart. It is hard to imagine anyone who has not, but apparently presidents are supposed to be above that sort of thing. In 1980 Ronald Reagan said that trees cause pollution—oops, here we go again.

Because of the fear of a slip, because the voters do not want to hear long, fact-filled speeches about complex issues, and because general-election campaigns are fights to attract the centrist voter, the candidates will rely on a stock speech that sets out the campaign theme as well as on their ability to string together several proven applause-getting lines. For reporters covering the candidate every day, it can be a mind-numbing experience. Nelson Rockefeller spoke so often of the "brotherhood of man and the fatherhood of God" that the reporters started referring to it as his BOMFOG speech. Occasionally this pattern is interrupted by a "major" address—that is, a carefully

composed talk on some critical issue, usually delivered before a live audience and designed to provide issue-related stories for the reporters to write.

If you dislike campaign oratory, put yourself in the candidate's shoes for a moment. Every word you say will be scrutinized, especially for slips of the tongue. Interest-group leaders and party activists will react sharply to any phrase that departs from their preferred policies. Your opponent stands ready to pounce on any error of fact or judgment. You must give countless speeches every day. The rational reaction to this state of affairs is to avoid controversy, stick to prepared texts and tested phrases, and shun anything that sounds original (and hence untested). You therefore wind up trying to sell yourself as much as or more than your ideas. Voters may *say* that they admire a blunt, outspoken person, but in a tough political campaign they would probably discover that this bluntness is a little unnerving.

Television is the most visible example of modern technology's effect on campaigns. Since 1960 presidential elections have been contested largely through television. Without television the campaign waged in 1992 by independent candidate Ross Perot might not have happened at all. Perot launched his candidacy with successive appearances on Cable News Network's call-in program "Larry King Live" and he bought several half-hour chunks of television time to air his views on the federal budget deficit. In early October, before the first of three televised debates featuring Perot, Republican incumbent George Bush, and Democratic challenger Bill Clinton, most national polls showed Perot with only 10 percent of the vote. But after the debates Perot's support in the polls doubled, and he ended up with about 19 percent of the votes cast on election day.

Less visible than television but perhaps just as important is the computer. The computer makes possible sophisticated direct-mail campaigning, and this in turn makes it possible for a candidate to address specific appeals to particular voters easily and to solicit persons for campaign contributions rapidly.

Whereas television is heard by everybody, and thus leads the candidate using it to speak in generalities to avoid offending anyone, direct mail is aimed at particular groups (college students, Native Americans, bankers, auto workers) to whom specific views can be expressed with much less risk of offending someone. So important are the lists of names of potential contributors to whom the computer sends appeals that a prized resource of any candidate, guarded as if it were a military secret, is "The List." Novices in politics must slowly develop their own lists or beg sympathetic incumbents for a peek at theirs.

The chief consequence of the new style of campaigning is not that, as some think, it is more manipulative than old-style campaigning (picnics with free beer and $5 bills handed to voters can be just as manipulative as TV ads), but rather that running the campaign has become divorced from the process of governing. Previously party leaders who ran the campaigns would take part in the government once it was elected, and since they were *party* leaders, they had to worry about getting their candidate *re*elected. Modern political consultants take no responsibility for governing, and by the time the next election rolls around, they may be working for someone else.

Money

All these consultants, TV ads, and computerized mailings cost money—lots of it (see Figure 8.1). A powerful California politician once observed that "money is the mother's milk of politics," and many people think that our democracy is drowning in it.

The 1992 presidential election cost $286 million, up from $177 million in 1988. The 1992 congressional races cost another $364 million. In total the candidates, parties, and taxpayers had to come up with $650 million to pick our national leaders. When that kind of money is spent, many people will cynically conclude that elections are being bought and sold. Clever television producers are being paid huge sums, so the theory goes, to put on TV ads that sell candidates as if they were boxes of soap.

But matters are a good deal more complicated and less sinister than the popular theory supposes. Money is important in politics as in everything else, but it is not obvious that candidates with the most money always win or that the donors of the money buy big favors in exchange for their big bucks. In Chapter 9 we will consider what, if anything, interest groups get for the money they give to politicians, and in Chapter 10 we shall summarize what we know about the effects of television advertising on elections. Here let us try to answer four questions: Where does campaign money come from? What rules gov-

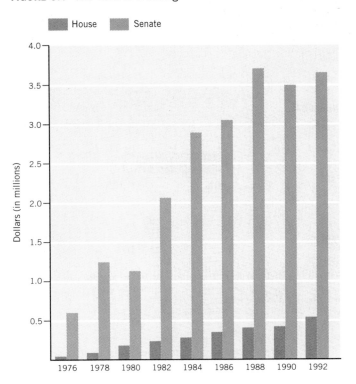

FIGURE 8.1 The Cost of Winning

SOURCES: For 1976–1988: *New York Times* (March 20, 1990): A10, reporting data from the Federal Election Commission. Copyright © 1990 by the New York Times Company. Reprinted by permission. For 1990–1992: Federal Election Commission Report, March 4, 1993.

ern how it is raised and spent? What has been the effect of campaign finance reform? What does campaign spending buy?

The Sources of Campaign Money

Presidential candidates get part of their money from private donors and part from the federal government; congressional candidates get all of their money from private sources.

In the presidential primaries, candidates raise money from private citizens and interest groups. The federal government will provide matching funds, dollar for dollar, for all money raised from individual donors who contribute no more than $250. Since every candidate wants as much of this "free" federal money as possible, each has an incentive to raise money from small, individual givers. (To prove they

FIGURE 8.2 Where the Money Comes From: Sources of Campaign Funds of All House and Senate Candidates, 1982 and 1990.

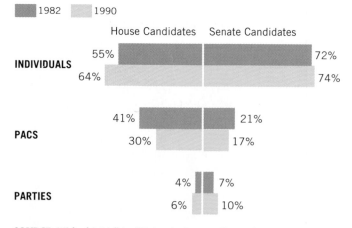

SOURCE: Michael J. Malbin, "Fixing the Race: Dollars and Sense in Campaigns," *The American Enterprise,* November/December 1991, p. 65. Reprinted with permission.

Congressional candidates get no governmental funds; all their money must come out of their own pockets or be raised from individuals, interest groups (PACs), or the political parties. Contrary to what many people think, most of that money comes—and has always come—from individual donors (see Figure 8.2). Because the rules sharply limit how much any individual can give, these donors tend not to be fat cats but people of modest means who contribute $100 or $200 per person.

Since the typical individual contribution is very small (and in no case larger than $1,000), some candidates have turned to rock bands and movie stars to put on benefit performances. If five thousand people will each pay $25 to hear a performance by the Slipped Disc, a lot of money can be raised in a hurry.

The limits on how much a PAC can give a candidate in any election is $5,000, but the typical PAC does not donate anything approaching the maximum amount; usually, it gives a few hundred dollars to each candidate it supports.

These figures conceal some important differences among kinds of candidates, however. As Table 8.1 shows, incumbent members of Congress running for reelection get over a third of their money from PACs and spend next to nothing out of their own pockets. Their challengers, by contrast, spend only half as much as the incumbent and are able to get only one-sixth of that from PACs. Challengers have to put up much more of their own money. As we shall see in

are serious candidates, they must first raise $5,000 in each of twenty states from such small contributors.) The government also gives a lump-sum grant to each political party to help pay the costs of its nominating convention. In the general election the government pays all the costs of each major-party candidate, up to a limit set by law (in 1992 that limit was $55 million per candidate).

TABLE 8.1   **Sources of Campaign Funds: All House and Senate Candidates in 1991–1992 by Incumbents, Challengers, and Open**

	Incumbents		Challengers		Open	
	Sum (millions)	Percent	Sum	Percent	Sum	Percent
Individuals	$151.7	50.5%	$107.0	58.5%	$96.6	55.1%
PACs	126.7	42.2	21.4	11.7	32.4	18.5
Candidates	1.0	0.3	10.5	5.7	6.8	3.9
Loans	9.6	3.2	37.0	20.2	33.6	19.2
Other	11.3	3.8	6.9	3.8	6.0	3.4
Totals	$300.3		$182.8		$175.4	

NOTE: The data on candidates' contributions are especially messy. They include direct personal contributions and loans to the campaign, but the campaign committees often repay loans from previous elections. In the end, loans from incumbents are almost always repaid by campaign committees, and direct contributions by candidates amount to a trace of the incumbents' totals.
SOURCE: *Federal Election Commission Report* (March 4, 1993).

the next section, these money problems weaken the ability of challengers to mount effective campaigns.

Campaign Finance Rules

During the 1972 presidential election, men hired by President Nixon's campaign staff broke into the headquarters of the Democratic National Committee in the Watergate office building. They were caught by an alert security guard. The subsequent investigation disclosed that the Nixon people had engaged in dubious or illegal money-raising schemes, including taking large sums from wealthy contributors in exchange for appointing them to ambassadorships. Many individuals and corporations were indicted for making illegal donations (since 1925 it had been against the law for corporations or labor unions to contribute money to candidates, but the law had been unenforceable). Some of the accused had given money to Democratic candidates as well as to Nixon.

To prevent these abuses, Congress passed in 1974 a new federal campaign finance reform law. It created a six-person Federal Election Commission (FEC) charged with enforcing a new, tougher set of restrictions on political spending as well as a system of public financing of presidential campaigns. The key provisions of this law are summarized in the box at right.

If you want to run for Congress today, you must report to the FEC every contribution you receive of $100 or more, and you cannot accept more than $1,000 from any individual during any election. (If you run in both the primary and the general election, you can take up to $1,000 in each campaign from the same person.) The law against taking money from corporations or labor unions was reaffirmed, but such organizations were allowed to form PACs that could raise money in voluntary contributions from their employees or members. (Trade associations, professional societies, and other groups were also allowed to form PACs.) No PAC can give more than $5,000 to any candidate in any election, with the primary and the general contest counted as separate elections.

Initially the law also set limits on how much an individual candidate could spend on his or her own campaign, but the Supreme Court ruled that this was an unconstitutional infringement of the First Amendment's guarantee of free speech.[5] The right to run for office and to express your views includes the

Major Federal Campaign-Finance Rules

General

- All federal election contributions and expenditures are reported to a six-person Federal Election Commission with power to investigate and prosecute violators.
- All contributions over $100 must be disclosed, with name, address, and occupation of contributor.
- No cash contributions over $100, no foreign contributions.
- No ceiling on amount a candidate or campaign may spend (unless a presidential candidate accepts federal funding).

Individual Contributions

- May not exceed $1,000 to any candidate in any election per year.
- May not exceed $20,000 per year to a national party committee or $5,000 to a political-action committee.
- No limit on expenditures for "independent advertising."

Political-Action Committees (PACs)

- A corporation, union, or other association may each establish one PAC.
- A PAC must register six months in advance, have at least fifty contributors, and give to at least five candidates.
- PAC contributions to a candidate may not exceed $5,000 per election, or to a national party, $15,000 per year.

Presidential Primaries

- Federal matching funds, dollar for dollar, are available for all money raised by candidates from individual donors giving $250 or less.
- To be eligible, a candidate must raise $5,000 in each of twenty states in contributions of $250 or less.

Presidential Election

- Federal government will pay all campaign costs of major-party candidates and part of the cost of minor-party candidates (those winning between 5 percent and 25 percent of the vote).

✪ Do American Elections Really Cost So Much?

*M*any people worry that elections in the United States are too costly. But compared to what? One way to answer that question is to see how our elections stack up against those held abroad. The data are hard to find and even harder to compare, but Howard Penniman has produced these estimates of the cost of a national election per eligible voter:

United Kingdom	$0.50
West Germany	3.20
UNITED STATES	3.25
(Congressional, $1.51)	
(Presidential, $1.74)	
Ireland	3.93
Israel	4.34

Elections are inexpensive in the United Kingdom, in part because the campaign is limited to three weeks. But the United States compares favorably to West Germany, Ireland, and Israel.

SOURCE: Howard Penniman, "U.S. Elections: Really a Bargain?" *Public Opinion* (June–July 1984): 51ff. Reprinted with permission of the American Enterprise Institute for Public Policy Research.

right to spend your own money on the effort. However, the Court let stand a limit of $50,000 on how much a presidential candidate could spend out of his pocket on his own campaign if he accepted federal financing. They reasoned that anybody taking the taxpayers' money was getting plenty of help in exercising his First Amendment rights, and so it was not unreasonable to restrict his own spending on that cause.

The law sets no limits on how much individuals or organizations can spend for "independent" political advertising on behalf of a candidate. To be independent an expenditure cannot be made at the request of or in cooperation or consultation with the candidate or the candidate's campaign organization. These independent expenditures are typically made by ideologically oriented PACs and sometimes take the form of "negative ads"—that is, advertisements attacking an opposing candidate for his or her position on the environment, abortion, or whatever.

No law regulating a powerful human desire, such as ambition for office, can ever be entirely successful,

and campaign finance rules are no exception. Though the law has ended many of the worst abuses, it leaves a number of loopholes that candidates can exploit. Among them are these:

- The political parties can solicit unlimited funds from individuals, corporations, and unions, provided that they spend the money on local party activities such as voter registration campaigns and get-out-the-vote drives and not on behalf of specific candidates. But of course a successful campaign by a party to get voters to the polls will tend to help the candidate of that party. The funds are called "soft money" as opposed to the hard money that must be reported to the FEC.

- Individual politicians, such as former Senator Alan Cranston of California, raised millions of dollars from contributors without regard to FEC limits by earmarking the money for voter-registration campaigns rather than for advertising on their own behalf. Among the big donors to Cranston's registration campaigns was Charles Keating, who was seeking Cranston's help in getting the federal government to go easy on a troubled savings-and-loan association that Keating ran so badly that he was later sent to prison.

- Many small contributions from different individuals or PACs can be bundled together and delivered at one time in order to increase the impact on the candidate of the contributions and, presumably, of the interests of the contributors.

The Effects of Reform

The intent of the reform was to get political fundraising out in the open and subject to clearly understood rules that minimized the chance of some fat cat's buying a pet politician. By and large the law has succeeded at that.

But the reform also had some unintended effects. First, by authorizing PACs to raise money the law made possible a vast increase in the amount of money spent on elections by special interests. Figure 8.3 shows how PACs have grown from just a few hundred in 1977 to over four thousand in 1993. During that same period their contributions to federal candidates rose from about $25 million to nearly $190 million.

FIGURE 8.3 Growth of PACs

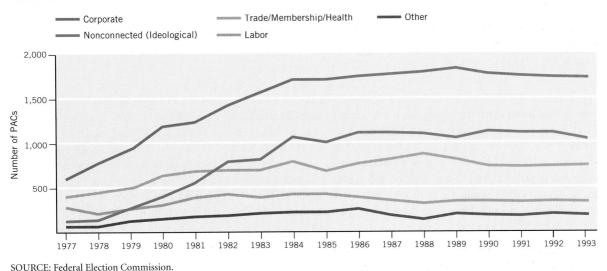

SOURCE: Federal Election Commission.

Second, the reform has shifted the control of campaign money away from the political parties and toward individual candidates, thus further weakening the power of the parties. Some people might think this is a good thing, but there is another side to the story. To the extent that people vote for parties rather than for individuals (and many people still do), the party ought to have some way of influencing the selection and behavior of its candidates. It is harder for this to occur when parties play so small a role in financing campaigns.

Third, the reforms provide an advantage to wealthy challengers. If you want to take on a well-entrenched incumbent and have no money of your own, you will find that the rules make raising the necessary funds a slow and painful process involving endless appeals to countless individuals to obtain small donations. It can easily take half a million dollars to mount a credible campaign; that adds up to a lot of phone calls and coffee parties. But if you can write a check for half a million dollars, you can spare yourself all the trouble.

Fourth, the reforms give an advantage to candidates with strong ideological appeal. Unless you are rich, the easiest way to get money from lots of small donors is to use direct-mail pieces that evoke powerful emotions such as feelings for or against abortion, gun control, school prayer, or the death penalty.

Never mind whether these are the most important issues; they generate cash.

Fifth, the reforms penalize people who start late in a campaign. Fund-raising takes a lot of time; if you decide at the last minute to run, you may discover you have no chance of raising the money you need before it is too late. Incumbents know this, so many of them spend their time in office raising huge war chests well in advance of the election in order to scare off would-be challengers.

Finally, the reforms help incumbents and hurt challengers. Incumbents find it easier to raise money from PACs, regardless of party and regardless of type of PAC. As we shall see in Chapter 9, corporate PACs are more likely to support incumbents of whatever party than they are to support Republicans.

Money and Winning

Money doesn't make much difference in presidential contests because, in the general election, both candidates have the same amount (not counting money spent by the parties—soft money that is about equally divided between the two parties).

In congressional races it is another matter. Scholars are not entirely agreed on the facts, but in general it seems that money does make a difference. There is strong evidence that how much the challenger spends

The 1992 Election

The presidential contest was over the day the Democrats nominated Governor Bill Clinton of Arkansas. Incumbent presidents, except those with extraordinary personal popularity, cannot survive an economic recession like the one that gripped this country in the early 1990s. And George Bush did not have that reservoir of personal popularity. Though Americans greatly admired the way he rallied American and allied forces to liberate Kuwait in Operation Desert Storm, the admiration was for his success and not for him.

Whatever chance the Republicans might have had for winning depended on the Democrats' choosing a candidate who appeared to be so far out of step with the public's core values that the people would vote against him or her in spite of hard times. The Democrats had made that mistake before. George McGovern was too liberal for the 1972 electorate, Michael Dukakis too aloof and technocratic for the 1988 electorate. Clinton was neither.

He had positioned himself as a reformist governor of a southern state with views on certain social issues that were not far from the mainstream of public opinion. Unlike Dukakis, he was not opposed to the death penalty; unlike Walter Mondale he was prepared to take a tough stance on welfare; unlike most congressional Democrats he did not clearly oppose U.S. participation in Desert Storm (but then he did not quite endorse it, either). Like any Democrat aspiring to the nomination, he supported the right to an abortion.

For a while it appeared that voter disgust with national politics might lead them to give enough support to independent candidate Ross Perot that he would carry enough states as to deny any candidate a clear Electoral College majority

and thus throw the decision into the House of Representatives. Perhaps because of his indecisiveness (he entered the race, withdrew, and then reentered), his initial popularity faded. Though he won 19 percent of the popular vote (a remarkably good showing for a third-party candidate), he carried no states and probably did not affect the outcome for Bush or Clinton anywhere.

Bush's only chance to defeat Clinton was on the character issue. Charges during the primary campaign about Clinton's marital infidelity did not stick, but new charges of his having taken extraordinary steps to evade the draft during the Vietnam war and organized antiwar protest demonstrations lingered in the fall. In the campaign, Clinton took pains to project a Middle American image, appearing with his running mate, Senator Al Gore of Tennessee, in small cities in the Midwest and the South and avoiding an overly close identification with such traditional Democratic constituencies as the leaders of labor unions and big-city blacks. Everywhere they went, Clinton and Gore attacked President Bush for his failure to produce an economic recovery.

Though he waged a skillful and energetic campaign, he did not have to win votes so much as he had to avoid losing any. From September on, the polls showed Clinton ahead in enough states to give him the presidency, provided he made no mistakes. He made none.

Clinton won 370 electoral votes (only 270 are needed for victory), carrying the Northeast, the Far West, and most of the states in the industrial Midwest. But there were clouds over his victory. Clinton got less than half the popular vote (43 percent) and, despite being a southerner, lost most of the southern states, including such big ones as Florida, North Carolina, and Texas to Bush.

The congressional races took on exceptional importance. Reapportionment after the 1990 census added many new seats to the California, Florida, and Texas delegations and caused big losses in Illinois, Michigan, New York, Ohio, and Pennsylvania. The state struggle over redistricting cut heavily into some traditionally Democratic districts in these and other states, a problem made worse for the Democrats by the tendency to create safe seats for black and Latino candidates, thus putting Anglo-white incumbents at a disadvantage.

In addition, popular resentment against Congress, intensified by the check-writing scandal in the House, caused many incumbents to feel deeply threatened. For all of these reasons, a record number of incumbents decided not to stand for reelection or were defeated in the primaries. Sixty-six representatives and eight senators retired or decided to run for other offices; nineteen representatives and one senator lost in the primaries. Many people thought that the anti-incumbency mood would carry over into the general election. It did, but to a very modest extent. In fact, 88 percent of the House and Senate incumbents who ran were reelected. With all the resignations, however, there were 110 new faces in the House, the biggest turnover since 1948.

Despite Bush's weaknesses, the Republicans gained nine seats in the House and lost only one in the Senate, leaving the party composition of the 103d Congress looking like this:

	House	Senate
Democrats	259	58
Republicans	175	42
Independent	1	

is important because the challenger usually must become known to the public. Buying name recognition is expensive. Gary Jacobson has shown that, other things being equal, in every congressional election since 1972, challengers who spent more money did better than those who spent less.[6] Jacobson also suggested that how much the incumbents spent was not very important, presumably because they had all the name recognition (as well as the other benefits of officeholding such as free mail and travel) that they needed. But other scholars, applying different statistical methods to the same facts, come to different conclusions. It now seems that, other things being equal, high-spending incumbents do better than low-spending ones.[7]

That money makes a difference does not mean it makes the only difference. In 1986 and 1988 the Republican challengers for Senate seats spent more money than the Democratic incumbents to whom they lost. Political party, incumbency, and issues affect the outcomes along with spending.

Incumbents find it easier to raise money than do challengers; incumbents provide services to their districts that challengers cannot; incumbents regularly send free ("franked") mail to their constituents while challengers must pay for their mailings; incumbents can get free publicity by sponsoring legislation or conducting an investigation. Thus it is hardly surprising that incumbents who run for election win in the overwhelming majority of races.

Many people think the campaign-finance system should be reformed once again—this time to undo some of the effects of the 1974 reforms. It will be very difficult for Congress to agree on any significant changes, however, because no matter what is done it will help some politicians and hurt others. Moreover, campaigning—whether by licking envelopes, making speeches, or giving money—is a valued and constitutionally protected right.

Some people would like to have public financing of congressional as well as presidential races. But since incumbent members of Congress already enjoy an enormous advantage, it would be difficult to design a public-financing law that did not perpetuate and even increase that advantage. For example, giving incumbents and challengers equal amounts of money might keep challengers at a disadvantage, since they often must spend more than the incumbent to overcome the latter's advantages.

What Other Countries Do

	Public Financing	Limits on Fund-Raising or Spending	Television
Britain	No	Yes	Free time, allocated according to party's strength in previous election
Denmark	Allowance to parties, based on strength in previous election	No	Parties given equal and free time on public stations
France	Reimbursement to candidates, according to votes received	Yes	Free and equal time to candidates
Italy	Reimbursement to candidates, according to votes received	No	Free and equal time to candidates on state-run stations, but parties control major private stations
Israel	No	No	Parties given equal and free time on public stations
Japan	No	Yes	Candidates given some free time for speeches: no negative advertising
Germany	Reimbursement to parties, according to votes received	No	Free time to candidates on public stations

SOURCE: *New York Times* (March 21, 1990): A12. Copyright © 1990 by the New York Times Company. Reprinted by permission.

Other people would like to restrict or even abolish campaign contributions from PACs. But even if that were constitutional, the money for the election must come from somewhere. If not from PACs, from whom? One answer is individuals, but that would require increasing the present $1,000 limit on what each person can give. Otherwise, with PAC spending banned, we would be back to the days before 1974 when money flowed into politics invisibly through hard-to-trace or even illegal channels.

Yet another way is to lower the cost of elections by shortening the campaign season, reducing the number of presidential primaries, or providing free or low-cost television for campaign speeches. Most

The Earthquake Election

Since 1934, every president has seen his party lose seats in Congress in midterm elections. No doubt President Clinton expected to take some losses too, but nothing could have prepared him for the electoral earthquake that hit on November 8, 1994. The Democrats lost 52 seats in the House and 8 in the Senate, giving Republicans control of both houses of Congress for the first time since 1954. To add insult to injury, one Democratic senator—Richard Shelby of Alabama—announced after the election that he was switching to the Republican party.

What happened? Explaining the 1994 election is a lot like explaining an earthquake—you feel the ground shake, you know something slipped, but the cause lies so deep in the earth you can't be sure why it moved. Here are some leading possibilities:

1. *The Economy.* Voters usually punish the president's party when the economy is bad. In 1994 voters who said that their standard of living had declined voted against the Democrats. But during the 1982 recession, when Ronald Reagan was in office, the Republicans lost only 26 seats in the House and actually gained one in the Senate. During the 1994 *recovery,* President Clinton's party lost twice as many House seats and 8 in the Senate. Why the difference? Perhaps it was because the voters had lost confidence in the ability of Democrats to manage the economy and had lost confidence in the president as a leader.

2. *Crime.* Rising rates of juvenile violence—gang killings, drive-by shootings, senseless murders to get a pair of Nike or Reebok sneakers—terrified people and convinced them that the country was on the wrong track. There is in fact not much the *federal* government can do about that, but whatever it can do the people became convinced that Republicans could do it better.

3. *The Southern Conversion.* The South was once solidly Democratic. Beginning in 1964, it started to give more support to Republican presidential candidates. Except for Jimmy Carter in 1976, the South went Republican in every election after 1964.* But for a long time, this shift of white Southerners to the Republican party took place mostly in presidential elections. In 1954, the last time the Republicans controlled the House before their 1994 victory, there were only 7 Republican representatives from the states of the old Confederacy. By 1994 that had changed dramatically—there were 63 Republican representatives from the South. The change had been occurring gradually, but in 1994 it accelerated sharply, with Republicans picking up 19 new Southern seats.

4. *"The Mess in Washington."* In his press conference the day after the election, President Clinton said that people were watching how Washington did business and didn't like what they saw. But for some reason that is not yet clear, the voters hold Democrats more responsible for that than they do Republicans. Maybe it is because the voters equated messy government with big government and so decided to vote against both the mess and the bigness—and the Democrats got labeled the party of big government. Or maybe it was because the Democrats who controlled Congress seemed to be the chief beneficiaries of the Washington mess, and so they became the chief victims of the voter backlash.

5. *The Quality of Candidates.* Veteran observers from both parties noted that in 1994 the Republicans fielded more experienced and more appealing candidates than they had in the past.

Even so, it is important to keep things in perspective. Though the Democrats suffered heavy losses, roughly nine out of every ten incumbent members of the House who stood for reelection were reelected. Many of the Republican gains came in races for open seats.

The defeat in Congress was only part of the story, however. The Republicans also won a majority of the governorships and increased their power in state legislatures. The number of Republican governors rose from 19 to 30, and the Republicans gained control of 15 more state legislative chambers without losing any.

In the Senate, Robert Dole (R., Kansas) became majority leader; in the House, Newt Gingrich (R., Georgia) became Speaker. During the campaign, Gingrich had persuaded several hundred Republican candidates to sign a "Contract with America" in which they pledged to vote for ten major proposals within the first hundred days of the 104th Congress. These included constitutional amendments requiring a balanced budget and imposing term limits on members of Congress and bills reforming welfare, strengthening the military, fighting crime, and cutting certain taxes.

Whether the Republicans can deliver on those promises remains to be seen.

---

*In 1968 the South backed George Wallace, a conservative independent. It amounted to the same thing as voting Republican.

TABLE 8.2 Pecentage of Popular Vote by Groups in Presidential Elections, 1960–1992

		National	Republicans	Democrats	Independents
1960	Kennedy	50%	5%	84%	43%
	Nixon	50	95	16	57
1964	Johnson	61	20	87	56
	Goldwater	39	80	13	44
1968	Humphrey	43	9	74	31
	Nixon	43	86	12	44
	Wallace	14	5	14	25
1972	McGovern	38	5	67	31
	Nixon	62	95	33	69
1976	Carter	51	11	80	48
	Ford	49	89	20	52
1980[a]	Carter	41	11	66	30
	Reagan	51	84	26	54
	Anderson	7	4	6	12
1984	Mondale	41	7	73	35
	Reagan	59	92	26	63
1988	Dukakis	46	8	82	43
	Bush	54	91	17	55
1992	Clinton	43	10	77	38
	Bush	38	73	10	32
	Perot	19	17	13	30

[a] The 1980 figures fail to add up to 100 percent because of missing data.
SOURCE: Gallup poll data compiled by Robert D. Cantor, *Voting Behavior and Presidential Elections* (Itasca, Ill.: F. E. Peacock, 1975), 35, Gerald M. Pomper, *The Election of 1976* (New York: David McKay, 1977), 61, and Gerald M. Pomper, *The Election of 1980* (Chatham, N.J.: Chatham House, 1981), 71, and *New York Times*–CBS Poll, November 5, 1992.

Americans no doubt think that campaigns are far too long, but they should remember that shorter ones might well make it even harder for challengers to defeat incumbents.

There are no easy answers, especially since it is almost impossible to think up a plan that will not appear to help one party and hurt the other.

What Decides the Election?

To the voter it all seems quite simple—he or she votes for "the best person" or maybe "the least-bad person." To scholars it is all a bit mysterious. How do voters decide who the best person is? What does *best* mean, anyway?

Party

One answer to these questions is party identification. People may say that they are voting for the "best person," but for many people the best person is always a Democrat or a Republican. Moreover we have seen in Chapter 5 that many people know rather little about the details of political issues. They may not even know what position their favored candidate has taken on issues that the voters care about. Given these facts, many scholars have argued that party identification is the principal determinant of how people vote.[8]

If it were only a matter of party identification, though, the Democrats would always win the presidency, since more people identify with the Democratic than the Republican party (that gap narrowed, however, in the early 1980s). But we know that the Democrats lost five of the seven presidential elections between 1968 and 1992. There are at least three reasons for this.

First, those people who consider themselves Democrats are less firmly wedded to their party than are Republicans wedded to theirs. Table 8.2 shows the percentage of people who identify themselves as Democrats or Republicans and who voted for various presidential candidates since 1960. At least 80 percent

The 1991–1992 recession was bad news for President Bush.

of the Republican voters supported the Republican candidate; indeed, if we omit the unusual 1964 election when Goldwater was the candidate, at least 84 percent of the Republican identifiers regularly voted Republican. By contrast there have been more defections among Democratic voters—in 1972, 33 percent supported Nixon, and in 1984, 26 percent supported Reagan.

The second reason, also clear in Table 8.2, is that the Republicans do much better than the Democrats among the self-described "independent" voters. In every election since 1952 (except 1964), the Republican candidate has won a larger percentage of the independent vote than the Democratic nominee; in fact the Republicans usually got a majority of the independents, who tend to be younger whites.

Finally a higher percentage of Republicans than of Democrats vote in elections. In every presidential contest in the last thirty years, those describing themselves as "strongly Republican" have been much more likely to vote than those describing themselves as "strongly Democratic."

Issues, Especially the Economy

Even though voters may not know a lot about the issues, that does not mean that issues play no role in elections or that voters respond irrationally to them.

For example, V. O. Key, Jr., looked at those voters who switched from one party to another between elections and found that most of them switched in a direction consistent with their own interests. As Key put it, the voters are not fools.[9]

Moreover voters may know a lot more than we suppose about issues that really matter to them. They may have hazy, even erroneous, views about monetary policy, Central America, and the trade deficit, but they are likely to have a very good idea as to whether unemployment is up or down, prices at the supermarket are stable or rising, or crime is a problem in their neighborhoods. And on some issues—such as abortion, school prayer, and race relations—they are likely to have some strong principles that they want to see politicians obey.

Contrary to what we learn in our civics lessons, representative government does not require voters to be well informed on the issues. If it were our duty as citizens to have accurate facts and sensible ideas about how best to negotiate with foreign adversaries, stabilize the value of the dollar, revitalize failing industries, and keep farmers prosperous, we might as well forget about citizenship and head for the beach. It would be a full-time job, and then some, to be a citizen. Politics would take on far more importance in our lives than most of us would want, given our need to earn a living and our belief in the virtues of limited government.

To see why our system can function without well-informed citizens, we must understand the difference between two ways in which issues can affect elections.

Prospective Voting   *Prospective* means "forward-looking"; we vote prospectively when we examine the views that the rival candidates have on the issues of the day and then cast our ballot for that person who we think has the best ideas for handling these matters. Prospective voting requires a lot of information about issues and candidates. Some of us do vote prospectively. Those who do tend to be political junkies. They are either willing to spend a lot of time learning about issues or so concerned about some big issue (abortion, school busing, nuclear energy) that all they care about is how a candidate stands on that question.

Prospective voting is more common among people who are political activists, who have a political ideology that governs their voting decision, or who are involved in interest groups with a big stake in the election. They are a minority of all voters, though (as we saw in Chapters 5 and 6) more influential than their numbers would suggest. Some prospective voters (by no means all) are organized into single-issue groups, to be discussed below.

Retrospective Voting *Retrospective* means "backward-looking"; retrospective voting involves looking at how things have gone in the recent past and then voting for the party that controls the White House if we like what has happened and voting against that party if we don't like what has happened. Retrospective voting does not require us to have a lot of information—we only need know whether things have, in our view, gotten better or worse.

Elections are decided by retrospective voters.[10] In 1980 they decided to vote against Jimmy Carter because inflation was rampant, interest rates were high, and we seemed to be getting the worst of things overseas. The evidence suggests rather clearly that they did not vote *for* Ronald Reagan; they voted for *an alternative* to Jimmy Carter. (Some people did vote for Reagan and his philosophy; they were voting prospectively, but they were in the minority.) In 1984 people voted for Ronald Reagan because unemployment, inflation, and interest rates were down and because we no longer seemed to be getting pushed around overseas. In 1980 retrospective voters wanted change; in 1984 they wanted continuity. In 1988 there was no incumbent running, but Bush portrayed himself as the candidate who would continue the policies that led to prosperity and depicted Dukakis as a "closet liberal" who would change those policies. In 1992 the economy had once again turned sour, and so voters turned away from Bush and toward his rivals, Clinton and Perot.

Though most incumbent members of Congress get reelected, those who lose do so, it appears, largely because they are the victims of retrospective voting. After Reagan was first elected, the economy went into a recession in 1981–1982. As a result Republican members of Congress were penalized by the voters, and Democratic challengers helped. But it is not just the economy that can hurt congressional candidates. Since 1860 every midterm election but one (1934) has witnessed a loss of congressional seats by the party holding the White House. Just why this should

be is not entirely clear, but it probably has something to do with the tendency of some voters to change their opinions of the presidential party once that party has had a chance to govern—which is to say, a chance to make some mistakes, disappoint some supporters, and irritate some interests.

Some scholars believe that retrospective voting is based largely on economic conditions. Figure 8.4 certainly provides support for this view. Each dot represents a presidential election (fifteen of them from 1932 through 1992). The horizontal axis is the percentage increase or decrease in per capita income (adjusted for inflation) during the election year. The vertical axis is the percentage of the two-party vote won by the party already occupying the White House. You can see that, as per capita income goes up (as you move to the right on the horizontal axis), the incumbent political party tends to win a bigger share of the vote.

Other scholars feel that matters are more complicated than this. As a result a small industry has grown up consisting of people who use different techniques to forecast the outcome of elections. If you know how

FIGURE 8.4 Economic Performance and Vote for the Incumbent President's Party

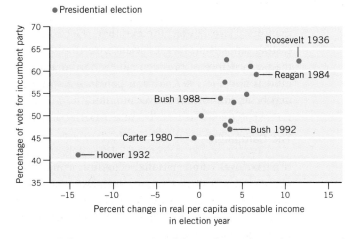

NOTE: Each dot represents a presidential election showing the popular vote received by the incumbent president's party. 1992 data do not include votes for independent candidate H. Ross Perot.

SOURCES: Economic data from Thomas Ferguson and Joel Rogers, "The Myth of America's Turn to the Right," *Atlantic Monthly* (May 1986), 50; election data from *CQ Guide to Elections,* 2d ed. Compiled by Professor John Zaller, Department of Political Science, UCLA. 1992 data from *Economic Report of the President,* 1993, 377, and *1993 World Almanac,* 73.

Radio talk shows have become an important way for like-minded people to discuss politics. This is Rush Limbaugh, a popular conservative talk-show host.

the president stands in the opinion polls several months before the election and how well the economy is performing, you can make a pretty good guess as to who is going to win the presidency. For congressional races predicting is a lot tougher because so many local factors affect these contests. Election forecasting remains an inexact science. As one study of the performance of presidential election forecasting models and the 1992 election concluded, "models may be no improvement over pundits."[11]

The Campaign

If party loyalty and national economic conditions play so large a role in elections, is the campaign just sound and fury, signifying nothing?

No. Campaigns can make a difference in three ways. First, they reawaken the partisan loyalties of voters. Right after a party's nominating convention selects a presidential candidate, that person's standing with voters of both parties goes way up in the polls. The reason is that the just-nominated candidate has received a lot of media attention during

summer months when not much else is happening. When the campaign gets under way, however, both candidates get publicity, and voters return to their normal Democratic or Republican affiliations.[12]

Second, campaigns give voters a chance to watch how the candidates handle pressure and give candidates a chance to apply that pressure. The two rivals, after promising to conduct a campaign "on the issues" without mudslinging, immediately start searching each other's personal history and records to find acts, statements, or congressional votes that can be shown in the worst possible light in newspaper or television ads. In 1988 George Bush asserted that as governor Michael Dukakis had vetoed a bill to make the Pledge of Allegiance mandatory in the Massachusetts schools; Dukakis retaliated by saying that Bush had to accept responsibility for some of the scandals of the Reagan administration because "a fish rots from the head." Many voters don't like these "negative ads"—but they work. As a result every politician constantly worries about how an opponent might portray his or her past record, a fact that helps explain why so many politicians never do or say anything that can't be explained in a thirty-second television spot.

Third, campaigns allow voters an opportunity to judge the character and core values of the candidates. Most voters don't study in detail a candidate's position on issues; even if they had the time, they know that you can't predict how politicians will behave just from knowing what a campaign manager has written in a position paper. The voters want some guidance as to how a candidate will behave once elected. They get that guidance by listening, not to the details of what a candidate says, but to the themes and tone of those statements. Is the candidate tough on crime and drugs? Are his or her statements about the environment sincere or perfunctory? Does the candidate favor having a strong military? Does the candidate care more about not raising taxes or more about helping the homeless?

The desire of voters to discern character, combined with the mechanics of campaigning—short radio and television ads and computer-targeted direct mail—lend themselves to an emphasis on themes at the expense of details. This tendency is reinforced by the expectations of ideological party activists and of single-issue groups.

Thematic campaigning, negative ads, and the demands of single-issue groups are not new; they are as old as the republic. In the nineteenth century the theme was slavery, the single-issue groups were abolitionists and their opponents, and their negative ads make the ones we have today sound like Sunday-school sermons. At the turn of the century the themes were temperance and votes for women; both issues led to no-holds-barred, rough-and-tumble campaigning. In the 1970s and 1980s new themes were advanced by fundamentalist Christians and by pro- and anti-abortion groups.

What has changed is not the tone of campaigning but the advent of primary elections. Once political parties picked candidates out of a desire to win elections. Today activists and single-issue groups influence the selection of candidates, sometimes out of a belief that it is better to lose with the "right" candidate than to win with the wrong one. In a five-candidate primary only 21 percent of the voters can pick the winner. Single-issue groups can make a big difference under these conditions even though they may not have much influence in the general election.

Union members were once heavily Democratic, but since Ronald Reagan began winning white union votes in 1980, these votes have been up for grabs.

Finding a Winning Coalition

Putting together a winning electoral coalition means holding on to your base among the committed partisans and attracting the swing voters who cast their ballots in response to issues (retrospectively or prospectively) and personalities.

There are two ways to examine the nature of the parties' voting coalitions. One is to ask what percentage of various identifiable groups in the population supported the Democratic or Republican candidate for president. The other is to ask what proportion of a party's total vote came from each of these groups. The answer to the first question tells us how *loyal* blacks, farmers, union members, and others are to the Democratic or Republican party or candidate; the answer to the second question tells us how *important* each group is to a candidate or party.

For the Democratic coalition, blacks are the most loyal voters. In every election but one since 1952, two-thirds or more of all blacks voted Democratic; since 1964 four-fifths have gone Democratic. At one time Jewish voters were almost as solidly Democratic, but in 1980 only a minority supported Jimmy Carter

(the rest split their votes between Reagan and John Anderson). Most Hispanics have been Democrats, though the label "Hispanic" conceals differences among Cuban-Americans (who often vote Republican) and Mexican-Americans and Puerto Ricans (who are strongly Democratic). The turnout among most Hispanic groups has been quite low (many are not yet citizens), so that their political power is not equivalent to their numbers.

The Democrats have lost their once strong hold on Catholics, southerners, and union members. In 1960 Catholics supported John F. Kennedy (a fellow Catholic), but they also have voted for Republicans Eisenhower, Nixon, and Reagan. Union members deserted the Democrats in 1968 and 1972, came back in 1980 and 1988, and divided about evenly between the two parties in 1952, 1956, and 1980. White southerners have voted Republican in national elections but Democratic in many local ones (see Table 8.3).

The Republican coalition is often described as the party of business and professional people. The loyalty of these groups to Republicans in fact is strong:

★ The Hispanic Vote

Some people call the Hispanic vote the "sleeping giant." In 1990 there were an estimated 22 million people of Hispanic origin in the United States, making them a potentially powerful voting bloc. But two things reduce this power considerably.

First, only about 2 million Hispanics voted in the 1980 and 1984 presidential elections. And in 1992, although they were about 9 percent of the population, they cast only 3 percent of the votes. The main reason for this low turnout is that many Hispanic citizens are not registered to vote. In addition, about one-third of all Hispanics are resident aliens and hence not entitled to register.

Second, the Hispanic vote is not homogeneous. Cuban-Americans, many of them concentrated in the Miami area, tend to be strongly Republican, while Mexican-Americans are strongly Democratic.

However, because the Hispanic vote is chiefly located in a few key states—California, Texas, and New York—any presidential candidate who succeeded in getting Hispanic voters to the polls would enjoy a big advantage. These three states have 119 electoral votes, almost half of the total number needed to win the presidency. Moreover, in 1990 there were nineteen Hispanic-majority congressional districts—seven in Texas, six in California, two each in New York and Florida, and one each in Arizona and Illinois. In these districts the Hispanic vote has already become crucial to winning election to Congress; it remains to be seen how or when the Hispanic vote will take on the same importance on the national level.

SOURCES: *National Journal* (November 19, 1983): 2410–2416; *New York Times* (July 18, 1986); *New York Times* (August 3, 1992): A14; *1993 World Almanac:* 73, 383

Both parties are trying to mobilize the potentially large Latino vote. Here, the Clinton campaign appeals to Mexican-Americans in Austin, Texas.

---

only in 1964 did they desert the Republican candidate to support Lyndon Johnson. Farmers have usually been Republican, but they are a volatile group, highly sensitive to the level of farm prices—and thus quick to change parties. They abandoned the Republicans in 1948 and 1964. Contrary to popular wisdom, the Republican party usually wins a majority of the votes of poor people (defined as those earning less than roughly $5,000 a year). Only in 1964 did most poor people support the Democratic candidate. This can be explained by the fact that the poor include quite different elements—low-income blacks

(who are Democrats) and many elderly, retired persons (who usually vote Republican).

In sum the loyalty of most identifiable groups of voters to either party is not overwhelming. Only blacks, businesspeople, and Jews usually give two-thirds or more of their votes to one party or the other; other groups display tendencies, but none that cannot be changed.

The contribution that each of these groups makes to the party coalitions is a different matter. Though blacks are overwhelmingly and persistently Democratic, they make up so small a portion of the total

TABLE 8.3 Who Likes the Democrats?

Pecentage of Various Groups Saying That They Voted for the Democratic Presidential Candidate, 1964–1992

		1964	1968[a]	1972	1976	1980[c]	1984	1988	1992[d]
Sex	Men	60%	41%	37%	53%	37%	37%	41%	41%
	Women	62	45	38	48	45	42	49	46
Race	White	59	38	32	46	36	34	40	39
	Nonwhite	94	85	87	85	82	90	86	82
Education	College	52	37	37	42	35	40	43	44
	Grade school	66	52	49	58	43	49	56	55
Occupation	Professional and business	54	34	31	42	33	37	40	NA
	Blue-collar	71	50	43	58	46	46	50	qNA
Age	Under 30	64	47	48	53	43	41	47	44
	50 and over	59	41	36	52	41[e]	39	49	50
Religion	Protestant	55	35	30	46	NA	NA	33[f]	33
	Catholic	76	59	48	57	40	44	47	44
	Jewish[b]	89	85	66	68	45	66	64	78
Southerners		52	31	29	54	47	36	41	42

[a] 1968 election had three major candidates (Humphrey, Nixon, and Wallace). [b] Jewish vote estimated from various sources; since the number of Jewish persons interviewed is often less than 100, the error in this figure, as well as that for nonwhites, may be large. [c] 1980 election had three major candidates (Carter, Reagan, and Anderson). [d] 1992 election had three major candidates (Clinton, Bush, and Perot). [e] For 1980–1992, refers to age 60 and over. [f] For 1988, white Protestants only.
SOURCE: Gallup poll data as tabulated in Jeane J. Kirkpatrick, "Changing Patterns of Electoral Competition," in *The New American Political System*, ed. Anthony King (Washington, D.C.: American Enterprise Institute, 1978), 264–256. Copyright © 1978 by the American Enterprise Institute. Reprinted by permision. 1980, 1984, 1988 and 1992 data from the *New York Times*–CBS News exit polls.

TABLE 8.4 The Contribution Made to Democratic Vote Totals by Various Groups, 1952–1988[a]

	1956	1960	1964	1968	1972	1976	1980	1984	1988	1992
Poor (income under $3,000 before 1980, $5,000 in 1990)	19%	16%	15%	12%	10%	7%	5%	8%	5%	5%
Black (and nonwhite)	5	7	12	19	22	16	22	24	15	23
Union member (or union member in family)	36	31	32	28	32	33	32	32	27	21
Catholic (and other non-Protestant)	38	47	36	40	34	35	32	47	43	46
South (including border states)	23	27	21	24	25	36	39	29	24	33
Central cities (12 largest metropolitan areas)	19	19	15	14	14	11	12	12	14	NA

[a] The figures shown represent the percentage of the party's vote in any specific election attributable to the group in question.
SOURCE: Extracted from figures presented by Robert Axelrod, "Communications," *American Political Science Review* (June 1981). Updated by Daron Shaw; ICPSR American National Election Study, 1992, Pre- and Post-Election Surveys.

electorate that only in recent years have they accounted for as much as one-fifth of the total Democratic vote (see Table 8.4). The groups that make up the largest part of the Democratic vote—Catholics, union members, southerners—are also the least dependable parts of that coalition.[13]

When representatives of various segments of society make demands on party leaders and presidential candidates, they usually stress their numbers or their loyalty, but rarely both. Black leaders, for example, sometimes describe the black vote as of decisive importance to Democrats and thus deserving of special consideration from a Democratic president. But blacks are so loyal that a Democratic candidate can almost take their votes for granted, and in any event they are not as numerous as other groups. Union leaders emphasize how many union voters there are, but a president will know that union leaders cannot "deliver" the union vote and that this vote may go to the president's opponent, whatever the leaders say. For any presidential candidate a winning coalition must be put together anew for each election. Only a few voters can be taken for granted or written off as a lost cause.

Election Outcomes

To the candidates and perhaps to the voter the only interesting outcome of an election is who won. To a political scientist the interesting outcomes are the broad trends in winning and losing and what they imply about the attitudes of voters, the operation of the electoral system, the fate of political parties, and the direction of public policy.

Figure 8.5 shows the trend in the popular vote for president since before the Civil War. From 1876 to 1896 the Democrats and Republicans were hotly competitive. The Republicans won three times, the Democrats twice in close contests. Beginning in 1896, the Republicans became the dominant party and, except for 1912 and 1916 when Woodrow Wilson, a Democrat, was able to win owing to a split in the Republican party, the Republicans carried every presidential election until 1932. Then Franklin Roosevelt put together what has since become known as the "New Deal coalition," and the Democrats became the dominant party. They won every election until 1952, when Eisenhower, a Republican and a popular military hero, was elected for two terms.

FIGURE 8.5 Partisan Division of the Presidential Vote in the Nation, 1824–1992

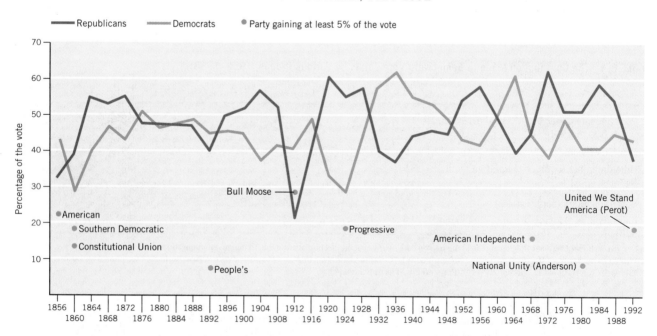

SOURCE: For 1824–1988: Historical Data Archive, Inter-University Consortium for Political Research, as reported in William H. Flanigan and Nancy H. Zingale, *Political Behavior of the American Electorate,* 3d ed., 32. Copyright © 1975 by Allyn and Bacon, Inc., Boston. Reprinted with permission of William C. Brown Publishers, Dubuque, Iowa. For 1992: Reprinted with permission from *The World Almanac and Book of Facts 1994:* 73. Copyright ©1993 Funk and Wagnalls Corporation.

Party Realignments

There have clearly been important turning points in the strength of the major parties, especially in the twentieth century, when for long periods we have not so much had close competition between two parties as we have had an alternation of dominance by one party and then another. To help explain these major shifts in the tides of politics, scholars have developed the theory of **critical** or **realigning periods.** During such periods a sharp, lasting shift occurs in the popular coalition supporting one or both parties. The issues that separate the two parties change, and so the kinds of voters supporting each party change. This shift may occur at the time of the election or just after as the new administration draws in new supporters.[14] There seem to have been five realignments so far, during or just after these elections: 1800 (when the Jeffersonian Republicans defeated the Federalists), 1828 (when the Jacksonian Democrats came to power), 1860 (when the Whig party collapsed and the Republicans under Lincoln came to power), 1896 (when the Republicans defeated William Jennings Bryan), and 1932 (when the Democrats under Roosevelt came into office). Some observers are struck by the fact that these realignments have occurred with marked regularity every twenty-eight to thirty-six years and have speculated on whether they are the result of inevitable cycles in American political life.

Such speculations need not concern us, for what is more important is to understand why a realignment occurs at all. That is not entirely clear. For one thing there are at least two kinds of realignments—one in which a major party is so badly defeated that it disappears and a new party emerges to take its place (this happened to the Federalists in 1800 and to the Whigs in 1856–1860); another in which the two existing parties continue but voters shift their support from one to the other (this happened in 1896 and 1932). Furthermore not all critical elections have been carefully studied.

The three clearest cases seem to be 1860, 1896, and 1932. By 1860 the existing parties could no longer straddle the fence on the slavery issue. The Republican party was formed in 1856 on the basis of clear-cut opposition to slavery; the Democratic party split in half in 1860, with one part (led by Stephen A. Douglas and based in the North) trying to waffle on

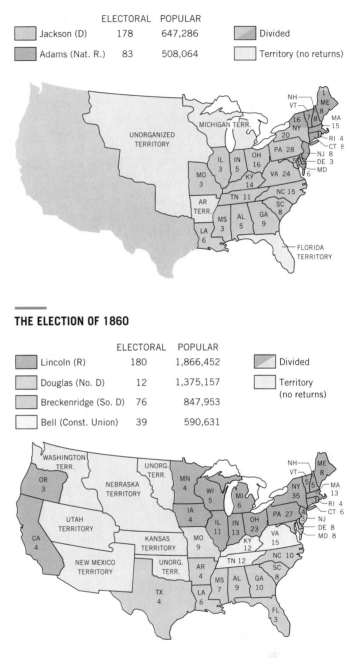

THE ELECTION OF 1828

	ELECTORAL	POPULAR	
Jackson (D)	178	647,286	Divided
Adams (Nat. R.)	83	508,064	Territory (no returns)

THE ELECTION OF 1860

	ELECTORAL	POPULAR	
Lincoln (R)	180	1,866,452	Divided
Douglas (No. D)	12	1,375,157	Territory (no returns)
Breckenridge (So. D)	76	847,953	
Bell (Const. Union)	39	590,631	

the issue, and the other (led by John C. Breckinridge and drawing its support from the South) categorically denying that any government had any right to outlaw slavery. The remnants of the Whig party, renamed the Constitutional Union party, tried to

THE ELECTION OF 1896

	ELECTORAL	POPULAR		
McKinley (R)	271	7,104,779		Divided
Bryan (D)	176	6,502,925		Territory (no returns)

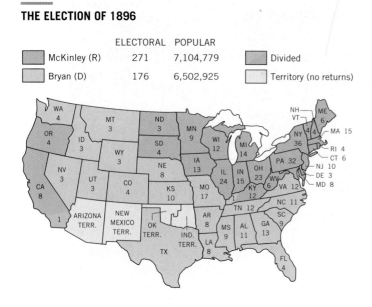

THE ELECTION OF 1932

	ELECTORAL	POPULAR
F.D. Roosevelt (D)	472	22,821,857
Hoover (R)	59	15,761,841

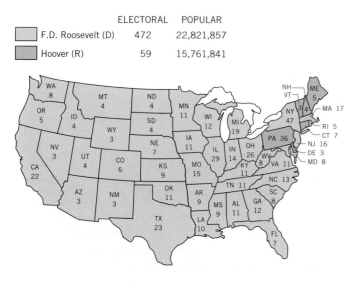

unite the nation by writing no platform at all, thus remaining silent on slavery. Lincoln and the antislavery Republicans won in 1860; Breckinridge and the proslavery Southern Democrats came in second. From that moment on, the two major political parties had acquired different sources of support and stood (at least for a decade) for different principles. The parties that had tried to straddle the fence were eliminated. The Civil War fixed these new party loy-

alties deeply into the popular mind, and the structure of party competition was set for nearly forty years.

In 1896 a different kind of realignment occurred. Economics rather than slavery was at issue. A series of depressions during the 1880s and 1890s fell especially hard on farmers in the Midwest and parts of the South. The prices paid to farmers for their commodities had been falling more or less steadily since the Civil War, making it increasingly difficult for them to pay their bills. A bitter reaction against the two major parties, which were straddling this issue as they had straddled slavery, spread like a prairie fire, leading to the formation of parties of economic protest—the Greenbackers and the Populists. Reinforcing the economic cleavages were cultural ones: Populists tended to be fundamentalist Protestants; urban voters were increasingly Catholic. Matters came to a head in 1896 when William Jennings Bryan captured the Democratic nomination for president and saw to it that the party adopted a populist platform. The existing Populist party endorsed the Bryan candidacy. In the election anti-Bryan Democrats deserted the party in droves to support the Republican candidate, William McKinley. Once again a real issue divided the two parties: the Republicans stood for industry, business, hard money, protective tariffs, and urban interests; the Democrats, for farmers, small towns, low tariffs, and rural interests. The Republicans won, carrying the cities, workers and businesspeople alike; the Democrats lost, carrying most of the southern and midwestern farm states. The old split between North and South that resulted from the Civil War was now replaced in part by an East versus West, city versus farm split.[15] It was not, however, only an economic cleavage—the Republicans had been able to appeal to Catholics and Lutherans who disliked fundamentalism and its hostility to liquor and immigrants.

This alignment persisted until 1932. Again change was triggered by an economic depression; again more than economic issues were involved. The New Deal coalition that emerged was based on bringing together into the Democratic party urban workers, northern blacks, southern whites, and Jewish voters. Unlike 1860 and 1896, it was not preceded by any third-party movement; it occurred suddenly (though some groups had begun to shift their allegiance in 1928) and gathered momentum throughout the 1930s. The Democrats, isolated since 1896 as

The 1896 election was a watershed in American politics—"a realigning election" that brought together new party coalitions. It pitted William McKinley, the Republican defender of the gold standard (left), against William Jennings Bryan, a fiery midwestern champion of strict religion and easy money (right).

a southern and midwestern sectional party, had now become the majority party by finding a candidate and a cause that could lure urban workers, blacks, and Jews away from the Republican party, where they had been for decades. It was obviously a delicate coalition—blacks and southern whites disagreed on practically everything except their liking for Roosevelt; Jews and the Irish bosses of the big-city machines also had little in common. But the federal government under Roosevelt was able to supply enough benefits to each of these disparate groups to keep them loyal members of the coalition and to provide a new basis for party identification.

These critical elections may have involved, not converting existing voters to new party loyalties, but recruiting into the dominant party new voters—young people just coming of voting age, immigrants just receiving their citizenship papers, and blacks just receiving, in some places, the right to vote. But there were also genuine conversions—northern blacks, for example, had been heavily Republican before

Roosevelt but became heavily Democratic after his election.

In short an electoral realignment occurs when a new issue of utmost importance to the voters (slavery, the economy) cuts across existing party divisions and replaces old issues that were formerly the basis of party identification. Some observers have speculated that we are due for a new party realignment as the tensions within the New Deal coalition become more evident. As the memory of Roosevelt and the Great Depression fades and as new voters come of age, the ability of the Democrats to keep within their party both people who are liberal and those who are conservative on social issues may decline.

Some people wondered whether the election of 1980, since it brought into power the most conservative administration in half a century, signaled a new realignment. Many of President Reagan's supporters began talking of their having a "mandate" to adopt major new policies in keeping with the views of the "new majority." But Reagan won in 1980 less because

Franklin Roosevelt greets Dr. George Washington Carver at Tuskegee Institute in Alabama. Blacks had long voted Republican; during the New Deal they shifted to the Democratic party. This change was part of the political realignment that occurred in the elections of 1932 and 1936.

of what he stood for than because he was not Jimmy Carter, and was reelected in 1984 primarily because people were satisfied with how the country was doing, especially economically.[16]

Just because we have had periods of one-party dominance in the past does not mean that we will have them in the future. Reagan's election could not

have been a traditional realignment because it left Congress in the hands of the Democratic party. Moreover some scholars are beginning to question the theory of critical elections, or at least the theory that they occur with some regularity.

Nevertheless one major change has occurred of late—the shift in the presidential voting patterns of the South. From 1972 through 1988 the South was more Republican than the nation as a whole. The proportion of white southerners describing themselves to pollsters as "strongly Democratic" fell from more than one-third in 1952 to about one-seventh in 1984. There has been a corresponding increase in "independents." As it turns out, southern white independents have voted overwhelmingly Republican in recent presidential elections.[17] If you lump independents together with the parties for which they actually vote, the party alignment among white southerners has gone from six-to-one Democratic in 1952 to about fifty-fifty Democrats and Republicans. If this continues, it will constitute a major realignment in a region of the country that is growing rapidly in size and political clout.

In general, however, the kind of dramatic realignment that occurred in the 1860s or after 1932 may not occur again because party labels have lost their meaning for a growing number of voters. For these people politics may *de*align rather than *re*align.

Party Decline

The evidence that parties are decaying, not realigning, is of several sorts. We have already noted (Chapter 7) that the proportion of people identifying with one or the other party declined between 1960 and 1980. Simultaneously the proportion of those voting a **split ticket** increased. Figure 8.6, for example, shows the steep increase in the percentage of congressional districts carried by one party for the presidency and by the other for Congress. Whereas in the 1940s one party would carry a given district for both its presidential and congressional candidates, today more than a third of the districts split their votes between one party's presidential candidate and the other's congressional candidate.

In 1988 more than *half* of all House Democrats were elected in districts that voted for Republican George Bush as president. This ticket splitting was greatest in the South, but common everywhere. If

FIGURE 8.6 Trends in Split-Ticket Voting for President and Congress, 1920–1992

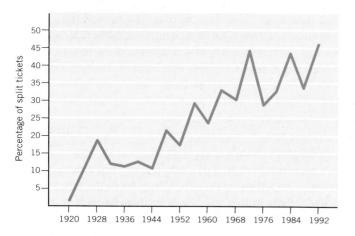

NOTE: The figure is the percentage of congressional districts carried by presidential and congressional candidates of different parties in each election year.

every district that voted for Bush had also elected a Republican to Congress, the Republican party would have held a two-to-one majority in the House of Representatives. Ticket splitting creates divided government—the White House and Congress controlled by different parties (see Chapter 12). Ticket splitting helped the Democrats keep control of the House of Representatives from 1954 to 1994.

Ticket splitting was almost unheard of in the nineteenth century, and for a very good reason. In those days the voter was either given a ballot by the party of his choice and he dropped it, intact, into the ballot box (thereby voting for everybody listed on the ballot), or he was given a government-printed ballot that listed in columns all the candidates of each party. All the voter had to do was mark the top of one column in order to vote for every candidate in that column. (When voting machines came along, they provided a single lever that, when pulled, cast votes for all the candidates of a particular party.) Progressives around the turn of the century began to persuade states to adopt the **office-bloc** (or "Massachusetts") **ballot** in place of the **party-column** (or "Indiana") **ballot**. This office-bloc ballot lists all candidates by office; there is no way to vote a straight party ticket by making one mark. Not surprisingly states using the office-bloc ballot show much more ticket splitting than those without it.[18]

The Effects of Elections on Policy

Cynics complain that elections are meaningless: no matter who wins, crooks, incompetents, or self-serving politicians still hold office. People of a more charitable disposition argue that elected officials are usually decent enough people but that public policy remains more or less the same no matter which official or which party is in office.

There is no brief and simple response to this latter view. Much depends on which office or policy we examine, something we shall do in greater detail in Part 4. One reason it is so hard to generalize about the policy effects of elections is that the offices to be filled by the voters are so numerous and the ability of the political parties to unite these officeholders behind a common policy is so weak that any policy proposal must run a gauntlet of potential opponents. Though we have but two major parties, and though only one party can win the presidency, each party is a weak coalition of diverse elements that reflect the many divisions in public opinion. The proponents of a new law must put together a majority coalition almost from scratch, and a winning coalition on one issue tends to be somewhat different—quite often dramatically different—from a winning coalition on another issue.

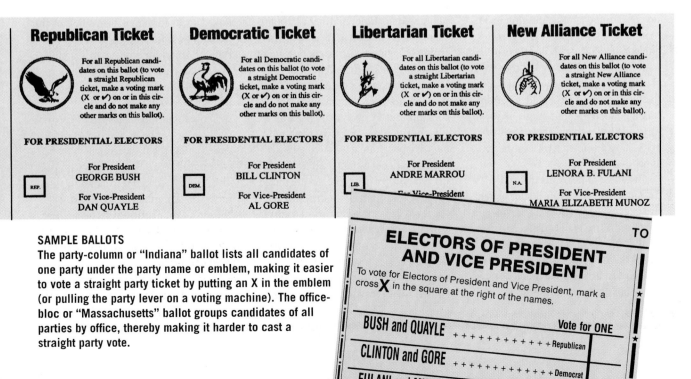

SAMPLE BALLOTS
The party-column or "Indiana" ballot lists all candidates of one party under the party name or emblem, making it easier to vote a straight party ticket by putting an X in the emblem (or pulling the party lever on a voting machine). The office-bloc or "Massachusetts" ballot groups candidates of all parties by office, thereby making it harder to cast a straight party vote.

Two Kinds of Campaign Issues: Position and Valence

There are at least two distinct kinds of campaign issues that have figured prominently in American elections. A **position issue** is one on which the rival parties or candidates reach out for the support of the electorate by taking different positions on a policy question that divides the electorate. Position issues have punctuated the history of presidential elections. Each of the great party realignments from 1860 onward was rooted in position issues. The party alignment that emerged from the Civil War was formed from a position issue of extraordinary power—should black Americans be enslaved or free? In the realignment of the 1890s the Republicans drew support from those who favored high rather than low tariffs on manufactured goods. In the 1930s the Democrats drew support from those who wanted to protect the interests of the poor and working class rather than those of the more affluent in American society. In the 1960s the New Deal coalition began to unravel around another position issue that divided the electorate along racial and regional lines—should there be laws to protect civil rights? And in the 1980s rivals for the presidency reached out for the support of the electorate in part by staking out different positions on yet another issue that sharply polarized voters—should women have legal access to abortion?

But some of the issues that powerfully move the electorate do not present two alternative positions that divide support for the two major parties and their candidates. There are issues on which voters choose parties and candidates not by their real or perceived differences on policy questions but by the degree to which they are linked in the voters' minds with conditions, goals, or symbols that are almost universally approved or disapproved by the electorate. The economy is a prime example of such a **valence issue.** We do not have one party advocating economic prosperity and the other advocating economic bad times—there is no constituency for economic distress. The issue of economic prosperity acquires its power as a valence issue from the fact that the parties or candidates may be very unequally linked in the public's mind with the universally approved condition of good times or the universally disapproved condition of bad times. The difference between electoral success and disaster may turn on each contender's ability to strengthen or weaken these perceptual bonds, or *valences*, in the public's mind.

Examples abound of valence issues that have powerfully moved the electorate. Corruption is a valence issue with a deep historical resonance in American politics. Many times in American political history—indeed, as recently as the House of Representatives' check-kiting scandal in 1992—there have been calls to "throw the rascals out." It should be obvious, however, that the impact of the corruption issue does not depend on what position the campaign rivals take: no party or candidate avowedly favors bribery. It depends rather on how closely the rival parties or candidates are linked in the public's mind with the universally approved value of honesty or the universally disapproved value of corruption. There is as little constituency for corruption as there is for economic bad times—or for a variety of other negative symbols that are staples of valence cam-paigns: irresolute leadership, unpatriotic beliefs, weak national defense, wasted tax dollars, and failure itself.

There are innumerable examples of valence campaigns in modern presidential elections. The valence issue of economic prosperity cost Martin Van Buren the presidency in 1840, when the electorate held him responsible for the misery that followed the panic of 1837. In 1964 the Democratic campaign was largely a valence campaign in which voters were encouraged to link a vote for the Republican candidate, Arizona senator Barry Goldwater, with negative symbols such as nuclear annihilation and a vote for President Lyndon B. Johnson with positive symbols such as carrying on the work of a beloved fallen president, John F. Kennedy. Four years later Richard Nixon made law and order a valence issue. In the shadow of Watergate, Jimmy Carter made honesty in government a valence issue in 1976. In 1980 Carter was the victim of a valence campaign that linked a vote for him with symbols of abject failure, from long gas lines to pictures of American hostages in Teheran. Ronald Reagan's campaign in 1984 was carefully designed to encourage voters to link the president with such positive symbols as patriotism, peace, and prosperity—"morning in America." Likewise, in 1988 the Bush campaign encouraged voters to link Bush with positive symbols such as respect for the American flag and his rival, Michael S. Dukakis, with negative symbols such as disrespect for the flag, water pollution, and fawning treatment of violent and remorseless criminals.

Presidential campaigns have always involved a mix of position and valence

issues, but the relative importance of valence issues has risen as the party alignments rooted in the powerful position issues of the past have weakened, and as modern image-making, image-carrying technologies such as television have proliferated.

THE VALENCE VICTORY OF 1992

Certainly, the valence strategy, tactics, and tempos of the 1992 presidential campaigns were consistent with the trend. The Clinton campaign was battered with charges of marital infidelity, draft dodging, and pot smoking. At their convention the Republicans depicted Clinton as "Slick Willie"and his wife as a power-hungry radical feminist who equated marriage with slavery, encouraged children to sue their parents, and eschewed family values. In the televised debates and up to election day, the Bush campaign, with some help from Ross

Perot's televised appeals, attempted to make Clinton into the unpatriotic, indecisive, fast-talking, failed governor of a small and insignificant state.

But Clinton's campaign strategists took a public relations hose to these valence fires. While continuing to stress the positive valences of change and better economic times, the Clinton campaign responded with what the *New York Times* termed "one of the most ambitious campaigns of political rehabilitation ever attempted. They proposed the construction of a new image for Mr. and Mrs. Clinton: an honest, plain-folks idealist and his warm and loving wife." As the paper explained, "Retooling the image of a couple who had been already in the public eye for five battering months required a campaign of behavior modification and media manipulation so elaborate that its outline ran to fourteen single-spaced pages."[*]

Known within the Clinton campaign as the General Election Project, the plan

called for the candidate to depict himself as the "agent of change." The message was to be delivered in town-hall style forums, on live television talk-shows, and in a series of speeches challenging specific special interests. The candidate was to appear on television playing the saxophone and poking fun at himself for saying he had tried marijuana but "didn't inhale." The plan also orchestrated events where the Clintons would "seem more warm and cuddly: 'events where Bill and Hillary can go on dates with the American people.' " It even called for staging an event where "Bill and Chelsea surprise Hillary on Mother's Day" and "joint appearances with her friends where Hillary can laugh, cry, do her mimickry."[†]

In the 1992 presidential campaign the electorate above all else decided that its deep concern about the economy was not adequately shared by the president and gave its support instead to the challenger who had posted the valence message "The Economy, Stupid" on the wall of his Little Rock campaign headquarters. President Clinton faces a number of difficult position choices on controversial social and foreign policy issues as well as difficult choices in managing the economy before he returns to the electorate in 1996. But if recent campaign history is any guide, he almost certainly will be judged by the electorate largely in valence terms rather than on the positions he takes on specific issues.

[*]Michael Kelley, "The Making of a First Family: A Blueprint," *New York Times* (November 14, 1992): 1.

[†]*Ibid.*, 9.

SOURCE: Adapted from Donald E. Stokes and John J. DiIulio, Jr., "The Setting: Valence Politics in Modern Elections," in Michael J. Nelson, ed., *The 1992 Elections* (Washington, D.C.: Congressional Quarterly Press, 1993), 6–9, 14–15, 19.

In a parliamentary system with strong parties such as that in Great Britain, an election can often have a major effect on public policy. When the Labour party won office in 1945, it put several major industries under public ownership and launched a comprehensive set of social services, including a nationalized health-care plan. Its ambitious and controversial campaign platform was converted, almost item by item, into law. When the Conservative party returned to power in 1951, it accepted some of these changes but rejected others (for example, it denationalized the steel industry).

American elections, unless accompanied by a national crisis such as war or a depression, rarely produce changes of the magnitude of those that occurred in Britain in 1945. The constitutional system within which our elections take place was designed to moderate the pace of change—to make it neither easy nor impossible to adopt radical proposals. But the fact that the system is intended to moderate the rate of change does not mean that it will always work that way.

The election of 1860 brought to national power a party committed to opposing the extension of slavery and southern secession; it took a bloody war to vindicate that policy. The election of 1896 led to the dominance of a party committed to high tariffs, a strong currency, urban growth, and business prosperity—a commitment that was not significantly altered until 1932. The election of that year led to the New Deal, which produced the greatest single enlargement of federal authority since 1860. The election of 1964 gave the Democrats such a large majority in Congress (as well as control of the presidency) that there began to issue forth an extraordinary number of new policies of sweeping significance—Medicare and Medicaid, federal aid to education and to local law enforcement, two dozen environmental and consumer-protection laws, the Voting Rights Act of 1965, a revision of the immigration laws, and a new cabinet-level Department of Housing and Urban Development.

The election of 1980 brought into office an administration determined to reverse the direction of policy over the preceding half-century; Reagan's administration succeeded in obtaining large tax cuts, significant reductions in spending (or in the rate of increase of spending) on some domestic programs, and changes in the policies of some regulatory agencies. The election of 1982, in which the Democrats made gains in the House of Representatives, stiffened congressional resistance to further spending cuts and stimulated renewed interest in tax increases as a way of reducing the deficit. Following the election of 1984 a major tax-reform plan was passed. After the 1992 election, President Clinton initiated a major reform of the health-care industry.

In view of all these new developments it is hard to argue that the pace of change in our government is always slow or that elections never make a difference. Studies by scholars confirm that elections are often significant, despite the difficulty of getting laws passed. One analysis of about fourteen hundred promises made between 1944 and 1964 in the platforms of the two major parties revealed that 72 percent were put into effect.[19]

Another study examined the party platforms of the Democrats and Republicans from 1844 to 1968 and all the laws passed by Congress between 1789 and 1968. By a complex statistical method, the author of the study was able to show that during certain periods the differences between the platforms of the two parties were especially large (1856, 1880, 1896, 1932) and that there was at about the same time a high rate of change in the kinds of laws being passed.[20] This study supports the general impression conveyed by history that elections can often be central to important policy changes.

Why then do we so often think that elections make little difference? It is because public opinion and the political parties enter a phase of consolidation and continuity between periods of rapid change. During this phase the changes are, so to speak, digested, and party leaders adjust to the new popular consensus that may (or may not) evolve around the merits of these changes. During the 1870s and 1880s Democratic politicians had to come to terms with the failure of the southern secessionist movement and the abolition of slavery; during the 1900s the Democrats had to adjust again, this time to the fact that national economic policy was going to support industrialization and urbanization, not farming; during the 1940s and 1950s the Republicans had to learn to accept the popularity of the New Deal.

Elections in ordinary times are not "critical," do not produce any major party realignment, are not fought out over a dominant issue, and provide the winners with no clear mandate. In most cases an election is little more than a retrospective judgment on the record of the incumbent president and the existing congressional majority. If times are good, incumbents win easily; if times are bad, incumbents may lose even though their opponents may have no clear plans for change. But even a "normal" election can produce dramatic results if the winner is a person such as Ronald Reagan, who has helped give to his party a distinctive political philosophy.

SUMMARY

Political campaigns have increasingly become personalized, with little or no connection to formal party organizations, as a result of the decay of parties, the rise of the direct primary and the electronic media, and campaign-finance laws. Candidates face the problem of creating a temporary organization that can raise money from large numbers of small donors, mobilize enthusiastic supporters, and win a nomination in a way that will not harm their ability to appeal to a broader, more diverse constituency in the general election. Campaigning has an uncertain effect on election outcomes, but election outcomes can have important effects on public policy, especially at those times—during critical or "realigning" elections—when new voters are coming into the electorate in large numbers, old party loyalties are weakening, or a major issue is splitting the majority party. Most people vote retrospectively rather than prospectively.

KEY TERMS

incumbent   *p. 184*

coattails (political)   *p. 185*

political-action committee   *p. 186*

general election   *p. 190*

primary election   *p. 190*

closed primary   *p. 190*

open primary   *p. 190*

blanket primary   *p. 190*

runoff primary   *p. 190*

presidential primary   *p. 190*

prospective voting   *p. 204*

retrospective voting   *p. 205*

critical *or* realigning periods   *p. 211*

split ticket (voting)   *p. 214*

office-bloc ballot   *p. 215*

party-column ballot   *p. 215*

straight ticket (voting)   *p. 215*

position issue   *p. 216*

valence issue   *p. 216*

SUGGESTED READINGS

Asher, Herbert. *Presidential Elections and American Politics.* 3d ed. Homewood, Ill.: Dorsey, 1984. A useful, brief analysis of how Americans have voted.

Burnham, Walter Dean. *Critical Elections and the Mainsprings of American Politics.* New York: Norton, 1970. An argument about the decline in voting participation and the significance of the realigning election of 1896.

Jacobson, Gary C. *The Politics of Congressional Elections.* 2d ed. Boston: Little, Brown, 1987. Careful analysis of how people get elected to Congress.

Kayden, Xandra. *Campaign Organization.* Lexington, Mass.: D. C. Heath, 1978. A close look at how political campaigns are organized, staffed, and led at the state level.

Malbin, Michael J., ed. *Money and Politics in the United States: Financing Elections in the 1980s.* Chatham, N.J.: Chatham House, 1984. Articles on the sources and uses of campaign money, with special attention to political parties and political action committees.

Page, Benjamin I. *Choices and Echoes in Presidential Elections.* Chicago: University of Chicago Press, 1978. Analyzes the interaction between the behavior of candidates and of voters in American elections.

Sorauf, Frank. *Money in American Elections.* Glenview, Ill.: Scott Foresman, 1988. The best summary of what we know about the sources and effects of campaign spending.

Sundquist, James L. *Dynamics of the Party System: Alignment and Realignment of Political Parties in the United States.* Rev. ed. Washington, D.C.: Brookings Institution, 1983. Historical analysis of realigning elections from 1860 to the nonrealignment of 1980.

9

Interest Groups

- ➤ **Reasons for proliferation of interest groups**
- ➤ **Rise of interest groups**
- ➤ **Kinds of interest groups**
- ➤ **Role of staff**
- ➤ **Responding to social movements**
- ➤ **Raising money**
- ➤ **The problem of bias**
- ➤ **Wielding influence**
- ➤ **Spending money**
- ➤ **Government regulation**

lmost every tourist arriving in Washington will visit the White House and the Capitol. Many will look at the Supreme Court building. But hardly any will walk down K Street, where much of the political life of the country occurs.

K Street? From the sidewalk it is just a row of office buildings, no different from what one might find in downtown Seattle or Kansas City. What's to see? But in these buildings, and in similar ones lining nearby streets, are the offices of the nearly seven thousand organizations that are represented in Washington.

It is doubtful whether there is any other nation in which so many organizations are represented in its capital. They are there to participate in politics. They are interest groups or, if you prefer, lobbies.

Explaining Proliferation

There are at least three reasons why interest groups are so common in this country. First, the more cleavages there are in society, the greater the variety of interests that will exist. In addition to divisions along lines of income and occupation found in any society, America is a nation of countless immigrants and many races. There are at least eighty-five religions that claim fifty thousand members or more. Americans live scattered over a vast land made up of many regions with distinctive traditions and cultures. These social facts make for a great variety of interests and opinions; as James Madison said in *Federalist* No. 10, "The latent causes of faction are thus sown in the nature of man."

Second, the American constitutional system contributes to the number of interest groups by multiplying the points at which such groups can gain access to the government. In a nation such as Great Britain where most political authority is lodged in a single official, such as the prime minister, there are only a few places where important decisions are made and thus only a few opportunities for affecting

Lobby

To **lobby** means to attempt to influence governmental decisions, especially legislation. A lobby is a group organized for this purpose.

The term came into vogue in the mid–seventeenth century to refer to a large anteroom near the English House of Commons wherein members of Parliament could be approached by people pleading their cases.

In the United States lobbyists were people who met members of Congress just outside the chambers of the House or Senate to argue their cause. In the nineteenth century *lobbyist* became synonymous with *vote buyer* because of the widespread belief that lobbyists were using money to corrupt legislators.

Today lobbying is no longer regarded as an inevitably corrupt activity and lobbyists in Washington are no longer embarrassed to refer to themselves by this term.

SOURCE: Adapted from William Safire, *Safire's Political Dictionary* (New York: Ballantine Books, 1978). Used by permission.

those decisions. But when political authority is shared by the president, the courts, and Congress (and within Congress, among two houses and countless committees and subcommittees), there are plenty of places where one can argue one's case. And the more chances there are to influence policy, the more organizations there will be that seek to exercise that influence.

This fact helps explain why in Great Britain there is often only one organization representing a given interest whereas in the United States there are several. In London only one major association represents farmers, one represents industry, one represents veterans, and one represents doctors. In the United States, by contrast, at least three organizations represent farmers (the American Farm Bureau Federation, the National Farmers' Union, and the Grange); and each of these is made up of state and county branches, many of which act quite independently of national headquarters. Though there is one major American labor organization, the AFL-CIO, it is in fact a loose coalition of independent unions (plumbers, steelworkers, coal miners), and some large unions, such as the Teamsters, were for many years not part of the AFL-CIO at all.

Third, the weakness of political parties in this country may help explain the number and strength of interest groups. Where parties are strong, interests work through the parties; where parties are weak, interests operate directly on the government. That at least is the theory. Though scholars are not certain of its validity, it is a plausible theory and can be illustrated by differences among American cities. Where, as in Chicago, the party—in this case, the Democratic party—has been very strong, labor unions, business associations, and citizens' groups have had to work with the party and on its terms. But where, as in Boston or Los Angeles, the parties are very weak, interest groups proliferate and play a large role in making policy.[1]

In Austria, France, and Italy, many if not most interest groups are closely linked to one or another political party. In Italy, for example, each party—Socialist, Communist, and Christian Democrat—has a cluster of labor unions, professional associations, and social clubs allied with it.[2] Though American interest groups often support one party (the AFL-CIO, for example, almost always backs Democratic candidates for office), the relationship between party and interest group here is not as close as it is in Europe.

The Birth of Interest Groups

The number of interest groups has grown rapidly since 1960. A study of Washington-based political associations revealed that roughly 70 percent of them established their Washington offices after 1960, and nearly half have opened their doors since 1970.[3]

The 1960s and 1970s were boom years for interest groups, but there have been other periods in our history when political associations were created in especially large numbers. During the 1770s many groups arose to agitate for American independence; during the 1830s and 1840s the number of religious associations increased sharply and the antislavery movement began. In the 1860s trade unions based on crafts emerged in significant numbers, farmers formed the Grange, and various fraternal organizations were born. In the 1880s and 1890s business associations proliferated. The great era of organization building, however, was in the first two decades of the twentieth century. Within this twenty-year period, many of the best-known and largest associations with an interest in national politics were formed: the Chamber of Commerce, the National Association of Manufacturers, the American Medical Association, the NAACP, the Urban League, the American Farm Bureau, the Farmers' Union, the National Catholic Welfare Conference, the American Jewish Committee, and the Anti-Defamation League. The wave of interest-group formation that occurred in the 1960s led to the emergence of environmental, consumer, and political-reform organizations such as those sponsored by consumer activist Ralph Nader.

The fact that associations in general, and political interest groups in particular, are created more rapidly in some periods than in others suggests that these groups do not arise inevitably out of natural social processes. There have always been farmers in this country, but there were no national farm organizations until the latter part of the nineteenth century. Blacks had been victimized by various white-supremacy policies from the end of the Civil War on, but the NAACP did not emerge until 1910. Men and women worked in factories for decades before industrial unions were formed.

At least four factors help explain the rise of interest groups. The first consists of broad economic developments that create new interests and redefine old ones. Farmers had little reason to become organized for political activity so long as most of them consumed what they produced. The importance of regular political activity became evident only after most farmers began to produce cash crops for sale in

The greater the activity of government—for example, in regulating the timber industry—the greater the number of interest groups.

W. E. B. Du Bois was one of the founders of the NAACP in 1910 and the editor of its magazine, *The Crisis*.

large, mass-membership unions did not exist until there arose mass-production industry operated by large corporations.

Second, government policy itself helped create interest groups. Wars create veterans, who in turn demand pensions and other benefits. The first large veterans' organization, the Grand Army of the Republic, was made up of Union veterans of the Civil War. By the 1920s these men were receiving about a quarter of a billion dollars a year from the government, and naturally had created organizations to watch over the distribution of this money. The federal government encouraged the formation of the American Farm Bureau Federation (AFBF) by paying for county agents who would serve the needs of farmers under the supervision of local farm organizations; these county bureaus eventually came together as the AFBF. The Chamber of Commerce was launched at a conference attended by President William Howard Taft.

Professional societies, such as those made up of lawyers and doctors, became important in part because state governments gave to such groups the authority to decide who was qualified to become a lawyer or a doctor. Workers had a difficult time organizing so long as the government, by the use of injunctions enforced by the police and by the army, prevented strikes. Unions, especially those in mass-production industries, began to flourish after Con-

markets that were unstable or affected by forces (the weather, the railroads, foreign competition) that farmers could not control. Similarly, for many decades most workers were craftspeople working alone or in small groups. Such unions as existed were little more than craft guilds interested in protecting their jobs and in training apprentices. The reason for

Almost any group today is prepared to stage a demonstration. Here, a group of senior citizens gather in front of the Capitol.

gress passed laws in the 1930s that prohibited the use of injunctions in private labor disputes, that required employers to bargain with unions, and that allowed a union representing a majority of the workers in a plant to require all workers to join it.[4]

Third, political organizations do not emerge automatically, even when government policy permits them and social circumstances seem to require them. Somebody must exercise leadership, often at substantial personal cost. These organizational entrepreneurs are found in greater numbers at certain times than at others. They are often young, caught up in a social movement, drawn to the need for change, and inspired by some political or religious doctrine. Antislavery organizations were created in the 1830s and 1840s by enthusiastic young people influenced by a religious revival then sweeping the country. The period from 1890 to 1920 when so many national organizations were created was a time when the college-educated middle class was growing rapidly. (The number of men and women who received college degrees each year tripled between 1890 and 1920.)[5] During this era, natural science and fundamentalist Christianity were locked in a bitter contest as the competing ideas of personal salvation and social progress, the Gospels and Darwinism, became the watchwords of rival social movements. The 1960s, when many new organizations were born, was a decade in which young people were powerfully influenced by the civil-rights and antiwar movements and when college enrollments more than doubled.

Finally, the more activities government undertakes, the more organized groups there will be that are interested in those activities. As can be seen from Table 9.1, most Washington offices representing corporations, labor unions, and trade and professional associations were established before 1960—in some cases many decades before—because it was during the 1930s or even earlier that government began making policies important to business and labor. The great majority of "public-interest" lobbies (those concerned with the environment or consumer protection), social-welfare associations, and organizations concerned with civil rights, the elderly, and the handicapped established offices in Washington after 1960. Policies of interest to these groups, such as the major civil-rights and environmental laws, were adopted after that date. In fact over half the "public-interest" lobbies opened their doors after 1970.

TABLE 9.1   Dates of Founding of Organizations Having Washington Offices

| | Percentage Founded | |
Organization	After 1960	After 1970
Corporations	14%	6%
Unions	21	14
Professional	30	14
Trade	38	23
Civil rights	56	46
Women / elderly / disabled	56	43
"Public interest"	76	57
Social welfare	79	51

SOURCE: Kay Lehman Schlozman and John T. Tierney, *Organized Interests and American Democracy* (New York: Harper & Row, 1985), 76. Copyright © 1986 by Kay Lehman Schlozman and John T. Tierney. Reprinted by permission of HarperCollins Publishers, Inc.

Kinds of Organizations

An **interest group** is any organization that seeks to influence public policy. When we think of an organization, we usually think of something like the Boy Scouts or the League of Women Voters—a group consisting of individual members. In Washington, however, many organizations do not have individual members at all, but are offices—corporations, law firms, public-relations firms, or "letterhead" organizations that get most of their money from foundations or from the government—out of which a staff operates. It is important to understand the differences between the two kinds of interest groups—"institutional" and "membership" interests.[6]

Institutional Interests

Institutional interests are individuals or organizations representing other organizations. General Motors, for example, has a Washington representative. Over five hundred firms have such representatives in the capital, most of which have opened their offices since 1970.[7] Firms that do not want to place their own full-time representative in Washington can hire a Washington lawyer or public-relations expert on a part-time basis. Between 1970 and 1980 the number

★ Quiz

What do the following interest groups have in common?

Amateur Softball Association
Barbecue Industry Association
Candy Wholesalers Association
Chocolate Manufacturers Association
Retinitis Pigmentosa Foundation
Sporting Goods Manufacturers Association

Hint: They were all in favor of the passage of the same law. What was that law?

Answer on page 227.

of lawyers in Washington more than tripled; Washington now has more lawyers (over 38,000) than Los Angeles, a city three times its size.[8] Another kind of institutional interest is the trade or governmental association, such as the National Independent Retail Jewelers or the National Association of Counties.

Individuals or organizations that represent other organizations tend to be interested in bread-and-butter issues of vital concern to their clients. Some of the people who specialize in this work can earn very large fees—top public-relations experts or Washington lawyers can charge $250 an hour or more for their time. Since they earn a lot, they are expected to deliver a lot.

Just what they are expected to deliver, however, varies with the diversity of the groups making up the organization. The American Cotton Manufacturers Institute represents southern textile mills. Those mills are few enough in number and similar enough in outlook to allow the institute to carry out clear policies squarely based on the business interests of its clients. For example, the institute works hard to get the federal government to adopt laws and rules that will keep foreign-made textiles from competing too easily with American-made goods. Sometimes the institute is successful, sometimes not, but it is never hard to explain what it is doing.

By contrast, the United States Chamber of Commerce represents thousands of different businesses in hundreds of different communities. Its membership is so large and diverse that the Chamber in Washington can speak out clearly and forcefully on only those relatively few matters in which all, or most, busi-

nesses take the same position. Since all businesses would like lower taxes, the Chamber favors that. On the other hand, since some businesses (those that import goods) want low tariffs and other businesses (those that face competition from imported goods) want higher tariffs, the Chamber says little or nothing about tariffs.

Institutional interests do not just represent business firms; they also represent governments, foundations, and universities. For example, the American Council on Education claims to speak for most institutions of higher education, the American Public Transit Association represents local mass-transit systems, and the National Association of Counties argues on behalf of county governments.

Membership Interests

It is often said that Americans are a nation of joiners, and so we take for granted the many organizations around us supported by the activities and contributions of individual citizens. But we should not take this multiplicity of organizations for granted; in fact their existence is something of a puzzle.

Americans join only certain kinds of organizations more frequently than do citizens of other democratic countries. We are no more likely than the British, for example, to join social, business, professional, veterans', or charitable organizations, and we are *less* likely to join labor unions. Our reputation as a nation of joiners arises chiefly out of our unusually high tendency to join religious and civic or political associations. About three times as many Americans as Britons say that they are members of a civic or political organization.[9]

This proclivity of Americans to get together with other citizens to engage in civic or political action reflects, apparently, a greater sense of political efficacy and a stronger sense of civic duty in this country. When Gabriel Almond and Sidney Verba asked citizens of five nations what they would do to protest an unjust local regulation, 56 percent of the Americans—but only 34 percent of the British and 13 percent of the Germans—said that they would try to organize their neighbors to write letters, sign petitions, or otherwise act in concert.[10] Americans are also more likely than Europeans to think that organized activity is an effective way to influence the national government, remote as that institution may seem.

And this willingness to form civic or political groups is not a product of higher levels of education in this country; at every level of schooling Americans are political joiners.[11]

But explaining the American willingness to join politically active groups by saying that they feel a "sense of political efficacy" is not much of an explanation; we might as well say that people vote because they think that their vote makes a difference. But one vote clearly makes no difference at all in almost any election; similarly one member, more or less, in the Sierra Club, the Christian Coalition, or the National Association for the Advancement of Colored People (NAACP) clearly will make no difference in the success of those organizations.

And in fact most people who are sympathetic to the aims of a mass-membership interest group do not join it. The NAACP, for example, enrolls as members only a tiny fraction of all blacks. This is not because people are selfish or apathetic, but because they are rational and numerous. A single black, for example, knows that he or she can make no difference in the success of the NAACP, just as a single nature enthusiast knows that he or she cannot enhance the power of the Sierra Club. Moreover, if the NAACP or

Bumper stickers are a sign of how many groups and causes Americans join.

the Sierra Club succeeds, blacks and nature lovers will benefit even if they are not members. Therefore rational people who value their time and money would no more join such organizations than they would attempt to empty a lake with a cup—unless they get something out of joining.

 Answer to Quiz

These organizations were all members of the National Daylight Saving Coalition.

For years the coalition lobbied Congress to lengthen the number of days during which daylight saving time would be in effect. In 1986 it was successful: Congress added three weeks to daylight saving, so that beginning in 1987 people in most states set their clocks ahead one hour on the first Sunday in April rather than the last Sunday, as previously.

Why did these interest groups join the coalition?

The businesses making sporting goods and barbecue equipment wanted more daylight saving so that they could sell more things for people to use outdoors in the evening.

The softball players wanted to start playing evening games earlier in the year so that they could get more games in during the season.

The Retinitis Pigmentosa Foundation is concerned about people who suffer from night blindness. With more daylight hours available during which to drive home from

work, these people would not have to worry so much about night blindness.

The chocolate manufacturers and the candy wholesalers joined the coalition in hopes of getting daylight saving time extended *later* in the year, not begun earlier. If daylight saving included Halloween, then it would stay light longer on that day; hence more parents would let their children go out trick-or-treating. This would result in the sale of more candy. These two organizations were unhappy that Congress decided to start daylight saving early instead of ending it later.

Some farm groups don't like daylight saving because it means that when farmers get up in the morning to milk cows, it is still dark out. Some western states don't like it either, and so (with congressional permission) Arizona, Hawaii, and most of Indiana don't observe the new law.

The point of the story: There is almost nothing that will not attract interest-group activity.

Among the services the American Association of Retired Persons provides the elderly is free assistance in preparing tax returns.

Incentives to Join

To get people to join mass-membership organizations, they must be offered an **incentive**—something of value they cannot get without joining. There are three kinds of these incentives.

Solidary incentives are the sense of pleasure, status, or companionship that arises out of meeting together in small groups. Such rewards are extremely important, but because they tend to be available only from face-to-face contact, national interest groups offering them often have to organize themselves as coalitions of small local units. For example, the League of Women Voters, the Parent-Teachers Association, the NAACP, the Rotary Club, and the American Legion all consist of small local chapters that support a national staff. It is the task of the local chapters to lure members and obtain funds from them; the state or national staff can then pursue political objectives by using these funds. Forming organizations made up of small local chapters is probably easier in the United States than in Europe because of the great importance of local government in our federal system. There is plenty for a PTA, an NAACP, or a League of Women Voters to do in its own community, and so its members can be kept busy with local affairs while the national staff pursues larger goals.

A second kind of incentive consists of **material incentives**—that is, money, or things and services

readily valued in monetary terms. Farm organizations have recruited many members by offering a wide range of services. The Illinois Farm Bureau, for example, offers to its members—and *only* to its members—a chance to buy farm supplies at discount prices, to market their products through cooperatives, and to purchase low-cost insurance. These material incentives help explain why the Illinois Farm Bureau has been able to enroll nearly every farmer in the state as well as many nonfarmers who also value these rewards.[12]

Similarly the American Association of Retired Persons (AARP) has recruited over 30 million members by supplying them with everything from low-cost life insurance and mail-order discount drugs to tax advice and group travel plans. About 45 percent of the nation's population that is fifty and older—one out of every four registered voters—belongs to the AARP. With an annual operating budget of over $200 million and a cash flow estimated at a whopping $10 billion, the AARP seeks to influence public policy in many areas, from health and housing to taxes and transportation.

The third—and most difficult—kind of incentive is the *purpose* of the organization. Many associations rely chiefly on this **purposive incentive**—the appeal of their stated goals—to recruit members. If the attainment of those goals will also benefit people who do not join, individuals who do join will have to be those who feel passionately about the goal, who have a strong sense of duty (or who cannot say no to a friend who asks them to join), or for whom the cost of joining is so small that they are indifferent to joining or not. Organizations that attract members by appealing to their interest in a coherent set of (usually) controversial principles are sometimes called **ideological interest groups**.

When the purpose of the organization, if attained, will principally benefit nonmembers, it is customary to call the group a **public-interest lobby.** (Whether the public at large will really benefit, of course, is a matter of opinion, but at least the group members think that they are working selflessly for the common good.)

Though some public-interest lobbies may pursue relatively noncontroversial goals (for example, persuading people to vote or raising money to house orphans), the most visible of such organizations are highly controversial. It is precisely the controversy that attracts the members, or at least those members who support one side of the issue. Many of these groups can be described as markedly liberal or decidedly conservative in outlook.

Perhaps the best known of the liberal public-interest groups are those founded by or associated with Ralph Nader. Nader became a popular figure in the mid-1960s after General Motors made a clumsy attempt to investigate and discredit his background at a time when he was testifying in favor of an auto-safety bill (see Chapter 15). Nader won a large out-of-court settlement against General Motors, his books began to earn royalties, and he was able to command substantial lecture fees. Most of this money was turned over to various organizations he created dealing with matters of interest to consumers. In addition he founded a group called Public Citizen that raised money by direct-mail solicitation from thousands of small contributors and sought foundation grants. Finally, he helped create Public Interest Research Groups (PIRGs) in a number of states, supported by donations from college students (some voluntary, some a compulsory assessment levied on all students at a given college) and concerned with organizing student activists to work on local projects.

Conservatives, though slow to get started, have also adopted the public-interest organizational strategy. As with such associations run by liberals, they are of two kinds: those that engage in research and

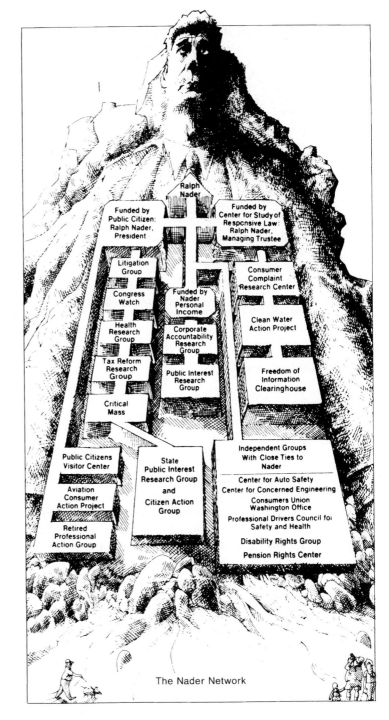

The Nader Network

lobbying and those that bring lawsuits designed to advance their cause. The boxes on page 230 and 231 list some examples of public-interest organizations that support liberal or conservative causes.

Membership organizations relying on purposive incentives, especially appeals to deeply controversial

Public-Interest Law Firms

A special kind of public-interest lobby is an organization that advances its cause by bringing lawsuits to challenge existing practices or proposed regulations. A public-interest law firm will act in one of two ways: First, it will find someone who has been harmed by some public or private policy and bring suit on his or her behalf. Second, it will file a brief with a court supporting somebody else's lawsuit (this is called an amicus curiae brief; it is explained in Chapter 14).

Here are some examples of liberal and conservative public-interest law firms:

Liberal	Conservative
American Civil Liberties Union	Atlantic Legal Foundation
Asian-American Legal Defense Fund	Criminal Justice Legal Foundation
Lawyers' Committee for Civil Rights	Landmark Legal Foundation
Mexican-American Legal Defense Fund	Mountain States Legal Foundation
NAACP Legal Defense and Education Fund	Pacific Legal Foundation
Natural Resources Defense Council	Washington Legal Foundation
Women's Legal Defense Fund	

purposes, tend to be shaped by the mood of the times. When an issue is hot—in the media or with the public—such organizations can grow rapidly. When the spotlight fades, the organization may lose support. Thus it has a powerful motive to stay in the public eye. To remain visible, public-interest lobbies devote a lot of attention to generating publicity by developing good contacts with the media and issuing dramatic press releases about crises and scandals.

Because of their need to take advantage of a crisis atmosphere, public-interest lobbies often do best when the government is in the hands of an administration that is *hostile*, not sympathetic, to their views. Environmentalist organizations could mobilize more resources when James Watt, an opponent of much of the environmental movement, was secretary of the interior than they could when Cecil D. Andrus, his proenvironmentalist predecessor, was in office. By the same token, many conservative interest groups were able to raise more money with the relatively liberal Jimmy Carter or Bill Clinton in the White House than with the conservative Ronald Reagan.

The Influence of the Staff

We often make the mistake of assuming that what an interest group does politically is simply to exert influence on behalf of its members. That is indeed the case when all the members have a clear and similar stake in an issue. But many issues affect different members differently. In fact, if the members joined to obtain solidary or material benefits, they may not care at all about many of the issues with which the organization gets involved. In such cases what the interest group does may reflect more what the staff wants than what the members believe.

Recall an example given in Chapter 1. A survey of the white members of a large labor union showed that one-third of them believed that the desegregation of schools, housing, and job opportunities had gone too fast; only one-fifth thought that it had gone too slowly. But among the staff members of the union, *none* thought that desegregation had gone too fast and over two-thirds thought that it had gone too slowly.[13] As a result the union staff aggressively lobbied Congress for the passage of tougher civil-rights laws even though most of the union's members did not feel that they were needed. The members stayed in the union for reasons unrelated to civil rights, giving the staff freedom to pursue its own goals.

The National Council of the Churches of Christ (NCC), an organization of various Protestant denominations claiming several million members, has spoken out frequently on political questions, generally by taking a strongly liberal position. But opinion surveys show that most white Protestants are relatively conservative, especially those in the South. Thus it is quite likely that the staff of the NCC does not, on many political questions, actually represent the majority of the churchgoers for whom it claims to speak.[14] It can ignore them because people join churches, by and large, for reasons other than how staff members in New York or Washington think.

Interest Groups and Social Movements

Because it is difficult to attract people with purposive incentives, interest groups employing them tend to arise out of social movements. A **social movement** is a widely shared demand for change in some aspect of the social or political order. The civil-rights movement of the 1960s was such an event, as was the environmentalist movement of the 1970s. A social movement need not have liberal goals. In the nineteenth century, for example, there were various nativist movements that sought to reduce immigration to this country or to keep Catholics or Masons out of public office. Broadly based religious revivals are social movements.

No one is quite certain why social movements arise. At one moment people are largely indifferent to some issue; at another moment many of these same people care passionately about religion, civil rights, immigration, or conservation. A social movement may be triggered by a scandal (an oil spill on the Santa Barbara beaches helped launch the environmental movement), the dramatic and widely publicized activities of a few leaders (lunch-counter sit-ins helped stimulate the civil-rights movement), or by the coming to age of a new generation that takes up a cause advocated by eloquent writers, teachers, or evangelists.

The Environmental Movement

Whatever its origin, the effect of a social movement is to increase the value some people attach to purposive incentives. As a consequence new interest groups are formed that rely on these incentives. In the box on page 232 are some examples. In the 1890s, as a result of the emergence of conservation as a major issue, the Sierra Club was organized. In the 1930s conservation once again became popular, and the Wilderness Society and the National Wildlife Federation took form. In the 1960s and 1970s environmental issues again came to the fore, and we see the emergence of the Environmental Defense Fund and Environmental Action.

This box contains the results of a survey of the members of these organizations. Note that the smallest organizations (Environmental Action and the Environmental Defense Fund) tended, at the time of this survey, to have the most liberal members. This is often the case with social movements. A movement will spawn many organizations (there are many more environmental organizations than those listed in this box). The most passionately aroused people will be the fewest in number, and they will gravitate toward the organizations that take the most extreme positions; as a result these organizations are small but vo-

 Think-Tanks in Washington

*T*hink-tanks are public-interest organizations that do research on policy questions and disseminate their findings in books, articles, conferences, op-ed essays for newspapers, and (occasionally) testimony before Congress. Some are nonpartisan and ideologically more or less neutral, but others—and many of the most important ones—are aligned with liberal or conservative causes. Here are some examples of each:

Liberal	*Conservative*
Center on Budget and Policy Priorities	American Enterprise Institute
Center for Defense Information	Cato Institute
Children's Defense Fund	Center for Strategic and International Studies
Economic Policy Institute	Competitive Enterprise Institute
Institute for Policy Studies	Ethics and Public Policy Center
Joint Center for Political and Economic Studies	Free Congress Foundation
Progressive Policy Institute	Heritage Foundation

Note that the labels "liberal" and "conservative," while generally accurate, conceal important differences among the think-tanks in each list.

ciferous. The more numerous and less-passionate people will gravitate toward more moderate, less-vociferous organizations, which will tend to be larger.

The Feminist Movement

There have been several feminist social movements in this country's history—in the 1830s, in the 1890s, in the 1920s, and in the 1960s. Each period has brought into being new organizations, some of which have endured to the present. For example, the League of Women Voters was founded in 1920 to educate and organize women for the purpose of using effectively their newly won right to vote.

Though a strong sense of purpose may lead to the creation of organizations, each will strive to find some incentive that will sustain it over the long haul. These permanent incentives will affect how the organization participates in politics.

There are at least three kinds of feminist organizations. First there are those that rely chiefly on solidary incentives, enroll middle-class women with

Profile of Five Environmental Organizations

"Environmentalists" are not all alike. There are well over a dozen major national environmentalist organizations. They differ in their goals, tactics, membership, and political ideology. Here are profiles of five such groups, ranging from (roughly) the most liberal to the most conservative:

	Environmental Action	Environmental Defense Fund	Sierra Club	Wilderness Society	National Wildlife Federation
Founded	1970	1967	1892	1935	1936
Membership	7,500	250,000	560,000	302,000	4,700,000
Budget	$1.2 million	$22 million	$38 million	$16.2 million	$100 million
Self-described ideology of members:					
Radical	10%	7%	4%	2%	2%
Liberal	72	67	57	51	21
Moderate	10	13	16	18	31
Conservative	9	13	23	29	47
Schooling of members:					
High school	7%	6%	7%	9%	34%
College	41	31	41	41	45
Postgraduate	52	63	53	50	22
Membership beliefs:					
Favor closing nuclear plants	40%	31%	22%	23%	10%
Government should redistribute income	72	63	53	55	42
Membership who were:					
Hunters	6%	5%	12%	13%	31%
Fishermen	22	22	33	34	53

SOURCE: Membership and budget figures as of January 1994, as reported by spokespersons for each organization. Membership characteristics and beliefs from a 1978 survey by Resources for the Future. Tabulations from John McAdams, Marquette University.

relatively high levels of schooling, and tend to support those causes that command the widest support among women generally. The League of Women Voters and the Federation of Business and Professional Women are examples. Both supported the campaign to ratify the Equal Rights Amendment (ERA), but as Jane Mansbridge has observed in her history of the ERA, they were uneasy with the kind of intense, partisan fighting displayed by some other women's organizations and with the tendency of more militant groups to link the ERA to other issues, such as abortion. The reason for their uneasiness is clear: to the extent to which they relied on solidary incentives, they had a stake in avoiding issues and tactics that would divide their membership or reduce the extent to which membership provided camaraderie and professional contacts.[15]

Second, there are women's organizations that attract members with purposive incentives. The National Organization for Women (NOW) and the National Abortion Rights Action League (NARAL) are two of the largest such groups, though there are many smaller ones. Because they rely on purposes, these organizations must take strong positions, tackle divisive issues, and employ militant tactics. Anything less would turn off the committed feminists who make up the rank and file and contribute the funds. But because these groups take controversial stands, they are constantly embroiled in internal quarrels between those who think that they have gone too far and those who think that they have not gone far enough, between women who want NOW or NARAL to join with lesbian and socialist organizations and those who want them to steer clear. Moreover, as Mansbridge showed, purposive organizations often cannot make their decisions stick on the local level (local chapters will do pretty much as they please).[16]

The third kind of women's organization is the caucus that takes on specific issues that have some material benefit to women. The Women's Equity Action League (WEAL) is one such. Rather than relying on membership dues for financial support, it obtains grants from foundations and government agencies. Freed of the necessity of satisfying a large rank-and-file membership, WEAL has concentrated its efforts on bringing lawsuits aimed at enforcing or enlarging the legal rights of women in higher education and other institutions. In electoral politics the National

Women's Political Caucus (officially nonpartisan, but generally liberal and Democratic) and the National Federation of Republican Women (openly supportive of the Republican party) work to get more women active in politics and elected or appointed to office.

The feminist movement has, of course, spawned an antifeminist movement, and feminist organizations have their counterpart antifeminist organizations. The campaign by NOW for the ERA was attacked by a women's group called STOP ERA; the proabortion position of NARAL has been challenged by the various organizations associated with the right-to-life movement. These opposition groups have their own tactical problems, which arise in large part from their reliance on different kinds of incentives. In Chapter 19 we shall see how the conflict between these opposing groups shaped the debate over the ERA.

The Union Movement

When social movements run out of steam, they leave behind organizations that continue the fight. But with the movement dead or dormant, the organizations often must struggle to stay alive. This has happened to labor unions.

The major union movement in this country occurred in the 1930s, when the Great Depression, popular support, and a sympathetic administration in Washington led to a rapid growth in union membership. In 1945 union membership peaked; at that time nearly 36 percent of all nonfarm workers were union members.

Since then union membership has fallen more or less steadily, so that by 1984 fewer than 19 percent of all workers were unionized (see Figure 9.1). This decline has been caused by several factors. There has been a shift in the nation's economic life away from industrial production (where unions have traditionally been concentrated) and toward service delivery (where unions have usually been weak). But accompanying this decline, and perhaps contributing to it, has been a decline in popular approval of unions. Approval has moved down side by side with a decline in union membership and union victories in elections held to see whether workers in a plant want to join a union. The social movement that supported unionism has faded.

FIGURE 9.1   The Decline in Union Membership

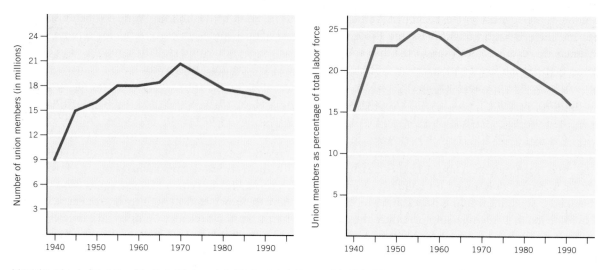

SOURCE: *Historical Statistics of the United States*, vol. 1, 178; *Statistical Abstract of the United States, 1990*, 419; and *Statistical Abstract of the United States, 1992*, 422.

But unions will persist because most can rely on incentives other than purposive ones to keep them going. In many industries they can require workers to join if they wish to keep their jobs, and in other industries workers believe that they get sufficient benefits from the union to make even voluntary membership worthwhile. And in a few industries, such as teaching and government, there has been a growth in union membership as some white-collar workers have turned to unions to advance their interests.

Funds for Interest Groups

All interest groups have some trouble raising money, but membership organizations have more trouble than most, especially membership organizations relying on appeals to purpose—to accomplishing stated goals. As a result the Washington office of a public-interest lobbying group is likely to be small, stark, and crowded, whereas that of an institutional lobby, such as the AFL-CIO or the American Council on Education, will be rather lavish.

To raise more money than members will supply in dues, lobbying organizations have turned to three sources that have become important in recent years: foundation grants, government grants, and direct-mail solicitation.

Foundation Grants

One study of eighty-three (primarily liberal) public-interest lobbying groups found that one-third of them received half or more of all their funds from foundation grants; one-tenth received over 90 percent from such sources.[17] Between 1970 and 1980 the Ford Foundation alone contributed about $21 million to liberal public-interest groups. Many of these organizations were law firms that, other than the staff lawyers, really had no members at all. The Environmental Defense Fund is supported almost entirely by grants from such foundations as the Rockefeller Family Fund. The more conservative Scaife foundations gave $1.8 million to a conservative public-interest group, the National Legal Center for the Public Interest.[18]

Federal Grants and Contracts

The expansion of federal grants during the 1960s and 1970s benefited interest groups as well as cities and states; the cutbacks in those grants during the early 1980s hurt interest groups even more than they hurt local governments. Of course the federal government usually does not give the money to support lobbying itself; it is given instead to support some project that the organization has undertaken. For example, the

National Alliance of Business received $20 million in 1980 from Washington, much of it for summer youth job programs and the like. But money for a project helps support the organization as a whole and thus enables the organization to press Congress for policies it favors (including, of course, policies that will supply it with more grants and contracts).

Before running for president in 1984, the Reverend Jesse Jackson had been heavily supported for several years by federal grants to his community-development organization, PUSH. Between 1978 and 1982 PUSH received in excess of $5 million from various federal agencies.

Since most public-interest groups pursue liberal policies, the Reagan administration became interested in saving money by reducing grants to interest groups and was particularly interested in cutting back on money being spent to lobby for liberal causes. Some writers called this an effort to "de-fund the left."

Direct Mail

If there is any one technique that is unique to the modern interest group, it is the sophistication with which mailings are used both to raise money and to mobilize supporters. By using computers, membership interest groups can mail directly to specialized audiences identified from lists developed by the staff or purchased from other organizations. Letters can be tailor-made, for example, to appeal to upper-income residents of Oregon who belong to the Sierra Club, live near the Columbia River, own four-wheel-drive vehicles, and thus might be interested in maintaining a local wilderness area.

A classic example of an interest group that was created and maintained by direct-mail solicitation is Common Cause, a liberal organization founded in 1970. Its creator, John Gardner, sent letters to tens of thousands of people selected from mailing lists it had acquired, urging them to join the organization and to send in money. Over two hundred thousand members were obtained in this way, each of whom mailed in dues (initially $15 a year) in return for nothing more than the satisfaction of belonging.

But raising money by mail costs money—lots of money. To bring in more money than it spends, the interest group must write a letter that will galvanize enough readers to send in a check. "Enough" usually

★ Who Gets the Money?

*I*f you give money in response to a direct-mail solicitation, don't assume that the money will go to support the cause in which you believe. It may just go to support the people who are in the business of producing direct-mail solicitations.

Representative Edward Markey of Massachusetts sent an emotional letter to people asking them to give money to support a freeze on nuclear weapons. Eula McNabb of Dallas, Texas, was impressed and sent in a $100 check, thinking that the money would help elect a nuclear freeze candidate. But that's not what happened. According to the *Washington Monthly*, the Markey organization (the U.S. Committee Against Nuclear War) raised $1.3 million from people like Ms. McNabb but spent only $40,000—just 3 percent of the total—on candidates. The rest went to pay for the mailing and to build up a mailing list of interested people to whom Markey could turn for money when he wanted to run for office.

This practice is not limited to liberal Democrats such as Markey. Conservatives, such as the Committee for the Survival of a Free Congress, have in the past given no more than 10 percent or 11 percent of what they raised to help political candidates; the rest went to overhead—offices, salaries, and the cost of direct-mail advertising.

SOURCE: Steven Waldman, "The Hiroshima Hustle," *Washington Monthly* (October 1986): 35–40; and Tina Rosenberg, "Diminishing Returns: The False Promise of Direct Mail," *Washington Monthly* (June 1983): 32–38.

amounts to at least 2 percent of the names on the list. Techniques include:

- Put a "teaser" on the outside of the envelope so that it won't be thrown out as "junk mail." If the letter is going to blacks, put a picture of some members of the Ku Klux Klan on the envelope.

- Arouse emotions, preferably by portraying the threat posed by some "devil." To environmentalists, a typical devil would be former Secretary of the Interior James Watt; to civil libertarians, former Moral Majority leader Jerry Falwell; to conservatives, Senator Ted Kennedy.

- Have the endorsement of a famous name; for liberals it is often Senator Kennedy; for conservatives it may be Ronald Reagan.

- Personalize the letter by instructing the computer to insert the recipient's name into the text of the letter to create the impression that it was written personally to him or her.

The Problem of Bias

Many observers believe that the interest groups active in Washington reflect an upper-class bias. There are two reasons for this belief: first, well-off people are more likely than poor people to join and be active in interest groups, and second, interest groups representing business and the professions are much more numerous and better financed than organiza-

TABLE 9.2 Organizational Membership and Social Class

	Percentage Who Are Members of an Organization or a Union, or Both
Total	53%
Education	
Grade school	35
Some high school	43
High school graduate	44
Some college	49
College graduate	60
Graduate school	80
Occupation	
Sales	39
Service	40
Clerical	41
Operative	48
Manager/administrator	51
Laborer	56
Crafts	64
Professional/technical	70
Income	
Under $6,000	29
$6,000–10,999	42
$11,000–15,999	52
$16,000 and over	65

SOURCE: 1976 Metropolitan Work Force Survey, as reported in Kay Lehman Schlozman and John T. Tierney, *Organized Interests and American Democracy* (New York: Harper & Row, 1986), 60. Copyright © 1986 by Kay Lehman Schlozman and John T. Tierney. Reprinted by permission of HarperCollins Publishers, Inc.

tions representing minorities, consumers, or the disadvantaged.

Doubtless both these facts are true. As we can see from Table 9.2, a survey of citizens done in 1976 shows that those with higher incomes, those whose schooling went through college or beyond, and those in professional or managerial jobs are much more likely to belong to a voluntary association than people with the opposite characteristics. Just as we would expect, higher-income people can afford more organizational memberships than lower-income ones; people in business and the professions find it both easier to attend meetings (they have more control over their own work schedules) and more necessary to do so than people in blue-collar jobs; and people with college degrees often have a wider range of interests than those without.

Of the nearly seven thousand groups that are represented in Washington, over half are corporations and another third are professional and trade associations. Only 4 percent are public-interest groups; fewer than 2 percent are civil-rights or minority groups.[19] About 170 organizations represented in Washington are concerned just with the oil industry.

But the question of an upper-class bias cannot be settled by these two facts taken alone. In the first place they only describe certain *inputs* into the political system; they say nothing about the *outputs*—that is, who wins and who loses on particular issues. Even if 170 interest groups are trying to protect the oil industry, this is important only if the oil industry in fact gets protected. Sometimes it does, sometimes it does not. At one time, when oil prices were low, oil companies were able to get Congress to pass a law that sharply restricted the importation of foreign oil; a few years later, after oil prices had risen and people were worried about energy issues, these restrictions were ended. In Chapter 15 the reader will find a theory that may help explain the circumstances under which business interests may exert more or less power.

In the second place business-oriented interest groups are often divided among themselves. Take one kind of business, farming. Once farm organizations seemed so powerful in Washington that scholars spoke of an irresistible "farm bloc" in Congress that could get its way on almost anything. Today dozens of agricultural organizations operate in the capital,

How Political Mail Piles Up

One day Daniel Aaron Schlozman of Massachusetts joined eight interest groups, four liberal and four conservative.

Over the next eighteen months, he received 248 pieces of mail, weighing a total of *eighteen pounds*. Included were 135 separate appeals for money.

Of the total, 63 pieces of mail were from organizations that he had not joined but that, apparently, had bought or borrowed mailing lists from organizations that he had joined. The conservative organizations allowed their mailing list to be used by other conservatives; the liberal organizations, by other liberals.

For example, by joining the National Conservative Caucus, he found himself on the mailing lists of Young Americans for Freedom, the Committee for the Survival of a Free Congress, the National Tax Limitation Committee, and the Senator Orrin Hatch Election Committee.

By joining Common Cause, he found himself on the mailing lists of the NAACP, the League of Women Voters, the National Organization for Women, the Campaign to Save the Massachusetts Bottle Bill, and the Union of Concerned Scientists.

But it didn't do any of these organizations much good. Daniel Schlozman was only four months old. His mother, Professor Kay Schlozman, a political scientist at Boston College, had enrolled him just to find out who shares mailing lists.

SOURCE: Adapted from Kay Lehman Schlozman and John T. Tierney, *Organized Interests and American Democracy* (New York: Harper & Row, 1986), 94–95.

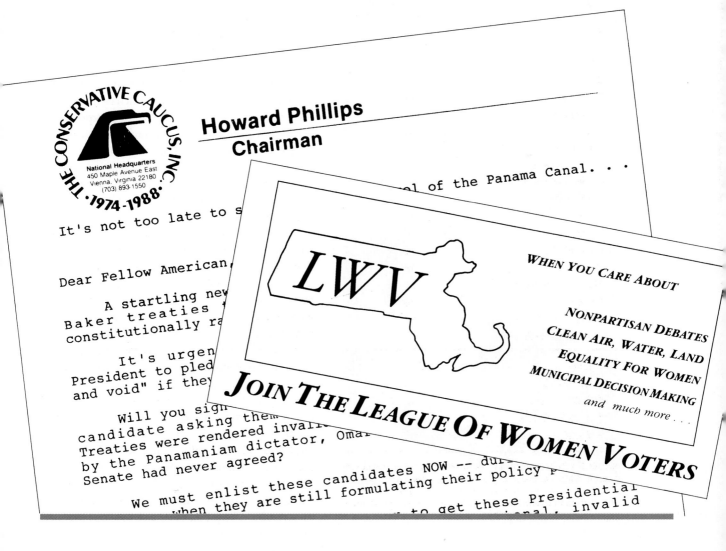

THE CONSERVATIVE CAUCUS, INC.

National Headquarters
450 Maple Avenue East
Vienna, Virginia 22180
(703) 893-1550

• 1974-1988 •

Howard Phillips
Chairman

It's not too late to s

...l of the Panama Canal. . .

Dear Fellow American,

A startling ne
Baker treaties
constitutionally ra

It's urgen
President to pled
and void" if they

Will you sign
candidate asking them
Treaties were rendered inval
by the Panamaniam dictator, Oma
Senate had never agreed?

We must enlist these candidates NOW -- du
when they are still formulating their policy
...to get these Presidential
...al, invalid

LWV

JOIN THE LEAGUE OF WOMEN VOTERS

WHEN YOU CARE ABOUT

NONPARTISAN DEBATES
CLEAN AIR, WATER, LAND
EQUALITY FOR WOMEN
MUNICIPAL DECISION MAKING
and much more . . .

Farmers once had great influence in Congress and could get their way with a few telephone calls. Today they often must use mass protest methods.

Willie Nelson performed at a rally—"FARM Aid II"—outside Austin, Texas, to draw attention to the problems of farmers.

with some (such as the Farm Bureau) attempting to speak for all farmers and others (such as the Tobacco Institute and Mid-America Dairymen) representing particular commodities and regions.

Farmers still have a great deal of influence, especially when it comes to blocking a bill that they oppose. But it is proving difficult for them to get a bill that they want passed by Congress. In part this political weakness reflects the decline in the number of farmers, and thus in the number of legislators who must take their interests into account. (Only 2.5 percent of all Americans live on farms—just one-sixth of the number who lived there thirty years ago.) In part their political weakness reflects the splits among the farmers themselves, with southern cotton growers often seeing things differently from midwestern wheat growers or New England dairy farmers. And to some extent it reflects the context within which interest-group politics must operate. In the 1950s few people thought that providing subsidies for farmers was too expensive—if indeed they knew of such programs at all. But in the 1980s consumers are acutely aware of food prices, and their legislators are keenly aware of the cost of farm-support programs.[20]

Whenever American politics is described as having an upper-class bias, it is important to ask exactly what this bias is. Most of the major conflicts in American politics—over foreign policy, economic affairs, environmental protection, or equal rights for women—are conflicts *within* the upper-middle classes; they are conflicts, that is, among politically active elites. As we saw in Chapter 5, there are profound cleavages of opinion among these elites. Interest-group activity reflects these cleavages.

Nonetheless it would be a mistake to ignore the overrepresentation of business in Washington. A student of politics should always take differences in the availability of political resources as an important clue to possible differences in the outcomes of political conflicts. But they are only clues, not conclusions.

The Activities of Interest Groups

Size and wealth are no longer entirely accurate measures of an interest group's influence—if indeed they ever were. Depending on the issue, the key to political influence may be the ability to generate a dramatic newspaper headline, mobilize a big letter-writing campaign, stage a protest demonstration, file a suit in federal court to block (or compel) some government action, or quietly supply information to key legislators. All of these things require organization, but only some of them require big or expensive organizations.

Information

Of all these tactics, the single most important one—in the eyes of virtually every lobbyist and every academic student of lobbying—is supplying credible information. The reason why information is so valuable is that, to busy legislators and bureaucrats, information is in short supply. Legislators in particular must take positions on a staggering number of issues about which they cannot possibly become expert.

Though there are nonpolitical sources of information, such as encyclopedias, they often do not provide the kind of detailed, specific, and up-to-date information that politicians need. This kind of information will ordinarily be gathered only by a group that has a strong interest in some issue. Lobbyists, for the most part, are not flamboyant, party-giving arm twisters; they are specialists who gather information (favorable to their client, naturally) and present it in as organized, persuasive, and factual a manner as possible. All lobbyists no doubt exaggerate, but few can afford to misrepresent the facts or mislead a legislator, and for a very simple reason: almost every lobbyist must develop and maintain the confidence of a legislator over the long term, with an eye on tomorrow's issues as well as today's. Misrepresentation or bad advice can embarrass a legislator who accepts it or repel one who detects it, leading to distrust of the lobbyist. Maintaining contacts and channels of communication is vital; to that end maintaining trust is essential.

To anticipate what will be said in Part 4, the value of the information provided by a lobbyist is often greatest when the issue is fairly narrow, involving only a few interest groups or a complex economic or technical problem. The value of information, and thus the power of the lobbyist, is likely to be least when the issue is one of broad and highly visible national policy.

Sometimes the nature of an issue or the governmental process by which an issue is resolved gives a great advantage to the suppliers of certain information and imposes a great burden on would-be suppliers of contrary information. In Part 4 we shall see in more detail how this happens with what will be called "client politics." For example, the Civil Aeronautics Board (CAB) once set airline fares and decided what airlines would fly to what cities. Historically the only organizations with any incentive to appear before the CAB and supply the necessary information were, naturally, the airlines. Until the CAB began to deregulate civil aviation, CAB decisions often tended to favor the established airlines.

For a long time only radio and television broadcasters had any incentive (or could afford) to appear before the Federal Communications Commission (FCC), which decides what broadcasters shall be licensed and on what terms. Owing to changes in the industry (such as the rise of cable and satellite television) and to the growth of consumer groups, FCC hearings are now often hotly contested. When the Federal Energy Administration (FEA) was trying to allocate scarce oil and gasoline supplies among competing users, it discovered that the information it needed was possessed only by the oil companies. (It later took steps to develop its own sources of data.)

Public officials not only want technical information; they also want political cues. A **political cue** is a signal telling the official what values are at stake in an

National Rifle Association: The Lobby That Can't Be Beat?

The National Rifle Association (NRA) was founded in 1871 as a group dedicated to providing shooting instruction. But in the 1960s and early 1970s, the NRA became a lobby dedicated primarily to opposing public policies that would restrict or abolish citizens' rights to own and use firearms for sporting and other legal purposes. By the 1980s the NRA's membership had increased from one million to nearly three million. Its members receive magazines, decals, and other direct benefits.

Throughout its lobbying history, the NRA has invoked the symbolic and legal authority of the last clause of the Constitution's Second Amendment: ". . . the right of the people to keep and bear Arms, shall not be infringed." In 1986 the NRA achieved one of its greatest lobbying victories when Congress passed the Firearm Owners Protection Act, which abolished the 1968 ban on interstate rifle and shotgun sales. The NRA's lobbying arm, the Institute for Legislative Action, has a budget that many other interest groups only dream of—$29 million in 1992. From 1983 to 1992, the NRA spent $8 million on congressional races in both direct contributions to their favored candidates and in independent expenditures supporting or opposing various candidates.

With millions of members, a big budget, and demonstrated political clout, the NRA has typified a lobby that can't be beat. However in the 1992 congressional races the NRA spent millions to defeat incumbents who had sponsored strict gun-control measures, but the incumbents won handily despite the NRA's efforts. At the state level the NRA lost a major battle to repeal New Jersey's ban on semiautomatic assault weapons and lost similar battles in Connecticut, Virginia, and other states. In 1992, the NRA's membership hovered around 2.6 million, down from its peak in the 1980s.

Why this apparent weakening in the NRA's political influence? Like any lobby, the NRA's influence depends not only on the size of its membership and financial clout, but on its consonance with public opinion and the strength of opposition lobbying groups. A 1992 poll found that 86 percent of the American public and 82 percent of the gun-owning public favored a national law that required a seven-day waiting period between the time a person applied to buy a handgun and the time it was sold. The same poll found that 79 percent of the general public and 76 percent of the gun-owning public favored a ban on assault weapons (semiautomatic military-style rifles that can hold up to

After Jim Brady was shot during an attempt to assassinate President Reagan, he (shown here with his wife, Sarah) become a symbol to and a leader of gun-control advocates. The 1993 bill was named after him.

thirty bullets). These are precisely the types of gun-control measures that the NRA *opposes*. Given this discrepancy between the NRA and public opinion it's not surprising that only 27 percent of the general public and 42 percent of gun owners expressed a favorable opinion of the NRA. At the same time, law enforcement groups like the Fraternal Order of Police and pro-gun-control lobbies such as Handgun Control, Inc., have joined forces to offset the influence of the NRA. With the force of public opinion behind them, these groups are beginning to undermine the impact of the NRA's anti-gun-control lobby.

As the NRA's recent history helps to illustrate, no lobby is all-powerful.

SOURCE: Peter H. Stone, "Under the Gun," *The National Journal* (June 5, 1993), 1334-1338; *New York Times*/CBS News poll, January 22–25, 1992, as presented in *The New York Times* (March 12, 1992), D21.

issue—who is for, who against a proposal—and how that issue fits into his or her own set of political beliefs. Some legislators feel comfortable when they are on the liberal side of an issue, and others feel comfortable when they are on the conservative side, especially when they are not familiar with the details of the issue. A liberal legislator will look to see whether the AFL-CIO, the NAACP, the Americans for Democratic Action, the Farmers' Union, and various consumer organizations favor a proposal; if so, that is often all he or she has to know. If these liberal groups are split, then the legislator will worry about the matter and try to look into it more closely. Similarly a conservative legislator will feel comfortable if the Chamber of Commerce, the Farm Bureau Federation, the American Medical Association, various business associations, and Americans for Constitutional Action are in agreement; he or she will feel less comfortable if such conservative groups are divided. As a result of this process lobbyists often work together in informal coalitions based on general political ideology.

One important way in which these cues are made known is by **ratings** that interest groups make of legislators. These are regularly compiled by the AFL-CIO (on who is prolabor), by the Americans for Democratic Action (on who is liberal), by the Americans for Constitutional Action (on who is conservative), by the Consumer Federation of America (on who is proconsumer), and by the League of Conservation Voters (on who is proenvironment). These ratings are designed to generate public support for (or opposition to) various legislators. They can be helpful sources of information, but they are sometimes biased by the arbitrary determination of what constitutes a liberal or a proconsumer or a conservative vote.

Public Support

Since conflict is the essence of politics, it may seem strange that politicians dislike controversy. But they do, and for perfectly human reasons: no one enjoys dealing with people who are upset or who find one's viewpoint objectionable or unworthy. Consequently most legislators tend to hear what they want to hear and to deal with interest groups that agree with them.[21] Two senators from the same state may

Lobbists don't confine their efforts to the lobby of the Capitol; here, one makes his case outside on the steps.

choose to listen to very different constituencies in that state and to take very different policy positions. Neither senator may feel "pressured" or "lobbied" because each has heard mostly from groups or persons who share his or her views. (Politicians define "pressure" as arguments and inducements supplied by somebody with whom they disagree.)

Members of an interest group will also tend to work primarily with legislators with whom they agree; lobbyists do not like to argue with people who are suspicious of them or who are unlikely to change their minds no matter what is said. For the lobbyist the key target is the undecided or wavering legislator or bureaucrat. Sometimes lobbyists will make a major effort to persuade the undecided legislator that public opinion is strongly inclined in one direction. A lobbyist will do this by commissioning public-

opinion polls, by stimulating local citizens to write letters or send telegrams, by arranging for constituents to pay personal visits to the legislator, or by getting newspapers to run editorials supporting the lobbyist's position.

Though most lobbying organizations cultivate the goodwill of government officials, there are important exceptions. Some groups, especially those that use an ideological appeal to attract supporters or that depend for their maintenance and influence on media publicity, will deliberately attack actual or potential allies in government in order to embarrass them. Ralph Nader is as likely to denounce as to praise those officials who tend to agree with him if their agreement is not sufficiently close or public. He did this with Senator Edmund Muskie, the author of the Clean Air Act, and with William Haddon, Jr., an early administrator of the National Highway Traffic Safety Administration. The head of the Fund for Animals is not reluctant to attack those officials in the Forest Service and the Interior Department on whose cooperation the fund must rely if it is to achieve its goals.[22] Sometimes, as we shall see in a later section, the use of threats instead of rewards extends to physical confrontations.

It is not clear how often public pressure works. Members of Congress are skilled at recognizing and discounting organized mail campaigns and feel that they can occasionally afford to go against even legitimate expressions of hostile public opinion. Only a few issues of great symbolic significance and high visibility are so important that a member of Congress would think that to ignore public opinion would mean losing the next election. In 1978 the proposed Panama Canal treaties were one such case; since the 1980s abortion has been another. Issues such as these can make or break a member of Congress.

Of late, interest groups have placed great emphasis on developing "grassroots" support. Sometimes it is impossible to develop such support, as when a complicated tax regulation of interest to only a few firms is being changed. But sometimes a proposed bill touches a public nerve such that even businesses can help generate an outpouring of mail: when the Food and Drug Administration announced it was going to ban saccharin on the grounds that it caused cancer in laboratory animals, the Calorie Control Council (closely tied to the Coca-Cola Company, a big user of saccharin in such soft drinks as Tab) ran newspaper ads denouncing the policy. The public, worried about losing access to an artificial sweetener important to dieters, responded with an avalanche of mail to Congress, which promptly passed a law reversing the ban.

What Would You Do?

MEMORANDUM

TO: P. B. Clark, president, Clark Corporation
FROM: Ellen Brown, vice president for public affairs,
      Clark Corporation
SUBJECT: Threat of tax increases

There is a real possibility that our taxes will be increased next year if the bill to be introduced in the next Congress passes. Given the reduced sales that we have had and the foreign competition that we face, higher taxes would hurt us badly. One or two plants might have to be closed and several hundred workers laid off. Profits would decline. I think it important to use whatever influence we have to avert this tax increase. As you know, we have formed a political-action committee (PAC) that makes campaign contributions to congressional candidates. We also have a lobbyist in Washington. Our political experts tell me that there are several alternative strategies we can follow:

1. Give the maximum campaign contribution (through the PAC) to candidates of whatever party are pledged to vote against the tax increase. We can give up to $5,000 to each candidate in both the primary and general elections, for a total of $10,000.
Advantages: (a) The money goes to people who are on our side. (b) The amount may be great enough to provide real help to our candidates.
Disadvantages: (a) If the candidates that we back lose, and we have given nothing to their victorious opponents, the victors will hold it against us and be less likely than ever to listen to our arguments. (b) The candidates that we do back may be criticized during the campaign for being "captives" of "special-interest" money (even though the amount that we can give them is so small as to make it unlikely that they will be our captives).

2. Give some money (perhaps $1,000 each) to all general-election candidates who have a good chance of winning.
Advantages: (a) No matter who wins, we will have some access to those persons. (b) No candidate can accuse any other of being the "captive" of a special interest.
Disadvantages: (a) Some of our money will go to people who oppose us. (b) The amounts are too small to make much difference in the election.

3. Give the maximum amount ($10,000) to every incumbent member of Congress who serves on a committee that writes tax legislation. Over 90 percent of House incumbents are reelected. Advantage: Some of these incumbent legislators oppose us, but by supporting them we at least get a chance to make our views heard.
Disadvantage: We will deny help to some challengers sympathetic to us who, with our help, might defeat some incumbents who oppose us.

Your decision: Option 1 ___   Option 2 ___   Option 3 ___

Next Congress to Act on Tax Legislation

Bill Would Increase Corporate Taxes

* * *

Washington, D.C. April 12—The members of Congress who will be elected this year will vote on a plan to reduce the federal deficit by raising taxes on corporations. The bill would increase taxes on

Usually, however, the public at large doesn't care that much about an issue, and so interest groups will try by direct-mail campaigns to arouse a small but passionate group to write letters or vote (or not vote) for specified candidates. Beginning in 1970, Environmental Action designated certain members of the House of Representatives as the "Dirty Dozen" because of their votes against bills that the lobbying group claimed were necessary to protect the environment. Of the thirty-one members of Congress so listed in various elections, only seven survived in office. Many members of Congress believe that the "Dirty Dozen" label hurts them with proenvironment voters in their districts, and though they are angry over what they feel is the unfair use of that label, they strive to avoid it if at all possible.

Money and PACs

Contrary to popular suspicions, money is probably one of the less-effective ways by which interest groups advance their causes. That was not always the case. Only a few decades ago, powerful interests used their bulging wallets to buy influence in Congress. The passage of the campaign-finance reform law in 1973 changed that. The law had two effects. First, it sharply restricted the amount that any interest could give to a candidate for federal office (see Chapter 8). Second, it made it legal for corporations and labor unions to form political-action committees (PACs) that could make political contributions.

The effect of the second change was to encourage the rapid growth of PACs. By 1989 more than four thousand existed, six times the number that existed in 1975. In 1988 they gave over $140 million to congressional candidates. Some people worry that the existence of all this political money has resulted in our having, as Senator Edward Kennedy put it, "the finest Congress that money can buy." More likely the increase in the number of PACs has had just the *opposite* effect. The reason is simple: with PACs so numerous and so easy to form, it is now probable that there will be money available on every side of almost every conceivable issue. As a result members of Congress can take money and still decide for themselves how to vote. As we shall see, there is not much scholarly evidence that money buys votes in Congress.

Indeed some members of Congress tell PACs what to do rather than take orders from them. Members will frequently inform PACs that they "expect" money from them; grumbling PAC officials feel that they have no choice but to contribute for fear of alienating the members. Moreover some members have created their *own* PACs—organizations set up to raise money from individual donors that is then given to favored political allies in and out of Congress or used to advance the members' own political ambitions. When Charles Rangel, congressman from New York, was hoping to be elected whip of the Democratic party in the House, he set up a PAC that made campaign contributions to fellow representatives in hopes that they might vote for him as whip. There are many other examples from both sides of the aisle. An ironic consequence of this is that a conservative Republican may give money to a PAC set up by a moderate Democrat who then gives the money to a liberal Democrat (or vice versa), with the result that the original donor winds up having his or her money go to somebody that he or she profoundly dislikes.

Almost any kind of organization—corporation, labor union, trade association, public-interest lobby, citizens group—can form a PAC. Over half of all PACs are sponsored by corporations, about a tenth by labor unions, and the rest by various groups, including ideological ones.

The rise of ideological PACs has been the most remarkable development in interest-group activity in recent years. They have increased in number at a faster rate than business or labor PACs, and in the 1980 and 1982 elections they raised more money than either business or labor. In the 1992 election there were more than one thousand ideological PACs; about one-third were liberal, about two-thirds conservative.[23]

Though the ideological PACs raised more money than business or labor ones, they spent less on campaigns and gave less to candidates. The reason for this anomaly is that an ideological PAC usually has to raise its money by means of massive direct-mail solicitations, expensive efforts that can consume all the money raised, and more. (By contrast a typical business or labor PAC solicits money from within a single corporation or union.) Even a well-run ideological PAC must spend fifty cents to raise a dollar; some spend much more than that.[24]

As Table 9.3 shows, of the twenty PACs that gave the most money to candidates in the 1992 election, most were labor unions, business organizations, and

TABLE 9.3   Spending by Political-Action Committees (PACs), 1991–1992

CONTRIBUTORS

The following table shows the twenty largest contributors to federal candidates in the 1992 election and the maximum they could have spent under proposed limits of $1,000 and $2,500 per candidate per election.

		Proposed Limits	
Organization	Actual Contribution	$1,000	$2,500
National Association of Realtors	$2,957,754	$934,924	$2,074,324
American Medical Association	2,910,486	920,550	2,064,660
Intl. Brotherhood of Teamsters	2,419,052	777,200	1,721,300
Association of Trial Lawyers of America	2,366,135	710,085	1,589,435
National Education Association	2,318,122	695,315	1,536,090
United Auto Workers	2,234,974	740,657	1,590,664
AFSCME	1,957,440	698,968	1,440,114
National Auto Dealers Association	1,752,625	733,925	1,437,525
National Rifle Association	1,730,946	575,942	1,247,350
National Association of Letter Carriers	1,706,777	686,075	1,286,235
Intl. Association of Machinists	1,588,696	577,875	1,166,900
American Institute of CPAs	1,525,863	648,150	1,181,354
Intl. Brotherhood of Electrical Workers	1,518,592	648,400	1,213,442
United Food and Commercial Workers	1,491,881	638,476	1,156,988
National Association of Federal Retirees	1,437,250	771,500	1,269,750
United Brotherhood of Carpenters	1,427,932	551,865	1,136,675
American Bankers Association	1,422,988	651,450	1,115,315
United Parcel Service Inc.	1,393,787	787,488	1,275,997
American Dental Association	1,392,958	687,950	1,215,045
National Association of Life Underwriters	1,348,600	646,650	1,074,150

SOURCE: James A. Barnes, "Sticky Wicket," *The National Journal* (May 8, 1993): 1111, reporting data from the Center for Responsive Politics through November 23, 1992. All rights reserved. Reprinted by permission.

CONTRIBUTIONS

Between January 1, 1991, and December 31, 1992, more than 3,000 PACs contributed some $189 million to federal candidates, divided as follows (in millions of dollars):

	Election			Incumbency			Party		
PAC Sponsor	Presidential	Senate	House	Incumbent	Challenger	Open	Democrat	Republican	Other
Corporations	$ .18	$21.2	$42.9	$49.8	$5.3	$8.2	$32.3	$32.0	$.20
Labor organizations	.34	8.8	30.7	23.6	7.7	8.4	37.5	1.9	.22
Ideological groups	.11	6.9	10.3	10.2	3.2	4.0	11.0	6.4	.30
Trade and professional groups	.10	12.4	38.7	37.5	4.7	9.0	30.0	21.4	.45
Other	.39	1.9	4.6	5.1	.57	.88	4.3	2.3	.04

SOURCE: Federal Election Commission Release (April 29, 1993): 1–3.

groups that represented doctors, lawyers, accountants, and retirees. Except for the National Rifle Association, none was an ideological PAC. There have been many proposals to cut the amount that PACs can give to candidates for federal office from a maximum of $5,000 to $2,500 per election. During the 1992 presidential election, Bill Clinton promised to cap such contributions at $1,000. The table shows the total amount that the top twenty PACs would have been able to give under each of these proposed limits. (If the $2,500 limit had been in effect in 1992, the ten PACs that gave the most money to congressional candidates would have been prohibited from giving $6.4 million or 29 percent of their contributions; if the $1,000 limit had been in effect it would have prohibited $14.9 million or two-thirds of their contributions.)

The data in the table also show that, as we learned in Chapter 8, incumbents received more PAC money than challengers and that, whereas labor PACs gave almost exclusively to Democrats, business PACs divided their contributions between Democrats and Republicans. The result of this pattern of spending is that, though business raises more political money than labor, Democratic candidates receive more PAC funds than do Republicans.

The popular image of rich PACs stuffing huge sums into political campaigns and thereby buying the attention and possibly the favors of the grateful candidates is a bit overdrawn. For one thing the typical PAC contribution is rather small. The average PAC donation to a House candidate is only a few hundred dollars and accounts for less than 1 percent of the candidate's total receipts. Most PACs spread small sums of money over many candidates, and despite their great growth in numbers and expenditures, PACs still account for only about one-third of all the money spent by candidates for the House.[25]

Moreover scholars have yet to find systematic evidence that PAC contributions generally affect how members of Congress vote. On most issues how legislators vote can be explained primarily by their general ideological outlook and the characteristics of their constituents; how much PAC money they have received turns out to be a small factor. On the other hand, when an issue arises in which most of their constituents have no interest and ideology provides little guidance, there is a slight statistical correlation between PAC contributions and votes. But even here the correlation may be misleading. The same groups that give money also wage intensive lobbying campaigns, flooding representatives with information,

The political action committee of the National Education Association—a teachers' union—is one of the biggest in the nation.

press releases, and letters from interested constituents. What these studies may be measuring is the effect of persuasive arguments, not dollars; no one can be certain.[26]

It is possible that money affects legislative behavior in ways that will never appear in studies of roll-call votes in Congress. Members of Congress may be more willing to set aside time in their busy schedules for a group that has given money than for a group that has not. What the money has bought is access: it has helped open the door. Or contributions might influence how legislators behave on the committees on which they serve, subtly shaping the way in which they respond to arguments and the facts on which they rely. No one knows, because the research has not been done.

In any event, if interest-group money makes a difference at all, it probably makes it on certain kinds of issues more than others. In Chapter 15 we define the kind of issues—we call them "client politics"—on which a given interest group is likely to be especially influential, whether by means of arguments, money, or both. After reading that chapter and considering the examples given there, it will be easier to put the present discussion of PAC money into context.

The "Revolving Door"

Every year, hundreds of people leave important jobs in the federal government to take more lucrative positions in private industry. Some go to work as lobbyists, others as consultants to business, still others as key executives in corporations, foundations, and universities. Many people worry that this "revolving door" may give private interests a way of improperly influencing government decisions. If a federal official uses his or her government position to do something for a corporation in exchange for a cushy job after leaving government, or if a person who has left government uses his or her personal contacts in Washington to get favors for private parties, then the public interest may suffer.

From time to time there are incidents that seem to confirm these fears. Michael K. Deaver, once the deputy chief of staff in the Reagan White House, was convicted of perjury in connection with a grand-jury investigation of his having used his former government contacts to help the clients of his public-rela-

Conflict of Interest

*I*n 1978 a new federal law, the Ethics in Government Act, codified and broadened the rules governing possible conflicts of interest among senior members of the executive branch. The key provisions were these:

The president, vice president, and top-ranking (GS-16 and above) executive-branch employees must each year file a public financial-disclosure report that lists:

- The source and amount of all earned income as well as income from stocks, bonds, and property; the worth of any investments or large debts; and the source of a spouse's income, if any.

- Any position held in business, labor, or certain nonprofit organizations.

Employment after government service is restricted. Former executive-branch employees may *not:*

- Represent anyone before their former agencies in connection with any matter that the former employees had been involved in before leaving the government.

- Appear before an agency, for two years after leaving government service, on matters that came within the former employees' official sphere of responsibility even if they were not personally involved in the matter.

- Represent anyone on any matter before their former agency, for one year after leaving it, even if the former employees had no connection with the matter while in the government.

In addition another law prohibits bribery—it is illegal to ask for, solicit, or receive anything of value in return for being influenced in the performance of one's duties.

Finally, an executive order forbids outside employment—an official may not hold a job or take a fee, even for lecturing or writing, if such employment or income might create a conflict, or an apparent conflict, of interest.

SOURCES: *National Journal* (November 19, 1977): 1796–1803; and *Congressional Quarterly Weekly Report* (October 28, 1978): 3121–3127.

tions firm. Lyn Nofziger, a former Reagan White House aide, was convicted of violating the Ethics in Government Act (see the box) by lobbying the White House, soon after he left it, on behalf of various businesses and labor unions.

Disruptive tactics have been a part of American politics since the Boston Tea Party. These gay-rights activists block a road near then-President George Bush's Maine home.

In 1988 federal investigators revealed evidence of corrupt dealings between some Defense Department officials and industry executives. Contractors and their consultants, many of whom were former Pentagon personnel, obtained favors from procurement officials, thereby getting an edge on their competitors.

How systematic is this pattern of abuse? We don't know. Studies of the revolving door in federal regulatory agencies have found no clear pattern of officials' tilting their decisions in hopes of landing a lucrative business job.[27]

Agencies differ in their vulnerability to outside influences. If the Food and Drug Administration is not vigilant, people in that agency who help decide whether a new drug should be placed on the market may have their judgment affected somewhat by the possibility that, if they approve the drug, the pharmaceutical company that makes it will later offer them a lucrative position.

On the other hand lawyers in the Federal Trade Commission who prosecute businesses that violate the antitrust laws may decide that their chances for getting a good job with a private law firm later on will increase if they are particularly vigorous and effective prosecutors. The firm, after all, wants to hire competent people, and winning a case is a good test of competence.[28]

Trouble

Public displays and disruptive tactics—protest marches, sit-ins, picketing, and violence—have always been a part of American politics. Indeed they were among the favorite tactics of the American colonists seeking independence in 1776.

Both ends of the political spectrum have used display, disruption, and violence. On the left feminists, antislavery agitators, coal miners, auto workers, welfare mothers, blacks, anti–nuclear power groups, public-housing tenants, the American Indian Movement, the Students for a Democratic Society, and the Weather Underground have created "trouble" ranging from peaceful sit-ins at segregated lunch counters to bombings and shootings. On the right the Ku Klux Klan has used terror, intimidation, and murder; parents opposed to forced busing of schoolchildren have demonstrated; business firms have used strong-arm squads against workers; right-to-life groups have blockaded abortion clinics; and an endless array of "anti-" groups (anti-Catholics, anti-Masons, anti-Jews, anti-immigrants, antisaloons, antiblacks, antiprotesters, and probably even anti-antis) have taken their disruptive turns on stage. These various activities are not morally the same—a sit-in demonstration is quite different from a lynching—but politically they constitute a similar problem for a government official.

An explanation of why and under what circumstances disruption occurs is beyond the scope of this book. To understand interest-group politics, however, it is important to remember that making trouble has since the 1960s become a quite conventional political resource and is no longer simply the last resort of extremist groups. Making trouble is now an accepted political tactic of ordinary middle-class citizens as well as of disadvantaged or disreputable people.

There is of course a long history of "proper" people's using disruptive methods. In a movement that began in England at the turn of the century and then spread here, feminists would chain themselves to lampposts or engage in what we now call "sit-ins" as part of a campaign to win the vote for women. The object then was much the same as the object of similar tactics today: to disrupt the workings of some institution so that it is forced to negotiate with you or, failing that, to enlist the sympathies of third parties (the media, other interest groups) who will come to your aid and press your target to negotiate with you or, failing that, to goad the police into making attacks and arrests so that martyrs are created.

The civil-rights and antiwar movements of the 1960s gave experience in these methods to thousands of young people and persuaded others of the effectiveness of such methods under certain conditions. Though these movements have abated or disappeared, their veterans and emulators have put such tactics to new uses—trying to block the construction of the Seabrook, New Hampshire, nuclear power plant, for example, or occupying the office of a cabinet secretary to obtain concessions for the handicapped.

Government officials dread this kind of trouble. They usually find themselves in a no-win situation. If they ignore the disruption, they are accused of being "insensitive," "unresponsive," or "arrogant." If they give in to the demonstrators, they encourage more demonstrations by proving that this is a useful tactic. If they call the police, they run the risk of violence and injuries, followed not only by bad publicity but by lawsuits. (When mass arrests were made during an antiwar demonstration in Washington, D.C., subsequent lawsuits were filed that were decided in favor of the protesters, and millions of dollars in damages had to be paid.)

Regulating Interest Groups

Interest-group activity is a form of political speech protected by the First Amendment to the Constitution: it cannot lawfully be abolished or even much curtailed. In 1946 Congress passed the Federal Regulation of Lobbying Act, which requires groups and individuals seeking to influence legislation to register with the secretary of the Senate and the clerk of the House and to file quarterly financial reports. The Supreme Court upheld the law but restricted its application to lobbying efforts involving direct contacts

Native Americans use protest with media appeal (here, a demonstration in front of Mt. Rushmore) to advance their cause.

with members of Congress.[29] More general "grass-roots" interest-group activity may not be restricted by the government. The 1946 act has had little practical effect. Not all lobbyists take the trouble to register, and there is no guarantee that the financial statements filed are accurate or complete. There is no staff in the Senate or House in charge of enforcing the law or of investigating violations of it.[30]

Several suggestions have been made for stricter or better-enforced laws. The issues involved are complex, and some important principles are at stake. One proposal, for example, would require that contributors to an interest group be disclosed, much as contributors to an election campaign must now be disclosed. But this could discourage people from giving money for fear of reprisals. Suppose you are an executive of the Ford Motor Company who happens to believe in tougher government controls on auto pollution. If you give money to the Environmental Defense Fund, and this becomes known, your career prospects at Ford might suddenly become a good deal dimmer. Matters get even tougher if you are a covert homosexual who gives money to a gay-rights group, only to have your name disclosed.

Even without disclosure rules, complex reporting requirements can place substantial burdens on smaller, less-affluent interest groups that might well find the cost and bother of filling out endless forms so great as to make it difficult or impossible for them to function. For example, one proposal would require any interest group that sends a letter to five hundred or more people or to twelve of its branches to send a copy of the letter to the comptroller general.[31] Such a rule would produce a blizzard of paperwork and give Congress access to essentially private correspondence. Needless to say, most lobbying groups oppose the requirements in this proposal. A comparable law in California has produced little beneficial effect.[32]

The significant legal constraints on interest groups come not from the current federal lobbying law (though that may change) but from the tax code and the campaign-finance laws. A nonprofit organization—which includes not only charitable groups but almost all voluntary associations that have an interest in politics—need not pay income taxes, and financial contributions to it can be deducted on the donor's income-tax return, provided that the organization does not devote a "substantial part" of its activities to "attempting to influence legislation."[33] Many tax-exempt organizations do take public positions on political questions and testify before congressional committees. If the organization does any serious lobbying, however, it will lose its tax-exempt status (and thus find it harder to solicit donations and more expensive to operate). Exactly this happened to the Sierra Club in 1968 when the Internal Revenue Service revoked its tax-exempt status because of its extensive lobbying activities. Some voluntary associations try to deal with this problem by setting up separate organizations to collect tax-exempt money—for example, the NAACP, which lobbies, must pay taxes, but the NAACP Legal Defense and Education Fund, which does not lobby, is tax-exempt.[34]

Finally, the campaign-finance laws, described in detail in Chapter 8, limit to $5,000 the amount any political-action committee can spend on a given candidate in a given election. These laws have sharply curtailed the extent to which any *single* group can give money, though they have increased the *total* amount that different groups are providing.

Beyond making bribery or other manifestly corrupt forms of behavior illegal and restricting the sums that campaign contributors can donate, there is probably no system for controlling interest groups that would both make a useful difference and leave important constitutional and political rights unimpaired. Ultimately the only remedy for imbalances or inadequacies in interest-group representation is to devise and sustain a political system that gives all affected parties a reasonable chance to be heard on matters of public policy. That, of course, is exactly what the Founders thought that they were doing. Whether they succeeded or not is a question to which we shall return at the end of this book.

SUMMARY

Interest groups in the United States are more numerous and more fragmented than those in nations such as Great Britain where the political system is more centralized. The goals and tactics of interest groups reflect not only the interests of their members but also the size of the groups, the incentives with which they attract supporters, and the role of the professional staffs. Because of the difficulty of organizing large numbers of people, a group purporting to speak for mass constituencies will often have to provide material benefits to members or acquire an affluent sponsor (such as a foundation). The chief source of interest-group influence is information; public support, money, and the ability to create "trouble" are also important. The right to lobby is protected by the Constitution, but the tax and campaign-finance laws impose significant restrictions on how money may be used.

KEY TERMS

lobby   *p. 222*

lobbyist   *p. 222*

interest group   *p. 225*

incentive   *p. 228*

SUGGESTED READINGS

Bauer, Raymond A., Ithiel de Sola Pool, and Lewis A. Dexter. *American Business and Public Policy*. New York: Atherton, 1963. A classic study of how business groups tried to shape foreign-trade legislation, set in a broad analysis of pressure groups and Congress.

Berry, Jeffrey M. *Lobbying for the People*. Princeton, N.J.: Princeton University Press, 1977. Analyzes more than eighty "public-interest" lobbies, with a detailed discussion of two.

Cigler, Allan J., and Burdett A. Loomis, eds. *Interest Group Politics*. 3d ed. 1991 Washington, D.C.: Congressional Quarterly Press, 1991. Essays on several interest groups active in Washington.

Lowi, Theodore J. *The End of Liberalism*. New York: Norton, 1969. A critique of the role of interest groups in American government.

Malbin, Michael J. *Money and Politics in the United States*. Chatham, N.J.: Chatham House, 1984. Excellent studies of PACs and of the influence of money in elections.

Mansbridge, Jane J. *Why We Lost the ERA*. Chicago: University of Chicago Press, 1986. Insightful analysis of the relationship between organizational incentives and tactics in the ERA campaign.

Olson, Mancur. *The Logic of Collective Action*. Cambridge, Mass.: Harvard University Press, 1965. An economic analysis of interest groups, especially the "free-rider" problem.

Sabato, Larry. *PAC Power*. New York: Norton, 1985. A full discussion of the nature and activities of political-action committees.

Schlozman, Kay Lehman, and John T. Tierney. *Organized Interests and American Democracy*. New York: Harper & Row, 1985. Comprehensive treatise on interest groups based on original research.

Truman, David B. *The Governmental Process*. 2d ed. New York: Knopf, 1971. First published in 1951, this was the classic analysis—and defense—of interest-group pluralism.

Wilson, James Q. *Political Organizations*. New York: Basic Books, 1973. A theory of interest groups emphasizing the incentives that they use to attract members.

10

The Media

All public officials have a love-hate relationship with newspapers, television, and the other media of mass communication. They depend on the media for the advancement of their careers and policies but fear the media's power to criticize, expose, and destroy. As political parties—and, especially, strong local party organizations—have declined, politicians have become increasingly dependent on the media. Their efforts to woo the press have become ever greater, and their expressions of rage and dismay when that courtship is spurned, ever stronger. At the same time, the media have been changing, especially in the kinds of people who have been attracted into leading positions in journalism and in the attitudes such people have brought with them. There has always been an adversary relationship between those who govern and those who write, but events of recent decades have, as we shall see, made that conflict especially keen.

The relationships between government and the media in this country are shaped by laws and understandings that accord the media a degree of freedom greater than that found in almost any other nation. Though many public officials secretly might like to control the media, and though no medium of communication in the United States or elsewhere is totally free of government influence, the press in this country is among the freest in the world. A study of ninety-four countries found only sixteen in which the press enjoyed a high degree of freedom; the United States was one of these.[1] Some democratic nations, such as France and Great Britain, place more restrictions on the communications media than are found here. The laws governing libel in England are so strict that public figures frequently sue newspapers for printing statements that tend to defame or ridicule them—and they collect. In the United States, as will be explained, the law of libel is loose enough to permit intense and even inaccurate criticism of anybody in the public eye. England also has an Official Secrets Act that can be used to punish any present or past public official who divulges to the press private

Newscaster Brit Hume of ABC News.

government business.[2] In this country, by contrast, the Freedom of Information Act, together with a long tradition of leaking inside stories and writing memoirs of one's public service, virtually guarantees that very little can be kept secret for very long.

Almost all American radio and television stations are privately owned, though they require government licenses (issued for seven- and five-year terms, respectively) to operate. In France broadcasting is operated by a government agency (Radiodiffusion-Télévision Française) under the control of the minister of information, who is not averse to using that control to protect the government's image. Until recently the French government had the power to ban the showing of any motion picture that was thought likely to "disturb the public order" or for other "reasons of state."[3] A French newspaper editor was heavily fined by a court for having written an article critical of the president of France.[4] While the federal government does impose rules on American broadcasters, it does not have the power to censor or dictate the contents of particular stories. As we shall see, though, its power to license broadcasters has been used, on occasion, to harass station owners who were out of favor with the White House.

The freedom from government control that comes with the private ownership of the mass media of communication has a price, of course: newspapers, magazines, and broadcast stations are businesses that must earn a profit. Some critics believe that the need for profit leads publishers and station owners to distort the news coverage of politics to satisfy the desires of advertisers, the pecuniary interests of stockholders, or the private ideology of the managers. This is much too simple a view, however. Every owner of a communications medium must satisfy the often competing interests of a number of distinct constituencies—advertisers, readers or viewers, editors and reporters, and organized external pressure groups. How each newspaper or broadcaster balances the preferences of these groups varies from case to case. Moreover the relative strength of these groups has changed over time. In general the history of American journalism, at least among newspapers, has been the history of the growing power and autonomy of editors and reporters.

Journalism in American Political History

Important changes in the nature of American politics have gone hand in hand with major changes in the organization and technology of the press. It is the nature of politics, being essentially a form of communication, to respond to changes in how communications are carried on. This can be seen by considering four important periods in journalistic history.

The Party Press

In the early years of the Republic, politicians of various factions and parties created, sponsored, and controlled newspapers to further their interests. This was possible because circulation was of necessity small (newspapers could not easily be distributed to large audiences owing to poor transportation) and newspapers were expensive (the type was set by hand and the presses printed copies slowly). Furthermore, there were few large advertisers to pay the bills. These newspapers circulated chiefly among the political and commercial elites who could afford the high subscription prices. Even with high prices, the newspapers, to exist, often required subsidies. That money frequently came from the government or from a political party.

During the Washington administration the Federalists, led by Alexander Hamilton, created the *Gazette of the United States.* The Republicans, led by Thomas Jefferson, retaliated by creating the *National Gazette* and made its editor, Philip Freneau, "clerk for foreign languages" in the State Department at $250 a year to help support him. After Jefferson became president, he induced another publisher, Samuel Harrison Smith, to start the *National Intelligencer,* subsidizing him by giving him a contract to print government documents. Andrew Jackson, when he became president, aided in the creation of the *Washington Globe.* By some estimates there were over fifty journalists on the government payroll during this era.[5] Naturally these newspapers were relentlessly partisan in their views. Citizens could choose among different party papers, but only rarely could they find a paper that presented both sides of an issue.

The Popular Press

Changes in society and technology made possible the rise of a self-supporting, mass-readership daily newspaper. The development of the high-speed rotary press enabled publishers to print thousands of copies

The *National Gazette,* edited by Philip Freneau, supported the Thomas Jefferson faction in national politics. Jefferson, as secretary of state, helped Freneau by giving him a job in the State Department. *The Gazette of the United States,* published by John Fenno, supported Jefferson's rival, Alexander Hamilton.

HOW SLOWLY NEWS TRAVELED, 1790

SOURCE: *Atlas of Early American History* (1976), 69. Adapted from map in Allan R. Pred, *Urban Growth and the Circulation of Information: The United States System of Cities, 1790–1840*, 37. By permission of Princeton University Press and Harvard University Press, © 1973 by the President and Fellows of Harvard College.

This map marks the average lag, in days, between the occurrence of an event in an outlying place and the published report of that event in the Philadelphia newspapers. The shaded areas show places with similar lag times. For example, it took over ten days in 1790 for news of an event in Boston to be published in Philadelphia. The numbers give lag times for locations beyond twenty days.

of a newspaper cheaply and quickly. The invention of the telegraph in the 1840s meant that news from Washington could be flashed almost immediately to New York, Boston, Philadelphia, and Charleston, thus providing local papers with access to information that once only the Washington papers enjoyed. The creation in 1848 of the Associated Press put the telegraphic dissemination of information to newspaper editors on a systematic basis. Since the AP provided stories that had to be brief and that went to newspapers of every political hue, it could not afford to be partisan or biased; to attract as many subscribers as possible, it had to present the facts objectively. Meanwhile the nation was becoming more urbanized, with large numbers of people brought together in densely settled areas. These people could support a daily newspaper by paying only a penny per copy and by patronizing merchants who advertised in its pages. Newspapers no longer needed political patronage to prosper, and soon such subsidies began to dry up. In 1860 the Government Printing Office was established, thereby putting an end to most of the printing contracts that Washington newspapers had once enjoyed.

The mass-based newspaper was scarcely nonpartisan, but the partisanship it displayed arose from the convictions of its publishers and editors rather than from the influence of its party sponsors. And these convictions blended political beliefs with economic interest. The way to attract a large readership was with sensationalism: violence, romance, and patriotism, coupled with exposés of government, politics, business, and society. As practiced by Joseph Pulitzer and William Randolph Hearst, founders of large newspaper empires, this editorial policy had great appeal for the average citizen and especially for the immigrants flooding into the large cities.

Strong-willed publishers could often become powerful political forces. Hearst used his papers to agitate for war with Spain when the Cubans rebelled against Spanish rule. Conservative Republican political leaders were opposed to the war, but a steady diet of newspaper stories about real and imagined Spanish brutalities whipped up public opinion in favor of intervention. At one point Hearst sent the noted artist Frederic Remington to Cuba to supply paintings of the conflict. Remington cabled back: "Everything is quiet. . . . There will be no war." Hearst supposedly replied: "Please remain. You furnish the pictures and I'll furnish the war."[6] When the battleship USS *Maine* blew up in Havana harbor, President William McKinley felt helpless to resist popular pressure, and war was declared in 1898.

For all their excesses, the mass newspapers began to create a common national culture, to establish the feasibility of a press free of government control or subsidy, and to demonstrate how exciting (and profitable) could be the criticism of public policy and the revelation of public scandal.

Magazines of Opinion

The growing middle class was often repelled by what it called "yellow journalism" and was developing, around the turn of the century, a taste for political reform and a belief in the doctrines of the progressive movement. To satisfy this market, a variety of national magazines appeared that, unlike those devoted to manners and literature, discussed issues of public policy. Among the first of these were the *Nation, Atlantic,* and *Harper's,* founded in the 1850s and 1860s; later there came the more broadly based mass-circulation magazines such as *McClure's, Scribner's,* and *Cosmopolitan.* They provided the means for developing a national constituency on behalf of certain issues, such as regulating business (or in the language of the times, "trust busting"), purifying municipal politics, and reforming the civil-service system. Lincoln Steffens and other so-called muckrakers were frequent contributors to the magazines, setting a pattern for what we now call "investigative reporting."

The national magazines of opinion provided an opportunity for individual writers to gain a nationwide following. The popular press, though initially under the heavy influence of founder-publishers, made the names of certain reporters and columnists household words. In time the great circulation wars between the big-city daily newspapers started to wane as the more successful papers bought up or otherwise eliminated their competition. This reduced the need for the more extreme forms of sensationalism, a change that was reinforced by the growing sophistication and education of the readers. And the founding publishers were gradually replaced by less-flamboyant managers. All of these changes—in circulation needs, in audience interests, in manage-

POLITICALLY P.S. SPEAKING

Muckraker

A **muckraker** is a journalist who searches through the activities of public officials and organizations, especially business firms, seeking to expose conduct contrary to the public interest.

Anyone who has been around stables knows that *muck* means manure; by extension it can refer to anything that is filthy or disgusting.

The word was first used in a political sense by President Theodore Roosevelt, who warned in a 1906 speech that antibusiness journalism could go too far. He said that "the men with the muckrakes are often indispensable to the well-being of society; but only if they know when to stop raking the muck, and to look upward to the celestial crown above them, to the crown of worthy endeavor."

Roosevelt was referring to a character named the Man with the Muck Rake in John Bunyan's book *Pilgrim's Progress;* this fellow was so preoccupied with raking the muck on the stable floor that he could never look any way but down.

SOURCE: Adapted from William Safire, *Safire's Political Dictionary* (New York: Ballantine Books, 1978). Used by permission.

rial style, in the emergence of nationally known writers—helped increase the power of editors and reporters and make them a force to be reckoned with.

Although politics dominated the pages of most national magazines in the late nineteenth century, today national magazines that focus mainly on politics and government affairs account for only a small and declining fraction of the national magazine market

FIGURE 10.1 Subject Areas of New Magazines Established in 1991

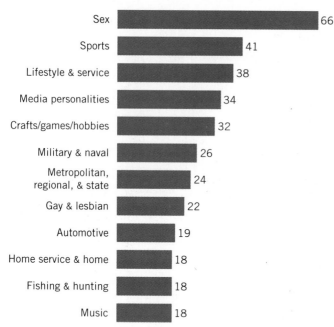

Sex	66
Sports	41
Lifestyle & service	38
Media personalities	34
Crafts/games/hobbies	32
Military & naval	26
Metropolitan, regional, & state	24
Gay & lesbian	22
Automotive	19
Home service & home	18
Fishing & hunting	18
Music	18

SOURCE: *The Public Perspective* (September/October 1992): 7, reporting data from *The Magazine Handbook* 64 (1992–1993). Reprinted by permission of *The Public Perspective*, a publication of the Roper Center for Public Opinion Research, University of Connecticut.

Two New York newspapers report on the stock market crash of October 19, 1987. The facts in both stories were essentially the same, but the use of photos and headlines made the *Times* coverage seem like a text-book while that of the *Daily News* looked like a soap opera.

(see Figure 10.1). Over five hundred new consumer magazines were established in 1991, but only a few of these covered the political scene. Among all magazines in circulation today only a fraction focus on politics—the majority of today's magazine focus on popular entertainment and leisure activities.

Electronic Journalism

Radio came on the national scene in the 1920s, television in the late 1940s. They represented a major change in the way news was gathered and disseminated, though few politicians at first understood the importance of this change. A broadcast permits public officials to speak directly to audiences without their remarks being filtered through editors and reporters. This was obviously an advantage to politicians, provided they were skilled enough to use it: they could in theory reach the voters directly on a national scale without the services of political parties, interest groups, or friendly editors.

But there was an offsetting disadvantage—people could easily ignore a speech broadcast on a radio or television station either by not listening at all or by tuning to a different station. By contrast the views of at least some public figures would receive prominent and often unavoidable display in newspapers, and in a growing number of cities there was only one daily paper. Moreover space in a newspaper is cheap compared to time on a television broadcast. Adding one more story, or one more name to an existing story, costs the newspaper little. By contrast less news can be carried on radio or television, and each news segment must be quite brief to avoid boring the audience. As a result the number of political personalities that can be covered by radio and television news is much smaller than is the case with newspapers, and the cost (to the station) of making a news item or broadcast longer is often prohibitively large.

Thus, to obtain the advantages of electronic media coverage, public officials must do something sufficiently bold or colorful to gain free access to radio and television news—or they must find the money to purchase radio and television time. The president of the United States, of course, is routinely covered by radio and television and can ordinarily get free time to speak to the nation on matters of importance. All other officials must struggle for access to the electronic media by making controversial statements, acquiring a national reputation, or purchasing expensive time.

As we discussed in Chapter 8, the rise of the talk show as a political forum has increased politicians' access to the electronic media, as has the televised "town meeting." But such developments need to be understood as part of a larger story.

Until recently, the "big three" television networks (ABC, CBS, and NBC) together claimed 80 percent or more of all viewers (see Table 10.1). Their evening newscasts dominated electronic media coverage of politics and government affairs. When it came to presidential campaigns, for example, the three networks were the only television games in town—they reported the primaries, broadcast the party conventions, and covered the general election campaigns, including any presidential debates. But over the last twenty-five years, the networks' evening newscasts changed in ways that made it harder for candidates to use them to get their messages across. For instance,

TABLE 10.1   Decline in Viewership of the Three Major Television Networks—ABC, CBS, and NBC

"Big Three" Networks: Average Shares of Prime-Time Viewing Audience

Year	Share
1961–1962	94%
1971–1972	91
1981–1982	83
1991–1992	63

Average Number of Households Tuned into the "Big Three" and Other Television Networks[a] During Prime Time, 1992

Network	Number (in thousands)
CBS	11,328
NBC	10,776
ABC	10,223
Fox	6,908
Independents	4,881
PBS	1,934
HBO	1,474
USA	1,382
TBS	1,289
ESPN	1,197
TNT	1,013
CNN	665
LIF	553
SHO	553
CMX	461
MTV	368

[a] Ten other networks not listed also had audiences of at least 100,000 households. Approximately 130 others together were viewed by about 2.7 million households.
SOURCE: Adapted from *The Public Perspective* (September/October 1992): 6, reporting data provided by Nielsen Media Research and NBC. Reprinted by permission of The Public Perspective, a publication of the Roper Center for Public Opinion Research, University of Connecticut.

the average **sound bite**—a video clip of a presidential contender speaking—dropped from about 42 seconds in 1968 to less than ten seconds in 1988.[7]

Today politicians have sources other than the network news for sustained and personalized television exposure. Cable television, early-morning news and

In 1933 White House press conferences were informal affairs, as when reporters gathered around Franklin Roosevelt's desk in the Oval Office. Today they are huge gatherings held either in a special conference room or (as here) outside in the Rose Garden.

entertainment programs, and prime-time "news magazine" shows have greatly increased and diversified politicians' access to the electronic media. Some of the most memorable moments of the 1992 presidential campaign—Ross Perot declaring his willingness to run for president on CNN's "Larry King Live" Bill Clinton playing the saxophone and joking about "not inhaling" on Fox's "Arsenio Hall Show"—occurred on cable television. And while the networks' evening news programs featured only small sound bites, their early-morning programs and news magazine shows featured lengthy interviews with the candidates.

Naturally, many politicians favor the call-in format, town-meeting setups, lengthy human interest interviews, and casual appearances on entertainment shows to televised confrontations on policy issues with seasoned network journalists who push, probe, and criticize. And naturally they favor being a part of visually interesting programs rather than traditional "talking heads" news shows. But what is preferable to candidates is not necessarily helpful to the selection process that voters must go through in choosing a candidate. No one has yet systematically analyzed

what, if any, positive or negative consequences these recent changes in politicians' access to the electronic media hold for campaigns, elections, or governance. Nor, for that matter, is there yet any significant research on the broader societal consequences of so-called narrowcasting—the proliferation of television and radio stations that target highly segmented listening and viewing audiences and the relative decline of electronic and print media that reach large and heterogeneous populations.

One thing is clear: most politicians crave the media spotlight, both on the campaign trail and in office. The efforts made by political candidates to get "visuals"—filmed stories—on television continue after they are elected. Since the president is always news, a politician wishing to make news is well advised to attack the president. Even better, attack him with the aid of a photogenic prop: when the late Senator John Heinz III of Pennsylvania wanted to criticize President Carter's bridge-repair program, Heinz had himself filmed making the attack, not in his office, but standing on a bridge.

In sum the transformations in the nature of journalism have altered significantly the way in which public officials and candidates can use communications. In the early era of the party press only a small number of better-off citizens regularly read newspapers, and those they read were typically highly partisan. This was a period in which politics consisted of competition among relatively small groups of notables and in which presidential candidates were nominated by legislators. The era of the mass newspaper made easier the emergence of mass politics: national conventions, the mobilization of voters at election time by broad appeals, mass rallies, and the development of strong party loyalties. The emergence of national magazines of opinion facilitated the development (discussed in Chapter 9) of national interest groups organized around policy questions and gave voice to the middle-class "reform" movement that agitated for a reduction in the role and power of political parties. Electronic journalism made it possible for politicians to develop personal followings independent of party structure, perhaps contributing to the decline of party loyalties and organization. Recent changes in the nature of politicians' access to the electronic media, many of them linked to the development of cable television and the diminishing importance of the "big three" networks, have ushered in a new era of electronic journalism.

In their effort to bring their message to the public directly without going through reporters, presidential candidates make increasing use of talk shows. Here, George Bush is interviewed by Larry King in 1992.

The Structure of the Media

The relationship between journalism and politics is a two-way street: though politicians take advantage as best they can of the media of communication available to them, these media in turn attempt to use politics and politicians as a way of both entertaining and informing their audiences. The mass media, whatever their disclaimers, are not simply a mirror held up to reality or a messenger that carries the news. There is inevitably a process of selection, of editing, and of emphasis, and this process reflects, to some degree, the way in which the media are organized, the kinds of audiences they seek to serve, and the preferences and opinions of the members of the media.

Degree of Competition

Contrary to popular belief, there has not been any significant decline in the number of daily newspapers in this country. There has been a decline, however, in the number of cities in which there are competing daily papers. There were competing newspapers in 60 percent of American cities in 1900, but in only 4 percent by 1972. The largest cities—New York, Chicago, Detroit, Philadelphia, Los Angeles, Washington, Atlanta, Boston—have at least two central-city newspapers, but most other cities have just one. This is partially offset by the fact that in many metropolitan areas, two or more neighboring cities will each have a newspaper whose readership overlaps. Residents of Manchester, New Hampshire, for example, can easily obtain the *Manchester Union Leader,* the *Boston Globe,* and the *Boston Herald.*

Radio and television, by contrast, are intensely competitive and becoming more so. Almost every American home has a radio and a television set. Though there are only five major television networks, there are over one thousand television stations, each of which has its own news programs. Local stations affiliated with a network are free to accept or reject network programs. There are more than eleven thousand cable TV systems serving over fifty million people (a typical cable can carry dozens of channels) and nearly ten thousand radio stations, some of which broadcast nothing but news whereas others develop a specialized following among blacks, Hispanics, or other minorities. Magazines exist for every conceivable interest. The number of news sources available to an American is vast—more than even dedicated readers and viewers can keep up with.

To a degree that would astonish most foreigners, the American press—radio, television, and newspapers—is made up of locally owned and managed enterprises. In Britain, France, Germany, Japan, Sweden, and elsewhere, the media are owned and operated with a national audience in mind. *The Times* of London may be published in that city, but it is read throughout Great Britain, as are the *Guardian,* the *Daily Telegraph,* and the *Daily Mirror.* Radio and television broadcasts are centrally planned and nationally aired.

The American newspaper, however, is primarily oriented to its local market and local audience, and there will typically be more local than national news in it. Radio and television stations accept network programming, but the early- and late-evening news programs provide a heavy diet of local political, social, and sports news. Government regulations developed by the Federal Communications Commission (FCC) are in part responsible for this. In general no one, including the networks, may own and operate more than one newspaper, one AM radio, one FM radio, or one television station in a given market. (In June 1993 the FCC granted its first waiver to this regulation when it permitted Rupert Murdoch to own and operate both WNYW-TV and the *New York Post* in New York. It did so on the grounds that New York City has three other large-circulation dailies and dozens of smaller newspapers—making it unlikely that the *Post* could monopolize the city's readership—and because closing the newspaper would have cost hundreds of jobs.) Nationally no one may own more than twelve television stations and twelve AM and twelve FM radio stations; and the networks may not compel a local affiliate to accept any particular broadcast. (In fact almost all network news programs are carried by the affiliates.) The result has been the development of a decentralized broadcast industry.

The National Media

The local orientation of much of the American communications media is partially offset, however, by the emergence of certain publications and broadcast services that constitute a kind of national press. The wire services—the Associated Press and United Press International—supply most of the national news that local papers publish. Certain news magazines—*Time, Newsweek, U.S. News & World Report*—have a national readership. The network evening news broadcasts produced by ABC, CBS, and NBC are carried by most television stations with a network affiliation. CNN—the Cable News Network—broadcasts national news around the clock. There are only three truly national newspapers, the *Wall Street Journal,* the *Christian Science Monitor,* and *USA Today,* but the *New York Times* and the *Washington Post* have acquired national influence because they are read daily by virtually every important official in Washington (and thus have become an important channel by which these officials keep track of one another) and because the television networks and many local newspapers use the stories that the *Times* and the *Post*

The national press wields great influence because it is read by presidents and virtually every other top government official. President Lyndon Johnson surveys his daily collection of newspapers in the Oval Office.

print. In fact one study found that the front page of the morning *Times* significantly shapes the contents of each network's evening news broadcasts.[8]

The existence of a national press is important for two reasons: First, government officials in Washington pay great attention to what these media say about them and their programs. They pay much less attention to what local papers and broadcasters say (if, indeed, they even know about their comments). Politicians read and worry about newspaper editorials, something that the average citizen rarely does. Second, reporters and editors for the national press tend to differ from those who work for the local press. They are usually better paid than most other journalists, they have often graduated from the most prestigious colleges and universities, and in general they have more liberal political views.[9] Above all they seek—and frequently obtain—the opportunity to write stories that are not merely accounts of a particular news event but that are "background," investigative, or interpretive stories about issues and policies.[10]

The national press plays the role of gatekeeper, scorekeeper, and watchdog for the federal government.

Gatekeeper As gatekeeper it can influence what subjects become national political issues, and for how long. Automobile safety, water pollution, and the quality of prescription drugs were not major political issues before the national press began giving substantial attention to these matters and thus helped place them on the political agenda (in ways described more fully in Chapter 15). When crime rates rose in the early 1960s, the subject was given little political attention in Washington, in part because the media did not cover it extensively. Media attention to crime increased in the late 1960s and early 1970s, slackened in the late 1970s, and rose again in the 1980s and 1990s. Throughout most of these years crime went up. In short *reality* did not change during this time; only the focus of media and political attention shifted. As we shall see later on in Chapter 20, elite opinion about the war in Vietnam also changed significantly as the attitude toward the war expressed by the national media changed.

Scorekeeper As scorekeepers the national media keep track of and help make political reputations,

note who is being "mentioned" as a presidential candidate, and help decide who is winning and losing in Washington politics. When Jimmy Carter, then a virtually unknown former governor of Georgia, was planning his campaign to get the Democratic nomination for president, he understood clearly the importance of being "mentioned." So successful was he in cultivating members of the national press that, between November 1975 and February 1976 before the first primary election was held, he was the subject of more stories in the *New York Times,* the *Washington Post,* and the *Columbus Dispatch* than any other

On Background

When politicians talk to the press, they set certain ground rules that the press (usually) observes. These rules specify who, if anyone, is quoted as the source of the story.

On the record. The official is quoted by name. For example: "I say that water runs downhill, and you can quote me on that."

Off the record. What the official says cannot be printed. For example: "Off the record, the head of my party is a complete wacko."

On background. What the official says can be printed, but it may not be attributed to him or her by name. For example: "A well-placed source said today that the sun will continue to rise in the East."

On deep background. What the official says can be printed, but it cannot be attributed to anybody. The reporter must say it on his or her own authority. For example: "In my opinion this administration secretly believes that two plus two equals five."

potential Democratic presidential candidate, even though most of the others (Henry Jackson, Hubert Humphrey, and George Wallace) were much better known. He did almost as well in getting mentioned on the three television networks.

The scorekeeper role of the media often leads the press to judge presidential elections as if they were horse races rather than choices among policies. Consider the enormous attention the media give to the Iowa caucuses and the New Hampshire primary election, despite the fact that these states produce only a tiny fraction of the delegates to either party's nominating convention and that neither state is representative of the nation as a whole. The results of the Iowa caucus, the first in the nation, are given great importance by the press. In 1988, the Iowa caucus received twice as much television coverage as did all the primaries and caucuses in the twenty "Super Tuesday" states put together, even though the Super Tuesday states chose over twenty times as many delegates as did Iowa. Consequently the coverage received by a candidate who does well in Iowa constitutes a tremendous amount of free publicity that can help him or her in the New Hampshire primary election. Doing well in that primary results in even more media attention, thus boosting the candidate for the next primaries. And so on.

The Maxims of Media Relations

*T*he importance of the national media to politicians has given rise to some shared understandings among officeholders about how one deals with the media. Some of these are caught in the following maxims:

- All secrets become public knowledge. The more important the secret, the sooner it becomes known.

- All stories written about me are inaccurate; all stories written about you are entirely accurate.

- The rosier the news, the higher-ranking the official who announces it.

- Always release bad news on Saturday night. Fewer people notice it.

- Never argue with a person who buys ink by the barrel.

For example: In 1984 Gary Hart won 15 percent of the Iowa caucus votes. Not many, you may think. But it placed him second, after Walter Mondale (who got a whopping 45 percent). The television networks "discovered" Hart, increasing their (free) news coverage of him by a factor of more than five. A "horse race" that once was portrayed as having a "clear leader" followed by several "also-rans" was now described as a "two-man race." Hart won the New Hampshire primary (to the surprise of almost everybody). The press increased its attention to Hart even more.[11]

There are other examples. In 1972 the press decided that George McGovern was the "man to watch" after *losing* the New Hampshire primary to Edmund Muskie (McGovern came in second). In 1968 Eugene McCarthy was described as having won a "moral victory" after losing to Lyndon Johnson in New Hampshire.

Watchdog But once the scorekeepers decide that you are the person to watch, they adopt their watchdog role. Before his New Hampshire victory in 1984, Hart's background went largely unexamined; after he had been declared a "front-runner," stories began appearing about how he had changed his name and altered his birth date by a year. In 1987, when Hart was already the front-runner for the 1988 Democratic presidential nomination, the press played its watchdog role right from the start. When rumors circulated that he was unfaithful to his wife, the *Miami Herald* staked out his apartment in Washington, D.C., and discovered that he had spent several evening hours there with an attractive young woman, Donna Rice. Soon there appeared other stories about his having taken Ms. Rice on a boat trip to Bimini. Not long thereafter Hart dropped out of the presidential race, accusing the press of unfair treatment. Then, in late 1987, Hart reentered the race only to drop out again after getting little popular support.

This close scrutiny is natural. The media have an instinctive—and profitable—desire to investigate personalities and expose scandals. To some degree all reporters probably share H. L. Mencken's belief that the role of the press is to "comfort the afflicted and afflict the comfortable." They tend to be tolerant of underdogs, tough on front-runners. Though some reporters develop close relations with powerful personages, many—especially younger ones—find the discovery of wrongdoing both more absorbing and more lucrative. Bob Woodward and Carl Bernstein, who wrote most of the Watergate stories for the *Washington Post,* simultaneously performed an important public service, received the accolades of their colleagues, and earned a lot of money.

Newspapers and television stations play these three roles in somewhat different ways. A newspaper can cover more stories in greater depth than a TV station and faces less competition from other papers. A TV station faces brutal competition, must select its programs in part for their visual impact, and must keep its stories short and punchy. As a result newspaper reporters have more freedom to develop their own stories but earn less money than television news broadcasters. The latter have little freedom (the fear of losing their audience is keen) but can make a lot of money (if they are attractive personalities who photograph well).

Rules Governing the Media

Ironically the least-competitive part of the media— the big-city newspapers—is almost entirely free from government regulation while the most competitive part—radio and television—must have a govern- ment license to operate and must conform to a variety of government regulations.

Newspapers and magazines need no license to publish, their freedom to publish may not be restrained in advance, and they are liable for punishment for what they do publish only under certain highly restricted circumstances. The First Amendment to the Constitution has been interpreted as meaning that no government, federal or state, can place "prior restraints" (that is, censorship) on the press except under very narrowly defined circumstances.[12] When the federal government sought to prevent the *New York Times* from publishing the Pentagon Papers, a set of secret government documents stolen by an antiwar activist, the Court held that the paper was free to publish them.[13]

Once something is published, a newspaper or magazine may be sued or prosecuted if the material is libelous or obscene or if it incites someone to commit an illegal act. But these are usually not very serious restrictions because the courts have defined *libelous, obscene,* and *incitement* so narrowly as to make it more difficult here than in any other nation to find the press guilty of such conduct. For example, for a paper to be guilty of libeling a public official or other prominent person, the person not only must show that what was printed was wrong and damaging but must show by "clear and convincing evidence" that it

Jeffrey Masson (here with an attorney) won his libel suit against Janet Malcolm, who he said defamed him in an essay in *The New Yorker* magazine.

Reporter Susan Wornick in Boston was arrested when she refused to divulge the name of a person who told her that police officers had broken into a drugstore. Eventually, the source revealed himself and the charges against her were dropped.

was printed maliciously—that is, with "reckless disregard" for its truth or falsity.[14] When in 1984 Israeli General Ariel Sharon sued *Time* magazine for libel, the jury decided that the story that *Time* had printed was false and defamatory, but that *Time* had not published it as the result of malice, and so Sharon did not collect any damages.

There are also laws intended to protect the privacy of citizens, but they do not really inhibit newspapers. In general your name and picture can be printed without your consent if they are part of a news story of some conceivable public interest. And if a paper attacks you in print, the paper has no legal obligation to give you space for a reply.[15]

It is illegal to use printed words to advocate the violent overthrow of the government if by your advocacy you incite others to action, but this rule has been applied to newspapers only rarely, and in recent years, never.[16]

Confidentiality of Sources

Reporters believe that they should have the right to keep confidential the sources of their stories. Some states agree and have passed laws to that effect. Most states and the federal government do not agree, so the courts must decide in each case whether the need of a journalist to protect confidential sources does or does not outweigh the interest of the government in gathering evidence in a criminal investigation. In general the Supreme Court has upheld the right of the government, in a properly conducted criminal investigation, to compel reporters to divulge information if it bears on the commission of a crime.[17]

The conflict is not only between a reporter and law-enforcement agencies, but often between a reporter and a person accused of a crime. Myron Farber, a reporter for the *New York Times*, wrote a series of stories that led to the indictment and trial of a physician on charges that he had murdered five patients. The judge ordered Farber to show him his notes to determine whether they should be given to the defense lawyers. Farber refused, arguing that revealing his notes would infringe upon the confidentiality that he had promised to his sources. Farber was sent to jail for contempt of court. On appeal the New Jersey Supreme Court and the United States Supreme Court decided against Farber, holding that the accused person's right to a fair trial includes the right to compel the production of evidence, even from reporters.

In another case the Supreme Court upheld the right of the police, with a warrant, to search newspaper offices. But Congress then passed a law forbidding such searches (except in special cases), requiring instead that the police subpoena the desired documents.[18]

Regulating Broadcasting

Although newspapers and magazines by and large are not regulated, broadcasting is regulated by the government. No one may operate a radio or television station without a license from the Federal Communications Commission, renewable every seven years for radio and every five for television. An application for renewal is rarely refused, but until recently the FCC required the broadcaster to submit detailed information about its programming and how it planned to

How to Read a Newspaper

Newspapers don't simply report the news, they report somebody's *idea* of what is news, written in language intended to *persuade* as well as inform. To read a newspaper intelligently, look for three things: what is covered, who are the sources, and how language is used.

Coverage Every newspaper will cover a big story, such as a flood, fire, or presidential trip, but newspapers can pick and choose among lesser stories. One paper will select stories about the environment, business fraud, and civil rights; another will prefer stories about crime, drug dealers, and "welfare cheats." What do these choices tell you about the beliefs of the editors and reporters working for these two papers? What do these people want you to believe are the important issues?

Sources For some stories, the source is obvious: "The Supreme Court decided . . . ," "Congress voted . . . ," or "the president said . . . ." For others, the source is not so obvious. There are two kinds of sources you should beware of; the first is an anonymous source. When you read phrases such as "a high official said today . . ." or "White House sources revealed that . . ." always ask yourself this question: Why does the source want me to

know this? The answer usually will be this: Because if I believe what he or she said, it will advance his or her interests. This can happen in one of three ways. First, the source may support a policy or appointment and want to test public reaction to it. This is called floating a **trial balloon**. Second, the source may oppose a policy or appointment and hope that by leaking word of it, the idea will be killed. Third, the source may want to take credit for something good that happened or shift blame on to somebody else for something bad that happened. When you read a story that is based on anonymous sources, ask yourself these questions: Judging from the tone of the story, is this leak designed to support or kill an idea? Is it designed to take credit or shift blame? In whose interest is it to accomplish these things? By asking these questions, you often can make a pretty good guess as to the identity of the anonymous source.

Some stories depend on the reader's believing a key fact, previously unknown. For example: "The world's climate is getting hotter because of man-made pollution," "drug abuse is soaring," "the death penalty will prevent murder," "husbands are more likely to beat up on their wives on Super Bowl Sunday." Each of these "facts" is either wrong, grossly exagger-

ated, or stated with excessive confidence. But each comes from an advocate organization that wants you to believe it because if you do you will take that organization's solution more seriously. Be skeptical of key facts if they come from an advocacy source. Don't be misled by the tendency of many advocacy organizations to take neutral or scholarly names, like "Center for the Public Interest" or "Institute for Policy Research." Some of these really are neutral or scholarly, but many aren't.

Language Everybody uses words so as to persuade people of something without actually making a clear argument for it. This is called using **loaded language**. For example: if you like a politician, call him "Senator Smith"; if you don't like him, refer to him as "right-wing (or left-wing) senators such as Smith." If you like an idea proposed by a professor, call her "respected"; if you don't like the idea, call her "controversial." If you favor abortion, call somebody who agrees with you "pro-choice" ("choice" is valued by most people); if you oppose abortion, call those who agree with you "pro-life" ("life," like "choice," is a good thing). The use of loaded language in a newspaper article can give you an important clue to deciphering the writer's own point of view.

---

serve "community needs" in order to get a renewal. Based on this information or on the complaints of some group, the FCC could use its powers of renewal to influence what the station put on the air. For example, it could induce stations to reduce the amount of violence shown, increase the proportion of "public-service" programs on the air, or alter the way in which it portrayed various ethnic groups.

Of late a movement has arisen to deregulate broadcasting, on the grounds that so many stations

are now on the air that competition should be allowed to determine how each station defines and serves community needs. In this view citizens can choose what they want to hear or see without the government's shaping the content of each station's programming. For example, since the early 1980s a station can simply submit a postcard requesting that its license be renewed, a request automatically granted unless some group formally opposes the renewal. In that case the FCC holds a hearing. As a result some of the old rules—for instance, that each hour on TV could contain only sixteen minutes of commercials—are no longer rigidly enforced.

The content of radio and television is still regulated in ways that newspapers and magazines are not. These include the following:

- **Equal time rule:** If a station sells time to one candidate for office, it must be willing to sell equal time for opposing candidates.

- **Right-of-reply rule:** If a person is attacked on a broadcast (other than in a regular news program), that person has the right to reply over that same station.

- **Political-editorializing rule:** If a broadcaster endorses a candidate, the opposing candidate has a right to reply.

For many years there was also in place the **fairness doctrine,** which required broadcasters to give time to opposing views if they broadcast a program giving one side of a controversial issue. In 1987 the FCC, believing that the doctrine inhibited the free discussion of issues, abolished it; Congress has tried to pass a law to reinstate it, but (so far) without success. Most broadcasters still follow the rule voluntarily.

Campaigning

When candidates wish to campaign on radio or television, the equal-time rule applies. A broadcaster must provide equal access to candidates for office and charge them rates no higher than the cheapest rate applicable to commercial advertisers for comparable time.

At one time this rule meant that a station or network could not broadcast a debate between the Democratic and Republican candidates for an office without inviting all other candidates as well—Libertarian, Prohibitionist, or whatever. Thus a presidential debate in 1980 could be limited to the major candidates, Reagan and Carter (or Reagan and Anderson), only by having the League of Women Voters sponsor it and then allowing radio and TV to cover it as a "news event." Now stations and networks can themselves sponsor debates limited to major candidates.

Though laws guarantee that candidates can buy time at favorable rates on television, not all candidates take advantage of this. The reason is that television is not always an efficient way to reach voters. A television message is literally "broad cast"—spread out to a mass audience without regard to the boundaries of the district in which a candidate is running. Presidential candidates, of course, always use television because their constituency is the whole nation. Candidates for senator or representative, however, may or may not use television, depending on whether the boundaries of their state or district conform well to the boundaries of a television market.

A **market** is an area easily reached by a television signal; there are about two hundred such markets in the country. Congressman Tim Roemer comes from a district in Indiana centered on the city of South Bend, which is also the hub of a distinct TV market. Roemer can use television effectively and relatively cheaply (dollars per viewer reached). By contrast, when Adam K. Levin ran for a congressional seat in New Jersey in 1982, he spent large sums on television ads on the only stations—those in New York City—that reach his district. But just 4 percent of the viewers of these stations live in Levin's district, and so most of the money was wasted. As a more experienced politician has commented, he "might as well give the money away at a bus station." Because of these factors, a far higher proportion of Senate than of House candidates buy television ads.[19]

The Effects of the Media on Politics

Everyone believes that the media have a profound effect, for better or for worse, on politics. Unfortunately very little scholarly evidence can prove or measure that effect. The reason for this discouraging gap between what everyone knows and what no one can prove is probably the fact that scholars have chiefly tried to measure the effect of the media on election outcomes. But as we have already seen (Chapter 8), elections—especially those for important, highly visible offices—are occasions when the voter is bombarded with all manner of cues from friends, family, interest groups, candidates, memories, and loyalties, as well as radio, television, and newspapers. It would be surprising if the effect of the media were very strong, or at least very apparent, under these circumstances.

Efforts to determine whether voters who watch a lot of television or who see candidates on television frequently vote differently from those who do not watch television at all (or who watch only nonpolitical messages) have generally proved unavailing.[20] This is quite consistent with studies of political propaganda generally. At least in the short run television and radio suffer from processes called **selective attention** (the citizen sees and hears only what he or she wants) and mental tune-out (the citizen simply ignores or gets irritated by messages that do not accord with existing beliefs). Radio and television may tend to reinforce existing beliefs, but it not clear that they change them.[21]

But if this is true, why do companies spend millions of dollars advertising deodorants and frozen pizza? And if advertising can sell these products, why not candidates? The answer is quite simple: citizens are not idiots. They can tell the difference between a deodorant and a Democrat, between a pizza and a Republican. If an ad persuades them to try a deodorant or a pizza, they will do so, knowing that not much is at stake, the costs are small, and if they do not like it, they can change brands in an instant. But they know that government is a more serious business, that one is stuck with the winning candidate for two, four, or even six years, and that as citizens they have accumulated a lot of information about the past behavior of the two major parties and their principal figures.

Local newspapers have generally endorsed Republican candidates for president throughout this century. Indeed only in 1964 did more newspapers endorse the Democrat (Johnson) than the Republican (Goldwater). Since the Democrats won eight of the fourteen presidential elections between 1932 and 1984, you might think that newspaper endorsements are worthless. They may have some value, however. A careful study of the effect of such endorsements on the 1964 presidential election found that, at least in the North, a newspaper endorsement may have added about five percentage points to what the Democratic candidate would otherwise have obtained.[22]

There are some elections, however, in which voters have few sources of information beyond what the media provide. Primary elections involving political unknowns and general elections for low-visibility offices (for example, tax assessor or superior court judge) may make voters dependent on newspaper and broadcast ads for information. Skillful ads may have a big effect on the results of these contests.

The major effects of the media, however, probably have much less to do with how people vote in an election and much more to do with how politics is conducted, how candidates are perceived, and how policies are formulated. National nominating conventions have been changed to fit the needs of television broadcasters. Some candidates have found it possible to win their party's nomination for senator or governor with expensive advertising campaigns that bypass the parties and ultimately weaken them. Unknown politicians can overnight acquire a national reputation by being shrewd enough—or lucky enough—to be at the center of an event heavily covered by the press.

In 1950 Estes Kefauver was a little-known senator from Tennessee. Then he chaired a special Senate investigating committee that brought before it various figures in organized crime. When these dramatic hearings were televised to audiences numbering in the millions, Kefauver became a household word

Senator Estes Kefauver pioneered the televised Senate investigation with hearings into organized crime and (pictured here) teenage drug addiction.

and, in 1952, a leading contender for the Democratic nomination for president. He was a strong vote getter in the primaries and actually led on the first ballot at the Chicago convention, only to lose to Adlai Stevenson.

The lesson was not lost on other politicians. From that time on developing through the media a recognized name and a national constituency became important to many senators. It also became, as we shall see in Part 4, a strategy whereby a variety of issues could be placed on the national agenda and pressed on Congress. Environmental and consumer issues benefited especially from the attention given them by the national press.

A survey of public opinion in North Carolina found that the issues that citizens believed to be important politically were very similar to the issues that newspapers and television newscasts had featured. Experiments conducted in New Haven, Connecticut, also showed that watching television news programs affected the importance people attached to various issues. TV influenced the political agenda.[23] On the other hand people are much less likely to take their cues from the media on matters that affect them personally. Everybody who is unemployed, the victim of crime, or worried about high food prices will identify these matters as issues whether or not the media emphasize them.[24] In short the media help set the political agenda on matters with which citizens have little personal experience but have much less influence on how people react to things that touch their lives directly.

The media also affect how we perceive certain issues and candidates. A study of the differences between voters who get their news primarily from television and those who get it chiefly from newspapers found that the two groups did not view political matters the same way. On a variety of issues newspaper readers thought that Gerald Ford was more conservative and Jimmy Carter more liberal than did television viewers. This difference persisted even after taking into account the fact that newspaper readers tend to have more schooling than do television viewers. Put another way, newspaper readers saw bigger differences between the 1976 presidential candidates than did television viewers.[25]

Another study found that television news stories affect the popularity of presidents and that television "commentary"—that is, the expression by newscasters of their personal opinions—tends to have a large effect, at least in the short run.[26] This will not come as a surprise to White House officials who spend almost every waking moment trying to get the television networks to say something nice about the president. The data support much anecdotal evidence on this score, such as Lyndon Johnson's belief that his war policy in Vietnam was doomed when Walter Cronkite, in his heavily watched CBS News programs, turned against the war.

Government and the News

Every government agency, every public official, spends a great deal of time trying to shape public opinion. From time to time somebody publishes an exposé of the efforts of the Pentagon, the White House, or some bureau to "sell" itself to the people, but in a government of separated powers, weak parties, and a decentralized legislature, any government agency that fails to cultivate public opinion will sooner or later find itself weak, without allies, and in trouble.

Prominence of the President

Theodore Roosevelt was the first president to raise to an art form the systematic cultivation of the press. From the day he took office he made it clear that he would give inside stories to friendly reporters and withhold them from hostile ones. He made sure that scarcely a day passed without the president's doing something newsworthy. In 1902 he built the West Wing of the White House and included in it, for the first time, a special room for reporters near his office, and he invited the press to become fascinated by the antics of his children. In return the reporters adored him. Teddy's nephew, Franklin Roosevelt, institutionalized this system by making his press secretary (a job created by Herbert Hoover) a major instrument for cultivating and managing, as well as informing, the press.[27]

Today the press secretary heads a large staff that meets with reporters, briefs the president on questions he is likely to be asked, attempts to control the flow of news from cabinet departments to the press, and arranges briefings for out-of-town editors (to bypass what many presidents think are the biases of the White House press corps).

All this effort is directed primarily at the White House press corps, a group of men and women who have a lounge in the White House itself where they wait for a story to break, attend the daily press briefing, or take advantage of a "photo op"—an opportunity to photograph the president with some newsworthy person.

No other nation in the world has brought the press into such close physical proximity to the head of its government. The result is that the actions of our government are personalized to a degree not found in most other democracies. Whether the president rides a horse, comes down with a cold, greets a Boy Scout, or takes a trip in his airplane, the press is there. The prime minister of Great Britain does not share his home with the press or expect to have his every sneeze recorded for posterity.

When President Theodore Roosevelt cultivated the media, reporters were usually unknown and poorly paid.

Coverage of Congress

Congress has watched all this with irritation and envy. It resents the attention given the president, but it is not certain how it can compete. The 435 members of the House are so numerous and play such specialized roles that they do not get much individual-ized press attention. In the past the House was quite restrictive about television or radio coverage of its proceedings. Until 1978 it prohibited television cameras on the floor except on purely ceremonial occasions (such as the annual State of the Union message delivered by the president). From 1952 to 1970 the House would not even allow electronic coverage of its

Every presidential action is a media event, as when Bill Clinton plays miniature golf.

FIGURE 10.2   Public Perception of Bias and Accuracy in the Media

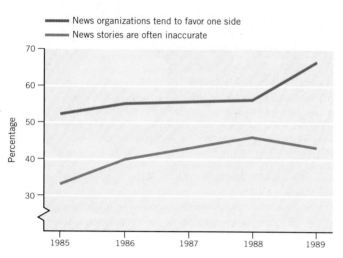

SOURCE: "The People and the Press," Part 5, *Los Angeles Times* (November, 1989): 13–14. Copyright © 1989, Los Angeles Times. Reprinted by permission.

TABLE 10.2   **Journalist Opinion versus Public Opinion**

	Journalists	The Public
Self-described ideology:		
Liberal	55%	23%
Conservative	17	29
Favor government regulation of business	49	22
U.S. should withdraw investments from South Africa	62	31
Allow women to have abortions	82	49
Allow prayer in public schools	25	74
Favor "affirmative action"	81	56
Favor death penalty for murder	47	75
Want stricter controls on handguns	78	50
Increase defense budget	15	38
Favor hiring homosexuals	89	55

SOURCES: *Los Angeles Times* poll of about 3,000 citizens and 2,700 journalists nationwide, as reported in William Schneider and I. A. Lewis, "Views on the News," *Public Opinion* (August–September1 1985): 7. Reprinted with permission of American Enterprise Institute for Public Policy Research.

committee hearings (except for a few occasions during those periods when the Republicans were in the majority). Significant live coverage of committee hearings began in 1974 when the House Judiciary Committee was discussing the possible impeachment of President Nixon.[28] Since 1979 cable TV (C-SPAN) has provided gavel-to-gavel coverage of speeches on the House floor.

The Senate has used television much more fully, heightening the already substantial advantage that senators have over representatives in getting the public eye. Although radio and television coverage of the Senate floor was not allowed until 1978 (when the debates on the Panama Canal treaties were broadcast live), Senate committee hearings have frequently been televised for either news films or live broadcasts ever since Estes Kefauver demonstrated the power of this medium in 1950. Since 1986 the Senate has allowed live television coverage of its sessions.

Senatorial use of televised committee hearings has helped turn the Senate into the incubator for presidential candidates. At least in most states, if you are a governor, you are located far from network television news cameras; the best you can hope for is that some disaster—a flood or a blizzard—will bring the cameras to you and focus them on your leadership. But senators all work in Washington, a city filled with cameras. No disaster is necessary to get on the air; only an investigation, a scandal, a major political conflict, or an articulate and telegenic personality.

Interpreting Political News

News stories, especially those about events of which we have no firsthand knowledge, are apt to be accepted without question. This may be particularly true of television news stories, since they enable us to judge not only what is said but how it is said.

Americans tell pollsters that they get most of their news from television, not newspapers, and regard TV as more reliable than the printed press. Though in general the public has a favorable view of the media, there has been a sharp increase of late in the proportion of Americans who think the media tend to favor one side of a story—from 53 percent in 1985 to 68 percent in 1989—and in the percentage who think stories are inaccurate (see Figure 10.2).

This is in sharp contrast to how the press sees itself. Two-thirds of all journalists think that the press deals fairly with all sides of political and social questions. Among the biggest losers in public confidence were Dan Rather and Ted Koppel; the biggest gainer was CNN (Cable News Network).

Bias is difficult to define and harder to measure, but in general the popular worry is that editors and reporters allow their personal political beliefs to influence the stories that they choose to run and to color the way in which they report them.

We do know that journalists are much more liberal than the public at large and that journalists working in the national media are the most liberal of all. In Table 10.2 we can see how the beliefs of some twenty-seven hundred journalists from around the country compare with those of about three thousand ordinary citizens. On most issues the journalists are more liberal. In Table 10.3 we see the views of the members of the "elite" or "national" media. Unfortunately this survey did not ask the same questions of the public as it did of the journalists. Nonetheless on such questions as abortion and affirmative action there is little doubt that the media elite are significantly to the left of the public. This is confirmed by a comparison of their voting patterns. In 1972, for example, when 61 percent of the American people voted for Richard Nixon, only 19 percent of the national media voted for him.[29]

Are News Stories Slanted?

The fact that reporters tend to have liberal views does not mean that their stories will inevitably have a liberal slant. Other factors influence how these stories are written, including the need to meet an urgent deadline, the desire to attract an audience, a professional obligation to be fair and tell the truth, and the need to develop sources among people holding different views. For example, whatever their views, the national media gave, according to a careful study, quite evenhanded treatment to both the Republican and Democratic presidential candidates during the 1980 campaign, although they gave quite decidedly anti-Reagan coverage during the 1984 campaign and appeared to have been consistently tougher on George Bush than on his 1992 campaign rivals, especially in the primaries (see Table 10.4).[30]

TABLE 10.3   The Political Attitudes of the Media Elite

	Percentage Agree
People with ability should earn more.	86%
Less regulation of business is good for the United States.	63
Government should reduce the income gap.	68
There should be a strong affirmative-action program for blacks.	80
A woman has a right to decide on an abortion.	90
Homosexuality is wrong.	25
The United States exploits the Third World and causes poverty.	56
U.S. use of resources is immoral.	57
The CIA should sometimes undermine hostile governments.	45

SOURCES: Survey of 240 journalists and broadcasters employed by the national media, reported in S. Robert Lichter and Stanley Rothman, "Media and Business Elites," *Public Opinion* (October–November 1981): 44.

TABLE 10.4   Negative Coverage in the 1992 Presidential Campaign

Percentages of Negative Remarks About the Candidates' Ability to Govern, Proposals, and Actions from All Interviews Aired on the Evening News Broadcasts of ABC, CBS, and NBC.

	Bush	Clinton	Perot
Primaries (January 1–June 2)	78%	59%	36%
Conventions (June 3–September 6)	62	55	60
General Election (September 7–November 2)	69	63	54

SOURCE: Adapted from Elizabeth Kolbet, "Maybe the Media Did Treat Bush Harshly," *The New York Times* (November 22, 1992): E3, reporting data from the Center for Media and Public Affairs.

Still it would be astonishing if strongly held beliefs had *no* effect on what is written or broadcast. To understand the circumstances under which a reporter's or editor's opinion is more or less likely to affect a story—and thus to be able to interpret intelligently what we read and hear—we must distinguish among these three *kinds* of stories:

1. **Routine stories:** These are public events regularly covered by reporters, involving relatively simple, easily described acts or statements. For example, the president takes a trip, a bill passes Congress, the Supreme Court rules on an important case.

2. **Feature stories:** These are public events knowable to any reporter who cares to inquire, but involving acts and statements not routinely covered by a group of reporters. Thus a reporter must take the initiative and select a particular event as newsworthy, decide to write about it, and persuade an editor to run it. Examples: an obscure agency issues a controversial ruling, an unknown member of Congress conducts an investigation, an interest group works for the passage of a bill.

3. **Insider stories:** Information not usually made public becomes public because someone with inside knowledge tells a reporter. The reporter may have worked hard to learn these facts, in which case we say it is "investigative reporting," or some official may have wanted a story to get out, in which case we call it a "leak."

Routine stories are covered in almost exactly the same way by almost all the media, differing only in their length, the kinds of headlines written, and the position the story occupies on the pages or the evening news. The wire services—AP and UPI—supply routine stories immediately to practically every daily newspaper in America. (The headlines and placement, however, can make a big difference in how the same story is perceived.) The political opinions of journalists have the least effect on these stories, especially if several competing journalists are covering the same story over a protracted period of time.

Even a routine news story can be incorrectly reported, however, if something dramatic or unique occurs. For example, toward the end of the Vietnam War the North Vietnamese army launched a massive, all-out attack on cities held by the South Vietnamese and their American allies. The attack failed—repulsed with heavy North Vietnamese casualties. But the news stories reported exactly the opposite: the North Vietnamese could move and fight at will, and the Americans were helpless to defend the cities or even their own fortified positions. Peter Braestrup, who later analyzed the Tet Offensive and its journal-istic coverage, painstakingly described the errors and omissions that led to the misleading versions published. He did not conclude that the political views of reporters explained the mistakes, and surely it would be difficult for any reporters, however fair, to grasp quickly and accurately an event as complex, dramatic, and violent as a major military struggle. But it is also probably the case that the antiwar attitudes of most reporters reinforced the interpretation of Tet that they wrote.[31]

Feature and insider stories must be selected, and thus someone must do the selecting. The grounds on which the selections are made include not only the intrinsic interest of a story but also the reporter's or editor's beliefs about what *ought* to be interesting. Among these beliefs are the political ideologies of the journalists. A liberal paper may well select for coverage stories about white-collar crime, consumerism, the problems of minorities, and environmentalism; a conservative paper might instead select stories about street crime, the decline of the central business district, and the need for family values.

Nor are selected stories rare. In order to compete with television, newspapers increasingly print feature stories, thereby becoming more like a magazine, with something for everybody. As a result a large part of a newspaper consists of precisely the kinds of stories that are most likely to be influenced by the ideological attitudes of reporters.

In one of the few studies of the effect of journalistic opinions on news stories, the authors found that in two examples of selected stories—articles concerning nuclear power and stories on the use of busing to integrate schools—the coverage provided by the national press reflected more the views of the press than those of experts or the public. But different segments of the media differed in how much slant they gave to their stories.

On nuclear power plants the vast majority of the stories in the *New York Times* gave a balanced view of the issue; the national news magazines (especially *Time* and *Newsweek*) and network television news programs, however, gave a predominately antinuclear slant to their stories. Moreover, though the great majority of scientists and engineers working in the field favor the rapid development of nuclear power plants, very few of the experts quoted on this subject by the national press favored nuclear power.[32]

The hostility between the press and the executive branch has been intensified by scandals: Watergate in the 1970s, the Iran-contra affair in 1988. Here, Lieutenant Colonel Oliver North testifies before Congress. In 1994, he was a candidate for the Senate from Virginia.

On school busing the majority of the stories run by the *New York Times,* the *Washington Post, Time,* and CBS News had a probusing slant.

If a nonroutine story is a major, complex, somewhat unique event, such as the congressional investigation of Irangate in 1987, all the media will cover it, but each part will choose what themes to emphasize and what questions to raise. Almost inevitably the media will put some "spin" on the story. (For example, was the star witness, Lieutenant Colonel Oliver North, a "hero," a "loose cannon," or a "Rambo"? It depended on whom you read.) If it is an offbeat story, it will be covered by one newspaper or TV station but not others; the very act of selection usually involves some political perspective. In evaluating feature and insider stories, every reader or viewer should keep these questions in mind:

- What beliefs or opinions led the editors to run this story?

- How representative of expert and popular opinion are the views of the people quoted in the story?

- What adjectives are being used to color the story?

Insider stories raise the most difficult questions of all—those of motive. When somebody inside government with private or confidential information gives a story to a reporter, that somebody must have a reason for doing so. But the motives of those who leak information are almost never reported. Sometimes the reporter does not know the motives. More often, one suspects, the reporter is dependent on his or her "highly placed source" and is reluctant to compromise it.

The reliance on the insider leak is as old as the Republic. At one time reporters were grateful for "background briefings" at which top government officials tried to put themselves in the best possible light while explaining the inner meaning of American policy. In the aftermath of Vietnam and Watergate, which weakened the credibility of "the Establishment," many reporters became even more interested in the leaks from insiders critical of top officials. In neither case were the motives of the sources discussed, leaving the reader or viewer to accept at face value whatever remarks are attributed to unnamed "highly placed sources" or "well-informed observers."

Why Do We Have So Many News Leaks?

American government is the leakiest in the world. The bureaucracy, members of Congress, and the White House staff regularly leak stories favorable to their interests. Of late the leaks have become geysers, gushing forth torrents of insider stories. Many people in and out of government find it depressing that our government seems unable to keep anything secret for long. Others think that the public has a right to know even more and that there are still too many secrets.

However you evaluate leaks, you should understand why we have so many. The answer is: the Constitution of the United States. Because we have separate institutions sharing powers, each branch of government competes with the others to get power. One way to compete is to try to use the press to advance your pet projects and to make the other side look bad. There are far fewer leaks in other democratic nations, in part because power is centralized in the hands of a prime minister who does not need to leak in order to get the upper hand over the legislature and because the legislature has too little information to be a good source of leaks. In addition we have no Official Secrets Act of the kind that exists in England; except for a few matters, it is not against the law for the press to receive and to print government secrets.

Even if the press and the politicians loved each other, the competition between the various branches of government would guarantee that we had plenty of news leaks. But since the Vietnam War, the Watergate scandal, and the Iran-contra affair, the press and the politicians have come to distrust one another. As a result journalists today are far less willing to accept at face value the statements of elected officials and far more likely to try to find somebody who will leak "the real story." We have come, in short, to have an **adversarial press**—that is, one that at least at the national level is suspicious of officialdom and eager to break an embarrassing story that will win for its author honor, prestige, and (in some cases) a lot of money.

This cynicism and distrust of government and elected officials have led to an era of attack journalism—seizing upon any bit of information or rumor that might call into question the qualifications or character of a public official. Media coverage of gaffes—misspoken words, misstated ideas, clumsy moves—has become a staple of political journalism. At one time, President Ford slipping down some stairs, Governor Dukakis dropping the ball while playing catch with a Boston Red Sox player, or Vice President Quayle misspelling the word *potato* would have been ignored, but now they are hot news items. (In fact one publication, the *Quayle Quarterly,* was devoted entirely to covering the gaffes of one man, Vice President Dan Quayle.) Attacking public figures has become a professional norm where once it was a professional taboo.

During the 1992 election, most of the national press clearly supported Bill Clinton. The love affair between Clinton and reporters lasted for several months after his inauguration. But when stories began to appear about Whitewater (an Arkansas real-estate deal in which the Clintons were once involved), the president's alleged sexual escapades while governor, and Hillary Rodham Clinton's profits in commodity trading, the press went into a feeding frenzy. The Clintons learned the hard way the truth of an old adage: If you want a friend in Washington, buy a dog.

Many people do not like this type of journalism, and the media's rising cynicism about the government is mirrored in the public's increasing cynicism

Because of satellite technology, it is now possible for television to cover a war right from the battle front. Here Peter Arnett of CNN broadcasts from Baghdad during the war against Iraq.

Tensions Mount between U.S. and Ruritania

U.S. 6th Fleet Maneuvering near African Nation

★ ★ ★

WASHINGTON, D.C. FEBRUARY 23—The State Department today denied Ruritanian claims that the United States is planning military action against Ruritania in the wake of Ruritanian-sponsored terrorist actions . . .

What Would You Do?

MEMORANDUM

TO: Editor in chief, *Washington Post*
FROM: Foreign news editor
SUBJECT: Ruritania

One of our best reporters has information that the United States plans to invade Ruritania three days from now. His source is a top military official who has been reliable in the past. As of now we do not think that any other newspaper has this story. As you know, opinion in the government is deeply divided over the wisdom of any action against Ruritania. So far all official sources in the White House and the State Department have denied that anything is underfoot. But we all know that the president is deeply upset by the continuation of Ruritanian-sponsored terrorism against U.S. personnel overseas. Your options are:

1. Print the story in tomorrow's edition.

<u>Advantages</u>: (a) This is important news, and we have an obligation to publish news. (b) We get a major scoop that no other newspaper can match. (c) In our editorials we have said that we think an invasion of Ruritania would be a mistake. This story, if printed now, may lead to a cancellation of the military action.

<u>Disadvantages</u>: (a) There is a small chance that we could be wrong and no invasion is planned. (b) We will be criticized for leaking military secrets. (c) If the invasion takes place despite our story, the United States may lose the element of surprise, and this may affect the outcome and cause additional casualties.

2. Do not print the story.

<u>Advantages</u>: (a) We avoid charges that we are leaking military secrets. (b) If an invasion occurs, we will not have alerted the enemy.

<u>Disadvantages</u>: (a) There is the possibility that another newspaper may learn of this story in the next two days; if we don't publish now, they may publish later and we will look foolish. (b) We will be failing in our duty to inform the people about the activities of their government. (c) The Ruritanians may already know of the planned invasion, and so our story will not have alerted them.

<u>Your decision</u>: Option 1 _____ Option 2 _____

FIGURE 10.3 Decline in Public Trust of the Media

QUESTION

Do you have more or less or about the same amount of confidence in the news media today as you did when you first began paying attention to news and current events?

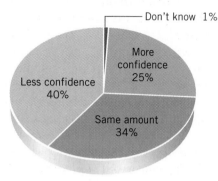

Don't know 1%
More confidence 25%
Less confidence 40%
Same amount 34%

QUESTION

Do you agree or disagree with this statement: "The news media give more coverage to stories that support their own point of view than to those that don't"?

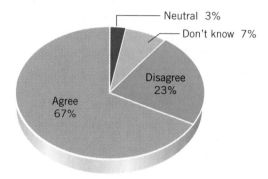

Neutral 3%
Don't know 7%
Disagree 23%
Agree 67%

QUESTION

Generally speaking, do you feel that the news media has too much or too little or the right amount of influence over what happens today?

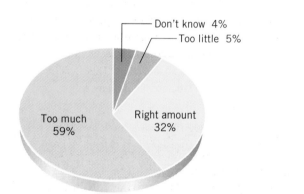

Don't know 4%
Too little 5%
Too much 59%
Right amount 32%

QUESTION

The Bill of Rights of the U.S. Constitution guarantees freedom of the press so that the news media can be a watchdog over the government and other powerful institutions. And the courts have ruled that the news media should be protected even in some cases when they have been unfair or inaccurate. Do you think the news media are careful to use this power responsibly?

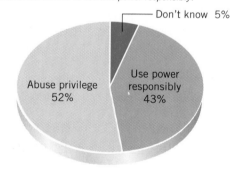

Don't know 5%
Abuse privilege 52%
Use power responsibly 43%

SOURCE: David Shaw, "Trust In Media Is on Decline," *Los Angeles Times* (March 31, 1993): A16, reporting data from a Times Poll conducted March 6–9, 1993. Copyright © 1993, Los Angeles Times. Reprinted by permission.

about the media. Figure 10.3 shows that most Americans have less confidence in the news media today than they did when they first came into political consciousness. Most people also believe that the press slants its coverage, has too much influence over events, and abuses its constitutional protections.

Furthermore, the public's confidence in big business has eroded along with its confidence in government, and the media are increasingly big business. As

noted earlier in this chapter, network television has become a highly competitive industry. Under these circumstances, every contribution to "market share" is vitally important, and the newsroom is no exception. In a highly competitive environment that is rich in information, those who aspire to reach a mass market must find a mass theme into which they can tap with visually dramatic, quick-tempo messages. In politics the theme is obvious: politics is a corrupt, self-serving enterprise. Many people encompass the profit-driven press in their antipolitical sentiments.

Given their experiences with Watergate and Irangate, given the highly competitive nature of national news gathering, and given their political ideology (which tends to put them to the left of the administration in power), American editors and reporters, at least at the national level, are likely to have an adversarial relationship with government for a long time to come. Given our constitutional system, there will always be plenty of people in government eager to help them with leaks hostile to one faction or another.

Government Constraints on Journalists

An important factor works against the influence of ideology and antiofficial attitudes—the need every reporter has for access to key officials. A reporter is only as good as his or her sources, and it is difficult to cultivate good sources if you regularly antagonize them. Thus Washington reporters must constantly strike a balance between expressing their own views (and risk losing a valuable source) and keeping a source (and risk becoming its mouthpiece).

The great increase in the number of congressional staff members has made striking this balance easier than it once was. Since it is almost impossible to keep anything secret from Congress, the existence of fifteen to twenty thousand congressional staffers means that there is a potential source for every conceivable issue and cause. Congress has become a gold mine for reporters. If a story annoys one congressional source, another source can easily be found.

The government is not without means to fight back. The number of press officers on the payroll of the White House, Congress, and the executive agencies has grown sharply in recent decades. Obviously these people have a stake in putting out news stories that reflect favorably on their elected superiors. They can try to do this with press releases, but adversarial journalists are suspicious of "canned news" (they use it nonetheless). Or the press officers can try to win journalistic friends by offering leaks and supplying background stories to favored reporters. (A **background story** is one that purportedly explains current policy and is given on condition that the source not be identified by name.) Finally, the press officers

can try to bypass the national press and reach directly the local press—the hometown newspapers and radio stations. Members of the local press are less likely to feel an adversarial attitude toward official Washington and perhaps are more likely to have a political ideology akin to that of the national administration.

The ultimate weapon in the government's effort to shape the press to its liking is the president's rewarding of reporters and editors who treat him well and his punishing of those who treat him badly. President Kennedy regularly called in offending reporters for brutal tongue lashings and favored friendly reporters with tips and inside stories. Johnson did the same, with special attention to television reporters. Nixon made the mistake of attacking the press publicly, thereby allowing it to defend itself with appeals to the First Amendment. (Kennedy's and Johnson's manipulative skills were used privately.) Probably every president tries to use the press with whatever means are at his disposal, but in the long run it is the press, not the president, who wins. Johnson decided not to run again in 1968, in part because of press hostility to him; Nixon was exposed by the press; Carter came to be disliked by national reporters. The press and the president need but do not trust one another; it is inevitably a stormy relationship.

SUMMARY

Changes in the nature of American politics have been accompanied by—and influenced by—changes in the nature of the mass media. The rise of mass-based political parties was facilitated by the emergence of mass-circulation daily newspapers. Political-reform movements depended in part on the development of national magazines catering to middle-class opinion. The weakening of political parties was accelerated by the ability of candidates to speak directly to constituents by radio and television.

The role of journalists in a democratic society poses an inevitable dilemma: if they are to serve well their functions as information gatherer, gatekeeper, scorekeeper, and watchdog, they must be free of government controls. But to the extent that they are free of such controls, they are also free to act in their own interests, whether political or economic. In the United States a competitive press largely free of government controls (except in the area of broadcast licenses) has produced both a substantial diversity of opinion and a general (though not unanimous) commitment to the goal of fairness in news reporting. The national media are in general more liberal than the local media, but the extent to which a reporter's beliefs affect reporting varies greatly with the kind of story—routine, feature, or insider.

KEY TERMS

muckraker *p. 257*

sound bite *p. 259*

trial balloon *p. 267*

loaded language *p. 267*

equal-time rule *p. 268*

right-of-reply rule *p. 268*

political editorializing rule *p. 268*

fairness doctrine *p. 268*

market (television) *p. 268*

selective attention *p. 269*

routine stories *p. 274*

feature stories *p. 274*

insider stories *p. 274*

adversarial press *p. 276*

background story (news) *p. 279*

SUGGESTED READINGS

Braestrup, Peter. *Big Story: How the American Press and Television Reported and Interpreted the Crises of Tet 1968 in Vietnam and Washington.* Boulder, Col.: Westview, 1977. 2 vols. A massive, detailed account of how the press reported one critical event; the factual accuracy or inaccuracy of each story is carefully checked.

Crouse, Timothy. *The Boys on the Bus.* New York: Random House, 1973. A lively, irreverent account by a participant of how reporters cover a presidential campaign.

Epstein, Edward J. *Between Fact and Fiction: The Problem of Journalism.* New York: Random House, 1975. Essays by a perceptive student of the press on media coverage of Watergate, the Pentagon Papers, the deaths of Black Panthers, and other major stories.

———. *News from Nowhere.* New York: Random House, 1973. Analysis of how television network news programs are produced and shaped.

Garment, Suzanne. *Scandal.* New York: Random House, 1991. A careful look at the role of the media (and others) in fostering the "culture of mistrust."

Graber, Doris A. *Mass Media and American Politics.* 3d ed. Washington, D.C.: Congressional Quarterly Press, 1989. A good summary of what we know about the press and politics.

Grossman, Michael Baruch, and Martha Joynt Kumar. *Portraying the President: The White House and the News Media.* Baltimore: Johns Hopkins University Press, 1981. How the White House is organized to handle the press and how the press is organized to cover the president.

Iyengar, Shanto, and Donald R. Kinder. *News That Matters.* Chicago: University of Chicago Press, 1987. The report of experiments testing the effect of television news on public perceptions of politics.

Lichter, S. Robert, Stanley Rothman, and Linda S. Lichter. *The Media Elite.* Bethesda, Md.: Adler & Adler, 1986. A study of the political beliefs of "elite" journalists and how those beliefs influence what we read and hear.

Linsky, Martin. *Impact: How the Press Affects Federal Policymaking.* New York: Norton, 1986. Study of how the national press affects the way in which federal officials make, discuss, and leak policy.

Patterson, Thomas W. *The Mass Media Election.* New York: Praeger, 1980. Analyzes what effect, if any, the media had on the 1976 election.

Robinson, Michael J., and Margaret A. Sheehan. *Over the Wire and on TV.* New York: Russell Sage Foundation, 1983. Analyzes how CBS News and United Press International covered the 1980 election.

PART THREE

Institutions of
Government

*"But the great security against a gradual
concentration of the several powers in
the same department consists in giving
to those who administer each department the necessary constitutional means
and personal motives to resist encroachments of the others."*

— FEDERALIST NO. 51

11

Congress

Senator Daniel Patrick Moynihan of New York once remarked that the United States is the only democratic government that has a legislative branch. Of course lots of democracies have parliaments that pass laws. What he meant is that among the large democracies of the world, only the United States Congress has great powers that it can exercise independently of the executive branch. To see why this is the case, we must understand the difference between a congress and a parliament.

The United States (along with most Latin American nations) has a congress; Great Britain (along with most Western European nations) has a parliament. A hint as to the difference between the two kinds of legislatures can be found in the original meanings of the words: *Congress* derives from a Latin term that means "a coming together," a meeting, as of representatives from various places. *Parliament* comes from a French word, *parler,* that means "to talk."

There is of course plenty of talking—some critics say that there is nothing *but* talking—in the United States Congress, and certainly members of a parliament represent to a degree their local districts. But the differences implied by the names of the lawmaking groups are real ones, with profound significance for how laws are made and how the government is run. These differences affect two important aspects of lawmaking bodies: how one becomes a member and what one does as a member.

Ordinarily a person becomes a member of a parliament (such as the British House of Commons) by persuading a political party to put his or her name on the ballot. Though usually a local party committee selects a person to be its candidate, that committee often takes suggestions from national party headquarters. In any case the local group selects as its candidate someone willing to support the national party program and leadership. In the election voters in the district choose not between two or three personalities running for office but between two or three national parties.

By contrast a person becomes a candidate for representative or senator in the United States Congress by running in a primary election. Except in a very few places, political parties exercise little control over the choice of who is nominated to run for congressional office. (This is the case even though the person who wins the primary will describe himself or herself in the general election as a Democrat or a Republican.) Voters select candidates in the primaries because of their personalities, positions on issues, or overall reputation; even in the general election, where the party label affects who votes for whom, many citizens vote "for the man" (or for the woman), not for the party. As a result of these different systems, a parliament tends to be made up of people loyal to the national party leadership who meet to debate and vote on party issues. A congress, on the other hand, tends to be made up of people who think of themselves as independent representatives of their districts or states and who, while willing to support their party on many matters, expect to vote as their (or their constitutents') beliefs and interests require.

Once they are in the legislature, members of a parliament discover that they can make only one important decision—whether or not to support the government. The government in a parliamentary system such as Britain's consists of a prime minister and various cabinet officers selected from the party that has the most seats in parliament. As long as the members of that party vote together, that government will remain in power (until the next election). Should members of a party in power in parliament decide to vote against their leaders, the leaders lose office and a new government must be formed. With so much at stake the leaders of a party in parliament have a powerful incentive to keep their followers in line. They insist that all members of the party vote together on almost all issues; if someone refuses, the penalty is often drastic: the party does not renominate the offending member in the next election.

Members of the United States Congress do not select the head of the executive branch of government—that is done by the voters when they choose a president. Far from making members of Congress less powerful, this makes them more powerful. Representatives and senators can vote on proposed laws without worrying that their votes will cause the government to collapse and without fearing that a failure to support their party will lead to their removal from the ballot in the next election. Congress has independent powers, defined by the Constitution, that it can exercise without regard to presidential preferences. Political parties do not control nominations for office, and thus they cannot discipline members of Congress who fail to support the party leadership. Because Congress is constitutionally independent of the president and because its members are not tightly disciplined by a party leadership, individual members of Congress are free to express their views and vote as they wish. They are also free to become involved in the most minute details of lawmaking, budget making, and supervision of the administration of laws. They do this through an elaborate and growing set of committees and subcommittees.

In short a parliament, such as that in Britain, is an assembly of party representatives who choose a government and who discuss major national issues. The principal daily work of a parliament is debate. A congress, such as that in the United States, is a meeting place of the representatives of local constituencies—districts and states. Members of the U.S. Congress can initiate, modify, approve, or reject laws, and they share with the president supervision of the ad-

The work of Congress takes place in committees. Here Gerald B. H. Solomon (R., N.Y.) and Joe Moakley (D., Mass.) confer at a meeting of the powerful House Rules Committee.

ministrative agencies of the government. The principal work of a congress is representation and action, most of which takes place in committee.

What this means in practical terms to the typical legislator is easy to see. Since members of the British House of Commons have little independent power, they get rather little in return. They are poorly paid, may have no offices of their own and virtually no staff, are allowed only small sums to buy stationery, and can make a few free local telephone calls. Each is given a desk, a filing cabinet, and a telephone, but not always in the same place.

A member of the United States House of Representatives, even the most junior one, has power and is rewarded accordingly. A representative earns a substantial salary ($129,500 a year as of 1992), receives generous retirement benefits, has at least a three-room suite of offices, is supplied with at least eighteen staff persons, can make thirty-three free trips to the home district each year, receives several thousand dollars for stationery and postage, and can mail newsletters and certain other documents to constituents free under the "franking privilege." Representatives with more seniority and senators receive even larger benefits—a senator from New York, for example, is allowed over $1 million a year to hire staff assistants. This example is not given to suggest that members of Congress are overrewarded but only that their importance, as individuals, in our political system can be inferred from the resources that they command.

The Evolution of Congress

The Framers chose to place legislative powers in the hands of a congress rather than a parliament for philosophical and practical reasons. They did not want to have all powers concentrated in a single governmental institution, even one that was popularly elected, because they feared that such a concentration could lead to rule by an oppressive or impassioned majority. At the same time they knew that the states were jealous of their independence and would never consent to a national constitution if it did not protect their interests and strike a reasonable balance between large and small states. Hence they created a **bicameral** (two-chamber) **legislature**—with a House of Representatives to be elected directly by the

The Powers of Congress

*T*he powers of Congress are found in Article I, section 8, of the Constitution.

- To lay and collect taxes, duties, imposts, and excises.
- To borrow money.
- To regulate commerce with foreign nations and among the states.
- To establish rules for naturalization (that is, becoming a citizen) and bankruptcy.
- To coin money, set its value, and punish counterfeiting.
- To fix the standard of weights and measures.
- To establish a post office and post roads.
- To issue patents and copyrights by inventors and authors.
- To create courts inferior to (that is, below) the Supreme Court.
- To define and punish piracies, felonies on the high seas, and crimes against the law of nations.
- To declare war.
- To raise and support an army and navy and make rules for their governance.
- To provide for a militia (reserving to the states the right to appoint militia officers and to train the militia under congressional rules).
- To exercise exclusive legislative powers over the seat of government (that is, the District of Columbia) and other places purchased to be federal facilities (forts, arsenals, dockyards, and "other needful buildings").
- To "make all laws which shall be necessary and proper for carrying into execution the foregoing powers, and all other powers vested by this Constitution in the government of the United States." (*Note:* This "necessary and proper," or "elastic" clause has been generously interpreted by the Supreme Court, as explained in Chapter 14.)

people and a Senate, consisting of two members from each state, to be chosen by the legislatures of each state. Though "all legislative powers" were to be vested in the Congress, those powers would be shared with a president (who could veto acts of Congress), limited to those explicitly conferred on the federal government, and, as it turned out, subject to the power of the Supreme Court to declare acts of Congress unconstitutional.

Although they designed these checks and balances to prevent legislative tyranny, the Framers nonetheless expected that Congress would be the dominant institution in the national government. And for at least a century and a half, it was, except for a few brief periods when activist presidents (such as Andrew Jackson, Abraham Lincoln, Theodore Roosevelt, and Woodrow Wilson) were able to challenge congressional supremacy. Until the twentieth century, and during some periods since, the major struggles for national political power have been *within* Congress over the rules and leadership of that body rather than between Congress and the president.

The struggles within Congress were generally over issues of great national significance—slavery, the admission of new states, the development of internal improvements, tariffs against foreign goods, and the regulation of business—but cutting across most of these substantive issues was a conflict over the distribution of power within the Congress itself. Two competing values were at stake: centralization versus decentralization. If Congress were to act quickly and decisively as a body, then there must be strong central leadership, restrictions on debate, few opportunities for stalling tactics, and minimal committee interference. If, on the other hand, the interests of individual members—and the constituencies that they represent—were to be protected or enhanced, then there must be weak leadership, rules allowing for delay and discussion, and many opportunities for committee activity.

Though there have been periods of strong central leadership in Congress, the general trend, especially in this century, has been toward decentralizing decision making and enhancing the power of the individual member at the expense of congressional leadership. This decentralization may not have been inevitable. Most American states have constitutional systems quite similar to the federal one, yet in many state legislatures, such as those in New York, Massachusetts, and Indiana, the leadership is quite powerful. In part the position of these strong state legislative leaders may be the result of the greater strength of political parties in some states than in the nation

as a whole. In large measure, however, it is a consequence of permitting state legislative leaders to decide who shall chair what committee and who shall receive what favors (see Chapter 24). Congress has left such matters to the workings of time (the seniority system), the decisions of large caucuses, or the rights of individual legislators.

The Period of the Founding

During the first three administrations—of George Washington, John Adams, and Thomas Jefferson—leadership in Congress was often supplied by the president or his cabinet officers. Alexander Hamilton, as secretary of the treasury, acted as Washington's leader in Congress, even though he was not a member of that body. Albert Gallatin, Jefferson's secretary of the treasury, performed essentially the same function, working through intermediaries.

Rather quickly, however, Congress began to assert its independence and to develop its own leadership. The House of Representatives was the preeminent institution, overshadowing the tiny Senate. It originated most legislation. Henry Clay, as Speaker of the House, was a powerful leader who appointed the members and chairmen of the committees and kept his party, the Democratic-Republicans, under reasonable control. The party caucus, dominated by Clay, was often influential in shaping policy questions before they were debated on the floor of the House. Indeed, during these early years, the caucus selected its party's candidate for president. For example, the Democratic-Republican caucus nominated Jefferson in 1804, James Madison in 1808 and again in 1812, and James Monroe in 1816. The caucus system of nomination enhanced the power of the House, for it meant that the president of the United States, though not elected by Congress, was nominated for that office by important members of Congress. This political fact of life helped make the presidents quite sensitive to congressional desires.

Decline of the House

In the late 1820s the preeminence of the House began to wane. Andrew Jackson asserted the power of the presidency by vetoing legislation that he did not like. The caucus system of nominations had fallen into

One of the most powerful Speakers of the House, Henry Clay, is shown here addressing the United States Senate around 1850.

disrepute and was replaced (as we saw in Chapter 7) with a system of national nominating conventions. Most important, the party unity necessary for a Speaker, or any other leader, to control the House was shattered by the issue of slavery. So divided were the parties over this question that the choice of a Speaker became a protracted struggle; one contest in 1856 took 133 ballots before the outcome was decided. A Speaker chosen under these circumstances could hardly wield much power.

During and after the Civil War the House reclaimed some of its lost stature, in part because the war eliminated the cleavage between the parties caused by the slavery issue. Most of the representatives from the proslavery states were absent—the South had seceded from the Union—and their seats remained vacant for several years after the end of the war. Opinion in the House was strongly antislavery and anti-South, and this view tended to unify the House. It was led by "Radical Republicans"—men from the North, such as Thaddeus Stevens of Pennsylvania, determined to punish the South for its secession—and their fierce ideology made them influential figures even when they did not always occupy formal positions of leadership. Perhaps the high-

water mark of their power came in 1868, when the House voted to impeach President Andrew Johnson, who was regarded as too "soft" on the South. (The Senate, by a margin of one vote, acquitted Johnson of the impeachment.)

The Importance of the Senate

During this period when the House had either weak leadership or leadership based on ideology rather than institutional power, the Senate was growing in stature. (The decision by Henry Clay in 1831 to move from the House to the Senate was symbolic of this shift.) One reason for the greater role of the Senate was the increasing importance of issues that the Senate was constitutionally required to deal with. Foreign affairs was one such issue: the Senate must approve all treaties.

Equally important, however, were various political circumstances that enhanced the Senate's role. One was the slavery issue in the years preceding the Civil War. The Senate had two senators from each state, and the admission of new states to the Union was carefully arranged to ensure that there would be equal numbers of senators from slave and free states.

Three powerful Speakers of the House: Thomas B. Reed (1889–1891, 1895–1899) (left), Joseph G. Cannon (1903–1911) (center), and Sam Rayburn (1941–1947, 1949–1953, 1955–1961) (right). Reed put an end to the filibuster in the House by refusing to allow dilatory motions and by counting as "present"—for purposes of a quorum—members in the House, even though they were not voting. Cannon further enlarged the Speaker's power by refusing to recognize members who wished to speak without Cannon's approval and increased the power of the Rules Committee, over which he presided. Cannon was stripped of much of his power in 1910. Rayburn's influence rested more on his ability to persuade than on his formal powers.

This meant that this great issue would be debated in a Senate where the two sides were equally matched. The Senate, unlike the House, had no rule limiting debate; hence slavery could be debated not only equally but at considerable length. As a result the great orators and statesmen of the time—Clay, Daniel Webster, John Calhoun—sought seats in the Senate.

Finally, senators were picked by state legislatures, not by the voters, and the Senate confirmed all major presidential appointments. This gave the Senate a crucial role in the development of local political parties. Often the most powerful party leaders in the various states became senators—men such as Roscoe Conkling, for example, an important party boss from New York. Many senators used their power to funnel jobs—political patronage—to their local party organizations.

Powerful as the Senate was, it was not tightly organized. Its individual members were too indepen-

dent, too securely based on their own local party organizations to tolerate strong central leadership. The small size of the Senate meant that relatively few rules were necessary to keep business moving in an orderly manner.

The Rise of Party Control in the House

During the period from 1889 to 1910, strong, partisan, central leadership emerged for the last time in the House of Representatives. This era was the high point of efforts to produce party government and a centrally controlled House. It began shortly after Thomas B. Reed of Maine was chosen by the Republicans to be Speaker. Reed used his power as Speaker and as leader of the Republican party caucus effectively. He selected all committee members and all committee chairmen, rewarding his supporters and punishing his opponents. He would not allow members to engage in dilatory tactics. He chaired the

Rules Committee, which decided what business would come up for a vote and what the limitations on debate should be. During his heyday an extraordinary amount of party unity was obtained—Republicans voted together as a block against the Democrats.

Not long after Reed resigned in 1899, another powerful man became Speaker, Joseph G. Cannon of Illinois. He sought to maintain the Reed tradition, but by now circumstances had changed. Whereas Reed had political views quite similar to those of most Republicans, Cannon was distinctly more conservative than many Republicans around the turn of the century. Moreover the desire of individual members to act independently was becoming more pronounced. Within a few years the revolt came.

The Shift to Committee Control

In 1910–1911 the House revolted against Cannon, voting to strip the Speaker of his right to appoint committee members or committee chairmen and to remove him from membership on the powerful Rules Committee. What power Cannon lost did not flow immediately into the hands of individual members, however. Three other sources of power emerged.

One was the party caucus. For a time the members of each political party in the House, meeting in their caucuses, would take positions on issues coming before the House and induce each member to support them. On occasion the leader of the caucus was an especially influential or respected figure, and the caucus was strong. But the caucus lacked any real sanctions, and soon its influence waned. Individual members increasingly discovered that they could defy it without penalty.

A second was the Rules Committee. Though the Speaker was no longer a member, the committee still decided what bills would come up for a vote, in what order, and under what restrictions on the length of debate and the right to offer amendments. From the time of Reed down to the present, the Rules Committee has used that power to boost certain bills and block others. A favored bill, for example, could be brought to the floor under a rule that said that debate would be limited to one hour, that no member could speak more than five minutes, and that no amendments could be offered without the support of the committee in charge of the bill. To those who favored these bills, it was an excellent device for ensuring that

action was taken; to the opponents of the bills, it was a "gag rule."

Third, the power of the chairmen of standing committees rose as the power of the Speaker fell. Until the 1970s these chairmen had substantial ability to decide what business the committees they chaired would take up, what bills would be sent out of the committees to the full House, and even what some of these bills would contain. In the days when these chairmen were chosen by the Speaker, they often used their power to follow his leadership or that of the party as a whole. But once the Speaker no longer appointed them, they acquired office strictly on the basis of seniority. The seniority principle, though later criticized, was at first seen as a reform. It meant that representatives could become committee chairmen automatically, subject neither to party control nor to leadership manipulation, simply by having served in Congress longer than anyone else of their party on the committee. When it later became apparent that the seniority system gave power to members of Congress whose political views were not shared by others on the same committees, the system was attacked.

The Decentralization of the House

In the early 1970s, the power of committee chairmen was reduced and that of individual members increased. Individual members obtained larger staffs and a voice in the selection of committee chairmen. Seniority was no longer sacrosanct: from time to time, a junior member became chairman of a committee. More subcommittees were created, thereby giving more members a chance to be chairman of something. Individual members, even the newest, became more assertive about introducing legislation.

All of these changes were made by the Democrats. When the Republicans assumed control after the 1994 elections, they retained many of these rules and added several of their own, many designed to insure more open debate. They also continued the policy of ignoring seniority in the selection of some committee chairmen. At the same time, however, the Republicans sought to enact a legislative program crafted under the direction of Speaker Newt Gingrich, thereby testing the idea that in the House power can be decentralized while policy leadership is centralized. Though the Speaker appears to have

THE WAY WE BECOME SENATOR NOWADAYS.

A cartoon from *Puck* in 1890 expressed popular resentment over the "Millionaires' Club," as the Senate had become known.

ten there was intense political maneuvering among the leaders of various factions, each struggling to win (and sometimes buy) the votes necessary to become senator. By the end of the nineteenth century, the Senate was known as the "Millionaires' Club," because of the number of wealthy party leaders and businessmen in it. There arose a demand for the direct, popular election of senators.

Naturally the Senate resisted, and without its approval the necessary constitutional amendment could not pass Congress. When some states threatened to demand a new constitutional convention, the Senate feared that such a convention would change more than just the way in which senators were chosen. A protracted struggle ensued, during which many state legislatures devised ways to ensure that the senators they picked would already have won a popular election. The Senate finally agreed to a constitutional amendment that required the popular election of its members, and in 1913 the Seventeenth Amendment was approved by the necessary three-fourths of the states. Ironically, given the intensity of the struggle over this question, no great change in the composition of the Senate resulted; most of those members who had first been chosen by state legislatures managed to win reelection by popular vote.

The other major issue in the development of the Senate was the filibuster. A **filibuster** is a prolonged speech, or series of speeches, made to delay action in a legislative assembly. It had become a common—and unpopular—feature of Senate life by the end of the nineteenth century. It was used by liberals and conservatives alike and for lofty as well as self-serving purposes. The first serious effort to restrict the filibuster came in 1917 after an important foreign-policy measure submitted by President Wilson had been talked to death by, as Wilson put it, "eleven willful men." Rule 22 was adopted by a Senate fearful of tying a president's hands during a wartime crisis. The rule provided that debate could be cut off if two-thirds of the senators present and voting agreed to a "cloture" motion (it has since been revised to allow sixty senators to cut off debate). Two years later it was first invoked successfully when the Senate voted cloture to end, after fifty-five days, the debate over the Treaty of Versailles. Despite the existence of Rule 22 the tradition of unlimited debate remains strong in the Senate.

gained some power in recent years, it remains the case that the House is a decentralized institution in which action occurs only after consensus is built among individual members.

The "Democratization" of the Senate

The Senate never created a position equivalent to that of the Speaker of the House, nor did it give to anyone else the power of a Reed or a Cannon. There was a Rules Committee, but not one that could control the Senate's business, which was always carried on under a tradition that allowed for unlimited debate. The major change in the Senate came not from a struggle over its internal control but from an attack on its membership. For more than a century after the Founding, members of the Senate were chosen by state legislatures. Though often these legislatures picked popular local figures to be senators, just as of-

Who Is in Congress?

With power so decentralized in Congress, the kind of person elected to it is especially important. Since each member exercises some influence, the beliefs and interests of each individual affect policy. Viewed simplistically, most members of Congress seem the same: the typical representative or senator is a middle-aged white Protestant male lawyer. If all such persons usually thought and voted alike, that would be an interesting fact, but they do not, and so it is necessary to explore the great diversity of views among seemingly similar people.

Sex and Race

Congress has gradually become less male and less white. Between 1950 and 1994, the number of women in the House increased from nine to forty-seven and the number of blacks from two to thirty-eight. There are also seventeen Hispanic members.

Until recently, the Senate had changed much more slowly (see Table 11.1). Before the 1992 election, there were no blacks and only two women in the Senate. But in 1992, four more women, including one black, Carol Mosely Braun of Illinois, were elected. Two more were elected in 1994. And a Native American, Ben Nighthorse Campbell of Colorado, became a senator.

The relatively small number of blacks and Hispanics in the House understates their influence, at least when the Democrats are in the majority. In 1994 four House committees were chaired by blacks and three by Hispanics. In the same year, however, no woman chaired a committee. The reason for the difference in power between minority and female representatives is that the former tend to come from safe districts and thus to have more seniority than the latter. Republican control of the House in 1995 reduced minority influence.

Incumbency

The most important change that has occurred in the composition of Congress, however, has been so gradual that most people have not noticed it. In the nineteenth century a large fraction—often a majority—

POLITICALLY P.S. SPEAKING

Filibuster

A filibuster is a technique by which a small number of senators attempts to defeat a measure by talking it to death—that is, by speaking continuously and at such length as to induce the supporters of the measure to drop it in order to get on with the Senate's business.

The right to filibuster is governed by the Senate's Rule 22, which allows for unlimited debate unless at least sixty senators agree to a motion to cut it off.

Originally *filibusterers* were sixteenth-century English and French pirates and buccaneers who raided Spanish treasure ships. The term came from a Dutch word, *vrijbuiter*, meaning "freebooter," which was converted into the English word *filibuster*.

The word came into use in America as a term for "continuous talking" in the mid–nineteenth century. One of its first appearances was in 1854, when a group of senators tried to talk to death the Kansas-Nebraska Act.

SOURCE: Adapted from William Safire, *Safire's Political Dictionary* (New York: Ballantine Books, 1978). Used by permission.

of congressmen served only one term. In 1869, for example, more than half the members of the House were serving their first term in Congress. Being a congressman in those days was not regarded as a career. This was in part because the federal government was not very important (most of the interesting political decisions were made by states); in part because travel to Washington, D.C., was difficult and the city

TABLE 11.1 Blacks and Women in Congress, 1951–1996

Congress	Senate		House	
	Blacks	Women	Blacks	Women
104th (1995–1996)	1	8	38	48
103d	1	6	38	47
102d	0	2	26	29
101st	0	2	24	25
100th	0	2	23	23
99th	0	2	20	22
98th	0	2	21	22
97th	0	2	17	19
96th	0	1	16	16
95th	1	2	16	18
94th	1	0	15	19
93d	1	0	15	14
92d	1	2	12	13
91st	1	1	9	10
90th	1	1	5	11
89th	0	2	6	10
88th	0	2	5	11
87th	0	2	4	17
86th	0	1	4	16
85th	0	1	4	15
84th	0	1	3	16
83d	0	3	2	12
82d (1951–1952)	0	1	2	10

SOURCE: *Congressional Quarterly Almanac,* various years.

The first Native American senator, Ben Nighthorse Campbell of Colorado.

was not a pleasant place in which to live; and in part because being a congressman did not pay well. Furthermore many congressional districts were highly competitive, with the two political parties fairly evenly balanced in each.

In this century the rate of turnover has declined, and Congress has become a full-time career for its members. From 1863 to 1969 the proportion of first-termers in the House fell from 58 percent to 8 percent, and then rose again to about 25 percent in 1992. In 1994 the typical representative had served in the House for just under five terms (see Figure 11.1).[1]

This low turnover has an important implication for our concept of democracy: most members of the

House face no serious electoral challenge. In almost every year since 1952 more than 90 percent of the incumbent representatives seeking reelection have been returned to office. In 1986 and 1988 they set a record—over 98 percent were reelected. Senators, on the other hand, face riskier elections: in this same period an average of only 75 percent of the incumbents were reelected.[2] Even in 1994, when Democrats lost control of Congress, about 90 percent of the House and Senate members running for reelection won. (Unfortunately for the Democrats, only 84 percent of them won compared to 100 percent of the Republicans.) Only in 1994 has there been a recent election in which incumbents did rather poorly, and that was the result of redistricting and the publicity given certain congressional scandals.

Furthermore the number of instances in which an incumbent representative faces a hotly contested election has been getting smaller. In 1948 most races where an incumbent representative was running were quite close—that is, the winner got less than 55 percent of the vote. By 1970, however, the winner in three-fourths of these contests got 60 percent or

FIGURE 11.1 Changing Percentage of First-Term Members in Congress

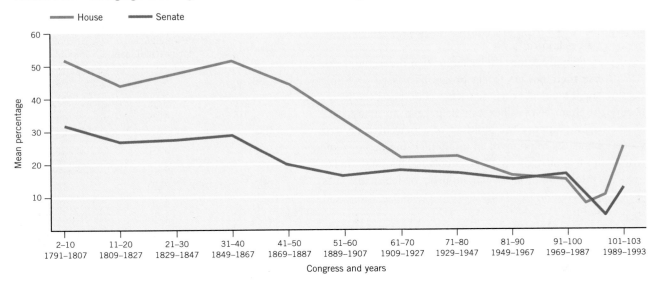

NOTES: 1989 freshman class in the House was the smallest in history. 1993 freshman class in the House was the largest since 1949.
SOURCES: Data for 90th through 103d Congresses are from *Congressional Quarterly Weekly Reports.* Data for 69th through 89th Congresses are adapted from Nelson W. Polsby, "The Institutionalization of the U.S. House of Representatives," *American Political Science Review* (March 1968), 146. Data for 1st through 68th Congresses are from Stuart A. Rice, *Quantitative Methods in Politics* (New York: Knopf, 1928), 296–297, as reported in Polsby, 146. Data for Senate are from N. J. Ornstein, T. J. Mann, and M. J. Malbin, *Vital Statistics on Congress, 1989–1990* (Washington, D.C.: CQ Press, 1990) pp. 56–57, 59–60.

more of the vote. Political scientists call districts that have close elections (in which the winner gets less than 55 percent) **marginal districts.** Of late, marginal districts have been much less common; House candidates who win tend to win by a large vote. Senators are a bit less secure: in fewer than half their races does the incumbent receive at least 60 percent of the vote.[3]

Why congressional seats should have become less marginal—that is, safer—is a matter on which scholars are not entirely in agreement. Some feel that it is the result of television and other ways of reaching the voters through the media. But challengers can go on television, too, so why should this benefit incumbents? Another possibility is that voters are becoming less and less likely to support whatever candidate wins the nomination of their own party. They are more likely, in short, to vote for the person rather than the party. And they are more likely to have heard of a person who is an incumbent: incumbents can deluge the voter with free mailings, travel frequently (and at public expense) to meet constituents, and get

FIGURE 11.2 Percentage of Incumbents Reelected to Congress

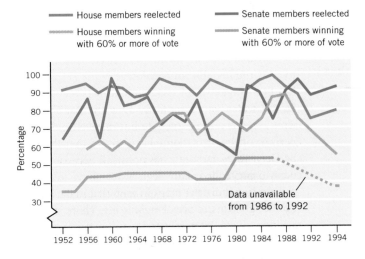

SOURCES: N. J. Ornstein, T. E. Mann, and M. J. Malbin, *Vital Statistics on Congress, 1989–1990* (Washington, D.C.: CQ Press 1990), 56–57, 59–60; *Congressional Quarterly Weekly Reports* (March 4, 1993).

their names in the newspaper by sponsoring bills or conducting investigations. Simply having a familiar name is important in getting elected, and incumbents find it easier than challengers to make their names known.

Finally, some scholars argue that incumbents can use their powers to get programs passed or funds spent to benefit their districts—and thereby to benefit themselves. They can help keep an army base open, support the building of a new highway (or block the building of an unpopular one), take credit for federal grants to local schools and hospitals, make certain that a particular industry or labor union is protected by tariffs against foreign competition, and so on.[4]

Probably all of these factors make some difference. Whatever the explanation, the tendency of voters to return incumbents to office means that in ordinary times no one should expect any dramatic changes in the composition of Congress.

Party

From 1933 to 1994 thirty-one congresses convened (a new Congress convenes every two years) and of these thirty-one, Democrats controlled both houses in twenty-five and at least one house in twenty-eight. Scholars differ in their explanations of why the Democrats have so thoroughly dominated Congress. Most of the research on the subject has focused on the reasons for Democratic control of the House.

As Table 11.2 shows, in every election from 1968 to 1992 the Republican percentage of the House vote has been higher than the Republican percentage of House seats. For example, in 1976 the Republicans won 42.1 percent of the vote but received only 32.9 percent of the seats. Some have argued that this gap between votes and seats has occurred because Democratic-controlled state legislatures have redrawn congressional district maps in ways that make it hard for Republicans to win House seats. There is some striking anecdotal evidence to support this conclusion. For example, following the 1990 census, the Democratic-controlled Texas legislature crafted a new congressional district map clearly designed to benefit Democrats. In 1992 Republicans won 48 percent of the House vote in Texas but received only 30 percent of the seats. Similarly, in 1984 Democrats in California won nine more congressional seats than did Re-

TABLE 11.2   Republican Vote-Seat Gap, 1968–1992

Year	Percentage of Popular Vote for Republican House Candidates	Percentage of House Seats Held by Republicans
1968	48.2%	44.1%
1970	44.5	41.4
1972	46.4	44.2
1974	40.5	33.1
1976	42.1	32.9
1978	44.7	36.3
1980	48.0	44.1
1982	43.3	38.2
1984	47.0	41.8
1986	44.6	40.7
1988	45.5	40.2
1990	45.0	38.4
1992	45.6	40.5

SOURCE: "House Republicans Scored A Quiet Victory in '92," *Congressional Quarterly* (April 17, 1993): 965, 966.

publicans even though the latter received about one hundred thousand more votes statewide. After 1990 California's congressional map was redrawn by a state court, and in 1992 Republican House candidates won 41 percent of the statewide vote and 42 percent of the seats.[5]

But partisan tinkering with district maps and other structural features of House elections is not a sufficient explanation of why Democrats have dominated the House. As one recent study concluded, "virtually all the political science evidence to date indicates that the electoral system has little or no partisan bias, and that the net gains nationally from redistricting for one party over another are very small."[6] To control the redistricting process, one party must control both houses of the legislature, the governor's office, and, where necessary, the state courts. These conditions simply do not exist in most states. And even if district lines were consistently drawn with scrupulous fairness, the Democrats would still win control of the House because they win more votes. As Figure 11.3 indicates, the Republican vote-seat gap is accounted for in part by the fact that Republicans tend to run best in high-turnout districts such as affluent white suburbs, while Democrats do especially well in low-turnout districts such as minority-dominated inner cities.

Congressional incumbents have come to enjoy certain built-in electoral advantages over challengers and the Democrats were in the majority as the advantages of incumbency grew. Studies suggest that the incumbency advantage was worth about two percentage points prior to the 1960s but has grown to seven to twelve points today.[7]

But as political scientist Gary C. Jacobson has observed, the historical Democratic dominance of the House cannot be explained simply by reference to incumbency advantages. Instead, Jacobson argues that "Democrats' continued dominance of the House (as well as of other lower offices) despite a string of Republican presidential victories is a consequence of electoral politics."[8] In comparison with the Republicans, the Democrats, he finds, generally have fielded better, more experienced congressional candidates, have more closely reflected district-level voters' policy preferences, and have been able to fashion winning, district-level coalitions from among national Democratic constituencies such as organized labor, civil rights activists, feminists, and environmentalists. This implies that more than mere changes in the structural features of House elections (incumbency advantages, partisan redistricting) would be necessary to close the GOP's vote-seat gap.

It is important to remember that from time to time major electoral convulsions do alter the membership of Congress. For example, in the election of

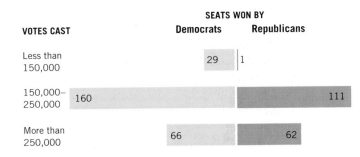

FIGURE 11.3 Results of 1992 House Election by Turnout

VOTES CAST	SEATS WON BY	
	Democrats	Republicans
Less than 150,000	29	1
150,000–250,000	160	111
More than 250,000	66	62

SOURCE: "House Republicans Scored a Quiet Victory in '92," *Congressional Quarterly* (April 17, 1993): 967.

1938 the Democrats lost seventy seats in the House; in 1942 they lost fifty; in 1950 they lost twenty-nine; and in 1966 they lost forty-eight. Despite these losses the Democrats retained a majority in the House elected in each of these years. In 1994, however, Republicans gained majorities in both the House and the Senate. Because members of Congress do not always vote along strict party lines, the size of that majority is important. The kinds of bills that get passed will be affected by how many conservative Democrats join with Republicans (the so-called **conservative coalition**). When the number of seats is rather evenly divided in Congress, one party may "control" Congress and still not be able to get all, or even most, of its legislative program approved.

The 110 new House members elected in 1992 made up the largest freshman class in decades.

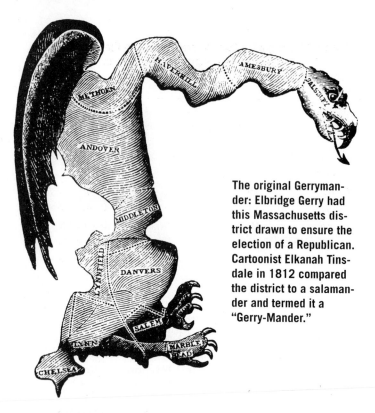

The original Gerrymander: Elbridge Gerry had this Massachusetts district drawn to ensure the election of a Republican. Cartoonist Elkanah Tinsdale in 1812 compared the district to a salamander and termed it a "Gerry-Mander."

Getting Elected to Congress

Who serves in Congress, and what interests are represented there, is affected by the mechanisms by which its members are elected. Each state is entitled to two senators who serve six-year terms and at least one representative who serves a two-year term. How many more representatives a state has depends on its population; what local groups these representatives speak for depends in part on how the district lines are drawn.

The Constitution says very little about how representatives will be selected except to require that they be inhabitants of the states from which they are chosen. It says nothing about districts and originally left it up to the states to decide who would be eligible to vote for representatives. The size of the first House was set by the Constitution at sixty-five members, and the apportionment of the seats among the states was spelled out in Article I, section 2. From that point on it has been up to Congress to decide how many representatives each state would have (provided that each had at least one).

Determining Fair Representation

Initially some states did not create congressional districts; all their representatives were elected at large. Others elected them from multimember as well as single-member districts. In time all states with more than one representative elected each from a single-member district. How those district boundaries were drawn, however, could profoundly affect the outcomes of elections. There were two problems. One was **malapportionment,** which results from having districts of very unequal sizes. If one district is twice as populous as another, twice as many votes are needed in the larger district to elect a representative. Thus a citizen's vote in the smaller district is worth twice as much as a vote in the larger.

The other problem was **gerrymandering,** which means drawing a district boundary in some bizarre or unusual shape to make it easy for the candidate of one party to win election in that district. In a state entitled to ten representatives, where half the voters are Democrats and half are Republicans, district lines could be drawn so that eight districts would have a slight majority of citizens from one party and two districts would have lopsided majorities from the other. Thus it can be made easy for one party to win eight of the ten seats.

Malapportionment and gerrymandering have been conspicuous features of American congressional politics. In 1962, for example, one district in Texas had nearly a million residents while another had less than a quarter-million. In California, Democrats in control of the state legislature drew district lines in the early 1960s so that two pockets of Republican strength in Los Angeles separated by many miles were connected by a thin strip of coastline. In this way most Republican voters were thrown into one district while Democratic voters were spread more evenly over several.

Hence there are four problems to solve in deciding who gets represented in the House:

1. establishing the total size of the House

2. allocating seats in the House among the states

3. determining the size of congressional districts within states

4. determining the shape of those districts

By and large Congress has decided the first two questions, and the states have decided the last two—but under some rather strict Supreme Court rules.

In 1911 Congress decided that the House had become large enough and voted to fix its size at 435 members. There it has remained ever since (except for a brief period when it had 437 members owing to the admission of Alaska and Hawaii to the union in 1959). Once the size was decided upon, it was necessary to find a formula for performing the painful task of apportioning seats among the states as they gained and lost population. The Constitution requires such reapportionment every ten years. A more or less automatic method was selected in 1929 based on a complex statistical system that has withstood decades of political and scientific testing. Under this system many states—such as New York, Ohio, Pennsylvania, and Illinois—lost representation in the House as other states grew more rapidly in population. The largest gainers have been California, Florida, and Texas (see Table 11.3). The average congressional district in 1990 had about 575,000 residents.

The states did little about malapportionment and gerrymandering until ordered to do so by the Supreme Court. In 1964 the Court ruled that the Constitution requires that districts be drawn so that, as nearly as possible, one person's vote would be worth as much as another's.[9] The Court rule, "one person, one vote," seems clear, but in fact leaves a host of questions unanswered. How much deviation from equal size is allowable? Should other factors be considered besides population? (For example, a state legislature might want to draw district lines to make it easier for blacks—or Italian-Americans or farmers or some other group with a distinct interest—to elect a representative; the requirement of exactly equal districts might make this impossible.) And the gerrymandering problem remains: districts of the same size can be drawn to favor one party or another. The courts have struggled to find answers to these questions, but they remain far from settled.

Majority-Minority Districts

Perhaps the most vexing legal questions concern **majority-minority districts**—congressional districts designed to make it easier for minority citizens to elect minority representatives. For many years

TABLE 11.3 Changes in State Representation in the House of Representatives after the 1990 Census

States	Number of Seats			Party Control of State, 1991
	Before Census	After Census	Change	
Gaining seats				
Arizona	5	6	+1	Split
California	45	52	+7	Split
Florida	19	23	+4	Democrats
Georgia	10	11	+1	Democrats
North Carolina	11	12	+1	Democrats
Texas	27	30	+3	Democrats
Virginia	10	11	+1	Democrats
Washington	8	9	+1	Split
Losing seats				
Illinois	22	20	−2	Split
Iowa	6	5	−1	Split
Kansas	5	4	−1	Split
Kentucky	7	6	−1	Democrats
Louisiana	8	7	−1	Democrats
Massachusetts	11	10	−1	Split
Michigan	18	16	−2	Split
Montana	2	1	−1	Split
New Jersey	14	13	−1	Democrats
New York	34	31	−3	Split
Ohio	21	19	−2	Split
Pennsylvania	23	21	−2	Split
West Virginia	4	3	−1	Democrat

NOTE: "Split" means that the same party does not control the governorship, House and Senate in that state.
SOURCE: U.S. Bureau of the Census.

geographically concentrated communities of blacks in the South and in many big cities throughout the country were carved up in ways that kept black politicians out of power. Even as recently as 1991, blacks constituted about 25 percent of the southern population but held barely 4 percent of the congressional seats in the South. In response, some southern states created majority-minority districts. For example, in 1991 the North Carolina General Assembly created two majority-black districts (shown on the

DISTRICTS 1 AND 12 IN NORTH CAROLINA

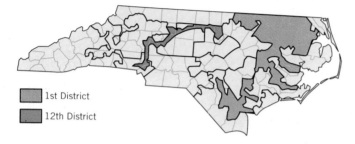

■ 1st District

■ 12th District

SOURCE: *Congressional Quarterly* (May 22, 1993): 1323.

map). One of these districts, the twelfth, was a 160-mile path no wider at some points than the interstate highway it traced.[10] The redistricting paid off. In 1992 Democratic Representatives Melvin Watt and Eva Clayton became the first blacks to represent North Carolina in Congress since 1901.[11] Similarly, New York City's X-shaped twelfth district snakes through a dozen different school districts and police precincts, and is only a block wide at one point. It was designed to pool Hispanic voters in Manhattan, the Queens, and Brooklyn.[12] In the 1992 Democratic primary in this district, a Hispanic challenger, Nydia M. Velasquez, defeated a Jewish incumbent, Stephen Solarz, and went on to win a House seat.

The constitutionality of majority-minority redistricting efforts has been called into question. In a 5-4 decision issued on June 28, 1993, in the case of *Shaw v. Reno,* the U.S. Supreme Court reinstated a suit by five white North Carolinians who maintained that the state's congressional map violated their Fourteenth Amendment right to "equal protection under the law."[13] The Court, however, did *not* invalidate North Carolina's map or rule in favor of the plaintiffs. Instead, it reversed the decision of a three-judge federal panel that had dismissed the complaint. In the Court's majority opinion, Justice Sandra Day O'Connor wrote that the plaintiffs were entitled to raise a question of constitutionality because the map "can be understood only as an effort to segregate voters into separate voting districts because of their race, and that the separation lacks sufficient justification." A "racial gerrymander," she noted, would be constitutionally permissible if a lower court determined that it was "narrowly tailored to further a compelling

governmental interest." But the Court did not specify the meaning of "compelling governmental interest."

In 1993 there were twenty Hispanic-majority districts and thirty-two black-majority districts nationwide. Many were represented by whites, and only some of them were created via the sort of redistricting that concerned the Court in *Shaw* v. *Reno.* But oddly configured majority-minority districts in Florida, Louisiana, and several other states could face constitutional challenges in the near future.[14]

Whatever the ultimate resolution of these constitutional issues, it is important to recognize that two conceptions of representation are at odds in the debate over majority-minority districts. The political theorist Hannah F. Pitkin has distinguished between **descriptive representation**—the statistical correspondence of the demographic characteristics of representatives with those of their constituents—and **substantive representation**—the correspondence between representatives' opinions and those of their constituents.[15]

To those who favor descriptive (also sometimes referred to as categorical) representation, majority-minority districts are desirable for their own sake, and creating them is a legitimate way of ensuring that citizens of a given racial or ethnic background are represented by persons of the same background. To those who favor substantive representation, however, the key question is whether representatives work to support the interests and opinions of the voters in their districts.

One challenging question is whether the substantive interests of minority voters will be represented by nonminority representatives in Congress. In a sophisticated analysis, political scientist Carol M. Swain has explored this question by studying the constituency relations and roll-call voting of black members of Congress from a variety of districts (historically black, newly black, heterogeneous, and primarily white), and of white members from districts with either a black majority or a significant black minority. Among other things, she found that liberal white members of Congress represented black interests as strongly as did black representatives (their voting records on key economic and other issues of import to the black community were virtually the same), and that "creating newly black districts will not significantly increase black substantive representation."[16]

Winning the Primary

Once the district lines are set, the other major procedural arrangement that affects the election of a candidate has to do with the system for getting one's name on the ballot. At one time the political parties nominated candidates and even printed ballots with the party slates listed on them. All the voter had to do was take the ballot of the preferred party and put it in the ballot box. Today, with rare exceptions, a candidate wins a party's nomination by gathering enough voter signatures to get on the ballot in a primary election, the outcome of which is often beyond the ability of political parties to influence. Candidates tend to form organizations of personal followings and win "their party's" nomination simply by getting more primary votes than the next candidate. It is quite unusual for an incumbent to lose a primary: from 1946 to 1988 only 6 percent of the incumbent senators and fewer than 2 percent of the incumbent representatives seeking reelection failed to win renomination in primaries. These statistics suggest how little opportunity parties have to control or punish their congressional members.

Nor are the voters much inclined to punish their members of Congress. We have already seen that typically over 90 percent of incumbent House members are reelected. Most newly elected members become strong in their districts very quickly; this is called the **sophomore surge.** It is the difference between the votes candidates get the first time they are elected (and thus become freshman members) and the votes they get when they run for reelection (in hopes of becoming sophomore members). Before the 1960s House candidates did not do much better the second time they ran than the first. Beginning then, however, the sophomore surge kicked in, so that today freshman candidates running for reelection will get 8 percent to 10 percent more votes than when they were first elected. Senate candidates also benefit now from a sophomore surge, though to a lesser degree.

The reason for this surge is that members of Congress have figured out how to use their offices to run *personal* rather than party campaigns. They make use of free ("franked") mail, frequent trips home, radio and television broadcasts, and the distribution of services to their districts to develop among their constituents a good opinion of *the members,* not their parties. They also cater to their constituents' distrust

TRIVIA
Congress

First woman in Congress	*Jeannette Rankin (Mont., 1916)*
First black in Congress	*Joseph H. Rainey (S.C., 1870)*
Longest session of Congress	*366 days (75th Congress, meeting from Jan. 3, 1940, to Jan. 3, 1941)*
Shortest length of time for states to ratify a constitutional amendment	*3 months, 7 days—26th Amendment*
Longest period of time to ratify an amendment	*203 years—27th Amendment*
Longest service in Congress by one member	*57 years, Carl Hayden of Arizona (15 years in House, 42 years in Senate), 1912–1969*
First member of the House to be elected president	*James Madison*
First member of the Senate to be elected president	*James Monroe*
The only woman to serve in the House at the same time as her son	*Frances Bolton, whose son was Oliver Bolton (served together 1953–1957, 1963–1965)*
Longest speech ever made in the Senate	*24 hours, 18 minutes, made on August 28–29, 1957, by Senator J. Strom Thurmond (D, S.C.), seeking to block a civil-rights bill*
First woman elected to the Senate for a full term who was not preceded in office by her husband	*Nancy Landon Kassebaum, elected in 1978 from Kansas*

Jeannette Rankin

Qualifications for Entering Congress and Privileges of Being in Congress

QUALIFICATIONS

Representative

- Must be twenty-five years of age (when seated, not when elected).
- Must have been a citizen of the United States for seven years.
- Must be an inhabitant of the state from which elected. (*Note:* custom, but *not* the Constitution, requires that a representative live in the district that he or she represents.)

Senator

- Must be thirty years of age (when, seated, not when elected).
- Must have been a citizen of the United States for nine years.
- Must be an inhabitant of the state from which elected.

JUDGING QUALIFICATIONS

Each house is the judge of the "elections, returns, and qualifications" of its members. Congress alone thus decides disputed congressional elections. On occasion it has excluded a person from taking a seat on grounds that the election was improper. Either house can punish a member—by reprimand, for example—or, by a two-thirds vote, expel a member.

PRIVILEGES

Members of Congress have certain privileges, the most important of which, conferred by the Constitution, is that "for any speech or debate in either house they shall not be questioned in any other place." This doctrine of "privileged speech" has been interpreted by the Supreme Court to mean that members of Congress cannot be sued or prosecuted for anything that they say or write in connection with their legislative duties.

When Senator Mike Gravel read the Pentagon Papers—some then-secret government documents about the Vietnam War—into the *Congressional Record* in defiance of a court order restraining their publication, the Court held that this was "privileged speech" and beyond challenge [*Gravel* v. *United States,* 408 U.S. 606 (1972)]. But when Senator William Proxmire issued a press release critical of a scientist doing research on monkeys, the Court decided that the scientist could sue him for libel because a press release was not part of the legislative process [*Hutchinson* v. *Proxmire,* 443, U.S. 111 (1979)

of the federal government by promising to "clean things up" if reelected. They run *for* Congress by running *against* it.[17]

To the extent that they succeed, they enjoy great freedom in voting on particular issues and have less need to explain away votes that their constituents might not like. If, however, any single-issue groups are actively working in their districts for or against abortion, gun control, nuclear energy, or tax cuts, muting the candidates' voting record may not be possible.

The way by which people get elected to Congress has two important effects. First, it produces legislators who are closely tied to local concerns (their districts, their states), and second, it ensures that party leaders will have relatively weak influence over them (because those leaders cannot determine who gets nominated for office).

The local orientation of legislators has some important effects on how policy is made. For example:

- Every member of Congress organizes his or her office to do as much as possible for people back home.

- If your representative serves on the House Public Works Committee, your state has a much better chance of getting a new bridge or canal than if you do not have a representative on this committee.[18]

- If your representative serves on the House Appropriations Committee, your district is more likely to get approval for a federal grant to improve your water and sewage-treatment programs than if your representative does not serve on that committee.[19]

Former House Speaker Thomas P. "Tip" O'Neill had this in mind when he said, "All politics is local politics." Some people think that this localism is wrong; in their view members of Congress should do what is best for "the nation as a whole." This argument is about the role of legislators: are they supposed to be *delegates* who do what their district wants or *trustees* who use their best judgment on issues without regard to the preferences of their district?

Naturally most members are some combination of delegate and trustee, with the exact mix depending on the nature of the issue. But some, as we shall see, definitely lean one way or the other. All members want to be reelected, but "delegates" tend to value this over every other consideration, and so seek out committee assignments and projects that will produce benefits for their districts. On the other hand "trustees" will seek out committee assignments that give them a chance to address large questions, such as foreign affairs, that may have no implications at all for their districts.

The Organization of Congress: Parties and Caucuses

Congress is not a single organization; it is a vast and complex collection of organizations by which the business of the legislative branch is carried on and through which its members form alliances. If we were to look inside the British House of Commons, we would find only one kind of organization of any importance—the political party. Though party organization is important in the United States Congress, it is only one of many important units. In fact other organizations have grown in number as the influence of party has declined.

The Democrats and Republicans in the House and the Senate are organized by party leaders. The key leaders in turn are elected by the full party membership within the House and Senate. The description that follows is confined to the essential positions.

Party Organization of the Senate

The majority party (in 1995, the Republicans) chooses one of its members—usually the person with the greatest seniority—to be president pro tempore of the Senate. It is largely an honorific position, required by the Constitution so that the Senate will have a presiding officer in the absence of the vice president of the United States, who is also, according to the Constitution, the president of the Senate. In fact presiding over the Senate is a tedious chore that neither the vice president nor the president pro tem relishes, and so the actual task of presiding is usually assigned to some junior senator.

The real leadership is in the hands of the **majority leader** (chosen by the senators of the majority party) and the **minority leader** (chosen by the senators of the other party). In addition the senators of each party elect a whip. The principal task of the majority leader is to schedule the business of the Senate,

usually in consultation with the minority leader. The majority leader has the right to be recognized first in any floor debate. A majority leader with a strong personality who is skilled at political bargaining may do much more. Lyndon Johnson, who was Senate majority leader for the Democrats during much of the 1950s, used his prodigious ability to serve the needs of fellow senators. He helped them with everything from obtaining extra office space to getting choice committee assignments, and in this way acquired substantial influence over the substance as well as the schedule of Senate business. Johnson's successor, Mike Mansfield, was a less assertive majority leader and had less influence.

The **whip** is a senator who helps the party leader stay informed about what party members are thinking, rounds up members when important votes are to be taken, and attempts to keep a nose count on how

POLITICALLY P.S. SPEAKING

Whip

A whip is a party leader who makes certain that party members are present for a vote and vote the way that the party wishes. In the British House of Commons, the whips produce strong party votes; in the U.S. Congress, whips are a lot less successful.

The word comes from *whipper-in,* a term from fox hunting denoting the person whose job it was to keep the hounds from straying off the trail. It became a political term in England in the eighteenth century, and from there came to the United States.

SOURCE: William Safire, *Safire's Political Dictionary* (New York: Ballantine Books, 1978). Used by permission.

```
DAVID E. BONIOR
    MICHIGAN
  MAJORITY WHIP

                    Congress of the United States
                         House of Representatives
                         Office of the Majority Whip
                         Washington, DC 20515-6503
  WHIP NOTICE INFORMATION                              APRIL 29, 1994

    Legislative Program - - 51600
    Floor Information - - 57400
    Whip Information - - 53130

    Dear Colleague:

         The program for the House of Representatives for Monday,
    May 2, 1994 is as follows:

  MONDAY, MAY 2

                       HOUSE MEETS AT NOON
                       NO LEGISLATIVE BUSINESS

  TUESDAY, MAY 3

                 HOUSE MEETS AT 10:30 A.M. FOR MORNING HOUR
                       HOUSE MEETS AT NOON
                            SUSPENSIONS
                             (2 BILLS)
               RECORDED VOTES ON SUSPENSIONS WILL BE POSTPONED
                   UNTIL THE END OF LEGISLATIVE BUSINESS

    1.  S.   2024    - -  Airport Improvement Program Temporary
                         Extension Act Of 1994
    2.  H.R. 3191    - -  National Flood Insurance Reauthorization

        H.R. 3254    - -  National Science Foundation
                         Authorization
                         (rule and general debate only)

  WEDNESDAY, MAY 4 AND THE BALANCE OF THE WEEK

                  HOUSE MEETS AT 2:00 P.M. ON WEDNESDAY
              HOUSE MEETS AT 11:00 A.M. ON THURSDAY AND FRIDAY

        H.R. 3254    - -  National Science Foundation
                         Authorization
                         (complete consideration)

        H.R. 2442    - -  Economic Development Reauthorization
                         Act of 1994
                         (subject to a rule)

        H.R. 4296    - -  Assault Weapons Ban Act
                         (subject to a rule)

        S.   636     - -  Access To Clinic Entrances Act
                         Conference Report

        H.Con.Res. 218 - -  Budget Resolution For FY 1995
                           Conference Report

         Conference reports may be brought up at any time.  Any further
    program will be announced later.

                                 Sincerely,

                                 David E. Bonior
                                 Majority Whip
```

This Whip Notice was issued by David Bonior (D., Mich.), majority whip of the 103d Congress, to inform party members and round up votes.

Daniel Patrick Moynihan (D., N.Y.) of the Senate Finance Committee.

the voting on a controversial issue is likely to go. The whip has several senators who assist him or her in this task.

Each party in the Senate also chooses a Policy Committee composed of a dozen or so senators who help the party leader schedule Senate business, choosing what bills are to be given major attention and in what order.

From the point of view of individual senators, however, the key party organization is the group that assigns senators to the standing committees of the Senate (listed on page 310). The Democrats have a Steering Committee that does this; the Republicans have a Committee on Committees. These assignments are especially important for newly elected senators: their political careers, their opportunities for favorable publicity, and their chances for helping their states and their supporters depend in great part on the committees to which they are assigned. For example, when Daniel Patrick Moynihan was elected to the Senate from New York in 1976, he waged an intensive and successful effort to get appointed to the Finance Committee. That body handles bills providing aid to cities and welfare recipients—two concerns of great importance to the big urban areas in Moynihan's state. When Lloyd Bentsen of Texas left the Senate to become the Clinton administration's secretary of the treasury, Moynihan succeeded him as chairman of the Finance Committee. During the 1960s many new senators fought to get on the Foreign Relations Committee because of the controversy

Party Leadership Structure

SENATE

President Pro Tempore Selected by majority party

Democrats

Majority Leader Leads the party

Majority Whip Assists the leader, rounds up votes, heads group of deputy whips

Chairman of the Conference Presides over meetings of all Senate Democrats

Policy Committee Schedules legislation

Steering Committee Assigns Democratic senators to committees

Democratic Senatorial Campaign Committee Provides funds, assistance to Democratic candidates for the Senate

Republicans

Minority Leader Leads the party

Assistant Minority Leader Assists the leader, rounds up votes

Chairman of the Conference Presides over meetings of all Senate Republicans

Policy Committee Makes recommendations on party policy

Committee on Committees Assigns Republican senators to committees

Republican Senatorial Committee Provides funds, advice to Republican candidates for the Senate

HOUSE

Speaker of the House Selected by majority party

Democrats

Majority Leader Leads the party

Majority Whip Assists the leader, rounds up votes, heads group of deputy and assistant whips

Chairman of the Caucus Presides over meetings of all House Democrats

Steering and Policy Committee Schedules legislation, assigns Democratic representatives to committees

Democratic Congressional Campaign Committee Provides funds, advice to Democratic candidates for the House

Republicans

Minority Leader Leads the party

Minority Whip Assists the leader, rounds up votes, heads large group of deputy and assistant whips

Chairman of the Conference Presides over meetings of all House Republicans

Committee on Committees Assigns Republican representatives to committees

Policy Committee Advises on party policy

National Republican Congressional Committee Provides funds, advice to Republican candidates for the House

Research Committee On request, provides information about issues

---

surrounding the war in Vietnam and the highly visible role of members of that committee in criticizing or defending American policy.

The key—and delicate—aspect of selecting party leaders, of making up the important party committees, and of assigning freshman senators to Senate committees is achieving ideological and regional balance. Liberals and conservatives in each party will fight over the choice of majority and minority leader, but factors in addition to ideology play

a part in the choice. These include personal popularity, the ability of the leader to make an effective television appearance, and who owes whom what favors.

Party Structure in the House

Though the titles of various posts are different, the party structure is essentially the same in the House as in the Senate. But leadership carries more power in the House than in the Senate because of the House rules. Being so large (435 members), the House must restrict debate and schedule its business with great care; thus leaders who do the scheduling and who determine how the rules shall be applied usually have substantial influence.

The Speaker is the most important person in the House. He is elected by whichever party has a majority and he presides over the meetings of that body. Unlike the president pro tem of the Senate, however, his position is anything but honorific. He is the principal leader of the majority party as well as the presiding officer of the entire House. Though Speakers-

as-presiders are expected to be fair, Speakers-as-party-leaders are expected to use their powers to help pass legislation favored by their party.

In helping his party, the Speaker has some important formal powers at his disposal: he decides who shall be recognized to speak on the floor of the House; rules whether a motion is relevant and germane to the business at hand; and decides (subject to certain rules) the committees to which new bills shall be assigned. He influences what bills are brought up for a vote and appoints the members of special and select committees (to be explained on page 309).

THE UNITED STATES CONGRESS

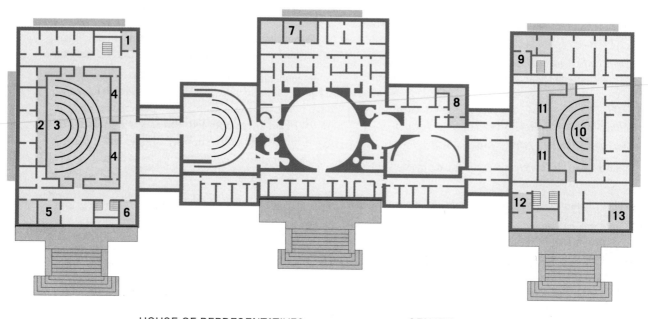

HOUSE OF REPRESENTATIVES

1. House Minority Whip
2. Lobby
3. House chamber
4. Cloakrooms
5. Speaker of the House
6. Ways and Means Committee
7. House Minority Leader

SENATE

8. Senate Minority Leader
9. Office of the Secretary
10. Senate chamber
11. Cloakrooms
12. Senate Majority Leader
13. Vice President

The House and Senate meet at opposite ends of the Capitol building. When there is a joint session of Congress—for example, to hear the president's State of the Union address—the senators sit with the representatives in the House chamber. Though the most important work of Congress goes on in committee meetings, which are held in office buildings behind the Capitol, some important political negotiations occur in the offices surrounding the chambers—especially in the cloakrooms (actually, lounges), the offices of the majority and minority leaders, of the Speaker and the vice president, and of the secretary of the Senate.

Since 1975 the Speaker has been able to nominate the majority-party members of the Rules Committee. He also has some informal powers: he controls some patronage jobs in the Capitol building and the assignment of extra office space. Even though far less powerful than in the days of Clay, Reed, and Cannon, the Speaker is still an important person to have on one's side. Sam Rayburn of Texas exercised great influence as Speaker, and Tip O'Neill, Jim Wright, Tom Foley, and Newt Gingrich have tried to do the same.

In the House, as in the Senate, the majority party elects a floor leader, called the majority leader. The other party also chooses a leader—the minority leader. Traditionally the majority leader becomes Speaker when the person in that position dies or retires—provided, of course, that the departing Speaker's party is still in the majority. Each party also has a whip, with several assistant whips in charge of rounding up votes from various state delegations. Committee assignments are made and the scheduling of legislation is discussed, by the Democrats, in a Steering and Policy Committee, chaired by the Speaker. The Republicans have divided committee assignments and policy discussions, with the former task assigned to a Committee on Committees and the latter to a Policy Committee. Each party also has a congressional campaign committee to provide funds and other assistance to party members running for election or reelection to the House.

The Strength of Party Structures

One important measure of the strength of party in Congress is the ability of party leaders to get their members to vote together on the rules and structure of Congress. When Newt Gingrich became Speaker of the Republican-controlled House in 1995, he proposed sweeping changes in House rules, many not popular with some Republican members. For example, he wanted no one to serve as a committee chairman for more than six years, for three committees to be abolished, and for other committees to lose either functions or members. He also wanted to pass over some senior members in picking committee chairmen. Though these moves adversely affected some Republican representatives, they all voted in favor of the new rules.[20] Of course, Gingrich would have not made these proposals unless he was certain he could get them adopted. But it was a measure of his influence and of his support among newly elected

Newt Gingrich (R., Ga.) is not only Speaker of the House but head of his party in that chamber. Dick Gephardt (D., Missouri) is the minority leader.

FIGURE 11.4   Party Voting in the House of Representatives, 1897–1991

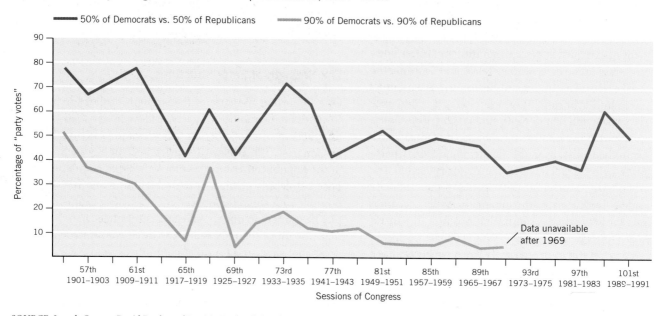

SOURCE: Joseph Cooper, David Brady, and Patricia Hurley, "The Electoral Basis of Party Voting: Patterns and Trends in the U.S. House of Representatives, 1887–1969," in *The Impact of the Electoral Process,* ed. Louis Maisel and Joseph Cooper (Beverly Hills, Calif.: Sage Publications, 1977), 139.

Republicans that even major changes in congressional procedures would get unanimous party support.[21] Getting support on proposed legislation is another, more difficult, matter.

The Senate, however, is another matter. As Barbara Sinclair has argued, in the last few decades the Senate has been transformed by changes in norms (informal understandings governing how members ought to behave toward their colleagues) without any far-reaching changes in the written Senate rules.[22] Compared to the Senate of the 1950s and 1960s, today's Senate is less party-centered, less leader-oriented, more hospitable to freshmen (who no longer have to "pay their dues" before assuming major roles as legislators), more heavily staffed, and more subcommittee-oriented.

Party Voting

The strength of the Congress's elaborate party machinery can also be crudely measured by the extent to which members of a party vote together in the House and Senate. A **party vote** can be defined in various ways; naturally the more stringent the definition, the less party voting we will observe. Figure 11.4 shows two measures of party voting in the House of Representatives during this century. By the strictest measure a party vote occurs when 90 percent or more of the Democrats vote together against 90 percent or more of the Republicans. A looser measure counts as a party vote in any case where at least 50 percent of the Democrats vote together against at least 50 percent of the Republicans. As is plain by either measure, the extent of party voting has fluctuated and is lower now than it was at the turn of the century. Nevertheless, there is some evidence of a trend toward greater party voting since the 1960s. In fact, since 1972 there has been a slow but steady increase in party voting, never dropping below 70 percent for either party since 1982, and reaching above 75 percent for the Republicans and 80 percent for the Democrats in recent years.

Specific issues tend to trigger an extraordinary degree of party voting. For example, in 1993 every single Republican in both the House and the Senate voted against the Clinton budget plan, the first budget plan offered by the first Democratic president since Jimmy Carter left office in 1980. This may be an extreme example, but it reflects the increasingly adversarial relationship between Democrats and Republicans, especially in the House.

Given the fact that political parties as organizations do not tightly control a legislator's ability to get elected, what is surprising is not that party votes are relatively rare, but that they occur at all. Why do congressional members of one party ever vote together against a majority of the other party? There are several reasons. First, members of Congress do not randomly decide to be Democrats or Republicans; these choices reflect some broad policy agreements, at least for most members. Democrats vote alike in part because they are ideologically alike.

Several interest groups tabulate the votes of legislators on important issues to see who is most and least favorable to their positions. By combining the scores given by many such organizations—including Americans for Democratic Action (liberal), Americans for Constitutional Action (conservative), the AFL-CIO, and the Chamber of Commerce—it is possible to rank each member of Congress from most to least liberal in three policy areas—economic affairs (taxes, job programs, and so forth), social questions (abortion, civil rights, school prayer), and foreign affairs (defense spending, support for military intervention). Democrats in the House and Senate have been much more liberal than Republicans in most recent years. So pronounced are the ideological differences between the parties that, even allowing for the existence of conservative southern Democrats, the average southern Democrat in the House is more liberal than the average northern Republican.

In addition to their personal views, members of Congress have other reasons for supporting their party's position at least some of the time. On many matters that come to a vote, members have little information and no opinion. They have no chance of becoming personally familiar with more than a small fraction of the hundreds of items with which Congress deals each session. They must get advice on how to vote, and it is only natural that Democrats look to Democratic leaders and fellow partisans for that advice, and Republicans look to Republicans.

Furthermore supporting the party position can work to the long-term advantage of a member inter-

"...AND FIGURES JUST IN SHOW 4 OUT OF 5 PEOPLE ARE FED UP WITH THE ELECTION!"

ested in rising in status and influence in Congress. As a number of recent studies have shown, though party leaders are weaker today than in the past, they are hardly powerless.[23] If you are a member of Congress who wants to get a committee assignment, obtain a favorable hearing for a bill, become chairman of an important subcommittee, or be taken seriously by other members in the party caucus, it pays not to insult, ignore, or challenge party leaders. Sam Rayburn, who served as Speaker for seventeen years (in the 1940s and 1950s), reputedly told freshman members of Congress that "if you want to get along, go along." That is less true today, but still good advice.

In short party *does* make a difference in Congress—not as much as it once did, and not nearly as much as it does in a parliamentary system, but party affiliation is still the most important thing to know about a member of Congress. Knowing whether a member is a Democrat or a Republican will not tell you everything about the member, but it will tell you more than any other single fact.

Caucuses

Congressional caucuses are a growing rival to the parties as a source of policy leadership. A **caucus** is an association of members of Congress created to advocate a political ideology or a regional or economic interest. In 1959 there were only four such caucuses; by the late 1980s there were over one hundred. The more important ones are these:

Caucus

A caucus is a closed meeting of the members of a political party, either to select a candidate for office or to agree on a legislative position.

The term is from an American Indian word meaning "elder" or "counselor." It quickly entered political usage in the United States, there being a Caucus Club in Boston as early as 1763.

The first national political caucuses were in Congress, where legislators would gather to select their party's candidate for president. Persons who did not get a caucus endorsement soon began denouncing the entire procedure, referring contemptuously to the "decrees of King Caucus." Popular resentment led in the 1830s to the creation of the nominating convention as a way of choosing presidential candidates.

Today congressional caucuses are organizations of legislators from a single party (Democrats or Republicans), with a common background (for example, women, blacks, Hispanics), sharing a particular ideology (liberals or conservatives), or having an interest in a single issue (such as mushrooms, steel mills, or the environment).

SOURCE: Adapted from William Safire, *Safire's Political Dictionary* (New York: Ballantine Books, 1978). Used by permission.

Democratic Study Group (DSG)   Organized in 1959 to facilitate communication and encourage unity among liberal Democrats, it chose the label Study Group to avoid offending nonliberal representatives. Though not an official party entity, it collects dues from its members, raises funds through mailings and banquets, employs a large staff, and publishes weekly reports and other materials on pending legislation. The DSG does not take a stand on specific bills, in part to avoid alienating members who might oppose that position and in part because on some questions there is no clearly "liberal" position. (It has been deeply split, for example, on gun control.)

Conservative Democratic Forum   Sometimes known as the Boll Weevils because most are from the South, these Democrats were a key part of the conservative coalition supporting presidents Reagan and Bush.

Wednesday Group   An organization of moderately conservative House Republicans, this group meets every Wednesday to discuss legislation.

State Delegations   Members from certain large states (California, New York, and Texas, among others) meet together on matters of common interest. Some such delegations vote together on many issues owing to the power of the local party organization. The Democratic representatives from Illinois, for example, are apt to vote together, especially the members from Cook County (Chicago). The powerful Democratic party organization in Cook County, once led by Richard J. Daley, usually decisively influences who gets nominated for national office.

Specialized Caucuses   Countless groups exist to advance racial, ethnic, regional, and policy interests. There is a Steel Caucus, a Mushroom Caucus, the Roller-and-Ball-Bearing Coalition, the Northeast-Midwest Economic Advancement Coalition, the Environmental Policy Committee, the Shipyard Coalition, and caucuses for women members, Spanish-speaking members, and blacks.

The Congressional Black Caucus (CBC) is one of the best known of the specialized caucuses. The CBC is typical of many in the way it functions. Some members are very active, others only marginally so. On certain issues it simply registers an opinion; on other issues it attempts to negotiate with leaders of other blocs so that votes can be traded in an advantageous way. It keeps members informed and often presses to have one of its members fill a vacancy on a regular congressional committee that has no blacks on it. The CBC was formed in 1971 by nine black members of the House. By 1993 the CBC had thirty-

Members of the Congressional Black Caucus. Speaking is Kweisi Mfume (D., Maryland).

eight members, nearly half of them newly elected. As the number of black members of Congress has grown, so has the strength of the CBC and its membership. For example, in 1990 one-quarter of all standing committees in the House were chaired by blacks. The CBC has established its own foundation, research group, and political action committee. By 1994, however, a problem loomed for the CBC: Two black Republicans, Gary Frank of Connecticut and J. C. Watt of Oklahoma, had been elected to the House. Both were more conservative than the other CBC members.

Some two dozen of the larger caucuses had staff paid for by Congress. When the Republicans took control of the House in 1995, they adopted a rule denying public funds to the caucuses. Now they must either give up their staffs or raise money from outside sources.

The Organization of Congress: Committees

The most important organizational feature of Congress is the set of legislative committees of the House and Senate. There the real work of Congress is done; in the chairmanship of these committees, and their subcommittees, most of the power in Congress is found. The number and jurisdiction of these committees are of the greatest interest to members of Congress, since decisions on these subjects determine what group of members, with what political views, will pass on legislative proposals, oversee the workings of agencies in the executive branch, and conduct investigations.

In a typical Congress the House and the Senate will each have two dozen committees and well over one hundred subcommittees. Periodically efforts have been made to cut the number of committees in order to give each a broader jurisdiction and reduce conflict between committees over a single bill. One such effort was the Legislative Reorganization Act of 1946. But as the number of committees declined, the number of subcommittees rose, leaving matters about as they once were.

There are three kinds of committees: **standing committees** (more or less permanent, continuing bodies with specified legislative responsibilities), **select committees** (groups appointed for a limited purpose, most of which last for only a few congresses), and **joint committees** (those on which both representatives and senators serve). An especially important kind of joint committee is the **conference committee** made up of representatives and senators appointed to resolve differences in the Senate and House versions of the same piece of legislation before final passage.

Standing Committees in 1995

SENATE

Major committees No senator is supposed to serve on more than two.*

Agriculture, Nutrition, and Forestry
Appropriations
Armed Services
Banking, Housing, and Urban Affairs
Budget
Commerce, Science, and Transportation
Energy and Natural Resources
Environment and Public Works
Finance
Foreign Relations
Governmental Affairs
Judiciary
Labor and Human Resources

Minor committees No senator is supposed to serve on more than one.*

Indian Affairs
Rules and Administration
Small Business
Veterans' Affairs

Select committees

Aging
Ethics
Intelligence

* Despite the rules, some senators in fact serve on more than two major committees.

HOUSE

Exclusive committees Member may not serve on any other committee, except Budget.

Appropriations
Rules
Ways and Means

Major committees Member may serve on only one major committee.

Agriculture
Banking and Financial Services
Commerce
Economic Opportunity
International Relations
Judiciary
National Security
Transportation and Infrastructure

Nonmajor committees Member may serve on one major and one nonmajor or two nonmajor committees.

Budget
Government Reform and Oversight
House Oversight
Public Lands and Resources
Technology and Competitiveness
Small Business
Standards of Official Conduct
Veterans' Affairs

Select committee
Intelligence

NOTE: Following the 1994 elections, the new Republican majority in the House reorganized the committee system, abolishing three committees and renaming and reorganizing several others. The three committees that were abolished in 1995 were the District of Columbia, Post Office and Civil Service, and Merchant Marine and Fisheries. The duties of the first two were transferred to the Government Reform and Oversight Committee; those of the third were distributed among the committees on National Security, Transportation and Infrastructure, and Public Lands and Resources.

Though members of the majority party could, in theory, occupy all seats on all committees, in practice they take the majority of the seats, name the chairman, and allow the minority party to have the remainder of the seats. The number of seats varies with the committee, from about six to over fifty. Usually the ratio of Democrats to Republicans on a committee roughly corresponds to their ratio in that house of Congress. In 1981 the Democrats held 56 percent of the House seats but tried to keep a two-to-one majority on key committees. After the Republicans complained, a compromise still left the Democrats overrepresented (with 66 percent of the seats on Ways and Means, 60 percent on Appropriations and Budget). A similar quarrel occurred in 1985.

Standing committees are the important ones because, with a few exceptions, they are the only ones that can propose legislation by reporting a bill out to the full House or Senate. Each member of the House usually serves on two standing committees, unless he or she is on an "exclusive" committee—Appropriations, Rules, or Ways and Means. In such a case the representative is limited to one. Each senator may serve on two "major" committees and one "minor" committee. (Major and minor Senate committees are indicated on page 310.)

When party leaders were strong, as under Speakers Reed and Cannon, committee chairmen were picked on the basis of loyalty to the leader. Now that this leadership has been weakened, seniority on the committee governs the selection of chairmen. Of late, however, even seniority has been under attack. In 1971 House Democrats decided in their caucus to elect committee chairmen by secret ballot. From then through 1991 they used that procedure to remove six committee chairmen. In 1975 three were deposed, in 1985 another, and in 1992 two more. When the Republicans took control of the House in 1995, they could have returned to the strict seniority rule, but they did not. House Speaker Gingrich passed over three senior representatives in favor of more junior ones as committee chairmen. Though most chairmen still get and hold their posts through seniority, these changes have made all chairmen worry about pleasing their rank-and-file members and the party leaders.

Traditionally the committees of Congress were dominated by the chairmen. They often did their

How Should Committee Chairmen Be Picked?

*T*here are essentially three methods by which committee chairmen could be selected in a legislature such as Congress. Each has its advantages and disadvantages.

Seniority Let the person with the most seniority on that committee chair the committee.

Advantages:

- Eliminates fights over selection.
- Makes it easier for legislators with unpopular views and for blacks and minorities to become chairmen.

Disadvantages:

- May result in incompetent people's chairing committees.
- Chairmen will be independent of party leadership.

Election by caucus Let the party members in the legislature elect committee chairmen.

Advantages:

- Chairmen will reflect views of party members.
- Autocratic chairmen can be replaced.

Disadvantages:

- Encourages bruising fights for chairmanships that can divide party.
- Committee chairmen not loyal to party leaders.

Appointment by party leaders Let party leaders (Speaker, majority leader, or minority leader) choose chairmen.

Advantages:

- Increases party discipline and accountability.
- Makes it easier for party program to be enacted.

Disadvantages:

- Makes party leaders very powerful.
- Can deny chairmanships to people out of favor with leaders.

most important work behind closed doors (though their hearings and reports were almost always published in full). In the early 1970s Congress further decentralized and democratized its operations by a series of changes that some members regarded as a "bill of rights" for representatives and senators, especially those with relatively little seniority. These changes were by and large made by the Democratic Caucus, but since the Democrats were in the majority, the changes, in effect, became the rules of Congress. The more important were as follows.

House

- Committee chairmen to be elected by secret ballot in party caucus.

- No member to chair more than one committee.

- All committees with more than twenty members to have at least four subcommittees (at the time, Ways and Means had no subcommittees).

- Committee and personal staffs to be increased in size.

- Committee meetings to be public unless members vote to close them.

Senate

- Committee meetings to be public unless members vote to close them.

- Committee chairmen to be selected by secret ballot at request of one-fifth of the party caucus.

- Committees to have larger staffs.

- No senator to chair more than one committee.

The effect of these changes, especially in the House, was to give greater power to individual members and to lessen the power of party leaders and committee chairmen. The decentralization of the House meant that it was much harder for chairmen to block legislation they did not like or to discourage junior members from playing a large role. House members were quick to take advantage of these enlarged opportunities. In the 1980s they proposed three times as many amendments to bills as they had in the 1950s.[24]

There was a cost to be paid for this membership empowerment, however. The 435 members of the House could not get much done if everyone talked as much as they liked and introduced as many amendments as they wished. And with the big increase in the number of subcommittees, many subcommittee meetings were attended by (and thus controlled by) only one person, the chairman. To deal with this, the Democratic leaders began reclaiming some of their lost power. They made greater use of restrictive rules that sharply limited debate and the introduction of amendments. Committee chairmen began casting proxy votes. (A *proxy* is a written authorization to cast another person's vote.) In this way a chairman could control the results of committee deliberations by casting the proxies of absent members.

Republican House members were angered by all of this. They suspected that restrictive rules and proxy voting were designed to keep them from having any voice in House affairs. When they took control of the House in 1995, they announced some changes:

- Proxy voting was banned.

- Committee chairmen were limited to six-year terms

- Floor debate would occur more often under open rules.

The endless arguments about rules illustrate a fundamental problem that the House faces. Closed rules, proxy voting, powerful committee chairmen, and strong Speakers make it easier for business to get done, put the House in a good bargaining position with the president and the Senate, and make it easier to reduce the number of special-interest groups with legislative power. But this system also keeps individual members weak. The opposite arrangements—open rules, weak chairmen, many subcommittees, meetings open to the public—help individual members be heard and increase the amount of sunshine shining on congressional processes. But if everyone is heard, no one is heard, because the noise is deafening and the speeches endless. And though open meetings and easy amending processes may be intended to open up the system to "the people," the real beneficiaries are the lobbyists.

Though committees are today shaped more by their members than by their chairmen, each still has a distinctive style. Richard F. Fenno found subtle but important differences among House and Senate committees. Some, such as the House Appropriations and Ways and Means committees and the Senate Foreign Relations and Human Relations committees, were attractive to members who wanted to influence public policy, who liked to become experts on important issues, and who valued having influence with their colleagues in Congress. Others, such as the House Merchant Marine and Fisheries Committee, the House Post Office and Civil Service Committee, and their Senate counterparts, were attractive to members who valued an opportunity to serve constituency groups and who worried more about solidifying their reelection prospects than about having influence with their congressional colleagues. Work on the first kind of committee—the Congress-oriented, policy-oriented type—does in fact give members more prestige and influence in Congress than work on the second kind, those that focus on external constituency concerns. The committee to which he or she is assigned thus importantly determines what sort of role a representative or senator will play.[25]

The Organization of Congress: Staffs and Specialized Offices

In 1900 representatives had no personal staff, and senators averaged fewer than one staff member each. As recently as 1935 the typical representative had but two aides. In 1994 the average representative had seventeen assistants and the average senator had forty. To the more than ten thousand individuals who served on the personal staffs of members of the 103d Congress must be added three thousand more who worked for congressional committees and yet another three thousand employed by various congressional research agencies. Congress has the most rapidly growing bureaucracy in Washington—the personal staffs of legislators increased more than five-fold from 1947 to 1989[26] (see Figure 11.5). Though some staffers perform routine chores, many help draft legislation, handle constituents, and otherwise shape policy and politics.

Everybody Wants to Get into the Act . . .

*T*he more complex the issues with which the government tries to cope, the greater the number of congressional committees that want to have a voice in the outcome.

In simpler times each bill went to only one committee; now, many claim jurisdiction. Twelve House committees have an interest in environmental legislation. Suppose you want to change the laws governing water pollution. You should be prepared to answer questions from these committees:

Agriculture
Appropriations
Energy and Commerce
Government Operations
Interior and Insular Affairs
Merchant Marine and Fisheries
Public Works and Transportation
Science, Space, and Technology
Small Business
Ways and Means

If you are the "drug czar"—that is, the director of the Office of National Drug Control Policy—you are in theory answerable to fifty-four committees and subcommittees in the House and twenty-one in the Senate. You may spend more time talking to Congress than fighting drugs.

SOURCES: *Washington Post* (May 12, 1989): A21; Roger H. Davidson and Walter J. Oleszek, *Congress and Its Members*, 3d ed. (Washington, D.C.: Congressional Quarterly Press, 1990), 212.

Tasks of Staff Members

Staff members assigned to a senator or representative spend most of their time servicing requests from constituents—answering mail, handling problems, sending out newsletters, and meeting with voters. In short a major function of a member of Congress's staff is to help constituents solve problems and thereby help that member get reelected. Indeed over the last two decades, a larger and larger portion of congressional staffs—now about one-third—work in the local (district or state) office of the member of Congress, rather than in Washington. Almost all members of Congress have such offices on a full-time basis; about half maintain two or more offices in their constituencies. Some scholars believe that this growth in constituency-serving staff helps explain why it is so hard to defeat an incumbent representative or senator.[27]

The legislative function of congressional staff members is also important. With each senator serving on an average of more than two committees and seven subcommittees and each representative serving on an average of six committees and subcommittees,

it is virtually impossible for members of Congress to become familiar in detail with all the proposals that come before them or to write all the bills that they feel ought to be introduced.[28] As the work load of Congress has grown (over six thousand bills are introduced, about six hundred public laws are passed, and uncounted hearings and meetings are held during a typical Congress), the role of staff members in devising proposals, negotiating agreements, organizing hearings, writing questions for members of Congress to ask of witnesses, drafting reports, and meeting with lobbyists and administrators has grown correspondingly.

Those who work for individual members of Congress, as opposed to committees, see themselves entirely as advocates for their bosses. As the mass media have supplanted political parties as ways of communicating with voters, the advocacy role of staff members had led them to find and promote legislation for which a representative or senator can take credit. This is the entrepreneurial function of the staff. While it is sometimes performed under the close supervision of the member of Congress, just as often a staff member takes the initiative, finds a policy, and then "sells" it to his or her employer. Lobbyists and reporters understand this completely and therefore spend a lot of time cultivating congressional staffers, both as sources of information and as consumers of ideas.

One reason for the rapid growth in the size and importance of congressional staffs is that a large staff creates conditions that seem to require an even larger staff. As the staff grows in size, it generates more legislative work. Subcommittees proliferate to handle all the issues with which legislators are concerned. But as the work load increases, legislators complain that they cannot keep up and need more help.

The increased reliance on staff has changed Congress, not because staffers do things against the wishes of their elected masters, but because the staff has altered the environment within which Congress does its work. In addition to their role as entrepreneurs promoting new policies, staffers act as negotiators. As a result members of Congress today are more likely to deal with one another through staff intermediaries rather than personally. Congress has thereby become less collegial, more individualistic, and less of a deliberative body.[29]

FIGURE 11.5   The Growth in Staff of Members and Committees in Congress, 1891–1989

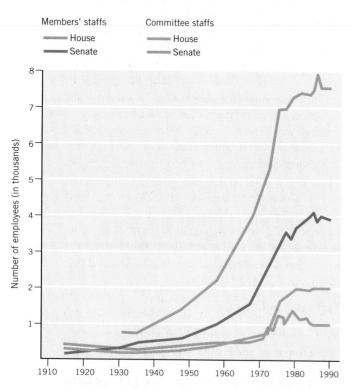

SOURCES: Ornstein et al., *Vital Statistics on Congress* (Washington, D.C.: American Enterprise Institute, 1984) from David C. Kozak and John D. Macartney, eds., *Congress and Public Policy*, 2d ed. (Chicago: Dorsey Press, 1987), 95; *Statistical Abstract of the United States* (1992): 264.

Staff Agencies

In addition to increasing the number of staff members, Congress has also created a set of staff agencies that work for Congress as a whole. These staff agencies have come into being in large part to give Congress specialized knowledge equivalent to what the president has by virtue of his position as chief of the executive branch.

Congressional Research Service (CRS)   Formerly the Legislative Reference Service, the CRS is part of the Library of Congress. Since 1914 it has responded to congressional requests for information and now employs nearly nine hundred people, many with advanced academic training, to respond to more than a quarter of a million questions each year. As a politically neutral body, it does not recommend policy, but it will look up facts and indicate the arguments for and against a proposed policy. CRS also keeps track of the status of every major bill before Congress and produces a summary of each bill introduced. This information is instantly available to legislators via computer terminals located in almost all Senate and most House offices.

General Accounting Office (GAO)   Created in 1921, this agency once performed primarily routine financial audits of the money spent by executive-branch departments. Today it also investigates agencies and policies and makes recommendations on almost every aspect of government—defense contracting, drug enforcement policies, the domestic security investigations of the FBI, Medicare and Medicaid programs, water-pollution programs, and so forth. Though the head of the GAO—the comptroller general—is appointed by the president (with the consent of the Senate), he or she serves for a fifteen-year term and is very much the servant of Congress rather than the president. The GAO employs about five thousand people, many of whom are permanently assigned to work with various congressional committees.

Office of Technology Assessment (OTA)   Established in 1972 to study and evaluate policies and programs with a significant use of or impact on technology, it has a staff of more than one hundred. Staff members look into such matters as a plan to build a pipeline to transport coal slurry. The agency as yet has had little impact.

Congressional Budget Office (CBO)   Created in 1974, the CBO advises Congress on the likely economic effect of different spending programs and provides information on the cost of proposed policies. This latter task has been more useful to Congress than the more difficult job of estimating future economic trends. The CBO prepares analyses of the president's budget and economic projections that often come to conclusions different from those of the administration, thus giving members of Congress arguments to use in the budget debates.

How a Bill Becomes Law

Some bills zip through Congress; others make their way slowly and painfully. Congress, an English observer once remarked, is like a crowd, moving either sluggishly or with great speed.

Bills that have sped through on the fast track include ones to reduce drug abuse, reform Defense Department procurement scandals, end mandatory retirement ages for older workers, and help the disabled. Those that have plodded through on the slow track include ones dealing with health care, tax laws, energy conservation, and foreign trade, as well as several appropriations bills.

Why the difference? Studying the list above gives some clues. Bills to spend a lot of money move slowly, especially during times (the 1980s and early 1990s) when the government is running up big deficits. Bills to tax or regulate businesses move slowly because so many different interests have to be heard and accommodated. On the other hand bills that seem to embody a clear, appealing idea ("stop drugs," "help old folks," "end scandal") gather momentum quickly, especially if the government doesn't have to spend a lot of its money (as opposed to requiring other people to spend *their* money) on the idea.

In the following account of how a bill becomes law, keep in mind the central fact that the complexity of these procedures ordinarily gives a powerful advantage to the opposition. There are many points at

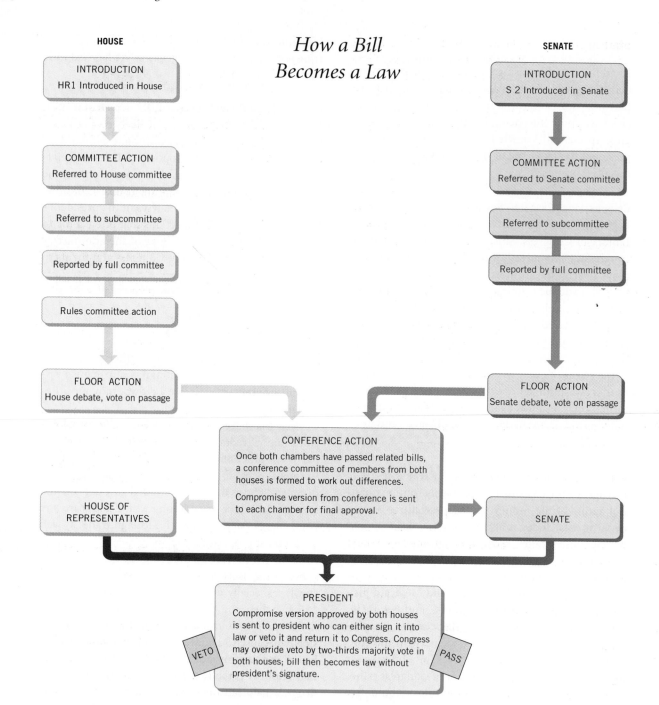

How a Bill Becomes a Law

HOUSE

INTRODUCTION
HR1 Introduced in House

COMMITTEE ACTION
Referred to House committee

Referred to subcommittee

Reported by full committee

Rules committee action

FLOOR ACTION
House debate, vote on passage

SENATE

INTRODUCTION
S 2 Introduced in Senate

COMMITTEE ACTION
Referred to Senate committee

Referred to subcommittee

Reported by full committee

FLOOR ACTION
Senate debate, vote on passage

CONFERENCE ACTION
Once both chambers have passed related bills, a conference committee of members from both houses is formed to work out differences.

Compromise version from conference is sent to each chamber for final approval.

HOUSE OF REPRESENTATIVES

SENATE

PRESIDENT
Compromise version approved by both houses is sent to president who can either sign it into law or veto it and return it to Congress. Congress may override veto by two-thirds majority vote in both houses; bill then becomes law without president's signature.

VETO

PASS

which action can be blocked. This does not mean that nothing gets done but that, to get something done, a member of Congress must *either* assemble slowly and painstakingly a majority coalition *or* take advantage of a temporary enthusiasm for some new cause that sweeps away the normal obstacles (for examples, see Chapter 15).

Introducing a Bill

Any member of Congress may introduce a bill—in the House simply by handing it to a clerk or dropping it in a box (the "hopper"); in the Senate by being recognized by the presiding officer and announcing the bill's introduction. Bills are numbered and sent to the printer: a House bill bears the prefix *H.R.*, a Senate bill the prefix *S*. A bill can be either a **public bill** (pertaining to affairs generally) or a **private bill** (pertaining to a particular individual, such as a person pressing a financial claim against the government or seeking special permission to become a naturalized citizen). Once private bills were very numerous; today many such matters have been delegated to administrative agencies or to the courts. If a bill is not passed by both houses and signed by the president within the life of one Congress, it is dead and must be reintroduced again during the next Congress. Pending legislation does not carry over from one Congress to the next. (A new Congress is organized every two years.)

We often hear that legislation is initiated by the president and enacted by Congress—the former proposes, the latter disposes. The reality is more complicated. Congress frequently initiates legislation; in fact, as we shall see in Chapter 15, most of the consumer and environmental-protection legislation passed since 1966 began in Congress, not in the executive branch. And even laws formally proposed by the president often represent presidential versions of proposals that have incubated in Congress. This was the case, for example, with some civil-rights laws and with the proposal that eventually became Medicare. Even when the president is the principal author of a bill, he usually submits it (if he is prudent) only after careful consultation with key congressional leaders. In any case the president cannot himself introduce legislation; he must get a member of Congress to do it for him.

One study showed that of ninety major laws passed between 1880 and 1945, seventy-seven were introduced without presidential sponsorship. In shaping the final contents, congressional influence was dominant in thirty-five cases, presidential influence in nineteen, and influence was mixed in the remaining thirty-six. Another study, covering the period 1940 to 1967, found that Congress was the major contributor to the contents of the laws passed in about half the cases.[30]

In addition to bills Congress can pass resolutions. A **simple resolution** (passed by either the House or the Senate) is used for such matters as establishing the rules under which each body will operate. A **concurrent resolution** settles housekeeping and procedural matters that affect both houses. Simple and

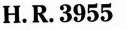

103D CONGRESS
2D SESSION

H. R. 3955

To increase the availability and continuity of health coverage for employees and their families, to prevent fraud and abuse in the health care delivery system, to reform medical malpractice liability standards, to reduce paperwork and simplify administration of health care claims, to promote preventive care, and for other purposes.

IN THE HOUSE OF REPRESENTATIVES

MARCH 3, 1994

Mr. ROWLAND (for himself, Mr. BILIRAKIS, Mr. SPRATT, Mr. BLILEY, Mr. TAUZIN, Mr. DUNCAN, Mr. PARKER, Mr. HASTERT, Mr. MONTGOMERY, Mr. BARTON of Texas, Mr. PETE GEREN of Texas, Mr. UPTON, Mr. SISISKY, Mr. MOORHEAD, Mr. TANNER, Mrs. VUCANOVICH, Mr. LAUGHLIN, Mr. GOSS, Mr. PICKETT, Mr. CRAPO, Mr. LANCASTER, Mr. GOODLATTE, Mr. HAYES, Mr. ZELIFF, Mrs. LLOYD, Mr. LINDER, Mr. BROWDER, Mr. CASTLE, Mr. ORTON, and Mr. YOUNG of Florida) introduced the following bill; which was referred jointly to the Committees on Energy and Commerce, Education and Labor, the Judiciary, and Ways and Means

APRIL 5, 1994

Additional sponsors: Mr. BREWSTER, Mr. LEWIS of Florida, Mr. DARDEN, Mr. FIELDS of Texas, Mr. NEAL of North Carolina, Mr. GREENWOOD, Mr. MORAN, Mr. KYL, Mr. CLEMENT, Mr. EWING, Mr. GLICKMAN, Mr. BALLENGER, Mr. STENHOLM, and Mr. CANADY

A BILL

To increase the availability and continuity of health coverage for employees and their families, to prevent fraud and abuse in the health care delivery system, to reform medical malpractice liability standards, to reduce paperwork and simplify administration of health care claims, to promote preventive care, and for other purposes.

A bill (H.R. 3955) as it looks after being introduced in the House.

concurrent resolutions are not signed by the president and do not have the force of law. A **joint resolution** requires the approval of both houses and the signature of the president; it is essentially the same as a law. A joint resolution is also used to propose a constitutional amendment; in this case it must be approved by a two-thirds vote of each house, but it does not require the signature of the president.

Study by Committees

A bill is referred to a committee for consideration by either the Speaker of the House or the presiding officer of the Senate. Rules govern which committee will get which bill, but sometimes a choice is possible; in the House the right of the Speaker to make such choices is an important component of his power. (His decisions can be appealed to the full House.) In 1963 a civil-rights bill was referred by the presiding officer of the Senate to the Commerce Committee in order to keep it out of the hands of the chairman of the Judiciary Committee, who was hostile to the bill. In the House the same piece of legislation was referred by the Speaker to the Judiciary Committee in order to keep it out of the grasp of the hostile chairman of the Interstate and Foreign Commerce Committee.

The Constitution requires that "all bills for raising revenue shall originate in the House of Representatives." The Senate can and does amend such bills, but only after the House has first acted. Bills that are not for raising revenue—that is, bills that do not change the tax laws—can originate in either house. In practice the House also originates appropriations bills—that is, bills directing how money shall be spent. Because of the House's special position on revenue legislation, the committee that handles those bills—the Ways and Means Committee—is particularly powerful.

Most bills die in committee. They are often introduced only to get publicity for the member of Congress or to enable the member to say to constituents or pressure groups that he or she "did something" on a matter concerning them. Bills of general interest—many of which will have been drafted in the executive branch even though introduced by a member of Congress—are assigned to a subcommittee for a hearing where witnesses appear, evidence is taken, and questions are asked. These hearings are used to inform members of Congress, to permit interest groups to speak out (whether or not they have anything helpful to say), and to build public support for a measure favored by the majority on the committee.

Though committee hearings are necessary and valuable, they also fragment the process of considering bills dealing with complex matters. Both power and information are dispersed in Congress, and thus it is difficult to take a comprehensive view of matters cutting across committee boundaries.

To deal with this problem, Congress has established a process whereby a bill may now be referred to several committees that simultaneously consider it in whole or in part. This process, called **multiple referral,** was used in 1977 to send President Carter's energy proposals to six different committees in both the House and Senate. An even bigger multiple referral was used for the 1988 trade bill, which was considered by fourteen committees in the House and nine

The Senate Judiciary Committee must act on all presidential nominations of federal judges and justices. Left to right: Orrin Hatch, Strom Thurmond, Joseph Biden, and Edward Kennedy.

in the Senate. The advantage of this procedure is that all views have a chance to be heard; the disadvantage is that it takes a lot of time and gives opponents a greater chance to kill or modify the bill. And if the different committees disagree about the bill, their members have to come together in a gargantuan joint meeting to iron out their differences. In these cases the advantages of the committee system—providing expert knowledge and careful deliberation—are often lost. About one-fourth of all House bills and resolutions now go through multiple referrals.

After the hearings the committee or subcommittee will "mark up" the bill—that is, make revisions and additions, some of which are extensive. These changes do not become part of the bill unless they are approved by the house of which the committee is a part. If a majority of the committee votes to report a bill out to the House or Senate, it goes forward. It is accompanied by a report that explains why the committee favors the bill and why it wishes to see its amendments, if any, adopted. Committee members who oppose the bill have an opportunity to include their dissenting opinions in the report.

If the committee does not report the bill out favorably, that ordinarily kills it. There is a procedure whereby the full House or Senate can get a bill that is stalled in committee out and onto the floor, but it is rarely used. In the House a **discharge petition** must be signed by 218 members; if the petition is approved by a vote of the House, the bill comes before it directly. In the Senate a member can move to discharge a committee of any bill and, if the motion passes, the bill comes before the Senate. During this century there have been over eight hundred efforts in the House to use discharge petitions; only two dozen have succeeded. Discharge is rarely tried in the Senate, in part because Senate rules permit almost any proposal to get to the floor as an amendment to another bill.

For a bill to come before either house, it must first be placed on a calendar. There are five such calendars in the House and two in the Senate (see the box).

Though the bill goes onto a calendar, it is not necessarily considered in chronological order or even considered at all. In the House the Rules Committee reviews most bills and adopts a rule that governs the procedures under which they will be considered by

Congressional Calendars

HOUSE

Union Calendar Bills to raise revenue or spend money
   Example: an appropriations bill

House Calendar Nonmoney bills of major importance
   Example: a civil-rights bill

Private Calendar Private bills
   Example: a bill to waive the immigration laws so that a Philadelphia woman could be joined by her Italian husband

Consent Calendar Noncontroversial bills
   Example: a resolution creating National Stenographers' Week

Discharge Calendar Discharge petitions

SENATE

Executive Calendar Presidential nominations, proposed treaties

Calender of Business All legislation

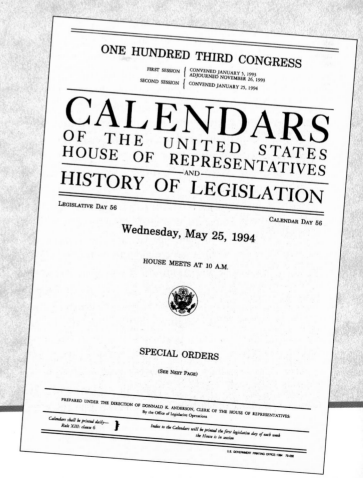

TABLE 11.4   Frequency of Open, Restrictive, and Closed Rules

	Congress					
Type of Rule	94th ('75–'76)	95th ('77–'78)	96th ('79–'80)	97th ('81–'82)	98th ('83–'84)	99th ('85–'86)
All measures						
Open	84.3%	83.9%	68.9%	71.2%	64.0%	55.4%
Restrictive	11.3	12.4	20.0	22.1	22.4	33.7
Closed	4.4	3.8	11.1	6.7	13.6	10.9
Number	248	186	180	104	125	101
Key vote measures						
Open	63.3%	70.6%	52.0%	23.5%	31.8%	13.6%
Restrictive	31.8	23.5	40.0	64.7	63.6	72.7
Closed	4.5	5.9	8.0	11.8	4.5	13.6
Number	22	17	25	17	22	22

SOURCES: Stanley Boch and Steven S. Smith, *Managing Uncertainty in the House of Representatives* (Washington, D.C.: Brookings Institution, 1988), 57. Reprinted with permission of the Brookings Institution. Richard E. Cohen, "Challenging the House's Traffic Cop," *The National Journal* (April 4, 1993): 1002.

the House. A **closed rule** sets a strict time limit on debate and forbids the introduction of any amendments from the floor, or forbids amendments except those offered by the sponsoring committee. Obviously such a rule can make it very difficult for opponents to do anything but vote yes or no on the measure. An **open rule** permits amendments from the floor. A **restrictive rule** permits some amendments but not others.

In the early 1970s, most bills were debated under open rules. In the 1980s, the Rules Committee—which is controlled by the Speaker—increasingly introduced bills for consideration under closed or restrictive rules in an effort to reduce the number of amendments from the floor (and, the Republicans claimed, to reduce Republican influence). By the end of the 1980s roughly half of all bills, and nearly three-fourths of all important ones, were debated under restrictive or closed rules (see Table 11.4). In 1992 only one-third of all bills were considered under an open rule.[31] In 1995 the Republicans came to power; we shall see whether they return to open rules.

The House has at least three ways of bypassing the Rules Committee: (1) a member can move that the rules be suspended, which requires a two-thirds vote; (2) a discharge petition, as explained above, can be filed; or (3) the House can use the "Calendar Wednesday" procedure.* These methods are not used very often, but they are available if the Rules Committee departs too far from the sentiments of the House.

No such barriers to floor consideration exist in the Senate. There bills may be considered in any order at any time whenever a majority of the Senate chooses. In practice the majority leader in consultation with the minority leader schedules bills for consideration.

---

*On Wednesdays the list of committees of the House is called more or less in alphabetical order and any committee can bring up for action a bill of its own already on a calendar. Action on a bill brought to the floor on Calendar Wednesday must be completed that day or the bill goes back to committee. Since major bills rarely can be voted on in one day, this procedure is not often used.

Floor Debate—The House

Once on the floor, the bills are debated. In the House all revenue and most other bills are discussed by the "Committee of the Whole," which is nothing more than whoever happens to be on the floor at the time. The quorum for the Committee of the Whole is only 100 members and thus easier to assemble than a quorum for the House itself, which the Constitution specifies as a majority, or 218 members. The Speaker does not preside but chooses another person to wield the gavel. The Committee of the Whole debates, amends, and generally decides the final shape of the bill, but technically cannot pass it. To do that, the Committee of the Whole reports the bill back to the House (that is, to itself!), which takes final action. During the debate in the Committee of the Whole, the committee sponsoring the bill guides the discussion, divides the time equally between proponents and opponents, and decides how long each member will be permitted to speak. If amendments are allowed under the rule, they must be germane to the purpose of the bill—extraneous matters (riders) are not allowed—and no one may speak for more than five minutes on an amendment. During this process people wishing to take time out to huddle about strategy or to delay action can demand a **quorum call**—a calling of the roll to find out whether the necessary minimum number of members is present. If a quorum is not present, the House must either adjourn or dispatch the sergeant at arms to round up missing members. The sponsoring committee almost always wins; its bill, as amended by it, usually is the version that the House passes.

Floor Debate—The Senate

Things are a good deal more casual in the Senate. Short of cloture (discussed below), there is no rule limiting debate, and members can speak for as long as they can stay on their feet. A senator's remarks need not be relevant to the matter under consideration (some senators have read aloud from the Washington telephone directory), and anyone can offer an amendment at any time. There is no Committee of the Whole. Amendments need not be germane to the purpose of the bill, and thus the Senate often attaches riders to bills.

Riders and Christmas Trees

A **rider** is a provision added to a piece of legislation that is not germane to the bill's purpose. The goal is usually to achieve one of two outcomes: either get the president (or governor) to sign an otherwise objectionable bill by attaching to it, as an amendment, a provision that the chief executive desperately wants to see enacted, or get the president to veto a bill that he would otherwise sign by attaching to it, as an amendment, a provision that the chief executive strongly dislikes.

A rider is a convenient way for a legislator to get a pet project approved that might not be approved if it had to be voted on by itself. The term can be traced back to seventeenth-century England.

When a bill has lots of riders, it becomes a **Christmas-tree bill.** In 1966, for example, the Foreign Investors Act, a bill designed to solve the balance-of-payments problem, had added to it riders giving assistance to hearse owners, the mineral ore business, importers of scotch whiskey, and presidential candidates.

SOURCE: Adapted from William Safire, *Safire's Political Dictionary* (New York: Ballantine Books, 1978). Used by permission.

In fact the opportunity to offer nongermane amendments gives a senator a chance to get a bill onto the floor without regard to the calendar or the schedule of the majority leader: he or she need only offer a pet bill as an "amendment" to a bill already under discussion. (This cannot be done to an appropriations bill.) Indeed the entire committee hearing process can be bypassed in the Senate if the House has already passed the bill. In that case a senator can get the House-passed measure put directly onto the Senate calendar without committee action. In 1957 and again in 1964 this was done with House-passed civil-rights bills to make certain that they would not be bottled up in the conservative Senate Judiciary Committee.

A Senate filibuster is difficult to break. The current **cloture rule** requires that sixteen senators sign a petition to move cloture. The motion is voted on two days after the petition is introduced; to pass, three-fifths of the entire Senate membership (sixty senators if there are no vacancies) must vote for it. If it passes, each senator is thereafter limited to one hour of debate on the bill under consideration. The total debate, including roll calls and the introduction of amendments, cannot exceed one hundred hours.

In recent years, both filibusters and cloture votes have become more common. The filibuster occurs more frequently because it is now easier to stage one. Often it consists, not of a senator's making a long speech, but of endless requests for the clerk to call the roll. More filibusters means more cloture votes, which are now easier to win since the 1975 change lowering the required number of supporters from two-thirds to three-fifths of all senators. During the 100th Congress (1987–1988), there were almost as many cloture votes—forty-three—as there had been in the half century after the procedure was invented. Since 1975, about 40 percent of all cloture votes have succeeded in cutting off debate.

Conservatives have used the filibuster to try to block civil-rights laws; liberals have used it to try to block decontrol of gas prices. Since both factions have found the filibuster useful, it seems most unlikely that it will ever be abolished, though it has been somewhat curtailed. One way to keep the Senate going during a filibuster is **double-tracking,** whereby the disputed bill is shelved temporarily so that the Senate can get on with other business. Because double-tracking permits the Senate to discuss and vote on matters other than the bill that is being filibustered, it is less costly to individual senators to stage a filibuster. In the past, before double-tracking, a senator and his allies had to keep talking around the clock to keep their filibuster alive. If they stopped talking, the Senate was free to take up other business. Opponents of the filibuster would bring cots and blankets to the Senate so that they could sleep and eat there, ready to take the floor the moment the filibuster faltered. But with double-tracking other business can go on while the stalled bill is temporarily set aside. As a result, the number of filibusters has sky-rocketed.

One rule is common to both houses: courtesy, often of the most exquisite nature, is required at all times. Members always refer to each other as "distinguished" even if they are mortal political enemies. Personal or ad hominem criticism is not tolerated, and there have been only a few cases of members' taking a punch at each other, and most of those occurred in the nineteenth century.

Methods of Voting

Some observers of Congress make the mistake of deciding who was for and who was against a bill by the final vote. This can be misleading—often a member of Congress will vote for final passage of a bill after having supported amendments that, if they had passed, would have made the bill totally different. To keep track of various members' voting records, therefore, it is often more important to know how they voted on key amendments than to know how they voted on the bill itself.

Finding that out is not always easy, though it has become more so in recent years. There are four procedures for voting in the House. A **voice vote** consists of the members' shouting "yea" or "nay"; a **division** (or standing) **vote** involves the members' standing and being counted. In neither a voice nor a standing vote are the names of members recorded as having voted one way or the other.

To learn how an individual votes, there must be either a recorded teller vote or a roll call. In a **teller vote** the members pass between two tellers, the yeas first and then the nays. Since 1971 a teller vote can be "recorded," which means that, at the request of twenty members, clerks write down the names of those favoring or opposing a bill as they pass the tellers. Since teller votes but not roll calls may be taken in the Committee of the Whole, the use of a recorded teller vote enables observers to find out how members voted in those important deliberations.

A **roll-call vote,** of course, consists of people's answering "yea" or "nay" to their names. It can be done at the request of one-fifth of the representatives present in the House. When roll calls were handled orally, it was a time-consuming process, since the clerk had to drone though 435 names. Since 1973 an electronic voting system has been in operation that permits each member, by inserting a plastic card into

The electronic voting system in the House of Representatives displays each member's name on the wall of the chamber. By inserting a plastic card in a box fastened to the chairs, a member can vote "yea," or "nay," or "present," and the result is shown opposite his or her name.

a slot, to record his or her own vote and to learn the total automatically. Owing to the use of recorded teller votes and the advent of electronic roll-call votes, the number of recorded votes has gone up sharply in the House. There were only seventy-three House roll calls in 1955; twenty years later there were over eight times as many. Voting in the Senate is much the same, only simpler: there is no such thing as a teller vote, and no electronic counters are used.

If a bill passes the House and Senate in different forms, the differences must be reconciled if the bill is to become law. If they are minor, the last house to act may simply refer the bill back to the other house, which then accepts the alterations. If the differences are major, it is often necessary to appoint a conference committee to iron them out. Only a minority of the bills requires a conference. Each house must vote to form such a committee. The members are picked by the chairmen of the House and Senate standing committees that have been handling the legislation, with representation given to the minority as well as the majority party. There are usually between three and fifteen members from each house. No decision can be made unless approved by a majority of *each* delegation.

Bargaining is long and hard; in the past it was also secret. Now some conference sessions are open to the public. Often—as with President Carter's en-

ergy bill—the legislation is substantially rewritten in conference. Complex bills can lead to enormous conferees. The 1988 trade bill went before a conference committee of two hundred members. Theoretically the conferees are not supposed to change anything already agreed to by both the House and Senate, but in the inevitable give-and-take even matters already approved may be changed.

In most cases the conference reports tend to favor, slightly, the Senate version of the bill. Several studies have suggested that the Senate wins in from 57 percent to 65 percent of the cases.[32] Whoever wins (and both sides always claim that they got everything out of the bargaining that they possibly could), conferees report their agreement back to their respective houses, which usually consider the report immediately. The report can be accepted or rejected; it cannot be amended. In the great majority of cases, it is accepted: the alternative is to have no bill at all, at least for that Congress. The bill, now in final form, goes to the president for signature or veto. If a veto is cast, the bill returns to the house of origin. There an effort can be made to override the veto. This requires that two-thirds of those present (provided that there is a quorum) must vote to override; this vote must be a roll call. If both houses override in this manner, the bill becomes law without the president's approval.

House-Senate Differences: A Summary

House	Senate
435 members serving two-year terms	100 members serving rotating six-year terms
House members have only one major committee assignment, thus tend to be policy specialists	Senators have two or more major committee assignments, tend to be policy generalists
Speaker's referral of bills to committee is hard to challenge	Referral decisions easy to challenge
Committees almost always consider legislation first	Committee consideration easily bypassed
Scheduling and rules controlled by majority party	Scheduling and rules generally agreed to by majority and minority leaders
Rules Committee powerful; controls time of debate, admissibility of amendments	Rules Committee weak; few limits on debate or amendments
Debate usually limited to one hour	Unlimited debate unless shortened by unanimous consent or by invoking cloture
Nongermane amendments may not be introduced from floor	Nongermane amendments may be introduced

How Members of Congress Vote

Voting on bills is not the only thing that a member of Congress does, but it is among the more important and is probably the most visible. Since leaders in Congress are not nearly so powerful as those in a typical parliament, since political parties have been declining in influence, and since Congress has gone to great lengths to protect the independence and power of the individual members, it is by no means obvious what factors will lead a representative or senator to vote for or against a bill or amendment.

There are at least three kinds of explanations: representational, organizational, and attitudinal. A *representational* explanation is based on the reasonable assumption that members want to get reelected, and therefore they vote to please their constituents. The *organizational* explanation is based on the equally reasonable assumption that since most constituents do not know how their legislator has voted, it is not essential to please them. But it *is* important to please fellow members of Congress whose goodwill is valuable in getting things done and in acquiring status and power in Congress. The *attitudinal* explanation is based on the assumption that there are so many conflicting pressures on members of Congress that they cancel one another out, leaving them virtually free to vote on the basis of their own beliefs.

Political scientists have studied, tested, and argued about these (and other) explanations for decades, and nothing like a consensus has emerged. Some facts have been established, however.

Representational View

The representational view has some merit under certain circumstances—namely, when constituents have a clear view on some issue and a legislator's vote on that issue is likely to attract their attention. Such is often the case on civil-rights laws: representatives with significant numbers of black voters in their districts are not likely to oppose civil-rights bills; representatives with few blacks in their districts, or with blacks who were prevented from voting (as in much of the South until the late 1960s), are comparatively free to oppose such bills. (Many representatives without black constituents supported civil-rights bills, partly out of personal belief and partly, perhaps, because certain white groups in their districts—organized liberals, for example—insisted on such support.)

One study of congressional roll-call votes and constituency opinion showed that the correlation between the two was quite strong on civil-rights bills. There was also a positive (though not as strong) correlation between roll-call votes and constituency opinion on social-welfare measures. Scarcely any correlation, however, was found between congressional votes and hometown opinion on foreign-policy measures.[33] Foreign policy is generally remote from the daily interests of most Americans, and public opinion about such matters can change rapidly. It is not surprising therefore that congressional votes and constituent opinion should be different on such questions.

From time to time an issue arouses deep passions among the voters, and legislators cannot escape the need either to vote as their constituents want, whatever their personal views, or to anguish at length about which side of a divided constituency to support. Gun control has been one such question, the ratification of the Panama Canal treaties another, and the use of federal money to pay for abortions a third. Some fortunate members of Congress get unambiguous cues from their constituents on these matters, and no hard decision is necessary; others get conflicting views, and they know that whichever way they vote, it may cost them dearly in the next election. Occasionally members of Congress in this fix will try to be out of town when the matter comes up for a vote. One careful study found that constituency influences were an important factor in Senate

votes,[34] but no comparable study has been done for the House.

You might think that members of Congress who won a close race in the last election—who come from a "marginal" district—would be especially eager to vote the way that their constituents want. Research so far has shown that is not generally the case. There seem to be about as many independent-minded members of Congress from marginal as from safe districts. Perhaps it is because opinion is so divided in a marginal seat that one cannot please everybody; as a result the representative votes on other grounds.

In general the problem with the representational explanation is that public opinion is not strong and clear on most measures on which Congress must vote. Many representatives and senators face constituencies that are divided on key issues. Some constituents go to special pains to make their views known (these interest groups were discussed in Chapter 9). But as we indicated, the power of interest groups to affect congressional votes depends, among other things, on whether a legislator sees them as united and powerful or as disorganized and marginal.

This does not mean that constituents rarely have a direct influence on voting. The influence that they have probably comes from the fact that legislators risk defeat should they steadfastly vote in ways that can be held against them by a rival in the next election. Though most congressional votes are not known to most citizens, blunders (real or alleged) quickly become known when an electoral opponent exploits them.

Still any member of Congress can choose the positions that he or she takes on most roll-call votes (and on all voice or standing votes, where names are not recorded). And even a series of recorded votes that are against constituency opinion need not be fatal: a member of Congress can win votes in other ways—for example, by doing services for constituents or by appealing to the party loyalty of the voters.

Organizational View

When voting on matters where constituency interests or opinions are not vitally at stake, members of Congress respond primarily to cues provided by their colleagues. This is the organizational explanation of their votes. The principal cue is party; as already

Senate to Vote on Abortion Amendment

Close Vote Expected on Plan to Ban Abortions

* * *

WASHINGTON, D.C. MARCH 10—The Senate tomorrow will vote on a proposed constitutional amendment to allow the states to decide whether abortions will be legal. Key senators, such as Matthew Wilson . . .

What Would You Do?

MEMORANDUM

TO: Senator Matthew Wilson
FROM: Kathy Nagle, Legislative assistant
SUBJECT: Abortion vote

As you know, the Senate will vote tomorrow on a constitutional amendment that, if passed by a two-thirds vote in Congress and ratified by three-fourths of the states, will reverse the 1973 Supreme Court decision in the case of <u>Roe</u> v. <u>Wade</u> and allow each state to decide for itself whether abortions shall be legal or illegal. If the constitutional amendment is ratified, this will make it possible for states to ban abortions. Many, but not all, will do this. The Senate vote is likely to be close, and so your vote may be of crucial importance. You have not taken a position on this issue as yet, partly because opinion in your state, Massachusetts, is so divided and partly because of your own uncertainty on the merits of this issue. Let me summarize the arguments:

1. Arguments in favor of the amendment: (a) As a Catholic, you are morally opposed to abortion. (b) The Catholic church in Massachusetts, led by the cardinal, has taken a strong position against abortion and in favor of the amendment. (c) Many legal scholars believe that the Court's decision in <u>Roe</u> v. <u>Wade</u> was wrong because it is not based on any explicit language in the Constitution that would prohibit states from controlling abortions. (d) The right-to-life movement is very active in Massachusetts and will support you if you vote for the amendment. If you oppose it, it will support your opponent in the next primary election—an election that is likely to be close anyway.

2. Arguments against the amendment: (a) Public-opinion polls show that a majority of the people believe that abortions should be legal, at least under most circumstances. (b) Some Catholics believe that the church is wrong in its opposition to abortion, and several Catholic politicians, such as Governor Mario Cuomo of New York, think that Catholic elected officials are not bound by church teachings in their official decisions. (c) Many legal scholars believe that <u>Roe</u> v. <u>Wade</u> rests on a "right of privacy" that is clearly implied by the Constitution. (d) The prochoice and women's movements are very active in Massachusetts and are strongly opposed to the amendment. They raise a lot of money for political campaigns and have powerful allies in the media (the <u>Boston Globe,</u> the television stations).

<u>Your decision:</u>   Vote yes _____   Vote no _____   Abstain _____

noted, what party a member of Congress belongs to explains more about his or her voting record than any other single factor. Additional organizational cues come from the opinions of colleagues with whom the member of Congress feels a close ideological affinity: for liberals in the House it is the Democratic Study Group; for conservatives it has often been the Republican Study Committee or the Wednesday Club. But party and other organizations do not have clear positions on all matters. For the scores of votes that do not involve the "big questions," a representative or senator is especially likely to be influenced by the members of his or her party on the sponsoring committee.

It is easy to understand why. Suppose you are a Democratic representative from Michigan who is summoned to the floor of the House to vote on a bill to authorize a new weapons system. You haven't the faintest idea what issues might be at stake. There is no obvious liberal or conservative position on this matter. How do you vote? Simple. You take your cue from several Democrats on the House Armed Services Committee that handled the bill. Some are liberal (such as Patricia Schroeder of Colorado), others are conservative (such as Sonny Montgomery of Mississippi). If Schroeder and Montgomery both support the bill, you vote for it unhesitatingly. If Schroeder and Montgomery disagree, you vote with whichever Democrat is generally closest to your own political ideology. If the matter is one that affects your state, you can take your cue from members of your state's delegation to Congress.

Attitudinal View

Finally, there is evidence that the ideology of a member of Congress affects how he or she votes. We have seen that Democratic and Republican legislators differ sharply on a liberal-versus-conservative scale. On both domestic and foreign-policy issues, many tend to be consistently liberal or conservative.[35]

This consistency isn't surprising; as we saw in Chapter 5, political elites think more ideologically than the public generally.

On many issues the average member of the House has opinions close to those of the average voter, as seen in Figure 11.6. Senators, by contrast, are often less in tune with public opinion. In the 1970s

they were much more liberal than voters; in the early 1980s, more conservative. Two senators from the same state often mobilize quite different bases of support. The result is that many states, such as California, Delaware, and New York, have been represented by senators with almost diametrically opposed views.

Of late the Senate has gone through three phases. In the first, during the 1950s and early 1960s, it was a cautious, conservative institution dominated by southern senators and displaying many of the features of a "club" that welcomed members into its inner circle only after they had displayed loyalty to its

FIGURE 11.6 Comparison of Public and Congressional Opinion on Policy Issues, 1978

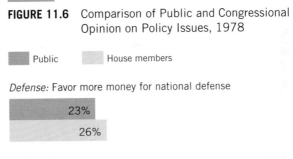

■ Public   ▨ House members

Defense: Favor more money for national defense

23%
26%

Arms control: Favor Strategic Arms Limitation Talks (SALT)

67%
74%

Health insurance: Favor national health insurance fully paid for by the government

47%
45%

Tax cut: Oppose a "large" federal income-tax cut

53%
51%

Abortion: Favor government paying for abortions for the poor

41%
35%

SOURCE: CBS–*New York Times* poll, as reported in Robert S. Erikson, Norman R. Luttbeg, and Kent L. Tedin, *American Public Opinion,* 2d ed. (New York: Wiley, 1980), 240.

gentlemanly (and in effect, conservative) customs. This was the era when the Senate was the graveyard of civil-rights bills.

The second period began in the mid-1960s as liberal senators rose steadily in number, seniority, and influence, helped along by the Johnson reforms that made it easier for junior senators to gain chairmanships. The decentralization of the Senate gave more power to individual senators, including liberals. In 1972 there were about twenty-four liberal senators, but among them they held forty subcommittee chairmanships.[36]

The third period began in the late 1970s and became most visible after the 1980 elections, when many liberals lost their seats to conservative Republicans. The conservatism of the present Senate is based more on ideology than on the rules of the southern "club" that characterized it in the 1950s.

The Democratic party is more deeply divided than the Republican. There are only a few liberal Republicans, but there are many conservative Democrats from the South and West. Southern Democrats often team up with Republicans to form a conservative coalition. In a typical year a majority of Republicans and southern Democrats will vote together against a majority of northern Democrats about 20 to 25 percent of the time. When the conservative coalition does form, it usually wins: between 1970 and 1982 it won about two-thirds of the votes on which it held together.[37] After the Reagan victory and the Republican gain of thirty-three seats in the House in 1981, the conservative coalition became even more effective, dominating key votes on the Reagan budget and tax plans.

Reforming Congress

Most citizens are less interested in why members of Congress vote the way they do than they are in whether Congress as an institution serves the public interest and fulfills its mission as a democratic body. In recent years a number of proposals have been made to reform Congress—term limitations, new ethics and campaign finance laws, and organizational changes intended to reduce the power and perks of members while making it easier for Congress to pass needed legislation in a timely fashion.

It is important to recognize that the kind of reform proposed depends not only on what is feasible but on an underlying idea of what Congress ought to be. For example, which of the two conceptions of democracy discussed in Chapter 1—direct or representative—should Congress embody? What definition of "the public interest" should Congress favor? And by what criteria should one decide whether a given piece of legislation is so badly needed that a failure to pass it promptly constitutes a failure of Congress?

Representative or Direct Democracy?

The Framers of the Constitution believed that representatives should refine, not reflect, public wishes. Today, however, many believe that elected officials should mirror, not mediate, the majority's views. Some would go so far as to bypass Congress entirely. A survey conducted in 1993 found that two-thirds of Americans favored having binding national referenda on policy questions, and about half favored selecting members of Congress randomly from lists of eligible voters. (One in six even supported the idea of auctioning seats in Congress to the highest bidders as a way of retiring the national debt.)[38] A more moderate vision of direct democracy in Congress would have citizen legislators serving short terms as the people's delegates (voting as a majority of their constituents want them to vote) with small staffs and no perks. In contrast, representative democracy in Congress would mean professional legislators serving as the people's trustees (consulting their constituents' views but voting their consciences) with expert staffs, no term limits, and such work-related perks (travel allowances, mailing privileges) as they required to fulfill their duties.

Any reforms that move Congress away from representative democracy and toward direct democracy could have far-reaching consequences. For example, it is unlikely that a Congress shaped largely as a direct democracy would have voted the way the House of Representatives did on June 21, 1990. On that day the House defeated a proposed constitutional amendment on protection of the American flag. Ten days before the House vote, the U.S. Supreme Court had struck down a Texas law against flag desecration. The public reaction to this ruling, which was widely interpreted to legalize and legitimize flag burning, was intensely negative. On the eve of the House vote, pollster George Gallup, Jr., reported that the "will of the public on making flag burning illegal appears to be both straightforward and remarkably stable."[39] Nevertheless, the House voted against the amendment. One study found that 87 percent of the legislators who voted against the amendment represented constituencies who supported it. This study also found that those who voted against the amendment were not punished by the voters for doing so in the 1992 congressional elections.[40]

Proper Guardians of the Public Weal?

Everyone agrees that Congress should serve the public interest, but what is the public interest? In *Federalist* No. 10 James Madison offered one answer. To him, the public interest—"the permanent and aggregate interests of the community"—was to be expressed concretely in national laws that transcended "local prejudices" and frustrated the "sinister designs" of factions.

In Madison's view the public interest was not the simple sum of whatever societal interests demanded from government. Instead, members of Congress were to be "proper guardians of the public weal," representatives who served "the great and aggregate interests" of the country. To Madison, the art of the public-spirited legislator was to know the true ends of the body politic and to effect reasonable compromises among competing societal interests via the legislative process. He held that "the regulation of these various and interfering interests" was the "principal task" of representatives, and he argued that a Congress fashioned institutionally as a representative rather than a direct democracy would be best able to balance contending societal interests without succumbing to the demands of factions.

Madison's conception of the public interest lives on in contemporary calls for reforming Congress to make the body less captive of so-called special interests, our modern term for factions. Some people believe that by outlawing political-action committees, fine-tuning congressional ethics regulations, or related measures Congress would become less accessible to special interests and more solicitous of the public interest.

The difficulty, however, is that one person's special-interest group is often another's professional association, trade group, or public-interest lobby. If you were a member of Congress, would you listen to the views of the National Abortion Federation, the U.S. Catholic Conference, both, or neither? Would you view the interests of the Meat Importers' Council of America as more or less important than the interests of the American Institute of Certified Public Accountants, the Bituminous Coal Operators Association, the Cement Kiln Recycling Association, or the American Political Science Association? Might you view the Southern Governors' Association as a faction but the National Governors' Association as a public-interest lobby? And what, as a committed "proper guardian of the public weal," would you make of the National Rifle Association or the American Association of Retired Persons?

A Decisive Congress or a Deliberative One?

Madison and the other Framers recognized that Congress, as a representative body designed to protect the public interest while balancing the competing views and interests of the citizenry, would normally proceed slowly. Congress was designed for deliberative, not decisive, action. It was intended to check and balance strong leaders in the executive branch, not automatically cede its authority to them. Its institutional mission was more to block or delay popular legislative action than it was to speed it along.

But many contemporary critics of Congress do not share the Framers' vision of what Congress ought to be. During the 1992 presidential campaign, for example, there was a great deal of talk about policy gridlock in Washington, D.C. Almost everyone agreed that the federal budget deficit needed to be reduced, but national policymakers could not agree on how to do it. Everyone admitted that the nation's health care system needed to be reformed, but no single plan gained widespread acceptance. And everyone insisted that America needed to strengthen its international trading position, but disagreements were rife over just how, if at all, this could be accomplished in our increasingly complex global economy.

Many wish to reform Congress in ways that might end "policy gridlock" by making Congress capable of speedily adopting sweeping changes in national policies. They see a need to reduce separation-of-powers barriers to joint executive-legislative action and to adopt other changes that would make the

CRITICAL ✦ THINKING

Limit Terms or Enlarge Congress?

The constitutionality of term limits on members of Congress has yet to be decided. Some reformers have advocated alternative measures that in their view would accomplish the same things that term limits would accomplish but without raising questions of constitutionality such as enlarging the House. Article I, section 2 of the Constitution allows no more than one representative for every thirty thousand inhabitants. The Antifederalists warned that such a low ratio of representatives to constituents would make the House a barony dominated by a few leaders and out of touch with the people. The first House had 65 members. Since 1913 the House has had 435 members; that number was fixed by law in 1929. But the nation's population has roughly doubled over the last seven decades. As a result, in 1992 each member of the House represents about

six hundred thousand persons. That ratio would have horrified the Antifederalists, and probably would have given the Framers of the Constitution second thoughts as well. It is also way out of line with the ratios in most other modern democracies such as Japan (1:238,600), Germany (1:120,000), France (1:96,300), and Great Britain (1:87,500).

To return to the Framers' original ratio would be to create a House of over eight thousand members. So far, no one has advocated doing that, but Michael Merrill and Sean Wilentz propose a return to the 1929 baseline, doubling the House to 870 members so that each member would represent about three hundred thousand rather than six hundred thousand citizens. Enlarging Congress, they argue, would "reduce the crushing load of constituent service for each member, encourage less expensive

campaigns, and mitigate the distracting and corrupting pursuit of PAC financing. Doubling the membership would make life all the more difficult (and costly) for special interests that lack a significant popular base among the citizenry."

Which strategy—limiting terms or enlarging Congress—do you favor? Which do you think is more likely to win popular support and be enacted into law? Which do you think stands a better chance of passing muster on constitutional terms? What are the likely drawbacks of each proposal? Short of such far-reaching reforms, what do you think can and should be done to change Congress?

SOURCE: Michael Merrill and Sean Wilentz, "The Big House: An Alternative to Term Limits," *The New Republic* (November 16, 1992): 16–17.

American political system more closely resemble a parliamentary system. The problem, however, is that a Congress that is capable of doing much good quickly is also capable of doing much bad quickly. A Congress that could move decisively to adopt wise budget, health, or trade policies could also move decisively to adopt unwise ones, and a Congress that can suddenly endorse and enact popular laws can do the same for unpopular ones. This is true whatever the subject—toxic waste disposal or civil service reform, environmental protection or mass transportation, juvenile justice or national defense.

As the reformers argue, there are costs associated with having congressional machinery that runs slowly on the precious fuel of political consensus. But there are benefits as well, not least among them the chance to identify competing interests, consider opposing ideas, weigh alternative approaches, and resist pressures to act where action may be premature, unwarranted, overly expensive, or socially divisive.

Imposing Term Limits

As explained in Chapter 2, the Antifederalists (those who opposed the new Constitution in the late 1780s) believed that a strong national government would grow corrupt, distant from the people, and contemptuous of states' rights. Among other measures to check the national government's power and ensure its responsiveness to the popular will, many Antifederalists believed that members of Congress should stand for election annually, and that no citizen should serve more than a few terms in Congress.

Today there are many Americans who have come to the view that the Antifederalists were right about the need for some type of term limits in Congress. When upwards of 95 percent of House incumbents are reelected, people worry that popular control of Congress has weakened, while state and local officials complain that there is no room for them to move up the political ladder. A 1992 survey showed that about 80 percent of Americans felt there should be a limit on the number of terms to which a senator or member of the House can be elected.[41]

The contemporary term-limit movement began in the fall of 1990 when term-limit measures passed in three statewide initiatives (California, Colorado, and Oklahoma). In 1991 voters in the state of Wash-

ington, home of former Speaker of the House Thomas Foley, also considered a term-limit initiative but Foley and others waged a successful campaign against the measure, which failed by a vote of 54 to 46 percent. The movement, however, gained speed again in 1992. By 1994 twenty-two states had voted, in most places by large majorities, to impose limits on the number of years their representatives could serve in Congress (see Table 11.5).

The effects of term limits on Congress would vary according to which type of term limits applied.[42] Proposals that would place a lifetime limit on legislative service would result in an amateur legislature. Let us assume, as many supporters of these measures do, that amateurs in Congress would act out of personal conviction rather than from the desire to be reelected. Reelection-minded professional politicians must be concerned about what their constituents think and want; principled amateur legislators need not be. Would a Congress composed of such legislators be good or bad, better or worse? The answer, of course, depends largely on whether you favor representative or direct democracy.

But whichever you favor, do not suppose that amateur legislators would eliminate policy gridlock: people who act out of conviction are more prone to disagree and less apt to compromise than people whose profession it is to practice the ABC's of democratic politics—making *a*lliances, striking *b*argains, and forging *c*ompromises.[43] In a diverse, pluralistic, and multicultural society, a politics of unbending

---

TABLE 11.5   Term-Limit Initiatives Passed in 1992

	Percent in Favor		Percent in Favor
Arizona	74%	Nebraska	68%
Arkansas	60	North Dakota	56
California	64	Ohio	66
Florida	77	Oregon	70
Michigan	59	South Dakota	64
Missouri	74	Washington	52
Montana	67	Wyoming	77

NOTE: In every state except North Dakota the measure included limits on the number of years that state legislators can serve as well.
SOURCE: *The American Enterprise* (January/February 1993): 97.

POLITICALLY **P.S.** SPEAKING

Pork Barrel

Before the Civil War it was the custom to take salt pork from barrels and distribute it to the slaves. Often the eagerness of the slaves to get the food would result in a rush on the barrels, in which each slave would try to get as much as possible.

By the 1870s members of Congress were using the term *pork* to refer to benefits for their districts and *pork barrel* to mean the piece of legislation containing those benefits.

Today the classic example of pork-barrel legislation is the rivers and harbors bill, which provides appropriations for countless dams, bridges, and canals to be built in congressional districts all over the country.

SOURCE: Adapted from William Safire, *Safire's Political Dictionary* (New York: Ballantine Books, 1978). Used by permission.

principle can be a recipe for political stalemate—or worse.

By the same token, do not suppose that all the amateur legislators would be true political novices. As should be obvious, the typical American is simply not well-positioned to quit work in order to spend a year or two in Washington, D.C. But there are people for whom such a brief tour of duty in Congress would be both feasible and desirable. With lifetime term limits many of tomorrow's citizen-legislators on Capitol Hill could well be yesterday's lawyer-lobbyists from K Street.

On the other hand, were term limits to take the form of limiting continuous service in one legislative branch without restricting eligibility for other elected offices, the probable result would be a Congress of office-hopping political professionals who must constantly prepare to run for the other chamber or some other office. In a Congress dominated by members who played electoral "musical chairs," it is probable that seniority would fade as the basis for distributing committee assignments, party leadership would change hands every few years, and individual members would probably keep one eye fixed on their next constituencies (local, regional, statewide, or national) and would have every incentive to act in ways that bring them public attention rather than work behind the scenes to get things done.

Finally, it remains to be decided whether term limits imposed by states are constitutional. The first clause of Article I, section 4 of the Constitution states that "the Times, Places and Manner of holding Elections for Senators and Representatives, shall be prescribed in each State by the Legislature thereof." But section 5 of Article I states that "Each House shall be the Judge of the Elections, Returns and Qualifications of its own Members." The core constitutional issue is whether the states can do more than set the "time, place and manner" of holding elections for Congress by setting "qualifications" for office other than those set by the Constitution.

Reducing Powers and Perks

To many term-limitation enthusiasts and other would-be reformers, Congress is grossly overstaffed and self-indulgent. It is quick to impose new laws on states, cities, businesses, and average citizens, but slow to apply those same laws to itself and its members. It is quick to pass **pork-barrel legislation**—bills that give tangible benefits (highways, dams, post offices) to constituents in the hope of winning their votes in return—but slow to tackle complex and controversial questions of national policy. The reformers' image of Congress is unflattering, but is it wholly unwarranted? Which calls to reduce congressional powers and perks amount to mere Congress-bashing and which came closer to being reasonable criticisms of a body that has lost its way as a representative institution?

Banning Legal Bribes As any baseball fan knows, tickets to an All-Star game are always hard to come by. But it was harder than usual to get a ticket to the 1993 All-Star game. Only ten thousand of the forty-six thousand seats at Orioles Park at Camden Yards in Baltimore were available to the public. But Congress was well-represented in the bleachers. Major league baseball owners gave members of Congress a special opportunity to purchase tickets for themselves and others. Over half of the five hundred and thirty-five representatives and senators took the tickets, despite the fact that Congress was in the midst of deciding whether major league baseball's long-standing exemption from federal antitrust laws should be rescinded. One member who did not take the tickets was Representative Jim Bunning of Kentucky. Bunning, a former All-Star player who threw a perfect game for the Philadelphia Phillies in 1964, wrote "No bribe" on the solicitation and sent it back.[44]

Reformers propose strict prohibitions on all such "legal bribes," gifts, or solicitations to members of Congress. Some would extend the ban to all congressional perks: discount hair cuts, discount dining services, cut-rate gym fees, cheap car washes, free airport parking, free picture framing, and the rest. No perk, however, is more treasured by members of Congress than the frank.

Fencing In the Frank Members of Congress are allowed by law to send material through the mail free of charge by substituting their facsimile signature (*frank*) for postage. But rather than using this **franking privilege** to keep their constituents informed about their government, most members use franked newsletters and questionnaires as campaign literature. That is why use of the frank soars in the months before an election. For example, more than 30 million newsletters were sent out in March 1992, the last month in which members facing June primaries could send franked mailings.[45] And two of the top three users of the frank during the first quarter of 1993 were both running at the time to fill the Senate seat vacated when Lloyd Bentsen became the Clinton Administration's secretary of the treasury.[46]

Thus, the frank amounts to a taxpayer subsidy of members' campaigns, a perk that bolsters the electoral fortunes of incumbents. Some reformers do not believe that it is possible to fence in congressional use of the frank for public education or other legitimate purposes and they propose abolishing it outright. Other reformers, however, argue that the frank can be fenced in by prohibiting mailings just before primaries and general elections (to dilute any electoral impact), and by placing a prominent notice on the front of every franked material, "Paid For At Taxpayer Expense."[47] Such measures could well change the politics of the postmark in ways that discourage members from abusing their franking privilege.

Placing Congress Under the Law For years Congress routinely exempted itself from many of the laws it passed that others had to obey. In defense of this practice, members said that if members of Congress were subject to, for example, the minimum wage laws, the executive branch, charged with enforcing these laws, would acquire excessive power over Congress. This would violate the separation of powers. But as public criticism of Congress grew and confidence in government declined, more and more people demanded that Congress subject itself to the laws that applied to everybody else. In 1995 the 104th Congress did this by passing a bill that would oblige Congress to obey ten or so important laws governing such things as civil rights, occupational safety, fair labor standards, and family leave. To avoid putting itself under the thumb of the executive branch, Congress created its own Office of Compliance to implement the necessary regulations. The law was pushed by the Republican majority, but many Democrats supported it. Whatever effect the law will have on the people who work for Congress, it has at least addressed a source of public anger.

Trimming the Pork Reformers are not alone in believing that Congress spends money on wasteful projects designed solely to win votes in home districts. Bills containing money for local dams, bridges, roads, and monuments are referred to disparagingly as pork-barrel legislation. When members act to "bring home the bacon," reformers complain, Congress misallocates tax dollars by supporting projects with trivial social benefits in order to bolster their reelection prospects. And now that the federal budget deficit has grown to such staggering dimensions, a favorite reform for restoring fiscal sanity is to "cut the pork."

No one can doubt the value of trimming unnecessary spending, but pork is not necessarily the villain it is made out to be. For example, the main cause of the budget deficit is the increase in spending on entitlement programs (like health care and interest on the national debt) without a corresponding increase in taxes. Spending on pork is a small fraction of spending on entitlements, and most categories of pork spending have decreased in the last ten or fifteen years. Furthermore, one person's pork is another person's necessity. No doubt some congressional districts get an unnecessary bridge or highway, but others get bridges and highways that are long overdue. The notion that every bridge or road a member of Congress gets for his or her district is wasteful pork is tantamount to saying that no member attaches any importance to merit. Opponents of pork assume that bridges and roads that are built as the result of a central plan (a plan drawn up in the executive branch) are inherently superior to bridges and roads built as a result of political bargaining. That may be true sometimes, but there is no reason to think it is always true.

Even if all pork were bad, it would still be necessary. Congress is an independent branch of government and each member is, by constitutional design, the advocate of his or her district or state. No member's vote can be won by coercion and few can be had by mere appeals to party loyalty or presidential needs. Pork is a way of obtaining consent. The only alternative is bribery, but bribery, besides being wrong, would benefit only the member whereas pork usually benefits voters in the member's district. If you want to eliminate pork, you must eliminate Congress by converting it into a parliament under the control of a powerful party leader or prime minister. In a tightly controlled parliament, no votes need be bought; they can be commanded. But members of such a parliament can do little to help their constituents cope with government or to defend them against bureaucratic abuses, nor can they investigate the conduct of the executive branch. The price of a citizen-oriented Congress is a pork-oriented Congress.

Cutting Committees   Congress is supposed to organize itself in ways that enable its members to deliberate, debate, and decide matters of national policy in the public interest. Instead, it often appears that Congress is organized mainly to afford each member a spot on numerous political feifdoms (committees) while keeping thousands of staff gainfully employed.

It is clear that congressional organization has been increasing in both size and complexity (see Table 11.6). The overall number of seats on House committees and subcommittees grew from 2,511 in 1982 to 3,177 in 1992, and the average number of member assignments grew during this period from 5.7 to 7.2. In the Senate in 1993 members averaged more than 11 committee and subcommittee assignments.[48] As two experts on the Congress, Thomas E. Mann and Norman J. Ornstein, have observed:

> *As the basic structure for a division of labor, the committee system serves several functions. It allows for simultaneous consideration of many important substantive matters without having to use shortcuts because of lack of time. . . . It allows multiple points of access for interests and individuals in society to approach Congress with their concerns. It enables Congress to legislate, investigate, and oversee executive behavior. . . . The ballooning number of committee assignments of members, leading to increasing conflicts in scheduling, a frenetic pace of legislative life, and a shorter attention span for members, accompanied by decreasing attendance at committee and subcommittee meetings and hearings and less real focus on important problems, has been one of the clearest and deepest problems we have seen emerge and grow.[49]*

To deal with these problems, Mann and Ornstein recommended strict limitations on committee assignments for members in both chambers: no member will be allowed to serve on more than two committees (one if exclusive) and four subcommittees in the House, and no more than two major committees, one minor committee, and four subcommittees in the Senate, with exceptions only for the Ethics Committee and temporary investigative panels. Except for Appropriations, no committee would be allowed more than six subcommittees. Under their plan, most select and joint committees would be abolished.[50]

Most reformers who advocate cutting committees also believe in downsizing staff. During the 1992 presidential campaign, Bill Clinton called for a 25 percent across-the-board cut in congressional staff, while George Bush called for a 33 percent cut. Most staff growth occurred in the 1960s and 1970s, a time when the White House was dramatically increasing

TABLE 11.6 Membership of House Standing Committees, 1983 and 1993

Committee	1983	1993	Percent Change
Agriculture	41	45	+10%
Appropriations	57	60	+5
Armed Services	44	55	+25
Banking	46	51	+11
Budget	31	43	+39
District of Columbia	11	11	None
Education and Labor	31	39	+26
Energy and Commerce	42	44	+5
Foreign Affairs	37	44	+19
Government Operations	39	42	+8
House Administration	19	19	None
Judiciary	31	35	+13
Merchant Marine	39	46	+18
Natural Resources	40	39	−3
Post Office	24	23	−4
Public Works	48	61	+27
Rules	13	13	None
Science and Technology	41	55	+34
Small Business	41	45	+10
Standards	12	14	+17
Veterans Affairs	33	35	+6
Ways and Means	35	38	+9

SOURCE: Thomas E. Mann and Norman J. Ornstein, *Renewing Congress: A Second Report* (Washington, D.C.: Brookings Institution and American Enterprise Institute, 1993), 18. Reprinted with permission of the Brookings Institution.

its own staff. Congressional staff sizes in the early 1990s were roughly equal to what they were in the early 1980s.[51] Staffers provide Congress with its own independent base of information and expertise, and the capacity to process mail and establish contacts with constituents. Thus, it is likely that a large across-the-board cut in congressional staff would make Congress more dependent on the executive branch and on interest groups for information and policy expertise, and less able to process constituent demands. As Mann and Ornstein conclude, any such "cut in staff would be a penny-wise, pound-foolish approach" to reform.[52]

Ethics and Congress

Most contemporary proposals to reform Congress are motivated at least in part by a belief that "congressional ethics" has become an oxymoron.* The Framers of the Constitution hoped that members of Congress would be virtuous citizens, but they feared that some would not. They had, as stated earlier, a rather sober view of human nature and designed the system of checks and balances in part to minimize the chance that anybody, by gaining corrupt influence over one part of the government, would be able to tyrannize over the other parts.

It could be argued that this very separation of powers made corruption more, rather than less, likely. If power were concentrated in one set of hands—say, those of a prime minister—nobody would have any incentive to bribe or even influence any other political figure; there is little that subordinate officials could do for that person. And though a favor seeker might try to influence the prime minister, few could pay the price of bribing someone with so much power. When bits and pieces of power are placed in many different hands, as in the United States, there are many opportunities to exercise influence: lots of officials have something that they could sell, and at a price that many favor seekers could afford.

For example, the appointive power is shared by the president and the Senate. Since the Senate will not confirm anybody for appointment to federal office who is personally obnoxious to either senator from the candidate's state (the rule of "senatorial courtesy"), the opportunity exists for an office seeker to try to influence a senator to get the desired appointment. The stage is also set for a senator, who may want the president to nominate a certain person, to delay some piece of presidential legislation until the nomination is made, or for the president to try to get a piece of legislation passed by offering to appoint the senator's campaign manager, brother-in-law, or law partner to a lucrative federal post.

Some of these attempts at influence may involve money, some may not. The point is that divided power means divided responsibility, and divided responsibility creates the possibility for evaded responsibility. It also creates the need to use influence to assemble enough power to get anything done. What the Constitution has separated, individuals must pull together; sometimes the pulling together involves mere persuasion, sometimes an exchange of favors, occasionally the payment of money.

Though the moral climate of American politics has improved in the last century, scandals continue. From 1941 to 1989 nearly fifty members of Congress faced criminal charges; most were convicted.[53] From 1981 to 1990 another forty or so were the object of charges of misconduct, including misuse of funds, having sex with minors, failing to disclose income, and accepting illegal gifts. The two most dramatic events were the 1980–1981 Abscam investigation and the 1989 Jim Wright hearings. In the former, six House members and one senator were convicted of having accepted money from an FBI agent posing as a wealthy Arab seeking political favors. In the latter, House Speaker Wright was found by the House Ethics Committee to have broken rules against taking certain gifts and exceeding limits on outside income. The Speaker resigned.

These scandals, together with the large amount of PAC money given to legislators, have led many people to conclude that "we have the best Congress money can buy." No doubt there are moral failings, as there would be among any group of 535 powerful men and women, but it is not clear that Congress is inherently corrupt. Since the Abscam investigation, only four House members have been indicted on criminal charges—lamentable, but not much different from the rate of theft in the population at large.

The more difficult issues are much deeper than brazen corruption:

- Members of Congress are elected to look out for their constituents. What limits, if any, should exist on how they go about this job?

- Congress has the right to judge and discipline its own members but insists that ethical cases in the executive branch be turned over to an independent special prosecutor. Shouldn't the same rules apply to both branches?

- Election campaigns are expensive, and somebody must pay the bill. If private fund-raising is out-

---

*An oxymoron is a phrase that combines contradictory terms ("deafening silence").

lawed or even sharply restricted, this could add to the already heavy burden that challengers must shoulder in running against incumbents. How can campaigns be paid for in ways that are both fair *and* honest?

In 1989 Congress adopted new ethics rules for itself. They differ somewhat between the House and Senate (under the Constitution each chamber can set its own rules). They include the following:

- *Disclosures:* Members must file a financial disclosure statement every year.

- *Honoraria:* Starting in 1991 House members could not accept fees for speaking. Senators can keep them, but only up to 27 percent of their salaries.

- *Campaign funds:* After 1992 House members first elected before 1980 were no longer able to keep surplus campaign funds for their personal use after they retire.

- *Lobbying:* Former members may not lobby Congress for one year after they retire.

- *Gifts:* House members may accept free meals and drinks but not other gifts worth more than $200 ($300 for senators) from any one person in any year. The annual limit will be adjusted for inflation.

- *Free travel:* Members may not accept travel paid for by private persons for more than four days of domestic travel per year (three days for the Senate) and seven days of international travel per year.

Other laws had already restricted the amount of money that any individual may contribute to a congressional election campaign and set rules for how those funds are to be handled (see Chapter 8).

The ethics code was based on the assumption that improper influence is associated with financial transactions, yet obviously that is not always the case. Many members of Congress who in the past earned substantial incomes from speaking and writing did not have their votes corrupted by such activities; other members of Congress who rarely take such fees may be heavily influenced, perhaps unduly so, by personal friendships and political alliances that have no direct monetary value at all. And no ethics code can address the bargaining among members of Con-

How Congress Raises Its Pay

*F*or over two hundred years Congress has tried to find a politically painless way to raise its own pay. It has managed to vote itself a pay increase twenty-three times in those two centuries, but usually at the price of a hostile public reaction. Twice during the nineteenth century a pay raise led to a massacre of incumbents in the next election.

Knowing this, Congress has invented various ways to get a raise without actually appearing to vote for it. These have included the following:

- voting for a tax deduction for expenses incurred as a result of living in Washington.

- creating a citizens' commission that could recommend a pay increase that would take effect automatically provided Congress did not vote *against* it, and

- linking increases in pay to decreases in honoraria (that is, in speaking fees).

In 1989 a commission recommended a congressional pay raise of over 50 percent (from $89,500 to $135,000) and a ban on honoraria. The House planned to let it take effect automatically. But the public wouldn't have it, demanding that Congress vote on the raise—and vote it down. It did.

Embarrassed by its maneuvering, Congress retreated. At the end of 1989 it voted itself (as well as most top executive and judicial branch members) a small pay increase (7.9 percent for House, 9.9 percent for the Senate) that also provided for automatic cost-of-living adjustments (up to 5 percent a year) in the future.

gress, or between members of Congress and the president, involving the exchange of favors and votes.

Moreover the ethics rules seem to favor people with inherited wealth or those who earned large sums before entering Congress. When the Senate voted in 1990 to limit the outside income its members could earn (mostly by writing and speaking) to 15 percent of their Senate salary, Senator Daniel Patrick Moynihan, who can earn a lot from writing and speaking, proposed an amendment to limit what

CRITICAL ★ THINKING

Ruling on Ethics in Congress: Ex-Members as Judges?

For several decades, both the House and Senate have used permanent committees as the primary vehicle for considering allegations of wrongdoing or violating ethical standards by members. But committees that consist of current lawmakers have an innate conflict of interest when judging their colleagues— that is, protecting a colleague from serious penalty, or seeing a colleague embarrassed, wounded, or removed from office. Also, having current lawmakers wrestle with ethics problems takes time away from their other duties. And no matter what they decide, ethics committees consisting of current lawmakers are always open to accusations of partisanship, score-settling, or foot-dragging.

For dealing with these drawbacks, Thomas E. Mann and Norman J. Ornstein propose that the House and Senate each designate pools consisting of a large number of former members, along with others whose experience and background make them appropriate persons to judge ethics issues involving members of Congress and their employees. Under their plan, the majority and minority leaders would each designate five members from the pool to sit as an ad hoc panel, which would then forward its recommendations to the internal ethics committees, and then, if necessary, to the House or Senate floors for consideration and votes.

Do you think such an ad hoc panel would be an improvement over the current system? How might the selection of panel members be politically motivated? Would a panel made up of individuals who are not serving in Congress be likely to apply ethical standards that are unrealistic or infeasible? Would Congress accept the rulings of an "outside" panel on its own members?

SOURCE: Thomas E. Mann and Norman J. Ornstein, *Renewing Congress: A Second Report* (Washington, D.C.: Brookings Institution and American Enterprise Institute, 1993), 18.

senators could receive from their "unearned income" (that is, their investments and inherited wealth) to 15 percent of their Senate salaries. It passed. Had the bill become law (which it did not, lacking presidential approval), it would have meant that the many Senate millionaires would have had either to leave their money to charity or leave the Senate. Moynihan reasoned that calling senators unethical if they made too much money by working, while calling them ethical if they did no work more arduous than collecting dividends, made no sense.

It might not have made sense to the Framers, either. Their object was not to create a simon-pure Congress, but to create one that was powerful, that would be composed of representatives who (at least in the lower house) could be closely checked by the voters, and that would offer manifold opportunities for competing interests and opinions to check one another. Their goal was liberty more than morality, though they knew that in the long run the latter was essential to the former.

SUMMARY:
THE OLD AND THE NEW CONGRESS

Over the last half century or so, Congress, especially the House, has evolved through three stages. The modern Congress is an uneasy combination of stages two and three.

During the first stage, lasting from the end of World War I until the early 1960s, the House was dominated by powerful committee chairmen who controlled the agenda, decided which members would get what services for their constituents, and tended to follow the leadership of the Speaker. Newer members were expected to be seen but not heard; power and prominence came only after a long apprenticeship. Congressional staffs were small, and so members dealt with each other face to face. In dealing with other members, it helped to have a southern accent: half of all committee chairmen in both the House and the Senate were from the South. Not many laws were passed over their objections.

The second stage emerged in the early 1970s in part as the result of trends already under way (for example, the steady growth in the number of staffers assigned to each member) and in part as a result of changes in procedures and organization brought about by younger, especially northern, members. Dissatisfied with southern resistance to civil-rights bills and emboldened by a sharp increase in the number of liberals who had been elected in the Johnson landslide of 1964, the House Democratic caucus adopted rules that allowed the caucus to select committee chairmen without regard to seniority, dramatically increased the number and staffs of subcommittees (for the first time, the Way and Means Committee was required to have subcommittees), authorized individual committee members (instead of the chairman) to choose the chairmen of these subcommittees, ended the ability of chairmen to refuse to call meetings, and made it much harder for those meetings to be closed to the public. The installation of electronic voting made it easier to require recorded votes, and so the number of times each member had to go on record rose sharply. The Rules Committee was instructed to issue more rules that would allow floor amendments.

At the same time the number of southern Democrats in leadership positions began to decline, and the conservatism of the remaining ones began to lessen. (In 1990 southerners held only a quarter of committee chairmanships in the House and none of the major party leadership posts.) Moreover northern and southern Democrats began to vote together a bit more frequently (though the conservative Boll Weevils remained a significant—and often swing—group).

These changes created a House ideally suited to serve the reelection needs of its members. Each representative could be an individual political entrepreneur, seeking publicity, claiming credit, introducing bills, holding subcommittee hearings, and assigning staffers to work on constituents' problems. There was no need to defer to powerful party leaders or committee chairmen. But because representatives in each party were becoming more alike ideologically, there was a rise in party voting. Congress became a career attractive to men and women skilled in these techniques, and these people entered Congress in large numbers. Their skill was manifest in the growth of the sophomore surge—the increase in their winning percentage during their first reelection campaign.

Even junior members could now make their mark on legislation. In the House more floor amendments were offered and were passed; in the Senate filibusters became more commonplace. Owing to multiple referrals and overlapping subcommittee jurisdictions, more members could participate in writing bills and overseeing government agencies.

But lurking within the changes that defined the second stage were others, less noticed at the time, that created the beginnings of a new phase. The third stage was an effort in the House to strengthen and centralize party leadership. The Speaker acquired the power to appoint a majority of the members of the Rules Committee. That body, worried by the flood of floor amendments, began issuing more restrictive rules. By the mid-1980s this had reached the point where Republicans were complaining that they were being gagged. The Speaker also got control of the Democratic Steering and Policy Committee (it assigns new members to committees) and was given the power to refer bills to several committees simultaneously.

These opportunities for becoming a powerful Speaker were not noticed while the affable Tip O'Neill of Massachusetts held that post, but when Jim Wright of Texas replaced O'Neill, he began making full use of those powers. Perhaps if he had not stumbled over his ethical problems, Wright might have succeeded in becoming the policy leader of the House, setting the agenda and getting much of it adopted. The replacement of Wright by Tom Foley of Washington signaled a return to a more accommodative leadership style. Foley's replacement, Republican Newt Gingrich, is a more assertive policy leader. The evolution of the House remains an incomplete story; it is not yet clear whether it will remain in stage two or find some way of moving decisively into stage three. For now it has elements of both.

Meanwhile the Senate remains as individualistic and decentralized as ever—a place where it has always been difficult to exercise strong leadership.

Though its members may complain that Congress is collectively weak, to any visitor from abroad it seems extraordinarily powerful, probably the most powerful legislative body in the world. Congress has always been jealous of its constitutional indepen-

How to Look Up Facts about Congress

To find out how Congress is organized, staffed, and run:

Congressional Quarterly, *Guide to Congress.* 3d ed. Washington, D.C.: Congressional Quarterly, 1982. One volume that covers almost everything.

Congressional Directory (published annually by Congress). Lists members of Congress, committee assignments, telephone numbers, maps of districts.

Congressional Staff Directory. Lists all staffers and gives biographical sketches.

To find out about the political inclinations and constituency characteristics of members of Congress:

Michael Barone et al. *The Almanac of American Politics.* Revised every two years, this is a candid description of districts, states, members of Congress, and how they vote.

Congressional District Data Book. Published by the Census Bureau, it compiles all relevant census data by congressional district.

To find out what is going on in Congress currently:

Congressional Quarterly Weekly Report. A weekly summary of issues, votes, politics. Commercially published.

Congressional Record. The official, verbatim account of what is said (after being revised by members of Congress who do the saying). Published daily by the Government Printing Office while Congress is in session.

To find out what Congress did in the past:

Congressional Quarterly Almanac. Published each year as a summary of issues, votes, and politics.

Congressional Quarterly: Congress and the Nation. 8 volumes, 1945–1992. Convenient compilation of past *Almanacs.*

To find out the exact wording of bills and laws:

United States Statutes at Large. Published by the Government Printing Office; the laws and volumes are chronologically arranged.

Digest of Public Bills. Published by Congressional Research Service.

dence and authority. Three compelling events led to Congress's reasserting its authority: the increasingly unpopular war in Vietnam; the Watergate scandals, which revealed a White House meddling illegally in the electoral process; and the advent of divided governments—with Republicans in control of the presidency and Democrats in control of Congress.

In 1973 it passed, over a presidential veto, the War Powers Act, giving it a greater voice in the use of American forces abroad (see Chapter 20). The following year it passed the Congressional Budget and Impoundment Control Act, which denied the president the right to refuse to spend money appropriated by Congress (see Chapter 12) and which allowed Congress to play a greater role in the budget process (see Chapter 16). It passed more laws to provide a legislative veto over proposed presidential actions, especially with respect to the sale of arms abroad (see Chapter 13). Not all these steps have withstood the tests of time or Supreme Court review, but taken together they symbolize the resurgence of congressional authority and helped set the stage for sharper conflicts between Congress and the presidency.

The claims that Congress became weak as the president grew stronger are a bit overdrawn. As we shall see in the next chapter, the view from the White House is quite different. Recent presidents have complained bitterly of their inability to get Congress even to act on, much less to approve, many of their key proposals and have resented what they regard as congressional interference in the management of executive-branch agencies and in the conduct of foreign affairs.

KEY TERMS

bicameral legislature   *p. 285*

filibuster   *p. 290*

marginal district   *p. 293*

conservative coalition   *p. 295*

malapportionment   *p. 296*

gerrymandering   *p. 296*

majority-minority districts   *p. 297*

descriptive representation   *p. 298*

SUGGESTED READINGS

Davidson, Roger H., and Walter J. Oleszek. *Congress and Its Members.* 3d ed. Washington, D.C.: Congressional Quarterly Press, 1990. Complete and authoritative account of who is in Congress and how it operates.

Dodd, Lawrence C., and Bruce I. Oppenheimer, eds. *Congress Reconsidered.* 4th ed. Washington, D.C.: Congressional Quarterly Press, 1989. Recent studies of congressional politics.

Malbin, Michael J., and Gerald Ginsberg, eds. *Limiting Legislative Terms.* Washington, D.C.: Congressional Quarterly, 1992. Good collection of essays on term limits.

Mann, Thomas E., and Norman J. Ornstein. *Renewing Congress.* 2 vols. Washington, D.C. Brookings Institution and American Enterprise Institute, 1993. Superb, up-to-date overview of what's really wrong with Congress and how to fix it.

Fenno, Richard F., Jr. *Congressmen in Committees.* Boston: Little, Brown, 1973. Study of the styles of twelve standing committees.

Maass, Arthur. *Congress and the Common Good.* New York: Basic Books, 1984. Insightful account of congressional operations, especially those involving legislative-executive relations.

Malbin, Michael J. *Unelected Representatives.* New York: Basic Books, 1980. Study of the influence of congressional staff members.

Mayhew, David R. *Congress: The Electoral Connection.* New Haven, Conn.: Yale University Press, 1974. Argues that a member of Congress's desire to win reelection shapes his or her legislative behavior.

Smith, Steven S., and Christopher J. Deering. *Committees in Congress.* Washington, D.C.: Congressional Quarterly, 1984. Analysis of how different kinds of congressional committees operate.

Sundquist, James L. *The Decline and Resurgence of Congress.* Washington, D.C.: Brookings Institution, 1981. A history of the fall and, after 1973, the rise of congressional power vis-à-vis the president.

12

The Presidency

Professor Jones speaks to his political-science class: "The president of the United States occupies one of the most powerful offices in the world. Presidents Kennedy and Johnson sent American troops to Vietnam, and President Bush sent them to Panama and to Saudi Arabia, all without war's being declared by Congress. President Nixon imposed wage and price controls on the country. Presidents Carter and Reagan between them selected most of the federal judges now on the bench; thus the political philosophies of these two men were stamped on the courts. No wonder people talk about our having an 'imperial presidency.' "

A few doors down the hall, Professor Smith speaks to her class: "The president, compared to the prime ministers of other democratic nations, is one of the weakest chief executives anywhere. President Carter signed an arms-limitation treaty with the Soviets, but the Senate wouldn't ratify it. President Reagan was not allowed even to test antisatellite weapons, and in 1986 Congress rejected his budget before the ink was dry. Regularly subordinates who are supposed to be loyal to the president leak his views to the press and undercut his programs before Congress. No wonder people talk about the president's being a 'pitiful, helpless giant.' "

Can Professors Jones and Smith be talking about the same office? Who is right? In fact they are both right. The American presidency is a unique office, with elements of great strength *and* profound weakness built into it by its constitutional origins.

The popularly elected president is an American invention. Of the roughly five dozen countries in which there is some degree of party competition and thus, presumably, some measure of free choice for the voters, only sixteen have a directly elected president, and thirteen of these are nations of North and South America. The democratic alternative is for the chief executive to be a prime minister, chosen by and responsible to the parliament. This system prevails in most Western European countries as well as in Israel and Japan. There is no nation with a purely presidential political system in Europe; France combines a directly elected president with a prime minister and parliament.[1]

Presidents and Prime Ministers

The parliamentary system of government, described at the beginning of Chapter 11, is a democratic alternative to a presidential one. The parliamentary system is twice as common as the presidential system and can be found in almost all the democratic nations of Europe—in England, Sweden, Denmark, Norway, Italy, The Netherlands, Germany—as well as in Japan and Israel. In a parliamentary system the chief executive, called the prime minister, is chosen not by the voters but by the legislature. The prime minister, in turn, selects the other ministers from the members of parliament. If the parliament has only two major parties, the ministers will usually be chosen from the majority party; if there are many parties (as in Italy), several parties may participate in a coalition cabinet. The prime minister remains in power as long as his or her party has a majority of the seats in the legislature or as long as the coalition he or she has assembled holds together. The voters choose who is to be a member of parliament—usually by voting for one or another party—but cannot choose who is to be the chief executive officer.

Whether a nation has a presidential or a parliamentary system makes a big difference in the identity and powers of the chief executive.

Presidents are often outsiders   People become president by winning elections, and sometimes winning is easier if you can show the voters that you are not part of "the mess in Washington." Prime ministers are selected from among people already in parliament, and so they are always insiders.

Jimmy Carter, Ronald Reagan, and Bill Clinton did not hold national office before becoming president. Franklin Roosevelt had been assistant secretary of the navy, but his real political experience was as governor of New York. Dwight Eisenhower was a general, not a politician. John F. Kennedy, Lyndon Johnson, and Richard Nixon had been in Congress, but only Nixon had had top-level experience in the executive branch (he had been vice president). George Bush had had a great deal of executive experience in Washington—as vice president, director of the CIA, and representative to China, whereas Bill Clinton's executive experience was as governor of Arkansas.

The prime minister of Great Britain may or may not have any real personal following at the time he or she is appointed. Winston Churchill was immensely popular in the country before he became the British prime minister in 1939, but Margaret Thatcher was largely unknown to the country when she became prime minister in 1979. But all British prime ministers have a lot of political experience.

Presidents choose cabinet members from outside Congress   Under the Constitution no sitting member of Congress can hold office in the executive branch. The persons chosen by a prime minister to be in the cabinet are almost always members of parliament.

Of the fourteen heads of cabinet agencies in the Clinton administration, only three had been members of Congress. The rest, as is customary with most presidents, were close personal friends or campaign aides, representatives of important constituencies (for example, farmers, blacks, or women), experts on various policy issues, or some combination of all three.

The prime minister of Great Britain, by contrast, picks all of his or her cabinet ministers from among members of Parliament. This is one way by which the prime minister exercises control over the legislature. If you were an ambitious member of Parliament, eager to become prime minister yourself some day, and if you knew that your main chance of realizing that ambition was to be appointed to a series of ever-more-important cabinet posts, then you would not be likely to antagonize the person doing the appointing.

Presidents have no guaranteed majority in the legislature   A prime minister's party (or coalition) always has a majority in parliament; if it did not, somebody else would be prime minister. A president's party often does not have a congressional majority; instead, Congress is often controlled by the opposite party, creating a divided government. Divided government means that cooperation between the two branches, hard to achieve under the best of circumstances, is often further reduced by partisan bickering.

Even when one party controls the White House and Congress, the two branches often work at cross purposes The U.S. Constitution created a system of separate branches sharing powers. The authors of the document expected that there would be conflict between the branches, and they have not been disappointed.

When Kennedy was president, his party, the Democrats, held a big majority in the House and the Senate. Yet Kennedy was frustrated by his inability to get Congress to approve proposals to enlarge civil rights, supply federal aid for school construction, create a Department of Urban Affairs and Housing, or establish a program of subsidized medical care for the elderly. During his last year in office, Congress passed only about one-fourth of his proposals. Carter did not fare much better; even though his Democrats controlled Congress, many of his most important proposals were defeated or greatly modified. Only Franklin Roosevelt (1933–1945) and Lyndon Johnson (1963–1969) had even brief success in leading Congress, and for Roosevelt most of that success was confined to his first term or to wartime.

Divided Government

In the forty years between 1952 and 1992, there were twenty congressional or presidential elections. Thirteen of the twenty produced **divided government**— that is, a government in which one party controlled the White House and a different party controlled one or both houses of Congress. When Bill Clinton became president in 1992, it was the first time since 1981 (and only the second time since 1969) that the same party was in charge of the presidency and Congress, creating a **unified government.**

Americans say they don't like divided government. They, or at least the pundits who claim to speak for them, think divided government produces partisan bickering, political paralysis, and policy gridlock. During the 1990 battle between President Bush and a Democratic Congress, one magazine compared it to a movie featuring the Keystone Kops, characters from the silent movies who wildly chased each other around while accomplishing nothing.[2] In the 1992 campaign, Bush, Clinton, and Ross Perot bemoaned the "stalemate" that had developed in Washington. When Clinton was sworn in as president, many commentators spoke approvingly of the "end of gridlock."

British Prime Minister John Major, unlike the president of the United States, knows that almost any bill he submits to his legislature will be approved.

There are two things wrong with these complaints. First, it is not clear that divided government produces a gridlock that is any worse than that which exists with unified government. Second, it is not clear that, even if gridlock does exist, it is always, or even usually, a bad thing for the country.

Does Gridlock Matter?

Despite the well-publicized stories about presidential budget proposals being ignored by Congress (Democrats used to describe Reagan and Bush budgets as "dead on arrival"), it is not easy to tell whether divided governments produce fewer or worse policies than unified ones. The scholars who have looked closely at the matter have, in general, concluded that divided governments do about as well as unified ones in passing important laws, conducting important investigations, and ratifying significant treaties.[3] Political scientist David Mayhew studied 267 important laws that were enacted between 1946 and 1990. These laws were as likely to be passed when different parties controlled the White House and Congress as when the same party controlled both branches.[4] For example, divided governments produced the 1946 Marshall Plan to rebuild war-torn Europe and the 1986 Tax Reform Act.

Why do divided governments produce about as much important legislation as unified ones? The main reason is that "unified government" is something of a myth. Just because the Democrats control the presidency and Congress does not mean that the Democratic president and the Democratic senators and representatives will see things the same way. For one thing, Democrats are themselves divided between conservatives (mainly from the South) and liberals (mainly from the Northeast and the West). They disagree about policy almost as much as Republicans and Democrats disagree. For another thing, the Constitution ensures that the president and Congress will be rivals for power and thus rivals in policy-making. That's what the separation of powers and checks and balances are all about.

As a result, periods of unified government often turn out not to be so unified. Democratic President Lyndon Johnson could not get many Democratic members of Congress to support his war policy in Vietnam. Democratic President Jimmy Carter could not get the Democratic-controlled Senate to ratify his strategic arms limitation treaty. Democratic President Bill Clinton could not get the Democratic Congress to go along with his policy on gays in the military or his original budget proposals; when the heavily revised budget did pass in 1993, it was by just one vote.

The only time there really is a unified government is when not just the same party but the same *ideological wing* of that party is in effective control of both branches of government. This was true in 1933 when Franklin Roosevelt was president and change-oriented Democrats controlled Congress and it was true again in 1965 when Lyndon Johnson and liberal Democrats dominated Congress. Both were periods when many major policy initiatives became law: Social Security, business regulation, Medicare, and civil rights. But these periods of ideologically unified government are very rare.

Is Policy Gridlock Bad?

An American president has less ability to decide what laws get passed than does a British prime minister. If you think that the job of a president is to "lead the country," that weakness will worry you. The only cure for that weakness is either to change the Constitution so that our government resembles that parliamentary system in effect in Great Britain or always to vote into office members of Congress who are not only of the same party as the president but agree with him on policy issues.

We suspect that even Americans who hate gridlock and want more leadership aren't ready to make sweeping constitutional changes or to stop voting for presidents and members of Congress from different parties. This unwillingness suggests that they like the idea of somebody being able to block a policy they don't like. Since all of us don't like something, we all have an interest in some degree of gridlock.

And we seem to protect that interest. In a typical presidential election, about one-fourth of all voters will vote for one party's candidate for president and the other party's candidate for Congress. As a result, about one-third of all congressional districts will be represented in the House by a person who does not belong to the party of the president who carried that district. Some scholars believe that voters split tickets deliberately in order to create divided government and thus magnify the effects of the checks and balances built into our system, but the evidence supporting this belief is not conclusive.

Gridlock, to the extent that it exists, is a necessary consequence of a system of **representative democracy.** Such a system causes delays, intensifies deliberations, forces compromises, and requires the creation of broad-based coalitions to support most new policies. This system is the opposite of **direct democracy.** If you believe in direct democracy, you believe that what the people want on some issue should become law with as little fuss and bother as possible. Political gridlocks are like traffic gridlocks—people get overheated, things boil over, nothing moves, and nobody wins except journalists who write about the mess and lobbyists who charge big fees to steer their clients around the tie-up. In a direct democracy, the president would be a traffic cop with broad powers to decide in what direction the traffic should move and to make sure that it moves that way.

Gridlock in History

The debate between advocates of direct and representative democracy has gone on since the founding of the republic. What is new is the greater frequency of divided government. Between 1900 and 1952, unified government was common (twenty-two out of twenty-six elections gave control over the White House and Congress to the same party). Since 1952, as we have seen, unified government has become a rarity and divided government has become common.

But if unified governments are not really unified—if in fact they are split by ideological differences within each party and by the institutional rivalries between the president and Congress—then this change is less important than it may seem. What *is* important is the relative power of the president and Congress. That has changed, and changed greatly.

The Evolution of the Presidency

In 1787 few issues inspired as much debate or concern among the Framers as the problem of defining the chief executive. The delegates feared anarchy and monarchy in about equal measure. When the Constitutional Convention met, the existing state constitutions gave most, if not all, power to the legislatures. In eight states the governor was actually chosen by the legislature, and in ten states the governor could not serve more than one year. Only in New York, Massachusetts, and Connecticut did governors have much power or serve for any length of time.

Some of the Framers proposed a plural national executive (that is, several people would each hold the executive power in different areas, or they would exercise the power as a committee). Others wanted the executive power checked, as it was in Massachusetts, by a council that would have to approve many of the chief executive's actions. Alexander Hamilton strongly urged the exact opposite: in a five-hour speech he called for something very much like an elective monarchy, patterned in some respects after the British kind. No one paid much attention to this plan or even, at first, to the more modest (and ultimately successful) suggestion of James Wilson for a single, elected president.

In time those won out who believed that the governing of a large nation, especially one threatened by foreign enemies, required a single president with significant powers. Their cause was aided, no doubt, by the fact that everybody assumed that George Washington would be the first president, and confidence in him—and in his sense of self-restraint—was widely shared. Even so, several delegates feared that the presidency would become, in the words of Edmund Randolph of Virginia, "the fœtus of monarchy."

Concerns of the Founders

The delegates in Philadelphia, and later the critics of the new Constitution during the debate over its ratification, worried about aspects of the presidency that were quite different from those that concern us today. In 1787–1789 some Americans suspected that the president, by being able to command the state militia, would use the militia to overpower state governments. Others were worried that, if the president

The first cabinet: left to right, Secretary of War Henry Knox, Secretary of State Thomas Jefferson, Attorney General Edmund Randolph, Secretary of the Treasury Alexander Hamilton, and President George Washington.

were allowed to share treaty-making power with the Senate, he would be "directed by minions and favorites" and become a "tool of the Senate."

But the most frequent concern was over the possibility of presidential reelection: Americans in the late eighteenth century were sufficiently suspicious of human nature and sufficiently experienced in the arts of mischievous government to believe that a president, once elected, would arrange to stay in office in perpetuity by resorting to bribery, intrigue, and force. This might happen, for example, every time the presidential election was thrown into the House of Representatives because no candidate had received a majority of the votes in the electoral college, a situation that most people expected to happen frequently.

In retrospect these concerns seem misplaced, even foolish. The power over the militia has had little significance; the election has gone to the House only twice (1800 and 1824). And though the Senate dominated the presidency off and on during the second half of the nineteenth century, it has not done so recently. The real sources of the expansion of presidential power—the president's role in foreign affairs, his ability to shape public opinion, his position as head of the executive branch, and his claims to have certain "inherent" powers by virtue of his office—were hardly predictable in 1787. And not surprisingly. There was nowhere in the world at that time, nor had there been at any time in history, an example of an American-style presidency. It was a unique and unprecedented institution, and the Framers and their critics can easily be forgiven for not predicting accurately how it would evolve. At a more general level, however, they understood the issue quite clearly. Gouverneur Morris of Pennsylvania put the problem of the presidency this way: "Make him too weak: the Legislature will usurp his powers. Make him too strong: he will usurp on the Legislature."

The Framers knew very well that the relations between the president and Congress and the manner in which the president is elected were of profound importance, and they debated both at great length. The first plan was for Congress to elect the president—in short, for the system to be quasi-parliamentary. But if that were done, some delegates pointed out, the Congress could dominate an honest or lazy president while a corrupt or scheming president might dominate Congress.

After much discussion it was decided that the president should be chosen directly by voters. But by which voters? The emerging nation was large and diverse. It seemed unlikely that every citizen would be familiar enough with the candidates to cast an informed vote for a president directly. Worse, a direct popular election would give inordinate weight to the large, populous states, and no plan with that outcome had any chance of adoption by the smaller states.

The Electoral College

Thus the electoral college was invented whereby each of the states would select electors in whatever manner it wished. The electors would then meet in each state capital and vote for president and vice president. Many Framers expected that this procedure would lead to each state's electors' voting for a favorite son, and thus no candidate would win a majority of the popular vote. In this event, it was decided, the House of Representatives should make the choice, with each state delegation casting one vote.

The plan seemed to meet every test: large states would have their say, but small states would be protected by having a minimum of three electoral votes no matter how tiny their populations. The small states together could wield considerable influence in the House, where, it was widely expected, most presidential elections would ultimately be decided. Of course it did not work out quite this way: the Framers did not foresee the role that political parties would play in producing nationwide support for a slate of national candidates.

Once the manner of electing the president was settled, the question of his powers was much easier to decide. After all, if you believe that the procedures are fair and balanced, then you are more confident in assigning larger powers to the president within this system. Accordingly the right to make treaties and the right to appoint lesser officials, originally reserved for the Senate, were given to the president "with the advice and consent of the Senate."

The President's Term of Office

Another issue was put to rest soon thereafter. George Washington, the unanimous choice of the electoral college to be the first president, firmly limited himself

President Corazon Aquino became president of the Philippines only after popular demonstrations and military support forced her predecessor, Ferdinand Marcos, to leave office amidst charges that he had presided over a rigged election. Free elections and peaceful transfers of power are rare in the world.

to two terms in office (1789–1797), and no president until Franklin D. Roosevelt (1933–1945) dared to run for more (though Ulysses S. Grant tried). In 1951 the Twenty-second Amendment to the Constitution was ratified, formally limiting all subsequent presidents to two terms. The remaining issues concerning the nature of the presidency, and especially the relations between the president and Congress, have been the subject of continuing dispute. The pattern of relationships that we see today is the result of an evolutionary process that has extended over more than two centuries.

The first problem was to establish the legitimacy of the presidency itself: that is, to assure, if possible, public acceptance of the office, its incumbent, and its powers, and to establish an orderly transfer of power from one incumbent to the next.

Today we take this for granted. When Bill Clinton was inaugurated in January 1993 as our forty-second president, George Bush, the forty-first president, quietly left the White House and went home. In the world today such an uneventful succession is unusual. In many nations a new chief executive comes to power with the aid of military force or as a result of political intrigue; his predecessor often leaves office disgraced, exiled, or dead. At the time that the Constitution was written, the Founders could only hope that an orderly transfer of power from one president to the next would occur. France had just undergone a bloody revolution; England in the not-too-distant past had beheaded a king; and in Poland the ruler was elected by a process so manifestly corrupt and so

America has witnessed a peaceful transfer of power, not only between leaders of different parties (such as Woodrow Wilson and William Howard Taft in 1913) but also after a popular leader is assassinated (Lyndon Johnson is sworn in after Kennedy's death).

The Electoral College

Each state is allotted by the Constitution as many electoral votes as it has senators and representatives in Congress. Thus no state has fewer than three electoral votes. (The District of Columbia also gets three even though it has no members of Congress.)

In each state each party runs a slate of electors pledged to that party's presidential and vice presidential candidates. The names of these electors usually do not appear on the ballots. The slate whose candidate wins more popular votes than any other is authorized to cast all the votes of that state in the electoral college.

This results in a "winner-take-all" effect. Since it is up to the state legislatures to decide how electors are chosen, they could devise systems that would produce a split in the state's electoral votes. Maine and Nebraska are the only states that have done this. In these two states, one electoral vote goes to the winner of the popular vote in each district, and two

electoral votes go to the top vote-getter statewide.

The winning slates of electors assemble in their state capitals about six weeks after the election to cast their ballots. Ordinarily this is a pure formality. Occasionally, however, an elector will vote for a presidential candidate other than the one who carried the state. Such "faithless electors" have appeared in nine elections since 1796. The most recent case was in 1988, when a West Virginia elector pledged to Michael Dukakis voted instead for Lloyd Bentsen.

The state electoral ballots are opened and counted before a joint session of Congress during the first week of January. The candidate with a majority of votes is declared elected.

If no candidate wins a majority, the House of Representatives chooses the president from among the three leading candidates, with each state casting one vote. By House rule, each state's vote is

allotted to the candidate preferred by a majority of the state's House delegation. If there is a tie within a delegation, that state's vote is not counted.

The House has had to decide two presidential contests. In 1800 Thomas Jefferson and Aaron Burr tied in the electoral college because of a defect in the language of the Constitution—each state cast two electoral votes without indicating which was for president and which for vice president. (Burr was supposed to be vice president and after much maneuvering, he was.) This problem was corrected by the Twelfth Amendment, ratified in 1804. The only House decision under the modern system was in 1824, when it chose John Quincy Adams over Andrew Jackson and William H. Crawford, even though Jackson had more electoral votes (and probably more popular votes) than his rivals.

The chief political effects of the electoral college are these: The winner-take-

---

open to intrigue that Thomas Jefferson, in what may be the first example of ethnic humor in American politics, was led to refer to the proposed American presidency as a "bad edition of a Polish king."

Yet by the time Abraham Lincoln found himself at the helm of a nation plunged into a bitter, bloody civil war, fifteen presidents had been elected, served their time, and left office without a hint of force being used to facilitate the process and with the people accepting the process—if not admiring all the presidents. This orderly transfer of authority occurred despite passionate opposition and deeply divisive elections (such as that which brought Jefferson to power). It did not happen by accident.

The First Presidents

Those who first served as president were among the most prominent men in the new nation, all active either in the movement for independence or in the Founding or in both. Of the first five presidents, four (all but John Adams) served two full terms. Washington and Monroe were not even opposed. The first administration had at the highest levels the leading spokesmen for all of the major viewpoints: Alexander Hamilton was Washington's secretary of the treasury (and was sympathetic to the urban commercial interests), and Thomas Jefferson was secretary of state (and more inclined toward rural, small-town, and

ELECTORAL VOTES PER STATE FOR 1992 ELECTION

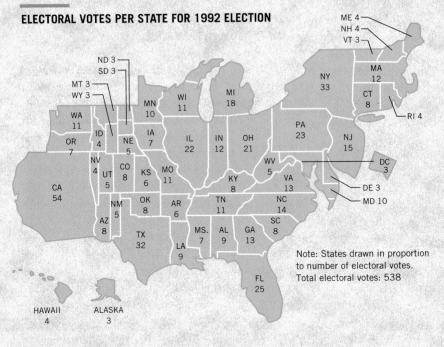

Note: States drawn in proportion to number of electoral votes. Total electoral votes: 538

dent seeking reelection has reason to be attentive to the needs of such states.

Proposals to alter or abolish the electoral college have been made, but none has come close to adoption. Among these are plans to elect the president by direct, national, popular vote; to divide each state's electoral votes in proportion to the popular vote received by each candidate in that state; to have electors chosen by congressional district rather than at large; and to retain the electoral system but abolish the office of elector and thus the chance of a faithless elector.

The issues and arguments are complex. Those who want to preserve the electoral college believe that it is important for the states to have a role in choosing the president and for the president to have an electoral reason to attend to state interests. Moreover, the electoral college helps maintain the two-party system. Those favoring direct popular election argue that the states are irrelevant in presidential elections and that each person's vote should count the same as every other person's regardless of where he or she lives.

all system probably discourages the emergence of serious third parties. The system encourages candidates to focus their campaigns on states, especially states whose vote may be in doubt. It especially encourages candidates to emphasize large, doubtful states. A candidate who carries the ten largest states wins 254 electoral votes, only 16 short of a majority. These states tend to be the most urbanized, industrialized, and politically competitive ones. A presi-

farming views). Washington spoke out strongly against political parties, and though parties soon emerged, there was a stigma attached to them: many people believed that it was wrong to take advantage of divisions in the country, to organize deliberately to acquire political office, or to make legislation depend upon party advantage. As it turned out, this hostility to party (or "faction," as it was more commonly called) was unrealistic: parties are as natural to democracy as churches to religion.

Establishing the legitimacy of the presidency in the early years was made easier by the fact that the national government had relatively little to do. It had, of course, to establish a sound currency and to settle the debt accrued during the Revolutionary War. The Treasury Department inevitably became the principal federal office, especially under the strong leadership of Hamilton. Relations with England and France were important—and difficult—but otherwise government took little time and few resources.

In appointing people to federal office, a general rule of "fitness" emerged: those appointed should have some standing in their communities and be well thought of by their neighbors. Appointments based on partisanship soon arose, but community stature could not be neglected.

The presidency was kept modest. Washington clearly had not sought the office and did not relish the exercise of its then modest powers. He traveled widely so that as many people as possible could see their new president. His efforts to establish a semiregal court etiquette were quickly rebuffed; the presidency was to be kept simple. Congress decided that not until after a president was dead might his likeness appear on a coin or on currency; no president until Eisenhower was given a pension on his retirement.

The president's relations with Congress were correct but not close. Washington appeared before the Senate to ask its advice on a proposed treaty with some Indian tribes. He got none, and instead was politely told that the Senate would like to consider the matter in private. He declared that he would be "damned if he ever went there again," and he never did. Thus ended the responsibility of the Senate to "advise" the president. Alexander Hamilton while secretary of the treasury tried to function as a prime minister, even attempting to appear before the House of Representatives to exercise personal leadership over his legislative program. The House would not let him enter its chamber (he had to buttonhole members in the lobby instead). Vetoes were sometimes cast by a president, but sparingly, and then only when the president believed that the law was not simply unwise but unconstitutional. Washington cast only two vetoes; Jefferson and Adams none.

The Jacksonians

At a time roughly corresponding to the presidency of Andrew Jackson (1829–1837), broad changes began to occur in American politics, which, together with the personality of Jackson himself, altered the relations between president and Congress and the nature of presidential leadership. As so often happens, few people at the time Jackson took office had much sense of what his presidency would be like. Though he had been a member of the House of Representatives and of the Senate, he was elected as a military hero, and an apparently doddering one at that. Sixty-one years old and seemingly frail, he nonetheless used the powers of his office as no one before him had.

Jackson vetoed twelve acts of Congress, more than all his predecessors combined and more than any subsequent president until Andrew Johnson thirty years later. His vetoes were not simply on constitutional grounds but on policy ones: he saw himself as the only official elected by the entire voting citizenry, and thus as the "Tribune of the People." None of his vetoes was overridden. He did not initiate many new policies, but he struck out against the ones that he did not like. He did so at a time when the size of the electorate was increasing rapidly, and new

President Andrew Jackson thought of himself as the "Tribune of the People," and symbolized this by throwing a White House party that anyone could attend. Hundreds of people showed up and ate or carried away most of a 1,400-pound block of cheese.

states, especially in the West, had entered the Union. (There were then twenty-four states in the Union, more than twice the original number.)

Jackson demonstrated what could be done by a popular president. He did not shrink from conflict with Congress, and the tension between the two branches of government that was intended by the Framers became intensified by the personalities of those in government: Jackson in the White House, and Henry Clay, Daniel Webster, and John Calhoun in Congress. These powerful figures walked the political stage at a time when bitter sectional conflicts—over slavery and commercial policies—were beginning to split the country. Jackson, though he was opposed to a large and powerful federal government and wished to return somehow to the agrarian simplicities of Jefferson's time, was nonetheless a believer in a strong and independent presidency. This view, though obscured by nearly a century of subsequent congressional dominance of national politics, was ultimately to triumph—for better or for worse.

The Reemergence of Congress

With the end of Jackson's second term, Congress quickly reestablished its power and, except for the wartime presidency of Lincoln and brief flashes of presidential power under James Polk (1845–1849) and Grover Cleveland (1885–1889, 1893–1897), the presidency for a hundred years was the subordinate branch of the national government. Of the eight presidents who succeeded Jackson, two (William H. Harrison and Zachary Taylor) died in office, and none of the others served more than one term. Schoolchildren, trying to memorize the list of American presidents, always stumble in this era of the "no-name" presidents. This is hardly a coincidence: Congress was the leading institution, struggling, unsuccessfully, with slavery and sectionalism.

It was also an intensely partisan era, a legacy of Jackson that lasted well into the twentieth century. Public opinion was closely divided. In nine of the seventeen presidential elections between the end of Jackson's term in 1837 and Theodore Roosevelt's election in 1904, the winning candidate received less than half the popular vote. Only two candidates (Lincoln in 1864 and Ulysses S. Grant in 1872) received more than 55 percent of the popular vote.

During this long period of congressional—and usually senatorial—dominance of national government, only Lincoln broke new ground for presidential power. Lincoln's expansive use of that power, like Jackson's, was totally unexpected. He was first elected in 1860 as a minority president, receiving less than 40 percent of the popular vote in a field of four candidates. Though a member of the new Republican party, he had been a member of the Whig party, a group that had stood for limiting presidential power. He had opposed America's entry into the Mexican War and had been critical of Jackson's use of executive authority. But as president during the Civil War, he made unprecedented use of the vague gift of powers in Article II of the Constitution, especially of those that he felt were "implied" or were "inherent" in the phrase, "take care that the laws be faithfully executed," and in the express authorization for him to act as commander in chief. Lincoln raised an army, spent money, blockaded southern ports, temporarily suspended the writ of habeas corpus, and issued an Emancipation Proclamation to free the slaves—all without prior congressional approval. He justified this, as most Americans probably would have, by the emergency conditions created by civil war. In this he acted little differently from Thomas Jefferson, who while president waged undeclared war against various North African pirates.

After Lincoln, Congress reasserted its power and became, during the Reconstruction of the South and for many decades thereafter, the principal federal institution. But it had become abundantly clear that a national emergency could equip the president with great powers and that a popular and strong-willed president could expand his powers even without an emergency. Except for the administrations of Theodore Roosevelt (1901–1909) and Woodrow Wilson (1913–1921), the president was, until the New Deal, at best a negative force—a source of opposition *to* Congress, not a source of initiative and leadership for it. Grover Cleveland was a strong personality, but for all his efforts he was able to do little more than veto bills that he did not like. He cast 414 vetoes—more than any other president until Franklin Roosevelt. A frequent target of his vetoes were bills to confer special pensions on Civil War veterans.

Today we are accustomed to thinking that the president formulates a legislative program to which

Congress then responds, but until the 1930s the opposite was more the case. Congress ignored the initiatives of such presidents as Grover Cleveland, Rutherford Hayes, Chester Arthur, and Calvin Coolidge. Woodrow Wilson in 1913 was the first president since John Adams to deliver personally the State of the Union address, and one of the first to develop and argue for a presidential legislative program.

Our popular conception of the president as the central figure of national government, devising a legislative program and commanding a large staff of advisers, is very much a product of the modern era and of the enlarged role of government. In the past the presidency only became powerful during a national crisis (the Civil War, World War I) or because of an extraordinary personality (Andrew Jackson, Theodore Roosevelt, Woodrow Wilson). Since the 1930s, however, the presidency has been powerful no matter who occupied the office and whether or not there was a crisis. Because government now plays such an active role in our national life, the president is the natural focus of attention and the titular head (whether he is the real boss is another matter) of a huge federal administrative system.

But the popular conception of the president as the central figure of national government belies the realities of present-day legislative-executive relations. In a thorough analysis of national policy-making from the Eisenhower years through the Reagan administration, Mark A. Peterson demonstrated that Congress, not the president, often took the lead in setting the legislative agenda.[5] For example, the 1990 Clean Air Act, like the 1970 Clean Air Act before it, was born and bred mainly by congressional, not presidential, action. Indeed, administration officials played almost no role in the legislative process that culminated in these laws.[6] When President Bush signed the 1990 bill at a stately ceremony in the East Room of the White House, he quipped, "Mission defined. Mission accomplished," but it is clear that it was members of Congress who had actually proposed and drafted "the several-inch stack of legislation" that Bush signed.[7] Likewise, although presidents dominated budget policymaking from the 1920s into the early 1970s, they no longer do. Instead, the "imperatives of the budgetary process have pushed congressional leaders to center stage."[8] Thus, as often as not, the Congress proposes, the president

disposes, and legislative-executive relations involve hard bargaining and struggle between these two branches of government.

The Powers of the President

Though the president, unlike a prime minister, cannot command an automatic majority in the legislature, he does have some formidable, albeit vaguely defined, powers. These are mostly set forth in Article II of the Constitution and are of two sorts: those he can exercise in his own right without formal legislative approval, and those that require the consent of the Senate or of Congress as a whole.

Powers of the President Alone

- Serve as commander in chief of the armed forces
- Commission officers of the armed forces
- Grant reprieves and pardons for federal offenses (except impeachment)
- Convene Congress in special sessions
- Receive ambassadors
- Take care that the laws be faithfully executed
- Wield the "executive power"
- Appoint officials to lesser offices

Powers of the President That Are Shared with the Senate

- Make treaties
- Appoint ambassadors, judges, and high officials

Powers of the President That Are Shared with Congress as a Whole

- Approve legislation

Taken alone and interpreted narrowly, this list of powers is not very impressive. Obviously the president's authority as commander in chief is important, but literally construed, most of the other constitutional grants seem to provide for little more than a president who is chief clerk of the country. A hundred years after the Founding, that is about how matters appeared to even the most astute observers. In 1884 Woodrow Wilson wrote a book about American politics entitled *Congressional Government*, in which he described the business of the president as "usually

An Army officer carrying what the White House calls "the football"—the briefcase containing the secret codes the president can use to launch a nuclear attack.

not much above routine," mostly "*mere* administration." The president might as well be an officer of the civil service. To succeed, he need only obey Congress and stay alive.[9]

But even as Wilson wrote, he was overlooking some examples of enormously powerful presidents, such as Lincoln, and was not sufficiently attentive to the potential for presidential power to be found in the more ambiguous clauses of the Constitution as well as in the political realities of American life. In Chapter 20 we shall see how the president's authority as commander in chief has grown—especially, but not only, in wartime—to encompass not simply the direction of the military forces but the management of the economy and the direction of foreign affairs as well. A quietly dramatic reminder of the awesome implications of the president's military powers occurs at the precise instant that a new president assumes office. An army officer carrying a locked briefcase moves from the side of the outgoing president to the side of the new one. In the briefcase are the secret codes and orders that permit the president to authorize the launching of American nuclear weapons.

The president's duty to "take care that the laws be faithfully executed" has become one of the most elastic phrases in the Constitution. By interpreting this broadly, Grover Cleveland was able to use federal troops to break a labor strike in the 1890s and Dwight Eisenhower to send troops to help integrate a public school in Little Rock, Arkansas, in 1957.

The greatest source of presidential power, however, is not found in the Constitution at all but in politics and public opinion. Increasingly since the 1930s Congress has passed laws that confer on the executive branch broad grants of authority to achieve some general goals, leaving it up to the president and his deputies to define the regulations and programs that will actually be put into effect. In Chapter 13 we shall see how this delegation of legislative power to the president has contributed to the growth of the bureaucracy. Moreover the American people—always in time of crisis, but increasingly as an everyday matter—look to the president for leadership and hold him responsible for a large and growing portion of our national affairs. The public thinks, wrongly, that the presidency is the "first branch" of government.

FIGURE 12.1 Growth of the White House Office, 1935–1985

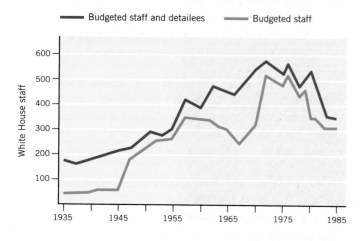

NOTE: Detailees are people who are employed by and paid by another federal agency but are assigned to work in the White House. Number of detailees for 1981 unavailable.

SOURCES: For 1935–1977: *Congressional Record* (April 13, 1978), 10111; for 1979–1985: annual reports filed by the White House with the House of Representatives Committee on Post Office and Civil Service, entitled "Aggregate Report on Personnel; Pursuant to Title 3, United States Code, Section 113"; and *Budget of the United States Government.* Reproduced from Samuel Kernell and Samuel Popkin, eds., *Chief of Staff* (Berkeley: University of California Press, 1986), 201.

The Office of the President

It was not until 1857 that the president was allowed to have a private secretary paid for with public funds, and it was not until after the assassination of President McKinley in 1901 that the president was given a Secret Service bodyguard. He was not able to submit a single presidential budget until after 1921, when the Budget and Accounting Act was passed and a Bureau of the Budget (now called the Office of Management and Budget) was created. Grover Cleveland personally answered the White House telephone, and Abraham Lincoln often answered his own mail.

Today, of course, the president has hundreds of people assisting him, and the trappings of power—helicopters, guards, limousines—are plainly visible. The White House staff has grown enormously. (Just how big the staff is, no one knows. Presidents like to pretend that the White House is not the large bureaucracy that it in fact has become.) Add to this the opportunities for presidential appointments to the cabinet, the courts, and various agencies, and the re-

sources at the disposal of the president would appear to be awesome. That conclusion is partly true and partly false, or at least misleading, and for a simple reason. If the president was once helpless for lack of assistance, he now confronts an army of assistants so large that it constitutes a bureaucracy that he has difficulty controlling (see Figure 12.1).

The ability of a presidential assistant to affect the president is governed by the rule of propinquity: in general, power is wielded by people who are in the room when a decision is made. Presidential appointments can thus be classified in terms of their proximity, physical and political, to the president. There are three degrees of propinquity: the White House Office, the Executive Office, and the cabinet.

The White House Office

The president's closest assistants have offices in the White House, usually in the West Wing of that building. Their titles often do not reveal the functions that they actually perform: "counsel," "counsellor," "assistant to the president," "special assistant," "special consultant," and so forth. The actual titles vary from one administration to another, but in general the men and women who hold them oversee the political and policy interests of the president. As part of his personal staff, these aides do not have to be confirmed by the Senate; the president can hire and fire them at will. In 1993 the Clinton White House had 500 staff members and a budget of $35.4 million.

There are essentially three ways in which a president can organize his personal staff—the "pyramid," "circular," and "ad hoc" methods. In a **pyramid structure,** used by Eisenhower, Nixon, Reagan, and Bush, most assistants report through a hierarchy to a chief of staff who then deals directly with the president. In a **circular structure,** used by Carter, cabinet secretaries and assistants report directly to the president. In an **ad hoc structure,** used by President Clinton, task forces, committees, and informal groups of friends and advisers deal directly with the president. For example, the Clinton administration's health-care policy planning was spearheaded not by Health and Human Services Secretary Donna E. Shalala, but by First Lady Hillary Rodham Clinton and a White House adviser, Ira Magaziner. Likewise, its initiative to reform the federal bureaucracy (the National Performance Review) was led not by Office of Management and Budget director Leon E. Panetta, but by an adviser to Vice President Gore, Elaine Kamarck.[10]

It is common for presidents to mix methods; for example, Franklin Roosevelt alternated between the circular and ad hoc methods in the conduct of his domestic policy, and sometimes employed a pyramidal structure when dealing with foreign affairs and military policy. Taken individually, each method of organization has advantages and disadvantages. A pyramid structure provides for an orderly flow of information and decisions but at the risk of isolating or misinforming the president. The circular method has the virtue of giving the president a great deal of information but at the price of confusion and conflict among cabinet secretaries and assistants. An ad hoc structure allows great flexibility, minimizes bureaucratic inertia, and generates ideas and information from disparate channels but at the risk of cutting the president off from the government officials who are ultimately responsible for translating presidential decisions into policy proposals and administrative action.

All presidents claim that they are open to many sources of advice, and some presidents try to guarantee that openness by using the circular method of staff organization. President Carter liked to describe his office as a wheel with himself as the hub and his several assistants as spokes. But most presidents discover, as did Carter, that the difficulty of managing the large White House bureaucracy and of conserving their own limited supply of time and energy makes it necessary for them to rely heavily on one or two key subordinates. Carter, in July 1979, dramatically altered the White House staff organization by elevating Hamilton Jordan to the post of chief of staff with the job of coordinating the work of the other staff assistants.

At first President Reagan adopted a compromise between the circle and the pyramid, putting the White House under the direction of three key aides. At the beginning of his second term in 1985, however, the president shifted to a pyramid, placing all his assistants under a single chief of staff (see Figure 12.2). Each assistant has, of course, others working for him or her, sometimes a large number. There are, at a slightly lower level of status, "special assistants to the president" for various purposes. (Being "special" means, paradoxically, being less important.)

Typically senior White House staff members are drawn from the ranks of the president's campaign staff—longtime associates in whom he has confi-

FIGURE 12.2 The Changing White House Office

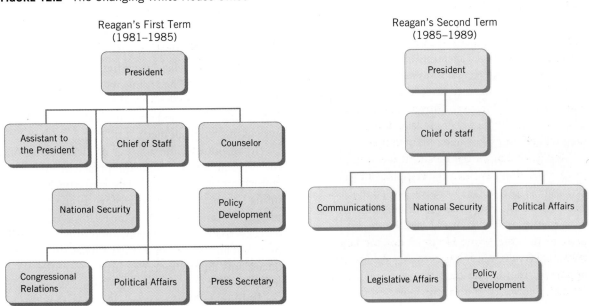

Reagan's First Term (1981–1985)

Reagan's Second Term (1985–1989)

The President:
Qualifications and Benefits

Qualifications

- A natural-born citizen (can be born abroad of parents who are American citizens).
- Thirty-five years of age.
- A resident of the United States for at least fourteen years (but not necessarily the fourteen years just preceding the election).

Benefits

- A nice house.
- A salary of $200,000 per year (taxable).
- Expense account of $50,000 per year (taxable).
- Travel expenses of $100,000 per year (tax-free).
- Pension, on retirement, equal to the pay of a cabinet member (taxable).
- Staff support and Secret Service protection on leaving the presidency.
- A White House staff of 400–500 persons.
- A place in the country — Camp David.
- A personal airplane — Air Force One.
- A fine chef.

Presidents deal with individual cabinet members, but rarely with the cabinet as a whole. Here, Secretary of State Jim Baker confers with President Bush.

dence. A few members, however, will be experts brought in after the campaign: such was the case, for example, with Henry Kissinger, a former Harvard professor who became President Nixon's assistant for national-security affairs. The offices that these men and women occupy are often small and crowded (Kissinger's was not much bigger than the one that he had while a professor at Harvard), but their occupants willingly put up with any discomfort in exchange for the privilege (and the power) of being *in* the White House. The arrangement of offices — their size, and especially their proximity to the president's Oval Office — is a good measure of the relative influence of the people in them.

To an outsider the amount of jockeying among the top staff for access to the president may seem comical or even perverse. The staff attaches enormous significance to whose office is closest to the president's, who can see him on a daily as opposed to a weekly basis, who can get an appointment with the president and who cannot, and who has a right to see documents and memoranda just before they go to the Oval Office. To be sure, there is ample grist here for Washington political novels. But there is also something important at stake: it is not simply a question of power plays and ego trips. Who can see the president and who sees and "signs off" on memoranda going to the president affect in important ways who influences policy and thus whose goals and beliefs become embedded in policy.

For example, if a memo from a secretary of the treasury who believes in free trade can go directly to the president, the president may be more likely to support free trade (low tariffs). On the other hand if that memo must be routed through the office of the assistant to the president for political affairs who is worried about the adverse effects of foreign competition on jobs in the American steel industry because the votes of steelworkers are important to the president's reelection campaign, then the president may be led to support higher tariffs.

Executive Office of the President

Agencies in the Executive Office report directly to the president and perform staff services for him but are not located in the White House itself. Their members may or may not enjoy intimate contact with him; some agencies are rather large bureaucracies. The top positions in these organizations are filled by presidential appointment, but unlike the White House staff positions, these appointments must be confirmed by the Senate.

The principal agencies in the Executive Office are:

- Office of Management and Budget (OMB)
- Central Intelligence Agency (CIA)
- Council of Economic Advisers (CEA)
- Office of Personnel Management (OPM)
- Office of the U.S. Trade Representative

Of all the agencies in the Executive Office of the President, perhaps the most important in terms of the president's need for assistance in administering the federal government is the Office of Management and Budget. First called the Bureau of the Budget when it was created in 1921, it became OMB in 1970 to reflect its broader responsibilities. Today it does considerably more than assemble and analyze the figures that go each year into the national budget that the president submits to Congress. It also studies the organization and operations of the executive branch,

The Myth and Reality of the White House Office

The myth The White House Office was created in the 1930s following recommendations made by the President's Commission on Administrative Management. The principles underlying those recommendations have been endorsed by almost every presidential chief of staff since then. The key ones are:

1. *Small is beautiful.* The presidential staff should be small. At first there were only six assistants.

2. *A passion for anonymity.* The president's personal assistants should stay out of the limelight.

3. *Honest brokers.* The presidential staff should not make decisions for the president; it should only coordinate the flow of information to the president.

The reality Increasingly the operations of the White House Office seem to reflect almost the exact opposite of these principles.

1. *Big is better.* The White House staff has grown enormously in size. Hundreds now work there.

2. *Get out front.* Key White House staffers have become household words—Henry Kissinger (under Nixon and Ford), H. R. Haldeman (under Nixon), Hamilton Jordan (under Carter), Donald Regan and Howard Baker (under Reagan), George Stephanopoulos (under Clinton).

3. *Be in charge.* Cabinet officers regularly complain that White House staffers are shutting them out and making all the important decisions. Congressional investigations have revealed the power of such White House aides as Haldeman, John Poindexter, and Lieutenant Colonel Oliver North.

Why the gap between myth and reality? The answer is—the people and the government. The people expect much more from presidents today; no president can afford to say, "We're too busy here to worry about that." The government is much more complex, and so leadership requires more resources. Even conservatives such as Ronald Reagan have been activist presidents.

SOURCE: Adapted from Samuel Kernell and Samuel L. Popkin, eds., *Chief of Staff* (Berkeley: University of California Press, 1986), 193–232.

Perks

Perks is the short form of *perquisites,* meaning "the fringe benefits of office." Among the perks of political office for high-ranking officials are limousines, expense accounts, free air travel, fancy offices, and staff assistants.

The word comes to us from Great Britain, probably in the 1960s, and was first applied to the fringe benefits given to top executives in business firms.

Among the kinds of perks are:

- Freebies (small gifts)

- Annie Oaklies (free tickets or passes to theatrical or sporting events)

- Junkets (free trips abroad)

SOURCE: Adapted from William Safire, *Safire's Political Dictionary* (New York: Ballantine Books, 1978). Used by permission.

devises plans for reorganizing various departments and agencies, develops ways of getting better information about government programs, and reviews proposals that cabinet departments want included in the president's legislative program.

OMB has a staff of over six hundred people, almost all career civil servants, many of high professional skill and substantial experience. Traditionally OMB has been a nonpartisan agency—experts serving all presidents, without regard to party or ideology. In recent administrations, however, OMB has

played a major role in advocating policies rather than merely analyzing them. David Stockman, President Reagan's OMB director, was the primary architect of the 1981 and 1985 budget cuts proposed by the president and enacted by Congress (described in Chapter 16). Stockman's proposals were often adopted over the objections of the affected department heads.

The Cabinet

The **cabinet** is a product of tradition and hope. At one time the heads of the federal departments met regularly with the president to discuss matters, and some people, especially those critical of strong presidents, would like to see this kind of collegial decision making reestablished. But in fact the cabinet is largely a fiction. Indeed the Constitution does not even mention the word (though the Twenty-fifth Amendment implicitly defines it as consisting of "the principal offices of the executive departments"). When Washington tried to get his cabinet members to work together, its two strongest members—Alexander Hamilton and Thomas Jefferson—spent most of their time feuding. The cabinet, as a presidential committee, did not work any better for John Adams or Abraham Lincoln, for Franklin Roosevelt or John Kennedy. Dwight Eisenhower is almost the only modern president who came close to making the cabinet a truly deliberative body: he gave it a large staff, held regular meetings, and listened to opinions expressed there. But even under Eisenhower, the cabinet did not have much influence over presidential decisions, nor did it help him obtain more power over the government.

By custom, cabinet officers are the heads of the fourteen major executive departments. These departments, together with the dates of their creation and the approximate number of their employees, are given in Table 12.1. The order of their creation is unimportant except in terms of protocol: where one sits at cabinet meetings is determined by the age of the department that one heads. Thus the secretary of state sits next to the president on one side and the secretary of the treasury next to him on the other. Down at the foot of the table are found the heads of the newer departments.

Though the president appoints, with the consent of the Senate, the heads of these cabinet departments, the power he obtains over them is sharply limited.

One reason is that he cannot appoint more than a tiny fraction of all of a department's employees. In only one small department, the Department of Education, can the president appoint at his discretion more than 3 percent of the employees. Table 12.2 shows the number of employees (and the percentage of all employees) presidentially chosen in each cabinet department. Even this number of presidential positions is an exaggeration, since many of the posts exempted from civil service are scientific or professional in nature and are occupied by persons who are not replaced by a new administration. A British prime minister has far fewer political appointments to make than an American president, but then a prime minister does not need so many because he or she does not have to compete with an independent Congress for influence over the bureaucracy.

But the main reason why the cabinet is a weak entity is that its members are heads of vast organizations that they seek to defend, explain, and enlarge. The secretary of Housing and Urban Development (HUD), for example, spends 99 percent of his or her time on departmental business and perhaps 1 percent (or even less) of the time speaking to the president about his business. It is hardly surprising that the HUD secretary is more of a representative of HUD *to* the president than his representative to HUD. Under these circumstances the HUD secretary is not especially interested in discussing policy at cabinet meetings with the secretary of the treasury: the latter probably wants the president to do things that are very different from what the former would like him or her to do.

Independent Agencies, Commissions, and Judgeships

The president also appoints people to four dozen or so agencies and commissions that are not considered part of the cabinet and that by law often have a quasi-independent status. The difference between an "executive" and an "independent" agency is not precise. In general it means that the heads of executive agencies serve at the pleasure of the president and can be removed at his discretion. On the other hand the heads of many independent agencies serve for fixed terms of office and can be removed only "for cause."

The president can also appoint federal judges, subject to the consent of the Senate. Judges serve for

TABLE 12.1 The Cabinet Departments

Departments	Created	Approximate Employment (1992)
State	1789	25,500
Treasury	1789	162,800
Defense[a]	1947	972,900
Justice	1789	91,700
Interior	1849	75,300
Agriculture[b]	1889	113,400
Commerce	1913	35,200
Labor	1913	19,700
Health and Human Services[c]	1953	128,800
Housing and Urban Development	1965	14,100
Transportation	1966	66,900
Energy	1977	19,700
Education	1979	4,900
Veterans Affairs	1989	229,000

[a] Formerly the War Department, created in 1789. Figures are for civilians only.
[b] Agriculture Department created in 1862; made part of cabinet in 1889.
[c] Originally Health, Education and Welfare; reorganized in 1979.
SOURCE: *Budget of the United States Government, Fiscal Year 1994*, 38.

TABLE 12.2 Number of Non–Civil Service Positions in Cabinet Departments, 1992

Department	Number of Non–Civil Service Positions	Percentage of All Positions in Each Department
State	454	1.70%
Treasury	287	0.17
Defense (civilians)	853	0.08
Justice	543	0.56
Interior	311	0.37
Agriculture	501	0.38
Commerce	399	1.10
Labor	214	1.20
Health and Human Services	541	0.40
Housing and Urban Development	188	1.40
Transportation	429	0.60
Energy	503	2.40
Education	252	4.90
Veteran Affairs	364	0.14

SOURCES: *United States Government Policy and Supporting Positions*, 1992, and *Federal Civilian Workforce Statistics, Employement, and Trends as of July 1992*.

Federal Agencies

Classified by Whether President Has Unlimited or Limited Right of Removal

"Executive" Agencies *Head can be removed at any time*

Action
Arms Control and Disarmament Agency
Commission on Civil Rights
Energy Research and Development Agency
Environmental Protection Agency
Federal Mediation and Conciliation Service
General Services Administration
National Aeronautics and Space Administration
Postal Service
Small Business Administration
All cabinet departments
Executive Office of the President

"Independent" or "Quasi-Independent" Agencies *Member serves for a fixed term*

Federal Reserve Board (14 years)
Consumer Product Safety Commission (6 years)
Equal Employment Opportunity Commission (5 years)
Federal Communications Commission (7 years)
Federal Deposit Insurance Corporation (6 years)
Federal Energy Regulatory Commission (5 years)
Federal Maritime Commission (5 years)
Federal Trade Commission (7 years)
Interstate Commerce Commission (7 years)
National Labor Relations Board (5 years)
National Science Foundation (6 years)
Securities and Exchange Commission (5 years)
Tennessee Valley Authority (9 years)

life unless they are removed by impeachment and conviction. The reason for the special barriers to the removal of judges is that they represent an independent branch of government as defined by the Constitution, and limits on presidential removal powers are necessary to preserve that independence.

Who Gets Appointed

As we have seen, a president can make relatively few appointments; furthermore he rarely knows more than a few of the people whom he does appoint. Unlike cabinet members in a parliamentary system, the president's cabinet officers and their principal deputies usually have not served with the chief executive in the legislature. Instead they come from private business, universities, "think tanks," foundations, law firms, labor unions, and the ranks of former and present members of Congress as well as past state and local government officials. A president is fortunate if most cabinet members turn out to agree with him on major policy questions. President Reagan made a special effort to ensure that his cabinet members were ideologically in tune with him, but even so Secretary of State Alexander Haig soon got into a series of quarrels with senior members of the White House staff and had to resign.

The men and women appointed to the cabinet and to the "subcabinet" (a loose term for those holding posts as deputy secretary or assistant secretary in the cabinet departments) will usually have had some prior federal experience. One study of over a thousand such appointments made by five presidents (Franklin Roosevelt through Lyndon Johnson) found that about 85 percent of the cabinet, subcabinet, and independent-agency appointees had some prior federal experience. In fact most were in government service (at the federal, state, or local levels) just before they received their cabinet or subcabinet appointment.[11] Clearly the executive branch is not, in general, run by novices.

Many of these appointees are what Richard Neustadt has called "in-and-outers": people who alternate between jobs in the federal government and ones in the private sector, especially in law firms and in universities. Cyrus Vance, before becoming secretary of state to President Carter, had been general counsel in the Defense Department, secretary of the army, and deputy secretary of defense under President Johnson. Before and after these federal jobs he was a member of a large Wall Street law firm. This pattern is quite different from that of parliamentary systems, where all the cabinet officers come from the legislature and are typically full-time career politicians.

At one time the cabinet had in it many people with strong political followings of their own—former senators and governors and powerful local party leaders. Under Franklin Roosevelt, Truman, and Kennedy, the postmaster general was the president's campaign manager. George Washington, Abraham Lincoln, and other presidents had to contend with cabinet members who were powerful figures in their own right: Alexander Hamilton and Thomas Jefferson worked with Washington; Simon Cameron (a Pennsylvania political boss) and Salmon P. Chase (formerly a governor of Ohio) worked for—and against—Lincoln. Before 1824 the post of secretary of state was regarded as a stepping-stone to the presidency; and even after that at least ten persons ran for president who had been either secretary of state or ambassador to a foreign country.[12]

Of late, however, a tendency has developed for presidents to place in their cabinets people known for their expertise or administrative experience rather than for their political following. This is in part because political parties are now so weak that party leaders can no longer demand a place in the cabinet and in part because presidents want (or think they want) "experts." A remarkable illustration of this is the number of people with Ph.D.'s who have entered the cabinet. President Nixon, who supposedly did not like Harvard professors, appointed two—Henry Kissinger and Daniel Patrick Moynihan—to important posts; Gerald Ford added a third, John Dunlop.

A president's desire to appoint experts who do not have independent political power is modified—but not supplanted—by his need to recognize various politically important groups, regions, and organizations. Since Robert Weaver became the first black to serve in the cabinet (as secretary of HUD under President Johnson), it is clear that it would be quite costly for a president *not* to have one or more blacks in his cabinet. The secretary of labor must be acceptable to the AFL-CIO, the secretary of agriculture to at least some organized farmers. Women have been in several cabinets since Franklin Roosevelt's; with the growing importance of the feminist movement, it is now essential that they be in every cabinet. Traditionally the interior secretary comes from the resource- and land-conscious West. And so on and on.

Secretary of Labor Frances Perkins (left), appointed by President Franklin Roosevelt, was the first woman cabinet member. When Robert Weaver (above) was made Secretary of Housing and Urban Development by President Johnson, he became the first black to hold a cabinet post.

Because political considerations must be taken into account in making cabinet and agency appointments and because any head of a large organization will tend to adopt the perspective of that organization, there is an inevitable tension—even a rivalry—between the White House staff and the department heads. Staff members see themselves as extensions of the president's personality and policies; department heads see themselves as repositories of expert knowledge (often knowledge of why something will *not* work as the president hopes). White House staffers, many of them young men and women in their twenties or early thirties with little executive experience, will call department heads, often persons in their fifties with substantial executive experience, and tell them that "the president wants" this or that or that "the president asked me to tell you" one thing or another. Department heads try to conceal their irritation and then maneuver for some delay so that they can develop their own counterproposals. On the other hand, when department heads call a White House staff person and ask to see the president, unless they are one of the privileged few in whom the president has special confidence, they are often told that "the president can't be bothered with that" or that "the president doesn't have time to see you."

Presidential Character

Every president brings to the White House a distinctive personality; the way the White House is organized and run will reflect that personality. Moreover the public will judge the president not only in terms of what he accomplished but also in terms of its perception of his character. Thus personality plays a more important role in explaining the presidency than it does in explaining Congress.

DWIGHT EISENHOWER brought an orderly, military style to the White House. He was accustomed to delegating authority and to having careful and complete staff work done for him by trained specialists. Though critics often accused him of having a bumbling, incoherent manner of speaking, in fact much of that was a public disguise—a strategy for avoiding being pinned down in public on matters where he wished to retain freedom of action. His private papers reveal a very different Eisenhower—sharp, precise, deliberate.

JOHN KENNEDY brought a very different style to the presidency. He projected the image of a bold, articulate, and amusing leader who liked to surround himself with talented amateurs. Instead of clear, hierarchical lines of authority, there was a pattern of personal rule and an atmosphere of improvisation. Kennedy did not hesitate to call very junior subordinates directly and tell them what to do, bypassing the chain of command.

LYNDON JOHNSON was a master legislative strategist who had risen to be majority leader of the Senate on the strength of his ability to persuade other politicians in face-to-face encounters. He was a consummate deal maker who, having been in Washington for thirty years before becoming president, knew everybody and everything. As a result he tried to make every decision himself. But the style that served him well in political negotiations did not serve him well in speaking to the country at large, especially when trying to retain public support for the war in Vietnam.

RICHARD NIXON was a highly intelligent man with a deep knowledge of and interest in foreign policy coupled with a deep suspicion of the media, his political rivals, and the federal bureaucracy. In contrast to Johnson, he disliked personal confrontations and tended to shield himself behind an elaborate staff system. Distrustful of the cabinet agencies, he tried first to centralize power in the White House and then to put into key cabinet posts former White House aides loyal to him. Like Johnson, his personality made it difficult for him to mobilize popular support. Eventually he was forced to resign under the threat of impeachment arising out of his role in the Watergate scandal.

GERALD FORD, before being appointed vice president, had spent his political life in Congress and was at home with the give-and-take, discussion-oriented procedures of that body. He was also a genial man who liked talking to people. Thus he preferred the circular to the pyramid system of White House organization. But this meant that many decisions were made in a disorganized fashion in which key people—and sometimes key problems—were not taken into account.

JIMMY CARTER was an outsider to Washington, and boasted of it. A former Georgia governor, he was determined not to be "captured" by Washington insiders. He also was a voracious reader with a wide

What Would You Do?

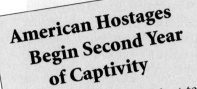

MEMORANDUM

TO: The president
FROM: National-security adviser
SUBJECT: Hostages

<u>The problem:</u>The six Americans held hostage in the Middle East are beginning their second year of captivity. One, a CIA officer with extensive knowledge of our intelligence apparatus in the region, is undergoing torture at an unknown location. It has been the policy of this administration not to negotiate with terrorists. Criticism of this refusal is being heard more frequently from hostage families and their sympathizers in Congress and the press. The terrorist groups are demanding that we end our support of Israel. A government in the region has secretly indicated that, in exchange for military supplies, it may be able to help win the release of "some" hostages.

<u>Your options:</u>
1. Maintain the "no-negotiations" policy but use quiet diplomacy with friendly nations in the region to see whether they can intercede with the terrorist groups on behalf of the hostages.

<u>Advantages:</u> (a) Our "no-negotiations" policy remains credible, and this will deter other terrorist groups from thinking that they can win concessions by capturing Americans. (b) This policy is consistent with our insistence that U.S. allies not negotiate with terrorists. <u>Disadvantages:</u> (a) There is no evidence that our traditional policy will get the hostages released. (b) Public sympathy for the hostages may increase, and this will lead to more criticism of this administration for failing to free captive Americans.

2. Secretly exchange arms for the release of Americans.

<u>Advantages:</u> (a) Some or all hostages may be released. (b) We may earn the goodwill of more moderate elements in the area and thereby increase our influence there. <u>Disadvantages:</u> (a) We may deliver arms and no hostages will be released. (b) If secret arms deliveries become public, we will be heavily criticized for abandoning our "no-negotiations" policy.

3. Use military units to find and free the hostages.

<u>Advantage:</u> The hostages may be freed without our having to make any concessions. <u>Disadvantages:</u> (a) The military is not optimistic that it can find and free the hostages, who are being kept in hidden, scattered sites. (b) The hostages may be killed during the rescue effort.

<u>Your decision:</u> Option 1_____Option 2_____Option 3_____

range of interests and an appetite for detail. These dispositions led him to try to do many things and to do them personally. Like Ford, he began with a circular structure; unlike Ford, he based his decisions on reading countless memos and asking detailed questions. His advisers finally decided that he was trying to do too much in too great detail, and toward the end of his term he shifted to a pyramid structure.

RONALD REAGAN was also an outsider, a former governor of California. But unlike Carter, he wanted to set the broad directions of his administration and leave the details to others. He gave wide latitude to subordinates and to cabinet officers, within the framework of an emphasis on lower taxes, less domestic spending, a military buildup, and a tough line with the Soviet Union. He was a superb leader of public opinion, earning the nickname of "The Great Communicator."

GEORGE BUSH lacked Reagan's speaking skills but was much more of a hands-on manager. Drawing on his extensive experience in the federal government (he had been vice president, director of the CIA, ambassador to the United Nations, representative to China, and member of the House), Bush made decisions on the basis of personal contacts with key foreign leaders and Washington officials.

BILL CLINTON was much like Carter in the attention he paid to the details of policy and his preference for informal, ad hoc organizational arrangements. Unlike Carter, he was an effective speaker who used those skills to try to get support for his policies. And unlike Reagan and Bush, he took office with little apparent interest in foreign affairs.

Professor James David Barber has attempted to study presidential personality systematically and use the results to predict presidential performance in office. Scholars are divided over whether this approach works, but none disputes the fact that personality affects how the White House is run.[13]

The Power to Persuade

The sketchy constitutional powers given the president, combined with the lack of an assured legislative majority, mean that he must rely heavily on persuasion if he is to accomplish much. Here the Constitution gives him some advantages: he and the vice president are the only officials elected by the whole nation, and he is the ceremonial head of state as well as the chief executive of the government. The president can use his national constituency and ceremonial duties to enlarge his power, but he must do so quickly: the second half of his first term in office will be devoted to running for reelection, especially if he faces opposition for his own party's nomination (as was the case with Carter and Ford).

The Three Audiences

The president's persuasive powers are aimed at three audiences. The first, and often the most important, is his Washington, D.C., audience of fellow politicians and leaders. As Richard Neustadt points out in his book *Presidential Power,* a president's reputation among his Washington colleagues is of very great importance in affecting how much deference his views receive and thus how much power he can wield.[14] If a president is thought to be "smart," "sure of himself," "cool," "on top of things," or "shrewd" and thus "effective," he *will* be effective. Franklin Roosevelt had that reputation, and so did Lyndon Johnson, at least for his first few years in office. Truman, Ford, and Carter often did not have that reputation, and they lost ground accordingly. Power, like beauty, exists largely in the eye of the beholder.

A second audience is composed of party activists and officeholders outside Washington—the partisan grassroots. These persons want the president to exemplify their principles, trumpet their slogans, appeal to their fears and hopes, and help them get reelected. Since, as we explained in Chapter 7, partisan activists increasingly have an ideological orientation toward national politics, these people will expect "their" president to make fire-and-brimstone speeches that confirm in them a shared sense of purpose and, incidentally, help them raise money from contributors to state and local campaigns.

The third audience is "the public," but of course that audience is really many publics, each with a different view or set of interests. A president on the campaign trail speaks boldly of what he will accomplish; a president in office speaks quietly of the problems that must be overcome. Citizens are often irritated at the apparent tendency of officeholders, including the president, to sound mealy-mouthed

Lyndon Johnson's great political skill was not his ability to make speeches but his knack for dealing effectively with people singly or in small groups. Left, his face shows the strain of making a public address; right, he relaxes while talking informally with reporters in the White House.

and equivocal. But it is easy to criticize the cooking when you haven't been the cook. A president learns quickly that his every utterance will be scrutinized closely by the media and by organized groups here and abroad, and his errors of fact, judgment, timing, or even inflection will be immediately and forcefully pointed out. Given the risks of saying too much, it is a wonder that presidents say anything at all.

In general presidents have made fewer and fewer impromptu remarks in the years since Franklin Roosevelt and have relied more and more on prepared addresses (from which errors can be culled in advance). The box on page 368 and Figure 12.3 show how press conferences have declined and how other ways of reaching the public have grown since Roosevelt's days.

Popularity and Influence

The object of all this talk is to convert personal popularity into congressional support for the president's

legislative programs (and improved chances for reelection). It is not obvious, of course, why Congress should care about a president's popularity. After all, as we saw in Chapter 11, most members of Congress are secure in their seats, and few need fear any "party bosses" who might deny them renomination. Moreover the president cannot ordinarily provide credible electoral rewards or penalties to members of Congress. By working for their defeat in the 1938 congressional election, President Roosevelt attempted to "purge" members of Congress who opposed his program, but he failed. Nor does presidential support help a particular member of Congress: most representatives win reelection anyway, and the few who are in trouble are rarely saved by presidential intervention. When President Reagan campaigned hard for Republican senatorial candidates in 1986, he, too, failed to have much impact.

For a while scholars thought that congressional candidates might benefit from the president's coattails: they might ride into office on the strength of the

How Presidents Go to the People

The three graphs in Figure 12.3 show how presidents have changed the way in which they "go public." The first graph shows the increase in public appearances by the president, from a dozen or so per year by Roosevelt to nearly a hundred per year by Bush, Reagan, Carter, and Nixon.

The number of presidential trips and broadcast addresses has also increased. The second graph shows that the number of radio and television speeches grew from a dozen or so per year by Roosevelt to more than a hundred per year by Bush (combining major and minor addresses).

Offsetting this increase has been the decline in the number of press conferences held per month. The third graph indicates that the number of press conferences held per month has decreased from a peak of almost seven when Franklin Roosevelt was in office to a low of less than one when Nixon, Carter, Reagan, and Bush were in office.

The reason? Broadcast speeches and public appearances allow the president to talk to the people *directly*; press conferences filter the president's words through the media.

SOURCE: Samuel Kernell, *Going Public* (Washington, D.C.: Congressional Quarterly Press, 1986), 69, 86, and 94. President Ford is omitted because he served so briefly in office.

popularity of a president of their own party. It is true, as can be seen from Table 12.3 on page 370, that a winning president will find that his party's strength in Congress increases.

But there are good reasons to doubt whether the pattern observed in Table 12.3 is the result of presidential coattails. For one thing there are some exceptions. Eisenhower won 57.4 percent of the vote in 1956, but the Republicans lost seats in the House and Senate. Kennedy won in 1960, but the Democrats lost seats in the House and gained but one in the Senate. When Nixon was reelected in 1972 with one of the largest majorities in history, the Republicans lost seats in the Senate.

Careful studies of voter attitudes and of how presidential and congressional candidates fare in the same districts suggest that, whatever may once have been the influence of coattails, their effect has de-

clined in recent years and is quite small today. The weakening of party loyalty and of party organizations, combined with the enhanced ability of members of Congress to build secure relations with their constituents, has tended to insulate congressional elections from presidential ones. When voters choose as members of Congress people of the same party as an incoming president, they probably do so out of a desire for a general change and as an adverse judgment about the outgoing party's performance as a whole, and not because they want to supply the new president with members of Congress favorable to him.[15] The big increase in Republican senators and representatives that accompanied the election of Ronald Reagan in 1980 was probably as much a result of the unpopularity of the outgoing president and the circumstances of various local races as it was of Reagan's coattails.

Nonetheless a president's personal popularity may have a significant effect on how much of his program Congress passes, even if it does not affect the reelection chances of those members of Congress. Though they do not fear a president who threatens to campaign against them (or cherish one who promises to support them), members of Congress do have a sense that it is risky to oppose too adamantly the policies of a popular president. Politicians share a sense of a common fate: they tend to rise or fall together. Statistically a president's popularity, as measured by the Gallup poll (see Figure 12.4), is associated with the proportion of his legislative proposals that are approved by Congress (see Figure 12.5). Other things being equal, the more popular the president, the higher the proportion of his bills that Congress will pass.[16]

The Decline in Popularity

Though presidential popularity is an asset, its value tends inexorably to decline. As can be seen from Figure 12.4, every president except Eisenhower lost popular support between his inauguration and the time that he left office, except when his reelection gave him a brief burst of renewed popularity. Truman was hurt by improprieties among his subordinates and by the protracted Korean War; Johnson was crippled by the increasing unpopularity of the Vietnam War; Nixon was severely damaged by the Watergate scandal; Ford was hurt by having pardoned Nixon for his

FIGURE 12.3 Public Appearances, Addresses, and Press Conferences by Presidents

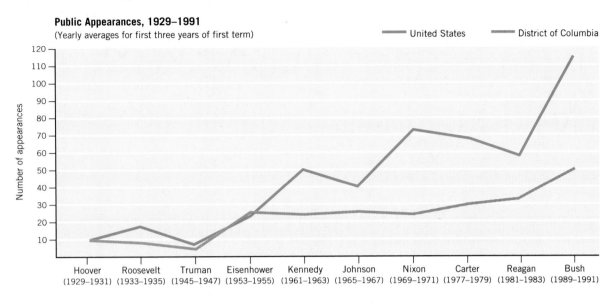

Public Appearances, 1929–1991
(Yearly averages for first three years of first term)

— United States   — District of Columbia

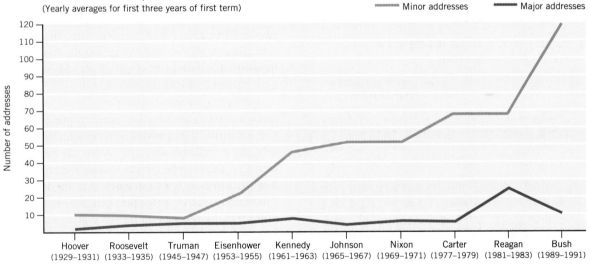

Presidential Addresses, 1929–1991
(Yearly averages for first three years of first term)

— Minor addresses   — Major addresses

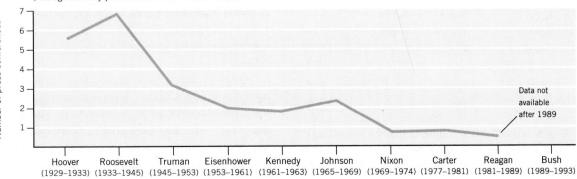

Press Conferences, 1929–1989
(Average monthly press conferences while in office)

Data not available after 1989

FIGURE 12.4 Presidential Popularity

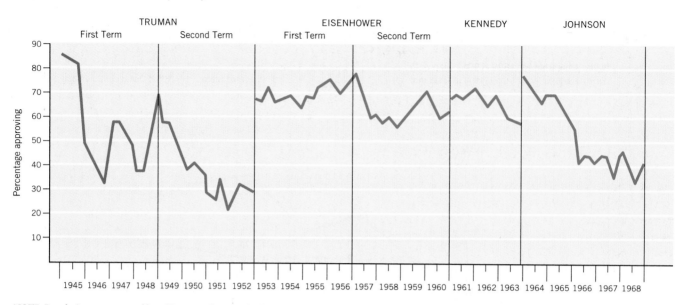

NOTE: Popularity was measured by asking every few months, "Do you approve of the way _____ is handling his job as president?"

SOURCE: Thomas E. Cronin, *The State of the Presidency* (Boston: Little, Brown, 1975), 110–111. Copyright © 1975 by Little, Brown and Company, Inc. Reprinted by permission. Updated with Gallup poll data, 1976–1993. Reprinted by permission of the Gallup Poll News Service.

TABLE 12.3 Partisan Gains or Losses in Congress in Presidential Election Years

Year	President	Party	Gains or Losses of President's Party in	
			House	Senate
1932	Roosevelt	Dem.	+90	+9
1936	Roosevelt	Dem.	+12	+7
1940	Roosevelt	Dem.	+7	−3
1944	Roosevelt	Dem.	+24	−2
1948	Truman	Dem.	+75	+9
1952	Eisenhower	Rep.	+22	+1
1956	Eisenhower	Rep.	−3	−1
1960	Kennedy	Dem.	−20	+1
1964	Johnson	Dem.	+37	+1
1968	Nixon	Rep.	+5	+7
1972	Nixon	Rep.	+12	−2
1976	Carter	Dem.	+1	+1
1980	Reagan	Rep.	+33	+12
1984	Reagan	Rep.	+16	−2
1988	Bush	Rep.	−3	−1
1992	Clinton	Dem.	−9	+1

SOURCES: Updated from Congressional Quarterly, *Guide to U.S. Elections*, 928; and *Congress and the Nation*, vol. IV (1973–1976), 28.

part in Watergate; Carter was weakened by continuing inflation, staff irregularities, and the Iranian kidnapping of American hostages; Bush was harmed by a protracted economic recession.

Because a president's popularity tends to be highest right after an election, political commentators like to speak of a "honeymoon," during which, presumably, the president's love affair with the people and with Congress can be consummated. Certainly Roosevelt enjoyed such a honeymoon. In the legendary "first hundred days" of his presidency, from March to June 1993, FDR obtained from a willing Congress a vast array of new laws creating new agencies and authorizing new powers. But those were extraordinary times: the most serious economic depression of this century had put millions out of work, closed banks, impoverished farmers, and ruined the stock market. It would have been political suicide for Congress to have blocked, or even delayed, action on measures that appeared designed to help the nation out of the crisis.

Other presidents, serving in more normal times, have not enjoyed such a honeymoon. Truman had little success with what he proposed; Eisenhower proposed little. Kennedy, Nixon, Ford, and Carter had some victories in their first year in office, but nothing that could be called a honeymoon. Only

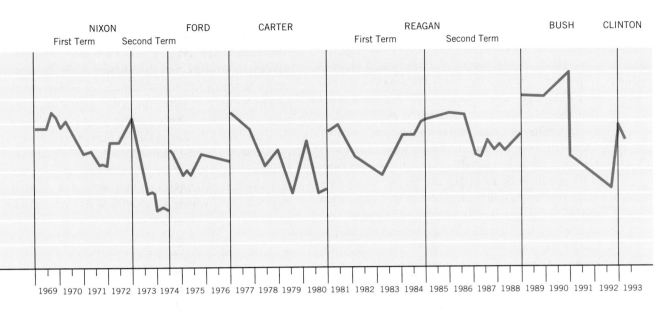

NIXON FORD CARTER REAGAN BUSH CLINTON

First Term Second Term First Term Second Term

1969 1970 1971 1972 1973 1974 1975 1976 1977 1978 1979 1980 1981 1982 1983 1984 1985 1986 1987 1988 1989 1990 1991 1992 1993

Lyndon Johnson enjoyed a highly productive relationship with Congress; until the Vietnam War sapped his strength he rarely lost. Reagan began his administration with important victories in his effort to cut expenditures and taxes (see Chapter 16), but in his second year in office he ran into trouble.

The decay in the reputation of the president and his party in midterm is evident in Table 12.4. Since 1934 in every off-year election the president's party has lost seats in one or both houses of Congress. The ability of the president to persuade is important but limited. However, he also has a powerful bargaining chip to play: the ability to say no.

The Power to Say No

The Constitution gives the president the power to veto legislation. In addition most presidents have asserted the right of "executive privilege" or the right to withhold information that Congress may want to obtain from the president or his subordinates, and some presidents have tried to impound funds appropriated by Congress. These efforts by the president to say no are not only a way of blocking action but also a way of forcing Congress to bargain with him over the substance of policies.

TABLE 12.4 Partisan Gains or Losses in Congress in Off-Year Elections

			Gains or Losses of President's Party in	
Year	President	Party	House	Senate
1934	Roosevelt	Dem.	+9	+9
1938	Roosevelt	Dem.	−70	−7
1942	Roosevelt	Dem.	−50	−8
1946	Truman	Dem.	−54	−11
1950	Truman	Dem.	−29	−5
1954	Eisenhower	Rep.	−18	−1
1958	Eisenhower	Rep.	−47	−13
1962	Kennedy	Dem.	−5	+2
1966	Johnson	Dem.	−48	−4
1970	Nixon	Rep.	−12	+1
1974	Ford	Rep.	−48	−5
1978	Carter	Dem.	−12	−3
1982	Reagan	Rep.	−26	0
1986	Reagan	Rep.	−5	−8
1990	Bush	Rep.	−9	−1
1994	Clinton	Dem.	−52	−9

SOURCES: Updated from Congressional Quarterly, *Guide to U.S. Elections*, 928; and *Congress and the Nation*, vol. IV (1973–1976), 28.

Veto

If a president disapproves of a bill passed by both houses of Congress, he may veto it in one of two ways. One is by a **veto message.** This is a statement that the president sends to Congress accompanying the bill, within ten days (not counting Sundays) after the bill has been passed. In it he sets forth his reasons for not signing the bill. The other is the **pocket veto.** If the president does not sign the bill within ten days *and* Congress has adjourned within that time, then the bill will not become law. Obviously a pocket veto can only be used during a certain time of the year—just before Congress adjourns at the end of its second session. At times, however, presidents have pocket-vetoed a bill just before Congress recessed for a summer vacation or to permit its members to campaign during an off-year election. In 1972 Senator Edward M. Kennedy of Massachusetts protested that this was unconstitutional, since a recess is not the same thing as an adjournment. In a case brought to federal court, Kennedy was upheld, and it is now understood that the pocket veto can only be used just before the life of a given Congress expires.

A bill that is not signed or vetoed within ten days while Congress is still in session becomes law automatically without the president's approval. A bill that has been returned to Congress with a veto message can be passed over the president's objections if at least two-thirds of each house votes to override the veto. A bill that has received a pocket veto cannot be brought back to life by Congress (since Congress has adjourned), nor does such a bill carry over to the next session of Congress. If Congress wants to press the matter, it will have to start all over again by passing the bill anew in its next session, and then hope that the president will sign it or that, if he does not, they can override his veto.

The president must accept or reject the entire bill; he does not have, as most governors do, the right to exercise a **line-item veto,** in which he approves of some provisions and disapproves of others. Congress can take advantage of this fact by putting provisions that a president wants into a bill that he does not like, thereby forcing him to sign the entire bill, objectionable parts and all, to get the provisions that he wants.

Nevertheless the veto power is a substantial one because Congress rarely has the votes to override it. From George Washington to George Bush, over 2,400

presidential vetoes were cast; less than 4 percent were overridden (see Table 12.5). Cleveland, Franklin Roosevelt, Truman, and Eisenhower made the most extensive use of vetoes, accounting for 70 percent of all vetoes ever cast. Often the vetoed legislation is revised by Congress and passed in a form suitable to the president. There is no tally of how often this happens, but it is frequent enough so that both branches of government recognize that the veto, or even the threat of it, is part of an elaborate process of political negotiation in which the president has substantial powers.

Executive Privilege

The Constitution says nothing about whether the president is obliged to divulge private communications between himself and his principal advisers, but presidents have acted as if they did have that privilege of confidentiality. The presidential claim is based on two grounds. First, the doctrine of the separation of powers means that one branch of government does not have the right to inquire into the internal workings of another branch headed by constitutionally named officers. Second, the principles of statecraft and of prudent administration require that the president have the right to obtain confidential and candid advice from subordinates; such advice could not be obtained if it would quickly be exposed to public scrutiny.

For almost two hundred years there was no serious challenge to the claim of presidential confidentiality. The Supreme Court did not require the disclosure of confidential communications to or from the president.[17] Congress was never happy with this claim but until 1973 did not seriously dispute it. Indeed in 1962 a Senate committee explicitly accepted a claim by President Kennedy that his secretary of defense, Robert S. McNamara, was not obliged to divulge the identity of Defense Department officials who had censored certain speeches by generals and admirals.

In 1973 the Supreme Court for the first time met the issue directly. A federal special prosecutor sought tape recordings of White House conversations between President Nixon and his advisers as part of his investigation of the Watergate scandal. In the case of *United States* v. *Nixon,* the Supreme Court, by a vote of eight to zero, held that while there may be a sound basis for the claim of executive privilege, especially where sensitive military or diplomatic matters are involved, there is no "absolute unqualified Presidential privilege of immunity from judicial process under all circumstances."[18] To admit otherwise would be to block the constitutionally defined function of the federal courts to decide criminal cases.

Thus Nixon was ordered to hand over the disputed tapes and papers to a federal judge so that the judge could decide which were relevant to the case at hand and allow those to be introduced into evidence. In the future another president may well persuade the Court that a different set of records or papers is so sensitive as to require protection, especially if there is no allegation of criminal misconduct requiring the production of evidence in court. As a practical matter it seems likely that presidential advisers will be able, except in unusual cases such as Watergate, to continue to give private advice to the president.

Impoundment of Funds

From time to time presidents have refused to spend money appropriated by Congress. Truman did not spend all that Congress wanted spent on the armed forces, and Johnson did not spend all that Congress made available for highway construction. Kennedy refused to spend money appropriated for new weapons systems that he did not like. Indeed the precedent for impounding funds goes back at least to the administration of Thomas Jefferson.

But what has precedent is not thereby constitutional. The Constitution is silent on whether the president *must* spend the money that Congress appropriates; all it says is that the president cannot spend money that Congress has *not* appropriated. The major test of presidential power in this respect occurred during the Nixon administration. Nixon wished to reduce federal spending. He proposed in 1972 that Congress give him the power to reduce federal spending so that it would not exceed $250 billion for the coming year. Congress, under Democratic control, refused. Nixon responded by pocket-vetoing twelve spending bills and then impounding funds appropriated under other laws that he had not vetoed.

Congress in turn responded by passing the Budget Reform Act of 1974, which, among other things, requires the president to spend all appropriated

TABLE 12.5 Presidential Vetoes, 1789–1993

	Regular Vetoes	Pocket Vetoes	Total Vetoes	Vetoes Overridden
Washington	2	—	2	—
Madison	5	2	7	—
Monroe	1	—	1	—
Jackson	5	7	12	—
Tyler	6	3	9	1
Polk	2	1	3	—
Pierce	9	—	9	5
Buchanan	4	3	7	—
Lincoln	2	4	6	—
A. Johnson	21	8	29	15
Grant	45	49	94	4
Hayes	12	1	13	1
Arthur	4	8	12	1
Cleveland	304	109	413	2
Harrison	19	25	44	1
Cleveland	43	127	170	5
McKinley	6	36	42	—
T. Roosevelt	42	40	82	1
Taft	30	9	39	1
Wilson	33	11	44	6
Harding	5	1	6	—
Coolidge	20	30	50	4
Hoover	21	16	37	3
F. Roosevelt	372	263	635	9
Truman	180	70	250	12
Eisenhower	73	108	181	2
Kennedy	12	9	21	—
L. Johnson	16	14	30	—
Nixon	24	18	42	6
Ford	53	19	72	12
Carter	13	18	31	2
Reagan	39	39	78	9
Bush	14	6	20	1
Clinton	0	0	0	0

SOURCES: *Statistical Abstract of the United States*, 1987, 235; Senate Library, *Presidential Vetoes* (Washington, D.C.: Government Printing Office, 1960), 199. Clinton figures through June 1993.

funds unless he first tells Congress what funds he wishes not to spend and Congress, within forty-five days, agrees to delete the items. If he wishes simply to delay spending the money, he need only inform

Congress, but Congress then can refuse the delay by passing a resolution requiring the immediate release of the money. Federal courts have upheld the rule that the president must spend, without delay for policy reasons, money that Congress has appropriated.

The President's Program

Imagine that you have just spent three or four years running for president, during which time you have given essentially the same speech over and over again. You have had no time to study the issues in any depth. To reach a large television audience, you have couched your ideas largely in rather simple—if not simple-minded—slogans. Your principal advisers are political aides, not legislative specialists.

You win. You are inaugurated. Now you must *be* a president instead of just talking about it. You must fill hundreds of appointive posts, but you know personally only a handful of the candidates. You must

deliver a State of the Union message to Congress only two or three weeks after you are sworn in. It is quite possible that you have never read, much less written, such a message before. You must submit a new budget; the old one is hundreds of pages long, much of it comprehensible only to experts. Foreign governments, as well as the stock market, hang on your every word, interpreting many of your remarks in ways that totally surprise you.

What will you do? What *will* you do?

The Constitution is not much help. It directs you to report on the state of the union and to recommend "such measures" as you shall judge "necessary and expedient." Beyond that you are charged to "take care that the laws be faithfully executed."

At one time, of course, the demands placed on a newly elected president were not very great because the president was not expected to do very much. The president, on assuming office, might speak of the tariff, or relations with England, or the value of veterans' pensions, or the need for civil-service reform, but was not expected to have something to say (and offer) to everybody. Today he is.

Putting Together a Program

To develop policies on short notice, a president will draw on several sources, each with particular strengths and weaknesses:

- Aides and campaign advisers

    Strength: Will test new ideas for their political soundness.

    Weakness: Will not have many ideas to test, being inexperienced in government.

- Federal bureaus and agencies

    Strength: Will know what is feasible in terms of governmental realities.

    Weakness: Will propose plans that promote own agencies and will not have good information on whether plans will work.

- Outside, academic, and other specialists and experts

    Strength: Will have many general ideas and criticisms of existing programs.

President Nixon justified his refusal to disclose tapes of conversations in the Oval Office by the argument that a president must have the private and candid views of his advisers, such as John Ehrlichman and Henry Kissinger (standing) and H. R. Haldeman (seated). The Supreme Court recognized this need but decided that tapes containing evidence bearing on possible criminal violations must be handed over to a judge.

Weakness: Will not know the details of policy or have good judgment as to what is feasible.

- Interest groups

Strength: Will have specific plans and ideas.

Weakness: Will have narrow view of the public interest.

There are essentially two ways for a president to develop a program. One, exemplified by President Carter, is to have a policy on almost everything. To do this Carter worked endless hours and studied countless documents, trying to learn something about, and then state his positions on, a large number of issues. The other method, illustrated by President Reagan, is to concentrate on three or four major initiatives or themes, and leave everything else to subordinates.

But even when a president has a governing philosophy, as did Reagan, he cannot risk plunging ahead on his own. He must judge public and congressional reaction to this program before he commits himself fully to it. Therefore he will often allow parts of his program to be "leaked" to the press, or to be "floated" as a trial balloon. Reagan's commitment to a 30 percent tax cut and larger military expenditures was so well known as to require no leaking, but he did have to float his ideas on Social Security and certain budget cuts to test popular reaction. His opponents in the bureaucracy did exactly the same thing, hoping for the opposite effect. They leaked controversial parts of the program in an effort to discredit the whole policy. This process of testing the winds by a president and his critics helps explain why so many news stories coming from Washington mention no person by name but only an anonymous "highly placed source."

In addition to the risks of adverse reaction, the president faces three other constraints on his ability to plan a program. One is the sheer limit of his time and attention span. Every president works harder than he has ever worked before. A ninety-hour week is typical. Even so, he has great difficulty keeping up with all the things that he is supposed to know and make decisions about. For example, Congress during an average year passes between four hundred and six hundred bills, each of which the president must sign, veto, or allow to take effect without his signature.

Scores of people wish to see him. Hundreds of phone calls must be made to members of Congress and others in order to ask for help, to soothe ruffled feathers, or to get information. He must receive all newly appointed ambassadors and visiting heads of state and in addition have his picture taken with countless people, from a Nobel Prize winner to a child whose likeness will appear on the Easter Seal.

The second constraint is the unexpected crisis. Franklin Roosevelt obviously had to respond to a depression and to the mounting risks of world war. But most presidents get their crises when they least expect them.

Truman

- Major strikes in the auto, steel, coal, railroad, and shipping industries
- Civil wars in Greece and Palestine
- South Korea invaded by North Korea
- Berlin put under siege by Soviet troops
- Truman's military aide charged with accepting improper gifts

Eisenhower

- Egypt seizes Suez Canal
- Revolts against communist rule in East Berlin, Poland, and Hungary
- Supreme Court outlaws school segregation
- USSR launches *Sputnik* satellite
- Presidential aide accused of accepting improper gifts

Kennedy

- Failure of Bay of Pigs invasion of Cuba
- Soviets put missiles in Cuba
- China invades India
- Federal troops sent to South to protect blacks

Johnson

- Vietnam War
- Black riots in major cities
- War between India and Pakistan
- Civil war in Dominican Republic
- Arab-Israeli war
- Civil-rights workers murdered in South

TRIVIA

Presidents

Only divorced president	*Ronald Reagan*
Only bachelor president	*James Buchanan*
Three presidents who died on the Fourth of July	*Thomas Jefferson (1826) John Adams (1826) James Monroe (1831)*
The shortest presidential term	*William Henry Harrison (one month)*
The longest presidential term	*Franklin D. Roosevelt (12 years and 1 month)*
The youngest president when inaugurated	*Theodore Roosevelt (42)*
The oldest president when first inaugurated	*Ronald Reagan (69)*
First president born in a hospital	*Jimmy Carter*
First presidential automobile	*Owned by William Howard Taft*
Only former presidents elected to Congress	*John Quincy Adams (to House) and Andrew Johnson (to Senate)*
Only president who never attended school	*Andrew Johnson*

John Adams

William Howard Taft and family

Nixon

- Watergate scandal
- Arab-Israeli war
- Value of dollar falls in foreign trade
- Arabs raise the price of oil

Carter

- OMB Director Bert Lance accused of improprieties
- Lengthy coal strike
- Seizure of American hostages in Iran
- Soviet invasion of Afghanistan

Reagan

- Poland suppresses Solidarity movement
- U.S. troops sent to Lebanon
- U.S. hostages held in Lebanon
- Civil war in Nicaragua
- Iran-contra crisis

Bush

- Soviet Union dissolves
- Iraq invades Kuwait
- China suppresses student rebellion in Tiananmen Square, Beijing

Clinton

- Murderous civil war continues in Bosnia and other parts of the former Yugoslavia
- North Korea resists inspections designed to detect possible manufacture of nuclear weapons
- Investigation of possible wrongdoing of President and Mrs. Clinton in Whitewater real estate development
- Charges of sexual harassment made against Clinton

The third constraint is the fact that the federal government and most federal programs, as well as the federal budget, can only be changed, except in special circumstances, marginally. The vast bulk of federal expenditures are beyond control in any given year: the money must be spent whether the president likes it or not. Many federal programs have such strong congressional or public support that they must be left intact or modified only slightly. And this means that most federal employees can count on being secure in their jobs, whatever a president's views on reducing the bureaucracy.

FIGURE 12.5 How the President Fares in Congress

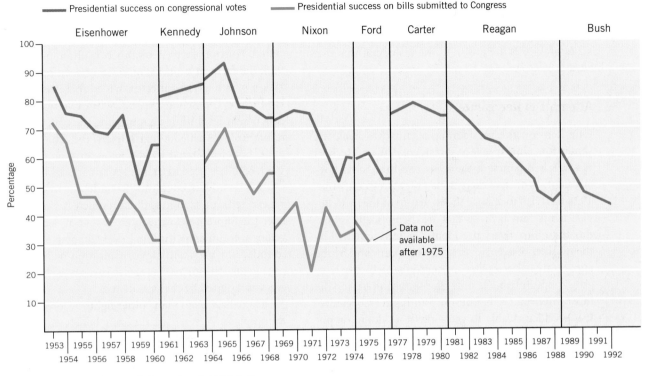

SOURCE: *Congressional Quarterly* (December 19, 1992): 3842.

The result of these constraints is that the president, at least in ordinary times, has to be selective about what he wants. He can be thought of as having a stock of influence and prestige the way that he might have a supply of money. If he wants to get the most "return" on his resources, he must "invest" that influence and prestige carefully in enterprises that promise substantial gains—in public benefits and political support—at reasonable costs. Each president tends to speak in terms of changing everything at once, calling his approach a "New Deal," a "New Frontier," a "Great Society," or the "New Federalism." But beneath the rhetoric he must identify a few specific proposals on which he wishes to bet his resources, mindful of the need to leave a substantial stock of resources in reserve to handle the inevitable crises and emergencies. In recent decades events have required every president to devote much of his time and resources to two key issues: the state of the economy and foreign affairs. What he manages to do in addition to this will depend on his personal views and his sense of what the nation, as well as his reelection, requires.

Measuring Success

There are two ways of measuring presidential success: by the proportion of the president's proposals approved by Congress (his "box score") and by the proportion of votes taken in Congress on which the president's position prevails. By the first method (the red line in Figure 12.5), the president usually wins less than half the time, even when his own party controls Congress. By the second method (the blue line in Figure 12.5), he does better: he is on the winning side perhaps three-fourths of the time. This latter measure is misleadingly high, however, because it ignores bills that the president favors that do not even come up for a vote and because it counts bills that he may reluctantly support after originally having opposed them. By contrast in Great Britain 96 percent of the prime minister's bills were passed by Parliament between 1957 and 1969. Judging by these two methods, the most successful recent president was Johnson, the least successful, Nixon. President Bush's 1992 success score of 43% is the lowest in the history of this vote study.

Attempts to Reorganize

One item on the presidential agenda has been the same for almost every president since Herbert Hoover: reorganizing the executive branch of government. With few exceptions every president since 1928 has tried to change the structure of the staff, departments, and agencies that are theoretically subordinate to him. Every president has been appalled by the number of agencies that report to him and by the apparently helter-skelter manner in which they have grown up. But this is only one—and often not the most important—reason for wanting to reorganize. If a president wants to get something done, or put new people in charge of a program, or recapture political support for a policy, it often proves easier to do so by creating a new agency or reorganizing an old one than by abolishing a program, firing a subordinate, or passing a new law. Reorganization serves many objectives and thus is a recurring theme of presidential leadership.

Between 1948 and 1961 the agency in charge of foreign aid was reorganized eight times. Between 1968 and 1973 the federal agency charged with enforcing narcotics laws was reorganized twice; in 1981 it was reorganized again and placed under the FBI. Truman and Eisenhower each created a national commission to recommend wholesale reorganizations of the executive branch, both chaired by former President Hoover. President Franklin Roosevelt appointed a commission on administrative management; over thirty years later President Nixon created another one. President Carter made reorganization a priority concern of his staff. From 1949 to 1977 one hundred and fourteen separate reorganization plans, some calling for small changes, some for large ones, were sent to Congress. About three-fourths were approved, many only after hard-fought battles. In modern times Presidents Johnson, Nixon, and Carter have been the most determined advocates of reorganization, though not necessarily the most successful.

Legally the president can reorganize his personal White House staff any time that he wishes. To reorganize in any important way the larger Executive Office of the President or any of the executive departments or agencies, however, Congress must first be consulted. For over forty years this consultation usually took the form of submitting to Congress a reorganization plan that took effect provided that neither the House nor the Senate passed, within sixty days, a concurrent resolution disapproving the plan (such a resolution was called a **legislative veto**). This procedure, first authorized by the Reorganization Act of 1939, could be used to change, but not create or abolish, an executive agency. In 1981 authority under that act expired, and Congress did not renew it. Two years later the Supreme Court declared that all legislative vetoes were unconstitutional (see Chapter 13), and so today any presidential reorganization plan would have to take the form of a regular law, passed by Congress and signed by the president.

There have been many bitter fights over reorganization plans. At stake are differing beliefs as to what an agency should do, who should head it, and what congressional committee should have power over it. The Department of Health, Education and Welfare was created by a reorganization plan in 1953, but to get the plan accepted, President Eisenhower had to promise to leave the Public Health Service and the Office of Education, nominally part of the new department, relatively autonomous. The first efforts to create a Department of Urban Affairs were blocked because key members of Congress objected to the prospect of a black's heading the agency (it was later created, and a black did head it). The law designed to create a Department of Transportation, which finally passed in 1966, involved one of the most difficult legislative struggles of President Johnson's administration: his chief domestic-policy aide later wrote that it took 15 percent of the aide's time and required daily presidential attention, and even then fell well short of a thorough restructuring of transportation agencies.[19]

What has been said so far may well give the reader the impression that the president is virtually helpless. That is not the case. The *actual* power of the president can only be measured in terms of what he can accomplish, and such an analysis requires that we first consider a number of concrete policies, as we shall do in Part 4. After that we shall return to the question of presidential power with a summary assessment. What this chapter has described so far is the office as the president finds it—the burdens, restraints, demands, complexities, and resources that he encounters on entering the Oval Office for the first time. Every president since Truman has commented feelingly on how limited the powers of the president seem from the inside compared to what they appear to be from the outside. Franklin Roosevelt spoke of his struggles with the bureaucracy in terms of punching a feather bed; Truman wrote that the power of the president was chiefly the power to persuade people to do what they ought to do anyway. After being in office a year or so, Kennedy spoke to interviewers about how much more complex the world appeared than he had first supposed. Johnson and Nixon were broken by the office and the events that happened there.

Yet Franklin Roosevelt helped create the modern presidency, with its vast organizational reach, and directed a massive war effort. Truman ordered two atomic bombs dropped on Japanese cities. Eisenhower sent American troops to Lebanon; Kennedy supported an effort to invade Cuba. Johnson sent troops to the Dominican Republic and to Vietnam; Nixon ordered an invasion of Cambodia; Reagan launched an invasion of Grenada and sponsored an antigovernment insurgent group in Nicaragua; Bush invaded Panama and sent troops to the Persian Gulf to fight Iraq. Obviously Europeans, Russians, Vietnamese, Cambodians, Dominicans, Panamanians, and Iraqis do not think of the American president as "helpless." In later chapters, especially Chapter 20, we shall return to this apparent paradox.

Presidential Transition

No president but Franklin Roosevelt has ever served more than two terms and, since the ratification of the Twenty-second Amendment in 1951, no president will do so again. But more than tradition or the Constitution escorts presidents from office. Only fourteen of the forty-one presidents since George Washington have been elected to a second term. Of the twenty-seven not reelected, four died in office during their first term. But the remainder either did not seek, or (more usually) could not obtain reelection.

Of the eight presidents who died in office, four were assassinated: Lincoln, Garfield, McKinley, and

Lame Duck

A **lame duck** is a politician whose power has diminished because he or she is about to leave office as a result of electoral defeat or statutory limitation (for example, the president can serve no more than two terms).

The expression was first used in eighteenth-century England, where it meant a "bankrupt businessman." Soon it was used to refer to "bankrupt" politicians. Perhaps they were called "lame ducks" because they had been shot on the wing and, though still alive, could no longer fly.

Not to be confused with a "sitting duck" (somebody who is an easy target).

SOURCE: Adapted from William Safire, *Safire's Political Dictionary* (New York: Ballantine Books, 1978). Used by permission.

Kennedy. At least six other presidents were the objects of unsuccessful assassination attempts: Jackson, Theodore Roosevelt, Franklin Roosevelt, Truman, Ford, and Reagan. (There may have been attempts on other presidents that never came to public notice; the attempts mentioned here involved public efforts to fire weapons at presidents.)

The presidents who served two or more terms fall into certain periods such as the Founding (Washington, Jefferson, Madison, Monroe) or wartime (Lincoln, Wilson, Roosevelt), or they happened to be in office during especially tranquil times (Monroe, McKinley, Eisenhower), or some combination of the

President Reagan, moments before he was shot on March 30, 1981, by a would-be assassin.

above. When the country was deeply divided, as during the years just before the Civil War and during the period of Reconstruction after it, it was the rare president who was reelected.

The Vice President

Eight times a vice president has become president because of the death of his predecessor. It first happened to John Tyler, who became president in 1841 when William Henry Harrison died peacefully after only one month in office. The question for Tyler and for the country was substantial: was Tyler simply to be the acting president and a kind of caretaker until a new president was elected, or was he to be *president* in every sense of the word? Despite criticism and despite what might have been the contrary intention of the Framers of the Constitution, Tyler decided on the latter course and was confirmed in that opinion by a decision of Congress. Ever since, the vice president has automatically become president, in title and in powers, when the occupant of the White House has died or resigned.

But if vice presidents frequently acquire office because of death, they rarely acquire it by election.

Since the earliest period of the Founding, when John Adams and Thomas Jefferson were each elected president after having first served as vice president under their predecessors, there have only been three occasions when a vice president was later able to win the presidency without his president's having died in office. One was in 1836, when Martin Van Buren was elected president after having served as Andrew Jackson's vice president; the second was in 1968, when Richard Nixon became president after having served as Eisenhower's vice president eight years earlier; the third was in 1988 when Bush succeeded Reagan. Many vice presidents who enter the Oval Office because their predecessors died are subsequently elected to terms in their own right—as happened to Theodore Roosevelt, Calvin Coolidge, Harry Truman, and Lyndon Johnson. But no one who wishes to become president should assume that to become vice president first is the best way to get there.

The vice presidency is just what so many vice presidents have complained about its being: a rather empty job. John Adams described it as "the most insignificant office that ever the invention of man contrived or his imagination conceived," and most of his successors would have agreed. Thomas Jefferson, almost alone, had a good word to say for it: "The second office of the government is honorable and easy, the first is but a splendid misery."[20] Daniel Webster rejected a vice presidential nomination in 1848 with the phrase, "I do not choose to be buried until I am really dead."[21] (Had he taken the job, he would have become president after Zachary Taylor died in office, thereby achieving a remarkable secular resurrection.) For all the good and bad jokes about the vice presidency, however, candidates still struggle mightily for it. John Nance Garner gave up the speakership of the House to become Franklin Roosevelt's vice president (a job he valued as "not worth a pitcher of warm spit"*), and Lyndon Johnson gave up the majority leadership of the Senate to become Kennedy's. Truman, Nixon, Humphrey, Mondale, and Gore all left reasonably secure Senate seats for the vice presidency.

The only official task of the vice president is to preside over the Senate and to vote in case of a tie. Even this is scarcely time-consuming, as the Senate chooses from among its members a president pro

---

* The word he actually used was a good deal stronger than *spit,* but historians are decorous.

tempore, as required by the Constitution, who (along with others) presides in the absence of the vice president. The vice president's leadership powers in the Senate are weak, especially when the vice president is of a different party from the majority of the senators. Presidents have from time to time found tasks for their vice presidents—attending the funerals of world figures, being the chairman of governmental commissions, and the like—but all in all the vice president can do little more than endorse whatever the president does, and wait. And if they should run for president after their former boss retires (as George Bush did in 1988), they have to walk the fine line between appearing loyal to the president and having opinions of their own. It isn't easy.

Problems of Succession

If the president should die in office, the right of the vice president to assume that office has been clear since the time of John Tyler. But two questions remain: What if the president falls seriously ill but does not die? And if the vice president steps up, who then becomes the new vice president?

The first problem has arisen on a number of occasions. After President James A. Garfield was shot in 1881, he lingered through the summer before he died. President Woodrow Wilson collapsed from a stroke and was a virtual recluse for seven months in 1919 and an invalid for the rest of his term. Eisenhower had three serious illnesses while in office; Reagan was shot during his first term and hospitalized during his second.

The second problem has arisen on eight occasions when the vice president became president owing to the death of the incumbent. In these cases no elected person was available to succeed the new president should he die in office. For many decades the problem was handled by law. The Succession Act of 1886, for example, designated the secretary of state as next in line for the presidency should the vice president die, followed by the other cabinet officers in order of seniority. But this meant that a vice president who becomes president could pick his own successor by choosing his own secretary of state. In 1947 the law was changed to make the Speaker of the House and then the president pro tempore of the Senate next in line for the presidency. But that created still other problems: a Speaker or a president pro tempore

is likely to be chosen because of his seniority, not his executive skill, and in any event might well be of the party opposite to that occupying the White House.

Both problems were addressed in 1967 by the Twenty-fifth Amendment to the Constitution. It deals with the disability problem by allowing the vice president to serve as "acting president" whenever the president declares that he is unable to discharge the powers and duties of his office or whenever the vice president and a majority of the cabinet declare that the president is incapacitated. If the president disagrees with the opinion of his vice president and a majority of the cabinet, then Congress decides the issue. A two-thirds majority is necessary to confirm that the president is unable to serve.

The amendment deals with the succession problem by requiring a vice president who assumes the presidency (after a vacancy is created by death or resignation) to nominate a new vice president. This person takes office if the nomination is confirmed by a majority vote of both houses of Congress. When

When President Woodrow Wilson suffered a stroke in 1919, his wife, Edith Galt Wilson, became the power behind the scenes. The Twenty-fifth Amendment is intended to solve the problem of presidential disability by providing for an orderly transfer of power to the vice president.

Six-Year Term for President

Delegates Divided on Big Issue

* * *

EUDORA, KANS. OCTOBER 15—Here at the convention called to propose amendments to the United States Constitution, the major issue facing the delegates is the proposal to limit the president to a single six-year term. Proponents of the measure claim . . .

What Would You Do?

MEMORANDUM

TO: Delegate James Nagle
FROM: Robert Gilbert, legal staff
SUBJECT: Six-year presidential term

The proposal to give the president a single six-year term is perhaps the most popular amendment now before the convention. Polls suggest that it is supported by a sizable percentage of the American people.

<u>Arguments for:</u>

1. Today a president no sooner learns the ropes after being elected for the first time than he or she has to start preparing for the next election. A six-year term will give the president a chance to govern for several years after learning how to be president. This will lessen the extent to which political pressures dictate what the president does.

2. Limited to a single term, the president need not cater to special-interest groups or the media in deciding on policy. He or she can concentrate on what is good for the country.

3. Many states have limited their governors to a single term.

<u>Arguments against:</u>

1. It is the need to win reelection that keeps the president (like any politician) attentive to what the people want. A president unable to succeed himself or herself will be tempted to ignore public opinion.

2. Limiting a president to a single term will not free him or her from the need to play to the media or special-interest groups, since the formal powers of the presidency are too weak to permit the incumbent to govern without the aid of Congress and the press.

3. There is no evidence that presidents (such as Dwight Eisenhower) who served a second term knowing that they could not run for reelection did a better or less "political" job in the second term than in the first.

<u>Your decision:</u> Favor amendment_____ Oppose amendment_____

there is no vice president, then the 1947 law governs: next in line are the Speaker, the Senate president, and the thirteen cabinet officers, beginning with the secretary of state.

The disability problem has not arisen since the adoption of the amendment, but the succession problem has. In 1973 Vice President Spiro Agnew resigned, having pleaded no contest to criminal charges. President Nixon nominated Gerald Ford as vice president and, after extensive hearings, he was confirmed by both houses of Congress and sworn in. Then on August 9, 1974, Nixon resigned the presidency—the first man to do so—and Ford became president. He nominated as his vice president Nelson Rockefeller, who was confirmed by both houses of Congress—again, after extensive hearings—and was sworn in on December 19, 1974. For the first time in history, the nation had as its two principal executive officers men who had not been elected to either the presidency or the vice presidency. It is a measure of the legitimacy of the Constitution that this arrangement caused no crisis in public opinion.

Impeachment

There is one other way—besides death, disability, or resignation—by which a president can leave office before his term expires, and that is by impeachment. Not only the president and vice president but also all "civil officers of the United States" can be removed by being impeached and convicted. As a practical matter civil officers—cabinet secretaries, bureau chiefs, and the like—will not be subject to impeachment because the president can remove them at any time and usually will if their behavior makes them a serious political liability. Federal judges, who serve for life and who are constitutionally independent of the president and Congress, have been the most frequent objects of impeachment.

An **impeachment** is like an indictment in a criminal trial: a set of charges against somebody, voted by (in this case) the House of Representatives. To be removed from office, the impeached officer must be convicted by a two-thirds vote of the Senate, which sits as a court, hears the evidence, and makes its decision under whatever rules it wishes to adopt. Fifteen persons have been impeached by the House, and seven have been convicted by the Senate. The last conviction was in 1989, when two federal judges were removed from office.

Only one president has been impeached—Andrew Johnson in 1868—but Richard Nixon almost surely would have been had he not first resigned. Johnson was not convicted on the impeachment, the effort to do so falling one vote short of the necessary two-thirds majority. Many historians feel that the effort to remove Johnson was entirely partisan and ideological in nature, for he was not charged with anything that they would regard as "high crimes and misdemeanors" within the meaning of the Constitution. The Congress detested Johnson's "soft" policy toward the defeated South after the Civil War and was determined to use any pretext to remove him. The charges against Nixon were far graver: allegations of illegal acts arising from his efforts to cover up his subordinates' involvement in the burglary of the Democratic National Committee headquarters in the Watergate building.

Some Founders may have thought that impeachment would frequently be used against presidents, but as a practical matter it is so complex and serious an undertaking that we can probably expect it to be reserved in the future only for the gravest forms of presidential misconduct. No one quite knows what a high crime or misdemeanor is, but most scholars agree that the charge must involve something illegal or unconstitutional, not just unpopular. Unless a president or vice president is first impeached and convicted, many experts believe that he is not liable to prosecution as would be an ordinary citizen. (No one is certain, because the question has never arisen.) President Ford's pardon of Richard Nixon meant that he could not be prosecuted under federal law for things that he may have done while in office.

Students may find the occasions of misconduct or disability remote and the details of succession or impeachment tedious. But the problem is not remote—succession has occurred nine times and disability at least twice—and what may appear tedious goes, in fact, to the heart of the presidency. The first and fundamental problem is to make the office legitimate. That was the great task George Washington set himself, and that was the substantial accomplishment of his successors. Despite bitter and sometimes violent partisan and sectional strife, beginning almost immediately after Washington stepped down, presidential succession has always occurred peacefully, without a military coup or a political plot. For centuries, in the bygone times of kings as well as in the present times of dictators and juntas, peaceful succession has been a rare phenomenon among the nations of the world. Many of the critics of the Constitution believed, in 1787, that peaceful succession would not happen in the United States either: somehow the president would connive to hold office for life or to handpick his successor. Their predictions were wrong, though their fears were understandable.

How Powerful Is the President?

Just as members of Congress bemoan their loss of power, so presidents bemoan theirs. Can both be right?

In fact they can. If Congress is less able to control events than it once was, it does not mean that the president is thereby more able to exercise control. The federal government *as a whole* has become more constrained so that it is less able to act decisively. The chief source of this constraint is the greater complexity of the issues with which Washington must deal.

It was one thing to pass a Social Security Act in 1935; it is quite another thing to keep the Social Security system adequately funded (see Chapter 17). It was one thing for the nation to defend itself when attacked in 1941; it is quite another to maintain a constant military preparedness while simultaneously exploring possibilities for arms control (see Chapter 21). It was not hard to give pensions to veterans; it seems almost impossible today to find the cure for drug abuse or juvenile crime.

In the face of modern problems, all branches of government, including the presidency, seem both big and ineffectual. Add to this the much closer and more critical scrutiny of the media and the proliferation of interest groups, and it is small wonder that both presidents and members of Congress feel that they have lost power.

Presidents have come to acquire certain rules of thumb for dealing with their political problems. Among them are these:

- *Move it or lose it.* A president who wants to get something done should do it early in his term, before his political influence erodes.

- *Avoid details.* President Carter's lieutenants regret having tried to do too much. Better to have three or four top priorities and forget the rest.

- *Cabinets don't get much accomplished; people do.* Find capable White House subordinates and give them well-defined responsibility; then watch them closely.[22]

SUMMARY

A president, chosen by the people and with powers derived from a written constitution, has less power than does a British prime minister, even though the latter depends entirely on the support of his or her party in Parliament. The separation of powers between the executive and legislative branches, the distinguishing feature of the American system, means that the president must deal with a competitor—Congress—in setting policy and even in managing executive agencies.

Presidential power, though still sharply limited, has grown from its constitutional origins as a result of congressional delegation, the increased importance of foreign affairs, and public expectations. But if the president today has more power, more is also demanded of him. As a result how effective he is depends not on any general grant of authority but on the nature of the issue that he confronts and the extent to which he can mobilize informal sources of power (public opinion, congressional support).

Though the president seemingly controls a vast executive-branch apparatus, in fact he appoints but a small portion of the officials, and the behavior of even these is often beyond his easy control. Moreover public support, high at the beginning of any new presidency, usually declines as the term proceeds. Consequently each president must conserve his power (and his energy and time), concentrating these scarce resources to deal with a few matters of major importance. Virtually every president since Franklin Roosevelt has tried to enlarge his ability to manage the executive branch—by reorganization, by appointing White House aides, by creating specialized staff agencies—but no president has been satisfied with the results.

The president, in dealing with Congress, can rely to some degree on party loyalty; thus presidents whose party controls Congress tend to have more of their proposals approved. But such loyalty is insufficient; every president must in addition cajole, award favors, and threaten vetoes to influence legislation. Few presidents can count on a honeymoon; most discover that their own plans are at the mercy of unexpected crises.

The extent to which a president will be weak or powerful will vary with the kind of issue and the circumstances of the moment. It is a mistake to speak of an "imperial presidency" or of an ineffectual one. A president's power is better assessed by considering how he behaves in regard to specific issues.

KEY TERMS

divided government   *p. 345*

unified government   *p. 345*

representative democracy   *p. 346*

direct democracy   *p. 346*

pyramid structure   *p. 356*

circular structure   *p. 356*

ad hoc structure   *p. 356*

perks   *p. 360*

cabinet   *p. 360*

veto message   *p. 372*

pocket veto   *p. 372*

line-item veto   *p. 372*

legislative veto   *p. 378*

lame duck   *p. 379*

impeachment   *p. 383*

SUGGESTED READINGS

General

Barber, James David. *The Presidential Character.* 3d ed. Englewood Cliffs, N.J.: Prentice-Hall, 1985. How a president's personality evolves and shapes his conduct in office.

Corwin, Edward S. *The President: Office and Powers.* 5th ed. New York: New York University Press, 1985. Historical, constitutional, and legal development of the office.

Cunliffe, Marcus. *American Presidents and the Presidency.* New York: American Heritage Press/McGraw-Hill, 1972. Readable history of the presidency, with shrewd insights and ample anecdotes.

Kernell, Samuel. *Going Public: New Strategies of Presidential Leadership.* Washington, D.C.: Congressional Quarterly Press, 1986. How presidents try to enlarge their power by taking their case to the public.

Neustadt, Richard E. *Presidential Power: The Politics of Leadership.* Rev. ed. New York: Wiley, 1976. How presidents try to acquire and hold political power in the competitive world of official Washington, by a man who has been both a scholar and an insider.

Peterson, Mark A. *Legislating Together: The White House and Congress from Eisenhower to Reagan.* Cambridge: Harvard University Press, 1990. Challenges the conventional view that "the president proposes, Congress disposes." Contains many excellent examples of bargaining and cooperation between Congress and the executive branch.

On Franklin D. Roosevelt

Burns, James MacGregor. *Roosevelt: The Lion and the Fox.* New York: Harcourt Brace, 1956.

Leuchtenberg, William E. *Franklin D. Roosevelt and the New Deal, 1932–1940.* New York: Harper & Row, 1963.

On Harry Truman

Hamby, A. L. *Beyond the New Deal: Harry S Truman and American Liberalism.* New York: Columbia University Press, 1973.

Truman, Harry S. *Memoirs.* 2 vols. Garden City, N.Y.: Doubleday, 1958.

On Dwight D. Eisenhower

Greenstein, Fred I. *The Hidden-Hand Presidency: Eisenhower as Leader.* New York: Basic Books, 1982.

On John F. Kennedy

Paper, Lewis J. *The Promise and the Performance: The Leadership of John F. Kennedy.* New York: Crown, 1975.

Sorenson, Theodore M. *Kennedy.* New York: Harper & Row, 1965.

On Lyndon B. Johnson

Kearns, Doris. *Lyndon Johnson and the American Dream.* New York: Harper & Row, 1976.

Evans, Rowland, and Robert Novak. *Lyndon B. Johnson: The Exercise of Power.* New York: New American Library, 1968.

On Richard M. Nixon

Ambrose, Stephen E. *Nixon—The Education of a Politician, 1913–1962.* New York: Simon and Schuster, 1987.

13

The Bureaucracy

There is probably not a man or woman in the United States who has not, at some time or other, complained about "the bureaucracy." Your letter was slow in getting to Aunt Minnie? The Internal Revenue Service took months to send you your tax refund? The Defense Department paid $400 for a hammer? The Occupational Safety and Health Administration told you that you installed the wrong kind of portable toilet for your farm workers? The "bureaucracy" is to blame.

For most people and politicians bureaucracy is a pejorative word implying waste, confusion, red tape, and rigidity. But for scholars—and for bureaucrats themselves—bureaucracy is a word with a neutral, technical meaning. A **bureaucracy** is a large, complex organization composed of appointed officials. By *complex* we mean that authority is divided among several managers; no one person is able to make all the decisions (see Figure 13.1). A large corporation is a bureaucracy; so also are a big university and a government agency. With its sizable staff, even Congress has become, to some degree, a bureaucracy.

What is it about complex organizations in general, and government agencies in particular, that leads so many people to complain about them? In part the answer is to be found in their very size and complexity. But in large measure the answer is to be found in the political context within which such agencies must operate. If we examine that context carefully, we will discover that many of the problems that we blame on "bureaucracy" are in fact the result of what Congress, the courts, and the president do.

Distinctiveness of the American Bureaucracy

Bureaucratic government has become an obvious feature of all modern societies, democratic and non-democratic. In the United States, however, three aspects of our constitutional system and political traditions give to the bureaucracy a distinctive character.

FIGURE 13.1   How Bureaucracy Grows: The Increasing Division of Authority in the Department of Labor

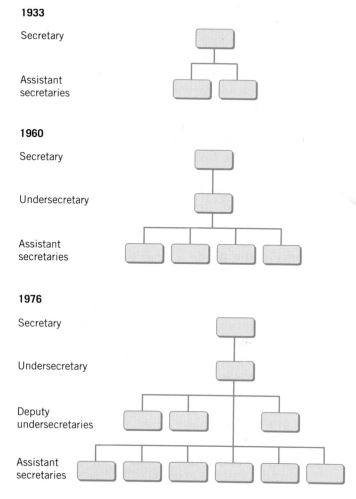

1933

Secretary

Assistant secretaries

1960

Secretary

Undersecretary

Assistant secretaries

1976

Secretary

Undersecretary

Deputy undersecretaries

Assistant secretaries

NOTE: Charts show political appointees above the level of bureau heads, U.S. Department of Labor, 1933, 1960, and 1976.

SOURCE: Hugh Heclo, "Issue Networks and the Executive Establishment," in *The New American Political System*, ed. Anthony King (Washington, D.C.: American Enterprise Institute, 1978). 114. Copyright © 1978 by the American Enterprise Institute. Reprinted by permission.

First, political authority over the bureaucracy is not in one set of hands but shared among several institutions. In a parliamentary regime, such as in Great Britain, the appointed officials of the national government work for the cabinet ministers, who are in turn dominated by the prime minister. In theory and to a considerable extent in practice, British bureaucrats report to and take orders from the ministers in charge of their departments, do not deal directly with Parliament, and rarely give interviews to the press. In the United States the Constitution permits both the president and Congress to exercise authority over the bureaucracy. Every senior appointed official has at least two masters: one in the executive branch and the other in the legislative. Often there are many more than two: Congress, after all, is not a single organization but a collection of committees, subcommittees, and individuals. This divided authority encourages bureaucrats to play one branch of government off against the other and to make heavy use of the media.

Second, most of the agencies of the federal government share their functions with related agencies in state and local government. Though some federal agencies deal directly with American citizens—the Internal Revenue Service collects taxes from them, the Federal Bureau of Investigation looks into crimes for them, the Postal Service delivers mail to them— many agencies work with other organizations at other levels of government. For example: the Department of Education gives money to local school systems; the Health Care Financing Administration in the Department of Health and Human Services reimburses states for money spent on health care for the poor; the Department of Housing and Urban Development gives grants to cities for community development; and the Employment and Training Administration in the Department of Labor supplies funds to local governments so that they can run job-training programs. In France, by contrast, government programs dealing with education, health, housing, and employment are centrally run, with little or no control exercised by local governments.

Third, the institutions and traditions of American life have contributed to the growth of what was called in Chapter 4 an "adversary culture," in which the definition and expansion of personal rights, and the defense of rights and claims through lawsuits as well as political action, are given central importance. A government agency in this country operates under closer public scrutiny and with a greater prospect of court challenges to its authority than in almost any other nation. Virtually every important decision of the Occupational Safety and Health Administration or of the Environmental Protection Agency is likely to be challenged in the courts or attacked by an affected party; in Sweden the decisions of similar agencies go largely uncontested.

The scope as well as the style of bureaucratic government differs. In most Western European nations the government owns and operates large parts of the economy: the French government operates the railroads and owns companies that make automobiles and cigarettes, and the Italian government owns many similar enterprises and also the nation's oil refineries. In just about every large nation except the United States, the telephone system is government-owned. Publicly operated enterprises account for about 12 percent of all employment in France but less than 3 percent in the United States.[1] As we shall see in Chapter 15, however, the United States government regulates privately owned enterprises to a degree not found in many other countries. Why we should have preferred regulation to ownership as the proper government role is an interesting question to which we shall return.

The Growth of the Bureaucracy

The Constitution made scarcely any provision for an administrative system other than to allow the president to appoint, with the advice and consent of the Senate, "ambassadors, other public ministers and consuls, judges of the Supreme Court, and all other officers of the United States whose appointments are not herein otherwise provided for, and which shall be established by law."[2] Departments and bureaus were not mentioned.

In the first Congress in 1789 James Madison introduced a bill to create a Department of State to assist the new secretary of state, Thomas Jefferson, in carrying out his duties. People appointed to this department were to be nominated by the president and approved by the Senate, but they were "to be removable by the president" alone. These six words, which would confer the right to fire government officials, occasioned six days of debate in the House. At stake was the locus of power over what was to become the bureaucracy. Madison's opponents argued that the Senate should consent to the removal of officials as well as their appointment. Madison responded that, without the unfettered right of removal, the president would not be able to control his subordinates,

and without this control he would not be able to discharge his constitutional obligation to "take care that the laws be faithfully executed."[3] Madison won, twenty-nine votes to twenty-two. When the issue went to the Senate, another debate resulted in a tie vote, broken in favor of the president by Vice President John Adams. The Department of State, and all cabinet departments subsequently created, would be run by people removable only by the president.

That decision did not resolve the question of who would really control the bureaucracy, however. Congress retained the right to appropriate money, to investigate the administration, and to shape the laws that would be executed by that administration—more than ample power to challenge any president who claimed to have sole authority over his subordinates. And many members of Congress expected that the cabinet departments, even though headed by people removable by the president, would report to Congress.

The government in Washington was at first minuscule. The State Department started with only nine employees; the War Department did not have eighty civilian employees until 1801. Only the Treasury Department, concerned with collecting taxes and finding ways to pay the public debt, had much power, and only the Post Office Department provided any significant service.

The Appointment of Officials

Small as the bureaucracy was, people struggled, often bitterly, over who would be appointed to it. From George Washington's day to modern times, presidents have found appointment to be one of their most important and difficult tasks. The officials that they select affect how the laws are interpreted (thus the political ideology of the job holders is important), what tone the administration will display (thus personal character is important), how effectively the public business is discharged (thus competence is important), and how strong will be the political party or faction in power (and thus party affiliation is important). Presidents trying to balance the competing needs of ideology, character, fitness, and partisanship have rarely pleased most people. As John Adams remarked, every appointment creates one ingrate and ten enemies.

Spoils System

The **spoils system** is another phrase for *political patronage*—that is, the practice of giving the fruits of a party's victory, such as jobs and contracts, to the loyal members of that party.

Spoils became a famous word when it was used in 1832 by Senator William Marcy of New York in a speech that he made defending the decision of President Andrew Jackson to appoint one of his supporters, Martin Van Buren, as ambassador to Great Britain. New York politicians, he said, "boldly preach what they practice.... If they are successful, they claim, as a matter of right, the advantages of success. They see nothing wrong in the rule, that to the victor belong the spoils of the enemy."

In fact both the word and the practice are much older than Marcy and Jackson. Thomas Jefferson had appointed his partisans to office when he won the presidency from John Adams. Though Jackson is remembered as a heavy user of spoils, in fact he only replaced about 20 percent of all the officeholders that he inherited from his predecessor.

By the late nineteenth century the spoils system was both more extensively used and sharply criticized. Ending the system and replacing it with appointments based on merit was a major goal of the progressive movement around the turn of the century.

Today most federal appointments are based on merit, but in many state governments there continues to be a heavy reliance on patronage.

SOURCE: Adapted from William Safire, *Safire's Political Dictionary* (New York: Ballantine Books, 1978). Used by permission.

Because Congress, during most of the nineteenth and twentieth centuries, was the dominant branch of government, congressional preferences often controlled the appointment of officials. And since Congress was, in turn, a collection of people who represented local interests, appointments were made with an eye to rewarding the local supporters of members of Congress or building up local party organizations. These appointments made on the basis of political considerations—patronage—were later to become a major issue. They galvanized various reform efforts that sought to purify politics and to raise the level of competence of the public service. Many of the abuses that the reformers complained about were real enough, but patronage served some useful purposes as well. It gave the president a way to ensure that his subordinates were reasonably supportive of his policies; it provided a reward that the president could use to induce recalcitrant members of Congress to vote for his programs; and it enabled party organizations to be built up to perform the necessary functions of nominating candidates and getting out the vote.

Though at first there were not many jobs to fight over, by the middle of the nineteenth century there were a lot. From 1816 to 1861 the number of federal employees increased eightfold. This expansion was not, however, the result of the government's taking on new functions but simply a result of the increased demands on its traditional functions. The Post Office alone accounted for 86 percent of this growth.[4]

The Civil War was a great watershed in bureaucratic development. Fighting the war led, naturally, to hiring many new officials and creating many new offices. Just as important, the Civil War revealed the administrative weakness of the federal government and led to demands by the civil-service-reform movement for an improvement in the quality and organization of federal employees. And finally, the war was followed by a period of rapid industrialization and the emergence of a national economy. The effects of these developments could no longer be managed by state governments acting alone. With the creation of a nationwide network of railroads, commerce among the states became increasingly important. The constitutional powers of the federal government to regulate interstate commerce, long dormant for want of much commerce to regulate, now became an important source of controversy.

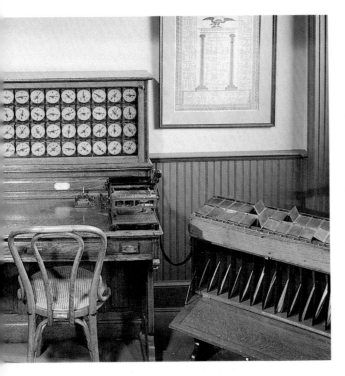

The Hollerith machine (left) was invented by Herman Hollerith (1860–1929) to help the government take the census. It analyzed statistical data by sorting and counting punched paper cards. Today, high-speed computers (right) read data optically and analyze them electronically.

A Service Role

From 1861 to 1901 new agencies were created, many to deal with particular sectors of society and the economy. Over two hundred thousand new federal employees were added, with only about half of this increase in the Post Office. A rapidly growing Pension Office began paying benefits to Civil War veterans; a Department of Agriculture was created in 1862 to help farmers; a Department of Labor was founded in 1882 to serve workers; and a Department of Commerce was organized in 1903 to assist businesspeople. Many more specialized agencies, such as the National Bureau of Standards, also came into being.

These agencies had one thing in common: their role was primarily to serve, not to regulate. Most did research, gathered statistics, dispensed federal lands, or passed out benefits. Not until the Interstate Commerce Commission was created in 1887 did the federal government begin to regulate the economy (other than by managing the currency) in any large way. Even the ICC had, at first, relatively few powers.

There were several reasons why federal officials primarily performed a service role. The values that had shaped the Constitution were still strong: these included a belief in limited government, the importance of states' rights, and the fear of concentrated discretionary power. The proper role of government in the economy was to promote, not to regulate; and a commitment to **laissez-faire**—a freely competitive economy—was strongly held. But just as important, the Constitution said nothing about giving any regulatory powers to bureaucrats. It gave to *Congress* the power to regulate commerce among the states. Now obviously Congress could not make the necessary day-to-day decisions to regulate, for example, the rates that interstate railroads charged to farmers and other shippers. Some agency or commission composed of appointed officials and experts would have to be created to do that. For a long time, however, the prevailing interpretation of the Constitution was that no such agency could exercise such regulatory powers unless Congress first set down clear standards that would govern the agency's decisions. As late as 1935 the Supreme Court held that a regulatory agency could not make rules on its own; it could only apply the standards enacted by Congress.[5] The Court's view was that the legislature may not delegate its powers to the president or to an administrative agency.[6]

These restrictions on what administrators could do were set aside in wartime. During World War I, for example, President Woodrow Wilson was authorized by Congress to fix prices, operate the railroads, manage the communications system, and even control the distribution of food.[7] This kind of extraordinary grant of power usually ended with the war.

Some changes in the bureaucracy did not end with the war. During the Civil War, World War I, World War II, the Korean War, and the war in Vietnam, the number of civilian (as well as military) employees of the government rose sharply. These increases were not simply in the number of civilians needed to help serve the war effort; many of the additional people were hired by agencies, such as the Treasury Department, not obviously connected with the war. Furthermore the number of federal officials did not return to prewar levels after each war. Though there was some reduction, each war left the number of federal employees larger than before.[8]

It is not hard to understand how this happens. During wartime almost every government agency argues that its activities have *some* relation to the war effort, and few legislators want to be caught voting against something that may help that effort. Hence in 1944 the Reindeer Service in Alaska, an agency of the Interior Department, asked for more employees because reindeer are "a valued asset in military planning."

A Change in Role

Today's bureaucracy is largely a product of two events: the Depression of the 1930s (and the concomitant New Deal program of President Roosevelt) and World War II. Though many agencies have been added since then, the basic features of the bureaucracy were set mainly as a result of changes in public attitudes and in constitutional interpretation that occurred during these periods. The government was now expected to play an active role in dealing with economic and social problems. In the late 1930s, the Supreme Court reversed its earlier decisions (see Chapter 14) on the question of delegating legislative powers to administrative agencies and upheld laws by which Congress merely instructs agencies to make decisions that serve "the public interest" in some area.[9] As a result it was possible for President Nixon to set up in 1971 a system of price and wage controls

based on a statute that simply authorized the president "to issue such orders and regulations as he may deem appropriate to stabilize prices, rents, wages, and salaries."[10] The Cost of Living Council and other agencies that Nixon established to carry out this order were run by appointed officials who had the legal authority to make sweeping decisions based on general statutory language.

World War II was the first occasion during which the government made heavy use of federal income taxes—on individuals and corporations—to finance its activities. Between 1940 and 1945 total federal tax collections increased from about $5 billion to nearly $44 billion. The end of the war brought no substantial tax reduction: the country believed that a high level of military preparedness continued to be necessary and that various social programs begun before the war should enjoy the heavy funding made possible by wartime taxes. Tax receipts continued, by and large, to grow. Before 1913, when the Sixteenth Amendment to the Constitution was passed, the federal government could not collect income taxes at all (it financed itself largely from customs duties and excise taxes). From 1913 to 1940 income taxes were small (in 1940 the average American paid only $7 in federal incomes taxes). World War II created the first great financial boom for the government, permitting the sustained expansion of a wide variety of programs and thus the support of a large number of administrators.[11]

The Federal Bureaucracy Today

No president wants to admit that he has increased the size of the bureaucracy. He can avoid saying this by pointing out that the number of civilians working for the federal government has not increased significantly in recent years and is about the same today (3.2 million persons) as it was in 1970, and less than it was during World War II.[12] This explanation is true but misleading, for it neglects the large and growing number of people who work *indirectly* for Washington as employees of private firms and state or local agencies that are largely, if not entirely, supported by federal funds. No one knows for certain, but there may be as many as four persons earning their living indirectly from the federal government for every one earning it directly. While federal employment has remained more or less stable, employment among federal contractors and consultants and in state and local governments has mushroomed.

The power of the federal bureaucracy cannot be measured by the number of employees, however. A bureaucracy of 5 million persons would have little power if each employee did nothing but type letters or file documents, whereas a bureaucracy of only one hundred persons would have awesome power if each member were able to make arbitrary life-and-death decisions affecting the rest of us. The power of the bureaucracy depends on the extent to which appointed officials have **discretionary authority**—that is, on their ability to choose courses of action and to make policies that are not spelled out in advance by laws. In Figure 13.3 we see how the volume of regulations issued and the amount of money spent have risen much faster than the number of federal employees who write the regulations and spend the money.

By this test the power of the federal bureaucracy has grown enormously. Congress has delegated substantial authority to administrative agencies in three areas: (1) paying subsidies to particular groups and organizations in society (farmers, veterans, scientists, schools, universities, hospitals); (2) transferring money from the federal government to state and local governments (the grant-in-aid programs described in Chapter 3); and (3) devising and enforcing regulations for various sectors of society and the economy. Some of these administrative functions, such as grants-in-aid to states, are closely monitored by Congress; others, such as the regulatory programs, usually operate with a greater degree of independence. These delegations of power, especially in the areas of paying subsidies and regulating the economy, did not become commonplace until the 1930s, and then only after the Supreme Court decided that such delegations were constitutional. In Chapter 15 we shall discuss how this power is used. For now it is

FIGURE 13.2 Characteristics of Federal Civilian Employees, 1960 and 1990

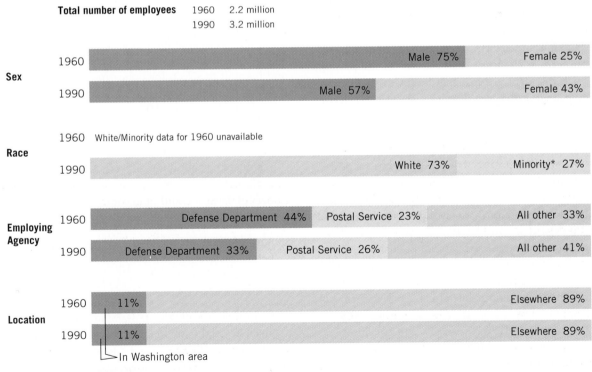

SOURCES: *Statistical Abstract of the United States, 1961*, 392–394; *Statistical Abstract of the United States, 1992*, 330–331.

FIGURE 13.3   Federal Government Growth: Money, Rules, and People

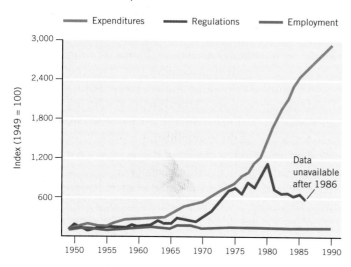

SOURCES: Hugh Heclo, "Issue Networks and the Executive Establishment," in *The New American Political System*, ed. Anthony King (Washington, D.C.: American Enterprise Institute, 1978), 90. Copyright © 1978 by the American Enterprise Institute. Reprinted by permission. Updated with the *Federal Register* and *Statistical Abstract of the United States.*

enough to know that appointed officials can decide, within rather broad limits, who shall own a television station, what safety features automobiles shall have, what kinds of scientific research shall be specially encouraged, what drugs shall appear on the market, which dissident groups shall be investigated, what fumes an industrial smokestack may emit, which corporate mergers shall be allowed, what use shall be made of national forests, and what price crop farmers and dairy farmers shall receive for their products.

If appointed officials have this kind of power, then how they use it is of paramount importance in understanding modern government. There are, broadly, four factors that may explain the behavior of these officials:

1. The manner in which they are recruited and rewarded.

2. Their personal attributes, such as their socioeconomic backgrounds and their political attitudes.

3. The nature of their jobs.

4. The constraints that outside forces—political superiors, legislators, interest groups, journalists—impose on their agencies.

Recruitment and Retention

About two-thirds of all appointed officials are part of the **competitive service.** This means that they are initially appointed only after they have passed a written examination administered by the Office of Personnel Management (OPM) or have met certain selection criteria (such as training, educational attainments, or prior experience) devised by the hiring agency and approved by OPM. Where competition for a job exists and candidates can be ranked by their scores or records, the agency must usually appoint one of the three top-ranking candidates.

The other one-third of the civilian employees are part of the excepted service—that is, they are not appointed on the basis of qualifications designed or approved by the Office of Personnel Management. Most of these, however, are also appointed on a nonpartisan basis but by various agencies that have merit-based appointment systems independent of the one run by the OPM. These include Postal Service employees, FBI agents, intelligence officers in the CIA, foreign-service officers in the State Department, and doctors in the Public Health Service and the Veterans Administration.

Some of the excepted employees—probably no more than 3 percent—are appointed on grounds other than or in addition to merit, narrowly defined. These legal exceptions exist to permit the president and his staff to select, for policy-making and politically sensitive posts, people who are in agreement with their policy views. These appointees are generally of three kinds:

1. Presidential appointments authorized by statute (cabinet and subcabinet officers, judges, U.S. marshals and U.S. attorneys, ambassadors, and members of various boards and commissions).

2. "Schedule C" jobs, which are described as having a "confidential or policy-determining character" below the level of cabinet or subcabinet posts (including executive assistants, special aides, and confidential secretaries).

3. Noncareer executive assignments (NEA jobs) given to high-ranking members of the regular competitive civil service, or to persons brought into the civil service at these high levels, who are deeply involved in the advocacy of presidential programs or who participate in policy making.

These three groups of excepted appointments constitute the patronage available to a president and his administration. In the nineteenth century practically every job was a patronage job. For example, when Grover Cleveland, a Democrat, became president in 1885, he replaced some forty thousand Republican postal employees with Democrats. In 1883, with the passage of the Pendleton Act, there began a slow but steady transfer of federal jobs from the patronage to the merit system. It may seem strange that a political party in power should be willing to relinquish its patronage in favor of a merit-based appointment system. Two factors made it easier for the Republicans in 1883 to pass the Pendleton Act: (1) public outrage over the abuses of the spoils system, highlighted by the assassination of President James Garfield by a man always described in the history books as a "disappointed office-seeker" (lunatic would be a more accurate term); and (2) the fear that if the Democrats came to power on a wave of anti-spoils sentiment, existing Republican officeholders would be fired. (The Democrats won anyway.)

The merit system spread to encompass most of the federal bureaucracy, generally with presidential support. Though presidents may have liked in theory the idea of hiring and firing subordinates at will, most felt that the demands for patronage were impossible either to satisfy or to ignore. Furthermore by increasing the coverage of the merit system a president could "blanket in" patronage appointees already holding office, thus making it difficult or impossible for the next administration to fire them.

The Buddy System The actual recruitment of civil servants, especially in middle- and upper-level jobs, is somewhat more complicated, and slightly more political, than the laws and rules might suggest. Though many people enter the federal bureaucracy by learning of a job, filling out an application, perhaps taking a test, and being hired, many also enter on a "name-request" basis. A **name-request job** is one that is filled by a person whom an agency has already identified. In this respect the federal government is not so different from private business. A person learns of a job from somebody who already has one, or the head of a bureau decides in advance whom he or she wishes to hire. The agency must still send a form describing the job to the OPM, but it also names the person whom the agency wants to ap-

A Day in the Life of a Bureaucrat

Here is how the Commissioner of the Social Security Administration (SSA), a high-level bureaucrat, spent a typical day:

5:45 A.M.	Arise.
6:50 A.M.	Leave for the office.
7:30 A.M.	Read newspapers.
8:00 A.M.	Meeting with deputy commissioner.
8:30 A.M.	Brief cabinet secretary on Social Security data.
9:45 A.M.	Decide how to respond to press criticisms.
10:05 A.M.	Leave for meeting in another building.
11:30 A.M.	Meet with top staff.
1:00 P.M.	Meet with bureau chiefs on half a dozen issues.
2:45 P.M.	Meet with a deputy to discuss next year's budget.
3:30 P.M.	Meet with business executive about use of computers in SSA.
4:30 P.M.	Meet with deputy in charge of Medicare to discuss plan for national health insurance.
5:10 P.M.	Catch up on phone calls; meet with committee concerned with drug abuse.
6:10 P.M.	Leave for home. Get out of attending a dinner meeting in Washington.

As is obvious, high-level bureaucrats spend most of their time discussing things in meetings. It is in such meetings that government policy is made.

SOURCE: Adapted from "A Day in the Life of a Government Executive," in *Inside the System*, 4th ed., ed. Charles Peters and Nicholas Leamann (New York: Holt, Rinehart and Winston, 1979), 205–213.

point. Sometimes the job is even described in such a way that the person named is the only one who can qualify for it. Occasionally this tailor-made, name-request job is offered to a person at the insistence of a member of Congress who wants a political supporter taken care of; more often it is made available because the bureaucracy itself knows whom it wishes to hire and wants to circumvent an elaborate search. This is the "buddy system."

The buddy system does not necessarily produce poor employees. Indeed it is frequently a way of hiring people known to the agency as being capable of handling the position. It also opens up the possibility of hiring people whose policy views are congenial to those already in office. Hugh Heclo refers to these recruitment patterns as "issue networks." Such networks are based on shared policy views, not (as once was the case) on narrow partisan affiliations. Bureaucrats in consumer-protection agencies, for example, recruit new staff from private groups with an interest in consumer protection, such as the various organizations associated with Ralph Nader, or from academics who have a proconsumer inclination.

There has always been an informal "old boys' network" among those who move in and out of high-level government posts; with the increasing appointment of women to these jobs, there has begun to emerge an old girls' network as well.[13] In a later section we will consider whether, or in what ways, these recruitment patterns make a difference.

Firing a Bureaucrat The great majority of bureaucrats who are part of the civil service and who do not hold presidential appointments have jobs that are, for all practical purposes, beyond reach. An executive must go through elaborate steps to fire, demote, or

suspend a civil servant. Realistically this means that no one is fired or demoted unless his or her superior is prepared to invest a great deal of time and effort in the attempt. In 1987 about 2,600 employees who had completed their probationary period were fired for misconduct or poor performance. That is about one-tenth of 1 percent of all federal employees. It is hard to believe that a large private company would fire only one-tenth of 1 percent of its workers in a given year. It's also impossible to believe that, as is often the case in Washington, it would take a year to fire anyone. To cope with this problem, federal executives have devised a number of stratagems for bypassing or forcing out civil servants with whom they cannot work—denying them promotions, transferring them to undesirable locations, or assigning them to meaningless work.

With the passage of the Civil Service Reform Act of 1978, Congress recognized that many high-level positions in the civil service have important policy-making responsibilities and that the president and his cabinet officers ought to have more flexibility in recruiting, assigning, and paying such people. Accordingly the act created a Senior Executive Service (SES) of about eight thousand top federal managers who could be hired, fired, and transferred more easily than ordinary civil servants. Moreover members of the SES would be eligible for substantial cash bonuses if they performed their duties well. (To protect the rights of SES members, anyone who is removed from the SES is guaranteed a job elsewhere in the government.)

Things did not work out quite as the sponsors of the SES had hoped. Though most eligible civil servants joined it, there was only a modest increase in the proportion of higher-ranking positions in agencies that were filled by transfer from another agency; the cash bonuses did not prove to be an important incentive (perhaps because the base salaries of top bureaucrats did not keep up with inflation); and hardly any member of the SES was actually fired. Two years after the SES was created, less than one-half of 1 percent of its members had received an unsatisfactory rating and none had been fired. Nor does the SES give the president a large opportunity to make political appointments: only 10 percent of the SES can be selected from outside the existing civil service. And no SES member can be transferred involuntarily.

Firing a Bureaucrat

*T*o fire or demote a member of the competitive civil service, these procedures must be followed:

1. The employee must be given written notice at least thirty days in advance that he or she is to be fired or demoted for incompetence or misconduct.

2. The written notice must contain a statement of reasons, including specific examples of unacceptable performance.

3. The employee has the right to an attorney and to reply, orally or in writing, to the charges.

4. The employee has the right to appeal any adverse action to the Merit Systems Protection Board (MSPB), a three-person, bipartisan body appointed by the president with the consent of the Senate.

5. The MSPB must grant the employee a hearing and the right to an attorney.

6. The employee has the right to appeal the MSPB decision to the United States Court of Appeals, which can hold new hearings.

One barrier to improving presidential control of the federal bureaucracy is that even the White House has become a large bureaucracy.

The Agency's Point of View   When one realizes that most agencies are staffed by people who were recruited by those agencies, sometimes on a name-request basis, and who are virtually immune from dismissal, it becomes clear that the recruitment and retention policies of the civil service work to ensure that most bureaucrats will have an "agency" point of view. Even with the encouragement for transfers created by the SES, very few persons appointed to the top three civil-service grades in a given agency come from other agencies.[14]

The Senior Executive Service may in time change this pattern, but for now most government agencies are dominated by people who have not served in any other agency and who have been in government service most of their lives. This fact has some advantages: it means that most bureaucrats are expert in the procedures and policies of their agencies and that there will be a substantial degree of continuity in agency behavior no matter which political party happens to be in power.

But the agency point of view has its costs as well. A political executive entering an agency with responsibility for shaping its direction will discover that he or she must carefully win the support of career subordinates. A subordinate has an infinite capacity for discreet sabotage and can make life miserable for a political superior by delaying action, withholding information, following the rule book with literal exactness, or making an "end run" around a superior to mobilize members of Congress who are sympathetic to the bureaucrat's point of view. For instance, when one political executive wanted to downgrade a bureau in his department, he found, naturally, that the bureau chief was opposed. The bureau chief spoke to some friendly lobbyists and a key member of Congress. When the political executive asked the congressman whether he had any problem with the contemplated reorganization, the congressman replied, "No, you have the problem, because if you touch that bureau, I'll cut your job out of the budget."[15]

TABLE 13.1 Percentage of Female, Black, and Total Minority Employment in the Federal Bureaucracy, by Rank, 1989–1990

Grade	Female (1989)	Black (1990)	All Minorities (1990)[a]
Lowest	74.8% (GS 1-6)	28.5% (GS 1-4)	42.1% (GS 1-4)
Moderate Low	53.5 (GS 7-10)	22.7 (GS 5-8)	33.3 (GS 5-8)
Moderate	32.9 (GS 11-12)	11.6 (GS 9-12)	21.3 (GS 9-12)
Moderate High	17.0 (GS 13-15)	6.4 (GS 13-15)	12.7 (GS 13-15)
Highest	9.1 (GS 16-18)	5.0 (Executive)	7.9 (Executive)
Totals	(NA)	16.6	27.3

[a] "All minorities" includes blacks, Hispanics, American Indians, Alaska natives, Asians, and Pacific Islanders.
SOURCE: *Statistical Abstract of the United States,1992*, 330, 333.

Personal Attributes

A second factor that might shape the way bureaucrats use their power is their personal attributes. These include their social class, education, and personal political beliefs. The federal civil service as a whole looks very much like a cross section of American society in the education, sex, race, and social origins of its members. But as with many other employers, women, blacks, and other minorities are most likely to be heavily represented in the lowest grade levels and tend to be underrepresented at the executive level (see Table 13.1). At the higher-ranking levels where the most power is found—say, in the supergrade ranks of GS-16 through GS-18—the typical civil servant is a middle-aged white male with a college degree whose father was somewhat more advantaged than the average citizen. In the great majority of cases this individual is in fact very different from the typical American in both background and personal beliefs.

Because the higher civil service is unrepresentative of the average American, some critics speculate that people holding these top jobs think and act in ways very different from most Americans. Depending on their politics, these critics have concluded that the bureaucracy is either more conservative or more liberal than the country it helps govern. Some critics believe that the upper-middle-class bureaucrats defend their class privileges.[16] Other critics, such as former President Nixon, argue that, since many members of the higher civil service were appointed by Democratic presidents and since these officials were trained by liberal faculty members in prestigious universities, the civil service favors liberal or leftist causes.[17]

A survey of the attitudes of some two hundred top-level, nonpolitical federal bureaucrats suggests that they are, in fact, somewhat more liberal than the average American voter but considerably less liberal than key members of the media (see Chapter 10). As we can see in Table 13.2, about 56 percent of those interviewed in 1982 described themselves as liberal and said that they had voted for the Democratic candidate for president in 1968, 1972, 1976, and 1980. By contrast a much smaller proportion of average voters think of themselves as liberals, and most voted for the Republican presidential candidate in 1968, 1972, and 1980. But on most specific policy questions, bureaucrats do not have extreme positions. For example, they don't think that the government should take over the big corporations, they support some amount of business deregulation, and a majority (by a slim margin) don't think that the goal of U.S. foreign policy has been to protect business.[18]

We can also see, however, that the kind of agency for which a bureaucrat works makes a difference. Those employed in "activist" agencies, such as the Federal Trade Commission, Environmental Protection Agency, and Food and Drug Administration, have much more liberal views than those who work for the more "traditional" agencies, such as the departments of Agriculture, Commerce, and the Treasury.

TABLE 13.2   Political Attitudes of High-Level Federal Bureaucrats

	Percentage Agreeing		
Attitude	All Bureaucrats	"Traditional" Agencies	"Activist" Agencies
I am a liberal.	56%	48%	63%
I voted for:			
Humphrey (1968)	72	67	76
McGovern (1972)	57	47	65
Carter (1976)	71	65	76
Carter (1980)	45	34	55
Less regulation of business is good for the U.S.	61	66	57
U.S. military should be the strongest in the world, regardless of cost.	25	31	19
Women should get preference in hiring.	34	28	40
Blacks should get preference in hiring.	44	35	53
Homosexuality is wrong.	47	54	40
Nuclear plants are safe.	52	58	46

SOURCE: Stanley Rothman and S. Robert Lichter, "How Liberal Are Bureaucrats?" Reprinted with permission from *Regulation* (November–December 1983). Copyright© 1983 by American Enterprise Institute.

This association between attitudes and kind of agency has been confirmed by other studies. Even when the bureaucrats come from roughly the same social backgrounds, their policy views seem to reflect the type of government work that they do. For example, people holding foreign-service jobs in the State Department tended to be more liberal than those coming from similar family backgrounds and performing similar tasks (such as working on foreign affairs) in the Defense Department.[19] It is not clear whether these differences in attitudes were produced by the jobs that they held or whether certain jobs attract people with certain beliefs. Probably both forces were at work.

Whatever the mechanism involved, there seems little doubt that different agencies display different political ideologies. A study done in 1976 revealed that Democrats and people with liberal views tended to be overrepresented in social-service agencies, whereas Republicans and people with conservative views tend to be overrepresented in defense agencies.[20]

Do Bureaucrats Sabotage Their Political Bosses?

Because it is so hard to fire career bureaucrats, it is often said that these people will sabotage any actions by their political superiors with which they disagree. And since civil servants tend to have liberal views, it has been conservative presidents and cabinet secretaries who have usually expressed this worry.

There is no doubt that some bureaucrats will drag their heels if they don't like their bosses, and a few will block actions they oppose. However, most bureaucrats try to carry out the policies of their superiors even when the personally disagree with them. When David Stockman was director of the Office of Management and Budget (OMB), he set out to make sharp cuts in government spending programs in accordance with the wishes of his boss, President Reagan. He later published a book complaining about all the people in the White House and Congress who worked against him.[21] But nowhere in the book is there any major criticism of the civil servants at

How to Get Rid of a Career Civil Servant Without Going Through the System

The frontal assault Tell him that he is no longer wanted and that if he quits, he will get a nice letter of recommendation and a farewell luncheon. If he won't quit but later wants to leave for a better job, he will get a nasty letter of recommendation.

The transfer technique Find out where in the country the civil servant does *not* want to live and threaten to transfer her there. Send Bostonians to Texas and Texans to Maine.

The special-assignment technique Useful for a family person who does not like to travel. Tell him that to keep his job he must inspect all the agency's offices in cities with less than twenty thousand population and bad motels. Even if he doesn't quit, at least you will have him out of the office.

The layering technique Put loyal subordinates in charge of disloyal ones or put the objectionable civil servant into an out-of-the-way post where you can ignore her.

SOURCE: Adapted from the "Federal Political Personnel Manual," printed in "Presidential Campaign Activities of 1972," Hearings before the Select Committee on Presidential Campaign Activities, Ninety-third Congress, 2d Session, vol. 19 (1974). This manual was produced by members of the Nixon administration, but in some version its principles have been applied by all administrations.

OMB. It appears that whatever these people thought about Stockman and Reagan, they loyally tried to carry out the Stockman policies.

Bureaucrats tend to be loyal to political superiors who deal with them cooperatively and constructively.

An agency head who tries to ignore or discredit them can be in for a tough time, however. The powers of obstruction available to aggrieved bureaucrats are formidable. Such people can leak embarrassing stories to Congress or to the media, help interest groups mobilize against the agency head, and discover a thousand procedural reasons why a new course of action won't work.

The exercise of some of those bureaucratic powers is protected by the Whistleblower Protection Act. Passed in 1989, the law creates an Office of Special Counsel charged with investigating complaints from bureaucrats that they were punished after reporting to Congress about waste, fraud, or abuse in their agencies.

It may seem odd that bureaucrats, who have great job security, would not always act in accordance with their personal beliefs instead of in accordance with the wishes of their bosses. Bureaucratic sabotage, in this view, ought to be very common. But bureaucratic cooperation with superiors is not odd, once you take into account the nature of a bureaucrat's job.

If you are a voter at the polls, your beliefs will clearly affect how you vote (see Chapter 5). But if you are the second baseman for the Boston Red Sox, your political beliefs, social background, and education will have nothing to do with how you field ground balls. Sociologists like to call the different things that people do in their lives "roles" and to distinguish between roles that are loosely structured (such as the role of voter) and those that are highly structured (such as that of second baseman). Personal attitudes greatly affect loosely structured roles and only slightly affect highly structured ones. Applied to the federal bureaucracy, this suggests that civil servants performing tasks that are routinized (such as filling out forms), tasks that are closely defined by laws and rules (such as issuing welfare checks), or tasks that are closely monitored by others (such as supervisors, special interest groups, or the media) will probably perform them in ways that can only partially be explained, if at all, by their personal attitudes. Civil servants performing complex, loosely defined tasks that are not closely monitored may carry out their work in ways powerfully influenced by their attitudes.

Among the loosely defined tasks are those performed by professionals, and so the values of these people may influence how they behave. An increasing number of lawyers, economists, engineers, and physicians are hired to work in federal agencies. These men and women have received extensive training that produces not only a set of skills but also a set of attitudes as to what is important and valuable. For example, the Federal Trade Commission (FTC), charged with preventing unfair methods of competition among businesses, employs two kinds of professionals—lawyers, organized into a Bureau of Competition, and economists, organized into a Bureau of Economics. Lawyers are trained to draw up briefs and argue cases in court and are taught the legal standards by which they will know whether they have a chance of winning a case or not. Economists are trained to analyze how a competitive economy works and what costs consumers must bear if the goods and services are produced by a monopoly (one firm con-

trolling the market) or an oligopoly (a small number of firms dominating the market).

Because of their training and attitudes, lawyers in the FTC prefer to bring cases against a business firm that does something clearly illegal, such as attending secret meetings with competitors to rig the prices that will be charged to a purchaser. These cases appeal to lawyers because there is usually a victim (the purchaser or a rival company) who complains to the government, the illegal behavior can be proved in a court of law, and the case can be completed rather quickly.

Economists, on the other hand, are trained to measure the value of a case not by how quickly it can be proved in court but by whether the illegal practice imposes larger or small costs on the consumer. FTC economists often dislike the cases that appeal to

---

 ## Learning Bureaucratese

A few simple rules, if remembered, will enable you to speak and write in the style of a government official.

- **Use nouns as if they were verbs.**
  Don't say, "We must set priorities"; say instead, "We must prioritize."

- **Use adjectives as if they were verbs.**
  Don't say, "We put the report in final form"; say instead, "We finalized the report."

- **Use several words where one word would do.**
  Don't say, "now"; say instead, "at this point in time."

- **Never use ordinary words where unusual ones can be found.**
  Don't say that you "made a choice"; say that you "selected an option."

- **No matter what subject you are discussing, employ the language of sports and war.**
  Never say, "progress"; say, "breakthrough." Never speak of a "compromise"; instead consider "adopting a fallback position."

- **Avoid active verbs.**
  Never say, "Study the problem"; say instead, "It is felt that the problem should be subjected to further study."

lawyers. The economists feel that the amount of money that such cases save the consumer is often small and that the cases are a distraction from the major issues—such as whether IBM unfairly dominates the computer business or whether General Motors is too large to be efficient. Lawyers, in turn, are leery of big cases because the facts are hard to prove, and they may take forever to decide (one blockbuster case can drag through the courts for ten years). In many federal agencies divergent professional values such as these help explain how power is used.

Culture and Careers

Unlike the lawyers and economists working in the FTC, the government bureaucrats in a typical agency don't have a lot of freedom to choose a course of action. Their jobs are spelled out not only by the laws, rules, and routines of their agency, but also by the informal understandings among fellow employees as to how they are supposed to act. These understandings are the *culture* of the agency.[22]

If you belong to the air force you could do a lot of things, but only one thing really counts: flying airplanes, especially advanced jet fighters and bombers. The culture of the air force is a pilots' culture. If you belong to the navy you have more choices: fly jet aircraft or operate nuclear submarines. Both jobs provide status and a chance for promotion to the highest ranks. By contrast, sailing minesweepers or transport ships (or worse, having a desk job and not sailing anything at all) is not a very rewarding job. The culture of the CIA emphasizes working overseas as a clandestine agent; staying in Washington as a report writer is not as good for your career. The culture of the State Department rewards skill in political negotiations; being an expert on international economics or embassy security is much less rewarding.

You can usually tell what kind of culture an agency has by asking an employee, "If you want to get ahead here, what sort of jobs should you take?" The jobs that are career enhancing are part of the culture; the jobs that are "not career enhancing" ("NCE" in bureaucratic lingo) are not part of it.

Being part of a strong culture is good—up to a point. It motivates employees to work hard in order to win the respect of their co-workers as well as the approval of their bosses. But a strong culture also makes it hard to change an agency. FBI agents for many years resisted getting involved in civil-rights or organized-crime cases, and diplomats in the State Department didn't pay much attention to embassy security. These important jobs were not a career-enhancing part of the culture.

Constraints

The biggest difference between a government agency and a private organization is the vastly greater number of constraints on the agency. Unlike a business firm, the typical government bureau cannot hire, fire, build, or sell without going through procedures set down in laws. How much money it pays its members is determined by statute, not by the market. Not only the goals of an agency but often its exact procedures are spelled out by Congress.

At one time the Soil Conservation Service was required by law to employ at least 14,177 full-time workers. The State Department is forbidden by law from opening a diplomatic post in Antigua or Barbuda but forbidden from closing a post anywhere else. The Agency for International Development (which administers our foreign-aid program) has been given by Congress thirty-three objectives and seventy-five priorities and must send to Congress 288 reports each year. When it buys military supplies, the Defense Department must give a "fair proportion" of its contracts to small businesses, especially those operated by "socially and economically disadvantaged individuals" and must buy from American firms even if, in some cases, buying abroad would be cheaper. Some of the more general constraints include:

- Administrative Procedure Act (1946): Before adopting a new rule or policy, an agency must give notice, solicit comments, and (often) hold hearings.

- Freedom of Information Act (1966): Citizens have the right to inspect all government records except those containing military, intelligence, or trade secrets or revealing private personnel actions.

- National Environmental Policy Act (1969): Before undertaking any major action affecting the environment, an agency must issue an environmental impact statement.

✪ So You Want a Big Job in Washington . . .*

*T*he White House or a cabinet secretary has just called to ask you to become an assistant secretary of defense. Wow! you say. A title, power, status, and a chance to do good! Before you call your mother to let her know how important you have become, think about what accepting that job involves.

Say you are an engineer working for a middle-sized company that does business with the Pentagon. This means that you know what needs to be done in Washington. You want to do a good job. You are honest and hard-working. Now here's what happens:

1. You will take a big pay cut.

2. Conflict-of-interest laws will require you to sell your stock in your present company and drop out of its pension plan. This will cost you a bundle.

3. You will have to pay your own moving expenses to Washington—the government won't pay, and it is against the law for your company to pay.

4. Since you will have to be confirmed by the Senate, your life will be put under a microscope. Every detail of your personal and professional affairs will become fair game for congressional staffers and newspaper reporters. If anybody has anything against you, the hearings could drag on for weeks.

5. Once in office you will discover that there are hundreds of rules telling you what you *can't* do and dozens of committees telling you what you *should* do.

6. Members of Congress will call asking favors, old friends will turn their backs on you for not doing them favors, the White House will demand party loyalty, and the press will leap on your every mistake—real or imagined.

7. When you get ready to leave government and go back to your company (assuming your old job is still open), you will by law be barred for life from lobbying the executive branch on matters in which you were personally and substantially involved while in office and barred for two years from lobbying the executive branch on matters that were under your official responsibility.

You won't be sure whether you will be allowed to have *any* conversations with people in government for at least two years. Under these circumstances your old company may not want you back. Now what do you do?

*With thanks to Dr. John S. Foster, Jr., who has gone through this.

- Privacy Act (1974): Government files about individuals, such as Social Security and tax records, must be kept confidential.

- Open Meeting Law (1976): Every part of every agency meeting must be open to the public unless certain matters (for example, military or trade secrets) are being discussed.

One of the biggest constraints on bureaucratic action is that Congress rarely gives any job to a single agency. Stopping drug trafficking is the task of the Customs Services, the FBI, the Drug Enforcement Administration, the Border Patrol, and the Defense Department (among others). Disposing of the assets of failed savings-and-loan associations is the job of the Resolution Funding Corporation, Resolution Trust Corporation, Federal Housing Finance Board, Office of Thrift Supervision in the Treasury Department, Federal Deposit Insurance Corporation, Federal Reserve Board, and Justice Department (among others).

The effects of these constraints on agency behavior are not surprising.

- The government will often act slowly. (The more constraints that must be satisfied, the longer it will take to get anything done.)

- The government will sometimes act inconsistently. (What is done to meet one constraint—for example, freedom of information—may endanger another constraint—for example, privacy.)

- It will be easier to block action than to take action. (The constraints ensure that lots of voices will be heard; the more voices that are heard, the more they may cancel each other out.)

- Lower-ranking employees will be reluctant to make decisions on their own. (Having many

TRIVIA

Famous Bureaucrats

The federal government has employed as bureaucrats people who were later to beome famous in other careers

Clara Barton, founder of the American Red Cross
Clerk in the U.S. Patent Office, 1854–1861

Alexander Graham Bell, inventor of the telephone
Special agent of the U.S. Census Bureau, 1890

Nathaniel Hawthorne, author
Weigher in the Boston Custom House, 1839–1841, and surveyor of the Port of Salem, Massachusetts, 1845–1849

Washington Irving, author
U.S. foreign service

Abraham Lincoln, president
Postmaster of New Salem, Illinois, 1833–1836

Knute Rockne, football coach
Clerk in Chicago Post Office, 1907–1910

James Thurber, humorist
Code clerk in State Department

James Whistler, painter
Draftsman, U.S. Coast Survey, 1854–1855

Walt Whitman, poet
Clerk, U.S. Department of the Interior, 1865

Clara Barton

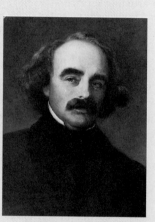

Nathaniel Hawthorne

constraints means having many ways to get into trouble; to avoid trouble, let your boss make the decision.)

- Citizens will complain of red tape. (The more constraints to serve, the more forms to fill out.)

These constraints do not mean that government bureaucracy is powerless, only that, however great its power, it tends to be clumsy. That clumsiness arises, not from the fact that the people who work for agencies are dull or incompetent, but from the complicated political environment in which that work must be done.

The moral of the story: The next time you get mad at a bureaucrat, ask yourself, Why would a rational, intelligent person behave that way? Chances are you will discover that there are good reasons for that action. You would probably behave the same way if you were working for the same organization.

Why So Many Constraints?   Government agencies behave as they do in large part because of the many different goals they must pursue and the complex rules they must follow. Where does all this red tape come from?

From us. From us, the people.

Every goal, every constraint, every bit of red tape, was put in place by Congress, the courts, the White House, or the agency itself responding to the demands of some influential faction. Civil-rights groups want every agency to hire and buy from women and minorities. Environmental groups want every agency to file environmental impact statements. Industries being regulated want every new agency policy to be formulated only after a lengthy public hearing with lots of lawyers present. Labor unions also want those hearings so that they can argue against industry lawyers. Everybody who sells something to the government wants a "fair chance" to make the sale, and so everybody insists that government contracts be awarded only after complex procedures are followed. A lot of people don't trust the government, and so they insist that everything it does be done in the sunshine—no secrets, no closed meetings, no hidden files.

If we want agencies to pursue their main goal with more vigor and less encumbering red tape, we would have to ask Congress, the courts, or the White

House to repeal some of these constraints. In other words, we would have to be willing to give up something we want in order to get something else we want even more But politics does not encourage people to make these trade-offs; instead it encourages us to expect to get everything—efficiency, fairness, help for minorities—all at once.

Agency Allies

Despite these constraints, government bureaucracies are not powerless. In fact some of them actively seek certain constraints. They do so because it is a way of cementing a useful relationship with a congressional committee or an interest group.

At one time scholars described the relationship among an agency, a committee, and an interest group as an **iron triangle.** For example, the Department of Veterans Affairs, the House and Senate committees on veterans affairs, and veterans' organizations (such as the American Legion) would form a tight, mutually advantageous alliance. The department would do what the committees wanted and in return get political support and budget appropriations; the committee members would do what the veterans' groups wanted and in return get votes and campaign contributions. Iron triangles are examples of what, in Chapter 15, will be called *client politics.*

Many agencies still have important allies in Congress and the private sector, especially those bureaus that serve the needs of specific sectors of the economy or regions of the country. The Department of Agriculture works closely with farm organizations, the Department of the Interior with groups interested in obtaining low-cost irrigation or grazing rights, and the Department of Housing and Urban Development with mayors and real-estate developers.

Sometimes these allies are so strong that they can defeat a popular president. For years President Reagan tried to abolish the Small Business Administration (SBA), arguing that its program of loans to small firms was wasteful and ridden with favoritism. But Congress, reacting to pressures from small-business groups, rallied to the SBA's defense. As a result Reagan had to oversee an agency that he didn't want.

But iron triangles are much less common today than once was the case. Politics of late has become far more complicated. For one thing, the number and variety of interest groups has increased so much in recent years that there is scarcely any agency that is not subject to pressures from several competing interests instead of only from one powerful interest. For another, the growth of subcommittees in Congress has meant that most agencies are subject to control by many different legislative groups, often with very different concerns. Finally, the courts have made it much easier for all kinds of individuals and interests to intervene in agency affairs.

As a result, nowadays government agencies face a bewildering variety of competing groups and legislative subcommittees that constitute, not a loyal group of allies, but a fiercely contentious collection of critics. The Environmental Protection Agency is caught between the demands of environmentalists and of industry organizations, the Occupational Safety and Health Administration between the pressures of labor and of business, and the Federal Communications Commission between the desires of broadcasters and of cable-television companies. Even the Department of Agriculture faces not a unified group of farmers but many different farmers split into rival groups, depending on the crops they raise, the regions in which they live, and the attitudes they have toward the relative merits of farm subsidies or free markets.

Political scientist Hugh Heclo has described the typical government agency today as embedded, not in an iron triangle, but in an **issue network.**[23] These issue networks consist of people in Washington-based interest groups, on congressional staffs, in universities and think tanks, and in the mass media who regularly debate government policy on a certain subject—say, health care or auto safety. The networks are contentious, split along political, ideological, and economic lines. When a president takes office, he often recruits key agency officials from those members of the issue network who are most sympathetic to his views.

When Jimmy Carter, a Democrat, became president, he appointed to key posts in consumer agencies people who were from that part of the consumerist issue network associated with Ralph Nader. Ronald Reagan, a conservative Republican, filled these same jobs with people who were from that part of the issue network holding free-market or antiregulation views.

When George Bush, a more centrist Republican, took office, he filled these posts with more centrist members of the issue network. Bill Clinton brought back the consumer activists.

Congressional Oversight

The main reason why some interest groups are important to agencies is that they are important to Congress. Not every interest group in the country has substantial access to Congress, but those that do and that are taken seriously by the relevant committees or subcommittees must also be taken seriously by the agency. Furthermore, even apart from interest groups, members of Congress have constitutional powers over agencies and policy interests in how agencies function.

Congressional supervision of the bureaucracy takes several forms. First, no agency may exist (except for a few presidential offices and commissions) without congressional approval. Congress influences—and sometimes determines precisely—agency behavior by the statutes it enacts.

Second, no money may be spent unless it has first been authorized by Congress. **Authorization legislation** originates in a legislative committee (such as Agriculture, Education and Labor, or Public Works) and states the maximum amount of money that an agency may spend on a given program. This authorization may be permanent, it may be for a fixed number of years, or it may be annual (that is, it must be renewed each year or the program or agency goes out of business).

Third, even funds that have been authorized by Congress cannot be spent unless (in most cases) they are also appropriated. Appropriations are usually made annually, and they originate not with the legislative committees but with the House Appropriations Committee and its various (and influential) subcommittees. An **appropriation** (money formally set aside for a specific use) may be, and often is, for less than the amount authorized. The Appropriations Committee's action thus tends to have a budget-cutting effect. There are some funds that can be spent without an appropriation, but in virtually every part of the bureaucracy each agency is keenly sensitive to congressional concerns at the time that the annual appropriations process is going on.

The Appropriations Committee and Legislative Committees

The fact that an agency budget must be both authorized and appropriated means that each agency serves not one congressional master but several, and that these masters may be in conflict. The real power over an agency's budget is exercised by the Appropriations Committee; the legislative committees are especially important when a substantive law is first passed or an agency first created or when an agency is subject to annual authorization.

The power of the Appropriations Committee in the past was rarely challenged: from 1947 through 1962, 90 percent of the House Appropriations Committee recommendations on expenditures were approved by the full House without change.[24] Furthermore the Appropriations Committee tends to recommend less money than an agency requests (though some specially favored agencies, such as the FBI, the Soil Conservation Service, and the Forest Service, have tended to get almost everything that they have asked for). Finally, the process of "marking up" (revising, amending, and approving) an agency's budget request gives to the Appropriations Committee, or one of its subcommittees, substantial influence over the policies that the agency follows.

Of late the appropriations committees have lost some of their great power over government agencies. This has happened in three ways:

First, Congress has created trust funds to pay for the benefits many people receive. The Social Security trust fund is the largest of these. In 1990 it took in about $260 billion in Social Security taxes and paid out about $220 billion in old-age benefits. There are several other trust funds as well. **Trust funds** operate outside the regular government budget, and the appropriations committees have no control over these expenditures. They are automatic.

Second, Congress has changed the authorization of many programs from permanent or multiyear to **annual authorizations.** This means that every year the legislative committees, as part of the reauthorization process, get to set limits on what these agencies can spend. This limits the ability of the appropriations committees to determine the spending limits. Before 1959 most authorizations were permanent or multiyear. Now a long list of agencies must be reauthorized every year—the State Department, NASA,

Representative Jamie L. Whitten (D., Miss.), long-time chairman of the House Appropriations Committee, was for over a half century a key congressional overseer of the bureaucracy.

military procurement programs of the Defense Department, the Justice Department, the Energy Department, and parts or all of many other agencies.

Third, the existence of huge budget deficits during the 1980s and early 1990s has meant that much of Congress's time has been taken up with trying (usually not very successfully) to keep spending down. As a result there has rarely been much time to discuss the merits of various programs or how much ought to be spent on them; instead attention has been focused on meeting a target spending limit (see Chapter 16). In 1981 the budget resolution passed by Congress mandated cuts in several programs before the appropriations committees had even completed their work.[25]

In addition to the power of the purse, there are informal ways by which Congress can control the bureaucracy. An individual member of Congress can call an agency head on behalf of a constituent. Most such calls merely seek information, but some result in, or attempt to second, special privileges for particular people. Congressional committees may also obtain the right to pass on certain agency decisions. This is called **committee clearance,** and though it is usually not legally binding on the agency, few agency

heads will ignore the expressed wish of a committee chairman that he or she be consulted before certain actions (such as transferring funds) are taken.

The Legislative Veto

For many decades Congress made frequent use of the legislative veto to control bureaucratic or presidential actions. A **legislative veto** is a requirement that an executive decision must lie before Congress for a specified period (usually thirty or ninety days) before it takes effect. Congress could then veto the decision if a resolution of disapproval were passed by either house (a "one-house veto") or both houses (a "two-house veto"). Unlike laws, such resolutions were not signed by the president. Between 1932 and 1980 about two hundred laws were passed providing for a legislative veto, many of them involving presidential proposals to sell arms abroad.

But in June 1983 the Supreme Court declared the legislative veto to be unconstitutional. In the *Chadha* case the Court held that the Constitution clearly requires in Article I that "every order, resolution, or vote to which the concurrence of the Senate and House of Representatives may be necessary" (with

"Laws" of Bureaucratic Procedure

Acheson's Rule   A memorandum is written not to inform the reader but to protect the writer.

Boren's Laws   When in doubt, mumble.
When in trouble, delegate.
When in charge, ponder.

Chapman's Rules of Committees
Never arrive on time, or you will be stamped a beginner.
Don't say anything until the meeting is half over; this
   stamps you as being wise.
Be as vague as possible; this prevents irritating others.
When in doubt, suggest that a subcommittee be appointed.

Meskimen's Law   There's never time to do it right but always time to do it over.

Murphy's Law   If anything can go wrong, it will.

O'Toole's Corollary to Murphy's Law   Murphy was an optimist.

Parkinson's First Law   Work expands to fill the time available for its completion.

Parkinson's Second Law   Expenditure rises to meet income.

Peter Principle   In every hierarchy, each employee tends to rise to his level of incompetence; thus, every post tends to be filled by an incompetent employee.

Robertson's Rule   The more directives you issue to solve a problem the worse it gets.

Smith's Principle   Never do anything for the first time.

---

certain minor exceptions) "shall be presented to the President of the United States," who must either approve it or return it with his veto attached. In short Congress cannot take any action that has the force of law unless the president concurs in that action.[26] At a stroke of the pen parts of some two hundred laws suddenly became invalid.

At least that happened in theory. In fact, since the *Chadha* decision, Congress has passed a number of laws that contain legislative vetoes despite the Supreme Court's having ruled against them! (Someone will have to go to court to test the constitutionality of these new provisions.)

Opponents of the legislative veto hope that future Congresses will have to pass laws that state much more clearly than before what an agency may or may not do. But it is just as likely that Congress will continue to pass laws stated in general terms and require that agencies implementing those laws report their plans to Congress so that it will have a chance to enact and send to the president a regular bill disapproving the proposed action. Or Congress may rely on informal (but scarcely weak) means of persuasion, including threats to reduce the appropriations of an agency that does not abide by congressional preferences.

Congressional Investigations

Perhaps the most visible and dramatic form of congressional supervision of an agency is the investigation. Since 1792, when Congress investigated an army defeat by a Native American tribe, congressional investigations of the bureaucracy have been a regular feature—sometimes constructive, sometimes destructive—of legislative-executive relations. The investigative power is not mentioned in the Constitution but has been inferred from the power to legislate. The Supreme Court has consistently upheld this interpretation, though it has also said that such investigations should not be solely for the purpose of exposing the purely personal affairs of private individuals and must not operate to deprive citizens of their basic rights.[27] Congress may compel a person to attend an investigation by issuing a subpoena; anyone who ignores the subpoena may be punished for contempt. Congress can vote to send the person to jail or can refer the matter to a court for further action. As explained in Chapter 12, the president and his principal subordinates have refused to answer certain congressional inquiries on grounds of "executive privilege."

Although many areas of congressional oversight—budgetary review, personnel controls, investigations—are designed to control the exercise of bureaucratic discretion, other areas are intended to ensure the freedom of certain agencies from effective control, especially by the president. In dozens of cases Congress has authorized department heads and bureau chiefs to operate independently of presidential preferences. Congress has resisted, for example, presidential efforts to ensure that policies to regulate pollution do not impose excessive costs on the economy, and interest groups have brought suit to prevent presidential coordination of various regulatory agencies. If the bureaucracy sometimes works at cross-purposes, it is usually because Congress—or competing committees in Congress—wants it that way.

Bureaucratic "Pathologies"

Everyone complains about bureaucracy in general (though rarely about bureaucratic agencies that everyone believes are desirable). This chapter should persuade you that it is difficult to say anything about bureaucracy "in general"; there are too many different kinds of agencies, kinds of bureaucrats, and kinds of programs to label the entire enterprise with some single adjective. Nevertheless many people who recognize the enormous variety among government agencies still believe that they all have some general features in common and suffer from certain shared problems or pathologies.

This is true enough, but the reasons for it—and the solutions, if any—are not often understood. There are five major (or at least frequently mentioned) problems with bureaucracies: red tape, conflict, duplication, imperialism, and waste. **Red tape** refers to the complex rules and procedures that must be followed to get something done. *Conflict* exists because some agencies seem to be working at cross-purposes with other agencies. (For example, the Agricultural Research Service tells farmers how to grow crops more efficiently, while the Agricultural Stabilization and Conservation Service pays farmers

POLITICALLY **P.S.** **SPEAKING**

Red Tape

As early as the seventh century, legal and government documents in England were bound together with a tape of pinkish red color. In the 1850s historian Thomas Carlyle described a British politician as "little other than a redtape Talking Machine," and later the American writer Washington Irving said of an American figure that "his brain was little better than red tape and parchment."

Since then **red tape** has come to mean "bureaucratic delay or confusion," especially that accompanied by unnecessary paperwork.

SOURCE: Adapted from William Safire, *Safire's Political Dictionary* (New York: Ballantine Books, 1978). Used by permission.

to grow fewer crops or to produce less.) *Duplication* (usually called "wasteful duplication") occurs when two government agencies seem to be doing the same thing, as when the Customs Service and the Drug Enforcement Administration both attempt to intercept illegal drugs being smuggled into the country. *Imperialism* refers to the tendency of agencies to grow without regard to the benefits that their programs confer or the costs that they entail. *Waste* means spending more than is necessary to buy some product or service.

These problems all exist, but they do not necessarily exist because bureaucrats are incompetent or power-hungry. Most exist because of the very nature of government itself. Take red tape: partly we encounter cumbersome rules and procedures because any large organization, governmental or not, must have some way of ensuring that one part of the organization does not operate out of step with another. Business corporations have red tape also; it is to a certain extent a consequence of bigness. But a great amount of governmental red tape is also the result of the need to satisfy legal and political requirements. Government agencies must hire on the basis of "merit," must observe strict accounting rules, must supply Congress with detailed information on their programs, and must allow for citizen access in countless ways. To meet each need, rules are necessary; to ensure that rules are obeyed, forms must be filled out.

Or take conflict and duplication: they do not occur because bureaucrats enjoy conflict or duplication. (Quite the contrary!) They exist because Congress, in setting up agencies and programs, often

These long lines of cars at the border between the United States and Mexico may be a symbol of "bureaucratic red tape" to some travelers, but they are a sign of "effective law enforcement" to people who want to cut off the flow of drugs and illegal immigrants.

wants to achieve a number of different, partially inconsistent goals or finds that it cannot decide which goal it values the most. Congress has 535 members and little strong leadership; it should not be surprising that 535 people will want different things and will sometimes succeed in getting them.

Imperialism results in large measure from government agencies' seeking goals that are so vague and so difficult to measure that it is hard to tell when they have been attained. When Congress is unclear as to exactly what an agency is supposed to do, the agency will often convert that legislative vagueness into bureaucratic imperialism by taking the largest possible view of its powers. It may do this on its own; more often it does so because interest groups and judges rush in to fill the vacuum left by Congress. As we saw in Chapter 3, the 1973 Rehabilitation Act was passed with a provision barring discrimination against the disabled in any program receiving federal aid. Under pressure from the disabled, that lofty but vague goal was converted by the Department of Transportation into a requirement that virtually every big-city bus have a device installed to lift people in wheelchairs on board.

Waste is probably the biggest criticism that people have of the bureaucracy. Everybody has heard stories of the Pentagon's paying $91 for screws that cost 3 cents in the hardware store. President Reagan's "Private Sector Survey on Cost Control," generally known as the Grace Commission, after its chairman, J. Peter Grace, publicized these and other tales in a 1984 report.

No doubt there is waste in government. After all, unlike a business firm worried about maximizing profits, in a government agency there are only weak incentives to keep costs down. If a business employee cuts costs, he or she often receives a bonus or raise, and the firm gets to add the savings to its profits. If a government official cuts costs, he or she receives no reward, and the agency cannot keep the savings—they go back to the Treasury.

But many of the horror stories are either exaggerations or unusual occurrences.[28] Most of the screws, hammers, and light bulbs purchased by the government are obtained at low cost by means of competitive bidding among several suppliers. When the government does pay outlandish amounts, the reason typically is that it is purchasing a new or one-of-a-

Abbreviations for Federal Government Agencies

ACDA	Arms Control and Disarmament Agency
ACIR	Advisory Commission on Intergovernmental Relations
BIA	Bureau of Indian Affairs
CEA	Council of Economic Advisers
CIA	Central Intelligence Agency
DEA	Drug Enforcement Administration
DOD	Department of Defense
DOJ	Department of Justice
DOL	Department of Labor
DOT	Department of Transportation
EEOC	Equal Employment Opportunity Commission
EOP	Executive Office of the President
EPA	Environmental Protection Agency
FAA	Federal Aviation Administration
FBI	Federal Bureau of Investigation
FCC	Federal Communications Commission
FDA	Food and Drug Administration
FDIC	Federal Deposit Insurance Corporation
FEC	Federal Election Commission
FRB	Federal Reserve Board
FTC	Federal Trade Commission
GAO	General Accounting Office
GSA	General Services Administration
HHS	Department of Health and Human Services
HUD	Department of Housing and Urban Development
ICC	Interstate Commerce Commission
INS	Immigration and Naturalization Service
IRS	Internal Revenue Service
NASA	National Aeronautics and Space Administration
NHTSA	National Highway Traffic Safety Administration
NIH	National Institutes of Health
NIJ	National Institute of Justice
NLRB	National Labor Relations Board
NRC	Nuclear Regulatory Commission

NSC	National Security Council
NSF	National Science Foundation
OMB	Office of Management and Budget
OPM	Office of Personnel Management
OSHA	Occupational Safety and Health Administration
SBA	Small Business Administration
SEC	Securities and Exchange Commission
TVA	Tennessee Valley Authority
USA	United States Army
USAF	United States Air Force
USCG	United States Coast Guard
USDA	United States Department of Agriculture
USMC	United States Marine Corps
USN	United States Navy
USPS	United States Postal Service
WHO	White House Office

kind item not available at your neighborhood hardware store—for example, a new bomber or missile. Just why Washington finds it so hard to keep costs down on these big-ticket items will be explained in Chapter 21.

Even when the government is not overcharged, it still may spend more money than a private firm in buying what it needs. The reason is red tape—the rules and procedures designed to ensure that when the government buys something, it will do so in a way that serves the interests of many groups. For example, it must often buy from American rather than foreign suppliers even if the latter charge a lower price; it must make use of contractors that employ minorities; it must hire only union laborers and pay them the "prevailing" (that is, the highest) wage; it must allow public inspection of its records; it frequently is required to choose contractors favored by influential members of Congress; and so on. Private firms do not have to comply with all these rules and thus can buy for less.

From this discussion it should be easy to see why these five basic bureaucratic problems are so hard to correct. To end conflicts and duplication, Congress would have to make some policy choices and set some clear priorities, but with all the competing demands that it faces, Congress finds it difficult to do that. You make more friends by helping people than by hurting them, and so Congress is more inclined to add new programs than to cut old ones, whether or not the new programs are in conflict with existing ones. To check imperialism, some way would have to be found to measure the benefits of government, but that is often impossible; government exists in part to achieve precisely those goals—such as national defense—that are least measurable. Furthermore what might be done to remedy some problems would make other problems worse: if you simplify rules and procedures to cut red tape, you are likely also to reduce the coordination among agencies and thus to increase the extent to which there is duplication or conflict. If you want to reduce waste, you will have to have more rules and inspectors—in short more red tape. The problem of bureaucracy is inseparable from the problem of government generally.

Just as people are likely to say that they dislike Congress but like their own member of Congress, they are also inclined to express hostility toward "the bureaucracy" but goodwill for that part of the bureaucracy with which they have dealt personally. In 1973 a survey of Americans found that over half had had some contact with one or more kinds of government agencies, most of which were either run directly or funded indirectly by the federal government. The great majority of people were satisfied with these contacts and felt that they had been treated fairly and given useful assistance. When these people were asked their feelings about government officials in general, however, they expressed much less favorable attitudes. Whereas about 80 percent liked the officials with whom they had dealt, only 42 percent liked officials in general.[29] This finding helps explain why government agencies are rarely reduced in size or budget: whatever popular feelings about the bureaucracy, any given agency tends to have many friends.

Reforming the Bureaucracy

The history of American bureaucracy has been punctuated with countless efforts to make it work better and cost less. There have been eleven major attempts in this century alone (see the box on page 413). The latest was the National Performance Review (NPR)—popularly called the plan to "reinvent government"—led by Vice President Al Gore and published in 1993.

The NPR differed from many of the preceding reform efforts in one important way. Most of the earlier ones suggested ways of increasing central (that is, presidential) control of government agencies: the Brownlow Commission (1936–1937) recommended giving the president more assistants, the Hoover Commission (1947–1949) suggested ways of improving top-level management, and the Ash Council (1969–1971) called for consolidating existing agencies into a few big "super departments." The intent was to make it easier for the president and his cabinet secretaries to run the bureaucracy. The key ideas were efficiency, accountability, and consistent policies.

The NPR, by contrast, emphasized customer satisfaction (the "customers" in this case being the citizens who come into contact with federal agencies). To the authors of the NPR, the main problem with the bureaucracy was that it had become too centralized, too rule-bound, too little concerned with making programs work, and too much concerned with avoiding scandal. The NPR report contained many

To dramatize the problem of bureaucracy, President Clinton and Vice President Gore spoke about reforming bureaucracy in front of huge piles of federal regulations.

Reforming the Federal Bureaucracy, 1905–1993

Keep Commission (1905–1909) Personnel management, government contracting, information management

President's Commission on Economy and Efficiency (1910–1913) Recommended creating a national executive budget

Joint Committee on Reorganization (1921–1924) Proposed ways of distributing executive functions among the departments

President's Committee on Administrative Management (1936–1937) Known as the Brownlow Commission after its chairman Louis Brownlow. Recommended creation of the Executive Office of the President. Famous conclusion: "The president needs help"

First Hoover Commission (1947–1949) Comprehensive review of the executive branch

Second Hoover Commission (1953–1955) Follow-up to the first Hoover commission; focused mainly on policy problems rather than organizational structure

Study commission on executive reorganization (1953–1968) Series of low-key reforms that produced small but significant changes

Ash Council (1969–1971) Proposed creation of new "super departments" to encompass existing departments

Carter reorganization effort (1977–1979) Attempted to reorganize agencies from the bottom up; new cabinet departments created independently of effort

Grace Commission (1982–1984) Large-scale, politically contentious effort to determine how government could be operated for less money

National Performance Review (1993–present) Attempt to "reinvent" government to improve its performance

SOURCE: Adapted from Ronald C. Moe, *Reorganizing the Executive Branch in the Twentieth Century* (Congressional Research Service, March 1992).

horror stories about useless red tape, excessive regulations, and cumbersome procurement systems that make it next-to-impossible for the agencies to do what they were created to do. (For example, before it could buy an ashtray the General Services Administration issued a nine-page document that described an ashtray and specified how many pieces it must break into should it be hit with a hammer.)[30] To solve these problems, the NPR called for less centralized management and more employee initiative, fewer detailed rules and more emphasis on customer satisfaction. It sought to create a new kind of organizational culture in government agencies, one more like that found in the more innovative, quality-conscious American corporations.

But making these changes is easier said than done. Most of the rules and red tape that make it hard for agency heads to do a good job are the result either of the struggle between the White House and Congress for control over the agencies or of the agencies' desire to avoid irritating influential voters. Silly as the rules for ashtrays may sound, they were written so that the government could say it had an "objective" standard for buying ashtrays. If it simply went out and bought ashtrays at a department store the way ordinary people do, it would risk being accused by the Acme Ashtray Company of buying trays from its competitor, the A-1 Ashtray Company, because of political favoritism.

The rivalry between the president and Congress for control of the bureaucracy makes bureaucrats nervous about irritating either branch, and so they issue rules designed to avoid getting into trouble even if these rules make it hard to do their job. Matters become even worse during periods of divided government when different parties control the White House and Congress. As we saw in Chapter 12, divided government may not have much effect on *making* policy, but it can have a big effect on *implementing* it. Republican presidents have tried to increase political control over the bureaucracy ("executive micromanagement") and Democratic Congresses have responded by increasing the number of investigations and detailed rule-making ("legislative micromanagement"). Divided government intensifies the crossfire between the executive and legislative branches, making bureaucrats dig into even deeper layers of red tape to avoid getting hurt.

This does not mean that reform is impossible, only that it is very difficult. Everyone in the White House and Congress is in favor of reform in principle; the trick is finding a practical solution that everyone can agree on. It might be easier to make desirable changes if the bureaucracy were accountable to but one master, say the president, instead of to several. But that situation, which exists in many parliamentary democracies, creates its own problems. When the bureaucracy has but one master, it often ends up having none: it becomes so powerful that it controls the prime minister and no longer listens to citizen complaints. A weak, divided bureaucracy, such as exists in the United States, may strike us as inefficient, but that very inefficiency may help protect our liberties.

SUMMARY

Bureaucracy is characteristic of almost all aspects of modern life, not simply the government. Government bureaucracies, however, pose special problems because they are subject to competing sources of political authority, must function in a constitutional system of divided powers and federalism, have vague goals, and lack incentive systems that will encourage efficiency. The power of bureaucracy should be measured by its discretionary authority, not by the number of its employees or the size of its budget.

War and depression have been the principal sources of bureaucratic growth, aided by important changes in constitutional interpretation in the 1930s that permitted Congress to delegate broad grants of authority to administrative agencies. With only partial success, Congress seeks to check or recover those grants by controlling budgets, personnel, and policy decisions and by the exercise of legislative vetoes. The uses to which bureaucrats put their authority can be explained in part by their recruitment and security (they have an agency orientation), their personal political views, and the nature of the tasks that their agencies are performing.

Many of the popular solutions for the problems of bureaucratic rule—red tape, duplication, conflict, agency imperialism, and waste—fail to take into account that these problems are to a degree inherent in any government that serves competing goals and is supervised by rival elected officials. Nevertheless, some reform efforts have succeeded in making government work better and cost less to operate.

KEY TERMS

bureaucracy   *p. 387*

spoils system   *p. 390*

laissez-faire   *p. 391*

discretionary authority   *p. 393*

competitive service   *p. 394*

name-request job   *p. 395*

iron triangle   *p. 405*

issue network   *p. 405*

authorization legislation   *p. 406*

appropriation   *p. 406*

trust funds   *p. 406*

annual authorizations   *p. 406*

committee clearance   *p. 407*

legislative veto   *p. 407*

red tape   *p. 409*

SUGGESTED READINGS

Burke, John P. *Bureaucratic Responsibility*. Baltimore: Johns Hopkins University Press, 1986. Examines the problem of individual responsibility—for example, when to be a "whistle blower"—in government agencies.

DiIulio, John J., ed. *Deregulating the Public Service: Can Government Be Improved?* Washington, D.C.: Brookings Institution Press, 1994. Essays by leading academics, public administrators, and journalists on how government personnel and procurement practices can be improved.

DiIulio, John J., Gerald Garvey, and Donald F. Kettl. *Improving Government Performance: An Owner's Manual*. Washington, D.C.: Brookings Institution Press, 1993. A concise overview of the history of federal bureaucracy and ideas about how to reform it.

Downs, Anthony. *Inside Bureaucracy*. Boston: Little, Brown, 1967. An economist's explanation of why bureaucrats and bureaus behave as they do.

Halperin, Morton H. *Bureaucratic Politics and Foreign Policy*. Washington, D.C.: Brookings Institution, 1974. Insightful account of the strategies by which diplomatic and military bureaucracies defend their interests.

Heclo, Hugh. *A Government of Strangers*. Washington, D.C.: Brookings Institution, 1977. Analyzes how political appointees attempt to gain control of the Washington bureaucracy and how bureaucrats resist those efforts.

Parkinson, C. Northcote. *Parkinson's Law*. Boston: Houghton Mifflin, 1957. Half-serious, half-joking explanation of why government agencies tend to grow.

Seidman, Harold, and Robert Gilmour. *Politics, Position, and Power*. 4th ed. New York: Oxford University Press, 1986. Perceptive account by a former insider of relations between the White House and the bureaucracy.

Tierney, John T. *Postal Reorganization*. Boston: Auburn House, 1981. A careful analysis of why it is so hard to manage our largest civilian bureaucracy, the Postal Service.

Wilson, James Q. *Bureaucracy: What Government Agencies Do and Why They Do It*. New York: Basic Books, 1989. A comprehensive review of what we know about bureaucratic behavior in the United States.

NOTE: Two important magazines regularly cover the workings of the Washington bureaucracy: the *National Journal* (which appears weekly and has a frequently published index to its articles) and *The Washington Monthly*, which is more irreverent.

14

The Judiciary

On July 1, 1987, President Ronald Reagan nominated Judge Robert Bork to be a justice of the United States Supreme Court. On October 23, 1987, after nearly four months of heated debate, the Senate voted, 58 to 42, to reject the nomination. Supporters of Bork argued that he would interpret the Constitution in a way that was faithful to the intent of its Framers. Opponents argued that Bork would interpret the Constitution in a way that would undermine civil rights. Both supporters and opponents produced long lists of prominent people and organizations that shared their views. The political struggle was intense, protracted, and televised. Millions of people watched the Judiciary Committee hearings. The final vote, with few exceptions, followed party lines.

Only in the United States would the selection of a judge produce so dramatic and bitter a conflict. The reason is simple: Only in the United States do judges play so large a role in making public policy.

One aspect of this power is **judicial review**—the right of the federal courts to declare laws of Congress and acts of the executive branch void and unenforceable if they are judged to be in conflict with the Constitution. Since 1789 the Supreme Court has declared over one hundred federal laws to be unconstitutional. In Britain, by contrast, Parliament is supreme, and no court may strike down a law that it passes. As the second Earl of Pembroke is supposed to have said, "A parliament can do anything but make a man a woman and a woman a man." All that prevents Parliament from acting contrary to the (unwritten) constitution of Britain are the consciences of its members and the opinion of the citizens. About sixty nations do have something resembling judicial review, but in only a few cases does this power mean much in practice. Where it means something—in Australia, Canada, Germany, India, and some other nations—one finds a stable, federal system of government with a strong tradition of an independent judiciary.[1] (Some other nations—France, for example—have special councils, rather than courts, that can under certain circumstances decide that a law is not authorized by the constitution.)

Judicial review is the federal courts' chief weapon in the system of checks and balances on which the American government is based. Today few people would deny to the courts the right to decide that a legislative or executive act is unconstitutional, though once that right was controversial. What remains controversial is the method by which such review should be conducted.

There are two competing views, each ardently pressed during the Bork fight (and later in the fight to confirm Clarence Thomas). The first holds that judges should only judge—that is, they should confine themselves to applying those rules that are stated in or clearly implied by the language of the Constitution. This is often called the **strict-constructionist approach.** The other argues that judges should discover the general principles underlying the Constitution and its often vague language, amplify those principles on the basis of some moral or economic philosophy, and apply them to cases. This is sometimes called the **activist approach.**

Note that the difference between strict-constructionist and activist judges is not necessarily the same as the difference between liberals and conservatives. Judges can be political liberals and still believe that they are bound by the language of the Constitution. A liberal justice, Hugo Black, once voted to uphold a state law banning birth control because nothing in the Constitution prohibited such a law. Or judges can be conservative and still think that they have the duty to use their best judgment in deciding what is good public policy. Rufus Peckham, one such conservative, voted to overturn a state law setting maximum hours of work because he believed that the Fourteenth Amendment guaranteed something called "freedom of contract," even though those words are not in the amendment.

Fifty years ago judicial activists tended to be conservatives and strict constructionists tended to be liberals; today the opposite is usually the case.

Chief Justice William H. Rehnquist

TABLE 14.1   Chief Justices of the United States

Chief Justice	Appointed by President	Years of Service
John Jay	Washington	1789–1795
Oliver Ellsworth	Washington	1796–1800
John Marshall	Adams	1801–1835
Roger B. Taney	Jackson	1836–1864
Salmon P. Chase	Lincoln	1864–1873
Morrison R. Waite	Grant	1874–1888
Melville W. Fuller	Cleveland	1888–1910
Edward D. White	Taft	1910–1921
William Howard Taft	Harding	1921–1930
Charles Evans Hughes	Hoover	1930–1941
Harlan Fiske Stone	F. Roosevelt	1941–1946
Fred M. Vinson	Truman	1946–1953
Earl Warren	Eisenhower	1953–1969
Warren E. Burger	Nixon	1969–1986
William H. Rehnquist	Reagan	1986–present

NOTE: Omitted is John Rutledge, who served for only a few months in 1795 and who was not confirmed by the Senate.

The Development of the Federal Courts

Most Founders probably expected the Supreme Court to have the power of judicial review (though they did not say that in so many words in the Constitution), but they did not expect federal courts to play so large a role in making public policy. The traditional view of civil courts was that they judged disputes between people who had direct dealings with each other—they had entered into a contract, for example, or one had dropped a load of bricks on the other's toe—and decided which of the two parties was right. The court then supplied relief to the wronged party, usually by requiring the other person to pay him or her money ("damages").

This traditional understanding was based on the belief that judges would find and apply existing law. The purpose of a court case was not to learn what the judge believes but what the law requires. The later rise of judicial activism occurred when judges questioned this traditional view and argued instead that judges do not merely find the law: they make the law.

The view that judges interpret the law and do not make policy made it easy for the Founders to justify the power of judicial review and led them to predict that the courts would play a relatively neutral, even passive, role in public affairs. Alexander Hamilton, writing in *Federalist* No. 78, described the judiciary as the branch "least dangerous" to political rights. The president is commander in chief and thus holds the "sword of the community"; Congress appropriates money and thus "commands the purse," as well as decides what laws shall govern. But the judiciary "has no influence over either the sword or the purse" and "can take no active resolution whatever." It has "neither force nor will but merely judgment," and thus is "beyond comparison the weakest of the three departments of power." As a result "liberty can have nothing to fear from the judiciary alone." Hamilton went on to state clearly that the Constitution intended to give to the courts the right to decide whether a law is contrary to the Constitution. But this authority, he explained, was not designed to enlarge the power of the courts but to confine that of the legislature.

Obviously things have changed since Hamilton's time. The evolution of the federal courts, especially the Supreme Court, toward the present level of activism and influence has been shaped by the political, economic, and ideological forces of three historical eras. From 1787 to 1865 nation building, the legitimacy of the federal government and slavery were the great issues; from 1865 to 1937 the dominant issue was the relationship between government and the economy; from 1938 to the present the major issues confronting the Court have involved personal liberty and social equality and the potential conflict between the two. In the first period the Court asserted the supremacy of the federal government; in the second it placed important restrictions on the powers of that government; and in the third it enlarged the scope of personal freedom and narrowed that of economic freedom.

National Supremacy and Slavery

"From 1789 until the Civil War, the dominant interest of the Supreme Court was in that greatest of all the questions left unresolved by the Founders—the nation-state relationship."[2] The answer that the Court gave, under the leadership of Chief Justice John Marshall, was that national law was in all instances the dominant law, with state law having to give way, and that the Supreme Court had the power to decide what the Constitution meant. In two cases of enormous importance—*Marbury* v. *Madison* in 1803 and *McCulloch* v. *Maryland* in 1819—the Court, speaking through decisions written by Marshall, held that the Supreme Court could declare an act of Congress unconstitutional, that the power granted to the federal government flows from the people and should be generously construed so that any laws "necessary and proper" to the attainment of constitutional ends would be permissible, and that federal law is supreme over state law even to the point that the state may not tax an enterprise (such as a bank) created by the federal government.[3]

The supremacy of the federal government was reaffirmed by other decisions. In one such decision in 1816 the Supreme Court rejected the claim of the Virginia courts that the Supreme Court could not review the decisions of state courts. The Virginia courts were ready to acknowledge the supremacy of the United States Constitution but believed that they had as much right as the United States Supreme Court to

Marbury v. Madison

*T*he story of *Marbury* v. *Madison* is often told but deserves another telling because it illustrates so many features of the role of the Supreme Court—how apparently small cases can have large results, how the power of the Court depends not simply on its constitutional authority but on its acting in ways that avoid a clear confrontation with other branches of government, and how the climate of opinion affects how the Court goes about its task.

When President John Adams lost his bid for reelection to Thomas Jefferson in 1800, he—and all members of his party, the Federalists—feared that Jefferson and the Republicans would weaken the federal government and turn its powers to what the Federalists believed were wrong ends (states' rights, an alliance with the French, hostility to business). Feverishly, as his hours in office came to an end, Adams worked to pack the judiciary with fifty-nine loyal Federalists by giving them so-called midnight appointments before Jefferson took office.

John Marshall, as Adams' secretary of state, had the task of certifying and delivering these new judicial commissions. In the press of business he delivered all but seventeen; these he left on his desk for the incoming secretary of state, James Madison, to send out. Jefferson and Madison, however, were furious at

John Adams

Adams' behavior and refused to deliver the seventeen. William Marbury and three other Federalists who had been promised these commissions hired a lawyer and brought suit against Madison to force him to produce the documents. The suit requested the Supreme Court to issue a writ of mandamus (from the Latin, "we command") ordering Madison to do his duty. The right to issue such writs had been given to the Court by the Judiciary Act of 1789.

Marshall, the man who had failed to deliver the commissions to Marbury and his friends in the first place, had become the chief justice and was now in a position to decide the case. These days a justice who had been involved in an issue before it came to the Court would probably disqualify himself or herself, but Marshall had no intention of letting others decide this question. He faced, however, not simply a partisan dispute over jobs but what was nearly a constitutional crisis. If he ordered the commission delivered, Madison might still refuse, and the Court had no way—if Madison was determined to resist—to compel him. The Court had no police force, whereas Madison had the support of the president of the United States. And if the order were given, whether or not Madison complied, the Jeffersonian Republicans in Congress would probably try to impeach Marshall. On the other hand, if Marshall allowed Madison to do as he wished, the power of the Supreme Court would be seriously reduced.

Marshall's solution was ingenious. Speaking for a unanimous Court, he announced that Madison was wrong to withhold the commissions, that courts could issue writs to compel public officials to do their prescribed duty—*but* that the Supreme Court had no power to issue such writs in this case because the

James Madison

law (the Judiciary Act of 1789) giving it that power was unconstitutional. The law said that the Supreme Court could issue such writs as part of its "original jurisdiction"—that is, persons seeking such writs could go *directly* to the Supreme Court with their request (rather than to a lower federal court and then, if dissatisfied, appeal to the Supreme Court). Article III of the Constitution, Marshall pointed out, spelled out precisely the Supreme Court's original jurisdiction; it did not mention issuing writs of this sort and plainly indicated that on all matters not mentioned in the Constitution, the Court would have only appellate jurisdiction. Congress may not change what the Constitution says; hence the part of the Judiciary Act attempting to do this was null and void.

The result was that a showdown with the Jeffersonians was avoided—Madison was not ordered to deliver the commissions—but the power of the Supreme Court was unmistakably clarified and enlarged. As Marshall wrote, "It is emphatically the province and duty of the judicial department to say what the law is." Furthermore, "a law repugnant to the Constitution is void."

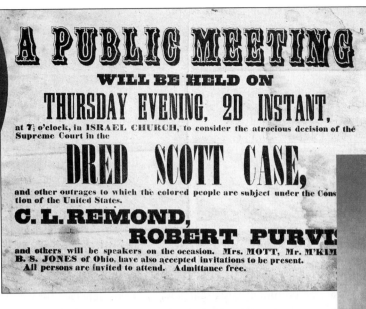

Roger B. Taney, chief justice from 1836 to 1864, wrote the *Dred Scott* decision, which asserted that blacks were not citizens of the United States. Dred Scott claimed that when his master brought him north to a free state, he ceased to be a slave. The public outcry against the decision, at least in the North, was intense, as is evident from this poster announcing a mass meeting "to consider the atrocious decision."

decide what the Constitution meant. The Supreme Court felt otherwise, and in this case and another like it the Court asserted its own broad powers to review any state court decision if that decision seemed to violate federal law or the federal Constitution.[4]

The power of the federal government to regulate commerce among the states was also established. When New York gave to Robert Fulton, the inventor of the steamboat, the monopoly right to operate his steamboats on the rivers of that state, the Marshall Court overturned the license because the rivers connected New York and New Jersey and thus trade on those rivers would involve *inter*state commerce, and federal law in that area was supreme. Since there was a conflicting federal law on the books, the state law was void.[5]

All of this may sound rather obvious to us today, when the supremacy of the federal government is largely unquestioned. In the early nineteenth century, however, these were almost revolutionary decisions. The Jeffersonian Republicans were in power and had become increasingly devoted to states' rights; they were aghast at the Marshall decisions.

President Andrew Jackson attacked the Court bitterly for defending the right of the federal government to create a national bank and for siding with the Cherokee Indians in a dispute with Georgia. In speaking of the latter case, Jackson is supposed to have remarked, "John Marshall has made his decision; now let him enforce it!"[6]

Though Marshall seemed to have secured the supremacy of federal over state government, another even more divisive issue had arisen; that, of course, was slavery. Roger B. Taney succeeded Marshall as chief justice in 1836. He was deliberately chosen by President Jackson because he was an advocate of states' rights, and he began to chip away at federal supremacy, upholding state claims that Marshall would have set aside. But the decision for which he is famous—or infamous—came in 1857, when, in the *Dred Scott* case, he wrote perhaps the most disastrous judicial opinion ever issued. A slave, Dred Scott, had been taken by his owner to a territory (near what is now St. Paul, Minnesota) where slavery was illegal under federal law. Scott claimed that since he had resided in a free territory, he was now a free man.

Taney held that Negroes were not citizens of the United States and could not become so, and that the federal law—the Missouri Compromise—prohibiting slavery in northern territories was unconstitutional.[7] The public outcry against this view was enormous, and the Court and Taney were discredited in (at least) northern opinion. A civil war was fought over what the Court mistakenly had assumed that it could treat as a purely legal question.

Government and the Economy

The supremacy of the federal government may have been established by John Marshall and a civil war, but the scope of the powers of that government or even of the state governments was still to be defined. During the period from the end of the Civil War to the early years of the New Deal, the dominant issue that the Supreme Court faced was to decide under what circumstances the economy could be regulated by state or nation.

The Court revealed a strong though not inflexible attachment to private property. In fact that attachment had always been there: the Founders thought that political and property rights were inextricably linked, and Marshall certainly supported the sanctity of contracts. But now, with the muting of the federal supremacy issue and the rise of a national economy with important unanticipated effects, the property question became the dominant one. In general the Court developed the view that the Fourteenth Amendment, adopted in 1868 primarily to protect black claims to citizenship from hostile state action, also protected private property and the corporation from unreasonable state action. The crucial phrase was: no state shall "deprive any person of life, liberty, or property, without due process of law." Once it became clear that a "person" could be a firm or a corporation as well as an individual, business and industry began to flood the courts with cases challenging various government regulations of these enterprises.

The Court quickly found itself in a thicket: it began passing on the constitutionality of virtually every effort by any government to regulate any aspect of business or labor, and its work load rose sharply. The activism of the courts was established in the 1880s and 1890s as the Court set itself up as the arbiter of what kind of regulation was permissible. In the first seventy-five years of this country's history, only 2 federal laws were held unconstitutional; in the next seventy-five years, 71 were.[8] Of the roughly 900 state laws held to be in conflict with the federal Constitution since 1789, about 800 were overturned after 1870. In one decade alone—the 1880s—5 federal and 48 state laws were declared unconstitutional.

Many of these decisions gave clear evidence of the Court's desire to protect private property: it upheld the use of injunctions to prevent labor strikes,[9] struck down the federal income tax,[10] sharply limited the reach of the antitrust law,[11] restricted the powers of the Interstate Commerce Commission to set railroad rates,[12] prohibited the federal government from eliminating child labor,[13] and prevented the states from setting maximum hours of work.[14] In 184 cases between 1899 and 1937, the Supreme Court struck down state laws for violating the Fourteenth Amendment, usually by economic regulation.[15]

But the Court also rendered decisions that authorized various kinds of regulation. It allowed states to regulate businesses "affected with a public interest,"[16] changed its mind about the Interstate Commerce Commission and allowed it to regulate railroad rates,[17] upheld rules requiring railroads to improve their safety,[18] approved state antiliquor laws,[19] approved state mine safety laws,[20] supported state workers' compensation laws,[21] allowed states to regulate fire-insurance rates,[22] and in time upheld a number of state laws regulating wages and hours. Indeed, between 1887 and 1910, in 558 cases involving the Fourteenth Amendment the Supreme Court upheld state regulations over 80 percent of the time.[23]

To characterize the Court as probusiness or antiregulation is both simplistic and inexact. More accurate, perhaps, is to characterize it as supportive of the rights of private property but unsure how to draw the lines that would distinguish "reasonable" from "unreasonable" regulation. Nothing in the Constitution clearly differentiated reasonable from unreasonable regulation, and the Court could invent no consistent principle of its own to make this determination. For example, what kinds of businesses are "affected with a public interest"? Grain elevators and railroads are, but are bakeries? Sugar refiners? Saloons? And how much of commerce is "interstate"—anything that moves? Or only something that actually crosses a state line? The Court found itself trying to make detailed judgments that it was not always competent to make and to invent legal rules where no clear legal rules were possible.

In one area, however, the Supreme Court's judgments were clear: the Fourteenth and Fifteenth Amendments were construed so narrowly as to give blacks only the most limited benefits of their provisions. In a long series of decisions the Court upheld segregation in schools and on railroad cars and permitted blacks to be excluded from voting in many states (see Chapter 19).

Government and Political Liberty

After 1936 the Supreme Court stopped imposing any serious restrictions on state or federal power to regulate the economy, leaving such matters in the hands of the legislatures. From 1937 to 1974 the Supreme Court did not overturn a single federal law designed to regulate business but did overturn thirty-six congressional enactments that violated personal political liberties. It voided as unconstitutional laws that restricted freedom of speech,[24] denied passports to communists,[25] permitted the government to revoke a person's citizenship,[26] withheld a person's mail,[27] or restricted the availability of government benefits.[28]

This new direction began when one justice changed his mind and continued as the composition of the Court changed. At the outset of the New Deal the Court was, by a narrow margin, dominated by justices who opposed the welfare state and federal regulation based on broad grants of discretionary authority to administrative agencies. President Franklin Roosevelt, who was determined to get just such legislation implemented, found himself powerless to alter the composition of the Court during his first term (1933–1937): because no justice died or retired, he had no vacancies to fill. After his overwhelming reelection in 1936, he moved to remedy this problem by "packing" the Court.

Roosevelt proposed a bill that would have allowed him to appoint one new justice for each one over the age of seventy who refused to retire, up to a total membership of fifteen. Since there were six men in this category then on the Supreme Court, he would have been able to appoint six new justices, enough to ensure a comfortable majority supportive of his economic policies. A bitter controversy ensued, but before the bill could be voted on, the Supreme Court, perhaps reacting to Roosevelt's big win in the 1936 elections, changed its mind. Whereas it had been striking down several New Deal measures by votes of five to four, now it started approving them by the same vote. One justice, Owen Roberts, had switched his position—the famous "switch in time that saved nine."

The "court-packing" bill was not passed, but it was no longer necessary. Justice Roberts had yielded before public opinion in a way that Chief Justice Taney a century earlier had not, thus forestalling an

The "nine old men": the Supreme Court in 1937, not long after President Franklin D. Roosevelt tried, unsuccessfully, to "pack" it by appointing six additional justices who would have supported his New Deal legislation. Justice Owen J. Roberts (standing at the left) changed his vote on these matters, and the Court ceased to be a barrier to the delegation of power to the bureaucracy.

U.S. DISTRICT AND APPELLATE COURTS

NOTE: Washington, D.C., is in a separate court. Puerto Rico is in the first circuit; the Virgin Islands are in the third; Guam and the Northern Mariana Islands are in the ninth.

SOURCE: Administrative Office of the United States Courts (January 1983).

assault on the Court by the other branches of government. Shortly thereafter several justices stepped down, and Roosevelt was able to make his own appointments (he made nine in all during his four terms in office). From then on the Court turned its attention to new issues—political liberties and, in time, civil rights.

With the arrival in office of Chief Justice Earl Warren in 1953, the Court began its most active period yet. Activism now arose to redefine the relationship of citizens to the government and especially to protect the rights and liberties of citizens from governmental trespass. Although the Court has always seen itself as protecting citizens from arbitrary government, before 1937 that protection was of a sort that conservatives preferred; after 1937 it was of a kind that liberals preferred.

The Structure of the Federal Courts

The only federal court that the Constitution requires is the Supreme Court, as specified in Article III. All other federal courts and their jurisdictions are creations of Congress. Nor does the Constitution indicate how many justices shall be on the Supreme Court (there were originally six, now there are nine) nor what its appellate jurisdiction shall be.

Congress has created two kinds of lower federal courts to handle cases that need not be decided by the Supreme Court: constitutional and legislative courts. A **constitutional court** is one exercising the judicial powers found in Article III of the Constitution, and therefore its judges are given constitutional protection: they may not be fired (they serve during "good behavior") nor may their salaries be reduced while they are in office. The most important of the constitutional courts are the **district courts** (a total of ninety-four, with at least one in each state, the District of Columbia, and the commonwealth of Puerto Rico) and the **courts of appeals** (one in each of eleven regions, or circuits, plus one in the District of Columbia). There are also certain specialized courts having constitutional status, such as the Court of International Trade, but we shall not be concerned with them.

A **legislative court** is one set up by Congress for some specialized purpose and staffed with people who have fixed terms of office and can be removed or have their salaries reduced. Legislative courts include the Court of Military Appeals and the territorial courts.

Selecting Judges

Since the judges on the constitutional courts serve for life and have the power of judicial review, how they are selected and what attitudes they bring to the bench are obviously important. All are nominated by the president and confirmed by the Senate. Almost invariably the president nominates a member of his own political party.

Party background does have some effect on how judges behave. A study by Robert A. Carp and C. K. Rowland of over twenty-seven thousand district court cases decided between 1933 and 1977 revealed that Democratic judges took somewhat more liberal positions than Republican ones. The biggest differences were in cases alleging discrimination based on race or sex and in those involving the rights of the accused in criminal prosecutions. In these matters Democratic judges reached a "liberal" decision 13 percent to 18 percent more frequently than Republican ones. Comparable findings have come from studies of appeals court and Supreme Court justices.[29] This is consistent with what we have already learned about public opinion: within political elites partisanship is associated with ideology, and this affects behavior.

But ideology does not determine behavior. So many other things shape court decisions—the facts of the case, prior rulings by other courts, the arguments presented by lawyers—that there is no reliable way of predicting how judges will behave in all mat-

How Partisanship Affects Judicial Attitudes

In 1984 over one hundred federal judges were interviewed to learn about their background and attitudes. Although they were about equal numbers of Democrats and Republicans, they were quite similar in social background. The overwhelming majority were white males; their average age was sixty. Most had attended a prestigious college. Despite these similarities, they expressed quite different political views and applied quite different judicial philosophies.

Attitudes	Judges Appointed by	
	Democrats	Republicans
Political ideology		
Liberal	75%	28%
Conservative	11	37
Policy positions		
Favor less government regulation of business	54	85
Government should reduce income gap between rich and poor	78	44
Special preference should be given to blacks in hiring	62	41
Special preference should be given to women in hiring	47	22
A woman has right to decide on abortion	81	80
Judicial philosophy		
Courts show too much concern for criminals	16	44
Judges should just apply the law, leave the rest to legislators	51	69
Judges need to supervise public bureaucracies	81	64

SOURCE: Althea K. Nagai, Stanley Rothman, and S. Robert Lichter, "The Verdict of Federal Judges," *Public Opinion* (November–December 1987): 52–56. Reprinted with the permission of the American Enterprise Institute for Public Policy Research, Washington, D.C.

ters. Presidents often make the mistake of thinking that they know how their appointees will behave, only to be surprised by the facts. Theodore Roosevelt appointed Oliver Wendell Holmes to the Supreme Court, only to remark later, after Holmes had voted

FIGURE 14.1　Female and Minority Judicial Appointments, 1963–1991

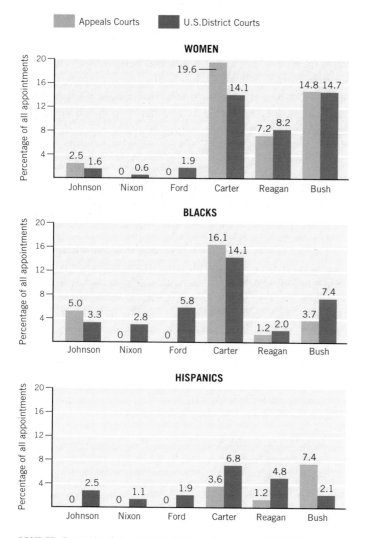

SOURCE: *Congressional Quarterly Weekly Report* (January 18, 1992): 112, reporting data gathered by Sheldon Goldman of University of Massachusetts (Johnson, Nixon, Ford) and Justice Department, Senate Judiciary Committee (Carter, Reagan, Bush).

ing the right to an abortion to be constitutionally protected.

Senatorial Courtesy　In theory the president nominates a "qualified" person to be a judge and the Senate passes on those "qualifications." In fact the tradition of senatorial courtesy gives heavy weight to the preferences of the senators from the state where a federal district judge is to serve. Ordinarily the Senate will not confirm a district court judge if the senator who is from that state and of the president's party objects. The senator can exercise this veto power by means of the "blue slip"—a blue piece of paper on which the senator is asked to record his or her views on the nominee. A negative opinion, or even failure to return the blue slip, usually kills the nomination. This means that as a practical matter the president nominates only persons recommended to him by the senator from that state. Someone once suggested that, at least with respect to district judges, the Constitution has been turned on its head. To reflect reality, he said, Article II, section 2, ought to read: "The senators shall nominate, and by and with the consent of the President, shall appoint" federal judges.

The "Litmus Test"　Of late, presidents have tried to exercise more influence on the selection of federal district and appellate court judges by getting the Justice Department to play an active role in finding and scrutinizing candidates to ensure that whomever they nominate not only is supported by their party's senators but also reflects the political and judicial philosophy of the president. President Carter sought out liberal, activist judges; President Reagan sought out conservative, strict-constructionist ones.

As far as we can tell, they succeeded. (See Figure 14.1.) Carter appointed more blacks and women than Reagan (though Reagan appointed the third highest percentage of women in history). We have no systematic data on the ideological differences between Carter and Reagan appointees, but every bit of impressionistic evidence suggests that Carter's were liberal and Reagan's conservative.*

---

* A survey of federal judges found that 75 percent of the Democrats, but only 28 percent of the Republicans, considered themselves to be liberals. See Althea K. Nagai, Stanley Rothman, and S. Robert Lichter, "The Verdict on Federal Judges," *Public Opinion* (November–December, 1987): 52.

in a way that Roosevelt did not like, that "I could carve out of a banana a judge with more backbone than that!" Holmes, who had plenty of backbone, said that he did not "give a damn" what Roosevelt thought. Richard Nixon, an ardent foe of court-ordered school busing, appointed Warren Burger to be chief justice. Burger promptly sat down and wrote the opinion upholding busing. Another Nixon appointee, Harry Blackmun, wrote the opinion declar-

This has led some to worry about the use of a political **litmus test**—a test of ideological purity—for judges. When conservatives are out of power (as they were under Carter), they complain about liberals' using a litmus test; when liberals are out of power (as they were under Reagan), they complain about conservatives' using it. People who are neither conservatives nor liberals wish that judges could be picked purely on the basis of "professional qualifications" without reference to ideology, but the courts are now so deeply involved in political issues that it is hard to imagine what a politically neutral set of professional qualifications might be.

The litmus-test issue is of greatest importance in selecting Supreme Court justices. Here there is no tradition of senatorial courtesy. The president takes a keen personal interest in the choices and, of late, has sought to find nominees who share his philosophy. In the Reagan administration there were bruising fights in the Senate over the nomination of William Rehnquist to be chief justice (he won) and Robert Bork to be an associate justice (he lost), with liberals pitted against conservatives. When President Bush nominated David Souter to be a justice, there were lengthy hearings as liberal senators tried to pin down Souter's views on issues such as abortion, but he refused to discuss matters that he might later have to judge. Clarence Thomas, another Bush nominee, also tried to avoid the litmus test by saying that he had not formed an opinion on the leading abortion cases. In his case, however, the litmus-test issue was overshadowed by sensational allegations from a former employee, Anita Hill, that Thomas had sexually harassed her.

Of the roughly 140 Supreme Court nominees presented to it, the Senate has rejected 27, though only 5 in this century.[30] These five cases are described in Table 14.2. The reasons for rejecting a Supreme Court nominee are complex—each senator may have a different reason—but have involved such matters as the nominee's alleged hostility to civil rights, questionable personal financial dealings, poor records as lower-court judges, and Senate opposition to the nominee's political or legal philosophy. Nominations of district court judges are rarely defeated because typically no nomination is made unless the key senators approve in advance.

There are exceptions. Some district court nominees have been controversial, and senators who have

Litmus Test

In chemistry a litmus test is a way of finding out whether a liquid is acid or alkaline. It involves exposing the fluid to an organic dye that turns red in acids, blue in alkalines.

The term is used in politics to mean a test of ideological purity, a way of finding out whether a person is a dyed-in-the-wool liberal or conservative. For liberals a litmus-test issue might be support for abortion or opposition to school prayer; for conservatives it might be holding the opposite of these views, or perhaps favoring tax cuts.

SOURCE: William Safire, *Safire's Political Dictionary* (New York: Ballantine Books, 1978). Used by permission.

displeased their constituents by their vote have paid a price. Senator Slade Gorton of Washington lost his 1986 reelection bid in part, it appears, because he had supported an unpopular court nominee.

The Jurisdiction of the Federal Courts

We have a dual court system—one state, one federal—and this complicates enormously the task of describing what kinds of cases federal courts may hear and how cases beginning in the state courts may end up before the Supreme Court. The Constitution lists the kinds of cases over which federal courts have jurisdiction (in Article III and the Eleventh Amendment); by implication all other matters are left to state courts. Federal courts can hear all cases "arising under the Constitution, the laws of the United States, and treaties" (these are **federal-question cases**), and cases involving citizens of different states (called **diversity cases**).

TABLE 14.2   Senate Rejections of Supreme Court Nominations in This Century

Nominee	Year	President	Action
John J. Parker	1930	Hoover	Rejected
Abe Fortas[a]	1968	Johnson	Withdrawn
Clement F. Haynsworth, Jr.	1969	Nixon	Rejected
G. Harold Carswell	1970	Nixon	Rejected
Robert Bork	1987	Reagan	Rejected

[a] Already on the Supreme Court, Fortas was nominated to be chief justice; when his nomination was blocked by a Senate filibuster, he resigned from the Court.

Some kinds of cases can be heard in either federal or state courts. For example, if citizens of different states wish to sue one another and the matter involves more than $50,000, they can do so in either a federal or a state court. Similarly if someone robs a federally insured bank, he or she has broken both state and federal law and thus can be prosecuted in state or federal courts, or both. Lawyers have become quite sophisticated in deciding whether, in a given civil case, their clients will get better treatment in state or federal court. Prosecutors often send a person who has broken both federal and state law to whichever court system is likelier to give the toughest penalty.

Sometimes defendants may be tried in both state and federal courts for the same offense. In 1992 four Los Angeles police officers accused of beating Rodney King were tried in a California state court and acquitted of assault charges. They were then prosecuted in federal court for violating King's civil rights. This time two of the four were convicted. Under the dual sovereignty doctrine, state and federal authorities can prosecute the same person for the same conduct. The Supreme Court has upheld this doctrine on two grounds: First, each level of government has the right to enact laws serving its own purposes.[31] As a result, federal civil-rights charges could have been brought against the officers even if they had already been convicted of assault in state court (though as a practical matter this would have been unlikely). Second, neither level of government wants the other to be able to block prosecution of an accused person who has the sympathy of the authorities at one level. For example, when certain southern state courts were in sympathy with whites who had lynched blacks, the absence of the dual sovereignty doctrine would have meant that a trumped-up acquittal in state court would have barred federal prosecution.

President Reagan's nomination of Robert H. Bork (left) was rejected by the Senate; that of Anthony Kennedy (right) was confirmed. Whether the two men actually differed in their judicial philosophy is unclear, but Bork, a former Yale Law School professor, had published many articles stating his commitment to a jurisprudence based on original intent, and this gave to his Senate critics ammunition lacking in the case of Kennedy.

The Jurisdiction of the Federal Courts

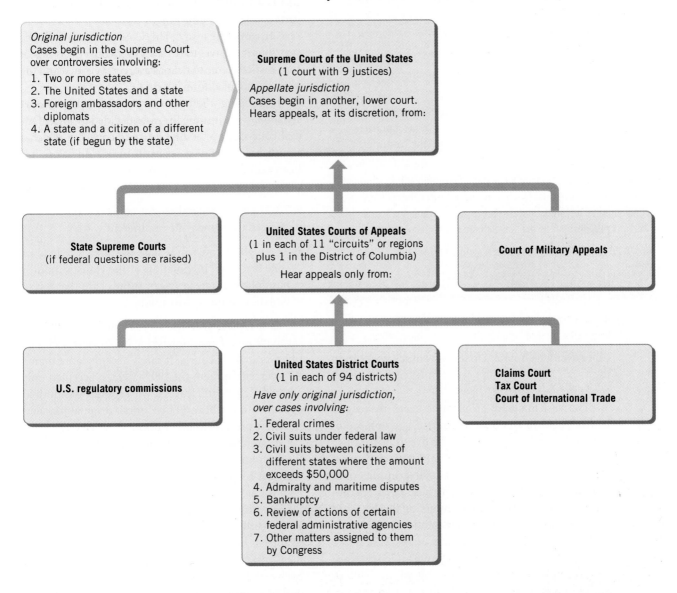

Original jurisdiction
Cases begin in the Supreme Court over controversies involving:

1. Two or more states
2. The United States and a state
3. Foreign ambassadors and other diplomats
4. A state and a citizen of a different state (if begun by the state)

Supreme Court of the United States
(1 court with 9 justices)

Appellate jurisdiction
Cases begin in another, lower court. Hears appeals, at its discretion, from:

State Supreme Courts
(if federal questions are raised)

United States Courts of Appeals
(1 in each of 11 "circuits" or regions plus 1 in the District of Columbia)

Hear appeals only from:

Court of Military Appeals

U.S. regulatory commissions

United States District Courts
(1 in each of 94 districts)

Have only original jurisdiction, over cases involving:

1. Federal crimes
2. Civil suits under federal law
3. Civil suits between citizens of different states where the amount exceeds $50,000
4. Admiralty and maritime disputes
5. Bankruptcy
6. Review of actions of certain federal administrative agencies
7. Other matters assigned to them by Congress

Claims Court
Tax Court
Court of International Trade

Furthermore a matter that is exclusively in the province of a state court—for example, a criminal case in which the defendant is charged with violating only a state law—can be appealed to the Supreme Court under certain circumstances described below. Thus federal judges can supervise state court rulings even when they have no jurisdiction over the original matter. Under what circumstances this should occur is the subject of long-standing controversy between the state and federal systems.

Some matters, however, are exclusively under the jurisdiction of federal courts. When a federal criminal law is broken—but not a state one—the case is heard in federal district court. If you wish to appeal the decision of a federal regulatory agency, such as the Federal Communications Commission, you can do so only before a federal court of appeals. And if you wish to declare bankruptcy, you do so in federal court. If there is a controversy between two state governments—say, California and Arizona sue each

Kinds of Law

The differences between *civil* and *criminal* law are not precise. Generally speaking:

- **Civil law** is the body of rules defining relationships among private citizens and consists of both statutes and the accumulated customary law embodied in judicial decisions (the "common law").

- **Criminal law** is the body of rules defining offenses that, though they harm an individual (such as murder, rape, robbery), are considered to be offenses against society as a whole and thus warrant punishment by and in the name of society.

You can go to prison if convicted of a crime but not if you lose a civil suit.

---

other over which state is to use how much water from the Colorado River—the case can be heard only by the Supreme Court.

The vast majority of all cases heard by federal courts begin in the district courts. The volume of business there is huge. In 1990 the five hundred or so district court judges received 218,000 civil cases (about 415 per judge) and 49,000 criminal ones (about 93 per judge). Most of these cases involve rather straightforward applications of the law, and few lead to the making of new public policy. Those that do affect the interpretation of the law or the Constitution can begin with seemingly minor events. For example, a major broadening of the Bill of Rights—requiring for the first time that all accused persons in *state* as well as federal criminal trials be supplied with a lawyer, free if necessary—began when impoverished Clarence Earl Gideon, imprisoned in Florida, wrote in pencil on prison stationery an appeal and sent it to the Supreme Court.[32]

The Supreme Court does not have to hear any appeal it does not want to hear. At one time it was required to listen to certain appeals, but Congress has changed the law so that now the Court can pick the cases it wants to consider.

It does this by issuing a **writ of certiorari.** *Certiorari* is a Latin word meaning, roughly, "made more certain"; lawyers and judges have abbreviated it to *cert.* It works this way: The Court considers all the petitions it receives to review lower court decisions. If four justices agree to hear a case, cert is issued and the case is scheduled for a hearing.

In deciding whether to grant certiorari, the Court tries to reserve its time for cases decided by lower federal courts or by the highest state courts in which a significant federal or constitutional question has been raised. For example, the Court will often grant certiorari when one or both of the following is true:

- Two or more federal circuit courts of appeal have decided the same issue in different ways.

- The highest court in a state has held a federal or state law to be in violation of the Constitution or has upheld a state law against the claim that it is in violation of the Constitution.

In a typical year the Court may consider over seven thousand petitions asking it to review decisions of lower or state courts. It rarely accepts more than 3 or 4 percent of them (in 1992–1993, it accepted only 1 percent). This still leaves it with about two hundred appeals it must hear. (The Court's original jurisdiction may produce another dozen or so cases.)

In exercising its discretion in granting certiorari, the Supreme Court is on the horns of a dilemma. If it grants it frequently, it will be inundated with cases. As it is, the work load of the Court has quintupled in the last fifty years. If, on the other hand, the Court grants certiorari only rarely, then the federal courts of appeals have the last word on the interpretation of the Constitution and federal laws, and since there are twelve of these staffed by about 168 judges, they may well be in disagreement. In fact this diversity of constitutional interpretation has happened: because the Supreme Court reviews only about 1 or 2 percent of appeals court cases, applicable federal law may be different in different parts of the country.[33] One proposal to deal with this dilemma is to devote the Supreme Court's time entirely to major questions of constitutional interpretation and to create a national court of appeals that would ensure that the twelve circuit courts of appeals are producing uniform decisions.[34]

In The Supreme Court of The United States
Washington D.C.
Clarence Earl Gideon
Petitioner | Petition for a writ
vs. | of Certiorari Directed
H.G. Cochran, Jr, as to The Supreme Court
Director, Divisions State of Florida.
of Corrections State No. 890 Misc.
of Florida CT. TERM 1961
U.S. SUPREME COURT

To The Honorable Earl Warren, Chief
Justice of the United States
Comes now The petitioner, Clarence
Earl Gideon, a citizen of The United States
of America, in proper person, and appearing
as his own counsel. Who petitions this
Honorable Court for a Writ of Certiorari
directed to The Supreme Court of The State
of Florida. To review the order and Judge-
ment of the court below denying the
petitioner a writ of Habeus Corpus.
Petitioner submits That The Supreme
Court of The United States has the authority
and jurisdiction to review the final Judge-
ment of The Supreme Court of The State
of Florida The highest court of The State
Under sec. 344 (B) Title 28 U.S.C.A. and
Because The "Due process clause" of the

Clarence Earl Gideon studied law books while in prison so that he could write an appeal to the Supreme Court. His handwritten appeal asked that his conviction be set aside because he had not been provided with an attorney. His appeal was granted.

Getting to Court

In theory the courts are the great equalizer in the federal government. To use the courts to settle a question, or even to alter fundamentally the accepted interpretation of the Constitution, one need not be elected to any office, have access to the mass media, be a member of an interest group, or be otherwise powerful or rich. Once the contending parties are before the court, they are legally equal.

It is too easy to believe this theory uncritically or to dismiss it cynically. In fact it is hard to get before the Supreme Court: it rejects over 96 percent of the applications for certiorari that it receives. And the costs involved in getting to the Court can be high. To apply for certiorari costs only $300 (plus forty copies of the petition), but if certiorari is granted and the case heard, the costs—for lawyers and for copies of the lower-court records in the case—can be very large. And by then one has already paid for the cost of the first hearing in the district court and probably one appeal to the circuit court of appeals. Furthermore the time it takes in federal court to settle a matter can be quite long.

But there are ways to make these costs lower. If you are indigent—without funds—you can file and be heard as a pauper for nothing; about half the petitions arriving before the Supreme Court are **in forma pauperis,** such as that from Gideon described earlier. If your case began as a criminal trial in the district courts and you are poor, the government supplies a lawyer at no charge. If the matter is not a criminal case and you cannot afford to hire a lawyer, interest groups representing a wide spectrum of opinion sometimes are willing to take up the cause if the issue in the case seems sufficiently important. The American Civil Liberties Union (ACLU) represents some people who believe that their freedom of speech or press has been abridged or that their constitutional rights in criminal proceedings have been violated.

But interest groups do much more than just help people pay their bills. Many of the most important cases decided by the Court got there because an interest group organized the case, found the plaintiffs, chose the legal strategy, and mobilized legal allies. The NAACP brought many of the key civil-rights cases on behalf of individuals. Although most of these interest groups in the past argued the liberal position, conservative interest groups of late have entered the courtroom on behalf of individuals. One helped sue CBS for televising a program that allegedly libeled General William Westmoreland, once the American commander in Vietnam. (Westmoreland lost the case.) And many important issues are raised by attorneys representing state and local governments. Several price-fixing cases have been won by state attorneys general on behalf of consumers in their states.

Fee Shifting

Unlike what happens in most of Europe, each party to a lawsuit in this country must pay its own way. (In England, by contrast, if you sue someone and lose, you pay the winner's costs as well as your own.) But various laws have made it easier to get someone else to pay. **Fee shifting,** as it is called, enables the **plaintiff** (the party that initiates the suit) to collect its costs from the defendant if the defendant loses, at least in certain kinds of cases. For example, if a corporation is found to have violated the antitrust laws, it must pay the legal fees of the winner. If an environmentalist group sues the Environmental Protection Agency, it can get the EPA to pay the group's legal costs. Even more important to individuals, Section 1983 of the *United States Code* allows a citizen to sue state and local government officials—say, a police officer or a school superintendent—who deprive the citizen of some constitutional right or withhold some benefit to which the citizen is entitled. If the citizen wins, he or she can collect money damages and lawyers' fees from the government. Citizens, more aware of their legal rights, have become more litigious, and a flood of such "Section 1983" suits has burdened the courts. The Supreme Court has restricted fee shifting to cases authorized by statute,[35] but it is clear that the drift of policy has made it cheaper to go to court—at least for some cases.

Standing

There is, in addition, a nonfinancial restriction on getting into federal court. To sue, one must have **standing,** a legal concept that refers to who is entitled to bring a case. It is especially important in determining who can challenge the laws or actions of government itself. A complex and changing set of rules governs standings; some of the more important ones are these:

- There must be an actual controversy between real adversaries. (You cannot bring a "friendly" suit against someone, hoping to lose in order to prove your friend right. You cannot ask a federal court for an opinion on a hypothetical or imaginary case, or ask it to render an advisory opinion.)

- You must show that you have been harmed by the law or practice about which you are complaining. (It is not enough to dislike what the government or a corporation or a labor union does; you must show that you were actually harmed by that action.)

- Merely being a taxpayer does not ordinarily entitle you to challenge the constitutionality of a federal governmental action. (You may not want your tax money to be spent in certain ways, but your remedy is to vote against the politicians doing the spending; the federal courts will generally require that you show some other personal harm before you can sue.)

Congress and the courts in recent years have made it easier to acquire standing. It has always been the rule that a citizen could ask the courts to order federal officials to carry out some act that they were under a legal obligation to perform or to refrain from some action that was contrary to law. A citizen can also sue a government official personally in order to collect damages if the official acted contrary to law. For example, it was for long the case that if an FBI agent broke into your office without a search warrant, you could sue the agent and, if you won, collect money. However, you cannot sue the government itself without its consent. This is the doctrine of **sovereign immunity.** For instance, if the army accidentally kills your cow while testing a new cannon, you cannot sue the government to recover the cost of the cow unless the government agrees to be sued. (Since testing cannons is legal, you cannot sue the army officer who fired the cannon.) By statute Congress has given its consent for the government to be sued in many cases involving a dispute over a contract or damage done as a result of negligence (for example, the dead cow). Over the years these statutes have made it easier to take the government into court as a defendant.

Even some of the oldest rules defining standing have been liberalized. The rule that merely being a taxpayer does not entitle you to challenge in court a government decision has been relaxed where the citizen claims that a right guaranteed under the First Amendment is being violated. The Supreme Court allowed a taxpayer to challenge a federal law that would have given financial aid to parochial (or church-related) schools on the grounds that this aid violated the constitutional requirement of separation between church and state. On the other hand another taxpayer suit to force the CIA to make public its budget failed because the Court decided that the taxpayer did not have standing in matters of this sort.[36]

Class-Action Suits

Under certain circumstances a citizen can benefit directly from a court decision, even though the citizen himself or herself has not gone into court. This can happen by means of a **class-action suit:** a case brought into court by a person on behalf not only of himself or herself but of all other persons in similar circumstances. Among the most famous of such cases is the school-desegregation decision of the Supreme Court in 1954, when it found that Linda Brown, a black girl attending the fifth grade in the Topeka, Kansas, public schools, was denied the equal protection of the laws (guaranteed under the Fourteenth Amendment) because the schools in Topeka were segregated. The Court did not limit its decision to Linda Brown's right to attend an unsegregated school but extended it—as Brown's lawyers from the NAACP had asked—to cover all "others similarly situated."[37] As we shall see in Chapter 19, it was not easy to design a court order that would eliminate segregation for black schoolchildren, but the principle was clearly established in this class action.

Since the *Brown* case, many other groups have been quick to take advantage of the opportunity created by class-action suits. By this means the courts could be used to give relief not simply to a particular person but to all those represented in the suit. A landmark class-action case was that which challenged the malapportionment of state legislatures (see Chapter 11).[38] In 1980 there were seven thousand class-action suits in the federal courts involving civil rights, the rights of prisoners, antitrust suits

against corporations, and other matters. These suits became more common partly because people were beginning to have new concerns that were not being met by Congress and partly because some class-action suits became quite profitable. The NAACP got no money from Linda Brown or from the Topeka Board of Education in compensation for its long and expensive labors, but beginning in the 1960s court rules were changed to make it financially attractive for lawyers to bring certain kinds of class-action suits.

Suppose, for example, you think that your telephone company overcharged you by $75. You could try to hire a lawyer to get a refund, but not many lawyers would take the case because there is no money in it. Even if you were to win, the lawyer would stand to earn no more than perhaps one-third of the settlement, or $25. Now suppose that you

Linda Brown was refused admission to a white elementary school in Topeka, Kansas. On her behalf the NAACP brought a class-action suit that resulted in the 1954 landmark Supreme Court decision, *Brown* v. *Board of Education*.

TABLE 14.3   Supreme Court Justices in Order of Seniority, 1994

Name (Birthdate)	Home State	Prior Experience	Appointed by (Year)
William H. Rehnquist, Chief Justice (1924)	Arizona	Justice: Assistant attorney general	Reagan (1986) as chief; Nixon (1971) as justice
John Paul Stevens (1916)	Illinois	Federal judge	Ford (1975)
Sandra Day O'Connor (1930)	Arizona	State judge	Reagan (1981)
Antonin Scalia (1936)	New York	Federal judge	Reagan (1986)
Anthony Kennedy (1936)	California	Federal judge	Reagan (1988)
David Souter (1939)	New Hampshire	State judge	Bush (1990)
Clarence Thomas (1948)	Georgia	Federal judge	Bush (1991)
Ruth Bader Ginsburg (1933)	New York	Federal judge	Clinton (1993)
Stephen Breyer (1938)	Massachusetts	Federal judge	Clinton (1994)

bring a class action against the company on behalf of everybody who was overcharged. Millions of dollars might be at stake; lawyers would line up eagerly to take the case because their share of the settlement, if they win, could be huge. The opportunity to win a profitable class-action suit, combined with the possibility of having the losing corporation pay attorneys' fees even when the damages awarded were not large, led to a proliferation of such cases.

In response to this increase in its work load, the Supreme Court decided in 1974 to tighten drastically the rules governing these suits. It held that it would no longer hear (except in certain cases defined by Congress, such as civil-rights matters) class-action suits seeking money damages unless each and every ascertainable member of the class was individually notified of the case. To do this is often prohibitively expensive (imagine trying to find and send a letter to every customer that may have been overcharged by the telephone company!), and so the number of such cases declined and the number of lawyers seeking them out dropped.[39]

In sum, getting into court depends on having standing and having resources. The rules governing standing are complex and changing, but generally have been broadened to make it easier to enter the federal courts, especially for the purpose of challenging the actions of the government. Obtaining the resources is not easy but has become easier because laws in some cases now provide for fee shifting, be-

cause private interest groups are willing to finance cases, and because it is sometimes possible to bring inexpensively a class-action suit that lawyers would find lucrative.

The Supreme Court in Action

If your case should find its way to the Supreme Court—and of course the odds are that it will not—you will be able to participate in one of the more impressive, sometimes dramatic ceremonies of American public life. The Court is in session in its white marble building for thirty-six weeks out of each year, from early October until the end of June. The nine justices read briefs in their individual offices, hear oral arguments in the stately courtroom, and discuss their decisions with one another in a conference room where no outsider is ever allowed.

Most cases, as we have seen, come to the Court on a writ of certiorari. The lawyers for each side may then submit their **briefs,** documents that set forth the facts, summarize the lower-court decision, give the arguments for the side represented by the lawyer, and discuss the other cases that the Court has decided that bear on the issue. Then the lawyers are allowed to present their oral arguments in open court. They usually summarize the briefs or emphasize particular points in them, and are strictly limited in time—usually to no more than a half hour. (The

This photo of the Supreme Court in session on February 8, 1932, may be the only one ever taken while the justices were actually hearing a case.

lawyer speaks from a lectern that has two lights on it. When the white light goes on, the attorney has five minutes remaining; when the red flashes, he or she must stop—instantly.) The oral arguments give the justices a chance to question the lawyers, sometimes searchingly.

Since the federal government is a party—as either plaintiff or defendant—to about half the cases that the Supreme Court hears, the government's top trial lawyer, the solicitor general of the United States, appears frequently before the Court. The solicitor general is the third-ranking officer of the Department of Justice, right after the attorney general and deputy attorney general. The solicitor general decides what cases the government will appeal from lower courts and personally approves every case that the government presents to the Supreme Court. In recent years the solicitor general has often been selected from the ranks of distinguished law-school professors.

In addition to the arguments made by lawyers for the two sides in a case, written briefs and even oral arguments may also be offered by "a friend of the court," or **amicus curiae.** An amicus brief is from an interested party not directly involved in the suit. For example, when Allan Bakke complained that he had been the victim of "reverse discrimination" when he was denied admission to a University of California medical school, fifty-eight amicus briefs were filed supporting or opposing his position. Before such briefs can be filed, both parties must agree or the Court must grant permission. Though these briefs sometimes offer new arguments, they are really a kind of polite lobbying of the Court that declare what interest groups are on which side. The ACLU, the NAACP, the AFL-CIO, and the United States government itself have been among the leading sources of such briefs.

These briefs are not the only source of influence on the justices' views. Legal periodicals such as the *Harvard Law Review* and the *Yale Law Journal* are frequently consulted, and citations to them often appear in the Court's decisions. Thus the outside world of lawyers and law professors can help shape, or at least supply arguments for, the conclusions of the justices.

The justices retire every Friday to their conference room, where in complete secrecy they debate the cases that they have heard. The chief justice speaks first, followed by the other justices in order of seniority. After the arguments they vote, traditionally in reverse order of seniority: the newest justice votes first, the chief justice last. In this process an able chief justice can exercise considerable influence—in guiding or limiting debate, in setting forth the issues, and in handling sometimes temperamental personalities. In deciding a case, a majority of the justices must be in agreement: if there is a tie, the lower-court decision is left standing. (There can be a tie among nine justices if one is ill or disqualifies himself or herself because of prior involvement in the case.)

Though the vote is what counts, by tradition the Court usually issues a written opinion explaining its decision. Sometimes the opinion is brief and unsigned (called a **per curiam opinion**); sometimes it is quite long and signed by the justices agreeing with it. If the chief justice is in the majority, he will either write the opinion or assign the task to a justice who agrees with him. If he is in the minority, the senior justice on the winning side will decide who writes the Court's opinion. There are three kinds of opinions— **opinion of the Court** (reflecting the majority's view), **concurring opinion** (an opinion by one or more jus-

tices who agree with the majority's conclusion but for different reasons that they wish to express), and **dissenting opinion** (the opinion of the justices on the losing side). Each justice has three or four law clerks (bright, recent graduates of the leading law schools) to help him or her review the many petitions that the Court receives, study cases, and write opinions.

Voting Patterns of the Court

Scholars have made elaborate and ingenious efforts to explain the pattern of voting of Supreme Court justices. The intricacies of these inquiries are best left to specialists, but the results can be summarized in general terms. They show that justices, like any group of men or women in politics, tend to take more or less consistent positions on public issues. They have a political philosophy. When the Court must decide a case that raises philosophical issues (and that occurs only part of the time), we should not be surprised to see rather clear voting blocs emerge.

During the 1970s and 1980s, there were often three such blocs: a liberal/activist bloc (led by former Justice William Brennan and including former Justice Thurgood Marshall and sometimes former Justice Harry Blackmun and former Justice Lewis Powell), a conservative/strict constructionist bloc (consisting of former Chief Justice Burger, Justice Rehnquist, and Justice O'Connor), and a swing bloc (composed of former Justice White and Justice Stevens).[40] The liberal bloc was usually in the minority but sometimes picked up enough swing votes to decide the issue.[41]

With the retirement of Powell, Brennan, Marshall, and Burger and the arrival of Justices Scalia, Kennedy, Souter, and Thomas, the liberal/activist bloc has more or less disappeared. There is now on many issues a conservative/strict-constructionist bloc of about six justices: Rehnquist, O'Connor, Scalia, Kennedy, Souter, and Thomas. But that bloc is not hard and fast; it split apart on the abortion issue, for example.

In 1993 Justice White retired, and Ruth Bader Ginsburg took his place. She was the first Supreme Court justice appointed by a Democratic president in twenty-six years. It is too early to tell how she will vote, but it is likely that she will be more liberal than most of her colleagues. In 1994 Justice Blackmun

The law clerks of Supreme Court justices are young men and women picked by the justices from among the highest-ranking recent law school graduates. Here, several clerks confer with Chief Justice Rehnquist.

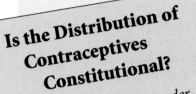

Is the Distribution of Contraceptives Constitutional?

Connecticut Statute under Review

* * *

WASHINGTON, D.C. MARCH 14, 1965— The United States Supreme Court is expected to decide during this term whether a Connecticut statute barring the distribution of contraceptive devices is constitutional. The law, passed in 1879, was used to convict an official of the Planned Parenthood Federation who gave contraceptives to a married couple . . .

What Would You Do?

MEMORANDUM

TO: Justice Saikia
FROM: Roberta Evans, law clerk
SUBJECT: Connecticut Statute barring distribution of contraceptive devices

The central issue is whether the Connecticut law violates any provisions of the U.S. Constitution. All justices agree that nothing in the Constitution refers to contraception or its regulation. Most justices agree that there is no explicit "right of privacy" in the Constitution that might be violated by enforcing the Connecticut law in a way that, as here, tells a married couple what they may or may not do in their bedroom. Justice Stewart has even referred to the statute as "an uncommonly silly law,"and a lot of your colleagues probably agree. But is the law unconstitutional?

<u>Justice Douglas thinks that it is.</u> His reasoning is that while there is no "right of privacy" mentioned in the Constitution, such a right can be inferred from the existence of "penumbras" that are formed by "emanations" from other provisions of the Bill of Rights. The First Amendment right of free association, for example, implies a right of privacy. The Fourth Amendment guarantee against unreasonable searches and seizures also implies such a right. In fact he thinks that the right of privacy is older than the Bill of Rights and ought to be understood as being implied by those amendments.

<u>Justice Black thinks that it is not.</u> It is our job to hold laws unconstitutional when they violate a right mentioned in the Constitution. However silly the Connecticut law may be, we cannot strike it down because we think that it violates some "penumbra" or "emanation." Striking down this law on these grounds is no different from striking down any law on the grounds that we don't like it, thereby substituting our views as to what should be social policy for the views of elected officials. If we do that, we are acting as a "supervisory agency" over "duly constituted legislative bodies." What is to prevent the Court from striking down (as it once tried to do) state laws regulating the hours and conditions of work because we find a "right of free enterprise" that "emanates" from the Constitution?

(The actual case was *Griswold* v. *Connecticut*. To learn how it came out, look it up: 381 U.S. 479 [1965].)

retired, and President Clinton nominated federal judge Stephen Breyer to replace him.

These voting blocs are important, but they are not the whole story and often not even a significant factor. During the 1992–1993 Court term, 43 percent of all the opinions of the Court were unanimous, the highest percentage in many decades. Even two justices who are as different philosophically as Scalia and Stevens voted the same way in 61 percent of the cases in 1992–1993.

The judicial philosophy of the justices, though important, does not prevent them from agreeing a lot of the time. The reason is that many cases have no "liberal" or "conservative" side, and even in those that do the justices must take into account the language of the law or the Constitution, the prior decisions (precedents) they have issued, and the facts of the case. And when philosophy plays a role, unexpected cleavages may develop, as when O'Connor and Kennedy broke ranks with Rehnquist and Scalia on the abortion question.

And in evaluating the Court, the student should remember that it is not the *results,* whether liberal or conservative, that ought to count; what should count is the quality of the judicial reasoning.

The Power of the Federal Courts

The great majority of the cases in federal courts have little or nothing to do with changes in public policy: people accused of bank robbery are tried, disputes over contracts are settled, personal-injury cases are heard, and the patent law is applied. In most instances the courts are simply applying a relatively settled body of law to a specific controversy.

The Power to Make Policy

The courts make policy whenever they reinterpret the law or the Constitution in significant ways, extend the reach of existing laws to cover matters not previously thought to be covered, or design remedies for problems that involve the judges' acting in administrative or legislative ways. By any of these tests the courts have become exceptionally powerful.

One measure of that power is the fact that more than 120 federal laws have been declared unconstitutional, although since 1937 relatively few of these had broad national significance. And as we shall see, on matters where Congress feels strongly, it can often get its way by passing slightly revised versions of the voided law.

Another measure, and perhaps a more revealing one, is the frequency with which the Court changes its mind. An informal rule of judicial decision making has been **stare decisis,** meaning "let the decision stand." It is the principle of precedent: a court case today should be settled in accordance with prior decisions on similar cases. (What constitutes a similar case is not always clear; lawyers are especially gifted at finding ways of showing that two cases are different in some relevant way.) There are two reasons why precedent is important. The practical reason should be obvious: if the meaning of the law continually changes, if the decisions of judges become wholly unpredictable, then human affairs affected by those laws and decisions become chaotic. A contract signed today might be invalid tomorrow. The other reason is at least as important: if the principle of equal justice means anything, it means that similar cases should be decided in a similar manner. On the other hand times change and the Court can make mistakes. As Justice Felix Frankfurter once said, "Wisdom too often never comes, and so one ought not to reject it merely because it comes late."[42]

However compelling the arguments for flexibility, the pace of change can become dizzying. By one count the Court since 1810 has overruled its own previous decisions in over 140 cases.[43] In fact it may have done it more often, because sometimes the Court does not say that it is abandoning a precedent, claiming instead that it is merely distinguishing the present case from a previous one.

A third measure of judicial power is the degree to which courts are willing to handle matters once left to the legislature. For example, the Court refused for a long time to hear a case about the size of congressional districts, no matter how unequal their populations.[44] The determination of congressional district boundaries was regarded as a **political question**— that is, as a matter that the Constitution left entirely to another branch of government (in this case, the Congress) to decide for itself. Then in 1962 the Court decided that it was competent after all to handle this matter, and the notion of a "political question" became a much less important (but by no means absent) barrier to judicial power.[45]

★ When the States Go Beyond the Supreme Court

*A*s the U.S. Supreme Court increasingly becomes a less activist body, interests as different as the abortion-rights movement and the National Rifle Association are looking to state courts and state constitutions for help. In many instances, the states have obliged by going beyond Supreme Court rulings. Here are some examples.

SOURCE: *National Journal* (October 5, 1991): 2400. Copyright © 1991 by National Journal, Inc. All rights reserved. Reprinted by permission.

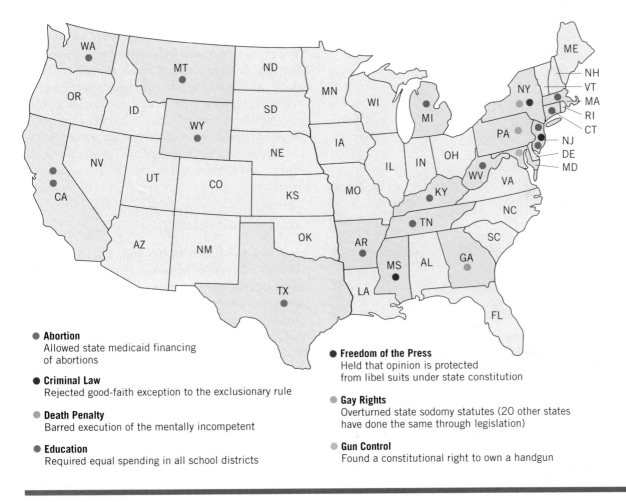

● **Abortion**
Allowed state medicaid financing of abortions

● **Criminal Law**
Rejected good-faith exception to the exclusionary rule

● **Death Penalty**
Barred execution of the mentally incompetent

● **Education**
Required equal spending in all school districts

● **Freedom of the Press**
Held that opinion is protected from libel suits under state constitution

● **Gay Rights**
Overturned state sodomy statutes (20 other states have done the same through legislation)

● **Gun Control**
Found a constitutional right to own a handgun

By all odds the most powerful indicator of judicial power can be found in the kinds of remedies that the courts will impose. A **remedy** is a judicial order setting forth what must be done to correct a situation that a judge believes to be wrong. In ordinary cases, such as one person's suing another, the remedy is straightforward: the loser must pay the winner for some injury that he or she has caused, or the loser must agree to abide by the terms of a contract he or she has broken, or the loser must promise not to do some unpleasant thing (such as dumping garbage on a neighbor's lawn). Today, however, judges design remedies that go far beyond what is required to do justice to the individual parties who actually appear in court. The remedies now imposed often apply to large groups and affect the circumstances under which thousands or even millions of people work, study, or live. For example, when a federal district judge in Alabama heard a case brought by a prison inmate in that state, he issued an order not simply to

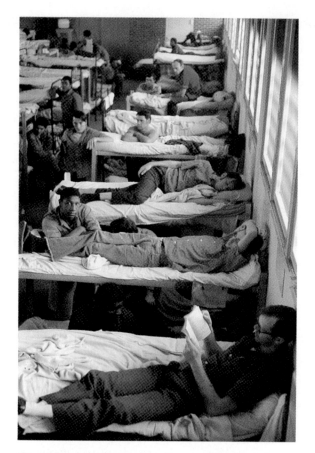

The activism of federal courts is exemplified by the sweeping orders they have issued designed to correct such problems as overcrowded prisons.

improve the lot of that prisoner but to revamp the administration of the entire prison system. The result was an improvement in the living conditions of many prisoners at a cost to the state of an estimated $40 million a year. Similarly a person who feels entitled to welfare payments that have been denied him or her may sue in court to get the money; the court order, however, will in all likelihood affect all welfare recipients. In one case certain court orders made an additional one hundred thousand people eligible for welfare.[46]

The basis for these sweeping court orders can sometimes be found in the Constitution; the Alabama prison decision, for example, was based on the judge's interpretation of the Eighth Amendment, which prohibits "cruel and unusual punishments."[47]

Others are based on court interpretations of federal laws. The Civil Rights Act of 1964 forbids discrimination on grounds of "race, color, or national origin" in any program receiving federal financial assistance. The Supreme Court interpreted that as meaning that the San Francisco school system was obliged to teach English to Chinese students unable to speak it.[48] Since a Supreme Court decision is the law of the land, the impact of that ruling was not limited to San Francisco. Local courts and legislatures elsewhere decided that that decision meant that classes must be taught in Spanish for Hispanic children. What Congress meant by the Civil Rights Act is not clear; it may or may not have believed that teaching Hispanic children in English rather than Spanish was a form of discrimination. What is important is that it was the Court, not Congress, that decided what Congress meant.

Views of Judicial Activism

Judicial activism has, of course, been controversial. Those who support it argue that the federal courts must correct injustices when the other branches of the federal government, or the states, refuse to do so. The courts are the institution of last resort for those without the votes or the influence to obtain new laws, and especially for the poor and powerless. State legislatures and the Congress, after all, tolerated segregated public schools for decades. If the Supreme Court had not declared segregation unconstitutional in 1954, it might still be law today.

Those who criticize the activist courts rejoin that judges usually have no special expertise in matters of school administration, prison management, or environmental protection; they are lawyers, expert in defining rights and duties but not in designing and managing complex institutions. Furthermore, however desirable court-declared rights and principles may be, implementing those principles means balancing the conflicting needs of various interest groups, raising and spending tax monies, and assessing the costs and benefits of complicated alternatives. Finally, judges are not elected; they are appointed and are thus immune to popular control. As a result, if they depart from their traditional role of making careful and cautious interpretations of what a law or the Constitution means and instead begin formulat-

CRITICAL ⬥ THINKING

A Debate: Constitutional Interpretation

⁊magine that you are at a debate between two people with opposed views on how judges should interpret the Constitution (and its amendments). Study carefully the words that these two persons use in explaining their views, and then try to imagine how they would answer the questions given below. Finally, try to decide which theory you favor and how you would answer those questions.

On the basis of *original intent*

A jurisprudence of original intent . . . is not difficult to describe. Where the language of the Constitution is specific, it must be obeyed. Where there is a demonstrable consensus among the framers and ratifiers as to a principle stated or implied by the Constitution, it should be followed. Where there is ambiguity as to the precise meaning or reach of a constitutional provision, it should be interpreted and applied in a manner so as to at least not contradict the text of the Constitution itself.

—Edwin Meese III, former attorney general of the United States (1985)

How do you think Mr. Meese would answer the following questions? How would you?

1. How do we discover what the Framers of the Constitution and its amendments really intended? What if the supporters of, say, the First Amendment disagreed as to its meaning?

2. What if the intentions of the Framers profoundly offend our sense of justice? For example, the authors of the Fourteenth Amendment did not intend for it to outlaw racially segregated schools, yet most people today believe that such schools should be regarded as an unconstitutional violation of that amendment (for details see Chapter 19).

On the basis of *contemporary meaning*

[T]he genius of the Constitution rests not in any static meaning it might have had in a world that is dead and gone, but in the adaptability of its great principles to cope with current problems and current needs. What the constitutional fundamentals meant to the wisdom of other times cannot be their measure to the vision of our times.

—William J. Brennan, Jr., former justice of the Supreme Court (1985)

How do you think Justice Brennan would answer the following questions? How would you?

1. Why should judges, who are not elected, decide what the "contemporary meaning" of the Constitution is? Shouldn't these questions be decided by elected legislators or by the people, through the amendment process?

2. What is the "vision of our times" that judges should follow? Should judges be free to pick *any* "vision"? Or only liberal ones? Or conservative ones?

---

ing wholly new policies, they become unelected legislators.

We shall not evaluate this argument until we have seen in greater detail (in Part 4) how the courts have behaved in various policy areas—civil liberties, civil rights, environmental protection, and economic regulation. Here we shall simply try to explain why activism has developed and what checks on it exist.

Some people think that we have activist courts because we have so many lawyers. The more we take matters to courts for resolution, the more likely it is that the courts will become powerful. It is true that

we have more lawyers in proportion to our population than most other nations. In 1982 there was 1 lawyer for every 400 Americans, but only 1 for every 1,600 Britons, every 3,400 French, and every 7,000 Japanese.[49] But that may well be a symptom, not a cause, of court activity. As we suggested in Chapter 4, we have an adversary culture based on an emphasis on individual rights and an implicit antagonism between people and government. Generally speaking, lawyers do not create cases; contending interests do, thereby generating a demand for lawyers. Furthermore we had more lawyers in relation to our

population in 1900 than in 1970, yet the courts seventy years ago were far less active in public affairs. In fact in 1932 there were more court cases (per 100,000 people) than in 1972.[50]

A more plausible reason for activist courts has been the developments (discussed earlier in this chapter) making it easier for people to get standing in courts, to pay for the costs of litigation, and to bring class-action claims. The courts and Congress have gone a long way toward allowing private citizens to become "private attorneys general." Making it easier to get into court increases the number of cases being heard. For example, in 1961 civil-rights cases, prisoner-rights cases, and cases under the Social Security laws were relatively uncommon in federal court. Between 1961 and 1990 the increase in the number of such matters was phenomenal: civil-rights cases rose over sixtyfold and prisoner petitions over fortyfold (see Figure 14.2). Such matters are the fastest-growing portion of the courts' civil work load.

Legislation and the Courts

An increase in cases will not by itself lead to sweeping remedies. For that to occur, the law must be sufficiently vague to permit judges wide latitude in interpreting it, and the judges must want to exercise that opportunity to the fullest. The Constitution is filled with words of seemingly ambiguous meaning—"due process of law," the "equal protection of the laws," the "privileges or immunities of citizens." Such phrases may have been clear to the Framers, but to the Court they have become equivocal or elastic. How the Court has chosen to interpret such phrases has changed greatly over the last two centuries in ways that can be explained in part by the personal political beliefs of the justices.

Increasingly Congress has passed laws that also contain vague language, thereby adding immeasurably to the courts' opportunities for designing remedies. Various civil-rights acts outlaw discrimination but do not say how one is to know whether discrimination has occurred or what should be done to correct it if it does occur. That is left to the courts and the bureaucracy. Various regulatory laws empower administrative agencies to do what the "public interest" requires but say little about how the public interest is to be defined. Laws intended to alleviate poverty or rebuild neighborhoods speak of "citizen participation" or "maximum feasible participation" but do not explain who the citizens are that should participate, or how much power they should have.

In addition to laws that require interpretation, other laws induce litigation. Almost every agency that regulates business will make decisions that cause the agency to be challenged in court—by business firms if the regulations go too far, by consumer or labor organizations if they do not go far enough. In 1988 the federal courts of appeals heard over three thousand cases in which they had to review the decision of a regulatory agency. In two-thirds of them the agency's position was supported; in the other third the agency was overruled.[51] Perhaps one-fifth of these cases arose out of agencies or programs that did not even exist in 1960. The federal government today is much more likely to be on the defensive in court than it was twenty or thirty years ago.

Finally, the attitudes of the judges powerfully affect what they will do, especially when the law gives them wide latitude. There have been very few studies of the attitudes of federal judges, but their decisions and opinions have been extensively analyzed—well enough, at least, to know that different judges often decide the same case in different ways. Conservative southern federal judges in the 1950s, for example, often resisted plans to desegregate public schools while judges with a different background authorized bold plans.[52] Some of the greatest disparities in judicial behavior can be found in the area of sentencing criminals.[53]

Checks on Judicial Power

No institution of government, including the courts, operates without restraint. The fact that judges are not elected does not make them immune to public opinion or to the views of the other branches of government. How important these restraints are will vary from case to case, but in the broad course of history they have been significant.

One restraint exists because of the very nature of courts. A judge has no police force or army; decisions that he or she makes can sometimes be resisted or ignored *if* the person or organization resisting is not highly visible and *if* the resister is willing to run the risk of being caught and charged with contempt of court. For example, long after the Supreme Court had decided that praying and Bible reading could not take place in public schools,[54] schools all over the country were still allowing prayers and Bible reading.[55] Years after the Court declared segregated schools to be unconstitutional, scores of school systems remained segregated. On the other hand, when a failure to comply is easily detected and punished, the courts' power is usually unchallenged. When the Supreme Court declared the income tax to be unconstitutional in 1895, income-tax collections promptly ceased. When the Court in 1952 declared illegal President Truman's effort to seize the steel mills in order to stop a strike, the management of the mills was immediately returned to their owners.

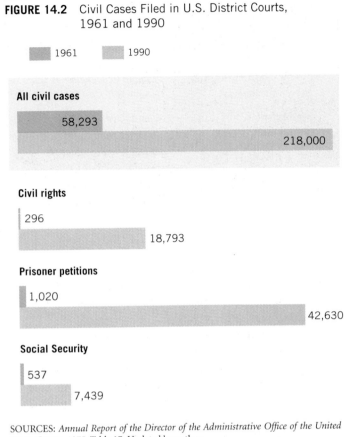

FIGURE 14.2 Civil Cases Filed in U.S. District Courts, 1961 and 1990

■ 1961   ■ 1990

All civil cases
58,293
218,000

Civil rights
296
18,793

Prisoner petitions
1,020
42,630

Social Security
537
7,439

SOURCES: *Annual Report of the Director of the Administrative Office of the United States Courts,* 1975, Table 17. Updated by author.

Congress and the Courts

Congress has a number of ways of checking the judiciary. It can gradually alter the composition of the judiciary by the kinds of appointments that the Senate is willing to confirm, or it can impeach judges that it does not like. (Fifteen federal judges have been the object of impeachment proceedings in our history, and nine others have resigned when such proceedings seemed likely. Of the fifteen who were impeached, seven were acquitted; four convicted, and one resigned. The most recent convictions were those of Alcee Hastings of Florida and Walter Nixon of Mississippi, both in 1989.)[56] In practice, however, confirmation and impeachment proceedings do not make much of an impact on the federal courts because simple policy disagreements are not generally regarded as adequate grounds for voting against a

The Supreme Court

Supreme Court justice who served the longest	*William O. Douglas: 36 years (1939–1975)*
Only Supreme Court justice to run for president	*Charles Evans Hughes (resigned from Court in 1916 to seek presidency; lost to Woodrow Wilson)*
Only president to become Supreme Court justice	*William Howard Taft (president, 1909–1913; chief justice of the United States, 1921–1930)*
First Catholic Supreme Court justice	*Roger B. Taney (1836–1864)*
First Jewish Supreme Court justice	*Louis Brandeis (1916–1939)*
First black Supreme Court justice	*Thurgood Marshall (1967–1991)*
First woman Supreme Court justice	*Sandra Day O'Connor (1981 to present)*
Only Supreme Court justice to have been impeached	*Samuel Chase (impeached by House in 1804; acquitted by Senate)*
Only Supreme Court justice whose grandson also served on the Court	*John Harlan (1877–1911), whose grandson, John Harlan, served from 1954 to 1971.*

Sandra Day O'Connor

Charles Evans Hughes

judicial nominee or for starting an impeachment effort.

Congress can alter the number of judges, though; and by increasing the number sharply, it can give a president a chance to appoint judges to his liking. A "court-packing" plan was proposed (unsuccessfully) by Franklin Roosevelt in 1937, specifically to change the political persuasion of the Supreme Court. In 1978 Congress passed a bill creating 152 new federal district and appellate judges to help ease the work load. This bill gave President Carter a chance to appoint over 40 percent of the federal bench. In 1984 an additional eighty-four judgeships were created; by 1988 President Reagan had appointed about half of all federal judges. In 1990 an additional seventy-two judges were authorized.

During and after the Civil War, Congress may have been trying to influence Supreme Court decisions when it changed the size of the Court three times in six years (raising it from nine to ten in 1863, lowering it again from ten to seven in 1866, and raising it again from seven to nine in 1869).

Congress and the states can also undo a Supreme Court decision interpreting the Constitution by amending that document. This happens, but rarely: the Eleventh Amendment was ratified to prevent a citizen from suing a state in federal court; the Thirteenth, Fourteenth, and Fifteenth were ratified to undo the *Dred Scott* decision regarding slavery; the Sixteenth was added to make it constitutional for Congress to pass an income tax; and the Twenty-sixth to give the vote to eighteen-year-olds in state elections. In 1983 a proposed amendment to authorize prayer in public schools failed to get the necesary two-thirds vote of the Senate.

On over thirty occasions Congress has merely repassed a law that the Court had declared unconstitutional. In one case a bill to aid farmers, voided in 1935, was accepted by the Court in slightly revised form three years later.[57] (In the meantime, of course, the Court had changed its collective mind about the New Deal.)

One of the most powerful potential sources of control over the federal courts, however, is the authority of Congress to decide what the entire jurisdiction of the lower courts and the appellate jurisdiction of the Supreme Court shall be. In theory Congress could prevent matters on which it did not want federal courts to act from ever coming before the courts. In 1868 just this happened. A Mississippi newspaper editor named McCardle was jailed by federal military authorities who had occupied the defeated South. McCardle asked the federal district court for a writ of habeas corpus to get him out of custody; when the district court rejected his plea, he appealed to the Supreme Court. Congress at that time was fearful that the Court might find the laws on which its Reconstruction policy was based (and under which McCardle was in jail) unconstitutional. To prevent that from happening, it passed a bill withdrawing from the Supreme Court appellate jurisdiction in cases of this sort. The Court conceded that Congress could do this and thus dismissed the case because it no longer had jurisdiction.[58]

Congress has threatened to withdraw jurisdiction on other occasions, and the mere existence of the threat may have influenced the nature of Court decisions. In the 1950s, for example, congressional opinion was hostile to Court decisions in the field of civil liberties and civil rights, and legislation was proposed that would have curtailed the Court's jurisdiction in these areas. It did not pass, but the Court may have allowed the threat to temper its decisions.[59] On the other hand, as congressional resistance to the Roosevelt court-packing plan shows, the Supreme Court enjoys a good deal of prestige in the nation, even among people who disagree with some of its decisions, and so passing laws that would frontally attack it would not be easy except perhaps in times of national crisis.

Furthermore laws narrowing jurisdiction or restricting the kinds of remedies that a court can impose are often blunt instruments that might not achieve the purposes of their proponents. Suppose that you, as a member of Congress, would like to prevent the federal courts from ordering schoolchildren to be bused for the purpose of achieving racial balance in the schools. If you denied the Supreme Court appellate jurisdiction in this matter, you would leave the lower federal courts and all state courts free to do as they wish, and many of them would go on ordering busing. If you wanted to attack that problem, you could propose a law that would deny to all federal courts the right to order busing as a remedy for racial imbalance. But the courts would still be free to order busing (and of course a lot of busing goes on even without court orders), provided that they did not say that it was for the purpose of achieving racial bal-

Police escorting black students being bused to a once all-white high school in Boston.

ance. (It could be for the purpose of "facilitating desegregation" or making possible "redistricting.") Naturally you could always make it illegal for children to enter a school bus for any reason, but then many children would not be able to get to school at all. Finally, the Supreme Court might well decide that if busing is essential to achieve a constitutional right, then any congressional law prohibiting such busing would itself be unconstitutional. Trying to think through how *that* dilemma would be resolved is like trying to visualize two kangaroos simultaneously jumping into each other's pouches.

Public Opinion and the Courts

Though not elected, judges read the same newspapers as members of Congress, and thus they, too, are aware of public opinion, especially elite opinion. Though it may be going too far to say that the

Supreme Court follows the election returns, it is nonetheless true that the Court is sensitive to certain bodies of opinion, especially of those elites—liberal or conservative—to which its members happen to be attuned. The justices will recall cases when, by defying opinion frontally, their predecessors very nearly destroyed the legitimacy of the Court itself. This was the case with the *Dred Scott* decision, which infuriated the North and was widely disobeyed. No such crisis exists today, but it is altogether possible that changing political moods affect the kinds of remedies that judges will think appropriate.

Opinion not only restrains the courts; it may also energize them. The most activist periods in Supreme Court history have coincided with times when the political system was undergoing profound and lasting changes. The assertion by the Supreme Court, under John Marshall's leadership, of the principles of national supremacy and judicial review occurred at the time when the Jeffersonian Republicans were coming to power and their opponents, the Federalists, were collapsing as an organized party. The proslavery decisions of the Taney Court came when the nation was so divided along sectional and ideological lines as to make almost any Court decision on

this matter unpopular. Supreme Court review of economic regulation in the 1890s and 1900s came at a time when the political parties were realigning and the Republicans were acquiring dominance that was to last for several decades. The Court decisions of the 1930s corresponded to another period of partisan realignment. (The meaning of a realigning election was discussed in Chapter 8.)

Since 1966 pollsters have been measuring how much confidence the public has in the Supreme Court. The results are shown in Figure 14.3. The percentage of people saying that they had a "great deal of confidence" in the Court fell sharply from 1966 to 1971, went up again around 1974, seesawed up and down for a few years, and then rose again after 1982. These movements seem to reflect the public's reaction not only to what the Court does but to what the government as a whole is doing. The decline in popular support in the late 1960s was probably the result of a spate of controversial Court decisions enlarging the rights of the accused; the upturn in the mid-1970s was probably caused by the Watergate scandal, an episode that simultaneously discredited the presidency and boosted the stock of those institutions (such as the courts) that seemed to be checking the

FIGURE 14.3 Patterns of Public Confidence in the Court, 1974–1994

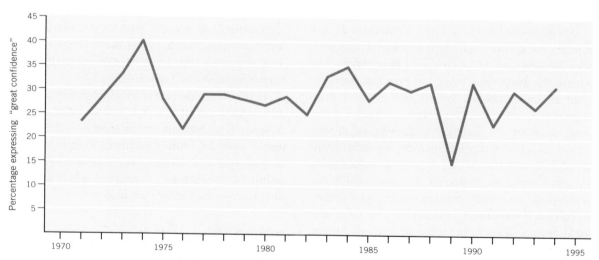

SOURCES: For 1966–1984: Gregory A. Caldeira, "Neither the Purse Nor the Sword: Dynamics of Public Confidence in the Supreme Court," *American Political Science Review* 80 (1988): 1213; for 1987–1991: *The Gallup Poll: Public Opinion 1991* (Wilmington, Del.: Scholarly Resources, Inc., 1992), 213. Reprinted by permission.

abuses of the White House. The upturn in the 1980s may reflect a general (albeit brief) restoration of public confidence in government.[60]

Though popular support is now lower for the Supreme Court than it was in the mid-1960s, this decline has so far not resulted in any legal checks being placed on it. In the 1970s and 1980s several bills were introduced in Congress that would have restricted the jurisdiction of federal courts over busing for purposes of racial integration or would have altered the Supreme Court's decisions regarding school prayer and abortion. None passed.

The changes that have occurred in the Court have been caused by changes in its personnel. Presidents Nixon and Reagan attempted to produce a less-activist Court by appointing justices who were more inclined to be strict constructionists and conservatives. To some extent they succeeded: Justices Kennedy, O'Connor, Rehnquist, and Scalia were certainly less inclined than Justice Thurgood Marshall to find new rights in the Constitution or to overturn the decisions of state legislatures. But there has as yet been no wholesale retreat from the positions staked out by the Warren Court. A Nixon appointee, Justice Blackmun, wrote the decision making antiabortion laws unconstitutional; and another Nixon appointee, Chief Justice Burger, wrote the opinion upholding court-ordered school busing to achieve racial integration (see Chapter 19). A Reagan appointee, Justice O'Connor, voted to uphold a right to an abortion. The Supreme Court has become somewhat less willing to impose restraints on police practices, and it has not blocked the use of the death penalty. But in general the major features of Court activism and liberalism during the Warren years—school integration, sharper limits on police practice, greater freedom of expression—have remained intact.

The reasons for the growth in court activism are clear. One is the sheer growth in the size and scope of government as a whole. The courts have come to play a larger role in our lives because Congress, the bureaucracy, and the president have come to play larger ones. In 1890 hardly anybody would have thought of asking the Congress—much less the courts—to make rules governing the participation of women in college sports or the district boundaries of state legislatures. Today such rules are commonplace, and the courts are inevitably drawn into interpreting them.

The other reason for increased activism is the acceptance by a large number of judges, conservative as well as liberal, of the legislative, or activist, view of the function of the courts. If courts once existed solely to "settle disputes," today they also exist in the eyes of their members to "solve problems."

SUMMARY

An independent judiciary with the power of judicial review—the right to decide the constitutionality of acts of Congress, the executive branch, and state governments—can be a potent political force in American life. That influence has been realized from the earliest days of the nation when Marshall and Taney put the Supreme Court at the center of the most important issues of the time. From 1787 to 1865 the Supreme Court was preoccupied with the establishment of national supremacy. From 1865 to 1937 it struggled with defining the scope of political power over the economy. In the present era it has sought to expand personal liberties.

The scope of the courts' political influence has increasingly widened as various groups and interests have acquired access to the courts, as the judges serving on them have developed a more activist stance, and as Congress has passed more laws containing vague or equivocal language. Whereas in other political arenas (the electorate, Congress, the bureaucracy) the influence of contending groups is largely dependent on their size, intensity, prestige, and political resources, the influence of contending groups before the courts depends chiefly on their arguments and the attitudes of the judges.

Though the Supreme Court is the pinnacle of the federal judiciary, most decisions, including many important ones, are made by the twelve courts of appeals and the ninety-four district courts. The Supreme Court can control its own work load by deciding when to grant certiorari. It has become easier for citizens and groups to gain access to the federal courts (through class-action suits, by amicus curiae briefs, by laws that require government agencies to pay legal fees, and because of the activities of private groups such as the NAACP and the ACLU).

At the same time, the courts have widened the reach of their decisions by issuing orders that cover whole classes of citizens or affect the management of major public and private institutions. However, the courts can overstep the bounds of their authority and bring upon themselves a counterattack from both public opinion and Congress. Congress has the right to control much of the courts' jurisdiction, but it rarely does so. As a result the ability of judges to make law is only infrequently challenged directly.

KEY TERMS

judicial review   *p. 417*

strict-constructionist approach   *p. 418*

activist approach   *p. 418*

constitutional court   *p. 424*

district courts   *p. 425*

courts of appeals   *p. 425*

legislative court   *p. 425*

litmus test   *p. 426*

federal-question cases   *p. 427*

diversity cases   *p. 427*

civil law   *p. 430*

criminal law   *p. 430*

writ of certiorari   *p. 430*

in forma pauperis   *p. 431*

fee shifting   *p. 432*

plaintiff   *p. 432*

standing   *p. 432*

sovereign immunity   *p. 432*

class-action suit   *p. 433*

brief   *p. 434*

amicus curiae   *p. 435*

per curiam opinion   *p. 436*

opinion of the Court   *p. 436*

concurring opinion   *p. 436*

dissenting opinion   *p. 436*

stare decisis   *p. 438*

political question   *p. 438*

remedy   *p. 439*

SUGGESTED READINGS

Abraham, Henry J. *The Judicial Process.* 6th ed. New York: Oxford University Press, 1993. An excellent, comprehensive survey of how the federal courts are organized and function.

Cardozo, Benjamin N. *The Nature of the Judicial Process.* New Haven, Conn.: Yale University Press, 1921. Important statement of how judges make decisions, by a former Supreme Court justice.

Carp, Robert A., and Ronald Stidham. *The Federal Courts.* Washington, D.C.: Congressional Quarterly Press, 1985. Excellent summary of the workings of the lower federal courts.

Ely, John Hart. *Democracy and Distrust.* Cambridge, Mass.: Harvard University Press, 1980. Effort to create a theory of judicial review that is neither strict-constructionist nor activist.

Hall, Kermit L., ed. *The Oxford Companion to the Supreme Court of the United States.* New York: Oxford University Press, 1992. Everything you ever wanted to know about the Supreme Court, its justices, and its major decisions, arranged in more than one thousand alphabetical entries.

Lasser, William. *The Limits of Judicial Power.* Chapel Hill, N.C.: University of North Carolina Press, 1988. Shows how the Court through history has withstood the political storms created by its more controversial decisions.

Lewis, Anthony. *Gideon's Trumpet.* New York: Random House, 1964. Fascinating account of how a pauper in jail persuaded the Supreme Court to change the rules governing criminal trials.

McCloskey, Robert G. *The American Supreme Court.* Chicago: University of Chicago Press, 1960. Superb brief history of the Court and its role in American politics and thought.

O'Brien, David M. *Storm Center: The Supreme Court and American Politics.* New York: Norton, 1986. Insightful survey of the workings of the Supreme Court.

Rabkin, Jeremy. *Judicial Compulsions.* New York: Basic Books, 1989. Explains (and argues against) the extensive Court intervention in the work of administrative agencies.

Wolfe, Christopher. *The Rise of Modern Judicial Review.* New York: Basic Books, 1986. An excellent history of judicial review from 1787 to the present.

PART FOUR

The Politics of Public Policy

"In the extended republic of the United States, and among the great variety of interests, parties, and sects which it embraces, a coalition of a majority of the whole society could seldom take place on any other principles than those of justice and the general good."

— FEDERALIST NO. 51

The Policy-Making Process

➤ Deciding what goes on the political agenda

➤ A model for explaining the politics of different policy issues

➤ Perceived costs and benefits of programs

➤ The case of business regulation

➤ Perception of policy costs and benefits

I f our political system handled all issues in the same way, this study of American government would be at an end. Now that we have seen how Congress, the presidency, the courts, the parties, the mass media, and other interest groups operate, we should be able to explain how policies get made (or not made). Some observers do argue that the system always operates more or less the same way—to serve corporate interests (the Marxist view), to manage conflict among organized groups (the pluralist view), to sustain the dominance of a pervasive bureaucracy (the Weberian view), and so on. In this part we shall look at how policies are actually made to see whether any of these generalizations are correct.

Consider some outcomes that need to be explained if we are to understand the political influence wielded by just one kind of institution—the business corporation. Certain oil companies were once able to persuade the government to restrict sharply the amount of foreign oil imported into the United States, to allow preferential tax treatment of their incomes, and to permit them to drill for new oil about anywhere that they liked. Today the restrictions on foreign oil imports have ended, the tax break that the oil companies enjoy has been reduced considerably (though it still exists), and their freedom to drill in certain places, particularly offshore, has been restricted.

Automobile manufacturers once faced virtually no federal controls on the product that they manufactured; now they face many. In the past some corporations have been regulated in ways that have increased their profitability (the airlines); others in ways that have reduced their profitability (the railroads); and still others in ways that may not have affected their profits much one way or another (electric utilities). These outcomes of government action or inaction are complicated. To understand why they happen, we need some theory of policy-making. This chapter will provide one; subsequent chapters will apply it.

Setting the Agenda

The most important decision that affects policy-making is also the least noticed: deciding what to make policy *about* or, in the language of political science, deciding what belongs on the **political agenda.** We take for granted that politics is about certain familiar issues such as taxes, energy, welfare, and civil rights. We forget that there is nothing inevitable about these issues—rather than some other ones—being on our agenda. At one time it was unconstitutional for the federal government to levy income taxes; energy was a nonissue because everybody (or at least everybody who could chop down trees for a fireplace) had enough; welfare was something for cities and towns to handle; and civil rights was supposed to be a matter of private choice rather than government action. Until the 1930s the national political agenda was quite short, and even in the 1950s many people would have been astonished or upset to be told that the federal government was supposed to worry about the environment, consumerism, or civil rights.

"He who decides what politics is about runs the country."[1] This is a statement of profound significance, though it exaggerates the extent to which somebody—some person—actually "decides" what politics is all about. The statement correctly suggests that at any given time certain shared beliefs determine what is legitimate (proper, right) for the government to do. This legitimacy is affected by several forces: shared political values (if many people believe that poverty is the result of individual failure rather than social forces, then there is no reason for a government program to combat poverty), the weight of custom and tradition (people will usually accept what the government has customarily done even if they are leery of what it proposes to do), the impact of events (wars and depressions alter our sense of the proper role of government), and changes in the way in which political elites think and talk about politics.

The Legitimate Scope of Government Action

Because many people believe that whatever the government now does, it ought to continue doing, and because changes in attitudes and the impact of events tend to increase the number of things that government does, the scope of legitimate government action is always getting larger. As a result the scope of what it is illegitimate for government to do steadily gets smaller. This means that today we hear far fewer debates about the legitimacy of a proposed government policy than we heard in the 1920s or 1930s. The existence of "big government" is sustained by these expanded beliefs about legitimacy and is not the consequence of some sinister power grab by politicians or bureaucrats. When President Gerald Ford, a Republican, ran for election in 1976, a favorite slogan of his was that a government big enough to give you everything that you want is also big enough to take away everything that you have. No doubt he thought that he was criticizing liberal Democrats. But it was his immediate predecessor, President Nixon, also a Republican, who had imposed peacetime wage-and-price controls and proposed a guaranteed annual income for every family, working or not working. It was another Republican president, Dwight Eisenhower, who had sent federal troops to Little Rock, Arkansas, to enforce a school-desegregation order. And it was yet another Republican president, Ronald Reagan, who was in office when federal payments to farmers grew to be six times larger than they had been in the 1970s. For better or worse the expansion of government has been the result, fundamentally, of a nonpartisan process.

Popular views on the legitimate scope of government action, and thus on the kinds of issues that ought to be on the political agenda, are changed by the impact of events. During wartime, especially during a war in which the United States has been attacked, the people expect the government to do whatever is necessary to win, whether or not such actions are clearly authorized by the Constitution. (As we saw in Chapter 13, the federal bureaucracy enjoys its most rapid growth in wartime.) A depression, such as the one that began in 1929, also leads people to expect the government to do something. As we shall see in Chapter 17, public opinion favored federal action to deal with the problems of the unemployed, the elderly, and the poor well in advance of the actual decisions of the government to take action. A coal-mine disaster leads to an enlarged role for the government in promoting mine safety. A series of airplane hijackings leads to a change in public opinion so great that what once would have been unthinkable—requiring all passengers at airports to be searched before boarding their flights—becomes routine. Most citizens probably oppose rationing; but let there be a sharp increase in gasoline prices and the demands for rationing become loud.

But sometimes, often dramatically, the government enlarges its agenda of policy issues without any crisis or widespread public demand. This may happen even at a time when the conditions at which a policy is directed are improving. There was no public demand for government action to make automobiles safer before 1966, when a law was passed imposing safety standards on cars. Though the number of auto fatalities (per 100 million miles driven) had gone up slightly just before the law was passed, the long-term trend in highway deaths had been more or less steadily downward. The Occupational Safety and Health Act was passed in 1970 at a time when the number of industrial deaths (per 100,000 workers) had been steadily dropping for almost twenty years.[2] Programs to combat urban poverty and unemployment were adopted in the mid-1960s at a time when the number of persons, black as well as white, living below the poverty line was declining, and when the adult unemployment rate—for blacks as well as whites—was lower than it had been at any time in the preceding ten years.[3]

It is not easy to explain why the government adds new issues to its agenda and adopts new programs when there is little public demand and when, in fact, there has been an improvement in the conditions to which the policies are addressed. In general the explanation may be found in the behavior of groups, the workings of institutions, and the opinions of political elites.

An oil spill on a beach is one event that changed the political agenda.

Groups Many policies are the result of small groups of people enlarging the scope of government by their demands. Sometimes these are organized interests (for example, corporations or unions); sometimes they are intense but unorganized groups (urban minorities). The organized groups often work quietly, behind the scenes; the intense, unorganized ones may take their causes to the streets.

Organized labor favored a tough federal safety law governing factories and other workplaces not because it was unaware that factory conditions had been improving but because the standards by which union leaders and members judged working conditions had risen even faster. As people became better

off, conditions that once were thought normal suddenly became intolerable. When Alexis de Tocqueville sought to explain the French Revolution, he observed that citizens are most restless and easily aroused not when they are living in abject poverty or under grinding repression but when they have started to become better off.[4] Social scientists sometimes refer to this as a sense of "relative deprivation."

On occasion a group expresses in violent ways its dissatisfaction with what it judges to be intolerable conditions. The black riots in American cities during the mid-1960s had a variety of causes, and people participated out of a variety of motives. For many, riots were a way of expressing pent-up anger at what they regarded as an unresponsive and unfair society. This sense of relative deprivation—of being worse off than one thinks one *ought* to be—helps explain why so large a proportion of the rioters were not uneducated, unemployed recent migrants to the city, but rather young men and women born in the North, educated in its schools, and employed in its factories.[5] Life under these conditions turned out to be not what they had come to expect or what they were prepared to tolerate.

The new demands of such groups need not result in an enlarged political agenda and do not when society and its governing institutions are confident of the rightness of the existing state of affairs. Unions could have been voted down on the occupational-safety bill; rioting blacks could have been jailed and ignored. At one time exactly this would have happened. But society itself had changed: many people who were not workers sympathized with the plight of the injured worker and distrusted the good intentions of business in this matter. Many whites felt that a constructive as well as a punitive response to the urban riots was required and thus urged the formation of commissions to study—and the passage of laws to deal with—the problems of inner-city life. These changes in the values and beliefs of people generally—or at least of people in key government positions—are an essential part of any explanation of why policies not demanded by public opinion nonetheless become part of the political agenda.

Institutions   Among the institutions whose influence on agenda-setting has become especially important are the courts, the bureaucracy, and the Senate.

The courts can make decisions that force the hand of the other branches of government. When in 1954 the Supreme Court ordered schools desegregated, Congress and the White House could no longer ignore the issue. Local resistance to implementing the order led President Eisenhower to send troops to Little Rock, Arkansas, despite his dislike for using force against local governments. When the Supreme Court in 1973 ruled that the states could not ban abortions during the first trimester of pregnancy, abortion suddenly became a national political issue. Right-to-life activists campaigned to reverse the Court decision or, failing that, to prevent federal funds from being used to pay for abortions. Pro-

choice activists fought to prevent the Court from changing its mind and to get federal funding for abortions. In these and many other cases the courts act like trip-wires: when activated, they set off a chain reaction of events that alters the political agenda and creates a new constellation of political forces.

The bureaucracy has acquired a new significance in American politics not simply because of its size or power but also because it is now a source of political innovation. At one time the federal government *reacted* to events in society and to demands from segments of society; ordinarily it did not itself propose changes and new ideas. Today the bureaucracy is so large, and includes within it so great a variety of experts and advocates, that it becomes a *source* of policy proposals as well as an implementer of those that become law. Daniel Patrick Moynihan called this the "professionalization of reform," by which he meant, in part, that the government bureaucracy had begun to think up problems for government to solve rather than simply to respond to the problems identified by others.[6] In the 1930s many of the key elements of the New Deal—Social Security, unemployment compensation, public housing, old-age benefits—were ideas devised by nongovernment experts and intellectuals here and abroad and then, as the crisis of the depression deepened, taken up by the federal government. In the 1960s, by contrast, most of the measures that became known as part of Lyndon Johnson's "Great Society"—federal aid to education, manpower development and training, Medicare and Medicaid, the "War on Poverty," the "safe-streets" act providing federal aid to local law-enforcement agencies—were developed, designed, and advocated by government officials, bureaucrats, and their political allies.

Chief among these political allies are United States senators and their staffs. Once the Senate was best described as a club that moved slowly, debated endlessly, and resisted, under the leadership of conservative southern Democrats, the plans of liberal presidents. With the collapse of the one-party South and the increase in the number of liberal activist senators, the Senate became in the 1960s an incubator for developing new policies and building national constituencies.[7] As the Senate became more conservative in the 1980s, it retained the initiative, but now on behalf of reversing some of the changes wrought earlier. The Senate has thereby become one of the sources of political change rather than, as the Founders intended, a balance wheel designed to moderate change.[8] That senators are tempted to run for president magnifies this tendency. When senators such as Edward M. Kennedy, George McGovern, Robert Dole, Gary Hart, Edmund Muskie, Joseph Biden, Albert Gore, and Paul Simon decide to try for the presidency, they have an incentive to seek out new issues and raise new proposals as a way of attracting attention.

Media   Finally, the national press can either help place new matters on the agenda or publicize those matters placed there by others. There was a close correlation between the political attention given in the Senate to proposals for new safety standards for industry, coal mines, and automobiles and the amount of space devoted to these questions in the pages of the *New York Times*. Newspaper interest in the matter, low before the issue was placed on the agenda, peaked at about the time that the bill was passed.[9] It is hard, of course, to decide which is cause and which effect. The press may have stimulated congressional interest in the matter or merely reported on what Congress had already decided to pursue. Nonetheless the press must choose which of thousands of proposals it will cover. The beliefs of editors and reporters led it to select the safety issue. In later chapters we shall discuss the kinds of issues in which the national press is important.

In short the political agenda can change because of changes in popular attitudes, elite interest, critical events, or government actions. An overly simple but essentially correct generalization might be this: popular attitudes usually change slowly, often in response to critical events; elite attitudes and government actions are more volatile and interdependent: they change more quickly, often in response to each other.

Making a Decision

Once an issue is on the political agenda, its nature affects the kind of politicking that ensues. Some issues provoke intense interest-group conflict; others allow one group to prevail almost unchallenged. Some

A crisis in the "Great Society": President Lyndon Johnson conferred with some of his advisers—Cyrus Vance (seated, right) and Robert S. McNamara (standing, right)—during the ghetto riots in Detroit in 1967.

issues involve ideological appeals to broad national constituencies; others involve quiet bargaining in congressional offices. We all know that private groups try to influence government policies; we often forget that the nature of the issues with which government is dealing influences the kinds of groups that become politically active.

One way to understand how an issue affects the distribution of political power among groups and institutions is to examine what appear to be the costs and benefits of the proposed policy. The **cost** is any burden, monetary or nonmonetary, that some people must bear, or think that they must bear, if the policy is adopted. The costs of a government spending program are the taxes that it entails; the costs of a school-desegregation plan may include the need to have children bused to schools away from home; the cost of a foreign-policy initiative may be the increased chance of having the nation drawn into war. The **benefit** is any satisfaction, monetary or nonmonetary, that people believe that they will enjoy if the policy is adopted. The benefits of a government spending program are the payments, subsidies, or contracts received by some people; the benefits of a school-desegregation plan include any improvement in educational opportunity, attainment, or motivation; the benefits of a foreign-policy initiative may include the enhanced security of the nation, the protection of a valued ally, or the vindication of some important principle such as human rights.

Two aspects of these costs and benefits should be borne in mind. First, it is the *perception* of costs and benefits that affects politics. People may think that the cost of an auto-emission-control system is paid by the manufacturer when it is actually passed on to the consumer in the form of higher prices and reduced performance. Political conflict over pollution control will take one form when people think that Ford and GM pay the costs and another when they think that the consumers pay.

Second, people take into account not only who benefits but whether it is *legitimate* for that group to benefit. When programs providing financial assistance to women with dependent children were first developed in the early part of this century, they were relatively noncontroversial because people saw the money as going to widows and orphans who deserved such aid. Later on giving aid to mothers with dependent children became controversial because some people now perceived the recipients not as deserving widows but as sexually loose women who had never married. Whatever the truth of the matter, the program had lost some of its legitimacy because the

beneficiaries were no longer seen as "deserving." By the same token, groups once thought undeserving, such as men out of work, were later thought to be entitled to aid, and thus the unemployment-compensation program acquired a legitimacy that it once lacked.

Politics is in large measure a process of raising and settling disputes over who *will* benefit or pay for a program and who *ought* to benefit or pay. Since beliefs about the results of a program and the rightness of those results are matters of opinion, it is evident that ideas are at least as important as interests in shaping politics. In recent years ideas have become especially important with the rise of issues whose consequences are largely intangible, such as abortion, school prayer, and racial integration.

Though perceptions about costs and benefits change, most people most of the time prefer government programs that provide substantial benefits to them at low cost. This rather obvious fact can have important implications for how politics is carried out. In a political system based on some measure of popular rule, public officials have a strong incentive to offer programs that confer—or appear to confer—benefits on people with costs that are either small in amount, remote in time, or borne by "somebody else." Policies that seem to impose high, immediate costs in return for small or remote benefits will be avoided, or enacted with a minimum of publicity,

Highway safety was always a problem, but it did not become an issue on the national political agenda until after politicians and policy entrepreneurs found a way to dramatize it.

or proposed only in response to a real or apparent crisis.

Ordinarily no president would propose a policy that would immediately raise the cost of fuel even if he were convinced that future supplies of oil and gasoline are likely to be exhausted unless higher prices reduce current consumption. But when a crisis occurs, such as the Arab oil price increases beginning in 1973, it becomes possible for the president to offer such proposals—as in varying ways did Nixon, Ford, and Carter. Even then, however, people are reluctant to see the price of fuel go up, and thus many are led to dispute the president's claim that an emergency actually exists. Walter Mondale probably lost votes when he promised in 1984 that, if elected, he would raise taxes in order to cut the deficit.

These entirely human responses to the perceived costs and benefits of proposed policies can be organized into a simple theory of politics.[10] It is based on the observation that the costs and benefits of a policy may be *widely distributed* (spread over many, most, or even all citizens) or *narrowly concentrated* (limited to a relatively small number of citizens or to some identifiable, organized group). For instance, a widely distributed cost would include an income tax, a Social Security tax, or a high rate of crime; a widely distributed benefit might include retirement benefits for all citizens, clean air, national security, or low crime rates. Examples of narrowly concentrated costs include the expenditures by a factory to reduce its pollution, government regulations imposed on doctors and hospitals participating in the Medicare program, or restrictions on freedom of speech imposed on a dissident political group. Examples of narrowly concentrated benefits include subsidies to farmers or merchant ship companies, the enlarged freedom to speak and protest afforded a dissident group, or protection against competition given to an industry because of favorable government regulation.

The perceived distribution of costs and benefits shapes the *kinds of political coalitions that will form*— but it will not necessarily determine *who wins*. A given popular majority, interest group, client, or entrepreneur may win or lose depending on its influence and the temper of the times.

In the remainder of this chapter we shall describe the politics of four kinds of policies and then illustrate each kind with examples drawn from government efforts to regulate business.

Majoritarian Politics: Distributed Benefits, Distributed Costs

Some policies promise benefits to large numbers of people at a cost that large numbers of people will have to bear (see Figure 15.1). For example, almost everybody will sooner or later receive Social Security benefits, and almost everybody who works has to pay Social Security taxes. Similarly defending the nation against military attack benefits everyone, and every taxpayer contributes to its cost. If government-sponsored research to find cures for cancer and heart disease is successful, a large proportion of the citizenry will benefit from a program that all taxpayers have been obliged to support.

Such **majoritarian politics** are usually not dominated by pulling and hauling among rival interest groups; instead they involve making appeals to large blocs of voters and their representatives in hopes of finding a majority. The reason why interest groups are not so important in majoritarian politics is that, as we saw in Chapter 9, citizens rarely will have much incentive to join an interest group if the policy that such a group supports will benefit everybody, whether or not they are members of the group. This is the "free-rider" problem. Why join a Committee to Increase (or Decrease) the Defense Budget when what you personally contribute to that committee makes little difference in the outcome and when you will enjoy the benefits of more (or less) national defense even if you have stayed on the sidelines?

Majoritarian politics may be controversial, but the controversy is usually over matters of cost or

FIGURE 15.1 A Way of Classifying and Explaining the Politics of Different Policy Issues

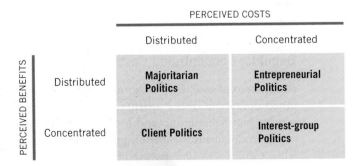

		PERCEIVED COSTS	
		Distributed	Concentrated
PERCEIVED BENEFITS	Distributed	**Majoritarian Politics**	**Entrepreneurial Politics**
	Concentrated	**Client Politics**	**Interest-group Politics**

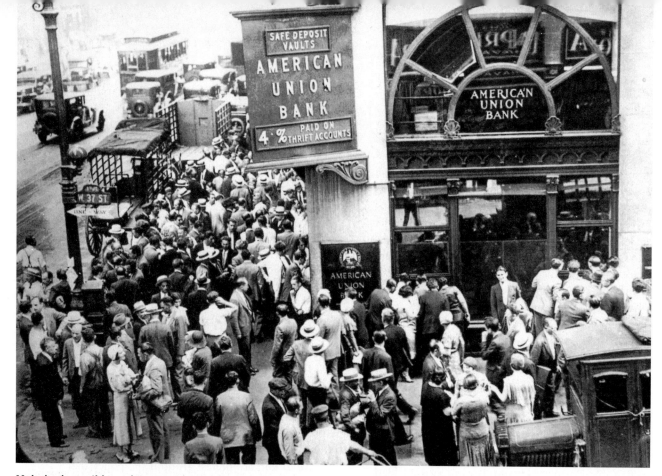

Majoritarian politics: widespread bank failures in the 1930s helped pave the way for laws regulating and insuring financial institutions.

ideology, not between rival interest groups. In the 1980s Congress passed three laws to reduce drug use. This was a majoritarian issue (that is, there were no interest groups active on behalf of drug dealers). The arguments were over such matters as the desirability of the death penalty for big traffickers. The military budget went up during the early 1980s and down in the late 1980s; the changes reflected different views on how much we should spend and the relationship between military spending and arms-control negotiations.

Interest-Group Politics: Concentrated Benefits, Concentrated Costs

In this second case, **interest-group politics,** a proposed policy will confer benefits on some relatively small, identifiable group and impose costs on another small, equally identifiable group. For example, when Congress in 1988 passed a bill requiring com-

panies to give sixty days' notice of a plant closing or a large-scale layoff, labor unions (whose members would benefit) backed the bill, and many business firms (which would pay the costs) opposed it.

Issues of this kind tend to be fought out by organized interest groups. Each side will be so powerfully affected by the outcome that it has a strong incentive to mobilize: union members who worry about layoffs will have a personal stake in favoring the notice bill; business leaders who fear government control of investment decisions will have an economic stake in opposing it.

Though many issues of this type involve money costs and money benefits, they can also involve intangible considerations. If the American Nazi party wants to march through a predominantly Jewish neighborhood carrying flags with swastikas on them, the community may organize itself to resist out of revulsion against the disgraceful treatment of Jews by Nazi Germany. Each side hires lawyers who fight the issue before the city council and in the courts.

Client Politics: Concentrated Benefits, Distributed Costs

With **client politics** some identifiable, often small group will benefit, but everybody—or at least a large part of society—will pay the costs. Because the benefits are concentrated, the group that is to receive those benefits has an incentive to organize and work to get them. But because the costs are widely distributed, affecting many people only slightly, those who pay the costs may be either unaware of any costs or indifferent to them because, per capita, they are so small.

This situation gives rise to client politics (sometimes called "clientele politics"); the beneficiary of the policy is the "client" of the government. For example, many farmers benefit substantially from agricultural price supports; each consumer, however, pays only a small amount of these subsidies in the form of higher taxes and higher food prices. Moreover the average consumer is unaware of how much higher his or her grocery bill is as a result of the government's paying certain farmers to produce less food than they otherwise would. In the same way, airlines for a long time benefited from the higher prices that they were able to charge on certain routes as a result of government regulations that restricted competition over prices. But the average passenger was either unaware that his or her costs were higher or did not think that the higher prices were worth making a fuss about.

Not all clients are economic interests. Localities can also benefit as clients when, for example, a city or county obtains a new dam, a better harbor, or an improved irrigation system. Some of these projects may be worthwhile, others may not; by custom, however, they are referred to as **pork-barrel projects.** Usually several pieces of "pork" are put into one barrel—that is, several projects are approved in a single piece of legislation, such as the "rivers and harbors" bill that Congress passes almost every year. Trading votes in this way attracts the support of members of Congress from each affected area; with enough projects a majority coalition is formed. This process is called **logrolling.**

Not every group that wants something from government at little cost to the average citizen will get it. Welfare recipients cost the typical taxpayer about

Logrolling

Among settlers in the American wilderness it was often necessary to cooperate in order to move logs off a piece of property that was to be farmed.

By the early nineteenth century *logrolling* had come to mean mutual aid among politicians, whereby one legislator supported another's pet project in return for the latter's support of his. Congressman B. F. Butler put it this way in 1870: "If you will vote for my interest, I will vote for yours. That is how these low tariffs are log rolled through."

Logrolling is the equivalent of the phrase, "You scratch my back and I'll scratch yours."

SOURCE: Adapted from William Safire, *Safire's Political Dictionary* (New York: Ballantine Books, 1978). Used by permission.

$190 per year; yet there is great resistance to increasing these benefits. The homeless have not organized themselves to get benefits; indeed most do not even vote. Yet benefits are being provided (albeit in modest amounts so far). These examples illustrate the importance of popular views as to the legitimacy of client claims as a factor in determining the success of client demands. As we shall see in Chapter 17, welfare recipients have never enjoyed much legitimacy in the public's eye, and so programs to increase their benefits have been hard to sell to Congress. The plight of the homeless, on the other hand, has aroused a good deal of sympathy and produced bipartisan agreement in 1987 on a bill providing emergency aid. Moreover that agreement seems to have persisted.

By the same token, groups can lose legitimacy that they once had. Farmers who grow tobacco once were supported simply because they were farmers, and thus both "deserving" and politically important. But when people began worrying about the health risks associated with using tobacco, a farmer who produced tobacco lost some legitimacy compared to one who produced corn or cotton. As a result it became harder to get votes for maintaining tobacco price supports and easier to slap higher taxes on cigarettes as well.

Entrepreneurial Politics: Distributed Benefits, Concentrated Costs

In **entrepreneurial politics** society as a whole or some large part of it benefits from a policy that imposes substantial costs on some small, identifiable segment of society. The antipollution and safety requirements for automobiles were proposed as ways of improving the health and well-being of all people at the expense (at least initially) of automobile manufacturers. Some members of Congress would like to reduce or end subsidies for farmers to cut the deficit or lower food prices. Others would like to abolish laws that require construction workers working on federal projects to be paid more than what the market would pay.

It is remarkable that policies of this sort are ever adopted, and in fact many are not. After all, the American political system creates many opportunities for checking and blocking the actions of others. The Founders deliberately arranged things so that it would be difficult to pass a new law; a determined minority therefore has an excellent chance of blocking a new policy. And any organized group that fears the loss of some privilege or the imposition of some burden will become a very determined minority indeed. The opponent has every incentive to work hard; the large group of prospective beneficiaries may be unconvinced of the benefit or regard it as too small to be worth fighting for.

Nonetheless policies with distributed benefits and concentrated costs are in fact adopted, and in recent decades with increasing frequency. A key ele-

ment in the adoption of such policies has been the work of people who act on behalf of the unorganized or indifferent majority. Such people, called **policy entrepreneurs,** are those both in and out of government who find ways of pulling together a legislative majority on behalf of interests that are not well represented in the government.

These policy entrepreneurs may or may not represent the interests and wishes of the public at large, but they do have the ability to dramatize an issue in a convincing manner. Ralph Nader is perhaps the best-known example of a policy entrepreneur or, as he might describe himself, a "consumer advocate." But there are other examples from both ends of the political spectrum, conservative as well as liberal.

Entrepreneurial politics can occur without the leadership of a policy entrepreneur if voters or legislators in large numbers suddenly become disgruntled by the high cost of some benefit that a group is receiving (or become convinced of the urgent need for a new policy to impose such costs). For example, voters may not care about government programs that benefit the oil industry when gasoline costs only 50 cents a gallon but care very much when the price rises to $2.00 a gallon, even if the government benefits had nothing to do with the price increase. By the same token, legislators may not worry much about the effects of smog in the air until a lot of people develop burning eyes and runny noses during an especially severe smog attack.

Likewise, most legislators did not worry very much about toxic or hazardous wastes until 1977 when the Love Canal dump site near Buffalo, New York, spilled some of its toxic waste into the backyards of an adjacent residential neighborhood and people were forced to leave their homes. Five years later, anyone who had forgotten about Love Canal was reminded of it when the town of Times Beach, Missouri, had to be permanently evacuated because it had become contaminated with the chemical dioxin. Only then did it become at all widely known that there were more than thirty thousand toxic waste sites nationwide that posed public safety risks. Although researchers have yet to find any conclusive evidence of health damage at either site, the Superfund program was born in 1980 of the political pressure that developed in the wake of these and other highly publicized tales of toxic waste dangers. Superfund was intended to force industries to clean up their own toxic waste sites. It also authorized the Environmental Protection Agency to act speedily, with or without cooperation from industries, in identifying and cleaning up any sites that posed a large or imminent danger.

Superfund has suffered a number of political and administrative problems and only 220 of the 1,300 sites initially targeted by the EPA actually have been cleaned up since the program went into effect.[11] However, Superfund is a good illustration of entrepreneurial politics in action. Special taxes on once largely unregulated oil and chemical companies have funded the program. Previously these companies enjoyed special tax privileges as beneficiaries of client politics; today they face special tax burdens as the targets of entrepreneurial politics.

For many reasons—including the enlarged political role of the media, the decentralization of Congress, and a change in the attitudes of many citizens—entrepreneurial politics has become more common and policy entrepreneurs have become more visible in recent decades.

The discovery of dioxin at Times Beach, Missouri, helped spur programs to clean up hazardous waste.

The Case of Business Regulation

Efforts by government to regulate business not only illustrate these four kinds of policy-making processes but also shed light on an issue that many people think is central to the study of politics—namely, the relationship between wealth and power.

To some observers the very existence of large corporations is a threat to popular rule. Economic power will dominate political power, they believe, for one or more of three reasons: first, because wealth can be used to buy influence; second, because politicians and business leaders have similar class backgrounds and thus similar beliefs about public policy; and third, because elected officials must defer to the preferences of business so as to induce corporations to keep the economy healthy and growing. Karl Marx, of course, proposed the most sweeping version of the view that economics controls politics; for him the state in a capitalist society was nothing more than the executive committee of the propertied classes.[12] But there are other non-Marxian or neo-Marxist versions of the same concern.[13]

To other observers politics, far from being subservient to economic power, is a threat to the very existence of a market economy and the values—economic growth, private property, personal freedom—that they believe such an economy protects. In this view politicians will find it in their interest, in their struggle for votes, to take the side of the nonbusiness majority against that of the business minority. The heads of large corporations, few in number but great in wealth, fear that they will be portrayed as a sinister elite on whom politicians can blame war, inflation, unemployment, and pollution. Defenders of business worry that corporations will be taxed excessively to pay for social programs that in turn will produce more votes for politicians. Just as bad, in this view, is the tendency of universities (on which corporations must rely for technical experts) to inculcate antibusiness values in their students.[14]

The theory of the policy-making process presented earlier in this chapter should suggest that neither of these two extreme views of business-government relations is entirely correct. These relations depend on many things, including the *kind* of policy being proposed. Instead of clenching our fists and shouting pro- or antibusiness slogans at each other, we should be able, after applying this theory to the available facts, to make more careful and exact statements of the following sort: "If certain conditions exist, then business-government relations will take certain forms."

Majoritarian Politics

Not all efforts to regulate business have pitted one group against another. From time to time laws are passed that reflect the views of a majority of voters that is neither imposing its will on a hostile business community nor acceding to the desires of a privileged industry.

Much of the antitrust legislation passed in this country, including the Sherman Act (1890) and parts of the Federal Trade Commission Act (1914) and the Clayton Act (1914), has been the result of majoritarian politics. Toward the end of the nineteenth century there arose a broadly based criticism of business monopolies (then called "trusts") and, to a lesser extent, of large corporations, whether or not they monopolized trade. The Grange, an organization of farmers, was especially outspoken in its criticism, and popular opinion generally—insofar as we can know it in an era without pollsters—seems to have been indignant about trusts and in favor of "trust busting." Newspaper editorials and magazine articles frequently dwelt on the problem.[15]

But though antitrust feeling was strong, it was also relatively unfocused: no single industry was the special target of this criticism (the Standard Oil Company came as close as any), and no specific regulation was proposed. In fact there was no general agreement about how to define the problem: for some it was monopoly; for others, sheer bigness; and for still others, the legal basis of the modern corporation. The bill proposed by Senator John Sherman did not clarify matters much: while it made it a crime to "restrain" or "monopolize" trade, it did not define these terms, nor did it create any new regulatory agency charged with enforcing the law.[16]

No doubt some large corporations worried about what all this would mean for them, but few felt sufficiently threatened to try very hard to defeat the bill. It passed the Senate by a voice vote and the House by a vote of 242 to 0.

Laws are not self-executing, and vague laws are especially likely to lie dormant unless political leaders work hard at bringing them to life. For the first decade or so after 1890, only one or two antitrust cases a year were filed in the courts. In 1904 President Theodore Roosevelt persuaded Congress to provide enough money to hire five full-time lawyers, and soon the number of prosecutions increased to about seven a year. Then in 1938 President Franklin Roosevelt appointed as head of the Antitrust Division of the Justice Department a vigorous lawyer named Thurman Arnold, who began bringing an average of fifty cases a year.[17] Today over four hundred lawyers in the division sift through complaints alleging monopolistic or other unfair business practices; though controversy exists over the kinds of cases that should be brought, there is no serious effort among either politicians or business leaders to abandon the commitment to a firm antitrust policy, the strongest such policy to be found in any industrial nation.

The antitrust laws were strengthened in 1914 by bills that created the Federal Trade Commission and

A policy entrepreneur in action: Howard Jarvis celebrating the passage of Proposition 13 to cut local property taxes in California (June 1978).

made (via the Clayton Act) certain specific practices, such as price discrimination, illegal. As with the earlier Sherman Act, the advocates of these measures had a variety of motives. Some proponents favored these laws because they would presumably help consumers (by preventing unfair business practices); other proponents supported them because they might help business (by protecting firms against certain tactics that competitors might employ). President Woodrow Wilson endorsed both of these bills and helped create a broad coalition on behalf of the legislation; the Federal Trade Commission Act and the Clayton Act passed Congress by lopsided majorities.[18]

As with the Sherman Act, there has been continual controversy about how these laws should be administered. But this controversy, like the debate over the initial passage of the laws, has not been dominated by interest groups.[19] The reason for the relative absence of interest-group activity is that these laws do not divide society into permanent and identifiable blocs of proponents and opponents. Any given business firm can be either helped or hurt by the enforcement of the antitrust laws. One year the XYZ Widget Company may be sued by the government to prevent it from unfairly advertising its widgets, and the next year the same XYZ Company may ask the government to prosecute its competitor for trying to drive XYZ out of business by selling widgets at prices below cost.

The amount of money that the federal government devotes to antitrust enforcement and the direction that those enforcement efforts take are determined more by the political ideology and personal convictions of the administration in power than by interest-group pressures. For example, in 1982 the Reagan administration decided that the benefits of trying to break up IBM were not worth the costs, and thus ended its antitrust prosecution of the giant computer firm. At the same time, it decided that it was desirable to break up American Telephone and Telegraph so that local phone companies became independent of AT&T while the long-distance services of AT&T would be required to compete with other companies.

In sum, as with most majoritarian policies, antitrust regulation tends to reflect broad philosophies of governance more than interest-group activity.

The Grange sought to warn farmers of the dangers of a railroad monopoly.

Interest-Group Politics

Organized interest groups are very powerful, however, when the regulatory policies confer benefits on a particular group and costs on another, equally distinct group.

In 1935 labor unions sought government protection for their right to organize, to bargain collectively with industry, and to compel workers in unionized industries to join the unions. Business firms opposed these plans. The struggle was fought out in Congress, where the unions won. The Wagner Act, passed that year, created the National Labor Relations Board (NLRB) to regulate the conduct of union organizing drives and to decide complaints of unfair labor practices brought by workers against management.

But the struggle was far from over. In 1947 management sought to reverse some of the gains won by unions by pressing for a law (the Taft-Hartley Act) that would make illegal certain union practices (such

Boycott

In 1880 an Irish landowner, Captain Boycott, was the target of an effort by the Irish Land League to get people to refuse to do business with him.

Today the term **boycott** refers to any concerted effort to get people to stop buying goods and services from a merchant or farmer in order to punish that person or to coerce him or her into changing policies.

The boycott has become a favored tool of interest-group politics. The Reverend Jesse Jackson has, in recent years, tried to get blacks to boycott certain businesses that had not, in his judgment, hired a sufficient number of black employees.

as the closed shop and secondary boycotts) and would authorize the president to obtain a court order blocking for up to eighty days any strike that imperiled the "national health or safety." Business won.

Business and labor fought round three in 1959 over a bill (the Landrum-Griffin Act) intended to prevent corruption in unions, to change the way in which organizing drives were carried out, and to prohibit certain kinds of strikes and picketing. Business won.

In each of these cases the struggle was highly publicized. The winners and losers were determined by the partisan composition of Congress (Republicans and southern Democrats tended to support

business, northern Democrats to support labor) and by the existence of economic conditions (a depression in 1935, revelations of labor racketeering in 1959) that affected opinion on the issue.

But the interest-group struggle did not end with the passage of the laws; it continued throughout their administration. The National Labor Relations Board, composed of five members appointed by the president, had to adjudicate countless disputes between labor and management over the interpretation of these laws. The losing party often appealed the NLRB decision to the courts, where the issue was fought out again. Moreover each president has sought to tilt the NLRB in one direction or another by whom he appoints to it. Democratic presidents favor labor and thus tend to appoint prounion board members; Republican presidents favor business and thus tend to appoint promanagement members. Since NLRB members serve five-year terms, a new president cannot immediately appoint all of the board's members, and so there is often a split on the board between two factions.

A similar pattern of interest-group influence is revealed by the history of the Occupational Safety and Health Act, passed in 1970. Labor unions wanted a strict bill with tough standards set by a single administrator; business organizations wanted a more flexible bill with standards set by a commission that would include some business representatives. After a long struggle labor won, and the Occupational Safety and Health Administration (OSHA), headed by a single administrator, was set up inside the Department of Labor.

As with the NLRB, conflict did not end with the passage of the law, and OSHA decisions were frequently appealed to the courts. The politics swirling about OSHA were all the more contentious because of the vast mandate of the agency: it is supposed to determine the safe limits for worker exposure to hundreds of chemicals and to inspect tens of thousands of workplaces to see whether they should be cited for violating any standards. During the Carter administration an OSHA administrator was appointed who was sympathetic to the labor view and thus set many standards and issued many citations; during the Reagan administration an administrator was selected who was admired by business because he set fewer standards and issued fewer citations.

Client Politics

Many people suppose that when government sets out to regulate business, the firms that are supposed to be regulated will in fact "capture" the agency that is supposed to do the regulating. But as we have already seen, certain kinds of policies—those that give rise to majoritarian and interest-group politics—do not usually lead to capture, because the agency either faces no well-organized, enduring opponent (as with majoritarian politics) or is caught in a cross fire of competing forces (as with interest-group politics).

But when a policy confers a benefit on one group at the expense of many other people, client politics arises and so agency "capture" is likely. More precisely nothing needs to be captured at all since the agency will have been created from the outset to serve the interests of the favored group. We sometimes think that regulations are always resisted. But a regulation need not be a burden; it can be a great benefit.

How this works can be seen close to home. State and city laws regulate the practice of law and medicine as well as a host of other occupations—barbers, beauticians, plumbers, dry cleaners, taxi drivers, and undertakers. These regulations are sometimes designed and always defended as ways of preventing fraud, malpractice, and safety hazards. But they also have the effect of restricting entry into the regulated occupation, thereby enabling its members to charge higher prices than they otherwise might.[20] Ordinarily citizens do not object to this, in part because they believe, rightly or wrongly, that the regulations in fact protect them and in part because the higher prices are spread over so many customers as to be unnoticed.

Much the same thing can be found at the national level. In the early 1930s the American dairy industry was suffering from rapidly declining prices for milk. As the farmers' incomes fell, many could no longer pay their bills and were forced out of business. Congress responded with the Agricultural Adjustment Act, which authorized an agency of the Department of Agriculture to regulate the milk industry. This agency, the Dairy Division of the Agricultural Marketing Service, would issue "market orders" that had the effect of preventing price competition among dairy farmers and thus kept the price of milk up. If this guaranteed minimum price leads to the production of more milk than people want to drink, then another part of the Agriculture Department—the Commodity Credit Corporation—stands ready to buy up the surplus with tax dollars.[21]

Consumers wind up paying more for milk than they otherwise would, but they have no way of knowing the difference between the regulated and unregulated price of milk (economists estimate that it amounts to between five and twenty-one cents per gallon).[22] Consumers have little incentive to organize politically to do much about it. The total cost, however, can be very high; in the 1980s it was $2 billion to $3 billion a year.

A similar system works with sugar. Sugar produced abroad, in countries such as Brazil and the Philippines, costs much less than sugar produced here, in states such as Louisiana. To keep the incomes

Client politics: to operate a New York taxi, the owner must have a medallion bolted to the hood. The number of medallions (and thus of taxis) is limited. This keeps competition down and prices up.

of U.S. sugar producers high, Congress decided to restrict the importation of cheap foreign sugar by imposing quotas. This costs the consumer money— maybe as much as $3 billion a year—but the extra cost per pound of sugar is not noticeable.[23]

From time to time various officials attempt to change the regulations that benefit a client group. But they must confront some sobering political facts. Dairy farmers are found scattered through scores of congressional districts; sugar-beet growers are concentrated in southern states that are important in any presidential election. Efforts have been made in Congress to cut milk subsidies and sugar quotas, but with only limited success.

Farmers are not the only group to enjoy a client relationship with a federal regulatory agency. Originally the Civil Aeronautics Board, established in 1938, regulated airlines in ways that prevented competition over prices and discouraged the creation of new airlines. (That has now changed.) The Federal Maritime Commission regulates the prices charged by American merchant ships engaged in international commerce in ways that tend to keep those prices higher than they would be in the absence of regulation.

Entrepreneurial Politics

During the 1960s and 1970s some two dozen consumer- and environmental-protection laws were passed, including laws that regulated the automobile industry, oil companies, toy manufacturers, poultry producers, the chemical industry, and pharmaceutical companies.*

When measures such as these become law, it is often because a policy entrepreneur has dramatized an issue, galvanized public opinion, and mobilized congressional support. Sometimes that entrepreneur is in the government (a senator or an outspoken bureaucrat); sometimes that entrepreneur is a private person (the best known, of course, is Ralph Nader). The motives of such entrepreneurs can be either self-serving or public-spirited; the policies that they embrace may be either good or bad. (Just because someone succeeds in regulating business does not mean that the public will necessarily benefit; by the same token just because business claims that a new regulation will be excessively costly does not mean that business will in fact have to pay those costs.)

An early example of a policy entrepreneur inside the government was Dr. Harvey Wiley, a chemist in the Department of Agriculture, who actively campaigned for what was to become the Pure Food and Drug Act of 1906. Later Senator Estes Kefauver held hearings that built support for the 1962 drug laws (and incidentally for his presidential bid), and Senator Edmund Muskie called attention to the need for air- and water-pollution-control legislation (and incidentally to his own 1972 presidential aspirations).

When a policy entrepreneur is outside the government, he or she will need a sympathetic ear within it. Occasionally the policy needs of the entrepreneur and the political needs of an elected official coincide. When Ralph Nader was walking the corridors of the Capitol looking for someone interested in auto safety, he found Senators Abraham Ribicoff and Warren Magnuson, who themselves were looking for an issue with which they could be identified.[24]

The task of the policy entrepreneur is made easier when a crisis or scandal focuses public attention on a problem. Upton Sinclair's book *The Jungle*[25] dramatized the frightful conditions in meat-packing plants at the turn of the century and helped pave the way for the Meat Inspection Act of 1906. The stock-market collapse of 1929 helped develop support for the Securities and Exchange Act. When some people who had taken a patent medicine (elixir of sulfanilamide) died as a result, the passage of the 1938 drug laws became easier. Oil spilled on the beaches of Santa Barbara, California, drew attention to problems addressed by the Water Quality Improvement Act of 1970.

The dramatic event need not be an actual crisis; in some cases a political scandal will do. Highway fatalities were not a matter of great concern to most citizens when Congress began considering the auto-safety act in 1965–1966, but support for the bill grew when it was revealed that General Motors had hired a private detective who made a clumsy effort to collect (or manufacture) gossip harmful to Ralph Nader, whose book *Unsafe at Any Speed* had criticized the safety of certain GM cars.

---

*The Motor Vehicle Air Pollution Control Act of 1965, the National Traffic and Motor Vehicle Safety Act of 1966, the Clean Air Act of 1970, the Water Quality Improvement Act of 1970, the Children's Protection and Toy Safety Act of 1969, the Wholesome Poultry Act of 1968, the Toxic Substances Control Act of 1976, and the 1962 amendments to the Pure Food and Drug Act.

Entrepreneurial politics: Upton Sinclair's book *The Jungle*, published in 1906, shocked readers about conditions in the meat-packing industry and helped bring about passage of the Meat Inspection Act of 1906.

In some cases no dramatic event at all is required for entrepreneurial politics to succeed. Most of the air- and water-pollution-control bills were passed despite the absence of any environmental catastrophe.[26] Support for such measures was developed by holding carefully planned committee hearings that were closely followed by the media. For example, by drawing attention to the profits of the pharmaceutical companies, Senator Kefauver was able to convince many people that these firms were insensitive to public needs. By drawing on information made available to him by environmentalists, Senator Muskie was able to capitalize on and help further a growing perception in the country during the early 1970s that nature was in danger.

Because political resistance must be overcome without the aid of a powerful economic interest group, policy entrepreneurs seeking to regulate an industry often adopt a moralistic tone, with their opponents portrayed as devils, their allies viewed with suspicion, and compromises fiercely resisted. When Senator Muskie was drafting an air-pollution bill, Ralph Nader issued a highly publicized report *attacking* Muskie, his nominal ally, for not being tough enough. This strategy forced Muskie—who wanted acclaim, not criticism, for his efforts—to revise the bill so that it imposed even more stringent standards.[27] Other allies of Nader, such as Dr. William

Haddon, Jr., and Joan Claybrook, got the same treatment when they later became administrators of the National Highway Traffic Safety Administration. They came under attack not only from the auto industry for designing rules that the companies thought were too strict but also from Nader for devising rules that he thought were not strict enough.

Once a policy entrepreneur manages to defeat an industry that is resisting regulation, he or she creates—at least for a while—a strong impetus for additional legislation of the same kind. A successful innovator produces imitators, in politics as in rock music. After the auto-safety law was passed in 1966, it became easier to pass a coal-mine-safety bill in 1969 and an occupational-safety-and-health bill in 1970.

The great risk faced by policy entrepreneurs is not that their hard-won legislative victories will later be reversed but that the agency created to do the regulating will be captured by the industry that it is supposed to regulate. The Food and Drug Administration (FDA), which regulates the pharmaceutical industry, fell victim during much of its history to precisely this kind of capture. Once the enthusiasm of its founders had waned and public attention had turned elsewhere, the FDA seemed to develop a cozy and rather uncritical attitude toward the drug companies. (In 1958 the head of the FDA received an award from the Pharmaceutical Manufacturers'

Association.)[28] In the mid-1960s, under the spur of renewed congressional and White House attention, the agency was revitalized. During the Reagan administration environmentalists worried that the leadership of the Environmental Protection Agency had been turned over to persons who were unduly sympathetic to polluters.

There are at least five reasons, however, why the newer consumer- and environmental-protection agencies may not be as vulnerable to capture as some critics contend. First, these agencies often enforce laws that impose specific standards in accordance with strict timetables, and so they have relatively little discretion. (The Environmental Protection Agency, for example, is required by law to reduce certain pollutants by a fixed percentage within a stated number of years.) Second, the newer agencies, unlike the FDA, usually regulate many different industries and so do not confront a single, unified opponent. The Occupational Safety and Health Administration, for example, deals with virtually every industry. Third, the very existence of these agencies has helped strengthen the hand of the "public-interest" lobbies that initially demanded their creation. Fourth, these lobbies can now call upon many sympathetic allies in the media who will attack agencies that are thought

to have a pro-business bias (witness the heavy criticism directed at James Watt, President Reagan's first secretary of the interior).

Finally, as explained in Chapter 14, it has become easier for groups to use the federal courts to put pressure on the regulatory agencies. These groups do not have to be large or broadly representative of the public; all they need are the services of one or two able lawyers. If the Environmental Protection Agency (EPA) issues a rule disliked by a chemical company, the company will promptly sue the EPA; if it issues a ruling that pleases the company, the Environmental Defense Fund or some similar group will sue.

Perceptions, Beliefs, Interests, and Values

The politics of business regulation provides a good illustration of the theory of policy-making offered in this book, but the reader should not be misled by a discussion of costs and benefits into thinking that all or even most of politics is about getting or losing money or that it is an easy matter to classify the costs and benefits of a policy and thus put it into the correct pigeonhole.

For one thing what constitutes a cost or a benefit is a matter of opinion, and opinions change. We have already said that it is the *perception* of costs and benefits that affects politics. If people think that laws requiring factories to install devices to remove from their smokestacks chemicals that contribute to acid rain can be implemented in ways that make the companies but not the consumers pay the bills, they will favor such measures, and the affected industries will oppose them. But if people believe that the cost of preventing acid rain will be borne by them—in the form of fewer jobs or higher prices—then these citizens may be less enthusiastic about such measures.

Some people favor having the government regulate the price of natural gas, and others oppose it. One reason for the conflict, obviously, is that people who use natural gas in their homes want to buy it cheaply, whereas people who work in the natural-gas industry want gas prices to go up so that they can earn more. Interests are clearly in conflict.

Yet some users may oppose regulating the price of gas because they believe that keeping the price of gas artificially low now will discourage exploration for new gas fields, thereby creating shortages—and

Agencies created by the use of entrepreneurial politics, such as those controlling the disposal of toxic wastes, must be wary of capture by the interests they are supposed to regulate.

The Savings-and-Loan Mess

Savings and loans (sometimes called "thrifts" or "S&Ls") were created primarily to help the average person borrow money to buy a house. Until the 1960s the president of an S&L followed the "3–6–3 Rule"; he paid depositors 3 percent interest, he lent money at 6 percent interest, and he played golf every day at three o'clock.

To prevent competition, the government limited by law the amount of interest an S&L could pay to a depositor. To protect the depositors, the federal government guaranteed their deposits up to some limit; in 1979, it was $40,000 per account.

This worked fine so long as interest rates did not go up very fast. But starting in the 1960s, other financial institutions began paying people higher interest on their savings than the S&Ls were allowed to pay. As a result people took their money out of the S&Ls and put them into money-market funds or certificates of deposit. The S&Ls were losing money, and so they went to Congress for help. They got it: they were allowed to pay higher interest in order to attract deposits.

But this competition for deposits only made matters worse. An S&L's income came from the interest it earned on the mortgage loans it had made. These mortgages, however, were often for twenty-five years. Many had been written in the low-interest days of the 1950s and paid the S&L only 6 percent. When the S&L began paying depositors 9 percent or 10 percent interest, it started to lose money. So the S&Ls went back to Congress and asked for permission to invest in things that would earn them a higher return than a home mortgage. Again Congress went along. Now the S&Ls could invest their depositors' money not just in home mortgages but in shopping malls, farmland, and high-yielding junk bonds. At the same time, federal regulators eased up on the S&Ls. Finally, Congress increased the size of the deposits guaranteed by the federal government from $40,000 to $100,000. One person or business could open accounts in any number of S&Ls and get the $100,000 guarantee on each.

Many S&Ls started paying sky-high interest rates to get new depositors. To earn enough money to pay this interest, they invested in high-risk deals—deals that would pay off handsomely *if* they worked out but would cause big losses if they didn't. Many didn't.

Why didn't the S&Ls worry that they might not make enough on their investments to pay off their depositors? Simple: the government had promised to pay off these depositors if anything went wrong. In effect the S&Ls were playing with free money. It was a recipe for disaster. Or if you were an unscrupulous S&L owner, it was party time.

Starting in the early 1980s, more and more S&Ls went bankrupt—they couldn't earn enough from their loans to pay what they owed their depositors. And so the federal government had to take over these failed thrifts and pay off the depositors. Soon there were hundreds of bankrupt thrifts, many concentrated in the Southwest. Some of these, such as Lincoln Savings and Loan, made big contributions to politicians to get them to persuade federal regulators not to declare these S&Ls insolvent. (The head of Lincoln, Charles Keating, was later convicted for mismanagement of his S&L, and the Senate Ethics Committee launched an investigation into the conduct of five senators whom Keating had approached.) But political influence could cover up the mess for only so long. As the federal regulators ran out of money with which to pay the depositors, Congress could no longer ignore the problem.

In 1989 Congress passed a law to bail out the system by paying $50 billion to close insolvent institutions and to pay off the depositors. (The law also reorganized and tightened federal regulation of the thrifts.) But by 1990 it was clear that much more money would be needed. It could cost each taxpayer $2,000 to end the mess—the biggest single bill ever presented to the American public.

---

much higher prices—in the future. Thus *beliefs* are also in conflict; in this case some users believe that it is more important to take the long view and worry about gas shortages ten years from now while others believe that what counts is how much you have to pay for natural gas today.

A political conflict is in large measure a struggle to make one definition of the costs and benefits of a proposal prevail over others; that is, it is a struggle to alter perceptions and beliefs. Material interests do play a part in all this: the more you stand to gain or lose in hard cash from a proposal, the harder it will be for someone else to change your mind about your position. But many, perhaps most, government proposals will not have an immediate, unambiguous impact on your pocketbook, and so your perceptions

Charles Keating's Lincoln Savings and Loan came to symbolize to many Americans the savings-and-loan debacle of the 1980s.

and beliefs about what will happen in the future become the prize for which political activists compete.

In that competition certain arguments enjoy a natural advantage over others. One might be called the here-and-now argument. What happens now or in the near future is more important to most people than what happens in the distant future. (Economists refer to this as the human tendency to "discount the future.") Thus most users of natural gas probably care more about present prices than future shortages, and so they will tend to favor price regulation today.

Another political tactic that enjoys a natural advantage might be called the cost argument. People seem to react more sharply to what they will lose if a policy is adopted than to what they may gain. Thus there will usually be strong opposition to putting a tax on imported oil even if the benefit gained will be to reduce our dependence on foreign oil.

Politicians know the value of the here-and-now and the cost arguments and so try to present their proposals in ways that take advantage of these sentiments. Regulations aimed at new drugs, for example, will emphasize the harm that will be prevented now from keeping dangerous drugs off the market, not the harm that may come later if life-saving drugs with some dangerous side effects are kept off the market. Plans to solve the problems of our Social Security system stress keeping intact the benefits now

received by people already retired, postponing into the future the tax increases necessary to pay for these benefits.

Policies are affected not only by our perceptions and beliefs about where our interests lie but also by our *values*—that is, by our conceptions of what is good for the country or for our community. Many whites, for example, want to see opportunities increased for blacks, not because such opportunities will make whites better off but because they think that it is the right thing to do. Many citizens worry about political conditions in Central America, not because they fear having to fight a war there or because they work for a company that does business there but because they wish a better life for people who live in that region and want them to be free of both right-wing and Marxist dictatorships. Some citizens oppose restrictions on the sale of obscene magazines and others favor those restrictions; neither group stands to benefit—those who oppose censorship usually don't plan to read the publications, and those who favor it would not thereby have their own lives improved—yet both groups often advocate their opposing views with great passion.

All this may seem obvious, but the reader should recall how often he or she assumes that people are only "looking out for themselves," and so politics is only about "who gets what." We all have a tendency to be a bit cynical about government—that is, to impute self-seeking motives to whoever is involved. Since there is plenty of self-interest in politics, this assumption is often a pretty good one. But following it blindly can lead us to ignore those cases in which ideas—beliefs, perceptions, and values—are the decisive forces in political conflict.

There are many examples of the power of ideas, even in conflicts that involve money interests. One—the Tax Reform Act of 1986—will be described in Chapter 16. Here, two other examples are noted: the deregulation of certain industries and the ending of certain taxpayer-financed agricultural subsidies.

Deregulation

In the 1980s several industries were deregulated over the objections of those industries. Airline fares were once set by the Civil Aeronautics Board. The airlines liked it that way—it kept competition down and prices up. But today airline fares are set by the mar-

Deregulation: Legislative Milestones

Act	Year	Key Elements
Railroad Revitalization and Regulatory Reform Act	1976	Allowed railroads limited rate-setting autonomy; was the first piece of deregulation legislation in the recent wave
Airline Deregulation Act	1978	Instructed the Civil Aeronautics Board to place maximum reliance on competition in its regulation of passenger service; provided that the board's authority over domestic fares and mergers end January 1, 1983, and that the CAB be abolished January 1, 1985
Staggers Rail Act	1980	Limited the Interstate Commerce Commission's jurisdiction over rates to those markets where railroads exercised market dominance; introduced price competition
Motor Carrier Act	1980	Allowed truckers to form subsidiaries and expand into additional regional markets; ended necessity of demonstrating public need; placed fewer restrictions on certain industry hauling practices; eased entry and introduced price competition
Depository Institution Deregulation and Monetary Control Act	1980	Allowed mutual savings banks to make commercial, corporate, and business loans equal to 5 percent of their assets; allowed payment of interest on demand deposits; removed interest-rate ceilings
Bus Deregulatory Reform Act	1982	Allowed companies to obtain operating authority without applying to ICC in many circumstances
Thrift Institutions Restructuring Act	1982	Authorized savings and loans to make commercial loans equal to 10 percent of their assets; allowed investments in nonresidential personal property and small-business investment companies

SOURCE: *Business Economics* magazine. Reprinted by permission of the National Association of Business Economists.

ket, with the result that in some (but not all) areas fares are lower than they once were. Not only did most airlines fight tooth and nail to prevent this deregulation from occurring, some couldn't adjust to the new era of competition and, like Eastern Airlines, went bankrupt.

Long-distance telephone services were once provided on a monopoly basis by AT&T; its prices were set by the Federal Communications Commission. Today there are several long-distance telephone systems—MCI, Sprint, AT&T—and prices are heavily influenced by competition. AT&T was not eager to have this happen, but it couldn't prevent it.

Once the number of trucking companies and the prices they charged were set by the Interstate Commerce Commission (ICC). The trucking companies and the Teamsters Union favored this pattern of regulation—as with the airlines, the system kept competition down and prices up. But then Congress changed the law, and the ICC decided to make it easy

for new truckers to enter the business and to allow market forces to set prices.

People who think that politics is simply the result of deals struck between certain favored industries and friendly or "captured" agencies would have a hard time explaining this period of deregulation. Client politics—the cozy relationship (or "iron triangle") between a private client, a government agency, and supportive Congress—was ended. How did it happen?

Martha Derthick and Paul Quirk, two political scientists, answered the question in their book, *The Politics of Deregulation*.[29] The key to that answer is the power of ideas. Academic economists were in agreement that regulating prices in industries that were, or could easily be made, competitive was a bad idea; the regulations hurt consumers by keeping prices artificially high. But academic ideas by themselves are powerless. In the three cases described above, key political leaders—Presidents Carter,

Ford, and Reagan, and Senators Edward Kennedy and Howard Cannon—accepted and acted on these ideas, albeit for very different reasons. The regulatory commissions—the CAB, the FCC, the ICC—were led by people who wanted to deregulate. In one case, the breakup of AT&T, a federal judge made many of the key decisions. Public opinion did not support deregulation, but it was concerned about inflation, and deregulation could be defended as a way of bringing prices down. Finally, the industries that fought to save their client relationships with government—the airlines, the trucking companies, the phone company—were not wildly popular businesses; once they were subjected to political criticism, they found that they had relatively few allies.

Reducing Subsidies

At one time the taxpayer shelled out a lot of money to help tobacco growers make money. Under that system, tobacco farmers who could not sell all the tobacco they were entitled to grow under a federal license could get a federal loan, using their unsold tobacco as collateral. If they did not pay back the loan, they got to keep the money, and the government was stuck with the bill.

Since tobacco farming is a key industry in certain states (such as Kentucky and North Carolina), the members of Congress from those states had a big stake in making certain that the subsidy program kept going. Since the program did not cost the average taxpayer too much and since, in any case, he or she had no idea of how much money went to pay for the program, most people had no incentive to organize to end the favored treatment of tobacco farmers.

They didn't, that is, until smoking became a well-publicized national health problem. Then many members of Congress from nontobacco states became upset about spending money to grow crops that contributed to cancer, heart disease, and emphysema. In 1982, when the tobacco-subsidy program was up for renewal, its congressional backers realized that they had to make concessions if the program were to survive. They did this by agreeing to a system in which the subsidies to the farmers would be paid for by the farmers themselves (in the form of mandatory contributions to a fund set up to pay for crop loans). The principle was to be "no net cost to the taxpayer" (except for administrative expenses).

Client politics was weakened when larger concerns (in this case, antismoking groups) were activated. Widely held beliefs ("smoking is bad for you") significantly reduced the influence of narrowly distributed benefits. The tobacco lobby lost again when the ban on smoking on all domestic airline flights was enacted in 1987.

Since the mid-1970s every president has put in place machinery to bring government regulation of industry under more central review. President Ford in 1974 ordered all regulatory agencies to assess the inflationary impact of their decisions. President Carter in 1978 directed each agency to consider alternative ways of achieving the goals of regulation. President Reagan in 1981 created a Task Force on Regulatory Relief and instructed those agencies under his control not to issue a regulation if, in the judgment of the Office of Management and Budget, its potential benefits to society did not outweigh its costs.[30] President Bush essentially continued the Reagan system.

Deregulation is opposed, of course, by groups that benefit from it. But it is controversial in at least two other ways. First, some members of the public do not like the results, especially if the world becomes more complicated as a result of relying on the market. Many people liked CAB control of the airlines, for example, because the higher prices kept the number of air travelers down, and so airports were less congested. Second, some people who favor deregulating *prices* oppose deregulating *processes*. **Process regulation** (sometimes called "social regulation") includes rules aimed at improving consumer or worker safety and reducing environmental damage. There are good and bad ways of achieving these goals, and much of the dispute about regulation concerns the question of means, not ends. The intensity of that dispute shows how important perceptions and beliefs are even when economic interests are at stake.

The Limits of Ideas

Ideas can be powerful, but there are limits to their power. There are many forms of client politics that persist—some because people agree that the client deserves to benefit, others because the conditions do not exist for mounting an effective challenge to the client.

Tobacco subsidies no longer are paid for by taxpayers, but dairy and other agricultural price supports still are. Regulations that increased above market levels the prices charged by airlines and trucking companies were successfully challenged; regulations that increased above market levels the prices charged by ocean-going freighters were not. The wages paid to airline pilots and truck drivers are no longer protected by federal rules; the wages paid to merchant seamen and construction workers employed on federal projects still are.

It is not entirely clear why it is easier to challenge client politics in some industries and occupations than in others. We can say, however, why client politics generally is harder to maintain free of challenge today than once was the case. That we shall do in Chapter 23, where we summarize what can be learned in the next few chapters about the politics of public policy.

SUMMARY

Policy-making involves two stages—placing an issue on the governmental agenda and deciding what to do about that issue once it is on the agenda. The agenda steadily expands as the result of historical crises, interest-group activity, the competition for votes, and the operation of key institutions, especially the courts, the bureaucracy, and the mass media.

Decision making requires that a majority coalition be formed. The kinds of coalitions that form will depend in large measure on the nature of the issue, especially the perceived distribution of costs and benefits. We have identified four kinds of coalitions, or distinctive political processes: majoritarian, client, interest-group, and entrepreneurial.

Government regulation of business illustrates the relationship between these four kinds of policies and the sorts of coalitions that will form in each instance. These case studies make clear that there is no single, simple answer to the question of how much influence business has over government (or vice versa).

The outcome of these political struggles will depend not only on who gains and who loses but on the perceptions, beliefs, and values of key political actors. The example of airline deregulation shows that changes in how people think can make a big difference even in the case of policies where money interests are at stake.

KEY TERMS

political agenda   *p. 452*

cost   *p. 455*

benefit   *p. 455*

majoritarian politics   *p. 457*

interest-group politics   *p. 458*

client politics   *p. 459*

pork-barrel projects   *p. 459*

logrolling   *p. 459*

entrepreneurial politics   *p. 460*

policy entrepreneurs   *p. 460*

boycott   *p. 464*

process regulation   *p. 472*

SUGGESTED READINGS

Derthick, Martha, and Paul J. Quirk. *The Politics of Deregulation.* Washington, D.C.: Brookings Institution, 1985. A brilliant analysis of how three industries—airlines, trucking, and telecommunications—were deregulated, often in the teeth of industry opposition.

Kingdon, John W. *Agendas, Alternatives, and Public Policies.* Boston: Little, Brown, 1984. An insightful account of how issues, especially those involving health and transportation, get on (or drop off) the federal agenda.

Lowi, Theodore J. "American Business, Public Policy, Case Studies, and Political Theory." *World Politics* 16 (July 1964). A theory of policy-making somewhat different from that offered in this book.

Nadel, Mark V. *The Politics of Consumer Protection.* 2d ed. Indianapolis, Ind.: Bobbs-Merrill, 1975. An analysis of the sources and uses of political influence in consumer legislation.

Noll, Roger G. *Reforming Regulation.* Washington, D.C.: Brookings Institution, 1971. A useful summary of the criticisms that economists make of many regulatory laws.

Polsby, Nelson W. *Political Innovation in America.* New Haven, Conn.: Yale University Press, 1984. Explains how eight policy innovations were adopted by the federal government.

Wilson, James Q., ed. *The Politics of Regulation.* New York: Basic Books, 1980. Analyzes regulatory politics in nine agencies and provides a fuller statement of the theory presented in this text.

16

Economic Policy

- ➤ Voters and the economy
- ➤ Economic theories
- ➤ Making economic policy
- ➤ The budget
- ➤ Taxes and tax reform

For decades the Republican party complained that the Democrats were big spenders. In 1981 a conservative Republican, Ronald Reagan, entered the White House. During his eight years in office federal spending steadily increased. When Democrat Jimmy Carter was president, federal outlays equaled about 22 percent of the gross national product. In 1987, under President Reagan, they amounted to nearly 24 percent (see Figure 16.1).

For decades Republicans complained that the Democrats spent more money than they took in from taxes. This deficit spending was driving up interest rates, threatening to cause a recession, and saddling future generations with a crushing national debt. During President Reagan's eight years in office the national debt more than doubled, increasing by an amount greater than the debt run up by all the preceding presidents since George Washington.

For decades many Democrats urged that taxes on corporations and affluent people be raised, and accused the Republicans of being the party of the rich. Republicans rejoined that businesses and the affluent were taxed so heavily that they were being discouraged from investing and producing economic growth. The Republicans sought to compensate for this by building into the tax laws various loopholes that would allow individuals and corporations to avoid part of this tax burden. In 1986 the Democrats voted to lower the tax rates on the rich and on corporations, and the Republicans voted to eliminate many of the tax loopholes enjoyed by the rich and by corporations. Then in 1993 the Democrats voted to raise taxes on the rich.

Welcome to the slightly unreal world of economic policy making.

A cynical reader might conclude that what politicians say means nothing and that as far as economic policy goes, they are all alike and equally unreliable. That would be a mistake. Democrats and Republicans, like people generally, do disagree about how the economy should be managed. But the policies that they support reflect not only their philosophical

FIGURE 16.1   Federal Outlays as a Percentage of Gross
National Product, 1869–1990

SOURCE: *Budget of the United States Government, Fiscal Year 1991*, A–332.

positions but also the demands of constituents, the changing theories and predictions of economists, and the limited and imperfect control that the government has over the direction of the economy.

From a political point of view there are three kinds of economic realities: the general health of the nation (as measured by employment, inflation, and growth in incomes), the level and distribution of taxes, and the amount and kind of government spending. Voters and interest groups judge the government on the basis of how well the economy is doing, how much they are paying in taxes, and how much they are getting from government spending programs. Economists may tell us that these three realities are closely intertwined, so that a change in taxes or spending will affect inflation or unemployment, and vice versa. But voters are not very interested in these relationships and theories; they are interested in results. They want economic growth, low taxes, high levels of government spending on most programs, and no budget deficit. This confronts the government with a problem: it may be impossible to achieve all of these results simultaneously. To see why, we shall look at these three economic realities.

Economic Health

Disputes about the economic well-being of the nation tend to produce majoritarian politics. This may seem strange, since each individual presumably cares most about his or her own material comfort. If that is the case, we would expect each voter to support politicians who offer programs to make that voter better off regardless of what those programs do to other voters. In fact people see connections between their own conditions and the economic health of the nation and tend to hold politicians responsible for those national conditions.

Everybody knows that just before an election politicians worry about the "pocketbook issue." We have seen in Chapter 8 that economic conditions are strongly associated with how much success the incumbent party has in holding on to the White House and to the seats held by the White House's party in Congress. But whose pocketbook are voters worried about?

In part, of course, it is their own. We know that low-income people are more likely to worry about unemployment and to vote Democratic, and higher income people are more likely to worry about inflation and to vote Republican.[1] We also know that people who tell pollsters that their families' finances have gotten worse are more likely than other people to vote against the incumbent president.[2] In 1980 about two-thirds of those who said that they had become worse off economically voted for Ronald Reagan, the challenger, while over half of those who felt that they had become better off voted for Jimmy Carter, the incumbent.[3] In 1992 people who felt economically pinched were more likely to vote for Clinton than for Bush. Clinton campaign aides often reminded each other, "It's the economy, stupid!"

But people do not simply vote their own pocketbooks. In any recession the vast majority of people will still have jobs; nevertheless these people will say that unemployment is the nation's biggest problem, and many of them will vote accordingly—against the incumbent during whose watch unemployment went up.[4] Why should employed people worry about other people's being unemployed?

By the same token, younger voters, whose incomes tend to go up each year, often worry more about inflation than do retired people living on fixed incomes, the purchasing power of which will go down with inflation.[5] In presidential elections those people who think that national economic trends are bad are much more likely to vote against the incumbent, *even when* their own personal finances have not worsened.[6]

When there are long lines at the unemployment office (as here in Detroit), the political party of the incumbent president is in trouble.

In technical language voting behavior and economic conditions are strongly correlated at the national level but not at the individual level, and this is true both in the United States and in Europe.[7] Such voters are behaving in an "other-regarding" or "sociotropic" way. In ordinary language voters seem to respond more to the condition of the national economy than to their own personal finances.

It is not hard to understand why this might be true. Part of the explanation is that people understand what government can and cannot be held accountable for. If you lose your job at the aircraft plant because the government has not renewed the plant's contract, you will be more likely to hold the government responsible than if you lost your job because you were always showing up drunk or because the plant moved out of town.

And part of the explanation is that people see general economic conditions as having indirect effects on them even when they are still doing pretty well. They may not be unemployed, but they may have friends who are, and they may worry that if unemployment grows worse, they will be the next to lose their jobs.

What Politicians Try to Do

Elected officials, who have to run for reelection every few years, are strongly tempted to take a short-run view of the economy and to adopt those policies that will best satisfy the self-regarding voter. They would dearly love to produce low unemployment rates and rising family incomes just before an election. Some scholars think that they do just this.

Since the nineteenth century the government has used money to affect elections. At first this mostly took the form of patronage passed out to the party faithful and money benefits given to important blocs of voters. The massive system of Civil War pensions for Union army veterans was run in a way that did no harm to the political fortunes of the Republican party. After the Social Security system was established, Congress voted to increase the benefits in virtually every year in which there was an election (see Chapter 17).

But it is by no means clear that the federal government can or will do whatever is necessary to reduce unemployment, cut inflation, lower interest rates, and increase incomes just to win an election.

For one thing the government does not know how to produce all these desirable outcomes. Moreover doing one of these things may often be possible only at the cost of not doing another. For example, reducing inflation can, in many cases, require the government to raise interest rates, and this in turn can slow down the economy by making it harder to sell houses, automobiles, and other things that are purchased with borrowed money.

If it were easy to stimulate the economy just before an election, practically every president would serve two full terms. But because of the uncertainties and complexities, presidents can lose elections over economic issues that they do not manage to the satisfaction of voters. Ford lost in 1976, Carter in 1980, and Bush in 1992. In all cases economic conditions played a major role.

All this means that politicians must make choices about economic policy, choices that are affected by uncertainty and ignorance. Those choices are importantly shaped by the ideological differences between the two political parties over what ought to be the principal goal of economic policy. Democrats and Republicans alike would prefer to have both low unemployment and no inflation, but if they must choose (and choose they must), then the Democrats attempt first to reduce unemployment and the Republicans attempt to reduce inflation.[8] This is no hard-and-fast rule; some say that Jimmy Carter, a Democrat, tried so hard to cut inflation in 1980 that he lost the support of many liberal Democrats, such as Edward Kennedy, who thought that he should be worrying more about creating jobs. But the general tendency seems clear: the Democratic party worries more about unemployment, the Republican party about inflation.

This tendency mirrors to some degree what Democratic and Republican voters want their parties to do. Polls regularly show that those who think of themselves as Democrats are much more worried about unemployment than those who think of themselves as Republicans.[9] (There is not as much of a difference between Democratic and Republican voters in worrying about inflation.) Because of these beliefs, voters concerned about unemployment not only are more likely to vote against the incumbent but also are more likely to vote Democratic.

Economic Theories and Political Needs

Policies aimed at improving the economy as a whole are examples of majoritarian politics. Benefits and costs are widely distributed, because a healthy economy benefits almost everybody and a stagnant one hurts almost everybody. As with most majoritarian issues, the president takes the lead and is held responsible for the results. Bur as we have seen, presidents do not always know what to do. The economy is an extraordinarily complex, poorly understood set of interrelationships. Nations (such as Marxist states) that have tried to run this machine by central commands have not done very well. Presidents thus become very dependent on the advice of experts who claim to have an idea as to how best to nudge the machine in the right direction. For better or worse, presidents (and governments) choose among competing economic theories.

There are at least four major theories about how best to manage the economy. Each theory, if fully stated, would be quite complicated; moreover many experts combine parts of one theory with parts of another. What follows is a highly simplified account of these theories that highlights their differences.

Monetarism

A monetarist, such as economist Milton Friedman, believes that inflation occurs when there is too much money chasing too few goods. Since the federal government has the power to create money (in ways to be described on page 484), inflation occurs when it prints too much money. When inflation becomes rampant and government tries to do something about it, it often cuts back sharply on the amount of money in circulation. Then a recession will occur, with slowed economic growth and an increase in unemployment. Since the government does not understand that economic problems result from its own start-and-stop habit of issuing new money, it will try to cure some of these problems by policies that make matters worse — such as having an unbalanced budget or creating new welfare programs. **Monetarism** suggests that the proper thing for government to do is to have a steady, predictable increase in the money supply at a rate about equal to the growth in the economy's productivity; beyond that it should leave matters alone and let the free market operate.

Keynesianism

John Maynard Keynes, an English economist who died in 1946, believed that the market will not automatically operate at a full-employment, low-inflation level. Its health will depend on what fraction of their incomes people save or spend. If they save too much, there will be too little demand, production will decline, and unemployment will rise. If they spend too much, demand will rise too fast, prices will go up, and shortages will develop. According to **Keynesianism**, the key is to create the right level of demand. This is the task of government. When demand is too little, the government should pump more money into the economy (by spending more than it takes in in taxes and by creating public-works programs). When demand is too great, the government should take money out of the economy by increasing taxes or cutting federal expenditures. There is no need for the government's budget to be balanced on a year-to-year basis; what counts is the performance of the economy. Keynesians, unlike monetarists, tend to favor an activist government.

Planning

Some economists have too little faith in the workings of the free market to be pure Keynesians, much less monetarists. They believe that the government should plan, in varying ways, some part of the country's economic activity. One form of **economic planning** is **price and wage control**, as advocated by John Kenneth Galbraith and others. In this view big corporations can raise prices (because the forces of competition are too weak to restrain them), and labor unions can force up wages (because management finds it easy to pass the increases along to consumers in the form of higher prices). Thus, during inflationary times, the government should regulate the maximum prices that can be charged and wages that can be paid, at least in the larger industries.

In the mid-1980s, however, inflation was not the problem that it once had been; instead the automakers were cutting car prices and labor unions were accepting wage reductions. This shift drew attention to a different form of economic planning. Called an **industrial policy**, it reflected the public's concern for the declining health of certain basic industries, such as steel and automobile manufacturing. People thought that these "smokestack" industries would not recover through market forces; what was needed

John Maynard Keynes

Milton Friedman

John Kenneth Galbraith

Arthur B. Laffer

At one time every U.S. dollar could be exchanged for gold. Today the dollar is backed chiefly by public confidence rather than by a precious metal.

market, far from having failed, had not been given an adequate chance. According to **supply-side theory**, what was needed was not planning but less government interference. In particular sharply cutting taxes would increase the incentive that people have to work, save, and invest. Greater investments would lead to more jobs and, if the earnings from these investments and jobs were taxed less, it would lessen the tendency of many individuals to shelter their earnings from the tax collector by taking advantage of various tax loopholes or by cheating on their income-tax returns. The greater productivity of the economy would produce more tax revenue for the government. Even though the tax *rates* would be lower, the total national income to which these rates are applied would be higher.

Ideology and Theory

Each economic theory has clear political consequences, and so it is no accident that people embrace one theory or another in part because of their political beliefs. If you are a conservative, monetarism or supply-side tax cuts will appeal to you because both imply that the government will be smaller and less intrusive. If you are a liberal, Keynesian economics will appeal to you because it permits (or even requires) the federal government to carry on a wide range of social-welfare programs. And if you are a socialist, planning will appeal to you because it is an alternative to the free market and the private management of economic resources.

Of course there are many exceptions to these patterns. Many advocates of so-called industrial policy are not socialists; some liberals have become skeptical of Keynesian economics; and quite a few conservatives think that supply-side economics is unrealistic. But in general one's economic theory tends to be consistent with one's political convictions.

"Reaganomics"

When Ronald Reagan became president in 1981, he set in motion changes in federal economic policies that were soon called **Reaganomics**. These changes were not dictated by any single economic theory but by a combination of monetarism, supply-side tax cuts, and domestic budget cutting. The president

instead was for the government somehow to direct or plan investments so that either these industries would recover or new and better industries would take their places. Advocates of this form of planning, such as Robert Reich (who became secretary of labor in the Clinton administration), often point to Japan as an example of a country in which the government does direct industrial investments.

Supply-Side Tax Cuts

Exactly the opposite remedy for declining American productivity was suggested by people who call themselves "supply siders." The view of economists such as Arthur Laffer and Paul Craig Roberts was that the

The White House Economy Doctors

Council of Economic Advisers
The president's own economic think tank; determines government's assumptions about the nation's economic performance in concert with OMB and Treasury.

Laura D'Andrea Tyson

President Clinton

The buck stops here . . .

Treasury Department
Sells and redeems government bonds, manages government cash flow, represents the United States in international economic summits and coordinates foreign exchange policy, manages tax policy, oversees banks and thrifts, oversees trade flows and collects tariffs.

Lloyd Bentsen

National Economic Council
New post to coordinate economic policy decisions among departments and agencies and advise the president. What, if anything, it will accomplish remains to be seen.

Robert Rubin

Office of Management and Budget
Writes the president's budget, manages agency spending, oversees regulatory policy.

Alice Rivlin

SOURCE: *Congressional Quarterly* (December 12, 1992): 3799.

wanted to achieve several goals simultaneously — to reduce the size of the federal government, to stimulate economic growth, and to increase American military strength. As it turned out for him (as for most presidents), the things that he wanted were not entirely consistent.

Spending on some domestic programs was reduced. These reductions slowed the rate of growth of federal spending on these programs but did not actually decrease the spending. Military spending was sharply increased (see Chapter 21). The money supply was held under control in order to combat inflation (at the price of allowing interest rates to rise). Finally, and most important, there were sharp across-the-board cuts in personal income taxes, but for many people these cuts were more than offset by increases in Social Security taxes.

The effect of lowering taxes while increasing spending was to stimulate the economy (by pumping more money into it) and to create large deficits. The stimulated economy resulted in a drop in the unemployment rate and a rise in business activity. The large deficits increased dramatically the size of the national debt. The effects of the tax cuts on productivity and investment were hard to estimate and remained a matter of controversy.

John Maynard Keynes, had he been alive, would have been startled. A conservative president (aided, of course, by Congress) created a massive budget deficit that helped reduce unemployment — just as

Are Economists Ever Right?

The jokes about them are endless. George Meany, a labor leader, once said that economics is the only profession in which you can rise to eminence without ever being right. Rudolph Penner, onetime head of the Congressional Budget Office (and himself an economist), quipped that economists can't even predict what happened in the past. What Paul Samuelson, a Nobel-prize-winning economist, once said about the stock market could also be said about economists: They have predicted nine of the last five recessions.

It is true that economists have not done a very good job of predicting which way the economy would move in the years ahead. In 1986, for example, the forecasts, made one year in advance by fifteen leading economic forecasters (two in the government, thirteen in the private sector), were in error by 25 percent in forecasting growth in the gross national product, by nearly 99 percent in forecasting price levels (that is, inflation), and by 19 percent in forecasting key interest rates.[1]

The government forecasters are the Office of Management and Budget (OMB), part of the executive branch, and the Congressional Budget Office (CBO), part of Congress. Both tend to make overly optimistic predictions. For example, both thought that economic growth in 1986 would be higher than it was, by an average of 44 percent.[2]

Does all this make economics useless? Not at all, any more than meteorology is useless despite the inability of meteorologists to predict the weather one year (or even one week) in advance. Today economists measure, with growing accuracy, what the economy is doing at any given moment. By contrast, when Herbert Hoover was president, we had no reliable information on how many people were unemployed or how much money workers were making.

Moreover economics reminds us of some sensible propositions that we forget at our peril: for example, that everything has a cost, or in popular parlance, there is no such thing as a free lunch. Finally, economists can use their concepts of price and cost to explain (and even predict) how parts of the economy will respond to specific changes in certain conditions. For instance, higher interest rates will cause less housing to be built.

SOURCES: [1]Charles Wolf, Jr., "Scoring the Economic Forecasters," *The Public Interest* (Summer 1987): 48–55, and Stephen K. McNees and John Ries, "The Track Record of Macroeconomic Forecasts," *New England Economic Review* (November–December 1983): 5–18. [2]Mark S. Kamlet, David C. Mowrey, and Tsai-Tsu Su, "Whom Do You Trust? An Analysis of Executive and Congressional Economic Forecasts," *Journal of Policy Analysis and Management* 6 (Spring 1987): 365–384, and *National Journal* (March 7, 1987): 552.

Keynes, a liberal, might have recommended. The Democrats, taken aback, began for the first time to argue against large budget deficits. In 1984 the Democratic presidential candidate, Walter Mondale, called for raising taxes to balance the budget—just as a traditional conservative might once have done.

The Machinery of Economic Policy-Making

Even if the president knew exactly the right thing to do, he would still have to find some way of doing it. In our government that is no easy task. The machinery for making decisions about economic matters is complex and not under the president's full control.

Within the executive branch three people other than the president are of special importance. Sometimes called the "troika,"* these are the chairman of the Council of Economic Advisers (CEA), the director of the Office of Management and Budget (OMB), and the secretary of the treasury.

The CEA, composed of three professional economists plus a small staff, has existed since 1946. In theory it is an impartial group of experts responsible for forecasting economic trends, analyzing economic issues, and helping prepare the economic report that the president submits to Congress each year. Though quite professional in tone, the CEA is not exactly im-

* From the Russian word for a carriage pulled by three horses.

partial in practice, since each president picks members sympathetic to his point of view. Kennedy picked Keynesians; Reagan picked supply siders and monetarists. But whatever its theoretical tilt, the CEA is seen by other executive agencies as the advocate of the opinion of professional economists, who, despite their differences, generally tend to favor reliance on the market.

OMB was originally the Bureau of the Budget, which was created in 1921 and made part of the executive office of the president in 1939; in 1970 it was renamed the Office of Management and Budget. Its chief function is to prepare estimates of the amount that will be spent by federal agencies, to negotiate with other departments over the size of their budgets, and to make certain (insofar as it can) that the legislative proposals of these other departments are in accord with the president's program. Of late it has acquired something of a split personality: it is in part an expert, nonpartisan agency that analyzes spending and budget patterns and in part an activist, partisan organization that tries to get the president's wishes carried out by the bureaucracy. Under President Reagan appointee David Stockman it became the device for making deep budget cuts in domestic spending.

The secretary of the treasury is often close to or drawn from the world of business and finance and is expected to argue the point of view of the financial community. (Since its members do not always agree, this is not always easy.) The secretary provides estimates of the revenue that the government can expect from existing taxes and what will be the result of changing tax laws, and represents the United States in its dealings with the top bankers and finance ministers of other nations.

A good deal of pulling and hauling takes place among members of the troika, but if that were the extent of the problem, presidential leadership would be fairly easy. The problem is far more complex. In 1978 one study found 132 separate government bureaus engaged in formulating economic policy. They regulate business, make loans, and supply subsidies. For example, as foreign trade becomes increasingly important to this country, the secretary of state (among many others) acquires an interest in economic policy. One-third of corporate profits come from overseas investments, and one-fourth of farm output is sold abroad.

The Fed   Among the most important of these other agencies is the board of governors of the Federal Reserve System (the "Fed"). Its seven members are appointed by the president, with the consent of the Senate, for fourteen-year, nonrenewable terms and may not be removed except for cause. (No member has ever been removed since it was created in 1913.) The chairman serves for four years. In theory, and to some degree in practice, the Fed is independent of both the president and Congress. Its most important function is to regulate, insofar as it can, the supply of money (both in circulation and in bank deposits) and the price of money (in the form of interest rates). In the box on page 484 are shown the means employed by the Fed to achieve this, and the structure of the Federal Reserve System over which it presides.

Just how independent the Fed may be is a matter of dispute. During the 1980 election Fed policies helped keep interest rates at a high level, a circumstance that did not benefit President Carter's reelection bid. On the other hand, whenever a president is

Defining Some Economic Terms

Fiscal policy   An attempt to use taxes and expenditures to affect the economy. A **budget deficit** means that the government spends more than it takes in, thus pumping more money into the economy. A **budget surplus** means that the government takes in more than it spends, thus draining money out of the economy.

Monetary policy   An attempt to use the amount of money and bank deposits and the price of money (the interest rate) to affect the economy.

Fiscal year (FY)   October 1 to September 30, the period of time for which federal government appropriations are made and federal books are kept. A fiscal year is named after the year in which it *ends* — thus "fiscal 1995" (or "FY 95") means the twelve-month period ending September 30, 1995.

The Federal Reserve Board

The Tools by Which the Fed Implements Its Monetary Policy

1. **Buying and selling federal government securities** (bonds, Treasury notes, and other pieces of paper that constitute government IOUs). When the Fed buys securities, it in effect puts more money into circulation and takes securities out of circulation. With more money around, interest rates tend to drop, and more money is borrowed and spent. When the Fed sells government securities, it in effect takes money out of circulation, causing interest rates to rise and making borrowing more difficult.

2. **Regulating the amount of money that a member bank must keep in hand as reserves** to back up the customer deposits it is holding. A bank lends out most of the money deposited with it. If the Fed says that it must keep in reserve a larger fraction of its deposits, then the amount that it can lend drops, loans become harder to obtain, and interest rates rise.

3. **Changing the interest charged banks** that want to borrow money from the Federal Reserve System. Banks borrow from the Fed to cover short-term needs. The interest that the Fed charges for this is called the *discount* rate. The Fed can raise or lower that rate; this will have an effect, though usually rather small, on how much money the banks will lend.

Federal Reserve Board (7 members)

- Determines how many government securities will be bought or sold by regional and member banks.
- Determines interest rates to be charged by regional banks and amount of money member banks must keep in reserve in regional banks.

Regional Federal Reserve Banks (12)

- Buy and sell government securities.
- Loan money to member banks.
- Keep percentage of holdings for member banks.

Member Banks (6,000)

- Buy and sell government securities.
- May borrow money from regional banks.
- Must keep percentage of holdings in regional banks.
- Interest rates paid to regional banks determine interest rates charged for business and personal loans and influence all bank interest rates.

Alan Greenspan, chairman of the Federal Reserve Board.

determined to change monetary policy, he usually can do so. For example, the term of Fed chairman Arthur F. Burns, appointed by President Nixon, came up for renewal in 1978. President Carter, seeking to influence Burns' decisions, held out the prospect of reappointing him chairman. When Burns balked, he was passed over, and G. William Miller was appointed in his stead. Presidents Truman, Johnson, and Nixon were all able to obtain changes in monetary policy. However, inducing the Fed to change its policy requires influence, of which no president has an unlimited supply.

Congress   The most important part of the economic policy-making machinery, of course, is Congress. It must approve all taxes and almost all expenditures; there can be no wage or price controls without its consent; and it has the ability to alter the policy of the nominally independent Federal Reserve Board by threatening to pass laws that would reduce its powers. And Congress itself is fragmented, with great influence wielded by the members of key committees, especially the House and Senate Budget Committees, the House and Senate Appropriations Committees, the House Ways and Means Committee, and the Senate Finance Committee.

In sum, no matter what economic theory the president may have, if he is to put that theory into effect he needs the assistance of (1) many agencies within the executive branch, (2) such independent agencies as the Federal Reserve Board, and (3) the various committees of Congress. Though members of the executive and legislative branches are united by their common desire to get reelected (and thus have a common interest in producing sound economic growth), each part of this system may also be influenced by different economic theories and will be motivated by the claims of interest groups.

The effect of these interest-group claims is clearly shown in the debate over trade restriction. Usually the economic health of the nation affects everyone in pretty much the same way—we are all hurt by inflation or helped by stable prices; the incomes of all of us tend to grow (or remain stagnant) together. In these circumstances the politics of economic health is majoritarian.

Now suppose, however, that most of us are doing pretty well but that the people in a few industries or occupations are suffering. That is exactly what happened in the 1980s when various forces combined to hurt such basic U.S. industries as steel and such important occupations as farming. Although economists differ over exactly what went wrong, in general these sectors of the economy were hurt by foreign competition (that is, foreign nations found it easy to sell things here), the rising value of the dollar (as a result U.S. companies and farmers found it hard to sell their products abroad), and overexpansion (many companies and farmers had gone heavily into debt to expand production beyond what the market would support).

Under these conditions the politics of economic health will pit one part of the country against another. People who want to buy things made abroad—German automobiles, Japanese computers, Taiwanese shoes—will oppose placing any restrictions on their ability to import these things. By contrast, people who make American automobiles, American computers, and American shoes will favor heavy restrictions (such as quotas or tariffs). Economic health becomes subject to interest-group politics.

In 1988 Congress responded to these competing pressures by passing a trade bill that put enough restrictions on foreign imports to satisfy the protectionists but not so many as to outrage the advocates of free trade. In the 1988 presidential election the worth of this legislation was a big issue, not only between the Democratic and Republican candidates, but among the primary candidates within each party.

Spending Money

If only the economic health of the nation mattered, then majoritarian politics would dominate, and so the president and Congress would both work to improve economic conditions. Although they still might work at cross-purposes because they held to different economic theories, the goal would be the same.

But the government must also respond to the demands from voters and interest groups. The trade bill was an example of that. While these demands are no less legitimate than the voters' general interest in economic health, they produce not majoritarian but client and interest-group politics.

The sources of this conflict can be seen in public-opinion polls. Consistently voters say that they want a balanced budget and lowered government spending. They believe that the government spends too much and that, if it wanted, it could cut spending. When the government runs a deficit, the reason is that (in the voters' eyes) it is spending too much, not that it is taxing too little. But these same polls show that the voters believe that the government should spend more on education, homelessness, child care, crime control, and almost anything else that one can think of (except "welfare" and "food stamps") (see Figure 16.2).

The voters are not irrational, thinking that they can have more spending and less spending simultaneously. Nor are they hypocrites, pretending to want less spending overall but more spending for particular programs. They are simply expressing a variety of concerns and a theory about spending. They want a limited government with no deficit; they also want good schools, cleaner air, better health care, and less crime. They believe that a frugal government could deliver what they want by cutting out waste. They may by wrong about that belief, but it is not obviously silly.

What this means for the government is easy to imagine. Politicians have an incentive to make two kinds of appeals: "Vote for me and I will keep government spending down and cut the deficit." "Vote for me and I will make certain that your favorite program gets more money." Some people will vote for the candidate because of the first appeal, some will vote for him or her because of the second. But acting on these two appeals is clearly going to lead to inconsistent policies. Where those inconsistencies become evident is in the budget.

The Budget

A **budget** is a document that announces how much the government will collect in taxes and spend in revenues and how those expenditures will be allocated among various programs. In theory the federal bud-

---

FIGURE 16.2 Do People Want More for Less?

The average citizen thinks that government spends too much. Most people don't want their taxes raised. But when asked about whether government should spend more, less, or about the same on various programs, the great majority favors spending the same or even more:

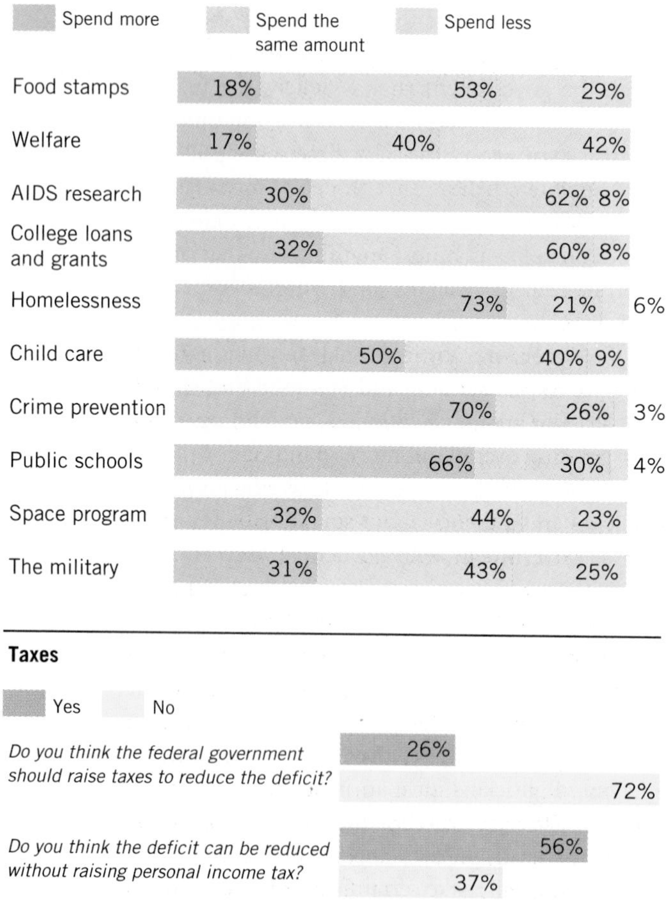

Legend: Spend more · Spend the same amount · Spend less

Food stamps	18%	53%	29%
Welfare	17%	40%	42%
AIDS research	30%	62%	8%
College loans and grants	32%	60%	8%
Homelessness	73%	21%	6%
Child care	50%	40%	9%
Crime prevention	70%	26%	3%
Public schools	66%	30%	4%
Space program	32%	44%	23%
The military	31%	43%	25%

Taxes

Legend: Yes · No

Do you think the federal government should raise taxes to reduce the deficit?	Yes 26%	No 72%
Do you think the deficit can be reduced without raising personal income tax?	Yes 56%	No 37%

SOURCES: On taxes, space program, and the military: *ABC-Washington Post* survey as reported in *National Journal* (April 18, 1987): 924, and (February 21, 1987): 444; on other programs: 1992 *NES Pre/Post-Election Study.*

---

get should be based on *first* deciding how much money you are going to spend and *then* allocating that money among different programs and agencies. That is the way in which a household makes up its budget: "We have this much in the paycheck and so we will spend X dollars on rent, Y dollars on food, and Z dollars on clothing, and what's left over on entertainment. If the amount of the paycheck goes down, we will cut something out—probably entertainment."

In fact the federal budget has typically been a list of everything that the government was going to spend money on, with only slight regard (sometimes no regard) for how much money is available to be spent. Instead of being a way of *allocating* money to be spent on various purposes, it was a way of *adding up* what in fact was being spent. Indeed there was no federal budget at all before 1921, and no unified presidential budget until the 1930s. Even after the president began submitting a single budget, the committees of Congress acted on it separately, adding to or subtracting from the amounts that he proposed. (Usually they followed his lead, but they were certainly free to depart from it as they wished.) If one committee wanted to spend more on housing, there was no effort made (in fact, there was no machinery for making an effort) to take that amount away from the committee that was spending money on health.

The Congressional Budget Act of 1974 changed this somewhat. Now after the president submits his budget in January, two budget committees—one in the House, one in the Senate—study the president's overall package and obtain an analysis of it from the Congressional Budget Office (CBO). Each committee then submits to its house a **budget resolution** that proposes a total budget ceiling and a ceiling for each of several spending areas (such as health or defense). Each May Congress adopts, with some modifications, these budget resolutions, intending them to be targets to guide the work of each legislative committee as it decides what should be spent in its area. During the summer the Congress then takes up the specific appropriations bills, informing its members as it goes along whether or not the spending proposed in these bills conforms to the May budget resolution. The object obviously is to impose some discipline on the various committees. After all the individual appropriations are decided, Congress then adopts a second budget resolution that "reconciles" the overall budget ceiling with the total resulting from the individual appropriations bills.

The loophole in this process is very large: there is nothing to prevent Congress from ignoring its first budget resolution, passed in May, and thereby making its second resolution, passed in September, simply reflect the total of all the individual spending bills that it has adopted. And sometimes Congress does just that. But the existence of this formal budget process has made a difference, despite the loophole: Congress is now conscious of how its spending decisions match up with an overall total that, for reasons of economic theory and practical politics, it wants to maintain.

When President Reagan took office, he and his allies in Congress took advantage of the Congressional Budget Act to start the controversial process of cutting federal spending. The House and Senate budget committees, with the president's support, used the first budget resolution in May 1981 not simply to set a budget ceiling that, as in the past, looked pretty much like the previous year's budget, but to direct each committee of congress to make *cuts*—sometimes deep cuts—in the programs for which it was responsible. These cuts were to be made in the authorization legislation (see Chapter 13) as well as in the appropriations.

The object was to get members of Congress to vote for a total package of cuts before they could vote on any particular cut. Republican control of the Senate and an alliance between Republicans and conservative southern Democrats in the House allowed this strategy to succeed. The first budget resolution ordered Senate and House committees to reduce federal spending during fiscal 1982 by about $36 billion—less than the president had first asked, but a large sum nonetheless. Then the individual committees set to work trying to find ways of making these cuts.

Note how the *procedures* used by Congress can affect the *policies* adopted by Congress. If the Reagan plan had been submitted in the old piecemeal way, it is unlikely that cuts of this size would have occurred at all, or in so short a time. The reason is not that Congress wants to ignore the president but that Congress reflects public opinion on economic policy. As stated at the beginning of the chapter, the public wants less total federal spending but more spent on specific federal programs. Thus if you allow the pub-

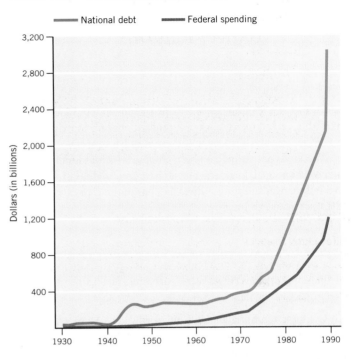

FIGURE 16.3 Trends in the National Debt

SOURCE: *Economic Reports of the President*, various years.

lic or Congress to vote first on specific programs, spending is bound to rise. But if you require Congress to vote first on a budget ceiling, then (unless it changes its mind as it goes along) total spending will go down, and tough choices will have to be made about the component parts of the budget.

That, at least, is the theory. It worked once, in 1981, but it did not work very well thereafter. During the rest of the Reagan years the budget process broke down in the warfare between the president and Congress. President Reagan represented the part of public opinion that wanted less government spending in general; most members of Congress represented the part of public opinion that wanted more spending on particular programs. The result was stalemate. In 1984 the budget resolution was not passed until late September (four months late); in 1985, not until August (three months late). The amount being spent in every year was far in excess of the amount coming in from tax revenues (see Figure 16.3). Part of this gap existed because taxes had been sharply cut in 1981. The responsibility was bipartisan—a Republican

Budget Reforms

*H*ardly anyone is satisfied with how the federal government makes spending decisions. It is complex, cumbersome, and time-consuming, and in the end does not produce a true budget but merely a list of appropriations only loosely related to how much money the government has to spend.

Two kinds of reforms have been proposed—procedural and constitutional. In general liberals have preferred the procedural changes and conservatives the constitutional ones, but there are many exceptions.

Procedural Changes

1. Have Congress vote on a budget and pass appropriations bills only once every two years. This would unclog the process and lighten the workload.

2. Combine appropriations and authorizing bills. At present separate committees must approve the authorization for a program and the appropriation for that program.

Constitutional Changes

1. Amend the Constitution to require a balanced budget. As of 1988 thirty-two states had passed resolutions asking Congress to call a constitutional convention to consider a balanced-budget amendment. This is only two states short of the number needed to force Congress to call such a convention, which would be the first since 1787. The amendment would allow an unbalanced budget in wartime or whenever an extraordinary majority in Congress voted for it. One version of the amendment would also limit increases in federal spending to some percentage of the increase in national income.

2. Amend the Constitution to give the president a line-item veto, now possessed by the governors of forty-three states. This would make it possible for the president to veto a specific item in a bill without vetoing the whole bill. Some legislators believe that a version of a line-item veto could be authorized by legislation.

president had proposed the tax cut and signed the spending bills, a majority of Senate Democrats had voted for the tax cut and the spending bills.

The deficit grew to the point that even politicians eager to please their constituents' demand for more services began to worry that the economy's health might be in peril. Accordingly in 1985 Congress changed the budget process once again by passing the Gramm-Rudman Balanced Budget Act (named after two of its sponsors, Senators Phil Gramm [Republican, Texas] and Warren Rudman [Republican, New Hampshire]).

Signed by President Reagan, the law created a plan whereby the budget would automatically be cut until there was no longer a deficit. Each year between 1986 and 1991 the deficit could not exceed a specified, declining amount. If Congress and the president could not agree on a spending plan within those targets, there would be automatic, across-the-board, percentage cuts—called a **sequester**—in federal programs except for certain exempt programs.* No one liked the idea of automatic budget cuts. Senator Rudman called it "a bad idea whose time has come."

In 1988 George Bush campaigned for the presidency on the slogan "Read my lips—no new taxes." But by 1990 it had become clear that the White House and Congress could not agree on spending cuts sufficient to meet the Gramm-Rudman limits for that year. As a result, Washington faced the prospect of a sequester of close to $100 billion. Everybody's favorite ox was going to be gored. The president and congressional leaders hastily called a summit meeting. After much shadow boxing the president's lips moved again, but this time they said that there would have to be "increased tax revenues."

The first summit agreement was rejected by Congress (one more measure of how little power congressional leaders have). After more backroom bargaining, a budget agreement was finally passed that increased taxes, cut defense spending, and put in place new budget procedures. The top tax rate went up from 28 percent to 31 percent, gasoline taxes were raised by ten cents a gallon, tax deductions were limited, and alcohol and tobacco taxes were increased.

---

* The exempt programs were Social Security, interest on the federal debt, veterans' benefits, food stamps, and various other welfare programs.

Hardly any domestic spending programs were cut; indeed, even after the defense cuts, total spending was scheduled to go up by almost 5 percent.[10]

The 1990 budget agreement was designed to permit the Democratic Congress and the Republican White House to get through the 1992 elections without having to make immediate spending cuts. The agreement did little either to cut the deficit or to calm the raging debate over tax increases versus spending cuts as the best means to reduce the deficit. That debate exploded into all-out partisan warfare in 1993 when the newly elected Democratic president, Bill Clinton, offered a new plan to achieve substantial deficit reduction.

The Clinton budget approved in August 1993 will achieve, it is claimed, an estimated total of $505 billion in deficit reduction over five years, about half of it in spending cuts ($255 billion) and the other half in tax increases ($250 billion). By comparison, tax increases were only about one third of the deficit reduction in the 1990 budget agreement. Among the key provisions of the 1993 budget bill are the following:

- An increase in the top tax rate from 31 percent to over 39 percent

- An increase in the portion of Social Security benefits subject to taxation from 50 percent to 85 percent for upper-income retirees

- About one quarter of all spending cuts ($56 billion) to come from Medicare

- About $21 billion added to expand the earned income-tax credit, which goes to poor, working families

- A 4.3-cent increase in the 14.1-cents-per-gallon federal gasoline tax

Politically, the most significant feature of the 1993 budget bill mirrors that of the 1990 budget agreement—namely, caps on appropriations that mandate area-specific cuts to finance new expenditures. The 1993 bill also capped discretionary spending at $539 billion in fiscal 1994 and allows such spending to increase to only $549 billion by 1998. In the early 1990s following the collapse of the Soviet Union there was much talk of a **peace dividend**— vast sums of money for domestic spending freed up

by cuts in post–Cold War defense spending. By most estimates, however, the defense cuts in the 1993 bill were not even enough to let existing domestic programs grow at the rate of inflation between 1994 and 1998, let alone to finance new programs. Thus, the 1990 and 1993 caps on domestic spending constituted a "hard freeze," meaning that any new domestic programs must be paid for by cost-saving reforms or the elimination of existing programs.

To say that Clinton had difficulty in getting the 1993 budget bill passed is an understatement. The final bill was hammered out in a grueling summer of negotiations. The president was forced to give ground on several major provisions of his original plan, including his call for a broad-based, $72 billion energy tax. During the often heated debate, Republicans insisted that the bill relied too much on taxes and not enough on spending cuts, while Democrats worried about the domestic spending caps and argued that the bill was not generous enough with the poor. Some members of both parties complained that, even if the plan's economic projections proved to be exactly on target, it would slow the deficit only temporarily through 1997; then the deficit would start galloping again.

When the political dust settled, the bill passed in the House on August 5 by a vote of 218–216. Not a single Republican voted for the package, and forty-one Democrats voted against it. The next day, the Senate adopted the bill by a razor-thin margin of 51–50, with Vice President Al Gore casting the tie-breaking vote. Once again not a single Republican voted for the bill. (It was the first time since 1945 that the majority party in Congress had passed major legislation without a single vote from the minority party.)

Under any circumstances cutting spending is no easy matter. Not only are there strong pressures supporting every government program, but also a large part of the federal budget consists of expenditures that represent past commitments that, politically and sometimes legally, cannot be altered. Politicians speak of these as "uncontrollable" because they involve contracts already signed, payments (such as Social Security) that are guaranteed by law, and interest on the national debt that must be paid if the government is to stay in business. In Figure 16.4 we see how rapidly spending on Social Security and Medicare

⭐ A Pawn in Party Politics?

*P*resident Clinton's 1993 deficit reduction plan passed 51–50 in the Senate. No one doubted that Vice President Al Gore, exercising his prerogative as president of the Senate, would cast the tie-breaker as he did. But the House vote was a genuine cliff-hanger, and for at least one member it was an intense personal drama. The Clinton plan passed 218–216 in the House because one freshman Democrat, Marjorie Margolies-Mezvinsky of Pennsylvania, switched her vote at the last minute. The first Democrat in 76 years to be elected from her heavily Republican district, Margolies-Mezvinsky had campaigned on a pledge not to vote for any tax increases. But once in Congress, she promised party leaders that she would support the Clinton plan if her vote proved necessary to pass it—an unlikely prospect at the time. When the moment of decision came, she was surrounded by these same party leaders, one urging her to "Just do what's right," another rubbing her back, and yet another easing the vote-switching green card into her hand. When she cast her deciding vote Republicans chanted "Goodbye Marjorie," a sarcastic forecast of defeat for her reelection bid in 1994.

Many other Democrats who stuck with the president on the budget bill did so in return for his support in obtaining special spending packages or other tangible benefits for their constituents. Interestingly, however, Margolies-Mezvinsky asked only that the president visit her district as the featured speaker at a conference on restricting the growth in entitlement spending. In December of 1993 Clinton appeared in Margolies-Mezvinsky's district, but he used the forum mainly to insist on the benefits of entitle-

ment spending and to advocate his health-care reform plan, which itself would expand entitlements.

Though it is not clear how Margolies-Mezvinsky's role in the 1993 budget war affected the voters in her district, she was nonetheless defeated in her bid for reelection in 1994.

---

has grown. Projections of the growth of federal spending suggest that Medicare expenditures will in time exceed Social Security and defense.

In 1985, a typical year, these relatively uncontrollable expenditures accounted for about *three-fourths* of all federal outlays. Of course some (such as Social Security) can be controlled if one is willing to reduce benefits promised to individuals, but such an action is quite risky. Most of the easily controllable expenditures are concentrated in the national-defense area, a fact that helps explain why there is greater variation from year to year in spending on defense than in spending on nondefense programs.

Just how difficult it is to cut federal spending is underscored by the fact that one year after President Reagan was inaugurated, the federal government was spending *more* than it was before he was elected. Although planned expenditures were cut, significantly affecting some domestic programs, this cut did not reduce total federal spending, or even total nondefense spending—it simply slowed the rate of increase.

Indeed it is almost impossible for any president to know by how much he *has* cut the budget. Federal programs contain countless provisions that automatically cause spending to increase or decrease depending on economic conditions that cannot be foreseen. For example, it has been estimated that a 1 percent increase in the unemployment rate will cause the government to spend $7 billion more than it had planned (in the form of unemployment and welfare benefits) and to take in $12 billion less than it had hoped (because people out of work do not pay taxes). In short a small change in unemployment can cause a $19 billion swing in the government budget. As someone has said, much of the government budget is on automatic pilot.

Levying Taxes

Tax policy reflects a various mixture of majoritarian politics ("What is a 'fair' tax law?") and client politics ("How much is in it for me?"). In the United States a fair tax law has generally been viewed as one that kept the overall tax burden rather low, that required everyone to pay something, and that required the better-off to pay at a higher rate than the less-well-off. The law, in short, was good if it imposed modest burdens, prevented cheating, and was mildly progressive.

Americans have had their first goal satisfied. The tax burden in the United States is lower than it is in most other democratic nations (see Figure 16.5). There is some evidence that they have also had their second goal met — there is reason to believe that Americans evade their income taxes less than do citizens of, say, France or Italy. (That is one reason why many nations rely more on sales taxes than we do — they are harder to evade.) Just how progressive our tax rates are is a matter of dispute; to determine whether the rich really pay at higher rates than the poor, one has to know not only the official rates but also the effect of deductions, exemptions, and exclusions (that is, of loopholes).

Keeping the burden low and the cheating at a minimum are examples of majoritarian politics: most people benefit, most people pay. The loopholes, however, are another matter — all manner of special interests can get some special benefit from the tax law that the rest of us must pay for but, given the complexity of the law, rarely notice. Loopholes are client politics, par excellence.

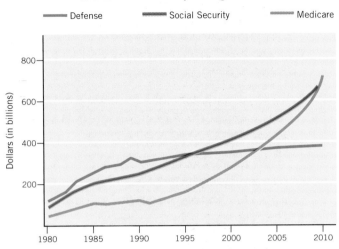

FIGURE 16.4 Where Will the Crunch Come? Projections of the Growth in Federal Spending

NOTE: Outyear defense projections are extrapolations of FY 1991–1995 presidential policy, which could change.

SOURCE: *Budget of the United States Government, Fiscal Year 1991*, 187.

Because of that, hardly any scholars believed that tax reform (dramatically reducing the loopholes) was politically possible. Every interest that benefited from a loophole — and these included not just corporations but universities, museums, states, cities, and investors — would lobby vigorously to protect it.

In 1986 a sweeping Tax Reform Act was passed. Many of the most cherished loopholes were closed or reduced. What happened? It is as if scientists who had proved that a bumblebee could not fly got stung by a flying bumblebee.

The Rise of the Income Tax

To understand what happened in 1986, one must first understand the political history of taxation. Until almost the end of the nineteenth century, there was no federal income tax (except for a brief period during the Civil War). The money that the government needed came mostly from tariffs (that is, taxes on goods imported into this country). And when Congress did enact a peace-time income tax, the Supreme Court in 1895 struck it down as unconstitutional.[11] To change this, Congress proposed, and in 1913 the states ratified, the Sixteenth Amendment, which authorized such a tax.

FIGURE 16.5   Tax Burdens in Twenty-two Democratic Nations

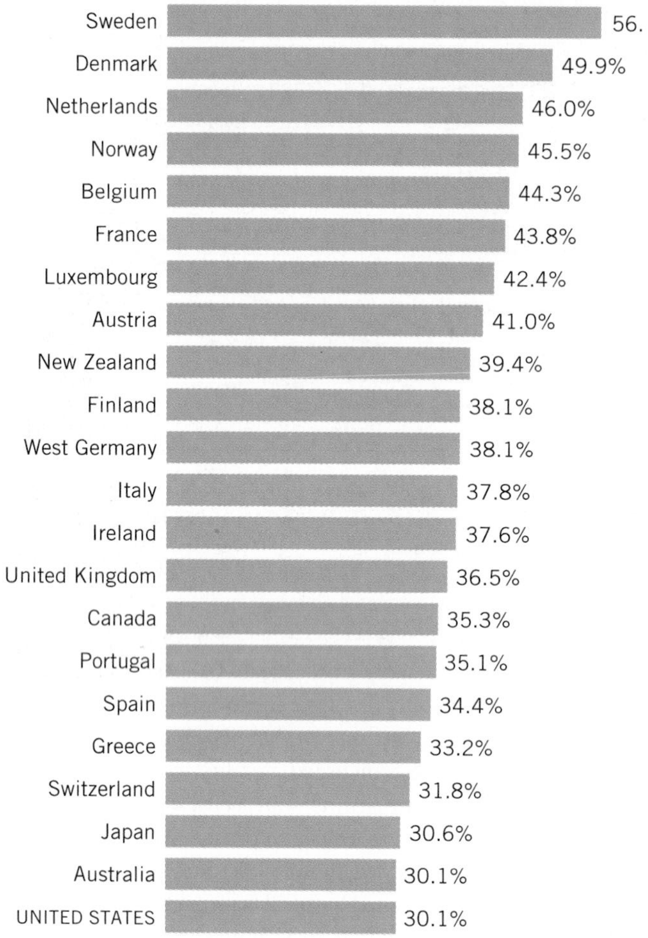

Nation	Percent
Sweden	56.
Denmark	49.9%
Netherlands	46.0%
Norway	45.5%
Belgium	44.3%
France	43.8%
Luxembourg	42.4%
Austria	41.0%
New Zealand	39.4%
Finland	38.1%
West Germany	38.1%
Italy	37.8%
Ireland	37.6%
United Kingdom	36.5%
Canada	35.3%
Portugal	35.1%
Spain	34.4%
Greece	33.2%
Switzerland	31.8%
Japan	30.6%
Australia	30.1%
UNITED STATES	30.1%

SOURCE: *Statistical Abstract of the United States*, 1992, 836.

For the next forty years or so tax rates tended to go up during wartime and go down during peacetime (see Figure 16.6). The rates were progressive—that is, the wealthiest individuals paid at a higher rate than the less affluent. For example, during World War II incomes in the highest bracket were taxed at a rate of 94 percent. (The tax rate in the highest bracket is called by economists the "marginal rate." This is the percentage of the last dollar that you earn that must be paid out in taxes.)

An income tax offers the opportunity for majoritarian politics to become class politics. The majority of the citizenry earn average incomes and control most of the votes. There is nothing in theory to pre-vent the mass of people from voting for legislators who will tax only the rich, who as a minority will always be outvoted. During the early decades of this century, that is exactly what the rich feared would happen. Since the highest marginal tax rate was 94 percent, you might think that that is in fact what did happen.

You would be wrong. Offsetting the high rates were the deductions, exemptions, and exclusions by which people could shelter some of their income from taxation. These loopholes were available for everyone, but they particularly helped the well-off. In effect a political compromise was reached during the first half of this century. The terms were these: the well-off, generally represented by the Republican party, would drop their bitter opposition to high marginal rates provided that the less-well-off, generally represented by the Democratic party, would support a large number of loopholes. The Democrats (or more accurately, the liberals) were willing to accept this compromise because they feared that if they insisted on high rates with no loopholes, the economy would suffer as people and businesses lost their incentive to save and invest.

For at least thirty years after the adoption of the income tax in 1913, only a small number of high-income people paid any significant amount in federal income taxes. The average citizen paid very little in such taxes until World War II. After the war, taxes did not fall to their prewar levels.

Most people did not complain too much because they, too, benefited greatly from the loopholes. They could deduct from taxable income the mortgage interest on their homes, state and local taxes, much of their medical-insurance premiums, and the interest that they paid on consumer loans (such as those used to buy automobiles). On the eve of the Tax Reform Act of 1986 an opinion poll showed that more people favored small cuts in tax rates coupled with many large deductions than favored big cuts in tax rates coupled with fewer and smaller deductions.[12]

Around each loophole interest groups organized. The average citizen may not have been part of these groups but was helped by them nonetheless. Home builders organized to support mortgage-interest deductions; universities, to support charitable-contribution deductions; health-insurance companies, to support medical-premium deductions; and automakers, to support consumer-interest deductions.

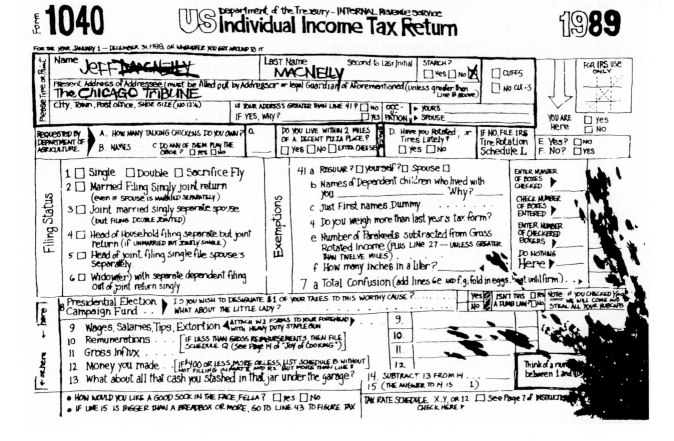

FIGURE 16.6 Federal Taxes on Income, Top Percentage Rates, 1913–1993

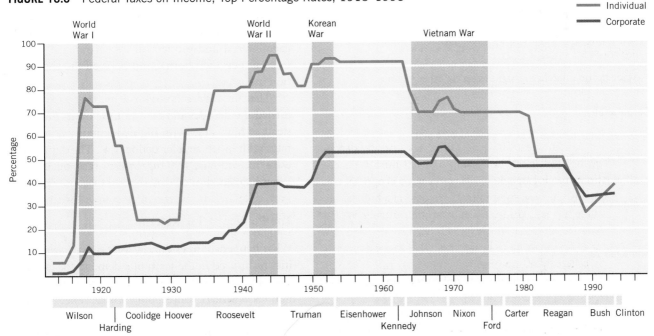

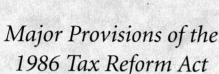

Major Provisions of the 1986 Tax Reform Act

Individuals

- Eliminated more than a dozen tax brackets, replacing them with two basic brackets: 15 percent and 28 percent. (Previously, the highest bracket was 50 percent.)

- Removed several million poor persons from the tax rolls altogether.

- Increased size of personal exemption and standard deduction for individuals and couples.

- Retained deductions for:

  Home mortgage interest

  State and local taxes

  Itemized charitable contributions

- Eliminated deductions for:

  Interest on consumer loans

  Sales taxes

  Many tax shelters

  Contributions to Individual Retirement Accounts (depending on income and whether covered by employer pension)

- Made tax on capital gains same as tax on other income

Corporations

- Lowered top tax rate from 46 percent to 34 percent

- Repealed the investment tax credit

- Eliminated many tax loopholes

- Stipulated that only 80 percent of business meals and entertainment can be deducted

Minimum Tax

- Both individuals and corporations would have to pay a minimum tax even when their deductions and exemptions would otherwise entitle them to pay no tax

In addition to these well-known loopholes there were countless others, not so well known and involving much less money, that were defended and enlarged through the efforts of other interest groups: for instance, oil companies supported the deduction for drilling costs, heavy industry supported the investment tax credit, and real-estate developers supported special tax write-offs for apartment and office buildings.

Until 1986 the typical tax fight was less about rates than about deductions. Rates were important but not as important as tax loopholes. "Loophole politics" was client politics. When client groups pressed for benefits, they could take advantage of the decentralized structure of Congress to find well-placed advocates who could advance these interests through low-visibility bargaining. In effect these groups were getting a subsidy from the federal government equal to the amount of the tax break. However, the tax break was even better than a subsidy because it did not have to be voted on every year as part of an appropriations bill: once part of the tax code, it lasted for a long time, and given the length and complexity of that code, scarcely anyone noticed that it was there.

Many of these loopholes could be justified by arguments about economic growth. Especially low tax rates on a certain kind of investment encouraged more investment of that kind. Deductions for mortgage interest and property taxes encouraged people to own their own homes and boosted the construction industry.

Then in 1986 a tax-reform bill was passed that turned the decades-old compromise on its head: instead of high rates with big deductions, we got low rates with much smaller deductions. The big gainers were individuals, the big losers were businesses. What happened?

The Politics of Tax Reform

What happened, in essence, is that majoritarian politics resurfaced in the form of a demand for fairness. The old system of loophole politics had created a situation in which some policy entrepreneurs could point to both real and imagined scandals that enabled them to mobilize majorities supporting change.

There were several kinds of entrepreneurs. Some were professional economists who had been writing for years about the inequities and inefficiencies of the old tax code. They complained that high tax rates discouraged investment and risk-taking by people who could not take advantage of any existing loopholes. They argued that many business decisions were being made, not on the basis of what was economically efficient, but on the basis of what worked under the tax law. They denounced the loopholes as "tax expenditures"—that is, subsidies to particular groups that had not passed through the normal legislative process of annually discussing a given appropriation. Over time the weight of this professional opinion on taxes was beginning to make itself felt, just as the weight of such opinion against airline regulation had made itself felt in the events leading up to deregulation in 1978 (see Chapter 15). In the government these economists found allies in the Treasury Department, the Council of Economic Advisers, and the Congress.

Another kind of entrepreneur comprised people who had an ideological commitment to supply-side economics. Then-Representative Jack Kemp was a leader of this group, whose members argued that low tax rates would spur economic growth. They won an initial victory in 1981 when the Reagan tax cut, which they endorsed, was enacted by Congress (it cut the average tax rate by about 23 percent). The 1986 legislation was seen as another step in that direction.

Still other entrepreneurs were those publicists and journalists who liked to produce stories about "tax cheats." These often took the form of lists of wealthy individuals or big corporations that had not paid anything in taxes that year. Usually they had paid no taxes for perfectly legal reasons—their deductions and exemptions were so large as to leave them owing no tax. To the American public, however, any affluent person or firm that paid no taxes was shirking its civic duty. The people supported the idea of deductions, but not when the system let somebody get off owing nothing. Opinion polls showed that a clear majority of the public thought that the existing tax law was "unfair."

For policy entrepreneurs to succeed, they must be able to motivate key politicians. In 1986 the motives were there. Representatives Kemp and Gephardt had presidential ambitions, and so they were willing to

Major Provisions of the 1993 Budget Reconciliation Act

Individuals

- Created a fourth tax bracket, increasing the effective top rate from 36 percent to 39.6 percent for upper-income taxpayers

- Phased out the personal exemption for upper-income taxpayers

- Raised the portion of Social Security benefits subject to taxation from 50 percent to 85 percent for individuals making more than $34,000 a year and couples making more than $44,000 a year

- Eliminated deductions for dues in any club organized for business, pleasure, recreation, or other social purposes

Corporations

- Increased top tax rate from 25 percent to 34 percent

- Reduced deductions for:

  Business meals

  Moving expenses

  Travel expenses

- Eliminated deductions for lobbying expenses

Minimum Tax

- Increased the minimum tax on individuals by creating a two-tiered rate structure: a 26 percent rate for the first $175,000 of a taxpayer's income and a 28 percent rate for income above $175,000

- Relaxed the minimum tax on business by changing the formula by which it is calculated

take up the cause in order to advance their candidacies. The chairman of the House Ways and Means Committee, Representative Dan Rostenkowski, wanted to be Speaker of the House and saw in support for comprehensive tax reform a way of becoming a stronger candidate for that job (as it turned out, he lost to Representative Jim Wright). The chairman of the Senate Finance Committee, Senator Bob Packwood, had been chagrined by press attacks labeling him "Senator Hackwood" for his prior support of various tax loopholes. The Democratic leadership in Congress wanted to overcome the adverse effect on public opinion created by the support that their 1984 presidential candidate, Walter Mondale, had given to raising taxes; tax reform seemed a good way of making people forget tax increases.

What may have sealed the victory was the behavior of the client groups who fought to keep their favorite loopholes. At congressional hearings on the bill they would sometimes applaud when, in the early negotiations, some pet loophole survived intact. Members of the Senate Finance Committee finally

rebelled at this, tore up the bill that they had been considering, and voted overwhelmingly for a new bill that eliminated many loopholes and cut rates. Within a few months the bill was passed and signed (for its provisions, see the box on page 494).

Tax politics had come full circle. The original 1913 tax law had been the product of majoritarian politics. Then, as the fight over rates intensified, subsequent versions of the law became more the product of client politics. In 1986 majoritarian politics reemerged to dominate the proceedings. As with airline deregulation, civil rights, and (as we shall see) foreign policy, ideas sometimes are more important than interests.

SUMMARY

There are three economic factors that make a difference to voters; the policies for each are formulated by a distinctive type of policy-making. The first is the economic health of the nation, the second the amount and kinds of government spending, and the third the level and distribution of taxes.

National economic health has powerful effects on the outcome of elections as much through people's perception of national conditions as from their worries about their own finances. The politics of inflation, unemployment, and economic growth tend to be majoritarian. The president is held responsible for national conditions. But he must meet that responsibility by using imperfect economic theories to manage clumsy government tools controlled by divided political authorities.

When economic ill health occurs in some industries and places but not others (as a result of such forces as foreign competition), the politics of economic health are shaped by interest-group politics. Firms that import foreign products or sell to foreign nations try to avoid trade restrictions, while firms and unions hurt by foreign competition try to impose such restrictions.

The amount of spending is theoretically determined by the budget, but in fact the nation has no meaningful budget. Instead the president and Congress struggle over particular spending bills whose amounts reflect interest-group and client pressures. In the 1980s those pressures, coupled with a large tax cut, led to a sharp increase in the size of the federal debt.

The general shape of federal tax legislation is determined by majoritarian politics, but the specific provisions (especially the deductions, exemptions, and exclusions) are the result of client-group politics. The Tax Reform Act of 1986 was a remarkable example of the reassertion of majoritarian politics over client-group pressures made possible by policy entrepreneurs and political incentives.

KEY TERMS

monetarism   *p. 478*

Keynesianism   *p. 479*

economic planning   *p. 479*

price and wage control   *p. 479*

industrial policy   *p. 479*

supply-side theory   *p. 480*

Reaganomics   *p. 480*

fiscal policy   *p. 483*

budget deficit   *p. 483*

budget surplus   *p. 483*

monetary policy   *p. 483*

fiscal year (FY)   *p. 483*

budget   *p. 486*

budget resolution   *p. 486*

sequester   *p. 488*

peace dividend   *p. 489*

SUGGESTED READINGS

Birnbaum, Jeffrey H., and Alan S. Murray. *Showdown at Gucci Gulch.* New York: Random House, 1987. Lively journalistic account of the passage of the Tax Reform Act of 1986.

Boskin, Michael J., and Aaron Wildavsky, eds. *The Federal Budget: Economics and Politics.* San Francisco: Institute for Contemporary Studies, 1982. Essays on how the budget is made, alternative means for controlling it, and trends in federal spending.

Kiewiet, D. Roderick. *Macroeconomics and Micropolitics.* Chicago: University of Chicago Press, 1983. Argues that citizens vote on the basis of their estimate of national economic conditions as well as their own financial circumstances.

Maisel, Sherman J. *Managing the Dollar.* New York: Norton, 1973. Nontechnical discussion, by a former member, of how the Federal Reserve Board works.

Pechman, Joseph A. *Federal Tax Policy.* 5th ed. Washington, D.C.: Brookings Institution, 1987. Description of federal tax policy and a discussion of the desirability of various changes.

Shick, Allen. *The Capacity to Budget.* Washington, D.C.: Urban Institute, 1990. Analysis of federal budget and spending policies.

Stein, Herbert. *Presidential Economics: The Making of Economic Policy from Hoover to Reagan and Beyond.* New York: Simon & Schuster, 1984. History, by a knowledgeable insider, of how economists participate in making federal economic policy, with special emphasis on the period since 1968.

Tufte, Edward R. *Political Control of the Economy.* Princeton, N.J.: Princeton University Press, 1978. Argues that there is a "political business cycle" caused by politicians' trying to stimulate the economy just before an election.

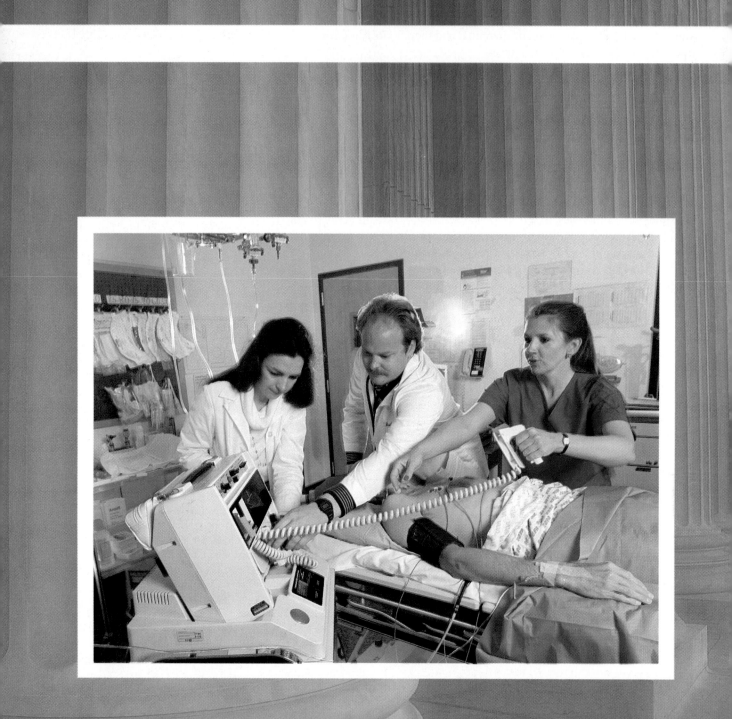

Social Welfare

Ask the average citizen to name the largest part of the federal budget, and chances are that he or she will answer, "military spending." Wrong. Since 1972 federal payments to individuals—Social Security, pensions, welfare, and other "transfer payments"—have been the largest single budget item. Since the late 1970s they have amounted to about one-half of all federal outlays (national defense amounts to about one-quarter). In 1985 defense spending, measured in "constant," or inflation-adjusted, dollars was about what it had been in 1970. During the same period payments to individuals more than doubled.

Some would infer from these facts that we already have a large and generous welfare state—perhaps one that is too large, too generous. Others would argue that these figures are misleading in that most of the money that the federal government sends to individuals does not go to the people who need it the most. Both observers are partially correct.

In this book we are not concerned with deciding what our welfare policies ought to be, only with explaining why they are what they are. But even sorting out this argument is difficult because there are literally hundreds of programs that involve the Treasury Department's sending a check each month to somebody (or as we shall see, sending it to some state agency that in turn sends it to an individual). To simplify matters, we shall discuss here the politics of only a few programs—the Social Security Act of 1935, the Economic Opportunity Act (or "War on Poverty") of 1964, the Medicare Act of 1965, the Family Assistance Plan (proposed in 1969 but not adopted), and the proposals for health-care reform. Two of them—Social Security and Medicare—account for about two-thirds of all federal welfare expenditures and thus have a major impact on the budget. The Family Assistance Plan, if it had been adopted, would have added billions more to these outlays.

These policies exemplify different kinds of political processes at work and reveal what is distinctive about the American approach to social welfare. At least three features of American welfare policy make it different from what one finds in most European democracies. First, Americans have generally taken a more restrictive view of who is entitled to receive government assistance. Second, we have been slower than other countries to adopt many of the components of the welfare state. Third, we have insisted that the states (and to a degree private enterprise) play a large role in running welfare programs.

Overview of Welfare Politics in the United States

The first distinctive feature of the American welfare state involves who is to benefit. To Americans, who benefits has been a question of who *deserves* to benefit. We have usually insisted that public support be given only to those who cannot help themselves. But what does it mean to say that a person "cannot" help himself or herself? Surely a disabled, blind, elderly woman deserted by her family cannot do much to help herself, but is she still deserving of public aid if she is merely disabled? Or merely elderly? And to what extent should we require that her family support her? As we shall see, American welfare policy since the 1930s has been fundamentally shaped by a slow but steady change in how we have separated the "deserving" from the "undeserving" poor.

That we have always thought this way may make us forget that there are other ways of thinking about welfare. The major alternative view is to ask not who deserves help but what each person's "fair share" of the national income is. Seen this way, the role of government is to take money from those who have a lot and give it to those who have only a little until each person has, if not the same amount, then at least a fair share. But defining a "fair share" is even more difficult than defining the "deserving poor." Moreover Americans have generally felt that giving money to people who were already working, or who could work if they chose, was unfair. In some nations, however, government policy is aimed at redistributing income from better-off to not-so-well-off persons without regard to who deserves the money.

Americans base their welfare policy on a concept of "help for the deserving poor" rather than on "redistribution to produce fair shares."[1] They have done so, one suspects, because they believe that citizens should be encouraged to be self-reliant, that people who work hard will get what they deserve, and that giving money to people who could help themselves will produce a class of "welfare chiselers." If Americans believed that success at work was a matter of luck rather than effort or was dictated by forces over which they had no control, they might support a different concept of welfare.

Moreover we have always been a bit uneasy about giving money to people. Though we recognize that many people through no fault of their own cannot buy groceries and thus need funds, we would prefer that, to the extent possible, people who deserve help be given *services* (education, training, medical care) rather than money. Throughout much of our history our welfare policies have reflected a general philosophical disposition in favor of providing services to deserving persons.

The second striking fact about American welfare policy is how late in our history it arrived (at least at the national level) compared to other nations. By 1935, when Congress passed the Social Security Act, at least twenty-two European nations already had similar programs, as did Australia and Japan.[2] Germany was the first to create a nationwide social security program when it developed sickness and mater-

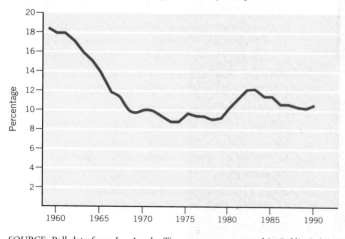

FIGURE 17.1 Family Poverty Rate, 1960–1990

Percentage of U.S. families living below the poverty line

SOURCE: Poll data from *Los Angeles Times* survey, as reported in *Public Opinion* (June–July 1985): 25; poverty data from *Statistical Abstract, 1987,* 442, 444.

nity insurance in 1883. Six years later it added old-age insurance and in 1927 unemployment insurance.

England offers perhaps the clearest contrast with the United States. In 1908 a national system of old-age pensions was set up, followed three years later by a plan for nationwide health and unemployment insurance.[3] England had a parliamentary regime in which a political party with liberal sentiments and a large majority had come to power. With authority concentrated in the hands of the prime minister and his cabinet, there was virtually no obstacle to instituting measures, such as welfare programs, that commended themselves to party leaders on grounds of either principle or party advantage. Furthermore the British Labour party was then beginning to emerge. Though the party was still small (it had only thirty seats in Parliament in 1908), its leaders included people who had been influential in formulating welfare programs that the leaders of the dominant Liberal party backed. And once these programs were approved, they were in almost all cases nationally run: there were no state governments to which authority had to be delegated or whose different experiences had to be accommodated.

Moreover the British in 1908 were beginning to think in terms of social classes, to accept the notion of an activist government, and to make welfare the central political issue. Americans at that time also had an activist leader, Theodore Roosevelt; there was a progressive movement; and labor was well along in its organizing drives. But the issues were defined differently in the United States. Progressives, or at least most of them, emphasized the reform of the political process—by eliminating corruption, by weakening the parties, and by improving the civil service—and attacked bigness by breaking up industrial trusts. Though some progressives favored the creation of a welfare state, they were a distinct minority. They had few allies in organized labor (which was skeptical of public-welfare programs) and could not overcome the general distrust of big government and the strong preference for leaving matters of welfare in state hands. In sum, what ordinary politics brought to England in 1908–1911, only the crisis politics of 1935 would bring to the United States. But once started, the programs grew. By 1983, almost one-third of all Americans received benefits from one or more social welfare programs.

President Lyndon Johnson signs the Medicare Act in 1965 in the company of Vice President Hubert Humphrey (standing) and former President Harry S Truman (seated).

The Great Depression: a breadline forms in a New York City street in December 1931.

The third factor involves the degree to which federalism has shaped national welfare policy. Since the Constitution was silent on whether Congress had the power to spend money on welfare and since powers not delegated to Congress were reserved to the states, it was not until the constitutional reinterpretation of the 1930s (see Chapter 14) that it became clear that the federal government could do anything in the area of social policy. At the same time federalism meant that any state so inclined could experiment with welfare programs. Between 1923 and 1933 thirty states enacted some form of an old-age pension. By 1935 all but two states had adopted a "mother's pension"—a program whereby a widow with children was given financial assistance, provided that she was a "fit mother" who ran a "suitable home." The poor were given small doles by local governments, helped by private charities, or placed in almshouses. Only one state, Wisconsin, had an unemployment-insurance program.

Politically the state programs had a double-edged effect: they provided opponents of a federal welfare system with an argument (the states were already providing welfare assistance), but they also supplied a lobby for federal financial assistance (state authorities would campaign for national legislation to help them out). Some were later to say that the states were the laboratories for experimentation in welfare policy. As we shall see, when the federal government entered the field in 1935, it did so in part by spending money through the states, thereby encouraging the formation in the states of a strong welfare bureaucracy whose later claims would be difficult to ignore.

Key Welfare Plans in Brief

Social Security Act of 1935

At the time that the Great Depression began in 1929, the job of providing relief to needy people fell to state and local governments or to private charities, and even these sources were primarily concerned with widows, orphans, and the elderly.[4] Hardly any state had a systematic program for supporting the unemployed, though many states provided some kind of help if it was clear that the person was out of work through no fault of his or her own. When the economy suddenly ground to a near standstill and the unemployment rate rose to include one-fourth of the work force, private charities and city relief programs were nearly bankrupt.

The election of 1932 produced an overwhelming congressional majority for the Democrats and placed Franklin D. Roosevelt in the White House. Almost immediately a number of emergency measures were adopted to cope with the depression by supplying federal cash to bail out state and local relief agencies and by creating public-works jobs under federal auspices. These measures were recognized as temporary expedients, however, and were unsatisfactory to those who believed that the federal government had a permanent and major responsibility for welfare. Roosevelt created a Cabinet Committee on Economic Security to consider long-term policies. It drew heavily on the experience of European nations and on the ideas of various American scholars and social workers, but understood that it would have to adapt these proposals to the realities of American

Senator Huey P. Long of Louisiana formed a "Share Our Wealth" movement that threatened the unity of the Democratic party. Left, in May 1935 he greets supporters of his effort to override President Roosevelt's veto of a veterans' bonus. Right, President Roosevelt meets with members of the Civilian Conservation Corps, which put unemployed young men to work; he feared that Long might challenge him in the 1936 election.

politics. Chief among these was the widespread belief that any direct federal welfare program might be unconstitutional. The Constitution nowhere explicitly gave to Congress the authority to set up an unemployment-compensation or old-age retirement program. And even if a welfare program was constitutional, it would be wrong because it violated the individualistic creed that people should help themselves unless they were physically unable to do so.

But failure by the Roosevelt administration to produce a comprehensive social security program, his supporters felt, might make the president vulnerable in the 1936 election to the leaders of various radical social movements. Huey Long of Louisiana was proposing a "Share Our Wealth" plan; Upton Sinclair was running for governor of California on a platform calling for programs to "End Poverty in California"; and Dr. Francis E. Townsend was leading an organization of hundreds of thousands of elderly people on whose behalf he demanded government pensions of $200 a month.

The plan that emerged from the cabinet committee was carefully designed to meet popular demands within the framework of popular beliefs and constitutional understandings. It called for two kinds of programs: (1) an **insurance program** for the unemployed and elderly to which workers would contribute and from which they would benefit when unemployed or upon retirement and (2) an **assistance program** for the blind, dependent children, and the aged. (Giving assistance as well as providing "insurance" for the aged was necessary because for the first few years the insurance program would not pay out any benefits.) The federal government would use its taxing power to provide the funds, but all of the programs (except for old-age insurance) would be administered by the states. Everybody, rich or poor, would be eligible for the insurance programs. Only the poor, as measured by a **means test** (a measure to determine that incomes are below a certain level), would be eligible for the assistance programs. Though bitterly opposed by some, the resulting Social Security Act passed swiftly and virtually unchanged through Congress. It was introduced in January 1935 and signed by President Roosevelt in August of that year.

TABLE 17.1   Beneficiaries of Major Government Transfer Programs, Selected Years, 1960–1990

Program	*Number of Recipients (in millions)*			
	1960	1970	1980	1990 (estimated)
Social Security	14.3	25.8	35.4	39.5
Medicare	0	19.9	27.5	33.2
Medicaid	0	14.5	21.6	25.8
School Lunch	13.6	22.4	26.6	25.0
Food Stamps[a]	4.3	8.5	19.3	25.4
Assisted Housing	1.6	3.5	10.6	14.0
Aid to Families with Dependent Children	3.0	7.4	10.6	10.9
Supplemental Security Income	2.8	2.9	3.7	4.2
Women, Infants, and Children Nutrition Program[a]	0	0.1	2.0	3.8
Veterans' Payments	4.0	4.7	4.7	3.6
Unemployment Insurance[b]	2.1	2.1	3.8	2.4[c]

[a] Predecessor programs included. [b] Weekly average insured unemployment. [c] 1987 data.
NOTE: Because some persons received benefits from two or more programs, the number of beneficiaries cannot be added up to determine the total number of persons receiving transfer payments.
SOURCE: The Urban Institute, 1990.

Economic Opportunity Act of 1964

When President Lyndon Johnson declared a War on Poverty, he did so not in the midst of a depression but at a time of prosperity. The program was aimed at a minority of the population—especially, but not exclusively, a black minority—that was not sharing in the general affluence.[5]

These "pockets of poverty" had recently been discovered by various writers and scholars. Michael Harrington's *The Other America*[6] and other studies, such as those of the economist Robert Lampman,[7] had called attention to poverty amid plenty. In both the Kennedy and Johnson administrations, key officials devised various programs aimed at what some considered a crisis in unemployment, inadequate schooling, juvenile delinquency, and urban squalor. Other people in and out of government felt that, in addition to conventional job-training and job-creation programs, a concerted effort should be made to mobilize the poor so that they could use their collective power to enlarge the opportunities open to them. Presidential assistants proposed dozens of different (and sometimes inconsistent) ideas in response to a presidential directive that a new approach to poverty be made ready for Johnson's 1964 State of the Union address.

The proposals might never have acquired any special sense of urgency save for two events. One was the civil-rights movement, which was steadily becoming stronger, with demonstrations in hundreds of American cities climaxed in August 1963 by a "March on Washington" of over two hundred thousand persons, mostly black. The march drew attention to black demands for jobs as well as for civil rights. The second event, two and a half months later, was the murder of President Kennedy in Dallas. It led many legislators to rally behind President Johnson and to treat favorably those Kennedy proposals that later became part of the Johnson program.

Unlike the Social Security Act, the Economic Opportunity Act provided services rather than money to its beneficiaries, calling for:

- Job Corps to train in camps young people who were chronically unemployed

- Literacy programs to teach English to adults not able to read or write

- Neighborhood Youth Corps to provide work experience to young people in cities

- A work-study program to subsidize the part-time employment of college students who came from poor families

- Community Action Program (CAP) to fund organizations that were to give residents in poor neighborhoods an opportunity for "maximum feasible participation" in planning and implementing service programs intended for their benefit

The bill passed Congress in the summer of 1964 on a nearly party-line vote, with most Democrats in favor and most Republicans opposed. But this vote was only the beginning of the political struggle. Unlike the Social Security Act, which authorized cash transfers that could be handled by relatively simple administrative arrangements, the Economic Opportunity Act authorized a complex, poorly understood set of services (training, teaching, organizing, counseling) that led to the creation of complicated and often controversial organizations in hundreds of American communities.

Much of the controversy arose because of the efforts in many cities to use the community-action programs as mechanisms for transferring political power from city halls or established agencies (such as schools and welfare offices) to neighborhood-based organizations of poor people or to leaders claiming to represent the poor. Mayors and school superintendents were frequently confronted by protest marches, sit-ins, and political campaigns organized by CAPs and paid for with federal funds. Not surprisingly the officials complained to their members of Congress, and efforts—many successful—were made to amend the Economic Opportunity Act to bring local CAPs more under the control of city hall.

Medicare Act of 1965

The idea of having the government pay the medical and hospital bills of the elderly and the poor had been discussed in Washington since the drafting of the Social Security Act in the 1930s. President Roosevelt and his Committee on Economic Security

Support for the Economic Opportunity Act was fueled by the 1963 March on Washington addressed by the Reverend Martin Luther King, Jr.

sensed that medical care would be very controversial, and so health programs were left out of the 1935 bill in order not to jeopardize its chances of passage.[8]

The proponents of the idea did not abandon it, however. Working mostly within the executive branch, they continued to press, sometimes publicly, sometimes behind the scenes, for a national healthcare plan. Democratic presidents, including Truman, Kennedy, and Johnson, favored it; Republican President Eisenhower opposed it; Congress was deeply divided on it. The American Medical Association attacked it as "socialized medicine." For thirty years key policy entrepreneurs, such as Wilbur Cohen, worked to find a formula that would produce a congressional majority.

The first and highest hurdle to overcome, however, was not Congress as a whole but the House Ways and Means Committee, especially its powerful

Major Social-Welfare Programs

INSURANCE, OR "CONTRIBUTORY," PROGRAMS

Old Age, Survivors, and Disability Insurance (OASDI)
Monthly payments to retired or disabled people and to surviving members of their families. This program, popularly called *Social Security,* is paid for by a payroll tax on employers and employees. *No means test.*

Medicare Federal government pays for part of the cost of hospital care for retired or disabled people covered by Social Security. Paid for by payroll taxes on employees and employers. *No means test.*

ASSISTANCE, OR "NONCONTRIBUTORY," PROGRAMS

Unemployment Insurance (UI) Weekly payments to workers who have been laid off and cannot find work. Benefits and requirements determined by states. Paid for by taxes on employers. *No means test.*

Aid to Families with Dependent Children (AFDC) Payments to families with children, either one-parent families or (in some states) two-parent families where the breadwinner is unemployed. Paid for partly by states and partly by federal government. *Means test.*

Supplemental Security Income (SSI) Cash payments to aged, blind, or disabled people whose income is below a certain amount. Paid for from general federal revenues. *Means test.*

Food Stamps Vouchers, given to people whose income is below a certain level, that can be used to buy food at grocery stores. Paid for out of general federal revenues. *Means test.*

Medicaid Pays medical expenses of persons receiving AFDC or SSI payments. *Means test.*

Earned Income Tax Credit Pays a cash subsidy (or tax credit) to poor working families. *Means test.*

chairman from 1958 to 1975, Wilbur Mills of Arkansas. A majority of the committee members opposed a national health-care program. Some members believed it wrong in principle; others feared that adding a costly health component to the Social Security system would jeopardize the financial solvency and administrative integrity of one of the most popular government programs. By the early 1960s a majority of the House favored a health-care plan, but without the approval of Ways and Means it would never reach the floor.

The 1964 elections changed all that. The Johnson landslide produced such large Democratic majorities in Congress that the composition of the committees changed. In particular the membership of the Ways and Means Committee was altered. Whereas before it had three Democrats for every two Republicans, after 1964 it had two Democrats for every one Republican. The House leadership saw to it that the new Democrats on the committee were strongly committed to a health-care program. Suddenly the committee had a majority favorable to such a plan, and Mills, realizing that a bill would pass and wanting to help shape its form, changed his position and became a supporter of what was to become Medicare.

The policy entrepreneurs in and out of the government who drafted the Medicare plan attempted to anticipate the major objections to it. First, the bill would apply only to the aged—those eligible for Social Security retirement benefits. This would reassure legislators worried about the cost of providing tax-supported health care for everybody. Second, the plan would cover only hospital expenses, not doctors' bills. Since doctors were not to be paid by the government, they would not be regulated by it; thus presumably the opposition of the American Medical Association would be blunted.

Unexpectedly, however, the Ways and Means Committee broadened the coverage of the plan beyond what the administration had thought was politically feasible. It added sections providing medical assistance, called Medicaid, for the poor (defined as those already getting public-assistance payments) and payment of doctors' bills for the aged (a new part of Medicare). The new, much-enlarged bill passed both houses of Congress with ease. The key votes pitted a majority of the Democrats against a majority of the Republicans.

Family Assistance Plan of 1969

Though most of the programs created by the Social Security Act proved quite popular, one—providing public assistance to families with dependent children (or AFDC)—became controversial as the number of welfare mothers grew rapidly in the 1960s. Between 1964 and 1969 the number of AFDC recipients increased by more than 60 percent while the costs more than doubled. This happened during a time of low and generally declining unemployment.[9]

AFDC was criticized for different reasons by different groups. Some objected to paying people public money if they were able to work and to subsidizing the families of men who were unwilling to support them. Others felt that the women needed the money but that in many states the benefits were too low (see Figure 17.2). (The states ran the program with federal financial assistance and decided how large the payments should be.) Others objected to the fact that intact poor families—that is, those with a mother and father both present in the home—were often excluded from any assistance, even though their incomes might be lower than those of single-parent families who were eligible for welfare payments. They thought that the program might even encourage families to break up. Still others felt that AFDC discouraged recipients from looking for jobs, since they lost their benefits if they went to work. And still others believed that the means tests used to find out whether a person was eligible were demeaning.

For some time economists and others had been advocating a "guaranteed annual income" or "negative income tax" to replace AFDC, which would put a floor under the incomes of all families, working or nonworking, single-parent or two-parent. President Nixon, at the urging of his urban affairs adviser, Daniel Patrick Moynihan, endorsed the concept, though he preferred calling it by a different name—the Family Assistance Plan (FAP). It was a bold step, and if it had been passed, it would have meant a radical departure from traditional American welfare concepts. Instead of helping only those who were disabled, retired, or unemployed, it would redistribute income by establishing a national minimum income below which no family, whether working or not, would be allowed to fall. To downplay its boldness, one early proponent half-seriously suggested calling the bill the "Honest Christian Anti-Communist Working Man's Family Allowance National Defense Human Resources Rivers and Harbors Act of 1969."[10]

The plan was complicated, a fact that did not help it. Every family with children would receive a guaranteed minimum income. All able-bodied recipients would be required either to work or to enter a job-training program. Any money that they earned would be offset against their FAP benefits, but at a rate less than dollar-for-dollar. Thus, as their job incomes rose, they would be able to keep some part of their FAP income as well, to a point (around $3,000 a year in job earnings) at which the FAP income would stop.

With the support of Wilbur Mills and other conservatives, FAP passed in the House. What appealed to conservatives was the hope that FAP would reduce welfare cheating, the knowledge that the federal government would assume a bigger share of the costs of welfare now borne by states and cities, and the belief

FIGURE 17.2   AFDC Benefits versus Poverty Line

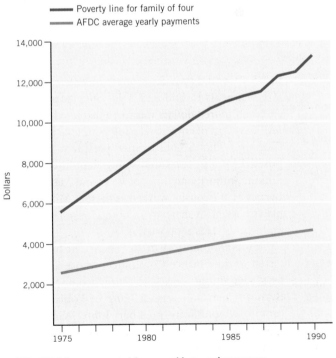

NOTE: AFDC figures converted from monthly to yearly payments.

SOURCE: *Statistical Abstract of the United States, 1992*, 370, 427.

Daniel Patrick Moynihan, who helped a Republican president write the Family Assistance Plan in 1969, was the Democratic sponsor of a major Senate welfare reform bill in 1988.

that FAP would provide stronger incentives for welfare recipients to find and hold jobs. (A penalty of several hundred dollars was to be deducted from the FAP payment of anyone refusing a suitable job or job training.) That a conservative president had proposed FAP also reassured many Republicans. The ranking minority member of Ways and Means, John Byrnes of Wisconsin, worked as hard as Mills for the plan's passage. A majority of both House Democrats and Republicans supported it.

It was another story in the Senate. The bill was referred to the Finance Committee, whose key members saw things very differently from Mills and Byrnes. Chairman Russell Long of Louisiana and ranking Republican member John Williams of Delaware thought that FAP would make the "welfare mess" even worse by adding a large number of people (some said as many as 14 million) to the welfare rolls, increasing welfare costs, and providing inadequate

work incentives. By now some liberal senators were also becoming skeptical. Their objections were precisely the opposite of those of the conservatives: FAP would not increase welfare benefits enough, too many people would be left in poverty, and the work incentives were too severe. Moreover liberal senators were suspicious of any welfare plan put forth by Nixon. Senator Fred Harris of Oklahoma, a liberal member of the Finance Committee, offered an amendment to raise substantially the benefits (and of course the costs).

By 1972 not only was the bill dead, but the idea underlying it was nearly dead as well. (In the presidential campaign that year Senator George McGovern offered a version of a guaranteed annual income that was poorly presented, quickly attacked, and hastily withdrawn.) In part the bill was defeated because there is no "welfare reform" capable of simultaneously keeping costs down, benefits high, and work incentives strong. President Carter discovered this when he introduced his own version of a guaranteed-income plan (the "Program for Better Jobs and Income"), only to encounter many of the same objections as those made against FAP. One variation of FAP did become law. A little-noticed provision in a 1975 tax law entitled working families with children to receive money from the government if their total income fell below a certain level. This program, called the **earned-income tax credit,** was in fact a "negative income tax" or guaranteed annual income. In 1988 the maximum amount it provided was $851 per year for eligible families with one child. The 1993 Budget Reconciliation Act increased the maximum credit to $2,038 and mandated further increases through 1996.

Two Kinds of Welfare Politics

These four programs illustrate two patterns of policy-making. The old-age pensions created by the Social Security Act of 1935 and the health-care benefits created by the Medicare Act of 1965 are examples of **majoritarian politics:** almost everybody benefits and almost everybody pays. The AFDC program and the Community Action Program (CAP) of the War on Poverty are examples of **client politics:** a relatively few people benefit, but everybody pays.

Majoritarian Politics

When both the benefits and the costs of a proposed program are widely distributed, the proposal will be adopted *if* the beneficiaries believe that their benefits will exceed their costs *and* if political elites believe that it is legitimate for the federal government to adopt the program.

Initially retirement benefits greatly exceeded the costs. Older people would be able to get an old-age pension or health care even though they had paid in taxes only a small fraction of what these benefits would cost. Social Security and Medicare seemed initially like the nearest thing to a free lunch. There were several reasons for this. First, the retirement benefits were initially set at a relatively low level, and so the taxes needed to pay for them were relatively small. (In 1937, a worker had to pay only 1 percent of his wages in Social Security—or FICA—taxes.) Second, the population was young enough so that lots of employed workers would pay for the benefits received by a relatively small number of retired persons. In 1950 there were fourteen workers paying Social Security taxes for every one retired person; even as late as 1960, there were five workers paying for every one person collecting. Third, people supporting Medicare vastly underestimated the actual costs of the program. One proponent said in 1965 that it would never cost more than $8 billion a year. Today the actual cost is more than thirteen times that.

The big debate in 1935 and in 1965 was not over whether the people wanted these programs—the polls showed that they did—but over whether it was legitimate for the federal government to run them.[11] In 1935 conservatives argued that as desirable as Social Security might be, nothing in the Constitution authorized the federal government to spend money for this purpose; welfare, they said, was a policy area reserved to the states. Liberals rejoined that the federal government had an obligation to help people avoid poverty in their old age. Besides, they said, as an "insurance" program, retirement benefits were not really a federal expenditure at all: Washington was merely collecting payments and holding them in a trust fund until the people who paid them were ready to retire. In the midst of the Great Depression and at a time when liberals had large majorities in Congress, it was an easy argument to make, and so

TABLE 17.2 Key Votes on Major Welfare Proposals in the House

Proposals	Democrats	Republicans
Social Security (1935)		
For	252	1
Against	45	95
Economic Opportunity (1964)		
For	204	22
Against	40	145
Medicare (1965)		
For	226	10
Against	63	128
Family Assistance Plan (1970)		
For	141	102
Against	83	72

the Social Security bill readily crossed over the legitimacy barrier.

In 1965 the same issues were raised. Conservatives argued that medical care was a private, not a governmental, matter and that any federal involvement would subject doctors and hospitals to endless red tape and harm the quality of the doctor-patient relationship. Liberals rejoined that the elderly had health needs that they could not meet without help and that only the federal government had the resources to provide that assistance. Because the 1964 elections, when Lyndon Johnson defeated Barry Goldwater, had swept into the House and Senate large majorities of liberal Democrats, there was no chance of a conservative coalition of Republicans and southern Democrats defeating Medicare, and so it passed.

As can be seen in Table 17.2, the votes in Congress on Social Security and Medicare followed party lines. Since the Democratic opponents of these bills were typically conservative southerners, the vote followed even more closely ideological lines.

Once the ideological issue had been settled and the benefits began to flow, it quickly became good politics to support frequent increases in the scope of the program and the size of the benefits. From 1950 to 1975 there was only one period (1959–1965) when Congress allowed more than two years to pass without either increasing retirement benefits or broadening the kinds of workers covered by the plan.[12]

It is not hard to see why. The House comes up for reelection every two years. Though some members no doubt voted to increase benefits out of a sincere conviction that the elderly needed more help, every member knew that it was a political asset to be able to say that he or she had voted to provide more benefits. By 1954 Social Security was so well established that a Republican president proposed to a Republican-controlled Congress that benefits be increased. The vote in the House was 356 in favor, 8 opposed.

Majoritarian politics remains good politics unless the costs to the voters begin to exceed their benefits. Though Social Security and Medicare were supposed to be insurance programs, in fact they are not. What a retired person takes out in benefits bears little relationship to what he or she has previously paid in taxes. These programs are in fact devices whereby people now working are taxed to provide benefits for people now retired.

Three things began to change the politics of these programs. First, Congress raised retirement benefits to the point where tax increases were necessary to pay for them. A tax that had taken only 1 percent of a worker's salary in 1935 was taking over 7.5 percent of

it by 1990. Second, older people began to live longer, and so the number of retired people who had to be supported increased. By 1975 only about three workers were paying taxes for every one person who was retired; early in the next century, the ratio will fall to about two to one. Third, the cost of health care began to shoot up. By 1985 the price of a hospital room was almost five times greater than it had been in 1970.

By 1977 Congress for the first time had to raise Social Security taxes without raising benefits. The bill carried the House by only twenty-six votes, a far cry from the nearly unanimous votes by which retirement bills had once passed. The days of easy votes on Social Security had come to an end.[13]

Client Politics

When the benefits of a proposal are to go to a relatively small group, but the public at large pays, we have client politics. Proposals to benefit clients will pass *if* the cost to the public at large is not perceived to be great *and* if the client receiving the benefit is thought to be "deserving."

Aid to Families with Dependent Children (AFDC) and the Community Action Program (CAP) of the War on Poverty have not cost much. The fed-

Aid to Families with Dependent Children (AFDC) became controversial as Americans began to see it as a program that chiefly aided unmarried black mothers.

eral government in 1990 spent less than $12 billion on AFDC, less than half what it spent on veterans' benefits and only a tenth of what it spent on Medicare. While it still existed, CAP cost less than half a billion dollars a year. The politics of these programs centers less on their cost than on the legitimacy of their beneficiaries.

When first enacted, AFDC was relatively noncontroversial. Originally it seemed intended to help deserving people. In 1935 the typical welfare mother was perceived to be a white woman living in a small town whose husband had been killed in a mining accident. Who could object to giving some modest help to a person who was the victim of circumstances? After all, it could happen to anyone. Thirty years later a welfare mother was perceived as being a never-married black woman living in a big-city public-housing project with children whose father had deserted them. This change in perception did not correspond to reality. Black women, though over-represented among AFDC recipients, have never been a majority of them. But in the public's mind "welfare," "black," and "illegitimacy" became linked, and thus a program that once was noncontroversial became deeply controversial. This controversy over AFDC helps explain some of the opposition to the Family Assistance Plan (FAP).[14] That program seemed to many people to be an attempt to tax hardworking people in order to give money to people unwilling to work hard.

Right or wrong, American values on this subject are quite clear. As can be seen in Table 17.3, both poor and nonpoor people believe that "welfare encourages husbands to avoid family responsibilities" and "poor young women often have babies so they can collect welfare." These poll data also indicate that Americans prefer to see poor people helped by giving them job training or even creating government jobs for them. This **service strategy** (providing training and education) is strongly preferred to an **income strategy** (giving people money)—unless, of course, the income can be called "insurance."[15]

Indeed some critics of welfare, such as Charles Murray, have argued that AFDC actually increases the number of people living in poverty. Murray claimed that high welfare benefits made it more attractive for some people to go on welfare than to look for a job and more attractive for some women to have babies than to get married. This kept them poor. Other scholars have criticized Murray's thesis. They

argued that there is no direct evidence that welfare encourages family breakup and suggested that the rise in the number of illegitimate children occurred during a period (the 1970s) when welfare benefits, in real (that is, inflation-adjusted) dollars, were going down.[16]

The popular preference for giving people "a hand, not a handout" explains why the War on Poverty was passed in 1964. It seemed to emphasize providing job training and providing services. But it turned out that some aspects of the antipoverty

TABLE 17.3 Attitudes Toward Poverty and Welfare

There is a remarkable similarity between the views of poor and nonpoor Americans on the nature of poverty, the government's obligation to help, and the likely causes of failure.

Question	Percentage Agreeing	
	Poor	Nonpoor
Most poor people:		
Prefer to stay on welfare	20%	25%
Prefer to earn own living	68	62
Poor young women often have babies so they can collect welfare	60	61
Welfare often encourages husbands to avoid family responsibilities	60	61
Antipoverty programs worked:		
Often	31	33
Seldom	56	59
Welfare benefits:		
Give poor people a chance to get started again	31	16
Encourage people to stay poor	43	61
Poor people find:		
It's very hard to get work	59	39
There are jobs available for anyone willing to work	31	59
Best thing to do about poverty is to:		
Give poor money	3	0
Provide services	6	6
Create government jobs	32	19
Provide job training	56	73

SOURCE: *Los Angeles Times* poll, as reported in I. A. Lewis and William Schneider, "Hard Times: The Public on Poverty," *Public Opinion* (June–July 1985): 6, 7, 59.

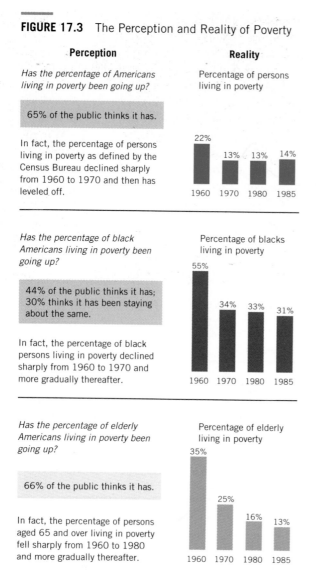

FIGURE 17.3   The Perception and Reality of Poverty

Perception	Reality

Has the percentage of Americans living in poverty been going up?

65% of the public thinks it has.

In fact, the percentage of persons living in poverty as defined by the Census Bureau declined sharply from 1960 to 1970 and then has leveled off.

Percentage of persons living in poverty

22% (1960) 13% (1970) 13% (1980) 14% (1985)

Has the percentage of black Americans living in poverty been going up?

44% of the public thinks it has; 30% thinks it has been staying about the same.

In fact, the percentage of black persons living in poverty declined sharply from 1960 to 1970 and more gradually thereafter.

Percentage of blacks living in poverty

55% (1960) 34% (1970) 33% (1980) 31% (1985)

Has the percentage of elderly Americans living in poverty been going up?

66% of the public thinks it has.

In fact, the percentage of persons aged 65 and over living in poverty fell sharply from 1960 to 1980 and more gradually thereafter.

Percentage of elderly living in poverty

35% (1960) 25% (1970) 16% (1980) 13% (1985)

SOURCE: *Congressional Quarterly Weekly* (January 18, 1992): 110, reporting data from the Joint Economic Committee.

program—in particular, the Community Action Program—involved a transfer of power rather than a distribution of services. CAP organizations in many cities conducted protest marches, sit-ins, and noisy demonstrations on behalf of their clients, and this created support for presidential efforts (by Nixon, Ford, and Reagan) to cut back on the program.

In short the clients of these programs never acquired in the public's mind the legitimacy necessary for their programs to prosper. As a result, whereas for forty years it was thought to be good politics to increase old-age benefits, it increasingly became considered bad politics to do anything but attack, investigate, and curtail the "welfare" (that is, AFDC and CAP) programs.

The Many Politics of Health-Care Reform

When Bill Clinton became president in 1993, he announced that a new federal health-care policy would be an important—perhaps *the* most important—item on his policy agenda. He was not the first president to say that. In 1935 Franklin D. Roosevelt endorsed the idea of compulsory national health insurance as part of his Social Security plan. Though Social Security—that is, pensions for the elderly—became law, the health insurance part was removed by Congress. The American Medical Association (AMA)—a powerful lobbying group for doctors—was strongly opposed, calling the plan "socialized medicine." In the late 1940s, Harry S Truman renewed the call for mandatory universal health insurance, but once again the opposition of doctors, joined by newly created private health insurance companies such as Blue Cross–Blue Shield, defeated the idea.

However in 1965 the federal government began playing a big role in health care with the passage of the Medicare Act. As we have seen, this provided federal money to help the elderly, regardless of their income, pay doctor and hospital bills. The powerful AMA lobby discovered an even more powerful force—the elderly and groups (such as labor unions) that spoke for the elderly. What once had been dismissed as socialism became reality.

Soon a new issue arose: the steeply rising cost of health care. Medicare and Medicaid meant that many people who had been reluctant to go to the hospital when they had to pay for it were now much more willing to go when somebody else paid for it. Moreover, the invention of new drugs and new medical technologies made health care far more expensive than once was the case. Finally, the life expectancy of Americans was rising, meaning that more and more people were living long enough to require costly and extended care. The cost of Medicare began shooting up. In 1970 it cost less than $8 billion; by 1990 it cost over $110 billion.

Several presidents tried to devise ways to control these costs. Richard Nixon urged the formation of national health maintenance organizations (HMOs) that would pay doctors fixed salaries rather than paying them a fee for each service performed. Jimmy Carter called for putting a cap on the amount of money hospitals could get from public and private insurance plans. During the Reagan administration the law was changed so that Medicare would reimburse hospitals a fixed amount, set in advance, for each service provided to each patient—so much for a heart bypass, so much for an appendectomy. Hospitals responded to these price controls by shifting the costs not covered by Medicare onto private patients and their private insurance companies—and total medical costs continued to soar.

When Clinton became president, he argued that the problem with health care was not only that it cost so much but that so many people were not covered by any private health insurance. Determined to create something like the universal, mandatory insurance system that presidents Roosevelt and Truman had once suggested, he formed a Task Force on National Health Care, headed by his wife, Hillary Rodham Clinton. In October 1993, the task force submitted its plan—a 1,342-page draft Health Security Act (HSA).

The Clinton plan, if passed, would be the single biggest change in domestic policy ever enacted. It would place about one-seventh of the entire economy under detailed federal regulation, require every employer to provide health insurance, supply health benefits to people not covered by an employer plan, oversee enrollments in medical schools, and set standards for what every health plan, public or private, offers subscribers.

Majoritarian versus Client Politics

In unveiling his plan, President Clinton faced a fundamental political dilemma. He wanted health care reform to be seen as a *majoritarian* issue—one in which everybody would benefit and almost everybody would pay and the perceived benefits would exceed the costs. But there was a problem with this strategy. Opinion polls showed that the great majority of Americans were happy with the health insur-

Hillary Rodham Clinton defending the president's health-care reform proposal.

ance programs they already had. This is not surprising: some 60 percent of Americans were already covered by health insurance supplied by their employer (or by the employer of a family member); another 24 percent were covered by Medicare and Medicaid. It is hard to make a majoritarian appeal to people who are happy with what they have. Why pay more for what already exists?

The alternative was to try *client* politics. About 15 percent of Americans—as many as 37 million people—were without health insurance at some time during the year. Many of these people still got health care (they could be found crowding the emergency rooms of many hospitals) but they were not guaranteed it. For client politics to be a winning strategy, the client group either has to have powerful allies in Congress or be seen as especially deserving. Many uninsured Americans were not in those categories—they were unemployed, poor, and members of minority groups. Though they may deserve care, it is hard to persuade the public to pay a lot of money to help people who are perceived to be marginal members of society.

The backers of Clinton's plan hit upon a strategy they hoped would solve this problem: downplay the client politics and make health care a majoritarian

issue by persuading people that, though they might be happy with the care they were *now* getting, they were in danger of losing it. Hence the name of the plan—the Health *Security* Act. The security argument was aimed at people who might feel insecure about their health coverage because they worried about losing their jobs, being cut off by their insurer, or not being able to afford future premiums. The timing could not have been better. HSA was unveiled in the midst of a recession when many people—especially people with white-collar jobs—were being laid off. To strengthen the majoritarian appeal of the plan, the president and Mrs. Clinton added a touch of *entrepreneurial* politics by attacking as undeserving certain groups that might have to pay a disproportionate share of the costs. These included drug manufacturers and insurance companies.

Not surprisingly for a proposal of this magnitude, it attracted many rivals. At about the same time the Clinton plan was unveiled, various members of Congress submitted their own proposed laws, some quite different from the Clinton plan. Some members of Congress offered a single-payer plan similar to that found in England and Canada. Under this plan, there would be no health insurance at all; instead, doctor and hospital bills would be paid directly by the federal government (the "single payer"). Clinton avoided this strategy because it sounded too

much like what once was called socialized medicine—all the doctors working for a government bureaucracy. Other members of Congress proposed a voluntary plan in which every employer would be encouraged to offer employees a health plan, but not necessarily one paid for by the employer. Clinton rejected this approach because it did not guarantee universal coverage for everyone. Clinton thought of his plan, called *managed competition,* as a compromise between these two alternatives.

Though it may have been a compromise, it was not an easily grasped one. The staggering length and complexity of the Clinton bill meant that hardly any citizen, and only some members of Congress, had any real grasp of how it might work. There is an old rule in congressional politics coined by Senator Daniel Patrick Moynihan: "If you have to explain it, you can't pass it."

As the debate began in 1994, the average citizen was less interested in hearing an explanation of the plan and more interested in getting clear answers to some practical questions:

1. *Would people have to pay higher taxes for benefits they already had?* The Clinton plan relied on "sin taxes" on cigarettes plus squeezing "waste, fraud, and abuse" out of the existing health-care system (just as President Reagan claimed that we could afford to pay for government while cutting taxes if we just squeezed the "waste, fraud, and abuse" out of government). Would this work?

2. *Would people retain the right to choose their own doctor?* No one could be certain. In some smaller states, just one health alliance would decide which health plans could operate. Plans that let patients choose their own doctor might be among the more expensive ones and would therefore get squeezed out. People liked choosing their own doctor and would be reluctant to give up what they regarded as a right.

3. *Would the United States continue to be in the forefront of developing new drugs and methods of treatment?* One of the reasons health costs have gone up is that medical technology has become more expensive. And one of the reasons it has become more expensive is that drug manufacturers and research firms can make large profits on new forms

of treatment. If prices—and profits—were controlled, would there still be as many medical advances? And if there were fewer such advances, would the quality of health care suffer?

4. *If all employers were required to provide health insurance, mostly at their own expense, would they cut back on the number of people they hired?* Many small firms didn't have health plans for their employees. Probably most of these employees would have liked to have health coverage, but they also liked to have their jobs. Some employers would have to cut back on employment—unless there was a ceiling on how much they would have to spend on health care. The Clinton plan proposed such a cap, but if employer contributions were capped, would there be enough money to run the system without rationing health care?

5. *Should there be one national plan or several state plans?* When Clinton proposed the HSA, several states were already developing their own ideas. Hawaii required all employers to provide health insurance to all full-time employees; Florida had created a number of health alliances somewhat similar to those Clinton proposed; Washington required that, starting in 1999, all residents have a minimum package of health benefits provided by a health alliance with a cap on the maximum premium that could be charged; Oregon had expanded its Medicaid program to cover everyone below the poverty line but not for all treatments. Much more would be known about what types of programs worked as these and other states continued to experiment. Some people felt that it was premature to enact a federal program before these lessons were learned on the state level.

By the end of 1994 the Clinton plan was dead and the Republicans had seized control of Congress.

Toward a New Welfare Politics

The biggest problem facing majoritarian welfare programs is their cost: who will pay, and how much will they pay? The biggest problem facing client-oriented welfare programs is their legitimacy: who should benefit, and how should they be served?

Costs

The supporters of Social Security and Medicare have spent most of their time since the mid-1970s trying to devise politically painless ways of maintaining existing benefits or providing new ones. It hasn't been easy.

By 1981 many people in Washington feared that the Social Security system was about to run out of money, especially since, beginning in 1972, the amount paid to each retired person automatically went up with inflation (that is, the payments were "indexed"). Liberals wanted to solve this problem by raising taxes; conservatives, by cutting benefits. After many false starts the two sides agreed to turn the matter over to a bipartisan commission. Its plan, adopted by Congress in 1983, both raised taxes and reduced (slightly) benefits for future retirees, mostly by gradually increasing the age at which people would become eligible for retirement benefits from sixty-five to sixty-seven.[17]

Medicare was a far tougher problem. It was politically impossible either to increase taxes by enough to pay for the rapidly escalating health costs of retired people or to cut those benefits by enough to make up for the shortfall.

The strategy Congress has followed is to try to control costs by imposing an ever-greater number of regulations and restrictions on what doctors and hospitals can charge. Doctors and hospitals don't like this, of course, and many economists warn that price controls won't work—one way or another, people will find a way to buy what they want, and doctors, to charge what they want. Nevertheless Congress works on the assumption that irritating physicians and economists is a lot better than outraging retired persons on Medicare.

The essence of the price-control system, adopted in 1983, is to replace the traditional way of paying hospitals (sending them a check to cover their customary costs) with a new policy of paying a flat fee for each particular treatment, from broken bones to brain tumors, regardless of what they cost. Doctors and hospitals that couldn't deliver the service for what the government would pay would have to swallow the extra cost themselves; if they could treat the patient for less, they could pocket the difference. Sounds good, but there is a hitch: some hospitals reacted to the price controls not by becoming more efficient but by scrimping on services and discharging patients "quicker but sicker."[18]

Despite the anguish of figuring out ways of delivering the most benefit for the lowest tax, Congress and the White House could not resist trying to create a new health benefit. The law was called the Medicare Catastrophic Coverage Act of 1988. It should have been called the Politically Catastrophic Act of 1988.

The idea was simple enough: elderly people are especially worried about having to pay for some medical catastrophe, such as cancer, a stroke, or Alzheimer's disease. These illnesses can quickly consume almost anyone's savings. Under the existing Medicare plan, the government paid your hospital bills for only 150 days in any given year. The catastrophic-illness bill dealt with this by guaranteeing that the government would pay your hospital bills for the whole year, every year, after you had paid a deductible. The cost of this additional coverage was to be paid for largely by the elderly themselves, with the increase in fees to be greatest for the more affluent.

The logic was simple: make those who benefit pay for the benefit. The problem was that the beneficiaries didn't think the new law provided any real benefit, certainly not one they wanted to pay for. They ex-

pressed their feelings in a tidal wave of opposition and within eighteen months Congress was forced to back down and to repeal the Medicare Catastrophic Coverage Act. The House vote to pass that act in 1988 had been 302 to 127; the House vote to repeal that act in 1989 was 352 to 63. It was the most dramatic reversal in the history of welfare legislation.

The cost problems of Medicare were nothing, however, compared to those of any new universal health plan, such as the one proposed by Clinton in 1993. To guarantee health care to everyone will cost a lot of money. Clinton claimed that much of that cost would be recovered through having a more efficient, streamlined system of paying medical bills, but not many members of Congress were convinced that the words *efficient* or *streamlined* were likely to be accurate descriptions of programs devised by the government. The Congressional Budget Office estimated that, were the Clinton plan to take effect between 1995 and 2000, the deficit would increase by about $70 billion.[19]

The problem is politically almost impossible to solve. People fear getting medical bills they can't pay. They also dislike paying new taxes. Nobody said majoritarian politics was always fun.

Legitimacy

Politicians who want to do more for poor people have to figure out some way of increasing the perceived legitimacy of those people, giving them socially approved services rather than a socially disapproved income, or concealing the extent to which the "undeserving poor" are the chief beneficiaries of any government program. There is little political credit to be gained from trying to increase AFDC payments or to start a large negative income tax. What else can be done?

One strategy is to reform AFDC so that people no longer see it as a program that encourages misconduct. In 1988 Congress, under the leadership of Senator Daniel Patrick Moynihan of New York, overhauled the welfare system in a way designed to satisfy public criticism of it without reducing the benefits. The key provisions of the Family Support Act of 1988 addressed the major criticisms of the old AFDC program—that it encouraged family breakups and discouraged gainful employment. The new law required the states to establish the paternity of children born

A food stamp. Over 25 million people use them to help pay the cost of food.

out of wedlock and to collect child-support payments from fathers who had deserted their families, by withholding child support from an absent parent's paycheck. In addition all states would have to enroll parents (usually mothers) receiving AFDC benefits in job-training and job-placement programs. (The law exempted from the work requirement parents who were ill, pregnant, or caring for a child under the age of three.) To permit welfare mothers to work, the states would have to supply them with child-care programs.

A measure of the success of this bill in addressing political concerns about welfare is that it passed both houses of Congress by lopsided majorities and was signed by President Reagan. Whether the program will meet those concerns well enough to permit benefits to be increased remains to be seen. President Clinton submitted a new welfare reform bill in mid-1994; its fate is uncertain.

Another strategy to provide politically acceptable help to poor people has been to emphasize services, especially schooling. The most popular example of this is Head Start, a federally funded program that provides preschool education to children (mostly ages three and four) from poor families. Begun in 1965, Head Start now enrolls about half a million children at two thousand locations.

Head Start is immensely popular among both liberals and conservatives because it meets the political criteria of both groups: it targets poor families (and so pleases liberals); it provides services rather than money (and so pleases conservatives); and it helps little children (and so pleases everybody). Moreover the hundreds of thousands of participating families are a political force that cannot be ignored. In 1990 President Bush called for more money for Head Start; Democrats in Congress allocated even more.

The Family Issue

The political power of Head Start coupled with the success President Reagan had in portraying Republicans as defenders of traditional family values has led liberal politicians to attempt to repackage a variety of welfare proposals as "family issues." At a party conference in 1988, congressional Democrats decided to try to win back the family issue from the Republicans. Helping people, they decided, is politically

much easier if the help can be described as "strengthening the family."[20]

There is no doubt that concern about family matters is strong among the public, especially among younger adults who are struggling to pay high housing prices and cope with raising children when both parents are working. To meet that concern, a number of proposals have been labeled family measures: increasing the minimum wage, providing government-supported day care, and requiring employers to allow their workers parental leave.

The political difficulty with the family strategy is that, while at a very general level it commands a great deal of support, at the level of specifics that support falls apart. Liberals and conservatives are divided over goals, values, and procedures. Liberals want a family policy that will meet the economic needs of families by providing government-funded and government-run child-care programs, leaving moral questions to private decisions; conservatives want a family policy to serve the moral needs of families by, for example, discouraging teenage pregnancy, leaving the economic needs to be met by tax cuts or tax credits that can be used to purchase child care from private suppliers. When President Bush vetoed a parental-leave bill in 1990, Democrats lacked the votes to override it. After Clinton was elected, the bill was passed again and he signed it into law.

The Homeless

No issue better illustrates the tensions within American social-welfare politics than the problem of the homeless. The streets and parks of many cities are filled with homeless people. That much is clear. Everything else is in dispute.

People disagree as to how many people are homeless, why they are homeless, and what should be done about it. Many liberals argue that there are millions of homeless people, that most of them are the victims of high housing costs or cuts in social services, and that the government should (at a minimum) not harass them and (at a maximum) provide them with shelter. Many conservatives, by contrast, argue that there are relatively few homeless people, that most of them are mentally ill or drug dependent, and that the government should use the criminal justice and mental-health systems to get them off the streets and into institutions.

Immigration has become a major political issue with the continued influx of undocumented aliens, such as these Mexicans waiting for a chance to slip through the fence into California near Tijuana.

When government is faced with a problem over which there is such profound disagreement, no one should be surprised to discover that it adopts a policy that satisfies neither group. In many cities the police enforce laws against public disorder but not against sleeping on the streets; local agencies supply shelters, but only during cold weather; health organizations offer treatment to mentally ill or drug-dependent people, but do not require it.

The federal government has so far limited its role to supplying money to the states and cities to help pay for the variety of local programs. Beginning in 1987, Congress has authorized spending about $600 million a year for emergency food, shelter, and health care for the homeless.

Immigrants

The social-welfare politics of homelessness pales in significance to the present and the potential social-welfare politics of immigration. In the early 1990s an estimated 1.25 million immigrants entered the country each year, most of them legally but some unknown fraction of them illegally (so-called undocumented aliens). Not since the early decades of this century has the United States experienced anything like this level of immigration.

The majority of these new immigrants are from Mexico, China, and Haiti and they are different in both culture and appearance from the descendants of European immigrants who make up the majority of all Americans. While many Americans of European ancestry cherish their grandparents' tales of how they came to this country, today's immigrants face a very different set of circumstances. This most recent influx of immigrants has occurred at a time when the economy has slowed down and many Americans are fearful about their economic future. Rather than landing on Ellis Island and spreading out across many states, an estimated 90 percent of today's immigrants are concentrated in six states: California, Florida, Illinois, New Jersey, New York, and Texas. California alone was the final destination of about half of all immigrants to the United States in the 1980s.

Most studies by economists indicate that the impact of immigration on the wages or unemployment rates of less-skilled workers is virtually nil. This holds even in such dramatic cases as the 1980 influx of some 125,000 Cubans to Miami, Florida. Although the Cuban immigration increased the city's labor force by almost 8 percent, it had virtually no deleterious economic effects on the city's less-skilled workers. Nevertheless, many Americans perceive that immigration harms American workers, and that immigrants who do not find jobs drain public coffers of billions of tax dollars. Especially with respect to illegal or undocumented aliens, many Americans are not inclined to number immigrants among the "deserving poor," nor to favor social-welfare policies that benefit immigrants at the expense of all taxpayers.

Research findings on the economic effects of immigration are mixed. Some studies contradict the view that immigrants take jobs from native-born workers and depress wages, but others estimate that a large fraction (by some estimates as much as one-third) of the decline in the earnings of low-skilled, native-born workers in the 1980s resulted from competition from low-skilled immigrants. Likewise, some studies show that immigrants pay more in taxes than they receive in government services, but others reach the opposite conclusion.[21] In any case, research alone will not decide the coming national debate over immigration and social-welfare policy. And it remains to be seen how government policy will settle with respect to the two historic oversimplifications in American thinking about immigrants—pitiable, huddled masses versus job-stealing aliens.

SUMMARY

We can explain welfare politics in America principally by two factors: who benefits and who pays, and the beliefs that citizens have about social justice. Neither factor is static: gainers and losers vary as the composition of society and the workings of the economy change, and beliefs about who deserves what are modified as attitudes toward work, the family, and the obligations of government change.

The benefits and costs of the policies help explain the popularity of two social-welfare programs and the controversy surrounding others. Social Security and Medicare provide widely distributed benefits and impose widely distributed costs. The politics surrounding their enactment and expansion have been majoritarian. The Aid to Families with Dependent Children (AFDC) program provides benefits to some at a cost to many. As a form of client politics, it is made especially controversial by the public perception of the program as one that helps an "undeserving" group. Proposals for health-care reform are essentially arguments about who pays and who benefits.

Popular beliefs about the meaning of social justice and thus about who "deserves" public aid help us understand not only why AFDC has become controversial but why the Family Assistance Plan was not enacted. It appeared to many to give money to people who were able to work.

The congressional (as opposed to the parliamentary) system of government means that greater political effort and more time are required for the adoption of a new welfare policy. Federalism means that the states will play a large role in determining how any welfare program is administered and at what level benefits are set.

KEY TERMS

insurance program   *p. 503*

assistance program   *p. 503*

means test   *p. 503*

earned-income tax credit   *p. 508*

service strategy   *p. 511*

income strategy   *p. 511*

SUGGESTED READINGS

Derthick, Martha. *Policymaking for Social Security.* Washington, D.C.: Brookings Institution, 1979. A detailed analysis of how the Social Security program grew.

Heclo, Hugh. *Modern Social Politics in Britain and Sweden.* New Haven, Conn.: Yale University Press, 1974. Comparative analysis of how social-welfare programs came to Britain and Sweden.

Mead, Lawrence. *Beyond Entitlement: The Social Obligations of Citizenship.* New York: Free Press, 1986. Argument for "workfare," a requirement that able-bodied people work as a condition of receiving welfare.

Moynihan, Daniel Patrick. *Maximum Feasible Misunderstanding.* New York: Free Press, 1969. Lively account of the intellectual and political origins of the Community Action Program of the War on Poverty.

———. *Family and Nation.* New York: Harcourt Brace Jovanovich, 1986. Argument for the importance of federal policy to aid families. Disputes the Murray thesis.

Murray, Charles. *Losing Ground: American Social Policy, 1950–1980.* New York: Basic Books, 1984. An argument that federal spending on the poor actually increased poverty during the 1960s and 1970s.

18

Civil Liberties

Dogs trained to sniff out drugs go down your high school corridors and detect marijuana in some lockers. The school authorities open and search your locker without permission or a court order. You are expelled from the school without any hearing. Have your liberties been violated?

Angry at what you consider unfair treatment, you decide to wear a cloth American flag sewn to the seat of your pants, and your fellow students decide to wear black armbands to class in protest against how you were treated. The police arrest you for wearing a flag on your seat, and the school punishes your classmates for wearing armbands contrary to school regulations. Have your liberties, or theirs, been violated?

You go into federal court to find out. We cannot be certain how the court would decide the issues in this particular case, but in similar cases in the past the courts have held that school authorities can use dogs to detect drugs in schools and that these officials can conduct a "reasonable" search of you and your effects if they have a "reasonable suspicion" that you are violating a school rule. But they cannot punish your classmates for wearing black armbands, they cannot expel you without a hearing, and the state cannot make it illegal to treat the flag "contemptuously" by, for example, sewing it to the seat of your pants.[1]

Your claim that these actions violated your constitutional rights would have astonished the Framers of the Constitution. They thought that they had written a document that stated what the federal government could do, not one that specified what state governments (such as school systems) could not do. And they thought that they had created a national government of such limited powers that it was not even necessary to add a list—a Bill of Rights—stating what that government was forbidden from doing. It would be enough, for example, that the Constitution did not authorize the federal government to censor newspapers; an amendment prohibiting censorship would be superfluous.

The people who gathered in the state ratifying conventions weren't so optimistic. They suspected—

rightly, as it turned out—that the federal government might well try to do things that it was not authorized to do, and so they insisted that a Bill of Rights be added to the Constitution. But even they never imagined that the Bill of Rights would affect what *state* governments could do. Each state would decide that for itself, in its own constitution. And if by chance the Bill of Rights did apply to the states, surely its guarantees of free speech and freedom from unreasonable searches and seizures would apply to big issues—the freedom to attack the government in a newspaper editorial, for example, or to keep the police from breaking down the door of your home without a warrant. The courts would not be deciding who can wear what kinds of armbands or under what circumstances a school can expel a student.

To understand the nature of civil liberties today, it is necessary to understand why the liberties mentioned in the Bill of Rights were thought to be important, how they came to apply to the states, and why they have grown in scope and meaning.

The Politics of Civil Liberties

The Bill of Rights is an important limitation on popular rule. It says that there are things that a government cannot do even if a majority wants them done. But why would the government, to say nothing of a popular majority, ever want to do these things? In our review of the politics of policy-making, we have repeatedly observed the ability of small but intensely motivated minorities to block action that would impose heavy costs on them. Milk producers for a long time resisted efforts that would reduce government subsidies for their products, and ship owners and merchant seamen have been able to block efforts to introduce more competition (and presumably lower prices) into their industry. The political system has facilitated this kind of client politics.

If a largely indifferent public permits various economic, occupational, or professional minorities to safeguard their own interests, why should other kinds of minorities—religious or ideological ones—require special constitutional protection? Just as the average citizen bears only slight costs created by the advantages enjoyed by milk producers or truck drivers, presumably the average citizen bears only slight (if

any) costs from the publication of a Communist party newspaper or from the refusal of a member of Jehovah's Witnesses to recite the pledge of allegiance to the flag. If costs are small and widely distributed, then one would expect that political activity to reduce those costs would be infrequent and often ineffective. Moreover some of these "costs"—such as the consequences of people's reading a Communist party newspaper—will occur in the distant future, if at all. Ordinarily people are not politically sensitive to such distant or hypothetical burdens.

Politics, Culture, and Civil Liberties

Why do the liberties claimed by some people ever become a major issue? There are three reasons. In two of the three the politics of civil liberties are similar to those of any other issue. First, there may be rights in conflict (in which case we have interest-group politics). Second, passions may be inflamed by a skilled policy entrepreneur (in which case we have entrepreneurial politics). But the third reason makes the politics of civil liberties different from most issues: the political culture described in Chapter 4 contains principles that are in conflict with one another. Most Americans accept that culture and thus accept the contradictions built into it. From time to time we tend to favor one part of that culture (say, a belief in "Americanism") over another part (say, a belief in personal freedom). When that happens, we find ourselves fighting over matters, such as the intentional burning of an American flag, with an intensity that seems out of proportion to what is actually at stake.

Rights in Conflict We often think of "civil liberties" as a set of principles that protect the freedoms of all of us all of the time. That is true—up to a point. But in fact the Constitution and the Bill of Rights contain a list of *competing* rights. That competition becomes obvious when one person asserts one constitutional right and another person asserts a different right. For example:

- Dr. Samuel H. Sheppard of Cleveland, Ohio, asserted his right to have a fair trial on the charge of having murdered his wife. Bob Considine and Walter Winchell, two radio commentators, as well as other reporters, asserted their right to broadcast

whatever facts and rumors they heard about Dr. Sheppard and his love life. Two rights in conflict.

- The United States government has an obligation to "provide for the common defense" and, in pursuit of that duty, has claimed the right to keep secret certain military and diplomatic information. The *New York Times* claimed the right to publish such secrets as the "Pentagon Papers" without censorship in exercise of the freedom of the press. A duty and a right in conflict.

- Carl Jacob Kunz delivered inflammatory anti-Jewish speeches on the street corners of a Jewish neighborhood in New York City, suggesting, among other things, that Jews be "burnt in incinerators." The Jewish people living in that area were outraged. The New York police commissioner revoked Kunz's license to hold public meetings on the streets. When he continued to air his views on the public streets, Kunz was arrested for speaking without a permit. Freedom of speech versus the preservation of public order.

Even in high school a disruptive student's right not to be a victim of arbitrary or unjustifiable expulsion is in partial conflict with the school's obligation to maintain an orderly environment in which learning can take place.

These struggles over rights follow much the same pattern as interest-group politics of the sort found in economic issues, even though the claims in question are those of individuals. Indeed formal interest groups organize even in the field of civil liberties. The Fraternal Order of the Police complains of restrictions on police powers, whereas the American Civil Liberties Union defends and seeks to enlarge those restrictions. Catholics have pressed for public support of parochial schools; Protestants and Jews have argued against it. Sometimes the opposed groups are entirely private; sometimes one or both are government agencies. (When the Supreme Court decided the cases given earlier, Sheppard, the *New York Times,* and Kunz all won.[2])

Policy Entrepreneurs   Just as a skilled policy entrepreneur can sometimes arouse legislators to act against the normally undisputed claims of an interest group, so also can such an entrepreneur sometimes arouse people to take action against the rights and liberties claimed by political or religious dissidents. The success of entrepreneurial politics, whether involving money interests or civil liberties, often depends on the existence of a crisis.

War has usually been the crisis that has facilitated entrepreneurial politics aimed at restricting the liberty of some minority. For example:

- The Sedition Act was passed in 1798, making it a crime to write, utter, or publish "any false, scandalous, and malicious writing" with the intention of defaming the president, Congress, or government or of exciting against the government "the hatred of the people." The occasion was a kind of half-war between the United States and France, stimulated by fear in this country of the violence following the French Revolution of 1789. The policy entrepreneurs were Federalist politicians who believed that Thomas Jefferson and his followers were supporters of the French Revolution and would, if they came to power, encourage here the kind of anarchy that seemed to be occurring in France.

- The Espionage and Sedition Acts were passed in 1917–1918, making it a crime to utter false statements that would interfere with the American military, to send through the mails material

A 1919 cartoon expresses popular fears of "reds" (that is, leftist radicals) threatening American institutions.

P O L I T I C A L L Y   **P.S.**   S P E A K I N G

McCarthyism

In 1950 Senator Joseph R. McCarthy of Wisconsin began making a long series of charges, usually unsubstantiated, that people working for various government agencies were communists. Since then anyone making a charge that unfairly impugns the motives, attacks the patriotism, or violates the rights of individuals is often criticized for engaging in **McCarthyism.** The word has become a synonym for "character assassination." Senator McCarthy was a conservative, and so liberals today are often quick to denounce conservative attacks on them as "McCarthyism." But increasingly conservatives have used the term against liberals, usually by modifying it to read "McCarthyism of the left."

SOURCE: Adapted from William Safire, *Safire's Political Dictionary* (New York: Ballantine Books, 1978). Used by permission.

"advocating or urging treason, insurrection, or forcible resistance to any law of the United States," or to utter or write any disloyal, profane, scurrilous, or abusive language intended to incite resistance to the United States or curtail war production. The occasion was World War I; the impetus was the fear that Germans in this country were spies and that radicals were seeking to overthrow the government. Under these laws more than two thousand persons were prosecuted (about half convicted) and thousands of aliens were rounded up and deported. The policy entrepreneur leading this massive crackdown, the so-called Red Scare, was Attorney General A. Mitchell Palmer.

• The Smith Act was passed in 1940, the Internal Security Act in 1950, and the Communist Control Act in 1954. These laws made it illegal to advocate the overthrow of the government by force or violence (Smith Act), required members of the Communist party to register with the government (Internal Control Act), and declared the Communist party to be part of a conspiracy to overthrow the government (Communist Control Act). The occasion was World War II and the Korean War, which, like earlier wars, inspired fears that Nazi and Soviet agents were trying to subvert the government. For the latter two laws the policy entrepreneur was Senator Joseph McCarthy, who attracted a great deal of attention with his repeated (and sometimes inaccurate) claims that Soviet agents were working inside the government.

• In 1968 a law was passed making it a federal crime to cross state lines or use interstate commerce in order to incite or organize a riot. The occasion was the wave of ghetto riots that had swept the country in the mid-1960s and the fear that some of the opponents of the war in Vietnam were going underground to organize violent attacks on governmental and other institutions. There was in this case no policy entrepreneur.

These laws had in common an effort to protect national security from the threats, real and imagined, posed by people who claimed to be exercising their freedom to speak, publish, organize, and assemble. In each case a real threat (a war or a riot) led the government to narrow the limits of permissible speech and activity. Almost every time such restrictions were imposed, the Supreme Court was called upon to decide whether Congress (or sometimes state legislatures) had drawn those limits properly. In most instances the Court tended to uphold the legislature. But as time passed and the war or crisis ended, popular passions abated.

Though uncommon, some use is still made of the sedition laws. In the 1980s various white supremacists and Puerto Rican nationalists were charged with sedition. In each case the government alleged that the accused had not only spoken in favor of overthrowing the government, they had actually engaged in violent actions such as bombings. Later in this chapter we shall see how the Court has increasingly restricted the power of the legislature to outlaw political

FIGURE 18.1   Annual Immigration, 1840–1990

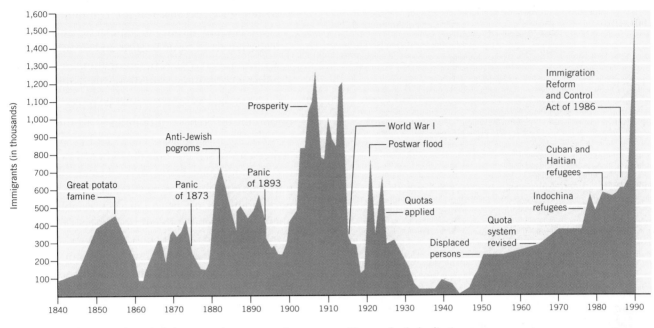

NOTE: Figures for 1989 and 1990 include persons who were granted permanent residence under the legalization program of the Immigration and Reform and Control Act of 1986.

SOURCES: For 1985–1990: *Statistical Abstract of the United States, 1992,* 10.

speech; to be found guilty of sedition now it is usually necessary to do something more serious than just talk about it.

Cultural Conflicts   In the main the United States was originally the creation of white European Protestants. Blacks were, in most cases, slaves, and Indians were not citizens. Catholics and Jews in the colonies composed a small minority, and often a persecuted one. The early schools tended to be religious—that is, Protestant—schools, many of them receiving state aid. It is not surprising that under these circumstances a view of America arose that equated "Americanism" with the values and habits of white Anglo-Saxon Protestants.

But immigration to this country brought a flood of new settlers, many of them coming from very different backgrounds (see Figure 18.1). In the mid–nineteenth century the potato famine led millions of Irish Catholics to migrate here. At the turn of the century religious persecution and economic disadvantage brought more millions of people, many

Catholic or Jewish, from southern and eastern Europe. In recent decades political conflict and economic want have led Hispanics (mostly from Mexico but increasingly from all parts of Latin America), Caribbeans, Africans, Middle Easterners, Southeast Asians, and Asians to cross our borders—some legally, some illegally (see Figure 18.2). Among them have been Buddhists, Catholics, Muslims, and the members of many other religious and cultural groupings.

Ethnic, religious, and cultural differences have given rise to different views as to the meaning and scope of certain constitutionally protected freedoms. For example:

- Many Jewish groups find it offensive for a creche (that is, a scene depicting the birth of Christ in a manger) to be displayed in front of the city hall at Christmastime, while many Catholics and Protestants regard it as an important part of our cultural heritage. Does the display violate the First Amendment requirement that the government pass no law "respecting an establishment of religion"?

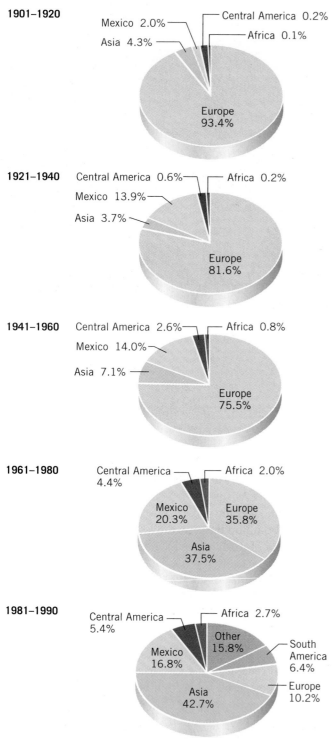

FIGURE 18.2 Changing Composition of U.S. Immigration, 1901–1980

1901–1920

Mexico 2.0%
Asia 4.3%
Central America 0.2%
Africa 0.1%
Europe 93.4%

1921–1940

Central America 0.6%
Mexico 13.9%
Asia 3.7%
Africa 0.2%
Europe 81.6%

1941–1960

Central America 2.6%
Mexico 14.0%
Asia 7.1%
Africa 0.8%
Europe 75.5%

1961–1980

Central America 4.4%
Mexico 20.3%
Asia 37.5%
Africa 2.0%
Europe 35.8%

1981–1990

Central America 5.4%
Mexico 16.8%
Asia 42.7%
Africa 2.7%
Other 15.8%
South America 6.4%
Europe 10.2%

SOURCES: For 1901–1980: Associated Press, adapted from a *Boston Globe* graphic by Steven Nelson. Reprinted courtesy of the *Boston Globe*. For 1981–1989: *Statistical Abstract of the United States, 1992,* 11.

• Many English-speaking people believe that public schools ought to teach all students to speak and write English, because it is our common heritage. Some Hispanic groups argue that schools should teach pupils in both English and Spanish, since Spanish is part of the Hispanic cultural heritage. Is bilingual education constitutionally required?

Even within a given cultural tradition there are important differences of opinion as to the balance between community sensitivities and personal self-expression. To some people the sight of a store carrying pornographic books or a theater showing a pornographic movie is deeply offensive; to others pornography is offensive but such establishments ought to be tolerated to ensure that laws restricting them do not also restrict politically or artistically important forms of speech; to still others pornography itself is not especially offensive. What forms of writing are entitled to constitutional protection?

Interpreting and Applying the First Amendment

The First Amendment contains the language that has been at issue in most of the cases to which we have thus far referred. It has roughly two parts: one protecting **freedom of expression** ("Congress shall make no law . . . abridging the freedom of speech, or of the press, or the right of people peaceably to assemble, and to petition the government for a redress of grievances") and the other protecting **freedom of religion** ("Congress shall make no law respecting an establishment of religion; or abridging the free exercise thereof"). In this section we shall discuss freedom of expression; in the next, freedom of religion.

Speech and National Security

The traditional view of free speech and press was expressed by William Blackstone, the great English jurist, in his *Commentaries,* published in 1765. A free press was essential to a free state, he wrote, but the freedom that the press should enjoy was a freedom from **prior restraint**—that is, freedom from censorship, or rules telling a newspaper in advance what it could publish. Once a newspaper published an article (or a person delivered a speech), that paper or speaker then had to take the consequences if what was written or said proved to be "improper, mischievous, or illegal."[3]

The U.S. Sedition Act of 1798 was in keeping with traditional English law. Like it, the act imposed no prior restraint on publishers; it did, however, make them liable to punishment after the fact. Indeed the act was an advance on the English law, because unlike the British model, it entrusted the decision to a jury, not a judge, and allowed the defendant to be acquitted if he or she could prove the truth of what had been published. Although several newspaper publishers were convicted under the act, none of these cases reached the Supreme Court. When Jefferson became president in 1801, he pardoned everyone who had been convicted under the Sedition Act. Though Jeffersonians objected vehemently to the law, their principal objection was not to the idea of holding newspapers accountable for what they published but to letting the *federal* government do this. Jefferson was perfectly prepared to have the *states* punish what he called the "overwhelming torrent of slander" by means of "a few prosecutions of the most prominent offenders."[4]

It was not for another century that the federal government attempted to define the limits of free speech and writing. Perhaps recalling the widespread opposition to the sweep of the 1798 act, Congress in 1917–1918 placed restrictions, not on publications that were critical of the government, but only on those that advocated "treason, insurrection, or forcible resistance" to federal laws or that attempted to foment disloyalty or mutiny in the armed services.

In 1919 this new law was examined by the Supreme Court when it heard the case of Charles T. Schenck, who had been convicted of violating the Espionage Act because he had mailed circulars to men eligible for the draft, urging them to resist. At issue was the constitutionality of the Espionage Act and, more broadly, the scope of Congress's power to control speech. One view held that the First Amendment prevented Congress from passing *any* law restricting speech; the other held that Congress could punish dangerous speech. For a unanimous Supreme Court, Justice Oliver Wendell Holmes announced a rule by which to settle the matter. It soon became known as the **clear-and-present-danger test:**

The question in every case is whether the words used are used in such circumstances and are of such a nature as to create a clear and present

Rights in conflict: some people object to pornographic books and videos being sold in their neighborhood; others think people have a right to patronize such stores.

danger that they will bring about the substantive evils that Congress has a right to prevent.[5]

The Court held that Schenck's leaflets did create such a danger, and so his conviction was upheld. In explaining why, Holmes said that not even the Constitution protects a person who has been "falsely shouting fire in a theatre and causing a panic." In this case things that might safely be said in peacetime may be punished in wartime.

The clear-and-present-danger test may have clarified the law, but it kept no one out of jail. Schenck went, and so did the defendants in five other cases in the period 1919–1927, even though during this time Holmes, the author of the test, shifted his position and began writing dissenting opinions in which he urged that the test had not been met and so the defendant should go free.

During the same period the Court for the first time came to grips with the power of state governments to punish speech. As we saw in Chapter 2, the Bill of Rights was originally intended only to limit the powers of the *federal* government. The adoption in 1868 of the Fourteenth Amendment, however, brought into the Constitution language that for the first time created the possibility that some or all of

MR. PRESIDENT
REMEMBER THE CONSTITUTION
"CONGRESS SHALL MAKE NO LAW---
ABRIDGING THE FREEDOM OF SPEECH.
OR OF THE PRESS-" THE POLITICAL
PRISONERS WHO BELEIVED IN THIS
GUARANTEE, ARE NOW SERVING 20
YEARS IN PRISON

Women picketed in front of the White House urging President Warren Harding to release political radicals arrested during his administration.

the Bill of Rights might now restrict *state* action. The key phrase was the **due-process clause:**

> *No state shall . . . deprive any person of life, liberty or property, without due process of law.*

For over half a century after 1868, the Supreme Court steadfastly denied that the due-process clause made the Bill of Rights applicable to the states. Therefore state legislatures could pass sedition laws or antiobscenity laws without fear of having them overturned by the Supreme Court.

Then in 1925 Benjamin Gitlow was convicted of violating the New York sedition law, one similar to the federal Sedition Act of 1918, by passing out some leaflets. The Supreme Court upheld his conviction but added a statement that changed constitutional history: freedom of speech and of the press were now among the "fundamental personal rights" that are protected by the due-process clause of the Fourteenth Amendment from infringements by *state* action.[6] Thereafter state laws involving speech, the press, and peaceful assembly were struck down by the

Supreme Court for being in violation of the freedom-of-expression guarantees of the First Amendment as made applicable to the states by the Fourteenth Amendment.[7]

The clear-and-present-danger test was a way of balancing the competing demands of free expression and national security. As the memory of World War I and the ensuing red scare evaporated, the Court began to develop other tests, ones that shifted the balance more toward free expression. Some of these tests are listed in the box on page 529.

But when a crisis reappears, as it did in World War II and the Korean conflict, the Court has tended to defer, up to a point, to legislative judgments about the need to protect national security. For example, it upheld the conviction of eleven leaders of the Communist party for having advocated the violent overthrow of the United States government, a violation of the Smith Act of 1940.

This conviction once again raised the hard question of the circumstances under which words can be punished. Hardly anybody would deny that actually *trying* to overthrow the government is a crime; the question is whether *advocating* its overthrow is a crime. In the case of the eleven Communist leaders, the Court said that the government did not have to wait to protect itself until "the *putsch* [rebellion] is about to be executed, the plans have been laid and the signal is awaited." Even if the communists were not likely to be successful in their effort, the Court held that specifically advocating violent overthrow could be punished. "In each case," the opinion read, the courts "must ask whether the gravity of the 'evil,' discounted by its improbability, justifies such invasion of free speech as is necessary to avoid the danger."[8]

But as the popular worries about communists began to subside and the membership of the Supreme Court changed, the Court began to tip the balance even farther toward free expression. By 1957 the Court made it clear that for advocacy to be punished, the government would have to show, not just that a person believed in the overthrow of the government, but that he or she was using words "calculated to incite" that overthrow.[9]

By 1969 the pendulum had swung to the point where the speech would have to be judged likely to incite "imminent" unlawful action. In this case Clarence Brandenburg, a leader of the Ku Klux Klan in Ohio, staged a cross-burning rally during which he

Even hateful symbols, such as this burning cross lit by members of the Ku Klux Klan, enjoy constitutional protection.

reviled blacks and Jews. The police told him to clear the street; as he left, he said, "We'll take the [expletive] street later." He was convicted of attempting to incite lawless mob action. The Supreme Court overturned the conviction, holding that any speech that does not call for illegal action is protected, and even speech that *does* call for illegal action is protected if the action is not "imminent" or there is reason to believe that the listeners will not take the action.[10]

This means that no matter how offensive or provocative some forms of political expression may be, this expression has powerful constitutional protections. In 1977 a group of American Nazis wanted to parade through the streets of Skokie, Illinois, a community with a large Jewish population. The residents, outraged, sought to ban the march. Many feared violence if it occurred. But the lower courts, under prodding from the Supreme Court, held that,

Testing Restrictions on Expression

*T*he Supreme Court has employed various standards and tests to decide whether a restriction on freedom of expression is constitutionally permissible.

1. Preferred position The right of free expression, though not absolute, occupies a higher, or more preferred, position than many other constitutional rights, such as property rights. This is still a controversial rule; nonetheless the Court always approaches a restriction on expression skeptically.

2. Prior restraint With scarcely any exceptions the Court will not tolerate a prior restraint on expression, such as censorship, even when it will allow subsequent punishment of improper expressions (such as libel).

3. Imminent danger Punishment for uttering inflammatory sentiments will be allowed only if there is an imminent danger that the utterances will incite an unlawful act.

4. Neutrality Any restriction on speech, such as a requirement that parades or demonstrations not disrupt other people in the exercise of their rights, must be neutral—that is, not favor one group more than another.

5. Clarity If you must obtain a permit to hold a parade, the law must set forth clear (as well as neutral) standards to guide administrators in issuing that permit. Similarly a law punishing obscenity must contain a clear definition of obscenity.

6. Least-restrictive means If it is necessary to restrict the exercise of one right to protect the exercise of another, the restriction should employ the least-restrictive means to achieve its end. For example, if press coverage threatens a person's right to a fair trial, the judge may only do what is minimally necessary to that end, such as transferring the case to another town rather than issuing a "gag order."

Cases cited, by item: (1) *United States* v. *Carolene Products,* 304 U.S. 144 (1938). (2) *Near* v. *Minnesota,* 283 U.S. 697 (1931). (3) *Brandenburg* v. *Ohio,* 395 U.S. 444 (1969). (4) *Kunz* v. *New York,* 340 U.S. 290 (1951). (5) *Hynes* v. *Mayor and Council of Oradell,* 425 U.S. 610 (1976). (6) *Nebraska Press Association* v. *Stuart,* 427 U.S. 539 (1976).

noxious and provocative as the anti-Semitic slogans of the Nazis may be, the Nazi party had a constitutional right to speak and parade peacefully.[11]

Similar reasoning led the Supreme Court in 1992 to overturn a Minnesota statute that made it a crime to display symbols or objects, such as a Nazi swastika or a burning cross, that are likely to cause alarm or resentment among an ethnic or racial group, such as Jews or blacks.[12] On the other hand, if you are convicted of actually hurting someone, you may be given a tougher sentence if it can be shown that you were motivated to assault them by racial or ethnic hatred.[13] To be punished for such a hate crime your bigotry must result in some direct and physical harm and not just the display of an odious symbol.

What Is Speech?

If most political speaking or writing is permissible, save that which actually incites someone to take illegal actions, what *kinds* of speaking and writing qualify for this broad protection? Though the Constitution says that the legislature may make "no law" abridging freedom of speech or the press, and though some justices have argued that this means literally *no* law, the Court has held that there are at least four forms of speaking and writing that are not automatically granted full constitutional protection: libel, obscenity, symbolic speech, and false advertising.

Libel A **libel** is a written statement that defames the character of another person. (If the statement is oral, it is called a slander.) In some countries, such as England, it is easy to sue another person for libel and to collect. In this country it is much harder. For one thing you must show that the libelous statement was false. If it was true, you cannot collect no matter how badly it harmed you.

A beauty-contest winner was awarded $14 million (later reduced on appeal) when she proved that *Penthouse* magazine had libeled her. The actress Carol Burnett collected a large sum from a libel suit brought against a gossip newspaper. But when Theodore Roosevelt sued a newspaper for falsely claiming that he was a drunk, the jury awarded him damages of only six cents.[14]

If you are a public figure, it is much harder to win a libel suit. A public figure such as an elected official, an army general, or a well-known celebrity must prove not only that the publication was false and damaging, but also that the words were uttered with "actual malice"—that is, with reckless disregard for their truth or falsity or with knowledge that they were false.[15] As we saw in Chapter 10, that is not easily done. General Ariel Sharon was able to prove that the statements made about him by *Time* magazine were false and damaging, but not that they were the result of "actual malice."

Obscenity Obscenity is not protected by the First Amendment. The Court has always held that obscene materials, because they have no redeeming social value and are calculated chiefly to appeal to one's sexual rather than political or literary interests, can be regulated by the state. The problem, of course, arises with the meaning of *obscene*. In one eleven-year period, 1957 to 1968, the Court decided thirteen major cases involving the definition of obscenity, which resulted in fifty-five separate opinions.[16] Some justices, such as Hugo Black, believed that the First Amendment protected all publications, even wholly obscene ones. Others believed that obscenity deserved no protection and struggled heroically to define the term. Still others shared the view of former Justice Potter Stewart, who objected to "hard-core pornography" but admitted that the best definition he could offer was "I know it when I see it."[17]

It is unnecessary to review in detail the many attempts by the Court at defining obscenity. The justices have made it clear that nudity and sex are not, by definition, obscene and that they will provide First Amendment protection to anything that has political, literary, or artistic merit, allowing the government to punish only the distribution of "hard-core pornography." Their most recent (1973) definition of this is as follows: to be obscene, the work, taken as a whole, must be judged by "the average person applying contemporary community standards" to appeal to the "prurient interest" or to depict "in a patently offensive way, sexual conduct specifically defined by applicable state law" and to lack "serious literary, artistic, political, or scientific value."[18]

After Albany, Georgia, decided that the movie *Carnal Knowledge* was obscene by contemporary local standards, the Supreme Court overturned the distributor's conviction on the grounds that the authorities in Albany failed to show that the film depicted "patently offensive hard-core sexual conduct."[19]

It is easy to make sport of the problems that the Court has faced in trying to decide obscenity cases (one conjures up images of black-robed justices leafing through the pages of *Hustler* magazine, taking notes), but these problems reveal, as do other civil-liberties cases, the continuing problem of balancing competing claims. One part of the community wants to read or see whatever it wishes; another part wants to protect private acts from public degradation. The first part cherishes liberty above all; the second values decency above liberty. The former fears that any restriction on literature will lead to pervasive restriction; the latter believes that reasonable people can distinguish (or reasonable laws can require them to distinguish) between patently offensive and artistically serious work.

Anyone strolling today through an "adult" bookstore must suppose that no restrictions at all exist on the distribution of pornographic works. This condition does not arise simply from the doctrines of the Court. Other factors operate as well, including the priorities of local law-enforcement officials, the political climate of the community, the procedures that must be followed to bring a viable court case, the clarity and workability of state and local laws on the subject, and the difficulty of changing the behavior of many people by prosecuting one person. The current view of the Court is that localities can decide for themselves whether to tolerate hard-core pornography; but if they choose not to, they must meet some fairly strict constitutional tests.

The protections given by the Court to expressions of sexual or erotic interest have not been limited to books, magazines, or films. Almost any form of visual or auditory communication will be considered "speech" within the meaning of the First Amendment. In one case even nude dancing was given protection as a form of "speech,"[20] although in 1991 the Court held that nude dancing was only "marginally" within the First Amendment, and so it upheld an Indiana statute that banned *totally* nude dancing.[21]

Of late some feminist organizations have attacked pornography on the grounds that it exploits and degrades women. They persuaded Indianapolis to pass an ordinance that defined pornography as portrayals of the "graphic, sexually explicit subordination of women" and allowed people to sue the producers of such material. Sexually explicit portrayals of women in positions of equality were not defined as pornography. The Court disagreed. In 1986 it affirmed a lower court ruling that such an ordinance was a violation of the First Amendment because it represented a legislative preference for one form of expression (women in positions of equality) over another (women in positions of subordination).[22]

One constitutionally permissible way to limit the spread of pornographic materials has been to establish rules governing where in a city they can be sold. When one city adopted a zoning ordinance prohibiting an "adult" movie theater from locating within one thousand feet of any church, school, park, or residential area, the Court upheld the ordinance, noting that the purpose of the law was not to regulate speech but to regulate the use of land. And in any case the adult theaters still had much of the city's land area in which to find a location.[23]

Symbolic Speech   You cannot ordinarily claim that an illegal act should be protected because that action is meant to convey a political message. For example, if you burn your draft card in protest against the foreign policy of the United States, you can be punished for the illegal act (burning the card) even if your intent was to communicate your beliefs. The Court reasoned that giving such **symbolic speech** the same protection as real speech would open the door to

"Symbolic speech": when young men burned their draft cards during the 1960s to protest the Vietnam War, the Supreme Court ruled that it was an illegal act for which they could be punished.

The toughest test of our commitment to political liberties is our willingness to tolerate the activities of groups that we find repellent.

permitting all manner of illegal actions—murder, arson, rape—if the perpetrator meant thereby to send a message.[24]

On the other hand, a statute that makes it illegal to burn the American flag is an unconstitutional infringement of free speech.[25] Why is there a difference between a draft card and the flag? The Court argues that the government has a right to run a military draft and so can protect draft cards even if this incidentally restricts speech. But the only motive that government has in banning flag burning is to restrict this form of speech, and that makes it improper. In 1989–1990 Congress refused to endorse a proposed constitutional amendment that, if ratified, would have reversed this Court ruling. It did pass a bill making flag-burning a crime, but the Supreme Court, consistent with its decision in an earlier Texas case, held that this law was an unconstitutional infringement of free speech.[26]

Who Is a Person?

If people have a right to speak and publish, do corporations, interest groups, and children have the same right? By and large the answer is "yes," though there are some exceptions.

When the attorney general of Massachusetts tried to prevent the First National Bank of Boston from spending money to influence votes in a local election, the Court stepped in and blocked him. The Court held that a corporation, like a person, has certain First Amendment rights.[27]

Similarly when the federal government tried to limit the spending of a group called Massachusetts Citizens for Life (an antiabortion organization), the Court held that such organizations have First Amendment rights.[28]

And when the California Public Utility Commission tried to compel one of the utilities that it regulates, the Pacific Gas and Electric Company, to enclose in its monthly bills to customers statements written by groups attacking the utility, the Supreme Court blocked the agency, saying that forcing it to disseminate political statements violated the firm's free-speech rights. "The identity of the speaker is not decisive in determining whether speech is protected," the Court said. "Corporations and other associations, like individuals, contribute to the 'discussion, debate, and the dissemination of information and ideas' that the First Amendment seeks to foster." In this case the right to speak includes the choice of what *not* to say.[29]

Even though corporations have some First Amendment rights, the government can place more limits on commercial than on noncommercial speech. The legislature can place restrictions on advertisements for cigarettes, liquor, and gambling; it can even regulate advertising for some less harmful products provided that the regulations are narrowly tailored and serve a substantial public interest.[30] If the regulations are too broad or do not serve a clear interest, then ads are entitled to some constitutional protection. For example, the states cannot bar lawyers from advertising or accountants from personally soliciting clients.[31]

Under certain circumstances, young people may have less freedom of expression than adults. In 1988 the Supreme Court held that the principal of a high school could censor articles appearing in the student-edited newspaper at Hazelwood High School. The newspaper was published using school funds and was part of a journalism class. The principal ordered the deletion of stories dealing with student pregnancies and the impact of parental divorce on students. The student editors sued, claiming their First Amendment rights had been violated. The Court agreed that students do not "shed their constitutional rights to freedom of speech or expression at the schoolhouse gate" and that they cannot be punished for expressing on campus their personal views. But students do not have exactly the same rights as adults if the exercise of those rights impedes the educational mission of the school. Students may lawfully say things on campus, as individuals, that they cannot say if they are part of school-sponsored activities, such as plays or school-run newspapers, that are part of the curriculum. School-sponsored activities can be controlled so long as the controls are "reasonably related to legitimate pedagogical concerns."[32]

Church and State

Everybody knows, correctly, that the plain language of the First Amendment protects freedom of speech and the press, though most people are not aware of how complex the law applying these terms has become. But many people also believe, wrongly, that the language of the First Amendment clearly requires the "separation of church and state." It does not.

What that amendment actually says is quite different and maddeningly unclear. It has two parts. The first, often referred to as the **free-exercise clause,** states that Congress shall make no law prohibiting the "free exercise" of religion. The second, which is called the **establishment clause,** states that Congress shall make no law "respecting an establishment of religion."

The Free-Exercise Clause

The free-exercise clause has been the clearer of the two, though by no means lacking in ambiguities. It obviously means that Congress cannot pass a law prohibiting Catholics from celebrating Mass, requir-ing Baptists to become Episcopalians, or preventing Jews from holding a *bar mitzvah.* Since the First Amendment has been applied to the states via the due-process clause of the Fourteenth Amendment, it means that state governments cannot pass such laws either. In general the courts have treated religion like speech: you can pretty much do or say what you want so long as it does not cause some serious harm to others.

Even some laws that do not appear on their face to apply to churches may be unconstitutional if their enforcement imposes particular burdens on churches or greater burdens on some churches than others. For example, a state cannot apply a license fee on door-to-door solicitors when the solicitor is a Jehovah's Witness selling religious tracts.[33] By the same token, the courts ruled that the city of Hialeah, Florida, cannot ban animal sacrifices by members of an Afro-Caribbean religion called Santeria. Since killing animals was generally not illegal (if it were, there could be no hamburgers or chicken sandwiches served in Hialeah restaurants and rat traps would be unlawful), the ban in this case was clearly directed against a specific religion and hence it was unconstitutional.[34]

Having the right to exercise your religion freely does not mean, however, that you are exempt from laws binding other citizens, even when the law goes against your religious beliefs. A man cannot have more than one wife, even if (as once was the case with Mormons) polygamy is thought desirable on religious grounds.[35] For religious reasons you may oppose being vaccinated or having blood transfusions, but if the state passes a compulsory vaccination law or orders that a blood transfusion be given to a sick child, the courts will not block them on grounds of religious liberty.[36] Similarly, if you belong to an Indian tribe that uses a drug, peyote, in religious ceremonies, you cannot claim that your freedom was abridged if the state decides to ban the use of peyote, provided the law applies equally to all.[37] Since airports have a legitimate need for tight security measures, begging can be outlawed in them even if some of the people doing the begging are part of a religious group (in this case, the Hare Krishnas).[38]

Unfortunately some conflicts between religious belief and public policy are even more difficult to settle. What if you believe on religious grounds that war

When a Hare Krishna hands out flowers, he is exercising his First Amendment rights.

is immoral? The draft laws have always exempted a conscientious objector from military duty, and the Court has upheld such exemptions. But the Court has gone further: it has said that people cannot be drafted even if they do not believe in a Supreme Being or belong to any religious tradition so long as their "consciences, spurred by deeply held moral, ethical, or religious beliefs, would give them no rest or peace if they allowed themselves to become part of an instrument of war."[39] Do exemptions on such grounds create an opportunity for some people to evade the draft because of their political preferences? In trying to answer such questions, the courts often have had to try to define a religion—no easy task.

And even when there is no question about your membership in a bona fide religion, the circumstances under which you may claim exemption from laws that apply to everybody else are not really clear. What if you, a member of the Seventh-day Adventists, are fired by your employer for refusing on religious grounds to work on Saturday, and then it turns out that you cannot collect unemployment insurance because you refuse to take an available job—one that also requires you to work on Saturday? Or what if you are a member of the Amish sect, which refuses, contrary to state law, to send its children to public schools past the eighth grade? The Court has ruled that the state must pay you unemployment compensation and cannot require you to send your children to public schools beyond the eighth grade.[40]

These last two decisions, and others like them, show that even the "simple" principle of freedom of religion gets complicated in practice and can lead to the courts' giving, in effect, preference to members of one church over members of another.

The Establishment Clause

What in the world did the members of the First Congress mean when they wrote into the First Amendment language prohibiting Congress from making a law "respecting" an "establishment" of religion? The Supreme Court has more or less consistently interpreted this vague phrase to mean that the Constitution erects a "wall of separation" between church and state.

That phrase, so often quoted, is not in the Bill of Rights nor in the debates in the First Congress that drafted the Bill of Rights; it comes from the pen of Thomas Jefferson, who was opposed to having the Church of England as the established church of his native Virginia. (At the time of the Revolutionary War there were established—that is, official, state-supported—churches in at least eight of the thirteen former colonies.) But it is not clear that Jefferson's view was the majority view.

During much of the debate in Congress the wording of this part of the First Amendment was quite different and much plainer than what finally emerged. Up to the last minute the clause was intended to read "no religion shall be established by law" or "no national religion shall be established." The meaning of those words seems quite clear: whatever the states may do, the federal government cannot create an official, national religion or give support to one religion in preference to another.[41]

But Congress instead adopted an ambiguous phrase, and so the Supreme Court had to decide what it meant. It has declared that these words do not simply mean "no national religion" but mean as well no

✪ Religious Issues on Which the Supreme Court Is Silent

Often the cases that the Supreme Court doesn't decide are just as important as the ones it does decide. Here are some cases involving claims of religious freedom that were decided by lower courts. Since the Supreme Court refused to hear an appeal of these decisions, the lower court decisions, at least for now, are the law.

Reading the Bible In a Colorado public school, classrooms occasionally have a silent reading period during which the students and teachers can read various books. One teacher silently read his Bible during this period. There is no evidence his students knew what he was reading; however the principal of the school told the teacher he could not read the Bible because *if* the students found out it might influence them to read the Bible also. A federal court upheld the principal.

Mentioning God A professor of physiology at the University of Alabama occasionally mentioned in class the importance to him of his Christian faith. He also gave an after-class lecture on "Evidences of God in Human Physiology." Attendance was optional. The university ordered him not to present any comments from a Christian perspective in class. A federal court upheld the university.

Spouse abuse and religion The New Orleans Baptist Theological seminary expelled a student when it learned from the police that he had abused his wife. The state courts ordered him reinstated because spouse abuse did not bear on his academic qualifications for a degree. The seminary argued that giving him a degree would entitle him to be a Baptist minister, and that spouse abuse was incompatible with a religious vocation. The seminary lost.

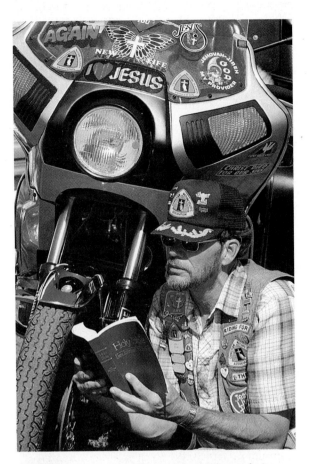

Americans, even a few bikers such as this one in Iowa, are more religious than the people of other industrialized nations, with the result that the Supreme Court must confront endless church-state issues.

SOURCE: Adapted from Michael McConnell, "Freedom From Religion?" *The American Enterprise* (January/February 1993): 32–43.

government involvement with religion at all, even on a nonpreferential basis. They mean, in short, erecting a "wall of separation" between church and state.[42] Though the interpretation of the establishment clause remains a topic of great controversy among judges and scholars, the Supreme Court has more or less consistently adopted this **wall-of-separation principle.**

Its first statement of this interpretation was in 1947. The case involved a New Jersey town that reim-bursed parents for the costs of transporting their children to school, including parochial (in this case Catholic) schools. The Court decided that this reimbursement was constitutional, but it made it clear that the establishment clause of the First Amendment applied (via the Fourteenth Amendment) to the states and that it meant, among other things, that the government cannot require a person to profess a belief or disbelief in any religion; it cannot aid one religion, some religions, or all religions; and it cannot spend any tax money, however small the amount might be, in support of any religious activities or institutions.[43] The reader may wonder, in view of the Court's reasoning, why it allowed the town to pay for busing children to Catholic schools. The answer that it gave is that busing is a religiously neutral activity, akin to providing fire and police protection to Catholic schools. Busing, available to public- and private-school children alike, does not breach the wall of separation.

Since 1947 the Court has applied the wall-of-separation theory to strike down as unconstitutional every effort to have any form of prayer in public schools, even if it is nonsectarian,[44] voluntary,[45] or limited to reading a passage of the Bible.[46] Since 1992 it has even been unconstitutional for a public school to ask a rabbi or minister to offer a prayer—an invocation or a benediction—at the school's graduation ceremony.[47] Moreover the Court has held that laws

A major free speech issue arises when parents object to the books their children are required to read in school, as here in Greenville, Tennessee.

prohibiting teaching the theory of evolution or requiring giving equal time to "creationism" are religiously inspired and thus unconstitutional.[48] A public school may not allow its pupils to take time out from their regular classes for religious instruction if this occurs within the schools, though "released-time" instruction is all right if it is done outside the public-school buildings.[49] The school-prayer decisions in particular have provoked a storm of controversy, but efforts to get Congress to propose to the states a constitutional amendment authorizing such prayers have failed.

Almost as controversial have been Court-imposed restrictions on public aid to parochial schools, though here the wall-of-separation principle has not been used to forbid any and all forms of aid. For example it is permissible for the federal government to provide aid for constructing buildings on denominational (as well as nondenominational) college campuses[50] and for state governments to loan free textbooks to parochial-school pupils,[51] grant tax-exempt status to parochial schools,[52] allow parents of parochial-school children to deduct their tuition payments on their income-tax returns,[53] and pay for a deaf child's sign-language interpreter at a Catholic school.[54] But the government cannot pay a salary supplement to teachers who teach secular subjects in parochial schools,[55] reimburse parents for the cost of parochial-school tuition,[56] supply parochial schools with services such as counseling,[57] give money with which to purchase instructional materials, or require that "creationism" (the Biblical doctrine that God created mankind) be taught in public schools.[58]

If you find it confusing to follow the twists and turns of Court policy in this area, you are not alone. The wall-of-separation principle has not been easy to apply, and with its membership undergoing change, the Court has begun to alter its position on church-state matters. (O'Connor, Rehnquist, and White have generally supported lowering—or perhaps perforating—the wall a bit.) The Court has tried to sort out the confusion by developing a three-part test to decide under what circumstances government involvement in religious activities is improper.[59] That involvement is constitutional if it meets these tests:

1. It has a secular purpose.

2. Its primary effect neither advances nor inhibits religion.

3. It does not foster an excessive government entanglement with religion.

No sooner had the test been developed than the Court decided that it was all right for the government of Pawtucket, Rhode Island, to erect a nativity scene as part of a Christmas display in a local park. But five years later it said that Pittsburgh could not put a nativity scene in front of the courthouse but could display a menorah (a Jewish symbol of Chanukah) next to a Christmas tree and a sign extolling liberty.[60]

Confused? It gets worse. Though the Court has struck down prayer in public schools, it has upheld prayers in Congress (since 1789, the House and Senate open each session with a prayer).[61] A public school cannot have a chaplain, but the armed services can. The Court has said that the government cannot "advance" religion, but it has not objected to the printing of the phrase "In God We Trust" on the back of every dollar bill.

It is obvious that despite its efforts to set forth clear rules governing church-state relations, the Court's actual decisions are hard to summarize. It is deeply divided—some would say deeply confused—on these matters, and so the efforts to define the "wall of separation" will continue to prove to be as difficult as the Court's earlier effort to decide what was interstate and what was local commerce (see Chapter 3).

Crime and Due Process

Whereas the central problem in interpreting the religion clauses of the First Amendment has been to decide what they mean, the central problems in interpreting those parts of the Bill of Rights that affect people accused of a crime have been to decide not only what they mean but how to put them into effect. It is not obvious what constitutes an "unreasonable search," but even if we settle that question, we still must decide how best to protect people against such searches in ways that do not unduly hinder criminal investigations.

There are at least two ways to provide that protection. One is to let the police introduce in court evidence relevant to the guilt or innocence of a person, no matter how it was obtained, and then, after the case is settled, punish the police officer (or his or her superiors) if the evidence was gathered improperly

(for example, by an unreasonable search). The other way is to exclude improperly gathered evidence from the trial in the first place, even if it is relevant to determining the guilt or innocence of the accused.

Most democratic nations, including England, use the first method; the United States uses the second. Because of this, many of the landmark cases decided by the Supreme Court have been bitterly controversial. Opponents of these decisions have argued that a guilty person should not go free just because the police officer blundered, especially if the mistake was minor.[62] Supporters rejoin that there is no way to punish errant police officers effectively other than by excluding tainted evidence; moreover nobody should be convicted of a crime except by evidence that is above reproach.[63]

The Exclusionary Rule

The American method relies on what is called the **exclusionary rule.** That rule holds that evidence gathered in violation of the Constitution cannot be used in a trial. The rule has been used to implement two provisions of the Bill of Rights—the right to be free from unreasonable searches or seizures (Fourth Amendment) and the right not to be compelled to give evidence against oneself (Fifth Amendment).*

Not until 1949 did the Supreme Court consider whether to apply the exclusionary rule to the states. In a case decided that year the Court made it clear that the Fourth Amendment prohibited the police from carrying out unreasonable searches and obtaining improper confessions but held that it was not necessary to use the exclusionary rule to enforce those prohibitions. It noted that other nations did not require that evidence improperly gathered had to be excluded from a criminal trial. The Court said that the local police should not improperly gather and use evidence, but if they did, the remedy was to sue the police department or punish the officer.[64]

But in 1961 the Supreme Court changed its mind about the use of the exclusionary rule. It all began

---

* We shall consider here only two constitutional limits—those bearing on searches and confessions. Thus we will omit many other important constitutional provisions affecting criminal cases, such as rules governing wiretapping, prisoner rights, the right to bail and to a jury trial, the bar on ex post facto laws, the right to be represented by a lawyer in court, the ban on "cruel and unusual" punishment, and the rule against double jeopardy.

How Would You Decide?

Suppose that you are on the Supreme Court. In each of the actual cases summarized below, you are asked to decide whether the First Amendment to the Constitution permits or prohibits a particular action. What would be your decision? (How the Supreme Court actually decided is given on page 541.)

CASE 1: Jacksonville, Florida, passed a city ordinance prohibiting drive-in movies from showing films containing nudity if the screen was visible to passersby on the street. A movie-theater manager protested, claiming that he had a First Amendment right to show such films even if they could be seen from the street. Who is correct?

CASE 2: Dr. Benjamin Spock wanted to enter Fort Dix Military Reservation in New Jersey to pass out campaign litera-

ture and discuss issues with service personnel. The military denied him access on grounds that regulations prohibit partisan campaigning on military bases. Who is correct?

CASE 3 A town passed an ordinance forbidding the placing of "For Sale" or "Sold" signs in front of homes in racially changing neighborhoods. The purpose was to reduce "white flight" and panic selling. A realty firm protested, claiming that its freedom of speech was being abridged. Who is correct?

CASE 4: A girl in Georgia was raped and died. A local television station broadcast the name of the girl, having obtained it from court records. Her father sued, claiming that his family's right to privacy had been violated, and pointed to a Georgia law that made it a crime to broadcast

the name of a rape victim. The television station claimed that it had a right under the First Amendment to broadcast the name. Who is correct?

CASE 5: Florida passed a law giving a political candidate the right to equal space in a newspaper that had published attacks on him. A newspaper claimed that this violated the freedom of the press to publish what it wants. Who is correct?

CASE 6: Zacchini is a "human cannonball" whose entire fifteen-second act was filmed and broadcast by an Ohio television station. Zacchini sued the station, claiming that his earning power had been reduced by the film because the station showed for free what he charges people to see at county fairs. The station replied that it had a First Amendment right to broadcast such events. Who is correct?

---

when the Cleveland police broke into the home of Dollree Mapp in search of drugs and, finding none, arrested her for possessing some obscene pictures that they found there. The Court held that this was an unreasonable search and seizure because the police had not obtained a search warrant, though they had ample time to do so. Furthermore such illegally gathered evidence could not be used in the trial of Mapp.[65] Beginning with this case—*Mapp* v. *Ohio*—the Supreme Court required the use of the exclusionary rule as a way of enforcing a variety of constitutional guarantees.

Search and Seizure

After the Court decided to exclude improperly gathered evidence, the next problem was to decide what evidence was improper. What happened to Dollree Mapp was an easy case: hardly anybody argued that it was reasonable for the police without a warrant to break into someone's home, ransack one's belong-

ings, and take whatever they could find that might be incriminating. But that left a lot of hard choices still to be made.

When can the police search you without its being unreasonable? Under two circumstances—when they have a search warrant and when they have lawfully arrested you. A **search warrant** is an order from a judge authorizing the search of a place; the order must describe what is to be searched and seized, and the judge can issue it only if he or she is persuaded by the police that good reason (**probable cause**) exists to believe that a crime has been committed and that the evidence bearing on that crime will be found at a certain location. (The police can also search a building if the occupant gives them permission.)

In addition you can be searched if the search occurs when you are being lawfully arrested. When can you be arrested? If a judge has issued an arrest warrant for you, if you commit a crime in the presence of a police officer, or if the officer has probable cause to believe that you have committed a serious crime (usually a felony). If you are arrested and no search warrant has been issued, the police, and not a judge, decide what they can search. What rules should they follow?

In trying to answer that question, the courts have elaborated a set of rules that are complex, subject to frequent change, and quite controversial. In general the police, after arresting you, can search:

• You
• Things in plain view
• Things or places under your immediate control

As a practical matter, "things in plain view" or "under your immediate control" mean the room in which you are arrested but not other rooms of the house.[66] If the police want to search the rest of your house or a car parked in your driveway, they will first have to go to a judge to obtain a search warrant. But if the police arrest a college student on campus for drinking under age and then accompany that student back to his or her dormitory room so that the student can get proof that he or she was old enough to drink, the police can seize drugs that are in plain view in that room.[67] And if marijuana is growing in plain view in an open field, the police can enter and search that field even though it is fenced off with a locked gate and a "No Trespassing" sign.[68]

But what if you are arrested while driving your car—how much of it can the police search? The answer has changed almost yearly. In 1979 the Court ruled that the police could not search a suitcase taken from a car of an arrested person and in 1981 extended this protection to any "closed, opaque container" found in the car.[69] But the following year the Court decided that all parts of a car, closed or open, could be searched if the officers had probable cause to believe that it contained contraband (that is, goods illegally possessed).[70]

In this confusing area of the law the Court is attempting to protect those places in which a person has a "reasonable expectation of privacy." Your body is one such place, and so the Court has held that the police cannot compel you to undergo surgery to remove a bullet that might be evidence of your guilt or innocence in a crime.[71] But the police can require you to take a Breathalyzer test to see whether you have been drinking while driving.[72] Your home is another place where you have an expectation of privacy, but a barn next to your home is not, nor is your back-

yard viewed from an airplane, nor is your home if it is a motor home that can be driven away, and so the police need not have a warrant to look into these places.[73]

If you work for the government, you have an expectation that your desk and files will be private; nonetheless your supervisor may search the desk and files without a warrant, provided that he or she is looking for something related to your work.[74] But bear in mind that the Constitution only protects you against *the government;* a private employer has a great deal of freedom to search your desk and files.

Some people had hoped that the Court would develop a general right of privacy so that nothing done in your home among consenting adults would be subject to government regulation. Support for this hope was given by the Court's decisions forbidding states from prohibiting the sale of contraceptives. But when the Court was asked to pass on the constitutionality of a Georgia statute that made it illegal to engage in homosexual activities, it held, by a narrow five-to-four vote, that the right to privacy does not extend to such activities, and so the Georgia statute may stand.[75]

Testing for Drugs and AIDS If the government can under some circumstances search your desk and files without a warrant, can it require you to undergo a test for AIDS or for drug use?

In the mid-1980s the deadly AIDS virus became a major public-health issue. Because it disproportionately affected homosexuals, testing people to see whether they had the disease raised fears among some that the tests would be used to discriminate against homosexuals in employment and the issuance of life insurance. But others worried that failing to test for the virus would cause people to be needlessly exposed to the risk of death. In 1987 President Reagan called for AIDS tests for new immigrants, federal prisoners, and certain other categories of people, but it will be some time before an authoritative court decision on the matter is reached.

Drug testing, however, has begun to work its way through the courts. In the wake of growing public concern about the spread of drug abuse, President Reagan in 1986 signed an executive order requiring many federal-government employees to be tested. Numerous private firms and major-league sports organizations had already required such testing of job applicants and athletes. There is no obvious constitutional reason why a *private* organization should not be able to test its members. But the Constitution restricts what the *government* may do; is drug testing by a government agency a proper or an improper "search" of a person?

At first some federal district courts took the view that the mandatory drug testing of, say, fire fighters was an unreasonable search unless the fire fighter who was tested had been suspected of some wrongdoing. But in 1989 the Supreme Court held that certain kinds of employees could be subjected to drug tests without a search warrant or even any individualized suspicion. These were employees involved in law enforcement (in particular, Customs Service agents) and railroad employees involved in accidents. In short, a concern for public safety or national security can justify government-ordered drug tests. Using the same reasoning, the Court has upheld state laws that authorize the police to set up roadblocks and randomly check drivers to see if they are sober.[76]

Confessions and Self-Incrimination

The constitutional ban on being forced to give evidence against oneself was originally intended to prevent the use of torture or "third-degree" police tactics to extract confessions. But it has since been extended to cover many kinds of statements uttered not out of

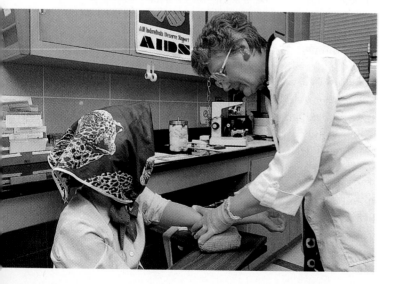

When can the government require that a person be tested for AIDS? As of early 1994, the courts hadn't decided.

fear of torture but from lack of awareness of one's rights, especially the right to remain silent, whether in the courtroom or in the police station.

For many decades the Supreme Court had held that involuntary confessions could not be used in federal criminal trials but had not ruled that they were barred from state trials. But in the early 1960s it changed its mind in two landmark cases—*Escobedo* and *Miranda*.[77] The story of the latter and of the controversy that it provoked is worth telling.

Ernesto A. Miranda was convicted in Arizona of the rape-kidnaping of a young woman. The conviction was based on a written confession that Miranda signed after two hours of police questioning. (The victim also identified him.) Two years earlier the Court had decided that the rule against self-incrimination applied to state courts.[78] Now the question arose, what constitutes an "involuntary" confession? The Court decided that a confession would be presumed involuntary unless the person in custody had been fully and clearly informed of his or her right to be silent, to have an attorney present during any questioning, and to have an attorney provided free of charge if he or she could not afford one. The accused may waive these rights and offer to talk, but the waiver must be truly voluntary. Since Miranda did not have a lawyer present when he was questioned and had not knowingly waived his right to a lawyer, the confession was excluded from evidence in the trial and his conviction was overturned.[79]

Miranda was tried and convicted again, this time on the basis of evidence supplied by his girlfriend, who testified that he had admitted to her that he was guilty. Nine years later he was released from prison; four years after that he was killed in a barroom fight. When the Phoenix police arrested the prime suspect in Ernesto Miranda's murder, they read him his rights from a "Miranda card."

Everyone who watches cops-and-robbers shows on television probably knows the "Miranda warning" by heart (see the box on page 542) since the police now read it routinely to people whom they arrest, both on and off television. It is not clear whether it has much impact on who does or does not confess or what effect, if any, it may have on the crime rate.

In time the Miranda rule was extended to mean that you have a right to a lawyer when you appear in a police lineup[80] and when you are questioned by a psychiatrist to determine whether you are competent

How the Court Decided

*T*he United States Supreme Court answered the questions on page 538 in the following way:

CASE 1: The drive-in movie won. The Supreme Court, 6–3, decided that the First Amendment protects the right to show nudity; it is up to the unwilling viewer on the public streets to avert his or her eyes.

Erznoznik v. Jacksonville,
422 U.S. 205 (1975)

CASE 2: The military won. The Supreme Court, 6–2, decided that military reservations are not like public streets or parks, and thus civilians can be excluded from them, especially if such exclusion prevents the military from appearing to be the handmaiden of various political causes.

Greer v. Spock, 424 U.S. 828 (1976)

CASE 3: The realtor won. The Supreme Court, 8–0, decided that the First Amendment prohibits the banning of signs, even of a commercial nature, without a strong, legitimate state interest. Banning the signs would not obviously reduce "white flight," and the government has no right to withhold information from citizens for fear that they will act unwisely.

Linmark Associates, Inc. v. Willingboro,
431 U.S. 85 (1977)

CASE 4: The television station won. The Court, 8–1, decided that the First Amendment protects the right to broadcast the names of rape victims obtained from public (that is, court) records.

Cox Broadcasting Corp. v. Cohn,
420 U.S. 469 (1975)

CASE 5: The newspaper won. The Supreme Court decided unanimously that the First Amendment prohibits the state from intruding into the function of editors.

Miami Herald Publishing Co. v. Tornillo,
418 U.S. 241 (1974)

CASE 6: Zacchini, the human cannonball won. The Supreme Court, 5–4, decided that broadcasting the entire act without the performer's consent jeopardized his means of livelihood even though the First Amendment would guarantee the right of the station to broadcast newsworthy facts about the act.

Zacchini v. Scripps-Howard Broadcasting Co.,
433 U.S. 562 (1977)

---

to stand trial.[81] The Court threw out the conviction of a man who had killed a child because the accused, without being given the right to have a lawyer present, had led the police to the victim's body.[82] You do not have a right to a Miranda warning, however, if, while in jail, you confess a crime to another inmate who turns out to be an undercover police officer.[83]

Relaxing the Exclusionary Rule

Cases such as *Miranda* were highly controversial and led to efforts in Congress to modify or overrule the decisions by statute—without much coming of the attempt. But as the rules governing police conduct became increasingly more complex, pressure mounted to find an alternative. Some thought that any evidence should be admissible, with the question of police conduct left to lawsuits or other ways of punishing official misbehavior. Others felt that the exclusionary rule served a useful purpose but had simply become too technical to be an effective deter-

rent to police misconduct (the police cannot obey rules that they cannot understand). And still others felt that the exclusionary rule was a vital safeguard to essential liberties and should be kept intact.

The courts themselves began to adopt the second position, deciding a number of cases in ways that retained the exclusionary rule but modified it by limiting its coverage (police were given greater freedom to question juveniles)[84] and by incorporating what was called a **good-faith exception.** For example, if the police obtain a search warrant that they believe is valid, the evidence that they gather will not be excluded if it later turns out that the warrant was defective for some reason (such as the judge's having used the wrong form).[85] And the Court decided that "overriding considerations of public safety" may justify questioning a person without first reading the person his or her rights.[86] Moreover the Court changed its mind about the killer who led the police to the place where he had disposed of his victim's body. After the man was convicted a second time and

The Miranda Rule

The Supreme Court has interpreted the due-process clause to require that local police departments issue warnings of the sort shown below to people whom they are arresting.

```
        PHILADELPHIA POLICE DEPARTMENT
      STANDARD POLICE INTERROGATION CARD

        WARNINGS TO BE GIVEN ACCUSED

We are questioning you concerning the
crime of (state specific crime).

    We have a duty to explain to
    you and to warn you that you
    have the following legal rights:

A.  You have a right to remain
    silent and do not have to say
    anything at all.

B.  Anything you say can and will
    be used against you in Court.

C.  You have a right to talk to a
    lawyer of your own choice
    before we ask you any questions,
    and also to have a lawyer here
    with you while we ask questions.

D.  If you cannot afford to hire a
    lawyer, and you want one, we
    will see that you have one
    provided to you free of charge
    before we ask you any questions.

E.  If you are willing to give us a
    statement, you have a right to
    stop any time you wish.

75-Misc.-3                        (Over)
(6-24-70)
```

Ernesto A. Miranda was convicted in Arizona of rape-kidnaping. When the Supreme Court overturned the conviction, it issued a set of rules—the "Miranda rules"—governing how police must conduct an arrest and interrogation.

again appealed, the Court in 1984 held that the body would have been discovered anyway; evidence will not be excluded if it can be shown that it would "inevitably" have been found.[87]

SUMMARY

Civil-liberties questions are in some ways like and in some ways unlike ordinary policy debates. Like most issues, civil-liberties problems often involve competing interests—in this case rights in conflict—and so we have groups mobilized on each side of issues involving free speech and crime control. Like some other issues, civil-liberties problems can also arise from the successful appeals of a policy entrepreneur, and so we have periodic reductions in liberty resulting from popular fears, usually aroused during or just after a war.

But civil liberties are unlike many other issues in at least one regard: more than struggles over welfare spending or defense or economic policy, debates about civil liberties reach down into our fundamental political beliefs and political culture, challenging us to define what we mean by religion, Americanism, and decency.

The most important of these challenges focuses on the meaning of the First Amendment: What is "speech"? How much of it should be free? How far can the state go in aiding religion? How do we strike a balance between national security and personal expression? The zigzag course followed by the courts in judging these matters has, on balance, tended to enlarge freedom of expression.

Almost as important has been the struggle to strike a balance between the right of society to protect itself from criminals and the right of people (including criminals) to be free from unreasonable searches and coerced confessions. As with free-speech cases, the courts have generally broadened the rights at some expense to the power of the police. But in recent years the Supreme Court has pulled back from some of its more sweeping applications of the exclusionary rule.

The resolution of these issues by the courts is political in the sense that differing opinions about what is right or desirable compete, with one side or another prevailing (often by a small majority). In this competition of ideas federal judges, though not elected, are often sensitive to strong currents of popular opinion. When entrepreneurial politics has produced new action against apparently threatening minorities, judges are inclined, at least for a while, to give serious consideration to popular fears and legislative majorities. And when no strong national mood is discernible, the opinions of elites influence judicial thinking (as described in Chapter 14).

At the same time, courts resolve political conflicts in a manner that differs in important respects from the resolution of conflicts by legislatures or executives. First, the very existence of the courts, and the relative ease with which one may enter them to advance a claim, facilitates challenges to accepted values. An unpopular political or religious group may have little or no access to a legislature, but it will have substantial access to the courts. Second, judges often settle controversies about rights not simply by deciding the case at hand but by formulating a general rule to cover like cases elsewhere. This has an advantage (the law tends to become more consistent and better known) but a disadvantage as well: a rule suitable for one case may be unworkable in another. Judges reason by analogy and sometimes assume that two cases are similar when in fact there are important differences. A definition of "obscenity" or of "fighting words" may suit one situation but be inadequate in another. Third, judges interpret the Constitution, whereas legislatures often consult popular preferences or personal convictions. However much their own beliefs influence what judges read into the Constitution, almost all of them are constrained by its language.

Taken together, the desire to find and announce rules, the language of the Constitution, and the personal beliefs of judges have led to a general expansion of civil liberties. As a result, even allowing for temporary reversals and frequent redefinitions, any value that is thought to hinder freedom of expression and the rights of the accused has generally lost ground to the claims of the First, Fourth, Fifth, and Sixth Amendments.

KEY TERMS

McCarthyism   *p. 524*

freedom of expression   *p. 526*

freedom of religion   *p. 526*

prior restraint   *p. 526*

clear-and-present danger test   *p. 527*

due-process clause   *p. 528*

libel   *p. 530*

symbolic speech   *p. 531*

free-exercise clause   *p. 533*

establishment clause   *p. 533*

wall-of-separation principle   *p. 535*

exclusionary rule   *p. 537*

search warrant   *p. 538*

probable cause   *p. 538*

good-faith exception   *p. 541*

SUGGESTED READINGS

Abraham, Henry J. *Freedom and the Court.* 5th ed. New York: Oxford University Press, 1988. Analysis of leading Supreme Court cases on civil liberties and civil rights.

Berns, Walter. *The First Amendment and the Future of American Democracy.* New York: Basic Books, 1976. A look at what the Founders intended by the First Amendment that takes issue with contemporary Supreme Court interpretations of it.

Clor, Harry M. *Obscenity and Public Morality.* Chicago: University of Chicago Press, 1969. Argues for the legitimacy of legal restrictions on obscenity.

Corwin, Edward S. *The Constitution and What It Means Today.* 14th ed. Revised by Harold W. Chase and Craig R. Ducat. Princeton, N.J.: Princeton University Press, 1978. A frequently updated analysis, section by section, of what the Constitution means in light of Court interpretations. A valuable reference.

Emerson, Thomas I. *Toward a General Theory of the First Amendment.* New York: Random House, 1966. Argues, contrary to Walter Berns (cited above), that the First Amendment confers an absolute protection on speech.

Levy, Leonard W. *Legacy of Suppression: Freedom of Speech and Press in Early American History.* Rev. ed. New York: Oxford University Press, 1985. Careful study of what the Founders and the early leaders meant by freedom of speech and press.

Pritchett, C. Herman. *Constitutional Civil Liberties.* Englewood Cliffs, N.J.: Prentice-Hall, 1984. An excellent summary and analysis of the constitutional law governing civil liberties.

19

Civil Rights

In 1830 Congress passed a law requiring all Indians east of the Mississippi River to move to the Indian Territory west of the river, and the army set about implementing it. In the 1850s a major political fight broke out in Boston over whether the police department should be obliged to hire an Irish officer. Until 1920 women could not vote in most elections. In the 1930s the Cornell University Medical School had a strict quota to limit the number of Jewish students who could enroll. In the 1940s the army, with the approval of President Franklin D. Roosevelt, removed all Japanese-Americans from their homes in California and placed them in relocation centers far from the coast.

In all such cases some group, usually defined along racial or ethnic lines, was denied access to facilities, opportunities, or services that were available to other groups. Such cases raise the issue of **civil rights.** That issue is not whether the government has the authority to treat different people differently, but only whether such differences in treatment are "reasonable." All laws and policies make distinctions—for example, the tax laws require higher-income people to pay taxes at a higher rate than lower-income ones—but not all distinctions are defensible. The courts have long held that classifying people on the basis of their income and taxing different classes at different rates is quite permissible because such classifications are not arbitrary or unreasonable and they are related to a legitimate public policy (that is, raising revenue). Increasingly, however, the courts have said that classifying people on the basis of their race or ethnicity is unreasonable—these are **suspect classifications**—and while not every law making such classifications will be ruled unconstitutional, they all will be subject to especially strict scrutiny.[1]

Given the theory of policy-making developed so far in this book, it may seem surprising that certain groups, particularly those that constitute only a small minority of the population, should require any special protection at all. We have seen how easy it is for many small groups—businesses, occupations,

545

United Farm Workers of America has been an important vehicle for mobilizing Hispanics in agricultural areas. The speaker here is Vilma Martinez.

unions—to practice client politics. They can obtain some special advantage (a grant, a license, a subsidy) or avoid some threatened regulation because, being small, they find it easy to organize and to escape general public notice. Yet Native Americans, blacks, Japanese-Americans, and Mexican-Americans are also relatively small groups whose demands seemingly place little burden on the majority population. Despite this, they have been more often the victims than the clients of the policy-making process.

To explain the victimization of certain groups and the methods by which they have begun to overcome that victimization, we shall consider chiefly the case of black Americans. Black-white relations have in large measure defined the problem of civil rights in this country; most of the landmark laws and court decisions have involved black claims. The strategies employed by or on behalf of blacks have typically set the pattern for the strategies employed by other groups. At the end of this chapter we shall look at the related but somewhat different issue of women's rights.

The Black Predicament

Though constituting more than 12 percent of the population, blacks until fairly recently could not in many parts of the country vote, attend integrated schools, ride in the front seats of buses, or buy homes in white neighborhoods.

One reason is that the perceived costs of granting these demands were not widely distributed among the public at large but instead were concentrated on some relatively small, readily organized, immediately affected group. Citizens generally may not feel threatened if a black moves into Cicero, Illinois; goes to school at Little Rock Central High School; or votes in Neshoba County, Mississippi—but at one time most whites (and even now some whites) in Cicero, Little Rock, and Neshoba County felt deeply threatened. In the language of this book civil rights in these places was not a matter of client politics but of competitive or interest-group politics. This was especially the case in those parts of the country, notably in the Deep South, where blacks were often in a majority. There the politically dominant white minority felt keenly the potential competition for jobs, land, public services, and living space posed by large numbers of people of another race. But even in the North, black gains often appeared to be at the expense of lower-income whites who lived or worked near them, not at the expense of upper-status whites who lived in suburbs.

The interest-group component of racial politics put blacks at a decided disadvantage: they were not allowed to vote at all in many areas, they could vote only with great difficulty in others, and even in those places where voting was easy, they often lacked the material and institutional support for effective political organizations. If your opponent feels deeply threatened by your demands and in addition can deny you access to the political system that will decide the fate of those demands, you are, to put it mildly, at a disadvantage. Yet from the end of Reconstruction down to the 1960s—for nearly a century—many blacks in the South found themselves in just such a position.

A second reason why the restrictions on black Americans continued for so long is that majoritarian politics worked to the disadvantage of blacks. Because of white attitudes, this was the case even when white and black interests were not directly in competition. To the dismay of those who prefer to explain political action by economic motives, people often attach greater importance to the intangible costs and benefits of policies than to the tangible ones. Thus, even though the average black represented no threat to the average white, antiblack attitudes—racism—produced some appalling actions. Between 1882 and 1946, 4,715 people, about three-fourths of them blacks, were lynched in the United States.[2] Some lynchings were carried out by small groups of vigilantes acting with much ceremony, but others were the actions of frenzied mobs. In the summer of 1911 a black charged with murdering a white man in Livermore, Kentucky, was dragged by a mob to the local theater, where he was hanged. The audience, which had been charged admission, was invited to shoot the swaying body (those in the orchestra seats could empty their revolvers, those in the balcony were limited to a single shot).[3]

Though public opinion in other parts of the country was shocked by such events, little was done: lynching was a local, not a federal, crime. It obviously would not require many lynchings to convince blacks in these localities that it would be foolhardy to try to vote or enroll in a white school. And even in those states where blacks did vote, popular attitudes were not conducive to blacks' buying homes or taking jobs on an equal basis with whites. Even among those professing to support equal rights, a substantial portion opposed black efforts to obtain them and federal action to secure them. In 1942 a national poll showed that only 30 percent of whites thought that black and white children should attend the same schools; in 1956 the proportion had risen to 49 percent, still less than a majority. (In the South white support for school integration was even lower—14 percent favored it in 1956, about 31 percent in 1963.) As late as 1956 a majority of southern whites were opposed to integrated public transportation facilities. Even among whites who generally favored integration, there was in 1963 (*before* the ghetto riots) considerable opposition to the black civil-rights movement: nearly half of the whites who were classified in a survey as moderate integrationists thought that demonstrations hurt the black cause; nearly two-thirds disapproved of actions taken by the civil-rights

movement; and over a third felt that civil rights should be left to the states.[4]

In short the political position in which blacks found themselves until the 1960s made it difficult for them to advance their own interests with any feasible legislative strategy: their opponents were aroused, organized, and powerful. Thus, if those interests were to be championed in Congress or state legislatures, blacks would have to make use of white allies. Though some such allies could be found, they were too few to make a difference in a political system, such as the one found in Congress, that gives a substantial advantage to strongly motivated opponents of any new policy. For that to change, one or both of two things would have to happen: additional allies would have to be recruited (a delicate problem, given that many white integrationists disapproved of aspects of the civil-rights movement), or the struggle would have to be shifted to a policy-making arena in which the opposition enjoyed less of an advantage.

Partly by plan, partly by accident, black leaders followed both of these strategies simultaneously. By

A segregated bus station in Durham, North Carolina, in 1940.

President Lyndon Johnson signs the Civil Rights Act of 1965 in the company of the Reverend Martin Luther King, Jr., and the Reverend Ralph Abernathy.

publicizing their grievances, but above all by developing a civil-rights movement that (at least in its early stages) dramatized the denial of essential and widely accepted liberties, blacks were able to broaden their base of support in both elite and public opinion and thereby to raise civil-rights matters from a low to a high position on the political agenda. By waging a patient, prolonged, but carefully planned legal struggle, black leaders shifted the key civil-rights decisions from Congress, where they had been stymied for generations, to the federal courts.

After this strategy had achieved some substantial successes—after blacks had been enfranchised and legal barriers to equal participation in political and economic affairs had been lowered—the politics of civil rights became more conventional. Blacks were able to assert their demands directly in the legislative and executive branches of government with reasonable (though scarcely certain) prospects of success. Civil rights became less a matter of gaining entry into the political system and more one of waging interest-group politics within that system. At the same time the goals of civil-rights politics were broadened. The struggle to gain entry into the system had focused on the denial of fundamental rights (to vote, to organize, to obtain equal access to schools and public facilities); since that entry the dominant issues have been manpower development, economic progress, and the improvement of housing and neighborhoods.

The Campaign in the Courts

The Fourteenth Amendment was both the opportunity and the problem. Adopted in 1868, it *seemed* to guarantee equal rights for all: "No state shall make or enforce any law which shall abridge the privileges or immunities of citizens of the United States; nor shall any state deprive any person of life, liberty, or property, without due process of law; nor deny to any person within its jurisdiction the equal protection of the laws."

CRITICAL ★ THINKING

The Black College Predicament

Howard University in Washington, D.C., a traditionally black college.

Until the Supreme Court desegregation rulings, blacks in most parts of the South could attend only segregated, all-black colleges. After a long struggle, blacks won admission to previously all-white colleges and universities.

This left an unanswered question: What should happen to the previously all-black schools, some of which had a long and illustrious history of providing education? Theoretically, whites would be free to enroll in traditionally black schools just as blacks were free to enter all-white ones, but in fact, very few whites applied to the all-black schools. Moreover, some black educators believe that attending a predominately black school is helpful to many black students, just as some female educators believe that going to an all-women college makes sense for many female students. The United Negro College Fund raises money for predominately black colleges.

But the Supreme Court, having ruled that separate schools are inherently unequal, opposed segregation. In 1992, it decided that the state-funded maintenance in Mississippi of eight universities, some of which were predominately black, was unconstitutional.* This ruling challenges public funding for all colleges and universities that have a predominately minority or female enrollment.

Should black colleges be abolished? Should colleges serving specific groups be banned even when no one is excluded from attending any school on the basis of race? Should blacks or women who prefer a more segregated environment be forced to attend mostly white and coeducational schools?

*United States v. Fordice, 112 S.Ct. 2727 (1992).

The key phrase was "equal protection of the laws." Read broadly, it might mean that henceforth the Constitution would be color-blind: no state law could have the effect of treating whites and blacks differently. Thus a law segregating blacks and whites into separate schools or neighborhoods would be unconstitutional. Read narrowly, "equal protection" might mean only that blacks and whites had certain fundamental legal rights in common, among them the right to sign contracts, to serve on juries, or to buy and sell property, but otherwise they could be treated differently.

Historians have long debated which view Congress held when it proposed the Fourteenth Amendment. What forms of racial segregation, if any, were still permissible? Segregated trains? Hotels? Schools? Neighborhoods?

The Supreme Court took the narrow view. Though in 1880 it declared unconstitutional a West Virginia law requiring juries to be composed only of white males,[5] it decided in 1883 that it was unconstitutional for Congress to prohibit racial discrimination in public accommodations such as hotels.[6] The difference between the two cases seemed, in the eyes of the Court, to be this: serving on a jury was an essential right of citizenship that the state could not deny to any person on racial grounds without violating the Fourteenth Amendment, but registering at a hotel was a convenience controlled by a private person (the hotel owner), who could treat blacks and whites differently if he or she wished.

The major decision that was to determine the legal status of the Fourteenth Amendment for over half a century was *Plessy* v. *Ferguson.* Louisiana had passed a law requiring blacks and whites to occupy separate cars on railroad trains operating in that state. When Adolph Plessy, who was seven-eighths white and one-eighth black, refused to obey the law,

he was arrested. He appealed his conviction to the Supreme Court, claiming that the law violated the Fourteenth Amendment. In 1896 the Court rejected his claim, holding that the law treated both races equally even though it required them to be separate. The equal-protection clause guaranteed political and legal but not social equality. "Separate-but-equal" facilities were constitutional because if "one race be inferior to the other socially, the Constitution of the United States cannot put them on the same plane."[7]

"Separate but Equal"

Thus began the **separate-but-equal doctrine.** Three years later the Court applied it to schools as well, declaring in *Cumming* v. *Richmond County Board of Education* that a decision in a Georgia community to close the black high school while keeping open the white high school was not a violation of the Fourteenth Amendment because blacks could always go to private schools. Here the Court seemed to be saying that not only could schools be separate, they could even be unequal.[8]

What the Court has made, the Court can unmake. But to get it to change its mind requires a long, costly, and uncertain legal battle. The National Association for the Advancement of Colored People (NAACP) was the main organization that waged that battle. Formed in 1909 by a group of whites and blacks in the aftermath of a race riot, the NAACP did many things—lobbying in Washington and publicizing black grievances, especially in the pages of *The Crisis,* a magazine edited by W. E. B. Du Bois—but its most influential role was played in the courtroom.

It was a rational strategy. Fighting legal battles does not require forming broad political alliances or changing public opinion, tasks that would have been very difficult for a small and unpopular organization. A court-based approach also enabled the organization to remain nonpartisan.

But it was a slow and difficult strategy. The Court had adopted a narrow interpretation of the Fourteenth Amendment. To get it to change its mind would require the NAACP to bring before it cases involving the strongest possible claims that a black was unfairly treated under circumstances sufficiently different from those of earlier cases so that the Court could either distinguish the new cases from the old ones or find some grounds for changing its mind.

POLITICALLY **P.S.** SPEAKING

Jim Crow

Thomas D. ("Daddy") Rice, a white entertainer, began around 1828 to stage a vaudeville sketch in which he blacked his face with burned cork and sang a ditty that acquired the title "Wheel About and Turn About and Jump, Jim Crow." Thus was born what later became the immensely popular minstrel shows, a burlesque by whites of black songs and speech mannerisms. The phrase **Jim Crow** from Rice's song soon came to be a slang expression for blacks and was later applied to laws and practices that segregated blacks from whites.

The steps in that strategy were these: First, persuade the Court to declare unconstitutional laws creating schools that were separate but obviously unequal. Second, persuade it to declare unconstitutional laws supporting schools that were separate but unequal in not-so-obvious ways. Third, persuade it to rule that racially separate schools were inherently unequal and hence unconstitutional.

Can Separate Schools Be Equal?

The first step was accomplished in a series of court cases stretching from 1938 to 1948. In 1938 the Court held that Lloyd Gaines had to be admitted to an all-white law school in Missouri because no black law school of equal quality existed in that state.[9] In 1948 the Court ordered the all-white University of Oklahoma Law School to admit Ada Lois Sipuel, a black, even though the state planned to build a black law school later. For education to be equal, it had to be available now.[10] It still could be separate, however: the university admitted Ms. Sipuel but required her to attend classes in a section of the state capitol, roped off from other students, where she could meet with her law professors.

The second step was taken in two cases decided in 1950. Heman Sweatt, a black, was treated by the University of Texas Law School much as Ada Sipuel had been treated in Oklahoma: "admitted" to the all-white school but relegated to a separate building. Another black, George McLaurin, was allowed to study for his Ph.D. in a "colored section" of the all-white University of Oklahoma. The Supreme Court unanimously decided that these arrangements were unconstitutional because, by imposing racially based barriers on the black students' access to professors, libraries, and other students, they created unequal educational opportunities.[11]

The third step, the climax of the entire drama, began in Topeka, Kansas, where Linda Brown wanted to enroll in her neighborhood school but could not because she was black and the school was by law reserved exclusively for whites. When the NAACP took her case to the federal district court in Kansas, the judge decided that the black school that Linda could attend was substantially equal in quality to the white school that she could not attend. Thus denying her access to the white school was constitutional. To change that, the lawyers would have to persuade the

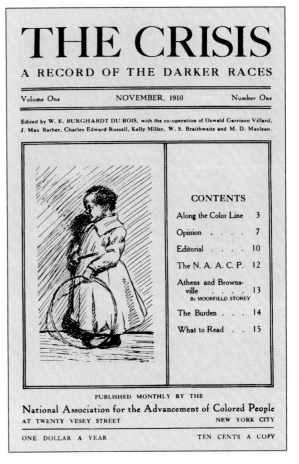

Shown above is the cover of the first issue of *The Crisis,* the magazine started by the NAACP in 1910 to raise black consciousness and publicize racist acts.

Supreme Court to overrule the district judge on the grounds that racially separate schools were unconstitutional even if they were equal. In other words, the separate-but-equal doctrine would have to be overturned by the Courts.

It was a risky and controversial step to take. Many states, Kansas among them, were trying to make their all-black schools equal to those of whites by launching expensive building programs. If the NAACP succeeded in getting separate schools declared unconstitutional, the Court might well put a stop to the building of these new schools. Blacks could win a moral and legal victory but suffer a practical defeat—the loss of these new facilities. Despite these risks the NAACP decided to go ahead with the appeal.

On September 25, 1957, troops of the 101st Airborne Division escorted nine black children into Little Rock (Arkansas) Central High School to begin its integration.

Brown v. Board of Education

On May 17, 1954, a unanimous Supreme Court, speaking through an opinion written and delivered by Chief Justice Earl Warren, found that "in the field of public education the doctrine of 'separate but equal' has no place" because "separate educational facilities are inherently unequal."[12] *Plessy* v. *Ferguson* was overruled, and "separate but equal" was dead.

The ruling was a landmark decision, but the reasons for it and the means chosen to implement it were as important and as controversial as the decision itself. There were at least three issues. First, how would the decision be implemented? Second, on what grounds were racially separate schools unconstitutional? Third, what test would a school system have to meet in order to be in conformity with the Constitution?

Implementation   The *Brown* case involved a class-action suit; that is, it applied not only to Linda Brown but to all others similarly situated. This meant that black children everywhere now had the right to at-

tend formerly all-white schools. This change would be one of the most far-reaching and disputatious events in modern American history. It could not be effected overnight or by the stroke of a pen. In 1955 the Supreme Court decided that it would let local federal district courts oversee the end of segregation by giving them the power to approve or disapprove local desegregation plans. This was to be done "with all deliberate speed."[13]

In the South "deliberate speed" turned out to be a snail's pace. Massive resistance to desegregation broke out in many states. Some communities simply defied the Court; some sought to evade its edict by closing their public schools. In 1956 over one hundred southern members of Congress signed a "Southern Manifesto" that condemned the *Brown* decision as an "abuse of judicial power" and pledged to "use all lawful means to bring about a reversal of the decision."

In the late 1950s and early 1960s the National Guard and regular army paratroopers were used to escort black students into formerly all-white schools and universities. It was not until the 1970s that resistance collapsed and most southern schools were integrated. The use of armed force convinced people that resistance was futile; the disruption of the politics and economy of the South convinced leaders that it was imprudent; and the voting power of blacks convinced politicians that it was suicidal. In addition federal laws began providing financial aid to integrated schools and withholding it from segregated ones. By 1970 only 14 percent of southern black schoolchildren still attended all-black schools.[14]

The Rationale As the struggle to implement the *Brown* decision continued, the importance of the rationale for that decision became apparent. The case was decided in a way that surprised many legal scholars. The Court could have said that the equal-protection clause of the Fourteenth Amendment makes the Constitution, and thus state laws, color-blind. Or it could have said that the authors of the Fourteenth Amendment meant to ban segregated schools. It did neither. Instead it said that segregated education is bad because it "has a detrimental effect upon the colored children" by generating "a feeling of inferiority as to their status in the community" that may "affect their hearts and minds in a way unlikely ever to be undone."[15] This conclusion was supported by a footnote reference to social-science studies of the apparent impact of segregation on black children.

Why did the Court rely on social science as much as or more than the Constitution in supporting its decision? Apparently for two reasons. One was the justices' realization that the authors of the Fourteenth Amendment may *not* have intended to outlaw segregated schools. The schools in Washington, D.C., were segregated when the amendment was proposed, and when this fact was mentioned during the debate, it seems to have been made clear that the amendment was not designed to abolish this segregation. When Congress debated a civil-rights act a few years later, it voted down provisions that would have ended segregation in schools.[16] The Court could not easily base its decision on a constitutional provision that had, at best, an uncertain application to schools. The other reason grew out of the first. On so important a matter the chief justice wanted to speak for a unanimous court. Some justices did not agree that the Fourteenth Amendment made the Constitution color-blind. In the interests of harmony the Court found an ambiguous rationale for its decision.

In 1963 Governor George Wallace of Alabama stood in the doorway of the University of Alabama to block the entry of black students. Facing him is United States Deputy Attorney General Nicholas Katzenbach.

Desegregation versus Integration That ambiguity led to the third issue. If separate schools were inherently unequal, what would "unseparate" schools look like? Since the Court had not said that race was irrelevant, an "unseparate" school could be either one that blacks and whites were free to attend if they chose or one that blacks and whites in fact attended whether they wanted to or not. The first might be called a desegregated school, the latter an integrated school. Think of the Topeka case. Was it enough that there was now no barrier to Linda Brown's attending the white school in her neighborhood? Or was it necessary that there actually be black children (if not Linda, then some others) going to that school together with white children?

As long as the main impact of the *Brown* decision lay in the South, where laws had prevented blacks from attending white schools, this question did not seem important. Segregation by law (**de jure segregation**) was now clearly unconstitutional. But in the North, laws had not kept blacks and whites apart; instead all-black and all-white schools were the result of residential segregation, preferred living patterns, informal social forces, and administrative practices (such as drawing school-district lines so as to produce single-race schools). This was often called segregation in fact (**de facto segregation**).

In 1968 the Supreme Court settled the matter. In New Kent County, Virginia, the school board had created a "freedom-of-choice" plan under which every pupil would be allowed without legal restriction to attend the school of his or her choice. As it turned out, all the white children chose to remain in the all-white school, and 85 percent of the black children remained in the all-black school. The Court rejected this plan as unconstitutional because it did not produce the "ultimate end," which was a "unitary, nonracial system of education."[17] In the opinion written by Justice William Brennan, the Court

Antibusing protesters buried a school bus (unoccupied) to dramatize their cause.

seemed to be saying that the Constitution required actual racial mixing in schools, not just the repeal of laws requiring racial separation.

This impression was confirmed three years later when the Court considered a plan in North Carolina under which pupils in Mecklenburg County (which includes Charlotte) were assigned to the nearest neighborhood school without regard to race. As a result about half the black children now attended formerly all-white schools, with the other half attending all-black schools. The federal district court held that this was inadequate and ordered some children to be bused into more distant schools in order to achieve a greater degree of integration. The Supreme Court, now led by Chief Justice Warren Burger, upheld the district judge on the grounds that the court plan was necessary to achieve a "unitary school system."[18]

This case—*Swann* v. *Charlotte-Mecklenburg Board of Education*—pretty much set the guidelines for all subsequent cases involving school segregation. The essential features of these rules are:

- To violate the Constitution, a school system, by law, practice, or regulation, must have engaged in discrimination. Put another way, a plaintiff must show an intent to discriminate on the part of the public schools.

- The existence of all-white or all-black schools in a district with a history of segregation creates a presumption of intent to discriminate.

- The remedy for past discrimination will not be limited to freedom of choice, or what the Court called "the walk-in school." Remedies may include racial quotas in the assignment of teachers and pupils, redrawn district lines, and court-ordered busing.

- Not every school must reflect the social composition of the school system as a whole.

Relying on *Swann,* district courts have supervised redistricting and busing plans in localities all over the nation, often in the teeth of bitter opposition from the community. In Boston the control of the city schools by a federal judge, W. Arthur Garrity, lasted for more than a decade and involved him in every aspect of school administration.

One major issue not settled by *Swann* was whether busing and other remedies should cut across city and county lines. In some places the central-city schools had become virtually all black. Racial integration could be achieved only by bringing black pupils to white suburban schools or moving white pupils into central-city schools. In a series of split-vote decisions the Court has announced this rule: intercity court-ordered busing will only be authorized when it has been shown that the suburban areas as well as the central city have in fact practiced school segregation. Where that cannot be shown, such intercity busing will not be required. The Court was not persuaded that intent had been proved in Atlanta, Detroit, Denver, Indianapolis, and Richmond, but it was persuaded in Louisville and Wilmington, and so intercity busing was ordered in the last two cities but not in the first five.[19]

The importance that the Court attaches to intent means that if a school system that was once integrated becomes all-black as a result of whites' moving to the suburbs, the Court will not require that district lines constantly be redrawn or new busing plans adopted to adjust to the changing distribution of population.[20] This in turn means that as long as blacks and whites live in different neighborhoods for whatever reason, there is a good chance that some schools in both areas will be heavily of one race. If mandatory busing or other integration measures cause whites to move out of a city at a faster rate than they otherwise would (a process often called "white flight"), then efforts to integrate the schools may in time create more single-race schools. Ultimately integrated schools will exist only in integrated neighborhoods or where the quality of education is so high that both blacks and whites want to enroll in the school even at some cost in travel and inconvenience.

Mandatory busing to achieve racial integration has been a deeply controversial program and has generated considerable public opposition. Surveys show a majority of people oppose it.[21] As recently as in 1992, 48 percent of whites in the Northeast and 53 percent of southern whites felt that it was "not the business" of the federal government to ensure "that black and white children go to the same schools."[22] Presidents Nixon, Ford, and Reagan opposed busing; all three supported legislation to prevent or reduce it, and Reagan petitioned the courts to reconsider busing plans. The courts refused to reconsider, and Congress has passed only minor restrictions on busing.

The reason why Congress has not followed public opinion on this matter is complex. It has been torn between the desire to support civil rights and uphold the courts and the desire to represent the views of its constituents. Because it faces a dilemma, Congress has taken both sides of the issue simultaneously.

During the 1970s the House of Representatives would pass bills restricting busing, whereupon the Senate would amend them by allowing busing if ordered by a court. The result was no policy at all. In 1981 the Senate approved a bill forbidding federal judges from ordering busing except in very narrow circumstances, but it never became law. Although a House version of these bills was adopted in 1982, it, too, never became law. Throughout the 1980s Congress did enact laws forbidding the use of federal funds to bus schoolchildren for purposes of racial integration; these laws had little effect, however, since a judge could still order states and cities to pay the costs. By the late 1980s busing was a dying issue in Congress, in part because no meaningful legislation seemed possible and in part because popular passion over busing had somewhat abated.

Then, in 1992, the Supreme Court made it easier for local school systems to reclaim control of their schools from the courts. In DeKalb County (a suburb of Atlanta), the schools had been operating under court-ordered desegregation plans for many years. Despite this effort full integration had not been achieved, largely because the neighborhoods increasingly had become either all-black or all-white. The Court held that the local schools could not be held responsible for segregation solely caused by segregated living patterns and so the courts would relinquish their control of the schools.[23]

The Campaign in Congress

The campaign in the courts for desegregated schools, though slow and costly, was a carefully managed effort to alter the interpretation of a constitutional provision. But to get new civil-rights laws out of Congress required a far more difficult and decentralized strategy, one that was aimed at mobilizing public opinion and overcoming the many congressional barriers to action.

The first problem was to get civil rights on the political agenda by convincing people that something had to be done. This could be achieved by dramatizing the problem in ways that shocked the

Rosa Parks was arrested for refusing to move to the segregated section at the back of a bus in Montgomery, Alabama.

consciences of those whites who were not racists but who were ordinarily indifferent to black problems. Brutal lynchings of blacks provided such shocks, but lynchings were becoming less frequent in the 1950s and obviously black leaders had no desire to provoke more lynchings just to get sympathy for their cause.

Those leaders could, however, arrange for dramatic confrontations between blacks claiming and whites denying some obvious right. Beginning in the late 1950s these confrontations began to occur in the form of sit-ins at segregated lunch counters and "freedom rides" on segregated bus lines. At about the same time, efforts were made to get blacks registered to vote in counties where whites had used intimidation and harassment to prevent it.

The best-known demonstration occurred in 1955–1956 in Montgomery, Alabama, where blacks, led by a young minister named Martin Luther King, Jr., boycotted the local bus system after it had a black woman, Rosa Parks, arrested because she refused to surrender her seat on a bus to a white man.

These early demonstrations were based on the philosophy of **nonviolent civil disobedience**—that is, peacefully violating a law, such as one requiring blacks to ride in a segregated section of a bus, and allowing oneself to be arrested as a result.

In 1960 black students from North Carolina Agricultural and Technical College staged the first "sit-in" when they were refused service at a lunch counter in Greensboro (left). Twenty years later, graduates of the college returned to the same lunch counter (right). Though prices had risen, the service had improved.

But the momentum of protest, once unleashed, could not be centrally directed or confined to nonviolent action. A rising tide of anger, especially among younger blacks, resulted in the formation of more militant organizations and the spontaneous eruption of violent demonstrations and riots in dozens of cities across the country. From 1964 to 1968 there were in the North as well as the South four "long, hot summers" of racial violence.

The demonstrations and rioting succeeded in getting civil rights on the national political agenda, but at a cost: many whites, opposed to the demonstrations or appalled by the riots, dug in their heels and fought against making any concessions to "law-breakers," "troublemakers," and "rioters." In 1964 and again in 1968 over two-thirds of the whites interviewed in opinion polls said that the civil-rights movement was pushing too fast, had hurt the black cause, and was too violent.[24]

In short there was a conflict between the agenda-setting and coalition-building aspects of the civil-rights movement. This was especially a problem since, in the 1960s, conservative southern legislators still controlled many key congressional committees that had for years been the graveyard of civil-rights legislation. The Senate Judiciary Committee was dominated by a coalition of southern Democrats and conservative Republicans, and the House Rules

Chronology of Major Events in the Civil Rights Movement, 1955–1968

Dec. 5, 1955	Blacks in Montgomery, Alabama, begin yearlong boycott of bus company; the Reverend Martin Luther King, Jr., emerges as leader.
Feb. 1, 1960	First sit-in demonstration. Black students at North Carolina Agricultural and Technical College sit in at dime-store lunch counter in Greensboro.
May 4, 1961	Freedom rides begin as blacks attempt to ride in white sections of interstate buses. Violence erupts, a bus is burned, U.S. marshals are dispatched to restore order.
Sept. 30, 1962	Violence greets effort of James Meredith, a black, to enroll in University of Mississippi.
Apr. 3, 1963	Demonstrations by blacks begin in Birmingham, Alabama; police retaliate.
June 12, 1963	Medgar Evers, Mississippi state chairman of NAACP, murdered in Jackson.
Aug. 28, 1963	March on Washington by 250,000 whites and blacks.
Fall 1963	Blacks boycott schools in several northern cities to protest *de facto* segregation.
June 1964	Three civil-rights workers killed in Neshoba County, Mississippi.
Summer 1964	First ghetto riots by blacks in northern cities, beginning in Harlem on July 18.
Jan. 2, 1965	King begins protest marches in Selma, Alabama; police attack marchers in February and March.
Aug. 11, 1965	Black riots in Watts section of Los Angeles and on West Side of Chicago.
June 6, 1966	James Meredith shot (but not killed) while on protest march in Mississippi.
Summer 1966	Black ghetto riots in Chicago, Cleveland, New York, and other cities; King leads protest marches in Chicago.
Summer 1967	Riots or violent demonstrations in 67 cities.
Apr. 4, 1968	Martin Luther King, Jr., murdered in Memphis, Tennessee.

FIGURE 19.1 Changing White Attitudes toward School
Integration

*Percentage of whites saying that they did not object to their children's
attending a school with a half-black, half-white enrollment.*

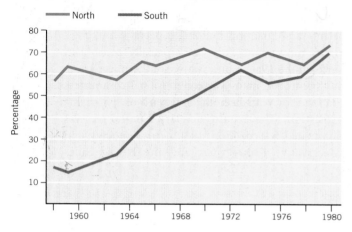

SOURCE: Howard Schuman, Charlotte Steeh, and Lawrence Bobo, *Racial Attitudes
in America* (Cambridge, Mass.: Harvard University Press, 1985), 69.

**This picture of a police dog lunging at a black during a
racial demonstration in Birmingham, Alabama, in May
1963 was one of the most influential news photographs
ever published. It was widely reprinted throughout the
world and frequently referred to in congressional
debates on the civil-rights bill of 1964.**

Committee was under the control of a chairman hostile to civil-rights bills, Howard Smith of Virginia. Any bill that passed the House faced an almost certain filibuster in the Senate. Finally, President John F. Kennedy was reluctant to submit strong civil-rights bills to Congress.

Four developments made it possible to break the deadlock. First, public opinion was changing. As Figure 19.1 shows, between 1959 and 1965 the proportion of southern whites who said that they were willing to have their children attend a school that was half black more than doubled (though it was still less than a majority), while the proportion of northern whites giving the same answer was high (over 60 percent) throughout that period. About the same change could be found in attitudes toward allowing blacks equal access to hotels and buses.[25] Of course support in principle for these civil-rights measures was not necessarily the same as support in practice; nonetheless there clearly was occurring a major shift in popular approval of at least the principles of civil rights. At the leading edge of this change were young, college-educated people.[26]

Second, certain violent reactions by white segregationists to black demonstrators were vividly portrayed by the media, especially television, in ways that gave to the civil-rights cause a powerful moral force. In May 1963 the head of the Birmingham police, Eugene "Bull" Connor, ordered his men to use attack dogs and high-pressure fire hoses to repulse a peaceful march by blacks demanding desegregated public facilities and increased job opportunities. The pictures of that confrontation (such as the one shown above) created a national sensation and contributed greatly to the massive participation, by whites and blacks alike, in the "March on Washington" that summer. About a quarter of a million people gathered in front of the Lincoln Memorial to hear the Reverend King deliver a stirring and widely hailed address, often called the "I Have a Dream" speech. The following summer in Neshoba County, Mississippi, three young civil-rights workers (two white and one black) were brutally murdered by Klansmen aided by the local sheriff. When the FBI identified the

In 1971 Jesse Jackson was arrested at a sit-in held to demand that a grocery chain hire more blacks. In 1984 he was a candidate for the Democratic nomination for president and addressed the Democratic National Convention in San Francisco.

murderers, the effect on national opinion was galvanic: no white southern leader could any longer offer persuasive opposition to federal laws protecting voting rights when white law-enforcement officers had killed students working to protect those rights. And the next year a white woman, Viola Liuzzo, was shot and killed while driving a car used to transport civil-rights workers. Her death was the subject of a presidential address.

Third, President John F. Kennedy was assassinated in Dallas, Texas, in November 1963. Many people originally (and wrongly) thought that he had been killed by a right-wing conspiracy; even after the assassin was caught and revealed to have left-wing associations, the shock of a president's murder in a southern city helped build support for the efforts by the new president, Lyndon B. Johnson (himself a Texan), to obtain passage of a strong civil-rights bill as a memorial to the slain president.

Fourth, the 1964 elections not only returned Johnson to office with a landslide victory, but also sent a huge Democratic majority to the House and retained the large Democratic margin in the Senate.

This made it possible for northern Democrats to outvote or outmaneuver southerners in the House.

The cumulative effect of these forces led to the enactment of five civil-rights laws between 1957 and 1968. Three (1957, 1960, and 1965) were chiefly directed at protecting the right to vote; one (1968) was aimed at preventing discrimination in housing; and one (1964), the most far-reaching of all, dealt with voting, employment, schooling, and public accommodations.

The passage of the 1964 act was the high point of the legislative struggle. Liberals in the House had drafted a bipartisan bill, but it was now in the House Rules Committee, where such matters had often disappeared without a trace. In the shock of Kennedy's murder a discharge petition was filed, with President Johnson's support, to take the bill out of committee and bring it to the floor of the House. But the Rules Committee, without waiting for a vote on the petition (which it probably realized that it would lose), sent the bill to the floor, where it passed overwhelmingly. In the Senate an agreement between Republican Minority Leader Everett Dirksen and

Key Provisions of Major Civil Rights Laws

1957   **Voting**   Made it a federal crime to try to prevent a person from voting in a federal election. Created the Civil Rights Commission.

1960   **Voting**   Authorized the attorney general to appoint federal referees to gather evidence and make findings about allegations that blacks were being deprived of their right to vote. Made it a federal crime to use interstate commerce to threaten or carry out a bombing.

1964   **Voting**   Made it more difficult to use devices such as literacy tests to bar blacks from voting.
Public accommodations   Barred discrimination on grounds of race, color, religion, or national origin in restaurants, hotels, lunch counters, gasoline stations, movie theaters, stadiums, arenas, and lodging houses with more than five rooms.
Schools   Authorized the attorney general to bring suit to force the desegregation of public schools on behalf of citizens.
Employment   Outlawed discrimination in hiring, firing, or paying employees on grounds of race, color, religion, national origin, or sex.
Federal funds   Barred discrimination in any activity receiving federal assistance.

1965   **Voter registration**   Authorized appointment by the Civil Service Commission of voting examiners who would require registration of all eligible voters in federal, state, and local elections, general or primary, in areas where discrimination was found to be practiced or where less than 50 percent of voting-age residents were registered to vote in 1964 election. The law was to have expired in 1970, but Congress has since extended it; it will expire in 2007.
Literacy tests   Suspended use of literacy tests or other devices to prevent blacks from voting.

1968   **Housing**   Banned, by stages, discrimination in sale or rental of most housing (excluding private owners who sell or rent their homes without the services of a real-estate broker).
Riots   Made it a federal crime to use interstate commerce to organize or incite a riot.

1972   **Education**   Prohibited sex discrimination in education programs receiving federal aid.

1988   **Discrimination**   If any part of an organization receives federal aid, no part of that organization may discriminate on the basis of race, sex, age, or physical handicap.

1991   **Discrimination**   Made it easier to sue over job discrimination and collect damages; overturned certain Supreme Court decisions.

President Johnson smoothed the way for passage in several important respects. The House bill was sent directly to the Senate floor, thereby bypassing the southern-dominated Judiciary Committee. Nineteen southern senators began an eight-week filibuster against the bill. On June 10, 1964, by a vote of seventy-one to twenty-nine, cloture was invoked and the filibuster ended—the first time in history that a filibuster aimed at blocking civil-rights legislation had been broken.

Since the 1960s congressional support for civil-rights legislation has grown—so much so, indeed,

Nearly six million blacks are registered to vote in the eleven southern states.

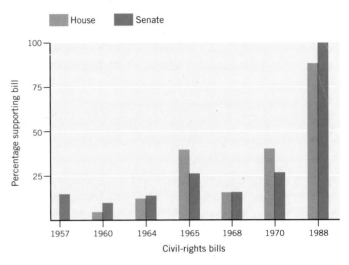

FIGURE 19.2. Growing Support among Southern Democrats in Congress for Civil-Rights Bills

SOURCES: Congressional Quarterly, *Congress and the Nation*, vols. I, II, III, VII.

that labeling a bill a civil-rights measure, once the kiss of death, now almost guarantees its passage. For example, in 1984 the Supreme Court decided that the federal ban on discrimination in education applied only to the "program or activity" receiving federal aid and not to the entire school or university.[27] In 1988 Congress passed a bill to overturn this decision by making it clear that antidiscrimination rules applied to the entire educational institution and not just to that part (say, the physics lab) receiving federal money. When President Reagan vetoed the bill (because, in his view, it would diminish the freedom of church-related schools), Congress overrode the veto. In the override vote *every* southern Democrat in the Senate and almost 90 percent of those in the House voted for the bill. This was a dramatic change from 1964, when over 80 percent of the southern Democrats in Congress voted against the Civil Rights Act (see Figure 19.2).

This change partly reflected the growing political strength of southern blacks. In 1960 less than one-third of voting-age blacks in the South were registered to vote; by 1971 more than half were, and by 1984 two-thirds were. In 1991 over seven thousand blacks held elective office in the South (see Table 19.1). But this was only half of the story. Attitudes among white political elites and members of Congress had also changed. This was evident as early as 1968, when Congress passed a law barring discrimination in housing even though polls showed that only 35 percent of the public supported the measure.

TABLE 19.1   Increase in Number of Black Elected Officials

Office	1970	1991
Congress and state legislatures	182	476
City and county offices	715	4,493
Judges and sheriffs	213	847
Boards of education	362	1,629
Total	1,472	7,445

SOURCES: *Statistical Abstract of the United States, 1990,* 260; *Statistical Abstract of the United States, 1992,* 267.

Women and Equal Rights

The political and legal efforts to extend the rights guaranteed to blacks were accompanied by efforts to expand the rights of women, but with an important difference: whereas blacks were arguing against a legal tradition intended explicitly to keep them in a subservient status, women had to argue against a tradition that claimed to be protecting them. For example, in 1908, the Supreme Court upheld an Oregon law that limited female laundry workers to a ten-hour workday against the claim that it violated the

Fourteenth Amendment. The Court justified its decision in this language:

> *The two sexes differ in structure of body, in the functions to be performed by each, in the amount of physical strength, in the capacity for long-continued labor, particularly when done standing, ... the self-reliance which enables one to assert full rights, and in the capacity to maintain the struggle for subsistence. This difference justifies a difference in legislation and upholds that which is designed to compensate for some of the burdens which rest upon her.*[28]

The feminist movement that resurfaced not long after the civil-rights movement questioned the claim that women differed from men in ways that justified differences in legal status. Congress responded by passing laws that required equal pay for work, prohibited discrimination on the basis of sex in employment and among students in any school or university receiving federal funds, and banned discrimination against pregnant women on the job.[29]

At the same time the Supreme Court was altering the standards that it applied to laws and practices that treated men and women differently. The traditional standard, as we saw in the 1908 case, reflected a kind of protective paternalism; under it no state law was ever held unconstitutional because of sex discrimination. In 1971, however, the Court overturned an Idaho statute that gave men preference over women in the appointment of administrators of the estates of deceased children. A unanimous Court set down a new test, the reasonableness standard: to be constitutionally permissible, any law that classifies people on the basis of sex "must be reasonable, not arbitrary, and must rest on some ground of difference having a fair and substantial relation to the object of the legislation so that all persons similarly circumstanced shall be treated alike."[30]

This was a milder test than the one that the Court had developed to judge racial classifications. The latter were always "suspect" and thus had to survive the **strict scrutiny** of the Court. In a later decision some justices wanted to abandon the standard of "reasonableness" applied to sex and replace it with the same standard governing laws involving race—that they are "inherently suspect." But there was no majority for this view.[31]

Under the "reasonableness" standard the courts have permitted some distinctions based on sex and have overturned others. Here are some examples.

Decisions barring differences based on sex

- A state cannot set different ages at which men and women legally become adults.[32]

- A state cannot set different ages at which men and women are allowed to buy beer.[33]

- Women cannot be barred from jobs by arbitrary height and weight requirements.[34]

- Employers cannot require women to take mandatory pregnancy leaves.[35]

Though many women have enlisted in the armed forces, the Supreme Court in 1981 held that Congress could exclude women from the draft.

- Girls cannot be barred from Little League baseball teams.[36]

- Business and service clubs, such as the Junior Chamber of Commerce and Rotary Club, cannot exclude women from membership.[37]

- Though women as a group live longer than men, an employer must pay them monthly retirement benefits equal to those received by men.[38]

- High schools must pay the coaches of girls' sports the same as they pay coaches of boys' sports.[39]

Decisions allowing differences based on sex

- A law that punishes males but not females for statutory rape is permissible; men and women are not "similarly situated" with respect to sexual relations.[40]

- All-boy and all-girl public schools are permitted if enrollment is voluntary and quality is equal.[41]

- States can give widows a property-tax exemption not given to widowers.[42]

- The navy may allow women to remain officers longer than men without being promoted.[43]

The lower federal courts have been especially busy in this area. They have said that public taverns may not cater to men only and that girls may not be prevented from competing against boys in noncontact high school sports; on the other hand hospitals may bar fathers from the delivery room. Women may continue to use their maiden names after marriage.[44]

Perhaps the most far-reaching cases defining the rights of women have involved the draft and abortion. In 1981 the Court held in *Rostker* v. *Goldberg* that Congress may require men but not women to register for the draft without violating the due-process clause of the Fifth Amendment.[45] In the area of national defense the Court will give great deference to congressional policy (Congress had already decided to bar women from combat roles). For many years women could be pilots and sailors but not on combat aircraft or combat ships. In 1993, the secretary of defense opened air and sea combat positions to all persons regardless of gender; only ground-troop combat positions are still reserved for men. The issue, as we shall see, played a role in preventing the ratification of the Equal Rights Amendment to the Constitution because of fears that it would reverse *Rostker* v. *Goldberg* and remains controversial.

Susan B. Anthony (standing) and Elizabeth Cady Stanton were early leaders of the women's rights movement. The long campaign to win for women the right to vote came to a victorious end in 1920 when the Nineteenth Amendment was ratified.

Opponents in the fight over the Equal Rights Amendment:
Phyllis Schlafly (left) opposed the ERA, and Eleanor Smeal
(right), then head of the National Organization for Women,
defended it.

The ERA

The extension to women, by law and court order, of a
wide range of rights was sufficiently steady to make it
seem for a while that the passage of an Equal Rights
Amendment (ERA) to the Constitution was a fore-
gone conclusion. That amendment, which had been
before Congress since 1923, read in its operative
clause as follows: "Equality of rights under the law
shall not be denied or abridged by the United States
or any State on account of sex."

When Congress in 1972 passed this amendment
and sent it to the states for consideration, the
prospects for its prompt ratification seemed excellent. It had sailed through Congress by votes of 84–8
in the Senate and 354–24 in the House; it had been
endorsed by every president from Harry Truman to
Jimmy Carter and by both political parties; opinion
polls showed the public to be in favor of it; and
women—the group to be benefited—accounted for
half the voting population.

The optimism of its backers appeared for the moment to be justified. Within the first year the legislatures of twenty-two states ratified the ERA, most by
overwhelming votes. By 1974–1975, however, it was
clearly in trouble: it barely squeaked through the
Montana senate and the North Dakota house, and
two states (Nebraska and Tennessee) voted to rescind
their earlier ratifications. By 1978 the ratification effort was stalled. Thirty-five states had ratified, three
short of the necessary three-fourths; three states had
rescinded their earlier ratifications; and repeated efforts to get the ERA ratified in such key states as Illinois and Florida had come to naught. Moreover the
time originally allowed for the ratification process—
until March 22, 1979—was about to expire.

Congress was persuaded to extend the period allowed for ratification to June 30, 1982, but to little
avail—none of the fifteen states refusing to ratify
changed its position. Thus the ERA is no longer before the states. How can this dramatic reversal in the
fortunes of this measure be explained?

What began as an apparently noncontroversial matter ended by being deeply controversial. That fact alone worked against it: since three-fourths of the states must ratify, the opponents need get only thirteen of the ninety-nine* state legislative houses to vote no. And legislators do not like to take positions on controversial matters, especially after it becomes evident that many of the supposed beneficiaries—in this case women—were themselves opposed. One issue that was particularly important was the draft: many legislators and voters otherwise favoring the ERA worried that its passage would require that women be drafted for combat duty. Proponents of the ERA, such as the National Organization for Women (NOW), had difficulty countering that argument. Another issue that was highly controversial was whether the ERA would eliminate laws that protected women in the workplace (such as maximum-hour or minimum-wage laws). This was a concern of the Mormon Church, and it was also a concern of the National Council of Catholic Women.

In the end the ERA became an issue that symbolized the conflict over a broad range of cultural values in the United States. Then a series of political events sealed the fate of the bill. In 1980 the Republican party withdrew its endorsement of the ERA, and the people elected as president a man known to oppose it. In 1982 a federal judge in Idaho held that Congress had acted unconstitutionally when it extended the deadline for ratification and refused to allow states to rescind their earlier ratifications. As of 1994, Congress had not produced the two-thirds majority necessary to resubmit the ERA to the states.

Abortion

As the struggle over the ERA faded, that over abortion intensified. Until 1973 it was up to the states to decide whether and under what circumstances women could obtain an abortion. For example, New York allowed abortion on demand during the first twenty-four weeks of pregnancy, but Texas banned abortion except in cases when the mother's life was threatened.

---

*Forty-nine states have two house (bicameral) legislatures; one state, Nebraska, has a one-house (unicameral) legislature.

By a seven-to-two vote, the Supreme Court, in the 1973 case of *Roe* v. *Wade,* struck down the Texas law (and all similar state laws).[46] The majority argued that the due-process clause of the Fourteenth Amendment implies a "right to privacy" that protects a woman's freedom to choose, during the first three months of pregnancy, whether to have an abortion. (During the second three months, or trimester, the states were allowed to regulate abortion procedures to protect the mother's health; during the final trimester, states might ban abortions.)

In reaching this decision, the Court denied that it was trying to decide when human life began—at the moment of conception, at the moment of birth, or somewhere in between. But that is not how critics of the decision saw things. To them, life began at conception, and so the human fetus was a "person" entitled to the equal protection of the laws guaranteed by the Fourteenth Amendment. People feeling this way began to use the slogans "right to life" and "pro-life." Supporters of the Court's action saw matters differently. In their view, no one could say for certain when human life began; what one could say, however, was that a woman was entitled to choose whether or not to have a baby. These people took the slogans "right to choose" and "pro-choice."

Almost immediately the congressional allies of pro-life groups introduced constitutional amendments to overturn *Roe* v. *Wade,* but none passed Congress. Nevertheless abortion foes did persuade Congress, beginning in 1976, to bar the use of federal funds to pay for abortions except where the life of the mother was at stake. This provision was known as the Hyde Amendment, after its sponsor, Representative Henry Hyde. The chief effect of the amendment was to deny the use of Medicaid funds to pay for abortions for low-income women. (In 1980 the Supreme Court upheld the constitutionality of the Hyde amendment.)[47] In the Bush administration, the government carried the spirit of this amendment one step further by barring the use of federal funds for family-planning clinics that provided abortion counseling. Called a "gag rule" by some, this policy was repealed by the Clinton administration.

Despite pro-life opposition, the Supreme Court for sixteen years steadfastly reaffirmed and even broadened its decision in *Roe* v. *Wade*. It struck down laws requiring, before an abortion could be per-

✪ The Constitutional Position of Abortion Laws as of 1994

*T*his is what the majority of the Court held in the 1992 *Casey* decision:

1. "It is a constitutional liberty of the woman to have some freedom to terminate her pregnancy. . . . No state may prohibit a woman from terminating her pregnancy" before the fetus becomes "viable."

2. After the fetus has become viable, a state may "regulate, and even proscribe, abortion except where it is necessary . . . for the preservation of the life and the health of the mother."

3. States may put restrictions on the right to an abortion, but these restrictions must not place an "undue burden" on the exercise of a woman's rights.

Planned Parenthood v. *Casey,* 112 S.Ct. 291 (1992).

---

formed, a woman to have the consent of her husband, an "emancipated" but underage girl to have the consent of her parents, or a woman to be advised by her doctor as to the facts about abortion.[48]

But in 1989, under the influence of justices appointed by President Reagan, it began in the *Webster* case to uphold some state restrictions on abortions. When that happened, many people predicted that in time *Roe* v. *Wade* would be overturned, especially if President Bush was able to appoint more justices. He appointed two (Souter and Thomas), but *Roe* survived. The key votes were cast by Justices O'Connor, Souter, and Kennedy. In 1992, in its *Casey* decision, the Court by a vote of 5–4 explicitly refused to overturn *Roe*, declaring that there was a right to an abortion. At the same time it upheld a variety of restrictions imposed by the state of Pennsylvania on women seeking abortion. These included a mandatory twenty-four-hour waiting period between the request for and the performance of an abortion, the obligation of teenagers to obtain the consent of one parent (or, in special circumstances, of a judge), and a state requirement that women contemplating an abortion be given pamphlets about alternatives to it. Similar restrictions had been enacted in many other

states, all of which looked to the Pennsylvania case for guidance as to whether they could be enforced. On the other hand, it struck down a state law that would have required a married woman to obtain the consent of her husband. In allowing these restrictions, the Court overruled some of its own earlier decisions.[49] The key provisions of the *Casey* decision are summarized in the box.

Women and the Economy

With the defeat of the ERA, women's organizations increasingly turned their attention to economic issues. Some women had begun to think of these matters as more important than the ERA because economic issues addressed the actual benefits that women might obtain from society rather than simply the legal claims that they could make on it.

A split had long existed among feminists on this score. One group, traditional liberals, wanted to press for equal rights; for them the ERA was the ultimate goal. If all legal barriers to female participation were struck down, then women would take advantage of their opportunities and advance themselves as far as their interests led them, they argued. But another group saw the economic status of women as perhaps more important than their legal one.

It has been illegal since 1964 to discriminate on the basis of sex in employment. Despite this the earnings of women are lower than those of men. Moreover one group of women—those with children sired by men who had deserted or divorced them—are especially vulnerable to economic hardship. Female-headed households are much more likely to be living in poverty than households headed by an intact couple. Finally, pregnant women have often found it necessary to give up their jobs if there is no provision for pregnancy leave.

These concerns reflect changes not only in political beliefs but in economic circumstances as well. In 1960 only about one-sixth of all married women with children under the age of six were in the labor force. By 1980 that proportion had risen to nearly half, and by 1991 it was nearly 60 percent. (Being "in the labor force" means that a person is either working at a job or looking for one.) In 1988 more than 60 percent of

A law passed in 1993 guarantees that employees of large firms can take unpaid pregnancy and child-care leave.

all working mothers made use of some form of day care for their children, either in the home of another person or in a group day-care center.[50] Mothers who had been deserted by or divorced from the fathers of their children were, in a significant fraction of cases, not receiving the child-support payments due them.

Women's organizations began pressing in the Congress and the courts for laws and rulings that would address these new interests, often referred to as women's-economic-equity issues. These took the form of demands for:

- **Government-funded day care.** In general liberals have favored generous programs of this sort (in order to help working mothers) while many conservatives have opposed them (in order to keep responsibility for raising children fixed on the family). In 1984 Congress passed and the president signed a compromise plan that authorized several million dollars in federal aid to states to support or provide information about local day-care services.

- **Child-support enforcement.** In 1984 Congress passed and the president signed a bill that requires the states to set up procedures for withholding from the paychecks of men and women (in those few cases where it is applicable to women) overdue court-ordered child-support payments to the spouses who have custody of their children. In 1988 this provision became part of the much larger welfare-reform plan discussed in Chapter 17.

- **Pregnancy leave.** In 1978 Congress passed a law amending the 1964 Civil Rights Act to prohibit employers from discriminating on the basis of pregnancy in the hiring, firing, or promoting of workers. It also required health and disability plans to cover pregnant workers. In 1987 the Supreme Court upheld state laws that required employers to provide parental leave to women and to guarantee that they could resume their jobs when their leave ended.[51] For several years efforts to enact a federal parental-leave law either failed in Congress or were blocked by presidential vetoes. In 1993, however, a law providing up to twelve weeks of unpaid leave to workers to deal with births, adoptions, or serious illnesses within their families was passed and signed by President Clinton.

A Nation of Immigrants

*A*s we approach the twenty-first century, immigration is bound to alter the American political, cultural, and legal landscapes in ways that can be only dimly perceived at present (see Chapters 4, 5, 6, 15, and 18). In the first decade of the twentieth century, immigration was virtually unrestricted and nearly 8.8 million persons, most of them from Europe, came to the United States. In the 1980s some 5.8 million people were admitted to the United States, and about 2.7 million who had resided here illegally were legalized under new federal immigration laws.

From 1911 to 1920, the average annual rate of immigration was 5.7 per 1,000 U.S. residential population. Between 1921 and 1930, the immigration rate dipped to 3.5. The adoption of restrictive immigration laws and uncompromising enforcement procedures kept the rate below 1.0 from 1931 to 1950. Despite a sharp increase in the number of people all around the world seeking to come to America because of famine, political persecution, civil war, and other reasons, the rate remained between 1.0 and 2.1 during the period 1951 to 1980. In the 1980s, however, changes both in immigration laws and in the enforcement of existing laws con-

tributed to a steady increase in the immigration rate. As the table below shows, the immigration rate climbed between 1984 and 1990, catapulting from 2.6 in 1988 to 6.1 in 1990. Most of today's immigrants come from Asia, Mexico, Central America, and Africa, not Europe, as we saw in Chapter 18.

These immigration trends presage a historic demographic shift and pose profound legal questions related to civil-rights laws and the meaning of citizenship. In the early 1990s, the many aspects of immigration law, policy, and practice remained largely unsettled. For example, state and federal courts were still undecided on the question of what obligations employers have in hiring aliens, legal and illegal. Even so, some things about the civil rights of aliens and the concomitant responsibilities of naturalized citizens were largely settled (see box on page 570).

Immigrants do not take only entry-level jobs; many bring important skills, such as these Vietnamese working in a dentist's office.

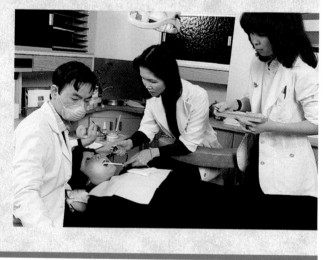

Year	Number	Rate[a]
1984	544,000	2.3
1985	570,000	2.4
1986	602,000	2.5
1987	602,000	2.5
1988	643,000	2.6
1989	1,091,000	4.4
1990	1,536,000	6.1

[a] Number of immigrants per 1,000 U.S. residential population.
SOURCE: Adapted from *Statistical Abstract of the United States, 1992*, 10.

• **Comparable worth.** The most controversial of the "economic-equity" proposals has involved the doctrine of "comparable worth." Since 1963 federal law has required that people receive "equal pay for substantially equal work." But this has left many women's groups dissatisfied on the grounds that women are concentrated in certain kinds of jobs that traditionally pay lower wages than the jobs men usually hold. For example, women tend to be nurses, secretaries, and sales clerks, whereas men tend to be plumbers, truck drivers, and bricklayers. Even if all nurses are paid equally and all plumbers are paid equally, plumbers may wind up earning more than nurses.

The doctrine of **comparable worth** would require salaries to be determined by the "worth" of the job, not by what it commands in the market. To measure "worth," each job must be ranked by an expert in terms of its intrinsic difficulty. Points are assigned based on the skill, training, and responsibility inherent in each job. For example, in San Jose, California, where the city government adopted a comparable-worth plan, it decided that painters (most of whom are men) are worth 173 points and secretaries (most of whom are women) are worth 177 points. Since secretaries on the average were earning much less than painters, the city agreed to raise the pay of the secretaries.[52]

Several other governments (including those of the states of Minnesota and Washington) have adopted comparable-worth plans for government employees, and many other states are studying the idea. The 1984 Democratic presidential platform endorsed comparable worth. But many critics argue that there is no objective way of comparing the worth of different jobs other than seeing what wages they can command in a free market. Moreover wage differences may have nothing to do with the sex or race of the job holder. For example, professors of law, medicine, and computer sciences earn more at most universities than do professors of history, Spanish, or fine arts. This would probably be true no matter what the race or sex of those holding these professorships, because lawyers, doctors, and computer scientists have job opportunities open to them outside the university that historians and Spanish instructors do not. Neither the Supreme Court nor Congress has yet spoken definitively on this question.

Affirmative Action

A common thread running through the politics of civil rights is the argument between equality of results and equality of opportunity.

Equality of Results   One view, expressed by most civil-rights and feminist organizations, is that the burdens of racism and sexism can be overcome only by taking race or sex into account in designing remedies. It is not enough to give rights to people; they must be given benefits. If life is a race, everybody

The Rights of the Disabled

*I*n 1990 the federal government passed the Americans with Disabilities Act (ADA), a sweeping law that extended many of the protections enjoyed by women and racial minorities to disabled persons.

WHO IS A DISABLED PERSON?

Anyone who *has* a physical or mental impairment that substantially limits one or more major life activities (for example, holding a job), anyone who has a *record* of such impairment, or anyone who is *regarded* as having such an impairment.

WHAT RIGHTS DO THE DISABLED HAVE?

Employment   May not be denied employment or promotion if, with "reasonable accommodation," they can perform the duties of that job. (Excluded from this protection are people who currently use illegal drugs, gamble compulsively, or are homosexual or bisexual.) Reasonable accommodation need not be made if this would cause "undue hardship" on the employer.

Government Programs   May not be denied access to government programs or benefits. In particular, new buses, taxis, and trains must be accessible to disabled persons, including those in wheelchairs.

Public Accommodations   The disabled must enjoy "full and equal" access to hotels, restaurants, stores, schools, parks, museums, auditoriums, and the like. To achieve equal access, owners of existing facilities must alter them "to the maximum extent feasible"; builders of new facilities must ensure that they are readily accessible to disabled persons unless this is structurally impossible.

Telephones   Directs the Federal Communications Commission to issue regulations to ensure that telecommunications devices for hearing- and speech-impaired people are available "to the extent possible and in the most efficient manner."

Congress   The rights under this law (unlike those under many other laws) apply to employees of Congress.

Rights Compared   The ADA does not enforce the rights of the disabled in the same way as the Civil Rights Act enforces the rights of blacks and women. Racial or gender discrimination must end *regardless of cost;* denial of access to the disabled must end unless "undue hardship" or excessive costs would result.

must be brought up to the same starting line (or possibly even to the same finish line). This means that the Constitution is not and should not be color-blind or sex-blind. In education this implies that the races must actually be mixed in the schools, by busing if necessary. In hiring it means that **affirmative action**—preferential hiring practices—must be used to find and hire women, blacks, and other minorities. Women should not simply be free to enter the labor force; they should be given the material necessities (for example, free day care) that will help them enter it. On payday workers' checks should reflect not just the results of people's competing in the marketplace but the results of plans designed to ensure that people earn comparable amounts for comparable jobs. Of late, affirmative action has been defended in the name of diversity or multiculturalism—the view that every institution (firm, school, or agency) and every

The Rights of Aliens

*A*merica is a nation of immigrants. Some have arrived legally, others illegally. An illegal, or undocumented, alien is subject to being deported. With the passage in 1986 of the Immigration Reform and Control Act, illegal aliens who have resided in this country continuously since before January 1, 1982, are entitled to amnesty—that is, they can become legal residents. However, the same legislation stipulated that employers (who once could hire undocumented aliens without fear of penalty) must now verify the legal status of all newly hired employees; if they knowingly hire an illegal alien, they face civil and criminal penalties.

Aliens—people residing in this country who are not citizens—cannot vote or run for office. Nevertheless, they must pay taxes just as if they were citizens. And they are entitled to many constitutional rights, even if they are in this country illegally. This is because most of the rights mentioned in the Constitution refer to "people" or "persons," not to "citizens." For example, the Fourteenth Amendment bars a state from depriving "*any person* of life, liberty, or property, without due process of law" or from denying "to *any person* within its jurisdiction the equal protection of the laws" [italics added]. As a result, the courts have held that:

- The children of illegal aliens cannot be excluded from the public school system.[1]
- Legally admitted aliens are entitled to welfare benefits.[2]
- Illegal aliens cannot be the object of reprisals if they attempt to form a labor union where they work.[3]

- The First Amendment rights of free speech, religion, press, and assembly and the Fourth Amendment protections against arbitrary arrest and prosecution extend to aliens as well as to citizens.[4]
- Aliens are entitled to own property.

The government can make rules that apply to aliens only, but they must justify the reasonableness of the rules. For example:

- The Immigration and Naturalization Service has broader powers to arrest and search illegal aliens than police departments have to arrest and search citizens.[5]
- States can limit certain jobs, such as police officer and school teacher, to citizens.[6]
- The president or Congress can bar the employment of aliens by the federal government.[7]
- States can bar aliens from serving on a jury.[8]
- Illegal aliens are not entitled to obtain a Social Security card.

[1] Plyler v. Doe, 457 U.S. 202 (1982).

[2] Graham v. Richardson, 403 U.S. 365 (1971).

[3] Sure-Tan v. National Labor Relations Board, 467 U.S. 883 (1984).

[4] Chew v. Colding, 344 U.S. 590 (1953).

[5] U.S. v. Brignoni-Ponce, 422 U.S. 873 (1975); INS v. Delgado, 466 U.S. 210 (1984); INS v. Lopez-Mendoza, 486 U.S. 1032 (1984).

[6] Cabell v. Chavez-Salido, 454 U.S. 432 (1982); Foley v. Connelie, 435 U.S. 291 (1978); Amblach v. Norwick, 441 U.S. 68 (1979).

[7] Hampton v. Mow Sun Wong, 436 U.S. 67 (1976).

[8] Schneider v. New Jersey, 308 U.S. 147 (1939).

college curriculum should reflect the cultural (that is, ethnic) diversity of the nation.

Equality of opportunities: The second view holds that if it was once wrong to use race or sex to discriminate against blacks and women, it is now wrong to use those labels to give preferential treatment to them. Doing the latter is **reverse discrimination.** The Constitution and laws should be color-blind and sex-neutral. In this view allowing children to attend the school of their choice is sufficient; busing them to attain a certain racial mixture is wrong. Eliminating barriers to job opportunities is right; using numerical "targets" and "goals" to place minorities and women in specific jobs is wrong. If people wish to compete in the market, they should be satisfied with the market verdict as to their worth.

These two views are intertwined with other deep philosophical differences. Supporters of equality of opportunity tend to have orthodox beliefs; they favor letting private groups behave the way that they want (and so may defend the right of a men's club to exclude women). Supporters of the opposite view are likely to be progressive in their beliefs and insist that private clubs meet the same standards as schools or business firms. Orthodox adherents of the opportunity view often attach great importance to the traditional role of the husband-wife family and so are skeptical of day care and federally funded abortions. Progressive adherents of the results view prefer greater freedom of individual choice in life-style questions and so take the opposite position on day care and abortions.

Of course the debate is more complex than this simple contrast suggests. Take, for example, the question of affirmative action. The advocates of both equality of opportunity and equality of results might agree that there is something odd about a factory or university that hires no blacks or women, and might press it to prove that its hiring policy is fair. Affirmative action in this case can mean *either* looking hard for qualified women and minorities and giving them a fair shot at the jobs *or* setting a numerical goal for the number of women and minorities that should be hired and insisting that they be hired. Persons who defend the second course of action call these goals "targets"; persons who criticize that course call them "quotas."

Government-subsidized job training programs are examples of compensatory action.

The issue has largely been fought out in the courts. Between 1978 and 1990 about a dozen major cases involving affirmative action were decided by the Supreme Court; in about half it was upheld, and in the other it was overturned. The different outcomes reflect two things—the differences in the facts of each case and the arrival onto the Court of three justices (Kennedy, O'Connor, and Scalia) appointed by a president, Ronald Reagan, who was opposed to at least the broader interpretation of affirmative action. As a result of these decisions, the law governing affirmative action is now complex and confusing.

Consider one issue: should the government be allowed to use a quota system to select workers, enroll students, award contracts, or grant licenses? In the *Bakke* decision in 1978, the Court said that the medical school of the University of California at Davis could not use an explicit numerical quota in admitting minority students but could "take race into account."[53] So no numerical quotas, right? Wrong. Two years later the Court upheld a federal rule that set aside 10 percent of all federal construction contracts for minority-owned firms.[54] All right, maybe quotas can't be used in medical schools, but they can be used in the construction industry. Not exactly. In 1989 the Court overturned a Richmond, Virginia, law that set aside 30 percent of its construction contracts for

For persons born in the United States, the rights of U.S. citizenship have been assured, in constitutional theory if not in everyday practice, since the passage of the Fourteenth Amendment in 1868 and the civil rights laws of the 1960s. The Fourteenth Amendment conferred citizenship upon "all persons born in the United States . . . and subject to the jurisdiction thereof." Subsequent laws also give citizenship to children born outside the United States to parents who are American citizens.

But immigrants, by definition, are not born with the rights of U.S. citizenship. Instead, those seeking to become U.S. citizens must, in effect, assume certain responsibilities in order to become citizens. The statutory requirements for naturalization, as they have been broadly construed by the courts, are as follows:

- Five years' residency, or three years if married to a citizen

- Continuous residency since filing of the naturalization petition.

- Good moral character, which is loosely interpreted to mean no evidence of criminal activity.

- Attachment to constitutional principles. This used to be interpreted to mean the ability to answer basic factual questions about American government (e.g., Who was the first president of the United States?), or a willingness to denounce any and all allegiances to the country of one's birth and its leaders (e.g., Italy and the King of Italy); it is now interpreted to be implicit in the act of applying for naturalization itself.

- Being favorably disposed to "the good order and happiness of the United States."[*]

Today about 97 percent of aliens who seek citizenship are successful in meeting these requirements and becoming naturalized citizens of the United States.

The Route to Citizenship

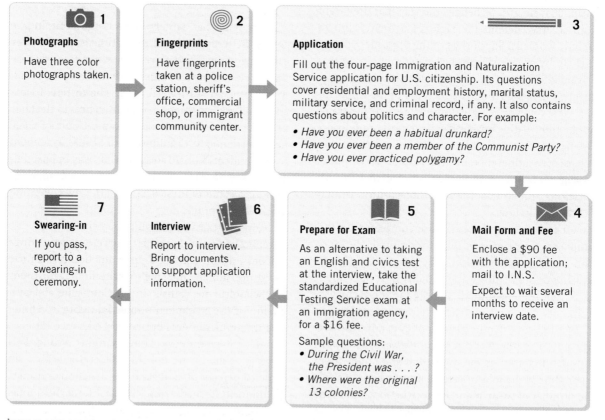

1 Photographs

Have three color photographs taken.

2 Fingerprints

Have fingerprints taken at a police station, sheriff's office, commercial shop, or immigrant community center.

3 Application

Fill out the four-page Immigration and Naturalization Service application for U.S. citizenship. Its questions cover residential and employment history, marital status, military service, and criminal record, if any. It also contains questions about politics and character. For example:

- *Have you ever been a habitual drunkard?*
- *Have you ever been a member of the Communist Party?*
- *Have you ever practiced polygamy?*

4 Mail Form and Fee

Enclose a $90 fee with the application; mail to I.N.S.

Expect to wait several months to receive an interview date.

5 Prepare for Exam

As an alternative to taking an English and civics test at the interview, take the standardized Educational Testing Service exam at an immigration agency, for a $16 fee.

Sample questions:
- *During the Civil War, the President was . . . ?*
- *Where were the original 13 colonies?*

6 Interview

Report to interview. Bring documents to support application information.

7 Swearing-in

If you pass, report to a swearing-in ceremony.

[*] 8 U.S.C. 1423, 1427 (1970); Girouard v. United States, 328 U.S. 61 (1946).

SOURCE: *The New York Times* (July 25, 1993): 33. Copyright © 1993 by The New York Times. Reprinted by permission.

minority-owned firms.[55] Well, maybe the Court just changed its mind between 1980 and 1989. No. One year later it upheld a federal rule that gave preference to minority-owned firms in the awarding of broadcast licenses.[56] Then in 1993 it upheld the right of white contractors to challenge minority set-aside laws in Jacksonville, Florida.[57]

It is too early to try to make sense of these twists and turns, especially since a deeply divided Court is still wrestling with these issues and Congress (as with the Civil Rights Act of 1991) is modifying or superseding some earlier Court decisions. But a few general standards seem to be emerging. In simplified form, they are:

- The courts will subject any quota system created by state or local governments to "strict scrutiny" and will look for a "compelling" justification for it.

- Quotas or preference systems cannot be used by state or local governments without first showing that such rules are needed to correct an actual past or present pattern of discrimination.[58]

- In proving that there has been discrimination, it is not enough to show that blacks (or other minorities) are statistically underrepresented among employees, contractors, or union members; you must identify the actual practices that have had this discriminatory impact.[59]

- Quotas or preference systems that are created by *federal* law will be given greater deference, in part because Section 5 of the Fourteenth Amendment gives to Congress powers not given to the states to correct the effects of racial discrimination.[60]

- It may be easier to justify in court a voluntary preference system (for example, one agreed to in a labor-management contract) than one that is required by law.[61]

- Even when you can justify special preferences in *hiring* workers, the Court is not likely to allow racial preferences to govern who gets *laid off*. A worker laid off to make room for a minority worker loses more than does a worker not hired in preference to a minority applicant.[62]

Complex as they are, these rulings still generate a great deal of passion. Supporters of the decisions barring certain affirmative-action plans hail these decisions as steps back from an emerging pattern of reverse discrimination. In contrast, civil-rights organizations have denounced those decisions that have overturned affirmative-action programs. In 1990 their congressional allies introduced legislation that would reverse several decisions. In particular this legislation would put the burden of proof on the employer, not the employee, to show that the underrepresentation of minorities in the firm's work force was the result of legitimate and necessary business decisions and not the result of discrimination. If the employer could not prove this, the aggrieved employee would be able to collect large damage awards. (In the past, he or she could only collect back pay.) In 1991 the bill was passed after being amended to forestall a veto by President Bush on the grounds that it would lead to quotas.

In thinking about these matters, most Americans distinguish between compensatory action and preferential treatment. They define **compensatory action** as "helping disadvantaged people catch up, usually by giving them extra education, training, or services." A majority of the public supports this. They define preferential treatment as "giving minorities preference in hiring, promotions, college admissions, and contracts." Large majorities oppose this.[63] These views reflect an enduring element in American political culture—a strong commitment to individualism ("nobody should get something without deserving it") coupled with support for help for the disadvantaged ("somebody who is suffering through no fault of his or her own deserves a helping hand").

Where does affirmative action fit into this culture? Polls suggest that if affirmative action is defined as "helping," people will support it, but if it is defined as "using quotas," they will oppose it.[64] The conflict in the courts over affirmative action—and the conflicting rulings the courts have issued—reflect this deeper conflict in American opinion.

SUMMARY

The civil-rights movement in the courts and in Congress profoundly changed the nature of black participation in politics by bringing southern blacks into the political system so that they could become an effective interest group. The decisive move was to enlist northern opinion in this cause, a job made easier by the northern perception that civil rights involved simply an unfair contest between two minorities—southern whites and southern blacks. That perception changed when it became evident that the court rulings and legislative decisions would apply to the North as well as to the South, leading to the emergence of northern opposition to court-ordered busing and affirmative-action programs.

By the time this reaction developed, the legal and political system had been changed sufficiently to make it difficult if not impossible to limit the application of civil-rights laws to the special circumstances of the South or to alter by legislative means the decisions of federal courts. Though the courts can accomplish little when they have no political allies (as revealed by the massive resistance to the early school-desegregation decisions), they can accomplish a great deal, even in the face of adverse public opinion, when they have some organized allies (as revealed by their ability to withstand antibusing moves).

The feminist movement has paralleled in organization and tactics many aspects of the black civil-rights movement, but with important differences. Women sought to repeal or reverse laws and court rulings that in many cases were ostensibly designed to protect rather than subjugate them. The conflict between protection and liberation was sufficiently intense to defeat the effort to ratify the Equal Rights Amendment.

The most divisive civil-rights issues in American politics are abortion and affirmative action. From 1973 to 1989 the Supreme Court seemed committed to giving constitutional protection to all abortions within the first trimester; since 1989 it has approved various state restrictions on the circumstances under which such abortions can be obtained.

There has been a similar shift in the Court's view of affirmative action. Though it will still approve some quota plans, it now insists that they pass strict scrutiny to ensure that they are used only to correct a proven history of discrimination, that they place the burden of proof on the party alleging discrimination, and that they be limited to hirings and not extended to layoffs. Congress has modified some of these rulings with new civil-rights legislation.

KEY TERMS

civil rights   *p. 545*

suspect classifications   *p. 545*

Jim Crow   *p. 550*

separate-but-equal doctrine   *p. 550*

de jure segregation   *p. 553*

de facto segregation   *p. 554*

nonviolent civil disobedience   *p. 556*

strict scrutiny   *p. 562*

comparable worth   *p. 568*

affirmative action   *p. 570*

equality of opportunities   *p. 571*

reverse discrimination   *p. 571*

compensatory action   *p. 573*

SUGGESTED READINGS

Flexner, Eleanor. *Century of Struggle: The Women's Rights Movement in the United States.* Rev. ed. Cambridge, Mass.: Harvard University Press, 1975. A historical account of the feminist movement and its political strategies.

Franklin, John Hope. *From Slavery to Freedom.* 5th ed. New York: Knopf, 1980. A survey of black history in the United States.

Freeman, J. *The Politics of Women's Liberation.* New York: Longmans, 1975. Good analysis of the organizational strategies of feminists.

Kluger, Richard. *Simple Justice.* New York: Random House/Vintage, 1977. Detailed and absorbing account of the school-desegregation issue, from the Fourteenth Amendment to the *Brown* case.

Mansbridge, Jane J. *Why We Lost the ERA.* Chicago: University of Chicago Press, 1986. Explains why the Equal Rights Amendment did not become part of the Constitution.

Orfield, Gary. *Congressional Power: Congress and Social Change.* New York: Harcourt Brace Jovanovich, 1975. Analysis of the legislative politics of the major civil-rights laws.

Pritchett, C. Herman. *Constitutional Civil Liberties.* Englewood Cliffs, N.J.: Prentice-Hall, 1984. Chapters 10 and 12 provide an excellent summary of the constitutional basis of civil rights.

Sindler, Allan P. *Bakke, DeFunis, and Minority Admissions.* New York: Longman, 1978. History and analysis of the landmark Supreme Court case on affirmative action and quotas in college admissions.

Wilhoit, Francis M. *The Politics of Massive Resistance.* New York: George Braziller, 1973. The methods—and ultimate collapse—of all-out southern resistance to school desegregation.

Woodward, C. Vann. *The Strange Career of Jim Crow.* New York: Oxford University Press, 1957. Brief, lucid account of the evolution of Jim Crow practices in the South.

Foreign Policy

When Iraq invaded Kuwait in August 1990, President Bush sent U.S. troops to the Persian Gulf, initially in small numbers to defend neighboring Saudi Arabia but later in large numbers to force Iraq out of Kuwait. He obtained the backing of the United Nations Security Council and the military support of many other nations.

This forced Americans once again to face a key foreign-policy issue: can the president send troops into combat on his own authority, or does he need a congressional declaration of war? President Bush said he did not need such a declaration, citing the action of previous presidents who had made war without it. Congress responded by quoting the Constitution, which gives to Congress the power "to declare war." On January 13, 1991, the immediate issue was settled when Congress passed (though by a narrow margin in the Senate) a resolution authorizing the president to use force in the Gulf. On January 16, we attacked. On March 3, Iraq gave up.

But the largest issue remains unsettled. Is our Constitution, or democratic politics generally, well suited to the needs of diplomacy in the modern age? Tocqueville said that the conduct of foreign affairs requires precisely those qualities most lacking in a democratic nation: "A democracy can only with great difficulty regulate the details of an important undertaking, persevere in a fixed design, and work out its execution in spite of serious obstacles. It cannot combine its measures with secrecy or await their consequences with patience."[1] In plain language, a democracy is forced to play foreign-policy poker with its cards turned up. As a result, aggressors, from Hitler to Saddam Hussein, will bluff us or misjudge us.

Others, however, find fault not with the system but with what they view as the reckless policies of American presidents. If Congress had been more involved, they say, we would not have gotten bogged down in Vietnam, tried to trade arms for hostages in Iran, or supported the rebels in Nicaragua.

Happily, most foreign-policy issues are not matters of war or peace. But the same issues can be found in them all: How great are the powers of the president? What role should Congress play? How important is public opinion? When do interest groups make a difference? To answer those questions we must first distinguish among foreign-policy issues that involve majoritarian, interest-group, and clientele politics.

Kinds of Foreign Policy

The majoritarian component of foreign policy includes those decisions (and nondecisions) that are perceived to confer widely distributed benefits and impose widely distributed costs. The decision to go to war is an obvious example of this. So, too, are the establishment of military alliances with Western Europe, the negotiation of a nuclear-test-ban treaty or a strategic-arms-limitation agreement, the response to the crisis posed by the Soviet blockade of West Berlin or the placement of Soviet offensive missiles in Cuba, the decision to aid the contras in Nicaragua, and the opening up of diplomatic relations with the People's Republic of China. These may be good or bad policies, but such benefits and such costs as they have accrue to the nation generally. Some argue that the costs of many of these policies are in fact highly concentrated—for example, soldiers bear the burden of a military operation—but that turns out, on closer inspection, not to shape the positions that people take on issues of war and peace. Though soldiers and their immediate families may feel the costs of a war to an especially high degree, public-opinion surveys taken during the Vietnam War show that whether a person had a family member in the armed forces did not significantly affect how he or she evaluated the

Domestic interest groups powerfully affect the making of foreign policy as when Jewish-Americans denounce Palestinian terrorists, and Arab-Americans support self-government for Palestinians.

foreign policy. If a multinational corporation is caught in a scandal, congressional investigations shake the usual indifference of politicians to the foreign conduct of such corporations. If presidential policies abroad lead to reversals, as when in 1986 presidential aides sought to trade arms for U.S. hostages in Iran and then use some profits from the arms sales to support the anti-Marxist contras fighting in Nicaragua, Congress becomes the forum for investigations and criticism. At such moments Congress often seeks to expand its power over foreign affairs.

In this chapter we will be chiefly concerned with foreign policy insofar as it displays the characteristics of majoritarian politics. Limiting the discussion in this way permits us to focus on the grand issues of foreign affairs—war, peace, and global diplomacy. It allows us to see how choices are made in a situation in which public majorities support but do not direct policy, in which opinion tends to react to events, and in which interest groups are relatively unimportant.

The president dominates the politics of grand diplomacy, as did President Carter when he announced the signing of the Camp David agreement between Egyptian President Anwar Sadat and Israeli Prime Minister Menachem Begin.

The Constitutional and Legal Context

The Constitution defines the authority of the president and of Congress in foreign affairs in a way that, as Edward Corwin put it, is an "invitation to struggle."[3] The president is commander in chief of the armed forces, but Congress must authorize and appropriate money for those forces. The president appoints ambassadors, but they must be confirmed by the Senate. The president may negotiate treaties, but the Senate must ratify these by a two-thirds vote. Only Congress may regulate commerce with other nations and "declare" war. (The Framers in an early draft had given Congress the power to "make" war but changed this to "declare" so that the president acting without Congress could take military measures to repel a sudden attack.) Because power over foreign affairs is shared by the president and Congress, conflict between them is to be expected.

Yet almost every American thinks instinctively that the president is in charge of foreign affairs, and what popular opinion supposes, the historical record confirms. Presidents have asserted the right to send troops abroad on their own authority in more than 125 instances.[4] Only five of the twelve major wars that this country has fought have followed a formal declaration of war by Congress.[5] The State Department, the Central Intelligence Agency, and the National Security Agency are almost entirely "presidential" agencies, with only modest congressional control. The Defense Department, though keenly sensitive to congressional views on weapons procurement and the location of military bases, is very much under the control of the president on matters of military strategy. While the Senate has since 1789 ratified well over a thousand treaties signed by the president, the president during this period has also signed around seven thousand executive agreements with other countries that do not require Senate ratification and yet have the force of law.[6]

Presidential Box Score

When the president seeks congressional approval for foreign-policy matters, he tends to win more often than when he asks for support on domestic matters. Between 1948 and 1964 Congress approved 73 percent of the president's defense measures, 71 percent of his treaty and foreign-aid proposals, 59 percent of

Shifting Patterns of Leadership in Foreign Policy

*D*epending on the personalities, skills, and interest of those involved, leadership in making American foreign policy may be found centered in the White House (the president and his national-security adviser) or in the State Department (the secretary of state).

Periods of White House dominance

President	Secretary of State
Franklin D. Roosevelt	Cordell Hull (1933–1944)
John F. Kennedy (and National Security Adviser McGeorge Bundy)	Dean Rusk (1961–1969)
Richard M. Nixon (and National Security Adviser Henry A. Kissinger)	William P. Rogers (1969–1973)

Periods of leadership by the secretary of state

Secretary of State	President
George O. Marshall (1947–1949) and Dean Acheson (1949–1953)	Harry S Truman
John Foster Dulles (1953–1959)	Dwight D. Eisenhower
Henry A. Kissinger (1973–1977)	Gerald R. Ford

Periods of tension between the White House and secretary of state

President	Secretary of State
Jimmy Carter	Cyrus Vance (1977–1980)
Ronald Reagan	George Shultz (1982–1989)

John F. Kennedy with Dean Rusk

his other foreign-policy measures—but only 40 percent of his domestic programs. One student of the presidency, Aaron Wildavsky, concluded that the American political system has "two presidencies"—one in domestic affairs that is relatively weak and closely checked, and another in foreign affairs that is quite powerful.[7] As we shall see, this view considerably overstates presidential power in certain areas.

By the standards of American government (limiting our attention to majoritarian issues of diplomacy and military deployment), the president is indeed strong, much stronger than the Framers in 1789 may have intended and certainly stronger than many members of Congress would prefer. Examples abound:

- 1801: Thomas Jefferson sent the navy to deal with the Barbary pirates.

- 1845: James K. Polk sent troops into Mexico to defend newly acquired Texas.

- 1861: Abraham Lincoln blockaded southern ports and declared martial law.

- 1940: Franklin D. Roosevelt sent fifty destroyers to England to be used against Germany, with which we were then technically at peace.

- 1950: Harry Truman sent American troops into South Korea to help repulse a North Korean attack on that country.

- 1960s: John F. Kennedy and Lyndon Johnson sent American forces into South Vietnam without a declaration of war.

- 1983: President Reagan without declaring war sent troops to overthrow a pro-Castro regime in Grenada.

- 1987: President Reagan sent the navy to protect oil tankers in the Persian Gulf.

- 1989: President Bush ordered the U.S. invasion of Panama to depose dictator Manuel Noriega.

- 1990: President Bush ordered troops to Saudi Arabia in response to Iraq's invasion of Kuwait.

However, by the standards of other nations, even other democratic ones, the ability of an American president to act decisively often appears rather modest. England was dismayed at the inability of Woodrow Wilson in 1914–1915 and Franklin Roosevelt in 1939–1940 to enter into an alliance when England was engaged in a major war with Germany. Wilson was unable to bring this country into the League of Nations. Gerald Ford could not intervene covertly in Angola in support of an anti-Marxist faction. President Reagan was heavily criticized in Congress for sending fifty-five military advisers to El Salvador and a few hundred marines to Lebanon.

By contrast the leaders of other democratic nations (to say nothing of totalitarian ones) are often able to act with much greater freedom. While Reagan was arguing with Congress over whether we should assign any military advisers to El Salvador, the president of France, François Mitterrand, ordered twenty-five hundred combat troops to Chad with scarcely a ripple of opposition. A predecessor of Mitterrand, Charles de Gaulle, brought France into the Common Market over the explicit opposition of the French Assembly and granted independence to Algeria, then a French colony, without seriously consulting the Assembly.[8] The British prime minister brought his country into the European Community Market despite popular opposition and can declare war without the consent of Parliament.[9]

After President Bush sent U.S. troops to the Persian Gulf in 1990, he began a long debate with Congress over whether he would need a formal declaration of war before the troops were sent into combat. And a treaty signed by the president is little more than his promise to try to get the Senate to go along. (He can sign executive agreements without Senate consent, but most of these are authorized in advance by Congress.)[10]

Evaluating the Power of the President

Whether one thinks the president too strong or too weak in foreign affairs depends not only on whether one holds a domestic or international point of view but also on whether one agrees or disagrees with his policies. Historian Arthur M. Schlesinger, Jr., thought that President Kennedy exercised commendable presidential vigor when he made a unilateral decision to impose a naval blockade on Cuba to induce the Soviets to remove missiles installed there. However, he viewed President Nixon's decision to extend United States military action in Vietnam into neighboring Cambodia as a deplorable example of the "imperial presidency."[11] To be sure, there were im-

portant differences between these two actions, but that is precisely the point: a president strong enough to do something that one thinks proper is also strong enough to do something that one finds wrong.

The Supreme Court has fairly consistently supported the view that the federal government has powers in the conduct of foreign and military policy beyond those specifically mentioned in the Constitution. The leading decision, rendered in 1936, holds that the right to carry out a foreign policy is an inherent attribute of any sovereign nation:

> *The power to declare and wage war, to conclude peace, to make treaties, to maintain diplomatic relations with other sovereignties, if they had never been mentioned in the Constitution, would have vested in the Federal Government as necessary concomitants of nationality.*[12]

The individual states have few rights in foreign affairs.

Moreover the Supreme Court has been most reluctant to intervene in disputes over the conduct of foreign affairs. When various members of Congress brought suit challenging the right of President Nixon to enlarge the war in Vietnam without congressional

In 1962 President Kennedy forced the Soviet Union to withdraw the missiles it had placed in Cuba after their presence was revealed by aerial photography.

Japanese-Americans awaiting transportation under military guard from their homes on the West Coast to relocation camps in the interior, where they remained for the duration of World War II.

How great the deference to presidential power may be is vividly illustrated by the actions of President Franklin Roosevelt in ordering the army to move over one hundred thousand Japanese—the great majority of them born in this country and citizens of the United States—from their homes on the West Coast to inland "relocation centers" for the duration of World War II. Though this action was a wholesale violation of the constitutional rights of citizens unprecedented in American history, the Supreme Court decided that in time of war with Japan and with the defenses of the West Coast weak, the president was within his rights to decide that people of Japanese ancestry might pose a threat to internal security; the relocation order was upheld.[16] (No Japanese-American was ever found guilty of espionage or sabotage.) One of the few cases in which the Court denied the president broad wartime powers occurred in 1952, when, by a five-to-four vote, it reversed President Truman's seizure of the steel mills—a move that he had made in order to avert a strike that, in his view, would have imperiled the war effort in Korea.[17]

Checks on Presidential Power

If there is a check on the powers of the federal government or the president in foreign affairs, it is chiefly political rather than constitutional. The most important check is Congress's control of the purse strings. In addition Congress has imposed three important kinds of restrictions on the president's freedom of action, all since Vietnam:

1. Limitations on the president's ability to give military or economic aid to other countries   For example, between 1974 and 1978 the president could not sell arms to Turkey because of a dispute between Turkey and Greece over control of the island of Cyprus. The pressure on Congress from groups supporting Greece was much stronger than that from groups supporting Turkey. In 1976 Congress prevented President Ford from giving aid to the pro-Western faction in the Angolan civil war. Until the method was declared unconstitutional, Congress for many years could use a legislative veto, a resolution disapproving of an executive decision (see Chapter 13), to block the sale by the president of arms worth more than $25 million to another country.

approval, the court of appeals handled the issue, as one scholar was later to describe it, with all the care of porcupines making love. The court said that it was a matter for the president and Congress to decide and that if Congress was unwilling to cut off the money to pay for the war, it should not expect the courts to do the job for it.[13]

The Supreme Court upheld the extraordinary measures taken by President Lincoln during the Civil War and refused to interfere with the conduct of the Vietnam War by Presidents Johnson and Nixon.[14] After Iran seized American hostages in 1979, President Carter froze Iranian assets in this country. To win the hostages' freedom, the president later agreed to return some of these assets and to nullify claims on them by American companies. The Court upheld the nullification because it was necessary for the resolution of a foreign-policy dispute.[15]

Despite predictions by critics that the United States would become bogged down in a long, costly ground war, the U.S. offensive against Iraq lasted only four days and took very few U.S. lives.

2. The War Powers Act Passed in 1973 over a presidential veto, this law placed the following restrictions on the president's ability to use military force:

- He must report in writing to Congress within forty-eight hours after he introduces U.S. troops into areas where hostilities have occurred or are imminent.

- Within sixty days after troops are sent into hostile situations, Congress must, by declaration of war or other specific statutory authorization, provide for the continuation of hostile action by U.S. troops.

- If Congress fails to provide such authorization, the president must withdraw the troops (unless Congress has been prevented from meeting as a result of an armed attack).

- If Congress passes a concurrent resolution (which the president may not veto) directing the removal of U.S. troops, the president must comply.

Under the War Powers Act the president has reported the use of troops to Congress on several occasions:

- President Ford three times sent armed forces to evacuate people from Communist-controlled areas in Cambodia and Vietnam.

- President Ford ordered the military to free the crew of the merchant ship *Mayaguez,* captured by Cambodia.

- President Carter sent troops (unsuccessfully) to rescue the Americans held hostage in Iran.

- President Reagan sent troops to try to restore order in Lebanon and to expel a pro-Cuban regime from the island of Grenada.

- President Bush invaded Panama.

No president has acknowledged the constitutionality of the War Powers Act. In its 1983 decision in the *Chadha* case the Supreme Court in effect struck down the part of the War Powers Act that authorizes the use of a legislative veto as well as all statutes authorizing legislative vetoes to control arms sales abroad.[18] The other parts of the War Powers Act—the notification provisions and the requirement that troops be withdrawn in sixty days unless war is formally declared—have not yet been tested in court.

Even if the law should be sustained by the courts, its practical political significance is unclear. Few members of Congress would challenge a military operation that was successful, as were the Panama and Grenada invasions. Some would rebuke the president for engaging in one that was swift and unsuccessful—but only after the fact. No one knows what effect the law would have if a president committed American forces to a protracted engagement of the sort that we had in Vietnam. Even after that war had become unpopular, Congress continued to appropriate money for its conduct. Not once from 1966 to 1973 did Congress cut off funds for the war or require the withdrawal of American troops by some specific date. When in 1982 President Reagan sent the marines ashore in Beirut, Lebanon, as a peacekeeping force, Congress after much discussion passed a joint resolution authorizing them to remain there for up to eighteen months. The president did not request this resolution, and it is not clear what would have happened had Congress not acted as it did. In time President Reagan withdrew the marines, not because of congressional demands but because the situation in Lebanon had deteriorated to the point where our military presence had little peacekeeping value.

3. Intelligence oversight Owing to the low political stock of President Nixon during the Watergate scandal and the revelations of illegal operations by the Central Intelligence Agency (CIA) within the United States, Congress required that the CIA notify appropriate congressional committees about any proposed covert action (between 1974 and 1980 it had to notify *eight* different committees). Today it must keep two groups, the House and the Senate Intelligence Committees, "fully and currently informed" of all intelligence activities, including covert actions. The committees do not have the authority to disapprove such actions.

However, from time to time Congress will pass a bill blocking particular covert actions. This happened when the Boland Amendment (named after its sponsor, Representative Edward Boland) was passed on several occasions between 1982 and 1985. Each version of the amendment prevented, for specifically

stated periods, intelligence agencies from supplying military aid to the Nicaraguan contras. One of the issues raised during the Iran-contra investigation was whether the aid supplied by the staff of the National Security Council was illegal because it was provided by an "intelligence agency" within the meaning of the law.

The Machinery of Foreign Policy

From the time that Thomas Jefferson took the job in Washington's first administration until well into this century, foreign policy was often made and almost always carried out by the secretary of state. No more. When America became a major world power during and after World War II, our commitments overseas expanded dramatically. With that expansion two things happened. First, the president began to put foreign policy at the top of his agenda and to play a larger role in directing it. Second, that policy was shaped by the scores of agencies (some brand-new) that had acquired overseas activities.

Today Washington, D.C., has not one State Department but many. The Defense Department has military bases and military advisers abroad. The Central Intelligence Agency has intelligence officers abroad, most of them assigned to "stations" that are part of the American embassy but not under the full control of the American ambassador there. The Departments of Agriculture, Commerce, and Labor have missions abroad. The Federal Bureau of Investigation and the Drug Enforcement Administration have agents abroad. The Agency for International Development has offices to dispense foreign aid in host countries. The United States Information Agency runs libraries, radio stations, and educational programs abroad.

Every new secretary of state bravely announces that he is going to "coordinate" and "direct" this enormous foreign-policy establishment. He never does. The reason is partly that the job is too big for any one person, partly that most of these agencies owe no political or bureaucratic loyalty to the secretary of state. If anyone is to coordinate them, it will have to be the president. But the president cannot keep track of what all these organizations are doing in the more than 140 nations and 50 international organizations where we have representatives, or what is going on in the more than 800 international conferences that we attend each year.

So he has hired a staff to do the coordinating for him. That staff is part of the National Security Council (NSC), a committee created by statute and chaired by the president whose members include (by law) the vice president and the secretaries of state and defense, and (by custom) the director of the CIA and the chairman of the Joint Chiefs of Staff, and (often) the attorney general. Depending on the president, the NSC can be an important body in which to hammer out foreign policy. Attached to it is a staff headed by the national-security adviser. That staff, which usually numbers a few dozen men and women, can be (again, depending on the president) an enormously powerful instrument for formulating and directing foreign policy.

Nominally that staff exists only to bring before the president a balanced account of the views of the heads of the major government agencies with a stake in foreign-policy decisions, to help the president choose among the options that these advisers identify, and to oversee the implementation of the presidential decision. These decisions are usually in the form of a National Security Decision Directive, or NSDD, signed by the president.

Presidents Truman and Eisenhower made only limited use of the NSC staff, but beginning with President Kennedy it has grown greatly in influence. Its head, the national-security adviser, has come to rival the secretary of state for foreign-policy leadership, especially when the adviser was a powerful personality such as Henry Kissinger. President Reagan attempted to downgrade the importance of the national-security adviser, but ironically it was one of his relatively low-visibility appointees, Admiral John Poindexter, and his subordinate, Lieutenant Colonel Oliver North, who precipitated the worst crisis of the Reagan presidency when, allegedly without informing the president, they tried to use cash realized from the secret sale of arms to Iran to finance the guerrillas fighting against the Marxist government of Nicaragua. The sale and the diversion became known, North was fired, a congressional investigation ensued, criminal charges were filed against Poindexter and North, and the president's political position was weakened.

Rivalry versus Cooperation: The President and the Senate

Because the Senate must ratify treaties and consent to the appointment of ambassadors and other high foreign-policy officials, it has the opportunity to play a large role in the conduct of foreign affairs. The key figure in the Senate is usually the chairman of the Senate Foreign Relations Committee.

Depending on personalities and circumstances, the president and the chairman have sometimes been able to work together closely but at other times have been bitter, outspoken rivals. In general cooperation occurs when there is a widely shared foreign-policy worldview; rivalry erupts when worldviews diverge.

Periods of shared worldviews and political cooperation

President	Chairman of Foreign Relations Committee
Franklin D. Roosevelt	Tom Connally (1941–1947, 1949–1953)
Harry S Truman	Arthur H. Vandenberg (1947–1949)

Periods of competing worldviews and political rivalry

President	Chairman of Foreign Relations Committee
Woodrow Wilson	Henry Cabot Lodge (1919–1924)
Lyndon B. Johnson	J. William Fulbright (1959–1975)
Richard M. Nixon	

Harry S Truman with Senator Arthur Vandenberg

Spook Speak

Spook Speak is the jargon used by the Central Intelligence Agency and other intelligence organizations to refer to their activities and procedures. The terms include:

- *Asset:* A foreign person who cooperates with the CIA by furnishing information or assistance, but who is not a CIA employee.
- *Black-bag job:* Secretly entering a home or office, without a warrant, to search it or plant a listening device.
- *Cover:* A false name and identity used to conceal the real identity of an intelligence officer or activity.
- *Covert action:* Secret or clandestine activity designed to influence events or governments abroad, including financial payments, propaganda, and military action.
- *Double agent:* An asset who is working both sides of the street, giving information or assistance to the intelligence service of one country while pretending to work for the service of another.
- *Family jewels:* The most important secrets (files or operations) of an intelligence agency.
- *Mole:* A person employed by one intelligence service who is actually spying on it for a hostile service.
- *Proprietary:* A private business firm that is actually owned and controlled by an intelligence agency: for example, an airline company that transports cargo for the CIA.
- *Safe house:* An innocent-appearing house or apartment used to hide intelligence officers or their assets.

SOURCE: Adapted from William Safire, *Safire's Political Dictionary* (New York: Ballantine Books, 1978). Used by permission.

But even in ordinary times the NSC staff is the rival of the secretary of state, except during that period in the Ford administration when Henry Kissinger held *both* jobs.

The way in which the machinery of foreign policy making operates has two major consequences for the substance of that policy. First, as former Secretary of State George Shultz asserted, "It's never over." Foreign-policy issues are endlessly agitated, rarely settled. The reason is that the rivalries *within* the executive branch intensify the rivalries *between* that branch and Congress. In ways already described Congress has steadily increased its influence over the conduct of foreign policy. Anybody in the executive branch who loses out in a struggle over foreign policy can take his or her case (usually by means of a well-timed leak) to a sympathetic member of Congress, who then can make a speech, hold a hearing, or introduce a bill.

The plan to have the NSC staff manage the Iran arms sale and the raising of private money for the contras may have been motivated by a desire to keep these controversial matters out of the leaky, conflict-ridden machinery by which foreign policy is normally made. If so, the effort was an exercise in futility; for no matter who carries out a policy, if it is controversial, it will become public. Americans often worry that their government is keeping secrets from them. In fact there are no secrets in Washington—at least not for long.

The interests of the various organizations making up the foreign-policy establishment profoundly affect the positions that they take. Because the State Department has a stake in diplomacy, it tends to resist bold or controversial new policies that might upset established relationships with other countries. Part of the CIA has a stake in gathering and analyzing information; that part tends to be skeptical of the claims of other agencies that their overseas operations are succeeding. Another part of the CIA conducts covert operations abroad; it tends to resent or ignore the skepticism of the intelligence analysts. The air force flies airplanes and so tends to be optimistic about what can be accomplished through the use of air power in particular and military power in general; the army, on the other hand, which must fight in the trenches, is often dubious about the prospects for military success.

Foreign Policy and Public Opinion

These organizational conflicts shape the details of foreign policy, but its broad outlines are shaped by public and elite opinion.

World War II was the great watershed. Before that time a clear majority of the American public opposed active involvement in world affairs by the United States. The public saw the costs of such involvement as substantially in excess of the benefits, and only determined, skillful leaders were able, as was President Roosevelt during 1939–1940, to affect in even a limited fashion the diplomatic and military struggles then convulsing Europe and Asia.

Our participation in the war produced a dramatic shift in popular opinion that endured for three decades, supplying broad (though often ambiguous) public support for an internationalist foreign policy. World War II had this effect, alone among all wars that we have fought, for several reasons. First, it was almost the only universally popular war in which we have been engaged, one that produced few, if any, recriminations afterward. Second, the war seemed successful: an unmitigated evil (the Nazi regime) was utterly destroyed; an attack on our own land (by Japan at Pearl Harbor) was thoroughly avenged. Third, that war ended with the United States recognized as the dominant power on earth, owing to its sole possession of the atomic bomb and its enormous military and economic productivity.

In 1937, 94 percent of the American public preferred the policy of doing "everything possible to keep out of foreign wars" to the policy of doing "everything possible to prevent war, even if it means threatening to fight countries that fight wars." In 1939, after World War II had begun in Europe but before Pearl Harbor was attacked, only 13 percent of Americans polled thought that we should enter the war against Germany. Just a month before Pearl Harbor only 19 percent felt that the United States should take steps, at the risk of war, to prevent Japan from becoming too powerful.[19] Congress reflected the noninterventionist mood of the country: in the summer of 1941, with war breaking out almost everywhere, the proposal to continue the draft passed the House of Representatives by only one vote.

The Japanese attack on Pearl Harbor on December 7 changed all that. Not only was the American war effort supported almost unanimously, not only did Congress approve the declaration of war with only one dissenting vote, but World War II—unlike World War I—produced popular support for an active assumption of international responsibilities that

The battleship *West Virginia* burning after being hit by Japanese warplanes at Pearl Harbor on December 7, 1941.

continued after the war had ended.[20] Whereas a majority after World War I opposed U.S. entry into the League of Nations, a clear majority after World War II favored our entry into the United Nations.[21]

This willingness to see the United States remain a world force persisted until the 1960s, when the inconclusive war in Vietnam led an increasing proportion of citizens to return to isolationist sentiments. The number of people thinking that we should "keep independent" in world affairs as opposed to "working closely with other nations" rose from 10 percent in 1963 to 22 percent in 1969.[22] Even so, as late as 1967, after more than two years of war in Vietnam, 44 percent of Americans believed that this country had an obligation to "defend other Vietnams if they are threatened by communism."[23]

But the support for an internationalist American foreign policy was, and is, highly general, heavily dependent on the phrasing of the question, the opinions expressed by popular leaders, and the impact of world events. Public opinion, while more internationalist than once was the case, is both mushy and volatile. Just prior to President Nixon's decision to send troops into Cambodia, only 7 percent of the people said that they supported such a move. After the troops were sent and Nixon made a speech explaining his move, 50 percent of the public said that they supported it.[24] Similarly only 49 percent of the

people favored a halt in American bombing of North Vietnam before President Johnson, in 1968, ordered such a halt; afterward 60 percent of the public said that it supported such a policy.[25]

Backing the President

Much of this volatility in specific opinions (as opposed to general mood) reflects the already-mentioned deference to the "commander in chief" and a desire to support the United States when it confronts other nations. Table 20.1 shows the proportion of people saying that they approve of the way in which the president is doing his job before and after various major foreign-policy events. Each foreign crisis increased the level of public approval of the president, often dramatically. The most vivid illustration of this was the Bay of Pigs fiasco: an American-supported, American-directed invasion of Cuba by anti-Castro Cuban émigrés was driven back into the sea. President Kennedy accepted responsibility for the aborted project. His popularity *rose*. (Comparable data for domestic crises tend to show no similar effect.)

This tendency to "rally 'round the flag" has been carefully studied and seems to operate on behalf of any president engaged in any foreign-policy initiative, whether force is used or not. One analysis of the standing of presidents in public opinion from Tru-

---

TABLE 20.1 Popular Reactions to Foreign-Policy Crises

Percentage of public saying that they approve of the way the president is handling his job

	Foreign-Policy Crisis	Before	After
1960	American U-2 spy plane shot down over Soviet Union	62%	68%
1961	Abortive landing at Bay of Pigs in Cuba	73	83
1962	Cuban missile crisis	61	74
1975	President Ford sends marines to rescue the *Mayaguez*	40	51
1979	American embassy in Teheran seized by Iranians	32	61
1980	Failure of military effort to rescue hostages in Iran	39	43
1983	U.S. invasion of Grenada	43	53
1989	U.S. invasion of Panama	71	80
1990	U.S. troops to Persian Gulf	60	75

SOURCE: Updated from Theodore J. Lowi, *The End of Liberalism* (New York: Norton, 1969), 184. Poll data are from Gallup poll. Time lapse between "before" and "after" samplings of opinion was in no case more than one month.

man through Johnson (1945–1968) found that, even allowing for the effects of ups and downs in the economy and the decay in presidential popularity that almost always occurs during a presidential term of office, every president enjoys a boost in popularity immediately after an international crisis or major diplomatic event.[26] There is at least one exception to this tendency. The revelation that the Reagan administration was trying to swap arms for hostages in Iran led to a *drop* in the president's popularity—perhaps because the effort had been secret and was revealed by critics of it.

If presidents derive more political rewards from playing a foreign-policy role rather than a domestic one, we would expect that most presidents would prefer the foreign-policy role and that some presidents might even deliberately manufacture diplomatic "successes" to bolster their sagging popularity. Most presidents since 1941 have in fact felt that their most important tasks were in the field of foreign affairs (though the realities of international problems probably have as much to do with that pattern as the political rewards of playing the diplomatic role). When presidents travel abroad, it is always as much for domestic political consumption as for any substantive effect. Since the rewards are so great, one wonders why any president would shun even risky international ventures.

One reason is that, though the president wins popular support during the early stages of an international crisis, that support tends to deteriorate if the crisis is not soon resolved or if a protracted and costly stalemate ensues. World War II is the only major war about which we have opinion data in which public support remained high throughout. World War I, though it commanded popular support at the time, led to bitter recriminations afterward; by 1937 nearly two-thirds of the American people thought that it was a mistake for the United States to have entered it.[27] Support for Truman's decision to send troops to Korea declined as the war went on: whereas initially about two-thirds of the people backed the decision, two years later only a bit more than a third thought that it had been a good idea.[28] Support for the decision of President Johnson to send troops to Vietnam followed almost exactly the same pattern: initial support gave way to mounting skepticism as the war dragged on inconclusively.[29] Though in retrospect

Americans returning home in 1981 after being held hostage by the Iranian government.

we think of Vietnam as bitterly controversial and Korea as much less so, in fact *public* opinion was pretty much the same in both cases. What was different is that *elite* opinion protested our involvement in Vietnam but not our participation in Korea.

The clearest lesson that history offers a president on the exercise of his war-making powers is this: either fight a popular crusade or fight only short wars that you win quickly. Given the edge enjoyed by Democrats in party identification, it is noteworthy that two of the five times since 1945 that a Republican has won the presidency have been in the midst of an unpopular war—Eisenhower in 1952 and Nixon in 1968. On a third occasion—Reagan in 1980—fifty-two Americans were being held hostage in Iran. It is not true that Democrats start wars and Republicans end them, but protracted military stalemates can help the party out of power get elected.

U.S. Marines escorting emergency food supplies to rural villages in Somalia.

Mass versus Elite Opinion

The average citizen tends to be rather uninformed about world affairs (except when the United States is directly and dramatically involved), to support the president in most of his undertakings, and to judge the success of those undertakings largely on practical grounds. By contrast members of the political elites tend to be well informed, to give much less support to the president, and to judge the success of his undertakings on philosophical rather than practical grounds.

In 1984, for example, fewer than half the voters knew that the United States was backing the government of El Salvador; a fifth thought, wrongly, that we

Vietnam split the country—and the youth—between those who thought the war immoral and those who thought it important to support our armed forces, whatever the value of the war.

were backing the rebels; and the rest did not know whom we were backing. In Nicaragua only a third thought, correctly, that we were supporting the rebels; a quarter thought, erroneously, that we were supporting the government.[30] Perhaps because of their lack of knowledge but more likely because of their innate caution, the voters have repeatedly indicated that they oppose sending American troops to El Salvador or anywhere else in Central America. But if past experience (such as the Grenada invasion) is any guide, they will give strong support to the president if he should decide to send in troops.

If troops are sent into the area, mass opinion will judge the success of the military action largely on pragmatic grounds. If we are successful, they will approve. If we suffer important defeats or the war drags on, they will reduce their approval. During Vietnam, for example, the average citizen reacted adversely to the war when American troops suffered losses or seemed to be on the defensive.[31]

Elite opinion, on the other hand, is better informed but more volatile and moralistic. Initially college-educated people gave *more* support to the war in Vietnam than those without college training; by the end of the war college-educated support had decreased dramatically (Figure 20.1). The reasons for that decline in support differed. Whereas the average citizen was upset when the United States seemed to be on the *defensive* in Vietnam, college-educated voters tended to be more upset when the United States was on the *offensive*.[32]

Though the average citizen did not want our military in Vietnam in the first place, he or she felt that we should support our troops once they were there. The average person also was deeply opposed to the antiwar protests taking place on college campuses. When the Chicago police roughed up antiwar demonstrators at the 1968 Democratic convention, public sentiment was overwhelmingly on the side of the police.[33] Contrary to myths much accepted at the time, younger people were *not* more opposed to the war than older ones (Figure 20.2). There was no "generation gap."

By contrast college-educated citizens, thinking at first that troops should be involved, soon changed their minds, decided that the war was wrong, and grew increasingly upset when the United States seemed to be enlarging the war (by, for example, invading Cambodia). College students protested

FIGURE 20.1 Trends in Support for the Vietnam War, by Education

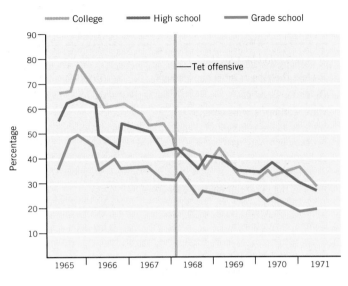

FIGURE 20.2 Trends in Support for the Vietnam War, by Age

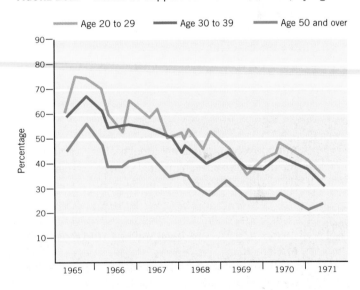

SOURCE: John E. Mueller, *War, Presidents, and Public Opinion* (New York: Wiley, 1973), 125, 139. Reprinted in 1985 by University Press of America, Lanham, Md., by permission of the author.

against the war largely on moral grounds, and their protests received more support from college-educated adults than from other citizens.

The cleavage between mass and elite opinion is even wider if you restrict the definition of *elite* to only

TABLE 20.2   How the Public and the Elite See Foreign Policy, 1990

	Percentage Agreeing	
	Public	Leaders
It is very important to:		
Protect the jobs of American workers	65%	39%
Defend U.S. allies	61	56
Have worldwide arms control	53	80
Improve living standard in under-developed nations	41	42
Protect the interests of U.S. business abroad	63	27
Prevent the spread of nuclear weapons	59	94
Improve the global environment	58	72
Contain communism	56	10
U.S. should send troops if:		
Soviets invade Europe	58	87
Iraq invades Saudi Arabia[a]	52	89
Arabs invade Israel	43	70
U.S. should give economic aid to:		
Soviet Union	40	71

[a] Question asked after Iraq invasion of Kuwait in August 1990.
SOURCE: *American Public Opinion and U.S. Foreign Policy,* 1991 (Chicago: Chicago Council on Foreign Relations, 1991), 15, 34, 37.

In the 1980s, American college campuses were the scene of demonstrations demanding that U.S. corporations end their investments in South Africa where blacks were subordinated to white rule by means of apartheid laws.

those involved in making foreign policy rather than including all college-educated people. In Table 20.2 we see the differences in foreign-policy views of a cross section of American citizens and a group of 341 leaders active in government, academia, the mass media, and various organizations concerned with foreign affairs.[34]

In general the leaders have a more liberal and internationalist outlook than the public: they are more likely to favor giving economic aid to other countries, defending our allies, reducing tariffs, and opposing oppressive regimes. The public, on the other hand, wants the United States to be less active overseas and worries about protecting the jobs of American workers. Accordingly it wants the United States to keep tariffs high, protect American jobs from foreign competition, protect American businesses abroad from foreign threats, and give less economic aid to other nations.

Cleavages among Foreign-Policy Elites

As we have seen, public opinion on foreign policy is permissive and a bit mushy: it supports presidential action without giving it much direction. Elite opinion therefore acquires extraordinary importance. Of course events and world realities are also important, but since events have no meaning except as they are perceived and interpreted by people who must react to them, the attitudes and beliefs of those people in and out of government who are actively involved in shaping foreign policy often assume decisive importance. Contrary to the views of people who think that some shadowy, conspiratorial group of insiders runs our foreign policy, the foreign-policy elite in this country is deeply divided.

That elite consists not only of those people with administrative positions in the foreign-policy field—

the senior officials of the State Department and the staff of the National Security Council—but also the members and staffs of the key congressional committees concerned with foreign affairs (chiefly the Senate Foreign Relations Committee and the House Foreign Affairs Committee) and various private organizations that help shape elite opinion, such as the members of the Council on Foreign Relations and the editors of two important publications, *Foreign Affairs* and *Foreign Policy.* To these must be added influential columnists and editorial writers whose work appears regularly in the national press. One could extend the list by adding ever-wider circles of people with some influence (lobbyists, professors, leaders of veterans' organizations); this would complicate without changing the central point: elite beliefs are probably more important in explaining foreign policy than in accounting for decisions in other policy areas.

How a Worldview Shapes Foreign Policy

These beliefs can be described in simplified terms as **worldviews** (or as some social scientists put it, as *paradigms*)—more or less comprehensive mental pictures of the critical problems facing the United States in the world and of the appropriate and inappropriate ways of responding to these problems. The clearest, most concise, and one of the most influential statements of one worldview that held sway for many years was an article published in 1947 in *Foreign Affairs,* entitled "The Sources of Soviet Conduct."[35] Written by a "Mr. X" (later revealed to be George F. Kennan, director of the Policy Planning Staff of the State Department and thereafter ambassador to Moscow), the article argued that the Russians were pursuing a policy of expansion that could only be met by the United States' applying "unalterable counterforce at every point where they show signs of encroaching upon the interests of a peaceful and stable world." This he called the strategy of "containment," and it became the governing principle of American foreign policy for at least two decades.

There were critics of the containment policy at the time—Walter Lippmann, in his book *The Cold War,* argued against it in 1947[36]—but the criticisms were less influential than the doctrine. A worldview is important precisely because it prevails over alternative views. One reason why it prevails is that it is broadly consistent with the public's mood. In 1947,

⭐ The Influence of the National Media

*B*etween 1964 and 1968 the position taken on the war in Vietnam by the major national magazines and the principal newspapers changed. In 1964 they tended to support the war effort; by 1968 they tended to oppose it.

During the same time the Survey Research Center (SRC) of the University of Michigan asked citizens for their positions on the war—once in 1964 and again in 1968.

As the table below shows, between 1964 and 1968 opinion of upper-middle-class and lower-middle-class people on the war effort changed much more than that of working-class people, *and* among the former, opinions changed the most among those who regularly read several magazines and newspapers.

For example: in 1964, 78 percent of those upper-middle-class people who regularly read many magazines and newspapers felt that we should take a stronger stand in Vietnam, even if it meant invading North Vietnam. By 1968 only 40 percent of this group felt that way, a shift of 38 percent. By contrast upper-middle-class people who did not regularly read several magazines and newspapers changed by only half as much—from 59 percent favoring a stronger stand in 1964 to 41 percent favoring it in 1968, an 18 percent shift. And among working-class people there was scarcely any media effect at all—a decline of 7 percent in the proportion favoring a stronger stand for both those who read a lot and those who did not.

Decline in Support for a Stronger Stand in Vietnam, by Social Class and Media Readership

	1964	1968	Change
Read several magazines and newspapers regularly			
Upper-middle class	78%	40%	−38
Lower-middle class	50	19	−31
Working class	55	48	−7
Do not read several magazines or newspapers			
Upper-middle class	59	41	−18
Lower-middle class	41	33	−8
Working class	45	38	−7

NOTE: Upper-middle class = white-collar workers earning over $10,000; Lower-middle-class = white-collar workers earning under $10,000; Working class = blue-collar workers. Omitted are nonwhites, southerners, and persons with no opinion on the war.
SOURCE: James D. Wright, "Life, Time and the Fortunes of War." Published by permission of Transaction, Inc., from *Transaction,* vol. 9, no. 3, copyright © January 1972 by Transaction, Inc.

The reading matter of the foreign-policy elite.

After the Soviet Union occupied Afghanistan in 1979, the United States sent military aid to the Afghan resistance, called the "Mujahideen." In 1988 Soviet troops began to withdraw from the country.

when Kennan wrote, popular attitudes toward the Soviet Union, favorable during World War II when Russia and America were allies, had turned quite hostile. In 1946 less than one-fourth of the American people believed that Russia could be trusted to cooperate with this country,[37] and by 1948 over three-fourths were convinced that the Soviet Union was trying not simply to defend itself but to become the dominant world power.[38]

Such a worldview was also influential because it was consistent with events at the time: Russia had occupied most of the previously independent countries of Eastern Europe and was turning them into puppet regimes. When governments independent of both the United States and the Soviet Union attempted to rule in Hungary and Czechoslovakia, they were overthrown by Soviet-backed coups. A worldview also becomes dominant because it is consistent with the prior experiences of the people holding it.

Three Worldviews   Every generation of political leaders comes to power with a foreign-policy worldview shaped, in large measure, by the real or apparent mistakes of the previous generation.[39] This pattern can

be traced back, some have argued, to the very beginnings of the nation. Frank L. Klingberg traces the alteration since 1776 of national "moods" (here called worldviews) that favored first "extroversion" (or an active, internationalist policy) and then "introversion" (a less-active, even isolationist posture).[40]

Since the 1920s American elite opinion has moved through three worldviews: isolationism, antiappeasement (or the "Munich–Pearl Harbor" paradigm), and the disengagement paradigm. **Isolationism** was the view adopted as a result of our unhappy experience in World War I. Our efforts to help European allies turned sour: thousands of American troops were killed in a war that seemed to accomplish little and certainly did not make, in Woodrow Wilson's words, the "world safe for democracy." In the 1920s and 1930s elite opinion (and popular opinion) opposed getting involved in European wars.

A meeting that named an era: In Munich, British Prime Minister Neville Chamberlain attempted to appease the territorial ambitions of Hitler. Chamberlain's failure brought World War II closer.

Containment (or **antiappeasement**) was the result of World War II. At a conference in Munich, efforts of British and French leaders to satisfy Hitler's territorial demands in Europe led not to "peace in our time" as Prime Minister Neville Chamberlain had claimed but to ever-greater territorial demands and ultimately to world war. This crisis brought to power men determined not to repeat their predecessors' mistakes: "Munich" became a synonym for weakness, and leaders such as Winston Churchill

POLITICALLY P.S. **SPEAKING**

Iron Curtain and Cold War

The **iron curtain** was neither iron nor a curtain; it was the political barrier, maintained by the Soviet Union, to free travel and communication between Eastern and Western Europe. In 1989 the iron curtain began to collapse. The phrase was given its present meaning by Winston Churchill in a speech that he delivered at Westminster College in Fulton, Missouri, on March 5, 1946: "From Stettin in the Baltic to Trieste in the Adriatic, an iron curtain has descended across the continent. Behind that line lie all the capitals of the ancient states of central and eastern Europe. . . ."

The **cold war** refers to the nonmilitary struggle between the United States (and its allies) and the former Soviet Union (and its allies). (A *cold war* is distinguished from a *hot,* or *shooting,* war.) The phrase was coined by journalist Herbert Bayard Swope in 1946 and popularized by columnist Walter Lippmann.

SOURCE: Adapted from William Safire, *Safire's Political Dictionary* (New York: Ballantine Books, 1978). Used by permission.

Alternative Worldviews of United States: Relations During the Cold War

Containment View

Communism is a monolithic threat.

If we don't intervene overseas, we may get dragged into war.

We must nip aggression in the bud.

Only American military superiority will contain Soviet expansionism and preserve peace.

> *Let every nation know that we shall pay any price, bear any burden, meet any hardship, support any friend, oppose any foe to assure the survival and success of liberty.*

President John F. Kennedy,
inaugural address, 1960

Disengagement or Vietnam View

Communism is a divided spastic.

If we do intervene overseas, we are sure to get into a war.

We are not the world's police force.

Only arms-limitation treaties and force reductions will preserve peace.

> *[It means] an even more positive commitment to coexistence with the Communist countries. It means a much more determined effort to get military competition with the Soviets under control. . . . It means abandoning the Sub-Imperial ambitions in the Third World and recognizing instead that there is little we can do to influence political development in this part of the world and less that we need to do now.*

John Kenneth Galbraith,
writing in *Esquire*, March 1972

SOURCE: Adapted from Michael Roskin, "From Pearl Harbor to Vietnam: Shifting Generational Paradigms and Foreign Policy," *Political Science Quarterly* 89 (Fall 1974): 576.

---

made antiappeasement the basis of their postwar policy of resisting Soviet expansionism. Churchill summed up the worldview that he had acquired from the Munich era in a famous speech delivered in 1946 in Fulton, Missouri, in which he coined the term *Iron Curtain* to describe Soviet policy in Eastern Europe.

Pearl Harbor was the death knell for isolationism. Senator Arthur H. Vandenberg of Michigan, a staunch isolationist before the attack, became an ardent internationalist not only during but after the war. He later wrote of the Japanese attack on Pearl Harbor on December 7, 1941: "That day ended isolationism for any realist."[41]

The events leading up to World War II were the formative experiences of those leaders who came to power in the 1940s, 1950s, and 1960s. What they took to be the lessons of Munich and Pearl Harbor were applied repeatedly—in building a network of defensive alliances in Europe and Asia during the late 1940s and 1950s, in operating an airlift to aid West

Berlin when road access to it was cut off by the Russians, in coming to the aid of South Korea, and finally in intervening in Vietnam. Most of these applications of the containment worldview were successful in the sense that they did not harm American interests, they proved welcome to allies, or they prevented a military conquest.

The disengagement (or Vietnam) view resulted from the experience of the younger foreign-policy elite who came to power in the 1970s. Unlike previous applications of the antiappeasement view, our entry into Vietnam had led to a military defeat and a domestic political disaster. There were three ways of interpreting that crisis: (1) we applied the correct worldview in the right place but did not try hard enough; (2) we had the correct worldview but tried to apply it in the wrong place under the wrong circumstances; (3) the worldview itself was wrong. By and large the critics of our Vietnam policy tended to draw the third lesson, and thus when they supplanted in office the architects of our Vietnam policy, they inclined toward a new worldview, based on the slogan "no more Vietnams." Critics of this view called it the "new isolationism," arguing that it would encourage Soviet expansion.

How elites think about Vietnam affects their foreign-policy views right down to the present. The answers to poll questions differ sharply depending on the respondents' opinion of the war in Vietnam. The foreign-policy leaders who thought that the war in Vietnam was "fundamentally wrong and immoral" were only half as likely as those who were not so critical of Vietnam to support the use of U.S. troops to protect South Korea from a North Korean invasion or to remove Soviet missiles from Nicaragua.[42]

To a great extent the foreign-policy elite who held the disengagement view came to power in the administration of President Jimmy Carter. They were replaced by leaders who held a different view during the administration of President Ronald Reagan. The elite that is out of power stays active by participating in the work of think tanks, foundations, and universities—liberal ones when conservatives are in power, conservative ones when liberals are in power.

Just how deep the cleavages in elite opinion can be is shown in Table 20.3. On virtually every issue there were huge differences in opinion between Reagan administration officials and foreign-policy leaders who were out of government. The Reagan officials

TABLE 20.3 Cleavages in the Elite: Reagan Administration Officials versus Other Foreign-Policy Leaders

	Percentage Agreeing	
	Reagan Officials	Other Leaders
In foreign policy Congress is too strong	77%	28%
Favor a nuclear freeze	40	82
Goal of containing communism is very important	86	40
Vietnam war was immoral	5	45
Favor military aid to rebels fighting communist-supported governments	100	48
Favor negotiating with terrorists	0	23
In Middle East I sympathize more with Israel	32	63
U.S. efforts to overthrow leftist government of Nicaragua were "excellent" or "good"	70	15

SOURCE: *American Public Opinion and U.S. Foreign Policy, 1987* (Chicago Council on Foreign Relations, 1987), 38.

worried about the power of Congress, thought that containing communism was very important, supported military aid to the contras in Nicaragua and to insurgents in other countries where they were opposing communist governments, and rejected the idea that the war in Vietnam was immoral. The foreign-policy elite not in office expressed very nearly the opposite of these views. When Bill Clinton became president, he brought to the White House attitudes shaped by his youthful opposition to American involvement in Vietnam.

The language of Vietnam continues to color discussions of foreign policy. Almost every military initiative since then has been debated in terms of whether it would lead us into "another Vietnam": sending the marines to Lebanon, invading Grenada, dispatching military advisers to El Salvador, supporting the contras in Nicaragua, helping South American countries fight drug producers, sending troops to the Persian Gulf to force Iraq to abandon its invasion of Kuwait, sending troops to Somalia, and using American air power in Bosnia.

Domino Theory

In 1954 President Eisenhower said that "you have a row of dominoes set up; you knock over the first one, and what will happen to the last one is that it will go over very quickly." He used this analogy to justify giving economic aid to South Vietnam to prevent it, and thus its Southeast Asian neighbors, from being taken over by communists.

Supporters of aid to South Vietnam accepted this **domino theory**; opponents of that aid denied the theory, arguing (as did novelist Norman Mailer) that these countries were not dominoes but "sand castles" that were being engulfed by a "tide of nationalism."

In the 1980s the domino theory was part of the argument about whether we should help El Salvador and support the contras in Nicaragua as a way of keeping Central America from being dominated by Marxist governments.

For the record: after South Vietnam fell to communist North Vietnam, two other nearby dominoes—Cambodia and Laos—also went communist, but Thailand did not.

SOURCE: Adapted from William Safire, *Safire's Political Dictionary* (New York: Ballantine Books, 1978). Used by permission.

The Beginning of a New Era

After more than forty years, the cold war ended. After nearly three-quarters of a century, the Soviet Union collapsed. A new era in American foreign policy began.

These dramatic changes started in 1985 when Mikhail Gorbachev became the Soviet leader. A dedicated Communist, he discovered that Communism was not working. The Soviet Union and its empire were on the brink of economic collapse. Neither the USSR nor its satellite governments in Eastern Europe could feed their people. In Poland a workers' movement, Solidarity, had challenged the government. Disparate ethnic groups inside the USSR were seething with discontent. Inefficiency and corruption were rampant.

Americans holding the antiappeasement view welcomed the fall of the iron curtain and the creation of freely elected governments in Czechoslovakia, East Germany, Hungary, and Poland, but warned that the Soviet Union remained a powerful and dangerously unpredictable force in the world. Gorbachev, they said, may have let go of his empire, but only out of economic necessity, not any fundamental change in Soviet thinking. Given this view, these elites urged the United States not to dismantle its armed forces, not to give direct economic aid to the USSR until it had created more democratic political institutions and a freer economic system, and to be wary of signing any further arms-reduction treaties until it was clear that the USSR had actually abandoned its efforts to impose its will on other nations.

Foreign-policy elites holding the disengagement outlook took a more optimistic view of the changes underway in Moscow. They argued that these changes fundamentally and irreversibly reduced the Soviet threat to the United States and that our policy should be based on that assessment. Since Europe was now safe from Soviet attack, our forces there could be dramatically reduced. Since the USSR no longer had the will to attack the United States, our ballistic missiles, designed to deter such an attack, could be cut back as well. Since the Soviet Union faced an economic crisis that, if not resolved, might lead to more dangerous leaders coming to power, the United States should give economic aid to Gorbachev.

These rival predictions were quickly put to the test in ways that surprised almost everybody. The strength of a worldview is that it draws lessons from history; the weakness of one is that it can be upset by an unexpected turn in history. This turn began on August 19, 1991, when certain top Soviet officials, including the head of the KGB (the Soviet secret police), launched a coup against Gorbachev. He was held captive in his summer home while KGB, military, and party leaders announced that they had assumed power. Boris Yeltsin, the president of Russia,

U.S. MILITARY INTERVENTION IN THE MIDDLE EAST

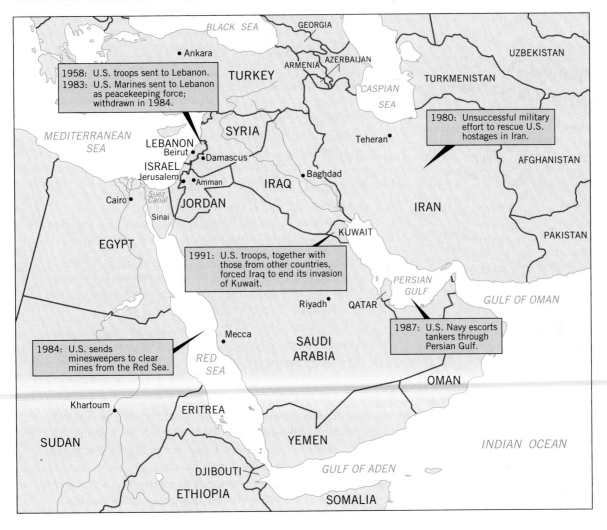

1958: U.S. troops sent to Lebanon.
1983: U.S. Marines sent to Lebanon as peacekeeping force; withdrawn in 1984.

1980: Unsuccessful military effort to rescue U.S. hostages in Iran.

1991: U.S. troops, together with those from other countries, forced Iraq to end its invasion of Kuwait.

1987: U.S. Navy escorts tankers through Persian Gulf.

1984: U.S. sends minesweepers to clear mines from the Red Sea.

denounced the coup and stated that he would not surrender certain Moscow government buildings to the forces controlled by the coup leaders. He called upon Western leaders not to recognize the new government being installed by the coup; they did not. He urged the people of Moscow to rally to his defense. And they did.

On August 21, two days after it began, the coup collapsed and Gorbachev was released. Soon thereafter the plotters were arrested. Yeltsin, whom many Western leaders had previously dismissed as a buffoon who drank too much, had become a hero.

Yeltsin (who as president of Russia headed the largest single part of the USSR) forced Gorbachev to relinquish his powers and his office. But more than Gorbachev was overthrown; the Soviet Union itself was abolished.

On December 8, the leaders of Russia, the Ukraine, and Byelorussia announced that the Soviet Union no longer existed and that each of them, along with several other regions of the former USSR, would become independent states with their own representation in foreign capitals. In order to provide some kind of union for the management of common

U.S. Troops Take Up Position Near Saba Border

★ ★ ★

WASHINGTON, D.C. MARCH 17—The American buildup of military forces near the Saba border continues with the arrival of the 82d Airborne Division and the 3d Armored Division. With more than 400,000 troops in the area, the president now has enough power to attack Saba and force it to abandon the occupied nation of Lophar. Debate rages in Washington over whether Congress will support such a move. It is not clear whether . . .

What Would You Do?

MEMORANDUM

TO: The President
FROM: The Attorney General
SUBJECT: Your power to wage war in the Persian Gulf

Once again a hostile power, The People's Republic of Saba, has invaded its neighbor in the Middle East. By so doing it has threatened many nations friendly to us in that region, placed in jeopardy large oil production facilities, and brought Israel within range of chemical, nuclear, and biological weapons. You have sent U.S. troops to defend the threatened nations. The United Nations Security Council has backed your action. If we fight, we have the ability to defeat Saba. As you know, Congress asserts that only it can authorize, by passing a declaration of war, any American attack on Saba. My staff is divided on this issue. Here, in summary, are the two positions:

1. <u>You should make clear to Congress that you have the right to attack Saba without a declaration of war.</u> Reasons: (a) Previous presidents have waged war without a declaration: Truman in defending South Korea, Johnson in defending South Vietnam, Reagan in invading Grenada, Bush in invading Panama. (b) Only if the president has the credible power to threaten an attack will the rulers of Saba have any incentive to negotiate a peaceful withdrawal. (c) If we do attack, our forces will have the advantage of surprise. (d) Public opinion will support our troops once they are in combat, whatever Congress may say.

2. <u>You should ask Congress for a declaration of war.</u> Reasons: (a) The Constitution clearly says that only Congress has the power to declare war. (b) If Congress is not asked to support you, popular support for your efforts will be undercut. (c) Saba will be more impressed by a united government. (d) When presidents have acted without a congressional declaration, they have usually wound up fighting an unwise war (as did Johnson in Vietnam).

<u>Your decision:</u> Option 1 _____ Option 2 _____

problems, including what to do with the massive Soviet armed forces, a Commonwealth of Independent States was formed. It was governed by a loose confederation (not too different from the Articles of Confederation under which the United States governed itself after declaring its independence from England). The once formidable Soviet Union had fragmented, dramatically altering the landscape of world politics.

America's Role in the New Era

The end of the cold war did not mean the end of American foreign-policy challenges. In some ways, the new challenges were more difficult to manage. Before, many people thought that it was only necessary to decide on the magnitude of the Soviet threat and prepare accordingly. With the collapse of the Soviet Union it became necessary to prepare for any number of hard-to-predict threats. These threats included the following:

- **More coups in Russia:** The coup that toppled Gorbachev may not be the last one. Yeltsin or one of his successors could be overthrown. Reactionary leaders desirous of ending Yeltsin's cooperation with the West could come to power, gaining control of the still formidable Russian armed forces and its arsenal of nuclear weapons.

- **Fighting within and among the remnants of the Soviet empire:** Ethnic warfare erupted in many regions within the former Soviet Union and between Serbs and Croatians within the former nation of Yugoslavia. These conflicts, especially in Yugoslavia, created the possibility that other nations might be drawn in.

U.S. MILITARY INTERVENTION IN CENTRAL AMERICA AND THE CARIBBEAN SINCE 1950

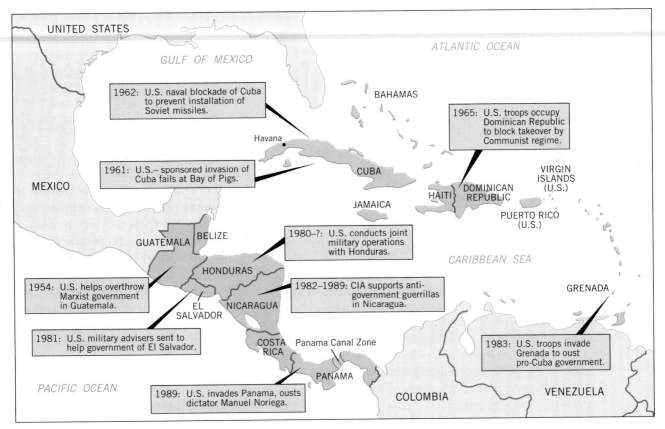

Third World

Originally a French term (*tiers monde*) referring to nations neutral in the cold war between the United Nations and the Soviet Union, the **Third World** now means almost any underdeveloped nation in Africa, Asia, Latin America, or the Middle East.

When the oil-producing nations, such as Saudi Arabia, became wealthy after having succeeded in raising oil prices in the early 1970s, some observers began to use a new phrase, the *Fourth World*, to refer to underdeveloped nations that had no oil reserves, and thus had to pay heavily for imported oil.

And some nations, such as Taiwan and the Republic of Korea, once thought to be Third World because they were underdeveloped, have made such startling economic progress that they are now referred to as the "newly industrialized nations" (NICs).

SOURCE: Adapted from William Safire, *Safire's Political Dictionary* (New York: Ballantine Books, 1978). Used by permission.

- **Ancient antagonisms in such explosive regions as the Middle East:** When there were two rival superpowers, there were limits to how far a Middle-Eastern nation might go in challenging its neighbors for fear of provoking a response from the United States or the USSR. With only one superpower, the United States, that was cutting back on its military strength, there were fewer checks on Middle Eastern military threats.

- **The spread of nuclear weapons:** Saddam Hussein tried to build his own nuclear bomb, and no doubt he and other nations will try again. Many people believe that such weapons exist in North Korea.

How the United States reacts to these possibilities will be heavily influenced by elite opinion. Some argue that the United States cannot be the "world's policeman" and so should cut back drastically on its armed forces. Others rejoin that, while the United States should not intervene everywhere, it is the only power capable of preventing the rise of regional aggressors (such as Saddam Hussein in Iraq) and so it must remain strong, albeit with armed forces organized and equipped in ways different from what was necessary when the USSR posed the major threat.

This disagreement reflects a long-lasting conflict between two worldviews. To some extent, the difference between the containment and the disengagement worldviews corresponds to the difference between conservatives and liberals. But not entirely: when Pat Buchanan, a conservative, challenged George Bush for the 1992 presidential nomination, he argued for the disengagement (or even the old isolationist) worldview. And when the army in Haiti overthrew its democratically elected president, some liberals, such as Senator John Kerry (D., Mass.), argued for a U.S. invasion to put the Haitian president back in power.

The Growing Role of the United Nations

The United Nations has had a long history of efforts to settle conflicts between member nations. Between 1948 and 1993, it sent more than thirty missions to monitor cease-fire agreements, observe national elections to make sure they were fair, or provide security for humanitarian operations. Most of these missions involved small numbers of troops contributed by United Nations members. Before 1991 it was rare for either the Soviet Union or the United States to provide any of these peacekeeping forces; the antagonism between the two great powers made such cooperation almost impossible and the presence of either one alone in a UN force would have undercut the UN's appearance of neutrality.

With the collapse of the Soviet Union and the end of the cold war, the United Nations is no longer dominated by the conflict between the United States and

UNITED NATIONS DEPLOYMENTS, 1993

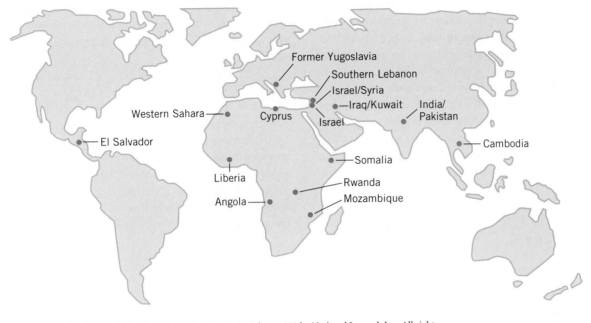

Former Yugoslavia
Southern Lebanon
Israel/Syria
Iraq/Kuwait
India/Pakistan
Western Sahara
Cyprus
Israel
El Salvador
Cambodia
Liberia
Somalia
Angola
Rwanda
Mozambique

the Soviet Union. The United Nations' military effort in Kuwait was organized and largely controlled by the United States and was not opposed by Russia. UN peacekeeping missions have also become more numerous. The UN played a role in sending troops that attempted to restore order in Somalia and that tried to protect humanitarian aid being shipped into what once was Yugoslavia. By 1993 U.S. troops were part of UN missions in seven different locations around the globe.

Some American leaders welcomed this development as the beginning of a new era in which the U.S. would use force in other parts of the world only, or chiefly, as part of a UN effort involving many nations. But other leaders worried that the U.S., as the sole remaining military superpower, ought not to let its forces be directed by an international organization in which the U.S. had but one vote.* The former leaders

* In the UN General Assembly the U.S. has one vote out of 184 members; in the Security Council the U.S. has one vote out of fifteen, but that one Security Council vote entitles it to block any action of which it disapproves.

United Nations peace-keeping forces, once a rarity, are becoming a fixture in many world trouble spots, such as Bosnia.

want the U.S. to work through the UN; the latter ones do not want to see U.S. policy controlled by other nations (many of which have dictatorial or hostile governments). As political conflict erupts around the globe with seemingly increasing frequency and intensity, the United States' relationship to the United Nations is likely to continue to be an important foreign-policy issue. Liberals, especially those with a disengagement worldview, often want the United States to use military force abroad only as part of a United Nations effort. Conservatives, especially those with an antiappeasement worldview, tend to favor acting without United Nations authority or controls.

SUMMARY

The great issues of national diplomacy are shaped by majoritarian politics. The president is the dominant figure, political ideology is important, and interest groups are only moderately important (unless the diplomatic issue involves differential costs and benefits, as it does when dealing with foreign trade).

But the majority opinion is weakly defined. It prefers that the United States mind its own business; when this country does become involved overseas, public opinion does not have strongly held views about most of our international activities except to urge that we put American interests, especially economic ones, first. However, in a crisis or the aftermath of a bold presidential initiative, popular opinion tends to follow the presidential lead.

Given the loose and permissive quality of public opinion, elite opinion is usually very important. Foreign-policy activists tend to hold to one or another rather well-defined worldview, or paradigm (ideology, if you prefer). Before World War II the elite view was *isolationist;* after Pearl Harbor and lasting until Vietnam it displayed the *containment* or antiappeasement perspective; since Vietnam it has been deeply divided between those who still favor containment and those who favor *disengagement* from military commitments.

Elite views are also shaped by the organizational interests of the machinery by which foreign policy is made. That machinery is so large and complex as to be beyond the control of the secretary of state, who is often reduced to being one player among many. Through the National Security Council and the national-security adviser, the president tries to coordinate that machinery, but sometimes he does so in ways that make the NSC staff an independent player with its own agenda.

These executive-branch divisions exacerbate the conflict between the president and Congress over the direction of foreign policy. Since the early 1970s Congress has become more assertive, passing laws (sometimes over presidential vetoes) that curb the president's ability to sell arms abroad or engage in covert operations (the Boland Amendments), that attempt to limit the president's ability to commit troops overseas (the War Powers Act), and that require the CIA to report to congressional committees.

KEY TERMS

worldviews   *p. 595*

isolationism   *p. 597*

containment (*or* antiappeasement)   *p. 597*

iron curtain   *p. 597*

cold war   *p. 597*

domino theory   *p. 600*

Third World   *p. 604*

SUGGESTED READINGS

Allison, Graham T. *Essence of Decision: Explaining the Cuban Missile Crisis.* Boston: Little, Brown, 1971. Shows how the decision made by a president during a major crisis was shaped by bureaucratic and organizational factors.

Blechman, Barry M., and Stephen S. Kaplan. *Force without War: U.S. Armed Forces as a Political Instrument.* Washington, D.C.: Brookings Institution, 1978. Describes how and with what effect American military power is used as an instrument of foreign policy.

Cohen, Benjamin J. *The Question of Imperialism.* New York: Basic Books, 1973. Careful analysis of theories claiming that economic motives control American foreign policy.

Destler, I. M. *Presidents, Bureaucrats, and Foreign Policy.* Princeton, N.J.: Princeton University Press, 1972. Analyzes the perennial struggle between the White House and the State Department.

Dougherty, James, and Robert Pfaltzgraff. *American Foreign Policy: FDR to Reagan.* New York: Harper & Row, 1986. Brief history of U.S. foreign policy since 1932.

Henkin, Louis. *Foreign Affairs and the Constitution.* New York: Norton, 1975. How the Supreme Court has interpreted the constitutional sources of the war and foreign-affairs powers.

Hilsman, Roger. *The Politics of Policymaking in Defense and Foreign Affairs.* Englewood Cliffs, N.J.: Prentice-Hall, 1987. Good review of the various theories of how foreign policy is made, by a scholar who was also a State Department official in the 1960s.

Kissinger, Henry. *White House Years.* Boston: Little, Brown, 1979. A brilliant insider's account of the politics and tactics of "high diplomacy" during the Nixon administration.

Mueller, John E. *War, Presidents, and Public Opinion.* New York: Wiley, 1973. Best summary of the relationship between presidential foreign-policy decisions and public opinion.

21

Military Policy

- ➤ How the military is organized
- ➤ Interservice rivalry
- ➤ The defense budget
- ➤ Defense spending
- ➤ What we get for our money
- ➤ The "$435 hammer"
- ➤ Congress versus the president

The politics of the military are captured in the movies about the military. In *Heartbreak Ridge* the American invasion of Grenada is a skillful maneuver of tough marines led by sergeant-major Clint Eastwood. But in *Platoon* land warfare is a bloody, confused, brutalizing experience of angry men and incompetent leaders. In *Top Gun* Tom Cruise, a sassy but superb naval aviator, flies an F-14 jet fighter with extraordinary precision. But in *Dr. Strangelove* pilots are dolts led by mindless generals and mad scientists.

The inconsistent images are matched by apparently inconsistent facts: in 1985 most Americans applauded the beautifully coordinated maneuver in which navy fighters forced down an Egyptian airliner carrying the terrorists who had hijacked a cruise ship; two years earlier most Americans were enraged by stories that "idiots" in the navy had paid $435 for a common hammer.

One interpretation of this imagery is that national defense is a vital function of the federal government whose goals and means are determined by debates about the international balance of power. As in any large venture, there are honest mistakes, agonizing struggles, and bureaucratic stupidities. In the language of this book defense policy making is an example of majoritarian politics, often reinforced by deep feelings of patriotism but sometimes fouled up by inevitable human error.

Another interpretation is that defense policy making is nothing but a gigantic boondoggle in which innocent men and women are exposed to unnecessary hazards by the pressures of client groups and the struggles of competing interests, all in the service of dubious national objectives that sometimes are merely a cloak for the economic imperialism of multinational corporations.

In the first view the benefits and costs of national defense are widely distributed: everybody is protected, and every taxpayer foots the bill. Accordingly the size and purposes of our military establishment will broadly reflect the realities of our international

After Palestinian terrorists hijacked the steamship *Achille Lauro* in the Mediterranean, they attempted to flee to Egypt on this airliner, but United States Navy jets forced it to land in Italy, where the hijackers were arrested and put on trial.

situation and the shape of public opinion. Before World War II we had a small standing army because there were no obvious threats to our security and because public opinion was isolationist. Since that time we have maintained a large military establishment because our role in the world has grown and public opinion has been concerned about the Soviet threat. We do not always agree about military matters—the debate over the wisdom of our intervention in Vietnam was bitter and lasting—but at least we are debating national purpose, not private advantage.

In the second view the only real beneficiaries of military spending are generals, admirals, big corporations, and members of Congress whose districts get fat defense contracts. Everyone pays, but only some well-placed clients benefit. The size of the defense budget reflects the lobbying skills of Pentagon bureaucrats, not the realities of any threat to the United States. Reductions in international tensions and the U.S.–Soviet arms race were frustrated by the stake that the **military-industrial complex** (the supposedly unified political bloc consisting of the Defense Department and industries that build military weapons) had in large defense budgets.

To understand what the people who hold these views are arguing about, we must first describe the structure of defense decision making and how the defense budget is determined. Then we'll turn to the politics of billion-dollar missiles and $435 hammers.

The Structure of Defense Decision Making

The formal structure within which decisions about national defense are made was in large part created after World War II, but it reflects concerns that go back at least to the time of the Founding. Chief among these is the persistent desire by citizens to ensure civilian control over the military.

The National Security Act of 1947 and its subsequent amendments created a Department of Defense (see Figure 21.1). It is headed by the secretary of defense, under whom serve the secretaries of the army, the air force, and the navy as well as the Joint Chiefs of Staff. The secretary of defense must be a civilian (though one former general, George C. Marshall, was allowed by Congress to be the secretary) who exercises, on behalf of the president, command authority over the defense establishment. The secretary of the army, the secretary of the navy,* and the secretary of the air force are subordinate to the secretary of defense. Unlike him, they do not attend cabinet meetings or sit on the National Security Council. In essence they manage the "housekeeping" functions of the various armed services under the general

---

* The secretary of the navy manages two services: the navy and the marine corps.

FIGURE 21.1 Department of Defense

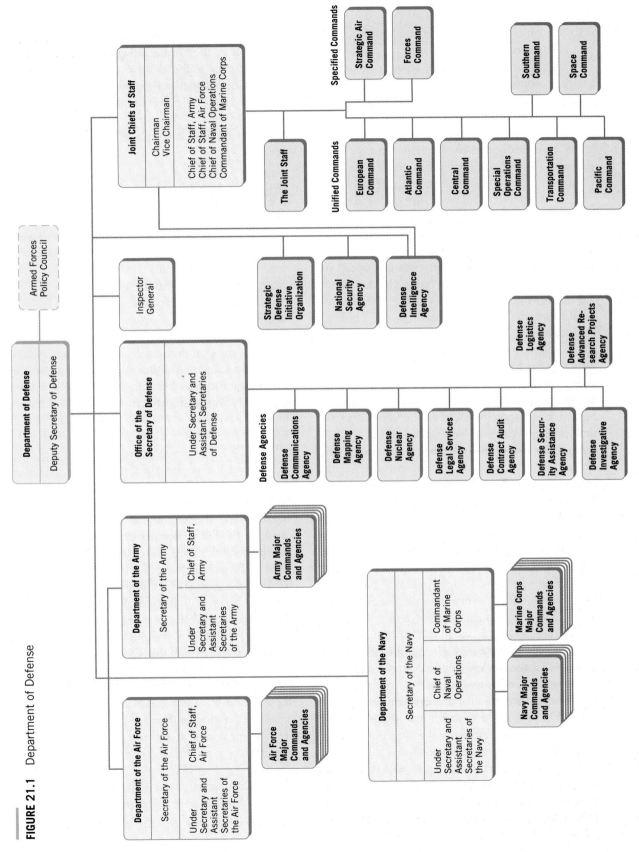

SOURCE: *The United States Government Manual, 1989/90,* 179.

direction of the secretary of defense and his deputy and assistant secretaries of defense.

The four armed services are separate entities; by law they cannot be merged or commanded by a single military officer, and each has the right to communicate directly with Congress. There are two reasons for having separate uniformed services functioning within a single department: the fear of many citizens that a unified military force might become too powerful politically, and the desire of each service to preserve its traditional independence and autonomy. The result, of course, is a good deal of interservice rivalry and bickering, but this is precisely what Congress intended when it created the Department of Defense. Rivalry and bickering, it was felt, would ensure that Congress would receive the maximum amount of information about military affairs and would enjoy the largest opportunity to affect military decisions.

Interservice rivalry has provided just this kind of opportunity to Congress. In 1948 the air force wanted to take over naval aviation; the navy counterattacked by criticizing the effectiveness of air force bombers and argued instead for building large aircraft carriers. When the navy was refused permission to build the "supercarriers" that it had in mind, several admirals resigned in protest. In the 1960s the navy and air force argued again, this time over a new fighter aircraft (the TFX), only one type of which was to be built. The air force wanted a plane to fly over long distances and to carry nuclear weapons; the navy wanted one to take off and land from aircraft carriers and to fly at high speed for short distances. The air force was seeking to enlarge the role of manned aircraft as a major part of our deterrent forces; the navy wanted to preserve the role of the carrier as a strategic force. In the 1970s another debate erupted, this time over whether the navy should build more large, nuclear-powered aircraft carriers or shift to smaller, oil-fueled ones.

Though disputes like these often employ the usual techniques of bureaucratic infighting—leaking information to the press, mobilizing sympathetic members of Congress, hiring rival civilian "experts"—they are not *merely* infighting, for they focus attention on major issues of defense policy.

Congress does not want a single military command headed by an all-powerful general or admiral, but neither does it want the services to be so autonomous or their heads so equal that coordination and efficiency suffer. In 1986 Congress passed and the president signed a defense-reorganization plan. Under its terms the power of officers who coordinate the activities of different services was increased. The 1947 structure was left in place, but with revised procedures.

Joint Chiefs of Staff   The Joint Chiefs of Staff (JCS) is a committee consisting of the uniformed heads of each of the military services (army, navy, air force, and marine corps), plus a chairman and a (nonvoting) vice chairman appointed by the president and confirmed by the Senate. The JCS is not part of the chain of military command; instead it serves an important advisory role in national defense planning. Before 1986 the JCS was a committee of equals. Since each service had one vote, the JCS operated by consensus: it rarely, if ever, made a decision opposed by any single service (and thus rarely made an important decision). Since 1986 the chairman of the Joint Chiefs has been designated the president's principal military adviser in an effort to give him more influence over the JCS. It remains to be seen whether the JCS will be any better equipped to make tough decisions under the new law than it was under the old.

Joint Staff   Assisting the JCS is a Joint Staff consisting of several hundred officers from each of the four services. The staff draws up plans for various military contingencies. Before 1986 each staff member was loyal to the service whose uniform he or she wore. As a result the staff was often "joint" in name only, since few members were willing to take a position opposed by their service for fear of being passed over for promotion. The 1986 law changed this in two ways: First, it gave the chairman of the JCS control over the Joint Staff; now it works for the chairman, not for the JCS as a group. Second, it required the secretary of defense to establish guidelines to ensure that officers assigned to the Joint Staff (or to other interservice bodies) were promoted at the same rate as officers whose careers were spent entirely with their own services.

Unified Commands   Most of the combat forces of the United States are assigned to one or another of eight "unified commands" or two "specified commands."

Five of the unified commands control our forces assigned to geographic areas—Europe, the Pacific (including the Far East and Southeast Asia), the Atlantic, Central America (called the Southern Command), and the Middle East (called the Central Command). Three handle specialized forces—space and its defense, transportation, and special operations (such as the army Rangers and navy Seal Teams). The specified commands are responsible for strategic missiles and bombers and for defense forces in the United States. Before 1986 these commands were often unified in name only: each service component (for example, the navy) would tend to take orders from its own brass in Washington rather than from the commander in chief (CINC) of the unified command. The 1986 law gave more power to the CINCs. The Central Command in the Middle East ("CentCom") was in charge of our forces fighting against Iraq.

The Services   Each military service is headed by a civilian secretary—one for the army, the navy (including the marine corps), and the air force—plus a senior military officer: the chief of staff of the army, the chief of naval operations, the commandant of the marine corps, and the chief of staff of the air force. The civilian secretaries are in charge of purchasing,

auditing, congressional relations, and public affairs. The military chiefs oversee the discipline and training of their uniformed forces and in addition represent their services on the Joint Chiefs of Staff.

The Chain of Command   Under the Constitution the president is the commander in chief of the armed forces. The chain of command runs from him to the secretary of defense (also a civilian), and from him to the various unified and specified commands. These orders may be transmitted through the Joint Chiefs of Staff or its chairman, but by law the chairman of the JCS does not have command authority over the combat forces. At the top, civilians are in charge.

No one yet knows how well the 1986 changes will work, though the quick victory in the 1991 Persian Gulf war was thought by some to be the answer. Critics of the Pentagon have been urging changes along these lines at least since 1947. But others say that unless the armed services are actually merged, interservice rivalry will continue. Still others argue that even the degree of coordination intended by the 1986 act is excessive; the country, in their view, is better served by having wholly autonomous services. What is striking is that many members of Congress who once would have insisted on this separation-of-services view without question voted for the 1986 law.

The Joint Chiefs of Staff as of April, 1994, left to right: General Carl E. Mundy, USMC; General Gordon R. Sullivan, USA; General Merrill A. Mc-Peak, USAF; Admiral Frank B. Kelso II, USN; General John M. Shalikashvili, USA, Chairman; Admiral William A. Owens, USN, Vice Chairman.

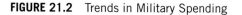

FIGURE 21.2 Trends in Military Spending

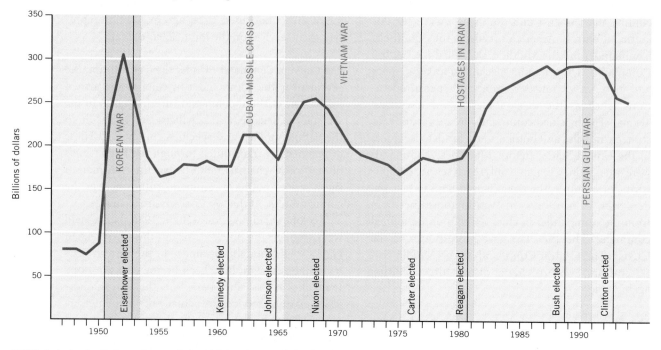

NOTE: Budget authority figures for years before 1985 have been recalculated to disregard the effect of inflation and show costs in 1985 dollars.

SOURCE: Adapted and updated from the *New York Times* (May 14, 1985). Copyright © 1985 by the *New York Times* Company. Reprinted by permission. Updated by the author.

The Defense Budget

There are two important things to know about the defense budget—how big it is and how it is divided up. The first reflects majoritarian politics, the second interest-group bargaining, with the "interests" in this case being the military services and their allies in Congress.

Total Spending

Throughout most of our history, the United States has not maintained large military forces during peacetime. For instance, the percentage of the gross national product (GNP) spent on defense in 1935, on the eve of World War II, was about the same as it was in 1870, when we were on the eve of nothing in particular.[1] We armed when a war broke out, then we disarmed when the war ended. But all of that changed in 1950.

In that year we rearmed to fight a war in Korea, but when it was over we did not completely disarm. The reason was our containment policy toward the Soviet Union. For about forty years—from the outbreak of the Korean War in 1950 to the collapse of the Soviet Union in 1990—American military spending was driven by our desire to contain the Soviet Union and its allies. The Soviet Union had brought under its control most of Eastern Europe; would it also invade Western Europe? Russia had always wanted access to the oil and warm-water ports of the Middle East; would it someday invade or subvert Iran? The Soviet Union was willing to help North Korea invade South Korea and North Vietnam to invade South Vietnam; would it next use an ally to threaten the United States? Soviet leaders supported "wars of national liberation" in Africa and Latin America; would they succeed in turning more and more nations against the United States?

To meet these threats the United States built up a military system that was designed to repel a Soviet

FIGURE 21.3 Public Sentiment on Defense Spending, 1960–1990

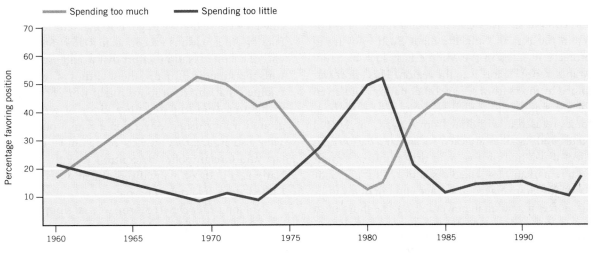

SOURCE: Gallup Poll data, reported by Kim Neighbor.

invasion of Western Europe and at the same time help allies resist smaller-scale invasions or domestic uprisings. Figure 21.2 depicts the dramatic increase in military spending in 1950. It also shows that even after we decided to have a large military force there were many ups and downs in the actual level of spending. After the Korean war was over, we spent less; when we became involved in Vietnam, we spent more; when the Soviet Union invaded Afghanistan we spent more again. These changes in spending tended to reflect changes in public opinion about the defense budget (see Figure 21.3).

Military spending in the United States rides a roller coaster. There is greater change in American defense outlays than in any other part of the federal budget. But until around 1991, any decreases in military spending were limited by the continuing fear of Soviet domination. For decades, America raised and lowered its defense spending, but always with an eye on the ever-increasing Soviet military budget.

Then, suddenly, the Soviet Union ceased to exist. The troops that once occupied Eastern Europe and Afghanistan withdrew to Russia; there were huge cuts in Russian military spending; and military and economic aid to its long-time ally, Cuba, was suspended. For the first time since 1950, American leaders were faced with defining the principles of our military policy (and thus the size of our defense budget) in the absence of a Soviet threat.

The debate that occurred, and is still continuing, largely reflected personal beliefs and political ideologies,[2] that is to say, *majoritarian* politics. Liberals demanded sharp cuts in defense spending, weapons procurement, and military personnel, arguing that, with the Soviet threat ended, it was time to collect our "peace dividend" and divert funds from the military to domestic social programs. Conservatives agreed that some military cuts were in order, but argued that the world was still a dangerous place and, therefore, that a strong (and well-funded) military remained essential to the nation's defense. This disagreement reflected different predictions about what the future would be like. Many liberals (and some conservatives, such as Pat Buchanan, who believed that America should "stay at home") argued that we could not afford to be the "world's policeman." Many conservatives (and some liberals) responded by saying that Russia was still a military powerhouse that might once again fall under the control of ruthless leaders and that many other nations hostile to the United States (such as Libya, North Korea, Iran, and Iraq) were becoming potential adversaries as they tried to build or acquire nuclear weapons and missile systems.

Saddam Hussein soon provided evidence that international aggression had by no means ended with the demise of the Soviet Union. In 1990, Iraq invaded and conquered Kuwait, a small oil-producing country in the Persian Gulf. President Bush, moving to protect our allies in the Middle East such as Saudi Arabia, sent U.S. forces to the region. This effort was joined by forces from several other nations and given the blessing of the United Nations. When the Iraqi forces refused to withdraw from Kuwait, the United States and its allies attacked in January of 1991. In short order Iraq's forces were driven out of Kuwait with remarkably few allied casualties. Although Saddam Hussein managed to salvage enough of his military forces to remain in power in Iraq, the short-lived war was viewed by most Americans as an astounding military success.

Operation Desert Storm (as it was called) postponed the debate over military spending but it did not end it. The U.S. victory was so swift and stunning that it convinced many people that this country could not be challenged by anyone. In this view, we

Saddam Hussein, ruler of Iraq.

could afford to rely on the "smart weapons" produced by our defense scientists and would not need a lot of men and women under arms. These people also came to believe that we ought not intervene in the affairs of other nations except, as in Desert Storm, as part of a United Nations effort that would provide us with the support of many allies. Critics of this view rejoined that smart weapons might work brilliantly in fighting Iraq but for other kinds of wars only ground troops using conventional arms would win. They also argued that the U.S. could not let its military and foreign policy be controlled by the United Nations, a body of many diverse interests where the United States had only one vote.

Not long after Desert Storm, we sent troops to aid the UN peacekeeping effort in Somalia, a country where millions of people were starving because a civil war had disrupted the economy and blocked the distribution of relief supplies sent from abroad. While this was going on, the former nation of Yugoslavia was collapsing into a civil war that produced unspeakable atrocities against innocent civilians. For a while, some American leaders thought we should intervene there, but eventually Washington decided against it.

Just as important as the debate over U.S. involvement in these world events was the reality of how defense spending is allocated within the overall federal budget. It is almost the only part of the federal budget that can easily be cut by the president and Congress. Presidents looking for money with which to reduce the deficit or finance new programs are irresistibly drawn to the defense budget. President Bush had begun to make cuts in military spending following the breakup of the Soviet Union. By 1993 the army was reduced from eighteen divisions to fourteen, the navy from 546 ships to 443; the air force from 24 wings of fighter planes to 16. President Clinton sought to make even deeper cuts. To do so he instructed his secretary of defense to conduct a "bottom-up" review of our defense needs. This review concluded that the biggest threat now facing the United States arose from the possibility of smaller, "regional" wars breaking out in various parts of the world—wars like the Iraqi invasion of Kuwait. The secretary and the Joint Chiefs of Staff decided that the United States had to have a military force capable of fighting two regional wars at the same time. The forces they proposed would reduce the army even further (to 10 divisions), the navy from 443 to 346 ships (including 12 aircraft carriers), and the air force from 16 to 13 fighter wings. Only the marine corps was spared deep cuts on the theory that the marines are especially trained and equipped to intervene in remote parts of the world (see Table 21.1). There were also to be cuts in the number of new weapons purchased.

But making big cuts in new weapons carries a risk: if the cuts are too deep, the companies with the ability to make these weapons will go out of business. For example, there are only two American companies able to build modern submarines and only a few able to build high-performance combat aircraft. The Pentagon plan, therefore, called for purchasing some submarines and aircraft that were not strictly necessary in order to keep these production lines, and the skilled workers employed by them, in existence. As we shall see, keeping a defense plant open is not simply a matter of defense policy; it also is a matter of interest-group and client politics.

By the end of 1993, Congress generally supported the Clinton plan, but with continuing demands for money to fund domestic programs or reduce the deficit and with many members of Congress concerned that our military forces were being cut either too fast or not fast enough, the debate about the level of military spending is likely to go on for many years.

TABLE 21.1 U.S. Military Forces Before and After the Breakup of the Soviet Union

Service	Before 1991	1993 Strength	1993 Reduction Plan
Army			
Active divisions	18	14	10
National Guard divisions	10	6	5
Navy			
Aircraft carriers	15	13	11
Training carriers	1	0	1
Ships	546	443	346
Air Force			
Active fighter wings	24	16	13
Reserve fighter wings	12	12	7
Marine Corps			
Active duty troops	197,000	182,000	174,000
Reserve troops	44,000	42,000	42,000
Strategic Nuclear Forces			
Ballistic missile submarines	34	22	18
Strategic bombers	301	201	Up to 184
ICBMs	1,000	787	500

SOURCE: *Congressional Quarterly Weekly Report* (September 4, 1993): 2350.

The Pentagon, headquarters of the United States armed forces.

Allocating Defense Dollars

Presidents may set, within limits, total military spending, but they have a much harder time changing the allocation of funds among the various services. If majoritarian politics governs the first decision, interest-group politics shape the second.

In the United States—and probably in every nation—the army, the navy, the marine corps, and the air force can each mobilize important political allies if threatened with a loss of resources relative to the other services. It is thus much easier for a president or secretary of defense to require that all services accept an across-the-board cut in budgets, equally applicable to all, than to compel one service to accept a cut while another service enjoys an increase.

The Joint Chiefs of Staff, composed of representatives of each service, usually will recommend unanimously policies that benefit all services equally and will accept (reluctantly) policies that penalize all equally. Members are obviously incapable of making choices that would favor one service over another. In any coordinating committee each member will tacitly agree to support the favored positions of every other member in exchange for support for his own favored position. Though there have been exceptions when the joint chiefs split on major issues, in general they follow this pattern.

This support for each service is reinforced by members of the congressional committees who handle its authorizations and appropriations. At one time each military service was overseen by separate committees in the House and the Senate, but after World War II these committees were merged into a single House Armed Services Committee and a single Senate Armed Services Committee. There remain within these committees strong congressional advocates of one or the other service. There is, for example, within the House Armed Services Committee a Subcommittee on Seapower whose members regularly support larger budget authorizations for the navy than even the Pentagon requests. In 1978 the subcommittee proposed a 68 percent increase in the Carter administration's request for funds with which to build navy ships.

As a result of these constraints, the share of the total defense budget going to each service changes very slowly. Each major service usually receives roughly a third of the defense budget. In peacetime the army share will be somewhat lower, since the number of soldiers tends to fluctuate between wartime and peacetime more than the number of sailors or air force personnel.

The key allocative decisions thus become incremental ones—decisions about what new things to add to a service's existing budget rather than decisions about transferring a function from one service to another. Usually these involve the purchase of major new weapons. Over one-third of the total defense budget is devoted to weapons research, development, and procurement. The more expensive of these weapons systems, such as the B-1 and B-2 bombers, the MX missile, the Trident nuclear submarine, and the M1 tank, become the subject of intense political debate involving the Pentagon, the White House, the Congress, and various interest groups. Interest groups include not only weapons manufacturers but scientists and private defense budget analysts in such think tanks as RAND, the Brookings Institution and the American Enterprise Institute.

In these debates many factors—strategic, economic, and political—come to the fore. The proposal to build the B-1 bomber, for example, involved arguments over whether we needed a supersonic intercontinental bomber; whether such a bomber, even if valuable, would cost too much; and whether making such an investment would have desirable effects on the economy of those states in which major components would be produced. Each year that funds were requested for developing the B-1, a prolonged discussion occurred, with frequently close votes in Congress. President Carter terminated the program, but President Reagan revived it, and the bombers were built.

The congressional role in deciding on weapons systems has changed somewhat over the years. Before World War II Congress often made, based on military advice, the most detailed decisions on what equipment to buy, what bases to open, and where ships and army units were to be located. During the war it retreated from this activist stance in deference to military opinion; the all-out nature of the war effort and the popularity of the cause dissuaded members of Congress from acting in a way that might be interpreted as hindering the fighting forces.

The national mood has changed with regard to military affairs. An enthusiastic parade celebrated the end of the war in Europe on May 7, 1945, and the role of the armed forces in that conflict. Forty years later protesters objected vehemently to money spent on weapons.

After the war Congress again became assertive, but typically in favor of different or larger military programs than those proposed by the president. For example, Congress favored a larger marine corps and a larger air force than President Truman. When Congress appropriated more money for these purposes than Truman wanted, he refused to spend it.

Congress was also deeply involved in postwar decisions regarding the B-36 bomber, the navy's "supercarriers," the choice among competing missile systems, and the building of new fighter aircraft such as the TFX. While a senator, John F. Kennedy criticized President Eisenhower's emphasis on strategic weapons (bombers and missiles armed with nuclear bombs) at the expense of conventional ground forces. After he became president in 1961, Kennedy began to build up these ground forces and encouraged the creation of the "Green Beret" special-forces units.

Throughout this period Congress was expanding its power to affect certain military decisions. In the 1950s it made military-construction appropriations subject to an annual authorization. In the 1960s it made the procurement of weapons systems subject to annual authorization.

During the latter part of the 1960s congressional interest in these matters sharpened and shifted its tone. Congress began to take a more critical stance toward the military. This reflected the growing unpopularity of the war in Vietnam, the increase in the influence of interest groups (such as liberal scientists with experience in weapons research) that opposed various new weapons systems, and a lessened popular confidence in military expertise. Unlike the late 1940s and early 1950s, when a decision to go ahead with the development of the hydrogen bomb could be made by the president acting alone without extensive congressional debate, since the late 1960s almost every new weapons system is subjected to intensive discussion.

For example, in 1969 the proposed antiballistic missile system barely survived congressional and interest-group opposition (in the Senate a motion to defeat the plan lost in a tie vote, fifty to fifty). Ultimately the president scaled down the plan to just one installation, and in 1975 Congress voted to close down even that facility.

In the 1980s the most controversial new weapon system was the strategic defense initiative (SDI), more popularly called "Star Wars." President Reagan proposed building a system that would intercept enemy missiles before they could reach this country. No one doubted that such a system would be complex and costly. The debate over it reflected both majoritarian politics, with heavy attention to philosophical and ideological issues, and interest-group politics, with keen rivalries among the armed services and prospective contractors.

The philosophical issues included the system's cost and feasibility as well as its likely success in actually knocking down enemy missiles or deterring an enemy from launching missiles. Conservatives argued that, though costly, it was feasible and a better way of protecting the United States than relying on our ability to blow up Soviet cities after they had attempted to blow up ours. Liberals argued that it was not feasible and that the system of "mutual assured destruction" (MAD), whereby each of the superpowers deterred the other through the threat of massive retaliation, had worked for many decades and would continue to work in the future.

The interest-group politics involved the armed services and the contractors. Many service leaders privately did not favor Star Wars because the program would cause a big change in their customary missions. The air force, for example, operated

the land-based intercontinental ballistic missiles (ICBMs) on which "mutual assured destruction" depended. If Star Wars were effective, the need for these missiles might be greatly reduced. But many defense contractors and the states in which they were located favored SDI because it held out the promise of big contracts.

For SDI, as for every other major new defense measure, congressional politics follows a two-stage process. In the first, members debate the merits of the proposal. Ideology plays a large role. If the proposal is adopted, then members maneuver to get contracts for their districts. Constituency interests play a large role. In the first stage strong conservatives will vote for increased military spending even though it may not benefit their district, and strong liberals will oppose it even if a bigger budget might be good for them. But in the second stage both wings of Congress work to get the benefits. For example, it is hard to find a senator more critical of defense spending than Edward Kennedy of Massachusetts. But when it comes to getting jet-engine contracts for the General Electric plant in Massachusetts, it is hard to find a more effective senator.

What Do We Buy for Our Money?

We buy people, of course—soldiers, sailors, airmen, and airwomen (see Table 21.1). They are the most expensive part of the defense budget. Then we buy hardware, of roughly two kinds—big-ticket items, like aircraft carriers and bombers, and small-ticket items, like hammers and screwdrivers. Each of these kinds of hardware has its own politics. Finally, we buy "readiness"—training, supplies, munitions, fuel, and food.

Personnel

From before World War II until 1973 the United States relied on the draft to obtain military personnel. Then, at the end of the Vietnam War, it replaced the draft with the all-volunteer force (AVF). After getting off to a rocky start, the AVF began to improve thanks to increases in military pay and rising civilian unemployment. Abolishing the draft had been politically popular: nobody likes being drafted, and even in congressional districts that otherwise are staunch supporters of a strong defense, the voters tell their representatives that they do not want to return to the draft.

If the armed forces continues to have 1.6 million people in uniform, Congress may have to consider reinstating the draft. The reason: the declining birth rate—the "baby bust"—means that between 1979 and 1990 there was a 13 percent drop in the number of young adults between the ages of eighteen and twenty-four, with another 7 percent decline projected by 1996.[3] That means that unless there is a high civilian unemployment rate or a big increase in military pay, the armed forces might not be able to meet their recruiting targets.

Of late the size of the armed forces has been shrinking; in 1994 there were 1.6 million men and women in uniform, down from 2.1 million just six years earlier. This decline may make finding recruits easier than it would have been had the armed forces remained at their cold war size.

The problem of finding recruits has been politically less important than the question of who shall be a recruit. There has been a steady increase in the percentage of women in the military (by 1990, they constituted 10 percent of the total). For a long time, however, they were barred by law from serving in combat roles. (What constitutes a "combat role" is a bit difficult to say, since even personnel far from the main fighting can be hit by an enemy bomb or artillery shell.) In 1993 Congress ended the legal ban on women being assigned to navy combat ships and air force fighter jets and by 1994 between four and five hundred women were serving on three aircraft carriers. Congress must still be consulted in advance if women are to serve in ground combat forces (such as in front-line infantry or tank units), but soon they may be in those positions as well.

The presence of homosexuals in the military has proved much harder to resolve. Until 1993 it was the long-standing policy of the U.S. armed forces to bar homosexuals from entering the military and to discharge them if they were discovered serving. Gay and lesbian rights organizations had long protested this exclusion. In 1993 a gay soldier won a lawsuit against the army for having discharged him; he settled for back pay and retirement benefits in exchange for a promise not to reenlist. In 1993 another judge or-

The military modified its ban on gays and lesbians serving in the armed forces: now the policy is "don't ask, don't tell."

dered the navy to reinstate a discharged sailor who had revealed on national television that he was a homosexual. In response to the growing controversy, presidential candidate Bill Clinton promised to lift the official ban on gays and lesbians serving in the military if he were elected to office.

Once in office he discovered that it was not that easy. Many members of the armed forces believed that knowingly serving alongside and living in close quarters with gays and lesbians would create unnecessary tension and harm military morale and unit cohesion. The Joint Chiefs of Staff opposed lifting the ban and several key members of Congress said they would try to pass a law reaffirming the ban. President Clinton was forced to settle for a compromise: "don't ask, don't tell." Under this policy, persons entering or serving in the military will not be asked to reveal their sexual orientation and will be allowed to serve provided they do not engage in homosexual conduct. If a person says he or she is a homosexual it will not be automatic grounds for a discharge but it may be grounds for launching an investigation to see whether rules against homosexual conduct have been violated.

In 1994 the new Pentagon rules designed to implement this policy went into effect. They are sure to lead to new lawsuits. For example, what constitutes homosexual conduct? Going to a gay bar? Holding hands in public with a person of the same sex?

Big-Ticket Hardware

Whenever the Pentagon buys a new submarine, airplane, or missile, we hear about **cost overruns.** In the 1950s actual costs were three times greater than estimated costs; by the 1960s things were only slightly better—actual costs were twice estimated costs.[4]

There are five main reasons for these overruns. First, it is hard to know in advance what something that has never existed before will cost once you build it. People who have remodeled their homes know this all too well. So do government officials who build new subways or congressional office buildings. It is no different with a B-2 bomber or a Trident submarine.

Second, people who want to persuade Congress to appropriate money for a new airplane or submarine have an incentive to underestimate the cost. To get the weapon approved, its sponsors tell Congress how little it will cost; once the weapon is under construction, the sponsors go back to Congress for additional money to cover "unexpected" cost increases. Similarly contractors who want the Pentagon to build their new device have an incentive to underestimate the costs and then increase them after the contract is granted.

Third, the Pentagon officials who decide what kind of new aircraft they want are drawn from the ranks of those who will fly it. These officers naturally want the best airplane (or ship or tank) that money can buy. As air force General Carl "Tooey" Spaatz once put it: "A second-best aircraft is like a second-best poker hand. No damn good."[5] But what exactly

The debate over defense spending usually centers on new weapons systems, such as these Bradley armored personnel carriers on maneuvers at Fort Hood, Texas.

is the "best" airplane? Is it the fastest one? Or the most maneuverable one? Or the most reliable one? Or the one with the longest range? Pentagon officials have a tendency to answer: "All of the above." Of course trying to produce all of the above is incredibly expensive (and sometimes impossible). But asking for the expensive (or the impossible) is understandable, given that the air force officers who buy it will also fly it. This tendency to ask for everything at once is called **gold plating.**

Fourth, many new weapons are purchased from a single contractor. This is called sole sourcing. A contractor is hired to design, develop, and build an airplane. As a result there is no competition, and so the manufacturer has no strong incentive to control costs. And if the sole manufacturer gets into financial trouble, the government, seeking to avoid a shutdown of all production, has an incentive to bail the company out.

Fifth, when Congress wants to cut the military budget, it often does so not by canceling a new weapons system but by stretching out the number of years during which it is purchased. Say that Congress wants to buy one hundred F-14s, twenty-five a year for four years. To give the appearance of cutting the budget, it will decide to buy only fifteen the first year and take five years to buy the rest. Or it will, say, build twenty now and then ask again next year for the authority to build more. But start-and-stop production decisions and stretching out production over more years drives up the cost of building each unit. If Ford built cars this way, it would go broke.

There are ways to cope with four of these five problems. You cannot do much about the first, ignorance, but you can do something about low estimates, gold plating, sole sourcing, and stretch-outs. If the Pentagon gave realistic cost estimates initially (verified perhaps by another agency), if the Pentagon were to ask industry to produce a weapon that met a few critical performance requirements (instead of meeting every requirement that one could think of), if two or more manufacturers were given contracts to compete in the design and development of the new weapon and then compete in its manufacture, if Congress would stop trying to "cut" the budget using the smoke-and-mirrors technique of stretch-outs, then we would hear a lot less about cost overruns.

And some of these things are being done. There is more competition and less sole sourcing in weapons procurement today than once was the case.[6] But the political incentives to avoid other changes are very powerful. Pentagon officers will always want "the best." They will always have an incentive to understate costs. Congress will always be tempted to use stretch-outs as a way of avoiding hard budget choices.

Small-Ticket Items

It may be easy to understand why jet fighters cost so much, but what about $435 hammers?

In fact there never was a $435 hammer. It was a myth. The myth grew out of a complicated feature of Pentagon accounting procedures, procedures exploited for publicity purposes by a member of Congress who thought that he had found an issue, and picked up on by news media fascinated by such a dramatic story. If you want to understand why somebody might think that the navy had paid $435 for a hammer, read the accompanying box on page 624.

The issue in buying small-ticket items is not the hammer problem, it is the coffee-maker problem. Everybody knows what a hammer is and where to buy one—for about $20, tops. But a coffee maker, *if it is especially designed to function on a military plane,* is another matter. If the plane is going to lurch about in rough air, if the coffee maker has to fit into an odd place, it will occur to somebody in the Pentagon that what is needed is a specially designed coffee maker.

Once somebody thinks like that, the coffee maker is purchased in the same way as a new jet fighter, and with results just as bad. The design is gold-plated (for example, "Let's have a coffee maker that can fly upside down"), the contract is let out to a sole source with no competition, the cost is underestimated, and the production run is limited to ten coffee makers. The result? A coffee maker that costs $7,600.[7]

Readiness

Presumably we have a peacetime military so that we will be ready for wartime. Presumably, therefore, the peacetime forces will devote a lot of their time and money to improving their readiness.

The $435 Hammer

For a long time the Pentagon paid its suppliers using an accounting method called the equal-allocation formula. Here is how it worked:

Suppose that you are selling the Pentagon equipment with which to fix a radar set. There are 250 of these parts, some extremely complex and costly (such as a piece of computer hardware) and others very simple and cheap (such as a hammer). Your total cost is the cost of manufacturing each item, plus your overhead costs. These overhead costs include the rent for your factory, the salary for your bookkeepers, and your taxes and insurance premiums. You want to charge the Pentagon an amount that will reimburse you for the cost of making these gadgets and for your overhead (plus a profit). How do you show overhead on the bill that you send to the government?

There are two ways. One is to figure out how much overhead was in fact needed to produce each of the 250 items. That is very complicated. The other way is simply to allocate your overhead equally to each item. If your total overhead is $100,000, under the "equal-allocation formula" you arbitrarily assign to each part an equal share of the overhead. That means that each part is billed to the government as if it were responsible for eating up $400 ($100,000 divided by 250 parts) of your overhead. The government may be paying the right price for the whole package of parts, but theoretically it is paying too little for the computer hardware and too much for the hammer. On the invoice it looks as though the hammer costs $435 because $400 of overhead was arbitrarily assigned to it. (Of course $35 may still be too much to pay for a hammer, but at least it is not totally outrageous.)

A sailor who gets the package of parts spots the $435 hammer price and wonders how anybody in his or her right mind could pay that much. He tells the press. A member of Congress picks up on the story. Nobody takes time to learn how the accounting rules work. And thus a myth is born.

The equal-allocation rule was eventually abolished. Now a different accounting system is in place. But whether there has been any real improvement in how the Pentagon buys hammers is unclear. The original hammer may have cost too much; no one knows. Future hammer purchases may cost too much; no one knows. The real problems in procurement—as described in the text—are left unattended.

SOURCE: Based on James Fairhall, "The Case for the $435 Hammer," *Washington Monthly* (January 1987): 47–52. See also Steven Kelman, "The Grace Commission: How Much Waste in Government?" *The Public Interest* (Winter 1985): 62–87.

Not necessarily. The politics of defense spending are such that readiness often is given a very low priority (see Figure 21.4). Here is why.

The Pentagon budget is very large. Frequently Congress will want to make cuts, especially during a period when the federal budget is running a big deficit and the former Soviet Union has collapsed. Where shall it make the cuts?

Client politics influences the decision. In 1990 Congress was willing to cut almost anything, provided it wasn't built or stationed in some member's district. That doesn't leave much. Plans to stop producing F-14 fighters for the navy were opposed by members from Long Island, where the Grumman manufacturing plant is located. Plans to kill the Osprey aircraft for the marines were opposed by members from the places where it was to be built. Plans to close bases were opposed by every member with a base in his or her district.

That leaves training and readiness. These things, essential to military effectiveness, have no constituencies and hence few congressional defenders. Moreover the savings from buying less fuel or having fewer exercises shows up right away, while the savings from canceling an aircraft carrier may not show up for years. Not surprisingly, training and readiness are usually what get the ax. In fiscal 1987 Congress cut heavily into readiness.[8] What *is* surprising is that some new weapons were canceled and some old bases closed. In January 1991 the secretary of defense startled everyone by terminating the contract to build an advanced tactical fighter (the A-12) for the navy on the grounds that the contractors (all well connected in Congress) had wasted too much money with too little to show for it.

Bases

At one time the opening and closing of military bases was pure client politics, which meant that a lot of bases were opened and hardly any were closed. Almost every member of Congress fought to get a base in his or her district, and *every* member fought to keep an existing base open. Even the biggest congressional critics of the U.S. military, people who would vote to take a gun out of a soldier's hand, would fight hard to keep a base in their district open and operating.

In 1988 Congress finally concluded that no base would ever be closed unless the system for making decisions was changed. It created a Commission on Base Realignment and Closure consisting of private citizens (originally twelve, later eight) who would consider recommendations from the secretary of defense. By law, Congress would have to vote within 45 days for or against the Commission's list as a whole without a chance to amend it. In 1989 Congress considered the Commission's first report, which called for closing 86 bases and slimming down five others. With no chance to pick the bases each member wanted to protect and knowing that the country had more bases than it needed, Congress let the report stand and the closings began.

In 1991 it went through the same process again, finally voting to accept (technically, voting not to block) a Commission report calling for closing 34 more bases and altering many others.

Congress, it appears, has finally figured out how to make some decisions that most members know are right but that each member individually finds it politically necessary to oppose.

Congress versus the Executive

Defense policy, like foreign policy, is an invitation to conflict. Until World War II, Congress made detailed decisions about what weapons to buy, what bases to build, and where troops should be sent. Even during the Civil War, Congress, restless with President

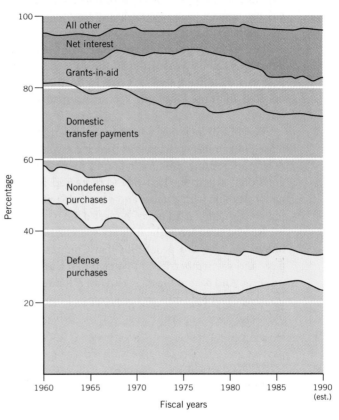

FIGURE 21.4 Distribution of Federal-Sector Expenditures by Category

SOURCE: *Budget of the United States Government, Fiscal Year 1988: Special Analyses,* B–6.

Lincoln's conduct of that struggle, attempted to influence his selection of commanding generals.

During World War II and for some time thereafter, Congress played a more passive role, deferring to the president and the military chiefs. But since the war in Vietnam, and especially since the Carter-Reagan arms buildup began, Congress has reasserted its interest in detailed decisions, something now called, by its critics, **micromanaging.**

The change is easily measured. In 1962 the Senate and House Armed Services Committees held 27 hearings and published 1,400 pages of testimony about the defense budget. In 1985 the two committees held 80 hearings and published 11,246 pages of testimony. The number of congressional subcommittees concerned with defense matters more than tripled from 1970 to 1985. The Military Reform Caucus has taken a keen interest in military policy even though only a quarter of its 133 members sit on defense-oversight committees. Whereas in 1977 the defense budget was debated in the House for two days and no amendment was offered, in 1986 it was debated for nine days and 116 amendments were offered.[9]

Part of this increased congressional interest in defense policy reflects changes in the executive branch. A large peacetime military is bound to attract congressional attention. Part of the increased interest had little to do with defense and a lot to do with serving constituents in an era of budget deficits. During the Reagan presidency the military spending bill was one of the few veto-proof bills that Congress could pass, and so members tried to attach to it a lot of pet projects. And part of the increased attention reflected the already-noted shifts in the ideology of members of Congress.

SUMMARY

The politics of defense, like that of everything else, is peculiarly American. Congress plays a much larger role in the details of military policy than does the parliament of a European democracy. The separation of powers among the branches of the U.S. government is a doctrine that is also applied to the military services, under the theory that divided and rivalrous armed forces are a better way of protecting civilian control than would be a unified and coordinated military.

Civilian control is vested in the president, who is commander in chief; the chain of command runs from him to the secretary of defense, who sends orders to the various unified commands. The Joint Chiefs of Staff is a planning and advisory body, not a centralized command. The 1986 defense-reorganization act increased somewhat the influence of the chairman of the Joint Chiefs and of the commanders of the unified commands.

Decisions regarding total military spending and the acquisition of new weapons systems are made by majoritarian politics, with a large role played by the ideology of the president and members of Congress, by international realities, and by public opinion. The allocation of contracts and (until the system was changed) the maintenance of military bases reflect interest-group politics.

The problems that we encounter in recruiting personnel, buying big-ticket and small-ticket items, and achieving readiness reveal the different kinds of defense politics at work. In general these decisions reflect a combination of ignorance (what will work?), organizational needs (the attractions of gold plating and the convenience of sole sourcing), and constituency pressures (avoid the draft, keep contractors happy, and cut the budget with stretch-outs and by underfunding readiness).

KEY TERMS

military-industrial complex   *p. 610*

cost overruns   *p. 622*

gold plating   *p. 623*

micromanaging   *p. 625*

SUGGESTED READINGS

Art, Robert J. *The TFX Decision: McNamara and the Military.* Boston: Little, Brown, 1968. An interesting case study of how the decision was made to acquire a controversial new fighter aircraft.

Cohen, Eliot. *Citizens and Soldiers.* Ithaca, N.Y.: Cornell University Press, 1985. An analysis of how the United States recruits soldiers, comparing the draft and the all-volunteer force.

Fox, J. Ronald. *The Defense Management Challenge: Weapons Acquisition.* Boston: Harvard Business School Press, 1988. A perceptive explanation of the problems in the way we acquire weapons systems, with suggestions for change.

Halperin, Morton. H. *Bureaucratic Politics and Foreign Policy.* Washington, D.C.: Brookings Institution, 1974. Analysis of how the tasks and missions of military and intelligence agencies affect the kind of positions that they take and the political strategies that they employ.

Rosen, Steven, ed. *Testing the Theory of the Military-Industrial Complex.* Lexington, Mass.: D.C. Heath/Lexington Books, 1973. Articles from different points of view on military-industry relations.

Sarkesian, Sam C., ed. *The Military-Industrial Complex: A Reassessment.* Beverly Hills, Calif.: Sage, 1972. Studies testing various aspects of the military-industrial complex theory.

22

Environmental Policy

Everybody loves the environment. A large majority of the American public believes that government should do more to protect it. Over 80 percent of college freshmen believe that the government is not doing enough to control pollution, far more than think the government is doing too little about disarmament, protecting the consumer, or controlling handguns.[1] No one wants to be called a "polluter."

Why, then, is environmental policy so controversial? There are three reasons. First, every governmental policy, including policies to protect the environment, creates both winners and losers. The losers are the people who must pay the costs without getting enough of the benefits. Sometimes those losers are influential interest groups. But sometimes the losers are average citizens. They may love the environment, but not enough to change the way they live in order to enhance it. For example, automobile exhausts are a major cause of smog, but not many people like the idea of being told to leave their cars at home and take the bus to work.

Second, many environmental issues are enmeshed in scientific uncertainty: the experts either do not know or they disagree about what is happening and how to change it. For example, some people worry that society is burning so much fuel (thus producing a lot of carbon dioxide) and cutting down so many trees (thus reducing the plants available to convert carbon dioxide back into oxygen) that the earth will soon become a greenhouse: the excess carbon dioxide in the earth's atmosphere will prevent heat from escaping, and so the earth will get warmer, with disastrous effects for humanity. But scientists do not know how large the greenhouse effect is, whether it will lead to a harmful amount of global warming, or (if it does) what should be done about it.[2]

Third, much environmental policy takes the form of entrepreneurial politics—mobilizing decision makers with strong, often emotional appeals in order to overcome the political advantages of the client groups that oppose a change. To make these appeals,

Everyone wants clean air, but few people are willing to give up the personal freedom that their automobiles afford them.

people who want change must stir up controversy and find villains. Many times this produces desirable changes. But it can also lead to distorted priorities. For example, it is much easier to make dramatic and politically powerful arguments about a pesticide that causes a minute increase in the risk of cancer than it is to dramatize the runoff into our rivers and oceans of polluted water from farms and city streets.

The American Context

Environmental policy, like welfare policy, is shaped by the unique features of American politics. Almost every industrialized nation has rules to protect the environment, but in this country the rules are designed and enforced in a way that would be baffling to someone in, say, Sweden or England.

First, environmental policy making here is much more adversarial than it is in most European nations. In this country there have been bitter and lasting conflicts over the contents of the Clean Air Act. Minimum auto-emission standards are uniform across the nation, regardless of local conditions (states can set higher standards if they wish). Many rules for improving air and water quality have strict deadlines and require expensive technology. Hundreds of inspectors enforce these rules, and hundreds of lawyers bring countless lawsuits to support or challenge this enforcement. Government and business leaders have frequently denounced each other for being unreasonable or insensitive. So antagonistic are the interests involved in environmental policy that it took thirteen years, from 1977 to 1990, to agree on a congressional revision of the Clean Air Act.

In England, by contrast, rules designed to reduce air pollution were written by government and business leaders acting cooperatively. The rules are neither rigid nor nationally uniform; they are flexible and allow plenty of exceptions to deal with local variations in business needs. Compliance with the rules depends mostly on voluntary action, not formal enforcement. Lawsuits are rare. Business and government officials do not routinely accuse each other of being unreasonable. You might think that all this sweetness and light was the result of having meaningless rules, but not so. As David Vogel has shown, the improvement in air and water quality in England has been at least as great as, if not greater than, in the United States.[3]

A second feature of environmental policy here is that, as in so many other policy areas, what is done depends heavily on the states. Though there are uniform national air-quality standards, how those standards are achieved is left to the states (subject to certain federal controls). Though sewage treatment plants are in large measure paid for by Washington, they are designed, built, and operated by state and local governments. Though radioactive waste must be disposed of somewhere, the states have a big voice in where that is. When Congress decided in 1982 to select places in which to dispose of such waste, it announced that sites would be chosen on the basis of "science." But of course no state wanted to get such wastes, so all objected. In the congressional committee that made the final decision in 1988, Nevada had the least influence, and so Nevada got the waste. In a federal system of government, "science" rarely makes allocative decisions; local politics usually does.

Federalism reinforces adversarial politics: one of the reasons environmental issues are so contentious in this country is that cities and states fight over what standards should apply where. But federalism is not the whole story. The separation of powers guarantees that almost anybody who wants to wield influence over environmental policy will have an opportunity to do so. In England, and in most European nations, the centralized, parliamentary form of government means that the opponents of a policy have less leverage.*

It would take a book almost as long as this one to describe all the environmental laws and regulations now in effect in this country and to discuss the endless controversies over how those rules should be changed or expanded. In Table 22.1 you can find a summary of some of the more important federal policies governing air and water pollution, environmental impact statements, and open spaces.

In this chapter we want to explain how environmental policy is made. Controversies over controlling pollution from stationary sources, such as factories and power plants, take the form of *entrepreneurial politics*—many people hope to benefit from rules that impose costs on a few firms. Policies intended to reduce air pollution caused by automobiles involve *majoritarian politics*—many people hope to benefit, but many people (anyone who owns a car) will have to pay the cost. The fight over acid rain has largely been a case of *interest-group politics*—regions hurt by acid rain (mainly in the Northeast) argue with regions that produce a lot of acid rain (mainly in the Midwest) about who should pay. Finally, there are examples of *client politics* at work—for example, when farmers manage to minimize federal controls over the use of pesticides. Most people are unaware of what food contains what pesticide or which, if any, are harmful; farmers are keenly aware of the economic benefits of pesticides and are well-organized to defend them.

---

* Here, environmental pressures are brought by interest groups; in Europe, where such groups have less influence, environmentalists form or enter political parties so as to be represented in the legislature.

TABLE 22.1 Major Federal Environmental Laws

1963	Clean Air Act
1964	Wilderness Act
1965	Highway Beautification Act
	Water Quality Act
1967	Air Quality Act
1968	Wild and Scenic Rivers Act
1969	National Environmental Policy Act
	Endangered Species Conservation Act
1970	Clean Air Amendments
	Water Quality Improvement Act
1972	Federal Water Pollution Control Act
	Marine Mammal Protection Act
	Marine Protection, Research, and Sanctuaries Act
	Coastal Zone Management Act
	Federal Environmental Pesticide Control Act
	Noise Control Act
1973	Endangered Species Act
1974	Safe Drinking Water Act
1976	Federal Land Policy and Management Act
	National Forest Management Act
	Resource Conservation and Recovery Act
	Toxic Substances Control Act
1977	Clean Air Act Amendments
	Clean Water Act
	Surface Mining Control and Reclamation Act
1978	Outer Continental Shelf Lands Act Amendments
1980	Comprehensive Environmental Response, Compensation, and Liability Act ("Superfund")
	Alaska National Interest Lands Conservation Act
1984	Hazardous and Solid Waste Amendments
1986	Safe Drinking Water Amendments
	Superfund Amendments and Reauthorization Act
1987	Water Quality Act
1988	Endangered Species Act Reauthorization
	Federal Insecticide, Fungicide, and Rodenticide Act Amendments
1990	Clean Air Act Amendments

SOURCE: *Congressional Quarterly Weekly Report* (January 20, 1990): 154.

Entrepreneurial Politics: Pollution from Factories

The environmental movement was created by entrepreneurial politics. Throughout the 1960s, public awareness of the problem of pollution had been growing, but any effort to pass tough laws to reduce pollution coming from stationary sources—such as factories, power plants, or oil fields—had to overcome the strategic political advantage enjoyed by the sources of pollution. These sources were well-organized to resist the costs of a cleanup, which might be high; the people who would benefit from the cleanup were numerous but unorganized.

On January 28, 1969, an oil well off the coast of California blew out, dumping thousands of gallons of oil on the beaches. Coming as it did at the end of the 1960s, when protest movements of every sort were commonplace, the event provided environmentalists with a horror story (the oil spill) and a demon (the oil companies) that could serve as rallying cries for a new environmental movement. On April 22, 1970, that movement came together around a national event—the first Earth Day celebration. By the end of the year, President Nixon had created, by executive order, an Environmental Protection Agency

(EPA), and Congress had passed a new Clean Air Act setting national air-quality standards that had to be met by certain deadlines.

Though the state governments were given the job of devising plans to achieve these standards (some states already had their own pollution-control laws), it was clear that factories and power plants would have to install expensive new equipment to cut down on the amount of pollutants they produced. Especially hard hit were steel mills, smelters, and electric utilities (particularly those that burned coal). These firms and organized coal producers (the National Coal Association) had for years been able to keep the federal government from adopting tough standards, but in 1970 the protests of utilities, firms, and producers were pretty much ignored.

The oil spill and Earth Day had generated bad publicity for any source of pollution, but headlines alone don't produce new laws. Members of Congress

 ## Major Environmental Issues

Smog

The Clean Air Act (passed in 1970; amended in 1977 and 1990)

- **Stationary sources:** EPA sets national air-quality standards; states must develop plans to attain them. If state plan is inadequate, EPA sets a federal plan. Local sources that emit more than a certain amount of pollutants must install pollution-control equipment.

- **Gasoline-powered vehicles:** Between 1970 and 1990, pollution from cars was cut by between 60 and 80 percent. Between 1991 and 1998 there must be another 30 percent reduction. All states must have an auto-pollution inspection system.

- **Cities:** Classifies cities in terms of how severe their smog problem is and sets deadlines for meeting federal standards.

Water

Clean Water Acts of various years state that there is to be no discharge of wastewater into lakes and streams without

a federal permit; to get a permit, cities and factories must meet federal discharge standards.

Toxic Wastes

EPA is to clean up abandoned dump sites with money raised by a tax on the chemical and petroleum industries and from general revenues. (Many thousands of such sites exist.)

Environmental Impact Statements

Since 1969, any federal agency planning a project that would significantly affect the human environment must prepare in advance an environmental impact statement (EIS).

Acid Rain

The Clean Air Act of 1990 requires a reduction of 10 million tons of sulfur dioxide (mostly from electric-generating plants that burn coal) by 1995. The biggest sources must acquire government allowances (which can be traded among firms) setting emission limits.

must be induced to act. The key congressional actor was Senator Edmund Muskie (D, Maine). He chaired the subcommittee that wrote environmental laws; just as important, he wanted to run for president in 1972. As Muskie began drafting the 1970 law, consumer activist Ralph Nader attacked him for offering proposals that Nader claimed were too weak and for "selling out" to industry.[4] Muskie in fact wanted a tough bill, but in the face of Nader's accusations and the publicity they generated, he had no choice but to make it tougher still. The Clean Air Act was signed into law in December 1970.

There are many other examples of policy entrepreneurs taking advantage of an aroused public opinion to put in place new laws, either by collaborating with congressional leaders or, as in the case of the Clean Air Act, by embarrassing them. In direct response to the Santa Barbara oil spill, Congress passed in 1970 a Water Quality Improvement Act that, among other things, made oil companies liable for up to $14 million in cleanup costs. Two years later it passed, over President Nixon's veto, a bill creating tough new standards and deadlines for reducing water pollution. Though strongly opposed by many industries, the bill required oil companies to install, by 1977, the "best practicable" technology for treating discharges into U.S. waterways and by 1983 to install the "best available" technology. The goal was to eliminate *all* pollutant discharges into U.S. waters by 1985. The EPA was to implement the law; in addition, citizens were given the right to sue the EPA if they believed it insufficiently vigorous in carrying out its duties.

All of these bills reflected the widespread national concern with environmental issues in the early 1970s. That concern arose almost overnight and caught politicians and interest groups by surprise. In May 1969 only 1 percent of the American people told pollsters that they thought pollution was an important national problem; one year later about 25 percent thought that. An estimated 20 million people participated in Earth Day, the membership of existing environmental organizations such as the Sierra Club and the Audubon Society rose dramatically, and several new organizations—Friends of the Earth, the Environmental Defense Fund, and others—were formed.[5] In the face of this groundswell, the lobbying

efforts of industry were mostly ineffective. As is often the case with entrepreneurial politics, leadership tended to come from Congress rather than from the president.

In the late 1980s and early 1990s the conditions existed for another wave of entrepreneurial politics aimed at environmental issues. The oil spill from the *Exxon Valdez* oil tanker off the Alaskan coast had much the same galvanizing effect as the Santa Barbara oil spill had twenty years earlier. In April 1990 there was another Earth Day celebration, this one even larger than the first in 1970. Public-opinion polls showed a growing number of Americans saying that the quality of the environment was worse than five years earlier and that "continuing environmental improvements must be made *regardless of cost*" (see Figure 22.1).

The difficulty with improving things "regardless of cost" is not only that the cost is likely to be very high, but that it will fall mostly on the average citizen, not on some special-interest group. The reason: the biggest single source of pollutants in the atmosphere is the automobile (see Figure 22.2). And that, as the next section shows, leads to a very different kind of politics.

FIGURE 22.1 Willing to Pay

QUESTION *Do you agree or disagree with the following statement? Protecting the environment is so important that requirements and standards cannot be too high, and continuing environmental improvements must be made regardless of cost.*

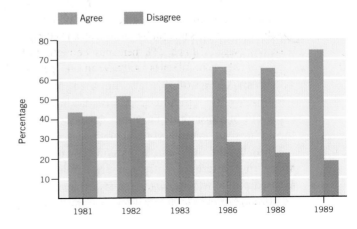

SOURCE: *Congressional Quarterly Weekly Report* (January 20, 1990): 142.

FIGURE 22.2 Sources of Toxins in the Air

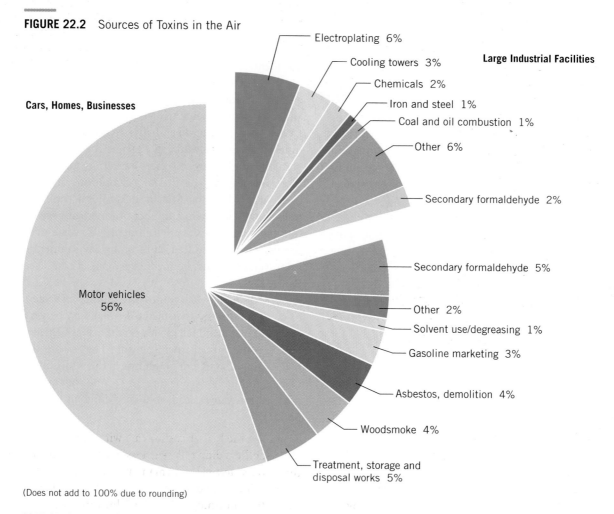

Electroplating 6%

Cooling towers 3%

Large Industrial Facilities

Chemicals 2%

Iron and steel 1%

Coal and oil combustion 1%

Other 6%

Secondary formaldehyde 2%

Cars, Homes, Businesses

Secondary formaldehyde 5%

Other 2%

Solvent use/degreasing 1%

Gasoline marketing 3%

Motor vehicles 56%

Asbestos, demolition 4%

Woodsmoke 4%

Treatment, storage and disposal works 5%

(Does not add to 100% due to rounding)

SOURCE: *Congressional Quarterly Weekly Report* (January 20, 1990): 143.

Majoritarian Politics: Pollution from Automobiles

The Clean Air Act of 1970 also imposed tough restrictions on the amount of pollutants that could come out of automobile tail pipes. Indeed, most of the debate over that bill centered on this issue.

Initially the auto-emissions control rules followed the pattern of entrepreneurial politics: an aroused public with media support demanded that automobile companies be required to make their cars less polluting. It seemed to be "the public" against "the interests," and the public won: by 1975 new cars would have to produce 90 percent less of two pollu-

tants (hydrocarbons and carbon monoxide), and by 1976, a 90 percent reduction in another (nitrous oxides). This was a tall order. There was no time to redesign automobile engines or to find an alternative to the internal combustion engine; it would be necessary to install devices (called catalytic converters) on exhaust pipes that would transform pollutants into harmless gases.

But a little-noticed provision in the 1970 law soon changed automobile pollution into majoritarian politics. That provision required states to develop land-use and transportation rules to help attain air-quality standards. What that meant in practice was that in any area where smog was still a problem even

In the wake of the *Exxon Valdez* oil spill, Americans began to express their concerns about the environment with renewed vigor.

after emission controls had been placed on new cars, there would have to be rules restricting the public's use of cars.

There was no way cities such as Denver, Los Angeles, and New York could get rid of smog just by requiring people to buy less-polluting cars—the increase in the number of cars or in the number of miles driven in those places outweighed the gain from making the average car less polluting. That meant that the government would have to impose such unpopular measures as bans on downtown parking, mandatory use of buses and carpools, and even gasoline rationing.

Efforts to do this failed. Popular opposition to such rules was too great, and the few such rules that were put into place didn't work. Congress reacted by postponing the deadlines by which air-quality standards in cities would have to be met; the EPA reacted by abandoning any serious effort to tell people when and where they could drive.[6]

Even the effort to clean up the exhausts of new cars was running into opposition. Some people

didn't like the higher cost of cars with catalytic converters; others didn't like the loss in horsepower that these converters caused (many people disconnected them). The United Auto Workers union began to worry that antismog rules would hurt the U.S. auto industry and cost them their jobs. Congress took note of these complaints and decided that despite a lot of effort, new cars could not meet the 90 percent emission-reduction standard by 1975–1976, and so in 1977 it amended the Clean Air Act to extend these deadlines by up to six years.

The Clean Air Act, when revised again in 1990, set new, tougher auto-emission control standards—but pushed back the deadline for compliance with them, in stages, to 1995. It reiterated the need for getting rid of smog in the smoggiest cities and proposed a number of ways to do it—but set the deadline for compliance in the worst area (Los Angeles) at twenty years in the future.

The public will support tough environmental laws when somebody else pays or when the costs are hidden (as in the price of a car); it will not give as much support when it believes that it *is* paying, especially when the payment takes the form of changing how and when it uses the family car. Here are more examples of each kind of majoritarian politics.

Majoritarian Politics When People Believe the Costs Are Low The National Environmental Policy Act (NEPA), passed in 1969, contained a provision requiring that an **environmental impact statement** (EIS) be written before any federal agency undertakes an activity that will "significantly" affect the quality of the human environment. (Similar laws have been passed in many states, affecting not only what government does but what private developers do.) Because it required only a "statement" rather than some specific action and because it was a pro-environment law, NEPA passed by overwhelming majorities.

As it turned out, the EIS provision was hardly innocuous. Opponents of virtually any government-sponsored project have used the EIS as a way of blocking, changing, or delaying the project. Hundreds of lawsuits have been filed to challenge this or that provision of an EIS or to claim that a project was not supported by a satisfactory EIS. In this way environmental activists have challenged the Alaska pipeline, a Florida canal, and several nuclear power plants, as well as countless dams, bridges, highways, and office buildings. Usually the agency's plan is upheld, but this does not mean that the EIS is unimportant: the EIS induces the agency to think through what it is doing, and it gives critics a chance to examine, and often to negotiate, the content of those plans.

Despite the grumbling of many people adversely affected by fights over an EIS (someone once complained that Moses would never have been able to part the Red Sea if he had had to file an EIS first), popular support for it remains strong because the public at large does not believe that it is paying a high price and believes that it is gaining a significant benefit.

Majoritarian Politics When People Believe the Costs Are High From time to time someone proposes that gasoline taxes be raised sharply. Such taxes would discourage driving, and this not only would conserve fuel but would reduce smog as well. Almost everyone would pay, but almost everyone would benefit. However, it is only with great difficulty that the public can be persuaded to support such taxes. The reason is that the people pay the tax first, and the benefit, if any, comes later. Unlike Social Security, where the taxes we pay now support cash benefits we get later, gasoline taxes support noncash benefits (cleaner air, less congestion) that many people doubt will ever appear or, if they do, will not be meaningful to them.[7]

When gasoline taxes have been raised, it has usually been because the politicians did not describe it as an environmental measure. Instead they promised that in return for the higher taxes they would provide some concrete benefits—more highways, more buses, or a reduction in the federal deficit (as happened with the gas tax hike of 1990 and again in 1993).

Interest-Group Politics: Acid Rain

Sometimes the rain, snow, or dust particles that fall onto the land are acidic. This is called **acid rain.** One source of that precipitation is burning fuel, such as certain types of coal, that contains a lot of sulfur. Some of the sulfur (along with nitrogen) will turn into sulfuric (or nitric) acid as it comes to earth. Steel mills and electric power plants that burn high-sulfur coal are concentrated in the Midwest and Great Lakes regions of the United States. The prevailing winds tend to carry those sulfurous fumes eastward, where some fall to the ground.

That much seems certain. Everything else has been surrounded by controversy. Many lakes and rivers in the eastern United States and in Canada have become more acidic and some forests in these areas have died back. Some part of this is the result of acid rain from industrial smokestacks, but some part of it is also the result of naturally occurring acids in the soils and rainfall. How much of the acidification is man-made and how much is a result of the actions of Mother Nature is unclear. Some lakes are not affected by acid rain; some are. Why some are affected more than others is unclear. The long-term effects of higher acid levels in lakes and forests are also unclear.

These scientific uncertainties were important because they provided some support for each side in a fierce interest-group battle. Residents of Canada and

New England complained bitterly of the loss of forests and the acidification of lakes, blaming it on midwestern smokestacks. Midwestern businesses, labor unions, and politicians denied that their smokestacks were the major cause of the problem (if, indeed, there was a problem) and argued that, even if they were the cause, they shouldn't have to pay the cost of cleaning up the problem.

Here was a classic case of two well-organized parties, one hoping to reap benefits and the other fearing to pay costs, locked in a struggle over a policy proposal. Even before people were aware that acid rain might be a problem, these two groups were fighting over how, if at all, sulfur emissions should be reduced. (In the early 1970s, sulfur coming out of smokestacks was believed to pose a health hazard.)

An attempt to deal with the issue in 1977 reflected the kind of bizarre compromises that sometimes result when politically opposed forces have to be reconciled. There were essentially two alternatives. One was to require power plants to burn low-sulfur coal. This would undoubtedly cut back on sulfur emissions, but it would cost money because, as can be seen in the map below, low-sulfur coal is mined mostly in the West, hundreds of miles away from the midwestern coal-burning industries. The other way would be to require power plants to install scrubbers—complicated and very expensive devices that would take sulfurous fumes out of the gas before it came out of the smokestack. In addition to their cost, the trouble with scrubbers was that they didn't always work and that they generated a lot of unpleasant sludge that would have to be hauled away and buried somewhere. Their great advantage, however, was that they would allow midwestern utilities to keep on using cheap, high-sulfur coal.

THE POLITICS OF ENERGY: SOURCES OF FOSSIL FUELS IN THE UNITED STATES

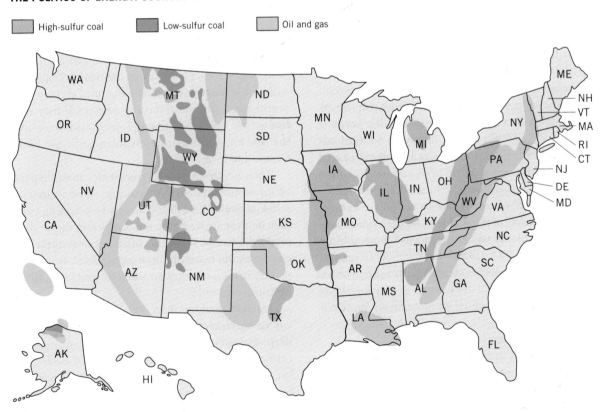

High-sulfur coal Low-sulfur coal Oil and gas

SOURCE: *Congressional Quarterly Weekly Report* (January 20, 1990): 160.

Acid rain may cause damage to forests.

Congress voted for the scrubbers for all new coal-burning plants, even if they burned low-sulfur coal. In the opinion of most economists, this was the wrong decision,[8] but it had four great political advantages. First, the jobs of miners in high-sulfur coal mines would be protected. They had powerful allies in Congress. Second, environmentalists liked scrubbers because they seemed like the definitive, technological "solution" to the problem, far preferable to relying on incentives to induce power plants to buy low-sulfur coal. Third, scrubber manufacturers liked the idea, for obvious reasons. Finally, some eastern governors liked scrubbers because if all new plants had to have them, it would be more costly, and thus less likely, for existing factories in their states to close down and move into the West.

The 1977 law in effect required scrubbers on new coal-burning plants—even ones located right next to mines where they could get low-sulfur coal. As two scholars later described the law, it seemed to produce "clean coal and dirty air."[9]

The 1977 bill did not solve much. Many of the scrubbers, as predicted, didn't work very well. And there remained the question of what to do about existing power plants and factories. In the early 1980s the Reagan administration took the position that too little was known to warrant strong action; more research was needed first. The Canadian government and members of Congress from the Northeast took a very different view, demanding that something be done immediately.

For thirteen years there was a political stalemate in Congress, as is often the case when strongly opposed interest groups fight it out. And when a solution was finally agreed upon, it was a compromise. President Bush proposed a two-step regulation. In the first phase 111 power plants would be required to reduce their emission of sulfur by a fixed amount. They could decide for themselves how to do it: buy low-sulfur coal, install scrubbers, or use some other technology. This would be done by 1995. In the second phase, with a deadline in the year 2000, there would be sharper emission reductions for many more plants, and this would probably require the use of scrubbers. To create some flexibility in how much each utility must cut its emissions, there was created a system of sulfur dioxide allowances that could be bought and sold. Coal miners complained that they would lose jobs during phase one, and so they were promised some financial compensation if they were laid off as a result of their employers' complying with the new limits. This compromise became part of the Clean Air Act of 1990.

Interest-group politics permeates many aspects of environmental policy making. When cities or states consider land-use controls and zoning ordinances, they are weighing the competing demands of established residents (who often want as little new growth in their communities as possible) against demands of developers who want to build additional housing.

Interest-group politics often lacks the moral fervor of entrepreneurial politics and rarely taps the deep streams of public opinion that are reflected in majoritarian politics. As environmental policy has become more complex and as people have adjusted to existing laws, however, new interest groups have been formed that have a stake in how things are done. As a result it becomes harder and harder to change existing policies. The heady victories of the early 1970s are hard to duplicate today because groups that were once unorganized are now well organized.

For example, there is now a large and growing industry that makes products designed to improve the environment. As we saw in the acid-rain controversy, industry can play an important role in supporting laws that favor their machines whether or not they are the best solution to the problem. Industry is far better organized today than in 1970 to use its employees and political allies to defend its interests. Similarly, public-interest groups, such as the Environmental Defense Fund, that did not exist in 1965 now compete with other environmental groups for money and publicity. Labor unions, such as the United Auto Workers, that once fought for tough air-pollution laws now are worried about whether some of these laws may cost them their jobs.

Despite the rise of all of these interests, the political momentum remains with the policy entrepreneurs. Environmentalism is seen as good politics (see Figure 22.3), and few members of Congress want to be caught on the wrong side of a vote on an environmental bill.

Client Politics: Agricultural Pesticides

Some client groups have so far escaped this momentum. One such group is organized farmers, who have more or less successfully resisted efforts to restrict, sharply, the use of pesticides or to control the runoff of pesticides from farmlands.

For a while it seemed as though farmers would also fall before the assaults of policy entrepreneurs. When Rachel Carson published *Silent Spring* in 1962, she set off a public outcry about the harm to wildlife caused by the indiscriminate use of DDT, a common pesticide. In 1972 the EPA banned the use of DDT.

That same year Congress directed the EPA to evaluate the safety of all pesticides on the market; unsafe ones were to be removed. However, that is easier said than done. One reason is that there are over fifty thousand pesticides now in use, with five thousand new ones introduced every year.[10] Testing all of these chemicals is a huge, vastly expensive, and very time-consuming job, especially since any health effects on people may not be observed for several years.[11]

FIGURE 22.3 Government Regulation

QUESTION *In general do you think there is too much, too little . . . government regulation and involvement in the area of environmental protection?**

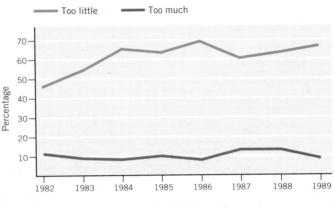

* Others responded "right amount" or "don't know."

SOURCE: *Congressional Quarterly Weekly Report* (January 20, 1990): 185.

Another reason is that pesticides have many beneficial uses; therefore someone has to balance the gains and the risks of using a given pesticide and compare the relative gains and risks of two similar pesticides.

But even if the science were easy, the politics would not be. American farmers are the most productive in the world, and most of them believe that they cannot achieve that output (and thus their present incomes) without using pesticides. These farmers are well organized to express their interests and well represented in Congress (especially on the House and Senate Agricultural Committees) to make those interests effective. Complicating matters is the fact that the subsidies the taxpayers give to farmers often encourage them to produce more food than they can sell and thus to use more pesticides than they really need. Though many of these chemicals do not remain in the crops that are harvested, large amounts sink into the soil, contaminating water supplies. But these problems are largely invisible to the public and are much harder to dramatize than, say, the discovery of a toxic-waste dump in Love Canal, New York.

Though attacked by environmental organizations, farm groups have been generally successful at practicing client politics. The EPA's budget for reviewing pesticides has been kept small (the longtime

Farm groups have been relatively successful in blocking efforts to remove pesticides from the market.

Environmentalists use the protection of an endangered species, such as the spotted owl, as a way of reducing timber harvests.

chairman of the House Appropriations Committee, Jamie Whitten, was a supporter of farmers and critic of environmentalists).[12] Very few pesticides have been taken off the market, and those that have tend to be ones that, because they are involved in some incident receiving heavy media coverage (such as the effect of DDT on birds), lend themselves to entrepreneurial politics.

A similar kind of client politics exists in the timber industry. Wood-product companies and loggers want access to forests under the control of the U.S. Forest Service. Though only 13 percent of all cut timber comes from these forests, and though two-thirds of the U.S. forest system are already off-limits to logging, environmentalists want further restrictions, especially in the mature forests of Oregon and Washington, and especially to prevent clear-cutting (that is, cutting down all the trees in a given area). But Congress has generally supported the timber industry by ordering the Forest Service to sell timber to the industry at below-market prices, in effect subsidizing the industry. Some activists hope to convert this client politics into entrepreneurial politics by demanding that clear-cutting in certain forests be stopped in order to protect endangered species, such as the spotted owl.

The Environmental Uncertainties

Making environmental policy strikes many people as easy—identify a problem, raise a fuss, defeat "the interests," and enjoy the benefits. In fact it is much harder than that to have a sane environmental policy.

First, what is the problem? Nobody likes smog, and human waste or oil slicks floating off our beaches are obviously bad. But many other problems are much less clear-cut. Science doesn't know whether we are experiencing a dangerous level of global warming or how bad (if bad at all) the greenhouse effect is. Pesticides that cause cancer in animals when given in megadoses may or may not cause cancer in people when consumed in nominal amounts.

Second, if there is a problem, what goals do we want to achieve? Reasonably clean air and water, of course, but how clean? Since the cost of removing from the air the last 10 percent of some pollutants is often greater than the cost of removing the first 90 percent, how clean is clean enough? If making air and water cleaner is costly in terms of jobs, energy, and economic growth, how big a price are we willing to pay? When the cost of gasoline shot up in 1973–1974, many voters became much less interested in nonpolluting cars if the devices that reduced the pollution also reduced the cars' gas mileage.

Third, how do we want to achieve our goals? Issuing rules and enforcing them in court often seem the easiest things to do, but they are not always the wisest. That **command-and-control strategy** assumes that the rule makers and rule enforcers know how to achieve the greatest environmental gain at the least cost. In fact no one knows how to do that because local circumstances, technological problems, and economic costs are so complex. Under what circumstances can we use incentives and market prices to get people voluntarily to clean up their act by using their best imagination?

All of these uncertainties have become part of the endless political controversies surrounding the administration of the Environmental Protection Agency. For example:

What Is the Problem? The EPA was given responsibility to administer certain laws governing air, water, and pesticides (among others). But it is rarely left alone to define these problems; any new environmental scandal leads to popular and congressional demands that it drop everything and solve that crisis. If toxic chemicals are found in Love Canal or Kepone in Virginia Beach, these dramatic discoveries put other, less dramatic, but often more important problems onto the back burner.

What Are Our Goals? When the EPA was told by Congress to eliminate *all* pollutants entering our waterways by 1985, to cut auto emissions by 90 percent within five years, and to eliminate smog in *all* cities, Congress should have known that these goals were utterly unrealistic. When the EPA realized that it could not achieve these goals, it was forced to ask for extensions in deadlines and for revisions in laws. This gave it the appearance of knuckling under to industry pressure.[13]

How Do We Achieve Our Goals? Initially the EPA was zealous about using a **command-and-control strategy** to improve air and water quality. For example, to reduce water pollution discharged from factories, the EPA issued rules broken down into 642 industry subcategories, and even then there was a lot of local variation that it could not take into account.[14] When the

Cleaning up the more than 1,200 major toxic waste sites nationwide will take decades.

Bruce Babbitt, secretary of the interior, has an un-enviable job: balancing demands for access to federal grazing land with demands for protecting those lands.

cost of doing this sort of thing got out of control, the EPA during the Carter administration began to devise incentives to replace some rules. These included offsets, bubbles, and banks.

- **Offsets:** If a company wants to open a new plant in an area with polluted air, it can do so if the pollution it generates is offset by a reduction in pollution from another source in that area. To get that reduction, the new company may buy an existing company and close it down.

- **Bubble standard:** A bubble is the total amount of air pollution that can come from a given factory. A company is free to decide which specific sources within that factory must be reduced and how to meet the bubble standard.

- **Pollution allowances** (or **banks**): If a company reduces its polluting emissions by more than the law requires, it can either use this excess to cover a future plant expansion or sell it to another company as an offset.

Once, only affected businesses complained about the high cost, slow progress, and legal complexity of environmental regulations. Increasingly, however, pro-environment interest groups and the government itself have become aware of the difficulties that arise when the government relies on a command-and-control strategy that is indifferent to costs and excessively reliant on lawsuits.

When the Clinton administration took office in 1993, it had the strong support of environmentalists. Vice President Gore was a visible and influential supporter of environmental protection; he had even written a book on the subject. Secretary of the Interior Bruce Babbitt was also a staunch environmentalist. But instead of just pushing ahead with more command-and-control policies, the new administration began to reexamine these approaches. It suggested, for example, that the Superfund law, intended to clean up toxic waste dumps, was in fact not cleaning up many sites; instead it was encouraging armies of lawyers to bring lengthy and costly lawsuits to determine who was responsible for the toxic waste.

American politics, though often messy, confusing, and conflict-ridden, sometimes changes as people learn from their experiences. Indeed, our political system causes learning (and undergoes change) precisely *because* it is messy, confusing, and conflict-ridden. Problems that once looked simple ("There is too much pollution") and policies that once sounded straightforward ("We'll tell people to stop polluting") must often be tempered and modified once they are tested by the complexities of reality.

The Results

Though Americans think that their environment has gotten worse, in fact many aspects of it have gotten better since 1970 (see Figure 22.4). There is now much less carbon monoxide, sulfur dioxide, and lead in the atmosphere than once was the case. It is less clear whether there have been equally noticeable improvements in water quality, in large part because much of the gunk that flows into our rivers, lakes, and oceans does not come from some fixed source (such as a sewer) that can be easily isolated; a lot comes from runoff from the ground as a result of rain washing pollutants off urban streets and farmlands and into the water.

FIGURE 22.4 Quality of Life

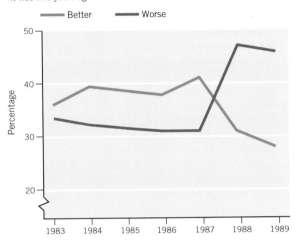

QUESTION

Overall quality of the environment around here: better or worse than it was five years ago?

—— Better —— Worse

SOURCE: *Congressional Quarterly Weekly Report* (January 20, 1990): 138.

Some states reserve a highway lane for people driving in carpools.

Hazardous waste is found at thousands of known locations (and perhaps hundreds more unknown ones). The cleanup job is so great that it will be years before much progress can be shown. Getting big reductions in dangerous pesticides requires first getting agreement on what is a dangerous pesticide and then finding a way of minimizing the harm to agriculture that would be caused by the reduction.

SUMMARY

Environmental issues illustrate all four styles of policy-making.

Entrepreneurial politics: an unorganized public is to benefit at the expense of a well-organized group. An example is the effort to reduce air and water pollution from stationary sources, such as factories. Such politics requires mobilizing the media, dramatizing the issue, and convincing members of Congress that their political reputations will suffer if they do not cast the right vote. To prevent client groups from taking over the implementation of these laws, the bills are written to make it easy to use the courts to force action.

Majoritarian politics: an unorganized public is to benefit at its own expense. Examples include reducing auto emissions by imposing transportation controls, raising gasoline taxes, and requiring environmental impact statements. Interest groups tend not to be the decisive players. Whether the proposal wins or loses depends on how the public generally evaluates the costs. They like environmental impact statements but oppose higher gasoline taxes and restrictions on private automobile use. Dramatizing a crisis tends to be less effective because the public at large, and not some small interest, must pay for any benefits.

Interest-group politics: two organized groups with a material stake in the outcome fight over who will pay and who will benefit. An example is the controlling of acid rain. When faced with two or more powerful interests, Congress tends not to pass broad, sweeping bills but to find workable compromises.

Client politics: an organized group gets a benefit; an unorganized public must pay. Examples include the use of agricultural pesticides and timber cutting in U.S. forests. Client politics depends on the client group's having strategically placed allies in Congress and on its potential opponents' being unable (by dramatizing a crisis, for example) to convert this policy system into a pattern of entrepreneurial politics.

In general, entrepreneurial politics has played the dominant role in most environmental issues. The prevalence of entrepreneurial politics in this arena is largely due to (1) the success of policy entrepreneurs in sensitizing public opinion to these matters and (2) the growth of a variety of public-interest lobbies with close ties to the media and with the ability to threaten recalcitrant legislators with attacks on their reputations.

Unlike economic or welfare issues, environmental issues lend themselves to entrepreneurial politics because the problems can be portrayed in life-threatening terms, the goals can be related to what most people believe is the good life, and the costs can be minimized, deferred, or (seemingly) placed on small groups.

KEY TERMS

environmental impact statement   *p. 636*

acid rain   *p. 636*

command-and-control strategy   *p. 641*

offsets   *p. 642*

bubble standard   *p. 642*

pollution allowances *or* banks   *p. 642*

SUGGESTED READINGS

Marcus, Alfred A. *Promise and Performance: Choosing and Implementing an Environmental Policy.* Westport, Conn.: Greenwood Press, 1980. Analysis of how the Clean Air Act passed and how the EPA was organized to implement it.

Meier, Kenneth J. *Regulation: Politics, Bureaucracy, and Economics.* New York: St. Martin's Press, 1985, chap. 6. Good brief overview of the laws and agencies that define our environmental policy.

Melnick, R. Shep. *Regulation and the Courts: The Case of the Clean Air Act.* Washington, D.C.: Brookings Institution, 1983. Thoughtful analysis of the extraordinary role played by the courts in implementing the Clean Air Act.

Rosenbaum, Walter A. *Environmental Politics and Policy.* 2d ed. Washington, D.C.: Congressional Quarterly Press, 1991. Analysis of the politics of environmental issues, including air and water pollution, the use of chemicals, nuclear power, and preserving open space.

Vogel, David. *National Style of Regulation: Environmental Policy in Great Britain and the United States.* Ithaca, N.Y.: Cornell University Press, 1986. An explanation of why environmental politics in the United States is so adversarial.

PART FIVE

The Nature of American Democracy

"Justice is the end of government.

It is the end of civil society.

It ever has been and ever will be pursued

until it be obtained,

or until liberty be lost in the pursuit."

— FEDERALIST NO. 51

23

Who Governs?

➤ What policies the government adopts

➤ The politics of various policies

➤ Evaluating the traditional theories of political power: Marxist, elitist, bureaucratic, pluralist

I t is time to try to answer the questions with which this book began. We want to know who governs and to what ends. In this chapter we shall try to answer the first question; in the next we shall say something about the second.

Describing, however precisely, government institutions and political organizations is a necessary but not sufficient condition for deciding who governs. Simply by choosing what to emphasize and what to leave out, one can write an account of the presidency that makes that institution seem "imperialistic" or a "pitiful, helpless giant" (to use the contrasting imagery of Arthur Schlesinger and Richard Nixon). And depending on what issues one picks, one can characterize Congress as a gathering of zealots that whoops new legislation through to passage in record time (as it did when it adopted a Social Security bill or a law outlawing mandatory-retirement practices in business) or depict it as an elephantine institution bogged down in its own convoluted procedures and internal quarrels (as it was when it labored for months over an energy bill and health-care reform).

Since we want to know who governs largely because our lives are affected by the distribution of political power, it seems only reasonable to try to answer the question of governance by examining, as systematically as we can, what policies the government adopts (or fails to adopt). A scheme for classifying public policies was presented in Chapter 15. It does not deserve to be called a theory, for there are many policies that do not fit well into the classification, and the distinctions that it suggests are crude and oversimplified. It does have at least two advantages: it requires us to look at a comprehensive list of policies (or nonpolicies) rather than permitting us to generalize about politics on the basis of a few issues in which we happen to be interested at the moment, and it calls attention to important ways in which those policies are thought to affect people (the distribution of perceived costs and benefits). Let us begin by summarizing what we have learned about the politics of making four kinds of policies and then use that information as evidence to evaluate the competing theories of political power that were described in Chapter 1.

Four Kinds of Politics

Majoritarian Politics

The costs and benefits of a proposed course of action are sometimes seen by people as being widely distributed: everybody, or almost everybody, or very broad groups of people stand to gain or lose in roughly the same way. We have seen several examples: the old-age and survivors' insurance provided under the 1935 Social Security Act, the medical benefits offered under the 1965 Medicare Act, the fair-business-competition requirements of the Sherman Antitrust Act of 1890 and the Federal Trade Commission Act of 1914, the general foreign-policy posture of the United States (internationalist or isolationist), the particular decisions to go to war in 1941, 1950, the 1960s, and 1991 (or *not* to go to war in 1914 or 1954), those features of macroeconomic policy that seem to contribute toward price stability and reasonably full employment, and the failure of attempts to reduce automobile use. All these policies, though different in substance, have in common the fact that similar political institutions and actors tend to play the leading roles.

Public Opinion Because matters like those listed above are highly visible and seem to affect the country as a whole, there usually is a discernible public opinion about them. Sometimes that opinion is quite specific, as when polls showed that a majority of Americans wanted something very much like what the Social Security and Medicare Acts ultimately provided. Sometimes that opinion provides only a general direction but no particular details to policy makers, as when the nation inclines toward internationalism or toward isolationism.

And sometimes that opinion may want things that turn out to be inconsistent, as when people want stable prices, full employment, and high levels of government spending—all at the same time. But policy makers are aware that public opinion does exist and that, even when it lacks detail or consistency, it is ignored only at a politician's peril. Citizens ex-

pect leadership and are willing to tolerate both delays and gambles in its exercise, but in the long run officials who ignore the thrust of opinion or devise policies that supply more costs than benefits are likely to suffer at the polls. The Republicans who opposed much of the New Deal misread public opinion or thought that they could defy it; they learned differently in the Democratic sweep of 1936. Democratic politicians were supported for a while in their military policy in Vietnam, but by 1968 a majority of people had decided that the policy was more burden than benefit and wanted a change. In 1980 the public was upset by inflation and the Iranian taking of American hostages; in 1992 they were concerned about the economy and crime.

The president and his principal advisers tend to play a leading, if not the dominant, role in majoritarian politics. People hold the president responsible for the economy, for national defense, for social welfare, and for foreign policy. Sometimes, as with foreign policy and military spending, that accountability is well taken, for the president, constitutionally and institutionally, plays the dominant role in these decisions. Sometimes, as with the state of the economy, the president may be as much victim as architect of the current state of affairs, but no matter: he must act as if he could control things because people believe that he should be able to control them.

Ideological Debate A proposal to adopt a wholly new program that applies to many people often precipitates an intense, sometimes ideological debate. Social Security and Medicare were enacted after just such a debate; the Family Assistance Plan was not enacted in consequence of such a debate. The struggles over neutrality versus interventionism in world affairs in 1939–1941, over strategic military doctrine in the 1960s and again in the 1970s, over policy toward Central America in the 1980s, over whether the nation should continue to follow Keynesian fiscal policy or adopt instead the big tax cuts suggested by supply-side economics—all these were genuine debates in which ideas as much as interests played a decisive role.

Worldview The outcome of such debates is often the institutionalization of a new worldview. In the 1950s the interventionists won out over the isolationists; the advocates of a federal social-welfare policy defeated the supporters of private charity and local relief programs; the critics of big business won at least a rhetorical advantage over the defenders of large industrial trusts. In these struggles a crisis often provided the decisive leverage: what the depression of 1929–1940 did for welfare policy, the attack on Pearl Harbor in 1941 did for foreign policy, and World War II did for fiscal policy. When the constraints of public opinion are loose, as they are in foreign policy, the worldview that is significant is that of policy elites who operate in or close to government. When the constraints are tighter, as they are in macroeconomic policy, elected officials discover that their freedom of action is narrowed. Incumbent politicians must balance national interests, as they define them, against the need to get reelected, which often leads them to fund certain programs—the "sacred cows"—more generously than others and to sweeten a general tax cut with specific benefits for particular groups.

But a crisis is not the only force that alters a popular or elite worldview. Higher education, the mass media, changing perceptions of the causes and consequences of various human problems—all have had an effect on people's ideas of what is desirable public policy. The history of welfare legislation provides a good example of how a worldview changes and evolves. It shows how a nation committed to a belief in self-reliance and the value of work has slowly modified (but not abandoned) those ideas as it came first to accept aid to the elderly and infirm (on an insurance basis), then to endorse aid to the unemployed and the indigent, and then to accept some limited forms of direct income support for the poor (whatever their age or work experience) in the form of food stamps.

But thus far this changing popular definition of social justice does not include large-scale income redistribution (as under a Family Assistance Plan or a negative income tax). And one particular form of welfare—Aid to Families with Dependent Children—is not seen to be a majoritarian policy at all, but one in which a client group ("them") benefits at the expense of society at large ("us").

Political Parties When Congress is adopting new majoritarian policies, political parties tend to be relatively important. Many of the key issues in social welfare, economic policy, and foreign affairs pit a substantial majority of Democrats against a substan-

The separation of powers can lead to stalemate, as when President Reagan repeatedly threatened to veto spending bills passed by a Democratic Congress.

tial majority of Republicans. In policies of this sort Congress has acted more like a parliament than an assemblage of independent legislators, debating broad issues in partisan and even ideological terms. Often no new policy can win if the parties are relatively evenly balanced in Congress, because, though Congress may debate in a parliamentary style, it lacks the parliamentary discipline to prevent a few defectors from one party or the other from blocking change. As a result the victory of a new idea often requires an election that gives one party an extraordinary majority.

A majoritarian policy once adopted *and* proved popular tends to lose its ideological significance and to attract bipartisan support, especially when government can readily increase the level of benefits to the public (as with Social Security and Medicare). However, if costs become very high—as they may have for Medicare—the "easy politics" of continual benefit increases may come under closer scrutiny.

Interest-Group Politics

When the costs of a policy are perceived to be concentrated in one distinct, relatively small group, and the benefits are seen as concentrated in a different, equally distinct and small group, interest-group politics dominates the policy-making process. Interest

Some "Rules" of Politics

H ere are some generalizations about American politics, distilled from what has been said in this book, offered in nervous awareness that our political system has a way of proving everybody wrong. (Before the 1960s it was a "rule" of politics that no Catholic could be elected president. John F. Kennedy took care of that.)

* Policies once adopted tend to persist, whatever their value. (It is easier to start new programs than to end old ones.)

* Almost all electoral politics is local politics. (Members of Congress who forget "home base" tend not to remain in Congress for long.)

* Whatever the size of their staff and budget, Congress and the White House will always be overworked. (More resources produce more work, which produces more resources.)

* Each branch of government tends to emulate the others. (Congress will become more bureaucratized to cope with an executive branch that is becoming more bureaucratized; judges will become more activist as Congress becomes more activist.)

* Proposals that seem to confer widespread and immediate benefits will be enacted whatever their long-term costs.

* Proposals that seem to confer delayed benefits will be enacted only if their costs are unknown, concealed, or deferred.*

* Nobody—businesspeople, bureaucrats, members of Congress, judges, professors—likes competition, and everybody will do whatever he or she can to reduce or eliminate it.

* "Planning" in government takes place after a crisis takes place.

* The mass media never cover a story about things that are going well. Thus the number of "problems" in society is a function of the number of reporters.

* If you want something, you are claiming a right; if your opponent wants something, he or she is protecting a vested interest.

_____

* This rule appears in William C. Mitchell, "The Anatomy of Public Failure: A Public Choice Perspective," paper no. 13 (Los Angeles: International Institute for Economic Research, 1978).

groups, of course, are active to some degree in almost all policies, but in issues of this sort they are the dominant political forces. Labor legislation—the National Labor Relations Act, the Taft-Hartley Act, the Landrum-Griffin Act, and other bills—are obvious examples of this. So also are the struggles between cable and over-the-air television broadcasters, between domestic ethnic groups over certain foreign-policy matters, and between importers and exporters over tariff laws and regulations. Similarly interest-group politics is evident in the tension between the Midwest and Northeast over acid rain, between opposed interests in cases involving rights in conflicts (such as the right to a fair trial versus the right to publish news), between parties competing before certain regulatory commissions (such as the Environmental Protection Agency or the Occupational Safety and Health Administration), and between blacks and whites in local communities with segregated schools.

Changing Cleavages in Society   The sources of interest-group policy proposals are to be found in changing economic and social cleavages in society. The rise of new technologies, the altered shape of markets, the rise and decline of regions, and changes in the organizational skills and resources of previously unorganized (or weakly organized) groups provide opportunities for new interest-group proposals. The debate over the Commerce Act of 1887 was set off by declining profits on the long-haul railroads, high monopolistic prices on many short-haul lines, rivalry among port cities for cheap access to the agricultural heartland of the country, and the rising importance of national and international markets for commercial farmers. Every interest had an incentive to organize for political action.

Though usually interest-group policies by their very nature stimulate the organization of all relevant interests, sometimes one group is able to block the organizing efforts of its rival. Many industries were able to do this in the nineteenth and early twentieth centuries with respect to would-be labor unions; whites were able to do this in many communities with respect to blacks and other racial minorities. These restraints on equality of organizational opportunity were made possible by the privileged access that one group already had to the coercive powers of the government. Industries could for many years count on the police and the army as allies in breaking strikes just as southern whites could use laws and administrative regulations to keep large numbers of blacks from voting.

That privileged power position was sustained by widely shared attitudes. Many people disapproved of unions or objected to strikes that seemed intended to win exclusive control by the union over entry into a particular job market. Similarly many citizens either were prejudiced against blacks or disapproved of black efforts to alter the distribution of political power. When these restraints on equal organizational opportunity existed, the disadvantaged group has had to employ a variety of tactics to change popular attitudes, attract legislative allies, and enlist the sympathy of the courts.

Political Parties   When a policy is proposed by one interest group and opposed by another of comparable political power, the political parties will often be deeply divided and, as a consequence, play little or no role in the resolution of the matter. The issue crosscuts partisan cleavages, and unlike parties in some European democracies, American parties are too weak to overcome such crosscutting pressures. The passage of the Commerce Act, for example, was not a partisan matter, and both Democrats and Republicans were split for decades over the question of civil rights. A few interest-group conflicts correspond to party lines—for example, labor-management issues have tended to parallel Democratic-Republican differences. But these are the exceptions.

Continuing Struggle   Interest-group politics does not end with the passage or defeat of the initial proposal. The struggle continues in other places—in the bureaucracy, before the courts, and in subsequent legislative sessions. The interest-group struggle that resulted in the passage of the National Labor Relations Act and the Occupational Safety and Health Act was transferred from the lobbies of Congress to the offices and corridors of the National Labor Relations Board and the Occupational Safety and Health Administration. Such agencies are less likely to be "captured" by any single interest than are those created as a result of client politics. Nor will the affected interest groups accept gracefully the decisions of the bureaucracy: appeals will be taken to the federal courts, and efforts will be made to get the law amended.

Public opinion and presidential leadership have some effect on the outcome of these struggles, but except in the formative stages that effect will ordinarily be weak. The public at large cannot possibly become so well informed or so concerned as to shape in important ways the conflict between well-organized, vitally involved opponents. The president can tilt the balance of power one way or another by whom he chooses to appoint to key bureaucratic agencies, but rarely does a president try to shape directly, deeply, or in detail the outcome of these conflicts. The public and the president are usually content to hope that the "right persons" are put in charge of refereeing interest-group conflicts. And except to report on the more important outcomes and occasional scandals associated with interest-group politics, the mass media rarely play an important role.

Client Politics

Sometimes the benefits of a policy are concentrated on one relatively small, easily organized group, and the costs are widely distributed over the public at large. In these cases client politics arises. We find this happening when the merchant marine receives a government subsidy, when veterans obtain special benefits, when farmers defeat efforts to curtail sharply the use of pesticides, and when various occupations are allowed by state licensing laws to govern themselves. Client politics is also at work when a community wishes to obtain a flood-control project or retain a military base, or when an economic or other interest obtains a "loophole" in the tax laws. Client politics need not involve obvious economic groups. We see client politics in action when teachers, organized as the National Education Association, seek the creation of a cabinet-level Department of Education, when organized Native Americans work to make certain that the Bureau of Indian Affairs is sensitive to their demands, when professors insist that only other professors decide on what research projects the National Science Foundation will spend its money, and when civil-rights groups dominate the work of the Office for Civil Rights.

Visibility   Client politics is low-visibility politics: neither the public at large nor (usually) the mass media have much interest in or knowledge about the policies involved. That can change, however. The regulations restricting the importation of foreign oil so that some oil companies are benefited became controversial because of the steep rise in oil prices in the early 1970s. The costs that consumers had to bear suddenly became so visible and so high that no client group in the oil industry could any longer hope that its benefits would go unnoticed. Similarly with the cost of electricity: for decades technological advances steadily reduced the cost of electricity. The public was indifferent to the fact that state utility commissions charged with regulating the price of electricity usually did so in a perfunctory manner. When electricity prices began rising steeply in the 1970s, however, consumers complained, and many state utility commissions began to take a tough line against utilities. Subsidies to tobacco farmers were largely ignored until many people became concerned about the harmful effects of cigarette smoking on health.

Noneconomic groups can also see their favored-client position deteriorate as a result of external forces. Extremist political groups may easily take advantage of the protection that they enjoy from the First Amendment during tranquil times; when a national crisis, such as a war, occurs, the public may suddenly decide that the costs of free speech have become too great and demand restrictions.

Political Parties   Political parties ordinarily play only a small role in client politics for an obvious reason: when a group makes an unopposed request, it would be foolhardy for most legislators to suppose that they had anything to gain by voting against it. Such measures typically pass with the support of lopsided majorities in both parties. Sometimes that outcome is facilitated by grouping a number of client proposals together in one package (a "pork barrel") so that there is something for everybody.

The political problem of a client group is ordinarily not that of winning a majority on the final vote but of getting its proposal brought up for a vote at all. Thousands of groups want things from the government; the limits of time and of congressional-committee interest reduce the number that will succeed. Finding a strategically placed congressional sponsor is essential. Because of the importance of having a

sponsor and the ease of avoiding publicity, many of the cases of political corruption occur in the arena of client politics. Some members of Congress think that they can charge for their services and get away with it. This is not to say that most or even many client-serving policies are the result of improper influence, but only that the conditions here are more conducive to such influence than they are in majoritarian politics.

Identifying the Clients   Occasionally a client-serving policy will be devised and proposed not by the client group itself but by a self-appointed (or "vicarious") representative. The Economic Opportunity Act of 1964 was intended to benefit the urban poor, especially in minority neighborhoods, but it was not carried through Congress by an organization representing the urban poor. This was done by professionals, bureaucrats, and political executives who thought that it was time to act on behalf of the poor. Because they framed their proposals in harmony with the existing consensus on how needy people should be helped (chiefly with services rather than money), and because their proposals seemed then to impose no costs on any other distinct segment of society, the easy passage of the Economic Opportunity Act revealed a kind of client politics. Conflict later erupted, however, when mayors discovered that the Community Action Programs were a challenge to the institutional authority of city hall. From then on the matter became one of interest-group politics.

Serving the Clients   Client-serving programs led to the creation of client-serving government agencies. Some scholars have spoken of such agencies as the Civil Aeronautics Board or the Federal Communications Commission as having been "captured" by the groups that they were supposed to regulate, but this is a misreading of history. These agencies and others like them were formed specifically to serve the interests of domestic aviation and radio broadcasting, just as the Veterans Administration (later renamed the Department of Veterans Affairs) was created to serve the interests of veterans. At the time that these laws were passed and for many years thereafter, people saw nothing wrong with such promotional ventures.

Important political changes have substantially reduced the freedom of action of client-serving agencies. The greater ease with which one can form and sustain groups purporting to represent mass or diffuse interests and the larger range of questions in which federal courts now intervene have made low-visibility client politics less common than in the past. Even tobacco farmers have had to accept lesser subsidies because of popular concerns over smoking. Consumer-advocate groups, environmental-protection groups, and organizations representing liberal and conservative causes use sophisticated fund-raising methods and take advantage of the easier access that plaintiffs have to courts (owing to changed rules on standing and provisions for fee shifting). By these methods such groups have reduced the extent to which diffuse interests go unrepresented in the arena of client politics but have created new problems because that representation is often inaccurate.

Moreover the proliferation of regulatory agencies in the government has resulted in the creation of off-setting pressure against some client interests. Client politics comes about because the majority of the people who must bear the costs (at a small per-person amount) of a client group's benefits have no incentive to organize to contest those benefits. The government, because it can sustain organizations through taxation rather than voluntary contributions, can create agencies to contest client claims. Thus the Antitrust Division of the Justice Department has challenged some of the practices of client-serving regulatory agencies, as when it criticized airline regulations for failing to promote competition.

Entrepreneurial Politics

Though opposition to client politics may eventually be institutionalized in the form of a new government agency, initially such opposition requires some form of entrepreneurial politics. An indifferent public can only be mobilized through skilled leadership that attracts substantial media attention. If real or imaginary threats to public well-being are pointed out, a congressional majority can be led to favor policies that will impose substantial costs on even a well-organized minority. This happened when congressional—and ultimately popular—majorities were led to support policies that set tough standards on air and water pollution or tightened the regulations on patent medicines and prescription drugs. It also happened when the public was aroused against socialists, anarchists, communists, and other radical political groups, and against high taxes.

Entrepreneurs can be found in the federal government, such as Dr. Harvey Wiley, the government chemist who dramatized the need for regulation of patent medicines, and Senator Estes Kefauver, who won headlines with his investigations of, first, organized crime and, later, the pharmaceutical industry. There were also Attorney General A. Mitchell Palmer and Senator Joseph McCarthy, who in different eras stimulated national passions directed at supposed subversives. Senator Bill Bradley and Representative Jack Kemp aroused interest in tax reform. Or the entrepreneurs can be found outside the federal government, as was Ralph Nader, who criticized various business practices; Upton Sinclair, who wrote about the conditions in meat-packing plants; and Howard Jarvis, who led a grassroots attack on high property taxes in California.

Compelling Symbols   Policy entrepreneurs must achieve by emotional appeals what appeals to narrow self-interest cannot. Thus the rationale for a new policy must be presented in dramatic terms and evoke powerful symbols in the public's mind—"clean air," "pure water," "Americanism," "sinister plots," "tax

Policy entrepreneurs can sometimes defeat client interests, as when cigarette companies were required to display health warnings on all packaging and advertisements.

Warning: The Surgeon General Has Determined That Cigarette Smoking Is Dangerous to Your Health.

cheats," "confiscatory taxes," and so on. Legislative and administrative action based on such appeals is often cast in equally bold terms, with strict standards, stern penalties, and short deadlines. Since the success of such proposals depends on arousing or taking advantage of a popular mood, the kinds of policies that can be adopted depend on the kinds of symbols to which people will respond. These symbols change from one generation to the next.

At one time atheists and communists seemed especially threatening forces; at another time people were largely indifferent to such groups. In an earlier era citizens might have accepted high levels of atmospheric pollution; in the modern era even low levels are a cause for popular concern. Some people may be indifferent to many deaths of coal miners caused by our dependence on coal as an energy source but be deeply upset by even the chance of accidents caused by a shift to nuclear power.

Sometimes no compelling symbol can be found. Advocates of strict gun control, for example, have found it difficult to mobilize an intense popular majority. This fact is sometimes explained by the power of the National Rifle Association. No doubt that group is influential, but so also have been the automobile industry, local pharmacists, and the American Medical Association. Nevertheless each of these groups has lost decisively on important issues because each was unable to defeat powerful symbolic appeals.

Promotion by the Media　The mass media are of great importance in entrepreneurial politics, especially key reporters and editors who decide to give serious attention to the proponent of a policy. Often a tacit alliance exists between a policy entrepreneur who supplies facts and arguments and a reporter who produces vivid feature stories. These stories often stimulate routine coverage of the issue by the press generally. Though political parties will play some role in this—one party is usually more sympathetic to the change than the other—that role is less significant than when majoritarian politics are involved. To the extent that the symbols are powerful, members of both parties feel compelled to pay them lip service.

Capture of the Agencies　The government agencies created as a result of entrepreneurial politics are often vulnerable to "capture" by the interest group ad-

versely affected by the policy. Since the policy adopted imposes significant costs on an organized group, that group has a strong incentive to weaken the administration of that policy. The pharmaceutical industry, for example, was from time to time able to weaken the enforcement of the food and drug laws by the Food and Drug Administration. In recognition of this possibility advocates of such laws will sometimes create agencies that will encourage interest-group competition (the regulations of the Environmental Protection Agency, for instance, impose costs on industries that must abide by them and create benefits for other industries that sell the equipment necessary to comply with the regulations).

The Courts　The courts play an important role in entrepreneurial politics. All affected parties, whether they be business firms or political movements, will seek court assistance in defending or resisting the new policy. Usually the courts have deferred to the popular mood, at least initially, and thus upheld new environmental regulations or new restrictions on free speech. In time, however, and especially as popular passions abate, the courts tend to evolve balancing tests to assess the fairness of the regulations following from the new policy.

Competing Theories of Political Power

In Chapter 1 we briefly sketched several competing theories of the distribution of political power in modern society. Each of these theories—the Marxist, the pluralist, the bureaucratic, the elitist—is an attempt to characterize the political system *as a whole.* From the evidence summarized earlier in this chapter, the reader may already have surmised what in fact is the case—that no single description of the entire political system seems adequate, as different policies tend to arise out of somewhat different political processes.

Of course there is one description of the entire system that is roughly accurate: ours is a representative democracy with a high degree of personal freedom in the area of speech and opinion. But though that says a great deal, it does not say everything; in particular it does not say much about the very different forms that "representative democracy" may take in particular policy areas. This point will become

It is hard to explain the importance of such issues as abortion by Marxist theories of politics.

clearer if we review the more familiar theories of politics in light of what we have learned about policy-making. We should bear in mind that even a fairly extensive review of policies will of necessity omit much that is important and that policies, perceptions of policies, and the political system itself are constantly changing.

Marxist Theory

Orthodox Marxist theory argues that the economic structure—and in particular the pattern of ownership of the means of production—shapes politics and determines political outcomes. The aspects of American policy-making most frequently cited in support of this view are foreign policy, defense policy, and economic regulation. With regard to foreign and defense policies we have seen that political considerations—public opinion, perceptions of international military and diplomatic necessities, and the worldview of government elites—and not corporate ones are the decisive factors. Political considerations account for at least the major diplomatic and military initiatives of this country and explain the overall level of defense spending. Economic regulations can be of very different kinds depending on whether they are the product of interest-group conflicts (the National Labor Relations Act), entrepreneurial skill (much environmental legislation), or client politics (an agency such as the Maritime Administration).

A Marxist—or more accurately an economic-determinist—theory of politics may be appropriate in the case where an economic client obtains a governmental advantage. An economic determinist can point to such client politics as maritime and dairy subsidies; price supports for large farmers; import quotas for sugar, beef, steel, and other products; and favorable tax treatment for various economic groups. But even with respect to client politics, economic determinism gives an incomplete explanation because a large and growing number of instances of client politics reflects the demands of noneconomic organizations. The most notable instances are those of ethnic, racial, and women's groups. The special status that such groups enjoy with the Office for Civil Rights, the Equal Employment Opportunity Commission, the Civil Rights Commission, and the Civil Rights Division of the Justice Department is not the result of their economic power, nor are the benefits that they seek exclusively economic.

Moreover even client politics takes place within the boundaries of public and elite opinion. One can easily explain in economic terms how the Civil Aeronautics Board (CAB) was created, since much of the work of that agency was directly beneficial to and protective of the major airline companies. It is harder to explain why the CAB was abolished and how the protected status of the airlines was removed over their intense opposition or how bills to increase competition among bankers, truckers, and securities brokers became law or why the auto industry was unable to prevent the passage of the Clean Air Act.

A Marxist might rejoin that the principal influence of economic, and especially corporate, power is not in the details of legislation but in the control of the agenda of politics, the shaping of the major thrust of policy (especially economic policy), and the distribution of political resources among potential participants in politics. There have been periods in American history where such influences have been important.

In an era of limited government, especially before the 1930s, many problems and practices never became political issues at all. Efforts to put them on the political agenda were met with the argument, often decisive, that it was wrong or illegitimate for the government to play any part in such matters as social welfare, income distribution, labor-management disputes, or the conditions of the workplace.

Since the 1930s, and in particular since the 1960s, it is hard to think of any problem, real or imagined, that has not found its way onto the political agenda. The "legitimacy barrier" has long since collapsed; politics today is not just about a few obviously public things but about nearly everything.

Similarly with the distribution of political resources: at one time access to such resources—money and votes—was sharply limited. The dollars were predominantly under the control of the wealthy, and the ballots heavily under the influence of party bosses and machines. Newcomers to politics often experienced difficulty in obtaining either. But in the modern era a remarkable transformation occurred. There was a wholesale redistribution of political resources without a prior redistribution of income:

- Nominations for office were awarded by primary elections rather than by party organizations.

- The partisan and elite media were in part replaced by the mass media.

- Racial and sexual barriers to voting were torn down.

- Issue organizations became easier to form and to maintain as a result of the role of private foundations, direct-mail fund-raising techniques, government grants and contracts, and fee shifting in court suits.

Moreover the making of economic policy was profoundly altered when elite opinion accepted the propriety of budget deficits and of public responsibility for the maintenance of a high-employment economy. Once the earlier constraints had been removed—the belief that balanced budgets were essential and that economic growth should be maintained by governmental aids to investment but not to consumption—public officials were free to pursue economic policies with an eye chiefly to their impact on majority opinion.

In sum, though many examples of policy-making are dominated by economic advantage, no simple theory of economic determinism offers an accurate comprehensive view of American politics.

Elitist Theory

In one sense almost all politics is elitist in that almost all government decisions are made by the few rather than the many. But elitist theory says more than this: it asserts that it is always the same elite that makes policy, whatever the nature of the issue; that this elite acts in concert or at least has a common social, economic, or occupational background; and that the elite is only weakly influenced, if influenced at all, by popular opinion.

One could describe client politics as a partial confirmation of elite theory. Obviously, when a few individuals—businesspeople, union leaders, professors, state welfare directors—acquire substantial influence over a broad policy area from which they benefit, they are an elite. But these examples illustrate the inherent ambiguity in elite theory. It makes all the difference whether a small group has power because it constitutes the direct *beneficiary* of some policy (as with dairy farmers, merchant seamen, or university research laboratories) or because it has certain general *characteristics* (wealth, prestige, social standing) that enable it to influence even policies that do not bear on the elite's material interests at all. Elite theory suggests that these personal attributes are the cause of its power.

Client politics should not be regarded as a confirmation of elite theory but as an illustration of how the distribution of the costs and benefits of a public policy differentially influences the abilities of the affected groups to shape that policy. The power of an activist federal judiciary is a better illustration of elite theory—not because judges are well paid or prestigious but because they are drawn from a profession (law) that provides them with cues and rewards that influence their decisions. Judges make decisions without being closely constrained by interest groups or voters but with considerable attention to the world of legal scholarship.

Foreign policy making is an especially interesting case of elite influence because here, unlike client politics, the power of the elite does not depend on its ability to win votes, mobilize interest groups, raise campaign funds, or represent ethnic or racial blocs. The influence of this elite depends on its members' being part of a group that shares certain ideas and that has acquired experience in managing or writing about foreign affairs. At one time the foreign-policy elite was also distinctive for its common social background—well-to-do, white, Anglo-Saxon Protestants who had attended Ivy League colleges. That is much less the case today. At present the members of the foreign-policy elite are distinctive more for their ideas than for their origins. These ideas are formed by experience, academic training, and personal ideology and tend to change from one generation to the next.

The most popular version of elitist theory today holds that career politicians in Congress make decisions without any serious regard for social reality or public opinion. But if that is true, how did these people get so much power? The answer, of course, is that we elected them to Congress, usually by big margins. Once, when people complained of elites, they had in mind business or labor leaders whom no one had elected. Today we complain of elites that the people have chosen.

Bureaucratic Theory

The bureaucratization of almost all aspects of life, public and private, is one of the dominant facts of modern society. Some have argued that the number, size, and influence of government bureaucracies have become so great that elected officials and their key advisers are almost powerless to affect policy: whatever top officials propose, the bureaucracy can subvert. Criticisms of the bureaucratic state have evoked a rich verbal imagery: "Leading the bureaucracy is like pushing a wet string." Or "Changing the bureaucracy is like moving a cemetery."

But it is as easy to overestimate as to underestimate bureaucratic power. Bureaucracy—that is, government by large organizations made up of appointed career officials—is most influential when the law confers on such officials wide discretion (or freedom to choose among alternative courses of action). Such broad discretion exists with respect to the procurement of weapons, the enforcement of civil-rights laws, the making of foreign policy, and the regulation of business enterprise.

Some of this discretionary authority is inevitable. There is no way, for example, that Congress could write into law the precise specifications of the fighter planes that the air force should buy or set the exact rates that railroads should charge for various classes of freight. But some discretion is the result of Congress's being unwilling to make choices that could, in fact, be made. Congress could, for example, clarify the ambiguous laws now governing methods for allocating TV licenses. Indeed it has tried to do this but found that congressional opinion is so divided that, willy-nilly, the choice must be left to judicial and administrative officials.

Bureaucrats have the least power when their task is specified by statute in exact language. This is the case in the area of the Social Security laws that tell the administrator exactly how much money is to be sent to what classes of people how often. Bureaucratic discretion is similarly narrow when it comes to providing benefits to veterans or to farmers. This is not to say that agencies working in these areas do not have bureaucratic problems, such as red tape or delays. They do, as do all large organizations, private or public. But those are very different problems from the

Despite the growth of the federal government, state and local governments retain more power here than in almost any other nation. This is the Texas legislature.

kinds that are created by the existence of bureaucratic discretion.

Congress has of late taken note of this and tried in some areas to reduce bureaucratic discretion. The clean-air and clean-water laws specify rather exact standards for pollution control; the Endangered Species Act gave (until it was revised in 1978) nearly absolute protection to such endangered creatures as spotted owls; the drug laws require the banning of certain foodstuffs and chemicals if they have *any* tendency to produce cancer. But if exact standards solve certain problems, they create others, such as the problem of keeping down the social cost of applying such strict standards.

There is at least one other way, besides exercising discretionary authority, in which bureaucracy has become more powerful. Increasingly the bureaucracy has become a source of the agenda of politics. The Economic Opportunity Act of 1964, the Medicare Act of 1965, proposals for new weapons systems, and many other important measures came not from private demands made on government but from government's generating demands on itself. Any presi-

dent who tries to formulate a legislative program quickly discovers that he is heavily dependent on the bureaucracy for most of his ideas, just as any president who tries to reorganize the executive branch soon learns that his chief opponents are his nominal subordinates, the bureau chiefs.

In short the power of bureaucracy may not depend so much on the kinds of politics (interest-group, client, or whatever) that led to its creation as on the clarity and consistency of the congressional laws governing it and on the political constraints that make it more concerned with following rules than serving people.

Pluralist Theory

The view that policies are made by conflict and bargaining among the organizations that represent affected groups is obviously an accurate description of what we have called interest-group politics. We have also seen the limits of the pluralist model: it overestimates the extent to which interest groups will form and be active. In client politics the large number of people who bear the widely distributed costs of a client-serving program have no incentive to organize and must rely instead on the vicarious (and perhaps inaccurate) representation supplied by "public-interest" lobbies. In majoritarian politics important decisions can be made as the result of direct presidential leadership of, and congressional response to, majority views, with interest groups playing only a marginal role.

With the rise of entrepreneurial politics and the collapse of some of the barriers to political participation, the pluralist theory has in a sense become more applicable to American government. Ironically, during the period (generally the 1950s) in which the theory was most influential, it was least accurate. Many interests (consumers, for example) were not represented in politics at all, and some groups in society (blacks, for example) were encountering barriers to political action. Today a greater variety of interests and of people is represented one way or another in Washington than ever before. Indeed some see in this an "atomization" of politics that has sharply reduced the power of government to do anything at all.[1]

But if the pluralist theory has become more descriptive of politics today, it still remains an incomplete one, not only because it does not take into account client or majoritarian politics but because it offers no clear explanation of the special nature of entrepreneurial politics. The policy entrepreneur as folk hero is not a new phenomenon, but it has become a commonplace one. This could not have happened without the rise of a national mass media and of a shift in beliefs among the upper middle class (or

at least that part of it called in Chapter 5 the "new class") in a direction that is supportive of certain kinds of entrepreneurship. Nor does pluralism take fully into account the extraordinary role played by the judiciary, an institution that can only with difficulty be described as a "group" with "interests." Rather the courts are a constitutionally based source of authority, the exercise of which depends crucially on the ideas and beliefs of its individual members.

SUMMARY

There is no single answer to the question "Who governs?" Everything depends on what policy is being proposed and on the opportunities that different proponents and opponents have to mobilize on their own behalf different parts of the fragmented institutions and processes of government. A crude classification can be made of some of the ways in which power is distributed by looking at the perceived costs and benefits of a policy. There are four types of policies: majoritarian, interest-group, client, and entrepreneurial.

Using these four types, we can evaluate the claims made by advocates of a Marxist, an elitist, a bureaucratic, and a pluralist theory of politics. No single theory is generally true, though some theories are correct in some cases. Any classification scheme and any evaluation of political theories must constantly be revised to account for changes in social reality, public perceptions of that reality, and ideas that people have about the proper purposes of government.

NAZIR MOHAMMED
ROBERT W THORNE
REED • NEAL S CROWDER
VENCILL • JAMES C WARD
PO • BOBBY JENE FIELDS
RE Jr • RANDY M RIGSBY
ART • MARCUS S STOEN
AM Jr • PATRICK D ERB
LL • PHILIP R JAMROCK
GREGORY S MORGAN
RDS • DAVID M SEXTON
UQUA • JAMES L GETTER
RAYMOND J SAATHOFF
S DEPAUL • CRAIG M DIX
WILLIAM G NEWBOULD
EELEY • BRYAN J SUTTON
NDT • JOHN R CHAMPLIN
GARCIA • JON M SPARKS
OLRIDGE • JACK L BARKER
LENDER • JOHN F DUGAN
D Jr • ROBERT P MARTIN
DLEY • JOHN L TRUESDELL
DAVID C LANCASTER
A SMALL • ANDRE B TIMS
AM • KARL W DRUZINSKI
COFSKI • WALTER R HALL
ROY • LARRY D LEAMON
Jr • ROGER W STAHL
AN AVANT

DALE A PEARCE • ...OR C STEPHENS • DAVID R WINKLE • E SNOWDEN • LAWRENCE R DANCE
LARRY J GAMMON • LARRY LEE ROBINSON • WAYNE R WILLIAMS • CHARLES L MARTIN • CHRISTOPHER M WINTERS
WILLIAM M GEORGE • DAVID P SOYLAND • THOMAS KUKOWSKI • LEONARD D MONTES
HERBERT S BARNES • GARY L HOLLINGSWORTH • DALE W DEHNKE • DANNY D ENTRICAN
JAMES D AGUILAR • ROBERT G BRUCE • PHILIP R DEARING • MIKLE E DIXON • JAMES E TORRENCE • GEORGE C YOSHONIS
GREGORY A SMITH • MARCUS E ARNESON • VINCENT M BENEDETTI • LOWELL T GLOSSUP • SCOTT H NEWPORT • RICHARD L BARBEE
CHARLES M CRAWFORD • ALVIN C CURRY • THOMAS F DELEHANT • MICKEY D LANG • HAROLD D WALLER
COLUMBUS V GROSS • BILLY D HERRING • RANDALL J GLASSPOOLE • JAMES E BODDIE
WILLIAM M KENEDY • CHARLES N KOWALK • WILLIAM H HJORTH • JOE F GAYOSSO • CHRISTOPHER J BIGLEY
STEVEN M MITCHELL • KARL J LAVALLEE • WILLIAM C JENNINGS • BILLY JOE JONES
OSIER L PRUITT • JOHN H NAJMOLA • ALBERTO A RAMIREZ • JAMES E TIGHE • ROBERT B LE CATES • DAVID B MATYKIEWICZ
GEORGE T TAYLOR Jr • BENNIE LEE NORTH • KENNETH G WESTERBERG • LEO C OATMAN • JEROME A OLSON
GARY A DORE • THOMAS R LUSHER • EDWARD W METCALF • WILLIAM T SMITH • J C SUMMERLIN
RALPH E POSEY • ROY G SHADDON • JAMES W PETERSON • HAROLD M CROWE
TOM R ADLER • PATRICK WEBER • ARMANDO MARIN ZEPEDA • RICHARD D PLUMM
LARRY R DEWEY • JIMMY D HUMPHRES • JOHN H GRUBER • RANDALL C SHORT • PHILIP D SHARP • HENRY D ADKINS
WILLIAM E ADAMS • GERALD M LUBBEHUSEN • ROY L MEADOWS • JACKIE DEAN STOGSDILL
MICHAEL D RIDDLE • MELVIN ROBINSON • JOHN D CURRAN • DENNIS C DURAND • ROY IGNACIO • JOHN W LITTLETON
HARVEY E HUMPHREY • LEROY J WESTRA • ROBERT L GREENSTREET • STEVEN W HENDRICKS
ROBERT L BROWN • STEPHEN CHAVIRA • PAUL D CARTER • JERRY FOY • THOMAS W KNUCKEY • PHILIP C TAYLOR
THOMAS G BLAIR Jr • STEPHEN G DAVIES • JOSEPH D ESPARZA • DONALD R MATHIS • PAUL D URQUHART
ROBERT K CAIN II • ERVIN B CHERRY • JOSE MARIA R ARREDONDO • WAYNE S CRAIG
STEVEN J KEARNS • CLINTON A MUSIL Sr • GARY J SHINN • AUGUSTUS ADAMS • JACK W BRUNSON
DEAN R ISAACS • LEON J JACKSON • PAUL G MAGERS • DENNIS L MEDUNA • GEORGE H GLAWSON Jr
ROBERT D McKINNEY • DON M RAMSEY • JAMES E SAXON • ANDREW C STRONG III • MARK R TAYLOR
DONALD L WANN • SCOTT W WYATT • EDWARD A WERMAN • KEVIN P FORCUM • DANNY R KING
ROBERT P SANCHEZ Jr • MICHAEL A LAMUSCA • GEORGE H POTTS • EDGAR D THOMAS • MICHAEL J VERSTRAETE
TERRY K BEGGS • RANDALL J BOYD • JOSE ANGEL SANCHEZ • DANIEL M BROWN • KIMBER L HALL
JAMES W MYLES • REY FRANCISCO TORRES-RAMOS • LEM CLARK • JOHN R JONES • WILLIAM J LAMMERS
LARRY LEE MILLER • DAVIS J MORGAN • WILLIAM K TAYLOR • BILLY H WYATT • EDMOND T BALLANCE
HAROLD E BARNARD • CARL W BORCHERS • MARTIN E LOVING • MICHAEL R STREET
...BAUMGARDNER • DAVID G BROWN • ANTHONY M EILERS • JERRY L THOMAS
...FARMER • HIAWATHA H WILLIAMS • JOHN R MICKLE • THOMAS E EPPERSON
...TON • HUGH ... EATON Jr • ROBERT L SIMMONS • JOHNNY ARTHUR
...WILL... BILLY • THOMAS J CONNIFF • JOHNNY...
...TY • CHE...LIE J BENTON • RALPH L CHURCH
...JAMES D JACKSON

24

To What Ends?

➤ Growth of government

➤ Competing interests

➤ Constraints on growth

➤ Rise of an activist government

➤ Disenchantment with government performance

➤ The influence of structure

➤ The influence of ideas

➤ Government reform

The most striking change in American government has been the dramatic expansion in the scope of its activities. Until well into the twentieth century, who ruled in Washington, or to what ends, made little difference in the lives of most citizens except in wartime or when a dispute arose over the management of the currency. National politics was not a career for many members of Congress; governors and mayors were more in the public eye than presidents; most citizens never came into contact with a federal official except when they received their mail.

When the federal establishment was relatively small, one could supply a fairly simple answer to the question of what ends the government served. If the Republicans were in power, the government sought high tariffs, tight money, and for a while the punishment of the southern states that had seceded from the Union. If the Democrats were in power, the government tended to lower tariffs, enlarge the money supply, and reach an accommodation with the South. From time to time circumstances altered this tidy pattern—a brief flirtation with "Manifest Destiny" and the acquisition of an overseas empire, the recurrence of various social issues such as temperance and the enfranchisement of women, the bitter struggle between labor and management over union organization, for example.

Today if one wants to know the objectives of government, the answer is "practically everything." The expansion of the scope of government has meant the proliferation of the goals of government. No single philosophy animates public policy because public policy is not responsive to any single set of interests or influenced by any single set of political resources. Washington has policies (such as highway construction and mortgage insurance) that make it easier to move out of cities, and policies (such as giving grants for neighborhood development) intended to encourage people to stay in cities. It has policies (such as pollution standards) designed to protect the environment even at the cost of economic growth,

661

and policies (such as tax deductions for investments) designed to stimulate economic growth. The government is formally committed to the goal of equal opportunity for all regardless of race and to programs that encourage employers to give special consideration to certain racial and ethnic groups in their hiring policies. In its foreign policy the government urges other nations to observe human rights and at the same time offers aid and alliances to nations that ignore fundamental rights.

Competing Interests

It is not perversity or stupidity that leads the federal government to pursue so many apparently inconsistent goals. Because the interests and opinions of people conflict, the policies of any government seeking to serve those interests and opinions will of necessity be inconsistent. People want different things. There is no "public opinion"; rather there are competing opinions of many different publics. As long as government is small, either the competing desires of people are reconciled by private arrangements (the market, voluntary agreements), or they are ignored. A large and active government might, of course, seek to be consistent, to follow a single philosophy, to serve some interests and not others. But if it is popularly elected, no such government will long survive.

A popular majority is a coalition of people who want different things from government; to win and hold that majority, a government must do many different things. But since it cannot do everything that a majority of the people want, it will lose the support of some, who will then join with others formerly in the minority to form a new majority coalition wanting a slightly different set of policies. A new government is elected, and the process starts over again. In the long run politicians win elections by promising to do things for people who either are not represented by or are disappointed by the party in power. Promises often become programs.

Politicians are not being venal when they try to win votes by making promises. They are being democratic. Politicians who fail to make promises (usually) fail to win elections; politicians who fail to deliver on their promises may not win reelection.

Restraints on the Growth of Government

For the better part of a century and a half democratic politics in this country did not produce a rapid growth in the power and scope of the federal government. There were three reasons for this. First, the prevailing interpretation of the Constitution sharply limited what policies the federal government could adopt. The Supreme Court restricted the authority of the government to regulate business and prevented it from levying an income tax. Most important, the Supreme Court refused, with some exceptions, to allow the delegation of broad discretionary power to administrative agencies. This changed somewhat in the early decades of this century and changed fundamentally in the 1930s.

But the Supreme Court could not have maintained this position for as long as it did if it had acted in the teeth of popular opposition. The second restraint on the growth of government was popular opinion. It was not thought legitimate for the federal government to intervene deeply in the economy (even the American Federation of Labor, led by Samuel Gompers, resisted federal involvement in labor-management issues). It was certainly not thought proper for Washington to upset racial segregation as it was practiced in both the North and the South.

It took constitutional amendments to persuade Congress that it had the authority to levy an income tax or to prohibit the sale of alcoholic beverages. Even in the 1930s public-opinion polls showed that as many as half the voters were skeptical of a federal unemployment-compensation program. Public opinion, of course, changed as a result of crises (such as the Great Depression), the spread of higher education, and other factors difficult to assess. Today people will quarrel about the *wisdom* of some government policy, but few any longer argue that the government has no *right* to enact the policy. Almost any policy—except for those that might restrict First Amendment and other fundamental freedoms—that can attract majority support can be enacted into law without a serious challenge to its legitimacy or constitutionality.

Third, the political system designed by the Framers was based on the assumption that the key

Washington, D.C., in 1858 and today.

problem was to prevent the government from doing too much. The separation of powers and other constitutional checks and balances were intended to make it difficult to enact a new policy unless that policy had broad support. No single faction would be able to dominate the government. For a long period things worked pretty much as intended: it was difficult to introduce significant new programs except in emergency circumstances or when approval was both enduring and widespread. But the same arrangements that make adopting new programs difficult make eliminating or revising old programs equally difficult. The very separation of powers that ensured that any new proposal would confront entrenched

critics also ensured that any existing programs would have entrenched defenders.

Ronald Reagan learned this when he took office in 1981 after promising to reduce the size of government. He did persuade Congress to cut taxes, but his plans to cut domestic spending resulted in only small declines in some programs and actual increases in many others. Though some programs, such as public housing, were hard hit, most were not, and agricultural subsidies increased dramatically. After Vice President Al Gore released his report on "reinventing government," not much happened. A large government has become a permanent fixture, mostly because that is what people want.

Consequences of Activist Government

It is tempting to make a sweeping judgment about a large and activist government, either praising it because it serves a variety of popular needs or condemning it because it is a bureaucratic affliction. Such generalizations are not entirely empty, but neither are they very helpful. The worth of any given program, or of any collection of programs, can be assessed only by a careful consideration of its costs and benefits, of its effects and side effects. But we may discover some general political consequences of the enlarged scope of government activity.

"Candidates night" in Strafford, Vermont: these traditions reveal the localism of American politics, even in an age of television.

First, as the government gets bigger, its members must spend more time managing the consequences—intended and unintended—of existing programs and less time debating at length new ideas. As a result all parts of the government, not just the executive agencies, become more bureaucratized. The White House Office and the Office of Management and Budget (OMB) grow in size and influence, as do the staffs of Congress. At the same time private organizations (corporations, unions, universities) that deal with the government must also become more bureaucratic. The government hires more people when it is running eighty programs concerned with employment than when it is running two. By the same token a private employer will hire (and give power to) more people when it is complying with eighty sets of regulations than when it is complying with two.

Second, the more government does, the more it will appear to be acting in inconsistent, uncoordinated, and cumbersome ways. When people complain of red tape, bureaucracy, stalemates, and confusion, they often assume that these irritants are caused by incompetent or self-seeking public officials. There is incompetence and self-interest in government just as in every other part of life, but these character traits are not the chief cause of the problem. As citizens, we want many different and often conflicting things. The result is the rise of competing policies, the division of labor among separate administrative agencies, the diffusion of accountability and control, and the multiplication of paperwork. And because Americans are especially energetic about asserting their rights, we must add to the above list of problems the regular use of the courts to challenge policies that we do not like.

Third, an activist government is less susceptible to control by electoral activity than a passive one. When the people in Washington did little, elections made a larger difference in policy than when they began to do a lot. We have pointed out in this book the extent to which political parties have declined in power and voters have reduced their voting turnout. There are many reasons for this, but an important one is often forgotten. If elections make less of a difference—because the few people for whom one votes can do little to alter the ongoing programs of government—then it may make sense for people to spend less time in party or electoral activity and to spend more time in interest-group activity aimed at specific agencies and programs.

The rapid increase in the number and variety of interest groups and their enlarged role in government is not pathological. It is a rational response to the fact that elected officials can tend to only a few things, and therefore we must direct our energies at the appointed officials (and judges) who tend to all other government matters. Every president tries to accomplish more, usually by trying to reorganize the executive branch. But no president and no reorganization plan can affect more than a tiny fraction of the millions of federal employees and thousands of government programs. "Coordination" from the top can at best occur selectively, for a few issues of exceptional importance.

Finally, the more government tries to do, the more things it will be held responsible for and the greater the risk of failure. From time to time in the nineteenth century, the business cycle made many people unhappy with the federal government—recall the rise of various protest parties—though then the government did very little. If federal officials were lucky, popular support would rise as soon as economic conditions improved. If they were unlucky and a depression lasted into the election campaign, they would be thrown out of office. Today, however, the government—and the president in particular—is held responsible for crime, drug abuse, abortion, civil rights, the environment, the elderly, the status of women, the decay of central cities, the price of gasoline, and international tensions in half a dozen places on the globe.

No government and no president can do well on all or even most of these matters most of the time. Indeed most of these problems, such as crime, may be totally beyond the reach of the federal government, no matter what its policy. It should not be surprising, therefore, that opinion surveys taken since the early 1960s have shown a steep decline in public confidence in government. There is no reason to believe that this represents a loss of faith in our form of government or even in the design of its institutions, but it clearly reflects a disappointment in, and even cynicism about, the performance of government.

Disenchantment with government performance is not unique to the United States; it appears to be a feature of almost every political system in which public opinion is accurately measured. The disenchant-

The Crime Bill

ment is in fact probably greater elsewhere. Americans who complain of high taxes might feel somewhat differently if they lived in Sweden, where taxes are nearly twice as high as here. Those who grouse about bureaucrats in this country probably have never dealt with the massive, centralized bureaucracies of Italy or France. People who are annoyed by congestion, pollution, and inflation ought to arrange a trip to Rome, Mexico City, or Tokyo. However frustrating private life and public affairs may be in this country, every year thousands living in other nations become immigrants to this country. Few Americans choose to emigrate to other places.

The enormous expansion of the scope and goals of the federal government has not been random or unguided. The government has tended to enlarge its powers more in some directions than in others; certain kinds of goals have been served more frequently than others. Though many factors shape this process of selection, two are of special importance. One is our constitutional structure, the other our political culture.

The Influence of Structure

To see the influence of structure, it is necessary to perform a mental experiment. Suppose that the Founders had adopted a centralized, parliamentary regime instead of a decentralized, congressional one. They had the British model right before their eyes. Every other European democracy adopted it. What

Political Proverbs

"If you can't stand the heat, get out of the kitchen."

—President Harry S Truman

"You scratch my back, I'll scratch yours."

—Attributed to Simon Cameron, secretary of
war in the cabinet of Abraham Lincoln

"To the victor belong the spoils of the enemy."

—Senator William Marcy of New York, 1832

"How you stand depends on where you sit."

—Attributed to Rufus Miles, formerly of
the U.S. Budget Bureau

"If it ain't broke, don't fix it."

—Bert Lance, director of the Office of
Management and Budget under
President Jimmy Carter

"Whenever you have to start explaining—you're in trouble."

—Representative Barber Conable of New York

SOURCE: Adapted from William Safire, *Safire's Political Dictionary* (New York: Ballantine Books, 1978). Used by permission.

difference would it have made had we followed the British example?

No one can be certain, of course, because the United States and Great Britain differ in many ways and not just in their political forms. At best our men-tal experiment will be an educated guess. But the following possibilities seem plausible.

A parliamentary regime of the British sort centralizes power in the hands of an elected prime minister with a disciplined partisan majority in the legislature and frees him or her from most of the constraints created by independent congressional committees or independent, activist courts. Had the Framers adopted a parliamentary system we might have seen in the United States:

- Quicker adoption of majoritarian policies, such as those in the area of social welfare. Broad popular desires would have been translated sooner into national policy when they were highly salient and conformed to the views of party leaders.

- More centralization of bureaucratic authority— more national planning, less local autonomy. More decisions would be made bureaucratically both because bureaucracies would be proportionately larger and because they would have wider discretionary authority delegated to them. (If the prime minister heads *both* the executive branch and the legislature, he or she sees no reason why decisions cannot be made as easily in one place as the other.)

- Fewer opportunities for citizens to challenge or block government policies of which they disapproved. Without independent and activist courts, without local centers (state and city) of autonomous power, a citizen would have less of a chance to organize to stop a highway or an urban-renewal project and hence fewer citizen organizations with these and similar purposes would exist.

- Local authorities would not have been able to prevent groups of citizens (such as blacks) from voting or otherwise participating in public life by maintaining at the local level segregated facilities that were illegal at the national level.

- If a situation like Watergate occurred, we would never know about it. No legislative investigating committees would be sufficiently independent of executive control to be able to investigate claims of executive wrongdoing.

- We probably would have fought in about the same number of wars and under pretty much the same circumstances.

- Taxes would be higher, and a larger share of our tax money would be collected at the national level. Thus we would find it harder to wage a "tax revolt" (since it is easier to block local spending decisions than national ones).

If this list of guesses is even approximately correct, it means that you would get more of some things that you want and less of others. In general it would have been easier for temporary majorities to govern and harder for individuals and groups to protect their interests.

The Founders would probably not be surprised at this list of differences. Though they could not have foreseen all the events and issues that would have led to these outcomes, they would have understood them, because they thought that they were creating a system designed to keep central power weak and to enhance local and citizen power. They would have been amazed, of course, at the extent to which central power has been enhanced and local power weakened, but if they visited Europe, they would learn that by comparison American politics remains far more sensitive to local concerns than does politics abroad.

The Influence of Ideas

The broadly shared political culture of Americans has also influenced the policies adopted by government. Paramount among these attitudes is the preoccupation with rights. More than the citizens of perhaps any other nation, Americans define their relations with one another and with political authority in terms of rights. The civil liberties protected by the Bill of Rights have been assiduously defended and their interpretation significantly broadened even while the power of government has been growing.

For example, we expect that the groups affected by any government program will have a right to play a role in shaping and administering that program. In consequence interest groups have proliferated. We think that citizens should have the right to select the nominees of political parties as well as to choose between the parties; hence primary elections have largely replaced party conventions in selecting candidates. Individual members of Congress assert their rights, and thus the power of congressional leaders and committee chairman has steadily diminished.

We probably use the courts more frequently than the citizens of any other nation to make or change public policy; in doing so, we are asserting one set of rights against a competing set. The procedural rules that set forth how government is to act—the Freedom of Information Act, the Privacy Act, the Administrative Procedure Act—are more complex and demanding than the rules under which any other democratic government must operate. Each rule exists because it embodies what somebody has claimed to be a right: the right to know information, to maintain one's privacy, to participate in making decisions, and to bring suit against rival parties.

The more vigorously we assert our rights, the harder it is to make government decisions or to manage large institutions. We recognize this when we grumble about red tape and bureaucratic confusion, but we rarely give much support to proposals to centralize authority or simplify decision making. We seem to accept whatever it costs in efficiency or effectiveness in order to maintain the capacity for asserting our rights.

We do not always agree on which rights are most important, however. In addition to the influence of the widely shared commitment to rights generally, government is also shaped by the views that certain political elites have about which rights ought to be given the highest priority. Elite opinion tends to favor freedom of expression over freedom to manage or dispose of property. Mass opinion, though it has changed a good deal in the last few decades, is less committed to the preferred position of freedom of expression. Rank-and-file citizens often complain that what the elite calls essential liberty should instead be regarded as excessive permissiveness. People who own or manage property often lament the extent to which the rights governing its use have declined.

The changes in the relative security of personal and property freedom are linked to a fundamental and enduring tension in American thought. Tocqueville said it best: Americans, he wrote, "are far more ardently and tenaciously attached to equality than to freedom." Though democratic communities have a "natural taste for freedom," that freedom is hard to preserve because its excesses are immediate and obvious and its advantages are remote and uncertain. The advantages of equality, on the other

A policy dilemma: nuclear power plants reduce our dependence on foreign and nonrenewable energy sources but sharpen our concerns over safety.

hand, are readily apparent, and its costs are obscure and deferred.[1]

Tocqueville may have underestimated the extent to which political liberties would endure because he did not foresee the determination of the courts to resist, in the long run if not the short, the passions of temporary majorities seeking to curtail such liberties. But he did not underestimate the extent to which in the economic and social realms Americans would decide that improving the conditions of life would justify restrictions on the right to dispose of property and manage private institutions. At first the conflict was between liberty and equality of opportunity; more recently it has become a conflict—among political elites if not within the citizenry itself—between equality of opportunity and equality of results.

The fact that decisions can be influenced by opinions about rights indicates that decisions can be in-

fluenced by opinions generally. As the political system has become more fragmented and more individualized as a result of our collective assertion of rights, it has come more under the sway of ideas. When political parties were strong and congressional leadership was centralized (as in the latter part of the nineteenth and the early part of the twentieth centuries), access to the decision-making process in Washington was difficult, and the number of new ideas that stood a chance of adoption was small. However, those proposals that could command leadership support were more easily adopted: though there were powerful organizations that could say no, those same organizations could also say yes.

Today these and other institutions are fragmented and in disarray. Individual members of Congress are far more important than congressional leaders. Political parties no longer control nominations for office. The media have given candidates direct access to the voters; campaign-finance laws have restricted, but not eliminated, the influence that interest groups can wield by spending money. Forming new, issue-oriented lobbying groups is much easier today than formerly, thanks to the capability of computers and direct-mail advertising.

These idea-based changes in institutions affect how policy is made. When there is widespread enthusiasm for an idea—especially among political elites but also in the public at large—new programs can be formulated and adopted with great speed. This happened when Lyndon Johnson's Great Society legislation was proposed, when the environmental- and consumer-protection laws first arrived on the public agenda, and when campaign-finance reform was proposed in the wake of Watergate. So long as such symbols have a powerful appeal, so long as a consensus persists, change is possible. But when these ideas lose their appeal—or are challenged by new ideas—the competing pressures make change extremely difficult. Environmentalism today is challenged by concerns about creating jobs and economic growth; social legislation is challenged by skepticism about its effectiveness and concern over its cost; campaign-finance reforms are, to some critics, merely devices for protecting incumbents.

This may all seem obvious to a reader raised in the world of contemporary politics. But it is different in degree if not in kind from the way in which politics was once carried out. In the 1920s, the 1930s, the

We often depend on voluntary associations to do what the government does in many other countries. Here the League of Women Voters helps people register to vote in Woodstock, New York.

1940s—even in the 1950s—people described politics as a process of bargaining among organized interests or "blocs," representing business, farming, labor, ethnic, and professional groups. With the expansion of the scope of government policy, there are no longer a few major blocs that sit astride the policy process. Instead thousands of highly specialized interests and constituencies seek above all to protect whatever benefits, intangible as well as tangible, they get from government. This vast array of specialized interests can often be mobilized (or overcome) to produce broad changes. In the 1960s and early 1970s there was change aplenty. But when enthusiasm wanes, when symbols lose their appeal, when ideologies are in conflict, the political process becomes slow, cautious, and localistic. This, of course, was what the Founders intended, but they intended it for a government far smaller and less active than what we now have.

We have a large government—and large expectations about what it can achieve. But the government finds it increasingly difficult to satisfy those expectations. The public acceptance of an activist role for government has been accompanied by a decline in public confidence in those who manage that government. We expect more and more from government but are less and less certain that we will get it, or get it in a form and at a cost that we find acceptable. This perhaps constitutes the greatest challenge to statesmanship in the years ahead: to find a way to serve the true interests of the people while restoring and retaining their confidence in the legitimacy of government itself.

Should the System Be Changed?

Some public-spirited citizens have concluded that the only way to serve the true needs of the people while bolstering their trust in government would be to change the system. The system, of course, has changed greatly over the last two centuries, so much so that one can speak intelligently about an Old System and a New System of American politics and government. The box on page 670 summarizes the differences between these two distinct styles of government.

Many people think that these evolutionary changes either don't go far enough or have made matters worse. They would like to see the Constitution amended. This is nothing new; almost from the day it was ratified, there have been debates over ways

How American Politics and Government Have Changed

Old System	New System
Congress:	
Chairmen relatively strong	Chairmen relatively weak
Small staffs	Large staffs
Few subcommittees	Many subcommittees
Interest groups:	
A few large blocs (farmers, business, labor)	Many diverse interests that form ad hoc coalitions
Rely on "insider" lobbying	Mobilize grass roots
Presidency:	
Small staff	Large staff
Reaches public via press conferences	Reaches public via radio and television
Courts:	
Allow government to exercise few economic powers	Allow government to exercise broad economic power
Take narrow view of individual freedoms	Take broad view of individual freedoms
Political parties:	
Dominated by state and local party leaders meeting in conventions	Dominated by activists chosen in primaries and caucuses
Policy agenda:	
Brief agenda	Long agenda
Key questions:	
Should the federal government enter a new policy area?	How can we fix or pay for an existing policy?
Key issue:	
Would a new federal program abridge states' rights?	Would a new federal program prove popular?

in which the Constitution might be improved. In general, there are today, as there were two hundred years ago, two kinds of critics—those who think the federal government is too weak and those who think it is too strong.

Reducing the Barriers to Action

To the first kind of critic, the chief difficulty with the Constitution is the separation of powers. By making every decision the uncertain outcome of the pulling and hauling between the president and Congress, the Constitution precludes the emergence, except perhaps in times of crisis, of the kind of effective national leadership the country needs. In this view our nation today faces a number of challenges that require prompt, decisive, and comprehensive action. Our position of international leadership and the need to find ways of stimulating economic growth (while reducing our dependence on foreign oil and conserving our environment) all require that the president be able to formulate and carry out policies free of some of the pressures and delays from interest groups and locality-oriented members of Congress.

This increase in presidential authority not only would make for better policies, these critics argue, but also it would help the voters hold the president and his party accountable for their actions. As matters now stand, nobody in government can be held responsible for policies: everybody takes the credit for successes and nobody takes the blame for failures. This is because the president, who tends to be the major source of new programs, cannot get his policies adopted by Congress without long delays and much bargaining, the result of which may be some watered-down compromise that neither the president nor Congress really likes but which each must settle for if anything is to be done at all.

Finally, critics of the separation of powers complain that the government agencies responsible for implementing a program are exposed to undue interference from members of Congress and the special interests that can capture a member's ear. In this view, the president is supposed to be in charge of the bureaucracy, but in fact he has to share that authority with countless legislators and legislative committees.

Not all critics of the separation of powers agree with all these points, nor do they all agree on what should be done about the problems. But they all have in common a fear that the separation of powers makes the president too weak and insufficiently accountable.

Their proposals for reducing the separation of powers include the following:

- Allow the president to appoint members of Congress to serve in the cabinet to create a closer alliance between the two branches of government (the Constitution forbids members from holding any federal appointive office while in Congress).

- Allow the president to dissolve a gridlocked Congress and call for a special election (elections now can be held only on the schedule determined by the calendar).

- Allow the Congress to require a president who has lost its confidence to face the country in a special election before his term would normally end.

- Require the presidential and congressional candidates to run as a team in each congressional district so that each voter would have to vote for the team as a whole. Thus a presidential candidate who carries a given district could be sure that the congressional candidate of his party would also win in that district.

- Have the president serve a single six-year term instead of being eligible for up to two four-year terms; this would presumably free him to lead without having to worry about reelection.

- Lengthen the terms of members of the House of Representatives from two to four years so that the entire House would stand for reelection at the same time as the president.

Some of these proposals are offered out of a desire to make the American system of government work a bit more like the British parliamentary system in which the prime minister is the undisputed leader of his or her majority in the British parliament. The parliamentary system is the major democratic alternative in the world today to the American separation-of-powers system. Another way of describing the aims of these reforms is that they would combine the somewhat greater centralization of power characteristic of the Old System of making policy with the larger agenda and bigger government characteristic of the New System.

Both the diagnosis and the remedies proposed by these critics of the separation of powers have been challenged. Many defenders of the present Constitution believe that other nations with a more unified political system, such as Great Britain, have done no better than the United States in dealing with the problems of economic growth, national security, and environmental protection. Moreover, they argue, close congressional scrutiny of presidential proposals has improved those policies more often than it has weakened them. Finally, congressional "interference" in the work of government agencies is a good way of ensuring that the average citizen can fight back against the bureaucracy. Without that so-called interference, citizens and interest groups might be helpless before big, powerful agencies.

Each of the proposals, defenders of the present system argue, would either make matters worse or have at best uncertain effects. Adding a few members of Congress to the president's cabinet would not help him much in getting his programs through Congress: of the 535 senators and representatives, only about half a dozen would probably be in the cabinet. Giving either the president or Congress the power to call a special election between the regular elections (every two or four years) would cause needless confusion and great expense: the country would live under the threat of being in a perpetual political campaign with even weaker political parties. Linking the fate of the president and representatives by having them run as a team in each district would reduce the stabilizing and moderating effect of having them separately elected: if a Republican presidential candidate won, he would have a Republican majority in the House; if a Democratic candidate won, he would have a Democratic majority. With a linked ticket we might expect dramatic changes in policy as the political pendulum swung back and forth. Giving the president a single six-year term would indeed free him from the need to worry about reelection, but it is precisely that worry that keeps the president reasonably concerned about what the American people want.

Finally, defenders of the present system simply do not agree that the separation of powers makes government inert. They marvel at the sweeping domestic- and foreign-policy initiatives taken during this century. How, they ask, can a governmental system capable of launching a New Deal, a Great Society, and a rocket to the moon, of mobilizing for World War I, World War II, and Vietnam, and of readying to impeach a president for violating his oath of office be characterized as antiquated or prone to inaction?

Defenders believe that problems in the system may result less from the separation of powers and more from the inability (or unwillingness) of key political leaders to work within it. They point, for example, to Jimmy Carter's first years in office. Carter did relatively little to persuade Congress to support his early domestic initiatives. His party had a majority in both houses of Congress but that did not seem to matter. Several of his efforts to court the press and the public were bungled. If the separation of powers, and not a lack of political skills, explains the policy stalemate suffered by President Carter, then how, defenders ask, did his immediate successor in the Oval Office, Ronald Reagan, succeed in getting Congress to act quickly on his major domestic proposals?

Increasing the Barriers to Action

The second kind of critic of the Constitution thinks the government does too much, not too little. Though the separation of powers at one time may have slowed the growth of government and moderated the policies it adopted, in the last few decades government has grown helter-skelter. The problem, these critics argue, is not that democracy is a bad idea, but that democracy can produce bad, or at least unintended, results if the government caters to the special-interest claims of the citizens rather than to their long-term values.

To see how these unintended results might occur, imagine a situation in which every citizen thinks the government is too big, taxes too heavily, and spends too much. Each citizen wants the government made smaller by reducing the benefits other people get—but not by reducing the benefits he or she gets. In fact this citizen may even be willing to see his or her own benefits cut, provided everybody else's are cut as well, and by a like amount.

But the political system attends to individual wants, which may or may not be in the public interest. It gives aid to farmers, contracts to industry, grants to professors, pensions to the elderly, and loans to students. As someone once said, the government is like an adding machine: during elections, candidates campaign by promising to do more for whatever group is dissatisfied with what the present officeholders are doing for it. As a result, most elections bring to office men and women who are com-

mitted to doing more for somebody. The grand total of all these additions is more for everybody. No politician has an incentive to do less for anybody.

Moreover, a big government is hard to manage. When the government tries to do too much, it does nothing well. To these critics, our government is big without being strong, fat but not effective.

To remedy this state of affairs, these critics suggest various mechanisms, but principally a constitutional amendment that would either set a limit on the amount of money the government could collect in taxes each year, or require that each year the government have a balanced budget (that is, not spend more than it collects in taxes), or both. In some versions of these plans, an extraordinary majority (say, 60 percent) of Congress could override these limits, and the limits would not apply in wartime.

The effect of such amendments, the proponents claim, would be to force Congress and the president to look at the big picture—the grand total of what they are spending—rather than just to operate the adding machine by repeatedly pushing the "add" button. If they could only spend so much during a given year, they would have to allocate what they spend among all the rival claimants, comparing the worth of each claimant to that of every other one. For example, if more money were spent on the poor, less would be spent on the military, or vice versa. In this way, we could no longer add to the national debt by continuing to run up big deficits.

Some critics of an overly powerful federal government think these amendments will not be passed or may prove unworkable. Instead they favor enhancing the president's power to block spending by giving him a line-item veto. The president must now sign or veto a bill as a whole, take it or leave it. Most state governors, with a line-item veto, can disapprove a particular part of a bill and approve the rest. The theory is that such a veto would better equip the president to stop unwarranted spending without vetoing the other provisions of a bill that he approves of.

Finally, some of these critics of a powerful government feel that the real problem arises not only from an excess of "adding-machine" democracy but also from the growth in the power of the federal courts. These critics would like to devise a set of laws or constitutional amendments that would narrow the authority of federal courts.

The opponents of these constitutional amendments argue that to restrict the level of taxes and to require a balanced budget are unworkable suggestions, even assuming—which they do not—that a smaller government is desirable. There is no precise, agreed-upon way to measure how much the government spends or to predict in advance how much it will receive in taxes during the year; thus defining and enforcing a "balanced budget" is no easy matter. The government has shown great ingenuity in spending money in ways that never appear as part of the regular budget (for example, Social Security).

The line-item veto may or may not be a good idea, these people argue, but we can't tell just by looking at the states that have it, because they differ markedly from the federal government in power and responsibilities. And if we tried it, we might discover that the president would use it not to spend less but to spend more—by threatening to veto something of modest cost that Congress wants in order to get Congress to vote for something expensive that the president wants.

Finally, proposals to curtail judicial power are thinly veiled attacks, the opponents argue, on the ability of the courts to protect essential citizen rights. If Congress and the people do not like the way the Supreme Court has interpreted the Constitution, they can always amend the Constitution to change that specific ruling. There is no need to adopt some general, across-the-board limitation on court powers.

Term Limits

As we suggested in Chapter 11, a change that might make our system either more or less democratic is to limit the number of terms that people can serve in Congress. Already, the president is limited to two terms. The most common proposal is to limit members of the House to six terms (a total of twelve years) and members of the Senate to two (also a total of twelve years). In 1992, the people in fourteen states adopted proposals that, if upheld in the courts, will impose term limits on their delegations to Congress.

But it is far from clear that the courts will uphold these measures. The Constitution makes Congress the sole judge of the qualifications of its members and limits the states to determining the time, place,

Four Simple Rules for Improving Government

1. **No law is valid unless the members of Congress voting for it have read it.** The Ninety-seventh Congress considered over ten thousand bills and enacted over five hundred. The tax bill alone ran to several hundred pages. What is your guess as to the number of these bills that the average member of Congress reads?

2. **No law or regulation is valid if it is incomprehensible to the average citizen.** Section 509(a) of the Internal Revenue Code reads as follows: "For purposes of paragraph (3), an organization described in paragraph (2) shall be deemed to include an organization described in section 501 (c) (4), (5), or (6) which would be an organization described in paragraph (2) if it were an organization described in section 501 (c) (3)." Any questions?

3. **No law is valid if it does not clearly state its goals and the means to attain them.** The law creating the Federal Communications Commission instructs it to award radio and television licenses on the following principle: to serve "the public interest, convenience, or necessity." Now you know.

4. **No law passed by Congress is valid if it does not apply to Congress itself.** For decades Congress exempted itself and its employees from many laws regulating the workplace, such as the minimum-wage and worker-safety laws. But in 1995 it voted to make itself subject to many of these. Will it continue to do this in the future?

SOURCE: Adapted from Irving Younger, "Socrates and Us," *Commentary* (December 1980): 46–49. Reprinted by permission. All rights reserved.

and manner of holding congressional elections. We will probably see a court challenge when these term limits begin to take effect.

It is also not clear what effect such limits might have. Proponents argue that it will once again make members of Congress "citizen legislators," not career politicians. Knowing that they can serve only twelve years, they will be free, at least toward the end of their last term in office, to do what is right rather than what is demanded by interest groups or required by their own desire for reelection.

But opponents argue that short-term legislators will never master the intricacies of federal politics and policies, and so they will become dependent on unelected staff members and Washington lobbyists. And they point to the many long-term legislators who are widely admired. Finally, they argue that the voters are the best judges of who should stay in office and so should have the right to keep reelecting their own representatives and senators if they wish.

There is no way to settle this issue by arguments or theories. We will learn what difference term limits make only if we try them. But there is a risk: if we try them and don't like them, it will be very hard to get rid of them. In any event, term limits may be hard to try because Congress doesn't want them and Congress must approve a constitutional amendment to impose them (unless, of course, two-thirds of the state legislatures call for a constitutional convention to consider them).

Who Is Right?

Some of the arguments of these various critics of the Constitution may strike you as plausible or even entirely convincing. But one should not make or re-make a Constitution based entirely on abstract reasoning or unproven factual arguments. Even when the Constitution was first written in 1787, it was not an exercise in abstract philosophy but rather an effort by the Framers to solve pressing, practical problems in the light of a theory of human nature, the lessons of past experience, and a close consideration of how governments in other countries had worked.

Just because the Constitution is now two hundred years old does not mean that it is out of date. The crucial questions are these: How well has it worked over the long sweep of American history? And how well has it worked compared to the constitutions of other democratic nations?

The only way to answer these questions is to study American government closely, with special attention to its historical evolution, the way it makes particular policies, and the practices of other nations. This book has provided only an introduction to the workings of American government and has said very little about how it works in comparison to other governments. Therefore, you should not try to make up your mind about what, if anything, needs to change in our Constitution from what you have learned here. Learn more.

PART SIX

State and Local Government

"The powers reserved to the several States will extend to all the objects which, in the ordinary course of affairs, concern the lives, liberties, and properties of the people, and the internal order, improvement, and prosperity of the State."

— FEDERALIST NO. 45

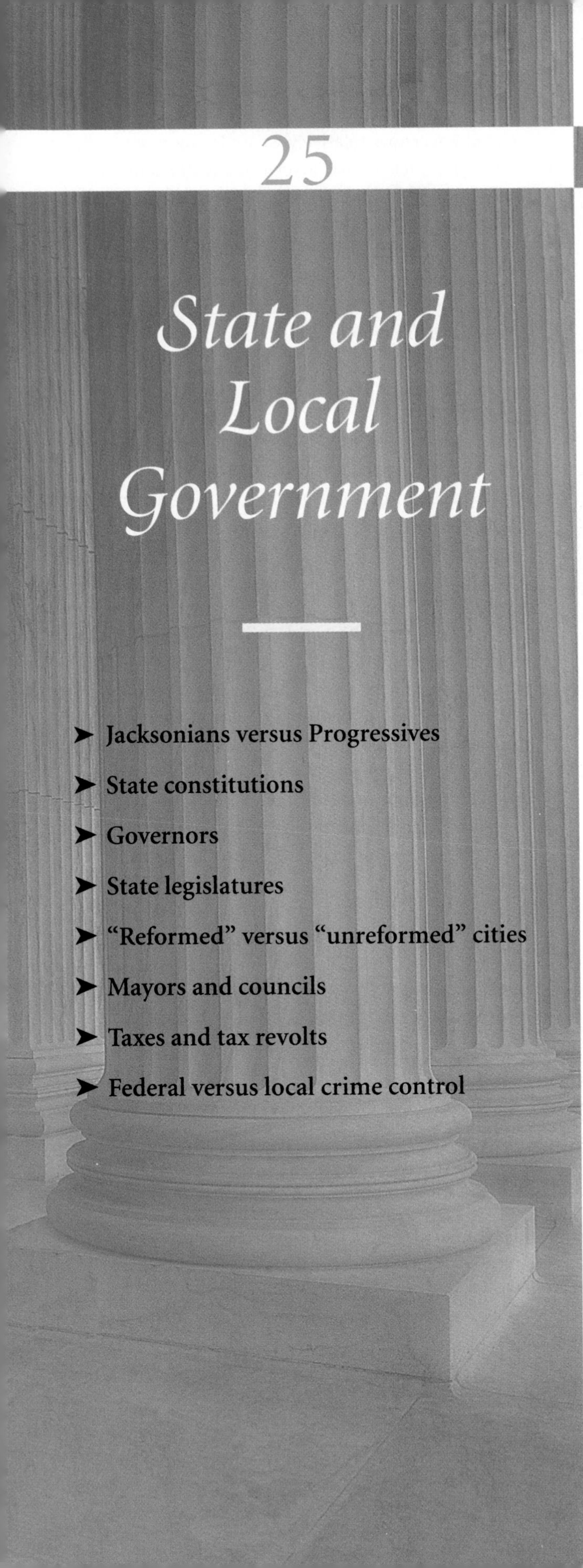

25

State and Local Government

➤ Jacksonians versus Progressives

➤ State constitutions

➤ Governors

➤ State legislatures

➤ "Reformed" versus "unreformed" cities

➤ Mayors and councils

➤ Taxes and tax revolts

➤ Federal versus local crime control

State governments are not miniature versions of the federal government, and municipal governments are not miniature versions of state ones. There is almost as much variation in the forms and operations of governments *within* the United States as between the United States and other democratic nations.

At all levels, government in the United States is in some sense democratic, but consider these variations on that theme:

• In the national government the president and vice president are the only elected executive officers; in most states the executive power is divided among several elected officials—a governor, attorney general, secretary of state, and treasurer. In some states the people even elect commissioners in charge of agriculture, insurance, education, and public utilities.

• In Congress party leaders have little influence over who becomes chairmen of the standing committees; in many state legislatures party leaders can select and dismiss committee chairmen almost at will.

• At the national level executive and legislative powers are divided between two separately elected branches of government; in many American cities the legislature (a city council) chooses the executive (a mayor or city manager).

• Federal judges are appointed by the president and confirmed by the Senate; many state judges are elected by the people.

• The people never vote directly on any matter decided by the national government; the people do vote directly on a host of matters decided by many state and local governments.

• The Constitution of the United States is brief, general, and rarely amended; the constitutions of many states are long, detailed, and frequently amended.

Andrew Jackson appealed to the people's distrust of strong executive powers that is built into many state constitutions.

The constitution and politics of each state, like those of the United States, have been profoundly shaped by important philosophical beliefs as to the nature and scope of government. These changing beliefs help explain the differences among state governments and between state and national governments.

State Constitutions and Political Philosophy

The Antifederalists may have lost their struggle to prevent the ratification of the United States Constitution, but the principles that they espoused—numerous elected officials, short terms of office, weak executives—triumphed in many states and cities.

The original thirteen states had been British colonies, ruled in most cases by a royal governor selected by the king. The American Revolution put an end to that and ushered in a period in which executive power was held in deep suspicion. Accordingly the new state constitutions vested most governmental authority in the legislatures and kept the newly

elected governors relatively weak. In many states the legislature picked the governor and the judges. In only a few states could the governor veto legislative acts. Though the legislatures were dominant in these new state governments, they were not, by modern standards, based on a wholly democratic electorate, for the right to vote was restricted by property and (sometimes) religious qualifications.

The Jacksonian Era

In the early nineteenth century the right to vote was significantly extended, the result in part of party competition and in part of rising land values that reduced the effect of the old property qualifications for voting. Soon most white males were eligible to vote. The mood of these voters was distinctly antigovernment. Many state constitutions were revised in the two decades preceding 1840 in ways intended to make state governments both democratic and weak. Property qualifications for voting were eliminated, and restrictions on the power of state governments were devised. For example, many legislatures were forbidden from meeting more often than once every two years or for more than a few weeks at a time. The theory was that if the politicians could not meet, they could not do much harm. Moreover, specific restrictions were placed on what kinds of laws the legislatures could pass. These included limits on the amount of debt that states could incur and prohibitions on raising the salaries of state officials or chartering private banks.

In some ways the powers of the governors were increased by filling the office through direct popular election, lengthening the term of office, and allowing governors to veto legislative acts. But these changes were not really intended to make the governor powerful; they were designed only to make the governor a more effective check on the legislature. In short, the principle of separation of powers was being vigorously pursued. To keep the governor weak, executive authority in state governments was divided among a host of elected officials—treasurers, auditors, secretaries of state, attorneys general, superintendents of education, even surveyors and state printers. In New York, for example, executive power was divided among a dozen or so elected officials. (It was ironic that this should be described as the era of "Jacksonian democracy," for the man in whose name the assault on executive authority was proceeding at the state level was himself substantially enlarging the power of the presidency at the national level.) Essentially the same changes were occurring at the local level. The power of mayors was reduced and that of city councils enlarged.

The result of all these changes was the radical decentralization of political authority at the state and local level. Whereas at the national level liberty was to be preserved by checks and balances among three branches of government, at the local level it was to be maintained by multiplying the number of elected officials and keeping each as weak as possible. This decentralization meant that for anything to get done at all in state or local government, a large number of legally independent elected officials would have to agree.

But unlike the national government, state and local governments had a lot of work to do. They had to pave streets, build city halls, run schools and jails, and deal with the poor and helpless. Some way had to be found for all the independent elected officials to agree on a program. The way was provided by the political party.

Political parties grew in power not only because they were needed to get voters out to the polls but also because they helped to make the decentralized government function. If a party in New York or New Jersey could elect a slate of candidates—say, for governor, lieutenant governor, treasurer, attorney general, state senator, and state representative—it could put into office people beholden to it. A party leader could make certain that a bill was enacted into law by inducing each party member holding office to support it. If somebody refused to go along, that official could be dropped from the party slate in the next election. Moreover party leaders often controlled valuable **patronage**—jobs, contracts, and money that could be given to or withheld from officeholders to reward or punish their party loyalty. Thus the local political parties, especially those that were party machines, came to dominate state and local government in many places.

The Progressive Response

The benefits of party government—in making certain that the decentralized government could function—were purchased at a price: corruption and in-

efficiency. Tammany Hall dominated the politics of New York City; the political machine of the Southern Pacific Railroad dominated California. Many upper-middle-class citizens thought that the costs of party or machine rule were too high and began a variety of efforts to reduce them. These efforts, called the **progressive movement,** began in earnest after the Civil War and reached a peak during the early years of the twentieth century. Though there were many differences among progressives, most shared a desire to purify politics and make government more efficient by attacking the sources of partisan influence.

Among the changes that they proposed were these:

- Make elections nonpartisan so that political parties will not play a role in them.

- Reduce the number of state officials so that executive authority is concentrated in the hands of the governor.

- Put the management of city affairs into the hands of an appointed, professional city manager.

- Reduce the size of state legislatures and city councils so that the close ties between legislators and local interests are reduced.

- Check the power of legislatures and city councils by giving the people the right to vote directly on important measures (the initiative, referendum, and recall, to be described).

- Eliminate patronage; make all appointments to administrative positions on the basis of merit.

In the early 1900s the progressives won power in a number of states, including California, Minnesota, and Wisconsin, where they proceeded to put their proposals into effect. They failed to make much headway in other states, such as Illinois, Massachusetts, and New York. But the struggle continues. From the beginning of the twentieth century right down to the present, much of the conflict in state and local government is between those who prefer the **Jacksonian model** of government and those who prefer the **progressive model.** The modern-day Jacksonians are those who want to have a lot of elected officials closely accountable to the voters, who believe that the average citizen and not some appointed expert should have the most authority, who want specific neighborhoods and not the "city as a whole"

California

California's politics reflects two deep divisions in the state—between north and south and between liberals and conservatives. Its congressional delegation, the largest in the nation, is perhaps the most divided ideologically: California Democrats are more liberal than Democrats elsewhere, and California Republicans are more conservative than Republicans elsewhere. The state's governors have ranged from the conservative Ronald Reagan to the liberal Jerry Brown. Today California has two Democratic senators, both of them women (Barbara Boxer and Dianne Feinstein). But for many years the state sent one Democrat and one Republican to the Senate.

The governor serves a four-year term to which he or she can be reelected. The governor shares authority with six other elected executive officers, an elected Board of Equalization, and several quasi-independent commissions (such as the one that runs the universities). The number of appointments that the governor can make is limited by a strong civil-service system, but he or she does have a line-item veto and substantial reorganization authority.

The legislature, which meets annually, is one of the most professionalized in the nation; its forty senators (who serve four-year terms) and eighty Assembly members (who serve two-year terms) are among the best paid and best staffed in the country. The speaker of the Assembly is very powerful, appointing all committee chairmen and most committee members. Since 1980 he has been Willie Brown, a black Democrat chosen with the support of Assembly Republicans as well as Democrats.

California's political parties are organizationally quite weak, a legacy of the progressive reforms begun in 1911. The real influence in elections comes, not from party leaders, but from elected officials and interest groups, professional campaign-management firms, newspaper endorsements, and television advertising.

The initiative, referendum, and recall are heavily used in California. During 1980–1983 eighty initiative measures were circulated to gather petition signatures; nine got on the ballot, and three were approved. The famous Proposition 13, which cut property taxes, was an initiative measure approved in 1978. So important are these petitions that firms have sprung up that are in the business of gathering signatures.

represented on city councils, and who expect legislators to intervene in government decisions on behalf of the interests of individual citizens. The modern-day progressives are those who prefer few elected officials, power concentrated more in executive than in legislative hands, greater reliance on experts, and city-council members elected from the city at large rather than from small districts.

In the late 1960s and early 1970s progressive sentiment was once again on the rise. Between 1965 and 1976 nine states adopted new constitutions and many others amended theirs; the new provisions tended to increase the authority of the governor. But similar changes were less apparent in city government. It may be that progressives were more successful at the state level because voters saw state issues (such as taxes and welfare programs) in terms of the need for greater efficiency and lower costs but saw city issues (such as school integration and neighborhood services) in terms of a need for greater citizen participation and closer checks on the power of experts. Moreover, Jacksonian systems are better adapted to giving representation to racial and ethnic groups (many of which tend, as we shall see, to be underrepresented in governments based on progressive principles), and it has been the cities, more than the states, that have been the arena of racial and ethnic politics.

The conflict between these two conceptions of politics, coupled with the normal struggles among competing interests, have given an amazing variety to state and local government in this country. Scarcely any other nation uses as many different political systems to manage local affairs. The continued existence of this variety is testimony to the special importance that Americans attach to local issues.

The Legal Basis of State and Local Government

That importance was evident in the debates over the initial ratification of the Constitution and the insistence of many that a Bill of Rights be added to it that would, in part, reaffirm the special place of the states. The Tenth Amendment specifies that "powers not delegated to the United States by the Constitution, nor prohibited by it to the States, are reserved to the States respectively, or to the people."

This amendment may have meant something at one time, but it does not mean much now. With only a few short-lived exceptions, the Supreme Court has refused to restrict the exercise of federal powers just because such powers intrude on powers reserved to the states. For example, in 1985 it decided that a mass-transit system in San Antonio, Texas, had to pay its workers in accordance with the federal Fair Labor Standards Act even though the system was owned by the city government.[1] In its opinion the Court majority suggested that it was up to the political process, not the courts, to decide what, if any, independence from federal control the cities and states should enjoy. Congress has the power to regulate interstate commerce even if that regulation interferes with state regulation of local commerce. Congress and the courts have interpreted the Constitution to permit a wider and wider exercise of federal power so that the things that are "reserved" as the exclusive powers of the states have become fewer and fewer.

But though the states have many fewer *exclusive* powers than they once had, they still have many powers that are *shared* with the federal government. In general the states can do anything that is not prohibited by the Constitution or preempted by federal policy and that is consistent with their own constitution. One generally recognized state power is the police power.

The **police power** refers to those laws and regulations, not otherwise unconstitutional, that promote health, safety, and morals. Thus the states can enact and enforce criminal laws, require children to attend school and citizens to be vaccinated, and restrict (subject to many limitations) the availability of pornographic materials or the activities of prostitutes and drug dealers. As a practical matter the most important activities of state and local governments involve public education, law enforcement and criminal justice, health and hospitals, roads and highways, public welfare, and control over the use of land.

The Constitutional Framework of State Government

How the states manage these functions is determined by state constitutions. Though they are like the federal Constitution in setting forth the offices that are to exist, the powers that they are to have, and the manner in which they are to be filled, these docu-ments are unlike the federal Constitution in going well beyond these structural matters to include all sorts of specific arrangements that one might suppose could be left to ordinary legislation. For example, the California constitution sets forth rules governing the duration of wrestling matches, and the Georgia constitution provides a $250,000 reward to the first person who strikes oil in the state. One reason that state constitutions are so detailed is that they are often easy to amend; usually an amendment requires only a two-thirds vote of the legislature (in fourteen states it requires only a simple majority vote) followed by a majority vote of the citizens in the next election. And in many states, such as California, voters can amend the constitution without going through the legislature if they can get enough signatures (California requires 8 percent of those who voted in the last gubernatorial election) to put a proposed amendment on the ballot. As a result the California constitution has been amended well over four hundred times.

Another reason for all this detail is that, since the early nineteenth century, citizens and interest groups have not trusted state government to do the right thing and so have told the government what to do or not to do by writing it into the constitution. If you were a small-town banker living in Illinois, for example, you might worry that someday the legislature might allow big-city banks to open branches in your town to compete with you. One way to prevent that would be to amend the constitution to prohibit branch banking. Exactly this was done, and so for many decades branch banking in the state of Illinois was unconstitutional.

States frequently write entirely new constitutions. Ten states have had five or more constitutions in their history. Louisiana has had eleven and Georgia ten. (The oldest state constitution still in effect, albeit much amended, is that of Massachusetts, adopted in 1780.)[2] But such changes are at times deeply controversial. In 1975 Texas tried unsuccessfully to adopt a new constitution. It was defeated by the voters in part because many people thought that the new constitution, by authorizing the legislature to meet annually, might lead to higher taxes—a worry that dates back at least to 1830.[3]

Twenty-one state constitutions provide for legislation by **initiative.** This is a method that allows voters to place legislative measures (and sometimes constitutional amendments) directly on the ballot by getting enough signatures (usually between 5 percent and 15 percent of those who voted in the last election) on a petition. Thirty-seven states also allow for the **referendum,** a procedure that enables voters to reject a measure adopted by the legislature. Often the legislature will handle controversial issues by means of a referendum: it will vote to enact the measure but require that, before it takes effect, it go before the voters at the next election. Sometimes the constitution specifies that certain kinds of legislation (for example, a tax increase) must be subject to a referendum whether the legislature wishes it or not. The **recall** is a procedure, in effect in fifteen states, whereby the voters can remove an elected official from office. If enough signatures are gathered on a petition, the official must go before the voters, who can vote to leave the person in office, remove the person from office, or remove the person and replace him or her with someone else.

The initiative, referendum, and recall show how far many state constitutions are from the federal one. The Founders would never have dreamed of giving voters these kinds of powers over federal lawmaking. As we saw in Chapter 2 of the text, the Constitution is based on a republican, not a democratic, principle:

Public education is one of the primary responsibilities of state and local government.

laws are to be made by the representatives of citizens, not by the citizens directly. The reason for this is to filter temporary popular passions through the medium of prolonged deliberation and discussion. Observers are divided over whether such filtering is also desirable at the state level.

The Constitutional Basis of Local Government

The existence of the states is guaranteed by the federal Constitution: no state can be divided without its consent, each state must have two representatives in the Senate, every state is assured of a republican form of government, and powers not exercised by the Congress are (theoretically) reserved to the states. But cities, towns, and counties enjoy no such protection. They exist at the pleasure of the states. Indeed states have frequently abolished certain kinds of local governments, such as independent school districts.

Most Americans live in cities. Legally a city is a **municipal corporation** that has been chartered by the state to exercise certain defined powers and provide certain specific services. There are two kinds of such charters: special-act charters and general-act charters. A **special-act charter** applies to a certain named city (for example, New York City) and lists what that city can and cannot do. A **general-act charter** applies to a number of cities that fall within a certain classification, usually based on city population. Thus in some states all cities over 100,000 population will be governed on the basis of one charter, while all cities between 50,000 and 99,999 population will be governed on the basis of a different one.

In accordance with the legal principle known as **Dillon's rule,** the terms of these charters are to be interpreted very narrowly. Under this rule (named after a lawyer who wrote a book on the subject in 1911), a municipal corporation can exercise only those powers expressly given it or those powers necessarily implied by, or essential to the accomplishment of, these stated powers.[4] Any doubts about what the city can do under its charter are to be resolved against the city. This means that a city cannot operate a peanut stand at the city zoo unless the state legislature has specifically given the city that power by law or charter.

City officials, needless to say, intensely dislike these restrictions and so argue in favor of a different kind of authorizing law, called a **home-rule charter.**

Such a charter, now in effect in many cities, especially larger ones, reverses Dillon's rule and allows the city government to do anything that is not prohibited by the charter or by state law. In theory the charter creates a form of government (or allows the city to choose among several forms), states what the government can do in general terms, lists some restrictions and prohibitions, and then allows the city to exercise its powers broadly: "You're on your own, govern yourself." In practice many home-rule charters have not been as flexible as this, since city laws (that is, ordinances) cannot be in conflict with state laws and the states often pass laws that interfere with what home-rule cities want to do.

You might think that everybody living in a city would like home rule, since that means that the people in the city can govern themselves. Not so. Many interest groups in a city—business, labor, civil-rights groups, and the like—often welcome the chance to get the state to pass a law requiring the city to do something contrary to what the city's voters want. Whether these groups will favor home rule depends on whether they think that they will win or lose in city politics. In this sense city-state relations are just like state-federal relations: the increase in the power and intrusiveness of higher levels of government is often the result of the activities of groups that lost out in the struggle for power at the lower level.

This page from the 1994 California ballot shows some of the measures voters had to decide as a result of the use of the initiative procedure.

NONPARTISAN BALLOT
COUNTY OF SACRAMENTO
June 7, 1994

MEASURES SUBMITTED TO VOTE OF VOTERS
STATE

Vote YES or NO

STATE MEASURE 1A

| 160 YES |
| 161 NO |

EARTHQUAKE RELIEF AND SEISMIC RETROFIT BOND ACT OF 1994. This act provides for a bond issue of two billion dollars ($2,000,000,000) to provide funds for an earthquake relief and seismic retrofit program.

Vote YES or NO

STATE MEASURE 1B

| 162 YES |
| 163 NO |

SAFE SCHOOLS ACT OF 1994. This act provides for a bond issue of one billion dollars ($1,000,000,000) to provide capital outlay for construction or improvement of public schools and the authorization to allocate bond funds and interest derived therefrom from the State School Building Aid Bond Law of 1952 for present-day public school construction or improvement.

Vote YES or NO

STATE MEASURE 1C

| 164 YES |
| 165 NO |

HIGHER EDUCATION FACILITIES BOND ACT OF JUNE 1994. To renew California's economic vitality and to regain our state's high quality of life, this act authorizes a bond issue of nine hundred million dollars ($900,000,000) for the strengthening, upgrading, and constructing of public colleges and universities throughout the state. These projects will create jobs and strengthen the state's economy by providing adult and student job training opportunities and by enabling public colleges and universities to prepare a well-trained and competitive workforce. They will repair and rebuild college classrooms, which will strengthen college campuses to prevent injuries in future earthquakes. They will provide alternatives to crime and gangs by ensuring access to higher education. They will improve the quality of learning at public campuses by improving classrooms and providing modern teaching technologies. Authorized projects for the 136 public campuses include, but are not necessarily limited to, earthquake and other health and safety improvements, upgrading of laboratories to keep up with scientific advances, improving and modernizing campus computer capabilities, and construction of classrooms and libraries. No moneys derived from the sale of the bonds will be expended for administrative overhead.

Vote YES or NO

STATE MEASURE 175

| 166 YES |
| 167 NO |

RENTERS' INCOME TAX CREDIT. LEGISLATIVE CONSTITUTIONAL AMENDMENT. Amends Constitution to provide qualified renters with an income tax credit of not less than $60 for individuals and $120 for others. Fiscal Impact: State costs of $100 million in 1995-96. Unknown but potential costs in the future, as the state would be prevented from making reductions in the renters' credit.

Cities are not, of course, the only kind of local government. As can be seen in Table 25.1, there are in this country over eighty-six thousand local governments, of which municipalities make up less than one-fourth. The other governments are these:

Counties These are the largest territorial units between a state and a city or town. Every state but two (Connecticut and Rhode Island) has a system of county government. (In Louisiana counties are called parishes; in Alaska they are called boroughs.) Numbering more than three thousand, county governments are especially important in rural areas where people do not live in incorporated cities or towns. Most are governed by an elected board of county supervisors or commissioners with a separately elected sheriff, county clerk, coroner, prosecutor (or district attorney), and various other officers. A few counties, especially those with a large, urbanized population (as in Nassau and Suffolk counties in New York), also elect a county executive who functions much like the mayor of a city, and some (as in Los Angeles County) appoint a professional county administrator who is in charge of the day-to-day running of county administrative affairs.

Towns and Townships In some eastern and midwestern states counties are divided into townships. Most have no separate government, but there are ex-ceptions. In New England and New York, town governments are important. A town was once a village (some are still called that) to which farmers from the surrounding area went to transact business. Such governmental business as they had was conducted by an annual gathering of all the citizens eligible to vote; these citizens would pass on proposals and choose officials to handle matters between town meetings. The New England **town meeting** continues that tradition in dozens of small towns across that region. As some of these towns grew in population, a meeting of all the adult citizens became impractical. A few of these towns became cities, but some preserved the town-meeting system, modifying it only by reducing the number of persons who attended to one or two hundred by having voters elect town-meeting representatives. This system is called the **representative town meeting.**

Special Districts There are more than thirty-three thousand special-district governments (sometimes called authorities) in the United States. They have specific responsibility for some single governmental function—handling sewage treatment and the supply of water, managing airports and bridges, or getting rid of mosquitoes. The biggest is the New York Port Authority, which operates airports, bridges, and bus terminals. Most are much smaller. The number of special-district governments has increased in recent years. Their proponents claim that they make possible more efficient management; their critics argue that they so diffuse responsibility for governmental functions as to make them hard to control.

School districts (there are more than fourteen thousand of them) are a familiar example of special-district government. Though arrangements vary from state to state, often the voters elect school-board members (the school board thus becomes a miniature legislature) who then choose a school superintendent (the executive). Where the progressive tradition is strong, the emphasis is on finding an "expert" school superintendent and giving him or her a great deal of power to run the schools on the basis of the best professional opinion. Where the Jacksonian tradition is strong, the emphasis is on finding a local person to be school superintendent and having the school board become deeply involved in the details of school management.

TABLE 25.1 Number of Governments in the United States

Type of Government	1992	1982	1972
Total	86,748	82,688	78,269
U.S. government	1	1	1
State governments	50	50	50
Local governments	86,697	82,637	78,218
County	3,043	3,041	3,044
Municipal	19,296	19,083	18,517
Township	16,666	16,748	16,991
School district	14,561	15,032	15,781
Special district	33,131	28,733	23,885

SOURCE: *Municipal Yearbook, 1986* (Washington, D.C.: International City Management Association) and *Governing* (April 1993): 15.

The Structure of State Government

Politically the essential difference among state governments is not whether they are big or small, urban or rural, but whether they embody the Jacksonian or the progressive philosophy of governance. Some states, such as California and Wisconsin, have governmental institutions that represent the high-water mark of progressive thinking—a strong governor, relatively few other elected executive officials, a more or less full-time and professionalized legislature, and a tradition of active (and expensive) governmental involvement in various policy areas such as welfare and education. Other states, such as Indiana, Louisiana, and Texas, were largely unaffected by the progressive movement and have institutions that reflect a desire for limited government by part-time officeholders: a weak governor who cannot serve more than one or two consecutive terms, many elected executive officials, a legislature that meets infrequently or for only a brief period, and a tradition of relatively limited (and less well funded) state activity.

To speak of two styles of state politics is, of course, to oversimplify matters greatly. California has some features of the Jacksonian system, such as an elected superintendent of instruction, and Texas has some features of the progressive system, such as a governor who can serve an unlimited number of terms. And state politics is changing—more and more states have moved in the progressive direction. Moreover, the states differ in many ways in addition to governmental systems—some have rural populations that want small government concerned about the needs of farmers; others have large urban populations that generate a wider variety of political demands. But the oversimplification is a useful one, for it reminds us that institutions make a difference in how politics works and that institutions arise out of competing philosophies as to what constitutes good government.

Governors

By considering various aspects of the formal (that is, legal) authority of governors—their tenure in office, their ability to appoint subordinates and reorganize the executive branch, and their budgetary and veto

Missouri

Missouri is a microcosm of the nation: it borders eight other states, straddles the North and South as well as the East and West, and contributed troops to both sides in the Civil War. Though it has a rural tradition, two-thirds of its population is now urbanized, notably in Kansas City and St. Louis, two big cities that are rivals in everything from baseball to state spending. The state includes rich farmland, the Ozark mountains, and such huge employers as McDonnell Douglas Aircraft, Anheuser-Busch beer, and Ralston Purina.

The outcome of all this variety is a tradition of conservative Democratic politics that almost always produces a Democratic state legislature, that once usually produced Democratic governors (but that elected Republicans in 1972, 1980, 1984, and 1988), and that supplied Republican majorities in four of the seven presidential elections between 1968 and 1992.

Missouri is a microcosm of the nation. From 1900 through 1992, it voted for the winner of every presidential election but one (1956).

The governor is elected for a four-year term but cannot serve more than two terms. He or she shares executive authority with (in addition to a lieutenant governor) four officials: a secretary of state, an attorney general, a treasurer, and an auditor.

Missouri senators (there are thirty-four) serve four-year terms, and members of the House (there are one hundred sixty-three) serve two-year terms. The legislature meets annually. Party politics tends to be more important in the House than the Senate. At one time rural legislators dominated affairs in the state capital of Jefferson City, but of late urban and suburban legislators from Kansas City and St. Louis have been gaining influence.

Personal incomes are not high in Missouri (in 1990 its per-capita income ranked twenty-fourth in the nation). This fact, combined with its political culture and institutions, has resulted in a low tax rate (the state ranks forty-third in the per-capita tax burden) and in relatively low rates of public spending (it ranks thirty-third in per-pupil spending on education).

New York

*T*raditionally the big split in New York politics has been between New York City and upstate. Part of it has been ideological (the city is more liberal than upstate) and part of it monetary (the city and the state disagree over who should pay for what services). The key figures in this struggle are the governor and the mayor of New York City.

For many years New York has had a series of strong governors, several of whom became presidential candidates. Elected for a four-year term to which they can be reelected, governors share their authority with only two other statewide officers (besides the lieutenant governor)—an attorney general and a controller. A governor can make many appointments, with a large supply of patronage at his disposal.

The legislature is among the best paid in the country. Its sixty-one senators and one hundred fifty members of the Assembly meet annually and are well organized along party lines. The Republicans control the Senate, the Democrats the Assembly. A great deal of power is wielded by the Senate president pro tem and the Assembly speaker, each of whom has considerable influence on committee assignments.

New York's Democratic and Republican parties have been neighborhood-based, patronage-fed organizations virtually since the founding of the Republic, though today the legendary Tammany Hall (the Democratic party of Manhattan) is but a pale shadow of its former self. In the city a reform movement that began in the late 1950s has gradually replaced the old-style bosses with younger, more issue-oriented activists and with black and Hispanic district leaders. Other parties—the Liberal, the Right-to-Life, and the Conservative—have also been influential in the state.

In New York City the Democratic party is an uneasy alliance among blacks, middle-income white ethnics, and liberal (often Jewish) activists. It has become strained by issues such as crime, taxes, and racial integration. Responding to popular concerns about crime and city services, Mayor Edward Koch put together a right-of-center, personality-based political coalition that elected him mayor for several terms, but by 1989 he could no longer hold his following together in the face of scandals among some associates. He lost to David Dinkins, who became the first black mayor of New York City. But after only one term in office, Dinkins was defeated by Republican Rudolph Guiliani, a white, who revived the old Koch political coalition.

Governor George Pataki of New York

powers—it is possible to distinguish between those who are relatively strong and those who are relatively weak. Thad L. Beyle did this and came up with the following ranking:

- *Very strong governors:* New Jersey, Pennsylvania, Utah, Hawaii, Maryland, Massachusetts, Minnesota, New York

- *Weak governors:* Mississippi, Texas, South Carolina, New Hampshire, North Carolina, Nevada[5]

The other governors were in between, with those in California and Connecticut tending toward the "very strong" end of the scale and those in Missouri, Ohio, and Virginia tending toward the "weak" end. Note that states with strong governors tend to be populous, urban states and those with weak ones tend to be rural or southern states. It is important to bear in mind, however, that these rankings are based only on legal authority; personal skill, the strength of political parties and interest groups allied with the governor, and the governor's use of the media all affect how much actual power he or she will have.

The typical governor, if there is such a thing, is elected for a four-year term but can serve for only two terms (in twenty-nine states). In the typical state the governor does *not* run as a team with the candidate for lieutenant governor, so that unlike the case of president and vice president, it is possible for the governor to be from one party and the lieutenant governor to be from a different one (this has happened in California and some other states). There is a growing tendency, however, to change the rules to require that the two candidates run as a team; that rule is now in effect in twenty-six states.

Most governors have the authority to prepare the state budget, veto legislation, take command of their state's National Guard, and grant pardons or clemency to persons convicted of a crime. In forty-three states the governor (unlike the president of the United States) can use a *line-item veto:* that is, he or she can veto one provision of some or all bills without vetoing the entire bill. In some states the governor can go even further than this—he or she can reduce the amount appropriated for a specific purpose. The legislature can override the line-item veto or the appropriation reduction, usually by a two-thirds vote.

The power of the governor to appoint other executive officers varies greatly from place to place. The limitations on the appointive power are of two kinds—constitutional and legal. The constitutional limitation arises from the requirement that certain executive offices be filled by direct election. About thirty states elect six or more executive officials in addition to the governor and lieutenant governor; these tend to be southern and midwestern states with a strong Jacksonian tradition. About twenty elect five or fewer; these tend to be eastern or far western states. Just Alaska and New Jersey follow the national practice of electing only the chief executive. Over the last quarter-century there has been a trend toward reducing the number of elected executive officers.

The political limitation arises from civil-service laws. In progressive states, such as California, these laws are very strong and restrict the governor from making more than a small number of appointments entirely at his or her discretion. In many Jacksonian states, such as Indiana, the civil-service laws are weak

As governor of California, Pete Wilson inherited a political system that gives the governor many formal powers but keeps political parties weak.

and the governor can make thousands of patronage appointments. Once again the link between constitutional philosophy and the appointive process is not perfect. Some states, such as Pennsylvania, that have powerful governors and only a few elected executives also have extensive opportunities for patronage appointments. And things are changing: whereas in 1958 only half of all state jobs were under civil service, today the great majority are.

Just as the constitutional base and political powers of the governor's office have been changing, so also has the kind of person who becomes governor. In the past a few governors, such as Al Smith in New York and Earl Warren in California, were important figures, but many were unimpressive time-servers who did little more than cut ribbons to open new public buildings and pose for the cameras. The states

In recent years, women have entered the statehouse as governors. (Top) Joan Finney of Kansas, (bottom) Ann Richards of Texas.

were not so much "laboratories of democracy" as havens for second-rate politicians. That seems to have changed.

A new breed of governor has come to the fore, bringing energy and intelligence to an office that has grown in both importance and power. Many new national policies have been modeled on ones pioneered in the states. For example, the Family Support Act of 1988, designed to encourage welfare recipients to become self-supporting, was based in part on work-oriented welfare programs begun by governors in California, Massachusetts, Michigan, New Jersey, and elsewhere. Federal efforts to improve education have grown out of meetings of the governors from states that have experimented with school reform plans. Three of the last four presidents—Jimmy Carter, Ronald Reagan, and Bill Clinton—came to the White House as former governors, as did thirteen presidents before them.

From 1970 until 1994, Democrats held a majority of the governorships, and they did this despite the increasing tendency of white Southerners to vote for Republican candidates. In 1994, that changed. Republicans lost none of the statehouses they already controlled and won eleven more while four Democratic incumbents were defeated. For the first time in a quarter century, Republicans had more governorships (thirty) than did the Democrats (nineteen) (see map). The Republicans now controlled the statehouses in eight of the ten largest states and in half of the Southern ones.

Until the 1994 election, Democrats had been doing a better job of winning governorships than of winning the presidency. There were several reasons for this. Presidential elections are often influenced more by the economic condition of the nation and the character of the candidates than by party loyalty. State elections, by contrast, are more likely to reflect traditional party allegiances; for a long time more voters have been Democratic than Republican. Another reason is that in most states gubernatorial elections are no longer held on the same day as presidential ones. In the 1930s thirty-three states chose their governors in the same election as they chose the president. In 1992 only twelve states did this. As a result the popularity of a Republican presidential candidate cannot readily be transferred to a Republican gubernatorial candidate—having the two chosen in differ-

PARTY CONTROL OF STATE GOVERNORSHIPS, 1995

19 Democratic   30 Republican   1 Independent

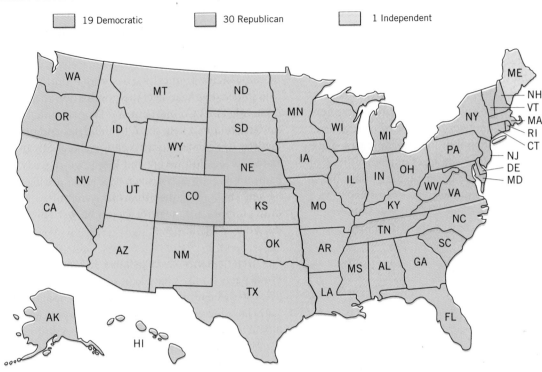

ent years cuts the president's coattails. Moreover, the president's party often loses popularity during off-year elections, just at the time when most governors are being elected.

Like most recent presidents, most governors face legislatures in which one or both houses are controlled by the opposition party. In 1952, about 80 percent of the states had a government in which the same party controlled the governor's office and both houses of the legislatures; by 1986, only about 40 percent had unified governments (see Figure 25.1). The main reason for the decline in unified state governments has been the inability of Republicans to elect state legislators. Once, a Republican governor could

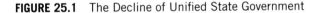

FIGURE 25.1 The Decline of Unified State Government

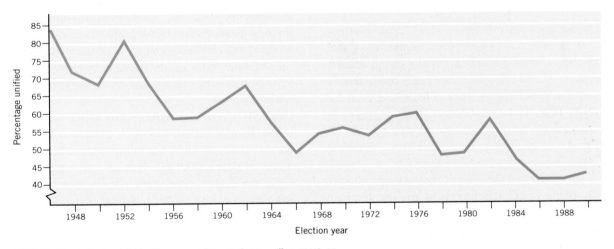

SOURCE: Morris Fiorina, *Divided Government* (New York: Macmillan, 1992), 25.

count on having a Republican-controlled legislature; no more. In 1993 eighteen states had Republican governors; in only three (Arizona, New Hampshire, and Utah) did the Republicans also control the legislatures. After the 1994 election, divided party control continued to be the rule rather than the exception. Before it, thirty-one states had divided rule; after it, twenty-eight did. Republican governors did make some progress; before the election, only three of them had legislatures of the same party, but after it fifteen did. Even so, Republican governors had to face legislatures with at least one house under Democratic control in such important states as California, New York, and Texas.

State Legislatures

State legislatures are not small-scale versions of Congress. Though all but Nebraska have two houses, the way in which they are elected, organized, and led often differs greatly from what one finds in Washington. A member of Congress represents a large (half-million population) district, is paid a good salary, has a large staff, and works at his or her job full-time; in many states exactly the opposite is true.

Elections and Electoral Districts   Many state legislators are not even chosen from single-member districts but rather from multimember ones. About a third of all members of the lower house of state legislatures (and about one-eighth of all state senators) are elected from districts that choose more than one legislator.[6] Until 1980, for example, three members of the Illinois house were chosen from each electoral district. Each voter in those districts could cast three votes, giving one to each of three candidates, or three to one candidate and none to any other, or some other combination. This meant that a passionate Republican could give all three of his or her votes to a single Republican candidate, and if enough other passionate Republicans did the same thing, a Republican could be elected from a district where the vast majority of voters were Democrats.

In most states the effect of multimember districts (as well as of other factors) is to give the dominant political party a big advantage—if it wins 55 to 60 percent of the popular vote in a state, it will win 65 to 70 percent of the legislative seats.[7]

Except in Nebraska, all state legislators run under a party label. Just as with members of Congress, they get on the ballot by winning a primary election. But in some states political parties play a much bigger role in deciding who gets the nomination than they do in others. In Connecticut and Pennsylvania, party leaders will often help recruit candidates and give to favored candidates a party endorsement. In other states, such as Minnesota and Washington, party organizations are much weaker, candidates are likely to be self-selected (rather than party-recruited), and only a minority of the primary candidates will be endorsed by party leaders.[8]

The Determinants of Legislative Elections   Traditional party loyalties have kept southern state legislatures overwhelmingly Democratic even though these states have increasingly voted for the Republican candidate for president and, of late, have begun to elect Republican governors in large numbers (there were three Republican governors in the South in 1993).

Outside the South state legislative elections tend to be influenced by some of the same forces that shape national elections. For example, since 1950 the president's political party has lost seats in the state legislatures (outside the South) in every election occurring between the regular presidential elections. This is strikingly similar to the losses that the president's party almost always suffers in congressional seats, and suggests that voters approach state legislative elections in much the same way as they approach congressional ones.

Further evidence of this is a fact discovered by political scientist John Chubb: the condition of the *national* economy has a strong effect on *state* legislative elections, just as it does on national ones.[9]

Once elected, legislators tend to be about as safe in most states as they are in the House of Representatives. In most years, about 90 percent of all state legislators who stand for reelection are reelected, just as in the House.[10] (However fewer state legislators stand for reelection, and so the turnover in membership is higher in state legislatures than in Congress.) But in 1992 public criticism of career politicians reduced the rate at which state legislators were reelected (down to "only" about 70 percent), just as it cut the reelection rate of members of Congress. Proposals to place term limits on state and national legislators passed in each of the fourteen states that had them on the ballot.

There are about 7,400 legislative seats in the American states; Democrats have won a majority of them in virtually every election for the last forty years, including 1994. The Republicans have closed the gap a bit, even in the South. In 1994 they took control of the lower houses in both North and South Carolina for the first time in this century. As of 1995, nineteen states were under Republican control, eighteen under Democratic sway, and twelve had divided party control. (One state, Nebraska, has a nonpartisan legislature. See map below.) In 1992 women and minorities made big gains in state capitols when 125 more women, 65 more blacks, and 27 more Hispanics entered office (see map on page 692).

Apportionment Once, many state legislatures were unrepresentative of the people of the state as a result of malapportionment. District lines were drawn so as to give an enormous advantage to some parts of the state, usually rural ones, at the expense of other parts,

usually urban and suburban ones. Before 1964, for example, a vote cast in a rural county would, on the average, be worth twice as much as one cast in a big city because in the former there would be only half as many voters per elected representative as in the latter.[11] In certain states the underrepresentation was much greater than these national averages suggest. Los Angeles County, with almost 40 percent of California's population, had but one state senator (out of forty). In 1964 the United States Supreme Court ruled, in the case of *Reynolds* v. *Sims*,[12] that the populations of each district in a given house of a state legislature had to be substantially equal. The rule to be followed was "one person, one vote."

As a result of this decision many state legislatures had to be redistricted. The consequences were often dramatic. In Georgia, for example, the number of representatives from urban areas increased by a factor of ten in the lower house of the legislature and by a factor of twenty in the upper house.[13] In other states the chief beneficiaries were suburban rather than urban voters. Moreover the partisan and racial

PARTY CONTROL OF LEGISLATIVE CHAMBERS, 1995

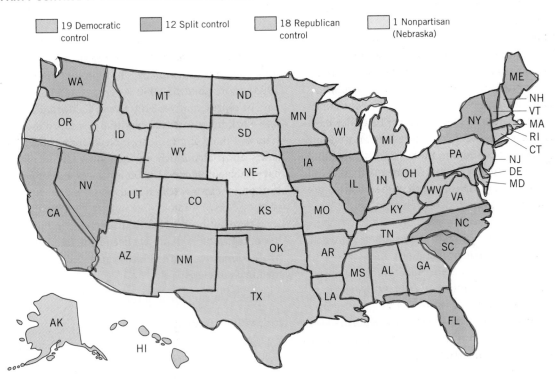

PERCENTAGE OF STATE LEGISLATORS WHO ARE WOMEN, 1993

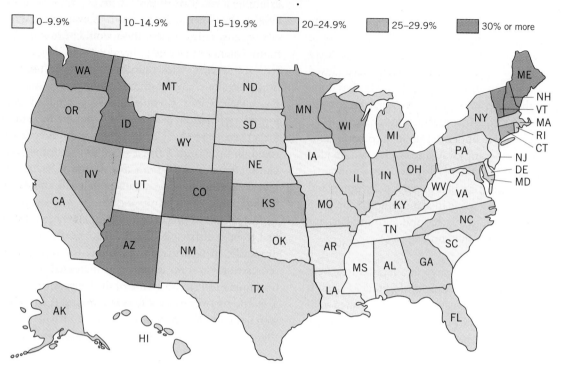

SOURCE: Rob Gurwitt, "Legislatures: The Faces of Change," *Governing* (February 1993): 30.

composition of state legislatures began to change. In the South Republicans (from suburban districts) and blacks (from urban districts) increased in number. Urban and suburban interests got more attention from state government, and rural interests got somewhat less. But some of these gains for big cities have proved to be short-lived. As people have moved out of large, older cities and into the suburbs, the continuing process of reapportionment means that many big cities have lost voting strength in their state capitols, and suburbs have gained strength.

Professional versus Amateur Legislators Though state legislative districts are about the same size within a given state, they of course differ greatly in size across states. A California legislative district may have 300,000 people in it while one in New Hampshire may have only 2,000.[14] Thus in California legislative politics is big business; in New Hampshire it is a folksy, friends-and-neighbors affair.

States differ not only in the size of their legislatures but in the extent to which being a legislator is a full-time job. California pays its representatives (as of 1993) more than $52,000 a year; New Hampshire pays its representatives $100 a year. California legislators work in an institution with a large, professional staff and many conveniences; New Hampshire legislators are pretty much on their own. Sixteen states pay their legislators $15,000 a year or more; seventeen pay them less (often much less) than $10,000 a year.

There has been a significant increase in the number of legislatures that have been professionalized. A **professional legislature** has some or all of the following characteristics:

- It meets during most of the year.

- Its members are relatively well paid.

- Its members regard being a legislator as their main job.

- Members and committees have sizable, year-round staffs.

California has a professional legislature, as do Illinois, Massachusetts, Michigan, Minnesota, New York, New Jersey, Ohio, Pennsylvania, and Wisconsin. By contrast, New Hampshire, Texas, Wyoming, and many other states have **amateur,** or part-time, legislatures. One of the striking features of professionalized legislatures is the low turnover among members. In eight of the ten professionalized legislatures listed above, turnover in the 1988 election was less than 10 percent.

The rise of the professional legislature means an increase in the number of legislators whose full-time occupation is politics. This fact may help explain why Democrats do better at winning elections to state legislatures than do Republicans. As Morris Fiorina and Alan Ehrenhalt have pointed out, the two parties differ in the kinds of people who are active in them.[15] Republican party activists are often older persons, especially lawyers, farmers, and business executives.

Conservative Republicans tend to be people who are suspicious of government, wishing that it were smaller. By contrast, Democratic party activists tend to be younger persons for whom politics (or work for various social movements involved in politics) has been a full-time career. Liberal Democrats tend to like government and want it to do more.

If this line of argument is correct, it means that Republicans will tend to be people who, because they have careers outside of politics, will find it easy to be part-time legislators but hard to be full-time ones. And it means that Republicans, because they think government should do relatively little, may enjoy serving in a legislature that does little but dislike serving in one that does a lot. As a result, Republicans will be less likely than Democrats to be vigorous, persistent, and skillful candidates for elective office, and so Democrats will win a larger-than-expected share of seats in the legislatures. The result will be a tendency to divided government—Republican governors who do not have a Republican legislature.

⭐ The People's Representatives Speak

When you have over a half-million elected officials at the state and local levels, you should not assume that they all will speak with the clarity and wisdom of Winston Churchill.

Take lawmakers in Michigan. Reporters covering that state's legislature have written down some of the flakier examples of official phrase making. Each exchange was heard by at least two reporters.

"There comes a time to put principle aside and do what's right."

"I don't see anything wrong with saving human life. That would be good politics, even for us."

"Some of our friends wanted it in the bill, some of our friends wanted it out. Jerry and I are going to stick with our friends."

"From now on, I'm watching everything you do with a fine-toothed comb."

"The chair would wish the members would refrain from talking about the intellectual levels of other members. That always leads to problems."

"Mr. Chairman, fellow members and guests. That's a goddamn lie."

"I don't think you appreciate how difficult it is to be a pawn of labor."

"Let's violate the law one more time."

"Now we've got them right where they want us."

"Mr. Speaker, what bill did we just pass?"

Party Organization Party leaders in Congress are important but have only a little power; they cannot choose committee chairmen or remove members from committees. But party leaders in many state legislatures often have a great deal of power.

A few states, mostly in the South (Alabama, Louisiana, Mississippi, South Carolina, and Texas), have no distinct majority and minority leaders, in part because there are so few Republicans in these legislatures as to make party organization almost meaningless. Nebraska has no party leaders because its state legislators are all elected on a nonpartisan ballot.

In the rest of the states the influence of party leaders varies considerably. In Massachusetts and California, for example, the speaker of the lower house handpicks committee members and committee chairmen. Chairmen who act against the speaker's wishes risk losing their chairmanships and all the accompanying powers and privileges. Similarly the speaker of the House in Michigan is a dominant figure; as one state legislator put it, "nothing happens without the speaker's approval."[16] In New York party discipline is quite strong; as one former speaker of the Assembly said, "never once in the fifteen years I've been here have we failed to get a Republican majority for a 'must' piece of legislation."[17] In a few states party caucuses not only meet regularly to decide what positions their parties will take on pending legislation; those decisions are binding on party members. But in other states party leaders have relatively little influence.

Party leaders derive their power not only from their ability to pick committee chairmen (posts that often carry higher salaries and more fringe benefits than ordinary legislative seats) but also from the legislative patronage that they have to dispense (a lot in states such as New York, New Jersey, and Pennsylvania) and from the campaign funds that they frequently control. In California, for example, the last few speakers of the Assembly (Jesse Unruh, Leo McCarthy, and Willie Brown) have raised millions of dollars from interest groups. The speakers then passed out this money to support the reelection campaigns of loyal legislators.

One would like to know how effective all this leadership is in producing party-line voting in the state legislatures. But we don't know: the research on this subject is too fragmentary to permit one to say much. It appears that in the legislatures of states such as California, Colorado, Rhode Island, and Pennsylvania there has been a high level of party voting and in states such as Montana, Washington, and Wyoming there has not been much.[18]

No one is quite certain why some states are more partisan than others, though it appears that the urbanized, industrialized states tend to have more party-line votes than do more rural states. But there are at least two qualifications that have to be made to this—and any other—generalization about legislative voting. One is that the patterns change over time. A second is that the concept of party is relatively meaningless in one-party states. In Alabama, Georgia, Louisiana, or Mississippi almost everybody in the legislature is a Democrat. The real cleavages in these states tend to be between urban and rural or liberal and conservative legislators, not between Democrats and Republicans.

Committees State legislatures, like Congress, have committees in which much of the real lawmaking work is done. But state committees are often much less important than their congressional counterparts, and for good reason. Where the party leaders are

 The Top Ten States in Spending

Educational Spending per Pupil (1991)	Average AFDC Monthly Payment (1991)
New Jersey	Alaska
Alaska	California
New York	Hawaii
Connecticut	Connecticut
District of Columbia	New York
Vermont	Vermont
Pennsylvania	Minnesota
Rhode Island	Rhode Island
Massachusetts	Washington
Maryland	Wisconsin

SOURCE: *Statistical Abstract of the United States, 1993,* 164, 382.

powerful, committee chairmen will be less powerful. One indication of committee weakness is the turnover in their membership—it is generally higher in the states than in Congress. Another is that seniority often counts for much less in picking a state committee chairman than it does in choosing a chairman in Congress.

In sum the legislatures of many of the bigger, industrialized, northern states tend to be more partisan, more highly organized, and more tightly led than is Congress, whereas legislatures in small, rural, and southern states tend to be somewhat less structured than Congress. Committees tend to be somewhat less important in the states than in Congress.

State Courts

In general the structure of state courts looks much like the federal system. There will be many trial courts in a given state and (usually) a single supreme court. In most states there will also be intermediate appeals courts. But when examined more closely, state courts turn out to be much more diverse and specialized than federal ones. Let us start at the bottom and work up.

Trial Courts   There are two kinds. First, there are minor courts (in cities they are usually called municipal courts; in rural areas they are sometimes called justices of the peace) that handle traffic tickets, small claims, and minor criminal offenses. Second, there are trial courts with broad jurisdiction over all criminal and civil matters. These are called, variously, superior courts, county courts, circuit courts, district courts, or courts of common pleas. (In New York they are called supreme courts, but they are not really supreme.) People charged with serious crimes are tried in these courts, and major lawsuits are settled here. At this level there may also be specialized courts to handle probate (that is, the wills and estates of deceased persons) and juvenile or family matters. Most general-jurisdiction trial courts are part of county government, though the judges may be selected by the governor.

Appeals Courts   At the top of the system there will be the state equivalent of the United States Supreme Court. In most states it is called the state supreme

As speaker of the Assembly, Willie Brown is probably the second most powerful person, next to the governor, in California politics.

court, but in Maine and Massachusetts it is called the Supreme Judicial Court and in Maryland and New York the Court of Appeals. (Two states have separate supreme courts for civil and criminal matters.) State supreme courts, like their federal counterpart, have the power to declare acts of state government to be unconstitutional. They can also claim that federal laws are unconstitutional, but such decisions almost always get reviewed by the United States Supreme Court. Between the highest court and the trial courts there will be, in most states, appeals courts on which several judges sit.

Choosing the Judges   There is a bewildering variety of methods for choosing judges. In general, states that reflect the Jacksonian tradition elect their judges, and states that embody the progressive tradition appoint theirs. The Jacksonians believe that election guarantees that the judges will be close to the people; the progressives argue that appointment ensures that the judges will be competent. But within this framework are countless combinations and exceptions.

Texts

Politics in Texas was traditionally a contest among Democrats whose campaigns were focused on the small towns and financed by big-city oil and banking money. But that is changing. Liberal Democrats, with support in the big cities and among ethnic minorities, have been growing in influence. In response, people who were once conservative Democrats increasingly have been campaigning and voting as Republicans, at least for statewide and national office. As a result, the old one-party politics of Texas has given way to two-party politics.

The emergence of a two-party Texas is especially important given its power in national affairs. It has the third-largest congressional delegation, two of its citizens have been president (Lyndon Johnson and George Bush), and in recent years it has produced two powerful speakers of the House (Sam Rayburn and Jim Wright), a Senate majority leader (Johnson), and two secretaries of the treasury (John Connally and Lloyd Bentsen).

Since 1978 both parties have had a good shot at winning the governorship; Republican William Clements won in that year, Democrat Mark White in 1982, Clements again in 1986, Democrat Ann Richards in 1990, and Republican George W. Bush in 1994. Currently both senators are Republican (Phil Gramm and Kay Bailey Hutchinson). In both houses of the state legislature, however, Democrats enjoy large majorities.

The governor serves a four-year term and can be reelected, but his or her executive authority must be shared with six other elected statewide officials and an elected Railroad Commission. The detailed, Jacksonian-style constitution places sharp limits on government power. The lieutenant governor is not elected on the same slate as the governor and enjoys considerable independent power as a result of his ability, as presiding officer of the Senate, to pick its committee members and chairmen. The speaker is equally influential in the House. The Texas legislature is a part-time venture, meeting only in odd-numbered years and paying its members $7,200 a year.

The state is fiscally conservative: it has no state income tax and it spends less per capita than most other states. The recession in the oil industry hurt the state in the 1980s, but in the 1990s it was enjoying an economic revival and industrial diversification.

To simplify matters a bit, let us look at five methods for picking judges:

1. *Partisan election.* In fifteen states judges run for office as Democrats or Republicans. Among the larger states that use this method are Illinois, New York, North Carolina, Pennsylvania, and Texas. In five of these states, including New York, partisan elections are used for some but not all courts.

2. *Nonpartisan election.* In sixteen states judges run for office in nonpartisan elections. Among the larger states using this method are Michigan, Minnesota, Ohio, and Wisconsin. Five of these states combine this method with another for different courts.

3. *Appointment by governor.* In ten states the governor appoints the judges. These include Maryland, Massachusetts, and New Jersey. Three of these states combine this method with another for different courts.

4. *Appointment by legislature.* In four states the judges are appointed by the legislature. These are Connecticut, Rhode Island (appeals judges only), South Carolina, and Virginia.

5. *"Missouri Plan."* In this system, used in whole or in part by sixteen states, the judge is first appointed and then must face the electorate at the end of his or her first term. The governor makes the appointment from a list of candidates produced by a screening committee of citizens and lawyers. When the judge completes the first term of office, his or her name goes on the ballot with the question, "Shall Judge A be retained in office?" There is no opponent (except in California, where trial-court judges, but not appellate judges, face an opponent). If more people vote "yes" than "no" on retaining the judge in office, the judge stays. Among the states using this plan are California, Colorado, Florida (appeals judges), Indiana (appeals judges), Iowa, Missouri, Nebraska, and Utah.[19]

Experts argue over what difference, if any, the selection method makes in the quality of judges. No one knows for certain, in part because people disagree as to what constitutes a good judge. We do know a few facts, however. First, not many people vote in those elections where judges are chosen. Second, most incumbent judges don't face an opponent when they stand for reelection. Third, the Missouri Plan results in the defeat of only a tiny proportion of all judges who run. Sometimes, though, that small fraction can include some celebrated cases. One such was Chief Justice Rose Bird of California, who in 1986 was defeated by a massive campaign to unseat her because of decisions that she had written preventing the carrying out of the death penalty in various criminal cases. Fourth, elected and appointed judges do not differ greatly in their decisions, though elected Democrats tend to be somewhat more liberal than elected Republicans.

Political Culture

These facts and figures, though important, do not capture the flavor of daily life in state government, because each has a style, or political culture, that is often quite distinctive. Alan Rosenthal suggests some of this with these thumbnail sketches:

> *In New York professional politics, political wheeling and dealing, and frantic activity are characteristic. In Virginia, one gets a sense of tradition, conservatism, and gentility, and the General Assembly has been described by its admirers as the "first men's club" in the state. Louisiana's politics are wild and flamboyant. By contrast, moderation and caution are features of Iowa. A strong disposition of compromise pervades Oregon. . . . In Kansas hard work, respect for authority, fiscal prudence, and a general conservatism and resistance to rapid social change are pervasive features of the state environment. Indiana is intensely partisan, Wyoming is mainly individualistic and Ohio is fundamentally conservative. In Hawaii the relatively recent political dominance of Japanese, and the secondary status of Chinese, native Hawaiians, and Haoles (whites) makes for tough ethnic politics. Yankee Republicans used to run Massachusetts, but now the Irish dominate. . . . Mormonism, of course, dominates Utah.[20]*

The Structure of Local Government

Just as states tend to reflect either the Jacksonian or the progressive political culture, so also do cities, especially big cities, differ in this way. Many scholars distinguish between **unreformed cities** and **reformed cities.** They do not mean by this that unreformed cities are bad and reformed ones good, only that in the latter case the progressive impulse has made greater headway. These differences can be summarized, in oversimplified form, as follows:

Unreformed (Jacksonian) city	Reformed (progressive) city
Elections partisan	Elections nonpartisan
City council elected from districts	City council elected at large
Executive powers in hands of mayor	Executive powers in hands of appointed city manager
Weak civil service	Strong civil service

In general unreformed large cities are found in the older states of the Northeast, while reformed cities are more characteristic of the younger states of the West and Southwest. Among cities that most nearly resemble the Jacksonian (or unreformed) model are Baltimore, Chicago, Cleveland, New York, Philadelphia, and St. Louis. Among those that most nearly approximate the progressive (or reformed) model are Cincinnati, Dallas, Kansas City, San Diego, and San Jose. Los Angeles and Detroit are interesting mixed cases. Los Angeles elects its council members by district and has no city manager, but it is nonpartisan and has a strong civil-service tradition. Detroit elects its council members at large but has a strong mayor.

Today some observers believe that a mixture of the two traditions is best suited for big-city governance. A strong elected mayor gives the city a single, visible symbol of popular desires and community attachments, and district elections ensure that neighborhoods will have a say in how things are done, but it is also necessary to have a nonpartisan civil service headed by a professional city administrator who serves under the mayor. In theory this would strike a balance between representation and efficiency. A few

TABLE 25.2   Forms of City and Town Government, 1992

Form of Government	All Cities
Mayor-council	15,125
Council-manager	3,131
Commission	351
Other	531
Total	19,138

SOURCE: U.S. Census Bureau, *1992 Census of Municipal Governments.*

cities have experimented with such combinations, but opinions differ as to their success.

Complicating the distinction between "reformed" and "unreformed" has been the controversy over the racial consequences of at-large elections. Originally at-large elections were favored by progressives because they would allow the "best people" to run for the city council without regard to where they lived in the city and without having to represent on the council the interests of a particular neighborhood; such council members would presumably be free to do what was good for the city "as a whole." Jacksonians opposed at-large elections precisely because they tended to result in elections' being won by well-known people (most of whom all lived in one part of town) who would not tend to the interests of particular neighborhoods.

Recently, however, the choice between at-large and district representation has been made more difficult because of the effect of each system on the chances that black (and other minority-group) representatives will get elected. The federal courts have interpreted the voting-rights laws to mean that it is not enough for blacks to have a chance to register, vote, and run for office; these laws also require that blacks (and other minorities) have a reasonable chance of *winning* the election. In a city where blacks are in the minority, few if any will be elected to the city council in an at-large election. In cities that use neighborhood districts, it is much easier for blacks to get elected. The federal courts have required many cities and counties (chiefly but not only in the South) to switch from at-large to district elections.

Mayor-Council Plan

The most common form of city government is one in which authority is vested in an elected mayor and council. It is typical of very small cities (those under 10,000 population) and very large cities (those over 250,000 population). (See Table 25.2.) A **mayor-council system** can be of two sorts. **Weak-mayor systems** have, as the name implies, a mayor who does not have much power over the administration of the system (he or she often must share executive authority with various boards and commissions) and does not have a lot of influence in the city council (see Figure 25.2). Often the mayor is chosen by the city council from among its members rather than being directly elected by the citizens. But even when directly elected, some mayors can be weak. The mayor of Los Angeles, for example, has relatively few appointive powers. The mayor can select the chief of police, but only from a short list produced by the civil-service system, and once selected the chief serves for a fixed term and reports to a separate police commission.

Strong-mayor systems have a directly elected mayor with substantial authority over the administrative branch of government and important budgetary powers (see Figure 25.3). The mayors of Boston and New York City are strong mayors. In general the larger cities have moved to increase the authority of their mayors, but this process has not moved as rapidly or as far as it has for governors.

FIGURE 25.2   Weak-Mayor–Council Form of Government

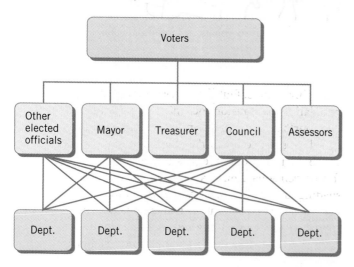

Council-Manager Plan

Under the **council-manager system** the people vote only for city-council members, who then appoint a professional city manager to take charge of most or all of the city's administration (see Figure 25.4). Usually elections in council-manager cities are nonpartisan and at-large, and civil service is quite strong. The council-manager plan is the most common form in middle-sized cities, those between 10,000 and 200,000 population. In some cities managers are in fact local politicians, but in most they have been specially trained for this career and often come to their job from another city.

Commission Plan

In a few cities government is in the hands of an elected commission that does not have a single head of the executive branch. Instead each commissioner takes responsibility for some part of city administration. One commissioner may oversee the fire and police departments; another may supervise roads and highways. The commission plan is not very popular, as it seems to make management more complex and leadership more divided, but a few big cities, including St. Paul, Tulsa, and Mobile, still have it.

Metropolitan Government

Some people think that the structure of governance in our big cities is out of date. In places such as Boston, Chicago, or St. Louis, the central city is run by one government and the surrounding suburbs are run by others. But the problems of the metropolitan area do not respect city boundaries. Crime, traffic congestion, and air pollution move across these political boundaries as if they did not exist. Moreover people in the suburbs often work and shop in the central cities but do not pay taxes there, and so the big cities must pay for programs aimed at slums, poverty, big welfare rolls, and run-down schools with money that is collected only from city residents.

People who worry about such matters advocate finding some way to govern the metropolitan area as a whole. One method is for the central city to annex the surrounding suburbs. Some cities have done just this. Houston has expanded its city limits so that it now encompasses a land area in excess of 565 square

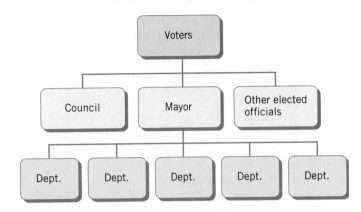

FIGURE 25.3 Strong-Mayor–Council Form of Government

SOURCE: Adapted from Institute of Public Affairs. The University of Texas at Austin, *Forms of City Government,* 7th ed. (Austin: 1968), 4.

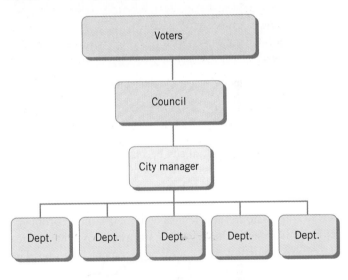

FIGURE 25.4 City-Manager Form of Government

miles. (By contrast Philadelphia, with about the same population as Houston, occupies a land area only one-fourth as large.) But **annexation** will be resisted by suburbs, especially in the older metropolitan areas. Boston, for example, has a land area of only forty-seven square miles and has no chance of persuading any of the surrounding towns to become part of the city. Annexation may be possible when suburban and central-city residents are about the same in race, social class, and political interest, but as

Bret Schundler, mayor of Jersey City, New Jersey.

Richard Riordan, mayor of Los Angeles.

soon as the central city becomes known for having a lower-income, minority population with many problems, white suburbanites are not likely to favor annexation.

Another way to deal with metropolitan problems is to strengthen county government or even to consolidate city and county government into one. The city and county of San Francisco are one and the same, as are (with some exceptions) the city of Boston and the county of Suffolk. New York City is the result of a merger, dating back to the turn of the century, of five counties (now called boroughs)—Brooklyn, the Bronx, Manhattan, Queens, and Staten Island. **City-county consolidation** today is unlikely for the same reason that annexation is unlikely.

County government can perform a major role even without consolidation by providing services on contract. In Los Angeles, for example, the county offers a variety of services that local communities can purchase by signing a contract. The Los Angeles

Sheriff's Office provides, for a fee, police protection to cities in the county that do not want the expense or bother of running their own police departments. Similar services are provided to many communities on Long Island in New York by the Nassau County government. This system offers the advantages of professional management and broad coverage without the political problems of merger.

A third way of managing metropolitan problems is to create a **metropolitan government.** This is a system for governing the entire area while leaving some autonomy in the hands of local governments. It is a kind of federal system, with the metropolitan-area government handling the areawide problems and city governments handling the local matters. Metropolitan governments have been created in Dade County (Miami), Florida, and Nashville, Tennessee, among other places. But most metropolitan areas have resisted this method because local communities want to be independent. Many people believe that they have a right to choose their own kind of town, and town government, just as they choose their own home and car. Suburban cities develop a distinctive lifestyle and want to preserve it.

In view of the problems with annexation, consolidation, and metropolitan government, the most common method of dealing with metropolitan problems is to create special districts or authorities to manage specific services, such as water supply, sewage treatment, airports and highways, or bus and subway systems. These districts can tax the residents throughout the area and can borrow money to build transportation or water systems. They often are quite efficient, but some people worry that they quickly become remote from popular control.

In general politics within most metropolitan areas is not under any kind of central leadership. Instead it is carried on by a process of conflict and bargaining among local governments. The arena in which the struggle proceeds is usually the state legislature, though an increasing number of metropolitan areas are creating councils of governments (sometimes known as COGs) in which mayors and city managers meet to see whether they can work out agreements on a voluntary basis.

Politics and Policies

Policy-making in the states differs from that in the federal government for at least two important reasons. First, most states have to work harder to live within their means than does Washington. In more than thirty states the constitution requires that the legislature pass a balanced budget. The Congress, by contrast, can vote for an unbalanced budget—that is, one that calls for spending more money than is coming in—any time it wants. It is more difficult for many states to borrow money than it is for the national government. In eleven states it takes an extraordinary majority in the legislature to authorize borrowing; in other states the voters must approve borrowing in a referendum. Neither provision applies to Congress. Owing to these and other factors, the total debt owed by all state governments is only about one-tenth of that owed by Washington. As a result, state politics is fiscally more constrained than national politics. Many governors lose elections because they raised taxes;[21] only rarely is a president defeated because of taxes. The reason: it is easier for a president to avoid new taxes by tolerating deficits.

Second, states (and cities) compete with one another to attract businesses, residents, and tourists. To do this they struggle to provide a "good business climate," which means, among other things, keeping taxes down, regulations simple, and costs under control. Because of political pressures for more services and regulations, some states lose out in this competition for jobs. For example, the high cost of doing business in California has caused many firms to move to Arizona, Nevada, Utah, and other less costly states. By contrast, the federal government does not have to do as much to maintain a good business climate. Though it worries a bit about foreign competition, even if an American firm decides to build a factory abroad, Washington can still tax the profits when they are brought back into this country.

States with a Jacksonian style of government are, it seems, a bit more likely to maintain a political climate attractive to business. A weak or divided state government will find it hard to raise taxes or impose new regulations; a state that, because of the progressive tradition, has a strong governor and a professionalized legislature will find it easier to do these things. Moreover, states with a Jacksonian style are more common in those parts of the country, such as the South, where a tradition of limited government is strong and where economic elites have great power.

Jacksonian states, especially those without many big cities, have emphasized limited government that business often finds attractive and labor finds unattractive. Progressive states, particularly those with a largely urbanized population, have tended to emphasize redistributing income and regulating business. For example, California and Wisconsin were among the first states to create and have been among the most generous in financing state universities, aid to families with dependent children (AFDC), and environmental protection laws.[22]

The same tendency can be found in city governments. Those with a "reformed" form of government (for example, council-manager) were among the first to fluoridate their water supplies[23] and have worked hardest to keep the police out of local politics and operating in accordance with whatever is thought to be "professional" police practice.[24]

Two Italian-American mayors: (left) Rudolph Giuliani of New York City, (right) Thomas Menino of Boston.

There are many exceptions to this generalization, however. Illinois has many features of the Jacksonian tradition, such as elected judges and patronage-oriented political parties, but it has not been reluctant to develop and pay for new programs. New York City has hardly been an example of a reformed city government, but it has been a pioneer in producing expensive schools, hospitals, and public-housing projects.

Politics and Representation

Progressive states and "reformed" cities not only differ in their tax and spending policies, they differ in how they represent citizens. As we have already seen, cities with at-large, nonpartisan elections make it harder for blacks and other spatially concentrated minorities to win office. Cities with district, partisan elections make it easier for such groups to enter office.

But the very "unreformed" cities that ease the entry of minorities into politics are also the cities that make it hard to adopt the kinds of programs that minorities often want. As a result, a political system that facilitates representation is often one that impedes change.

For example: Blacks are politically very liberal—they want the government to do a lot about their concerns regarding integration, reducing poverty, and enhancing education. And like every racial or ethnic group, they want their share of elected and appointed offices. But the institutions most likely to adopt liberal policies are ones in which political authority is centralized, tax monies are ample, experts are influential, and local interests are kept in the background—precisely the kinds of institutions that will underrepresent racial or neighborhood interests. Cities with at-large, nonpartisan elections are likely to have fewer black elected officials (relative to the size of the black population) than cities with district-based, partisan elections. Blacks have most frequently come to power in unreformed cities with a weak tax base, a decaying array of municipal services, and a relatively small supply of trained experts.

Moreover the old political machines that once made governing possible in the unreformed cities—the Daley machine in Chicago, Tammany Hall in New York—have been so weakened by a combination of political reform and ethnic conflict that, just as blacks begin to take control in the old cities, they discover that the traditional instrument of municipal power, the party, is no longer of much value. Harold

Washington, a black, became mayor of Chicago and immediately became embroiled in a struggle with white aldermen and ward committeemen representing the remnants of the old Daley machine. Washington triumphed, leading to a period in which racial politics largely replaced machine politics. After Washington died in 1987, a new election in which voters cast their ballots along racial lines resulted in the election of a white mayor, Richard Daley, son of the old boss. Though the younger Daley had his father's name, he did not have his power. Eventually another black will probably become mayor of Chicago, but that person will not be able to run the city as it was once run.

Of course blacks have also come to power in cities without a tradition of machine politics. Tom Bradley became mayor of Los Angeles, Coleman Young mayor of Detroit, and Marion Barry mayor of Washington, D.C. (By 1993 there were black mayors in 356 American cities and Hispanic mayors in 202.) They have had to negotiate alliances with other interests, such as downtown businesspeople and white liberals, in order to govern. It is difficult, however, for these mayors to increase their formal authority. The mayor of Los Angeles (until 1993 Tom Bradley, now Richard Riordan) would no doubt like to get tighter control over many quasi-independent boards, commissions, and administrators, but this is not easily done, and so the pursuit of any political agenda will confront many roadblocks.

Taxes and Tax Revolts

Politics in states and cities is often dominated by issues of taxing and spending not only because government at these levels must try harder to live within their means but for three other reasons as well.

First, states and cities provide services—schooling, law enforcement, fire protection, hospital care, road maintenance—directly to the citizen. Voters can see and even touch what state and local government does; they can only guess about much of what the federal government does. Because state and local services are so close to the daily lives of the people, the quality of these services is often a hot political issue.

Second, state and local taxes are more visible than federal ones. The voters must write checks to pay the

★ Where Do You Pay the Most Taxes?

State and local tax payments in 1990 for a family of four earning $25,000 per year:

Portland, Oregon	$3,457
Milwaukee, Wisconsin	$3,436
Philadelphia, Pennsylvania	$3,192
Detroit, Michigan	$2,980
Baltimore, Maryland	$2,826
Newark, New Jersey	$2,800
New York, New York	$2,647
Providence, Rhode Island	$2,641
Cleveland, Ohio	$2,484
Washington, D.C.	$2,372
Honolulu, Hawaii	$2,112

SOURCE: *Statistical Abstract of the United States, 1992, 303.*

property taxes on which cities rely for about three-fourths of their revenue. Voters pay cash at the checkout counter for the sales taxes on which the states rely for about half their revenues (see Figure 25.5). The federal income tax, by contrast, is mostly collected by withholding it from our paychecks. It is money we never see, and often we can look forward to getting a refund after we file our tax return.

Third, many state and local taxes do not reflect how much money people earn. People must pay the same sales tax whether they are rich or poor. People must pay their property taxes whether they earned a lot of money that year or were laid off and earned next to nothing. By contrast, how much we pay in federal income taxes depends on how much we earn—in good years we pay more, in poor years we pay less.

These factors mean that city and state politicians are more likely than federal ones to be hit by demands for more services or lower taxes. People want more police on the streets but don't want to pay for them. Often some compromise can be worked out, but sometimes the voters' anger at their tax bills makes any compromise impossible. When that happens we have a **tax revolt**—a citizen-initiated demand for lower taxes.

This is especially likely to occur when property taxes have been rising faster than personal income. Suppose you bought a modest home at a time when you could afford the taxes. Then your neighborhood or city became very popular, with people moving in by the thousands trying to buy houses. The price of your home suddenly skyrockets. The local tax assessor keeps raising the stated value of your home, and that means the property taxes you pay go up even if the tax *rate* has not changed. But during all of this your income has not gone up. As a result, you discover you can't afford to pay your property taxes. So you join a tax revolt.

Probably the first and certainly the best known of these revolts was Proposition 13, a measure adopted by the voters of California in 1978. Under it property taxes had to be limited to 1 percent of the market value of the land or house. Property assessments could not go up by more than 2 percent a year, and new state taxes would require a two-thirds vote of the legislature. Many cities had to reduce their taxes, and some had to reduce their services (some were able to maintain services by adopting nonproperty taxes, assessing fees for various services, or increasing governmental efficiency). The state government, which at the time had a budget surplus, also came to the aid

FIGURE 25.5 Where the Money Comes From and Where the Money Goes, 1990

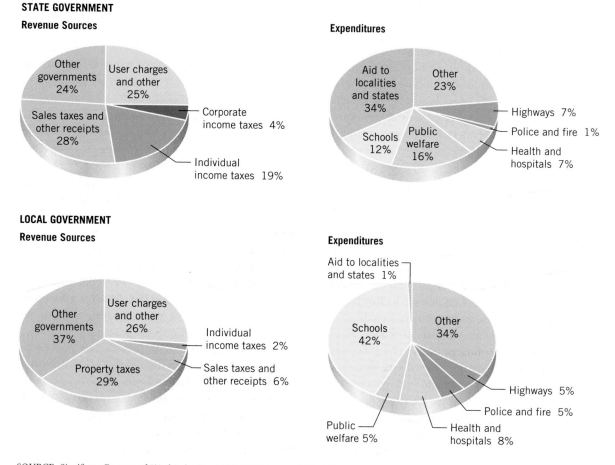

STATE GOVERNMENT
Revenue Sources

- Other governments 24%
- User charges and other 25%
- Sales taxes and other receipts 28%
- Corporate income taxes 4%
- Individual income taxes 19%

Expenditures

- Aid to localities and states 34%
- Other 23%
- Schools 12%
- Public welfare 16%
- Highways 7%
- Police and fire 1%
- Health and hospitals 7%

LOCAL GOVERNMENT
Revenue Sources

- Other governments 37%
- User charges and other 26%
- Individual income taxes 2%
- Property taxes 29%
- Sales taxes and other receipts 6%

Expenditures

- Aid to localities and states 1%
- Schools 42%
- Other 34%
- Highways 5%
- Police and fire 5%
- Health and hospitals 8%
- Public welfare 5%

SOURCE: *Significant Features of Fiscal Federalism, 1992* (Washington, D.C.: Advisory Commission on Intergovernmental Relations, 1992), Tables 5, 9, 61, 77, 79.

of local governments by increasing its share of the costs of certain programs. As a result more and more of California's public expenditures were being paid for out of state income and sales taxes.

In the wake of Proposition 13 several other states adopted tax-limitation or spending-limitation measures. Massachusetts voters enacted Proposition 2½, and Missouri and Texas amended their constitutions to restrict the growth in revenues (Missouri) or expenditures (Texas) to the rate of growth in personal income. Other states adopted similar plans.

State and local governments tried to cope with tax revolts and declining federal aid in several ways. They began to tighten up the administration of their programs in hopes of saving money. In some places they reduced services (several cities laid off many police officers). They charged fees for various services, such as participating in the school band, that once were paid for out of taxes. They turned over some previously public services, such as trash collection, to private contractors who operated on a fee-for-service basis. And more than forty states created state-run lotteries, earmarking a portion of the state's profits for aid to education or subsidies for city and town governments. In 1990 lottery sales were nearly $20 billion, with the states retaining about 40 percent of the proceeds.

State Policies and Federal Politics: The Case of Crime Control

The importance of the decisions made by state and local governments and the diversity in the ways in which those decisions are made are two of the most distinctive features of the American political system. We often quote a maxim familiar to all elected officials: "all politics is local politics." This is not literally true—a lot of important decisions are made with an eye chiefly on their national or international implications. But it is true enough for many policies and especially true for electoral politics.

State or local governments, after all, is where most members of Congress and many members of the national administration get their start. (For example, between 1950 and 1980 one-fourth of all ex-governors who stayed in politics wound up in Congress and 40 percent were appointed to federal administrative posts.) They learn politics by practicing local politics. In so doing, they learn that to get and keep national office, one must be seen as serving local interests.

As we have seen, the states and the federal government are locked in a continuing struggle over policy. The states want Washington to pay for new programs but to let the states decide what those programs should consist of and how they should be run. Washington wants the states to pay a larger share, but it hopes to decide what programs will be supported by this money. The balance of power has continually shifted back and forth between them, with different laws, political personalities, and changes in public opinion influencing their repositioning. One of the most vivid examples of this ever-changing relationship is in the area of crime control.

You might think that crime control would always have been on the federal agenda. After all, America has always had crime and crime is an ideal issue for majoritarian politics: if crime is reduced, all of us (except criminals) benefit and all of us (especially criminals) pay. Any president or member of Congress would be delighted to take credit for reducing crime.

But before the late 1960s, crime was rarely on the federal agenda. There were two reasons for this. First, many people thought the national government had no constitutional right to play a role in crime control. Criminal laws were passed by state legislatures and enforced by city police chiefs and county prosecutors. Nowhere did the Constitution give to Washington the power to have a police force or pass laws making local behavior—stealing, killing, raping—federal crimes. We are so used to having a Federal Bureau of Investigation (FBI) that we forget that it did not exist until the 1920s and then it was controversial because people worried about creating a "national police force." When Congress passed a law against prostitution in 1910 it had to justify its enactment by relying on the commerce clause of the Constitution. Since Congress could regulate interstate commerce, it could regulate prostitutes who moved across state lines. It used a similar justification for a law banning the interstate transportation of stolen vehicles. When the infant son of the heroic aviator Charles Lindbergh was kidnapped in 1932, there was a demand that Congress do something. It responded by making

Among the most difficult problems state and local governments must struggle with are illegal drugs (left, Texas state police confiscate bags of cocaine) and the homeless (right, police question a street person).

it a federal offense to transport a kidnapped person across state lines.

The second limitation on the federal role came from the widespread assumption that local matters ought to be handled by local authorities. Local politicians reinforced this view by defending "states' rights." One reason for this position was the fear in many southern states that if the federal government started passing criminal laws it might make civil-rights violations (which were part of the underpinning of many political systems at that time) a federal crime. But there was another reason: Americans had not yet come to expect that Washington would, should, or could do much about local matters.

The role of the federal government in crime slowly grew as the power to regulate interstate commerce was more broadly interpreted by the Supreme Court (see Chapter 3), making it possible to apply federal criminal statutes to more and more local ac-

tivities. For example, the Consumer Credit Protection Act of 1968 made loan sharking* a federal crime. When this law was challenged, the Supreme Court said that even if loan sharking was a purely local activity, it might "affect" interstate commerce and so Congress was entitled to regulate it.[26]

The growing crime rate and political opportunism also drove this growth of federal power. In the early 1960s, the number of reported crimes began to rise dramatically, an increase that within ten years had doubled the rate of violent crime. This increase hit the big cities especially hard, and America had become a nation of city dwellers. In 1964 Republican Barry Goldwater ran against President Lyndon Johnson on a platform that, among other things, accused

---

* A loan shark is a person who loans money to people at illegally high interest rates and enforces repayment of the loan by the threat of force.

the Democrats of tolerating "crime in the streets." Goldwater lost, but Johnson responded to the Goldwater attack by appointing a national commission to make recommendations on how to improve law enforcement. Four years later Richard Nixon defeated Hubert Humphrey after a campaign that made "law and order" a key issue. Nixon carried out his campaign pledge to get tough on crime by appointing "law and order" attorneys to the Justice Department and by strengthening the federal drug enforcement agency.

Crime has been on the national agenda ever since. During the 1980s, Congress passed at least one new crime or drug control bill every two years (see box on page 708). In 1993 President Clinton signed the Brady bill, requiring a five-day waiting period for the purchase of a handgun, and other legislation designed to put more police officers on the streets of the cities. In the 1960s and early 1970s, crime was an issue pressed by Republicans, but of late it has become a bipartisan issue with many of the toughest proposals coming from some Democrats in Congress.

Crime: Rhetoric Versus Reality

There are two main problems with the enlarged federal role in crime control. First, the vast majority of the people and money involved in fighting crime are still to be found at the local level. Second, nobody—not the president, not any police chief, not any judge, not any professor—really knows how to cut the crime rate dramatically, or at least cut it dramatically while still preserving our essential freedoms.

In 1990, state and local governments spent nearly nine dollars on crime control for every one dollar spent by the federal government. There are thirteen times as many inmates in state prisons as there are in federal ones. The vast majority of law enforcement officers are local police officers. Even the Washington, D.C., police force is under the control of a mayor, not Congress or the president. The president cannot appoint a single police chief. Washington has become a partner of the states in the war on crime, but it is still very much a junior partner, and that is not likely to change.

Washington has spent billions of dollars and passed many get-tough crime bills, but crime rates have been largely unaffected by any of this. There are many reasons for our inability to design an effective crime-control strategy for a free society. It is rather easy to steal something, hit someone, or sell drugs when no police officer is looking. Even doubling or tripling the number of officers on the street will not make it much more likely that a criminal will be caught in the act. Most of us don't steal, hit, or deal in drugs; the reasons some people do are varied and complex.

Many criminals come from homes that are broken, unhappy, or abusive, but the government doesn't know how to create intact, happy, and caring families. Many criminals have parents who are criminals or who abuse alcohol and drugs, yet it is very hard for the government to prevent the problems of parents from becoming the problems of their children. The moral values that keep some individuals from engaging in criminal acts are not shared by all members of our society, and morality is not something that can be easily created by plan.

In some communities the lack of jobs and the evident success of drug dealers have reduced the incentive to find legitimate work and increased the rewards and glamour of crime and drug dealing. It is not easy to create jobs in such neighborhoods; businesses don't want to locate there because the crime rate is high. In many crime-ridden neighborhoods, gangs often rule the streets, shooting their rivals and sometimes killing innocent bystanders. It is not easy, however, to break up these gangs because they provide safety and income for their members—safety that the police can't provide and income that local businesses can't supply.

All this makes for a difficult kind of majoritarian politics. When you create a Social Security program and pay benefits to retired people, the rate of poverty among the elderly goes down. When you pass an environmental law requiring that less polluting engines be installed in new automobiles, the amount of pollution in the air goes down. But when you pass an anti-crime bill, the crime rate does not necessarily go down.

This means that the options Washington has are rather few: make speeches denouncing crime (but criminals don't listen), spend more money on crime control (but federal money is only a drop in the national crime-control bucket), or make penalties for breaking federal laws more severe (but most

Major Federal Anti-Crime Laws, 1980–1993

Comprehensive Crime Control Act (1984)
Established the Sentencing Commission to produce sentencing guidelines for federal judges that would provide greater "certainty and fairness" in punishing those who broke federal laws.

Anti-Drug Abuse Act (1986)
Toughened penalties for drug dealers and other federal offenders, made it easier to seize the assets (money, homes, cars, etc.) of convicted drug dealers, and provided money for state and local governments to combat crime and drug abuse.

Anti-Drug Abuse Act (1988)
Created the Office of National Drug Control Policy (commonly known as the "Drug Czar"), specified how money should be allocated between treatment and enforcement, authorized the death penalty for drug dealers who commit murders, required that contractors doing work for the federal government certify that they have a drug-free work place, and denied federal benefits (such as the right to live in public housing) to drug dealers.

Crime Control Act (1990)
Addressed a wide range of criminal activities including international money laundering, drug-free school zones, and prohibitions on the sale of drug paraphernalia.

Anti-Car Theft Act (1992)
Made car-jacking (stealing a car from its driver at gun point) a federal crime.

Brady Bill (1993)
Required that anyone purchasing a hand gun wait five days before taking delivery so that a mandatory records check can be made to see if purchaser has a criminal record.

Crime Act (1994)
Expanded federal death penalty; mandated life imprisonment for federal criminals convicted of three violent or drug offenses; banned certain assault weapons; and authorized $8 billion to hire 100,000 more police officers, $8 billion to build prisons for state offenders, and $7 billion for various crime prevention programs.

criminals are prosecuted under state laws). Because a president can do so little about crime, he is always vulnerable to political attack in an election if he has the bad luck to be in office when crime rates are high or rising. And since the early 1960s, every president has been in that unenviable position.

The Changing Face of Crime-Control Policy

Given the fact that the states and localities will always play the lead role in crime control, Washington has been limited to trying various combinations of three different strategies:

1. *It has supplied help—money, technical assistance, computerized information, fingerprint records, and statistics—to local law enforcement agencies.* The federal government has funded research on new crime-control techniques, coordinated some local investigations that cut across state lines, and investigated criminal organizations that were too big to be investigated by local authorities.

2. *It has made some things that were once just state crimes into federal crimes.* For example, Washington has made bank robbery, car-jacking, and drug dealing federal crimes. This means that the FBI and the Drug Enforcement Administration (DEA) can get involved in investigating these matters; with respect to drug trafficking, even the military has been involved. And it means that federal prosecutors can try some cases and, on occasion, get tougher penalties imposed than can state prosecutors. The federal government has also passed laws especially aimed at organized crime so that federal investigators can bring charges against gangsters who may have corrupted or overpowered local authorities.

3. *It has brought under some degree of federal regulation activities that may contribute to crime.* For example, Washington controls who and what kinds of products (such as drugs) can enter the country, it has rules for buying handguns and certain other weapons, and it inspects the flow of money through banks to see if any of it is the result of fraud, organized crime, or drug trafficking.

During the late 1960s and most of the 1970s, Washington emphasized the first of these strategies.

This was done through the Law Enforcement Assistance Administration (LEAA), created in 1968, and its successor agencies, such as the National Institute of Justice (NIJ), the Bureau of Justice Statistics (BJS), and the Bureau of Justice Assistance (BJA), all located in the U.S. Department of Justice. The LEAA, NIJ, and BJA were essentially funding agencies that shipped federal money to states, counties, and cities to help them fight crime. They were specifically prohibited from getting involved in the direction or operation of local law enforcement. The law creating LEAA, for example, barred any federal official from directing, supervising, or controlling any local police force or state law enforcement agency.

As a check-writing machine, LEAA was a great success. Between 1969 and 1977, it sent about $8 billion to the states and localities. But crime continued to go up, and so it came as no surprise when, in the 1976 election campaign, Democratic candidate Jimmy Carter attacked Republican presidents Richard Nixon and Gerald Ford for having presided over a crime wave and for LEAA's failure to do anything about it. LEAA was in particular criticized for letting local authorities buy almost anything they wanted with federal dollars. After Carter was elected, LEAA was reorganized and its budget sharply cut; most of its functions were transferred to NIJ and later BJA, but with nowhere near as much money as LEAA once had. But crime rates continued to rise.

Now President Carter was vulnerable to attack on the crime issue, and in the 1980 campaign Republican candidate Ronald Reagan was quick to go on the offensive. Reagan and his successor, George Bush, began to shift federal crime-control policies toward the second and third strategies listed above. With bipartisan support in Congress, Washington began to emphasize direct federal involvement in law enforcement. It did this by expanding the number of local crimes that were now also federal crimes, toughening the sentences violating federal criminal statutes, and (especially) getting federal agencies more deeply involved in combatting drug trafficking.

Since the 1960s, governors and mayors had wanted Washington to send them money to combat crime. They got money from LEAA until it was abolished by Ronald Reagan; then, between 1989 and 1992, Washington nearly quadrupled (from $118 million to $423 million) the amount of drug-fighting money it was sending to the states and cities each year. Traditionally the states had not wanted direct federal involvement in enforcing the laws, except for the cooperation of the FBI, but increasingly they began asking for more direct federal involvement. If they thought that the state penalty for, say, car-jacking or drug dealing was too lenient, they urged the federal government either to make this a federal crime or, if it was already a federal offense, increase the penalties. That way, a person arrested for such a crime could be subjected to federal prosecution. The states also pressed Washington to get the military involved in stopping international drug trafficking.

For all of the changes that have occurred since the 1960s, law enforcement remains a local matter. Of the three areas of possible involvement—making policy, administering justice, and supplying funds—the federal government has sometimes emphasized one, sometimes another, but never has it taken the lead in all three. The localism of American politics—a localism supported by constitutional tradition and (more importantly) public sentiment—is clearly evident in the independence state and local governments continue to exercise in fighting crime. Though the federal government has expanded its supportive role in recent decades, crime control remains the province of local police officers and state troopers, who have very little connection to the policies of Washington.

SUMMARY

State and local governments tend to reflect variations on two different views of the public interest: a Jacksonian tradition that seeks to keep government close to the people (leading to many elected offices, weak governors and mayors, small electoral districts, a suspicion of experts, detailed constitutions, and patronage politics) and a progressive, or "reformed" tradition that seeks to make government stronger and more efficient (leading to strong governors, appointed city managers, large electoral districts, professionalized legislatures, nonpartisan elections, brief constitutions, and a comprehensive civil service in which expertise is rewarded).

State government is by no means a small version of national government, as can be seen by the many executive and judicial posts that are filled, at the state level, by popular election and by the much greater strength of party leaders in many state legislatures. Local government shows an even greater variety, with large and small cities governed under the mayor-council system, middle-sized cities governed by the council-manager form, and some places governed by town meetings, representative town meetings, or commissions.

Within these institutions there is a struggle among rival interests and preferences shaped, in great part, by a concern over taxes and the competitive economic position of states and localities. They also continually negotiate with the federal government over crime control and many other matters, looking to increase federal funding without giving up their autonomy.

KEY TERMS

SUGGESTED READINGS

Banfield, Edward C., and James Q. Wilson. *City Politics.* Cambridge, Mass.: Harvard University Press, 1963. An argument about how political culture or ethos shapes the politics of American cities.

Council of State Governments. *Book of the States.* Lexington, Ky.: Council of State Governments, annual. Yearly publication of facts and figures on state government.

Elazar, Daniel J. *American Federalism: A View from the States.* 3d ed. New York: Harper & Row, 1984. Insightful discussion of state political cultures.

Fesler, James W., ed. *The Fifty States and Their Local Governments.* New York: Knopf, 1967. Though dated, it remains a good source on the constitutional background of state and local government.

Gray, Virginia, Herbert Jacob, and Robert Albritton, eds. *Politics in the American States.* 5th ed. Glencoe, Ill.: Scott Foresman, 1992. An excellent collection of articles on state governmental institutions, processes, and policies.

International City Managers Association. *Municipal Yearbook.* Washington, D.C.: ICMA, annual. A yearly publication with facts and figures about American local government.

Pierce, Neal R., and Jerry Hagstrom. *The Book of America: Inside 50 States Today.* New York: Norton, 1983. A lively and informative account by two first-class journalists of how each of the fifty states is governed.

Rosenthal, Alan. *The Third House.* Washington, D.C.: CQ Books, 1993. Examines lobbying in state governments; many vivid examples.

Appendix

The Declaration of Independence

In Congress, July 4, 1776

The Unanimous Declaration of the Thirteen United States of America

When, in the course of human events, it becomes necessary for one people to dissolve the political bands which have connected them with another, and to assume, among the powers of the earth, the separate and equal station to which the laws of nature and of nature's God entitle them, a decent respect to the opinions of mankind requires that they should declare the causes which impel them to the separation.

We hold these truths to be self-evident: That all men are created equal; that they are endowed by their Creator with certain unalienable rights; that among these are life, liberty, and the pursuit of happiness; that, to secure these rights, governments are instituted among men, deriving their just powers from the consent of the governed; that whenever any form of government becomes destructive of these ends, it is the right of the people to alter or to abolish it, and to institute new government, laying its foundation on such principles, and organizing its powers in such form, as to them shall seem most likely to effect their safety and happiness. Prudence, indeed, will dictate that governments long established should not be changed for light and transient causes; and accordingly all experience hath shown that mankind are more disposed to suffer, while evils are sufferable, than to right themselves by abolishing the forms to which they are accustomed. But when a long train of abuses and usurpations, pursuing invariably the same object, evinces a design to reduce them under absolute despotism, it is their right, it is their duty, to throw off such government, and to provide new guards for their future security. Such has been the patient sufferance of these colonies; and such is now the necessity which constrains them to alter their former systems of government. The history of the present King of Great Britain is a history of repeated injuries and usurpations, all having in direct object the establishment of an absolute tyranny over these states. To prove this, let facts be submitted to a candid world.

He has refused to assent to laws, the most wholesome and necessary for the public good.

He has forbidden his governors to pass laws of immediate and pressing importance, unless suspended in their operation till his assent should be obtained; and, when so suspended, he has utterly neglected to attend to them.

He has refused to pass other laws for the accommodation of large districts of people, unless those people would relinquish the right of representation in the legislature, a right inestimable to them, and formidable to tyrants only.

He has called together legislative bodies at places unusual, uncomfortable, and distant from the depository of their public records, for the sole purpose of fatiguing them into compliance with his measures.

He has dissolved representative houses repeatedly, for opposing, with manly firmness, his invasions on the rights of the people.

He has refused for a long time, after such dissolutions, to cause others to be elected; whereby the legislative powers, incapable of annihilation, have returned to the people at large for their exercise; the state remaining, in the mean time, exposed to all dangers of invasions from without and convulsions within.

He has endeavored to prevent the population of these states; for that purpose obstructing the laws for naturalization of foreigners; refusing to pass others to encourage their migration hither, and raising the conditions of new appropriations of lands.

He has obstructed the administration of justice, by refusing his assent to laws for establishing judiciary powers.

He has made judges dependent on his will alone, for the tenure of their offices, and the amount and payment of their salaries.

He has erected a multitude of new offices, and sent hither swarms of officers to harass our people and eat out their substance.

He has kept among us, in times of peace, standing armies, without the consent of our legislatures.

He has affected to render the military independent of, and superior to, the civil power.

He has combined with others to subject us to a jurisdiction foreign to our constitution, and unacknowledged by our laws, giving his assent to their acts of pretended legislation:

For quartering large bodies of armed troops among us:

For protecting them, by a mock trial, from punishment for any murders which they should commit on the inhabitants of these states;

For cutting off our trade with all parts of the world;

For imposing taxes on us without our consent;

For depriving us, in many cases, of the benefits of trial by jury;

For transporting us beyond seas, to be tried for pretended offenses;

For abolishing the free system of English laws in a neighboring province, establishing therein an arbitrary government, and enlarging its boundaries, so as to render it at once an example and fit instrument for introducing the same absolute rule into these colonies;

For taking away our charters, abolishing our more valuable laws, and altering fundamentally the forms of our governments;

For suspending our own legislatures, and declaring themselves invested with power to legislate for us in all cases whatsoever.

He has abdicated government here, by declaring us out of his protection and waging war against us.

He has plundered our seas, ravaged our coasts, burned our towns, and destroyed the lives of our people.

He is at this time transporting large armies of foreign mercenaries to complete the works of death, desolation, and tyranny already begun with circumstances of cruelty and perfidy scarcely paralleled in the most barbarous ages, and totally unworthy the head of a civilized nation.

He has constrained our fellow-citizens, taken captive on the high seas, to bear arms against their country, to become the executioners of their friends and brethren, or to fall themselves by their hands.

He has excited domestic insurrections among us, and has endeavored to bring on the inhabitants of our frontiers the merciless Indian savages, whose known rule of warfare is an undistinguished destruction of all ages, sexes, and conditions.

In every stage of these oppressions we have petitioned for redress in the most humble terms; our repeated petitions have been answered only by repeated injury. A prince, whose character is thus marked by every act which may define a tyrant, is unfit to be the ruler of a free people.

Nor have we been wanting in our attentions to our British brethren. We have warned them, from time to time, of attempts by their legislature to extend an unwarrantable jurisdiction over us. We have reminded them of the circumstances of our emigration and settlement here. We have appealed to their native justice and magnanimity; and we have conjured them, by the ties of our common kindred, to disavow these usurpations, which would inevitably interrupt our connections and correspondence. They, too, have been deaf to the voice of justice and of consanguinity. We must, therefore, acquiesce in the necessity which denounces our separation, and hold them, as we hold the rest of mankind, enemies in war, in peace friends.

We, therefore, the representatives of the United States of America, in General Congress assembled, appealing to the Supreme Judge of the world for the rectitude of our intentions, do, in the name and by the authority of the good people of these colonies, solemnly publish and declare, that these United Colonies are, and of right ought to be, FREE AND INDEPENDENT STATES; that they are absolved from all allegiance to the British crown, and that all political connection between them and the state of Great Britain is, and ought to be, totally dissolved; and that, as free and independent states, they have full power to levy war, conclude peace, contract alliances, establish commerce, and do all other acts and things which independent states may of right do. And for the support of this declaration, with a firm reliance on the protection of Divine Providence, we mutually pledge to each other our lives, our fortunes, and our sacred honor.

JOHN HANCOCK [*President*]
[*and fifty-five others*]

The Constitution of the United States

Preamble

We the People of the United States, in Order to form a more perfect Union, establish Justice, insure domestic Tranquility, provide for the common defence, promote the general Welfare, and secure the Blessings of Liberty to ourselves and our Posterity, do ordain and establish this Constitution for the United States of America.

ARTICLE I.

Bicameral Congress

Section 1. All legislative Powers herein granted shall be vested in a Congress of the United States, which shall consist of a Senate and House of Representatives.

Membership of the House

Section 2. The House of Representatives shall be composed of Members chosen every second Year by the People of the several States, and the Electors in each State shall have the Qualifications requisite for Electors of the most numerous Branch of the State Legislature.

No person shall be a Representative who shall not have attained to the age of twenty five Years, and been seven Years a Citizen of the United States, and who shall not, when elected, be an Inhabitant of that State in which he shall be chosen.

Representatives and direct Taxes shall be apportioned among the several States which may be included within this Union, according to their respective Numbers, which shall be determined by adding to the whole Number of free Persons, including those bound to Service for a Term of Years, and excluding Indians not taxed, three fifths of all other Persons.[1] The actual Enumeration shall be made within three Years after the first Meeting of the Congress of the United States, and within every subsequent Term of ten Years, in such Manner as they shall by Law direct. The Number of Representatives shall not exceed one for every thirty Thousand, but each State shall have at Least one Representative; and until such enumeration shall be made, the State of New Hampshire shall be entitled to chuse three, Massachusetts eight, Rhode-Island and Providence Plantations one, Connecticut five, New-York six, New Jersey four, Pennsylvania eight, Delaware one, Maryland six, Virginia ten, North Carolina five, South Carolina five, and Georgia three.

When vacancies happen in the Representation from any State, the Executive Authority thereof shall issue Writs of Election to fill such Vacancies.

Power to impeach

The House of Representatives shall chuse their Speaker and other Officers; and shall have the sole Power of Impeachment.

Membership of the Senate

Section 3. The Senate of the United States shall be composed of two Senators from each State, *chosen by the Legislature thereof,*[2] for six Years; and each Senator shall have one Vote.

Immediately after they shall be assembled in Consequence of the first Election, they shall be divided as equally as may be into three Classes. The Seats of the Senators of the first class shall be vacated at the Expiration of the second Year, of the second Class at the Expiration of the fourth Year, and of the third Class at the Expiration of the sixth Year, so that one third may be chosen every second Year; *and if Vacancies happen by Resignation, or otherwise, during the Recess of the Legislature of any State, the Executive thereof may*

NOTE: The topical headings are not part of the original Constitution. Excluding the Preamble and Closing, those portions set in italic type have been superseded or changed by later amendments.
1. Changed by the Fourteenth Amendment, section 2.
2. Changed by the Seventeenth Amendment.

make temporary Appointments until the next Meeting of the Legislature, which shall then fill such Vacancies.[3]

No Person shall be a Senator who shall not have attained to the Age of thirty Years, and been nine Years a Citizen of the United States, and who shall not, when elected, be an Inhabitant of that State for which he shall be chosen.

The Vice President of the United States shall be President of the Senate, but shall have no Vote, unless they be equally divided.

The Senate shall chuse their other Officers, and also a President pro tempore, in the Absence of the Vice President, or when he shall exercise the Office of President of the United States.

Power to try impeachments

The Senate shall have the sole Power to try all Impeachments. When sitting for that Purpose, they shall be on Oath or Affirmation. When the President of the United States is tried the Chief Justice shall preside: And no Person shall be convicted without the Concurrence of two thirds of the Members present.

Judgment in Cases of Impeachment shall not exceed further than to removal from Office, and disqualification to hold and enjoy any Office of honor, Trust or Profit under the United States: but the Party convicted shall nevertheless be liable and subject to Indictment, Trial, Judgment and Punishment, according to Law.

Laws governing elections

Section 4.   The Times, Places and Manner of holding Elections for Senators and Representatives, shall be prescribed in each State by the Legislature thereof; but the Congress may at any time by Law make or alter such Regulations, except as to the Places of chusing Senators.

The Congress shall assemble at least once in every Year, and such Meeting shall be on the *first Monday in December, unless they shall by Law appoint a different Day.*[4]

Rules of Congress

Section 5.   Each House shall be the Judge of the Elections, Returns and Qualifications of its own Members, and a Majority of each shall constitute a Quorum to do Business; but a smaller number may adjourn from day to day, and may be authorized to compel the Attendance of absent Members, in such Manner, and under such Penalties as each House may provide.

Each House may determine the Rules of its Proceedings, punish its Members for disorderly Behaviour, and, with the Concurrence of two thirds, expel a Member.

Each House shall keep a Journal of its Proceedings, and from time to time publish the same, excepting such Parts as may in their Judgment require Secrecy; and the Yeas and Nays of the Members of either House on any question shall, at the Desire of one fifth of those Present, be entered on the Journal.

Neither House, during the Session of Congress, shall, without the Consent of the other, adjourn for more than three days, nor to any other Place than that in which the two Houses shall be sitting.

Salaries and immunities of members

Section 6.   The Senators and Representatives shall receive a Compensation for their Services, to be ascertained by Law, and paid out of the Treasury of the United States. They shall in all Cases, except Treason, Felony and Breach of the Peace, be privileged from Arrest during their Attendance at the Session of their respective Houses, and in going to and returning from the same; and for any Speech or Debate in either House, they shall not be questioned in any other Place.

3. Changed by the Seventeenth Amendment.
4. Changed by the Twentieth Amendment, section 2.

Bar on members of Congress holding federal appointive office

No Senator or Representative shall, during the Time for which he was elected, be appointed to any civil Office under the Authority of the United States, which shall have been created, or the Emoluments whereof shall have been encreased during such time; and no Person holding any Office under the United States, shall be a Member of either House during his Continuance in Office.

Money bills originate in House

Section 7.   All Bills for raising Revenue shall originate in the House of Representatives; but the Senate may propose or concur with Amendments as on other Bills.

Procedure for enacting laws; veto power

Every Bill which shall have passed the House of Representatives and the Senate, shall, before it become a Law, be presented to the President of the United States; If he approve he shall sign it, but if not he shall return it, with his Objections to that House in which it shall have originated, who shall enter the Objections at large on their Journal, and proceed to reconsider it. If after such Reconsideration two thirds of that House shall agree to pass the Bill, it shall be sent, together with the Objections, to the other House, by which it shall likewise be reconsidered, and if approved by two thirds of that House, it shall become a Law. But in all such Cases the Votes of both Houses shall be determined by yeas and Nays, and the Names of the Persons voting for and against the Bill shall be entered on the Journal of each House respectively. If any Bill shall not be returned by the President within ten Days (Sundays excepted) after it shall have been presented to him, the Same shall be a Law, in like Manner, as if he had signed it, unless the Congress by their Adjournment prevent its Return, in which Case it shall not be a Law.

Every Order, Resolution, or Vote to which the Concurrence of the Senate and House of Representatives may be necessary (except on a question of Adjournment) shall be presented to the President of the United States; and before the Same shall take Effect, shall be approved by him, or being disapproved by him, shall be repassed by two thirds of the Senate and House of Representatives, according to the Rules and Limitations prescribed in the Case of a Bill.

Powers of Congress
—*taxes*

Section 8.   The Congress shall have Power To lay and Collect Taxes, Duties, Imposts and Excises, to pay the Debts and provide for the common Defence and general Welfare of the United States; but all Duties, Imposts and Excises shall be uniform throughout the United States.

—*borrowing*

To borrow Money on the credit of the United States;

—*regulation of commerce*

To regulate Commerce with foreign Nations, and among the several States, and with the Indian Tribes;

—*naturalization and bankruptcy*

To establish an uniform Rule of Naturalization, and uniform Laws on the subject of Bankruptcies throughout the United States;

—*money*

To coin Money, regulate the Value thereof, and of foreign Coin, and fix the Standard of Weights and Measures;

—*counterfeiting*

To provide for the Punishment of counterfeiting the Securities and current Coin of the United States;

—*post office*

To establish Post Offices and post Roads;

—*patents and copyrights*

To promote the Progress of Science and useful Arts, by securing for limited Times to Authors and Inventors the exclusive Right to their respective Writings and Discoveries;

—*create courts*

To constitute Tribunals inferior to the Supreme Court;

—*punish piracies*

To define and punish Piracies and Felonies committed on the high Seas, and Offences against the Law of Nations;

—*declare war*

To declare War, grant Letters of Marque and Reprisal, and make Rules concerning Captures on Land and Water;

—create army and navy

To raise and support Armies, but no Appropriation of Money to that Use shall be for a longer Term than two Years;

To provide and maintain a Navy;

To make Rules for the Government and Regulation of the land and naval Forces;

—call the militia

To provide for calling forth the Militia to execute the Laws of the Union, suppress Insurrections and repel Invasions;

To provide for organizing, arming, and disciplining, the Militia, and for governing such Part of them as may be employed in the Service of the United States, reserving to the States respectively, the Appointment of the Officers, and the Authority of training the Militia according to the discipline prescribed by Congress;

—govern District of Columbia

To exercise exclusive Legislation in all Cases whatsoever, over such District (not exceeding ten Miles square) as may, by Cession of Particular States, and the Acceptance of Congress, become the Seat of the Government of the United States, and to exercise like Authority over all Places purchased by the Consent of the Legislature of the State in which the Same shall be, for the Erection of Forts, Magazines, Arsenals, dock-Yards and other needful Buildings;—And

—"necessary-and-proper" clause

To make all Laws which shall be necessary and proper for carrying into Execution the foregoing Powers, and all other Powers vested by this Constitution in the Government of the United States, or in any Department or Officer thereof.

Restrictions on powers of Congress

—slave trade

Section 9. The Migration or Importation of such Persons as any of the States now existing shall think proper to admit, shall not be prohibited by the Congress prior to the Year one thousand eight hundred and eight, but a Tax or duty may be imposed on such Importation, not exceeding ten dollars for each Person.

—habeas corpus

The Privilege of the Writ of Habeas Corpus shall not be suspended, unless when in Cases of Rebellion or Invasion the public Safety may require it.

—no bill of attainder or ex post facto law

No bill of Attainder or ex post facto Law shall be passed.

No Capitation, or other direct, Tax shall be laid, *unless in Proportion to the Census or Enumeration herein before directed to be taken.*[5]

—no interstate tariffs

No Tax or Duty shall be laid on Articles exported from any State.

—no preferential treatment for some states

No Preference shall be given by any Regulation of Commerce or Revenue to the Ports of one State over those of another; nor shall Vessels bound to, or from, one State, be obliged to enter, clear or pay Duties in another.

—appropriations

No Money shall be drawn from the Treasury, but in Consequence of Appropriations made by Law; and a regular Statement and Account of the Receipts and Expenditures of all public Money shall be published from time to time.

—no titles of nobility

No Title of Nobility shall be granted by the United States: And no Person holding any Office of Profit or Trust under them, shall, without the Consent of the Congress, accept of any present, Emolument, Office, or Title, of any kind whatever, from any King, Prince, or foreign State.

Restrictions on powers of states

Section 10. No State shall enter into any Treaty, Alliance, or Confederation; grant Letters of Marque and Reprisal; coin Money; emit Bills of Credit; make any Thing but gold and silver Coin a Tender in Payment of Debts; pass any Bill of Attainder, ex post facto Law, or Law impairing the Obligation of Contracts, or grant any Title of Nobility.

No State shall, without the Consent of the Congress, lay any Imposts or Duties on Imports or Exports, except what may be absolutely necessary for executing its inspection Laws; and the net Produce of all Duties and Imposts, laid by any State on Imports or

---

5. Changed by the Sixteenth Amendment.

Exports, shall be for the Use of the Treasury of the United States; and all such Laws shall be subject to the Revision and Controul of the Congress.

No State shall, without the Consent of Congress, lay any Duty of Tonnage, keep Troops, or Ships of War in time of Peace, enter into any Agreement or Compact with another State, or with a foreign Power, or engage in War, unless actually invaded, or in such imminent Danger as will not admit of delay.

ARTICLE II.

Office of president

Section 1.   The executive Power shall be vested in a President of the United States of America. He shall hold his Office during the Term of four Years, and, together with the Vice President, chosen for the same Term, be elected, as follows

Election of president

Each State shall appoint, in such Manner as the Legislature thereof may direct, a Number of Electors, equal to the whole Number of Senators and Representatives to which the State may be entitled in the Congress: but no Senator or Representative, or Person holding an Office of Trust or Profit under the United States, shall be appointed an Elector.

The Electors shall meet in their respective States, and vote by Ballot for two Persons, of whom one at least shall not be an Inhabitant of the same State with themselves. And they shall make a List of all the Persons voted for, and of the Number of Votes for each; which List they shall sign and certify, and transmit sealed to the Seat of the Government of the United States, directed to the President of the Senate. The President of the Senate shall, in the Presence of the Senate and House of Representatives, open all the Certificates, and the Votes shall then be counted. The Person having the greatest Number of Votes shall be the President, if such Number be a Majority of the whole Number of Electors appointed; and if there be more than one who have such Majority, and have an equal Number of Votes, then the House of Representatives shall immediately chuse by Ballot one of them for President; and if no Person have a Majority, then from the five highest on the List the said House shall in like Manner chuse the President. But in chusing the President, the Votes shall be taken by States, the Representation from each State having one Vote; a quorum for this Purpose shall consist of a Member or Members from two thirds of the States, and a Majority of all the States shall be necessary to a Choice. In every Case, after the Choice of the President, the Person having the greatest Number of Votes of the Electors shall be the Vice President. But if there should remain two or more who have equal Votes, the Senate shall chuse from them by Ballot the Vice President.[6]

The Congress may determine the Time of chusing the Electors, and the Day on which they shall give their Votes, which Day shall be the same throughout the United States.

Requirements to be president

No Person except a natural born Citizen, or a Citizen of the United States, at the time of the Adoption of this Constitution, shall be eligible to the Office of President; neither shall any person be eligible to that Office who shall not have attained to the Age of thirty five Years, and been fourteen Years a Resident within the United States.

In Case of the Removal of the President from Office, or of his Death, Resignation, or Inability to discharge the Powers and Duties of the said Office, the Same shall devolve on the Vice President, and the Congress may by Law provide for the Case of Removal, Death, Resignation or Inability, both of the President and Vice President, declaring what Officer shall then act as President, and such Officer shall act accordingly, until the Disability be removed, or a President shall be elected.[7]

6. Superseded by the Twelfth Amendment.
7. Modified by the Twenty-fifth Amendment.

Pay of president

The President shall, at stated Times, receive for his Services, a Compensation, which shall neither be encreased nor diminished during the Period for which he shall have been elected, and he shall not receive within that Period any other Emolument from the United States, or any of them.

Before he enter on the Execution of his Office, he shall take the following Oath or Affirmation:—"I do solemnly swear (or affirm) that I will faithfully execute the Office of President of the United States, and will to the best of my Ability, preserve, protect and defend the Constitution of the United States."

Powers of president
—commander in chief

—pardons

—treaties and
  appointments

Section 2.   The President shall be Commander in Chief of the Army and Navy of the United States, and of the Militia of the several States, when called into the actual Service of the United States; he may require the Opinion, in writing, of the principal Officer in each of the executive Departments, upon any Subject relating to the Duties of their respective Offices, and he shall have Power to grant Reprieves and Pardons for Offences against the United States, except in Cases of Impeachment.

He shall have Power, by and with the Advice and Consent of the Senate, to make Treaties, provided two thirds of the Senators present concur; and he shall nominate, and by and with the Advice and Consent of the Senate, shall appoint Ambassadors, other public Ministers and Consuls, Judges of the supreme Court, and all other Officers of the United States, whose Appointments are not herein otherwise provided for, and which shall be established by Law: but the Congress may by Law vest the Appointment of such inferior Officers, as they think proper, in the President alone, in the Courts of Law, or in the Heads of Departments.

The President shall have Power to fill up all Vacancies that may happen during the Recess of the Senate, by granting Commissions which shall expire at the End of their next Session.

Relations of president with
Congress

Section 3.   He shall from time to time give to the Congress Information of the State of the Union, and recommend to their Consideration such Measures as he shall judge necessary and expedient; he may, on extraordinary Occasions, convene both Houses, or either of them, and in Case of Disagreement between them, with Respect to the Time of Adjournment, he may adjourn them to such Time as he shall think proper; he shall receive Ambassadors and other public Ministers; he shall take Care that the Laws be faithfully executed, and shall Commission all the Officers of the United States.

Impeachment

Section 4.   The President, Vice President and all civil Officers of the United States, shall be removed from Office on Impeachment for, and Conviction of, Treason, Bribery, or other high Crimes and Misdemeanors.

ARTICLE III.

Federal courts

Section 1.   The judicial Power of the United States, shall be vested in one supreme Court, and in such inferior Courts as the Congress may from time to time ordain and establish. The Judges, both of the supreme and inferior Courts, shall hold their Offices during good Behaviour, and shall, at stated Times, receive for their Services, a Compensation, which shall not be diminished during their Continuance in Office.

Jurisdiction of courts

Section 2.   The judicial Power shall extend to all Cases, in Law and Equity, arising under this Constitution, the Laws of the United States, and Treaties made, or which shall be made, under their Authority;— to all Cases affecting Ambassadors, other public Ministers and Consuls;—to all Cases of admiralty and maritime Jurisdiction;—to Controversies to which the United States shall be a Party;—to Controversies between two or more States;—*between a State and Citizens of another State;*[8]—between Citizens of different States;—between Citizens of the same State claiming Lands under Grants of different States, and between a State, or the Citizens thereof, and foreign States, Citizens or Subjects.

—original

—appellate

In all Cases affecting Ambassadors, other public Ministers and Consuls, and those in which a State shall be Party, the supreme Court shall have original Jurisdiction. In all the other Cases before mentioned, the supreme Court shall have appellate Jurisdiction, both as to Law and Fact, with such Exceptions, and under such Regulations as the Congress shall make.

The Trial of all Crimes, except in Cases of Impeachment, shall be by Jury; and such Trial shall be held in the State where the said Crimes shall have been committed; but when not committed within any State, the Trial shall be at such Place or Places as the Congress may by Law have directed.

Treason

Section 3.   Treason against the United States, shall consist only in levying War against them, or in adhering to their Enemies, giving them Aid and Comfort. No Person shall be convicted of Treason unless on the Testimony of two Witnesses to the same overt Act, or on Confession in open Court.

The Congress shall have Power to declare the Punishment of Treason, but no Attainder of Treason shall work Corruption of Blood, or Forfeiture except during the Life of the Person attainted.

ARTICLE IV.

Full faith and credit

Section 1.   Full Faith and Credit shall be given in each State to the public Acts, Records, and judicial Proceedings of every other State. And the Congress may by general Laws prescribe the Manner in which such Acts, Records and Proceedings shall be proved, and the Effect thereof.

Privileges and immunities

Section 2.   The Citizens of each State shall be entitled to all Privileges and Immunities of Citizens in the several States.

Extradition

A person charged in any State with Treason, Felony, or other Crime, who shall flee from Justice, and be found in another State, shall on Demand of the executive Authority of the State from which he fled, be delivered up, to be removed to the State having Jurisdiction of the Crime.

No Person held to Service or Labour in one State, under the Laws thereof, escaping into another, shall, in Consequence of any Law or Regulation therein, be discharged from such Service or Labour, but shall be delivered up on Claim of the Party to whom such Service or Labour may be due.[9]

Creation of new states

Section 3.   New States may be admitted by the Congress into this Union; but no new State shall be formed or erected within the Jurisdiction of any other State; nor any State be formed by the Junction of two or more States, or Parts of States, without the Consent of the Legislatures of the States concerned as well as of the Congress.

Governing territories

The Congress shall have Power to dispose of and make all needful Rules and Regulations respecting the Territory or other Property belonging to the United States; and nothing in this Constitution shall be so construed as to Prejudice any Claims of the United States, or of any particular State.

8. Modified by the Eleventh Amendment.
9. Changed by the Thirteenth Amendment.

Protection of states

Section 4. The United States shall guarantee to every State in this Union a Republican Form of Government, and shall protect each of them against Invasion; and on Application of the Legislature, or of the Executive (when the Legislature cannot be convened) against domestic Violence.

ARTICLE V.

Amending the Constitution

The Congress, whenever two thirds of both Houses shall deem it necessary, shall propose Amendments to this Constitution, or, on the Application of the Legislatures of two thirds of the several States, shall call a Convention for proposing Amendments, which, in either Case, shall be valid to all Intents and Purposes, as Part of this Constitution, when ratified by the Legislatures of three fourths of the several States, or by Conventions in three fourths thereof, as the one or the other Mode of Ratification may be proposed by the Congress; Provided that no Amendment which may be made prior to the Year One thousand eight hundred and eight shall in any Manner after the first and fourth Clauses in the Ninth Section of the first Article; and that no State, without its Consent, shall be deprived of its equal Suffrage in the Senate.

ARTICLE VI.

Assumption of debts of Confederation

All Debts contracted and Engagements entered into, before the Adoption of this Constitution, shall be as valid against the United States under this Constitution, as under the Confederation.

Supremacy of federal laws and treaties

This Constitution, and the Laws of the United States which shall be made in Pursuance thereof; and all Treaties made, or which shall be made, under the Authority of the United States, shall be the Supreme Law of the Land; and the Judges in every State shall be bound thereby, any Thing in the Constitution or Laws of any State to the Contrary notwithstanding.

No religious test

The Senators and Representatives before mentioned, and the Members of the several State Legislatures, and all executive and judicial Officers, both of the United States and of the several States, shall be bound by Oath or Affirmation, to support this Constitution; but no religious Test shall ever be required as a Qualification to any Office or public Trust under the United States.

ARTICLE VII.

Ratification procedure

The Ratification of the Conventions of nine States, shall be sufficient for the Establishment of this Constitution between the States so ratifying the Same.

Done in Convention by the Unanimous Consent of the States present the Seventeenth Day of September in the Year of our Lord one thousand seven hundred and Eighty seven and of the Independence of the United States of America the Twelfth In witness whereof We have hereunto subscribed our Names,

G⁰:ASHINGTON—*Presid*ᵗ.
and deputy from Virginia

New Hampshire	JOHN LANGDON NICHOLAS GILMAN	*Connecticut*	Wᴹ. SAM.ᴸ JOHNSON ROGER SHERMAN
Massachusetts	NATHANIEL GORHAM RUFUS KING	*New York*	ALEXANDER HAMILTON

New Jersey	WIL: LIVINGSTON DAVID BREARLEY W.ᴹ PATERSON JONA: DAYTON	*Maryland*	JAMES MᶜHENRY DAN OF Sᵀ THO.ˢ JENIFER DANᴸ CARROLL
		Virginia	JOHN BLAIR— JAMES MADISON JR.
Pennsylvania	B FRANKLIN THOMAS MIFFLIN ROBᵀ MORRIS GEO. CLYMER THO.ˢ FITZSIMONS JARED INGERSOLL JAMES WILSON GOUV MORRIS	*North Carolina*	W.ᴹ BLOUNT RICHᴰ DOBBS SPAIGHT HU WILLIAMSON
		South Carolina	J. RUTLEDGE CHARLES COTESWORTH PINCKNEY CHARLES PINCKNEY PIERCE BUTLER
Delaware	GEO: READ GUNNING BEDFORD jun JOHN DICKINSON RICHARD BASSETT JACO: BROOM	*Georgia*	WILLIAM FEW ABR BALDWIN

[The first ten amendments, known as the "Bill of Rights," were ratified in 1791.]

AMENDMENT I.

Freedom of religion, speech, press, assembly

Congress shall make no law respecting an establishment of religion, or prohibiting the free exercise thereof, or abridging the freedom of speech, or of the press; or the right of the people peaceably to assemble, and to petition the Government for a redress of grievances.

AMENDMENT II.

Right to bear arms

A well regulated Militia, being necessary to the security of a free State, the right of the people to keep and bear Arms, shall not be infringed.

AMENDMENT III.

Quartering troops in private homes

No Soldier shall, in time of peace be quartered in any house, without the consent of the Owner, nor in time of war, but in a manner prescribed by law.

AMENDMENT IV.

Prohibition against unreasonable searches and seizures

The right of the people to be secure in their persons, houses, papers, and effects, against unreasonable searches and seizures, shall not be violated, and no Warrants shall issue, but upon probable cause, supported by Oath or affirmation, and particularly describing the place to be searched, and the persons or things to be seized.

AMENDMENT V.

Rights when accused; "due-process" clause

No person shall be held to answer for a capital, or otherwise infamous crime, unless on a presentment or indictment of a Grand Jury, except in cases arising in the land or naval forces, or in the Militia, when in actual service in time of War or public danger; nor shall any person be subject for the same offence to be twice put in jeopardy of life or limb; nor shall be compelled in any criminal case to be a witness against himself, nor be deprived of life, liberty, or property, without due process of law; nor shall private property be taken for public use, without just compensation.

AMENDMENT VI.

Rights when on trial

In all criminal prosecutions, the accused shall enjoy the right to a speedy and public trial, by an impartial jury of the State and district wherein the crime shall have been committed, which district shall have been previously ascertained by law, and to be informed of the nature and cause of the accusation; to be confronted with the witnesses against him; to have compulsory process for obtaining witnesses in his favor, and to have Assistance of Counsel for his defence.

AMENDMENT VII.

Common-law suits

In Suits at common law, where the value in controversy shall exceed twenty dollars, the right of trial by jury shall be preserved, and no fact tried by a jury, shall be otherwise reexamined in any Court of the United States, than according to the rules of the common law.

AMENDMENT VIII.

Bail; no "cruel and unusual" punishments

Excessive bail shall not be required, nor excessive fines imposed, nor cruel and unusual punishments inflicted.

AMENDMENT IX.

Unenumerated rights protected

The enumeration in the Constitution, of certain rights, shall not be construed to deny or disparage others retained by the people.

AMENDMENT X.

Powers reserved for states

The powers not delegated to the United States by the Constitution, nor prohibited by it to the States, are reserved to the States respectively, or to the people.

AMENDMENT XI.
[*Ratified in 1795.*]

Limits on suits against states

The Judicial power of the United States shall not be construed to extend to any suit in law or equity, commenced or prosecuted against one of the United States by Citizens of another State, or by Citizens or Subjects of any Foreign State.

AMENDMENT XII.
[*Ratified in 1804.*]

Revision of electoral-college procedure

The Electors shall meet in their respective states and vote by ballot for President and Vice President, one of whom, at least, shall not be an inhabitant of the same state with themselves; they shall name in their ballots the person voted for as President, and in distinct ballots the person voted for as Vice President, and they shall make distinct lists of all persons voted for as President, and of all persons voted for as Vice President, and of the number of votes for each, which lists they shall sign and certify, and transmit sealed to the seat of the government of the United States, directed to the President of the Senate;—The President of the Senate shall, in the presence of the Senate and House of Representatives, open all the certificates and the votes shall then be counted;—The person having the greatest number of votes for President, shall be the President, if such number be a majority of the whole number of Electors appointed; and if no person have such majority, then from the persons having the highest numbers not exceeding three on the list of those voted for as President, the House of Representatives shall choose immediately, by ballot, the President. But in choosing the President, the votes shall be taken by states, the representation from each state having one vote; a quorum for this purpose shall consist of a member or members from two-thirds of the states, and a majority of all the states shall be necessary to a choice. *And if the House of Representatives shall not choose a President whenever the right of choice shall devolve upon them, before the fourth day of March next following, then the Vice President shall act as President, as in the case of the death or other constitutional disability of the President.*—[10] The person having the greatest number of votes as Vice President, shall be the Vice President, if such number be a majority of the whole number of Electors appointed, and if no person have a majority, then from the two highest numbers on the list, the Senate shall choose the Vice President; a quorum for the purpose shall consist of two-thirds of the whole number of Senators, and a majority of the whole number shall be necessary to a choice. But no person constitutionally ineligible to the office of President shall be eligible to that of Vice President of the United States.

AMENDMENT XIII.
[*Ratified in 1865.*]

Slavery prohibited

Section 1. Neither slavery nor involuntary servitude, except as a punishment for crime whereof the party shall have been duly convicted, shall exist within the United States, or any place subject to their jurisdiction.

Section 2. Congress shall have power to enforce this article by appropriate legislation.

AMENDMENT XIV.
[*Ratified in 1868.*]

Ex-slaves made citizens

Section 1. All persons born or naturalized in the United States and subject to the jurisdiction thereof, are citizens of the United States and of the State wherein they reside. No State shall make or enforce any law which shall abridge the privileges or immunities of citizens of the United States; nor shall any State deprive any person of life, liberty, or property, without due process of law; nor deny to any person within its jurisdiction the equal protection of the laws.

**"Due-process" clause applied to states
"Equal-protection" clause**

Reduction in congressional representation for states denying adult males the right to vote

Section 2. Representatives shall be apportioned among the several States according to their respective numbers, counting the whole number of persons in each State, excluding Indians not taxed. But when the right to vote at any election for the choice of electors for President and Vice President of the United States, Representatives in Congress, the Executive and Judicial officers of a State, or the members of the Legislature thereof, is denied to any of the male inhabitants of such State, being *twenty-one*[11] years of age, and citizens of the United States, or in any way abridged, except for participation in rebellion, or other crime, the basis of representation therein shall be reduced in the proportion which the number of such male citizens shall bear to the whole number of male citizens twenty-one years of age in such State.

Southern rebels denied federal office

Section 3. No person shall be a Senator or Representative in Congress, or elector of President and Vice President, or hold any office, civil or military, under the United States, or under any State, who, having previously taken an oath, as a member of Congress, or as an officer of the United States, or as a member of any State legislature, or as an executive or judicial officer of any State, to support the Constitution of the United States, shall have engaged in insurrection or rebellion against the same, or given aid or comfort to the enemies thereof. But Congress may by a vote of two-thirds of each House, remove such disability.

---

10. Changed by the Twentieth Amendment, section 3.
11. Changed by the Twenty-sixth Amendment.

Rebel debts repudiated

Section 4.   The validity of the public debt of the United States, authorized by law, including debts incurred for payment of pensions and bounties for services in suppressing insurrection or rebellion, shall not be questioned. But neither the United States nor any State shall assume or pay any debt or obligation incurred in aid of insurrection or rebellion against the United States, or any claim for the loss or emancipation of any slave; but all such debts, obligations and claims shall be held illegal and void.

Section 5.   The Congress shall have power to enforce, by appropriate legislation, the provisions of this article.

AMENDMENT XV.
[*Ratified in 1870.*]

Blacks given right to vote

Section 1.   The right of citizens of the United States to vote shall not be denied or abridged by the United States or by any State on account of race, color, or previous condition of servitude.

Section 2.   The Congress shall have power to enforce this article by appropriate legislation.

AMENDMENT XVI.
[*Ratified in 1913.*]

Authorizes federal income tax

The Congress shall have power to lay and collect taxes on incomes, from whatever source derived, without apportionment among the several States, and without regard to any census or enumeration.

AMENDMENT XVII.
[*Ratified in 1913.*]

Requires popular election of senators

The Senate of the United States shall be composed of two Senators from each State, elected by the people thereof, for six years; and each Senator shall have one vote. The electors in each State shall have the qualifications requisite for electors of the most numerous branch of the State legislatures.

When vacancies happen in the representation of any State in the Senate, the executive authority of such State shall issue writs of election to fill such vacancies: Provided, That the legislature of any State may empower the executive thereof to make temporary appointments until the people fill the vacancies by election as the legislature may direct.

This amendment shall not be so construed as to affect the election or term of any Senator chosen before it becomes valid as part of the Constitution.

AMENDMENT XVIII.
[*Ratified in 1919.*]

Prohibits manufacture and sale of liquor

Section 1.   *After one year from the ratification of this article the manufacture, sale, or transportation of intoxicating liquors within, the importation thereof into, or the exportation thereof from the United States and all territory subject to the jurisdiction thereof for beverage purposes is hereby prohibited.*

Section 2.   *The Congress and the several States shall have concurrent power to enforce this article by appropriate legislation.*

Section 3. *This article shall be inoperative unless it shall have been ratified as an amendment to the Constitution by the legislatures of the several States, as provided in the Constitution, within seven years from the date of the submission hereof to the States by the Congress.*[12]

AMENDMENT XIX.
[*Ratified in 1920.*]

Right to vote for women

The right of citizens of the United States to vote shall not be denied or abridged by the United States or by any State on account of sex.

Congress shall have power to enforce this article by appropriate legislation.

AMENDMENT XX.
[*Ratified in 1933.*]

Federal terms of office to begin in January

Section 1. The terms of the President and Vice President shall end at noon on the 20th day of January, and the terms of Senators and Representatives at noon on the 3d day of January, of the years in which such terms would have ended if this article had not been ratified; and the terms of their successors shall then begin.

Section 2. The Congress shall assemble at least once in every year, and such meeting shall begin at noon on the 3d day of January, unless they shall by law appoint a different day.

Emergency presidential succession

Section 3. If, at the time fixed for the beginning of the term of the President, the President elect shall have died, the Vice President elect shall become President. If a President shall not have been chosen before the time fixed for the beginning of his term, or if the President elect shall have failed to qualify, then the Vice President elect shall act as President until a President shall have qualified; and the Congress may by law provide for the case wherein neither a President elect nor a Vice President elect shall have qualified, declaring who shall then act as President, or the manner in which one who is to act shall be selected, and such person shall act accordingly until a President or Vice President shall have qualified.

Section 4. The Congress may by law provide for the case of the death of any of the persons from whom the House of Representatives may choose a President whenever the right of choice shall have developed upon them, and for the case of the death of any of the persons from whom the Senate may choose a Vice President whenever the right of choice shall have devolved upon them.

Section 5. Sections 1 and 2 shall take effect on the 15th day of October following the ratification of this article.

Section 6. This article shall be inoperative unless it shall have been ratified as an amendment to the Constitution by the legislatures of three-fourths of the several States within seven years from the date of its submission.

AMENDMENT XXI.
[*Ratified in 1933.*]

Repeals Prohibition

Section 1. The eighteenth article of amendment to the Constitution of the United States is hereby repealed.

12. Repealed by the Twenty-first Amendment.

Section 2.   The transportation or importation into any State, Territory, or possession of the United States for delivery or use therein of intoxicating liquors, in violation of the laws thereof, is hereby prohibited.

Section 3.   This article shall be inoperative unless it shall have been ratified as an amendment to the Constitution by conventions in the several States, as provided in the Constitution, within seven years from the date of the submission hereof to the States by the Congress.

AMENDMENT XXII.
[Ratified in 1951.]

Two-term limit for president

Section 1.   No person shall be elected to the office of the President more than twice, and no person who has held the office of President, or acted as President, for more than two years of a term to which some other person was elected President shall be elected to the office of the President more than once. But this Article shall not apply to any person holding the office of President when this Article was proposed by the Congress, and shall not prevent any person who may be holding the office of President, or acting as President, during the term within which this Article becomes operative from holding the office of President or acting as President during the remainder of such term.

Section 2.   This Article shall be inoperative unless it shall have been ratified as an amendment to the Constitution by the legislatures of three-fourths of the several States within seven years from the date of its submission to the States by the Congress.

AMENDMENT XXIII.
[Ratified in 1961.]

Right to vote for president in District of Columbia

Section 1.   The District constituting the seat of Government of the United States shall appoint in such manner as the Congress may direct:

A number of electors of President and Vice President equal to the whole number of Senators and Representatives in Congress to which the District would be entitled if it were a State, but in no event more than the least populous State; they shall be in addition to those appointed by the States, but they shall be considered, for the purposes of the election of President and Vice President, to be electors appointed by a State; and they shall meet in the District and perform such duties as provided by the twelfth article of amendment.

Section 2.   The Congress shall have power to enforce this article by appropriate legislation.

AMENDMENT XXIV.
[Ratified in 1964.]

Prohibits poll taxes in federal elections

Section 1.   The right of citizens of the United States to vote in any primary or other election for President or Vice President, for electors for President or Vice President, or for Senator or Representative in Congress, shall not be denied or abridged by the United States or any State by reason of failure to pay any poll tax or other tax.

Section 2.   The Congress shall have power to enforce this article by appropriate legislation.

AMENDMENT XXV.
[*Ratified in 1967.*]

Presidential disability and succession

Section 1.   In case of the removal of the President from office or of his death or resignation, the Vice President shall become President.

Section 2.   Whenever there is a vacancy in the office of the Vice President, the President shall nominate a Vice President who shall take office upon confirmation by a majority vote of both Houses of Congress.

Section 3.   Whenever the President transmits to the President pro tempore of the Senate and the Speaker of the House of Representatives his written declaration that he is unable to discharge the powers and duties of his office, and until he transmits to them a written declaration to the contrary, such powers and duties shall be discharged by the Vice President as Acting President.

Section 4.   Whenever the Vice President and a majority of either the principal officers of the executive departments or of such other body as Congress may by law provide, transmit to the President pro tempore of the Senate and the Speaker of the House of Representatives their written declaration that the President is unable to discharge the powers and duties of his office, the Vice President shall immediately assume the powers and duties of the office as Acting President.

Thereafter, when the President transmits to the President pro tempore of the Senate and the Speaker of the House of Representatives his written declaration that no inability exists, he shall resume the powers and duties of his office unless the Vice President and a majority of either the principal officers of the executive department[s] or of such other body as Congress may by law provide, transmit within four days to the President pro tempore of the Senate and the Speaker of the House of Representatives their written declaration that the President is unable to discharge the powers and duties of his office. Thereupon Congress shall decide the issue, assembling within forty-eight hours for that purpose if not in session. If the Congress, within twenty-one days after receipt of the latter written declaration, or, if Congress is not in session, within twenty-one days after Congress is required to assemble, determines by two-thirds vote of both Houses that the President is unable to discharge the powers and duties of his office, the Vice President shall continue to discharge the same as Acting President; otherwise, the President shall resume the powers and duties of his office.

AMENDMENT XXVI.
[*Ratified in 1971.*]

Voting age lowered to eighteen

Section 1.   The right of citizens of the United States, who are eighteen years of age or older, to vote shall not be denied or abridged by the United States or by any State on account of age.

Section 2.   The Congress shall have power to enforce this article by appropriate legislation.

AMENDMENT XXVII.
[*Ratified in 1992.*]

Congressional pay raises

No law varying the compensation for the services of the Senators and Representatives shall take effect, until an election of Representatives shall have intervened.

The Federalist No. 10

November 22, 1787

James Madison

TO THE PEOPLE OF THE STATE OF NEW YORK.

Among the numerous advantages promised by a well constructed Union, none deserves to be more accurately developed than its tendency to break and control the violence of faction. The friend of popular governments, never finds himself so much alarmed for their character and fate, as when he contemplates their propensity to this dangerous vice. He will not fail therefore to set a due value on any plan which, without violating the principles to which he is attached, provides a proper cure for it. The instability, injustice and confusion introduced into the public councils, have in truth been the mortal diseases under which popular governments have every where perished; as they continue to be the favorite and fruitful topics from which the adversaries to liberty derive their most specious declamations. The valuable improvements made by the American Constitutions on the popular models, both ancient and modern, cannot certainly be too much admired; but it would be an unwarrantable partiality, to contend that they have as effectually obviated the danger on this side as was wished and expected. Complaints are every where heard from our most considerate and virtuous citizens, equally the friends of public and private faith, and of public and personal liberty; that our governments are too unstable; that the public good is disregarded in the conflicts of rival parties; and that measures are too often decided, not according to the rules of justice, and the rights of the minor party; but by the superior force of an interested and over-bearing majority. However anxiously we may wish that these complaints had no foundation, the evidence of known facts will not permit us to deny that they are in some degree true. It will be found indeed, on a candid review of our situation, that some of the distresses under which we labor, have been erroneously charged on the operation of our governments; but it will be found, at the same time, that other causes will not alone account for many of our heaviest misfortunes; and particularly, for that prevailing and increasing distrust of public engagements, and alarm for private rights, which are echoed from one end of the continent to the other. These must be chiefly, if not wholly, effects of the unsteadiness and injustice, with which a factious spirit has tainted our public administrations.

By a faction I understand a number of citizens, whether amounting to a majority or minority of the whole, who are united and actuated by some common impulse of passion, or of interest, adverse to the rights of other citizens, or to the permanent and aggregate interests of the community.

There are two methods of curing the mischiefs of faction: the one, by removing its causes; the other, by controlling its effects.

There are again two methods of removing the causes of faction: the one by destroying the liberty which is essential to its existence; the other, by giving to every citizen the same opinions, the same passions, and the same interests.

It could never be more truly said than of the first remedy, that it is worse than the disease. Liberty is to faction, what air is to fire, an aliment without which it instantly expires. But it could not be a less folly to abolish liberty, which is essential to political life, because it nourishes faction, than it would be to wish the annihilation of air, which is essential to animal life, because it imparts to fire its destructive agency.

The second expedient is as impracticable, as the first would be unwise. As long as the reason of man continues fallible, and he is at liberty to exercise it, different opinions will be formed. As long as the connection subsists between his reason and his self-love, his opinions and his passions will have a reciprocal influence on each other; and the former will be objects to which the latter will attach themselves. The diversity in the faculties of men from which the rights of property originate, is not less an insuperable obstacle to a uniformity of interests. The protection of these faculties is the first object of Government. From the protection of different and unequal faculties of acquiring property, the possession of different degrees and kinds of property immediately results: and from the influence of these on the sentiments and views of the respective proprietors, ensues a division of the society into different interests and parties.

The latent causes of faction are thus sown in the nature of man; and we see them every where brought into different degrees of activity, according to the different circumstances of civil society. A zeal for different opinions concerning religion, concerning Government and many other points, as well of speculation as of practice; an attachment to different leaders ambitiously contending for pre-eminence and power; or to persons of other descriptions whose fortunes have been interesting to the human passions, have in turn divided mankind into parties, inflamed them with mutual animosity, and rendered them much more disposed to vex and oppress each other, than to cooperate for their common good. So strong is this propensity of mankind to fall into mutual animosities, that where no substantial occasion presents itself, the most frivolous and fanciful distinctions have been sufficient to kindle their unfriendly passions, and excite their most violent conflicts. But the most common and durable source of factions, has been the various and unequal distribution of property. Those who hold, and those who are without property, have ever formed distinct interests in society. Those who are creditors, and those who are debtors, fall under a like discrimination. A landed interest, a manufacturing interest, a mercantile interest, a monied interest, with many lesser interests, grow up of necessity in civilized nations, and divide them into different classes, actuated by different sentiments and views. The regulation of these various and interfering interests forms the principal task of modern Legislation, and involves the spirit of party and faction in the necessary and ordinary operations of Government.

No man is allowed to be a judge in his own cause; because his interest would certainly bias his judgment, and, not improbably, corrupt his integrity. With equal, nay with greater reason, a body of men, are unfit to be both judges and parties, at the same time; yet, what are many of the most important acts of legislation, but so many judicial determinations, not indeed concerning the rights of single persons, but concerning the rights of large bodies of citizens, and what are the different classes of legislators, but advocates and parties to the causes which they determine? Is a law proposed concerning private debts? It is a question to which the creditors are parties on one side, and the debtors on the other. Justice ought to hold the balance between them. Yet the parties are and must be themselves the judges; and the most numerous party, or, in other words, the most powerful faction must be expected to prevail. Shall domestic manufactures be encouraged, and in what degree, by restrictions on foreign manufactures? are questions which would be differently decided by the landed and the manufacturing classes; and probably by neither, with a sole regard to justice and the public good. The apportionment of taxes on the various descriptions of property, is an act which seems to require the most exact impartiality; yet, there is perhaps no legislative act in which greater opportunity and temptation are given to a predominant party, to trample on the rules of justice. Every shilling with which they over-burden the inferior number, is a shilling saved to their own pockets.

It is in vain to say, that enlightened statesmen will be able to adjust these clashing interests, and render them all subservient to the public good. Enlightened statesmen will not always be at the helm: Nor, in many cases, can such an adjustment be made at all, without taking into view indirect and remote considerations, which will rarely prevail over the immediate interest which one party may find in disregarding the rights of another, or the good of the whole.

The inference to which we are brought, is, that the *causes* of faction cannot be removed; and that relief is only to be sought in the means of controlling its *effects*.

If a faction consists of less than a majority, relief is supplied by the republican principle, which enables the majority to defeat its sinister views by regular vote: It may clog the administration, it may convulse the society; but it will be unable to execute and mask its violence under the forms of the Constitution. When a majority is included in a faction, the form of popular government on the other hand enables it to sacrifice to its ruling passion or interest, both the public good and the rights of other citizens. To secure the public good, and private rights, against the danger of such a faction, and at the same time to preserve the spirit and the form of popular government, is then the great object to which our enquiries are directed: Let me add that it is the great desideratum, by which alone this form of government can be rescued from the opprobrium under which it has so long labored, and be recommended to the esteem and adoption of mankind.

By what means is this object attainable? Evidently by one of two only. Either the existence of the same passion or interest in a majority at the same time, must be prevented; or the majority, having such co-existent passion or interest, must be rendered, by their number and local situation, unable to concert and carry into effect schemes of oppression. If the impulse and the opportunity be suffered to coincide, we well know that neither moral nor religious motives can be relied on as an adequate control. They are not found to be such on the injustice and violence of individuals, and lose their efficacy in proportion to the number combined together; that is, in proportion as their efficacy becomes needful.

From this view of the subject, it may be concluded, that a pure Democracy, by which I mean, a Society, consisting of a small number of citizens, who assemble and administer the Government in person, can admit of no cure for the mischiefs of faction. A common passion or interest will, in almost every case, be felt by a majority of the whole; a communication and concert results from the form of Government itself; and there is nothing to check the inducements to sacrifice the weaker party, or an obnoxious individual. Hence it is, that such Democracies have ever been spectacles of turbulence and contention; have ever been found incompatible with personal security, or the rights of property; and have in general been as short in their lives, as they have been violent in their deaths. Theoretic politicians, who have patronized this species of Government, have erroneously supposed, that by reducing mankind to a perfect equality in their political rights, they would, at the same time, be perfectly equalized and assimilated in their possessions, their opinions, and their passions.

A republic, by which I mean a government in which the scheme of representation takes place, opens a different prospect, and promises the cure for which we are seeking.

Let us examine the points in which it varies from pure democracy, and we shall comprehend both the nature of the cure and the efficacy which it must derive from the union.

The two great points of difference, between a democracy and a republic, are, first, the delegation of the government, in the latter, to a small number of citizens, elected by the rest; secondly, the greater number of citizens, and greater sphere of country, over which the latter may be extended.

The effect of the first difference is, on the one hand, to refine and enlarge the public views, by passing them through the medium of a chosen body of citizens, whose wisdom may best discern the true interest of their country, and whose patriotism and love of justice, will be least likely to sacrifice it to temporary or partial considerations. Under such a regulation, it may well happen, that the public voice, pronounced by the representatives of the people, will be more consonant to the public good, than if pronounced by the people themselves, convened for the purpose. On the other hand the effect may be inverted. Men of factious tempers, of local prejudices, or of sinister designs, may by intrigue, by corruption, or by other means, first obtain the suffrages, and then betray the interest of the people. The question resulting is, whether small or extensive republics are most favorable to the election of proper guardians of the public weal, and it is clearly decided in favor of the latter by two obvious considerations.

In the first place, it is to be remarked that, however small the republic may be, the representatives must be raised to a certain number, in order to guard against the cabals of a few; and that however large it may be, they must be limited to a certain number, in order to guard against the confusion of a multitude. Hence, the number of representatives in the two cases not being in proportion to that of the constituents, and being proportionally greatest in the small republic, it follows, that if the proportion of fit characters be not less in the large than in the small republic, the former will present a greater option, and consequently a greater probability of a fit choice.

In the next place, as each Representative will be chosen by a greater number of citizens in the large than in the small Republic, it will be more difficult for unworthy candidates to practise with success the vicious arts, by which elections are too often carried; and the suffrages of the people being more free, will be more likely to center on men who possess the most attractive merit, and the most diffusive and established characters.

It must be confessed, that in this, as in most other cases, there is a mean, on both sides of which inconveniences will be found to lie. By enlarging too much the number of electors, you render the representatives too little acquainted with all their local circumstances and lesser interests; as by reducing it too much, you render him unduly attached to these, and too little fit to comprehend and pursue great and national objects. The Federal Constitution forms a happy combination in this respect; the great and aggregate interests being referred to the national, the local and particular, to the state legislatures.

The other point of difference is, the greater number of citizens and extent of territory which may be brought within the compass of Republican, than of Democratic Government; and it is this circumstance principally which renders factious combinations less to be dreaded in the former, than in the latter. The smaller the society, the fewer probably will be the distinct parties and interests composing it; the fewer the distinct parties and interests, the more frequently will a majority be found of the same party; and the smaller the number of individuals composing a majority, and the smaller the compass within which they are placed, the more easily will they concert and execute their plans of oppression. Extend the sphere, and you take in a greater variety of parties and interests; you make it less probable that a majority of the whole will have a common motive to invade the rights of other citizens; or if such a common motive exists, it will be more difficult for all who feel it to discover their own strength, and to act in unison with each other. Besides other impediments, it may be remarked, that where there is a consciousness of unjust or dishonorable purposes, communication is always checked by distrust, in proportion to the number whose concurrence is necessary.

Hence it clearly appears, that the same advantage, which a Republic has over a Democracy, in controlling the effects of factions, is enjoyed by a large over a small Republic—is enjoyed by the Union over the States composing it. Does this advantage consist in the substitution of Representatives, whose enlightened views and virtuous sentiments render them superior to local prejudices, and to schemes of injustice? It will not be denied, that the Representation of the Union will be most likely to possess these requisite endowments. Does it consist in the greater security afforded by a greater variety of parties, against the event of any one party being able to outnumber and oppress the rest? In an equal degree does the increased variety of parties, comprised within the Union, increase this security? Does it, in fine, consist in the greater obstacles opposed to the concert and accomplishment of the secret wishes of an unjust and interested majority? Here, again, the extent of the Union gives it the most palpable advantage.

The influence of factious leaders may kindle a flame within their particular States, but will be unable to spread a general conflagration through the other States: a religious sect, may degenerate into a political faction in a part of the Confederacy but the variety of sects dispersed over the entire face of it, must secure the national Councils against any danger from that source: a rage for paper money, for an abolition of debts, for an equal division of property, or for any other improper or wicked project, will be less apt to pervade the whole body of the Union, than a particular member of it; in the same proportion as such a malady is more likely to taint a particular county or district, than an entire State.

In the extent and proper structure of the Union, therefore, we behold a Republican remedy for the diseases most incident to Republican Government. And according to the degree of pleasure and pride, we feel in being Republicans, ought to be our zeal in cherishing the spirit, and supporting the character of Federalists.

PUBLIUS

The Federalist No. 51

February 6, 1788

James Madison

TO THE PEOPLE OF THE STATE OF NEW YORK.

To what expedient then shall we finally resort for maintaining in practice the necessary partition of power among the several departments, as laid down in the constitution? The only answer that can be given is, that as all these exterior provisions are found to be inadequate, the defect must be supplied, by so contriving the interior structure of the government, as that its several constituent parts may, by their mutual relations, be the means of keeping each other in their proper places. Without presuming to undertake a full development of this important idea, I will hazard a few general observations, which may perhaps place it in a clearer light, and enable us to form a more correct judgment of the principles and structure of the government planned by the convention.

In order to lay a due foundation for that separate and distinct exercise of the different powers of government, which to a certain extent, is admitted on all hands to be essential to the preservation of liberty, it is evident that each department should have a will of its own; and consequently should be so constituted, that the members of each should have as little agency as possible in the appointment of the members of the others. Were this principle rigorously adhered to, it would require that all the appointments for the supreme executive, legislative, and judiciary magistracies, should be drawn from the same fountain of authority, the people, through channels, having no communication whatever with one another. Perhaps such a plan of constructing the several departments would be less difficult in practice than it may in contemplation appear. Some difficulties however, and some additional expense, would attend the execution of it. Some deviations therefore from the principle must be admitted. In the constitution of the judiciary department in particular, it might be inexpedient to insist rigorously on the principle; first, because peculiar qualifications being essential in the members, the primary consideration ought to be to select that mode of choice, which best secures these qualifications; secondly, because the permanent tenure by which the appointments are held in that department, must soon destroy all sense of dependence on the authority conferring them.

It is equally evident that the members of each department should be as little dependent as possible on those of the others, for the emoluments annexed to their offices. Were the executive magistrate, or the judges, not independent of the legislature in this particular, their independence in every other would be merely nominal.

But the great security against a gradual concentration of the several powers in the same department, consists in giving to those who administer each department, the necessary constitutional means, and personal motives, to resist encroachments of the others. The provision for defense must in this, as in all other cases, be made commensurate to the danger of attack. Ambition must be made to counteract ambition. The interest of the man must be connected with the constitutional right of the place. It may be a reflection on human nature, that such devices should be necessary to control the abuses of government. But what is government itself but the greatest of all reflections on human nature? If men were angels, no government would be necessary. If angels were to govern men, neither external nor internal controls on government would be necessary. In framing a government which is to be administered by men over men, the great difficulty lies in this: You must first enable the government to control the governed; and in the next place, oblige it to control itself. A dependence on the people is no doubt the primary control on the government; but experience has taught mankind the necessity of auxiliary precautions.

This policy of supplying by opposite and rival interests, the defect of better motives, might be traced through the whole system of human affairs, private as well as public. We see it particularly displayed in all the subordinate distributions of power; where the constant aim is to divide and arrange the several offices in such a manner as that each may be a check on the other; that the private interest of every individual, may be a sentinel over the public rights. These inventions of prudence cannot be less requisite in the distribution of the supreme powers of the state.

But it is not possible to give each department an equal power of self defense. In republican government the legislative authority, necessarily, predominates. The remedy for this inconveniency is, to divide the legislature into different branches; and to render them by different modes of election, and different principles of action, as little connected with each other, as the nature of their common functions, and their common dependence on the society, will admit. It may even be necessary to guard against dangerous encroachments by still further precautions. As the weight of the legislative authority requires that it should be thus divided, the weakness of the executive may require, on the other hand, that it should be fortified. An absolute negative, on the legislature, appears at first view to be the natural defense with which the executive magistrate should be armed. But perhaps it would be neither altogether safe, nor alone sufficient. On ordinary occasions, it might not be exerted with the requisite firmness; and on extraordinary occasions, it might be prefidiously abused. May not this defect of an absolute negative be supplied, by some qualified connection between this weaker department, and the weaker branch of the stronger department, by which the latter may be led to support the constitutional rights of the former, without being too much detached from the rights of its own department?

If the principles on which these observations are founded be just, as I persuade myself they are, and they be applied as a criterion, to the several state constitutions, and to the federal constitution, it will be found, that if the latter does not perfectly correspond with them, the former are infinitely less able to bear such a test.

There are moreover two considerations particularly applicable to the federal system of America, which place that system in a very interesting point of view.

First. In a single republic, all the power surrendered by the people, is submitted to the administration of a single government; and usurpations are guarded against by a division of the government into distinct and separate departments. In the compound republic of America, the power surrendered by the people, is first divided between two distinct governments, and then the portion allotted to each, subdivided among distinct and separate departments. Hence a double security arises to the rights of the people. The different governments will control each other; at the same time that each will be controlled by itself.

Second. It is of great importance in a republic, not only to guard the society against the oppression of its rulers; but to guard one part of the society against the injustice of the other part. Different interests necessarily exist in different classes of citizens. If a majority be united by a common interest, the rights of the minority will be insecure.

There are but two methods of providing against this evil: The one by creating a will in the community independent of the majority, that is, of the society itself, the other by comprehending in the society so many separate descriptions of citizens, as will render an unjust combination of a majority of the whole, very improbable, if not impracticable. The first method prevails in all governments possessing an hereditary or self appointed authority. This at best is but a precarious security; because a power independent of the society may as well espouse the unjust views of the major, as the rightful interests, of the minor party, and may possibly be turned against both parties. The second method will be exemplified in the federal republic of the United States. While all authority in it will be derived from and dependent on the society, the society itself will be broken into so many parts, interests and classes of citizens, that the rights of individuals or of the minority, will be in little danger from interested combinations of the majority. In a free government, the security for civil rights must be the same as for religious rights. It consists in the one case in the multiplicity of interests, and in the other, in the multiplicity of sects. The degree of security in both cases will depend on the number of interests and sects; and this may be presumed to depend on the extent of country and number of people comprehended under the same government. This view of the subject must particularly recommend a proper federal system to all the sincere and considerate friends of republican government: Since it shows that in exact proportion as the territory of the union may be formed into more circumscribed confederacies or states, oppressive combinations of a majority will be facilitated, the best security under the republican form, for the rights of every class of citizens, will be diminished; and consequently, the stability and independence of some member of the government, the only other security, must be proportionally increased. Justice is the end of government. It is the end of civil society. It ever has been, and ever will be pursued, until it be obtained, or until liberty be lost in the pursuit. In a society under the forms of which the stronger faction can readily unite and oppress the weaker, anarchy may as truly be said to reign, as in a state of nature where the weaker individual is not secured against the violence of the stronger: And as in the latter state even the stronger individuals are prompted by the uncertainty of their condition, to submit to a government which may protect the weak as well as themselves: So in the former state, will the more powerful factions or parties be gradually induced by a like motive, to wish for a government which will protect all parties, the weaker as well as the more powerful. It can be little doubted, that if the state of Rhode Island was separated from the confederacy, and left to itself, the insecurity of rights under the popular form of government within such narrow limits, would be displayed by such reiterated oppressions of factious majorities, that some power altogether independent of the people would soon be called for by the voice of the very factions whose misrule had proved the necessity of it. In the extended republic of the United States, and among the great variety of interests, parties and sects which it embraces, a coalition of a majority of the whole society could seldom take place on any other principles than those of justice and the general good; and there being thus less danger to a minor from the will of the major party, there must be less pretext also, to provide for the security of the former, by introducing into the government a will not dependent on the latter; or in other words, a will independent of the society itself. It is no less certain than it is important, notwithstanding the contrary opinions which have been entertained, that the larger the society, provided it lie within a practicable sphere, the more duly capable will be of self government. And happily for the *republican cause,* the practicable sphere may be carried to a very great extent, by a judicious modification and mixture of the *federal principle.*

PUBLIUS

Presidents and Congresses, 1789–1994

Year	President and vice president	Party of president	Congress	House Majority party	House Minority party	Senate Majority party	Senate Minority party
1789–1797	**George Washington** John Adams	None	1st	38 Admin	26 Opp	17 Admin	9 Opp
			2d	37 Fed	33 Dem-Rep	16 Fed	13 Dem-Rep
			3d	57 Dem-Rep	48 Fed	17 Fed	13 Dem-Rep
			4th	54 Fed	52 Dem-Rep	19 Fed	13 Dem-Rep
1797–1801	**John Adams** Thomas Jefferson	Federalist	5th	58 Fed	48 Dem-Rep	20 Fed	12 Dem-Rep
			6th	64 Fed	42 Dem-Rep	19 Fed	13 Dem-Rep
1801–1809	**Thomas Jefferson** Aaron Burr (to 1805) George Clinton (to 1809)	Dem-Rep	7th	69 Dem-Rep	36 Fed	18 Dem-Rep	13 Fed
			8th	102 Dem-Rep	39 Fed	25 Dem-Rep	9 Fed
			9th	116 Dem-Rep	25 Fed	27 Dem-Rep	7 Fed
			10th	118 Dem-Rep	24 Fed	28 Dem-Rep	6 Fed
1809–1817	**James Madison** George Clinton (to 1813) Elbridge Gerry (to 1817)	Dem-Rep	11th	94 Dem-Rep	48 Fed	28 Dem-Rep	6 Fed
			12th	108 Dem-Rep	36 Fed	30 Dem-Rep	6 Fed
			13th	112 Dem-Rep	68 Fed	27 Dem-Rep	9 Fed
			14th	117 Dem-Rep	65 Fed	25 Dem-Rep	11 Fed
1817–1825	**James Monroe** Daniel D. Tompkins	Dem-Rep	15th	141 Dem-Rep	42 Fed	34 Dem-Rep	10 Fed
			16th	156 Dem-Rep	27 Fed	35 Dem-Rep	7 Fed
			17th	158 Dem-Rep	25 Fed	44 Dem-Rep	4 Fed
			18th	187 Dem-Rep	26 Fed	44 Dem-Rep	4 Fed
1825–1829	**John Quincy Adams** John C. Calhoun	Nat-Rep	19th	105 Admin	97 Jack	26 Admin	20 Jack
			20th	119 Jack	94 Admin	28 Jack	20 Admin
1829–1837	**Andrew Jackson** John C. Calhoun (to 1833) Martin Van Buren (to 1837)	Democrat	21st	139 Dem	74 Nat Rep	26 Dem	22 Nat Rep
			22d	141 Dem	58 Nat Rep	25 Dem	21 Nat Rep
			23d	147 Dem	53 AntiMas	20 Dem	20 Nat Rep
			24th	145 Dem	98 Whig	27 Dem	25 Whig
1837–1841	**Martin Van Buren** Richard M. Johnson	Democrat	25th	108 Dem	107 Whig	30 Dem	18 Whig
			26th	124 Dem	118 Whig	28 Dem	22 Whig
1841	**William H. Harrison*** John Tyler	Whig					
1841–1845	**John Tyler** (VP vacant)	Whig	27th	133 Whig	102 Dem	28 Whig	22 Dem
			28th	142 Dem	79 Whig	28 Whig	25 Dem
1845–1849	**James K. Polk** George M. Dallas	Democrat	29th	143 Dem	77 Whig	31 Dem	25 Whig
			30th	115 Whig	108 Dem	36 Dem	21 Whig
1849–1850	**Zachary Taylor*** Millard Fillmore	Whig	31st	112 Dem	109 Whig	35 Dem	25 Whig
1850–1853	**Millard Fillmore** (VP vacant)	Whig	32d	140 Dem	88 Whig	35 Dem	24 Whig
1853–1857	**Franklin Pierce** William R. King	Democrat	33d	159 Dem	71 Whig	38 Dem	22 Whig
			34th	108 Rep	83 Dem	40 Dem	15 Rep

NOTES: Only members of two major parties in Congress are shown; omitted are independents, members of minor parties, and vacancies.
Party balance as of beginning of Congress.
Congresses in which one or both houses are controlled by party other than that of the president are shown in color
During administration of George Washington and (in part) John Quincy Adams, Congress was not organized by formal parties; the split shown is between supporters and opponents of the administration.

ABBREVIATIONS: **Admin** = Administration supporters; **AntiMas** = Anti-Masonic; **Dem** = Democratic; **Dem-Rep** = Democratic-Republican; **Fed** = Federalist; **Jack** = Jacksonian Democrats; **Nat Rep** = National Republican; **Opp** = Opponents of administration; **Rep** = Republican; **Union** = Unionist; **Whig** = Whig.

* Died in office.

| | | | | House | | Senate | |
| | President and | Party of | | Majority | Minority | Majority | Minority |
Year	vice president	president	Congress	party	party	party	party
1857–1861	**James Buchanan**	Democrat	35th	118 Dem	92 Rep	36 Dem	20 Rep
	John C. Breckinridge		36th	114 Rep	92 Dem	36 Dem	26 Rep
1861–1865	**Abraham Lincoln***	Republican	37th	105 Rep	43 Dem	31 Rep	10 Dem
	Hannibal Hamlin (to 1865)		38th	102 Rep	75 Dem	36 Rep	9 Dem
	Andrew Johnson (1865)						
1865–1869	**Andrew Johnson**	Republican	39th	149 Union	42 Dem	42 Union	10 Dem
	(VP vacant)		40th	143 Rep	49 Dem	42 Rep	11 Dem
1869–1877	**Ulysses S. Grant**	Republican	41st	149 Rep	63 Dem	56 Rep	11 Dem
	Schuyler Colfax (to 1873)		42d	134 Rep	104 Dem	52 Rep	17 Dem
	Henry Wilson (to 1877)		43d	194 Rep	92 Dem	49 Rep	19 Dem
			44th	169 Dem	109 Rep	45 Rep	29 Dem
1877–1881	**Rutherford B. Hayes**	Republican	45th	153 Dem	140 Rep	39 Rep	36 Dem
	William A. Wheeler		46th	149 Dem	130 Rep	42 Dem	33 Rep
1881	**James A. Garfield***	Republican	47th	147 Rep	135 Dem	37 Rep	37 Dem
	Chester A. Arthur						
1881–1885	**Chester A. Arthur**	Republican	48th	197 Dem	118 Rep	38 Rep	36 Dem
	(VP vacant)						
1885–1889	**Grover Cleveland**	Democrat	49th	183 Dem	140 Rep	43 Rep	34 Dem
	Thomas A. Hendricks		50th	169 Dem	152 Rep	39 Rep	37 Dem
1889–1893	**Benjamin Harrison**	Republican	51st	166 Rep	159 Dem	39 Rep	37 Dem
	Levi P. Morton		52d	235 Dem	88 Rep	47 Rep	39 Dem
1893–1897	**Grover Cleveland**	Democrat	53d	218 Dem	127 Rep	44 Dem	38 Rep
	Adlai E. Stevenson		54th	244 Rep	105 Dem	43 Rep	39 Dem
1897–1901	**William McKinley***	Republican	55th	204 Rep	113 Dem	47 Rep	34 Dem
	Garret A. Hobart (to 1901)		56th	185 Rep	163 Dem	53 Rep	26 Dem
	Theodore Roosevelt (1901)						
1901–1909	**Theodore Roosevelt**	Republican	57th	197 Rep	151 Dem	55 Rep	31 Dem
	(VP vacant, 1901–1905)		58th	208 Rep	178 Dem	57 Rep	33 Dem
	Charles W. Fairbanks		59th	250 Rep	136 Dem	57 Rep	33 Dem
	(1905–1909)		60th	222 Rep	164 Dem	61 Rep	31 Dem
1909–1913	**William Howard Taft**	Republican	61st	219 Rep	172 Dem	61 Rep	32 Dem
	James S. Sherman		62d	228 Dem	161 Rep	51 Rep	41 Dem
1913–1921	**Woodrow Wilson**	Democrat	63d	291 Dem	127 Rep	51 Dem	44 Rep
	Thomas R. Marshall		64th	230 Dem	196 Rep	56 Dem	40 Rep
			65th	216 Dem	210 Rep	53 Dem	42 Rep
			66th	240 Rep	190 Dem	49 Rep	47 Dem
1921–1923	**Warren G. Harding***	Republican	67th	301 Rep	131 Dem	59 Rep	37 Dem
	Calvin Coolidge						
1923–1929	**Calvin Coolidge**	Republican	68th	225 Rep	205 Dem	51 Rep	43 Dem
	(VP vacant, 1923–1925)		69th	247 Rep	183 Dem	56 Rep	39 Dem
	Charles G. Dawes		70th	237 Rep	195 Dem	49 Rep	46 Dem
	(1925–1929)						
1929–1933	**Herbert Hoover**	Republican	71st	267 Rep	167 Dem	56 Rep	39 Dem
	Charles Curtis		72d	220 Dem	214 Rep	48 Rep	47 Dem
1933–1945	**Franklin D. Roosevelt***	Democrat	73d	310 Dem	117 Rep	60 Dem	35 Rep
	John N. Garner		74th	319 Dem	103 Rep	69 Dem	25 Rep
	(1933–1941		75th	331 Dem	89 Rep	76 Dem	16 Rep
	Henry A. Wallace		76th	261 Dem	164 Rep	69 Dem	23 Rep
	(1941–1945)		77th	268 Dem	162 Rep	66 Dem	28 Rep
	Harry S Truman (1945)		78th	218 Dem	208 Rep	58 Dem	37 Rep
1945–1953	**Harry S Truman**	Democrat	79th	242 Dem	190 Rep	56 Dem	38 Rep
	(VP vacant, 1945–1949)		80th	245 Rep	188 Dem	51 Rep	45 Dem
	Alben W. Barkley		81st	263 Dem	171 Rep	54 Dem	42 Rep
	(1949–1953)		82d	234 Dem	199 Rep	49 Dem	47 Rep

* Died in office.

Year	President and vice president	Party of president	Congress	House		Senate	
				Majority party	Minority party	Majority party	Minority party
1953–1961	**Dwight D. Eisenhower**	Republican	83d	221 Rep	211 Dem	48 Rep	47 Dem
	Richard M. Nixon		84th	232 Dem	203 Rep	48 Dem	47 Rep
			85th	233 Dem	200 Rep	49 Dem	47 Rep
			86th	283 Dem	153 Rep	64 Dem	34 Rep
1961–1963	**John F. Kennedy***	Democrat	87th	263 Dem	174 Rep	65 Dem	35 Rep
	Lyndon B. Johnson						
1963–1969	**Lyndon B. Johnson**	Democrat	88th	258 Dem	177 Rep	67 Dem	33 Rep
	(VP vacant, 1963–1965)		89th	295 Dem	140 Rep	68 Dem	32 Rep
	Hubert H. Humphrey		90th	247 Dem	187 Rep	64 Dem	36 Rep
	(1965–1969)						
1969–1974	**Richard M. Nixon**†	Republican	91st	243 Dem	192 Rep	57 Dem	43 Rep
	Spiro T. Agnew††		92d	254 Dem	180 Rep	54 Dem	44 Rep
	Gerald R. Ford§						
1974–1977	**Gerald R. Ford**	Republican	93d	239 Dem	192 Rep	56 Dem	42 Rep
	Nelson A. Rockefeller§		94th	291 Dem	144 Rep	60 Dem	37 Rep
1977–1981	**Jimmy Carter**	Democrat	95th	292 Dem	143 Rep	61 Dem	38 Rep
	Walter Mondale		96th	276 Dem	157 Rep	58 Dem	41 Rep
1981–1989	**Ronald Reagan**	Republican	97th	243 Dem	192 Rep	53 Rep	46 Dem
	George Bush		98th	269 Dem	165 Rep	54 Rep	46 Dem
			99th	253 Dem	182 Rep	53 Rep	47 Dem
			100th	257 Dem	178 Rep	54 Dem	46 Rep
1989–1993	**George Bush**	Republican	101st	262 Dem	173 Rep	55 Dem	45 Rep
	Dan Quayle		102d	267 Dem	167 Rep	56 Dem	44 Rep
1993–	**Bill Clinton**	Democrat	103d	258 Dem	176 Rep	57 Dem	43 Rep
	Albert Gore, Jr.		104th	230 Rep	204 Dem	53 Rep	47 Dem

* Died in office. † Resigned from the presidency. †† Resigned from the vice presidency. § Appointed vice president.

References

Chapter 1   *The Study of American Government*

1. Aristotle, *Politics,* iv, 4, 1290[b]. More precisely Aristotle's definition was this: democracy is a "constitution in which the free-born and poor control the government—being at the same time a majority." He distinguished this from an oligarchy, "in which the rich and well-born control the government—being at the same time a minority." Aristotle listed several varieties of democracy, depending on whether, for example, there was a property qualification for citizenship.
2. Joseph A. Schumpeter, *Capitalism, Socialism, and Democracy,* 3d ed. (New York: Harper Torchbooks, 1950), 269. (This book was first published in 1942.)
3. Karl Marx and Friedrich Engels, "The Manifesto of the Communist Party," in *The Marx-Engels Reader,* 2d ed., ed. Robert C. Tucker (New York: Norton, 1978), 469–500.
4. C. Wright Mills, *The Power Elite* (New York: Oxford University Press, 1956).
5. Richard Rovere, *The American Establishment* (New York: Harcourt Brace, 1962).
6. H. H. Gerth and C. Wright Mills, eds., *From Max Weber: Essays in Sociology* (London: Routledge & Kegan Paul, 1948), 232–235.
7. Among the authors whose interpretations of American politics are essentially pluralist is David B. Truman, *The Governmental Process,* 2d ed. (New York: Knopf, 1971).
8. Alexis de Tocqueville, *Democracy in America,* ed. Phillips Bradley (New York: Knopf, 1951), vol. 2, book 2, ch. 8, 122.
9. Derek C. Bok and John T. Dunlop, *Labor and the American Community* (New York: Simon & Schuster, 1970), 134.

Chapter 2   *The Constitution*

1. Quoted in Bernard Bailyn, *The Ideological Origins of the American Revolution* (Cambridge, Mass.: Harvard University Press, 1967), 61, n. 6.
2. Quoted in Bailyn, *op. cit.,* 135–137.
3. Quoted in Bailyn, *op. cit.,* 77.
4. Quoted in Bailyn, *op. cit.,* 160. Italics in the original.
5. *Federalist* No. 37.
6. Gordon S. Wood, *The Creation of the American Republic* (Chapel Hill: University of North Carolina Press, 1969). See also *Federalist* No. 49.
7. Letter of George Washington to Henry Lee (October 31, 1787). In John C. Fitzpatrick, ed., *Writings of George Washington* (Washington, D.C.: Government Printing Office, 1939), vol. 29, 34.
8. Letters of Thomas Jefferson to James Madison (January 30, 1787) and to Colonel William S. Smith (November 13, 1787), in Bernard Mayo,

ed., *Jefferson Himself* (Boston: Houghton Mifflin, 1942), 145.
9. *Federalist* No. 51.
10. *Federalist* No. 48.
11. *Federalist* No. 51.
12. *Ibid.*
13. *Ibid.*
14. "The Address and Reasons of Dissent of the Minority of the State of Pennsylvania to Their Constituents," in *The Anti-Federalist,* ed. Cecelia Kenyon (Indianapolis, Ind.: Bobbs-Merrill, 1966), 39.
15. Max Farrand, *The Framing of the Constitution of the United States* (New Haven, Conn.: Yale University Press, 1913), 185.
16. See, for example, John Hope Franklin, *Racial Equality in America* (Chicago: University of Chicago Press, 1976), ch. 1, esp. 12–20.
17. Max Farrand, *The Records of the Federal Convention of 1787,* 4 vols. (New Haven, Conn.: Yale University Press, 1911–1937).
18. Theodore J. Lowi, *American Government: Incomplete Conquest* (Hinsdale, Ill.: Dryden Press, 1976), 97.
19. Article I, section 2, para. 3.
20. Article I, section 9, para. 1.
21. Article IV, section 2, para. 3.
22. Charles A. Beard, *An Economic Interpretation of the Constitution* (New York: Macmillan, 1913), esp. 26–51, 149–151, 324–325.
23. Forrest McDonald, *We the People* (Chicago: University of Chicago Press, 1958); Robert E. Brown, *Charles Beard and the Constitution* (Princeton: Princeton University Press, 1956).
24. Robert A. McGuire, "Constitution Making: A Rational Choice Model of the Federal Convention of 1787," *American Journal of Political Science* 32 (May 1988): 483–522. See also Forrest McDonald, *Novus Ordo Seclorum* (Lawrence, Kan.: University of Kansas Press, 1985), 221.
25. McDonald, *Novus Ordo Seclorum,* 202–221.
26. Robert A. McGuire and Robert L. Ohsfeldt, "Economic Interests and the American Constitution: A Quantitative Rehabilitation of Charles A. Beard," *Journal of Economic History* 44 (June 1984): 509–519.
27. Lloyd N. Cutler, "To Form a Government," *Foreign Affairs* (Fall 1980), 126–143.

Chapter 3   *Federalism*

1. William H. Riker, "Federalism," in *Handbook of Political Science,* ed. Fred I. Greenstein and Nelson W. Polsby (Reading, Mass.: Addison-Wesley, 1975), vol. 5, 101.
2. David B. Truman, "Federalism and the Party System," in *Federalism: Mature and Emergent,*

ed. Arthur MacMahon (Garden City, N.Y.: Doubleday, 1955), 123.
3. Harold J. Laski, "The Obsolescence of Federalism," *New Republic* (May 3, 1939), 367–369.
4. Riker, *op. cit.,* 154.
5. Daniel J. Elazar, *American Federalism: A View from the States* (New York: Crowell, 1966), 216.
6. Martin Diamond, "The Federalists' View of Federalism," in *Essays in Federalism,* ed. George C. S. Benson (Claremont, Calif.: Institute for Studies in Federalism, 1961), 21–64; and Samuel H. Beer, "Federalism, Nationalism, and Democracy in America," *American Political Science Review* 72 (March 1978): 9–21.
7. United States v. Sprague, 282 U.S. 716 (1931).
8. Garcia v. San Antonio Metropolitan Transit Authority, 105 S. Ct. 1005 (1985), overruling National League of Cities v. Usery, 426 U.S. 833 (1976).
9. McCulloch v. Maryland, 4 Wheat. 316 (1819).
10. This was in part overruled in Pollock v. Farmers' Loan & Trust Co, 157 U.S. 429 (1895); overruled in South Carolina v. Baker, No. 94 (1988).
11. Texas v. White, 7 Wall. 700 (1869).
12. Champion v. Ames, 188 U.S. 321 (1903).
13. Hoke v. United States, 227 U.S. 308 (1913).
14. Clark Distilling Co. v. W. Md. Ry., 242 U.S. 311 (1917).
15. Hipolite Egg Co. v. United States, 220 U.S. 45 (1911).
16. United States v. E. C. Knight Co., 156 U.S. 1 (1895).
17. Paul v. Virginia, 8 Wall. 168 (1869).
18. Veazie Bank v. Fenno, 8 Wall. 533 (1869).
19. Brown v. Maryland, 12 Wheat. 419 (1827).
20. Wickard v. Filburn, 317 U.S. 111 (1942); NLRB v. Jones & Laughlin Steel Corp., 301 U.S. 58 (1937).
21. Kirschbaum Co. v. Walling, 316 U.S. 517 (1942).
22. Goldfarb v. Virginia State Bar, 421 U.S. 773 (1975); Flood v. Kuhn, 407 U.S. 258 (1972).
23. United States v. California, 332 U.S. 19 (1947).
24. Morton Grodzins, *The American System* (Chicago: Rand McNally, 1966), 49–50.
25. Morton Keller, *Affairs of State* (Cambridge, Mass.: Harvard University Press, 1977), 310, 381–382.
26. Edward C. Banfield, "Making a New Federal Program: Model Cities, 1964–1968," in *Policy and Politics in America,* ed. Allan P. Sindler (Boston: Little, Brown, 1973), 124–158.
27. Neal R. Pierce, "Partnership for City Aid," *Boston Globe* (March 30, 1978).
28. Samuel H. Beer, "The Modernization of American Federalism," *Publius* 3 (Fall 1973), esp. 74–79; and Beer, "Federalism . . . ," *op. cit.,* 18–19.

29. Calculated from *Special Analyses: Budget of the U.S. Government, Fiscal Year 1979* (Washington, D.C.: Government Printing Office, 1978), 187.
30. Quoted in *National Journal* (September 18, 1976), 1321.
31. R. Douglas Arnold, "The Local Roots of Domestic Policy," in *The New Congress,* ed. Thomas E. Mann and Norman J. Ornstein (Washington, D.C.: American Enterprise Institute, 1981), 268.
32. Congressional Budget Office, *Federal Constraints on State and Local Government Actions* (Washington, D.C.: Government Printing Office, 1979).
33. Civil Rights Act of 1871, as amended in 1875: *United States Code,* Title 42, section 1983.
34. Maine v. Thiboutot, 448 U.S. 1 (1980).
35. Catherine H. Lovell et al., *Federal and State Mandating on Local Governments* (Riverside, Calif.: University of California at Riverside Graduate School of Public Administration, 1979), 71.
36. *United States Code,* Title 23, section 131 (1976).
37. *Congressional Record* 126 (February 5, 1980), S1009–S1013.
38. *Ibid.,* S1010.
39. *Statistical Abstract of the United States, 1990,* 371.
40. Charles Murray, "Does Welfare Bring More Babies?" *The American Enterprise* (Jan./Feb. 1994): 55.
41. David R. Cameron and Richard I. Hofferbert, "The Impact of Federalism on Education Finance: A Comparative Analysis," *European Journal of Political Research* 2 (1974): 240, 245.
42. Jeffery L. Pressman and Aaron B. Wildavsky, *Implementation* (Berkeley, Calif.: University of California Press, 1973).

Chapter 4 *American Political Culture*

1. Alexis de Tocqueville, *Democracy in America,* ed. Phillips Bradley (New York: Knopf, 1951), vol. 1, 288. (First published in 1835.)
2. *Ibid.,* vol. 1, pp. 319–320.
3. *Ibid.,* vol. 1, p. 319.
4. Donald J. Devine, *The Political Culture of the United States* (Boston: Little, Brown, 1972), 185; Herbert McClosky and John Zaller, *The American Ethos: Public Attitudes toward Capitalism and Democracy* (Cambridge, Mass.: Harvard University Press, 1984), ch. 3, esp. 74–75.
5. McClosky and Zaller, *op. cit.,* 74–77.
6. *Ibid.,* 66.
7. Gunnar Myrdal, *An American Dilemma: The Negro Problem in Modern Democracy* (New York: Harper, 1944), intro. and ch. 1.
8. Frank R. Westie, "The American Dilemma: An Empirical Test," *American Sociological Review* 30 (August 1965): 536–537.
9. Eric L. McKitrick, "Party Politics and the Union and Confederate War Efforts," in *The American Party Systems,* 2d ed., ed. William Nisbet Chambers and Walter Dean Burnham (New York: Oxford University Press, 1975), 117–121.
10. McClosky and Zaller, *op. cit.,* 174.
11. Sidney Verba and Gary R. Orren, *Equality in America: The View from the Top* (Cambridge, Mass.: Harvard University Press, 1985), 146–147.
12. McClosky and Zaller, *op. cit.,* 82–84.
13. *Ibid.,* 93, 95.
14. Verba and Orren, *op. cit.,* 74; McClosky and Zaller, *op. cit.,* 126.
15. Verba and Orren, *op. cit.,* 72, 254.
16. Donald Kinder and David Sears, "Symbolic Racism versus Racial Threats to the Good Life," *Journal of Personality and Social Psychology* 40 (1981): 414–431.
17. Paul M. Sniderman and Michael Gray Hagen, *Race and Inequality: A Study in American Values* (Chatham, N.J.: Chatham House, 1985), 111.
18. *Ibid.,* 37–38.
19. Theodore Caplow and Howard M. Bahr, "Half a Century of Change in Adolescent Attitudes: A Replication of a Middletown Survey by the Lynds," *Public Opinion Quarterly* 43 (1979): 1–17, table 1.
20. Kay Schlozman and Sidney Verba, *Insult to Injury* (Cambridge, Mass.: Harvard University Press, 1979). See also Jennifer L. Hochschild, *What's Fair? American Beliefs about Distributive Justice* (Cambridge, Mass.: Harvard University Press, 1981), ch. 5.
21. Thomas J. Anton, "Policy-Making and Political Culture in Sweden," *Scandinavian Political Studies* 4 (1969): 88–100; M. Donald Hancock, *Sweden: The Politics of Post-Industrial Change* (Hinsdale, Ill.: Dryden Press, 1972); Sten Johansson, "Liberal-Democratic Theory and Political Processes," in *Readings in the Swedish Class Structure,* ed. Richard Scarse (New York: Pergamon Press, 1976); Steven J. Kelman, *Regulating America, Regulating Sweden: A Comparative Study of Occupational Safety and Health Policy* (Cambridge, Mass.: MIT Press, 1981), 118–123.
22. Lewis Austin, *Saints and Samurai: The Political Culture of American and Japanese Elites* (New Haven, Conn.: Yale University Press, 1975).
23. Gabriel Almond and Sidney Verba, *The Civic Culture* (Princeton, N.J.: Princeton University Press, 1963), 169, 185. See also Gabriel Almond and Sidney Verba, eds., *The Civic Culture Revisited* (Boston: Little, Brown, 1980).
24. Gordon Heald, "A Comparison between American, European, and Japanese Values," as quoted in Richard Rose, "Public Confidence, Popular Consent: A Comparison of Britain and the United States," *Public Opinion* (February–March 1984), 11.
25. Gallup International Poll for the European Value System Study, 1982.
26. Paul M. Sniderman, *A Question of Loyalty* (Berkeley: University of California Press, 1981).
27. Seymour Martin Lipset, *The First New Nation* (New York: Doubleday Anchor Books, 1967), 170–171.
28. Verba and Orren, *op. cit.,* 255.
29. Max Weber, *The Protestant Ethic and the Spirit of Capitalism,* trans. Talcott Parsons (New York: Scribner's, 1930). (First published in 1904.)
30. Erik H. Erikson, *Childhood and Society* (New York: Norton, 1950), ch. 8.
31. The phrase "culture war" is from James Davison Hunter, *Culture Wars: The Struggle to Define America* (New York: Basic Books, 1991). This discussion draws heavily on Professor Hunter's analysis.
32. *Ibid.,* 96–97, 116–117. See also Robert Lerner, Stanley Rothman, and S. Robert Lichter, "Christian Religious Elites," *Public Opinion* 11 (March/April 1989): 54–58.
33. Schlozman and Verba, *op. cit.,* 218–224, 237.
34. Arthur H. Miller, "Political Issues and Trust in Government: 1964–1970," *American Political Science Review* 68 (September 1974): 95–272. These data were updated from figures supplied by the Survey Research Center, University of Michigan.
35. Jack Citrin, "Comment: The Political Relevance of Trust in Government," *American Political Science Review* 68 (September 1974): 973–988; James S. House and William M. Mason, "Political Alienation in America, 1958–1968," *American Sociological Review* 40 (April 1975): 123–147; Seymour Martin Lipset and William Schneider, *The Confidence Gap: Business, Labor, and Government in the Public Mind* (New York: Free Press, 1983), ch. 12.
36. Citrin, *op. cit.,* 975.
37. Robert E. Lane, "The Politics of Consensus in the Age of Affluence," *American Political Science Review* 59 (December 1965): 874–875; Lane, "The Decline of Politics and Ideology in a Knowledgeable Society," *American Sociological Review* 31 (October 1966): 649–662; Lipset and Schneider, *op. cit.,* 14–15.
38. Arthur Miller, "Is Confidence Rebounding?" *Public Opinion* (June–July 1983), 16–20.
39. Lipset and Schneider, *op. cit.,* 21–22; Warren E. Miller, "Crisis in Confidence II—Misreading the Public Pulse," *Public Opinion* (October–November 1979), 12–13.
40. Data from the Survey Research Center, University of Michigan. See also Norman H. Nie, Sidney Verba, and John R. Petrocik, *The Changing American Voter* (Cambridge, Mass.: Harvard University Press, 1976), 125–128.
41. Samuel H. Barnes and Max Kaase, eds., *Political Action: Mass Participation in Five Democracies* (Beverly Hills, Calif.: Sage, 1979), 541–542, 574.
42. James W. Prothro and Charles M. Grigg, "Fundamental Principles of Democracy: Bases of Agreement and Disagreement," *Journal of Politics* 22 (Spring 1960): 275–294.
43. Herbert McClosky and Alida Brill, *Dimensions of Tolerance: What Americans Believe about Civil Liberties* (New York: Russell Sage Foundation, 1983), 124.
44. *Ibid.,* 62, 66, 70, 118, 131.
45. *Ibid.,* 435; James A. Davis, "Communism, Cohorts, and Categories: American Tolerance in 1954 and 1972–1973," *American Journal of Sociology* 81 (1975): 491–513; and Clyde A. Nunn, Harry J. Crockett, Jr., and J. Allen Williams, Jr., *Tolerance for Nonconformity: A National Survey of Changing Commitment to Civil Liberties* (San Francisco, Calif.: Jossey-Bass, 1978). But compare the different conclusion in John L. Sullivan, James Pierson, and George E. Marcus, *Political Tolerance and American Democracy* (Chicago: University of Chicago Press, 1982).

Chapter 5 *Public Opinion*

1. George W. Bishop, Alfred J. Tuchfarber, and Robert W. Oldendick, "1984: How Much Can We Manipulate and Control People's Answers to Public Opinion Surveys?" paper delivered at the 1984 annual meeting of the American Political Science Association; Howard Schuman and S. Presser, *Questions and Answers in Attitude Surveys* (New York: Academic Press, 1981), ch. 5.

2. Data from the National Election Survey, 1986, as tabulated by Professor John Zaller, University of California at Los Angeles.

3. M. Kent Jennings and Richard G. Niemi, "The Transmission of Political Values from Parent to Child," *American Political Science Review* 62 (March 1968): 173.

4. Robert D. Hess and Judith V. Tomey, *The Development of Political Attitudes in Children* (Chicago: Aldine, 1967), 90.

5. Several studies of child-parent agreement on party preference are summarized in David O. Sears, "Political Behavior," in *The Handbook of Social Psychology*, 2d ed., ed. Gardner Lindzey and Elliot Aronson (Reading, Mass.: Addison-Wesley, 1969), vol. 5, 376.

6. Norman H. Nie, Sidney Verba, and John R. Petrocik, *The Changing American Voter* (Cambridge, Mass.: Harvard University Press, 1976), ch. 4.

7. Robert S. Erikson and Norman R. Luttbeg, *American Public Opinion: Its Origins, Content, and Impact* (New York: Wiley, 1973), 197; and Seymour Martin Lipset, *Revolution and Counterrevolution*, rev. ed. (Garden City, N.Y.: Doubleday Anchor Books, 1970), 338–342.

8. *The Baron Report* (June 18, 1984).

9. ICPSR American National Election Study, 1992: Pre- and Post-Election Surveys.

10. Alexander M. Astin, *Four Critical Years: Effects of College on Beliefs, Attitudes, and Knowledge* (San Francisco: Jossey-Bass, 1978), 36–38.

11. Institute of Politics, Harvard University, *Campaign '84 and Beyond* (1986), 12.

12. Erikson and Luttbeg, *op. cit.*, 138; Terry S. Weiner and Bruce K. Eckland, "Education and Political Party: The Effects of College or Social Class?" *American Journal of Sociology* 84 (1979): 911–928.

13. Astin, *op. cit.*, 38.

14. John Zaller, "The Effects of Political Awareness on Public Opinion and Voting Behavior," *American Political Science Review*, forthcoming.

15. Everett Carl Ladd, Jr., and Seymour Martin Lipset, *The Divided Academy: Professors and Politics* (New York: McGraw-Hill, 1975), 26–27, 55–67, 184–190.

16. *Statistical Abstract of the United States, 1984*, 144.

17. J. L. Spaeth and Andrew M. Greeley, *Recent Alumni and Higher Education* (New York: McGraw-Hill, 1970), 100–110; and Erland Nelson, "Persistence of Attitudes of College Students Fourteen Years Later," *Psychological Monographs* 68 (1954): 1–13.

18. Kenneth A. Feldman and Theodore M. Newcomb, *The Impact of College on Students* (San Francisco: Jossey-Bass, 1969), vol. 1, 99–100, 312–320.

19. John McAdams, "Testing the Theory of the New Class," *Sociological Quarterly* 28 (1987): 23–49.

20. M. Kent Jennings, "Residues of a Movement: The Aging of the American Protest Generation," *American Political Science Review* 81 (1987): 367–382.

21. Kay Lehman Schlozman and Sidney Verba, *Insult to Injury: Unemployment, Class, and Political Response* (Cambridge, Mass.: Harvard University Press, 1979), 115–118; David Butler and Donald Stokes, *Political Change in Great Britain* (New York: St. Martin's Press, 1969), 70, 77; Erikson and Luttbeg, *op. cit.*, 184; *National Journal* (November 8, 1980), 1878.

22. V. O. Key, Jr., *Public Opinion and American Democracy* (New York: Knopf, 1961), 122–138.

23. Richard E. Dawson, *Public Opinion and Contemporary Disarray* (New York: Harper & Row, 1973), ch. 4.

24. Seymour Martin Lipset, "Two Americas, Two Value Systems: Blacks and Whites," *Working Papers in Political Science* P–91–1, Hoover Institution, Stanford University (November 1991): 18.

25. *Ibid.*, 15.

26. *Ibid.*, 16.

27. Nie, Verba, and Petrocik, *op. cit.*, 253–256.

28. Schlozman and Verba, *op. cit.*, 172.

29. Susan Welch and Lorn Foster, "Class and Conservatism in the Black Community," paper delivered at the 1986 annual meeting of the American Political Science Association. See also Franklin D. Gilliam, Jr., "Black America: Divided by Class?" *Public Opinion* (February–March 1986): 53–57.

30. Linda S. Lichter, "Who Speaks for Black America?" *Public Opinion* (August–September 1985): 41ff.

31. Bruce Cain and Roderick Kiewiet, "California's Coming Minority Majority," *Public Opinion* (February–March 1986): 50–52.

32. F. Chris Garcia et al., "The Effects of Ethnic Partisanship on Electoral Behavior: An Analysis and Comparison of Latino and Anglo Voting in the 1988 United States Presidential Election," paper delivered at the Annual Meeting of the American Political Science Association, September 3–6, 1992.

33. Robert Suro, "Poll Finds Hispanic Desire to Assimilate," *The New York Times* (December 15, 1992), A18, citing the findings of the National Latino Survey led by Rodolfo O. de la Garza.

34. Nie, Verba, and Petrocik, *op. cit.*, 247–250.

35. Philip E. Converse, "The Nature of Belief Systems in Mass Publics," in *Ideology and Discontent*, ed. David Apter (New York: The Free Press of Glencoe, 1964), 206–261.

36. Christopher H. Achen, "Mass Political Attitudes and the Survey Response," *American Political Science Review* 69 (December 1975): 1218–1231.

37. Seymour Martin Lipset and Earl Raab, *The Politics of Unreason* (New York: Harper & Row, 1970), ch. 11; James A. Stimson, "Belief Systems: Constraint, Complexity, and the 1972 Election," *American Journal of Political Science* 19 (1975): 393–417; and Herbert McClosky and John Zaller, *The American Ethos* (Cambridge, Mass.: Harvard University Press, 1984), ch. 8.

38. William S. Maddox and Stuart A. Lilie, *Beyond Liberal and Conservative* (Washington, D.C.: Cato Institute, 1984), 5, 68, 96, 104.

39. Zaller, *op. cit.*; and Stimson, *op. cit.* See also Allen H. Barton and R. Wayne Parsons, "Measuring Belief System Structures," *Public Opinion Quarterly* 41 (1977): 159–180.

40. McAdams, *op. cit.*

41. Seymour Martin Lipset and David Riesman, *Education and Politics at Harvard* (New York: McGraw-Hill, 1975), ch. 8.

42. McAdams, *op. cit.*

43. *Ibid.*

44. John Zaller, *The Nature of Mass Opinion* (Cambridge: Cambridge University Press, 1992).

Chapter 6 *Political Participation*

1. David Glass, Peverill Squire, and Raymond Wolfinger, "Voter Turnout: An International Comparison," *Public Opinion* (December–January 1984): 49–55. See also G. Bingham Powell, Jr., "Voting Turnout in Thirty Democracies: Partisan, Legal, and Socio-Economic Influences," in *Electoral Participation: A Comparative Analysis*, ed. Richard Rose (Beverly Hills, Calif.: Sage Publications, 1980).

2. Morton Keller, *Affairs of State* (Cambridge, Mass.: Harvard University Press, 1977), 523.

3. United States v. Reese, 92 U.S. 214 (1876); United States v. Cruikshank, 92 U.S. 556 (1876); and Ex parte Yarbrough, 110 U.S. 651 (1884).

4. Guinn and Beall v. United States, 238 U.S. 347 (1915).

5. Smith v. Allwright, 321 U.S. 649 (1944).

6. Schnell v. Davis, 336 U.S. 933 (1949).

7. Congressional Quarterly, *Congress and the Nation*, vol. 3: 1969–1972 (Washington, D.C.: Congressional Quarterly, 1973), 1006; and *Statistical Abstract of the United States, 1975*, 450.

8. *Historical Statistics of the United States: Colonial Times to 1970*, part 2, 1071–1072.

9. Walter Dean Burnham, "The Changing Shape of the American Political Universe," *American Political Science Review* 59 (March 1965): 11; and William H. Flanigan and Nancy H. Zingale, *Political Behavior of the American Electorate*, 3d ed. (Boston: Allyn & Bacon, 1975), 15.

10. Burnham, *op. cit.*; E. E. Schattschneider, *The Semisovereign People* (New York: Holt, Rinehart and Winston, 1960), chs. 5, 6.

11. Keller, *op. cit.*, 523.

12. *Ibid.*, 524.

13. Philip E. Converse, "Change in the American Electorate," in *The Human Meaning of Social Change*, ed. Angus Campbell and Philip E. Converse (New York: Russell Sage Foundation, 1972), 263–338.

14. Michael W. Traugott and John P. Katosh, "Response Validity in Surveys of Voting Behavior," *Public Opinion Quarterly* 43 (1979): 359–377; Aage R. Clausen, "Response Validity: Vote Report," *Public Opinion Quarterly* 32 (1969): 588–606.

15. Sidney Verba and Norman H. Nie, *Participation in America* (New York: Harper & Row, 1972), 118–119.

16. Lester W. Milbrath and M. L. Goel, *Political Participation*, 2d ed. (Chicago: Rand McNally, 1977), 98–116; Raymond E. Wolfinger and Steven J. Rosenstone, *Who Votes?* (New Haven, Conn.: Yale University Press, 1980); W. Russell Neuman, *The Paradox of Mass Politics* (Cambridge, Mass.: Harvard University Press, 1986), ch. 4.

17. Wolfinger and Rosenstone, *op. cit.*, esp. 102; and John P. Katosh and Michael W. Traugott, "Costs and Values in the Calculus of Voting," *American Journal of Political Science* 26 (1982): 361–376.

18. David C. Leege and Lyman A. Kellstedt, *Rediscovering the Religious Factor in American Politics* (Armonk, N.Y.: M. E. Sharpe, 1993), 129–131.

19. Verba and Nie, *op. cit.*, 151–157; and Milbrath and Goel, *op. cit.*, 120.

20. Jack Citrin, "The Alienated Voter," *Taxing and Spending* (October 1978), 1–7; Austin Ranney, "Nonvoting is Not a Social Disease," *Public Opinion* (October–November 1983): 16–19; Glass, Squire, and Wolfinger, *op. cit.*

21. Dunn v. Blumstein, 405 U.S. 330 (1972).

22. Wolfinger and Rosenstone, *op. cit.*

23. Richard G. Smolka, *Election Day Registration: The Minnesota and Wisconsin Experience* (Washington, D.C.: American Enterprise Institute, 1977), 5.

24. Gary R. Orren, "The Linkage of Policy to Participation," in *Presidential Selection,* ed. Alexander Heard and Michael Nelson (Durham, N.C.: Duke University Press, 1987).

25. Glass, Squire, and Wolfinger, *op. cit.*, 52.

26. Powell, *op. cit.*; Robert W. Jackman, "Political Institutions and Voter Turnout in Industrial Democracies," *American Political Science Review* 81 (1987): 405–423.

27. Roy Texeira, "Will the Real Nonvoter Please Stand Up?" *Public Opinion* (July/August 1988): 43; Texeira, "Registration and Turnout," *Public Opinion* (January/February 1989): 12.

28. Richard A. Brody, "The Puzzle of Political Participation in America," in *The New American Political System,* ed. Anthony King (Washington, D.C.: American Enterprise Institute, 1978), 315–323; and Charles Lewis Taylor and Michael C. Hudson, *World Handbook of Political and Social Indicators,* 2d ed. (New Haven, Conn.: Yale University Press, 1972), table 3.1.

29. Richard Smolka, quoted in William J. Crotty, *Political Reform and the American Experiment* (New York: Crowell, 1977), 86–87.

30. Sidney Verba et al., "Race, Ethnicity, and the Resources for Participation: the Role of Religion," paper delivered at the 1992 Annual Meeting of the American Political Science Association, September 3–6, 1992.

Chapter 7 *Political Parties*

1. Leon D. Epstein, "Political Parties," in *Handbook of Political Science,* ed. Fred I. Greenstein and Nelson W. Polsby (Reading, Mass.: Addison-Wesley, 1975), vol. 4, 230.

2. Quoted in Henry Adams, *History of the United States of America during the Administrations of Jefferson and Madison,* abridged edition, ed. Ernest Samuels (Chicago: University of Chicago Press, 1967), 147.

3. Robert Kuttner, "Fat and Sassy," *The New Republic* (February 23, 1987), 21–23.

4. Morton Keller, *Affairs of State* (Cambridge, Mass.: Harvard University Press, 1977), 239.

5. Quoted in Keller, *op. cit.,* 256.

6. Martin Shefter, "Parties, Bureaucracy, and Political Change in the United States," in *The Development of Political Parties,* Sage Electoral Studies Yearbook, vol. 4, ed. Louis Maisel and Joseph Cooper (Beverly Hills, Calif.: Sage Publications, 1978).

7. James Q. Wilson, *The Amateur Democrat: Club Politics in Three Cities* (Chicago: University of Chicago Press, 1962).

8. Samuel J. Eldersveld, *Political Parties: A Behavioral Analysis* (Chicago: Rand McNally, 1964), 278, 287.

9. Robert H. Salisbury, "The Urban Party Organization Member," *Public Opinion Quarterly* 29 (Winter 1965–1966): 550–564.

10. *Ibid.,* 557, 559.

11. Eldersveld, *op. cit.;* and J. David Greenstone, *Labor in American Politics* (New York: Knopf, 1969), 187.

12. David R. Mayhew, *Placing Parties in American Politics* (Princeton, N.J.: Princeton University Press, 1986), chs. 2, 3.

13. *Boston Globe* (July 9, 1984), 1.

14. William Nisbet Chambers and Walter Dean Burnham, eds., *The American Party Systems: Stages of Political Development,* 2d ed. (New York: Oxford University Press, 1975), 6.

15. Williams v. Rhodes, 393 U.S. 23 (1968).

16. James Q. Wilson, *Political Organizations* (New York: Basic Books, 1973), ch. 12; and Samuel Stouffer, *Communism, Conformity, and Civil Liberties* (Garden City, N.Y.: Doubleday, 1955).

17. On 1972 and 1976 see Jeane Kirkpatrick, *The New Presidential Elite* (New York: Russell Sage Foundation and Twentieth Century Fund, 1976), 297–315; on 1980 see *New York Times* (August 13, 1980).

18. Nelson W. Polsby, *Consequences of Party Reform* (New York: Oxford University Press, 1983), 9–11, 64.

19. *Ibid.,* 158. But compare John G. Geer, "Voting in Presidential Primaries," paper delivered to the 1984 annual meeting of the American Political Science Association.

20. Michael J. Malbin, "Democratic Party Rules Are Made to be Broken," *National Journal* (August 23, 1980), 1388.

21. Kirkpatrick, *op. cit.,* ch. 4.

22. Kirkpatrick, *op. cit.*

Chapter 8 *Elections and Campaigns*

1. Fred Barnes, "Charade on Main Street," *The New Republic* (June 15, 1987), 15–17. See also Hugh Winebrenner, *The Iowa Precinct Caucuses: The Making of a Media Event* (Ames, Iowa: Iowa State University Press, 1987).

2. Arthur H. Miller *et al.,* "A Majority Party in Disarray: Policy Polarization in the 1972 Election," *American Political Science Review* 70 (1976): 757.

3. Thomas E. Patterson and Robert D. McClure, *The Unseeing Eye: The Myth of Television Power in National Politics* (New York: Putnam, 1976); and Xandra Kayden, *Campaign Organization* (Lexington, Mass.: D. C. Heath, 1978), ch. 6.

4. Gerald M. Pomper *et al., The Election of 1980* (Chatham, N.J.: Chatham House, 1981), 75, 105–107.

5. Buckley v. Valeo, 424 U.S. 1 (1976).

6. Gary C. Jacobson, *The Politics of Congressional Elections,* 2d ed. (Boston, Mass.: Little, Brown, 1987), 49.

7. Donald Philip Green and Jonathan S. Krasno, "Salvation for the Spendthrift Incumbent: Reestimating the Effects of Campaign Spending in House Elections," *American Journal of Political Science* 32 (1988): 884–960; Stephen Ansolabehre, "Winning is Easy But It Sure Ain't Cheap," Working Paper 90-1, Center for American Politics and Public Policy, UCLA (1990); Robert S. Erikson and Thomas R. Palfrey, "The Puzzle of Incumbent Spending in Congressional Elections," *Social Science Working Paper* 806 (California Institute of Technology, August 1992).

8. Angus Campbell, Philip E. Converse, Warren E. Miller, and Donald E. Stokes, *The American Voter* (New York: Wiley, 1960), ch. 8.

9. V. O. Key, Jr., *The Responsible Electorate* (Cambridge, Mass.: Harvard University Press, 1966).

10. Morris P. Fiorina, *Retrospective Voting in American National Elections* (New Haven, Conn.: Yale University Press, 1981).

11. Jay P. Greene, "Forewarned Before Forecast: Presidential Election Forecasting Models and the 1992 Election," *P.S.: Political Science and Politics* (March 1993): 20.

12. In 1988, Dukakis led Bush by 17 percent in polls taken shortly after Dukakis was nominated, only to see Bush win handily. In 1980 Carter led Reagan in the early polls.

13. Robert Axelrod, "Where the Votes Come From: An Analysis of Electoral Coalitions, 1952–1968," *American Political Science Review* 66 (1972): 11–20; and Axelrod, "Communication," *American Political Science Review* 68 (1974): 718–719.

14. Walter Dean Burnham, *Critical Elections and the Mainsprings of American Politics* (New York: Norton, 1970), 10.

15. James L. Sundquist, *Dynamics of the Party System* (Washington, D.C.: Brookings Institution, 1973), ch. 7.

16. Edward G. Carmines and James A. Stimson, "Issue Evolution, Population Replacement, and Normal Partisan Change," *American Political Science Review* 75 (March 1981): 107–118; and Gregory Markus, "Political Attitudes in an Election Year," *American Political Science Review* 76 (September 1982): 538–560.

17. Ray Wolfinger and Michael G. Hagen, "Republican Prospects: Southern Comfort," *Public Opinion* (October–November 1985), 8–13. But compare Richard Scammon and James A. Barnes, "Republican Prospects: Southern Dis-

comfort," *Public Opinion* (October–November 1985), 14–17.

18. Jerrold G. Rusk, "The Effect of the Australian Ballot Reform on Split-Ticket Voting: 1876–1908," *American Political Science Review* 64 (December 1970): 1220–1238.

19. Gerald M. Pomper, *Elections in America* (New York: Dodd, Mead, 1971), 178.

20. Benjamin Ginsberg, "Elections and Public Policy," *American Political Science Review* 70 (March 1976): 41–49.

Chapter 9   *Interest Groups*

1. L. Harmon Zeigler and Hendrik van Dalen, "Interest Groups in the States," in *Politics in the American States,* 2d ed., ed. Herbert Jacob and Kenneth N. Vines (Boston: Little, Brown, 1974), 122–160; and Edward C. Banfield and James Q. Wilson, *City Politics* (Cambridge, Mass.: Harvard University Press, 1963), chs. 18, 19.

2. Joseph LaPalombara, *Interest Groups in Italian Politics* (Princeton, N.J.: Princeton University Press, 1964).

3. Kay Lehman Schlozman and John T. Tierney, "More of the Same: Washington Pressure Group Activity in a Decade of Change," *Journal of Politics* 45 (1983): 356.

4. The use of injunctions in labor disputes was restricted by the Norris–La Guardia Act of 1932; the rights to collective bargaining and to the union shop were guaranteed by the Wagner Act of 1935.

5. *Historical Statistics of the United States, Colonial Times to 1970,* vol. 1, 386.

6. The distinction is drawn from Kay Lehman Schlozman and John T. Tierney, *Organized Interests and American Democracy* (New York: Harper & Row, 1985).

7. Jeffrey M. Berry, *The Interest Group Society* (Boston: Little, Brown, 1984), 20–21.

8. *Ibid.,* 24, 130.

9. Gabriel A. Almond and Sidney Verba, *The Civic Culture* (Princeton, N.J.: Princeton University Press, 1963), 302; Derek C. Bok and John T. Dunlop, *Labor and the American Community* (New York: Simon & Schuster, 1970), 49; *Statistical Abstract of the United States, 1975,* 373.

10. Almond and Verba, *op. cit.,* 194.

11. *Ibid.,* 207.

12. Mancur Olson, Jr., *The Logic of Collective Action* (Cambridge, Mass.: Harvard University Press, 1965), 153–157.

13. Bok and Dunlop, *op. cit.,* 134.

14. Henry J. Pratt, *The Liberalization of American Protestantism* (Detroit: Wayne State University Press, 1972), ch. 12; Gerhard Lenski, *The Religious Factor* (Garden City, N.Y.: Doubleday, 1961), ch. 4.

15. Jane J. Mansbridge, *Why We Lost the ERA* (Chicago: University of Chicago Press, 1986), ch. 10. See also Joyce Gelb and Marian Lief Palley, *Women and Public Choices* (Princeton, N.J.: Princeton University Press, 1982), ch. 3; Jo Freeman, *The Politics of Women's Liberation* (New York: McKay, 1975), ch. 3; Maren Lockwood Carden, "The Proliferation of a Social Move-

ment: Ideology and Individual Incentives in the Contemporary Feminist Movement," *Research in Social Movements,* vol. 1 (1978), 179–196; and Dom Bonafede, "Still a Long Way to Go," *National Journal* (September 13, 1986), 2175–2179.

16. Mansbridge, *op. cit.,* 130–131.

17. Jeffrey M. Berry, *Lobbying for the People* (Princeton, N.J.: Princeton University Press, 1977), 71–76.

18. Berry, *Interest Group Society, op. cit.,* 88.

19. Schlozman and Tierney, *Organized Interests and American Democracy, op. cit.,* table 5–4.

20. *New York Times* (December 8, 1983), 1.

21. Raymond A. Bauer, Ithiel de Sola Pool, and Lewis Anthony Dexter, *American Business and Public Policy* (New York: Atherton, 1963), ch. 30.

22. Berry, *Lobbying for the People, op. cit.,* 136–140.

23. Margaret Ann Latus, "Assessing Ideological PACs: From Outrage to Understanding," in *Money and Politics in the United States,* ed. Michael Malbin (Chatham, N.J.: Chatham House, 1984), 143; and data supplied by the Federal Election Commission, March 1992.

24. *Ibid.,* 144.

25. Malbin, *op. cit.,* table A.8, 290–291.

26. Michael J. Malbin, "Looking Back at the Future of Campaign Finance Reform: Interest Groups and American Elections," in Malbin, *Money and Politics, op. cit.,* 248; James B. Kau and Paul H. Rubin, *Congressmen, Constituents and Contributors* (Boston: Martinus Nijhoff, 1982); Henry W. Chappell, Jr., "Campaign Contributions and Voting on the Cargo Preference Bill: A Comparison of Simultaneous Models," *Public Choice* 36 (1981): 301–312; W. P. Welch, "Campaign Contributions and Voting: Milk Money and Dairy Price Supports," *Western Political Quarterly* 35 (1982): 478–495; John R. Wright, "PACs, Contributions, and Roll Calls: An Organizational Perspective," *American Political Science Review* 79 (1985): 400–414. But compare Benjamin Ginsberg and John C. Green, "The Best Congress Money Can Buy," in Ginsberg and Alan Stone, eds., *Do Elections Matter?* (Armonk, N.Y.: M. E. Sharpe, 1986), 75–89.

27. William T. Gormley, "A Test of the Revolving Door Hypothesis at the FCC," *American Journal of Political Science* 23 (1979): 665–683; Paul J. Quirk, *Industry Influence in Federal Regulatory Agencies* (Princeton, N.J.: Princeton University Press, 1981); and Jeffrey E. Cohen, "The Dynamics of the 'Revolving Door' on the FCC," *American Journal of Political Science* 30 (1986): 689–708.

28. Suzanne Weaver, *Decision to Prosecute* (Cambridge, Mass.: MIT Press, 1977), 154–163.

29. United States v. Harriss, 347 U.S. 612 (1954).

30. Hope Eastman, *Lobbying: A Constitutionally Protected Right* (Washington, D.C.: American Enterprise Institute, 1977), 30.

31. One such bill was S. 1785, 95th Congress. See Eastman, *op. cit.,* 10.

32. Eastman, *op. cit.,* 20–21.

33. *United States Code,* Title 26, section 501(c)(3).

34. James Q. Wilson, *Political Organizations* (New

York: Basic Books, 1973), 321.

Chapter 10   *The Media*

1. R. L. Lowenstein, *World Press Freedom, 1966* (Columbia, Mo.: Freedom of Information Center, 1967), publication No. 11.

2. D. E. Butler, "Why American Political Reporting Is Better than England's," *Harper's* (May 1963), 15–25.

3. *New York Times* (March 15, 1975).

4. *New York Times* (January 28, 1974).

5. Douglass Cater, *The Fourth Branch of Government* (Boston: Houghton Mifflin, 1959), 76; and William L. Rivers, "The Press as a Communication System," in *Handbook of Communication,* ed. Ithiel de Sola Pool *et al.* (Chicago: Rand McNally, 1973), 522–526.

6. Quoted in F. L. Mort, *American Journalism, 1690–1960,* 3d ed. (New York: Macmillan, 1962), 529, as cited in Rivers, *op. cit.,* 526.

7. Kiko Adatto, *Picture Perfect: The Art and Artifice of Public Image Making* (New York: Basic Books, 1993).

8. Edward Jay Epstein, *News from Nowhere: Television and the News* (New York: Random House, 1973), 37.

9. Allen H. Barton, "Consensus and Conflict among American Leaders," *Public Opinion Quarterly* 38 (Winter 1974–1975): 507–530.

10. Paul H. Weaver, "The New Journalism and the Old—Thoughts after Watergate," *The Public Interest* (Spring 1974), 67–88.

11. William C. Adams, "Media Coverage of Campaign '84: A Preliminary Report," *Public Opinion* (April–May 1984), 9–13.

12. Near v. Minnesota, 283 U.S. 697 (1931).

13. *New York Times* v. United States, 403 U.S. 713 (1971).

14. *New York Times* v. Sullivan, 376 U.S. 254 (1964).

15. Miami Herald Publishing Co. v. Tornillo, 418 U.S. 241 (1974).

16. Yates v. United States, 354 U.S. 298 (1957).

17. Branzburg v. Hayes, 408 U.S. 665 (1972).

18. Zurcher v. *Stanford Daily,* 436 U.S. 547 (1978), overturned by the Privacy Protection Act of 1980 (P.L. 96–440).

19. *National Journal* (April 16, 1983), 787.

20. Thomas E. Patterson and Robert D. McClure, *The Unseeing Eye: The Myth of Television Power in National Elections* (New York: Putnam, 1976); and Herbert Asher, *Presidential Elections and American Politics* (Homewood, Ill.: Dorsey Press, 1976), 239–240 (and studies cited therein).

21. David O. Sears and Richard E. Whitney, "Political Persuasion," in Pool, *op. cit.,* 253–289.

22. Robert S. Erikson, "The Influence of Newspaper Endorsements in Presidential Elections: The Case of 1964," *American Journal of Political Science* 20 (May 1976): 207–233.

23. Maxwell E. McCombs and Donald R. Shaw, "The Agenda Setting Function of the Mass Media," *Public Opinion Quarterly* 36 (Summer 1972): 176–187; Shanto Iyengar and Donald R. Kinder, *News That Matters* (Chicago: University of Chicago Press, 1987).

24. G. Ray Funkhouser, "The Issues of the Sixties," *Public Opinion Quarterly* 37 (Spring 1973): 62–75.

25. Joseph Wagner, "Media Do Make a Difference: The Differential Impact of Mass Media in the 1976 Presidential Race," *American Journal of Political Science* 27 (August 1983): 407–430.

26. Benjamin I. Page, Robert Y. Shapiro, and Glenn R. Dempsey, "What Moves Public Opinion?" *American Political Science Review* 81 (March 1987): 23–43.

27. George Jergens, "Theodore Roosevelt and the Press," *Daedalus* (Fall 1982), 113–133; and Henry Fairlie, "The Rise of the Press Secretary," *New Republic* (March 18, 1978), 20–23.

28. Michael J. Robinson, "A Twentieth Century Medium in a Nineteenth Century Legislature: The Effects of Television on the American Congress," in *Congress in Change*, ed. Norman J. Ornstein (New York: Praeger, 1975), 240–261.

29. S. Robert Lichter and Stanley Rothman, "Media and Business Elites," *Public Opinion* (October–November 1981), 42–46.

30. Michael J. Robinson, "Just How Liberal Is the News? 1980 Revisited," *Public Opinion* (February–March 1983), 55–60; Maura Clancey and Michael J. Robinson, "The Media in Campaign '84: General Election Coverage," *Public Opinion* (December–January 1985); Elizabeth Kolbet, "Maybe the Media Did Treat Bush Harshly," *The New York Times* (November 22, 1992), E2.

31. Peter Braestrup, *Big Story* (Boulder, Col.: Westview Press, 1977), 2 vols.

32. S. Robert Lichter, Stanley Rothman, and Linda S. Lichter, *The Media Elite: America's New Powerbrokers* (Bethesda, Md.: Adler & Adler, 1986), 179, 213.

Chapter 11   *Congress*

1. H. Douglas Price, "Careers and Committees in the American Congress," in *The History of Parliamentary Behavior*, ed. William O. Aydelotte (Princeton, N.J.: Princeton University Press, 1977), 28–62; John F. Bibby, Thomas E. Mann, and Norman J. Ornstein, *Vital Statistics on Congress, 1980* (Washington, D.C.: American Enterprise Institute, 1980), 53–54; Thomas E. Cavanaugh, "The Dispersion of Authority in the House of Representatives," *Political Science Quarterly* 97 (1982–1983): 625–626; *Congressional Quarterly Weekly Reports*.

2. David R. Mayhew, *Congress: The Electoral Connection* (New Haven, Conn.: Yale University Press, 1974); Bibby, Mann, and Ornstein, *op. cit.*, 14–15.

3. Bibby, Mann, and Ornstein, *op. cit.*, 16.

4. Mayhew, *op. cit.*; Morris P. Fiorina, *Congress: Keystone of the Washington Establishment* (New Haven, Conn.: Yale University Press, 1977).

5. Rhodes Cook, "House Republicans Scored a Quiet Victory in '92," *Congressional Quarterly* (April 17, 1993), 966.

6. Bruce E. Cain and David Butler, "Redrawing District Lines: What's Going On and What's At Stake," *The American Enterprise* (July/August 1991), 37.

7. Gary C. Jacobson, "The Persistence of Democratic House Majorities: Structure or Politics," paper delivered at the 1990 Annual Meeting of the American Political Science Association (San Francisco, California, August 30–September 2, 1990): 2.

8. *Ibid.*

9. Wesberry v. Sanders, 376 U.S. 1 (1964).

10. Linda Greenhouse, "Court Questions Districts Drawn To Aid Minorities," *New York Times* (June 29, 1993), A1, A12.

11. Dave Kaplan, "Constitutional Doubt is Thrown on Bizarre-Shaped Districts," *Congressional Quarterly* (July 3, 1993), 1761–1763.

12. John Leo, "Electioneering By Race," *U.S. News and World Report* (September 28, 1992), 33.

13. Kaplan, *op. cit.*; Greenhouse, *op. cit.*

14. Holly Idelson, "Supreme Court Considers Racially Conscious Map," *Congressional Quarterly* (April 24, 1993), 1034; Kaplan, *op. cit.*; Greenhouse, *op. cit.*

15. Hannah F. Pitkin, *The Concept of Representation* (Berkeley: University of California Press, 1967).

16. Carol M. Swain, *Black Faces, Black Interests: The Representation of African-Americans in Congress* (Cambridge, Mass.: Harvard University Press, 1993), 207.

17. Richard F. Fenno, Jr., "U.S. House Members and Their Constituencies: An Exploration," *American Political Science Review* 71 (September 1977), 883–917, esp. 914.

18. John A. Ferejohn, *Pork Barrel Politics* (Stanford, Calif.: Stanford University Press, 1974).

19. Douglas Arnold, *Congress and the Bureaucracy* (New Haven, Conn.: Yale University Press, 1979).

20. *Congressional Quarterly Weekly Report*, December 3, 1994, pp. 3430–3435.

21. In 1993, the 103rd Congress also contained a lot of newly elected Democratic members eager to change House rules. But they voted for the old rules and procedures because that is what their party leaders wanted.

22. Barbara Sinclair, *The Transformation of the United States Senate* (Baltimore, Md.: Johns Hopkins University Press, 1989).

23. Gary C. Cox and Matthew D. McCubbins, *Legislative Leviathan* (Berkeley: University of California Press, 1993); David W. Rhode, *Parties and Leaders in the Postreform House* (Chicago: University of Chicago Press, 1991).

24. Steven S. Smith, "Revolution in the House: Why Don't We Do It on the Floor?" discussion paper No. 5 (Washington, D.C.: Brookings Institution, September 1986).

25. Richard F. Fenno, Jr., *Congressmen in Committees* (Boston: Little, Brown, 1973).

26. Bibby, Mann, and Ornstein, *op. cit.*, 65–74.

27. Fiorina, *op. cit.*,

28. Bibby, Mann, and Ornstein, *op. cit.*, 60.

29. Michael J. Malbin, "Delegation, Deliberation, and the New Role of Congressional Staff," in *The New Congress*, ed. Thomas E. Mann and Norman J. Ornstein (Washington, D.C.: American Enterprise Institute, 1981), 134–177, esp. 170–171.

30. Lawrence H. Chamberlain, "The President, Congress, and Legislation," in *The Presidency*, ed. Aaron Wildavsky (Boston: Little, Brown, 1969), 444–445; Ronald C. Moe and Steven C. Teel, "Congress as a Policy-Maker: A Necessary Reappraisal," *Political Science Quarterly* 85 (September 1970), 443–470.

31. Richard E. Cohen, "Challenging the House's Traffic Cop," *The National Journal* (April 4, 1993), 1002.

32. Malcolm E. Jewell and Samuel C. Patterson, *The Legislative Process in the United States*, 3d ed. (New York: Random House, 1977), 439.

33. Warren E. Miller and Donald E. Stokes, "Constituency Influence in Congress, in *Elections and the Political Order*, ed. Angus Campbell *et al.* (New York: Wiley, 1966), 359.

34. John E. Jackson, *Constituencies and Leaders in Congress* (Cambridge, Mass.: Harvard University Press, 1974).

35. Jerrold E. Schneider, *Ideological Coalitions in Congress* (Westport, Conn.: Greenwood Press, 1979), 134, 195.

36. Michael Foley, *The New Senate: Liberal Influence on a Conservative Institution, 1959–1972* (New Haven, Conn.: Yale University Press, 1980), 242.

37. *Congressional Quarterly Weekly Report* (January 15, 1983), 102.

38. Based on results of interviews with one thousand randomly selected Americans conducted by the American Talk Issues Foundation, March 10–15, 1993.

39. As quoted in Edward L. Lascher *et al.*, "Policy Views, Constituency Pressure, and Congressional Action on Flag Burning," *Public Choice* 6 (1993), 90.

40. *Ibid.*, 98.

41. Survey by NBC News/*Wall Street Journal*, April 11–14, 1992, as reported in *The American Enterprise* (January/February 1993), 97.

42. Michael J. Malbin and Gerald Benjamin, eds., *Limiting Legislative Terms* (Washington, D.C.: Congressional Quarterly Press, 1992).

43. *Decisionmaking in the Federal Government: The Wallace S. Sayre Model*, 20–21.

44. Steve Goldstein, "All-Star Tickets Find Their Way to Congress," *The Philadelphia Inquirer* (July 14, 1993), A1, A8.

45. Thomas E. Mann and Norman J. Ornstein, *Renewing Congress: A Second Report* (Washington, D.C.: Brookings Institution and American Enterprise Institute, 1993), 71–72.

46. As reported in *New York Times* editorial, "Postmark Politics," July 13, 1993, p. A18.

47. Mann and Ornstein, *op. cit.*, 72.

48. *Ibid.*, 18.

49. *Ibid.*, 15–17.

50. *Ibid.*, 15–31.

51. *Ibid.*, 68–69.

52. *Ibid.*, 69.

53. *Congressional Quarterly Weekly Report* (February 9, 1980), 323–342.

Chapter 12 *The Presidency*

1. Jean Blondel, *An Introduction to Comparative Government* (New York: Praeger, 1969), as cited in Nelson W. Polsby, "Legislatures," in *Handbook of Political Science,* ed. Fred I. Greenstein and Nelson W. Polsby (Reading, Mass.: Addison-Wesley, 1975), vol. 5, 275.

2. Donald F. Kettl, *Deficit Politics: Public Budgeting in Its Institutional and Historical Context* (New York: Macmillan, 1992), 13.

3. Morris P. Fiorina, *Divided Government* (New York: Macmillan, 1992), 86–111.

4. David Mayhew, *Divided We Govern: Party Control, Lawmaking, and Investigations, 1946–1990* (New Haven, CT: Yale University Press, 1991), 76.

5. Mark A. Peterson, *Legislating Together: The White House and Congress from Eisenhower to Reagan* (Cambridge: Harvard University Press, 1990).

6. Richard E. Cohen, *Washington At Work: Back Rooms and Clean Air* (New York: Macmillan, 1992), 154–155.

7. *Ibid.,* 169.

8. Kettl, *op. cit.,* 138.

9. Woodrow Wilson, *Congressional Government* (New York: Meridian Books, 1956), 167–168, 170. (First published in 1885.)

10. Stephen Hess, *Organizing the Presidency* (Washington, D.C.: Brookings Institution, 1976), 3; R. W. Apple, "Clinton's Refocusing," *The New York Times* (May 6, 1993), A22; Michael K. Frisby, "Power Switch," *The Wall Street Journal* (March 26, 1993), A1, A7.

11. David T. Stanley *et al., Men Who Govern* (Washington, D.C.: Brookings Institution, 1967), 41–42, 50.

12. Daniel J. Elazar, "Which Road to the Presidency?" in *The Presidency,* ed. Aaron Wildavsky (Boston: Little, Brown, 1969), 340.

13. James David Barber, *The Presidential Character: Predicting Performance in the White House,* 3d ed. (Englewood Cliffs, N.J.: Prentice-Hall, 1985).

14. Richard E. Neustadt, *Presidential Power,* rev. ed. (New York: Wiley, 1976), ch. 4.

15. Walter D. Burnham, "Insulation and Responsiveness in Congressional Elections," *Political Science Quarterly* 90 (Fall 1975): 412–413; George C. Edwards III, *Presidential Influence in Congress* (San Francisco: Freeman, 1980), 70–78; Warren E. Miller, "Presidential Coattails: A Study in Political Myth and Methodology," *Public Opinion Quarterly* 19 (Winter 1955–1956): 368; and Miller, "The Motivational Basis for Straight and Split Ticket Voting," *American Political Science Review* 51 (June 1957): 293–312.

16. Edwards, *op. cit.,* 86–100; Douglas Rivers and Nancy L. Rose, "Passing the President's Program: Public Opinion and Presidential Influence in Congress," paper delivered at the 1981 annual meeting of the Midwestern Political Science Association.

17. Marbury v. Madison, 1 Cranch 137 (1803).

18. United States v. Nixon, 418 U.S. 683 (1974).

19. Joseph A. Califano, Jr., *A Presidential Nation* (New York: Norton, 1975), 51.

20. Marcus Cunliffe, *American Presidents and the Presidency* (New York: American Heritage Press/McGraw-Hill, 1972), 63, 65.

21. *Ibid.,* 214.

22. Adapted from Paul C. Light, *The President's Agenda* (Baltimore, Md.: Johns Hopkins University Press, 1982), 217–225.

Chapter 13 *The Bureaucracy*

1. Charles E. Lindblom, *Politics and Markets* (New York: Basic Books, 1977), 114.

2. Article II, section 2, para. 2.

3. Article II, section 3.

4. Calculated from data in *Historical Statistics of the United States: Colonial Times to 1970* (Washington, D.C.: Government Printing Office, 1975), vol. 2, 1102–1103.

5. Panama Refining Co. v. Ryan, 293 U.S. 388 (1935).

6. Hampton Jr. & Co. v. United States, 276 U.S. 394 (1928).

7. Edward S. Corwin, *The Constitution and What It Means Today,* 13th ed. (Princeton, N.J.: Princeton University Press, 1973), 151.

8. Bruce D. Porter, "Parkinson's Law Revisited: War and the Growth of American Government," *Public Interest* (Summer 1980), 50–68.

9. See the cases cited in Corwin, *op. cit.,* 8.

10. *U.S. Statutes,* vol. 84, sec. 799 (1970).

11. *Historical Statistics of the United States,* vol. 2, 1107.

12. *Statistical Abstract of the United States, 1975* (Washington, D.C.: Government Printing Office, 1975), 242.

13. Hugh Heclo, "Issue Networks and the Executive Establishment," in *The New American Political System,* ed. Anthony King (Washington, D.C.: American Enterprise Institute, 1978), 87–124.

14. *National Journal* (July 18, 1981), 1296–1299.

15. Quoted in Hugh Heclo, *A Government of Strangers* (Washington, D.C.: Brookings Institute, 1977), 225.

16. J. Donald Kingsley, *Representative Bureaucracy* (Yellow Springs, Ohio: Antioch Press, 1944).

17. See Richard P. Nathan, *The Plot That Failed: Nixon and the Administrative Presidency* (New York: Wiley, 1975).

18. Stanley Rothman and S. Robert Lichter, "How Liberal Are Bureaucrats?" *Regulation* (November–December, 1983), 17–18.

19. Kenneth Meier and Lloyd Nigro, "Representative Bureaucracy and Policy References: A Study of the Attitudes of Federal Executives," *Public Administration Review* 36 (July–August 1976): 458–467; Bernard Mennis, *American Foreign Policy Officials* (Columbus, Ohio: Ohio State University Press, 1971).

20. Joel D. Aberbach and Bert A. Rockman, "Clashing Beliefs within the Executive Branch: The Nixon Administration Bureaucracy," *American Political Science Review* 70 (June 1976): 456–468.

21. David Stockman, *The Triumph of Politics* (New York: Harper and Row, 1986).

22. James Q. Wilson, *Bureaucracy* (New York: Basic Books, 1989), ch. 6.

23. Heclo, "Issue Networks and the Executive Establishment," *op. cit.,* 87–124.

24. Richard F. Fenno, Jr., *The Power of the Purse* (Boston: Little, Brown, 1966), 450, 597.

25. John E. Schwartz and L. Earl Shaw, *The United States Congress in Comparative Perspective* (Hinsdale, Ill.: Dryden Press, 1976), 262–263; *National Journal* (July 4, 1981), 1211–1214.

26. Immigration and Naturalization Service v. Chadha, 103 S. Ct. 2764 (1983); Maine v. Thiboutot, 100 S. Ct. 2502 (1980).

27. See cases cited in Corwin, *op. cit.,* 22.

28. Steven Kelman, "The Grace Commission: How Much Waste in Government?" *Public Interest* (Winter 1985), 62–87.

29. Daniel Katz *et al., Bureaucratic Encounters* (Ann Arbor: Survey Research Center, University of Michigan, 1975), 63–69, 118–120, 184–188.

30. *From Red Tape to Results: Creating a Government That Works Better and Costs Less,* report of the National Performance Review, Vice President Al Gore, September 7, 1993.

Chapter 14 *The Judiciary*

1. Henry J. Abraham, *The Judicial Process,* 3d ed. (New York: Oxford University Press, 1975), 279–280.

2. Robert G. McCloskey, *The American Supreme Court* (Chicago: University of Chicago Press, 1960), 27.

3. Marbury v. Madison, 5 U.S. 137 (1803); and McCulloch v. Maryland, 17 U.S. 316 (1819).

4. Martin v. Hunter's Lessee, 14 U.S. 304 (1816); and Cohens v. Virginia, 19 U.S. (1821).

5. Gibbons v. Ogden, 22 U.S. (1824).

6. Quoted in Albert J. Beveridge, *The Life of John Marshall* (Boston: Houghton Mifflin, 1919), vol. 4, 551.

7. Dred Scott v. Sandford, 60 U.S. 393 (1857).

8. Abraham, *op. cit.,* 286.

9. *In re* Debs, 158 U.S. 564 (1895).

10. Pollock v. Farmers' Loan & Trust Co., 157 U.S. 429 (1895).

11. United States v. Knight, 156 U.S. 1 (1895).

12. Cincinnati, N.O. & T.P. Railway Co. v. Interstate Commerce Commission, 162 U.S. 184 (1896).

13. Hammer v. Dagenhart, 247 U.S. 251 (1918).

14. Lochner v. New York, 198 U.S. 45 (1905).

15. McCloskey, *op. cit.,* 151.

16. Munn v. Illinois, 94 U.S. 113 (1877).

17. Dayton-Goose Creek Railway Co. v. United States, 263 U.S. 456 (1924).

18. Atchison, Topeka, and Santa Fe Railroad Co. v. Matthews, 174 U.S. 96 (1899).

19. Mugler v. Kansas, 123 U.S. 623 (1887).

20. St. Louis Consolidated Coal Co. v. Illinois, 185 U.S. 203 (1902).

21. New York Central Railroad Co. v. White, 243 U.S. 188 (1917).

22. German Alliance Insurance Co. v. Lewis, 233 U.S. 389 (1914).

23. Morton Keller, *Affairs of State* (Cambridge, Mass.: Harvard University Press, 1977), 369. See also Mary Cornelia Porter, "That Commerce Shall Be Free: A New Look at the Old Laissez-

Faire Court," in *The Supreme Court Review,* ed. Philip B. Kurland (Chicago: University of Chicago Press, 1976), 135–159.

24. Chief of Capitol Police v. Jeannette Rankin Brigade, 409 U.S. 972 (1972).

25. Aptheker v. Secretary of State, 378 U.S. 500 (1964).

26. Trop v. Dulles, 356 U.S. 86 (1958); Afroyim v. Rusk, 387 U.S. 253 (1967); and Schneider v. Rusk, 377 U.S. 163 (1964).

27. Lamont v. Postmaster General, 381 U.S. 301 (1965); and Blount v. Rizzi, 400 U.S. 410 (1971).

28. Richardson v. Davis, 409 U.S. 1069 (1972); U.S. Department of Agriculture v. Murry, 413 U.S. 508 (1973); Jimenez v. Weinberger, 417 U.S. 628 (1974); and Washington v. Legrant, 394 U.S. 618 (1969).

29. Robert A. Carp and C. I. Rowland, *Policymaking and Politics in the Federal District Courts* (Knoxville, Tenn.: University of Tennessee Press, 1983), 38; Sheldon Goldman, "Voting Behavior on the United States Courts of Appeals, Revisited," *American Political Science Review* 69 (1975): 491–506; C. Heal Tate, "Personal Attribute Models of the Voting Behavior of U.S. Supreme Court Justices," *American Political Science Review* 75 (1981): 355–367.

30. Henry J. Abraham, *Justices and Presidents* (New York: Oxford University Press, 1974), 75.

31. United States v. Lanza, 260 U.S. 377 (1922). Cf. Abbate v. United States, 359 U.S. 187 (1959) and Bartkus v. Illinois, 359 U.S. 121 (1989).

32. Gideon v. Wainwright, 372 U.S. 335 (1963). The story is told in Anthony Lewis, *Gideon's Trumpet* (New York: Random House, 1964).

33. Erwin Griswold, "Rationing Justice: The Supreme Court's Case Load and What the Court Does Not Do," *Cornell Law Review* 60 (1975): 335–354.

34. Paul A. Freund, *Report of the Study Group on the Caseload of the Supreme Court* (Washington, D.C.: Federal Judicial Center, 1972).

35. Alyeska Pipeline Service Co. v. Wilderness Society, 421 U.S. 240 (1975).

36. Flast v. Cohen, 392 U.S. 83 (1968), which modified the earlier Frothingham v. Mellon, 262 U.S. 447 (1923); United States v. Richardson, 418 U.S. 166 (1947).

37. Brown v. Board of Education of Topeka, 347 U.S. 483 (1954).

38. Baker v. Carr, 369 U.S. 186 (1962).

39. See Louise Weinberg, "A New Judicial Federalism?" *Daedalus* (Winter 1978), 129–141.

40. "The Supreme Court, 1989 Term," *Harvard Law Review* 104 (1990): 360. See also Lawrence Baum, *The Supreme Court,* 2d ed. (Washington, D.C.: Congressional Quarterly Press, 1985), 139–139.

41. "The Supreme Court, 1989 Term," *op. cit.,* 360.

42. Quoted in Abraham, *The Judicial Process, op. cit.,* 330.

43. A. P. Blaustein and A. H. Field, "Overruling Opinions in the Supreme Court," *Michigan Law Review* 47 (1958): 151; Henry J. Abraham, *The Judicial Process,* 4th ed. (New York: Oxford University Press, 1980), 349.

44. Colegrove v. Green, 328 U.S. 549 (1946).

45. The Court abandoned the "political question" doctrine in Baker v. Carr, 369 U.S. 186 (1962), and began to change congressional-district apportionment in Wesberry v. Sanders, 376 U.S. 1 (1964).

46. Donald L. Horowitz, *The Courts and Social Policy* (Washington, D.C.: Brookings Institution, 1977), 6.

47. Gates v. Collier, 349 F. Supp. 881 (1972).

48. Lau v. Nichols, 414 U.S. 563 (1974).

49. *International Directory of Bar Associations,* 4th ed. (Chicago: American Bar Foundation, 1983).

50. Joel B. Grossman and Austin Sarat, "Litigation in the Federal Courts: A Comparative Perspective," *Law and Society Review* 9 (Winter 1975): 321–346.

51. Administrative Office of the U.S. Courts, *Annual Report, 1988,* 109.

52. Jack W. Peltason, *Fifty-Eight Lonely Men: Southern Federal Judges and School Desegregation* (New York: Harcourt Brace, 1961).

53. Anthony Patridge and William B. Eldridge, *The Second Circuit Sentencing Study* (Washington, D.C.: Federal Judicial Center, 1974).

54. Abington School District v. Schempp, 374 U.S. 203 (1963).

55. Robert H. Birkby, "The Supreme Court and the Bible Belt," *Midwest Journal of Political Science* 10 (1966): 3.

56. *Ibid.,* 41–42.

57. *Ibid.,* 332.

58. *Ex parte* McCardle, 74 U.S. 506 (1869).

59. Walter F. Murphy, *Congress and the Court* (Chicago: University of Chicago Press, 1962); and C. Herman Pritchett, *Congress versus the Supreme Court* (Minneapolis: University of Minnesota Press, 1961).

60. Gregory A. Caldeira, "Neither the Purse Nor the Sword: Dynamics of Public Confidence in the U.S. Supreme Court," *American Political Science Review* 80 (1986): 1209–1226. See also Joseph T. Tannenhaus and Walter F. Murphy, "Patterns of Public Support for the Supreme Court: A Panel Study," *Journal of Politics* 43 (1981): 24–39.

Chapter 15 *The Policy-Making Process*

1. E. E. Schattschneider, *The Semisovereign People* (New York: Holt, Rinehart and Winston, 1960), 68.

2. Jack L. Walker, "Setting the Agenda in the U.S. Senate: A Theory of Problem Selection," *British Journal of Political Science* 7 (1977): 343, 441.

3. *Statistical Abstract of the United States, 1975* (Washington, D.C.: Government Printing Office, 1975), 342–343, 349.

4. Alexis de Tocqueville, *The Old Regime and the French Revolution,* trans. Gilbert Stuart (Garden City, N.Y.: Doubleday Anchor Books, 1955), 176–177. (First published in 1856.)

5. David O. Sears and J. B. McConahay, *The Politics of Violence* (Boston: Houghton Mifflin, 1973). Compare Abraham H. Miller *et al.,* "The New Urban Blacks," *Ethnicity* 3 (1976): 338–367.

6. Daniel Patrick Moynihan, *Maximum Feasible Misunderstanding* (New York: Free Press, 1969), ch. 2.

7. Nelson W. Polsby, "Goodbye to the Senate's Inner Club," in *Congress in Change: Evolution and Reform,* ed. Norman J. Ornstein (New York: Praeger, 1975), 208–215.

8. *Federalist* No. 62.

9. Walker, *op. cit.,* 434, 439, 441.

10. This is a revised version of a theory originally presented in James Q. Wilson, *Political Organizations* (New York: Basic Books, 1973), ch. 16. There are other ways of classifying public policies, notably that of Theodore J. Lowi, "American Business, Public Policy, Case Studies, and Political Theory," *World Politics* 16 (July 1964).

11. Donald F. Kettl, *Sharing Power: Public Governance and Private Markets* (Washington, D.C.: Brookings Institution, 1993). Lawrence J. Hajna, "Superfund: Costly Program Under Fire," *Courier-Post* (February 13, 1994), 6A.

12. Edward S. Greenberg, *Serving the Few: Corporate Capitalism and the Bias of Government Policy* (New York: Wiley, 1974).

13. Charles E. Lindblom, *Politics and Markets* (New York: Basic Books, 1977).

14. Joseph Schumpeter, *Capitalism, Socialism, and Democracy* (New York: Harper & Row, 1950).

15. Louis Galambos, *The Public Image of Big Business in America, 1880–1940* (Baltimore, Md.: Johns Hopkins University Press, 1975).

16. Suzanne Weaver, *Decision to Prosecute: Organization and Public Policy in the Antitrust Division* (Cambridge, Mass.: MIT Press, 1977); Robert H. Bork, *The Antitrust Paradox* (New York: Basic Books, 1978).

17. Richard A. Posner, *Antitrust Law: An Economic Perspective* (Chicago: University of Chicago Press, 1976), 25.

18. Alan L. Seltzer, "Woodrow Wilson as 'Corporate-Liberal': Toward a Reconsideration of Left Revisionist Historiography," *Western Political Quarterly* 30 (June 1977): 183–212.

19. Weaver, *op. cit.,* and Robert A. Katzmann, *Regulatory Bureaucracy: The Federal Trade Commission and Antitrust Policy* (Cambridge, Mass.: MIT Press, 1980).

20. Charles R. Plott, "Occupational Self-Regulation: A Case Study of the Oklahoma Dry Cleaners," *Journal of Law and Economics* 8 (October 1965): 195–222.

21. Paul H. MacAvoy, ed., *Federal Milk Marketing Orders and Price Supports* (Washington, D.C.: American Enterprise Institute, 1977).

22. *Ibid.,* 111.

23. *Congressional Quarterly Weekly Report* (April 21, 1990), 1184–1188.

24. Paul J. Halpern, "Consumer Politics and Corporate Behavior: The Case of Automobile Safety" (unpublished Ph.D. dissertation, Harvard University, 1972).

25. Upton Sinclair, *The Jungle* (New York: Doubleday, Page and Co., 1906).

26. Mark V. Nadel, *The Politics of Consumer Protection* (Indianapolis, Ind.: Bobbs-Merrill, 1971), 143–144.

27. Alfred A. Marcus, *Promise and Performance: Choosing and Implementing an Environmental Policy* (Westport, Conn.: Greenwood Press, 1980).

28. Nadel, *op. cit.,* 66–80.
29. Martha Derthick and Paul J. Quirk, *The Politics of Deregulation* (Washington, D.C.: Brookings Institution, 1985).
30. Executive Orders 11821 (1974), 12044 (1978), and 12291 (1981).

Chapter 16 *Economic Policy*

1. Edward R. Tufte, *Political Control of the Economy* (Princeton, N.J.: Princeton University Press, 1978), 84; Douglas A. Hibbs, Jr., "The Mass Public and Macroeconomic Performance: The Dynamics of Public Opinion toward Unemployment and Inflation," *American Journal of Political Science* 23 (1979): 705–731.
2. D. Roderick Kiewiet, *Macroeconomics and Micropolitics: The Electoral Effect of Economic Issues* (Chicago: University of Chicago Press, 1983); Morris P. Fiorina, "Economic Retrospective Voting in American National Elections: A Micro-Analysis," *American Journal of Political Science* 22 (1978): 426–443; Donald R. Kinder and D. Roderick Kiewiet, "Sociotropic Politics: The American Case," *British Journal of Political Science* 11 (1981): 129–161.
3. *New York Times*—CBS News poll cited in Douglas A. Hibbs, Jr., "President Reagan's Mandate from the 1980 Elections: A Shift to the Right?" *American Politics Quarterly* 10 (1982): 387–420.
4. Hibbs, "The Mass Public . . . ," *op. cit.*
5. *Ibid.*
6. Kiewiet, *op. cit.*
7. Michael S. Lewis-Beck, "Comparative Economic Voting: Britain, France, Germany, Italy," *American Journal of Political Science* 30 (1986): 315–346.
8. Douglas A. Hibbs, Jr., "Political Parties and Macroeconomic Policy," *American Political Science Review* 71 (1977): 1467–1487.
9. Kiewiet, *op. cit.,* 69.
10. *Congressional Quarterly Weekly Report* (November 3, 1990), 3710–3717; *National Journal* (November 3, 1990), 2674.
11. Pollock v. Farmers' Loan & Trust Co., 157 U.S. 429, 158 U.S. 601 (1895).
12. NBC News/*Wall Street Journal* poll, as reported in *National Journal* (July 12, 1986), 1741.

Chapter 17 *Social Welfare*

1. For a general discussion see Charles E. Gilbert, "Welfare Policy," in *Handbook of Political Science,* ed. Fred I. Greenstein and Nelson W. Polsby (Reading, Mass.: Addison-Wesley, 1975), vol. 6, ch. 4.
2. Congressional Quarterly, *Congress and the Nation, 1945–1964* (Washington, D.C.: Congressional Quarterly Service, 1965), 1225.
3. Harold E. Raynes, *Social Security in Britain: A History* (London: Pitman, 1960), ch. 18. See also Hugh Heclo, *Modern Social Politics in Britain and Sweden* (New Haven: Yale University Press, 1974).
4. Histories of the 1935 act include Edwin E. Witte, *The Development of the Social Security Act*

(Madison: University of Wisconsin Press, 1962). A different view, offering a neo-Marxist interpretation of the act, can be found in Frances Fox Piven and Richard A. Cloward, *Regulating the Poor* (New York: Pantheon, 1971).
5. The development of the War on Poverty is told in Daniel Patrick Moynihan, *Maximum Feasible Misunderstanding* (New York: Free Press, 1969), and James Sundquist, *Politics and Policy* (Washington, D.C.: Brookings Institution, 1968).
6. Michael Harrington, *The Other America* (Baltimore, Md.: Penguin Books, 1962).
7. The Lampman work was given wide circulation in the government by the Joint Economic Committee of the U.S. Congress in the late 1950s.
8. The development of Medicare is described in Sundquist, *op. cit.,* and Theodore Marmor, "Doctors, Politics, and Health Insurance for the Aged: The Enactment of Medicare," in *Cases in Contemporary American Government,* ed. Allan Sindler (Boston: Little, Brown, 1969).
9. The development of FAP is the subject of several studies: Daniel Patrick Moynihan, *The Politics of a Guaranteed Income* (New York: Random House, 1973); Kenneth M. Bowler, *The Nixon Guaranteed Income Proposal* (Cambridge, Mass.: Ballinger, 1974); and Vincent J. Burke and Vee Burke, *Nixon's Good Deed—Welfare Reform* (New York: Columbia University Press, 1974).
10. Quoted in Bowler, *op. cit.,* 47.
11. Michael E. Schiltz, *Public Attitudes toward Social Security, 1935–1965,* Research Report No. 3, Social Security Administration, U.S. Department of Health, Education, and Welfare (Washington, D.C.: Government Printing Office, 1970), 36, 98, 128, 140.
12. Alicia H. Munnell, *The Future of Social Security* (Washington, D.C.: Brookings Institution, 1977), appendix.
13. Martha Derthick, "How Easy Votes on Social Security Came to an End," *Public Interest* (Winter 1979), 96.
14. Moynihan, *The Politics of a Guaranteed Annual Income, op. cit.,* 268–269.
15. Schiltz, *Public Attitudes Toward Social Security, op. cit.,* ch. 4, pp. 154–165.
16. Charles Murray, *Losing Ground: American Social Policy, 1950–1980* (New York: Basic Books, 1984). A critique of Murray is William J. Wilson, *The Truly Disadvantaged* (Chicago: University of Chicago Press, 1987), esp. chs. 3 and 4.
17. *Congressional Quarterly Weekly Report* (March 26, 1983), 596–600.
18. Congressional Quarterly, *Congress and the Nation,* Vol. VII, 1985–1988 (Washington, D.C.: Congressional Quarterly, 1990), 551.
19. Congressional Budget Office, *An Analysis of the Administration's Health Proposal* (February 8, 1994), xiii.
20. Julie Kosterlitz, "Family Fights," *National Journal* (June 2, 1990), 1333–1337.
21. G. J. Borjas, R. B. Freeman, and L. F. Katz, "Labor Market Effects of Immigration and Trade," in George J. Borjas and Richard B. Freeman, *Immigration and the Work Force* (Chicago: University of Chicago Press, 1992), 242–243.

Chapter 18 *Civil Liberties*

1. Zamora v. Pomeroy, 639 F. 2d 662 (1981); Goss v. Lopez, 419 U.S. 565 (1975); Tinker v. Des Moines Community School District, 393 U.S. 503 (1969); Smith v. Goguen, 415 U.S. 566 (1974); New Jersey v. T.L.O. 469 U.S. 325 (1985).
2. Sheppard v. Maxwell, 384 U.S. 333 (1966); New York Times Co. v. United States, 403 U.S. 713 (1971); and Kunz v. New York, 340 U.S. 290 (1951).
3. William Blackstone, *Commentaries,* vol. IV (1765), 151–152.
4. Jefferson's remarks are from a letter to Abigail Adams (quoted in Walter Berns, *The First Amendment and the Future of American Democracy* [New York: Basic Books, 1976], 82) and from a letter to Thomas McKean, governor of Pennsylvania, February 19, 1803 (Paul L. Ford, ed., *The Writings of Thomas Jefferson: 1801–1806,* vol. 8 [New York: Putnam, 1897], 218).
5. Schenck v. United States, 249 U.S. 47 (1919), 52.
6. Gitlow v. New York, 268 U.S. 652 (1925), 666.
7. Fiske v. Kansas, 274 U.S. 380 (1927); Stromberg v. California, 283 U.S. 359 (1931); Near v. Minnesota, 283 U.S. 697 (1931); De Jonge v. Oregon, 299 U.S. 353 (1937).
8. Dennis v. United States, 341 U.S. 494 (1951), 510ff. The test was first formulated by Judge Learned Hand of the Court of Appeals: see Dennis v. United States, 183 F.2d 201 (1950), 212.
9. Yates v. United States, 354 U.S. 298 (1957).
10. Brandenburg v. Ohio, 395 U.S. 444 (1969).
11. Village of Skokie v. National Socialist Party, 432 U.S. 43 (1977); 366 N.E.2d 349 (1977); and 373 N.E.2d 21 (1978).
12. R.A.V. v. City of St. Paul, 112 S. Ct. 2538 (1992).
13. Wisconsin v. Mitchell, No. 92–515 (1993).
14. C. Herman Pritchett, *Constitutional Civil Liberties* (Englewood Cliffs, N.J.: Prentice-Hall, 1984), 100.
15. *New York Times* v. Sullivan, 376 U.S. 254 (1964); but compare Time, Inc., v. Firestone, 424 U.S. 448 (1976).
16. Henry J. Abraham, *Freedom and the Court,* 4th ed. (New York: Oxford University Press, 1982), p. 193, fn 189.
17. Justice Stewart's famous remark was made in his concurring opinion in Jacobellis v. Ohio, 378 U.S. 184 (1964), 197.
18. Miller v. California, 413 U.S. 15 (1973).
19. Jenkins v. Georgia, 418 U.S. 153 (1974).
20. Schad v. Borough of Mt. Ephraim, 452 U.S. 61 (1981).
21. Barnes v. Glen Theatre, 111 S. Ct. 2456 (1991).
22. American Booksellers Association v. Hudnut, 771 F.2d 323 (1985), affirmed at 475 U.S. 1001 (1986).
23. Renton v. Playtime Theatres, 475 U.S. 41 (1986). See also Young v. American Mini-Theatres, Inc., 427 U.S. 50 (1976).
24. United States v. O'Brien, 391 U.S. 367 (1968).
25. Texas v. Johnson, 109 S. Ct. 2533 (1989).
26. The Court had earlier held unconstitutional statutes that made it illegal to mutilate the flag [Street v. New York, 394 U.S. 576 (1967)], deface the flag [Spence v. Washington, 418 U.S.

405 (1974)], or treat the flag contemptuously by, for example, sewing it to the seat of your pants [Smith v. Goguen, 415 U.S. 566 (1974)]. U.S. v. Eichman, 496 U.S. 310 (1990).

27. First National Bank of Boston v. Bellotti, 435 U.S. 765 (1978).

28. Federal Election Commission v. Massachusetts Citizens for Life, Inc., 479 U.S. 238 (1986).

29. Pacific Gas and Electric Co. v. Public Utilities Commission, 475 U.S. 1 (1986). Some limitations on corporate speech have been upheld, including a state law prohibiting a firm from spending money on candidates for elective office. Austin v. Michigan Chamber of Commerce, 100 S. Ct. 1391 (1990).

30. Board of Trustees of the State University of New York v. Fox, 492 U.S. 469 (1989).

31. Bates v. State Bar of Arizona, 433 U.S. 350 (1977); Edenfield v. Bane, 113 S. Ct. 1792 (1993).

32. Hazelwood School District v. Kuhlmeier, et al. 484 U.S. 260 (1988).

33. Murdock v. Pennsylvania, 319 U.S. 105 (1943).

34. Church of the Lukumi Babalu Aye v. City of Hialeah, No. 91–948 (1993).

35. Reynolds v. United States, 98 U.S. 145 (1878).

36. Jacobson v. Massachusetts, 197 U.S. 11 (1905).

37. Employment Division, Department of Human Resources of Oregon v. Smith, 110 S. Ct. 1595 (1990).

38. Society for Krishna Consciousness v. Lee, 112 S. Ct. 2701 (1992).

39. Welsh v. United States, 398 U.S. 333 (1970); Pritchett, *op. cit.*, 140–141.

40. Sherbert v. Verner, 374 U.S. 398 (1963); Wisconsin v. Yoder, 406 U.S. 205 (1972); Hobbie v. Unemployment Appeals Commission of Florida, 480 U.S. 136 (1987); Estate of Thornton v. Caldor, Inc., 472 U.S. 703 (1985).

41. Berns, *op. cit.*

42. Pritchett, *op. cit.*, 145–147.

43. Everson v. Board of Education, 330 U.S. 1 (1947).

44. Engel v. Vitale, 370 U.S. 421 (1962).

45. Lubbock Independent School District v. Lubbock Civil Liberties Union, 669 F.2d 1038.

46. School District of Abington Township v. Schempp, 374 U.S. 203 (1963).

47. Lee v. Weisman, 112 S. Ct. 2649 (1992).

48. Epperson v. Arkansas, 393 U.S. 97 (1968); McLean v. Arkansas Board of Education, 529 F. Supp. 1255 (1982).

49. McCollum v. Board of Education, 333 U.S. 203 (1948); Zorach v. Clauson, 343 U.S. 306 (1952).

50. Tilton v. Richardson, 403 U.S. 672 (1971).

51. Board of Education v. Allen, 392 U.S. 236 (1968).

52. Walz v. Tax Commission, 397 U.S. 664 (1970).

53. Mueller v. Allen, 463 U.S. 388 (1983).

54. Zobrest v. Catalina Foothills School District, No. 92–94 (1993).

55. Lemon v. Kurtzman, 403 U.S. 602 (1971).

56. Committee for Public Education v. Nyquist, 413 U.S. 756 (1973).

57. Meek v. Pittenger, 421 U.S. 349 (1975) and

Wolman v. Walter, 433 U.S. 229 (1977).

58. Edwards v. Aguillard, 482 U.S. 578 (1987).

59. Lemon v. Kurtzman, 403 U.S. 602 (1971).

60. Lynch v. Donnelly, 465 U.S. 668 (1984); Allegheny v. ACLU, 109 S. Ct. 3086 (1989).

61. Marsh v. Chambers, 492 U.S. 573 (1983).

62. Stephen R. Schlesinger, *Exclusionary Injustice: The Problem of Illegally Obtained Evidence* (New York: Dekker, 1975).

63. Yale Kamisar, "Does (Did) (Should) the Exclusionary Rule Rest on a 'Principled Basis' Rather Than an 'Empirical Proposition'?" *Creighton Law Review* 16 (1982–1983): 565–667.

64. Wolf v. Colorado, 338 U.S. 25 (1949).

65. Mapp v. Ohio, 367 U.S. 643 (1961).

66. Chimel v. California, 395 U.S. 752 (1969).

67. Washington v. Chrisman, 455 U.S. 1 (1982).

68. Oliver v. United States 466 U.S. 170 (1984).

69. Arkansas v. Sanders, 442 U.S. 753 (1979); Robbins v. California, 453 U.S. 420 (1981).

70. United States v. Ross, 456 U.S. 798 (1982).

71. Winston v. Lee, 470 U.S. 753 (1985).

72. South Dakota v. Neville, 459 U.S. 553 (1983); Schmerber v. California, 384 U.S. 757 (1966).

73. United States v. Dunn, 480 U.S. 294 (1987); California v. Ciraolo, 476 U.S. 207 (1986); California v. Carney, 471 U.S. 386 (1985).

74. O'Connor v. Ortega, 480 U.S. 709 (1987).

75. Bowers v. Hardwick, 478 U.S. 186 (1986).

76. National Treasury Employees Union v. von Rabb, 489 U.S. 656 (1989); Skinner v. Railway Labor Executives' Association, 489 U.S. 602 (1989); Michigan v. Sitz, 496 U.S. 444 (1990).

77. Escobedo v. Illinois, 378 U.S. 478 (1964); Miranda v. Arizona, 384 U.S. 436 (1966).

78. Malloy v. Hogan, 378 U.S. 1 (1964).

79. Miranda v. Arizona, 384 U.S. 436 (1966).

80. Gilbert v. California, 388 U.S. 263 (1967); Kirby v. Illinois, 406 U.S. 682 (1972).

81. Estelle v. Smith, 451 U.S. 454 (1981).

82. Brewer v. Williams, 430 U.S. 387 (1977).

83. Illinois v. Perkins, 496 U.S. 292 (1990).

84. Fare v. Michael C., 442 U.S. 707 (1979).

85. United States v. Leon, 468 U.S. 897 (1984); Massachusetts v. Sheppard, 468 U.S. 981 (1984).

86. New York v. Quarles, 467 U.S. 649 (1984). See also Arizona v. Fulminante, 111 S. Ct. 1246 (1991).

87. Nix v. Williams, 467 U.S. 431 (1984).

Chapter 19 *Civil Rights*

1. United States v. Carolene Products Co., 304 U.S. 144 (1938); San Antonio Independent School District v. Rodriguez, 411 U.S. 1 (1973).

2. Gunnar Myrdal, *An American Dilemma* (New York: Harper, 1944), ch. 27.

3. Richard Kluger, *Simple Justice* (New York: Random House/Vintage Books, 1977), 89–90.

4. Paul B. Sheatsley, "White Attitudes toward the Negro," in *The Negro American,* ed. Talcott Parsons and Kenneth B. Clark (Boston: Houghton Mifflin, 1966), 305, 308, 317.

5. Strauder v. West Virginia, 100 U.S. 303 (1880).

6. Civil Rights Cases, 109 U.S. 3 (1883).

7. Plessy v. Ferguson, 163 U.S. 537 (1896).

8. Cumming v. Richmond County Board of Education, 175 U.S. 528 (1899).

9. Missouri *ex rel.* Gaines v. Canada, 305 U.S. 337 (1938).

10. Sipuel v. Board of Regents of the University of Oklahoma, 332 U.S. 631 (1948).

11. Sweatt v. Painter, 339 U.S. 629 (1950); McLaurin v. Oklahoma State Regents for Higher Education, 339 U.S. 637 (1950).

12. Brown v. Board of Education of Topeka, 347 U.S. 483 (1954).

13. Brown v. Board of Education of Topeka, 349 U.S. 294 (1955). This case is often referred to as "Brown II."

14. Frederick S. Mosteller and Daniel P. Moynihan, eds., *On Equality of Educational Opportunity* (New York: Random House, 1972), 60–62.

15. Brown v. Board of Education of Topeka, 347 U.S. 483 (1954).

16. C. Herman Pritchett, *Constitutional Civil Liberties* (Englewood Cliffs, N.J.: Prentice-Hall, 1984), 250–251, 261.

17. Green *et al.* v. County School Board of New Kent County, 391 U.S. 430 (1968).

18. Swann v. Charlotte-Mecklenburg Board of Education, 402 U.S. 1 (1971).

19. Busing *within* the central city was upheld in Armour v. Nix, 446 U.S. 930 (1980); Keyes v. School District No. 1, Denver, 413 U.S. 189 (1973); Milliken v. Bradley, 418 U.S. 717 (1974); Board of School Commissioners of Indianapolis v. Buckley, 429 U.S. 1068 (1977); and School Board of Richmond v. State Board of Education, 412 U.S. 92 (1972). Busing *across* city lines was upheld in Evans v. Buchanan, 423 U.S. 963 (1975), and Board of Education v. Newburg Area Council, 421 U.S. 931 (1975).

20. Pasadena City Board of Education v. Spangler, 427 U.S. 424 (1976).

21. See, for example, Herbert McClosky and John Zaller, *The American Ethos* (Cambridge, Mass.: Harvard University Press, 1984), 92, 100; and data reported in Chapter 5 of this text.

22. NES, *1952–1990 Cumulative Data File, 1992 NES Pre/Post Election Study* (1992).

23. Freeman v. Pitts, 112 S. Ct. 1430 (1992).

24. Robert S. Erikson and Norman R. Luttbeg, *American Public Opinion* (New York: Wiley, 1973), 49; and Hazel Erskine, "The Polls: Demonstrations and Race Riots," *Public Opinion Quarterly* 31 (Winter 1967–1968): 654–677.

25. Howard Schuman, Charlotte Steeh, and Lawrence Bobo, *Racial Attitudes in America* (Cambridge, Mass.: Harvard University Press, 1985), 69, 78–79.

26. *Ibid.*, 102, 110, 127–135.

27. Grove City College v. Bell, 465 U.S. 555 (1984).

28. Mueller v. Oregon, 208 U.S. 412 (1908).

29. Equal Pay Act of 1963; Civil Rights Act of 1964, Title VII, and 1978 amendments thereto; Education Amendments of 1972, Title IX.

30. Reed v. Reed, 404 U.S. 71 (1971).

31. Frontiero v. Richardson, 411 U.S. 677 (1973).

32. Stanton v. Stanton, 421 U.S. 7 (1975).

33. Craig v. Boren, 429 U.S. 190 (1976).

34. Dothard v. Rawlinson, 433 U.S. 321 (1977).

35. Cleveland Board of Education v. LaFleur, 414

U.S. 632 (1974).

36. Fortin v. Darlington Little League, 514 F.2d 344 (1975).

37. Roberts v. United States Jaycees, 468 U.S. 609 (1984); and Board of Directors of Rotary International v. Rotary Club of Duarte, 481 U.S. 537 (1987).

38. Arizona Governing Committee for Tax Deferred Annuity and Deferred Compensation Plans v. Norris, 463 U.S. 1073 (1983).

39. E.E.O.C. v. Madison Community Unit School District No. 12, 818 F.2d 577 (1987).

40. Michael M. v. Superior Court, 450 U.S. 464 (1981).

41. Vorchheimer v. School District of Philadelphia, 430 U.S. 703 (1977).

42. Kahn v. Shevin, 416 U.S. 351 (1974).

43. Schlesinger v. Ballard, 419 U.S. 498 (1975).

44. Bennett v. Dyer's Chop House, 350 F. Supp. 153 (1972); Morris v. Michigan State Board of Education, 472 F.2d 1207 (1973); Fitzgerald v. Porter Memorial Hospital, 523 F.2d 716 (1975); Kruzel v. Podell, 226 N.W.2d 458 1975).

45. Rostker v. Goldberg, 453 U.S. 57 (1981).

46. Roe v. Wade, 410 U.S. 113 (1973).

47. Harris v. McRae, 448 U.S. 297 (1980); Beal v. Doe, 432 U.S. 438 (1977); Maher v. Roe, 432 U.S. 464 (1977).

48. Planned Parenthood Federation of Central Missouri v. Danforth, 428 U.S. 52 (1976); Bellotti v. Baird, 443 U.S. 622 (1979); Akron v. Akron Center for Reproductive Health, 462 U.S. 416 (1983); Thornburgh v. American College of Obstetricians and Gynecologists, 476 U.S. 747 (1986). But compare with Planned Parenthood Association of Kansas City v. Ashcroft, 462 U.S. 476 (1983).

49. Planned Parenthood v. Casey, 112 S. Ct. 2791 (1992).

50. *Statistical Abstract of the United States, 1992* (Washington, D.C.: Government Printing Office, 1987), 374, 388.

51. California Federal Savings and Loan Association v. Guerra, 479 U.S. 272 (1987).

52. John R. Bunzel, "To Each According to Her Worth?" *Public Interest,* no. 67 (Spring 1982): 77–93.

53. Regents of the University of California v. Bakke, 438 U.S. 265 (1978).

54. Fullilove v. Klutznick, 448 U.S. 448 (1980).

55. City of Richmond v. J.A. Croson Co., 488 U.S. 469 (1989).

56. Metro Broadcasting v. FCC, 497 U.S. 547 (1990).

57. Northeastern Florida Contractors v. Jacksonville, 91–1721 (1993).

58. Firefighters Local Union No. 1784 v. Stotts, 467 U.S. 561 (1984); Wygant v. Jackson Board of Education, 476 U.S. 267 (1986); City of Richmond v. J.A. Croson Co., 488 U.S. 469 (1989).

59. Local No. 28 of the Sheet Metal Workers' International Association v. Equal Employment Opportunity Commission, 478 U.S. 421 (1986); Wards Cove Packing Co. v. Atonio, 490 U.S. 642 (1989); Price Waterhouse v. Hopkins, 490 U.S. 228 (1989). (Note: Wards Cove and Price were both superseded in part by the Civil Rights Act of 1991, as discussed in the text of memo above.)

60. Fullilove v. Klutznick, 448 U.S. 448 (1980); Metro Broadcasting v. FCC, 497 U.S. 547 (1990).

61. United Steelworkers of America v. Weber, 443 U.S. 193 (1979); Johnson v. Santa Clara County Transportation Agency, 480 U.S. 616 (1987).

62. Wygant v. Jackson Board of Education, 476 U.S. 267 (1986); U.S. v. Paradise, 480 U.S. 149 (1987).

63. Seymour Martin Lipset and William Schneider, "An Emerging National Consensus," *The New Republic* (October 15, 1977), 8–9.

64. Poll data cited in John R. Bunzel, "Affirmative Re-Actions," *Public Opinion* (February–March 1986), 45–49.

Chapter 20 *Foreign Policy*

1. Alexis de Tocqueville, *Democracy in America,* vol. 1, ed. Phillips Bradley (New York: Knopf, 1951), 235.

2. Richard Lau, Thad A. Brown, and David O. Sears, "Self-Interest and Civilians' Attitudes toward the Vietnam War," *Public Opinion Quarterly* 42 (1978): 464–481.

3. Edward S. Corwin, *The President: Office and Powers* (New York: New York University Press, 1940), 200.

4. Louis Henkin, *Foreign Affairs and the Constitution* (New York: Norton, 1972), 53, 306 n 43.

5. Louis W. Koenig, *The Chief Executive,* 3d ed. (New York: Harcourt Brace Jovanovich, 1975), 217.

6. Louis Fisher, *President and Congress* (New York: Free Press, 1972), 45; United States v. Belmont, 301 U.S. 324 (1937).

7. Aaron Wildavsky, "The Two Presidencies," in *The Presidency,* ed. Wildavsky (Boston: Little, Brown, 1969), 231.

8. Bernard E. Brown, "The Decision to End the Algerian War," in *Cases in Comparative Politics,* ed. James B. Christoph (Boston: Little, Brown, 1965), 154–180; Roy C. Macridis, "De Gaulle and NATO," in *Modern European Governments,* ed. Macridis (Englewood Cliffs, N.J.: Prentice-Hall, 1968), 92–115; and Schwartz and Shaw, *op. cit.,* 235–236.

9. Peter G. Richards, *Parliament and Foreign Affairs* (London: George Allen & Unwin, 1967), 37–38; and John E. Schwartz and L. Earl Shaw, *The United States Congress in Comparative Perspective* (Hinsdale, Ill.: Dryden Press, 1976), 235.

10. Loch Johnson and James M. McCormick, "The Making of International Agreements: A Reappraisal of Congressional Involvement," *Journal of Politics* 40 (1978): 468–478.

11. Arthur M. Schlesinger, Jr., *A Thousand Days: John F. Kennedy in the White House* (Boston: Houghton Mifflin, 1965), chs. 30, 31. Schlesinger, at p. 841, described Kennedy's actions as a "brilliantly controlled," "matchlessly calibrated" combination of "nerve and wisdom." His view of Nixon's actions was a good deal less charitable in *The Imperial Presidency* (Boston: Houghton Mifflin, 1974), ch. 7.

12. United States v. Curtiss-Wright Export Co., 299 U.S. 304 (1936).

13. Mitchell v. Laird, 488 F.2d 611 (1973).

14. Prize Cases, 67 U.S. 635 (1863); Mora v. McNamara, 389 U.S. 934 (1964); Massachusetts v. Laird, 400 U.S. 886 (1970).

15. Dames and Moore v. Regan, 435 U.S. 654 (1981).

16. Korematsu v. United States, 323 U.S. 214 (1944).

17. Youngstown Sheet & Tube Co. v. Sawyer, 343 U.S. 579 (1952).

18. Immigration and Naturalization Service v. Chadha, 103 S. Ct. 2764 (1983).

19. Robert S. Erikson and Norman R. Luttbeg, *American Public Opinion* (New York: Wiley, 1973), 50–51.

20. William R. Caspary, "The `Mood Theory': A Study of Public Opinion and Foreign Policy," *American Political Science Review* 64 (June 1970): 536–547.

21. Erikson and Luttbeg, *op. cit.,* 52.

22. John E. Mueller, *War, Presidents, and Public Opinion* (New York: Wiley, 1973), 110.

23. *Ibid.,* 112.

24. Milton J. Rosenberg, Sidney Verba, and Philip E. Converse, *Vietnam and the Silent Majority* (New York: Harper & Row, 1970), 26–27.

25. Erikson and Luttbeg, *op. cit.,* 155.

26. Mueller, *op. cit.,* ch. 9.

27. *Ibid.,* 169.

28. *Ibid.,* 45–47.

29. *Ibid.,* 54–56.

30. ABC–*Washington Post* poll as cited in *National Journal* (July 28, 1984), 1450.

31. Howard Schuman, "Two Sources of Antiwar Sentiment in America," *American Journal of Sociology* 78 (1973): 513–536.

32. *Ibid.*

33. Philip E. Converse, Warren E. Miller, Jerrold G. Rusk, and Arthur C. Wolfe, "Continuity and Change in American Politics: Parties and Issues in the 1968 Election," *American Political Science Review* 63 (December 1969): 1083–1105; and John P. Robinson, "Public Reaction to Political Protest: Chicago, 1968," *Public Opinion Quarterly* 34 (Spring 1970): 1–9.

34. Chicago Council on Foreign Relations, *American Public Opinion and U.S. Foreign Policy, 1983* (Chicago: Council on Foreign Relations, 1983), 13, 25, 37.

35. X, "The Sources of Soviet Conduct," *Foreign Affairs* 25 (July 1947): 566.

36. Walter Lippmann, *The Cold War* (New York: Harper Brothers, 1947).

37. Erikson and Luttbeg, *op. cit.,* 52.

38. Mueller, *op. cit.,* 40.

39. Michael Roskin, "From Pearl Harbor to Vietnam: Shifting Generational Paradigms and Foreign Policy," *Political Science Quarterly* 89 (Fall 1974): 567.

40. Frank L. Klingberg, "The Historical Alternation of Moods in American Foreign Policy," *World Politics* 4 (1952): 239–273.

41. Roskin, *op. cit.,* 567.

42. *American Public Opinion and U.S. Foreign Policy, 1987* (Chicago: Chicago Council on Foreign Relations, 1987), 33.

Chapter 21   *Military Policy*

1. Stanley Lieberson, "An Empirical Study of Military-Industrial Linkages," in *Testing the Theory of the Military Industrial Complex,* ed. Steven Rosen (Lexington, Mass.: D. C. Heath/Lexington Books, 1973), 74.

2. Arnold Kanter, "Congress and the Defense Budget: 1960–1970," *American Political Science Review* 66 (1972): 129–143.

3. *National Journal* (March 8, 1986), 580.

4. Robert J. Art, "Why We Overspend and Underaccomplish: Weapons Procurement and the Military-Industrial Complex," in Rosen, *op. cit.,* 249.

5. Quoted in Robert J. Art, *The TFX Decision: McNamara and the Military* (Boston: Little, Brown, 1968), 126.

6. Bill Keller, "Competition: A Pentagon Battlefield," *New York Times* (May 12, 1985), section 3, p. 1.

7. James Fairhall, "The Case for the $435 Hammer," *Washington Monthly* (January 1987), 50.

8. Harry Summers, "Nuts, Bolts, & Death," *Washington Monthly* (January 1987), 51–52.

9. David C. Morrison, "Chaos on Capitol Hill," *National Journal* (September 27, 1986), 2302–2307.

Chapter 22   *Environmental Policy*

1. Alexander W. Astin, et al., *The American Freshman: National Norms for 1989* (Los Angeles: UCLA Graduate School of Education, 1989), 89.

2. On the greenhouse effect, see Philip D. Jones and Tom L. Wigley, "Global Warming Trends," *Scientific American* (August 1990), 84–91; Gordon J. MacDonald, "Scientific Basis for the Greenhouse Effect," *Journal of Policy Analysis and Management* 7 (1988): 425–444; S. Fred Singer, *Global Warming: Do We Know Enough to Act?* Paper 104, Center for the Study of American Business, Washington University (March 1991).

3. David Vogel, *National Styles of Regulation* (Ithaca, N.Y.: Cornell University Press, 1986), 19–30.

4. Alfred Marcus, *Promise and Performance: Choosing and Implementing an Environmental Policy* (Westport, Conn.: Greenwood Press, 1980), ch. 2; Charles O. Jones, *Clean Air* (Pittsburgh, Penn.: University of Pittsburgh Press, 1975).

5. David Vogel, *Fluctuating Fortunes: The Political Power of American Business* (New York: Basic Books, 1989), 65.

6. R. Shep Melnick, *Regulation and the Courts: The Case of the Clean Air Act* (Washington, D.C.: Brookings Institution, 1983), ch. 9.

7. Pietro S. Nivola, *The Politics of Energy Conservation* (Washington, D.C.: Brookings Institution, 1986), 11–12, 244–247.

8. Robert W. Crandall, "Pollution, Environmentalists, and the Coal Lobby," in Roger G. Noll and Bruce M. Own, eds., *The Political Economy of Deregulation* (Washington, D.C.: American Enterprise Institute, 1983), 84–96; and Crandall, *Controlling Industrial Pollution* (Washington, D.C.: Brookings Institution, 1983).

9. Bruce A. Ackerman and William T. Hassler, *Clear Coal/Dirty Air* (New Haven, Conn.: Yale University Press, 1981).

10. Meier, *op. cit.,* 159.

11. Robert Dorfman, "Lessons of Pesticide Regulation," in Wesley A. Magat, ed., *Reform of Environmental Regulation* (Cambridge, Mass.: Ballinger, 1982), 13–30.

12. *Congressional Quarterly Weekly Report* (January 12, 1990), 166–170.

13. R. Shep Melnick, "Deadlines, Cynicism, and Common Sense," *The Brookings Review* (Fall 1983), 21–24.

14. Meier, *op. cit.,* 156–157.

Chapter 23   *Who Governs?*

1. Anthony King, "The American Polity in the Late 1970s: Building Coalitions in the Sand," in *The New American Political System,* ed. King (Washington, D.C.: American Enterprise Institute, 1978), 391; and James Q. Wilson, "American Politics, Then and Now," *Commentary* (February 1979), 39–46.

Chapter 24   *To What Ends?*

1. Alexis de Tocqueville, *Democracy in America,* ed. Phillips Bradley (New York: Knopf, 1951), vol. 2, book 2, ch. 1.

Chapter 25   *State and Local Government*

1. Garcia v. San Antonio Metropolitan Transit Authority, 105 S. Ct. 1005.

2. *Book of the States, 1984–1985* (Lexington, Ky.: Council of State Governments, 1985), 221.

3. Beryl E. Pettus and Randall W. Bland, *Texas Government Today* (Homewood, Ill.: Dorsey Press, 1979).

4. John F. Dillon, *Commentaries on the Law of Municipal Corporation,* 5th ed. (Boston: Little, Brown, 1911), vol. 1, sec. 237.

5. Thad L. Beyle, "Governors," in *Politics in the American States,* 4th ed., ed. Virginia Gray, Herbert Jacob, and Kenneth N. Vines (Boston: Little, Brown, 1983), 202.

6. Samuel C. Patterson, "Legislators and Legislatures in the American States," in Gray, Jacob, and Vines, *op. cit.,* 141.

7. Patterson, *op. cit.,* 142.

8. Richard J. Tobin and Edward Keynes, "Institutional Differences in the Recruitment Process: A Four-State Study," *American Journal of Political Science* 19 (1975): 671–676, quoted in Patterson, *op. cit.,* 144.

9. John E. Chubb, "Institutions, the Economy, and the Dynamics of State Elections," Brookings Discussion Paper no. 7 (Washington, D.C.: Brookings Institution, 1986).

10. Patterson, *op. cit.,* 148–149, 153.

11. Paul T. David and Ralph Eisenbergh, *Devaluation of the Urban and Suburban Vote* (Charlottesville, Va.: University of Virginia Bureau of Public Administration, 1961), 8, cited in Thomas R. Dye, *Politics in States and Communities* (Englewood Cliffs, N.J.: Prentice-Hall, 1969), 122.

12. 377 U.S. 533 (1964).

13. Timothy G. O'Rourke, *The Impact of Reapportionment* (New Brunswick, N.J.: Transaction Books, 1980), ch. 7.

14. Patterson, *op. cit.,* 145.

15. Morris Fiorina, *Divided Government* (New York: Macmillan, 1992); Fiorina, "Divided Government in the American States," paper presented to the Midwestern Political Science Association (March 1993); Alan Ehrenhalt, *The United States of Ambition: Politicians, Power, and the Pursuit of Office* (New York: Random House/Times Books, 1991).

16. Quoted in Patterson, *op. cit.,* 161.

17. Quoted in Alan Rosenthal, *Legislative Life: People, Process, and Performance in the States* (New York: Harper & Row, 1981), 168.

18. Sarah McCally Morehouse, *State Politics, Parties and Policy* (New York: Holt, Rinehart and Winston, 1981), 295.

19. Adapted from Herbert Jacob, "Courts," in Gray, Jacob, and Vines, *op. cit.,* 238.

20. Rosenthal, *op. cit.,* 112–113.

21. Larry Sabato, *Goodbye to Good-Time Charlie: The American Governorship Transformed,* 2d ed. (Washington, D.C.: Congressional Quarterly Press, 1983), 108–109; Beyle, *op. cit.,* 215.

22. Virginia Gray, "Politics and Policy in the American States," in Gray, Jacob, and Vines, *op. cit.,* ch. 1.

23. Donald B. Rosenthal and Robert L. Crain, "City Government and Fluoridation," in *City Politics and Public Policy,* ed. James Q. Wilson (New York: Wiley, 1968).

24. James Q. Wilson, *Varieties of Police Behavior* (Cambridge, Mass.: Harvard University Press, 1968), 257–277.

25. Perez v. United States, 404 U.S. 146 (1971).

Photograph Credits

Illustrations other than political cartoons by Patrice Rossi, Rossi & Associates. Maps by Maryland Carto-Graphics, Inc. Politically Speaking cartoons by Peter Wallace. Background photograph on all part and chapter pages by Robert Llewellyn.

Chapter 1

p. 2, John Elk III / Stock, Boston; p. 5, Rob Nelson / Picture Group; p. 6, David Burnett / Contact Press Images; p. 7, Randy Taylor / Sygma; p. 8, George A. Robinson / f/Stop Pictures, Inc.; p. 9, David Young-Wolff / PhotoEdit; p. 10 (left), The Granger Collection; (right), German Information Center; p. 12, Focus on Sports; p. 14 (top), Gilles Peress / Magnum; (bottom), Gary McCracken / Pensacola News Journal.

Chapter 2

p. 16, Norman R. Rowan / Stock, Boston; p. 18, Library of Congress; p. 19, Private Collection; p. 21 (right), Rare Books Division, New York Public Library, Astor, Lenox and Tilden Foundations; p. 22, Dennis Degnan / Uniphoto; p. 23, Free Library of Philadelphia; p. 24 (left), The Bettmann Archive; (right), American Antiquarian Society; p. 25 (top left), Library of Congress; (top center), U.S. Government Printing Office; (top right), Bowdoin College Museum of Art, Brunswick, Maine. Bequest of the Honorable James Bowdoin III; (bottom left), Library of Congress; (bottom center), Harvard College Library; (bottom right), The New Jersey Bank; p. 26 (top left), Library of Congress; (bottom left), New York Historical Society; (center), American Antiquarian Society; (right), Library of Congress; p. 33, The Washington University Gallery of Art; p. 37, Chicago Historical Society; p. 38, © 1987 G. B. Trudeau. Reprinted with permission of Universal Press Syndicate. All rights reserved; p. 39 (left), The Bostonian Society; (right), National Collection of Fine Arts, Smithsonian Institution; p. 43, Gary Brookins, Richmond Times-Dispatch; p. 45, Seth Resnick / Stock, Boston.

Chapter 3

p. 48, John Eascott / Yva Momatiuk / The Image Works; p. 51, Rhoda Sidney / The Image Works; p. 52 (left), The Granger Collection; (right), Bob Daemmrich / The Image Works; p. 55, Bowdoin College Museum of Art, Brunswick, Maine. Bequest of the Honorable James Bowdoin III; p. 58, The Granger Collection; p. 60, Office of Public Information, University of California, Berkeley; p. 64, Rick Friedman / The Picture Group; p. 69, Marion Bernstein; p. 70 (left), J. P. Laffont / Sygma; (right), Christopher Little / Outline Press; p. 73, Alon Reininger / Contact Press Images.

Chapter 4

p. 78, Joe Sohm / The Image Works; p. 80, The Granger Collection; p. 81, (left), Charles Harbutt / Magnum; (center), Jim McHugh / Sygma; (right), Sylvia Johnson / Woodfin Camp & Associates; p. 82, The Bettmann Archive; p. 83, UPI / Bettmann Newsphotos; p. 86, Les Stone / Sygma; p. 89, Alan Oddie / PhotoEdit; p. 91 (top), State Historical Society of Wisconsin, Neg. no. R20345; (bottom left), M. Hayman / Photo Researchers, Inc.; (bottom right), Alan Carey / The Image Works; p. 92, Claudio Edinger / Liaison International; p. 94, Kenneth Jarecke / Contact Press Images; p. 95 (left), Jean-Claude Lejeune; (right), Charles Gatewood / Magnum; p. 96, UPI / Bettmann Newsphotos; p. 97, Richard Levine.

Chapter 5

p. 102, Bob Daemmrich / Stock, Boston; p. 104, J. Toppling / Liaison International; p. 107, Drawing by Richter; © 1991 The New Yorker Magazine, Inc.; p. 108, John Emmons / Photoreporters; p. 115, © 1980 G. B. Trudeau. Reprinted with permission of Universal Press Syndicate. All rights reserved; p. 116, Bob Daemmrich Photos; p. 119, J. Sohm / The Image Works; p. 124, Judy G. Rolfe / Uniphoto; p. 125 (left), Allan Tannenbaum / Sygma; (right), Misha Erwitt / Magnum; p. 126, Tony Savino / Sygma; p. 128, Mark Reinstein / Uniphoto.

Chapter 6

p. 130, Peter Southwick / Stock, Boston; p. 133, Washington Secretary of State; p. 134, Abby Aldrich Rockefeller Folk Art Center, Williamsburg, Virginia; p. 135 (left), The Granger Collection; p. 137, Library of Congress; p. 139, Roger Maass / SIPA; p. 142, The Granger Collection; p. 143, The League of Women Voters; p. 144, Bob Daemmrich / Stock, Boston; p. 145, Bruce Kliewe / The Picture Cube.

Chapter 7

p. 150, Martin Simon / Saba Press; p. 153, Paul Conklin; p. 154, Peter Menzel / Stock, Boston; p. 156, Tennessee State Library and Archives; p. 158, Burt Glinn / Magnum; p. 159, UPI / Bettmann Newsphotos; p. 160, Jesse Nemorofsky / Photoreporters; p. 161 (left), AP / Wide World Photos; (right), The Bettmann Archive; p. 162, Robert John Mihovil / Photoreporters; p. 163, Library of Congress; p. 166, By permission of Houghton Library, Harvard University; p. 168, Photo Courtesy of CBN; p. 169 (left), Mike Greenlar / The Image Works; (right), James Colburn / Photoreporters; p. 170, Henri Dauman / Magnum; p. 172, Bruno Barbey / Magnum; p. 173, Bill Schorr / Reprinted by permission of UFS, Inc.; p. 176 (top), Library of Congress; (bottom), The Bettmann Archive.

Chapter 8

p. 182, Charles Gupton / Stock, Boston; p. 186 (both), Smithsonian Institution, Division of Political History; p. 188, Steve Liss / Liaison International; p. 189, Diego Goldberg / Sygma; p. 190, State of Wisconsin Elections Board; p. 191, Library of Congress; p. 192 (top), The Bettmann Archive; (bottom left), UPI / Bettmann Newsphotos; (bottom right), Joe Sohm / Uniphoto; p. 193, National Broadcasting Company; p. 194, Steve Lehman / Saba Press; p. 204, Michael Newman / PhotoEdit; p. 206, Shepard Sherbell / Saba Press; p. 207, Michael Evans / Sygma; p. 208, Bob Daemmrish / The Image Works; p. 213 (left), The Granger Collection; (right), Historical Pictures Service; p. 214, UPI / Bettmann Newsphotos; p. 215 (top), Indiana State Election Board; (bottom) Commonwealth of Massachusetts Secretary of State; p. 217, Reed Saxon / Wide World.

Chapter 9

p. 220, Bob Daemmrich / The Image Works; p. 223 (both), Michael Schumann / Saba Press; p. 224 (top), Historical Pictures Service; (bottom), Terry Ashe / Uniphoto; p. 227, Michael Newman / PhotoEdit; p. 228, Barry Staver; p. 238 (top), J. P. Laffont / Sygma; (bottom), Bob Daemmrich / Stock, Boston; p. 240, John Ficara / Sygma; p. 241, Paul Conklin; p. 246, Courtesy National Education Association; p. 248, Bruce Allen / Photoreporters; p. 249, Rick Smolan / Stock, Boston.

Chapter 10

p. 252, Colburn / Photoreporters; p. 254, Dirck Halstead / Liaison International; p. 255, By permission of Houghton Library, Harvard University; p. 258, University Microfilms International, Ann Arbor; p. 260 (left), UPI / Bettmann Newsphotos; (right), Paul S. Conklin / Uniphoto; p. 261, Bob Daemmrich / Stock, Boston; p. 262, Lyndon Baines Johnson Library; p. 265, J. Patrick Forden / Sygma; p. 266, Molly Lynch / WCVB TV; p. 269, UPI / Bettmann Newsphotos; p. 271 (top), Brown Brothers; (bottom), Les Stone / Sygma; p. 275, Terry Ashe / Uniphoto; p. 276, William Johnson / Stock, Boston.

Chapter 11

p. 282, Mark Reinstein / The Image Works; p. 284, Kathy McLaughlin / The Image Works; p. 287, Library of Congress; p. 288 (left), Library of Congress; (center), Library of Congress; (right), AP / Wide World Photos; p. 290, New York Public Library / Astor, Lenox and Tilden Foundations; p. 292, James Colburn / Photoreporters; p. 295, R. Michael Jenkins / Congressional Quarterly; p. 296, The Bettmann Archive; p. 299, UPI / Bettmann Newsphotos; p. 302 (left), House of Representatives Majority Whip's Office; (right), Mark Reinstein / Uniphoto; p. 305 (left), James Colburn / Photoreporters; (right); Cynthia Johnson / Liaison International; p. 307, © Wayne Stayskal, Tampa Tribune; p. 309, Terry Ashe / Liaison International; p. 317, House of Representatives Clerk's Office; p. 318, James Colburn / Photoreporters; p. 319, House of Representatives Majority

Whip's Office; p. 323 *(both)*, Keith Jewell / U.S. House of Representatives; p. 329, © 1994 National Forum, Inc. All rights reserved. By Chas Fagan; p. 334, Mark Cullum / Birmingham News.

Chapter 12

p. 342, David Burnett / Contact Press Images; p. 345, UPP / Photoreporters; p. 347, The Bettmann Archive; p. 349 *(top)*, Noel-Figaro / Liaison International; *(center)*, Library of Congress; *(bottom)*, AP / Wide World Photos; p. 352, The Granger Collection; p. 355, Wally McNamee / Woodfin Camp & Associates; p. 358 *(top)*, AP / Wide World Photos; *(bottom)*, White House Photo Office; p. 363 *(left)*, Franklin D. Roosevelt Library; *(right)*, Lyndon Baines Johnson Library; p. 367 *(left)*, Wally McNamee / Washington Post; *(right)*, UPI / Bettmann Newsphotos; p. 374, Fred Maroon / Louis Mercier; p. 376 *(left)*, The Granger Collection; p. 381, Michael Evans / The White House; p. 381, Historical Pictures, Inc.

Chapter 13

p. 386, Bob Daemmrich / Stock, Boston; p. 391 *(left)*, Smithsonian Institution; *(right)*, Mark Mangold / Bureau of the Census; p. 397, Jeff MacNelly. Reprinted by permission: Tribune Media Services; p. 401, Frank & Ernest reprinted by permission of NEA, Inc.; p. 404 *(left)*, National Archives; *(right)*, National Portrait Gallery, Smithsonian Institution. Transfer from the National Gallery of Art, Gift of Andrew Mellon, 1942; p. 407, Paul Conklin; p. 410, Rick Brown / Stock, Boston; p. 413, James Colburn / Photoreporters.

Chapter 14

p. 416, Robert C. Shafer / Uniphoto; p. 418, Wally McNamee / Woodfin Camp & Associates; p. 420 *(top)*, National Portrait Gallery / Smithsonian Institution; *(bottom)*, Library of Congress; p. 421 *(left)*, Library of Congress; *(center)*, The Granger Collection; *(right)*, New-York Historical Society; p. 423, The Bettmann Archive; p. 428 *(left)*, Wally McNamee / Woodfin Camp & Associates; *(right)*, Terry Ashe / Liaison International; p. 431 *(left)*, National Archives; *(right)*, Flip Schulke / Life Magazine © 1964, Time, Inc.; p. 433, Carl Iwasaki / Life Magazine © 1954, Time, Inc.; p. 435, Erich Solomon / Magnum; p. 436, Ken Heinen; p. 440, Alex Webb / Magnum; p. 442, Tank McNamara © 1978 / Universal Press Syndicate; p. 444 *(left)*, Brown Brothers; *(right)*, UPI / Bettmann Newsphotos; p. 445, Owen Franken / Stock, Boston.

Chapter 15

p. 450, James Colburn / Photoreporters; p. 453, Peter Menzel / Stock, Boston; p. 455, Lyndon Baines Johnson Library; p. 456, Mark Antman / The Image Works; p. 458, Brown Brothers; p. 461, James Finley / Liaison International; p. 462, Ken Rogers / Black Star; p. 465, Susan McCartney / Photo Researchers, Inc.; p. 467 *(left)*, The Bettmann Archive; *(right)*, Brown Brothers; p. 468, Jeffrey D. Smith / Woodfin Camp & Associates; p. 470, AP / Wide World Photos.

Chapter 16

p. 474, Jim Pickerell / Stock, Boston; p. 477, © Alon Reininger / Contact Press Images; p. 479 *(from left to right)*, UPI / Bettmann Newsphotos; Karen Vismara / Black Star; UPI / Bettmann Newsphotos; Tony Korody / Sygma; p. 480, Tom McHugh / Photo Researchers, Inc.; p. 481 *(clockwise from top)*, Mark Reinstein / Uniphoto; James Colburn / Photoreporters; Jeffrey Markowitz / Sygma; Larry Downing / Sygma; Mark Reinstein / Uniphoto; p. 484, Terry Ashe / Uniphoto; p. 490; March Nighswander / Wide World; p. 493, Jeff MacNelly. Reprinted by permission, Tribune Media Services; p. 496, Jeff MacNelly. Reprinted by permission, Tribune Media Services.

Chapter 17

p. 498, Wernher Krutein / Liaison International; p. 501, Yoichi Okamoto / Lyndon Baines Johnson Library; p. 502, UPI / Bettmann Newsphotos; p. 503 *(left)*, UPI / Bettmann Newsphotos; *(right)*, AP / Wide World Photos; p. 505, AP / Wide World Photos; p. 508, Gwendolyn Stewart; p. 510, Kevin Horan / Picture Group; p. 513, Terry Ashe / Liaison International; p. 514, © Jimmy Margulies / The Record, New Jersey, Reprinted by permission.; p. 516, Kevin Horan / Picture Group; p. 518, Alon Reininger / Contact Press Images.

Chapter 18

p. 520, Bryce Flynn / Picture Group; p. 523, The Granger Collection; p. 527, Ellis Herwig / Stock, Boston; p. 528, The Bettmann Archive; p. 529, William Campbell / Sygma; p. 531, From In Opposition © 1968, Benedict Fernandez; p. 532, Les Stone / Sygma; p. 534, Owen Franken / Stock, Boston; p. 535, Max Winter / Stock, Boston; p. 536, Rob Nelson / Picture Group; p. 540, Doug Menuez / Picture Group; p. 542 *(inset)*, Ludd Keaton, Courtesy The Arizona Republic.

Chapter 19

p. 544, Rob Nelson / Black Star; p. 546, Julia E. Brody / Stock, Boston; p. 547, Library of Congress; p. 548, Yoichi Okamoto / Lyndon Baines Johnson Library; p. 549, Dennis Brack / Black Star; p. 550, By permission of Houghton Library, Harvard University; p. 551, By permission of Houghton Library, Harvard University; p. 552, UPI / Bettmann Newsphotos; p. 553, Steve Shapiro / Black Star; p. 554, Ted Crowell / Black Star; p. 556, AP / Wide World Photos; *(bottom left)*, UPI / Bettmann Newsphotos; *(bottom right)*, AP / Wide World Photos; p. 558, AP / Wide World Photos; p. 559 *(both)*, AP / Wide World Photos; p. 561, Peter Blakely / Picture Group; p. 562, Topham / The Image Works; p. 563 *(left)*, Smithsonian Institution, Division of Political History; *(right)*, Photoworld / FPG International; p. 564 *(left)*, UPI / Bettmann Newsphotos; *(right)*, AP / Wide World Photos; p. 567, David J. Sams / Stock, Boston; p. 568, J. P. Laffont / Sygma; p. 571, Rhoda Sidney / The Image Works.

Chapter 20

p. 576, Frank Fournier / Contact Press Images; p. 578 *(left)*, Gilles Peress / Magnum; *(right)*, Bert Miller / Black Star; p. 579, Bob Daemmrich / The Image Works; p. 580, Bill Gentile / Picture Group; p. 581, David Burnett / Black Star; p. 582, UPI / Bettmann Newsphotos; p. 583, UPI / Bettmann Newsphotos; p. 584, National Archives; p. 585, Bill Gentile / SIPA; p. 587, AP / Wide World Photos; p. 589, U.S. Navy; p. 591, Bryce Flynn / Picture Group; p. 592 *(top)*, Alexandra Avakian / Contact Press Images; *(bottom left)*, Burt Glinn / Magnum; *(bottom right)*, Paul Conklin; p. 594, John Chiasson / Liaison International; p. 596 *(top)*, Mark Corsey; *(bottom)*, Tony O'Brien / Picture Group; p. 597, The Bettmann Archive; p. 598 *(left)*, Henri Dauman / Magnum; *(right)*, Michael D. Sullivan / Black Star; p. 605, Art Zamur / Liaison International.

Chapter 21

p. 628, Don Jones / Liaison International; p. 610, Franco Zechim / Liaison International; p. 613, Department of Defense photo by Helene C. Stikkel; p. 616, Pierre Perrin / Liaison International; p. 617, Robert Llewellyn; p. 619 *(left)*, UPI / Bettmann Newsphotos; *(right)*, AP / Wide World Photos; p. 621, Lisa Quinones / Black Star; p. 622, Peter Silva / Picture Group.

Chapter 22

p. 628, Alan Odie / PhotoEdit; p. 630, John Lawlor / Tony Stone Images; p. 635, AP / Wide World Photos; p. 638, John Elk III / Stock, Boston; p. 640 *(top)*, Grant Heilman / Grant Heilman Photography; *(bottom)*, William Campbell / Sygma; p. 641, Bill Horsman / Stock, Boston; p. 642, Wally McNamee / Sygma; p. 643, Stephen Frisch / Stock, Boston.

Chapter 23

p. 646, Uniphoto; p. 649, AP / Wide World Photos; p. 653, Kevin Horan / Picture Group; p. 655, Susan Steinkamp / Picture Group; p. 658, Bob Daemmrich / The Image Works.

Chapter 24

p. 660, Matthew Borkoski / Stock, Boston; p. 663 *(top)*, Stacy Pick / Stock, Boston; *(bottom)*, Library of Congress; p. 664, Thomas Ames, Jr. / f/Stop Pictures; p. 665, Mike Ramirez / Copley News Service; p. 668, Tony O'Brien / Picture Group; p. 669, Mark Antman / The Image Works; p. 673, Alan Carey / The Image Works; p. 674, By permission of Mike Luckovich and Creators Syndicate.

Chapter 25

p. 676, Lisa Quinones / Black Star; p. 678, National Archives; p. 682, Pat Valenti / Tony Stone Images; p. 683, County of Sacramento Voter Registration and Elections; p. 686, Anders Krusberg / Photoreporters Inc., p. 687, AP / Wide World Photos; p. 688 *(top)*, Eli Reichman; *(bottom)*, AP / Wide World Photos; p. 695, California Legislature; p. 700 *(left)*, Mayor's Office, Jersey City, N.J.; *(right)*, Bart Bartholemew / Black Star; p. 702 *(left)*, Allan Tannenbaum / Sygma; *(right)*, Rick Friedman / Black Star; p. 706 *(left)*, Bob Daemmrich / The Image Works; *(right)*, Matthew Neal McVay / Stock, Boston.

Glossary

Acid rain   Precipitation in the form of rain, snow, or dust particles, the increased acidity of which is caused by environmental factors such as pollutants released into the atmosphere. (22)

Activist   An individual, usually outside of government, who actively promotes a political party, philosophy, or issue he or she cares about. (6)

Activist approach (judicial)   The view that judges should discern the general principles underlying the Constitution and its often vague language and assess how best to apply them in contemporary circumstances, in some cases with the guidance of moral or economic philosophy. (14)

Ad hoc structure   A method of organizing a president's staff in which several task forces, committees, and informal groups of friends and advisers deal directly with the president. (12)

Adversarial press   A national press that is suspicious of officialdom and eager to break an embarrassing story about a public official. (10)

Affirmative action   The requirement, imposed by law or administrative regulation, that an organization (business firm, government agency, labor union, school, or college) take positive steps to increase the number or proportion of women, blacks, or other minorities in its membership. (19)

Amateur legislature   A state legislature consisting of part-time representatives whose primary job is outside of government. *See also* Professional legislature (25)

Amendment (constitutional)   Change in, or addition to, a constitution. Amendments are proposed by a two-thirds vote of both houses of Congress or by a convention called by Congress at the request of two-thirds of the state legislatures and ratified by approval of three-fourths of the states. (2)

Amicus curiae   A Latin term meaning "a friend of the court." Refers to interested groups or individuals, not directly involved in a suit, who may file legal briefs or make oral arguments in support of one side. (14)

Annexation (city)   A policy of incorporating an area into an adjoining city. (25)

Annual authorizations   *See* Authorization legislation (13)

Antifederalists   Opponents of a strong central government who campaigned against ratification of the Constitution in favor of a confederation of largely independent states. Antifederalists successfully marshaled public support for a federal bill of rights. After ratification, they formed a political party to support states' rights. *See also* Federalists (2)

Appropriation   A legislative grant of money to finance a government program. *See also* Authorization (13)

Articles of Confederation   A constitution drafted by the newly independent states in 1777 and ratified in 1781. It created a weak national government that could not levy taxes or regulate commerce. In 1789 it was replaced by our current constitution in order to create a stronger national government. (2)

Assistance program   A government program financed by general income taxes that provides benefits to poor citizens without requiring contributions from them. (17)

Australian ballot   A government-printed ballot of uniform size and shape to be cast in secret that was adopted by many states around 1890 in order to reduce the voting fraud associated with party-printed ballots cast in public. (6)

Authority   The right to use power. (1)

Authorization legislation   Legislative permission to begin or continue a government program or agency. An authorization bill may grant permission to spend a certain sum of money, but that money does not ordinarily become available unless it is also appropriated. Authorizations may be annual, multiyear, or permanent. *See also* Appropriation (13)

Background story (news)   A public official's explanation of current policy provided to the press on the condition that the source remain anonymous. (10)

Benefit   Any satisfaction, monetary or nonmonetary, that people believe they will enjoy if a policy is adopted. *See also* Cost (15)

Bicameral legislature   A lawmaking body made up of two chambers or parts. The U.S. Congress is a bicameral legislature composed of a Senate and a House of Representatives. (11)

Bill of attainder   A law that declares a person, without a trial, to be guilty of a crime. The state legislatures and Congress are forbidden to pass such acts by Article I of the Constitution. (2)

Bill of Rights   The first ten amendments to the U.S. Constitution, containing a list of individual rights and liberties, such as freedom of speech, religion, and the press. (2)

Blanket primary   A primary election that permits all voters, regardless of party, to choose candidates. A Democratic voter, for example, can vote in a blanket primary for both Democratic and Republican candidates for nomination. (8)

Block grants   Grants of money from the federal government to states for programs in certain general areas rather than for specific kinds of programs. *See also* Grants-in-aid; Categorical grants (3)

Boycott   A concerted effort to get people to stop buying goods and services from a company or person in order to punish that company or to coerce its owner into changing policies. (15)

Brief   A legal document prepared by an attorney representing a party before a court. The document sets forth the facts of the case, summarizes the law, gives the arguments for its side, and discusses other relevant cases. (14)

Bubble standard   The total amount of air pollution that can come from a given factory. A company is free to decide which specific sources within that factory must be reduced and how to meet the bubble standard. (22)

Budget   A document that announces how much the government will collect in taxes and spend in revenues and how those expenditures will be allocated among various programs. (16)

Budget deficit A situation in which the government spends more money than it takes in from taxes and fees. (16)

Budget resolution A proposal submitted by the House and Senate budget committees to their respective chambers recommending a total budget ceiling and a ceiling for each of several spending areas (such as health or defense) for the current fiscal year. These budget resolutions are intended to guide the work of each legislative committee as it decides what to spend in its area. (16)

Budget surplus A situation in which the government takes in more money than it spends. (16)

Bureaucracy A large, complex organization composed of appointed officials. The departments and agencies of the U.S. government make up the federal bureaucracy. (13)

Bureaucratic theory (politics) A theory that appointed civil servants make the key governing decisions. (1)

Bureaucrats (government) The appointed officials who operate government agencies from day to day. (1)

Cabinet By custom, the cabinet includes the heads of the fourteen major executive departments. (12)

Categorical grants A federal grant for a specific purpose defined by federal law: to build an airport, for example, or to make welfare payments to low-income mothers. Such grants usually require that the state or locality put up money to "match" some part of the federal grant, though the amount of matching funds can be quite small. *See also* Grants-in-aid; Block grant (3)

Caucus (congressional) An association of members of Congress created to advocate a political ideology or a regional, ethnic, or economic interest. (11)

Caucus (nominating) An alternative to a state primary in which party followers meet, often for many hours, to select party candidates. (7)

Checks and balances The power of the legislative, executive, and judicial branches of government to block some acts by the other two branches. *See also* Separation of powers (2)

Christmas-tree bill *See* Riders (11)

Circular structure A method of organizing a president's staff in which several presidential assistants report directly to the president. (12)

City-county consolidation A policy of merging city and county governments into one. For example, the city and county of San Francisco are the same. (25)

Civic competence A belief that one can affect government policies. (4)

Civic duty A belief that one has an obligation to participate in civic and political affairs. (4)

Civil law The body of rules defining relationships among private citizens. It consists of both statutes and the accumulated customary law embodied in judicial decisions (the "common law"). *See also* Criminal law (14)

Civil rights The rights of citizens to vote, to receive equal treatment before the law, and to share equally with other citizens the benefits of public facilities (such as schools). (19)

Class consciousness An awareness of belonging to a particular socioeconomic class whose interests are different from those of others. Usually used in reference to workers who view their interests as opposite to those of managers and business owners. (4)

Class-action suit A case brought into court by a person on behalf of not only himself or herself but all other persons in the country under similar circumstances. For example, in *Brown* v. *Board of Education of Topeka, Kansas,* the Court decided that not only Linda Brown but all others similarly situated had the right to attend a local public school of their choice without regard to race. (14)

Clear-and-present danger test A legal interpretation that reconciled two views of the First Amendment right of free speech, the first that Congress could not pass any law to restrict speech and the second that it could punish harms caused by speech. Proposed by Supreme Court Justice Oliver Wendell Holmes in 1919, it held that Congress could only punish speech that created a "clear and present danger" of bringing about the actions that Congress is authorized to prevent. (18)

Client politics The politics of policy making in which some small group receives the benefits of the policy and the public at large bears the costs. Only those who benefit have an incentive to organize and press their case. (15)

Closed primary A primary election limited to registered party members. Prevents members of other parties from crossing over to influence the nomination of an opposing party's candidate. *See also* Open primary; Primary election (8)

Closed rule An order from the House Rules Committee in the House of Representatives that sets a time limit on debate and forbids a particular bill from being amended on the legislative floor. *See also* Open rule; Restrictive rule (11)

Cloture rule A rule used by the Senate to end or limit debate. Designed to prevent "talking a bill to death" by filibuster. To pass in the Senate, three-fifths of the entire Senate membership (or sixty senators) must vote for it. *See also* Filibuster (11)

Coalition An alliance among different interest groups (factions) or parties to achieve some political goal. An example is the coalition sometimes formed between Republicans and conservative Democrats. (2)

Coattails (political) The tendency of lesser-known or weaker candidates to profit in an election by the presence on the ticket of a more popular candidate. (8)

Cold War Refers to the nonmilitary struggle between the United States (and its allies) and the former Soviet Union (and its allies) following World War II. (A cold war is distinguished from a *hot* or *shooting war*.) (20)

Command-and-control strategy A strategy to improve air and water quality, involving the setting of detailed pollution standards and rules. (22)

Committee clearance The ability of a Congressional committee to review and approve certain agency decisions in advance and without passing a law. Such approval is not legally binding on the agency, but few agency heads will ignore the expressed wishes of committees. (13)

Comparable worth   A doctrine that would require salaries to be determined by the "worth" of the job, not by what it commands in the market. (19)

Compensatory action   An action designed to help members of disadvantaged groups, especially minorities and women, catch up, usually by giving them extra education, training, or services. (19)

Competitive service   The government offices to which people are appointed on grounds of merit as ascertained by a written examination or by having met certain selection criteria (such as training, educational attainments, or prior experience). *See also* Excepted service (13)

Concurrent resolution   An expression of congressional opinion without the force of law that requires the approval of both the House and Senate but not of the president. Used to settle housekeeping and procedural matters that affect both houses. *See also* Simple resolution; Joint resolution (11)

Concurring opinion   A Supreme Court opinion by one or more justices who agree with the majority's conclusion but for different reasons. *See also* Opinion of the Court; Dissenting opinion (14)

Conditions of aid   Federal rules attached to the grants that states receive. States must agree to abide by these rules in order to receive the grant. (3)

Confederation or **Confederal system**   A political system in which states or regional governments retain ultimate authority except for those powers that they expressly delegate to a central government. The United States was a confederation from 1776 to 1787 under the Articles of Confederation. *See also* Federalism; Unitary system (2)

Conference committees   *See* Joint committees (11)

Congressional campaign committee   A party committee in Congress that provides funds to members who are running for reelection or to would-be members running for an open seat or challenging a candidate from the opposition party. (7)

Conservative coalition   An alliance between Republicans and conservative Democrats. (11)

Conservative   In general, a person who favors more limited and local government, less government regulation of markets, more social conformity to traditional norms and values, and tougher policies toward criminals. *See also* Liberal (5)

Constitutional Convention   A meeting of delegates in 1787 to revise the Articles of Confederation, which produced a totally new constitution still in use today. (2)

Constitutional court   A federal court exercising the judicial powers found in Article III of the Constitution and whose judges are given constitutional protection: they may not be fired (they serve during "good behavior") nor may their salaries be reduced while they are in office. The most important constitutional courts are the Supreme Court, the ninety-four district courts, and the courts of appeals (one in each of eleven regions plus one in the District of Columbia). *See also* District courts; Courts of appeals; Federal-question cases (14)

Containment or **Antiappeasement**   The view that the United States should contain aggressive nations (such as the former Soviet Union). *See also* Isolationism (20)

Cost   Any burden, monetary or nonmonetary, that some people must bear, or think that they must bear, if a policy is adopted. *See also* Benefit (15)

Cost overruns   Actual costs that are several times greater than estimated costs. These occur frequently among private contractors producing new weapons for the Pentagon. (21)

Council-manager system   A system in which people vote only for city-council members, who then appoint a professional city manager to take charge of most or all of the city's administration. Elections in council-manager cities are usually nonpartisan. This plan is most common in cities with a population between 10,000 and 200,000. (25)

Courts of appeals   The federal courts with authority to review decisions by federal district courts, regulatory commissions, and certain other federal courts. Such courts have no original jurisdiction; they can hear only appeals. There are a total of twelve courts of appeals in the United States and its territories. *See also* Constitutional courts; District courts (14)

Criminal law   The body of rules defining offenses that, though they harm an individual (such as murder, rape, and robbery), are considered to be offenses against society as a whole and as a consequence warrant punishment by and in the name of society. *See also* Civil law (14)

Critical or **Realigning periods**   Periods during which a sharp, lasting shift occurs in the popular coalition supporting one or both parties. The issues that separate the two parties change, and so the kinds of voters supporting each party change. (8)

Cue (political)   A signal telling a congressional representative what values (e.g., liberal or conservative) are at stake in a vote—who is for, who against a proposal—and how that issue fits into his or her own set of political beliefs or party agenda. (9)

De facto segregation   Racial segregation in schools that occurs, not because of laws or administrative decisions, but as a result of patterns of residential settlement. To the extent that blacks and whites live in separate neighborhoods, neighborhood schools will often be segregated "de facto." *See also* De jure segregation (19)

De jure segregation   Racial segregation that occurs because of laws or administrative decisions by public agencies. When state laws, for example, required blacks and whites to attend separate schools or sit in separate sections of a bus, "de jure" segregation resulted. *See also* De facto segregation (19)

Delegated powers   Powers expressly granted to the national government by the Constitution. These powers, found in Article I, section 8, include the authority to provide for the common defense, to coin money, and to regulate commerce. *See also* Concurrent powers; Implied powers (2)

Democracy   A term used to describe a political system in which the people are said to rule, directly or indirectly. *See also* Democratic centralism; Participatory democracy; Representative democracy (1)

Democratic centralism A government said to be democratic if its decisions will serve the "true interests" of the people whether or not the people affect the decision making or select the decision makers. Using this definition, various authoritarian regimes have claimed to be "democratic." *See also* Direct or participatory democracy; Representative democracy (1)

Descriptive representation A correspondence between the demographic characteristics of representatives and those of their constituents. (11)

Dillon's rule A legal principle that holds that the terms of city charters are to be interpreted narrowly. Under this rule (named after a lawyer who wrote a book on the subject in 1911), a municipal corporation can exercise only those powers expressly given it or those powers necessarily implied by, or essential to the accomplishment of, these stated powers. (25)

Direct or **Participatory democracy** A political system in which all or most citizens participate directly by either holding office or making policy. The town meeting, in which citizens vote on major issues, is an example of participatory democracy. (1)

Discharge petition A device by which any member of the House, after a committee has had a bill for thirty days, may petition to have it brought to the floor. If a majority of the members agree, the bill is discharged from the committee. The discharge petition was designed to prevent a committee from killing a bill by holding it for too long. (11)

Discretionary authority The extent to which appointed bureaucrats can choose courses of action and make policies that are not spelled out in advance by laws. (13)

Dissenting opinion A Supreme Court opinion by one or more justices in the minority to explain the minority's disagreement with the Court's ruling. *See also* Opinion of the Court; Concurring opinion (14)

District courts The lowest federal courts where federal cases begin. They are the only federal courts where trials are held. There are a total of ninety-four district courts in the United States and its territories. *See also* Courts of appeals; Constitutional courts; Federal-question cases (14)

Diversity cases Cases involving citizens of different states over which the federal courts have jurisdiction as described in the Constitution. *See also* Federal-question cases (14)

Divided government A government in which one party controls the White House and another party controls one or both houses of Congress. *See also* Unified government (12)

Division vote A congressional voting procedure in which members stand and are counted. *See also* Voice vote; Teller vote; Roll call (11)

Domino theory An influential theory first articulated by President Eisenhower holding that if an important nation were to fall into communist hands, other neighboring countries would follow suit. Eisenhower used the metaphor of a row of dominoes falling in sequence to illustrate his point. (20)

Double-tracking A procedure to keep the Senate going during a filibuster in which the disputed bill is shelved temporarily so that the Senate can get on with other business. *See also* Filibuster; Cloture rule (11)

Dual federalism A constitutional theory that the national government and the state governments each have defined areas of authority, especially over commerce. (3)

Due-process clause Protection against arbitrary deprivation of life, liberty, or property as guaranteed in the Fifth and Fourteenth Amendments. (18)

Earned-income tax credit A provision of a 1975 tax law that entitles working families with children to receive money from the government if their total income falls below a certain level. (17)

Economic planning An economic philosophy that assumes that the government should plan, in varying ways, some part of the country's economic activity. For instance, in times of high inflation, it suggests that the government regulate the maximum prices that can be charged and wages that can be paid, at least in the larger industries. Another form of planning, called *industrial policy*, would have the government planning or subsidizing investments in industries that need to recover or in new industries that could replace them. (16)

Elite (political) An identifiable group of persons who possess a disproportionate share of some valued resource—such as money or political power. (1)

Elitist theory (politics) A theory that a few top leaders make the key decisions without reference to popular desires. (1)

Entrepreneurial politics Policies benefiting society as a whole or some large part that impose a substantial cost on some small identifiable segment of society. *See also* Policy entrepreneurs (15)

Environmental impact statement A report required by federal law that assesses the possible effect of a project on the environment if the project is subsidized in whole or part by federal funds. (22)

Equal-time rule A rule of the Federal Communications Commission (FCC) stating that if a broadcaster sells time to one candidate for office, he or she must be willing to sell equal time to opposing candidates. (10)

Equality of opportunities A view that it is wrong to use race or sex either to discriminate against or give preferential treatment to blacks or women. *See also* Reverse discrimination (19)

Establishment clause A clause in the First Amendment to the Constitution stating that Congress shall make no law "respecting an establishment of religion." (18)

Ex post facto law A Latin term meaning "after the fact." A law that makes criminal an act that was legal when it was committed, or that increases the penalty for a crime after it has been committed, or that changes the rules of evidence to make conviction easier; a retroactive criminal law. The state legislatures and Congress are forbidden to pass such laws by Article I of the Constitution. (2)

Exclusionary rule A rule that holds that evidence gathered in violation of the Constitution cannot be used in a trial. The rule has been used to implement two provisions of the Bill of Rights—the right to be free from unreasonable searches or seizures (Fourth Amendment) and the right not to be compelled to give evidence against oneself (Fifth Amendment). *See also*

Good-faith exception (18)

External efficacy *See* political efficacy. (4)

Faction According to James Madison, a group of people who seek to influence public policy in ways contrary to the public good. (2)

Fairness doctrine A former rule of the Federal Communications Commission (FCC) that required broadcasters to give time to opposing views if they broadcast a program giving one side of a controversial issue. (10)

Feature stories Media reports about public events knowable to any reporter who cares to inquire, but involving acts and statements not routinely covered by a group of reporters. Thus a reporter must take the initiative and select a particular event as newsworthy, decide to write about it, and persuade an editor to run it. (10)

Federal system A system in which sovereignty is shared so that on some matters the national government is supreme and on others the state, regional, or provincial governments are supreme. (3)

Federal-question cases Cases concerning the Constitution, federal law, or treaties over which the federal courts have jurisdiction as described in the Constitution. *See also* Diversity cases (14)

Federalism A political system in which ultimate authority is shared between a central government and state or regional governments. *See also* Confederation; Unitary state (2)

Federalist Papers A series of eighty-five essays written by Alexander Hamilton, James Madison, and John Jay (all using the name "Publius") that were published in New York newspapers in 1787–1788 to convince New Yorkers to adopt the newly proposed Constitution. They are classics of American constitutional and political thought. (2)

Federalists Supporters of a stronger central government who advocated ratification of the Constitution. After ratification they founded a political party supporting a strong executive and Alexander Hamilton's economic policies. *See also* Antifederalists (2)

Fee shifting A law or rule that allows the plaintiff (the party that initiates the lawsuit) to collect its legal costs from the defendant if the defendant loses. *See also* Plaintiff (14)

Filibuster An attempt to defeat a bill in the Senate by talking indefinitely, thus preventing the Senate from taking action on it. From the Spanish *filibustero* which means a "freebooter," a military adventurer. (11)

Fiscal policy An attempt to use taxes and expenditures to affect the economy. (16)

Fiscal year The period from October 1 to September 30 for which government appropriations are made and federal books are kept. A fiscal year is named after the year in which it ends—thus "fiscal 1995" (or "FY 95") refers to the twelve-month period ending September 30, 1995. (16)

Franking privilege The ability of members of Congress to mail letters to their constituents free of charge by substituting their facsimile signature (frank) for postage. (11)

Free-exercise clause A clause in the First Amendment to the Constitution stating that Congress shall make no law prohibiting the "free exercise" of religion. (18)

Freedom of expression The constitutional rights of Americans to "freedom of speech, or of the press, or the right of people peaceably to assemble, and to petition the government for a redress of grievances" as outlined in the First Amendment to the Constitution. (18)

Freedom of religion The religious rights of Americans outlined in the First Amendment to the Constitution. The amendment states that "Congress shall make no law respecting an establishment of religion; or abridging the free exercise thereof." (18)

Gender gap Differences in the political views and voting behavior of men and women. (5)

General election An election used to fill an elective office. *See also* Primary election (8)

General-act charter A charter that applies to a number of cities that fall within a certain classification, usually based on city population. Thus in some states, all cities with populations over 100,000 will be governed on the basis of one charter, while all cities with populations between 50,000 and 99,999 will be governed by a different one. *See also* Special-act charter (25)

Gerrymandering Drawing the boundaries of political districts in bizarre or unusual shapes to make it easy for candidates of the party in power to win elections in those districts. (11)

Gold plating The tendency of Pentagon officials to ask weapons contractors to meet excessively high requirements. (21)

Good-faith exception Admission at a trial of evidence that is gathered in violation of the Constitution if the violation results from a technical or minor error. *See also* Exclusionary rule (18)

Grandfather clause A clause added to registration laws allowing people who did not meet registration requirements to vote if they or their ancestors had voted before 1867 (before blacks were legally allowed to vote). This was to exempt poor and illiterate whites from registration requirements established to keep former slaves from voting. The Supreme Court declared the practice unconstitutional in 1915. (6)

Grants-in-aid Federal funds provided to states and localities. Grants-in-aid are typically provided for airports, highways, education, and major welfare services. *See also* Categorical grants; Block grant (3)

Great Compromise or **Connecticut Compromise** A compromise at the Constitutional Convention in 1787 that reconciled the interests of small and large states by allowing the former to predominate in the Senate and the latter in the House. Under the agreement, each state received two representatives in the Senate, regardless of size, but was allotted representatives on the basis of population in the House. (2)

Home-rule charter A charter that allows the city government to do anything that is not prohibited by the charter or by state law. (25)

Ideological party A party that values principled stands on issues above all else, including winning. It claims to have a comprehensive view of American society and government radically different from that of the established parties. (7)

Ideological-interest group A political organization that attracts members by appealing to their political convictions with a coherent set of (usually) controversial principles. (9)

Impeachment A formal accusation against a public official by the lower house of a legislative body. Impeachment is merely an accusation and not a conviction. Only one president, Andrew Johnson in 1868 was ever impeached. He was not, however, convicted for the Senate failed by one vote to obtain the necessary two-thirds vote required for conviction. (12)

In forma pauperis A procedure whereby a poor person can file and be heard in court as a pauper, free of charge. (14)

Incentive (political) A valued benefit obtained by joining a political organization. (9)

Income strategy A policy of giving poor people money to help lift them out of poverty. (17)

Incumbent The person currently in office. (8)

Industrial policy *See* Economic planning (16)

Initiative A procedure allowing voters to submit a proposed law to a popular vote by obtaining a required number of signatures. *See also* Referendum (25)

Insider stories Information not usually made public that becomes public because someone with inside knowledge tells a reporter. The reporter may have worked hard to learn these facts, in which case it is called "investigative reporting," or some official may have wanted a story to get out, in which case it is called a "leak." (10)

Insurance program A self-financing government program based on contributions that provide benefits to unemployed or retired persons. (17)

Interest group An organization of people sharing a common interest or goal that seeks to influence the making of public policy. (9)

Interest-group politics The politics of policy making in which one small groups bears the costs of the policy and another small group receives the benefits. Each group has an incentive to organize and to press its interest. *See also* Majoritarian politics; Client politics (15)

Internal efficacy *See* political efficacy (4)

Iron Curtain A metaphor first used by Winston Churchill to describe a military and political barrier maintained by the former Soviet Union to prevent free travel and communication between Eastern and Western Europe. (20)

Iron triangle A close relationship between an agency, a congressional committee, and an interest group that often becomes a mutually advantageous alliance. *See also* Issue network; Client politics (13)

Isolationism The view that the United States should withdraw from world affairs, limit foreign aid, and avoid involvement in foreign wars. *See also* Containment (20)

Issue network A network of people in Washington-based interest groups, on congressional staffs, in universities and think tanks, and in the mass media who regularly discuss and advocate public policies—say, health care or auto safety. Such networks are split along political, ideological, and economic lines. (13)

Jacksonian model (government) A model of government favored by those who want many elected officials closely accountable to the voters, who believe that average citizens rather than appointed experts should have the most authority, who want specific neighborhoods and not the "city as a whole" represented on city councils, and who expect legislators to intervene on behalf of individual citizen interests. *See also* Progressive model (25)

Jim Crow A slang expression for African Americans that emerged in the 1820s and came to signify the laws and governmental practices designed to segregate blacks from whites, especially in the American South. (19)

Joint committees Committees on which both representatives and senators serve. An especially important kind of joint committee is the *conference committee* made up of representatives and senators appointed to resolve differences in the Senate and House versions of the same piece of legislation before final passage. *See also* Standing committees; Joint committees (11)

Joint resolution A formal expression of congressional opinion that must be approved by both houses of Congress and by the president. Joint resolutions proposing a constitutional amendment need not be signed by the president. *See also* Concurrent resolution; Simple resolution (11)

Judicial review The power of the courts to declare acts of the legislature and of the executive to be unconstitutional and hence null and void. (2, 14)

Keynesianism An economic philosophy that assumes that the market will not automatically operate at a full-employment, low-inflation level. It suggests that the government should intervene to create the right level of demand by pumping more money into the economy (when demand is low) and taking it out (when demand is too great). (16)

Laissez-faire An economic theory that government should not regulate or interfere with commerce. (13)

Lame duck A politician who is still in office after having lost a reelection bid. (12)

Legislative court A court that is created by Congress for some specialized purpose and staffed with judges who do not enjoy the protection of Article III of the Constitution. Legislative courts include the Court of Military Appeals and the territorial courts. (14)

Legislative veto The rejection of a presidential or administrative-agency action by a vote of one or both houses of Congress without the consent of the president. In 1983 the Supreme Court declared the legislative veto to be unconstitutional. (12)

Legitimacy Political authority conferred by law, public opinion, or constitution. (1)

Liberal In general, a person who favors a more active federal government for regulating business, supporting social welfare, and protecting minority rights, but who prefers less regulation of private social conduct. *See also* Conservative (5)

Libertarians People who wish to maximize personal liberty on both economic and social issues. They prefer a small weak government that has little control over either the economy or the personal lives of citizens. (5)

Line-item veto   The power of an executive to veto some provisions in an appropriations bill while approving others. The president does not have the right to exercise a line-item veto and must approve or reject an entire appropriations bill. *See also* Pocket veto; Veto message (2, 12)

Literacy test   A requirement that citizens pass a literacy test in order to register to vote. It was established by many states to prevent former slaves (most of whom were illiterate) from voting. Illiterate whites were allowed to vote by a "grandfather clause" added to the law saying that you could vote, even though you did not meet the legal requirements, if you or your ancestors voted before 1867. (6)

Litmus test   In chemistry, a way of finding out whether a liquid is acid or alkaline. The term is used in politics to mean a test of ideological purity, a way of finding out whether a person is a dyed-in-the-wool liberal or conservative or what his or her views are on a controversial question. (14)

Loaded language   Words that reflect a value judgment, used to persuade the listener without making an argument. For example, if someone likes a politician, he might call him "the esteemed Senator Smith"; if he doesn't like him, he might refer to him as "right-wing or radical senators such as Smith." (10)

Lobby   An interest group organized to influence governmental decisions, especially legislation. To *lobby* is to attempt to influence such decisions. A *lobbyist* is a person attempting to influence government decisions on behalf of the group. (9)

Lobbyist   *See* Lobby (9)

Logrolling   Mutual aid among politicians, whereby one legislator supports another's pet project in return for the latter's support of his. The expression dates from the days when American pioneers needed help from neighbors in moving logs off of land to be farmed. (15)

Majoritarian politics   The politics of policy making in which almost everybody benefits from a policy and almost everybody pays for it. *See also* Interest-group politics; Client politics (15)

Majority leader   The legislative leader elected by party members holding the majority of seats in the House of Representatives or the Senate. *See also* Minority leader (11)

Majority-minority districts   Congressional districts designed to make it easier for citizens of a racial or ethnic minority to elect representatives. (11)

Malapportionment   Drawing the boundaries of political districts so that districts are very unequal in population. (11)

Mandates   Rules imposed by the federal government on the states as conditions for obtaining federal grants or requirements that the states pay the costs of certain nationally defined programs. (3)

Marginal district   Political districts in which the candidate elected to the House of Representatives wins in a close election, typically with less than 55% of the vote. (11)

Market (television)   An area easily reached by a television signal. There are about two hundred such markets in the country. (10)

Marxist theory (politics)   A theory that those who control the economic system also control the political one. (1)

Material incentives   Benefits that have monetary value; including money, gifts, services, or discounts received as a result of one's membership in an organization. (9)

Mayor-council system   The most common form of city government in which authority is vested in an elected mayor and council. It is typical of very small cities (those under 10,000 population) and very large cities (those over 250,000 population). (25)

McCarthyism   Making a charge that unfairly or dishonestly tarnishes the motives, attacks the patriotism, or violates the rights of individuals, especially of political opponents. Refers to the numerous unsubstantiated accusations of communism made against public and private individuals by Senator Joseph McCarthy in the 1950s. (18)

Means test   An income qualification that determines whether one is eligible for benefits under government programs reserved for lower-income groups. (17)

Metropolitan government   A government for a metropolitan area that includes county, city, and suburban governments. (25)

Micromanaging   A term used to criticize congressional involvement in reviewing the detailed decisions of the executive branch. (21)

Middle America   A phrase coined by the late Joseph Kraft in a 1968 newspaper column to refer to Americans who have moved out of poverty but are not yet affluent and who cherish traditional middle-class values. (5)

Military-industrial complex   An alleged alliance among key military, governmental, and corporate decision makers involved in weapons procurement and military support systems. The phrase was coined by Dwight D. Eisenhower who warned Americans about its dangers. (21)

Minority leader (floor leader)   The legislative leader elected by party members holding a minority of seats in the House of Representatives or the Senate. *See also* Majority leader (11)

Monetarism   An economic philosophy that assumes inflation occurs when there is too much money chasing too few goods. Monetarism suggests that the proper thing for government to do is to have a steady, predictable increase in the money supply at a rate about equal to the growth in the economy's productivity. (16)

Monetary policy   An attempt to alter the amount of money in circulation and the price of money (the interest rate) to affect the economy. (16)

Motor-voter bill   A bill passed by Congress in 1993 to make it easier for Americans to register to vote. The law, which goes into effect in 1995, requires states to allow voter registration by mail, when one applies for a driver's license, and at state offices that serve the disabled or poor. (6)

Muckraker   A journalist who searches through the activities of public officials and organizations seeking to expose conduct contrary to the public interest. The term was first used by President Theodore Roosevelt in 1906 to warn that antibusiness journalism, while valuable, could be excessively negative. (10)

Mugwumps or **Progressives**   The faction in the Republican party of the 1890s to the 1910s composed of reformers who opposed the use of patronage and party bosses and favored the leadership of experts. After 1910, they evolved into a nonpartisan "good government" movement that sought to open up the political system and curb the abuses of parties. *See also* Political machine (7)

Multiple referral   A congressional process whereby a bill may be referred to several committees that consider it simultaneously in whole or in part. For instance, the 1988 trade bill was considered by fourteen committees in the House and nine in the Senate simultaneously. (11)

Municipal corporation   A legal term for a city. It is chartered by the state to exercise certain powers and provide certain services. *See also* Special-act charter; General-act charter (25)

Name-request job   A job to be filled by a person whom a government agency has identified by name. (13)

National chairman (party)   A paid, full-time manager of a party's day-to-day work who is elected by the national committee. (7)

National committee   A committee of delegates from each state and territory that runs party affairs between national conventions. (7)

National convention   A meeting of party delegates elected in state primaries, caucuses, or conventions that is held every four years. Its primary purpose is to nominate presidential and vice-presidential candidates and to ratify a campaign platform. (7)

Necessary-and-proper clause or **Elastic clause**   The final paragraph of Article 1, section 8, of the Constitution, which authorizes Congress to pass all laws "necessary and proper" to carry out the enumerated powers. Sometimes called the "elastic clause" because of the flexibility that it provides to Congress. (3)

Nonviolent civil disobedience   A philosophy of opposing a law one considers unjust by peacefully violating it and allowing oneself to be punished as a result. (19)

Norm   A standard of right or proper conduct that helps determine the range of acceptable social behavior and policy options. (5)

Nullification   A theory first advanced by James Madison and Thomas Jefferson that the states had the right to "nullify" (that is, declare null and void) a federal law that, in the states' opinion, violated the Constitution. The theory was revived by John C. Calhoun of South Carolina in opposition to federal efforts to restrict slavery. The North's victory in the Civil War determined once and for all that the federal union is indissoluble and that states cannot declare acts of Congress unconstitutional, a view later confirmed by the Supreme Court. (3)

Office-bloc ballot   A ballot listing all candidates for a given office under the name of that office; also called a "Massachusetts" ballot. *See also* Party-column ballot (8)

Offsets   An environmental rule that a company in an area with polluted air can offset its own pollution by reducing pollution from another source in the area. For instance, an older company that can't afford to pay for new anti-pollution technologies may buy pollution credits from a newer company that has reduced its source of pollution below the levels required by law. (22)

Open primary   A primary election that permits voters to choose on election day the party primary in which they wish to vote. They may vote for candidates of only one party. *See also* Blanket primary; Closed primary; Primary election; Presidential primary (8)

Open rule   An order from the House Rules Committee in the House of Representatives, that permits a bill to be amended on the legislative floor. *See also* Closed rule; Restrictive rule (11)

Opinion of the Court   A Supreme Court opinion written by one or more justices in the majority to explain the decision in a case. *See also* Concurring opinion; Dissenting opinion (14)

Orthodox (social)   People who believe that moral rules are derived from the commands of God or the laws of nature, commands and laws that are relatively clear, unchanging, and independent of individual moral preferences. They are likely to believe that traditional morality is more important than individual liberty and should be enforced by government and communal norms. *See also* Progressive (social) (4)

Party vote   There are two measures of such voting. By the strictest measure, a party vote occurs when 90 percent or more of the Democrats in either house of Congress vote together against 90 percent or more of the Republicans. A looser measure counts as a party vote any case where at least 50 percent of the Democrats vote together against at least 50 percent of the Republicans. (11)

Party-column ballot   A ballot listing all candidates of a given party together under the name of that party; also called an "Indiana" ballot. *See also* Office-bloc ballot (8)

Patronage   *See* Political machine (25)

Peace dividend   Vast sums of money that some assumed would be freed up for domestic spending by cuts in post-Cold War defense spending. (16)

Per curiam opinion   A brief, unsigned opinion issued by the Supreme Court to explain its ruling. *See also* Opinion of the Court (14)

Perks   A short form of perquisites meaning the "fringe benefits of office." Among the perks of political office for high-ranking officials are limousines, expense accounts, free air travel, fancy offices, and staff assistants. (12)

Personal following   The political support provided to a candidate on the basis of personal popularity and networks. (7)

Plaintiff   The party that initiates a lawsuit to obtain a remedy for an injury to his or her rights. (14)

Pluralist theory (politics)   A theory that competition among all affected interests shapes public policy. (1)

Plurality system   An electoral system, used in almost all American elections, in which the winner is the person who gets the most votes, even if he or she does not receive a majority of the votes. (7)

Pocket veto   One of two ways for a president to disapprove a bill sent to him by Congress. If the president does not sign the bill within ten days of his receiving it and Congress has adjourned within that time, the bill does not become law. *See also* Veto message; Line-item veto (12)

Police power   The power of a state to promote health, safety, and morals. (25)

Policy entrepreneurs   Those in and out of government who find ways of pulling together a legislative majority on behalf of unorganized interests. *See also* Entrepreneurial politics (15)

Political action committee (PAC)   A committee set up by and representing a corporation, labor union, or special-interest group that raises and spends campaign contributions on behalf of one or more candidates or causes. (8)

Political agenda A set of issues thought by the public or those in power to merit action by government. (15)

Political culture A broadly shared way of thinking about political and economic life that reflects fundamental assumptions about how government should operate. It is distinct from *political ideology* which refers to a more or less consistent set of views about the policies government ought to follow. Up to a point, people sharing a common political culture can disagree about ideology. *See also* Political ideology (4)

Political efficacy, sense of A citizen's belief that he or she can understand and influence political affairs. This sense is divided into two parts— internal efficacy (confidence in a citizen's own abilities to understand and take part in political affairs) and external efficacy (a belief that the system will respond to a citizen's demands). (4)

Political elite *See* Elite (political) (5)

Political ideology A more or less consistent set of views as to the policies government ought to pursue. *See also* Political culture (4)

Political machine A party organization that recruits its members by dispensing *patronage*—tangible incentives such as money, political jobs, an opportunity to get favors from government—and that is characterized by a high degree of leadership control over member activity. (7)

Political party A group that seeks to elect candidates to public office by supplying them with a label—a "party identification"—by which they are known to the electorate. (7)

Political question An issue that the Court refuses to consider because it believes the Constitution has left it entirely to another branch to decide. Its view of such issues may change over time, however. For example, until the 1960s, the Court refused to hear cases about the size of congressional districts, no matter how unequal their populations. In 1962, however, it decided that it was authorized to review the constitutional implications of this issue. (14)

Political-editorializing rule A rule of the Federal Communications Commission that if a broadcaster endorses a candidate, the opposing candidate has a right to reply. (10)

Poll A survey of public opinion. *See also* Random sample (5)

Poll tax A requirement that citizens pay a tax in order to register to vote. It was adopted by many states in order to prevent former slaves (most of whom were poor) from voting. It is now unconstitutional. *See also* Grandfather clause; Literacy test (6)

Pollution allowances or **Banks** A reduction in pollution below that required by law that can be used to cover a future plant expansion or sold to another company whose pollution emissions are above the legal requirements. (22)

Populists People who hold liberal views on economic matters and conservative ones on social matters. They prefer a strong government that will reduce economic inequality, regulate businesses, and impose stricter social and criminal sanctions. The name and views have their origins in an agriculturally-based social movement and party of the 1880s and 1890s that sought to curb the power of influential economic interests. (5)

Pork-barrel legislation Legislation that gives tangible benefits (highways, dams, post offices) to constituents in several districts or states in the hope of winning their votes in return. (11)

Pork-barrel projects *See* Pork-barrel legislation (15)

Position issue An issue dividing the electorate on which rival parties adopt different policy positions to attract voters. *See also* Valence issue (8)

Power The ability of one person to get another person to act in accordance with the first person's intentions. (1)

Presidential primary *See* Primary election (8)

Price-and-wage control *See* Economic planning (16)

Primary election (direct primary) An election prior to the general election in which voters select the candidates who will run on each party's ticket. Before presidential elections, a *presidential primary* is held to select delegates to the presidential nominating conventions of the major parties. *See also* Closed primary; Open primary (8)

Prior restraint The traditional view of the press' s free speech rights as expressed by William Blackstone, the great English jurist. According to this view, the press is guaranteed freedom from censorship—that is, rules telling it in advance what it can publish. After publication, however, the government can punish the press for material that is judged libelous or obscene. (18)

Private bill A legislative bill that deals only with specific, private, personal, or local matters rather than with general legislative affairs. The main kinds include immigration and naturalization bills (referring to particular individuals) and personal-claim bills. *See also* Public bill (11)

Probable cause *See* Search warrant (18)

Process regulation Rules regulating manufacturing or industrial processes, usually aimed at improving consumer or worker safety and reducing environmental damage. (15)

Professional legislature A state legislature that meets during most of the year, consists of legislators who are well paid and regard their position as their main job, and that provides legislators and legislative committees with sizable, year-round staffs. *See also* Amateur legislature (25)

Progressive (social) People who believe that moral rules are derived in part from an individual's beliefs and the circumstances of modern life. They are likely to favor government tolerance and protection of individual choice. (4)

Progressive model A model of government favored by those who prefer to have few elected officials, power concentrated more in executive than in legislative hands, greater reliance on experts, and city-council members elected from the city at large rather than from small districts. (25)

Progressive movement A movement that began in earnest after the Civil War and reached a peak during the early years of the twentieth century. Its principal aims were to purify politics and make government more efficient by attacking the sources of partisan influence. *See also* Mugwumps or progressives (25)

Prospective voting Voting for a candidate because one favors his or her ideas for addressing issues after the election. (Prospective means "forward-looking.") *See also* Retrospective voting (8)

Public bill   A legislative bill that deals with matters of general concern. A bill involving defense expenditures is a public bill; a bill pertaining to an individual's becoming a naturalized citizen is not. *See also* Private bill (11)

Public-interest lobby   A political organization the stated goals of which will principally benefit nonmembers. (9)

Purposive incentive   The benefit that comes from serving a cause or principle from which one does not personally benefit. (9)

Pyramid structure   A method of organizing a president's staff in which most presidential assistants report through a hierarchy to the president's chief of staff. (12)

Quorum call   A calling of the roll in either house of Congress to see whether the number of representatives in attendance meets the minimum number required to conduct official business. (11)

Random sample   A sample selected in such a way that any member of the population being surveyed (e.g., all adults or voters) has an equal chance of being interviewed. (5)

Ratings   An assessment of a representative's voting record on issues important to an interest group. Such ratings are designed to generate public support for or opposition to a legislator. (9)

Reaganomics   The federal economic policies of the Reagan Administration elected in 1981. These policies combined a monetarist fiscal policy, supply-side tax cuts, and domestic budget-cutting. Their goal was to reduce the size of the federal government and stimulate economic growth. *See also* Supply-side theory; Monetarism (16)

Recall   A procedure, in effect in fifteen states, whereby the voters can vote to remove an elected official from office. (25)

Red tape   Complex bureaucratic rules and procedures that must be followed to get something done. (13)

Referendum   The practice of submitting a law to a popular vote at election time. The law may be proposed by a voter's initiative or by the legislature. *See also* Initiative (25)

Reformed cities   Cities based on the progressive model of government. They have nonpartisan elections, a city council elected at large, a strong civil service, and their executive powers in the hands of an appointed city manager. *See also* Unreformed cities (25)

Registered voters   People who are registered to vote. While almost all adult American citizens are theoretically eligible to vote, only those who have completed a registration form by the required date may do so. (6)

Religious tradition   The moral teachings of religious institutions on religious, social and economic issues. (5)

Remedy   A judicial order preventing or redressing a wrong or enforcing a right. (14)

Representative democracy   A political system in which leaders and representatives acquire political power by means of a competitive struggle for the people's vote. This is the form of government used by most nations that are called democratic. (1)

Representative town meeting   A town meeting that consists of one- to two-hundred town meeting representatives elected by all voters eligible to vote in the town. *See also* Town meeting (25)

Republic   A form of democracy in which power is vested in representatives selected by means of popular competitive elections. *See also* Representative democracy (2)

Restrictive rule   An order from the House Rules Committee in the House of Representatives that permits certain kinds of amendments but not others to be made to a bill on the legislative floor. *See also* Closed rule; Restrictive rule (11)

Retrospective voting   Voting for or against the candidate or party in office because one likes or dislikes how things have gone in the recent past. (Retrospective means "backward-looking.") *See also* Prospective voting (8)

Revenue sharing   A law providing for the distribution of a fixed amount or share of federal tax revenues to the states for spending on almost any government purpose. Distribution was intended to send more money to poorer, heavily taxed states and less to richer, lightly taxed ones. The program was ended in 1986. (3)

Reverse discrimination   Using race or sex to give preferential treatment to some people. (19)

Riders   Amendments on matters unrelated to a bill that are added to an important bill so that they will "ride" to passage through the Congress. When a bill has lots of riders, it is called a Christmas-tree bill. (11)

Right-of-reply rule   A rule of the Federal Communications Commission that if a person is attacked on a broadcast (other than in a regular news program), that person has the right to reply over that same station. (10)

Roll call or **Record vote**   A congressional voting procedure that consists of members answering "yea" or "nay" to their names. When roll calls were handled orally, it was a time-consuming process in the House. Since 1973 an electronic voting system permits each House member to record his or her vote and learn the total automatically. *See also* Voice vote; Division vote; Teller vote (11)

Routine stories   Media reports about public events that are regularly covered by reporters and that involve simple, easily described acts or statements. For example, the president takes a trip or Congress passes a bill. (10)

Runoff primary   A second primary election held in some states when no candidate receives a majority of the votes in the first primary; the runoff is between the two candidates with the most votes. Runoff primaries are common in the South. (8)

Sampling error   The difference between the results of two surveys or samples. For example, if one random sample shows that 60 percent of all Americans like cats and another random sample taken at the same time shows that 65 percent do, the sampling error is 5 per cent. *See also* Sampling (5)

Search warrant   An order from a judge authorizing the search of a place; the order must describe what is to be searched and seized, and the judge can only issue it if he or she is persuaded by the police that good reason (probable cause) exists that a crime has been committed and that the evidence bearing on the crime will be found at a certain location. (18)

Select committees   Congressional committees appointed for a limited time and purpose. *See also* Standing committees; Joint committees (11)

Selective attention Paying attention only to those parts of a newspaper or broadcast story with which one agrees. Studies suggest that this is how people view political ads on television. (10)

Separate-but-equal doctrine The doctrine, established in *Plessy v. Fergusson* (1896), in which the Supreme Court ruled that a state could provide "separate but equal" facilities for blacks. (19)

Separation of powers A principle of American government whereby constitutional authority is shared by three separate branches of government—the legislative, the executive, and the judicial. *See also* Checks and balances (2)

Sequester Automatic, across-the-board cuts in certain federal programs that are triggered by law when Congress and the president cannot agree on a spending plan. (16)

Service strategy A policy of providing poor people with education and job training to help lift them out of poverty. (17)

Shays's Rebellion A rebellion in 1787 led by Daniel Shays and other ex–Revolutionary War soldiers and officers to prevent foreclosures of farms as a result of high interest rates and taxes. The revolt highlighted the weaknesses of the Confederation and bolstered support for a stronger national government. (2)

Silent majority A phrase used to describe people, whatever their economic status, who uphold traditional values, especially against the counterculture of the 1960s. (5)

Simple resolution An expression of opinion either in the House of Representatives or the Senate to settle housekeeping or procedural matters in either body. Such expressions are not signed by the president and do not have the force of law. *See also* Concurrent resolution; Joint resolution (11)

Social movement A widely shared demand for change in some aspect of the social or political order. The civil-rights movement of the 1960s was such an event as are broadly based religious revivals. A social movement may have liberal or conservative goals. (9)

Social status or **Socio-economic status** A measure of one's social standing obtained by combining factors such as education, income, and occupation. (5)

Solidary incentives The social rewards that lead people to join local or state political organizations. People who find politics fun and want to meet others who share their interests are said to respond to solidary incentives. (7, 9)

Sophomore surge An increase in the votes that congressional candidates usually get when they first run for reelection. (11)

Sound bite A brief statement no longer than a few seconds used on a radio or television news broadcast. (10)

Sovereign immunity A doctrine that a citizen cannot sue the government without its consent. By statute Congress has given its consent for the government to be sued in many cases involving a dispute over a contract or damage done as a result of negligence. (14)

Sovereignty Supreme or ultimate political authority; a sovereign government is one that is legally and politically independent of any other government. (3)

Special-act charter A charter that defines the powers of a certain named city and lists what that city can and cannot do. *See also* General-act charter (25)

Split-ticket (voting) Voting for candidates of different parties for various offices in the same election. For example, voting for a Republican for senator and a Democrat for president. *See also* Straight-ticket voting (8)

Spoils system Another phrase for political patronage—that is, the practice of giving the fruits of a party's victory, such as jobs and contracts, to the loyal members of that party. (13)

Sponsored party A local or state political party that is largely staffed and funded by another organization with established networks in the community. One example is the Democratic party in and around Detroit which has been developed, led, and to a degree financed by the political-action arm of the United Auto Workers union. (7)

Spots (campaign) Short television advertisements used to promote a candidate for government office. *See also* Visual (8)

Standing A legal concept establishing who is entitled to bring a lawsuit to court. For example, an individual must ordinarily show personal harm in order to acquire standing and be heard in court. (14)

Standing committee A permanently established legislative committee that considers and is responsible for legislation within a certain subject area. Examples are the House Ways and Means Committee and the Senate Judiciary Committee. *See also* Select committees; Joint committees (11)

Stare decisis A Latin term meaning "Let the decision stand." The practice of basing judicial decisions on precedents established in similar cases decided in the past. (14)

Straight-ticket voting Voting for candidates who are all of the same party. For example, voting for Republican candidates for senator, representative, and president. *See also* Split-ticket voting (8)

Strict constructionist approach (judicial) The view that judges should decide cases on the basis of the language of the Constitution. (14)

Strict scrutiny The standard by which the Supreme Court judges classifications based on race. To be accepted, such a classification must be closely related to a "compelling" public purpose. (19)

Strong-mayor system A system with a directly elected mayor who has substantial authority over the administrative branch of government and important budgetary powers. *See* Weak-mayor system (25)

Substantive representation The correspondence between representatives' opinions and those of their constituents. *See also* Descriptive representation (11)

Superdelegates Party leaders and elected officials who become delegates to the national convention without having to run in primaries or caucuses. Party rules determine the percentage of delegate seats reserved for party officials. (7)

Supply-side theory An economic philosophy that holds that sharply cutting taxes would increase the incentive that people have to work, save, and invest. Greater investments would lead to more jobs, a more productive economy, and more tax revenues for the government. (16)

Suspect classifications Classifications of people on the basis of their race and ethnicity. The courts have ruled that laws classifying people on these grounds will be subject to "strict scrutiny." (19)

Symbolic speech   An act that conveys a political message, such as burning a draft card to protest the draft. (18)

Tax revolt   A citizen-initiated movement to limit or reduce taxes. (25)

Teller vote   A congressional voting procedure in which members pass between two tellers, the "yeas" first and then the "nays." Since 1971 the identities of members in a teller vote can be "recorded." *See also* Voice vote; Division vote; Roll call (11)

Third World   Originally a French term *(tiers monde)* referring to nations neutral in the cold war between the United States and the former Soviet Union. The term now refers to the group of developing nation in Africa, Asia, Latin America, and the Middle East. *See also* Cold War (20)

Town meeting   A meeting of all town citizens to vote on budgets and proposals. *See also* Representative town meeting (25)

Trial balloon (political)   Information provided to the media by an anonymous public official as a way of testing the public reaction to a possible policy or appointment. (10)

Trust funds   Funds for government programs that are collected and spent outside the regular government budget; the amounts are determined by preexisting law rather than by annual appropriations. The Social Security trust fund is the largest of these. *See also* Appropriations (13)

Two-party system   An electoral system with two dominant parties that compete in state or national elections. Third parties have little chance of winning. (7)

Unalienable rights   Rights thought to be based on nature and Providence rather than on the preferences of people. (2)

Unified government   A government in which the same party controls both the White House and both houses of Congress. When Bill Clinton became president in 1993, it was the first time since 1981 (and only the second time since 1969) that the same party was in charge of the presidency and Congress. *See also* Divided government (12)

Unitary system   A system in which sovereignty is wholly in the hands of the national government so that subnational political units are dependent on its will. *See also* Federalism; Federal system (3)

Unreformed cities   Cities based on the Jacksonian model of government. They have partisan elections, a city council elected from districts, and their executive powers are in the hands of the mayor. *See also* Reformed cities (25)

Valence issue   An issue on which voters distinguish rival parties by the degree to which they associate each party or candidate with conditions, goals, or symbols the electorate universally approves or disapproves of. Examples of such issues are economic prosperity and political corruption. *See also* Position issue (8)

Veto message   One of two ways for a president to disapprove a bill sent to him by Congress. The veto message must be sent to Congress within ten days after the president receives it. *See also* Pocket veto; Line-item veto (12)

Visual (campaign)   A campaign activity that appears on a television news broadcast. *See also* Spots (8)

Voice vote   A congressional voting procedure in which members shout "yea" in approval or "nay" in disapproval; allows members to vote quickly or anonymously on bills. *See also* Division vote; Teller vote; Roll call (11)

Voting-age population   The citizens who are eligible to vote after reaching a minimum age requirement. In the United States, a citizen must be at least eighteen years old in order to vote. (6)

Wall-of-separation principle   A Supreme Court interpretation of the Establishment clause in the First Amendment that prevents government involvement with religion, even on a nonpreferential basis. (18)

Weak-mayor system   A mayor-council system in which the mayor does not have much power over the administration of the system (he or she often must share executive authority with various boards and commissions) and does not have a lot of influence in the city council. *See also* Strong-mayor system (25)

Whip   A senator or representative who helps the party leader stay informed about what party members are thinking, rounds up members when important votes are to be taken, and attempts to keep a nose count on how the voting on controversial issues is likely to go. (11)

White primary   The practice of keeping blacks from voting in primary elections (at the time, the only meaningful election in the one-party South was the Democratic primary) through arbitrary implementation of registration requirements and intimidation. Such practices were declared unconstitutional in 1944. (6)

Work ethic   A belief in the importance of hard work and personal achievement. (4)

Worldviews (foreign policy)   More or less comprehensive mental pictures of the critical problems facing the United States in the world and of the appropriate and inappropriate ways of responding to these problems. (20)

Writ of certiorari   A Latin term meaning "made more certain." An order issued by a higher court to a lower court to send up the record of a case for review. Most cases reach the Supreme Court through the writ of certiorari, issued when at least four of the nine justices feel that the case should be reviewed. (14)

Writ of habeas corpus   A Latin term meaning "you shall have the body." A court order directing a police officer, sheriff, or warden who has a person in custody to bring the prisoner before a judge and show sufficient cause for his or her detention. The write of habeas corpus was designed to prevent illegal arrests and imprisonment. (2)